# YEARS OF RENEWAL

Henry Kissinger was born in Germany, arrived in the United States in 1938 and became a US citizen in 1943. He graduated from Harvard in 1950 and from 1954 to 1969 he was a member of the faculty of Harvard University, in both the Department of Government and the Center for International Affairs. From 1969 to 1975 he served as Assistant to the President for National Security Affairs and from 1973 to 1977 he was Secretary of State. Among the awards Dr Kissinger has received are the Nobel Peace Prize in 1973, the Presidential Medal of Freedom in 1977 and the Medal of Liberty in 1986.

### ALSO BY HENRY KISSINGER

White House Years

Years of Upheaval

A World Restored: Castlereagh, Metternich
and the Restoration of Peace, 1812–1822

Diplomacy

Observations: Selected Speeches and Essays, 1982–1984

For the Record: Selected Statements, 1977–1980

American Foreign Policy: Three Essays

Problems of National Strategy: A Book of Readings

The Troubled Partnership: A Re-Appraisal of the Atlantic
Alliance

The Necessity for Choice: Prospects of American Foreign Policy

Nuclear Weapons and Foreign Policy

# YEARS OF RENEWAL

## Henry Kissinger

PHOENIX
PRESS

5 UPPER SAINT MARTIN'S LANE
LONDON
WC2H 9EA

A PHOENIX PRESS PAPERBACK

First published in 1999 by Simon & Schuster, USA
First published in Great Britain
by Weidenfeld & Nicolson in 1999
This paperback edition published in 2000
by Phoenix Press,
a division of The Orion Publishing Group Ltd,
Orion House, 5 Upper St Martin's Lane,
London WC2H 9EA

Copyright © 1999 Henry A. Kissinger

Designed by Amy Hill
Maps by Paul J. Pugliese

A CIP catalogue record for this book
is available from the British Library.

Printed and bound in Great Britain by
Clays Ltd, St Ives plc

ISBN 1 84212 042 5

# CONTENTS

## Part One: THE NIXON LEGACY

## Part Five: COLLAPSE IN INDOCHINA, TRAGEDY OF THE KURDS

## Part Six: THE ATLANTIC RELATIONSHIP

# LIST OF MAPS

# FOREWORD

For five and a half tumultuous years, I had the honor of serving first as National Security Adviser and then as Secretary of State to President Richard M. Nixon. I was then invited to continue in office by President Gerald R. Ford.

This volume is an account of the period in which Gerald Ford healed the nation and launched it on a course that, in subsequent administrations, culminated in victory in the Cold War and a dominant role in shaping the structure of the world. In the brief period of thirty months vouchsafed to him in office, Ford navigated his country through a series of extraordinary events: ethnic conflicts in Cyprus and Lebanon; a decisive step toward Middle East peace; a major agreement on strategic arms control; the end of America's ordeal in Indochina; a worldwide energy crisis; the signing of the Helsinki Final Act at the first European Security Conference, now generally recognized as a turning point of the Cold War; Soviet and Cuban depredations in Africa; the transition to majority rule in Southern Africa; a new permanent arrangement for the Panama Canal; and the first G-7 economic summit among the great industrial democracies. This is why Ford's presidency will be remembered as ushering in an age of renewal.

After completing two volumes of memoirs on the Nixon years, I waited for over a decade before beginning this account of the Ford presidency. I did so in large part to permit the evaluation of the entire period of my government service from a philosophical perspective rather than according to the tactics of the moment. For the deepest debates of the time concerned the national purpose—for which the growing obsession with sensational media and congressional exposés was a surrogate.

As I reviewed the source material, the Ford presidency emerged less as the ending of a period than as an overture to what is now described as the "new world order." Local ethnic conflicts began to take on large international dimensions and have proliferated since the end of the Cold War; the debate over the role of human rights in foreign policy started in earnest then and has continued since; victory in the Cold War was foreshadowed, if not yet recognized, as the Brezhnev regime began to stagnate internally; today's Middle East diplomacy could be drawn from a script of the Ford period with only some of the names of the principal actors changed; with respect to the Kurdish relations with Iraq, even the names have remained the same; the complexities of long-range China policy began to emerge; the relative roles of Congress and the executive branch in the conduct of foreign policy have still not yet been settled. Obviously history has not stood still, and the collapse of the Soviet Union has opened new dimensions not imaginable in the mid-1970s.

As I wrote in the foreword to the first volume of this series, the perspective of the participant in great events risks merging the impulse to defend with the compulsion to explain. I have sought to the extent possible to do the latter and to explain not only what we did but why. This does not prove that our decisions were always wise. But it may help the reader to see how the interaction of circumstances and statesmen's convictions shapes events.

In my archival research, I have relied on my copies of official records deposited since 1977 in the Library of Congress. The originals of these official records are in the files of either the State Department, the National Archives (for the Nixon period), or the Gerald R. Ford Library. I want to thank Samuel R. Berger, President Clinton's Assistant for National Security Affairs, and Deputy Assistant Major General Donald L. Kerrick for reviewing and clearing all excerpts from classified material. The deletions they requested have been made.

This book could not have been written without the invaluable assistance of dedicated associates. Foremost among them are Peter W. Rodman and Rosemary Neaher Niehuss. Associate, confidant, and friend of many decades, Peter did indispensable research, particularly with respect to Indochina, Europe, China, and Southern Africa. In addition, he reviewed the entire manuscript for content, accuracy, and style.

Rosemary Niehuss, trusted associate since my government service, did key substantive research on the Middle East and Lebanon. In addition, she supervised the entire research effort, served as the liaison to the Library of Congress, and coordinated the production process with the publisher.

Gina Goldhammer went over the entire manuscript indefatigably several times with a fine editorial eye and is responsible for many invaluable improvements.

Fredrica Friedman reviewed the early chapters and offered useful comments.

I cannot say enough for the dedication of Jody Iobst Williams and Theresa Cimino Amantea. Jody typed the entire manuscript more times than I can count from my nearly indecipherable handwriting and made extremely helpful editorial suggestions. Theresa organized the interaction of research, fact-checking, publisher's and author's schedules with extraordinary efficiency and unflagging good cheer. Gratitude is also due to Suzanne McFarlane, who had to shoulder additional tasks to ensure the smooth operation of my office while her colleagues were working on this book.

I have imposed on other associates who had served with me in government and on friends familiar with particular subject matter to check my account against their recollections and to assist with research.

William Hyland helped organize the mass of material on East-West relations and arms control and made valuable comments on the chapters dealing with these subjects. Mary E. Brownell did much of the research on Cyprus and Latin America and reviewed the Latin American chapters for accuracy. Samuel Halpern assisted on research for the intelligence chapter. Politimi Kelekis, Mollie Megan Smith, and Cathy Snider Buchanan helped with research from unclassified sources.

The following friends and colleagues read parts of the manuscript: Brent Scowcroft, Lawrence Eagleburger, and L. Paul Bremer III (especially on the Nixon legacy and the *Mayaguez* chapter); William D. Rogers (on Latin America); Harold Saunders, Hermann Eilts, and Alfred Atherton, Jr. (on the Middle East); Richard Helms and Samuel Halpern (on intelligence); Stephen Bosworth and Robert Hormats (on energy); Frank Wisner, Walter Cutler, Peggy Dulany, and Faye Wattleton (on Africa); Peter Flanigan, William F. Buckley, Norman Podhoretz, and the late Eric Breindel (on the analysis of Nixon and the debate with the neoconservatives). The comments of all these individuals were extremely constructive, helpful, and much appreciated.

Richard Valeriani, who was a member of the traveling press party, refreshed my memory with anecdotes dealing with my Southern Africa diplomacy.

My wife, Nancy, ever supportive, read most of the manuscript and made many incisive comments.

I want to thank Dr. James H. Billington, the Librarian of Congress, and James H. Hutson, Chief, David Wigdor, Assistant Chief, of the Library's Manuscript Division—home of my official papers—and its staff for efficient and friendly cooperation.

Kenneth G. Hafeli of the Gerald R. Ford Library was extremely helpful with locating official White House photographs. Many of these were taken by David Hume Kennerly, a Pulitzer Prize–winning photojournalist who served President Ford as chief official White House photographer. Others came from a collection of official State Department photographs.

No author could wish for a more supportive and patient publisher than Simon & Schuster. As editor, friend, and adviser, Michael Korda made innumerable wise and subtle suggestions in his inimitable tactful and thoughtful manner. Gypsy da Silva supervised the copyediting, indexing, photographs, and maps with enormous patience and matching efficiency. John Cox as line editor and Fred Chase as copy editor were impeccable. Jim Stoller and Andrew Jakabovics were vigilant proofreaders.

Needless to say, any shortcomings of this volume are my own.

I have dedicated this book to the memory of my mother, Paula Stern Kissinger. She had shared the period of writing with me as she had all other important events of my life and had looked forward to publication with characteristic buoyancy. She passed away, aged ninety-seven, just as the book was going into galleys.

# 1

# A FORD, NOT A LINCOLN

## *The Changing of the Guard*

Gerald Rudolph Ford was an uncomplicated man tapped by destiny for some of the most complicated tasks in the nation's history. The first nonelected President, he was called to heal the nation's wounds after a decade in which the Vietnam War and Watergate had produced the most severe divisions since the Civil War. As different as possible from the driven personalities who typically propel themselves into the highest office, Gerald Ford restored calm and confidence to a nation surfeited with upheavals, overcame a series of international crises, and ushered in a period of renewal for American society.

A year before his inauguration, it would not have occurred to Ford that he was about to be thrust into the presidency. The highest office to which he had ever aspired was that of Speaker of the House of Representatives, and that had appeared out of reach because of the Democratic Party's apparently invulnerable majority in Congress. Ford had, in fact, decided to retire after the next election in November 1974. Suddenly, in October 1973, Richard Nixon appointed him Vice President in the wake of Spiro Agnew's resignation. "I'm a Ford, not a Lincoln," Ford said modestly when he assumed that responsibility on December 6, 1973.

Having never felt obliged to participate in the obsessive calculations of normal presidential candidates, Ford was at peace with himself. To a world concerned lest America's domestic torment impair its indispensable leadership during what was still the height of the Cold War, he provided a sense of restored purpose. On his own people, Ford's matter-of-fact serenity bestowed the precious gift of enabling the generations that followed to remain blissfully unaware of how close to disaster their country had come in a decade of tearing itself apart.

The ever-accelerating pace of history threatens to consume memory. Even those of us who experienced firsthand the disintegration of the Nixon Administration find ourselves struggling to reconstruct the sense of despair that suffused the collapsing presidency and the sinking feeling evoked by seemingly endless revelations of misconduct, by the passionate hostility of the media, and by the open warfare between the executive and legislative branches of our government.

In my dual role of National Security Adviser and Secretary of State, my constant nightmare as Watergate accelerated was that, sooner or later, some foreign adversary might be tempted to test what remained of Nixon's authority and discover that the emperor had no clothes. Probably the greatest service rendered by the Nixon Administration in those strange and turbulent final months was to have prevented any such overt challenge. For even as it approached dissolution, the Nixon Administration managed to navigate the Arab-Israeli War of 1973, diminish the Soviet position in the Middle East by sponsoring two disengagement agreements, and conduct successfully a complicated triangular diplomacy with Moscow and Beijing.

The disintegration of executive authority in the democratic superpower did not lead to a collapse of our international position as any standard textbook on world politics would have predicted, partly because the sheer magnitude of the disintegration of presidential authority was unimaginable to friend and adversary alike. Together with the prestige Nixon had accumulated over five years of foreign policy successes, we were able to sustain what came close to a policy of bluff. In October 1973 at the end of the Middle East War, it even saw us through an alert of our military forces, including of the nuclear arsenal. But with every passing month, the sleight of hand grew more difficult. We were living on borrowed time.

As the impeachment proceedings gathered momentum, Nixon's personal conduct began to mirror his political decline. He kept fully abreast of the various foreign policy issues and at no point failed to make the key decisions. But, as time went on, Watergate absorbed more and more of Nixon's intellectual and emotional capital. As day-to-day business became trivialized by the increasingly apparent inevitability of his downfall, I felt enormous sympathy for this tormented man whose suffering was compounded by his knowledge that his tragedy was largely self-inflicted. Yet by early July 1974, I, like the other few survivors of Nixon's entourage, was so drained by the emotional roller coaster that I was half hoping for some merciful end to it all.

The brutal process of attrition seemed both endless and incapable of being ended. Even when, on July 24, the Supreme Court ordered the White House tapes to be turned over to the special prosecutor, I was so inured to daily crises that I doubted anything conclusive would emerge. On July 25, I escorted the new German Foreign Minister Hans-Dietrich Genscher to the summer White House at San Clemente for a meeting with the President. After an hour with a ravaged-looking Richard Nixon the next day, Genscher asked the question tormenting me as well: "How long can this go on?"

On July 31, Al Haig, then Nixon's chief of staff, requested an urgent meeting during which he informed me that one of the tapes the Supreme Court had ordered to be turned over to the special prosecutor was indeed the long-sought "smoking gun"—the conclusive proof of Nixon's participation in the cover-up. Haig would not divulge the contents.

Even at the edge of the precipice, the surreal aspect of Watergate continued. The White House decided to release the tape on August 5 in order to be able to put its own "spin" on it. The day before, my friend Diane Sawyer—at the time, assistant to Nixon's press secretary, Ron Ziegler, and now a national television personality—came to my office to check some public relations detail on an unrelated foreign policy matter. She had not heard the tape, she said, but she was beginning to believe that a climax would never come and that we were doomed to bleed to death slowly. "As likely as not," she said, "the tape will be drowned out by the background noise."

Clever, beautiful Diane turned out to be wrong. On the tape, Nixon was clearly heard instructing his chief of staff, H. R. "Bob" Haldeman, to use the CIA to thwart an FBI investigation into the Watergate burglary. This proof of an attempted obstruction of justice provided the catharsis for the Watergate affair. I have elsewhere described in detail the outburst that followed its release—the Cabinet revolt, the decision of senior Republicans to abandon the President, and my meetings with Nixon, including the melancholy encounter in the Lincoln Sitting Room on his next-to-last night in the White House —all of it culminating in Nixon's decision forty-eight hours later to resign, effective at noon on August 9.[1] In these pages, I will confine myself to my interaction with the President-to-Be, Gerald R. Ford.

On the morning of the tape's release, Nixon telephoned with a bizarre request: would I call the Vice President and ask him to invite key southern members of Congress to a briefing by me on foreign policy? Nixon did not explain his purpose, but obviously he thought it might persuade these representatives to vote against impeachment.

I had first met Gerald Ford some ten years before when, as a Harvard professor, I invited him to address a seminar on defense policy I was conducting under the joint auspices of the Harvard Law School and the Graduate School of Public Administration (now the John F. Kennedy School of Government). Ford discussed congressional control of the defense budget, a subject he knew well from his service as the ranking Republican on the Defense Subcommittee of the House Committee on Appropriations. Although (and perhaps because) his presentation was delivered in the unassuming style of Grand Rapids rather than the convoluted jargon of the academic world, he left an extremely favorable impression on students who, in the prevailing atmosphere of the incipient anti-Vietnam protest, were anything but benevolently disposed toward advocates of a strong defense.

After I became Nixon's National Security Adviser, Ford, in his capacity as Minority Leader of the House of Representatives, attended occasional White House briefings. His interventions were sensible, supportive, and good-humored. For the eight months of his vice presidency, Ford conducted himself with dignity and loyalty to the President. He remained aloof from Watergate controversies and displayed no designs on the highest office. Roughly once a month, I would brief him about major foreign policy developments. General Brent Scowcroft, then my deputy, saw him more frequently. Ford would limit himself to asking clarifying questions—the appropriate course of conduct for a Vice President, who, since he has no clear-cut area of responsibility, should make any suggestions he may have directly to the President and not to a subordinate.

I have never asked Ford what went through his mind when I called him on that fateful morning of August 5 with Nixon's request that he invite the southern congressmen to a foreign policy briefing. And he has never volunteered a comment. By then, we now know, a small group to advise him on the inevitable transition had already been formed. Did he think I was trying to bring myself to his attention? Did he believe Nixon was seeking to embarrass him? Whatever he may have thought, Ford played it straight. He would do what the President asked, he said, but—demonstrating that he had seen through Nixon's stratagem—he added that it would have little influence on the impeachment vote (which I had not mentioned). Matters had gone too far; foreign policy issues would not affect the decision of the House of Representatives.

The tape having been released, Ford took the unprecedented step on August 6 of dissociating from the President at a Cabinet meeting. He would no longer defend the President's position on Watergate, he said, and indeed he would not have done so in the past had he known what was on the tape. Publicly he would maintain silence on the matter on the ground that he was a "party in interest"—pointedly reminding everyone that he was next in line for Nixon's office. But Ford stressed that even though he was dissociating from the President, he would continue to support Nixon's policies:

> Everyone here recognizes the difficult position I'm in. No one regrets more than I do this whole tragic episode. I have deep personal sympathy for you, Mr. President, and your fine family. But I wish to emphasize that had I known what has been disclosed in reference to Watergate in the last twenty-four hours, I would not have made a number of the statements I made either as Minority Leader or as Vice President. I came to a decision yesterday and you may be aware that I informed the press that because of commitments to Congress and the public, I'll have no further comment on the issue because I'm a party in interest. I'm sure there will be impeachment in the House. I can't predict the Senate outcome. I will make no comment concerning this. You have given us the finest foreign policy this country has ever had. A super job, and the people appreciate it. Let me assure you that I expect to continue to support the Administration's foreign policy and the fight against inflation.[2]

I did not speak with Ford at that meeting or, indeed, until Nixon had decided to resign. It was now certain that Ford would become President. In that turbulent week of Nixon's resignation, I had no time to speculate on how it would affect my own position. Before I could address the subject, Ford took the decision out of my hands by telephoning me on the morning of August 8 after Nixon had informed him of his plans to resign. Ford asked me to come to see him and, in his unassuming way, left the time up to me. In the course of the same conversation, he asked me to stay on and in a way that made it sound as if I would be doing him a favor by agreeing. The conversation went as follows:

FORD: Good morning.

KISSINGER: Mr. Vice President.

FORD: How are you, Henry?

KISSINGER: Fine.

FORD: I just finished talking with the President, and he gave me his decision, and we spent about an hour and twenty minutes over there. During the course of the conversation, he indicated that you were the only one in the Cabinet with whom he had shared his decision.

KISSINGER: That is right.

FORD: I would hope we could get together sometime this afternoon at your convenience. I have no plans other than to start getting ready.

KISSINGER: Would 3:00 suit you, Mr. Vice President?

FORD: That would be fine, Henry. I would appreciate it very much and whatever your schedule is—mine is totally flexible.

KISSINGER: After the President talked to me yesterday, I prepared some tentative suggestions for your consideration. Might I bring those along?

FORD: Absolutely.

KISSINGER: They are things that need to be done in the next two days.

FORD: I will be delighted to see you and bring anything along that you want, Henry.

KISSINGER: Right. One other technical thing. Can we say to the press that I am coming over to see you, or had you rather announce that? It is not particularly necessary. We can just avoid it altogether.

FORD: I see no reason why you can't say that you are coming over to see me. I see no harm in that.

KISSINGER: We would not say anything else.

FORD: I think it important actually that it be announced— so announce it, Henry.

KISSINGER: I think from the foreign policy point of view it
would have a calming effect.

FORD: Why don't you state it or have it released and in any
way that you think would be helpful? Don't hesitate to
embellish it.

KISSINGER: I think the best thing, if you agree, is to say
you have called me, and you have asked me to come to
see you, and I am coming to see you at 3:00.

FORD: Very good, Henry.

KISSINGER: I pray for you, and you know the whole world
depends on you, Mr. Vice President.

FORD: I know that, Henry, and I will talk to you more about
it. As I have inferred in our previous conversations, I
really want you to stay and stand with me in these
difficult times.

KISSINGER: You can count on me, Mr. Vice President. We
will have a chance to talk about it.

FORD: I wanted to get that in now so there is no doubt
about it.

KISSINGER: I am very, very appreciative of your thought-
fulness in mentioning it.

FORD: We will see you at 3:00 then.

Dramatic events are not always ushered in by dramatic dialogue.
As I reread this conversation from the perspective of two decades, I am
struck by its matter-of-fact tone and concerns. At the time, I was
affected by the understated way in which Ford conveyed Nixon's decision which would make him President, without rhetorical flourishes
and without mentioning the emotional impact on himself. And I was
moved by his tact in so swiftly putting an end to any personal uncertainty I might be experiencing.

The atmosphere of the conversation carried over into our meeting
that afternoon. It took place in the Vice President's large office in the
Old Executive Office Building, which, before World War II, had been
assigned to the Secretary of the Navy. This gingerbread edifice is physically separated from the White House by a narrow passageway incongruously named West Executive Avenue and much more so by the
nearly unbridgeable chasm of difference in actual power. As a general
rule, the policymakers have offices in the White House; supporting
staffs are installed in the Old Executive Office Building. In that respect,

the location of the Vice President's office accurately reflects his real power.*

In less bureaucratic times—until 1947—the Old Executive Office Building used to house the State Department as well as the Army and Navy Departments earlier. Each of these alone would today overflow its patrician corridors. No building in Washington has offices better calculated to stimulate reflection. The ceilings are high, the proportions vast by contemporary standards. The larger offices have exterior balconies, many with views of the White House lawn.

During my meeting with Ford in the afternoon of August 8, I sat on a sofa near the balcony, Ford on an easy chair with his back to the window. He seemed casual and calm, neither grandiloquent nor pretentiously humble. He opened the conversation by saying that he intended to announce even before he had taken the oath of office—in fact, that very evening—that I would be staying. Ford added that he had felt comfortable with me ever since our first meeting at Harvard. Artlessly, he added that he felt confident we would "get along." I replied that it was my job to get along with him, not the other way around.

With this, we turned to the practical problems of the transition. To avoid confusion abroad, it was important to establish a sense of continuity in our foreign policy, at least for an interim period until the new President could determine what changes, if any, he wished to make. To this end, I had brought along a transition plan, the essential feature of which was to put before every government around the world a personal presidential message. In addition, I recommended that the new President meet with all the ambassadors accredited to Washington so that they could report their personal impressions to their governments. These two steps were designed to prevent the various capitals from basing their initial judgments on rumor and speculation. Since it was physically impossible to see each ambassador individually, I proposed that Ford meet them in regional groups, allotting about an hour to each. The first group would be NATO ambassadors, followed by Latin America, the Middle East, Africa, and Southeast Asia. Since the nations of Northeast Asia did not fit any grouping, and since Japan was an indispensable ally and China a key element in our triangular diplomacy, I recommended that their diplomatic representatives be received individually. (Anatoly Dobrynin, the Soviet ambassador, was on home leave; he

---

* Beginning with Walter Mondale under President Carter, Vice Presidents have received an additional office in the West Wing of the White House near the President's office.

would be received as soon as he returned.)[3] Finally, there would be separate meetings with the ambassadors of South Korea and South Vietnam —two countries on behalf of which American blood had been shed. Their ultimate safety depended on making sure that their adversaries understood the new President's commitment to their security.

Ford took some time to look over the various documents. He invited John O. "Jack" Marsh, Jr., a longtime associate whom he was to appoint counselor, to join our meeting. After some desultory discussion, Ford agreed to the draft letters and to the meetings with the ambassadors. He demurred only when I handed him another document listing outstanding commitments, including some sensitive understandings with other governments. One of these had not yet been implemented and was, in fact, somewhat ambiguous. I told Ford that, if he felt uncomfortable with it, I could delay carrying it out: "They will blame me, not you," I said. But passing the buck was not a trait of this President-to-Be: "No, I will make that decision," Ford said.

Perhaps the most lasting impact of that first conversation was its aftermath. For the first time since I came to the White House, I left the presidential presence without afterthoughts, confident that there was no more to the conversation than what I had heard. Nixon was one of the most gifted of American Presidents, prepared to make tough decisions and courageous in doing so. But he needed solitude for such an act. Face-to-face, Nixon was obsessively incapable of overruling an interlocutor or even disagreeing with him, as I shall elaborate in a subsequent chapter. Since one could never be certain that Nixon might not undo what he appeared to have just decided, wariness occasionally verging on paranoia prevailed among his entourage.

With Ford, what one saw was what one got. Starting with that first meeting, I never encountered a hidden agenda. He was sufficiently self-assured to disagree openly, and he did not engage in elaborate maneuvers about who should receive credit. Having been propelled so unexpectedly into an office he revered but never thought he would hold, he felt no need to manipulate his environment. Ford's inner peace was precisely what the nation needed for healing its divisions.

## The New President

The morning of August 9, 1974, witnessed one of the most dramatic moments in American history. At 9:30 in the East Room of the White House, President Nixon bade farewell to his staff, culminating the greatest rupture of the American domestic consensus since the Civil War.[4] At 12:03 that same day, in the same room, Gerald R. Ford was sworn in as the thirty-eighth President of the United States. The seats had been rearranged so that when Ford spoke, he was facing in a different direction than Nixon had, symbolizing a new beginning.

Nixon's parting speech was an elegy of anguish. Usually so disciplined, he talked in a rambling, occasionally disjointed manner about the dreams of his youth, about his mother and family, and about the importance of putting into practice Theodore Roosevelt's injunction never to shirk the political arena. Having devoted so much of his effort to self-control all his life, Nixon seemed impelled to put on display the passions and dreams he had publicly suppressed for so long; he even wore glasses for the first time in public. For a staff drained by the unraveling of the presidency, it was almost too much to have to witness —in this, Nixon's last act as President—such a baring of the inner self of this anguished figure refusing to admit defeat, even as his life's work was in shambles.

When, two and a half hours later, Gerald Ford took the oath of office, he declared calmly and confidently that "our long national nightmare" was over.[5] And his audience, exhausted by struggling for nearly a year and a half against a premonition of catastrophe and by the emotional wringer of Nixon's parting speech, placed its hopes on this unpretentious man from Grand Rapids into whose hands an extraordinary twist of fate had placed America's destiny.

As it happened, I played a conspicuous if technical role in the two resignations that had made Ford's ascent to the presidency possible. At 11:35 A.M., General Haig handed me Nixon's formal resignation addressed to me in my role as Secretary of State in the National Security Adviser's office at the White House. All presidential appointments are countersigned by the Secretary of State and, by the same token, resignations of the President and Vice President are made to the Secretary of State as well. This is a vestige of the days when the Founding Fathers had designed that position to include major domestic functions—somewhat similar to the prime minister in the French Fifth Republic. When the letters of resignation of Spiro Agnew as Vice President on October 10, 1973, and of Richard Nixon as President on August 9, 1974, were formally addressed to me, I achieved what one must hope will remain the permanent record for receiving high-level resignations.

By the time of Agnew's forced resignation, Nixon's original entourage had been decimated, and the remnants were like shipwrecked sailors thrown together on some inaccessible island. In these circumstances, I became privy to the President's ruminations regarding the political choices before him—a subject matter from which I had previously been excluded. He enunciated three criteria affecting his decision on the new Vice President: who would make the best President, who would be easiest to confirm without provoking further Watergate problems, and who would provide the least incentive for the advocates of impeachment to do away with Nixon.

Of the potential candidates, Nixon considered former Texas Governor and Secretary of the Treasury John B. Connally by far the best qualified for the presidency, with New York Governor Nelson A. Rockefeller a close second in ability though not in terms of his attractiveness to Nixon. Connally, of whose brash self-confidence Nixon stood in awe and the only person about whom I never heard Nixon make a denigrating comment, would surely have been his first choice had he not been the subject of an investigation (which ultimately led to his indictment). Still confident of surviving Watergate, Nixon wanted to make sure that, despite Connally's obvious handicap, the ultimate vice presidential choice would not blight Connally's prospects for the 1976 Republican presidential nomination—by which time the latter's legal troubles would presumably be behind him.

Nixon's strong feelings about Connally would have been sufficient to eliminate Rockefeller's prospects even if Nixon could have brought himself to appoint the political adversary of a lifetime. Rockefeller's fatal handicap in Nixon's eyes—at least the one Nixon stressed to me as Nelson's lifelong friend—was that Rockefeller's nomination would utterly divide the Republican Party. (Nixon was to say later that he had also considered Ronald Reagan but had rejected him because he could not be confirmed. If so, he never mentioned it to me.)

Through this process of elimination, Gerald Ford emerged as Nixon's choice. He would prove easy to confirm and be, in Nixon's words, an "adequate" Vice President. In addition to being acceptable to Congress, Ford carried another benefit in Nixon's eyes: his lack of experience on the executive level would give Congress pause in any plan to impeach Nixon. On several occasions, the President mused that Congress would not dare to assume responsibility for replacing him with a man who had so little background in international affairs.

As it turned out, the choice of Vice President had no impact on Nixon's impeachment for, by then, Watergate had gathered its own momentum. Ford was nominated on October 13, 1973, and easily confirmed. And his elevation to President ten months later was welcomed with universal relief.

When Ford took the oath of office, no one—not even the new President—could know whether he would be equal to the monumental task bequeathed to him. Without any executive experience, he assumed the presidency at a moment as desperate as our nation has known outside of wartime. Lacking a popular mandate and in the wake of the traumas of Vietnam and Watergate, Ford was handed the responsibility for his country's renewal. And Providence smiled on Americans when—seemingly by happenstance—it brought forward a President who embodied our nation's deepest and simplest values.

In no other country are personal relations so effortless as in small-town America; nowhere else is there to be found the same generosity of spirit and absence of malice. The quintessential product of this environment, Gerald Ford performed his task of overcoming America's divisions and redeeming its faith so undramatically and with such absence of histrionics that his achievements have so far been taken far too much for granted. Only very recently have some journalists who used to mock him begun to reevaluate his period in office.[6]

To a great extent, this neglect was because Ford bore so little resemblance to the prototype of the political leader of the Television Age. The media and many of his colleagues were at a loss when it came to fitting him into the familiar stereotypes. The modern presidential candidate ends up making a kind of Faustian bargain: a full-scale national primary campaign costs a minimum of $15 million for television and print media advertising. But the money must be raised within strict limits defined by law. To remain credible, a candidate feels obliged to devote most of his energies for the better part of three years to accumulating a war chest from fragmented and disparate constituencies. In that process, his principal incentive—approaching an imperative—is to try to be all things to all people. What starts as a tactic, over the course of the grueling campaign easily and imperceptibly turns into a defining characteristic. National recognition is achieved at the price of nearly compulsive personal insecurity.

The age of the computer and of television has compounded this insecurity. When the visual image replaced the written word as the principal means of understanding the world, the process of learning was transformed from an active to a passive mode, from a participatory act to assimilating predigested data. One learns from books via concepts that relate apparently disparate events to each other and require analytical effort and training. By contrast, pictures teach passively; they evoke impressions which require no act by the viewer, emphasize the mood of the moment, and leave little room for either deductive reasoning or the imagination. Concepts are permanent; impressions are fleeting and in part accidental.

The new technology has fundamentally altered the way in which the modern political candidate perceives his role. The great statesmen of the past saw themselves as heroes who took on the burden of their societies' painful journey from the familiar to the as yet unknown. The modern politician is less interested in being a hero than a superstar. Heroes walk alone; stars derive their status from approbation. Heroes are defined by inner values, stars by consensus. When a candidate's views are forged in focus groups and ratified by television anchorpersons, insecurity and superficiality become congenital. Radicalism replaces liberalism, and populism masquerades as conservatism.

A curious blend of brittleness and flamboyance thus defines the modern political persona: brittleness verging on obsequiousness in the quest for mass approval, flamboyance turning into panic when the public's mood shifts. Far more concerned with what to say than with what to think, the modern political leader too frequently fails to fulfill the role for which he is needed most: to provide the emotional ballast when experience is being challenged by ever-accelerating change. The inability to fulfill these emotional needs lies behind the curious paradox of contemporary democracy: never have political leaders been more abject in trying to determine the public's preferences, yet, in most democracies, respect for the political class has never been lower.

In the United States, the dividing line between the new and old style of politics coincides roughly with the advent of the Kennedy Administration. A young and untested Senator achieved the presidency by eloquence and by his capacity to exploit the still novel medium of television. John F. Kennedy's presidency was too brief to require him to choose between heroism and stardom, or even to be conscious of the choice. Kennedy was able to practice both modes, unintentionally mortgaging the tenure of his immediate successors who fell prey to the illusion that no choice needed to be made.

Lyndon Johnson, well grounded in traditional politics, tore himself apart in his quest for the kind of adulation Kennedy had evoked but which was destined to be beyond reach for a President of Johnson's generation. Immortalized by his untimely death, Kennedy, for his admirers, served as the embodiment of dreams turned legacy. Johnson's vain attempt to play the same role lured him into craving approbation from those who would never accept him.

The case of Nixon proved even more stark. No modern president was more solitary, more studious, or spent so much of his time alone, reading or outlining options on his ubiquitous yellow legal pads. If ever there was a man from out of the age of books, it was Richard M. Nixon. He understood foreign policy better than almost any other practicing political figure of his era. And yet, as the tapes of his conversations and the blizzard of notes emanating from his office are made public, it will become apparent that he spent an exorbitant amount of his time in the hopeless quest to elicit the adulation of those he identified as the Eastern Establishment, of which—in his mind—Kennedy had been the superstar.

Nixon's convictions, while firm and—in foreign policy—carefully thought out, did not seem able to sustain him unless they resonated not just with public acclaim but with the approval of the classes he admired and despised at the same time. His actions were in the mold of heroes, but Nixon doomed them by a frantic quest for stardom shading into efforts to vindicate his perception of the ruthlessness of his rivals.

Gerald Ford was about as different as possible from what has become the familiar political persona. Having risen through the ranks of his party in the House of Representatives—a career dependent on day-to-day practical relations with his peers—Ford was immune to the modern politician's chameleon-like search for ever-new identities and to the emotional roller coaster this search exacts. Far too unassuming to think of himself as heroic, Ford would have been embarrassed had anyone suggested that Providence had imposed on him just such a role.

Cartoonists had great fun with Ford's occasionally fractured syntax. They forgot—if they were ever aware—that being articulate is not the same as having analytical skill, which Ford had in abundance. For a national leader, courage and devotion to principle are, in any case, the more important qualities.

Ford was well aware of his relative lack of suavity and, unlike the modern political leader, was not embarrassed to admit it. "I am not one of those oratorical geniuses," he said to me on the telephone on January 15, 1975. "There is no point in my trying to be one. I just have to be myself." A week later, he returned to the subject after a press conference in which he thought he could have done better (a view I did not share). Unlike most political leaders of the Television Age, Ford blamed himself, not the media:

> I came away feeling myself it could have been a lot better. . . . I get mad as hell, but I don't show it, when I don't do as well as I think I should. . . . If you don't strive for the best, you never make it.

Ford was always himself, and he always did his best; in the process, he saved the cohesion and dignity of his country.

## The Domestic Crisis

During the Watergate period, I sometimes indulged in a fantasy about its end, much as a parched voyager crossing a desert imagines the bliss of a beckoning oasis. For me, it was a moment when international crises would end or at least moderate, and domestic controversy would be replaced by a new national consensus. But as happens occasionally to the desert wanderer, these visions turned into a mirage.

The irony of Ford's presidency was that however much he might dedicate himself to the renewal of his society, the patterns of confrontation that had evolved over a decade could not be eliminated overnight. Indeed, it sometimes seemed as if the United States had become addicted to crises and could not do without the periodic fix of some discovery or investigation. The media had been geared to uncovering large-scale malfeasance; that, at least, is where fame beckoned. And Congress was more concerned with inhibiting executive discretion than with nonpartisan national security policy, or else it identified the two.

In this atmosphere, Ford was never vouchsafed the honeymoon traditionally set aside for new Presidents. From his first day in office, he had to face in several directions at once. International crises have their own momentum, only marginally influenced in the short term by domestic politics. If anything, the attention of the world, momentarily deflected by the drama unfolding in Washington, returned to normalcy and that, in practice, signaled an intensification of foreign challenges.

On Cyprus a precarious cease-fire between Greeks and Turks

achieved in the last days of the Nixon administration collapsed on the fourth day of Ford's presidency and threatened to escalate at any moment into military conflict between two indispensable NATO allies. In the very week of Ford's inauguration, the foreign ministers of Egypt, Saudi Arabia, and Syria, and Jordan's King Hussein were preparing to come to Washington to begin exploring the next phase of the Middle East peace process. Their visits could not be delayed because their counterparts from Israel and Jordan had already been received by Nixon in the weeks before the change in the presidency, and postponement would have fueled accusations of deliberate foot-dragging.

On other fronts, the American delegation negotiating strategic arms control with the Soviets required new instructions. Ratification of a trade agreement with the Soviet Union was awaiting the resolution of the conflict between the executive branch and Congress about whether Most Favored Nation status for the Soviet Union should be conditional on the easing of emigration regulations for Soviet Jews.

In addition, other more important—if less urgent—issues were waiting for the new President. Perhaps the most fateful challenge to the industrial democracies was their collective demoralization due to the quadrupling of energy prices. Only concerted action could avoid financial panic and political deterioration in Western Europe, and the time had come to begin the process of taking charge of our common future. Sub-Cabinet officials of the industrial democracies were meeting even then to establish an International Energy Agency to enable the countries they represented to conserve energy, share supplies in an emergency, and create a financial safety net if the oil producers should seek to use their huge petrodollar surpluses to pressure the consumers of oil.

Beyond these tactical issues, the conduct of foreign policy in the Ford presidency became especially complex due to a legacy Nixon was wont to call a "new structure of peace." The Cold War was, of course, still in full swing, and the Soviet Union continued to loom as a major threat, menacing in its nuclear potential, maintaining its ideological pretensions, and capable of taking advantage of the domestic divisions of its superpower rival.

The Nixon Administration had systematically sought to change the context of the Cold War. This was not because we had become blind to Soviet ideology; rather we had concluded that the Soviets' ideological reach was collapsing. In two generations of Communist history, no Communist Party had ever won a free election. The only allies of the Soviet Union were in Eastern Europe, and they were being held in line by what amounted to Soviet military occupation. Once our opening to China was completed, the Soviet Union faced a coalition of all the industrial nations in the world in tacit alliance with the most populous nation. Sooner or later this equation would work in favor of the democracies, provided they could contain Soviet adventures by deterrence and give the Soviets a chance to reduce confrontation by opportunities for cooperation.

No new President since Harry S Truman inherited quite the same gamut of foreign policy challenges in his first few weeks in office, and none since Lincoln in so uncongenial a domestic environment. Almost all the contending forces in the United States found it difficult to disenthrall themselves from the internal battles of the past decade. Especially the veterans of the Vietnam protest movement, committed to the proposition that foreign policy was a morality play in which the United States was assigned the role of villain, were nostalgic for the struggles which had been the seminal experience of their lives.

No other society has so conceived itself to be the product of a uniquely moral vision as America's. Freed by geography from the necessities of geopolitics as well as from its temptations, the United States has been permeated by the conviction that political issues— especially with respect to foreign policy—could be equated with choices between good and evil. Americans have always perceived their society as in pursuit of perfection in world affairs, rewarded when it fulfills this promise, punished when it falls short. Wilsonianism distilled this conviction into the unprecedented theory that wars are caused not so much by struggles for power as that these struggles reflect domestic moral failings, specifically the degree to which a society falls short of the democratic ideal. In a world of democracies, conflicts would be settled by international law. Alliances would be based on the principle of collective security, which bases defense less on the balance of power than on a coalition of the righteous against the lawless. All these assumptions were being ground down in the stark mountains and lush rice paddies of Vietnam.

In terms of its historic traditions and its values, the United States had entered Indochina for highly moral reasons: the conviction that democratic institutions, being universally applicable, could be transplanted successfully to half of a divided country eight thousand miles away in the midst of a murderous civil war and that the principles which had restored Europe would prove equally applicable to the fledgling politics of Southeast Asia.[7] As these hopes turned into illusions, the American leading classes tore themselves apart. Critics attacked not so much errors of judgment as the validity of American experience. They blamed the mounting frustrations on the failure of the entire political system and on ethical flaws in need of being expurgated root and branch.

So it happened that a majority of the Old Establishment—the men and women who had set the direction and tone for American foreign policy for a generation—came to insist on the defeat of their own country in order to purify it. In the 1920s, isolationism had turned the United States inward in the widespread belief that the country was too ethical to expose itself to the imperfections of the world at large. In the course and aftermath of the Vietnam War, isolationism took the form of the proposition that we were too depraved to participate in international politics.

As liberals veered into pacifism, radicalism, and protest, conservatives turned into crusaders. They had heretofore supported the containment policy on traditional American grounds: as a means of transforming the Soviet system to democracy. As containment was collapsing in Southeast Asia, some conservatives were spurred by the national humiliation into an attack not on the protest movement but on the administration the protesters were assaulting and paralyzing. Interpreting the looming defeat as a symbol of America's ideological retreat, they blamed the foreign policy establishment for inadequate moral vigilance and, once the war was safely over, urged a determined assault (at least of the rhetorical kind) on Communism itself and a deliberate policy of confrontation with the Soviet Union.

Traditional conservatives were reinforced by new recruits from the opposite side of the barricades. Rejecting the protest movement's turn toward radicalism, some eminent liberals joined their erstwhile adversaries in the conservative camp. Self-styled "neoconservatives," these were primarily intellectuals who injected into the debate an element of ideological passion well exercised from their previous sectarian battles on the left. They had been on the opposite side of the Vietnam debate and hence gave no credit to Nixon for exertions on behalf of an honorable extrication. Nor had they any experience with the fragility of our domestic consensus, which, in fact, they had done so much to weaken. Hence they felt less restrained to urge new crusades than those of us who, battle-scarred by Vietnam and Watergate, sought to stabilize the environment and restore confidence before courting major new confrontations.

Caught in the maelstrom of these conflicting currents, the new Ford Administration found itself a target of criticism from all sides. The reaction to Vietnam and Watergate had polarized the country. Liberals wanted the United States to withdraw from the world and tend to our domestic improvement; conservatives began to clamor for an ideological crusade. In the eyes of the liberals, America's international involvements went too far; for conservatives, the United States was not assertive enough. That debate continued throughout the Ford Administration and underlay most of the confrontations with Congress. It has, in various incarnations, continued to this day.

## Ford and Congress

Normally a Vice President acceding to office can count on the support of his own party. But by the time Ford took the oath of office, the Republican Party had first been divided by Vietnam and then demoralized by Watergate. The same was true to a considerable extent on the Democratic side. That Ford had been appointed rather than elected as Vice President and that he would have to stand for reelection within twenty-seven months of coming to office imposed a straitjacket never before faced by a new President. That many in both parties expected him to be defeated in that election was a further blow to presidential authority.

The pressures were compounded because Ford, though shaped by his experiences in Congress and dedicated to close executive-congressional relations, came into office while these relations were undergoing a revolutionary change. In that sense, it was the Ford Administration which paid the ultimate price for Watergate.

In November 1972, Nixon had prevailed with the second-largest landslide in American history in a national election fought on philosophical issues as clearly drawn as any in this century. Neither George McGovern nor Nixon was a charismatic personality. But their substantive disagreements could not have been more explicit: Nixon's strong foreign policy protecting the existing dividing lines in the Cold War against McGovern's neopacifism and distrust of American power; Nixon's moderate conservatism affirming traditional American values against McGovern's tacit endorsement of the lifestyles and ethos of the radical protest movement. Nixon won that de facto referendum by 61 percent of the popular vote.

Within less than a year, Watergate had wiped out the results of that election. It amounted to a revolution no less sweeping for having been made possible by presidential misconduct. Three months after Ford's inauguration, a McGovernite majority representing views over-whelmingly rejected by the American people two years earlier was returned to Congress. This was due far less to a change in the public's fundamental views than to its outraged reaction to Watergate.

The result was a serious decline in relations between the legislative and executive branches. Heretofore chairmen of the Senate and House committees had been the balance wheel between the branches of the government. But the McGovernite upheaval weakened the seniority system and hence the authority of the committee chairmen. This forced the executive branch into direct negotiations with individual Senators and Congressmen. Legislative staffs grew in both size and influence. As the range and magnitude of congressional intervention in foreign policy increased, the capacity of the individual Senator and, even more, of the individual Congressman to keep himself informed diminished. The role of staff advisers was magnified—a fact which special interest groups quickly recognized and exploited.

A significant proportion of the new staffers had been recruited from the executive branch, where, for one reason or another, they had failed to fulfill their ambitions. From the safe haven of Capitol Hill, they were able to second-guess the administration on an ad hoc basis, free of the constraints of a sense of continuity and of long-term foreign policy perspective that are inseparable from high-level policymaking. The executive branch thus found itself in endless negotiations, both internally and with congressional staffs seeking to influence the most minute tactical detail of policy.

Paradoxically, Congress felt more free to challenge Ford than it had Nixon. For a while, Watergate had constrained congressional chal-lenges to foreign policy because some of Nixon's critics feared being deflected from their quarry by the charge of weakening national secu-rity. More importantly, Congress was restrained during the later part of Watergate by genuine patriotism—a sense of responsibility lest the national tragedy tempt foreign adversaries to foment a major crisis.

Nixon's resignation seemed to still these concerns. A collective mania for ever more sweeping investigations descended over Congress, of which the intelligence investigations were the most sensational, exposing every covert operation in which the United States had en-gaged during a period of over twenty years. These consumed an exor-bitant amount of time of the top officials of the Ford Administration in servicing the committees and in agreeing on how to deal with classified documents.

In this new atmosphere, Congress felt more free to legislate specific policies than it ever had before. However virulent congressional opposition had been to the Vietnam War, Congress had confined its critique to "sense of the Congress" resolutions, which are not obligatory. But in the twenty-nine months of the Ford Administration, Congress legislated an arms embargo on Turkey, cut off aid to Cambodia and eviscerated it for Vietnam, and legislated a prohibition against any military role in Angola. The micromanagement went so far that, at one point, Congress voted antiaircraft missiles for Jordan only on the condition that they be in fixed positions. (The refusal of wheels was more humiliating than meaningful because, as King Hussein pointed out at the time, it was an easy matter to acquire such wheels in the markets of the Arab world.)

## Ford and the National Interest

Ford reacted to the seemingly inexhaustible volume of challenges without either self-pity or doubt about the good faith of his political adversaries. Liberal critics were urging confrontations on human rights, and neoconservatives were celebrating their recent conversion by urging a new, nonelected President to precipitate a series of showdowns with the Soviet Union at a moment when Soviet policy was still relatively restrained and Congress was gutting the defense budget.

Ford viewed his role not unlike that of a doctor ministering to a patient just recovering from a debilitating illness. He therefore resisted demands for exhausting posturing and prescribed a regimen of building and conserving strength. He judged the patient's challenge to be in the nature of a marathon race, and he would not allow him to dissipate his strength in a series of sprints designed for the gallery. And he was reinforced in this attitude because Congress had just legislated cuts in the 1974 defense budget, necessitating a reduction of ready Air Force wings and causing a deterioration of naval readiness. The Army had been cut by five divisions from its peak in the Vietnam period.

Ford thought it essential to prove to the American people that crisis and confrontation were a last resort, not an everyday means of conducting foreign policy. Both of us were convinced that we stood to win the marathon for which we were girding. With its creaky economy, the Soviet Union would, in the end, not be able to compete with a coalition we were assembling of all the industrial democracies cooperating with China, the world's most populous country. And that is essentially what happened.

Dedicated to the proposition that his presidency should be a time of healing (as he would entitle his memoirs),[8] Ford displayed personal goodwill to friend and foe alike. At times, I thought his apparent equanimity excessive, especially when his reluctance to impose penalties made resistance to presidential authority appear free of risk. In retrospect, I have come to appreciate Ford's self-restraint, for it gradually drained the American political system of its accumulated poison and created the conditions for the restoration of faith in American institutions. In the end, societies thrive not on the victories of factions but on their reconciliations.

That Ford had courage and leadership ability was demonstrated by a series of actions during the first month of his presidency. On his second day in office, Secretary of Defense James Schlesinger and I called on him for a decision that could not be delayed. In the far reaches of the northern Pacific, a Soviet submarine had sunk at a depth of sixteen thousand feet several years earlier. In pursuit of an intelligence coup, the CIA had commissioned the building of the *Glomar Explorer*, which presented itself to the world as an oceanic research vessel but was in fact equipped with a device that lowered steel claws to the ocean floor, capable of lifting the submarine into the ship's body. The *Glomar Explorer* was in place and all set to lift the submarine on the day Ford took the oath of office. A Soviet trawler was hovering nearby, raising a number of issues: Did the new President want to risk relations with the Soviet Union for the sake of an intelligence coup? Was there a danger that the trawler would interfere with the operation, inviting a clash though the *Glomar Explorer* was undefended? Ford asked how long the Soviet trawler had been there. When told that it had been on station for weeks, he ordered the salvage to begin because, he argued, conditions would be no more propitious a week later. Unfortunately, on raising the submarine, one claw broke, and part of the submarine was lost.

That Ford would march to his own drummer and not to the advice of his experts became evident five days after his inauguration when the Soviet ambassador, Anatoly Dobrynin—having hurriedly returned from home leave—presented himself at the Oval Office. To the amazement of both State Department experts and the NSC staff, Ford used the occasion to ask for the release of a Soviet seaman (from Lithuania, then a Soviet republic). Four years earlier, the sailor had sought asylum on an American Coast Guard vessel, the commander of which had inexplicably ordered him returned by force to the Soviet ship. The result of this bureaucratic bungle was that the unfortunate refugee was being held in a Soviet jail.

Ford's request was entirely unscripted. There was not the remotest legal basis for urging the release of a Soviet citizen being held in a Soviet prison. Fortunately for the seaman and the cause of human rights, Ford's goodwill coincided with the Soviet desire for a favorable start to its relationship with the new President. The request was granted, and the seaman found himself miraculously transported from a Soviet prison to an American haven.

Of greater long-range significance was Ford's handling of Nixon's pardon. Nixon seemed nearly certain to be indicted by the special prosecutor—a painful prospect for the United States and for the fallen President. Such a spectacle would have been gravely damaging to America's standing in the world. And those of us who knew Nixon felt certain that he would never get through a trial or even an indictment without grave physical and psychological repercussions. Yet given the risks a pardon posed for Ford, it was a tricky subject to initiate with the new President, particularly for me as one of Nixon's close associates. I finally overcame my hesitations when, in the second week of Ford's presidency, Bryce Harlow called on me to express his own deep concern.

Harlow had been President Eisenhower's assistant for congressional relations and served briefly in the same capacity in the Nixon White House—until he ran afoul of Bob Haldeman. His wisdom, charm, and intelligence had made Harlow one of the most respected figures in the permanent Washington Establishment. He had often advised me on how to navigate the shoals of high-level politics. Now Harlow argued that putting Nixon on trial would further divide the American people and probably compound the emotional disintegration of a President who, with all his faults, had rendered distinguished service for the country.

The conversation with Harlow gave me the pretext to raise the subject with Ford. I passed on Harlow's views and endorsed them. In response to Ford's questions about the psychological impact of a trial on Nixon, I argued that equally important was the impact on the world, where the former President was highly respected. Ford mentioned that some of his advisers thought he should wait until an indict-ment was actually handed down. I replied that I could not judge the domestic situation, but delay would surely complicate both the international impact and Nixon's personal despair.

Ford made no further comment, and I did not hear from him again on the subject until the afternoon of Saturday, September 7, 1974, when he telephoned to inform me of his decision to pardon Nixon the following morning. The time had come, Ford said, to lay the past to rest and, in a spirit of Christian forgiveness, to permit Nixon to live out the remainder of his days in dignity. Ford did not invite my com-ments. Though the decision probably cost him his own election to the presidency, I am convinced that it was a courageous and humane act which was necessary if the nation was ever to be liberated from the traumas of the previous decade.

This unflinching sense of the national interest enabled Ford in his twenty-nine months in office to navigate his country through a series of crises which could have filled a two-term presidency. He kept the ethnic conflict in Cyprus and a similar one in Lebanon from escalating into international war. He managed the collapse of Indochina with dignity and restraint and successfully used military power to free an American ship, the *Mayaguez*, captured by the murderous Cambodian Khmer Rouge. Ford achieved major progress on strategic arms control with the Soviet leaders in Vladivostok in 1974 and a breakthrough in the Middle East peace process when Israel and Egypt signed the Sinai interim agreement of 1975. Over passionate opposition, he concluded the Final Act of the European Security Conference, widely credited today with contributing to the collapse of the Soviet empire. Ford urged the American initiative to bring majority rule to southern Africa and supported a diplomacy which led to its ultimate success. And he originated a program of cooperation on energy among the industrial democracies which has lasted to this writing and has become institu-tionalized in the economic summits which have become key compo-nents of the contemporary international order.

Other Presidents were to receive the credit for winning the Cold War. But I am certain the time will come when it is recognized that the Cold War could not have been won had not Gerald Ford, at a tragic period of America's history, been there to keep us from losing it.

# PART ONE

# THE NIXON
# LEGACY

# 2

# THE MAN AND
# THE ORGANIZATION

## *At the Edge of Greatness*

On Nixon's forlorn next-to-last evening in the White House, he
and I were together in the Lincoln Sitting Room, reflecting on his
place in history. "History," I said, "will treat you more kindly than
your contemporaries." Nixon was characteristically skeptical: "It depends who writes the history."

It is difficult to write about Richard Nixon, who combined intelligence, patriotism, and courage with self-destructive flaws as in a Greek
tragedy. The hatred he evoked in his political opponents was extraordinary even by the turbulent standards of American democracy. I served
as his principal adviser on foreign policy for five and a half years and,
when we were both in town, often saw him several times a day. Yet, to
some extent, I still remain mystified by the personality of the perhaps
most complex President of the twentieth century.

One of the questions posterity will surely ask is what it was about
Nixon that caused passions to run quite so deep. Was it because almost
everything one could say about Richard Nixon was both true and yet
somehow wrong? He was politically astute and highly intelligent yet
prone to self-destructive acts; exceptionally analytical yet done in by
yielding to ill-considered impulse; deeply patriotic yet wont to hazard
his achievements on tawdry practices; possessed of a considerable capacity to feel guilt coupled with an instinct to gravitate toward actions
guaranteed to evoke these very feelings; an outstanding judge of people
except of those whose actions could affect his own interests; successful

in the gregarious profession of politics although introverted, almost reclusive.

Nobody who dealt with Nixon regularly has ever doubted that here was a man capable of imposing his will on circumstances. But he could not handle face-to-face disagreements and would go to extraordinary lengths to achieve his aims by indirection. Nixon aspired to greatness and came close to it, at least in the conduct of foreign policy. Yet he ruined his presidency by acts as unnecessary as they were unworthy.

It would take a poet of Shakespearean dimension to do justice to the extraordinary, maddening, visionary, and debilitating personality of Richard Nixon—at once thoughtful and quirky, compassionate and insensitive; sometimes fiercely loyal, at other times leaving in his wake the casualties of abandoned old associates. Yet ultimately Nixon's obvious and unending struggle with himself proved so unsettling, even threatening, because deep down one could never be certain that what one found so disturbing in Nixon might not also be a reflection of some suppressed flaw within oneself.

I will always be deeply grateful to Richard Nixon for giving me the opportunity to serve the country which rescued my family from Nazi tyranny. He appointed me as his assistant for national security affairs even though all my previous political activities had been on behalf of Nelson A. Rockefeller, his principal rival for over a decade. Rare is the modern President who entered office under such brutally inauspicious circumstances—asked to end a war in which his predecessors had involved our country without a strategy for either victory or extrication, and which, now out of office, too many of them in apparent quest of expiation seemed determined that the United States should simply abandon without regard for those who had staked their lives on our word.

Inevitably our personal relationship exhibited the ambivalences Nixon inspired in his entourage. Nixon, who treated acquaintances with wary aloofness and even close associates as foils, provided few emotional footholds. His oblique, indirect method of government and his tendency to foment conflicts among his subordinates could be nerve-racking. Occasionally I would relieve the tension with exasperated comments. For his part, Nixon resented the publicity I attracted, starting with the secret trip to China on which he sent me in 1971. Presidents do not take kindly to assistants who compete with them for public attention—especially when some of Nixon's closest advisers were arguing that I was upstaging him deliberately. While the word "deliberately" was inaccurate, it is certainly true that I did not exactly resist the media's favors.

Nevertheless, and despite some mutual misgivings, Nixon and I worked extremely well together. Face-to-face, he always treated me with conspicuous courtesy. Though we were not emotionally close, I was touched by his vulnerability and often moved by his inner torments, as in the period just prior to his resignation (when I might well have been as close to Nixon as anyone, except his immediate family, ever got) or on the last evening of his China trip when, on a veranda in Shanghai, Nixon mused about his hopes for a peaceful world.[1]

I genuinely admired Nixon's contribution to America's foreign policy. The endless speculation about which of us contributed to what specific aspect of it misses the point. Whatever my advice, it was Nixon who made the final decisions, Nixon who, in 1971, assumed responsibility for sending me secretly to China and who would have borne the brunt of failure, and again Nixon who, in 1972, assumed the risks of responding to Hanoi's offensive by blockading North Vietnam, an ally of the Soviet Union, two weeks before a summit scheduled for Moscow and six months before a presidential election.

Nixon could have greatly eased his presidency by simply abandoning our allies in Indochina and placing the onus for the debacle on the Kennedy and Johnson Administrations; he was surely given incentives to do so when the American architects of the war constantly harassed him to travel the road of unilateral and unconditional extrication, unembarrassed by the fact that, under their aegis, our forces and our casualties were increasing until the very day they left office. Believing such a course to be dishonorable and against the national interest, Nixon played the hand he had been dealt and achieved a settlement the critics had declared unattainable—though it ultimately unraveled through a combination of North Vietnamese implacability and a congressional cutoff of aid to Indochina, as I shall describe in a later chapter. Even while extricating our country from Vietnam, Nixon managed to forge new policies toward China, strategic arms limitations, American-European relations, and the Middle East peace process. Often controversial, these policies in their essence nevertheless set the course for the remainder of the Cold War and beyond.

Nixon's single most important quality was the ability to make bold decisions. That attribute was all the more remarkable because he was not by nature daring and by no means a happy warrior. On the contrary, he made his major decisions with a joylessness verging on despair, as if he was doomed by some malign destiny to have so much anguish brought to naught despite all the meticulous reflection and all the notepads crammed with options.

One of the paradoxes of the Nixon presidency is that the evidence on the tapes pictures him as impulsive, even reckless. But the Nixon with whom I worked on foreign policy reached his major decisions only after almost maddening deliberation. He might act intuitively, but he did not do so impulsively. Every significant foreign policy decision was preceded by weeks of solitary reflection and apparent indecision. Sequestered in his hideaway in the Old Executive Office Building with the curtains drawn, Nixon would work out on a pad of yellow sheets permutations of the options I generally had submitted to him. And since, in any major decision, the pros and cons are closely balanced and unanimity among advisers is rare, he would muse endlessly about how to overrule fractious subordinates. But once he had overcome his premonitions of catastrophe and found someone (usually Bob Haldeman or John Mitchell) to bring the bad news to the overruled associates, Nixon would almost invariably take a big leap.

Afterward Nixon would retire to Camp David for a few days to recover from the ordeal but also to make it that much more difficult for opponents of the decision to reach him. It was hardly the decision-making process recommended in public administration textbooks, and it was emotionally exhausting for all the participants—including, especially, Nixon. But Presidents could do worse than to place on their desks the dictum Nixon would invoke on such occasions: "You pay the same price for doing something halfway as for doing it completely. So you might as well do it completely."

## The President and His Adviser

The French political philosopher Raymond Aron once told me that exaggerating my influence was the American intellectuals' and media's alibi for their animosity toward Nixon. During a period of major accomplishment, Nixon's legion of enemies may well have given me disproportionate credit as a means of depriving the hated President of claims to a lasting legacy. In a strange way, some of Nixon's traditional supporters on the right strengthened the media's message by blaming me for what they considered Nixon's retreat from his original conservative vocation. At the same time, some of Nixon's entourage, in order to garner more credit for their chief—and occasionally Nixon himself—described me as a mere staff assistant, a kind of puppet pulled by strings in the hands of the master manipulator.

Both versions—that of the dominant adviser and that of the domineering President—misstate reality. The breakthroughs of the Nixon Administration were due to the fact that both Nixon and I subordinated our reservations to close collaboration based on mutual respect. The Quaker's son from Yorba Linda and the son of a secondary school teacher in Bavaria complemented each other's qualities in a special way. Nixon had the best personal acquaintance with contemporary leaders around the world of any American political figure I have met. Foreign policy was his hobby, and he deepened his understanding of it by frequent travel. I had a better knowledge of history and of the conceptual side of geopolitics. Nixon operated by flashes of insight to which he clung with remarkable persistence. My forte was to translate general goals into long-range strategies—a task for which Nixon lacked the requisite patience.

Nixon had an instinct for the jugular. With respect to several key decisions, though I came to view their necessity somewhat before he did, once Nixon decided to act, he went frequently beyond my recommendations. In 1970, after the North Vietnamese forces stationed in Cambodia broke out of their base areas and threatened to take over the entire country, Nixon and I were studying ways to neutralize the North Vietnamese offensive in Cambodia and prevent the whole country from being turned into a vast base area aimed at South Vietnam. I recommended an assault on Parrot's Beak, the Communist base area closest to Saigon; after hesitating for nearly a month, Nixon opted for attacking every base area along the Vietnamese-Cambodian border. In 1972, when we were discussing resuming the bombing of the Hanoi-Haiphong area to break the deadlock in the Vietnam peace talks, I recommended the established method by fighter planes; Nixon ordered the use of B-52s (I was not opposed to B-52s in principle; their use simply had not occurred to me). In 1973, when I tried to organize the Pentagon's civilian reserve air fleet for an airlift to Israel, Nixon overcame Pentagon foot-dragging by ordering a military airlift and using the giant C-5 planes. In each case, Nixon's decision was vindicated by events.

Nixon was less hands-on with respect to diplomacy. He took an intense interest in strategy, but the give-and-take of diplomacy, the slow advance by accumulating nuances, made him restless. Nixon would carefully go over the various negotiating options, and he would skim the detailed reports of the actual negotiations. He would make insightful comments, especially on the memoranda outlining strategy. But the version of some spinmeisters of an eagle-eyed President spotting drafting flaws in evolving negotiations is nonsense.

In the end, the cooperation between the President and the National Security Adviser worked not just because we complemented each other's strengths (and perhaps reinforced each other's weaknesses with respect to our sensitivity to criticism and proclivity for sudden diplomatic coups) but above all because Nixon and I viewed international relations from a nearly identical perspective. Both of us believed that we were in trouble in Vietnam because our predecessors had launched the United States into an enterprise in a distant region for worthy causes but without adequately assessing the national interest and the likely cost. In a more complex world—of a China returned to international affairs, a resurgent Europe, a more flexible Soviet Union—the United States needed a long-term strategy that would avoid the congenital oscillation between overextension and abdication. America's historic idealism had to be leavened with an assessment of national interest, and our approach to international relations had to move from episodic interventions to a strategic design which took account of the requirement of equilibrium. This was then—and probably still is at this writing—a minority view in a society which, never having experienced national tragedy, identifies the quest for peace with the missionary vocation of the spreading of its own domestic values around the world.

## Nixon and the Establishment

In the folklore of his enemies, Nixon was portrayed as an obsessive anti-Communist and as a standard-bearer of right-wing conservatism. This was far from his own perception. Privately Nixon placed himself in a position well within Establishment orthodoxy. Having been closely associated with both Richard Nixon and Nelson Rockefeller, the latter beloved of the Establishment, I found no significant difference in their approach to foreign policy—only in their personalities and in their respective attitudes toward the Establishment. In the course of one of his rambling discourses with me in 1970, Nixon argued that there were only three possible directions for American foreign policy: the conservative, whose dominant personality was Ronald Reagan; the liberal, whose most attractive representative was Hubert Humphrey; and the moderate, which he believed he himself embodied. The conservative policy, Nixon argued, would be belligerent without being effective and, being intellectually too "thin," would risk the support of American public opinion as well as that of our allies. The liberal position would "sell us out" and run the risk of war imposed by a frustrated right once the American public realized that the United States was losing ground. The American people, Nixon insisted, were not "losers" and would demand a strong, even violent, reaction to military defeats or even diplomatic setbacks. The moderate foreign policy for which he stood, Nixon averred, was "the only bulwark for international stability." Rockefeller would have endorsed nearly every word of that statement. (Nixon turned out to be wrong in his assessment of Reagan, though perhaps not of the dominant conservative trend. At the time he made that statement, the neoconservative intellectual wing did not yet exist.)

Unlike Rockefeller, however, Nixon did not consider himself a member of the Establishment (although, in the case of Rockefeller, these ties were more a matter of entitlement than of any emotional linkage). As for Nixon, he felt ignored, even ostracized, by the elite before and throughout his period in office. He ascribed this rejection to his vocal anti-Communism of the 1950s and to his having brought down that epitome of the Eastern aristocracy, Alger Hiss. Reacting with bitter resentment, Nixon's conversation was suffused with outrage at the hypocrisy and implacable hostility of what he summed up with the epithet "Georgetown cocktail set" and the Council on Foreign Relations. The Establishment was the "enemy," and enemies should be "kicked in the groin."

If one deduced from Nixon's disdainful, belligerent, and occasionally spiteful comments about the Establishment that here was a President on a crusade to destroy it, one would have been far off the mark. Behaving more like the rejected lover than a sworn enemy, Nixon was eager to be admitted into the club, not to destroy it. His ambivalent reverence for the Establishment came to expression when Harvard students occupied the university's administrative center, University Hall. Nixon told me that he was happy it had happened at Harvard. At first I thought he was gloating at the discomfiture of his enemies. In fact, he had something else in mind: "Harvard is the leading university in the country. It will set an example for how to handle student upheavals." Nixon was incredulous when I told him that, in my view, no one would know after two days who had done what to whom. At the conclusion of the first volume of my memoirs, I wrote: "What would have happened had the Establishment about which he [Nixon] was so ambivalent shown him some love? Would he have withdrawn deeper into the wilderness of his resentments, or would an act of grace have liberated him?"[2]

Nixon's inveterate enemies have much to answer for; from the first, they never gave him the benefit of any doubt. And within less than a year of Nixon's taking the oath of office, the people he considered the elite of the country were organizing—or acquiescing in—massive demonstrations that paralyzed Washington with nary a word of understanding for the besieged President who was, after all, trying to deal with dilemmas they had left him.

Nevertheless, the President is the symbol of national unity. This imposes an obligation to rise above the level of adversaries pursuing some special interest and to submerge the day-to-day battles in some more embracing national purpose. While in office, Nixon never managed any such act of grace.

As an erstwhile refugee who was for decades self-conscious about my German accent, I had some understanding of Nixon's fear of rejection. The difference between us was in the way each of us dealt with this concern. Nixon tried to preempt rejection by assuming a posture of hostility. But I did not consider the intellectual Establishment as some strange, unapproachable enemy. It was part of a world I knew well and from which I had emerged into prominence. This was why, throughout my government career, I sought to stay in touch with the academic world. During the various protest marches in Washington, college students and their faculties converged on parks and other public places such as Lafayette Square to the north of the White House or the Ellipse to the south of it. I would send staff members out to invite student and faculty leaders to my office for a dialogue, and rarely did a week pass—especially in my first two years in office—without some visit from one faculty or student group or another.

Ironically, the quest for dialogue achieved, if anything, the opposite of its intended purpose. For it laid the groundwork for a permanent misunderstanding between me and the intellectual community—especially the part of it represented by the Harvard faculty. At first, the academic community interpreted my eagerness to exchange views as a sign of sympathy for its point of view and as proof that I was being overruled by a bellicose, unbalanced President. When it gradually realized that I was basically on Nixon's side, many liberal intellectuals began to treat me as an opportunistic traitor to their cause.

So it happened that, by the end of the Nixon Administration, the President and I found ourselves being harassed by what had originally been our normal constituencies. Liberals accused me of abandoning them in quest of power; conservatives thought that Nixon had been seduced by visions of Establishment legitimacy.

In this atmosphere, the extrication from Vietnam took on the character of a civil war. Nixon had inherited the war in Southeast Asia. Over 540,000 American troops had been sent to a part of the world as geographically and culturally remote from the United States as it is possible to be on this globe. When Nixon took office, their numbers were still being increased according to a schedule established in the Johnson Administration. We found no plans for withdrawal nor a White House—approved negotiating strategy.

We were nevertheless prepared to assume the responsibility for extricating the United States from this debacle and never blamed our predecessors for the mess. We would not, however, leave the country for which nearly forty thousand Americans had already died by turning over to Communist rule tens of millions who had staked their lives on our word. But that for four years remained the ineradicable North Vietnamese precondition to any cease-fire.

Yet as soon as they left office, the very people who had saddled Nixon with these tragic dilemmas either acted as if they were innocent bystanders or, more frequently, began harassing the Nixon Administration for failing to achieve in four months what they had never endeavored to accomplish in four years. High officials of the Johnson Administration participated in protest demonstrations as if the obstacle to peace was the White House rather than the intransigence of the North Vietnamese—something they, better than anyone, should have known to be the underlying cause of the deadlock. Within a year, they were pressing us for concessions never even hinted at while they were in office. In 1968, the Democratic convention split over the so-called Peace Platform and fought out this division in the streets of Chicago. By the fall of 1969, Nixon had accepted and offered the key elements of this platform. Yet that was the time of the most massive antiwar demonstrations.[3]

The irony is that the self-righteous demonstrators were, in effect, arguing expediency in the form of peace for us at any price. They demanded an end to their own personal anguish over the war and would brook no policy short of unconditional withdrawal—which we believed was risking the lives of the American troops amidst seven hundred thousand Communist forces and nearly a million armed South Vietnamese unlikely to be tolerant of being abandoned. Nixon simply could not understand how the favored of our society could embrace defeat with such insouciance or urge with so much passion the abandonment of millions to whom we had given our word. He withdrew unilaterally 150,000 troops a year. By the end of his first term, he had withdrawn over 500,000 troops and reduced casualties from 14,600 in 1968 to 300 in 1972 while keeping South Vietnam independent. Yet Nixon was accused of "killing Americans needlessly," motivated by some inexplicable blood lust.

Nixon interpreted these attacks as the Establishment's permanent vendetta against him. What he (and I) did not understand was that the radical protest movement was not an arm of the Establishment. Rather, the radicals considered the traditional liberal Establishment as their ultimate enemy, were bent on extirpating it and with their tactics succeeded in intimidating it into acquiescence. Besieged, Nixon reacted with grandiloquently inflammatory statements against what was, in fact, a cowering Establishment.

Strangely enough, while talking blood feud, Nixon held the touching belief that the civil war conditions were the result of some historic misunderstanding which I—a Harvard professor, a member of the Council on Foreign Relations, and a friend of Nelson Rockefeller— might somehow help to overcome. In pursuit of that mirage, a flood of presidential missives descended on my office with instructions to brief the press or Establishment leaders and, at the same time, to punish recalcitrants. Punishment usually consisted of instructions that I refuse to receive specific journalists, even though they were the same ones who, on alternate days, I was being urged to court. These tasks fell to me not because of some special faith in my skill in dealing with the media—I had, in fact, never held a press conference before being appointed National Security Adviser. It was an expression of Nixon's belief that the elite's hostility was due, above all, to class prejudice which I, with my assumed Establishment ties, might help ameliorate.

The defining moment for both sides came with the disclosure of the Pentagon Papers in June 1971. The event has achieved a nearly liturgical status and is still invoked at many ceremonial events as a classic demonstration of heroic journalism defying an oppressive government. One hesitates to challenge well-established orthodoxy, but Nixon's side of the story deserves expression.

When seven thousand pages of highly classified documents appear in the pages of leading newspapers, it is far from axiomatic that the President's only obligation should be to the First Amendment to the exclusion of other basic American principles—especially in wartime when several hundred thousand Americans were still at risk. Presidential concern became—in Nixon's eyes (and mine)—a duty because the publication of the Pentagon Papers occurred at a moment when preparations were under way for my secret trip to China, and confidential talks were taking place in Paris to end the war in Vietnam. Both of these extremely delicate enterprises stood to be jeopardized by a demonstration that the American executive authority was declining and that Washington's ability to maintain confidential discussions was falling into doubt.

That Nixon's primary concern was to protect the national interest as he saw it is emphasized by an almost never mentioned fact: not one page of the Pentagon Papers was embarrassing to Nixon or to his administration; every last one of them came from the files of Nixon's predecessors, especially the Kennedy and Johnson Administrations.

I first learned of the disclosures from the Sunday *New York Times* of June 13, 1971, while I was on the West Coast. Because all the documents were from Defense Department files, I assumed that the leaks had been instigated by someone in the Defense Department to embarrass our predecessors in government. I called Al Haig, then my deputy, and asked him to warn Secretary of Defense Melvin Laird against letting his people use official documents for political ends; continuity would be lost by such tactics. Haig asked me how many documents I thought were involved. When I guessed the number to be around twenty, Haig replied: "How would at least seven thousand grab you?" Soon afterward, the perpetrators of the hemorrhage identified themselves.

A cynical President could have publicly deplored the publication while using it to demonstrate the extent of the mess he had inherited. But when the issue was national security, Nixon was not cynical. The sadness is that, instead of fighting for the principle, he turned a valid case into yet another skirmish in his vendetta with the media. Going into civil court to argue for an injunction against publication was unwise and futile, but it was neither unethical nor dishonorable. There is no excuse, however, for the extralegal methods employed against Daniel Ellsberg, who had leaked the documents, especially for the break-in into the office of his psychiatrist. Nor were discussions of such acts (as revealed in the tapes) as breaking into the Brookings Institution, where a set of the documents was believed to be kept, compatible with the dignity and moral stature of the presidency—no matter that they were never carried out.

The breach was never healed while Nixon was in the Oval Office. Not until a decade later would a defeated and disgraced Nixon avow his refusal to wither in exile by reemerging from San Clemente and, by the end of his life, reaching a kind of armistice with his erstwhile tormentors. He did so by dint of thoughtful public commentaries and private meetings with the Washington foreign policy community. Did Nixon earn something close to the status of elder statesman because, defeated, he was no longer a threat? Or did Nixon's overtures—for he clearly took the first step—finally liberate both sides from their obsessions?

Whatever the answers, in death, Nixon contributed to a healing never vouchsafed during his contentious career. Amazingly, in light of the disgrace that had befallen him, Nixon's funeral in April 1994 turned into a national occasion attended by all the surviving former Presidents, and the incumbent President Bill Clinton, a former Vietnam protester, delivered a moving eulogy.

## Nixon the Person

In the mythology of his traducers—and of some film portraits—Richard Nixon was a man given to histrionics, to shouting his prejudices at cowed subordinates, and to dominating his environment by conveying his views with great, even overpowering insistence—frequently under the influence of alcohol. Nothing could be further from the real Richard Nixon—at least the Richard Nixon with whom I dealt.

For example, the portrayals of Nixon drinking himself into incoherence with a bottle ever at his side are simply absurd. In my experience, Nixon never took any liquor during working hours or in the Oval Office. Only his closest associates ever saw him drink in any context. The trouble was that Nixon could not hold even a small quantity of alcohol. Two glasses of wine were quite enough to make him boisterous, just one more to grow bellicose or sentimental with slurred speech. Alcohol had a way of destroying the defenses he had so carefully constructed to enable him to succeed in a profession based on a conviviality unnatural to him. These episodes occurred rarely, always at night and almost never in the context of major decisions. The few of us who actually witnessed such conduct never acted on what he might have said; we felt we owed the President another chance to consider whatever the issue was.

The Richard Nixon with whom I worked on a daily basis for five and a half years was generally soft-spoken, withdrawn, and quite shy. When talking to me or to George Shultz, he rarely, if ever, used the graphic language that proved so startling in the transcripts of his conversations with the political side of the White House. Nixon was capable of dominating a conversation only by conducting a monologue, never in a genuine dialogue. To passive admirers or people who sought his views, Nixon could appear overpowering and confident. But Nixon abhorred face-to-face disagreements of any kind. In his many conversations with me, he would ask many perceptive questions. And he would frequently make very astute observations. He was quite capable of changing his mind upon reflecting on a counterargument. But these were separate events. I cannot remember—nor have I encountered in my records—any real dialogue in which we argued clashing points of view.

The way differences between us were handled was that I would register more or less passively some comment of Nixon's. Sometime later, I would revert to the same point without ascribing it to him and state my contrary view. After yet another interval, Nixon would either reaffirm his original position or change it without acknowledging the disagreement between us.

Since this was a method involving a considerable risk of misunderstanding, I conducted most of the major policy discussions with Nixon and almost every presentation of options by memorandum. Relieved of the presence of the interlocutor, Nixon felt no inhibitions about reading contrary views. And he felt free to state his response crisply and to issue unambiguous orders. Future historians removed from the passions of the moment will find a study of these voluminous memoranda far more rewarding than the dialogues on the tapes.

The reason for Nixon's diffidence in face-to-face encounters was the opposite of arrogance: it was a reflection of his abiding fear of being rejected. Others more knowledgeable about Nixon's early years may be better able to explain this handicap—for such it was—in a man of such intelligence and possessed of extraordinary powers of persuasion. Or the even greater anomaly that Nixon seemed more paralyzed by the prospect of rejection than by its actuality. Once the worst had, in fact, occurred and the dreaded (and half-anticipated) debacle had finally taken place, Nixon displayed extraordinary fortitude, willpower, and resilience. His book, *Six Crises,* a staple of his private conversation, recounts some of these disasters overcome, though many more lay ahead.[4] After losing to John F. Kennedy in 1960 and after the California voters had rebuffed his bid for governor in 1962, Nixon came back to be elected President in 1968. Then, after resigning from the presidency, he returned from exile in San Clemente and reestablished himself as a serious participant in the national dialogue (unlike Spiro Agnew, who, after his resignation, dropped out of sight).

To spare himself face-to-face controversies as much as possible, Nixon avoided office appointments wherever possible unless they were carefully orchestrated set-piece encounters. Those of us in the inner circle faced no more daunting task than to persuade Nixon to meet some individual he did not already know or to see someone who might produce an unpleasant situation—that is, anyone whose opinion Nixon did not know in detail beforehand.

The reverse side of this fear of being rejected—its ballast, so to speak—was Nixon's romantic image of himself as a fearless manipulator, marching to his own drummer, unaffected either by turmoil around him or contrary advice on the part of his Cabinet and staff. Sometimes this was indeed the case, but more often Nixon would exhaust his entourage with phone calls seeking reassurance. His quest to receive sole credit for every achievement and to have it perceived as an entirely solitary act explains why Nixon rarely, if ever, had an approving word to say about any of his associates—as *The Haldeman Diaries* demonstrate.[5] Subconsciously at least, Nixon sought to enhance his eminence by denigrating his associates, thereby magnifying his own solitude.

Another aspect of this cult of the "tough guy" was that, in conversations with his entourage, Nixon might generate a series of extravagant propositions that, in his heart, he never expected to be implemented. Some of the more bloodcurdling orders on the tapes released thus far have their origin in this proclivity—as I believe to have been the origin of Watergate itself. Nixon was convinced, and repeated on many occasions, that during the 1960 presidential campaign, his office and airplane had been bugged by the Kennedy camp. And I suspect he felt that his near-certain victory in 1972 would not be complete until he had demonstrated his own ability to play by the same rules as he imagined the admired and feared Kennedy clan to have done.[6]

In foreign policy, these tough-guy orders were much less frequent, though, when they occurred, they could be unsettling (after a few months with Nixon, I was able to distinguish between what he intended to be carried out immediately and what he deserved to be given an opportunity to reconsider). For example, on a Saturday night in August 1969, a TWA plane with Americans aboard was hijacked and flown to Damascus airport. I reported this fact to Nixon, who was in San Clemente with his two friends, Charles "Bebe" Rebozo and Robert Abplanalp. Obviously trying to impress his pals, Nixon issued a curt-sounding order: "Bomb the airport of Damascus." I was certain the order would never survive the night and called Secretary of Defense Mel Laird to tell him what had happened. The two aircraft carriers in the Mediterranean were out of range, and bombing a country is not a simple matter of giving an order; targets have to be selected, a diplomatic scenario prepared, and press guidance developed. So Laird and I decided to carry out the letter of the order by implementing the first steps and leaving the other measures for the morning. Laird ordered the carriers to be moved to the vicinity of Cyprus without conveying the purpose, enabling us to respond truthfully to the hourly presidential inquiries by stating that the carriers were indeed moving into position. Laird has told me that he backed me up by stating in his conversations with the President that no time was being lost, since weather conditions prevented aerial operations.

The next morning, at my regular briefing, I brought Nixon up to date on the events of the previous twenty-four hours, including the fact that the Sixth Fleet carriers were now near Cyprus. "Did anything else happen?" Nixon innocently asked. When I replied in the negative, the President—without moving a facial muscle—said, "Good." I never heard another word about bombing Damascus.

It remained only to close the books on the movement of the carriers, which had surely been noted by Soviet intelligence, and without withdrawing the implied threat. That professionals' professional, Under Secretary of State U. Alexis Johnson, who knew about the movements but not the presidential orders, helped draft guidance for the State and Defense Departments. It read: "Elements of the Sixth

Fleet are continuing essentially the movements which had been planned for them. However, they have been made aware of the fact that tensions have been increased as a result of hijacking. This was done to assure readiness."

The matters that Nixon put forward as orders but in reality made subject to reconsideration did not always reach such a portentous level. For example, in November 1970, Nixon had been the first head of state to announce his attendance at the memorial service for President de Gaulle at Notre Dame cathedral. Because this led to a deluge of other high-level delegations, the French treatment of Nixon in the media and by the government was extraordinarily cordial. Widespread approval is a heady experience for any political leader but was especially so for Nixon. On the flight over, I had convinced the President to overrule Haldeman, who wanted Nixon to return immediately after the memorial service. I had warned that not to attend President Pompidou's reception for heads of delegations would be taken as an affront. Haldeman, perhaps peeved that I had interfered in his scheduling prerogative, had suggested filling the interim with lunch at Maxim's. In high spirits the evening of our arrival in Paris, Nixon reverted to Haldeman's idea. I protested that the French would be outraged if we went from Notre Dame to Maxim's. Nixon, rarely ready to concede to face-to-face disagreements, turned to Ambassador Arthur Watson, and said: "Reserve a table; tell them we won't have any wine. No appeal."

When Nixon said "no appeal," it meant that he was very unsure of himself. Haldeman and Watson left the room to implement the order, and I followed them out. I stressed that lunch in a fashionable restaurant would undo all the good produced by the President's early announcement of his attendance, and the order not to serve wine would only call more attention to the incongruity. Haldeman said, with a smile: "It is now a foreign policy problem," which meant that this fierce enforcer of Nixon's wishes agreed with me but preferred to let me bear the brunt. I told Watson to wait. If all hell broke loose, he would be the victim; if Nixon persisted, I would take responsibility for the delay, and there would still be plenty of time to make the reservation in the morning.

As I was briefing Nixon on the appointed day, he asked what would happen after the memorial service. I suggested that he might want to review the list of heads of state and government attending President Pompidou's reception at the Elysée later in the afternoon. There was a trace of a smile as Nixon said: "That's right."

The veterans of Nixon's entourage generally knew how to interpret or, if need be, to calibrate presidential pronouncements. But newcomers found it difficult going. In 1971, John Scali, a former television reporter fresh from having joined the White House staff as a presidential communications adviser, conveyed what he considered to be a presidential request that I should order Secretary of State William Rogers to attack Senator Edward Kennedy in the media. The mere fact that the order came through Scali told me that its intent had been to impress the messenger rather than that it be carried out. Nixon would not confront Rogers on such an issue and, had he really wanted action, he would have addressed either Haldeman, Mitchell, or John Ehrlichman (who handled domestic issues). The result was the following exchange:

> SCALI: The President is anxious for Rogers to take on Teddy Kennedy.
>
> KISSINGER: Rogers won't do it.
>
> SCALI: Just let me tell you. I talked to him twice; he said he is going to talk to you with the President at 11:45. I understand he will also see you.
>
> KISSINGER: I have gone through this with him a thousand times. He will not do it.
>
> SCALI: I am doing this at the instruction of the President.
>
> KISSINGER: That's a beautiful statement. He will not do it.
>
> SCALI: Well, I hope you will reflect to the Secretary of State the President's strong feeling that he should do it. I know what the President will say.
>
> KISSINGER: No you don't. The President will let him slide off. I will not talk against it, but I am not at all sure by the time he gets through he won't have made it worse.
>
> SCALI: I know how determined the President is that he should do it. . . . He wants it done.
>
> KISSINGER: If you can get the President to order it, it will be done.

The trouble arose when members of the Nixon entourage with less access and therefore less experience with exuberant presidential statements got into the Oval Office. When the full extent of Watergate became apparent in April 1973, I asked permanent elder statesman

Bryce Harlow how it could have happened: "Some damn fool got into the Oval Office and did as he was told," Harlow remarked.

Most Presidents are preoccupied with how history will treat them. For Nixon, it was an extension of his permanent nightmare that, in the end, all his efforts—the self-discipline, the strong decisions wrung from nagging self-doubt—would vanish into thin air, defeated by the hostility of contemporaries and the indifference of historians. At regular intervals, Nixon would send me lengthy memoranda on how to interpret for posterity the various actions in which he had been involved. The purpose of these memoranda was less to affect immediate publicity—they were too complex for that—than to influence the judgment of history by becoming part of the permanent record.

Two such instances dealt with China policy. The first, dated March 9, 1972, covered the drafting of the Shanghai Communiqué, which was issued at the end of Nixon's visit to China in February 1972. In this communiqué, for the first time in the modern (or, for all I know, the entire) history of diplomacy, the two sides stated opposing views on many subjects before enunciating a series of agreements. Nixon's memorandum explained the reasons why he had allegedly chosen this approach. He had been led to the decision to put a moderate American position before the Chinese people, Nixon argued, by his experience when he visited Moscow as Vice President in 1959. Having been given an opportunity to address the Soviet people, Nixon had deliberately chosen a conciliatory tone to create the maximum contrast between the description of the United States by Soviet propagandists and the utterances of the American Vice President. Nixon urged me to read *Six Crises* as well as the Moscow speech to understand his reasoning in choosing the same approach for the Shanghai Communiqué:

> Having gone through that experience I was determined that in this document, which would be the first time Chinese leaders, and cadres, and to a certain extent even Chinese masses, would ever hear the American position expressed, I had to make the strongest possible effort to set it in a tone which would not make it totally incredible when they heard it. It would not have been credible, of couse, had we set forth our position in more aggressive terms because twenty-two years of propaganda at the other extreme would have made it impossible for the reader of the communiqué, or those who heard it read on radio, to believe it at all if the tone was too harsh.

The second memorandum, dated March 14, 1972 is contained in the Notes.[7] Signed by Haldeman but, in language and content, clearly dictated by Nixon, it outlined the qualities the President had displayed in Beijing. Presenting his meetings with Chinese leaders as monumental confrontations, I was asked to detail Nixon's careful preparation, knowledge, humor, debating skill, toughness, abstinence, candor, and stamina.

The fascinating aspect of both memoranda is their recasting of reality into a romantic picture of the President-hero dominating all around him—even though the President had to be aware that I knew better. But I provided only the occasion, not the real target audience, which was posterity. In fact, Nixon had not been involved in the drafting of the Shanghai Communiqué at all. The part to which he referred was drafted in October 1971 during my second visit to China. The chosen format of stating opposing views had not been an American idea but originated with Premier Zhou Enlai as a way to avoid a set of platitudes pretending to nonexistent agreements and in order to highlight whatever genuine agreements were reached. I thought it a brilliant idea and went along with it. My staff and I had drafted the text dealing with the American position; Nixon had approved it upon my return with no significant comment.

As for Nixon's meetings with Mao and Zhou during the China summit in 1972, these were not at all confrontational, consisting of conceptual explanations of each side's positions with respect to the geopolitical situation. They were designed to enable the world's most populous nation and the world's most advanced industrial society to coordinate their international strategy. Nixon conducted the American side of the dialogue thoughtfully, analytically, and eloquently without any notes.

Nixon's achievements, in fact, transcended his version of them. Who drafted what parts of the communiqué was far less important than that Nixon had been the President to open the way to China, knew how to cast the resulting dialogue in geopolitical terms, and had presented the American view of world affairs in a masterful way. (Whether he had displayed stamina, abstinence, and humor in the process would surely be lost in the background noise of history.) History has shown that Nixon had no need for these embellishments, for it has already accorded him his due as one of the most creative American Presidents in the field of foreign policy.

From the perspective of Nixon's place in history, his relationship with me was not without irony. In order to establish White House preeminence and to convey the sense that all decisions were made in the Oval Office rather than in the State Department, Nixon had for years conferred extraordinary authority on me. Confident that he could regulate the public impact of an assistant, he used me frequently as his spokesman on foreign policy strategy on a background basis, which, by the then existent rules, meant that the briefings were ascribed to a White House spokesman. In an extraordinary demonstration of personal confidence, he had asked me to conduct all the major negotiations: with North Vietnam, for the trip to China, for the Moscow summit, and with the various Middle Eastern parties.

Nixon never imagined that his own staff assistant would achieve an independent celebrity, on occasion approaching his own. He did not permit me to be seen on television until my secret trip to China in July 1971 and, up until the end of his first term in October 1972, had insisted that my voice not be heard lest my foreign accent disturb "the good citizens of Peoria" (in his words). On the eve of his reelection, Nixon asked me to respond to Hanoi's leak of the imminent Vietnam settlement.

Suddenly I emerged as a major public figure in my own right. I surely had not planned this; others will have to judge to what extent I encouraged it. But it had to be painful to Nixon to be obliged to share the cover of *Time* magazine's coveted "Man of the Year" issue for 1972 or to see me receive the 1973 Nobel Peace Prize on which he had set his heart. Conscious of this, I appealed repeatedly to Hedley Donovan, then *Time*'s editor-in-chief, to make Nixon the sole "Man of the Year." Donovan ended my entreaties by saying that, if I made one more phone call, he would make *me* sole "Man of the Year."

Some of Nixon's associates retaliated by leaking stories of my alleged emotional instability, or of irresolution in crises, or of having uttered the phrase "peace is at hand" without authorization to gain partial credit for Nixon's electoral victory, and similar derogatory comments suggesting that I was but a tool of the master puppeteer.[8] After he left office, Nixon himself occasionally participated in spreading that myth in his characteristically elliptical manner—usually by volunteering in the course of an interview a disavowal of some purported charge made against me (and about which he had not been asked).

In the perspective of time, if not of the moment, it was both exasperating and understandable. And when all was said and done, these were glancing blows that did not affect our close day-to-day cooperation while in office and our mutual regard on substance afterward. Like others close to Nixon, I was sometimes maddened by his endless maneuvering and his opaqueness. But I was also touched by his demonstration of personal confidence where it mattered and in pursuit of what was, when all was said and done, a serious joint attempt to define and to sustain the national interest in a time of crisis and division.

## The Taping System

No decision of Nixon's contributed more to his ultimate downfall than the installation of a taping system which recorded every word uttered in the Oval Office, in Nixon's hideaway in the Old Executive Office Building, and in the Cabinet Room for almost three years. Unlike a similar system of Lyndon Johnson's that could only be activated if the President pushed a button on his desk, Nixon's was self-activating, meaning that he lost control over what was being recorded. This was because Haldeman considered Nixon not mechanically adept enough to be entrusted with pressing a button unobtrusively.

What makes that decision all the more bizarre is that Johnson had shown Nixon his taping system during the presidential transition and that Nixon had ordered it removed as soon as he took over the Oval Office because he considered it an outrageous invasion of privacy. At the beginning of his term, Nixon would occasionally mention Johnson's taping system as an example of paranoia.

What caused Nixon to change his mind and to install a much more intrusive and less controllable system of his own has never been explained. Since I did not know of its existence until after Haig became chief of staff—that is, some six weeks before the public disclosure—I can only speculate as to Nixon's and Haldeman's motives. Part of the reason surely had to do with the siege mentality which enveloped the White House, especially after the Cambodian crisis in the spring of 1970. The taping system had been installed to show Nixon in masterful control, carefully planning his moves and dominating events, rather than as the bellicose hard-liner of the mythology of his critics. A subsidiary motive may have been to help Nixon write his memoirs.

But verbatim office conversations are the worst way to demonstrate coherence. Even with a less complex personality than Richard Nixon, it would be difficult years after the event to disentangle the sarcastic from the genuine, the tentative from the serious, the fleeting thought from the carefully worked out proposition. That was a particular problem with this master of the oblique and the indirect. In order to survive, those of us working daily with Nixon had become experts at observing his convoluted method of making his points by means of carom shots and at learning to distinguish the ostensible direction of his remarks from their ultimate intent. But years after the events, how well would journalists or researchers be able to make such distinctions or even to understand that they needed to be made?

For his entourage, Nixon's musings or occasional random orders were part of the landscape—background noise, so to speak. They were not treated as guides to action but as expressions of a mood, a way for the President to let off steam. A conversation with Haldeman in the summer of 1972 provides an example of how his closest advisers reacted to presidential instructions. The occasion for it was my request that Haldeman schedule some meeting or other:

> HALDEMAN: You'll have to ask Alex [Butterfield] about that. I'm not allowed to muddy my hands with mundane matters like the schedule.
>
> KISSINGER: Oh, really.
>
> HALDEMAN: I've been ordered to stay out of such things.
>
> KISSINGER: What are you doing?
>
> HALDEMAN: I haven't figured that out yet. I'm trying to understand that part of it. It's something about there's nobody to really run things, and so I've got to stop running things so that I can run things.
>
> KISSINGER: [laughter]
>
> HALDEMAN: At the moment, it's a little abstract, and I'm not quite sure exactly how it all sorts out.
>
> KISSINGER: Well, it sorts out with you doing the schedule.
>
> HALDEMAN: Well, I piled all the schedule stuff on Alex today, and he trudged in, went over it all with the President, and got it all worked out.
>
> KISSINGER: That will last for forty-eight hours.
>
> HALDEMAN: That's what I figured. About that long at best.
>
> KISSINGER: Then he'll scream at you for having inflicted Alex on him.
>
> HALDEMAN: And then I'll say, "But Mr. President—"
>
> KISSINGER: He says, "You don't understand. Now write it down."

HALDEMAN: He says, "I don't care what I said, that's not
what I meant."

To the uninitiated researcher or journalist decades later, the flotsam
and jetsam on tape seem set in concrete, portentous presidential pronouncements, a key to the actions of our thirty-seventh President.
Some of those released sound like appalling invitations to an abuse of
power—even when they were not meant to be carried out. And there
is no excuse for some of Nixon's language or for his various schemes,
even when they were not implemented—as I suspect the vast majority
were not.

The tapes are therefore difficult to assess on at least three levels:
First, the real intent of Nixon is not easy to determine. Is he showing
off? Is he manipulating his interlocutor? Does he want action? Is he
letting off steam in imaginary retaliation against critics? What else was
said on other occasions and by whom? What does the written record
show?

Nixon was at his best in written policy memoranda or when making marginal comments on the written submissions of others. But these
have been overshadowed by the tapes, which—at least those chosen
for publication—show Nixon at his worst: manipulative and grandiloquent all at once.

Second, the tapes bring out the worst in Nixon's interlocutors as
well—as in part they were meant to do. It is easy enough for outsiders
to prescribe heroic resignations when one hears a principle being
violated verbally. But in any White House, there is a court atmosphere nearly inseparable from the sheer power concentrated in the
modern presidency. However draining the assignment, a high-level
presidential assistant knows that he could not be doing anything more
significant and fulfilling. He will therefore be reluctant to jeopardize
this opportunity by debating a point of no practical consequence with
the President—and especially not with one like Nixon who had a way
of reacting neuralgically to face-to-face disagreements.

The compromise was to evade orders incompatible with one's principles but not to argue about Nixon's random monologues outside
one's area of jurisdiction (and even within that area, it was more
prudent to resist via a memorandum or a conversation with Haldeman
or Mitchell than by direct confrontation). In retrospect, this can be
made to appear as obsequiousness, and sometimes it may well have
been, but subjectively it more often represented a balancing of how to
make the best contribution to national policy.

Third, the tapes fail to provide a context. On seminal issues such as Vietnam and Watergate which evolved gradually, many observations made at an earlier stage (say at the beginning of Watergate when its full extent was not yet clear) would not have been repeated later on. For example, in December 1997, more than twenty years after the fact, several journals had great fun with a comment of mine to Nixon in early 1973 to the effect that his foreign policy achievements would be remembered far longer than Watergate. They neglected to mention that the statement was made before John Dean had gone to the prosecutor, before Haldeman and Ehrlichman were forced to resign, and before the full extent of the transgressions had become public. Even so, I still believe that my judgment will stand the test of time, and I repeated it to Nixon long after he had left office and was in no position to do anything for me.

Despite all these qualifications, the tapes do show one very real and unfortunate aspect of the Nixon presidency: the manipulativeness at the heart of the taping system. Since only Nixon and Haldeman and a few technicians knew of its existence, they believed they could arrange tableaus to enhance Nixon's historical record or to provide a basis for shifting blame if things went wrong. In retrospect, I can think of several conversations in which I participated that seem to have had this as their principal purpose. For example, on the day the mining of North Vietnam's harbors was about to take place, Nixon and Haldeman arranged a dialogue in the Executive Office hideaway, the principal objective of which must have been to get me on tape as a strong supporter of what was, in fact, already in train. Since it was too late to affect any decisions, the purpose seems to have been to create a record to counteract any attempt by the media to portray me as the restraining element on a bellicose Nixon or perhaps, in case of failure, to present me as the driving force behind a debacle.[9]

But in the course of a busy day, successful manipulations must have been rare indeed. After Haig told me about the taping system in May 1973 and warned me to be careful, I had a personal experience with this very difficulty. In the course of the six more weeks that the system remained in operation, I noticed no change in what I was saying in my daily contacts with the President. It was simply too strenuous to censor oneself and to worry about how a conversation might appear in retrospect.

Inevitably the outcome of the taping system was diametrically different from what was intended. The designers may have believed that they would someday edit the tapes or their transcripts, perhaps after Nixon had retired. But they overlooked the crucial reality expressed to me by a psychiatrist who had given up taping his patients because he found that "it takes an hour to listen to an hour." In Nixon's case, it would have taken several years to listen to the tapes—a daunting assignment. And even if it were to prove possible, recreating their contexts would have represented a nearly insurmountable hurdle.

One can only guess at the impact of these tapes had they ended up in Nixon's presidential library as he had intended. There some unwary professor or graduate student would have happened onto this mélange of remarks made by courtiers seeking attention, serious policy proposals, and presidential outbursts ranging from the profound to the outrageous. Nixon would then have succeeded in the improbable feat of committing suicide after his death.

Thus the overall effect of the taping system was not only to damage severely Nixon's immediate reputation, it complicated any objective analysis of his presidency. Because the tapes possess so much immediate, almost salacious, interest, they detract from serious consideration of what is far more important for the understanding of the period: the vast number of memoranda that were the real basis for decisions, at least in the foreign policy area. The tapes offer tidbits, but they rarely provide any information as to the context or who else said what about the same subject at a different time or place. They are not easily compared even to statements on the same subject by the person speaking. Ironically, Nixon's obsession with the historical record came close to destroying the ability of historians to render an accurate account of his presidency.

## The Operation of the Nixon White House

That a man with such a complex psychological makeup could for three decades have projected himself into a leadership role in politics and reached the very apex represents a tour de force of willpower for which there are few parallels. Nixon was only able to do so by means of procedures permitting him to skirt his inhibitions and brace himself for the act of governing.

Every White House reflects to some extent the personal traits of the President. But Nixon's were so singular as to require a whole set of unprecedented arrangements that sought to reconcile paradoxically incompatible traits. Nixon was decisive and courageous but nearly obsessively reluctant to settle disagreements face-to-face. Those of us who dealt with him on a daily basis were only too well aware that Nixon was quite capable of undoing some pronouncement he had made to an associate or visitor with another set of comments later to another associate or visitor that augmented his options and prepared a hedge for unexpected setbacks.

Nixon abhorred large meetings, especially those in which he might be asked to arbitrate between conflicting points of view—no matter that this happens to be one of the principal tasks of a President. On the other hand, he wanted to be informed about the nature of the issues before him, and he insisted on having them settled in accordance with his preferences. How to convey orders the President refused to communicate thus turned into an exercise not taught in schools of public administration. It was an assignment that tested the nervous equilibrium of his staff assistants daily.

Nixon solved this conundrum—at least on his end—by installing a system of decision-making that relied heavily on memoranda rather than on face-to-face meetings. And he dealt with personal encounters through three staff assistants: John Ehrlichman, counsel to the President, for domestic policy; me for national security policy; and Bob Haldeman as chief of staff. Wherever possible, Nixon avoided holding meetings with Cabinet members and heads of agencies unless they were primarily informational or one of his assistants—and occasionally Attorney General John Mitchell—had already more or less prenegotiated the outcome. If a Cabinet member refused to play by these rules, he would find access to the President more and more restricted.

This is why one of these assistants (or his representative) was invariably present at presidential meetings, partly as a buffer in case the agreed framework broke down and, even more importantly, to assure that those responsible for the follow-up would know what had actually been said. Nixon's emotional resistance to having to disappoint a supplicant was so great that there was always the danger of being saddled with some unfulfillable promise. (And if Nixon had been alone, an accurate account was hard to come by.) Acquiescence in an interlocutor's point of view—in any case, usually phrased so artfully as to mean less than it implied—frequently ended as soon as the door closed behind the visitor.

Nixon set in motion a fierce competition among his advisers while guarding the mystery of his own ultimate destinations. He was determined that foreign policy be conducted from the Oval Office, but he never said as much to his Secretary of State. He would send me off on secret back-channel negotiations without informing Bill Rogers—and while complaining to Haldeman about the Kissinger-Rogers feud which he himself never ceased stoking. The result was that the State Department would often pursue a course of action that was in direct conflict with what I was doing on behalf of the President and of which the department was unaware. The practical consequence was that the party being overruled blamed the outcome on some malign influence —as time went on, most often on me.

There is no doubt that I had a significant role in first shaping the decisions and then explaining them to the media. But, in the end, nobody could move Nixon in directions contrary to his views or to-ward objectives he had not considered carefully on the yellow pads which served as his surrogates for dialogue. For my part, my work too often left me feeling as if I was sitting in the cab of a train, hurtling toward a collision with another, while the man in the control tower looked on, refusing to throw a switch, expecting one of the conductors to step on the brakes at the last moment.

The atmosphere was summed up in a comment I made in late 1971 to John Osborne, in many ways then the dean of the Washington journalists. In reply to his observation that I was the director of the play (i.e., American foreign policy), I said: "I am either the director of this play or an actor in some other play whose plot they haven't told me yet."

The experience of being permanently in an eerie no-man's-land was so unnerving that I had decided to resign as soon as the Vietnam accords were firmly in place, toward the end of the first year of Nixon's second term. In early 1973, I had started preliminary discussions re-garding a fellowship at All Souls College in Oxford.

Because Nixon's method of governing guaranteed incessant bu-reaucratic competition and disagreements, he was obliged to institute ad hoc procedures for adjudicating controversies. Sometimes he would ask Haldeman—more rarely, John Mitchell—to settle the disputes he both fomented and resented. Or else the contestants would appeal to Haldeman as the associate closest to Nixon. But Haldeman was nei-ther particularly interested in substance nor knowledgeable about for-eign policy; his métier was public relations, and he tended to treat bureaucratic disputes as trifling deviations from the main message, in the process driving the contestants into even greater frenzy.

Nixon's reputation for "trickiness" resulted from his need to balance his abhorrence for direct confrontation against his even stronger inward drive to live up to his foreign policy convictions. Preposterous as this may sound, what passed for trickiness was Nixon's way of being principled.

Still, reconciling the requirements of the bureaucratic machinery with Nixon's personal work habits proved a daunting task which was never completely resolved. It is in the nature of the bureaucracy to generate documents requiring decisions. But many of these decisions —especially arcane, esoteric aspects of arms control—bored Nixon. He preferred to concentrate on the core issues: the ultimate directions of national policy, the social basis of the protest movement, long-range policies toward Europe, China, the Middle East, and the Soviet Union. As a result, one of the many paradoxes surrounding Nixon was that, though a classic workaholic in terms of the sheer time spent in the office, he did not devote much of that time to problems of governance. Nixon tended to work only in spurts; sustained efforts, especially on routine matters, exhausted him physically and made him extremely irritable. He also had no hobbies to occupy his free time.

Spending much of what would normally be considered personal time in his hideaway in the Old Executive Office Building or at Camp David, Nixon would sit in an easy chair, his feet on a hassock, the shades drawn, commenting on conceptual rather than action memoranda and making notes on his yellow pads. To relieve the inner tension, he would call in one of his advisers to go over his notes and/or to recount again and again the battles of his earlier years, from the Alger Hiss case through the California election of 1962. These grinding conversations could go on for hours while the designated listener, frantic over the work and telephone calls piling up back in the office, yearned for some catastrophe to divert the President and permit one to get back to one's regular chores.

A conversation with Haldeman illustrates the dilemma for Nixon's advisers, whose incentives soon became exactly the opposite of the normal assistant's ambition, which is to log the maximum amount of time with the President. Nixon's aides by contrast tried to cut down their time with the President. In the process, they revealed something less creditable about themselves: the degree to which the emotionally exhausting White House atmosphere had robbed them of sensitivity for the obvious and all-encompassing loneliness of their President, who needed them as much to fill the emptiness of his life as for practical advice.

In early June 1972, Haldeman, who had already spent some days at Camp David with Nixon, tried to lure me to go there so that he could have a break:

> HALDEMAN: Are you coming up to glorious Camp David?
>
> KISSINGER: I was afraid—I guess I can't escape it.
>
> HALDEMAN: You want to escape it?
>
> KISSINGER: Well, if I can leave early in the morning, it's all right. . . . What does he have on his mind?
>
> HALDEMAN: I think he just wants to talk.
>
> KISSINGER: Okay, I'll come up.
>
> HALDEMAN: I haven't talked to him today. I wanted to check with you. If it's a real problem for you, I'll see if we can smooth it down.
>
> KISSINGER: But your judgment is that it's better for me to come up?
>
> HALDEMAN: If you can do it without really throwing you into a problem, yeah. . . .
>
> KISSINGER: . . . Do I have dinner with him then or with you or—
>
> HALDEMAN: I think so, yeah.
>
> KISSINGER: The three of us?
>
> HALDEMAN: The two of you.
>
> KISSINGER: No, you join us.
>
> HALDEMAN: No, no . . . I never eat with the big boys.

Though Nixon was generally leery of visitors, he did enjoy foreign guests. Presidential visitors from abroad rarely come to negotiate. Rather they seek reassurance or confirmation of a general course of action. This allowed Nixon to concentrate on presenting our overall strategy or his analysis of a particular situation, both of which he did masterfully. But even in his area of expertise, he would not meet a visitor without meticulous preparation to minimize the prospects of some unwanted or unanticipated direct confrontation.

My staff would prepare detailed memoranda explaining the purpose of the visit, the physical arrangements, what the foreign interlocutor was likely to say, our recommendations for the best response, the optimum outcome, and the dangers to avoid. Nixon would commit to memory either the entire memorandum or the part he thought useful. Since Nixon did not like to admit that he needed any staff assistance in foreign policy—and, indeed, he had an extraordinarily broad knowledge of the field—he never brought the staff memorandum to the meeting. Instead he would hold forth as if extemporaneously, not without sometimes skating as close as he dared—and closer than I sometimes considered wise—to the very subjects our memorandum had warned represented the areas of thinnest ice. Nixon liked to live dangerously and to show off his skill on the high wire.

On one occasion, the arrangement went awry, and it was the vaunted NSC staff system, not Nixon, that misfired. As part of some U.N. celebration, the Prime Minister of Mauritius had been invited to Washington. Mauritius is a subtropical island located in the Indian Ocean off the coast of South Africa. It enjoys plenty of rainfall and a verdant agriculture; its relations with the United States were excellent. Somehow my staff gained the impression that the visitor was from Mauritania, an arid desert state in West Africa which had broken diplomatic relations with us in 1967 as an act of solidarity with its Muslim brethren in the aftermath of the Middle East War.

This misconception produced an extraordinary dialogue. Coming straight to the point, Nixon suggested that the time had come to restore diplomatic relations between the United States and Mauritius. This, he noted, would permit resumption of American aid, and one of its benefits might be assistance in dry farming, in which Nixon maintained the United States had special capabilities. The stunned visitor, who had come on a goodwill mission from a country with, if anything, excessive rainfall, tried to shift to a more promising subject. He inquired whether Nixon was satisfied with the operation of the space tracking station the United States maintained on his island. Now it was Nixon's turn to be discomfited as he set about frantically writing on his yellow pad. Tearing off a page, he handed me a note which read: "Why the hell do we have a space tracking station in a country with which we do not have diplomatic relations?"

## The National Security Council System

When Nixon's eccentricities have been accounted for, they must be balanced against the fact that, in the field of foreign policy, he achieved almost everything he set out to do. In the end, Nixon not only succeeded in recasting much of the foreign policy he found when

entering office but in institutionalizing it in the sense that every succeeding administration, however different its rhetoric, returned to the
main themes of the Nixon strategy—and some version of his NSC
system.

The process was neither as secretive nor as solitary as the caricatures drawn by Nixon's detractors describe it.[10] Side by side with the
somewhat surreal atmosphere in the Nixon White House, there existed
an extraordinarily systematic and wide-ranging National Security
Council process. No administration prepared for negotiations more
meticulously or planned its long-range policies more systematically
than did Richard Nixon's, especially during his first term. Whenever
the research of that history moves from the quest for the odd secret
memorandum or tape to the actual documentation of serious policy
choices, it will discover a sustained effort by the Nixon Administration
to think about America's long-range interests in a way that involved
all the agencies. And negotiations—including secret ones—were, in
the overwhelming number of cases, documented by verbatim records
and long analytical memoranda. Since the advent of the Freedom of
Information Act and of the culture of unrestrained leaking, no succeeding administration has dared to keep such a full record of its
internal deliberations and international negotiations.

Moreover, few if any administrations have gone to comparable
lengths to explain the rationale for their foreign policy to the American
public, the international community, and to Congress. For four consec-
utive years, the NSC staff spent exhausting weeks preparing a summary of the concepts and strategies underlying American foreign
policy. In addition, while in the White House, I gave weekly backgrounders. As Secretary of State, I visited thirty-eight states and made
a major speech on some conceptual problem in each, in addition to
holding press conferences and making television appearances. As Secretary of State, I testified formally and informally before scores of
congressional committees. Anyone reading the annual reports and
major speeches would have before them an accurate and detailed road
map of our foreign policy design.

The trouble was that the material in our annual reports was practically embargoed by the national media, which, in effect, covered only
the part dealing with Vietnam. To a lesser extent, this was also the
case with my "heartland speeches." The charge of Nixon's alleged
secretiveness—which was true with respect to tactics—ignores the vast
educational effort as to strategy, in effect suppressed by the media's

deprecatory attitude toward long-range design and its obsession with crises.

Most of a President's time is taken up by various supplicants: heads of departments pressing their case; foreign leaders urging a course of action or seeking guidance; spokesmen for domestic constituencies advocating their special interests or those of their ethnic groups. These points of view are largely tactical and geared to specific situations. Long-term issues make their way onto the President's agenda only with difficulty and then usually as a result of some interdepartmental controversy. The outcome too often reflects the overriding desire to keep peace in the bureaucracy or with Congress, with conclusions phrased in platitudes that enable the various agencies to interpret them in light of their own initial preferences, thereby starting the cycle all over again.

This is why the conduct of the presidency almost of necessity involves a depletion of intellectual capital. Paradoxically, Nixon's abhorrence of face-to-face meetings enabled his administration to deal with one of the most important challenges of modern government: to husband the President's time—his most precious commodity—so as to give him the opportunity for reflection. Nixon's schedule was carefully managed to allow time for the conceptual problems that interested him and the solution of which represented his greatest strength. The tactics of diplomacy and the details of negotiations bored him. But Nixon made the basic strategic decisions, if not crisply at least in a timely fashion, and prided himself—correctly—on his ability to "get ahead of the power curve."

The Nixon Administration NSC system has been described as growing out of a "coup" during the 1968–69 transition by which Nixon, aided—if not manipulated—by me, centralized power in the White House. The word "coup" is surely inappropriate because, in the American system of government, power is inherently centralized in the White House. And it implies that there existed some accepted procedure inherited by each President. In fact, major foreign policy decisions in each administration have almost invariably been made by the President. Franklin Delano Roosevelt, for example, operated a process at least as centralized as Nixon's and far less systematic.

Nixon's decision-making process operated on two levels: the White House staff system peculiar, indeed idiosyncratic, to him described earlier, and the NSC machinery consisting of the National Security Council and a plethora of supporting interagency subcommittees. The talk about coup comes from defenders of an essentially parochial concern: which department should chair the various subcommittees of the NSC. In the Johnson Administration, the State Department had been in the chair—though, in the absence of NSC meetings, this concerned status rather than substance. Nixon moved the chairmanship into the White House, raising State Department hackles, though no one outside of Foggy Bottom much cared.

The architect of this change was General Andrew Goodpaster, whom Nixon knew and respected from the time he had served as staff secretary of the Eisenhower White House.[11] Nixon asked him to devise a new NSC structure because, on entering office, the President found that the NSC machinery had fallen into disuse; Johnson made his decisions at Tuesday lunches attended only by three or four principals with no sustained preparatory staff work or systematic follow-up. Goodpaster was charged with reviving the NSC system on a basis that produced the widest range of options for the President. Goodpaster argued that, so long as the interdepartmental subgroups were chaired by the State Department, they would never enlist genuine cooperation from the Pentagon and other agencies. He therefore recommended that the National Security Adviser or his deputy chair the interdepartmental subcommittees. Eisenhower strongly endorsed this proposal when Goodpaster and I called on him at Walter Reed Army Hospital in December 1968. Nixon accepted Goodpaster's (and Eisenhower's) recommendations to the extreme dismay of State Department professionals, who blamed me for the loss of an essentially meaningless prerogative (never since regained in any subsequent administration). The best proof of the utility of the Nixon NSC system is that, adjusted to the personality of the incumbent President, it has in its main outlines been preserved by all successor administrations.

The Goodpaster blueprint produced an NSC system meticulous in assembling the options and open in developing its strategy but opaque with respect to implementation. The various departments participated fully and made major contributions to the development of the options. But Nixon reserved for himself the final decision and to act alone if necessary. He treated the formal interdepartmental system in much the same way some senior professors deal with their research assistants. He absorbed the product without necessarily committing himself to the perceptions of his subordinates. For the better part of Nixon's first term—until my secret trip to China—the NSC process concentrated almost exclusively on long-range strategic options.

A network of geographic interdepartmental groups at the assistant secretary level met in the White House Situation Room under my chairmanship to generate option papers for the various regions. These then moved through a Senior Review Group at the deputy secretary level to the formal National Security Council, where Nixon would hear directly the views of his principal Cabinet advisers. Crises were handled on a daily basis by the Washington Special Actions Group (so named for a reason which now escapes me), consisting of the Senior Review Group, augmented by additional military and intelligence specialists. Given Nixon's preference of memoranda over interacting with individuals, he would spend an extraordinary amount of time on these background papers, frequently writing comments in the margins. The Nixon Administration's breakthroughs with China, the Soviet Union, arms control, and in the Middle East would not have been possible without the options produced by this network.

Where criticism of Nixon's decision-making apparatus is valid is with respect to the way it restricted participation in the implementation of decisions. This was due to a combination of the resistance of the bureaucracy to departing from the conventional (liberal) wisdom and Nixon's reluctance to overrule them head-on, as well as his compulsiveness about garnering the sole credit for foreign policy breakthroughs.

The Foreign Service has the best personnel among American public officials—dedicated, well informed, and, if led decisively, highly disciplined. But they start from the conviction that their elected or appointed chiefs could probably not have passed the Foreign Service examination. Hence they consider it their duty to persuade the Secretary and the President to their point of view and, failing that, to maneuver bureaucratically and with the media in such a way that their superior knowledge prevails by indirection. Their convictions are conventionally Wilsonian; diplomacy and power are often treated as discrete realms—and diplomacy as separate from any other area of national policies. Nixon was not wrong in believing that their instinctive reaction was to find him and his approach based on national interest uncongenial.

The supercilious attitude of some State Department officials toward Nixon can be illustrated by the reaction of the deputy chief of mission (DCM) in Tokyo when he heard a rumor to the effect that Nixon, in a conversation with Prime Minister Eisaku Sato in 1969, had hinted that the United States would not object to Japanese acquisition of nuclear weapons. There was not a smidgen of truth to that report; no contemporary document records such an utterance by Nixon either to Japanese leaders or to his associates. Instead of inquiring in Washington as to the accuracy of that report and, on that basis, either refuting the rumor authoritatively or—if accurate—supporting the President's policy or resigning, the DCM took it upon himself to take care of the matter on his own: "We just quietly sabotaged the whole thing."[12] Only the conviction, reminiscent of what the Bourbons felt about the Bonapartes, that Nixon was somehow illegitimate can explain so cavalier an attitude.

The single most important reason why this latent tension was never resolved was the appointment of William P. Rogers as Secretary of State. I say this not to deprecate Rogers's exceptional decency and human qualities nor his abundant common sense. His influence was benign and always moderate. Throughout he behaved with a dignity shaming to those who systematically undercut him. In retrospect, I am not proud of the way I participated in Nixon's deliberate effort to marginalize the man who at the time was considered by most observers to be the President's closest friend.

Nevertheless, it was a major mistake to appoint a close friend to a post which, in the Nixon scheme of things, was bound to be highly subordinate. Given Nixon's determination to dominate foreign policy both in conception and in the public perception—which he had announced in the campaign—he needed a Secretary of State who acted as either a principal negotiator of policies developed at the White House (like Warren Christopher for Clinton) or as the principal spokesman with Congress and the media (as Mel Laird for the Nixon Defense Department). But William Rogers was not sufficiently well versed in foreign policy to assume the first role, and he was too major a figure to confine himself to the second. As a matter of fact, Rogers had never been subordinate to Nixon to that—or, indeed, to any— degree. Quite the contrary, Rogers was the strong personality to whom Nixon had generally turned when he was in trouble and who supplied balance and reassurance during crises in Nixon's life.

This raised a double dilemma: Rogers found it psychologically difficult to play the subsidiary role that Nixon had in mind for him; Nixon found it impossible to insist on it directly. The result was a whole series of stratagems by which Nixon achieved by indirection what he would not bring himself to order personally. Rogers, in turn, took the position that he would carry out without question any direct order—something which his long experience with Nixon must have taught him could not possibly be forthcoming.

In a way, the two old friends were maneuvering against each other without ever coming to grips with the real issues dividing them or even that they were maneuvering. It began during Nixon's first week in office when he excluded Rogers from the greater part of his introductory meeting with Soviet Ambassador Anatoly Dobrynin. It continued on every presidential trip. Nixon would insist that a separate program be set up for the Secretary of State so that he alone, assisted only by the National Security Adviser, conducted the major conversations with his opposite number. As time went on, Nixon drew more and more of the key negotiations into the White House.

Though I surely facilitated these measures, they could hardly have been carried out toward an old friend had they not reflected the President's wishes. Why then did Nixon put Rogers into the one Cabinet post where he would never be granted any real authority and for which he had no real preparation? Had Nixon put his old friend into a position so unsuited to his temperament and background because, for once, he wanted to be the dominating partner and to show Bill Rogers, on whom he had always called when he felt weak, just how strong he really could be? And this perhaps subconscious attitude may well have been given impetus because Nixon occasionally hinted—without elaborating—that when they were both practicing law, Rogers had outmaneuvered him in competing for a client.

Whatever the underlying reason, Nixon found himself with a Secretary of State who was in no position to manage for him the department that Nixon believed to be both ideologically hostile and socially condescending. Rogers had spent his career in the legal profession; he had not dealt with foreign policy in any systematic way. His general view of foreign policy never strayed far from that of the *New York Times* editorial page, which was also close to the dominant opinion in the State Department. He therefore did not have the conviction to impose Nixon's will on his department, but he was also sufficiently unsure about foreign policy to challenge Nixon openly. The result of that strange relationship between the President and his Secretary of State was to unleash all the tendencies of self-will and of liberal bias in the State Department that Nixon had been determined to discipline or to overcome.

Marginalizing the Secretary of State was the worst way of dealing with Nixon's dual purpose of establishing White House preeminence and obtaining State Department support for a new approach to foreign policy. The Foreign Service, sensing the discomfort of the Secretary and explaining its exclusion from decision-making to itself with the myth that its views were somehow being kept from the President, resorted to massive leaks or procrastination—the idea being to give Nixon a second chance to see the light. The President, in turn, interpreted these obstructions as a form of class warfare and as yet another example of the East Coast Establishment's unending battle against him.

As a result of this ever latent conflict, NSC meetings under Nixon had a somewhat theoretical, almost academic, character. The President would verbally navigate between the different positions without tipping his hand, occasionally interjecting a sarcastic comment or philosophical rumination that involved no operational consequences. He almost never issued a directive on the spot, not even in the absence of a dispute or when a decision was urgently needed. Wherever possible —and he was extraordinarily ingenious in making it possible—Nixon would convey his decisions by memorandum from the Oval Office.

Whenever the President felt stymied by departmental self-will or was reluctant to overrule Rogers, he would have recourse to the backchannel—a direct negotiation through White House communications, bypassing regular diplomatic channels and forums. After a while, the backchannel proved so convenient that what had started as a procedure for getting around bureaucratic deadlocks became a way of life. At the same time, the raw material for the negotiations, however secret, invariably grew out of the interdepartmental option papers. Once I became Secretary of State, almost all key positions in the State Department were held by Foreign Service officers, and the backchannel ceased.

A few examples of the backchannel negotiations will show that the impetus for them was not Nixon's failure to consult experts but his indirect method of imposing coherence on departments and experts who were thwarting his policies and whose views he understood only too well.

Secret talks with North Vietnam Politburo member Le Duc Tho had been initiated during the Johnson Administration by Averell Harriman and Cyrus Vance, the official American negotiators at the Paris meetings. Nixon continued these private talks for two reasons. He did not want to have to choose formally among the various negotiating options presented by the interdepartmental process because he was convinced—correctly—that the losing party was likely to leak its position, especially if it was the "softer" option, thereby magnifying his already serious domestic challenges. Nor was the State Department, battle-scarred by years of civil strife, eager to share the opprobrium for an outcome which was bound to be extremely painful and controversial. Even when Le Duc Tho showed up in Paris for his periodic visits, the State Department proposed no initiatives and seemed quite content to let the White House carry the burden of the dialogue.

The negotiations were, in any event, not all that "secret." The State Department, surely in a position to suspect that something was going on when Le Duc Tho sat in Paris, never inquired—a very uncharacteristic posture. Summaries of the negotiations (sometimes quite selective) were sent to David Bruce when he was the head of the delegation in Paris and to Ambassador Ellsworth Bunker in Saigon. The Defense Department supplied the presidential plane flying me to France for weekend negotiations. And, after the event, Secretary of Defense Melvin Laird claimed that he had been familiar with the substance of the negotiations from intelligence sources—a statement which, if accurate, raises the unsettling question why these reports were never sent to the White House or were kept from me there.

By contrast, Nixon pursued the opening to China, from the beginning a key goal of his diplomacy, initially through normal diplomatic channels.[13] In 1954, Beijing and Washington had agreed that Warsaw would serve as their official contact point. But there had been no contact since the Cultural Revolution—the better part of a decade. In 1969, Nixon ordered our ambassador in Warsaw, the extremely competent Walter Stoessel, to initiate talks with the Chinese at the first opportunity—if necessary, by approaching a Chinese diplomat at a diplomatic reception.

After an abortive beginning—during which an unprepared Chinese chargé d'affaires literally ran away from Stoessel's first approach—the Warsaw channel warmed up. When, at an early stage, the Chinese hinted strongly that Beijing would welcome an American emissary, the State Department submitted a long memorandum emphasizing the technical aspects—for example, transportation, communication, and diplomatic status—of such a visit. It also suggested an agenda for the talks embracing such topics as U.N. membership for China, the future of Taiwan, trade and travel restrictions, and arms control—without placing any of these issues in a geopolitical context. The memorandum concluded by proposing that American embassies in Tokyo, Taipei,

Moscow, London, Paris, Ottawa, Rome, Canberra, Wellington, as well as our consulate general in Hong Kong, be authorized to brief their hosts.

The State Department proposal, reflecting the conventional approach, would have aborted our policy before an American emissary could reach Beijing or would have saddled him with so many conditions and second thoughts as to guarantee a stalemate. With dramatic disclosures and a public uproar certain, Nixon sighed: "We'll kill this child before it is born." He was therefore relieved when, as a gesture to protest the American incursions into Cambodia in 1970, Beijing broke off communications via Warsaw. We used the hiatus to seek a more flexible channel.

When we found such an intermediary in Pakistan, Nixon was able to send me to China in July 1971 unencumbered by preconditions on either side. My assignment was to develop an agenda which would lead to a presidential visit to begin settling the fundamental issues between the two countries. It would have been impossible to move with such decisiveness and on so broad a front through regular channels. As on Vietnam, I can recall no State Department inquiry seeking to reactivate the Warsaw channel; the subject was obviously too controversial for those bitter days.

Whereas the backchannel negotiations on Vietnam and China grew out of Nixon's concern over leaks and departmental timidity, those concerning Soviet-American arms control negotiations represented an attempt by the President to break a deadlock that had developed in the regular channels. After the Strategic Arms Limitation Talks (SALT) opened in November 1969, the Soviets sought to confine discussions to antiballistic missile systems which we were building; Moscow refused to discuss restraints on Soviet offensive arsenals to which it was adding nearly two hundred missiles a year. This one-sided Soviet proposal would have constrained American weapons capable of blunting the growing Soviet blackmail potential and in which, moreover, we were technologically ahead of the Soviet Union while producing a growing edge in Soviet offensive weapons because we had stopped our offensive buildup. Nixon refused this proposition and insisted on dealing with limitations on offensive and defensive weapons simultaneously.

Despite the one-sided nature of the Soviet proposals, congressional and media pressures to move toward the Soviet position multiplied. In the fetid atmosphere of our domestic debate, diplomatic deadlocks were almost automatically blamed on the alleged bad faith of the Nixon Administration. Our official negotiators, eager for some break-through, were moving toward a "compromise" whereby defensive weapons would be limited first and offensive weapons dealt with in a follow-on negotiation. Convinced that such an approach would forfeit our leverage and still reluctant as ever to confront his subordinates head-on, Nixon solved the problem by bypassing them. In October 1970, the President authorized me to send a verbal note to Soviet Prime Minister Alexei Kosygin via Dobrynin stressing that the White House would not approve any agreement which excluded offensive weapons, whatever might transpire in the formal negotiations. At the same time, Nixon offered to accelerate the Geneva talks if the Soviets agreed to link limitations on offensive and defensive deployments. After the So-viet leadership had agreed to the principle, Dobrynin and I worked out an understanding which was announced on May 20, 1971—the first breakthrough in the Strategic Arms Limitation Talks.[14]

A few other deadlocks—especially on whether to include subma-rine-launched missiles—were similarly dealt with in the backchannel. The talks that led to a guarantee of access to the beleaguered city of Berlin were likewise given a decisive impetus in the White House backchannel—though because this was a four-power negotiation, the procedures were even more complicated.

State Department opposition took on acute form during the India-Pakistan crisis of 1971 when the State Department, which was a full par-ticipant in all discussions, in effect sabotaged Nixon's decision to demonstrate to China that we supported our strategic partners in times of crisis. It was three months since my visit to Beijing arranged by Paki-stan. India, determined to humiliate Pakistan over Bangladesh, had made a de facto alliance with the Soviet Union and was now using force to achieve Bangladesh's independence in full knowledge that we had al-ready conceded the principle and were working on implementing it.

Nixon ordered a diplomatic tilt toward Pakistan to prevent a forc-ible dismemberment of West Pakistan and to show China that we would resist Soviet-backed military intervention. The State Depart-ment representatives at daily interagency meetings argued passionately that India was a more important country than Pakistan—a judgment we did not challenge. But, at that moment, our incipient China policy was more important than Indian goodwill. We judged that it would be easier to restore our relations with India than to remain inactive to-ward a challenge that might be viewed in Beijing as a rehearsal for pressure against China. I am not trying to refight the substantive argument; the issue was discipline and coherence. The responsible State Department assistant secretaries were passionately opposed and have expressed this in many forums. But their real complaint is not that they were ignored or bypassed but that they were overruled. From Nixon's point of view (and mine), once the President had rejected the State Department position, the debate should have ended. Instead, it was moved by leaks into the media and Congress.

I have devoted this much space to a discussion of how diplomacy was conducted in the Nixon Administration because it explains the origin and rationale for our procedures. A combination of elaborate interdepartmental groups and dramatic diplomatic forays through various backchannels produced a novel mix for most of Nixon's first term that was both dramatic and effective. Other Presidents had employed special emissaries, occasionally even on secret missions. Woodrow Wilson and Colonel Edward House, Franklin Roosevelt and Harry Hopkins are good examples. But no previous President had similarly combined personal diplomacy with systematic backup. The interdepartmental process produced option papers from among which Nixon and I were able to select the courses of action most compatible with our overall strategy without necessarily informing the authors of the decision until we had achieved a diplomatic breakthrough.

But the same method spawned many of the controversies which followed. For a few years, the system worked well. Since the departments were as yet unaware of the secret negotiations, they put forward their genuine views as part of the NSC process. Almost every proposal advanced in the presidential back channel thus had its backup within the interdepartmental process. None was ever generated by Nixon or me in a vacuum. For example, the formula in the February 1972 Shanghai Communiqué that "acknowledged" the indivisibility of China without as yet recognizing Beijing dated back to a position paper prepared in 1954 for Secretary of State John Foster Dulles which had been lying dormant in the files since then.

As it turned out, the procedures of the Nixon Administration worked best on single-issue negotiations and before the departments had come to understand that the actual management of many negotiations had slipped out of their hands. Once they caught on, it became apparent that hell hath no fury like a bypassed negotiator. The very individuals who had pressed us for greater negotiating flexibility so long as they thought they were in charge turned against agreements reached without their participation.

Within the NSC process, Nixon and I had generally sided with the harder line in interdepartmental controversies. But once the negotiations became public, an astonishing and totally unexpected reversal of roles took place. With no department having any real stake in the negotiations, each felt at liberty to claim how much they could have improved the outcome. The concessions we had extracted were taken for granted while compromises achieved with great difficulty were described as inadequate. The White House and I as the principal negotiator were now being charged with excessive flexibility, even "softness," by the very people who had a year earlier chastised us for being obstacles to diplomatic progress. The White House first under Nixon and later under Ford was thereby gradually deprived of its traditional bureaucratic safety net.

The first hint of the new bureaucratic lineup emerged during Nixon's visit to China in February 1972 while we were negotiating what later came to be known as the Shanghai Communiqué. Fearful of leaks and eager to receive sole credit for what he had every right to believe had been brought about through his own initiative, Nixon rejected the participation of State Department officers in the negotiating sessions between Foreign Minister Qiao Guanhua and myself. (For once I had urged the inclusion of the responsible assistant secretary, the extremely able, disciplined, and well-informed Marshall Green, who would be needed to shepherd the result through its various implementation phases.)

As a result, the State Department did not see a draft of the communiqué until twenty-four hours before it was to be published. Inevitably Marshall Green objected to some formulations he either would have succeeded in modifying or accepted in the give-and-take of a negotiation. Since we were eager to avoid domestic controversy or damaging leaks of a disagreement within Nixon's traveling party, we asked our Chinese counterparts for a special negotiating session at midnight following a formal banquet to propose some of Green's modifications. After a few hours of strained dialogue, the Chinese negotiators accepted several changes which, while altering little of substance, improved precision and mollified the State Department by giving it a stake in the outcome.

What had been an embarrassment in China turned into a full-scale bureaucratic stalemate in the aftermath of the Moscow summit of May 1972. The negotiations on SALT, however facilitated by the back channel, also revealed its limits. For SALT involved too many vested interests of both the Defense Department and the uniformed military to allow these issues to be settled conclusively in the backchannel. As a result, both the open and backchannel negotiations often took place simultaneously, imposing nerve-racking requirements of coordination on the NSC staff. Once the Soviets caught on, they sometimes tried to play the two channels against each other by putting into the open channel some proposals Nixon had already rejected in the backchannel.

A climax of sorts occurred when I was in Moscow secretly in April 1972 to prepare for Nixon's summit in May. (The Soviets had insisted on the visit being secret, another example of their sometimes compulsive insistence on establishing equivalence with China.) Three negotiations were going on simultaneously: the "frontchannel" SALT negotiation in Helsinki, headed by Ambassador Gerard Smith; the still secret negotiation between First Secretary Leonid I. Brezhnev and me in Moscow to prepare a summit agenda; and other discussions headed by General Scowcroft, who was openly in Moscow to prepare the technical aspects of Nixon's visit. Just as I was leaving for Moscow, the Soviets put into the Helsinki front channel a proposal Nixon had already rejected in the back channel. Nixon, in Camp David (partly to avoid having to tell his Secretary of State about my mission), lost track of who was saying what to whom. Some testy exchanges between Haig and me followed until my return when I was able to straighten out the misunderstanding.[15]

But the underlying problem remained. Once the departments realized that the White House could and would break the deadlocks, they lost their incentive to press for flexibility. By Nixon's second term, his bureaucratic options were becoming constrained by the very successes of his first term. Every NSC meeting turned into a confrontation between the President (or me as his surrogate) and a united front of departmental opposition. Once I became Secretary of State in addition to National Security Adviser, my dual position turned into yet another handicap because it deprived me of a crucial mediating function. In a normal administration, it is the departments which carry the burden for publicly defending controversial decisions while the President basks in the glow of popular ones. By the end of the Nixon Administration, the opposite situation prevailed: the onus for most of the controversial decisions was shifted either to the President or to me.

Gerald Ford paid the price for Richard Nixon's attempt to conform policymaking to one of the most complex and convoluted personalities produced by the American political system. It was a tour de force unsustainable indefinitely, requiring endless juggling on the part of the National Security Adviser and a deft high-wire act by the President. In the end, the insistence on solitary efforts prevented Nixon's policymaking from reaching that special added dimension toward which he was groping: "Will I ever be known for anything but competence?" Nixon once asked me.

The answer was that Nixon was flirting with greatness, but a President's ultimate achievement can never be a purely personal effort. Rather it resides in that intangible ability to inspire one's society and one's associates to aim for what they had always regarded as being beyond their reach. This Nixon was unable to do. His vision of the statesman as a romantic loner diminished his associates, and his perception that he was somehow living in a hostile environment—not always incorrect—caused him to spend more time fending off dangers than seeking to transcend them. Had Nixon wanted to culminate what he had begun so creatively and imaginatively in his first term, he would have had to return to more normal governmental processes in his second term. Yet I doubt that he could ever have brought himself to take direct charge of the machinery of government, and he was therefore bound to fall somewhat short of his conceptions.

## Epilogue

The transition to Ford marks the end of my official relationship to Nixon. Still, a few concluding pages about our subsequent dealings are in order.

After resigning from the presidency, Nixon lived for another two decades. The first few years in exile were excruciatingly difficult for him. Few except his closest friends telephoned him, and he disappeared from the public debate except in the sensational stories regarding his alleged abuses of power. During this period, he and I often spoke on the telephone, and I visited him once in San Clemente. While I was still in office, when major events occurred, I would brief him; when I was under attack—which happened more and more frequently—he would call with supporting and usually very insightful comments.[16]

In February 1980, Nixon moved to New York and launched a spectacular career of reinventing himself as elder statesman. I hosted a small dinner to welcome him. For the first time, he sought to engage the Establishment. He would invite key representatives of the media and industry for an evening of discussion that usually turned into a briefing; he would send thoughtful little notes to authors of articles or books that caught his attention. Patiently and tenaciously, Nixon earned himself a position as a senior commentator whom, in the end, the incumbent Presidents—be it Ronald Reagan, George Bush, or Bill Clinton—found it to their benefit to consult.

Nixon began to deliver public speeches. I attended a few of them and marveled at how he used the occasion to overwhelm his audience. Pushing the lectern ostentatiously out of the way, he would deliver an hour-long speech forcefully and extemporaneously. Only the few Nixon cognoscenti in the audience understood just how much the sheer effort of it had cost him. They knew that, if it was an important group, he would have written out the speech beforehand or at least made a full outline and probably rehearsed parts of it before a mirror. They were participating in an extraordinary feat of memory and self-discipline, not a spontaneous effusion.

In April 1987, Nixon and I wrote a joint article. In it we raised questions about the proposal to withdraw intermediate-range nuclear weapons from Europe because we feared it might lead to the unilateral denuclearization of Western Europe and to a fissure within the Atlantic Alliance.[17] We met or talked on the average of about once a month throughout this period, invariably for a discussion of the international situation. In 1988, Nixon hosted a dinner in my honor to which he invited former NSC associates and a few others. Beyond that, there was little social contact.

As Nixon developed new roots, he demonstrated the adage that, after a certain age, personalities rarely change. He continued to play his cards close to his vest even when the issues we might be discussing were no longer of ultimate importance or, indeed, of any importance. A good example was a conversation about where Nixon should reside in New York. A close mutual friend had told me that Nixon had put down a deposit on a cooperative apartment on Madison Avenue. Yet when we chatted about his planned move to New York, Nixon asked for my recommendation on a suitable residence as if all choices were still open and as if I was still working on a White House option paper. Not wanting to spoil his game, I reviewed the various avenues with him, making sure to put Madison Avenue far down on the list. Nixon rejected Fifth Avenue because of the tourists and the East River because "Pat hates water," which was news to me. He walked me through the pros and cons of every avenue until, by a process of elimination, we reached Madison Avenue, which, by this point in the conversation, Nixon had elevated from a choice to a necessity. It was a nostalgic experience, reminiscent of many far more important occasions when I had seen Nixon turn an interlocutor into an accomplice. (As it happened, the co-op board—bizarrely—rejected Nixon's application.)

Throughout, Nixon continued to suffer from what he considered the disproportionate recognition accorded to me. He dealt with it in characteristically romantic fashion by inventing the epic tale of how, at crucial turning points, it had been he who had stiffened my spine, reined me in, or overruled me. In April 1990, *Time* published an interview with Nixon in which he implied that I had pushed the Vietnam peace settlement in 1972 to help him win the election (and perhaps claim some credit for his electoral victory); that the "peace is at hand" press conference had been unnecessary—indeed he would have preferred not to discuss negotiations publicly at all; and that all along I had been more trusting of the North Vietnamese than he.[18]

For once I decided to confront Nixon directly in a letter, the full text of which is in the Notes.[19] I began with a reaffirmation of the importance of our relationship to my life:

> I read your interview in *Time* with a mixture of melancholy and amazement.
>
> Melancholy because I shall always be grateful to you for giving me the opportunity to serve my adopted country and repay it for the safe haven from persecution for my family and me. And I shall forever consider it a privilege to have worked for a President whose role in foreign policy was seminal in charting the main directions of everything that followed since. . . .
>
> Amazement because a host of factual inaccuracies escalated previous incorrect innuendos. If you wish, I would be happy to make available to John Taylor [Nixon's assistant] the various memoranda, telephone conversations and other documentation that leave no doubt of the inaccuracy of these assertions. . . .

I then reminded Nixon that, on the day of the "peace is at hand" news conference, Hanoi had published the text of the agreement as it stood and had demanded that we sign it; that some response had been unavoidable, and that my statements had been approved in the Oval

Office in detail. Nixon, I pointed out, had been as committed as I to try to end the war as soon as possible; indeed, he had personally warned Soviet Foreign Minister Andrei Gromyko in late September 1972 that the October 8 meeting with Le Duc Tho at which the breakthrough occurred would be the last opportunity to settle before the election.

I ended the letter on a reassuring, conciliatory, and even affectionate note that gave Nixon major credit, as he deserved, for the upheavals in the Communist world that had just taken place:

> None of these tactical issues will affect what I believe must be the verdict of history: that in a desperate hour you vindicated America's honor with a foreign policy which, under your leadership, set the basic directions culminating in the revolutionary changes of last year.

Nixon answered in characteristically indirect fashion. Having put forward one romantic version of history to *Time* magazine, he now put forward another one to me, this one involving my wife, Nancy. He had not meant to imply, he said, that I was on the "soft" side on whether to negotiate with Hanoi; this was the invention of the *Time* journalists. The contrary was true; if anything, I had been more of a hawk than he. As for our relative optimism regarding the prospects for negotiations with Hanoi, this was a tactical issue on which I had turned out to be right:

> As you will of course recall, you often told me, as I have noted in my diaries, that Nancy believed that in view of McGovern's way-out position, our continuing to take a hard-line on negotiations was politically helpful rather than harmful. While I shared that view, I often told you that if we could get the right deal before the election, we should do so regardless of what we thought the political consequences might be. If we couldn't get the right deal, we should refuse to make an agreement even though we thought that the political effect would be negative. I believed that you shared that view then and still do.
>
> There was only one area where we had a significant difference of opinion. I felt that you had more confidence in the negotiating process than I had. On the other hand, as I

noted in my *Memoirs*, I had to admit, once you negotiated the Paris Peace Agreement, that you were right and I was wrong on this score.

After this exchange, we resumed our normal relationship. Nixon invited me to share the platform with him at a number of Nixon Library conferences. I saw Nixon for the last time in January 1994 when I was one of the speakers in Yorba Linda at the launching of the Nixon Center, a new foreign policy think tank now located in Washington. Former key Cabinet members spoke briefly: Bill Simon as master of ceremonies; George Shultz about Nixon's domestic legacy; Bill Rogers about Nixon's political legacy; and I about his foreign policy legacy. Nixon concluded the event with a graceful speech to a large and friendly audience. At the lunch following, I toasted Nixon on behalf of his former Cabinet.

A few months later, in April 1994, Richard Nixon died.

We had lived together through periods of hope and of despair, through fleeting moments of triumph and long domestic travails. Nixon could be exasperating, maddening, even treacherous. But the overriding feeling evoked by his death was one of sorrow. I was well aware of Nixon's compulsive insecurity; at times, I had been its target. Yet, paradoxical as it sounds, Nixon's endless machinations were apt to be forgiven especially by those closest to him and therefore most likely to be damaged by his wiles because we were also familiar with the sweep of his aspirations and aware that his most tormenting battles were with himself.

At that melancholy moment, I recalled an occasion when, from the summer White House in San Clemente, Nixon invited Bebe Rebozo and me to accompany him to his birthplace in nearby Yorba Linda. Once there, the President noticed that a Secret Service car and a press pool had followed us. Outraged, Nixon commanded privacy for himself in a loud and insistent voice—an event so extraordinary that both the Secret Service and the press violated all their standing orders and obliged. Enchanted by his unprecedented freedom, Nixon decided to take his guests on a journey through his youth—never mind that he and I, holding most of the nation's secrets, were now being guarded by only a single Secret Service agent who doubled as our driver.

As Nixon showed us the gasoline station his family had owned in Whittier, the hotel where he had been selected to run for Congress in a seemingly hopeless race, and Whittier College where he recalled some of his professors affectionately, he was far gentler, more at ease, and more genuine than I had ever seen him. On the spur of the moment, Nixon decided to prolong the adventure by taking us to Los Angeles to show us, by way of contrast, the house in which he had lived for two years in the 1960s as a successful lawyer before he began his final quest for the presidency. There was only one difficulty. Nixon recalled the house being in one of the canyons behind the Beverly Hills Hotel, but, try as he might, he could not find it, even after searching for an hour in every conceivable canyon and development. And, in the process, the agitated, tense Nixon with whom I was so familiar reemerged. On the way to the presidency, Nixon had traveled many roads, but he had never managed to discover where he really belonged.

And yet it was this man, ridden by insecurities and assaulted on all sides, who had held fast to a concept of national honor, determined to prove that the greatest free nation had no right to abdicate. With a romantic and even lofty notion of the hero-statesman, he sought to overcome his nation's oscillation between overcommitment and withdrawal. Though in the end he fell short of fulfilling his highest aspirations, Nixon's goals were worthy even when the execution was occasionally flawed.

This is why his funeral on April 27, 1994, became a national occasion attended by all surviving Presidents, including Bill Clinton. And my eulogy came from the heart:

> When I learned the final news, by then so expected yet so hard to accept, I felt a deep loss and a profound void. In the words of Shakespeare: "He was a man, take him for all in all, I shall not look upon his like again." . . .
>
> . . . So let us now say goodbye to our gallant friend. He stood on pinnacles that dissolved into precipices. He achieved greatly and suffered deeply. But he never gave up. In his solitude, he envisaged a new international order that would reduce lingering enmities, strengthen historic friendships, and give new hope to mankind—a vision where dreams and possibilities conjoined.
>
> Richard Nixon ended a war, and he advanced the vision of peace of his Quaker youth. He was devoted to his family, he loved his country, and he considered service his honor. It was a privilege to have been allowed to help him.

# 3

# CONTROVERSY OVER DÉTENTE

If Harry Truman was the architect of the core institutions that won the Cold War and Ronald Reagan provided the impetus for the end game, Richard Nixon was the pivotal figure in the middle period. It was during his presidency that the main lines of American policy for the final two decades of the Cold War were put in place side by side with the extrication from the Vietnam tragedy.

By the end of Nixon's presidency, the United States had withdrawn its forces from Vietnam on honorable terms. The threat of a Soviet blockade that had been hanging over Berlin for twenty-five years had been removed by an agreement with the Soviet Union guaranteeing access to that beleaguered city. The process of strategic arms limitations with the Soviet Union had begun. China had been brought into Great Power diplomacy, essentially on America's side. That move had transformed Moscow's geopolitical position overnight because it consolidated a tacit coalition of all the world's major powers against it. A Middle East war had been surmounted, and the Soviet political and strategic position in that region was being eroded with each passing month. A peace process between Israel and its Arab neighbors under American auspices was under way. Probably the most abiding tribute to Nixon's legacy is that most of the relationships and strategies launched during his presidency have sustained the foreign policy of all of his successors to this writing.

It is equally true that, by the summer of 1974 when Gerald Ford took over, Nixon's foreign policy had become nearly as controversial as his personality. Liberals chastised the President—and me—for inadequate attention to human rights. Conservatives depicted the administration as overeager for accommodation with the Soviet Union in the name of détente, which, in their view, compounded bad policy with French terminology.

Each of these criticisms owed something to the discomfort evoked by Nixon's ambiguous personality, but the overriding cause was that his foreign policy raised two fundamental philosophical challenges. Nixon sought to extricate the United States from Vietnam on terms he defined as honorable at a time when most of the intellectual and much of the political community wanted to get out of Indochina essentially unconditionally and the radical protesters preferred humiliation to honor or, more precisely, equated humiliation with honor.

Even more importantly for Nixon was that he was presiding over the transition of America's role in the world from domination to leadership. For much of the postwar period, the United States was preeminent because of its nuclear predominance and economic strength. By the time Nixon entered office, our nuclear monopoly was dwindling, Europe was regaining vitality, Asia was entering the international arena, and Africa was being swept by independence movements. Dominance can be based on power; leadership requires building consensus. But an attempt to balance rewards and penalties inseparable from consensus-building ran counter to the prevailing Wilsonianism, which tried to bring about a global moral order through the direct application of America's political values undiluted by compromises with "realism."

Over two decades later, as these lines are being written, many of the themes of the debates of the 1970s have reappeared in the contemporary argument over America's role in the world and especially its China policy. In this sense, the controversy over détente with the Soviet Union that blighted the Ford presidency was the forerunner of the contemporary post–Cold War debate over the direction of American foreign policy.

## What Was Détente?

A nation's foreign policy inevitably reflects an amalgam of the convictions of its leaders and the pressures of the environment. To understand the Nixon Administration approach to East-West relations —and the controversy that Ford inherited—it is necessary to describe the situation in which Nixon found himself.

Richard Nixon entered office in the midst of one of the gravest foreign policy crises in American history. Over 540,000 American troops were fighting in Vietnam, and our country was tearing itself apart over what Professor Walter A. McDougall of the University of Pennsylvania has brilliantly described as America's first "Great Society war."[1] By this he meant that Vietnam was the first American war fought for no military objective. Rather, the strategic goal was not to lose in order to give South Vietnam time to create democratic institutions and social programs that would win the war for the hearts and minds of the population. Such a goal for a divided country, independent for only a decade, and in a society governed by colonialism for a century was a prodigious challenge in itself. What is certain is that the process required a time span of stalemated war beyond the psychological endurance of the American public.

To end such a war would have been bitter and difficult under the best of circumstances. American forces found themselves amidst three quarters of a million South Vietnamese allied forces and a comparable force of infiltrated North Vietnamese divisions and local guerrillas. A sudden unilateral withdrawal, for which our predecessors—who had never entertained the idea while in office—and the antiwar demonstrators were clamoring, had the potential of leaving American forces trapped between allies resentful of betrayal and adversaries determined to prevail.

Yet America's deepest challenge was not the technical aspect of withdrawal; it was a moral issue even when presented in realistic guise. Nixon would not abandon the tens of millions who, in reliance on the words of his two Democratic predecessors, had cast their lot with ours. We argued on the basis of the national interest that, as the leader of the Western Alliance, our credibility toward both friend and foe was at stake. But beyond "realistic" considerations, Nixon also had laid down a moral marker that defined the limit of his strong desire to extricate the United States from Indochina. He was prepared to display considerable flexibility in negotiations with Hanoi—going beyond what had ever been suggested, even by the "doves" in Johnson's presidency.[2] There was only one concession we would never make on geopolitical and, above all, on moral grounds—to impose a Communist government on peoples who had joined the anti-Communist cause in reliance on America's word. That, however, was the demand from which Hanoi would not budge and on which the peace movement came increasingly to insist.

The so-called peace movement, wrapping itself in the cloak of morality, insisted that there was only one ethical issue, which was peace on whatever terms, and that the fate of the population was irrelevant to that goal (or, in its more sophisticated version, that the peoples of Indochina would be better off if we abandoned them). In pursuit of what amounted to unconditional and unilateral withdrawal, the protestors sought to impose their views by mass demonstrations designed to paralyze the government. The protesters considered the very terms of honor and credibility abominations, the empty slogans of a flawed society which would repeat its errors over and over again until it was made to taste the bitter dregs of futility and humiliation. An "honorable" peace to unite the country was precisely the outcome which the protest movement sought to prevent. In its view, American presumption and vainglory had caused the tragedy in Indochina. It rejected the invocation of America's role in preserving the global equilibrium as a symptom of a national obsession with power, and it denied that Nixon had a moral right to invoke the term "honor."

To be sure, the Establishment figures never went quite this far. Paralyzed by the futility of what they had wrought, they simply wished to extirpate the Vietnam War from their consciousness and to submerge their mistakes in collective amnesia. The practical result of their emotional abdication was that they would not support any American negotiating position rejected by Hanoi, thereby depriving the American negotiators of a floor on which to stand.

At this writing, a generation has grown up which has no personal memories of the passions of the period. Some of its survivors suppress their memories; others devote themselves to revisionist history. But the fact that many, if not most, of the American foreign policy elite were promoting—or acquiescing in—an American abandonment of the premises of previous Cold War policy affected the future evolution of American foreign policy profoundly.

Pressures from abroad paralleled the domestic ones. Most of America's North Atlantic allies were extremely skeptical about the war in Indochina. By the time Nixon took office, they had begun to question whether America's alleged bellicosity might not threaten, rather than safeguard, their own security. A number of European leaders felt quite free to present themselves to their publics as apostles of peace whose primary mission was to moderate American intransigence in the conduct of the Cold War.

All this was happening less than a year after the Soviet Union had occupied Czechoslovakia in order to overthrow a *Communist* regime aspiring to a measure of autonomy from Moscow. Leonid Brezhnev had proclaimed the doctrine (bearing his name) which asserted Moscow's right to impose ideological orthodoxy on the Communist world. Backed by a rapidly growing arsenal of nuclear weapons, the Kremlin was projecting an image of ideological militancy and military strength.

Such was the context of stalemate, tension, and frustration inherited by Nixon. For us to have launched the grandiloquent anti-Soviet crusade which our critics later (though not at the time) chastised us for not undertaking would only have driven our domestic crisis out of control. For, at the time Nixon entered office, the American public was drained by twenty years of Cold War exertions and the increasing frustrations with Vietnam. It had lived through two Berlin crises, the Korean War, Soviet invasions of Hungary and Czechoslovakia, and the Cuban Missile Crisis, and had already sustained over 35,000 casualties in Indochina. Americans were growing tired of defending distant frontiers against a seemingly irreconcilable ideological opponent in a protracted conflict with no end in sight.

Throughout his career, Nixon's critics had portrayed him as an unregenerate Cold Warrior. But now that he was President, the liberals who dominated Congress and the media urged him to act to end the Cold War with policies as if he were one of their own. A widespread and vocal consensus, which had many supporters within the bureaucracy, pressed the new administration to initiate immediate negotiations with Moscow on trade, cultural and scientific exchanges, and, above all, arms control. Each of these, we were told insistently by Nixon's historic adversaries, should be pursued on its own merits; any agreement with the Soviets, however limited, would contribute to an easing of Soviet suspicions and thereby reduce the danger of war. A "get-acquainted" summit meeting between Soviet and American leaders was perhaps the most popular proposal of all.

The conservatives remained sullenly silent. Shell-shocked by Vietnam and the domestic upheaval, they provided no counterweight to the liberal onslaught. A good example was the reaction of my close and trusted friend, William Buckley, when I asked him to help mobilize conservative opinion to counter the anti-Vietnam protest movement: "It is too late," Buckley said. "That horse has left the barn."

Another case in point was a memorandum from Deputy Secretary of Defense David Packard in early 1970. Departing from the typical Pentagon position, Packard recommended a new and urgent arms control initiative for the purpose of concluding an agreement by "mid-

October or, at the latest, November." Otherwise the congressional "squeeze on the national budget" was "likely" to cause "large reductions in defense programs, including strategic forces."[3]

In the absence of a counterweight to the liberal consensus, the dominant theme of the public discourse was peace: how to achieve it in Vietnam, how to preserve it in the world at large through immediate East-West negotiations, how to protect it at home from the Nixon Administration's alleged hard-line proclivities. At that time, of course, the neoconservatives who would later accuse us of softness on Communism were still on the radical side of the dividing line, adding their voice to the clamor for accommodation.

Nixon thus confronted a dual challenge: 1) to manage the extrication from Vietnam in a way that preserved American leadership and fulfilled our moral obligations; and 2) to define a role for the United States in the post-Vietnam period that avoided the extremes between abdication and heroic posturing.

Wilsonianism had involved the United States in Indochina by means of universalist maxims which had proved successful in Europe and were now applied literally in Asia. These were that the building of democracy could take place in the same time frame as the conduct of a guerrilla war; indeed, that the war need not be won and only be kept from being lost, drawing us into a conflict which could have no military end. And the traditional conservative version of Wilsonianism supplied no philosophical counterweight. Its vision of some apocalyptic showdown with the Soviet Union left us musclebound in the face of the actual Cold War challenges which our adversaries were careful to keep below the threshold of all-out confrontation.

Wilsonianism rejects peace through balance of power in favor of peace through moral consensus. It sees foreign policy as a struggle between good and evil, in each phase of which it is America's mission to help defeat the evil foes challenging a peaceful order. Having prevailed, the United States can then devote itself to fostering the underlying harmony (in the internationalist version) or cultivate its own virtues (in the isolationist version) until the next discrete crisis arises —perceived not as a disturbance of the equilibrium but as a deviation from the moral order. Such a foreign policy tends to be segmented into a series of episodes and not perceived as a continuum requiring constant attention and adjustment, a quest for absolutes rather than as the shaping of reality by means of nuances.

The Nixon Administration strove for a more differentiated approach. Though he admired Woodrow Wilson, nothing in Nixon's personal experience led him to share the conviction that great ideas could be realized in one grand ideological assault. Both Nixon and I enlisted our firm anti-Communist convictions in the service of a complex strategy designed to achieve our objective in stages, each of which by definition was bound to fall short of the ultimate ideal and could therefore be castigated as amoral. We viewed foreign policy as a continuing process with no terminal point, unlike the dominant view among liberals and conservatives, who were seeking a series of climaxes, each of which would culminate its particular phase and obviate the need for a continuing exertion.

It was not that either Nixon or I rejected the crucial role of the American democratic ideal either in our domestic cohesion or in giving impetus to our foreign policy. It was that we did not believe that ideal could be translated as a kind of mechanical blueprint for day-to-day foreign policy. Our values were needed to provide the moral fortitude to act in the face of the ambiguous choices and uncertain outcomes, which is how historical decisions present themselves to the policymaker. To avoid either overextension or abdication, the United States needed, in addition, the guide of a concept of the national interest. This we defined in Nixon's very first annual foreign policy report to Congress on February 18, 1970:

> Our objective, in the first instance, is to support our *interests* over the long run with a sound foreign policy. The more that policy is based on a realistic assessment of our and others' interests, the more effective our role in the world can be. We are not involved in the world because we have commitments; we have commitments because we are involved. Our interests must shape our commitments, rather than the other way around.[4]

These general considerations led to a strategy which had the following components: (1) to extricate from Vietnam under honorable conditions; (2) to confine the dissent of the protest movement to Indochina; (3) to seize the high ground of the peace issue by a strategy that demonstrated to the American public that, even while pursuing the Cold War, we would do our utmost to control its dangers and gradually to overcome it; (4) to broaden the diplomatic chessboard by including China in the international system; (5) to strengthen our alliances; (6) and, from that platform, to go on the diplomatic offensive, especially in the Middle East.

Détente was one aspect of the overall strategy. An unfortunate label implying European antecedents, détente was designed to control a relationship conceived as adversarial, not to conjure up the blissful nirvana from which all tensions had automatically been removed, as later caricatures of it implied. Throughout, Nixon and I considered the Soviet Union ideologically hostile and militarily threatening. At once an empire and a cause, it was the only other power capable of intervention globally, the source of most postwar international crises, and the sole country capable of attacking the United States.[5]

Years later, Nixon's critics, attacking from the right, alleged that he was "soft" on the Soviet global threat. They misunderstood the danger he faced. What most concerned the Nixon Administration at that stage was that the Politburo might come to view America's turmoil over Vietnam (and later Watergate) as an opportunity to destabilize Europe and other strategic regions. The challenge was less the Soviet nuclear menace (which we were confident we would continue to deter) than that the Politburo might rely on its conventional superiority to spark a crisis and then, taking its cue from Hanoi's tactics, alternate military pressures with peace offensives designed to mobilize the already powerful peace movements against an allegedly bellicose administration in Washington.

We were determined not to wait passively behind our ramparts while protest tore our country apart and our alliances weakened in the face of a diplomacy defined by our adversaries and paralyzed by the protest movement. Instead, we strove for a strategy which calibrated the benefits of restraint and the penalties to recklessness to keep Soviet leaders from mounting a challenge during our period of national turmoil. And if the calibration failed, the very effort would at least have demonstrated to the American people that the resulting crisis was caused by the Soviet Union—thereby bolstering support for a strong response. In short, we treated America's travail over Vietnam as a temporary weakness which, once overcome, would enable us to prevail over the Soviet system when geopolitical isolation and a stagnant economy had exhausted its ideological zeal.

A briefing memorandum I sent to Nixon prior to Brezhnev's visit to the United States in 1973 reflected this analysis:

> Almost certainly, Brezhnev continues to defend his détente
> policies in Politburo debates in terms of a historic conflict

with us as the main capitalist country and of the ultimate
advantages that will accrue to the USSR in this conflict.
Brezhnev's gamble is that as these policies gather momentum
and longevity, their effects will not undermine the very system from which Brezhnev draws his power and legitimacy.
*Our goal on the other hand is to achieve precisely such
effects over the long run.* [emphasis added][6]

We judged the Soviet Union, seemingly so monolithic and so eager
to demonstrate its military power, as in fact being rent by vast systemic
upheavals. Such astute observers as Andrei Amalrik (whose article I
gave to Nixon to read) were already calling attention to the fact that
the Soviet empire was facing profound and congenital vulnerabilities.[7]
In the more than fifty years of its history, the Soviet leadership had
never managed a legitimate succession. Leaders had either died in
office (like Lenin and Stalin) or had been replaced by coup-like procedures (like Khrushchev). In each case, succession was followed by a
purge. And the growth of Soviet military potential was draining the
economy and driving it into stagnation. This is why, in the Alastair
Buchan Lecture in June 1976, I said: "We have nothing to fear from
competition: . . . if there is an economic competition, we won it long
ago . . . In no part of the world and under no other system do men
live so well and in so much freedom. If performance is any criterion,
the contest between freedom and Communism, of which so much was
made three decades ago, has been won by the industrial democracies."[8]

In the process, the Soviet international position was growing more
complicated. Tensions between Moscow and Beijing were escalating.
Within weeks of Nixon's inauguration, we learned of military clashes
along the Ussuri River, which demarcates the boundary between China
and the Soviet Union's maritime provinces at the edge of Siberia. Soviet
military forces all along the four-thousand-mile frontier with China
were being reinforced. Even before we established contact with Beijing,
we had calculated that the fear of a two-front war would impose
growing restraints on the Soviet Union's pressures on Europe as well
as provide new diplomatic opportunities for the United States—as
indeed it did.

Upheavals in Hungary and Czechoslovakia and a near-revolution
in Poland in 1970 dramatized the tenuousness of the Soviet hold over
its satellites. It had become popular to joke that the Soviet Union was
the only state entirely surrounded by hostile Communist countries.

In the Middle East, the Soviet Union had been arming its Arab allies for a war it was well within our capacity to prevent them from winning. Therefore, our strategy in the Middle East sought to oblige the Soviet Union and its radical Arab allies to dissociate from each other or to moderate their diplomacy.

Far from conducting détente from a perception of weakness, the Nixon Administration was convinced that it had little to fear and much to gain from a flexible diplomacy in which the rigid Soviet system was bound to find itself increasingly at a disadvantage. Deprived of its ideological card, the Soviets' creaky economy, aging leadership, and dearth of true allies cast it in the role of simply another power player and not a very effective one at that.

This view was put forward publicly in the first annual presidential report to Congress on foreign policy:

> [T]he lessons of the last two decades must have left their imprint on the leadership in the Kremlin—in the recognition that Marxist ideology is not the surest guide to the problems of a changing industrial society, the worldwide decline in the appeal of ideology, and most of all in the foreign policy dilemmas repeatedly posed by the spread of Communism to states which refuse to endure permanent submission to Soviet authority—a development illustrated vividly by the Soviet schism with China.[9]

To be effective, a strategic assessment needs to be translated into an operating policy. This effort ran up against the perennial American controversy regarding the purpose of diplomacy. The then-dominant liberal group viewed negotiations as an end in itself almost regardless of content. The very act of dialogue, it argued, "eased the atmosphere"; each agreement facilitated the path for further progress until a spirit of reconciliation had supplanted the suspicions of the Cold War and made some of the issues that had dominated it less central.

The Nixon Administration rejected this approach. We were prepared for an intense period of negotiation, but we were not willing to let our adversaries choose the agenda or the conditions. Progress on issues of concern to Moscow had to coincide with progress in areas of concern to us. Therefore we insisted that individual negotiations, as on trade or arms control, take place in an atmosphere of Soviet political restraint, especially with regard to such long-standing trouble spots as Berlin, the Middle East, and Indochina. Two weeks after his inauguration, on February 4, 1969, Nixon sent a letter to this effect to his senior Cabinet Secretaries on the National Security Council:

> I am convinced that the great issues are fundamentally inter-related. I do not mean this to establish artificial linkages between specific elements of one or another issue or between tactical steps that we may elect to take. But I do believe that crisis or confrontation in one place and real cooperation in another cannot long be sustained simultaneously.
>
> I believe that the Soviet leaders should be brought to understand that they cannot expect to reap the benefits of cooperation in one area while seeking to take advantage of tension or confrontation elsewhere. Such a course involves the danger that the Soviets will use talks on arms as a safety valve on intransigence elsewhere.[10]

The Nixon Administration's negotiating strategy toward the Kremlin differed from conventional wisdom in two important respects. Unlike the liberals, it did not justify its East-West diplomacy by a presumed change in Soviet motivations. In the President's annual report on foreign policy cited above, we explicitly rejected the proposition that Communist leaders "have already given up their beliefs or are just about to do so. . . ."[11] But unlike the conservatives, who feared that agreements might weaken American vigilance, we argued that the Soviet Union was more vulnerable than the free world to a long period of peace and more likely to face fundamental changes as a result of it.

We did not view the Soviet Union as a monolith but as an amalgam of ideological, nationalist, and imperialistic tendencies. It had been placed on the defensive by the combination of Khrushchev's revelations of Stalin's crimes and the Soviet repression of upheavals in Eastern Europe. In light of its vulnerable economy and geopolitical isolation, we intended to nudge the Soviet colossus into transforming itself from a cause into a state capable of being influenced by traditional calculations of reward and punishment, thereby at first easing the Cold War and ultimately transcending it.

By the end of Nixon's first term, we had vindicated the strategy of moving forward on a broad front. The Soviet Union was being constrained from geopolitical adventures by the stick of our opening to China and the carrot of prospects of increased trade. In 1971, we helped channel West German Chancellor Willy Brandt's *Ostpolitik* into a direction compatible with Allied cohesion by using the back channel to help negotiate the linking of West German recognition of the East German Communist regime to a guarantee of free access to Berlin, thereby ending for the rest of the Cold War Soviet harassment of the city's access routes. In 1972, we were able to step up military pressure on Hanoi without Soviet interference. The Soviets went ahead with the planned summit despite the mining of Vietnamese harbors and the renewal of bombing of North Vietnam because they prized the benefits of a visit by Nixon more than ideological ties with Hanoi. And that restraint was reinforced by the Soviet knowledge that, in conditions of American-Soviet confrontation, the German parliament would never ratify the treaties with the U.S.S.R. accepting the postwar frontiers. It was also in 1972 that Soviet military forces were expelled from Egypt—as we had predicted in 1970. By the end of 1973, the United States was dominating Middle East diplomacy. A strategic arms agreement freezing the Soviet numerical missile buildup without modifying any established American program had been negotiated. Linkage had prevailed.[12]

## *The Attack on Nixon's Foreign Policy: The Liberal Challenge*

At this high point of Nixon's and perhaps of American postwar foreign policy, the national consensus broke down. Beginning in 1972 and continuing for the remainder of Nixon's term, a monumental domestic debate over the nature and the priorities of American foreign policy broke out. With brief interruptions, it has continued to this writing.

Many factors combined to produce this totally unexpected state of affairs. Perhaps the most fundamental was that Nixon and I underestimated the impact on the public psyche of the sharp difference between our approach to foreign policy and the Wilsonianism which had become dominant in the twentieth century. For his part, Nixon embittered the emerging debate by stressing in his public speeches (though not in our annual reports to Congress) domestic political rather than conceptual explanations for his foreign policy. Coolly convinced that the best way to isolate his liberal opponents was, in effect, to steal their program, Nixon could not resist rubbing it in that it was he— the despised, ostensibly reactionary Cold Warrior—who had, in fact, fulfilled much of the liberal agenda on negotiating with the adversary.

This tactic infuriated the liberals, who moved ever further away from Nixon by searching for such "moral" causes as human rights and more sweeping arms control proposals where they thought Nixon could not follow them. And it lost him the support of the traditional conservatives who might well have gone along with a justification of our policy for what it was—a way of managing the Cold War—but who considered co-opting liberal slogans as opportunism and began to look elsewhere for heroes. By being too adaptable, Nixon found himself caught between the two groups he was seeking to outmaneuver: the liberals, who accused him of being too Cold War-oriented, and the traditional conservatives, who charged him with being too opportunistic.

The liberals, having advocated greater East-West contacts, arms control, and increased trade for at least a decade, would have been normally supportive of these policies now that they were actually being implemented. And under the leadership of any President other than Richard Nixon, they probably would have eventually endorsed the substance of our policies, even while differing with the geopolitical approach with which we were justifying them. But Nixon had been anathema to the liberal community for more than two decades; the blood feud ran too deep.

The liberals' first line of defense was to invoke all of their standard critiques. Nixon's policy, they argued, was not going far enough and was indeed a subterfuge for continuing the Cold War. But given the broad front on which Nixon was proceeding, this argument held little attraction for any but confirmed Nixon-haters.

So it happened that, in the course of 1972, the liberals' attack veered in an entirely new direction which enabled them to maintain their traditional moral critique. Though they had hitherto insisted that East-West trade, arms control, and cultural exchanges were vital to ameliorating the superpower conflict and therefore needed to be pursued in their own right, the liberals now declared war on the Soviet internal system. Unembarrassed by their previous rejection of the concept of linkage of foreign policy issues to each other, they now resurrected linkage with a vengeance by insisting that all agreements be linked to changes in Soviet *domestic* practices.

Shifts in the editorial position of the *New York Times* mirrored this metamorphosis. Over the course of a few months in the fall of 1972, they moved from unconditional advocacy of East-West trade and arms control—and attacks on linkage—into a stern criticism of any agreement that did not dismantle the Soviet domestic structure. On

September 13, 1972, the *Times* was espousing its traditional liberal view that expanded trade "is sufficiently beneficial to both sides that it ought to be considered . . . on its own merits, independent of particular secondary disputes in other areas." [13]

Within two months, on November 25, 1972, in what was a complete reversal, the *Times* was cautioning its readers that "it will be a serious mistake if American business, the Nixon Administration, or, for that matter, Soviet officials, become so eager to expand Soviet-American trade as to forget the continuing sensitivity of the American people—and of Congress—to Soviet political behavior both inside and outside the USSR's borders." [14]

## The Conservative Critique

The liberals' reversal of position was soon being echoed by various conservative groups. Convinced that the Cold War was a life-and-death ideological struggle, conservatives had never been comfortable with a wide-ranging negotiation with the Soviet Union because the mere fact of it implied some degree of common interest with the Communist adversary. In their view, so long as Communism retained its grip, any hope for restraint in Soviet conduct was chimerical. The conservatives would have been most comfortable with some variation of the original Acheson-Dulles containment posture of waiting behind "positions of strength" for the eventual collapse of Communism within the Soviet Union and preferably in China as well. [15]

The conservatives' split from Nixon was a pity because we did not differ with their analysis of the nature of the Soviet system. Where we disagreed was in assessing its implications for American foreign policy. Nixon and I believed that refusing to negotiate with the Kremlin would spread the virulence of the anti-Vietnam protest movement into every aspect of American foreign policy and deeply, perhaps fatally, divide our alliances. Far better, we thought, to seize the initiative and control the diplomatic process. In the meantime, we would keep open the possibility that what had begun as tactics might evolve into a more reliable pattern of coexistence.

Nixon's disagreement with the traditional conservatives was in the nature of a family quarrel; they resented seeing their historic paladin adopt the tactics and even some of the rhetoric of his erstwhile liberal opponents. In time, especially had Watergate not supervened, they might well have been reconciled if Nixon had elaborated his strategic design to his traditional supporters—as he surely would have in an undamaged second term.

What drove conservative disquiet into outright opposition was the emergence of the so-called neoconservatives. That they claimed even part of the conservative label for themselves was something of an anomaly, since, nearly without exception, their leading representatives had started out on the liberal side, most of them on its radical wing. They had disdained Nixon, passionately opposed the Vietnam War, objected to our military budget as too Cold War–oriented, and pressed for a more conciliatory approach toward the Soviet Union.[16]

Starting in the summer of 1972 and extending over the period of a year, this group grew disillusioned with the turn American liberalism was taking. They found distasteful the radicalism and lifestyles of the Democratic convention that had nominated George McGovern in 1972. And ever since the Soviet invasion of Czechoslovakia, they had become increasingly disenchanted with the Soviet Union. The 1973 Middle East War completed their conversion to geopolitical realities. They interpreted that war as a Soviet-Arab conspiracy against Israel and the industrial democracies and concluded that the challenge was best resisted in the name of opposition to détente.

Once they changed sides, their anti-Communism was intense, often eloquent. And they demonstrated a considerable affinity for strategy honed by years of ideological warfare on the left side of the barricades.

Many of the neoconservatives were (or have become) personal friends. I respect Norman Podhoretz, Midge Decter, and Irving Kristol for their important intellectual and moral contributions, and I like them enormously on a personal level. I had long been an admirer also of Daniel Patrick "Pat" Moynihan—even though his label as a "conservative" proved to be somewhat temporary. When I was appointed Secretary of State, I offered him the position of counselor in the State Department. I had recommended him to Nixon for the ambassadorship to India and to Ford as ambassador to the United Nations. From this last position, Moynihan went on to launch his political career, partly on the basis of opposition to my alleged views on East-West relations or at least in his idiosyncratic interpretation of them.

However painful their critiques might occasionally have proved when I was in office, these individuals and their colleagues made significant contributions to American thinking on foreign policy. They brought a much needed intellectual rigor and energy to the debate, which helped to overcome the dominance of liberal conventional wisdom. Once they reached office in the Reagan Administration, they conducted a strong and successful national strategy.

But there was also a reverse side to the single-mindedness with which they pursued their newfound convictions. When the neoconservatives first appeared on the scene, their defining experience was their own ideological conversion to the pursuit of the Cold War. Tactics bored them; they discerned no worthy goals for American foreign policy short of total victory. Their historical memory did not include the battles they had refused to join or the domestic traumas to which they had so often contributed from the radical left side of the barricades. When the neoconservatives moved to the radical right, they packed in their bags their visceral dislike of Nixon even though technically they were now on the same side. And they distorted the subsequent debate by a touch of amnesia about their own role in the seminal battles of which Vietnam was a symbol, if not a cause.

Vietnam accelerated what the United States would have experienced in any event—albeit more gradually: that power in the world was becoming more diffused and isolation for America increasingly impossible. As the twenty-first century approached, the United States would have to exercise its influence as the single most important and coherent part of an international system but no longer as the predominant country it had been at the beginning of the Cold War. The great initiatives of the early Cold War had been presented as "solutions" to the challenge they were addressing, often with a terminal date. Henceforth what was needed was a permanent American participation depending more on the ability to accumulate nuances than on engineering final outcomes in a brief period.

The realization was dawning that idealism could lead to overextension as much as bad calculation. Yet traditional American Wilsonianism rebelled against the verity that great goals in foreign policy generally must be approached in imperfect stages. And the frustrations of Vietnam compounded the disillusionment. The radical opponents of the Vietnam War had ascribed the failures in Indochina to a moral defect and had preached the cure of abdication to enable the United States to concentrate on self-improvement. The neoconservatives reversed the lesson, seeing in moral regeneration the key to reengagement. Nixon and I agreed with the neoconservative premise, but we also believed that the simple Wilsonianism of the early 1960s had lured us into adventures beyond our capacities and deprived us of criteria to define the essential elements of our national purpose. Those of us who had been mauled by the Vietnam protest were deeply concerned—perhaps obsessed—with avoiding a repetition of this paralysis. We therefore searched for a more sober approach to American foreign policy that would—as we repeatedly stated—avoid the oscillations between abdication and overextension that had marked the previous period.

The neoconservatives insisted that such an approach did not do justice to the moral dynamism of a society that had turned its back on the callous calculations of the Old World. In the process, they put forward not so much a new dispensation—as they claimed—but a return to a militant, muscular Wilsonianism. The fundamental aim of foreign policy as they saw it was the eradication of the evil represented by the Soviet Union without confusing the issue with tactics.

Where Nixon (and I) saw the greatest danger in creeping Soviet expansionism abetted by the Soviet superiority in conventional forces, interior lines of communication, and the umbrella of a vast and growing strategic nuclear force, the neoconservatives' stated nightmare was some apocalyptic showdown, perhaps nuclear, over world domination. The Nixon team viewed the conflict with Moscow as a long-term geopolitical contest in which, together with our allies, we would wear down the Soviet system. The neoconservatives argued that it was possible to overcome Communism with a burst of ideological élan.

Since many of the neoconservatives considered even the NATO alliance as more an impediment to than an enhancement of American power, they saw far less value in defeating Soviet geopolitical encroachments on distant battlefields, such as Angola or Indochina, than in facing down the Soviet ideological or nuclear threat in some kind of definitive confrontation. This is why most neoconservatives failed to support the Ford Administration when Congress cut off aid to the desperate peoples of South Vietnam and Cambodia and to the African forces resisting the Soviet/Cuban intervention in Angola.

The neoconservatives' inward necessity to break with their past made them oblivious to the context in which their prescriptions had to be carried out and made it impossible to incorporate the real lessons of Vietnam into the national consciousness. Whatever the theoretical validity of the neoconservative argument, the United States, just emerging from Vietnam, in the midst of Watergate and later with a non-elected President, was not in a position to conduct a crusade; in fact, the attempt to do so would have torn the country apart even further. By depicting the diplomatic strategy of the Nixon and Ford Administrations as a form of appeasement and our resistance to Communist expansion in various theaters as a diversion from the main struggle, the neoconservatives undercut the real foreign policy debate.

Until well into Ford's term in office, congressional and media pressures were coming predominantly from the liberal side of the political spectrum. Senate Majority Leader Mike Mansfield periodically led drives to pull American troops out of Europe; Senate Foreign Relations Committee Chairman J. William Fulbright was challenging the alleged militarization of American foreign policy; Senators Frank Church and Walter Mondale were attacking the intelligence community. Some liberal Senators, such as Republicans Jacob Javits and John Sherman Cooper and Democrat Hubert Humphrey, endorsed our arms control policies but shrank from the defense programs necessary to give us leverage in the negotiations.

In the early 1970s, the option of what later became the Reagan policy did not exist. The obstacle to such a policy was not the Nixon or the Ford Administration but the liberal Congress and media. By training their fire on first Nixon and then Ford, the neoconservatives provided an alibi to those whose pressures had prevented a more favorable outcome in Indochina and whose legislation then caused its collapse and mandated an end to the Soviet/Cuban onslaught in Angola. The focal point of the foreign policy debate for the neoconservatives has been the moment at which they appeared on the scene, and they have so concentrated on a largely tactical disagreement with fellow conservatives that they have made it difficult to come to grips with the real lessons of the Vietnam tragedy.

Even after the neoconservatives had achieved major influence with the Reagan ascendancy, they continued their assault by insisting on a version of history that lures the United States away from the need to face complexity. According to this version of history, a group of accommodation-prone, European-influenced leaders was overcome by the knights-errant who had suddenly appeared on the scene and had prevailed in short order by proclaiming the distinction between good and evil and the revolutionary role of democratic principles.

Reality was more complex then and has become even more so at this writing. Ronald Reagan and his associates deserve much credit for

the denouement of the Cold War. But the United States will not harvest
the intellectual lessons of their success if it ascribes its victory in the
Cold War to rhetorical posturing. Reagan's policy was, in fact, a canny
reassertion of the geopolitical strategies of the Nixon and Ford Administrations clothed in the rhetoric of Wilsonianism—a quintessentially
American combination of pragmatism and idealism.[17] In an important
sense, the victories of the 1980s derived from a Reaganite variant—
not a rejection—of the strategies of the 1970s.

The Reagan Administration did not abjure practical arrangements;
for example, it signed a communiqué with China in which it accepted
limitations on arms supplies to Taiwan. And, at Reykjavik, Reagan
came within a hair of agreeing to the abandonment of all nuclear
arsenals—a gamble on arms control Nixon would never have considered. In its operating policies in the Middle East, Southern Africa, and
Central America and on missile defense, the Reagan Administration
followed a course to a great extent charted by Nixon or Ford, which is
why I and all former members of the national security team of both
the Nixon and Ford Administrations supported the key elements of
the Reagan foreign policy.

Nixon, Ford, and Reagan conducted policies that sought simultaneously to contain the Soviet Union, shrink its influence, and work
with it as this process unfolded. But whereas Nixon had sought to
legitimize these policies by their practical success, Reagan proved to
have a better instinct for America's emotions by justifying his course
in the name of American idealism. Nixon attempted to teach the
virtues of the national interest by evoking what he called a "structure
of peace"; Reagan understood better that the American people are
moved more by purpose than structure, and his policy declaration
resonated with classic Wilsonianism based on democratic virtue. As a
result, he won broader support for high defense budgets and geopolitical reengagement than Nixon was able to achieve or could have
achieved in his time with the same appeal. (Reagan, of course, led a
nation that had largely recovered from the Vietnam trauma and had
grown disgusted with the humiliations of the Iran hostage crisis.)

The fact is that both Reagan's inspirational approach and Nixon's
geopolitical perspicacity are needed to conduct a long-range foreign
policy in the twenty-first century. Nixon, under the pressure of circumstances and perhaps his personality, probably overemphasized the tactical element. But Reagan's disciples today, neglecting that Reagan
inherited a psychologically recovered American people ready for a

stronger course as well as a Soviet Union weakened by overextension (and by Nixon's foreign policy legacy), seek to telescope a historical process into one climactic presidency. They thereby postpone the synthesis without which we will never fully grasp our challenge and the consensus that would be theirs if they could only leaven their righteousness with an understanding that history did not begin on the date of their conversion.

As the Nixon Administration was ending, neither the President nor I understood the depth of the neoconservative challenge. We considered ourselves philosophically close to the neoconservatives and divided from them primarily by a tactical difference. The divide arose, in our view, from a differing strategic perspective, not from a debate over "tough" versus "soft" options, as the neoconservatives claimed.

As time went on, it became increasingly clear that the differences went much deeper. On one level, there was an element of personal rivalry inseparable from politics. Many of the converts to conservatism had been activists in Democratic politics, which meant that they sought not only to develop ideas but aspired to implement them in the political world. Newly arrived in the conservative camp, they needed space for that ambition. Nothing was more natural than to elevate tactical differences into a matter of principle, thereby necessitating replacement of the group shaping existing Republican foreign policy.

But there was, in fact, a philosophical difference—though it took me over a decade to understand it. Our clash with the neoconservatives was not over the nature of Communism, on which we were very close, but over the relationship of moral values to the conduct of international politics. I thought moral goals important, even decisive, in finding the fortitude to navigate a series of difficult choices, in any one of which the pros and cons were evenly balanced and the outcome likely to be imperfect. The neoconservatives believed that values could be translated directly into operating programs.

Absent Watergate, a successful Nixon presidency might well have been able to use the high-wire acts of his first term to amalgamate the ideological convictions of the neoconservatives with the geopolitical insights of his own approach. But in the supercharged atmosphere of 1973–74, the attacks on Nixon's foreign policy—especially on détente —began to merge with Watergate. Nixon lost his leverage in Congress and thereby the carrots and sticks without which there was no sustaining any serious Soviet policy. He never achieved maneuvering room for the sort of dialogue that might have reconciled him with both his erstwhile conservative supporters and the emerging neoconservatives. Since the attendant debate was deprived of a strong presidential voice, I was alone to face the onslaught. This turned my role into a political issue—an uncomfortable and, in the long run, unsustainable position for a Secretary of State. Damaged by Watergate, the President was in no position to resist what amounted to a revolt of the traditional Wilsonianism against his administration's emphasis on the national interest.

The irony of it was that Soviet Ambassador Anatoly Dobrynin understood our strategy far better than our neoconservative critics. He wrote in his memoirs:

> Underlying their policy toward the Soviet Union was a combination of deterrence and cooperation, a mosaic of short-term and long-term considerations. Both Nixon and Kissinger sought to create a more stable and predictable strategic situation without reducing the high level of armaments, which remained the basis of a policy that was essentially based on military strength, and on the accommodation of national interests only when they found it desirable to do so. Their arms control efforts thus disguised this policy of strength, but only slightly. Essentially, neither the President nor his closest aide proved able (or wanted) to break out of the orbit of the Cold War, although their attitude was more pragmatic and realistic than other Cold Warriors in the White House.[18]

## Senator Henry Jackson and Détente: Strategy and Arms Control

Had the controversy remained largely theoretical, the uneasy alliance between liberal and conservative critics of Nixon would probably have broken down over their clashing interpretations of the evolving international situation.

What prevented this from happening was the emergence of Henry "Scoop" Jackson as a leader capable of forging a platform which both the liberals and conservatives could support. Democratic Senator from the state of Washington since 1952, Jackson had been Nixon's first choice for Secretary of Defense. He had turned it down in part because he was hoping to run for President in the 1970s. Jackson was popular with the labor movement and had the respect of the conservatives because he was a staunch champion of a strong national defense. He had courageously stood by both the Johnson and Nixon Administrations on Vietnam. And, in 1969, he had managed the narrow Senate victory which approved the Nixon Administration's missile defense program.

Later on, the fate of that program became one of the causes of Jackson's disenchantment. He came to believe that he had been misled about the resoluteness with which Nixon and Defense Secretary Melvin Laird would defend the original "Safeguard" program. Opponents of missile defense in Congress reduced the originally planned twelve missile defense sites each year until only two were left in the 1972 defense budget. Jackson argued that the administration had not defended its own program with requisite conviction. Given the characteristic opaqueness of both Laird and Nixon, Jackson probably had some justification for his claim—though at worst Nixon and Laird had acquiesced in congressional pressures they had deemed to be overwhelming in order to salvage the rest of the defense budget.

Through all controversies, I maintained a high regard for Scoop Jackson. During Nixon's first term, I occasionally had dinner at his house to brief him on our policy. And Jackson was an indispensable ally in the endless grinding battle to rescue the defense budget from congressional depredations—an extremely courageous stand given the prevailing trend within the Democratic Party of the 1970s.

A man of high principle, Jackson found it impossible to reconcile himself to Nixon's tactic of seeming to adopt the rhetoric of his domestic opponents, especially regarding negotiations with the Soviet Union. Though Jackson's aims remained parallel to Nixon's and Ford's —and he sometimes admitted it[19]—the Senator was enough of a politician to understand that if he wanted to be a credible contender for the Democratic presidential nomination in 1976, he would have to dissociate from Richard Nixon.

Jackson was stubborn and persistent. Once launched on a course, he was not to be deflected. And he was spurred on by the extraordinary Richard Perle, who became his principal staffer. Perle, who had not participated in the debates of the 1960s, was a passionate anti-Communist and one of the ablest geopolitical minds I have encountered. He now emerged as the chief designer of Jackson's strategy of confrontation with Nixon. Far too intelligent not to have realized that some of the charges he was making were more cynical than substantive, Perle proved as steadfast as he was ingenious in pursuing his larger aim: to stymie the administration's arms control policies by submerging them in technical controversies, to block trade with the Soviet Union by making it dependent on changes in Soviet emigration policies, and to isolate the administration by accusing it of indifference to human rights. By using such code words as "strategic equality" and "free emigration," Jackson, with Perle's indispensable assistance, took his stand on two issues which effectively put us on the defensive. On each issue, he skillfully transformed administration successes into liabilities by an extraordinary ability to manipulate vague, symbolic allegations.

Who could be opposed to the principles of "equality" in strategic armaments or to the desirability of free emigration from the Soviet Union? Absent Watergate, no serious observer would have believed that Nixon, with his strong anti-Communist record, would knowingly settle for inequality. The trouble lay in the elusive meaning of that term. Since the strategic forces of the two sides had been designed on the basis of radically different criteria and technologies, the very definition of "equality" lent itself, as I shall explain below, to endless controversy and obfuscation—a circumstance which Jackson and Perle deftly wove into a de facto veto over the actual negotiations.

The issue of Jewish emigration from the Soviet Union was even more arbitrary. The Nixon Administration had quietly introduced the issue into Soviet-American diplomacy and had succeeded in raising the number of emigrants from four hundred in 1968 to 35,000 in 1972. At that point, the Soviets imposed an exit tax on emigrants, triggering Jackson—who had played no role in our previous efforts—into the fray. He demanded not only that the exit tax be removed (which we supported) but also that the number of emigrants be tripled on pain of Congress denying Soviet trade Most Favored Nation (MFN) status.

Jackson never explained what made him think that the Soviet Union, which he was accusing of aiming for world domination with its strategic nuclear program, would submit to so public a challenge to its domestic structure without resistance—especially on an issue on which it had gone far to accommodate our demands. Jackson's pressures were generating a crisis with Moscow at the precise moment when the American presidency was facing its period of greatest weakness since the Civil War, and the American Congress was systematically reducing our military budget.

Jackson's assault gained momentum because Nixon was extremely reluctant to accept the fact that the Senator had turned into an adversary. Our first instinct was to try to meet Jackson's criticisms. Thus when he introduced a Senate resolution in 1972 calling for "equality" in strategic arms control, I assigned two staff members to help him draft it, intending to use it as leverage against the Soviets in the next round of negotiations. Only gradually and very reluctantly did we come to understand that Jackson's various pressures were designed to gut rather than improve our East-West policy. We agreed with Jackson's suspicions regarding Soviet motivations, but we rejected the notion that, in a diplomatic contest with the rigid old men in the Kremlin, we were bound to lose—if only because it was so contrary to our own experiences with them.

The biggest impact of the Jackson assault was to make it that much more difficult for the United States to come to grips with the changed military environment into which the new technology had projected it. Jackson and his neoconservative supporters spawned the myth that Nixon was sacrificing American military security on the altar of arms control theory. The facts were more complex. Nixon faced three interrelated challenges: (1) an altered strategic environment caused by the growth of the Soviet missile force and the explosion of technology; (2) congressional resistance to high defense budgets; and (3) the negotiations on arms control, which had wide popular and media support and were needed to sustain adequate defense budgets.

Nixon had always been a defense hawk and remained so throughout his presidency. No Pentagon defense budget was ever reduced by the Nixon White House; no existing weapons system was ever abandoned in a Nixon-led negotiation. Where we differed with Jackson and the neoconservatives was with respect to their apparent belief that arms control negotiations could, by themselves, alter strategic realities. They were asking arms control to undo what had, in large part, been brought about by unilateral American decisions over the course of a decade and to make up for congressional refusal to back some necessary strategic programs, such as missile defense. These were impossible tasks for any negotiator, and they obfuscated the real strategic challenge facing the President.

The fact was that, long before arms control was invented, the evolution of nuclear strategy had been in the direction of the dead end produced by the widening gap between the destructiveness of the nuclear arsenals and any political purpose to which they might be put. That condition had become inescapable by the time the Nixon Administration took office.

From the beginning of the Cold War, the Soviet Union had benefited from the general impression that it possessed a vast superiority in conventional weapons. Its ruthless repression of the Berlin uprisings of 1953, the Hungarian revolution in 1956, and the Czechoslovak reform of 1968 reinforced the aura associated with the seemingly overwhelming numbers of the Red Army. But until the early 1970s, Soviet conventional strength was counterbalanced by America's superiority in long-range nuclear striking power. That American edge was now gradually declining as a result of progress in Soviet nuclear technology. It happened in three stages.

The first was in the era of America's atomic monopoly from 1945 to 1950 when the United States had the capacity to devastate the Soviet Union in defense of vital American interests without any fear of significant retaliation.

The second stage, lasting from the early 1950s to about 1970, began when the Soviet Union developed nuclear weapons of its own. Nevertheless, so long as the Soviet capacity to deliver these weapons remained rudimentary and America's strategic forces remained so much larger and more capable, we retained what was technically called a "first-strike" capability—that is, in response to a Soviet conventional attack, we would be able to destroy the Soviet strategic forces and war-making capability with tolerable losses on our side.

The third stage began when the Soviet leaders reacted to the humiliation of bowing to our first-strike capability in the 1962 Cuban Missile Crisis by creating a large arsenal of long-range strategic missiles of their own. In less than ten years, the Soviets built 1,400 missiles in concrete silos to replace their previous force of some 210 highly vulnerable and rather clumsy missiles standing in the open. At this point, the cost of strategic nuclear war began to involve unacceptable levels of destruction for both sides, whatever the numerical edge of one side or the other.

These dilemmas deepened when, in 1962, Secretary of Defense Robert McNamara adopted the strategy of "assured destruction," which based deterrence on the calculation of a level of civilian devastation that would be theoretically unacceptable to the Soviet Union. This essentially academic concept presupposed unlimited willingness to threaten civilian casualties; minimum estimates involved tens of millions. This professorial strategy calculated everything except the willingness to resort to it. Inevitably it created a huge gap between our awesome military capacity and the moral convictions of almost any foreseeable American leader. A deliberate all-out attack on civilian targets offended the most jaded moral sensibilities, while, at prevailing levels of strategic forces, an attempt to wipe out the opponent's strategic capability would almost surely trigger a retaliation on our own civilian targets.

To the degree that these nuclear dilemmas raised American inhibitions to resort to nuclear war, they increased the Soviet potential to engage in blackmail, a problem which would inevitably mount as the Soviet nuclear arsenal multiplied. As nuclear strategy metamorphosed into a form of self-deterrence, the Soviet conventional preponderance once again emerged as a dominant threat.

This was the real strategic dilemma facing the Nixon Administration as nuclear warheads multiplied on both sides—not the arms control agreements being negotiated at Geneva which reflected them and could not undo them. Nor have they ever done so in any of the successor administrations. Nixon took a series of steps to improve the strategic equation: he ordered a shift in emphasis of war-planning away from civilian and toward military targets; and he built up our strategic forces by pushing the deployment of multiple warheads and proposing a ballistic missile defense to Congress—a forerunner of Reagan's 1983 Strategic Defense Initiative (SDI), albeit on the basis of less adequate technology.

The revision of war-planning proved laborious. Secretary Laird was too preoccupied with preventing congressional depredations against the defense budget to give the attention necessary to adaptations of strategic concepts. In addition, the combination of congressional pressures on the military budget and of a technology generating ever more weapons systems caused the military services to be far more concerned with protecting their favorite projects than with developing a new overall strategy. While fighting for its life against a hostile Congress, the Pentagon was in no mood to risk its existing programs on theoretical controversies over the use of strategic weapons. The revision of the Single Integrated Operational Plan (SIOP), or strategic war plan, consumed the better part of Nixon's period in office. And, by the time it was completed under Secretary James Schlesinger five years later, the increase in the number of weapons and improvements in technology prevented a significant reduction in civilian casualties even when the number of targets was reduced.

The buildup of American strategic forces faced determined congressional opposition in the Vietnam era. The Nixon Administration did succeed in fending off congressional attempts (led by liberal Republican Senator Edward Brooke) to stop the testing of multiple warheads—in technical terms, Multiple Independently Targetable Reentry Vehicles, or MIRVs—which was essential to balance the emerging Soviet advantage in the number of long-range missile forces, then and for the decade to come still equipped with single warheads. Since the funds for the project had been authorized during the Johnson Administration, Congress could not muster a majority to stop it. That did not, however, keep a sizable minority from harassing us on the basis of an assumption for which there was not a shred of evidence: that, if we forswore testing, the Soviet Union would follow suit.

Congress proved more successful in its opposition to the Anti-Ballistic Missile (ABM) defense system, which had been put forward by Nixon in April 1969 for both strategic and philosophical reasons. In an age of growing nuclear stockpiles, Nixon considered it irresponsible to leave the American people totally exposed to such foreseeable contingencies as accidents, small-scale nuclear attacks, or to the dangers arising from the growing nuclear capability of emerging nuclear powers. And he wanted to disabuse the Soviets of any temptations to risk a limited nuclear attack.

But the majority of defense scientists, the peace movement, and most of the media had grown committed to the unprecedented— and nihilistic—proposition that the total vulnerability of the civilian population was essential for a nation's security. Making both nuclear powers totally vulnerable would, they argued, cause them to recoil from the brink. Nixon's ABM system was soon being violently attacked for several largely incompatible reasons: that it would not work; that it would work too well and tempt a Soviet preemptive attack; that it would somehow damage relations with Moscow, never mind that the Soviet Union had long since deployed a missile defense system of its own—albeit not a very effective one.

Like water dripping onto a stone, the constant invocation of this dogma eventually carried the day in Congress as it has in essence ever since. In 1969, Nixon's program of twelve defense sites passed the Senate by only one vote—the Vice President's. In subsequent years, as noted, its opponents in Congress whittled down the program by annually cutting out a few ABM sites until only two remained in the 1972 budget. (Two decades later, the Reagan SDI program was to suffer the same fate.) Trapped into a system which no longer made any strategic sense, the Pentagon reluctantly began to treat strategic defense as one of our few remaining bargaining chips with which to curtail further Soviet offensive deployments.

In the face of all these obstacles, the Nixon and Ford Administrations did bring about a significant increase of American strategic power. By building 500 new ICBMs (each with three warheads), the Minuteman III, and 500 new submarine-launched missiles with ten to fourteen warheads each (the Poseidon), the United States increased the number of its warheads from 1,700 in 1970 to 7,000 in 1978. A new submarine—the Trident—with longer range and more powerful weapons was approved, and construction began in 1975. An entirely new intercontinental missile, the MX, was developed. The B-52s were completely rebuilt, and two new supersonic bombers—the B-1 and the stealthy B-2—were developed, as was a panoply of long-range cruise missiles saved by Nixon (on my recommendation) from the Pentagon budget ax in 1973. Indeed, the vast majority of the offensive weapons in the American strategic arsenal twenty years later had originated during the Nixon and Ford periods.

What slowed down the buildup was not arms control but congressional opposition, not just in the 1970s but even during the Reagan buildup ten years later. When the B-1 bomber was approved in the Nixon Administration, 240 had been planned; congressional pressures over ten years cut the number to 95. When the Ford Administration approved the MX, 200 had been planned; twenty years later, 50 have been deployed. The B-2 stealth bomber was slashed from 132 to 20, and the Nixon ABM program from 12 sites to zero; the Reagan SDI program has never been funded beyond a research effort.

The ultimate nuclear dilemma was that, even after all the buildup, the strategic arsenals were useful primarily to deter nuclear attacks and for little else. This frustration came to expression in an exasperated challenge I threw out—unwisely but correctly—at a press conference at the end of the Moscow summit of 1974: "What in the name of God is strategic superiority? What is the significance of it . . . at these levels of numbers? What do you do with it?"[20]

The theoretical answer was the destruction of the enemy retaliatory force in a first strike and the fending off of retaliation through missile defense. But in the real world, that capacity has never been developed, and the execution of it involved risks and calculations so complex as to be beyond the psychological capacity of most foreseeable policymakers. Neither the Nixon Administration nor any of its successors solved this conundrum.

The debate inherited by Gerald Ford was well summed up by an Australian scholar, Coral Bell:

> On the right, excess expectation runs to an assumption, or at any rate an argument, that the Russians can and should be made to pay for détente by a remodelling of their entire behaviour, international and domestic: that they can be made to refrain from competing in areas whose future is ambiguous, like Angola, to relax their grip on their buffer-zone in Eastern Europe, and to behave with more liberalism towards their own citizenry, all for the sake of détente. No doubt all these things are desirable, and not just from a Western point of view. But from the point of view of the Soviet political elite it might seem less dangerous and embarrassing simply to return to the full cold war, and that might logically be their preferred option if the bargain were presented solely on those terms.
>
> On the left, excess expectation assumes that in a détente situation the normal modes of conserving the Western power base can and should be neglected or abandoned: that arms budgets should be cut, the capacity for covert operations dismantled and in general the security necessities of international politics disregarded.
>
> These are, in my view, equal and opposite errors. They confuse a strategy with the end towards which it is directed. Détente does not mean that the power contest has ended: it only proposes a mode by which it may be made less dangerous and pointed in a more creative direction.[21]

# 4

# JACKSON, ARMS CONTROL, AND JEWISH EMIGRATION

## Arms Control

When Nixon entered office, he was far from a zealot on arms control. If anything, he considered it as a bargaining chip to be used to help extricate the United States from Vietnam.[1] He procrastinated in opening negotiations to see what political concessions delay might extract from Moscow.

Three considerations convinced Nixon to authorize the opening of negotiations on November 3, 1969. The first was that, in order to compensate for his generally hard line on Vietnam, the Middle East, defense, and other issues, some concrete demonstration of his administration's commitment to peace was necessary. This is why Nixon announced the opening of talks in a speech seeking to rally support behind his Vietnam policy. Second, congressional pressures on the defense budget turned the Pentagon—for a fleeting moment—into supporters of mutual arms limitations. Third, Nixon was becoming concerned about the buildup of Soviet strategic forces, which were being increased at the rate of about two hundred missiles a year, while Congress was gutting every effort to augment our own strategic forces.

The opening of negotiations brought us face-to-face with the problem of how to define equality. For the nuclear forces of the two sides had been built on the basis of divergent technologies and concepts of security. In the 1960s, before SALT had been invented, the United States, by its own choice, had stopped building additional intercontinental missiles and concentrated instead on such qualitative improvements as multiple warheads. In addition, the United States relied on long-range bombers, for which the Soviets had no modern counterpart, as well as on aircraft based overseas and on carriers.

For its part, in the wake of the Cuban Missile Crisis, the Soviet Union had launched a vast program of land- and submarine-based missiles, which, by the 1970s, began to exceed the number of American missiles. Nevertheless, because of our lead in multiple warheads, the United States would possess a three-to-one edge in warheads throughout the 1970s and a substantial numerical advantage well into the 1980s. That advantage would gradually decline as the Soviets placed multiple warheads on their own missiles. By the late 1980s, Soviet MIRV numbers would exceed those of the United States—unless we built more and larger missiles, such as the MX, which we had on the drawing boards. It was therefore entirely a matter of our own decision whether we would close the emerging numerical gap. Throughout any foreseeable period, the United States would possess a vast advantage in heavy bombers.

The conceptual problem with any arms control negotiation is that its outcome represents but a single snapshot of a rapidly evolving technological and strategic equation. The parties have to find a way not only to take account of the existing balance of forces but to maintain the agreed relationship throughout a period in which the arms race was shifting from the quantitative to the qualitative plane.

Until about 1970, the arms race had been largely about numbers. So long as each missile carried only one warhead, a quantitative edge on the order of three-to-one would be required for even a theoretically successful surprise attack. (This assumed that, even with high accuracy, two warheads would be assigned to each concrete-encased missile launcher and that some missiles would be held back as reserves for follow-on missions.) Thus, the Soviets would require 3,000 *accurate* missiles to have the least confidence of destroying our land-based missiles and we about 4,500 to destroy the Soviet land-based force. Such a force could only be developed over a long period of time—long enough to ensure a suitable response—and it was almost certainly financially out of reach. In the early 1970s, the Soviet Union possessed less than half the required number of single-warhead missiles, and most of them were not very accurate.

The advent of multiple warheads revolutionized the strategic equation. From then on, a first-strike capability could be achieved—at least theoretically—by adding warheads to existing individual missiles without increasing the number of launchers. Some of our submarine-launched missiles were capable of carrying as many as fourteen relatively small warheads (each, however, larger than the bombs which destroyed Hiroshima and Nagasaki). The problem was that, with both sides capable of installing over 10,000 warheads on existing missile launchers (plus, on the American side, a fleet of some 500 heavy bombers), there would be more weapons than conceivable targets. General George S. Brown, then Chairman of the Joint Chiefs of Staff, told Ford at an NSC meeting on October 7, 1974, that we had limited the number of MIRVs on our submarine-launched missiles because of a paucity of targets. Once it became possible to assign several warheads to each enemy missile launcher and still have thousands of warheads left, a first strike against the land-based forces again became conceivable.

Not surprisingly, the talks deadlocked almost immediately. Even in the absence of ideological and geopolitical disagreements, it was intellectually difficult to put forward a proposal which would actually improve the evolving situation. Moreover, in view of the congressional reluctance to approve new American strategic weapons, the Soviet Union had little incentive to accept limitations on its own offensive strategic programs.

In the end, the Nixon Administration achieved some leverage by means of the ironic fact that Soviet leaders turned out to have more confidence in American technology than did our domestic critics. Far from ruining SALT—as congressional opponents argued—ballistic missile defense provided the key that unlocked the door to offensive limitations, just as it did for Reagan fifteen years later. The Soviet leaders feared that, even if an American missile defense was not fully effective against an all-out surprise attack, it might work against the inevitably disorganized retaliation from the residual forces left after an American first strike. And it might also render limited blackmail attacks too difficult to calculate and to plan. The Soviets' fear of even our first-generation defense was magnified by its potential to be upgraded.

Hoping—not unreasonably in the conditions of the period—that Congress would do their work for them, Soviet negotiators insisted that any agreement be confined to limiting defensive weapons—a classic Kremlin ploy to freeze the weapons that concerned them while putting no constraints on the two hundred new Soviet missiles being built each year, which happened to be our principal worry. As noted earlier, the deadlock was finally broken in May 1971 after Nixon insisted in the back channel that he would never accept an agreement confined to defensive weapons. After that, and with many hiccups —mostly produced by Soviet attempts to evade offensive limitations —two arms control agreements were signed on the occasion of the Moscow summit of May 1972.

Though the technical provisions were complex, the overall concept was straightforward enough. First, a permanent agreement with certain escape clauses limited ballistic missile defense to two sites in each country—the same number to which Congress had already confined us. These were too few to provide for a continental defense. Second, an interim agreement lasting five years, from 1972 until 1977, froze offensive missile deployments at existing levels. Heavy bombers were not limited so as to enable us to deploy the newly developed supersonic B-1 bomber and because the Soviets had no genuinely long-range bomber nor a program for one. During the interim period, a permanent and more comprehensive agreement would hopefully be negotiated.

At first, the agreement was well received but, as time went on, criticism mounted. Liberal frustrations with Nixon merged with the conservative distrust of any deal with the Soviet Union. The portion of the agreement dealing with missile defense proved relatively noncontroversial at the time, though I regretted that our domestic divisions should have obliged us to accept vulnerability as a permanent fixture of our strategy.

To our surprise, criticism focused on the agreement freezing offensive deployments, which had put an end to the Soviet offensive buildup of two hundred missiles a year and did not require the United States to abandon a single existing or planned program. The criticism had two aspects: that the agreement had granted a numerical advantage to the Soviets and that it rendered our strategic forces vulnerable to surprise attack.

Both charges were more a reflection of the acrimony of our national divisions than of any serious analysis. The numerical inequality in missile launchers had not been "granted" by our SALT negotiators but established unilaterally by the Joint Chiefs of Staff and the Defense Secretaries of two administrations of both parties before SALT negotiations had even been conceived. To put it crudely, the United States stopped building additional missiles because its most senior defense officials had become convinced that the country's security required no more. The 1972 interim agreement (SALT I) neither shaped nor altered this conviction, which has been maintained for nearly three decades since. Not even the hawkish Reagan Administration sought to increase our missile forces. And whatever inequality did exist in the numbers of missile launchers was more than made up by America's advantage in multiple warheads and heavy bombers.

The Pentagon had never requested any increase in the total number of missiles. Neither the Nixon nor the Ford White House ever disapproved or discouraged any Defense Department proposal for augmenting American strategic forces either before or after the SALT agreement. On the contrary, the Nixon and Ford Administrations used the SALT agreements to justify modernization of our strategic forces —causing Senator Stuart Symington to grumble at the time the agreement was being presented to the Senate Foreign Relations Committee that he doubted we could financially afford another such arms limitation agreement.

The charge that the interim offensive agreement (SALT I) "granted" an advantage to the Soviets was basically demagoguery. In November 1974 (as we shall see in Chapter 10), Ford did negotiate at Vladivostok the equal levels that were so stridently demanded by Henry Jackson and his supporters. Though allowed 2,500 launchers under the Vladivostok ceilings, the defense planners of *all* succeeding administrations adhered to the SALT I limits. Three administrations later, our totals were in fact slightly lower than they had been under Nixon, and even the hawkish Reagan Administration did not alter them. The following chart demonstrates that twenty years after the "inequality" debate, the ratios of the two missile forces were still what they had been when the interim agreement was signed and, if anything, the "missile gap" had grown slightly larger:

|  | 1972 | | 1991 | |
| --- | --- | --- | --- | --- |
|  | U.S. | U.S.S.R. | U.S. | U.S.S.R. |
| ICBM * Launchers | 1,000 | 1,618 | 1,000 | 1,451 |
| SLBM † Launchers | 710 | 740‡ | 608 | 942 |
| Total Missile Launchers | 1,710 | 2,358 | 1,608 | 2,393 |
| Heavy Bombers² | 525 | 140 | 307 | 177 |
| Total Strategic Launchers | 2,235 | 2,498 | 1,915 | 2,570 |
| Total Missile Warheads | 1,710 | 2,358 | 8,658 | 10,463 |

* Intercontinental ballistic missile
† Submarine-launched ballistic missile
‡ Up to 950 allowed if 210 older ICBM launchers were dismantled.

The second charge against the arms control policies of the Nixon Administration—that it tempted a Soviet surprise attack—was even more out of touch with reality.

The surprise attack scenario went as follows. By placing ten warheads on its 300 heavy missiles, the Soviet Union would be able to destroy all of America's 1,000 land-based missiles and perhaps a third of our missile-carrying submarines in port at any one time. The United States would then be left with only some 450 submarine-launched warheads and the surviving bomber force with a total of perhaps 3,000 to 4,000 warheads, while the Soviet residual force might approach four times that number. Under these conditions, it was claimed that the American President could be intimidated into holding back his remaining retaliatory force and into accepting Soviet terms.[3]

The scenario substituted overwrought technical terminology for plausibility. The various disaster scenarios assumed that Soviet leaders were prepared to stake the survival of their society and political system on a number of wild gambles:

- that the Soviets were technically able to launch several hundred missiles simultaneously even though they had never test-fired more than three at a time and these only from test sites, never from operational silos. (Some of the more dramatic scenarios even predicted that the Soviets would first evacuate their cities to blunt our counterblow while the United States remained passive.)
- that American missiles would not be launched on warning even though there might be a thirty- to forty-five-minute interval in which to determine whether an all-out attack was under way.
- that Soviet operational missiles had the same accuracy as test missiles—a risky assumption in light of the fact that, in a surprise attack, they would need to be fired in a north–south direction, whereas all test missiles (of both sides) had been fired in an east–west direction to avoid creating the impression of a surprise attack thereby triggering retaliation. (This was, of course, a vivid demonstration of the precariousness of counting on surprise.)
- that the aged leaders of a moribund society would have enough confidence to gamble that an American President would refrain from using the thousands of warheads which, even under the most pessimistic scenario, would survive a surprise attack.

Finally, none of these hypothetical scenarios would be available even to the most demented Soviet leader until about a decade *after*

*SALT I expired*, or more than enough time in which to take counter-measures. These could involve increasing the survivable United States forces by putting more warheads on existing missiles, developing a larger missile with more warheads and greater explosive power, or building new weapons with altogether different characteristics not limited by SALT I, such as cruise missiles. And there was always the option of missile defense. With the exception of missile defense, which was emasculated by Congress, all of these steps were, in fact, either taken or initiated in the Nixon Administration and were elaborated by Ford *before* SALT I expired.

No wonder the professional military never endorsed any of these frantic scenarios. What they thought of the strategic balance was expressed in a letter from the Chairman of the Joint Chiefs of Staff, General George Brown, to Senator William Proxmire in 1977 shortly after Ford had left office:

> The Joint Chiefs of Staff do not agree that the Soviet Union
> has achieved military superiority over the United States. . . .
> [U.S. strategic forces] are considered sufficient to achieve US
> objectives today.[4]

By fixating on a single and remote danger, Henry Jackson and his neoconservative allies managed to deflect the domestic debate from America's real security problem in the 1970s, which was, not an all-out nuclear attack on the United States; it was rather that an emerging strategic stalemate might tempt the Soviet Union into exploiting its superiority in *conventional* weapons for geopolitical encroachment or blackmail. Strategic arms control should have been treated as a component of overall national strategy. Yet the liberals clung to arms control as a panacea, and the conservatives imagined SALT I to be the cause, not the result, of our own unilateral procurement decisions made for more than a decade.

The actual strategic equation, in fact, gave the United States a much greater capacity than the Soviet Union to carry out doomsday scenarios. For even under SALT I conditions, the Soviet strategic forces were far more vulnerable to an American first strike than their American counterparts. That was because only about 30 percent of America's strategic forces were land-based, as compared to 90 percent of the Soviet Union's. And American submarine-launched missiles were far more efficient and accurate than those of the Soviets. With the right mix of MXs and Minuteman IIIs, the United States could have made the Soviet land-based force as vulnerable as our critics claimed the American strategic forces were and to much more devastating effect on the Soviet overall strategic capability. None of our successors ever proposed such a mix.

Thus, by the time Nixon left office, arms control discussions were slipping into an intellectual never-never land. Détente was under attack by liberals for being excessively focused on military security and by conservatives for being inadequately concerned with it, by liberals for demonstrating too little commitment to arms control and by conservatives for displaying too much. Defense programs were just barely being pushed through Congress with conservative help over liberal opposition, while arms control measures narrowly prevailed with liberal support against conservative opposition. Jackson and his supporters deserve much credit for having helped to stem the assault of the Vietnam protest against national defense. But they were paralyzing America's Soviet policy.

## Jewish Emigration from the Soviet Union

Emigration from the Soviet Union had never been either a foreign policy or a domestic issue until the Nixon Administration introduced it into the Soviet-American dialogue. I first discussed Jewish emigration with Soviet Ambassador Anatoly Dobrynin in 1969. I kept my approach low-key, since, until then, the subject had been raised only by private Jewish groups. Calling attention to the small number being permitted to leave in 1968—it was less than four hundred—I pointed out that any increase would be noted by the administration and would have a favorable impact on our assessment of Soviet intentions. Somewhat to our surprise, Jewish emigration from the Soviet Union gradually rose nearly a hundredfold in five years, from four hundred in 1968 to nearly 35,000 in 1973.

To ensure that the positive trend in emigration continued, the Nixon Administration never claimed public credit, not even during the 1972 presidential election campaign. Thus we found ourselves almost helpless when our policy was suddenly hijacked by Jackson.

What triggered Jackson's assault was a Kremlin decision in August 1972 to levy an "exit tax" on all emigrants, allegedly to compensate the Soviet state for what it had spent on the emigrants' education. The practical effect would be a substantial reduction in the numbers emigrating. Why the Soviet Union should have chosen to jeopardize American goodwill at that high point of East-West relations has never been adequately explained. Dobrynin's claim—that the decision had been made by some middle-level official—is not credible given the compulsively centralized Communist system and the interest the Nixon Administration had shown in the subject. More likely, top Soviet leaders, shaken by Egyptian President Anwar Sadat's voluble disappointment with the results of the 1972 summit and his expulsion of Soviet advisers in retaliation, were trying to avoid the additional accusation that their laxness on Jewish emigration was tacitly strengthening Israel (where a majority of the emigrants were then settling).

Whatever the explanation, the exit tax unleashed an assault on the successful policy which we had been conducting without fanfare for four years and in an almost ostentatiously nonpolitical fashion. The vehicle for launching the assault became the pending Senate approval of the 1972 agreement granting Most Favored Nation status to the Soviet Union in return for Moscow's paying Lend-Lease debts dating back to the Second World War. Concluding MFN had been urged on us since the early days of the Nixon Administration, especially by liberal Congressmen, Senators, and the media.

In the supercharged post–Vietnam/Watergate atmosphere, the term Most Favored Nation sounded incendiary because it implied that some new and somehow special favor was being bestowed on the Soviet Union (twenty years later, the same issue was to arise with respect to China). In fact, MFN is a technical term signifying that a country is being granted the same treatment already available to all other nations with which the United States maintains normal commercial relations (there were over one hundred of these in 1974, about 160 at this writing).

Only its refusal to repay wartime Lend-Lease credits had kept the Soviet Union from obtaining MFN status earlier. In September 1972, Secretary of Commerce Peter G. Peterson concluded a negotiation settling both issues. Given the backward state of Soviet industry, MFN was not expected to lead to a significant increase in Soviet-American trade. Its principal benefit was psychological as a symbol of equality for Soviet leaders, who, though claiming to represent the vanguard of history, nevertheless seemed obsessed by the fear that they were not being accorded appropriate status.

The agreement on MFN supplied Senator Jackson with a legislative vehicle to bring matters to a head. On October 4, 1972, he offered an amendment to a measure renewing the President's negotiating authority on trade. The Jackson Amendment prohibited Most Favored Nation status for any Communist country which restricted emigration. When, on April 10, 1973, Nixon submitted to Congress the Lend-Lease settlement together with the proposed MFN status for the Soviet Union, the battle was joined.

We were convinced that the issue would be settled quickly and amicably, for we still considered Jackson an ally and treated our disagreements with him as largely tactical. This is why we initially indulged him and sought to turn his amendment into leverage for inducing the Soviets to lift the exit tax. After several discussions between Dobrynin and myself, the Soviet embassy, on March 30, 1973, delivered a memorandum to my office marked "Confidential for the President." Though it described emigration practices as a strictly domestic Soviet matter, the Kremlin informed Nixon that henceforth the exit tax would be levied only in "unusual" cases involving state security; in all others, only "insignificant" duties would be collected.

Our response showed the extent to which Jackson had succeeded in turning Jewish emigration from the Soviet Union into an American domestic issue. We asked Moscow to allow us to communicate the message to Congress and to the Israeli government as well. Protesting volubly that Israel had no standing whatsoever with respect to Soviet emigration practices, the Kremlin nevertheless gave ground, leaving it to the discretion of the President "to decide how to use our communication and whom he will inform about its contents." We thought we were home free.

On April 18, our illusions about Jackson's purposes vanished; that date marked the watershed for his open and increasingly implacable opposition to our policies. Nixon had invited congressional leaders to a meeting in the Roosevelt Room of the White House to inform them of the Soviet communication. We had expected the briefing to end the matter, perhaps even to elicit some recognition for what we considered to be a diplomatic coup.

Jackson, however, had lost interest in the immediate issue of the exit tax. Having discovered a weapon with which to challenge Nixon's Soviet policy, he was not about to sheathe it. The Soviet reply, the Senator declared icily, was inadequate. To be eligible for MFN, the Soviet Union would have to *guarantee* a *minimum* number of exit visas and ease restrictions on emigration for *all* nationalities. Jackson did not stipulate what minimum number he had in mind, but clearly it would be significantly larger than the already unprecedented figure of nearly 35,000 being allowed to leave in 1973.

Jackson's demand to add conditions to a signed agreement in which the Soviets had accepted our stated terms (the repayment of Lend-Lease debts) was an invitation to a confrontation. And Jackson was organizing it at a moment when Nixon's authority was visibly declining. For that was the very week in which John Dean went to the prosecutor and Watergate exploded in Nixon's face.

Nor could it have eluded the Senator that he was honing an issue ideally suited to his own presidential ambitions. Inside the Beltway, Jackson was recognized as a canny tactician and respected as a man of principle. But to secure the Democratic nomination three years hence, he would have to find a way to win primaries in New York and California, and this obliged him to try to soften his hawkish image by appealing to the increasingly dominant liberal wing of his party.

In the face of daily televised Watergate hearings, Nixon felt too weakened to take on Jackson and his allies. The trade bill was shelved for the first half of 1973 and again in the fall because of the East-West tensions resulting from the Middle East War. Jackson and I therefore did not meet until March 6, 1974, to see whether some compromise was possible.

By then Nixon was on his way to impeachment, and Jackson had no incentive to ease the pressure on the President by striking a deal. A dialogue of the deaf was inevitable. No matter that I had told Jewish leaders on many occasions that I would not object if Jackson received the credit for any modifications in Soviet emigration practices.[5]

In the meantime, Jackson had raised the importance of the emigration issue to the symbolic level. He was determined to use it to demonstrate that the Nixon Administration's approach to the entire gamut of East-West relations had been wrong all along both in concept and in method. A public clash with the President and Secretary of State would allow him to show that more concessions could be achieved by confrontation than by diplomacy. Jackson's hand was strengthened enormously when Andrei Sakharov, the eminent Soviet scientist and human rights champion, published a letter endorsing Jackson's legislation.

My first meeting with Jackson was exploratory. At the second, on March 15, he began to show his hand. The Senator demanded a written Soviet guarantee that 100,000 emigrants would be permitted to leave annually (nearly three times the highest number which had ever been permitted to leave). Jackson saw to it that the figure was leaked, forcing me into appearing either too weak to put it forward or too incompetent to achieve it. (In keeping with hardball inside-the-Beltway practice, Jackson's staff blamed me for the leak—though I could have had no conceivable motive to maneuver myself into thus demonstrating my impotence.) To assure himself of adequate maneuvering room even at the extravagant numbers he had proposed, Jackson refused to guarantee that MFN status would be granted even if the quota were met. Instead, he confined himself to the enigmatic statement that such a concession might permit him to "consider" the "possibility" of a compromise. The implication was that he had additional demands in his pocket.

A catch-22 situation was being cleverly created for Nixon and for me, who, at this stage of the President's travail, was in effect the sole negotiator on his behalf. Compromise being the lifeblood of the Senate, there was little hope of congressional support unless I showed a willingness to explore Jackson's proposals. But if I went along with his numbers and demand for a signed Soviet guarantee, I would be destroying the prospects for an agreement with the Soviet Union on this or any other subject.

Trying to work my way out of this dilemma, I promised—probably unwisely—Senators Jacob Javits from New York and Abraham Ribicoff from Connecticut, who comprised the Senate's negotiating team headed by Jackson, that I would attempt to find a way around the Soviet refusal to submit their domestic practices to congressional scrutiny. During my visit to Moscow set for March 24–28, 1974, I proposed to initiate a dialogue with Soviet Foreign Minister Andrei Gromyko to elicit a definition of the Soviet emigration practices to which Brezhnev's statement of the previous year had referred. I would then seek to translate these into an increase in overall numbers of emigrants and convey my understanding of Soviet intentions in a letter to the Senators. In this manner, the Soviets would be able to avoid formally submitting their emigration practices to congressional scrutiny while Congress would receive indirectly the assurances it required.

It was an ingenious formula, and it might have worked had there been a willingness on the part of the Senators to save Soviet face. But to impress their constituencies, the Senators needed to demonstrate that they had managed to extort from the reluctant Soviet leaders and the "soft" administration guarantees which would not have been extended without their pressure.

This attitude was bound to abort the broader scheme, for the Soviets would never agree to a right of emigration defined by Congress; they had only gone along with us in the first place to secure American goodwill in other areas. My compromise that we communicate the administration's understanding of Soviet intentions to Congress was therefore destined to land us in endless controversy. Congress would no doubt interpret our communication as a commitment while Soviet leaders would reject any claim that they had undertaken a legal obligation.

The Senators' insistence that MFN for the Soviet Union be renewed annually would further have the effect of holding the administration permanently hostage. With each renewal, new demands could be raised that, sooner or later, would prove to be more than the traffic could bear. At that point, the administration was sure to be accused of either deception or weakness, especially since the first renewal would come up as the 1976 election and the New York primary, crucial for Jackson, approached. Working together, the Senators and the administration could easily have achieved respectable improvements in the already dramatically improving Soviet emigration figures. Locked in confrontation, the near certainty of a blowup outweighed any conceivable benefit, jeopardizing not only emigration but all the other achievements of four years of a patient and, on the whole, successful East-West diplomacy.

For a few weeks, my scheme seemed to hold promise. At meetings with me in Moscow in March and again in Geneva in April 1974, Gromyko, while far from enthusiastic, reiterated Brezhnev's assurance that no legal obstacles would be placed in the way of Jewish emigration; that there would be no harassment of applicants; and that the total would be in proportion to the number of applications. He formalized Brezhnev's assurance that rejections would not exceed 1.6 percent. However grudgingly, Gromyko agreed that a target figure of 45,000—some 25 percent above the highest previous level—was a "reasonable" projection. He added sarcastically that the Soviet government would, however, stop short of forcing its citizens to emigrate in order to please the American Congress.

These numbers were treated with contempt by Jackson and his staff. Richard Perle continued to insist on an annual quota of 100,000 emigrants; Jackson—playing the good cop—offered as a "concession" the proposition that the figure was a "target" rather than a "precondition." After a while, it appeared that, by "target," he had meant a "compromise" at around seventy-five thousand, or more than twice the maximum number thus far granted exit visas. While the American side thus negotiated with itself as if it were in our power to determine levels of Jewish emigration, the actual number of emigrants began to fall, being cut in half each of the years that we were debating the Jackson Amendment.

Even so, the relentless Senator kept coming up with new demands. Jackson claimed that exit visas were being granted preferentially to would-be emigrants in the provinces where a lower educational and cultural level prevailed and fewer to the intellectual elite from Moscow. This "harassment," argued Jackson, had to end as one of the preconditions of MFN. Javits summed up the Senators' consensus: "The idea is that the Secretary go back and talk some more." The assignment was simplicity itself—to implement an agreement already signed by the American Secretary of Commerce, I was to triple Jewish emigration from the highest level it had ever reached and to prescribe the geographic distribution of the emigrants; in return, the Soviet Union would receive the same trade treatment already being unconditionally enjoyed by over one hundred other nations but, unlike those others, be subject to an annual congressional review.

To close any remaining loophole for improved commercial relations with the Soviet Union, Jackson set about restricting credits as well as trade. On June 30, 1974, the President's authority to use the facilities of the Export-Import Bank came up for renewal, as it had biannually without controversy for two decades. Jackson and his senatorial ally, Illinois Democrat Adlai Stevenson III, used this opportunity to place a double lock on East-West economic relations by introducing an entirely new amendment. Though Stevenson formally sponsored the amendment, he gave public credit for it to Jackson. The amendment made all Ex-Im loans to the Soviet Union in excess of $50 million subject to congressional approval and established an absolute ceiling of $300 million for the combined total of *all* loans to the Soviet Union. With Jackson and his allies systematically eliminating presidential flexibility in East-West diplomacy, Soviet-American economic relations were, after two years of Washington-Moscow cooperation in a number of areas, significantly worse than they had been at any previous period of the Cold War.

By now the issue of Jewish emigration had become entwined with Nixon's fate. At the end of June 1974, he left for his last summit with Brezhnev. The trip to Moscow was also destined to be his last foreign journey as President. Nixon's critics indulged the fantasy that he might try some spectacular sleight of hand to avert his impending impeachment. In fact, he had no such ideas. Not then—nor since—has a shred of evidence surfaced that Nixon contemplated any deal that could only have tarnished a foreign policy record of which he was rightly proud. Nevertheless, Jackson, determined that Nixon have no negotiating room while in Moscow, announced two days before the President's departure that he was about to put forward another new set of conditions with respect to Jewish emigration. He did not specify what these might be, but the mere announcement of it put an end to any efforts to settle the issue of Jewish emigration until after Nixon resigned five weeks later.

By the end of Nixon's presidency, his East-West policies were under relentless and nearly continuous attack. A confrontational and grandiose strategy was being urged first on a President facing impeachment and then on a nonelected successor at a moment when the United States was deeply divided and a hostile, pacifist Congress was restricting his authority to take military action and assaulting every new weapons system. It was a heavy responsibility to put such a burden on a new President who sought most of all to restore confidence while defusing a battery of crises, both domestic and foreign.

# 5

# CHINA AND ITS LEADERS

The speed and scale of modern communications will make it increasingly difficult for future historians to render an accurate account of contemporary international relations. Until the advent of the typewriter and the copy machine, the drafting of documents was a laborious process, limiting official papers to important matters of substance. And until the advent of the telegraph, communications were too slow for detailed tactical directions. Instructions to diplomats were, of necessity, conceptual. The foreign offices of even the Great Powers could do little more than convey general objectives and strategy; the appropriate tactics had to be improvised on the spot. Diplomatic reports, in turn, were obliged to be similarly conceptual. They needed to explain the relationship between what had occurred and the strategy that had been conveyed. At times—albeit rarely—a change in strategy could be requested by the diplomat. In either case, diplomatic documents were largely analytical.

Technology has revolutionized the conduct as well as the content of diplomacy. Preparing a document, reproducing it, then distributing it within minutes all over the world is now accomplished at the touch of a button. Bureaucracies have grown so bloated that a large proportion—perhaps the majority—of documents deal with housekeeping or internal interagency disputes. They illuminate not so much geopolitical objectives or strategy as bureaucratic turf battles.

Future historians will always be in danger of becoming confused not only by the profusion of documents but also by their character. Detailed instructions are now relayed so easily and quickly that Presidents and foreign ministers prefer to focus their communications on

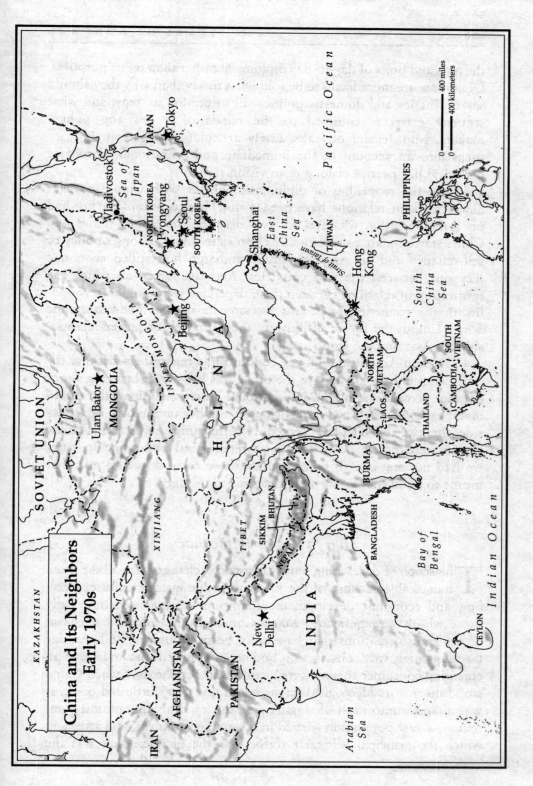

China and Its Neighbors
Early 1970s

SOVIET UNION

KAZAKHSTAN

MONGOLIA
Ulan Bator ★

INNER MONGOLIA

XINJIANG

C H I N A

Vladivostok

Sea of Japan

JAPAN
Tokyo ★

NORTH KOREA
Pyongyang ★

South Korea
Seoul ★

Shanghai

East China Sea

Strait of Taiwan

TAIWAN

Pacific Ocean

PHILIPPINES

Hong Kong

South China Sea

Beijing ★

TIBET

SIKKIM
BHUTAN

NEPAL

BANGLADESH

BURMA

LAOS

NORTH VIETNAM

THAILAND

CAMBODIA

SOUTH VIETNAM

Bay of Bengal

Indian Ocean

New Delhi ★

INDIA

AFGHANISTAN

PAKISTAN

IRAN

Arabian Sea

CEYLON

0    400 miles
0    400 kilometers

the nuts and bolts of day-to-day diplomacy rather than on its purposes. Diplomats are more likely to be told what to say than why they should say it. Tactics and domestic politics substitute for strategy, and what strategy exists is confined to the minds of a few top policy-makers, who, fearful of leaks, rarely articulate or share it. History turns into an account of the immediate and sensational, devoid of historical perspective or long-term vision.

Since the reopening of diplomatic contact with China in 1971, Sino-American relations have been a notable exception. Having had no communication whatever for two decades, the United States and China started with a substantially clean slate. Mao Zedong's policy of self-reliance and an American trade embargo had stifled economic relations between the two countries. And the issues on which the restoration of relations between them depended were primarily geopolitical: the countries' respective assessments of the threat from the Soviet Union; the future of Taiwan; the definition of power relationships in Asia and the world.

The Sino-American dialogue concentrated on strategy because the only claim either side had on the other was by way of bringing about parallel perceptions of the international situation. Of all the diplomatic exchanges in which I participated—either on my own or alongside the two Presidents I served—the meetings with the Chinese leaders were the most consistently conceptual and long-range. In truth, we had nothing else to talk about in those early days and no other means to build the ties we were determined to forge.

## Two Styles of Diplomacy

The scope of developing Sino-American exchanges was all the more remarkable because of the vast gulf in the history, culture, ideology, and economic development separating the two societies. Only those who have experienced Mao's China can appreciate that chasm or the transformations that have since been wrought. The latter-day bustling cities, vast construction booms, numbing traffic jams, and an emerging consumer society were inconceivable in the days when China stood out for its ideological fervor based on Mao's little red book. It was a world unto itself of stagnating industry, drab agricultural communes, a vast population garbed in a standard uniform, and streets in which the principal vehicular traffic was the bicycle. That was the

China I encountered in those distant days when Richard Nixon of the strident anti-Communist rhetoric and Mao Zedong of the pithy and contemptuous anti-capitalist slogans came together to launch their geopolitical revolution.

Nixon was driven by the desire to extricate the United States from Vietnam, to create a counterweight to Soviet expansionism, and to draw the sting from the militant peace movement at home by unveiling a grand design for peace. Mao shared Nixon's concern over Soviet expansionism; indeed, he had every reason to believe that China might well become the next target. For no Communist leader was then challenging Moscow's doctrinal preeminence more rigorously than Mao. And if the Brezhnev Doctrine of 1968, which had proclaimed that Moscow had the right to bring any backsliding Communist state to heel by military force, had any obvious application, it was to Mao's China. That China and the United States should seek rapprochement in the early 1970s was therefore imposed on each of them by their necessities. That it occurred with such speed and in so straight a line was due to the ability of the leaders on both sides to subordinate ideology to mutual interests.

Such an approach required a greater intellectual adjustment for the American side than for the Chinese. Mao was far too subtle not to have understood that the United States had no conceivable interest in defending his right to doctrinal Communist heterodoxy. A return to classical patterns of Chinese statecraft was the only possible basis for cooperation with the United States.

China, the so-called Middle Kingdom, had been supreme in the region relevant to it for the greatest part of its history. When threatened, China would see to its security by balancing the surrounding states—which it regarded as barbarian—against each other. A rule of thumb was that the distant barbarian was usually safer to deal with than one nearby. In 1969, it required no great acumen to divine that the principal threat to China's security was the Soviet Union, a million of whose troops were massing on China's borders; the principal question in Mao's mind was almost certainly whether the United States, the distant barbarian, would understand its own interests.

Nixon's philosophical problem was more complex. He was the chief executive of a country built by peoples who had turned their back on the institutions, practices, and values of the societies from which they had emigrated. That made belief in the superior virtue of the American political experience a national faith, and it was reinforced by a propitious geography. Secure between two great oceans, the United States was for two hundred years the only major country without powerful neighbors and therefore without the experience of any direct threat to its security. The balance of power as practiced in Europe was decried as either irrelevant or dangerous; equilibrium was deemed less important than a moral and legal consensus.

When, in the Shanghai Communiqué of 1972, Mao and Nixon pledged their countries to oppose hegemony in Asia (a year later extended to the entire world), it marked a far more significant departure from prevailing American Wilsonianism than from Chinese traditions. Even when not spelled out in detail, resistance to hegemony implies a policy of balancing power, of preventing any one nation from marshaling the resources and manpower conducive to world domination. The unspoken but unavoidable implication was that China and the United States were jointly engaged in counterbalancing Soviet power.

In fact, our strategic objective was even more complicated: it was to transform the two-power world of the Cold War into a triangle and then to manage the triangle in such a way that we would be closer to each of the contenders than they were to each other, thereby maximizing our options. Such emphasis on geopolitics and equilibrium was unprecedented for an American President, at least since the days of Theodore Roosevelt.

In the process of executing our strategy, we were necessarily exposed to the Chinese style of statecraft. Before my secret trip to Beijing, we thought that we could apply our experience with Soviet methods to the Chinese. We quickly discovered the vast cultural gap between Moscow and Beijing. Soviet diplomats represented a society which had historically prevailed through brute force rather than consensus and had created a multinational empire sustained by military power. The Soviet Union (and Imperial Russia before it) had very few allies beyond the reach of its armies. The Russian negotiating style mirrored these realities—being less an effort to persuade than to wear down the interlocutor through persistence and intimidation.

By contrast, Chinese diplomats represent a society which has been culturally dominant in the world known to it. Chinese diplomacy insinuates rather than bullies. The interlocutor is flattered by being admitted to the Chinese "club," albeit as only a guest member. The standard welcoming speech for visitors to Beijing greets "old friends" as near-members to the Chinese club and welcomes "new friends" as if they were applicants for membership. The proclamation of friendship makes it that much more difficult to disagree on those issues which the Chinese declare—usually at an early stage of a negotiation—as matters of principle and therefore beyond compromise. In the Sino-American relationship, such principles have always included China's unity and its corollary, the insistence that Taiwan is a part of China.

For Soviet negotiators, who tended to behave as if diplomacy were trench warfare, there was no such thing as a minor issue. Every problem or formulation was treated as having equal significance and fought over with a grim persistence if only to establish some future claim should it later become necessary to abandon it. Chinese leaders—at least in the early stages of Sino-American relations—used concessions on nonessentials to establish a reputation for reliability in the long term.[1] And they have taken great pains ever since to show that Chinese friendship is not a transitory phenomenon by the meticulous attention they have paid to retired statesmen around the world who, while in office, had fostered closer ties with China. (A good example is when Mao sent a plane to bring Nixon to China in 1976 at a time when political figures in the United States avoided contact with the former President.)

American policymakers tend to oscillate between the pragmatic and the missionary, between the practical and the idealistic. On the Chinese side, this gap is likely to be bridged by careful geopolitical analysis—a strategic view sustained with great persistence. American negotiators are inclined to appeal to legal concepts and pay great heed to legally binding documents. Chinese statesmen believe that what sustains agreements is building a consensus on common interests; lacking that consensus, legal obligations cannot, in the Chinese view, survive for long. They therefore generally proceed by making their case in the form of some parable drawn from their five-thousand-year history.

Very different concepts of time are involved between the two societies. Asked when a certain event occurred, the American will cite a date; the Chinese will refer to a dynasty. Of the fourteen Chinese dynasties, seven have lasted longer than the entire history of the United States, and three were in place just as long. Whereas the American sense of time is precise and the perspective is relatively short, the Chinese sense of time is proximate and the perspective, in most cases, far longer. Chinese historical references tend to mystify all but the most expert Americans. Our references to our own history tend to be viewed by the Chinese as primarily illustrating an insufficient national experience hardly warranting an informed judgment.

Cultural differences notwithstanding, the Sino-American dialogue remained unusually consistent and geared to long-range considerations starting in the Nixon Administration and continuing since, in every succeeding administration. It has, in many ways, been the most consistent and bipartisan American foreign policy of the twentieth century.

## Mao Zedong

Chairman Mao Zedong, Premier Zhou Enlai, and later Deputy Premier Deng Xiaoping were my day-to-day interlocutors, but Mao overshadowed all his colleagues by the near-religious awe in which he was held—or which his associates deemed it wise to affect. The other Chinese leaders invariably buttressed their arguments with extensive quotations from the Chairman, conferring legitimacy on their pronouncements and perhaps security on their persons. By the same token, they were always extraordinarily deferential in his presence.

The atmosphere of remoteness and of all-encompassing, at times menacing, dominance was reinforced by the manner in which meetings with Mao materialized. The Chairman resided in the Imperial City in a style as remote and exalted as any of the emperors he was wont to deride. Appointments with him were never scheduled in advance; they simply sprang into being like divine acts. Each of my five meetings with Mao was signaled by a stirring among my Chinese interlocutors, followed by the appearance of Assistant Foreign Minister Wang Hairong, reputed to be Mao's niece. For a few minutes, my clearly agitated Chinese counterparts would continue to act as if nothing unusual was happening. Then Zhou or Deng would put away his papers and say: "Chairman Mao is expecting you." Whether the American delegation was ready for the encounter did not seem to be worthy of consideration.

Accompanied by Zhou (or Deng, in my last two conversations), I would set off for Mao's residence in a Chinese car. No American security personnel were permitted to accompany me, and the press was notified only afterward. The Chinese proved adept at shaping the public image they wanted to evoke by the pictures they would release and by the adjectives they used to describe the meetings. When Mao was seen beaming in the photograph and the communiqué spoke of a farsighted meeting, the message was that Sino-American relations were flourishing. After another meeting, a smiling Mao was pictured wagging a finger at me so that the overall impact was that of a benign, somewhat put-upon teacher conveying the message that the Sino-American relationship might require some additional tending.

Mao's residence was approached through a red gate on Xichang'an Jie, part of the eight-lane, east–west axis carved from where the ancient city walls had stood until the Communist victory in the civil war. Today the traffic on this avenue is in permanent gridlock though, in the early days of Sino-American relations, it was almost nonexistent. The few official cars and the mass of bicycles seemed lost on it. Once inside the Imperial City, the road hugged a lake, on the other side of which stood a series of residences for high officials. They had all been built in the first flush of Sino-Soviet friendship and reflected the heavy Stalinist architecture of the period.

Mao's residence looked no different though it stood slightly apart from the rest. On my first two visits, a small anteroom was almost completely taken up by a Ping-Pong table which later disappeared. I was, in any event, always taken directly to Mao's study. Whereas most heads of state are surrounded by accoutrements intended to convey the majesty of their society, Mao's surroundings strove for the opposite impression. The all-powerful ruler of the world's most populous nation wished to be perceived as a scholar-statesman who had no need to buttress his authority with the traditional symbols of majesty.

Mao's study was of modest size. Bookshelves bursting with bound volumes and what appeared to be manuscripts tied together with string covered three walls. More books were piled on tables and sometimes on the floor. On my first few visits, a simple wooden bed stood in a corner.

Mao would rise from a semicircle of easy chairs in the center of the room, a female attendant standing close by (and, on my last visit, holding him up), for by the time I met him, Mao had already suffered several of the strokes which eventually disabled him. He would fix upon me a smile both penetrating and slightly mocking as if to warn that it would be futile to attempt to deceive this specialist in human duplicity. And since "barbarians" always ran the risk of missing the point, Mao would occasionally use an anecdote to emphasize the impossibility of tricking him—for example, at our meeting of November 12, 1973:

The President of South Yemen approached me. He said he wanted to sever diplomatic relations with the Soviet Union. He asked me my opinion. I was not taken in and said he must be prudent. Now they are tying themselves very closely to the Soviet Union.

Even as Mao's physical condition became progressively more impaired, he exuded greater concentrated willpower and determination than any leader I have encountered—with the possible exception of Charles de Gaulle. He moved only with difficulty, and his speech deteriorated from meeting to meeting until, during our last conversation, aides had to write down what the sounds he uttered might mean, whereupon he would either nod or shake his head before the interpreter was able to proceed.

Despite these handicaps, Mao always conducted his conversations in the form of a Socratic dialogue. Eschewing the soliloquies with which heads of state tend to present their case, he would generally begin with a question, quite often in a needling tone. With deceptive casualness, Mao would then offer a few pithy comments ranging from the philosophical to the sarcastic and gradually expanding the subject matter.

The following exchange from my November 1973 meeting illustrates the point. Opening the conversation, Mao inquired into the subjects discussed by Zhou and me but quickly turned this into a defiant discussion of Soviet ambitions:

MAO: What did you discuss?

ZHOU: Expansionism.

KISSINGER: That's correct.

MAO: Who's doing the expanding, him? [indicating me]

ZHOU: He started it, but others have caught up.

KISSINGER: The Foreign Minister criticizes us from time to time for the sake of equilibrium, but I think he knows the real source.

MAO: But that expansionism is a pitiful one. You should not be afraid of them.

KISSINGER: We are not afraid of them, Mr. Chairman. Every once in a while we have to take some strong measures as we did two weeks ago.

MAO: Those were not bad, those measures [referring to the
U.S. alert during the Middle East War].
KISSINGER: The problem in the Middle East is to prevent
it now from being dominated by the Soviet Union.
MAO: They can't possibly dominate the Middle East because, although their ambition is great, their capacities
are meager.

The cumulative effect of Mao's tangential observations was to
convey a mood and to indicate a route of march while ostensibly
leaving the tactical decisions in Zhou's control. When, in February
1972, Nixon tried to draw Mao into a discussion of specific countries,
the Chairman replied: "They should be discussed with the Premier
[Zhou Enlai]. I discuss the philosophical questions."

That was actually only true when Mao sought to separate himself
from an as yet uncertain outcome. Once the Shanghai Communiqué
had defined the framework for Sino-American relations, his utterances
grew increasingly direct. On my October 1975 trip to Beijing, Mao
picked up on a banality I had uttered to Deng before meeting the
Chairman to the effect that Sino-American relations were in good
shape because neither side wanted anything from the other. That was
too pedestrian for Mao, seeking a coordinated strategy toward the
Soviet Union:

> If neither side had anything to ask from the other, why
> would you be coming to Beijing? . . . [And] why . . . would
> we want to receive you and the President?

In December of the same year, Mao chose a parable as a way of
conveying his displeasure with what he considered ineffective American resistance to Soviet and Cuban moves in Angola—though these
had, in fact, been imposed on us by acts of Congress:

> The world is not tranquil, and a storm—the wind and rain
> —are coming. And at the approach of the storm, the swal-
> lows are busy . . . but the flapping of their wings cannot
> obstruct the coming of the storm.[2]

Mao could be quite brutal as well. Also in December 1975, President Ford tried out one of his favorite phrases on Mao: "I always say

it is possible to disagree without being disagreeable." This pronouncement utterly stumped the interpreter, it being linguistically impossible
to make that juxtaposition in Chinese. Mao brought the subject to a
close: "Why would you always say that?" (Had he understood the
phrase, he would no doubt have objected to it even more strongly.)

Mao's conversations with us were divided into two subjects: increasingly precise elaborations of his views on the need to develop a
common international strategy, and ever more elliptical references to
China's internal conditions. On international affairs, he followed a
geopolitical and insistently nonideological approach. One of Mao's
first observations on Nixon's visit to China in February 1972 was that:

> People like me sound a lot of big cannons. . . . [T]hings like
> "the whole world should unite and defeat imperialism, revi-
> sionism, and all reactionaries and establish socialism."

He laughed uproariously at the implication that anyone might be
taking seriously a slogan which had been scrawled for decades on
placards and on the walls of public buildings all over China. With
similar glee, Mao volunteered that he preferred dealing with conservative Western leaders such as Richard Nixon, Edward Heath, or Georges
Pompidou because the conservatives were more suspicious of the Soviet
Union than their leftist opponents, who were sentimental, unrealistic,
and vulnerable to Communist peace offensives:

> I like rightists. People say you are rightists, that the Republi-
> can Party is to the right, that Prime Minister Heath is also
> to the right. . . . I am comparatively happy when these peo-
> ple on the right come into power.

It was fortunate for Sino-American relations that the Nixon Administration was Mao's first American interlocutor. Almost any other
group—most especially the McGovernite Democrats of the late 1960s
and early 1970s—would not have been able to bring themselves to
base the relationship so explicitly on unsentimental strategic and geopolitical considerations. At the time of Nixon's February 1972 visit,
the United States still recognized Taiwan as the legitimate government
of China; we were, in effect, paying a visit to a capital we did not
recognize. We were also at war with North Vietnam, then China's

ostensible ally and beneficiary of its economic assistance as well as some military aid.

Mao wasted no time unraveling these complexities. Taiwan would not be permitted to stand in the way of Sino-American rapprochement, nor would Indochina. "The issue [of Taiwan] is not an important one," Mao said offhandedly in the first few minutes of his meeting with Nixon, as if he were lubricating a social chat with some self-evident observation. "The issue of the international situation is an important one." And Mao quickly put to rest America's nightmare legacy of the Korean War—the fear of Chinese intervention in Vietnam, which had for a decade constrained every American administration in the conduct of the war in Indochina. He declared flatly that Chinese armies would not cross their frontiers—presumably regardless of what happened in Indochina (which Mao pointedly never specifically mentioned):

> At the present time, the question of aggression from the United States or aggression from China is relatively small. . . . You want to withdraw some of your troops back on your soil; ours do not go abroad.

In subsequent conversations, Mao elaborated on the general comments he had made to Nixon. In November 1973, he invited me to a nearly three-hour tour d'horizon of the international situation. Combining query with allusion and alternating bonhomie with mocking challenge, Mao sketched in broad strokes his conception of how to contain the Soviet Union globally. He set the tone in his opening banter in which he described two meetings with Soviet Premier Alexei Kosygin nearly ten years apart. Beneath the jocular tone lurked a query about American tactics vis-à-vis the Soviet Union and a warning that China, once aroused, would prove an implacable adversary:

> MAO: Kosygin came himself, and that was in 1960. I declared to him that we were going to wage a struggle against him for ten thousand years. [laughter]
>
> INTERPRETER: The Chairman was saying ten thousand years of struggle.
>
> MAO: . . . This time [1969] I made a concession to Kosygin. I said that I originally said this struggle was going to go on for ten thousand years. On the merit of his coming

to see me in person, I will cut it down by one thousand years. [laughter] And you must see how generous I am. Once I make a concession, it is for one thousand years.

And then there was another time . . . and a Mr. Bordeoloski came also to speak on behalf of the Soviet Union. This time I again made a concession of a thousand years. [laughter] You see, my time limit is becoming shorter and shorter.

And the fifth time the Romanian President Ceauşescu came—that was two years ago—and he again raised the issue, and I said, "this time no matter what you say, I can make no more concessions." [laughter]

KISSINGER: We must adopt Chinese tactics.

MAO: There is now some difference between you and us. I do not speak with such ease now because I've lost two teeth. And there is a difference between your and our activities, that is, we just hit back at everything that comes. . . .

KISSINGER: I explained to the Prime Minister, going in the car or elsewhere, that our tactics are more complex and maybe less heroic, but our strategy is the same. We have no doubt who is the principal threat in the world today.

MAO: What you do is a Chinese kind of shadow boxing. [laughter] We do a kind of shadow boxing which is more energetic.

ZHOU: And direct in its blows.

KISSINGER: That is true, but where there is a real challenge, we react as you do.

MAO: I believe in that. And that is why your recent trip to the Arab world was a good one [my first visit after the Middle East War].

In Mao's view—subsequently largely borne out by events—the Soviet Union was not a real, only a mock, superpower. It had "stretched its hands too far," and its industrial capacity would not be able to sustain its global ambitions. Therefore, Moscow was certain to lose the geopolitical struggle, provided the countries around the Soviet periphery cooperated in thwarting Moscow's designs and did not permit themselves to be defeated one by one. It was the Chinese version of containment:

MAO: Their ambitions are contradictory with their capacity.

KISSINGER: That may be true.

MAO: Beginning from their Pacific Ocean, there is the United States, there is Japan, there is China, there is South Asia, and westward there is the Middle East, and there is Europe, and the Soviet forces that are deployed along the lines through Siberia way up to the Kurile Islands only account for one fourth of their forces.

ZHOU: East of the Urals.

KISSINGER: A little closer to one half. Two fifths maybe. . . .

MAO: . . . They have to deal with so many adversaries. They have to deal with the Pacific. They have to deal with Japan. They have to deal with China. They have to deal with South Asia, which also consists of quite a number of countries. And they only have a million troops here—not enough even for the defense of themselves and still less for attack forces. But they can't attack unless you let them in first, and you first give them the Middle East and Europe so they are able to deploy troops eastward. And that would take over a million troops.

KISSINGER: That will not happen. I agree with the Chairman that if Europe and Japan and the U.S. hold together—and we are doing in the Middle East what the Chairman discussed with me last time—then the danger of an attack on China will be very low.

MAO: We are also holding down a portion of their troops, which is favorable to you in Europe and the Middle East. For instance, they have troops stationed in Outer Mongolia, and that had not happened as late as Khrushchev's time. At that time they had still not stationed troops in Outer Mongolia, because the Chenpao Island incident [the Sino-Soviet border clash] occurred after Khrushchev. It occurred in Brezhnev's time.

KISSINGER: It was 1969. That is why it is important that Western Europe and China and the U.S. pursue a coordinated course in this period.

MAO: Yes.

KISSINGER: Because in that case, nobody will be attacked.

To implement that concept of what is perhaps best described as active containment, Mao next reviewed the countries around the Soviet periphery which could contribute to this task and analyzed what was needed to strengthen them as if there could be no other constraints on a joint policy than the national interest. David Bruce, then head of our liaison office in Beijing, who had dealt with Churchill, de Gaulle, and Konrad Adenauer, described Mao's presentation as the most extraordinary tour de force in his experience.

This conversation took place in November 1973, the very moment when critics in the United States were accusing the Nixon Administration of insufficient vigilance vis-à-vis the Soviet threat. While Mao's analysis of Soviet motivations paralleled that of the conservative and neoconservative critics, he differed with them on the appropriate strategy. The most vocal of Nixon's critics believed that the Soviet Union was preparing some ultimate apocalyptic showdown, and they therefore urged the United States to gear its policies toward meeting that threat instead of dissipating its strength on geopolitical contests around the Soviet periphery. But defeating Soviet thrusts where they occurred was exactly what Mao was proposing as the best strategy for defeating Soviet expansionism. In pursuit of that goal, Mao insisted that a Sino-American strategic partnership did not require formal agreement. An appropriate understanding by each side of the requirements of its national interest would suffice:

> Each side has its own means and acted out of its own necessity. That has resulted in our two countries acting hand in hand. . . . So long as the objectives are the same, we would not harm you nor would you harm us.

Because of their commitment to the creation of a de facto anti-Soviet coalition, Mao (and Zhou) were solicitous about America's relations with Europe and Japan. They urged me to ease the controversies generated by our 1973 proposal for a "Year of Europe"; in the view of my Chinese interlocutors, the foreseeable benefits of the proposed American-European joint declarations were not worth the discord they were generating.[3] Mao and Zhou proved especially solicitous about American-Japanese relations. After years of condemning our security treaty with Japan, they now described it as a means of containing the Soviet Union and preventing the resurgence of Japanese militarism.

The nascent strategic partnership did not preclude differences in the tactics being pursued by the two sides. China was the most vulnerable party of the strategic triangle, and Mao knew it—despite all his bravado that China was immune to pressure and implacable in the defense of its principles. Under direct threat and with little scope for diplomatic maneuver, Mao treated the Soviet Union as a relentless enemy to be confronted verbally, politically, and militarily at every opportunity.

But the Nixon and later the Ford Administrations governed a society traumatized by a decade of war and domestic division. Both Presidents had as their top priority restoring confidence in the purposes and design of our foreign policy. America's national interest required us to maneuver in a way that would position us closer to each of the Communist giants than they were to each other. Since we considered China the weaker and the more exposed, we were clearly tilting toward Beijing. And Mao was made well aware of the inevitable implication of the Nixonian approach that, if necessary, we would resist the changes in the global balance of power inherent in a Soviet attack on China whatever our tactical maneuvers in the interim. We would do so not because of any legal obligations but in pursuit of our interpretation of the national interest. In the meantime, however, we were determined to preserve a measure of freedom of maneuver and to reserve the final decision for actual, not conjectural, challenges.

Mao, who understood our design far better than our domestic critics did, could not be expected to be enthusiastic about the application of Chinese statecraft to China. He would surely have preferred to be on the side of the strategic triangle that had the greater options. And he did not fail to let us know that he saw through our design, as I shall describe in Chapter 28. But he was experienced enough to understand that we were entitled to tactics appropriate to our situation in pursuit of parallel strategies.

The blueprint of Sino-American relations established by Nixon and Mao remained remarkably consistent through five administrations of both parties: a parallel strategy with China for preventing "hegemony"—in other words, preservation of the global balance of power against the Soviet threat; avoidance of challenges by either side to the vital interests of the other; acceptance by the United States of the principle of one China and disavowal of a two-China or one-China, one-Taiwan policy; and deferral by China of pressing the Taiwan issue. Mao stated these priorities in November 1973:

> We can do without Taiwan for the time being and let it come
> after one hundred years. Do not take matters of this world
> so rapidly. Why is there need to be in such great haste? It is
> only such an island with a population of a dozen or more
> million [corrected by Zhou to 16 million]. . . . As for your
> relations with us, I think they need not take one hundred
> years.

Mao's geopolitical, single-minded, and essentially nonideological foreign policy stood in stark contrast to the dominant role he assigned to ideology at home. When we first encountered Mao, he was the unchallenged leader of a revolution which had claimed tens of millions of victims in the name of historical truth, yet he was assailed by premonitions of the potentially ephemeral nature of his achievements. Two contradictory impulses seemed to be undermining the revolutionary élan: the persistence of traditional Chinese values, and the stagnation built into the Communist state itself. When Nixon began their meeting by stating that Mao had transformed an ancient civilization, Mao sounded the first theme:

> I haven't been able to change it. I have only been able to
> change a few places in the vicinity of Beijing.

After a lifetime of titanic struggle to uproot Chinese society, there was not a little pathos in Mao's resigned recognition of the stubborn imperviousness of Chinese culture. Through the millennia, Chinese rulers have governed a society far more populous than any other, often by assertions of absolute power. But the sheer numbers of the Chinese people, their irrepressible individualism, and the priority they assign to the family have imposed a limit on government. The rulers could never be sure that their orders to this teeming, entrepreneurial, and family-oriented people were, in fact, being carried out. Chinese governments were occasionally driven to extremes of absolutism by their premonitions of their ultimate impotence, as, for example, when Mao strapped the entire population into uniform. Yet, in the end, a kind of pluralism would assert itself time and again, not as the result of a political philosophy preaching liberty but—like a powerful stream surrounding and finally swamping all obstacles—due to the lifestyle and spirit of the individual Chinese.

The family, not the state, has been the fundamental unit of Chinese life, and preservation and enhancement of the family's future have proven to be the raison d'être of Chinese society. Families would bend, like so much bamboo, to a prevailing wind, but they would not break. The limits of their pliability were established by their pervasive common sense, geared to their assessment of the requirements of survival and well-being of the family. In the end, even the most powerful Chinese rulers ran up against this paradoxical mass—at once obedient and independent, submissive and self-reliant, imposing limits less by defining issues than by hesitating to carry out orders deemed to be unreasonable.

When I first encountered high Maoist officials, I learned to my astonishment that, prior to the Communist takeover, many families had sent their sons abroad, each to a different country, as a form of insurance against all possible outcomes of the civil war. One son would stay with the Communists, another would go to the United States, occasionally a third could be found in Taiwan. This is how it happened that several senior Chinese officials I encountered (including one Chinese ambassador to Washington) had brothers in the United States—a condition that, in the Soviet Union, would have precluded government service and, under Stalin, might have been life-threatening.

Ironically, the family structure is now being imperiled more by China's birth control policies than it ever was by Communist ideology. Families limited to one child will give rise to generations in which there are no uncles, aunts, cousins, or any of the vast network of obligations and mutual support systems that have hitherto defined the traditional Chinese family unit. An only child will lack the broad context of contemporaries to help socialize him and will find it harder to adjust to the competition and discipline by which the reverence for achievement and learning was historically inculcated in China. Poignantly, the birth control policy is driven by necessity—by limits on resources in relation to the population—rather than by ideology.

That Communist practice should have been curbed by some of the historic tendencies of China's culture magnified the frustrations and ultimately the rage of Mao's last years. Millions had died to implement his quest for egalitarian virtue. Yet at the end of the aged Chairman's life, he came up against the reality that a centrally planned state was turning the Communist bureaucracy into a feudal class as pervasive as the one he had eradicated. For bureaucratic prerogatives were now legitimized by the true faith.

Rebelling against the nightmare that one result of his victory had been to re-create the Chinese tradition of an all-embracing mandarin class, Mao launched ever more fierce campaigns to save his people from themselves. With each passing decade, the fading Chairman would launch yet another purge against the huge, bloated bureaucracies he had established, and then destroyed, thereby requiring even larger bureaucracies to bring the resulting chaos under control.

In the course of these assaults upon his own system, Mao kept circling back to a dilemma as ancient as China itself. Modernity and especially technology intrinsically threaten any society's claims to uniqueness. And uniqueness had always been the distinctive claim of Chinese society. To preserve it, China had refused to imitate the West in the nineteenth century, risking colonization and incurring humiliation. A century later, one objective of Mao's Cultural Revolution— from which, indeed, it derived its name—had been to eradicate precisely those elements of modernization which threatened to submerge China in universal culture. This was why Mao purged Deng Xiaoping in 1966, together with all other proponents of modernization. Destroying his own disciples became a ritual of Mao's vast enterprise and a way of imposing his own version of virtue on Chinese society. For a decade, the aging Chairman renounced all the tools of progress, including education, closing the universities, recalling his ambassadors from abroad, and sending the graduates of universities to work in the fields so that they would experience the new revolutionary spirit and hopefully pass it on when they returned home.

In February 1973, a year after my first encounter with Mao, the physically frail but intellectually still vigorous Chairman seemed to have recognized this dilemma. In one of his elliptical references, Mao warned me against Chinese women and their radical views. Referring to the Jackson-Vanik Amendment before the American Congress on behalf of increased Jewish emigration from the Soviet Union, Mao offered to supply the United States with an unlimited number of Chinese women. This was his way, he said, of avoiding potential disaster for his own country.

At first I thought he was joking, and he actually had to repeat the comment several times before I understood that he was referring to the radicalism of his wife, Jiang Qing, and her entourage. Mao went on to say that he was ending the Cultural Revolution. The Chinese would have to go to school abroad, especially since their language was itself an obstacle to modernization. The Chinese people, he added, were "very obstinate and conservative." Ever the radical, he continued: "If the Soviet Union would throw its bombs and kill all those over thirty who are Chinese, that would solve the problem for us." But that was another way of saying that the problem was insoluble.

Within a year, Mao reversed himself. In early 1974, Zhou was for all practical purposes retired and, two years later, Deng was purged a second time to be replaced by Hua Guofeng and the Gang of Four. Reform gave way to Maoist orthodoxy. When I saw Mao for the last time in 1975, he concluded the meeting with a whimsical and melancholy bit of irony that embraced all his ambivalence about what he had wrought. Explaining why it was just as well that Taiwan's status remain unchanged for a while, he said:

> God blesses you, not us. God does not like us because I am
> a militant warlord, also a Communist.

## Zhou Enlai

It fell to Zhou Enlai, the Premier, to rescue continuity and consistency from beneath the shadow of this towering, driven, conflicted personality and against the backdrop of Mao's ever present temptation to institutionalize permanent upheaval. Graceful, suave, and elegant, Zhou was my principal interlocutor during the first three years of Sino-American relations. After my secret trip in July 1971 and before liaison offices were established in each capital in 1973, we were obliged to exchange messages first through Pakistan, then through the Chinese Embassy in Paris via the American military attaché, General Vernon Walters, and finally through China's U.N. Mission in New York. The dialogue between the two sides followed no established diplomatic precedent. Sending messages was technically so complicated and personal meetings so infrequent that we had, in effect, no choice except to concentrate on fundamentals.

Zhou demonstrated the priority he attached to the American relationship by appearing to have limitless time available for our dialogues. On my typical sojourns in Beijing, we would meet for eight hours each day from around 4:00 P.M. until midnight. Zhou delicately alternated the venue between the Great Hall of the People and my own residence in one of the ponderous state guest houses. It was his way of suggesting that the United States delegation was "at home," as it were, on Chinese soil and that meetings would alternate between the "home turf" of each side. During these lengthy sessions, which included meals, Zhou never permitted himself to be interrupted by any other business. No phone calls or notes were passed to him. Indeed, no phone was even in sight, a state of affairs that would be unthinkable—nay, impermissible—in Washington and that I warned Zhou could not be repeated whenever he was in a position to pay a reciprocal visit. Zhou seemed determined to convey that he had no more important task than to nurture China's relationship with the United States.

Zhou's conduct of the substantive negotiations reinforced the mood he worked so meticulously to create. Despite the fact that American forces were still on Taiwan, the issue of China's unification, though always raised in principle, was invariably deferred. Similarly, even though our meetings coincided with the most intensive American bombing of Vietnam in four years, Indochina was mentioned only elliptically and then usually to dissociate China from the events at its border. Early on, Zhou insisted that China owed Vietnam a degree of sympathy but not for security reasons nor because of a common Communist ideology. Rather it was a kind of repayment of a historical legacy:

> The debt we owe them was incurred by our ancestors. We
> have since liberation no responsibility because we overthrew
> the old system. Still, we feel a deep and encompassing sym-
> pathy for them.

Sympathy, of course, was not the same as political—still less, military—support. The statement that whatever obligation existed was the result of history was a delicate way of assuring us that no current vital Chinese national interest was involved in Vietnam. Like Mao, Zhou was at pains to stress—and more explicitly than Mao— that China would not send soldiers abroad, hence would neither intervene in Indochina nor threaten other American interests militarily. Though Brezhnev occasionally implied (if not very forcefully) that America's conduct of the war in Vietnam might impair Soviet- American relations, Zhou never even hinted at such a prospect.

As for Laos and Cambodia, Zhou dissociated China even further by claiming to know nothing about them; hence China did not even have historical obligations there:

> When we were making our revolution, we did not know
> anything about that country [Laos]. Although there have

been many writings in our historical books about the country called the Land of the Vientiane, which, in Chinese, means literally "the land of the ten thousand elephants." The same is the case with Cambodia.

Once the Southeast Asian problems had been pushed to the margins of the agenda, Zhou and I could concentrate on the geopolitical aspects of Sino-American relations. This would depend crucially on our ability to orchestrate parallel contributions to the global, and especially to the Asian, balance of power. That task was all the more subtle because to announce parallel policies was certain to evoke a firestorm. The Sino-American strategic partnership would have to come into being by means of tacit understandings based on parallel views regarding the details of the balance of power. These would, in effect, implement the general declarations against hegemony contained in the Shanghai Communiqué.

The first sentence Zhou uttered to me was to remind me of John Foster Dulles's refusal to shake hands with him at Geneva in 1954—a deeply rankling experience. Close behind was: "Our word counts." He understood—just as Nixon did—that our nascent strategic cooperation would have to be sustained by intangibles. Zhou eschewed the "salami tactics" by which so many diplomats try to impress their publics or their superiors—of adopting some extreme opening positions, then negotiating backward toward a compromise. The difficulty with this approach is that its outcomes more often reflect endurance rather than substance and that it prolongs negotiations because the inerlocutor never knows what position is the final one.

During my secret trip to Beijing in July 1971, Zhou Enlai interposed Huang Hua, who was to become ambassador to the U.N. and later Foreign Minister, to negotiate the communiqué. Assuming it to be a negotiation in the Soviet mold, I suggested that we each put forward our optimum outcome and then see what compromises might be required. Huang Hua replied that a much better approach would be to begin by explaining our necessities to each other—specifically what each side required in order to prepare its people for the announcement that a secret trip had taken place and that Nixon would visit China.

After a couple of hours of dialogue in which each side explained its imperatives, we parted, agreeing to present our respective drafts the next morning. As it happened, Huang Hua's text turned out to be less complicated—and in a way more favorable toward our point of view

—than our own, which, in the end, we never did put forward. The concessions Zhou had made to our needs were more than outweighed by the gain in confidence they engendered.

Another example of Zhou's style emerged in October 1971 during the preliminary negotiation for what later became the Shanghai Communiqué. Zhou proposed that we forgo the customary artful language designed to gloss over existing differences. No one familiar with the history of Sino-American relations would take seriously a document in which the leaders of the two sides pretended after only one encounter that they had agreed on all international issues. Far better, suggested Zhou, that each side clearly state its actual—if necessarily contrasting—views on a number of issues. This, he argued, would avoid confusion both at home and internationally while lending additional emphasis to whatever agreements might be reached.

Though I agreed to this approach, the first version of the Chinese presentation of their position struck me as too ideological and confrontational. I therefore suggested that several especially aggressive sentences be removed. Applying traditional negotiating methods, I offered to eliminate an equal number of sentences in the American draft. Zhou replied: "Give your two sentences to your President if you wish. I don't want them . . . all you have to do is to convince me why our language is embarrassing." Zhou did, in fact, remove some of the offending phraseology from the Shanghai Communiqué. (Nothing ever being wasted in China, it reappeared in the first speech by the Chinese Foreign Minister at the U.N. where, being made unilaterally, it went unnoticed.)

In this manner, within less than two years, China and the United States moved toward a high degree of cooperation and on the basis of perhaps the fullest and frankest discussions of overall strategy with a foreign government of my period in government service (other than with Britain). I had no illusions that Zhou, survivor of the Long March and of decades in Mao's entourage, would—if Chinese interests required it—prove as implacable an opponent as he was a thoughtful collaborator. But Zhou played an indispensable role at that particular juncture when both countries faced a common danger and their national interests dictated that they harmonize their policies without being deflected by peripheral issues.

Mao would introduce the basic concepts of the Chinese view in the way a composer might sketch the major themes of his opera in the overture. It was Zhou's task to mount the actual performances by turning Mao's parables and allusions into operational policies. When it came to discussing China's strategic imperatives, Zhou was far less defiant and less insistent on China's ability to stand alone than was his driven Chairman. Mao was too proud to affirm any degree of Chinese dependence on foreigners even when his policy was based on it. Zhou took the importance of American support for granted but insisted that a country could sustain its morale only by relying on itself in the first instance. Only in this manner could it be worthy of outside assistance:

> China is not a warlike or aggressive nation. But at the same time we must maintain constant preparations against all eventualities, because we must always be prepared against some surprise incident in case something happens. In Chinese, "We must be prepared against one case in ten thousand. . . ."
>
> And it can be only in this way that we will be able to maintain our self-confidence and also gain the mutual assistance of others. . . .
>
> So with regard to this problem [Soviet expansionism] you have said that you think it is best to prevent the event before it happens. Of course that would be good if it can be done. And that will call for joint efforts, that is, to envisage all aspects. But if we ourselves did not make our own preparations ourselves, that would not be right.

In his relationship with Mao, Zhou always took great care to emphasize that he was the subordinate, whether Mao was present or not. It was the only prudent course, considering the fate of predecessors who had been destroyed by Mao once they had reached the position of "heir apparent" in the Chinese hierarchy. Wherever possible, even when it required a stretch, Zhou would flesh out his observations with quotes from Mao, and he invariably described every new initiative as having been decreed by Mao.

Zhou spoke of China's domestic problems in the passive tone of an observer even though, as Premier, he was, in fact, charged with implementing these very policies. Like Mao, he praised the Chinese language for having unified the country though, again like Mao, he considered it an obstacle to modernization. China had much to learn from the United States, he would say, because America had "the courage to use young people" in its government. Yet at no point did Zhou suggest that he considered it his mission to bring about the reforms he described as being so necessary. With some melancholy, Deng was to say later that, though Zhou had undoubtedly eased the fate of many, he had never actually tried to reverse the policies which had caused the suffering in the first place.

And that was precisely how Zhou himself described his role during the Cultural Revolution at our first encounter in July 1971. It was Zhou who introduced the subject, insisting that if I was going to deal with China, I needed to learn about the Cultural Revolution. He described it as an upheaval propelled by Mao's determination to prevent the emergence of a new mandarin class. But that crusade was driven into excess by ideological zeal. A society brought up on faith in a single historical truth suddenly found itself riven by factions, all calling themselves Red Guards, each insisting that they represented the one and only truth as they carried their controversies into street battles. Zhou described how he, the Premier, had been held prisoner in his office for several days by one faction of Red Guards. At that point, fifty years of struggle and sacrifice seemed to have been all in vain. Yet, in the end, Zhou had conquered his doubts and had come to understand that "Mao was wiser; he had the courage to look further into the future."

Zhou never explained what that future was or why it called for such stupendous suffering. Whether, in fact, he shared Mao's vision of it or not, Zhou had clearly decided that fate had vouchsafed him no higher task than to mitigate the handiwork of his awesome master.

Starting in mid-1973, Zhou's role began to wane. The reason for it remains unclear; the Chinese always jealously guard the secrecy of their internal deliberations. (I have always believed that the collapse of Zhou's mediating role on Cambodia was a contributing factor.) Whatever the reason, the burden of the pressures on Zhou was brought home to me at a dinner in the Great Hall of the People in November 1973. In a general conversation, I made the observation that China seemed to me to have remained essentially Confucian in its belief in a single, universal, generally applicable truth as the standard of individual conduct and social cohesion. All that Communism had done, I suggested, was to establish Marxism as the content of that truth.

I cannot recall what possessed me to make this statement, which, however accurate, surely did not take into account Mao's periodic digs at Confucians who were alleged to be impeding his policies. Zhou exploded, the only time I saw him lose his temper. Confucianism, he said, was a doctrine of class oppression while Communism represented a philosophy of liberation. With uncharacteristic insistence, he kept up the assault on Confucianism, no doubt to some degree so as to have it on record for the benefit of Nancy Tang, the interpreter, who was close to Jiang Qing, Mao's wife, and Wang Hairong, Mao's niece.

In early 1974, Zhou disappeared from all dealings with Americans. Shortly thereafter, it was announced that he had entered a hospital. No Chinese official mentioned him to us again so long as Mao was alive. Henceforth the long tour d'horizon with Mao in November 1973 (described earlier in this chapter) would serve as the bible Chinese officials invariably invoked to support their positions.

I saw Zhou for the last time in late November 1974. Barely settled in the state guest house, I was whisked off, accompanied by my wife and children, to see Zhou in what was described as a hospital. Located in the same general vicinity of the former Imperial City as Mao's residence, it looked to the medically untrained eye no different from any other Soviet-model Chinese guest house. No medical equipment was in evidence, and Zhou, suave as ever, appeared physically unchanged. Yet he steered clear of any substantive discussion, rebuffing every attempt to engage him by saying that doctors had warned him against strain. He did not explain why substantive conversation would prove more taxing than social chitchat. But the symbolism was plain: Zhou was no longer my officially approved interlocutor.

Zhou's death in January 1976 was briefly turned by many Chinese into an occasion to affirm the humane side of the revolution. Large throngs gathered in Tiananmen Square to mourn his passing. Mao—or his entourage—interpreted these demonstrations as being directed against Maoist orthodoxy or perhaps as an attempt to create a competing icon. Counterdemonstrations were organized, and Deng, the embodiment of the reform movement, was purged a second time.

By the time I returned to China for a private visit in 1979, Deng had returned to power, and Zhou had been rehabilitated. I was conspicuously received by Zhou's wife. A museum in Tiananmen Square traced the evolution of Zhou's career, displaying replicas of his office (which I had never seen) and of his home. It attracted large crowds.

Afterward, Zhou's person again receded from public view though he remained a respected figure. In the summer of 1995—after President Lee Teng-hui of Taiwan was issued a visa to visit the United States only one month after the American Secretary of State had assured Beijing of the contrary—relations between Washington and Beijing fell into a deep freeze. China's ambassador to Washington, Li Daoyu, was recalled, and Beijing refused to accredit a new American ambassador.

Arranged months earlier, a trip by me to China, beginning July 1, 1995, happened to coincide with this tense moment. The Chinese government used the occasion to revive Zhou's memory to demonstrate its continued interest in good relations with the United States. I was invited to accept an honorary degree from Nankai University in Tianjin where Zhou had studied. The ceremony consisted of speeches praising Zhou's role in establishing ties with the United States. Later, at a photo opportunity in front of a statue of the late Premier, I was greeted by a friendly crowd of students—surely the only pro-American demonstration in China at the time.

## Deng Xiaoping

In 1974, at the very end of the Nixon period, Deng Xiaoping became my principal interlocutor. Though I intend to treat my dealings with him during the Ford Administration at the appropriate point in the chronology, the story of Nixon's China legacy would not be complete without an account of his administration's first encounter with the remarkable figure of Deng Xiaoping.

We knew very little about Deng when he suddenly reappeared as a major figure in the Chinese leadership. Our intelligence analysts informed us that he had been secretary general of the Communist Party until he was purged in 1966, charged with being a "capitalist roader." We also learned that he had recently been restored to the Central Committee of the Communist Party through Mao's personal intervention and against the opposition of the radicals in the Politburo. Though Mao's wife, Jiang Qing, had publicly snubbed Deng shortly after his return to Beijing, he was important enough to Mao for the Chairman—uncharacteristically—to apologize to Deng for his treatment during the Cultural Revolution. This included working in a factory as a manual laborer, being kept in detention when not working, and seeing his son rendered a paraplegic after being hounded by Red Guards and falling or being pushed out of a window as a result.

The same reports also told us that, in speaking to a delegation of Australian scientists, Deng had struck what was to become one of his dominant themes in the decades ahead: China was a poor and developing country in need of scientific and educational exchanges with advanced countries such as Australia. Deng had advised his Australian visitors that in their travels through China they should look at the backward side of the country and not only at its achievements. Our intelligence reports concluded that Deng had been brought in to strengthen Zhou's presumably reformist tendencies rather than as a counterweight to the Premier.

As soon as we met Deng, we realized that this last assessment was certainly wrong, for he wasted no time in distancing himself from Zhou. Deng arrived in New York in April 1974 as part of a Chinese delegation to the Sixth Special Session of the U.N. General Assembly dealing with economic development. We paid no particular attention to him since Foreign Minister Qiao Guanhua was the official head of the delegation. Deng did not ask to see me, but neither did he leave New York even after Qiao Guanhua had delivered the official Chinese speech. Believing him to be clearly subordinate to Zhou and primarily interested in economics, I did not even invite Deng and his delegation to dinner until about a week later when a scheduled address to the General Assembly brought me to New York.

It immediately became evident who was the real head of the Chinese delegation and—even more important—that, far from having been restored to ease Zhou's burden, Deng's assignment was, in fact, to replace him. Several friendly references about Zhou went unacknowledged; allusions to remarks of the Premier were answered by similar quotes from the far less extensive repertoire of my conversations with Mao. Indeed, Zhou's name was never volunteered by any member of the Chinese delegation.

To make sure we got the message, Deng, apropos nothing at all, suddenly reverted to my last conversation with Zhou by asking whether I was familiar with Confucius. Reluctant to provoke another outburst like Zhou's, I replied evasively, whereupon Deng took it upon himself to educate me:

> Confucius, in short, was an expert in keeping up the rites, and very conservative. His ideology has been binding the Chinese for over two thousand years. These ideas have a deep influence on the ideology of the people. If we wish to emancipate the people's ideology from old thinking, we must remove Confucius. This is a move to emancipate the people's thinking.

I asked whether the debate in China was theoretical or practical, specifically whether it was "directed against individuals, living individuals, rather than against ancient individuals." Deng minced no words in confirming that the anti-Confucian campaign had an eminently contemporary purpose:

> When you criticize a conservative ideology, then, naturally, it will affect some working staffs—some people who represent the conservative ideology being attacked.

As time went on, I developed enormous regard for this doughty little man with the melancholy eyes who had stuck to his cause in the face of extraordinary vicissitudes and who would, in time, transform his country far beyond any of his predecessors. Mao's overthrow of traditional China had created a united country, but it had also left a vacuum, as he himself indicated when telling Nixon that he had really changed only Beijing. But out of the wreckage of the Cultural Revolution, Deng fashioned a modernization that is likely to turn China into an economic superpower during the twenty-first century and will surely transform the political structure. His socialist market economy abandoned all but Mao's most formal liturgy. He based his reform on market economics—which he called socialist market economics—and friendly relations with the United States.

At that initial meeting in April 1974, none of us considered Deng as a major, much less a seminal, figure. He acted as if he were on a training mission on how to deal with Americans, with whom he had had no previous contact. Speaking in terse phrases, he never strayed— except for the reference to Confucius—from the framework sketched by Mao in his long talk with me five months earlier. Appearing to be still only feeling his way, Deng took care to quote frequently from that conversation. The difference was in nuance and style, reflecting Deng's preference for the specific over the allusive. Commenting on what he considered America's global overextension, Deng warned that we ran the risk of stretching out our hands to the point where we would wind up with "ten fleas under ten fingers." He supported Mao's thesis that the Soviets were "feinting in the East so as to be able to strike in the West"—which was the Chairman's way of boosting his leverage by suggesting that the United States was the more threatened party. But when I pointed out that it was fruitless to discuss whether the focal point of Soviet strategy was Europe or Asia because "wherever the focal point is, the next one is obvious," Deng saw no point in debating the issue. Experience, he said, would settle it:

We have talked to the Japanese—our Japanese friends—
about this point. They do not seem to realize this. They
seem to think that the Soviet intentions in the East do not
include them.

In other words, Deng would work with us on coalition-building.

Mao and Zhou had rarely gone beyond speaking in terms of *parallel* policies. Where Zhou had confined himself to welcoming unilateral American efforts to create a united anti-Soviet front, Deng referred to a *"joint"* strategy, such that "we work together with you to fix the bear in the north." In this spirit, he urged us to be more sensitive toward our European allies: "If you were to show more consideration for the Europeans, would there not be a better result?"

Shortly after my initial encounter with Deng, the disintegration of the Nixon presidency and the arrival of Ford necessitated a hiatus of some six months in high-level Beijing-Washington exchanges. In that interim, we demonstrated our continued commitment to Nixon's China policy by meticulously briefing Huang Zhen, head of the Chinese Liaison Office in Washington, about our view of events as they unfolded. In that spirit, Ford had received Huang Zhen in the Oval Office three hours after his inauguration to affirm his commitment to what Nixon had started. Nevertheless, we could not help notice that, during the annual session of the U.N. General Assembly in September 1974, Qiao Guanhua delivered a speech which edged close to treating the United States and the Soviet Union as nearly equal threats to the peace.

This was no accident. The vitality of the Sino-American relationship depended on a recognition of parallel interests and a mutual ability to support each other. It would suffer whenever the perceptions of the respective national interests began to diverge or when the ability to implement common views was impaired. Too many domestic upheavals had occurred in the United States not to have had some effect on China's perception of the effectiveness of the Sino-American strategic partnership. China's interest in that partnership presupposed a United States committed to preserving the global equilibrium and sufficiently cohesive to implement its strategic convictions. Yet within twelve months, the Chinese had witnessed the disintegration of our executive power in the wake of Watergate and were now obliged to get to know a new President whom none of their current top leaders had even met. Congress was challenging presidential powers over Indochina, Cyprus, war powers, and intelligence activities. All this eroded confidence in American staying power, while the controversy over détente raised questions about the very direction of American Cold War policy.

As Ford took office, what was at issue was not the design of China policy but our ability to continue to give it meaning.

# PART TWO

# FORD AT THE HELM

# 6

# THE NEW PRESIDENCY

## The Transition

No chief executive of any advanced industrial democracy conducts his office in so personal a manner as the American President. There are few limitations on his executive branch appointments; upon taking office, he is in a position to fill nearly three thousand positions down through the level of deputy assistant secretary of each department and a whole host of special assistants. The Cabinet serves at the President's discretion, and there is no requirement that it approve—or, for that matter, even discuss—his decisions. The fewest, if indeed any, major foreign policy decisions of any administration are put before the Cabinet except in the form of a general briefing. The underlying assumption is that Cabinet decisions are bound to leak because its membership is too diverse.

As a result, sensitive foreign policy discussions take place in the National Security Council (NSC) or its subordinate interagency committees. The NSC is composed by statute of the President, the Vice President, the Secretary of State, and the Secretary of Defense, with the Chairman of the Joint Chiefs of Staff and the Director of Central Intelligence Agency as statutory advisers. NSC meetings include as well whomever the President chooses to invite—invariably the National Security Adviser and often the Secretary of the Treasury, the Attorney General, and other senior officials conversant with the matter at hand. Even this forum is advisory; the President is not bound by its views. In my experience, neither Nixon nor Ford ever asked for a vote. And Nixon would ostentatiously announce his decisions by memorandum from the Oval Office, thus emphasizing the National Security Council's purely advisory role.

The interregnum of nearly three months that our system grants a new President between his election and inauguration is barely long enough to staff the administration and prepare its agenda. The hiatus provides the last respite that the newly elected President is likely to experience in office. With ingratiating solicitude, the bureaucracy volunteers a flood of information which the President-elect, not yet required to make decisions, can absorb (or not), free from the burden of having to settle raging controversies between the various agencies or departments. As yet unmarked with the double meanings and sacramental nuances of the bureaucratic debates, the President-elect, for perhaps the last time, is able to give priority to substance over management.

In the name of continuity, the top echelon of the administration in the process of being replaced puts forward projects for which time has run out. The incoming group, as yet unmarred by bureaucratic battle scars, responds with a mixture of disdain for its predecessors and an exuberant faith in its own ability to bring about major transformations. And the media are as yet mercifully restrained. Since few, if any, decisions are actually being made, journalists do not feel obliged to exercise their prerogative to select and emphasize information that sustains their preferences. Top media representatives spend much of their energy "developing sources," as they like to call it, or "apple-polishing" likely leakers, as less charitable observers view it.

Presidential transitions are thus enveloped in an aura of simultaneous expectation and uncertainty: expectation because they are a time of catharsis and renewal; uncertainty because they puncture continuity and occasionally uproot forests in order to ascertain whether the roots of the trees are still intact.

This pattern is telescoped brutally whenever the Vice President accedes to the highest office through some mishap that ends a President's tenure prematurely. Faced with a sudden transition, the new President is obliged to continue for a time with his predecessor's personnel and procedures. However well intentioned, these will have been selected on the basis of criteria which match up with the psychology or the needs of the new chief executive only in the rarest of cases, since presidential tickets usually result from balancing different wings of the winning party. Inevitably, the inherited personnel are gradually replaced. In anticipation of this upheaval, the first months of an administration formed by the Vice President are a period of internal tension rather than the wave of hope that sweeps in a newly elected President.

The changeover from Nixon to Ford was particularly complex. As the first nonelected Vice President, Ford did not have the benefit of having gone through a presidential campaign at the side of his predecessor, garnering the refracted aura of having been part of the original winning ticket. And Ford inherited an administration demoralized by nearly two years of the buffeting and catastrophes surrounding the Watergate crisis. Like all Vice Presidents succeeding to the presidency, he had neither the stable of policy advisers nor the kind of political machine that propels an elected President into office.

After several weeks, Ford changed almost the entire domestic policy staff he had inherited from Nixon, including the press office. Alexander Haig was moved from chief of staff to NATO commander and replaced by Donald Rumsfeld, a friend of Ford's from their service in the House of Representatives. Over the next eighteen months, all Cabinet officers except two (Bill Simon at Treasury and I at State) were replaced, as well as the Director of the Central Intelligence Agency. In other words, Ford had to navigate the ship of state with a constantly changing crew through one of our nation's gravest domestic storms and political divisions, some of which have persisted to this day.

Ford's human qualities eased the pain for those whose public careers were ending and brought a new style and tone to what had been a beleaguered administration. His approach to decision-making was almost diametrically the opposite of his predecessor's. Nixon was fascinated by strategic options and devoted a great deal of his time to studying and discussing them. Details of execution bored him, and he followed negotiations only in the most general way (his spinmeisters' version notwithstanding). Ford, by contrast, would settle on goals in one or two crisp meetings in which everyone responsible for implementing the decision was given an opportunity to express his views. Afterward he would permit himself no second thoughts.

Ford was far more intimately involved in the execution of policy than Nixon ever was. Nixon's intricate maneuvers proved uncongenial to Ford, who, though eager to identify his choices when action was called for, was not given to studying long-range, hence conjectural, options. And he preferred oral to written presentations. Nixon's elaborate system of interdepartmental geographic groups at the assistant secretary level fell into disuse. Interdepartmental deliberations were now handled at the deputy secretary level in the Senior Review Group or in its crisis management equivalent, the Washington Special Actions Group, whence they moved directly to the National Security Council. And they were usually triggered by the need to reach some decision.

Ford neither feared controversy among his advisers nor objected to having his preconceptions challenged. Presiding with magnanimous goodwill, he never lost his temper, asked perceptive questions, and made clear decisions, most often at the end of the meeting. He would make himself available for discussion—as Nixon almost never did—with the officials who were being overruled. Ford did not brood over decisions and, once he had made up his mind, he would not be deflected, least of all by domestic political considerations.

Ford's associates never needed to fear that he might be leaving other colleagues with some different impression from their own. There was none of that almost surreal uncertainty about the President's ultimate intentions that had made service in the Nixon White House such an emotional roller coaster. Disagreements did not lead to competing conspiracies; Ford would have them out in front of him, and there was no ambiguity about the outcome.

Still, transparency did not guarantee harmony. From the start, Ford had to overcome that intangible nuance of difference in the reaction of Cabinet members to a newly elected President to whom they owed their appointment compared to a nonelected President without executive experience who had retained them in office and whom most experts did not expect to be reelected. The singular interpretations of Ford's instructions by CIA Director William Colby regarding Angola and the congressional intelligence investigations or by Secretary of Defense James Schlesinger during the *Mayaguez* incident—to be discussed in later chapters—owed much to their (perhaps subconscious) conviction that they understood the nuances of the national interest better than Ford.

When presidential decisions went against them, fractious officials were tempted to engage in endless rear-guard actions. An overruled department would withdraw to the next line of defense, which was an exegesis of how to interpret the presidential decisions. Disputes over strategic arms limitation strategy were therefore never finally settled, partly because they involved substantial philosophical issues for which the technical debates were surrogates, partly because some of the key players were sensitive to the growing influence of the conservative wing of the party which opposed Ford.

## The Ford Team

Every President tends to surround himself with a staff with whose personalities and habits he has become familiar through a period of joint service. But unlike most presidential staffs or even those of traditional Vice Presidents succeeding in office, Ford's entourage—Robert T. Hartmann, Philip Buchen, and L. William Seidman—had never carried out or even aspired to any role at the executive level. Hartmann had served as Ford's legislative assistant in the House of Representatives; Phil Buchen was a lawyer and Bill Seidman a managing partner of an international accounting firm, both hailing from Grand Rapids. Their principal qualifications in Ford's eyes were familiarity, not expertise; they understood his thinking, and he trusted them. Their distinguishing qualities were character and decency. Their drawback was that nothing in Grand Rapids had prepared them for the atmosphere of war of all against all which described Washington in the aftermath of Vietnam and Watergate. Stunned by congressional and media assaults on the new administration, they sometimes acted as if they were not involved in a political battle so much as in clearing up some terrible personal misunderstanding. This in turn could tempt those they were trying to placate into believing that attacks on the Ford presidency were free of the normal political risks associated with dealing with a staff toughened by years of a national campaign.

However reluctant the new arrivals were to confront Congress or the media, they felt more free to do battle with the executive departments. The Cabinet members demonstrably lacked the lifetime record of close association with Ford of his Grand Rapids friends. Because the White House staff has only one client—the President—it tends to flaunt its special concern for him. A certain amount of tension is therefore built into these relationships even inside the Ford White House.

Hartmann in particular appointed himself protector of Ford's special virtues against the allegedly self-serving vestiges of the Nixon era. During the collapse of Indochina in 1975, Hartmann strove mightily to have Ford receive credit for "ending" the Vietnam War by rejecting all requests for additional funds. He seemed oblivious to the fact that his proposal amounted to pulling out unilaterally, rapidly, and unconditionally—the same outcome the radical wing of the peace movement had been urging for nearly a decade. Nor would the radicals share whatever credit was to be achieved with a President in effect appointed by Nixon. Similarly, before Ford left in late July 1975 for the European Security Conference in Helsinki, Hartmann tried to pull the sting from the conservative attacks that we were abandoning Eastern Europe by blaming me for the entire enterprise. But while a President can always dismiss his Secretary of State, he is in no position to dissociate from him while keeping him in office, especially on the eve of a major international conference that is now generally recognized as one of the turning points of the Cold War.

Though such incidents were annoying, they amounted over Ford's term in office to minor episodes. Hartmann—and the rest of the Grand Rapids group—lacked the energy and surely the malice of their counterparts in the Nixon White House. After some months, Hartmann confined himself—or was confined by Ford—to speechwriting and surfaced on policy issues only to the extent of making sure that his chief was receiving adequate credit.

Phil Buchen's role was more pervasive. Every President I have observed has had somewhere in his entourage some associate who, because he is perceived to have no ulterior motive, is in a position to act as the presidential conscience. As Haldeman had incarnated Nixon's romantic image of the overpowering hero-president, so Phil Buchen embodied Ford's commitment to conciliation and healing.

The gaunt, white-haired Buchen, who held the title of counsel to the President, seemed to have stepped out of one of Frank Capra's movies about the small-town America of the 1930s. Loathing confrontations, his bearing exuded disbelief in irreconcilable differences. To some of us battle-hardened veterans of the Vietnam protest, Buchen sometimes seemed to drive the search for compromise to the point of appeasement and, by depriving them of all risk, to encourage the very assaults on executive authority that he was supposed to quell. By taking the White House out of direct confrontations with Congress, he left the agencies—especially the CIA—in the immediate line of fire and therefore extremely vulnerable.

Though at the time I strongly disagreed with Buchen's noncombative proclivities—even while feeling great affection for him personally —I now think, with the perspective of the decades, that he may have embodied a deeper intuitive wisdom. If Ford was to achieve renewal, he would need to balance every victory in the domestic arena against the deepening divisions incurred by continuing domestic strife. Buchen performed his role with dignity and class and, having completed his government service, chose not to return to Grand Rapids after Ford left office. Instead he remained in Washington—a city noted for its difficulty in accommodating those no longer holding power. Buchen has borne the fate of obscurity with the same grace for which even his opponents always respected him.

By far the most formidable new arrival in the Ford White House was Donald Rumsfeld, whom Ford brought back from his post as NATO ambassador when Al Haig departed as chief of staff. After the so-called Halloween Massacre of November 1975 when Ford dismissed Schlesinger, Rumsfeld was appointed as Secretary of Defense. He had earned Ford's respect while they served together in Congress and Ford's gratitude for having helped to manage Ford's election as Minority Leader in 1965.

Rumsfeld afforded me a close-up look at a special Washington phenomenon: the skilled full-time politician-bureaucrat in whom ambition, ability, and substance fuse seamlessly. Rumsfeld had served briefly on the domestic side of the Nixon White House; there he skillfully avoided involving himself in the controversies of an embattled presidency. In those days, he often evinced a certain empathy for the sentiments of the young protesters, even while he expressed disdain for their political program. In early 1973, Nixon assigned Rumsfeld to Brussels as NATO ambassador, where he could establish foreign policy credentials without participating in the Vietnam and Watergate debates.

By the time Rumsfeld returned to Washington in the fall of 1974, the national mood had changed. As a veteran of the political wars, Rumsfeld understood far better than I that Watergate and Vietnam were likely to evoke a conservative backlash and that what looked like a liberal tide after the election of the McGovernite Congress in fact marked the radical apogee. As Ford's chief of staff, Rumsfeld was determined to help Ford survive the political wars without suffering too many lasting wounds himself. He navigated skillfully between the liberal orgy of investigating every aspect of past foreign policy and the conservative and neoconservative critique of the Ford policy toward the Soviet Union as inherited from Nixon.

Charming, tough, and capable of being quite decisive, Rumsfeld neither explicitly supported nor explicitly defied the critics of Ford's foreign policy. As Secretary of Defense, he thwarted new diplomatic initiatives or military moves by a rigorous insistence on bureaucratic procedures and playing the devil's advocate with respect to every new proposal, as I shall discuss in a later chapter. Whether this was because Rumsfeld disagreed with the formal positions Ford and I were encouraging, or because of his judgment of the political landscape, or, most likely, a combination of both is impossible to settle conclusively at this remove. Whichever the motive—and they were all honorable—Rumsfeld was skillful at deflecting every controversial issue into some bureaucratic bog or other. But as the 1976 election approached, a prolonged internal controversy was not sustainable. Delay thus put disputed diplomatic issues on ice for the remainder of 1976.

John Osborne, generally considered among the wisest of Washington commentators, reported on Rumsfeld's relations with his senior colleagues as follows:

> It was only in the twilight weeks, when Ford people loosened up and were more willing to talk than they had previously been, that I began to comprehend the depth and ferocity of the animosities. Donald Rumsfeld, whom I respected during his turn at the head of the White House staff and respect now, was the center and target of much of the distrust. Nelson Rockefeller was convinced that Rumsfeld deliberately frustrated his efforts to contribute to domestic policy formulation, engineered the pressures upon Rockefeller to withdraw from consideration for the 1976 vice presidential nomination, and beguiled Gerald Ford into firing Secretary of Defense James Schlesinger and CIA Director William Colby, replacing Schlesinger with Rumsfeld at Defense and Colby with George Bush at CIA, and depriving Secretary of State Henry Kissinger of his White House base and status as assistant for national security affairs on November 2 and 3, 1975. Of the persons named, only Rockefeller asserted on the record that Rumsfeld did all this in the interest of placing himself in line for the 1976 vice presidential nomination. Kissinger, Schlesinger and Secretary of the Treasury William Simon, who detested the White House staff under Rumsfeld and his successor, Richard Cheney, as thoroughly as Rockefeller did, shared the suspicions of Rumsfeld and found them believable. But they did not speak of them as accepted fact in the way that Rockefeller did. This welter of suspicion and

hatred—the word hatred is justified—was discussed on and
off the record with all of the principals named here and with
President Ford during the final weeks of the administration.[1]

With the passage of time, I grew more mellow about Rumsfeld's
brilliant single-mindedness, especially after I left government and was
no longer in his line of fire. He was tough, capable, personally attractive, and knowledgeable. I came to believe that if he ever reached the
presidency, he might be a more comfortable chief executive than Cabinet colleague—indeed, he had the makings of a strong President.

But somewhere along the way, this talented political leader abandoned his quest for power. Just when Rumsfeld seemed well positioned
to make a run for the presidency, he gave up the pursuit. Were the
conditions not propitious, or had running for the presidency become
too draining even for someone of Rumsfeld's determination? Or had
the reason for his tenacious procrastination all along been a congenital
dread of a setback which made him recoil before the last hurdle because he could not bear the idea of failure? By the time Don Rumsfeld
abandoned electoral politics, I genuinely thought it was a pity.*

Rumsfeld's relations with Schlesinger, whom he replaced, had been
no better than with me or other Cabinet Secretaries, and he inherited
from him an ongoing turf battle with me. But my tensions with Schlesinger were different than those with Rumsfeld. Schlesinger was basically an academic who would occasionally fight intellectual battles
using political means—though never very comfortably. Rumsfeld
might invoke systems analysis in his battles, but he was more a political
leader than an analyst. I was convinced that, at the end of the day,
Schlesinger and I would come to an understanding because, in truth,
our disagreements were essentially esoteric and technical or else bureaucratic.

Schlesinger and I, in fact, went back a long way. I had met him
when we were both "defense intellectuals"; I was then a professor at
Harvard, he a brilliant analyst at the RAND Corporation. At that
time, our views coincided on all essentials, the principal difference
being that I was more concerned with geopolitical and he with technological challenges. In government, I had very high regard for his perfor-

---

* In the 1996 presidential campaign, Rumsfeld was drafted as senior adviser to GOP nominee
Robert Dole. It is difficult to predict what would have laid in store for him had Dole won. In
1998, Rumsfeld chaired an important bipartisan, congressionally-established commission that
produced a thoughtful assessment of the ballistic-missile threat to the United States.

mance as assistant director and later acting director of the Budget Bureau, for defense matters, to which he brought his own unusual blend of economic and strategic insight. When Schlesinger was promoted to chairman of the Atomic Energy Commission in 1971, I greatly admired the way he handled the protests against American underground tests in the Aleutian Islands as allegedly too dangerous. He simply moved his entire family to the test site and stayed there with them throughout the testing. Appointed Secretary of Defense in the summer of 1973 after a brief stint as CIA director, Schlesinger made outstanding contributions to the revision of strategic doctrine and fought tenaciously and effectively on behalf of an adequate defense program in the face of congressional opposition.

I had strongly supported Schlesinger's appointment as Secretary of Defense; it never occurred to me that we might wind up in conflict. Nor was Schlesinger without justifiable grievances. The arms control negotiations during Nixon's first term had ridden roughshod over too many established prerogatives, including those of the Pentagon, whose interests and strategies were directly involved. For example, at the end of the Nixon Administration, the backchannel Strategic Arms Limitation Talks (SALT) were still being conducted in the presidential channel without a Defense Department representative on my negotiating team. So long as I was acting as Nixon's personal adviser and he was using the backchannel to the Kremlin to break Washington's bureaucratic deadlocks, this practice had had a rationale. (I made sure to clear our position with the Chairman of the Joint Chiefs of Staff. But this is not the same as participating in the negotiations.)

But once I became Secretary of State, it was not only insensitive to exclude the department primarily affected by arms control talks, it was bureaucratically reckless. It is axiomatic that those who have not participated in the give-and-take of the diplomatic process become the heroes of retrospective analysis. Unaware of the hurdles surmounted, they can afford to concentrate on the concessions that were made rather than on the achievements these had elicited. With a free shot at the outcome, they tend to foster the fantasy of a negotiation in which all concessions are made by the other side. In the real world of diplomacy, this never happens. And, in fact, when I did add a Defense Department representative on my last SALT negotiation with Brezhnev in January 1976, James P. Wade proved invaluable both in shaping the proposals and in trying to convince his colleagues that they were in the national interest. By then, however, it was too late.

However justified Schlesinger's grievances were initially, he let them run out of proportion. He resented my close relationship with Ford and mistakenly saw me as the principal obstacle to comparable intimacy with the President. What had started out as a perhaps legitimate grievance turned step by step into a systematic effort to reduce my influence. Whether the issue was Cyprus or arms control, supplies for Israel during the Middle East War, the *Mayaguez* crisis or East-West relations, Schlesinger behaved as if he were the leader of the opposition to me in a parliamentary system.

Schlesinger did not help matters by the professorial tone, verging on condescension, he tended to adopt toward the Presidents he served. At an NSC meeting in June 1974 prior to Nixon's departure for the Moscow summit, Schlesinger proposed a SALT agreement in which all the concessions would have to be made by the Soviets. When Nixon asked how he might accomplish this trick, Schlesinger replied: "You can be very persuasive; you have great forensic skills." On October 7, at an NSC meeting chaired by Ford on the same subject, the new President, in the course of disputing a Schlesinger argument, said: "I would like to debate you on the floor of Congress on that point." Schlesinger shot back: "Not if you go into the details"—implying that Ford did not know what he was talking about.

On arms control issues, though intellectually too fastidious to go all the way over to Scoop Jackson's camp and restrained to some extent by his Cabinet position, Schlesinger nevertheless abetted Jackson by not challenging Richard Perle's numbers games. Occasionally Schlesinger would even publicly endorse some arcane technical objection Jackson or Perle had invented—as he did just before Nixon left for the June 1974 summit in Moscow.[2] Schlesinger was motivated in part by his dependence on Jackson's support in the annual congressional battle over the defense budget. And, once he launched his confrontational course with the White House, he could not afford to veer off without risking the loss of his principal political ally, who also happened to be his President's principal critic—an unprecedented and, in the long run, untenable state of affairs.

Schlesinger's deputy, William P. Clements, as well as General George Brown, Chairman of the Joint Chiefs of Staff, did their utmost to mitigate the resulting tensions. Yet it was a losing battle when it came to the debate on arms control; Schlesinger was in his element balancing weapons systems designed by each superpower before the concept of arms control existed on the basis of different, even incommensurable, criteria, and Jackson, as the second-ranking member of the Armed Services Committee, dominated the congressional process.

Schlesinger and I made periodic attempts to end the feud. On July 26, 1974, two weeks before Nixon's resignation, I called Schlesinger:

> KISSINGER: I really think, whatever our personal feelings may be, that within this present crisis you and I cannot leave the impression to foreign countries that we are at each other's throats.
>
> SCHLESINGER: Couldn't agree more, couldn't agree more.
>
> KISSINGER: And that is my attitude.
>
> SCHLESINGER: That's fine. I had told [military aide, Major General John] Wickham to chat with Scowcroft—that if this were the case, that it was unproductive for such a thing to take place.
>
> KISSINGER: It can't take place. Why would I do it? First of all, I honestly do not believe that there are great philosophical differences between us.
>
> SCHLESINGER: Well, I certainly haven't detected them.

At that point, with the Nixon presidency disintegrating, I even appealed to Senator John Stennis, the venerable chairman of the Senate Armed Services Committee, to help compose the differences:

> KISSINGER: I don't want to get you involved in the middle here because the issue isn't what the past was. The issue is that with our President being under the attack he is, we cannot have foreign governments see the two senior officials who have to handle crises in disagreement.
>
> STENNIS: Well, I think you're a thousand percent right, and you're going more than halfway in trying to remedy that situation.
>
> KISSINGER: . . . I was wondering whether you as a patriot and as somebody who is the chairman of that committee might not give Schlesinger a call and give him your impression of my testimony. You can hook it to that. So then you're not mixing into anything.
>
> STENNIS: I'll certainly do it, and I'm glad to. And I'm interested in it and concerned about it for the country's sake, and I just—I'll talk to him along that line and tell him that you and I were very frank at the table there, and you were with all of us and so forth.

KISSINGER: But that I supported him. So that he doesn't think that I went to his committee behind his back.

STENNIS: Oh no, he couldn't think that. Remember I brought this up.

KISSINGER: That's right and, as you recall, I strongly supported him.

STENNIS: Yes sir.

KISSINGER: And also I want to tell you, Mr. Chairman, if you ever find anything being done either by me or the State Department that you think makes an unnecessary point in this, call me up and let me know, and it will be remedied immediately.

It did not take. As soon as Ford became President, the battle started again, leaving the impression to all the world that there were significant philosophical differences. In a normal administration, such a conflict would have ended quickly with the dismissal of one or both of the contestants. But the gradual disintegration of Nixon's presidency and Ford's initial need for continuity—and his desire to placate Henry Jackson—kept the drama running until November 1975, when Ford suddenly replaced Schlesinger.

Ironically, Schlesinger's principal grievance—that I impeded relations between him and Ford—was based on a misapprehension. Schlesinger happened to be one of the very few people who made Ford extremely uncomfortable, as he has explained at length in his memoirs.[3] Already as Vice President, Ford had objected to Schlesinger's handling of congressional relations. Then, within a week of his inauguration, Ford was taken aback by a news story quoting Schlesinger as saying that, at the climax of the Nixon resignation tragedy, he had instructed the Joint Chiefs of Staff to check presidential orders with him to forestall any coup attempt by the President. Ford considered this a low blow and an attack on the authority of the commander-in-chief. He checked its accuracy with the Joint Chiefs of Staff, who denied the existence of the directive but not the fact of the quotation.

Afterward Ford resented not only Schlesinger's brusque comments at NSC meetings but also his tendency to arrive at the Oval Office with his tie loosened and to drop into an easy chair, draping one leg over the armrest. Ford summed up his own shrewd assessment of the internal relationships when I apologized for the amount of the President's time taken up by the internecine sparring: "Jim's fight is not with you but with me. He thinks I am stupid, and he believes you are running me, which he resents. This conflict will not end until I either fire Jim or make him believe *he* is running me." A few months later, Ford chose the first option.

As Ford's presidency matured, General Brent Scowcroft became the indispensable balance wheel of the national security machinery. Scowcroft joined the National Security Council staff as my deputy when Al Haig, who had held the post through Nixon's first term, was nominated to be the Army's vice chief of staff in November 1972. Haig had started out as my military adviser when I arrived in Washington at Nixon's side in 1969. Since ending the Vietnam War would be one of the principal tasks of the Nixon presidency, I tried to recruit a professional officer who had served in Vietnam to help me find my way through the military complexities of Indochina. The various services eager to place a high-level representative recommended a group of outstanding officers with heavily academic backgrounds. But I felt already sufficiently familiar with the academic approach and decided what I needed was a combat officer. My friend, Dr. Fritz Kraemer (see Chapter 27), recommended Haig, who was then teaching at West Point, thus supplying both academic and combat experience. Energetic, intelligent, and dedicated, Haig soon became indispensable, and I appointed him as my deputy after one year.

As Nixon's first term progressed, the backchannel negotiations assigned to me took me away from Washington a good deal of the time. For Nixon, the temptation to pit subordinates against each other proved irresistible. Haig undoubtedly rationalized his difficult and sometimes ambiguous role to himself as helping me do my job more effectively. Nor have Haig's maneuvers at the end of Nixon's first term diminished my admiration for his extraordinarily distinguished service to me and later in even more responsible positions, especially his vital role in holding the country together amidst the disintegrating Nixon presidency.[4]

By the time Haig left for the Pentagon, the position of NSC deputy had become one of the key posts in Washington. Not surprisingly, the Pentagon presented me with a truly imposing list of candidates, all of whom went on to very high positions in their various services. Yet I wanted for deputy someone who was not already part of the high-level Pentagon bureaucratic game.

It was my good fortune to discover such a person on the White House staff. Brent Scowcroft was then serving in the largely anonymous yet highly responsible position of military aide to the President, one of whose duties is to ensure that the war plans are always available to the President wherever he may find himself. Since this aide is obliged to travel with the President, I had many opportunities to exchange views with Scowcroft. Meticulous in expression, tenacious in the pursuit of argument, and highly intelligent, this unassuming Mormon from Utah with a Columbia Ph.D. had impressed me with his deep knowledge of East European and Soviet affairs. He made a particular impact on me when, with a courage verging on foolhardiness, he stood up to Haldeman, then at the apex of his power, over some technical issues I have since forgotten.

Scowcroft proved the perfect choice. His strengths lay in careful analysis and sound judgment. If he erred, it was on the side of an opportunity missed; on his watch, avoidable errors had a high probability of being discovered. We complemented each other's strong points. My approach to strategic analysis was probably more sweeping; Scowcroft was surely more meticulous in assessing the nuances of execution. His role became all the more important on September 22, 1973, when I was sworn in as Secretary of State while retaining the post of National Security Adviser.

As eager as I was to undertake the dual role, it was decidedly an anomalous arrangement. As head of the State Department, I (or a deputy) had to present its point of view at interdepartmental meetings or at the National Security Council—occasionally in conflict with the views of the other departments. But as National Security Adviser, I was charged with representing the President's needs, chief of which was that all options—including those with which I disagreed—be presented fully and fairly. When, in my capacity as National Security Adviser, I chaired interdepartmental meetings, the State Department's position was anomalous. It was recognized that the deputy secretary of state was, in fact, articulating my views, which I was then supposed to present to the President evenhandedly with the others. That this worked at all for twenty-two months was largely due to the unassailable fairness of Scowcroft, who in fact, if not in title, assumed many of the functions of the National Security Adviser.

In November 1975, Ford ended my dual role by appointing Scowcroft as National Security Adviser (as I will describe in a subsequent chapter). This had the potential of turning into a difficult transition, but Scowcroft's tact and integrity averted any tension. I had total confidence that he would represent my views fairly to the President, the President's views accurately to me, and his own views precisely to both of us, whether we liked them or not. He gave Ford his independent judgment in dealing with foreign policy issues without ever giving me the feeling that he was competing with my responsibilities as Secretary of State. Scowcroft acted as the balance wheel of the national security process, and he has remained a national asset and personal friend since.*

No account of my service in the Ford Administration would be complete without a discussion of Nelson Rockefeller, whom Ford selected as his Vice President on August 20, 1974. Rockefeller was one of the seminal influences on my life. We met in the summer of 1955 when he was an assistant to President Eisenhower and invited me, a first-year instructor at Harvard, to join a panel of experts he was setting up to ponder the nation's future. It was in the aftermath of the Geneva summit of July 1955 between President Eisenhower, British Prime Minister Anthony Eden, French Prime Minister Edgar Faure, and Nikolai Bulganin and Nikita Khrushchev on the Soviet side. Our panel was asked to recommend foreign policy initiatives for the post-Stalin era.

Rockefeller entered the room with his trademark gregariousness, slapping backs, calling us by the best approximation of our first names that he could remember. He was at once outgoing and remote, using bonhomie as a way of keeping people at a distance without appearing condescending. Embracing everyone in a kind of universal bear hug allows no one a special claim. Intoxicated by our proximity to power, we panelists—all of us academicians—sought to impress Rockefeller with our practical acumen and offered tactical advice on how to manipulate events. After we were finished, the smile left his face, and Nelson's eyes assumed the hooded look signifying that we were now turning to the things that mattered. He had not brought us down here, he said, "to tell me how to maneuver. . . . *Your* job is to tell me what is right."

The challenge, as apparently naive as it was rare in internal governmental discussions, turned out to be the political essence of Nelson Rockefeller. Third-generation scion of a famous family, he had been raised on the conviction that each generation of Rockefellers had to reearn the family's enormous wealth by public service. For Rockefeller

* President Reagan appointed Scowcroft as chairman of task forces on strategic forces modernization and later to study what had gone wrong in the Iran-Contra affair. And, under President Bush, Scowcroft performed as National Security Adviser with the same distinction.

and his brothers, simple ambition for high office was not enough; they had to justify their role by actions serving their country and reflecting America's deepest values. Each Rockefeller brother had selected some specialty to which he devoted his resources and energy: John concentrated on population; David on international affairs, New York City, and art; Laurance on the environment and sciences; and Nelson first on Latin America, then on national politics and always on art.

But Nelson's political quest was innately different from the exertions of his brothers. They were in a position to create the institutions they wanted to foster. But to be effective in politics, one must hold an existing office, which cannot be reached without some element of self-seeking. Nelson became governor of New York because the state's Republicans had chosen him as their standard-bearer—someone with the means and the charisma to reclaim the state capital from the dominant Democrats. He did not have to vie for the office in the kind of personal rivalry that the presidential primaries would require in later times.

This way of reaching a high position fulfilled Nelson's sense of duty. Once nominated, he was able to put his extraordinary gift for campaigning into the service of a set of ideas he had been instrumental in evoking. His was the last generation of politician who emphasized substance over electoral technique. Modern politicians would think Rockefeller hopelessly naive in his belief that high office had to be earned by advancing the best program. He had never heard of focus groups. When I joined Nelson's staff on a part-time basis in 1957, we spent three evenings a week and many Sundays engaged in what the contemporary politician would consider a waste of time: meeting with leading experts to define the national goals in a variety of fields, both foreign and domestic.

Ten years earlier, when presidential candidates were still being selected by professional politicians, such an approach might have worked on the national level. In the age of primaries, it represented a diversion and a handicap. Thus, there was something foreordained in Rockefeller's repeated failure to win his party's nomination for the nation's highest office. Many years later, at a reunion of Rockefeller campaign veterans, I remarked that textbooks would one day be written about our ingenuity in failing to achieve our goal of nominating Nelson Rockefeller. Each time, some new way was found: withdrawing from the race when Rockefeller should have stayed in (in 1960 and 1968); staying in when he should have withdrawn (1964).

Rockefeller failed to gain his party's nomination not *despite* the fact that he was a Rockefeller but *because* of it. Nelson's entire upbringing made him recoil from ever acting as if his desire to serve was based on naked ambition. Already so privileged, he felt that he had no right to ask anything for himself as an individual. And so this superb campaigner who genuinely liked people eschewed the personal pursuit of delegates. Instead, he sought to reach the presidency by trying to present to the nation the most sweeping vision of its future and the best available blueprints for attaining it—as if the competition were for some academic prize. While others specialized in pursuing delegates, Rockefeller stubbornly practiced a touching faith in the power of ideas.

But that was not quite the way our boisterous political process works, at least not in the period in which Rockefeller appeared as a national figure. In each political campaign, his research staff was larger —and more professional—than his political one, which was usually dominated by facile speechwriters rather than hard-boiled political operatives or by Rockefeller family staffers expert at keeping their charge out of the public eye and disdainful of self-promotion.

Of course, an important element of Nelson's failed quest was the shift in the Republican Party toward a more conservative ideology and in its power base from the Northeast to the South and Southwest. Rockefeller, who had received his first governmental post from Franklin Delano Roosevelt, believed in the spirit—if not all the policies—of the New Deal: that those in power owe compassion and concern for the less fortunate. In foreign policy, he was always a strong defender of the national interest—in practice, frequently more hard-line than his conservative critics.

The emerging leaders of the Republican Party were not sympathetic to this product of the Eastern Establishment which had shaped the party through the Eisenhower Administration. And Rockefeller was never prepared to make the liturgical concessions to win them over—even when, as time went on, he developed increasing reservations about the welfare state.

Rockefeller bore his disappointments with the attitude that no one is entitled to a particular position but everyone has an obligation to help the country—represented by the President, of whatever party. On one occasion, I reported to Nelson that, in a conversation with President Kennedy, I had pointed out a number of policy mistakes. Nelson asked whether I had offered any remedy and, when I replied that I had confined myself to analysis, he grew impatient: "Always remember," he said, "that Presidents are overwhelmed with problems. Your obligation is to help them find solutions."

This was why he reacted with generosity to my service in the administration of Richard Nixon, his nemesis, who had defeated him twice for the nomination. I had initially hesitated to accept Nixon's offer to become National Security Adviser and had asked for a week to reflect, partly to be able to consult Rockefeller, who was unreachable in Venezuela. Rockefeller cut my doubts short by insisting not only that I accept but that, in my new position, I be fully Nixon's man. Rockefeller never asked me to transmit any concerns or requests to Nixon and used other channels when necessary. (Nor did Nixon ever ask me to intercede with Rockefeller.) Nelson's attitude toward my service in Washington came to expression in 1973 during a graceful toast at my fiftieth birthday party: "Henry and I tried for ten years to help shape policy in Washington. I am so proud that one of us finally has the opportunity."

The vice presidency did not come to Nelson Rockefeller until he had abandoned all political ambitions. Having been elected governor of New York four times, he resigned in 1973 to enable his lieutenant governor to position himself for the following year's election. Rockefeller was already making plans for his new role as a private citizen when Ford offered him the office.

The choice did credit to both Ford's determination to appoint the most qualified individual and to Rockefeller's credo that a presidential request was a summons to duty. The appointment annoyed the conservatives and gained nothing for Ford among liberals, who were afraid that so high-powered an addition to the Ford team might enhance the President's prospects if he ran for election in his own right in 1976.

Rockefeller's experience as Vice President would have demoralized a lesser man. Nominated in August 1974, he was not sworn in until December 19 because the Democratic Congress wanted to keep him off the campaign trail during the congressional elections that November. The hearings were tortuous and prolonged, publicizing the Rockefeller finances in excruciating detail. Once confirmed, Rockefeller quickly learned that the American system grants the Vice President prestige but little authority. When he tried to play a role as presiding officer of the Senate, Senator James Allen of Alabama, the Senate's most skilled parliamentarian, insisted that, while the Vice President has the right to break a deadlock with a casting vote, he could not participate in the Senate's deliberations. And the White House staff systematically undercut Rockefeller's role as vice chairman of the Domestic Council, to which Ford had appointed him.

Rockefeller thus found himself confined to those functions usually delegated to Vice Presidents: spot assignments that establish no permanent bureaucratic base and foreign visits to locations just short of those requiring personal presidential attention. His most important assignment was to chair a committee of distinguished outsiders to look into alleged transgressions by the intelligence services—a mission that ended in June 1975. Afterward Rockefeller attended many inaugurations and funerals; he once jokingly told me that he had taken to reading the obituary pages to determine whether some state funeral might require his presence. Less than a year after being confirmed, Rockefeller was induced to take himself off the ticket for the 1976 vice presidential nomination. Ford encouraged that conclusion—records and recollections are unclear on that point—because his staff had convinced him that he would not be able to win the nomination if Rockefeller stayed on the ticket because that would lose him the votes of all the southern delegations. (In the event, Ford lost them anyway.)

Despite this demeaning experience, Rockefeller continued to serve with dedication and without ever criticizing Ford either publicly or privately. He became an indispensable personal adviser to the President, whom he continued to like and respect. Ford trusted him, and Nelson provided me with invaluable moral support and practical advice in trying times—as will be seen throughout this volume. He gave an extraordinary impetus to the Ford Administration, demonstrating by his conduct in adversity the ideal of service that fate never fully vouchsafed him to fulfill in the public arena.

## Ford and His Secretary of State

Ford made his heterogeneous team pull together, and he did so with methods that were peculiarly his own. He did not deliver himself of philosophical homilies or impose an extended personal biography on his interlocutors. Bureaucratic rivalries ended at the door of the Oval Office because Ford simply would not listen to them. I never heard him make critical comments about associates, nor would he have welcomed them from others.

My relations with the President reflected Ford's operating procedure. When he and I were both in town, we would meet every morning, generally with Scowcroft in attendance. The agenda was unvarying: we would discuss the President's daily intelligence brief, which I could be sure he would have read (unlike Nixon, who, deeply suspicious of the CIA, had frequently ignored it). I would sketch the pros and cons of imminent decisions and of some long-range issues. Ford would either state his views or give instructions, both without flourish. Time permitting, he would give me his matter-of-fact estimate of the domestic political situation.

The atmosphere was cordial and businesslike. Ford hated gossip and never indulged in it. He also did not like to discuss lower-level bureaucratic maneuvers. Thus, whatever the stories circulating in the Washington rumor mill, whatever the "revelations" of columnists reading tea leaves to determine who is up or down in the Washington hierarchy, they never originated in the Oval Office, nor would they have been well received there.

This mood of mutual confidence was especially important for the President's relations with his Secretary of State because Ford's inauguration signaled an inevitable change in my status. During Nixon's last year, the political establishment had developed second thoughts about Watergate's potentially damaging international impact and sought to insulate foreign policy from our domestic conflicts. In pursuit of this effort, a role almost amounting to surrogate President for foreign policy fell to me by an instinctive, tacit consensus. For the last months of Nixon's presidency, I met, at his request, with the congressional leadership once a month at the State Department—a role always reserved for the President in normal circumstances.

It had been a precarious and inherently transitory position, and it evaporated—as it should have—as soon as Ford took office. The American system of separation of powers resists exorbitant influence, especially on the part of appointed officials. In the normal course of events, the more prominent a Cabinet member, the more fire he draws. The party in opposition will concentrate its attacks on the best-known personalities in order to weaken the incumbent administration and also to garner the maximum of publicity. This had certainly been the fate of Dean Acheson and John Foster Dulles. I had been spared so long as Nixon was the principal target.

With Nixon's resignation, I became a "normal" Secretary of State and lost my special status. Throughout the Ford Administration, I was

both close to the President but also "controversial" on a host of issues
—from Indochina to détente. Some of these differences were genuine,
others contrived. A tacit coalition of various grievances was forming
of all those who had felt excluded by me from the various negotiations,
the opponents of particular outcomes, and philosophical critics of the
Nixon foreign policy. Ford stood by me staunchly and never let himself
be driven from the course we had charted together.

Some in Ford's entourage occasionally tried to build up their boss
by claiming that I had been overruled on this or that issue or that my
influence was waning. They did not understand the nature of our
relationship or, indeed, of any successful relationship between a President and a Secretary of State. While in office, I told John Osborne
that Presidents and their Secretaries of State need to have a shared
fundamental philosophy on key issues. The question of dominance
can therefore never arise; irreconcilable differences are by definition
excluded—or else the Secretary of State must leave.[5] I am certain
that Dean Acheson—the Secretary I most admired in the postwar
generation—would have spoken similarly.

After his defeat and before he left office, Ford said much the same
thing to John Osborne:

> OSBORNE: This also concerns Kissinger and your relation-
> ship with him. During the two and a half years of your
> presidency, did you ever overrule Kissinger or go against
> his recommendations, his preferences of what he
> wanted to do, in any major, substantive matter of for-
> eign policy?
>
> FORD: There was never any time that there was an impasse
> we could not resolve, where I thought he was right and
> I was wrong, or vice versa. There was never any rupture,
> never a misunderstanding. Sure, there were differences.
> But there was never any major difference that wasn't
> resolved by a shift here or a change there.
>
> OSBORNE: I have a strong notion that that is just about
> what Kissinger would say in answer to that question.
>
> FORD: I think that is about what Henry would say.
>
> OSBORNE: I think you said publicly and you emphasized to
> me in the last talk we had that, if you were elected,
> you would certainly want Kissinger to remain as your
> secretary of state, if he were willing to serve.

FORD: If I were the elected president today, I would strongly urge him to stay on as secretary of state.[6]

This was the team at Ford's side as he began his presidency. And within forty-eight hours of taking the oath of office, he was tested by a crisis on Cyprus carrying with it the risk of war between Greece and Turkey, two NATO allies.

# 7

# CYPRUS, A CASE STUDY IN ETHNIC CONFLICT

The Cyprus crisis turned out to be a seminal event for Ford's presidency. Its origins went back centuries; the passions ran so deep as to be almost beyond the comprehension of anyone not belonging to either of the two ethnic groups. But Cyprus was the forerunner of conflict between ethnic groups, which has become increasingly common and threatening in the decades since. It also had the effect of launching the Ford Administration into an immediate and totally unanticipated clash with Congress.

In the first four months of the Ford presidency, Congress cut off military aid to Turkey, a strategically indispensable ally and host to twenty-six surveillance installations from which the United States was monitoring Soviet missile and nuclear testing. Once a pattern of congressional macromanagement was established, comparable measures followed in short order: the Jackson-Vanik and the Stevenson Amendments in December 1974, severely restricting trade and credits to the Soviet Union; the cutoff of aid to Indochina in March 1975; the prohibition against assistance to groups in Angola resisting a Cuban expeditionary force in December 1975; and a host of restrictions on various other activities. The trend to limit presidential discretion in foreign policy has continued—if not accelerated—in the interval.

It was a cruel twist of fate that threw a nonelected President so precipitously into the maelstrom of Greek-Turkish passions. It was all the more unjust since Ford was deeply committed to close executive-legislative cooperation and was not responsible for the decisions that had evoked the conflict between these two branches in the first place.

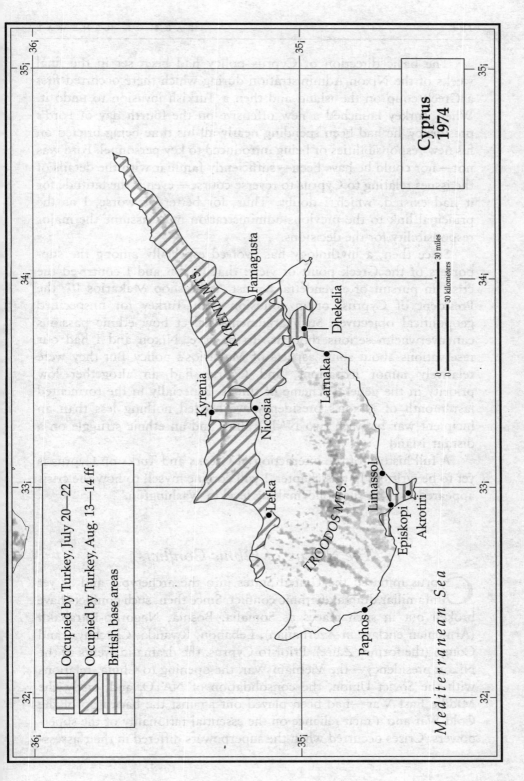

**Cyprus
1974**

Mediterranean Sea

KYRENIA MTS.

TROODOS MTS.

Famagusta

Dhekelia

Kyrenia

Nicosia

Larnaka

Lefka

Limassol

Episkopi

Akrotiri

Paphos

Occupied by Turkey, July 20—22

Occupied by Turkey, Aug. 13—14 ff.

British base areas

30 miles

30 kilometers

The basic direction of Cyprus policy had been set in the final weeks of the Nixon Administration during which there occurred first a Greek coup on the island and then a Turkish invasion to undo it. When Turkey launched a new offensive on the fourth day of Ford's presidency, he had been spending nearly all his time being briefed on his new responsibilities or being introduced to key personnel. Ford was not—nor could he have been—sufficiently familiar with the details of the issues relating to Cyprus to reverse course—even if the latitude for it had existed, which I doubt. Thus, for better or worse, I as the principal link to the previous administration must assume the major responsibility for the decisions.

Since then, a mythology has evolved especially among the supporters of the Greek point of view: that Nixon and I contrived the crisis in pursuit of a vendetta against Archbishop Makarios III, the President of Cyprus, or in collusion with Turkey for unspecified geopolitical objectives. Such arguments reflect how ethnic passions can overwhelm serious thought. To be sure, Nixon and I had our reservations about some aspects of Makarios's policy. But they were relatively minor irritations, and Cyprus had an altogether low priority in the general scheme of things. Especially in the tormented last month of Nixon's presidency, we needed nothing less than an incipient war between two NATO allies and an ethnic struggle on a distant island.

A full history of the interaction of Greeks and Turks on Cyprus is yet to be written. In this chapter, I will confine myself to how the crisis appeared to us at the policymaking level in Washington.

## The Nature of Ethnic Conflicts

Cyprus initiated the United States into the archetypal and as yet unfamiliar drama of ethnic conflict. Since then, such conflicts have broken out in such places as Somalia, Bosnia, Nagorno-Karabakh (Armenian enclave in Azerbaijan), Lebanon, Rwanda, Chechnya, and Congo (the former Zaire). Prior to Cyprus, the dramatic events of the Nixon presidency—the Vietnam War, the opening to China, relations with the Soviet Union, the consolidation of NATO, and, lastly, the Middle East War—had been played out against the backdrop of the Cold War and a tacit reliance on the essential rationality of the superpowers. Crises occurred when the superpowers differed in their assessment of risks, and they were settled when that calculus of risks and rewards was again made to coincide either by threats or diplomacy.

Throughout the period of the Cold War, the superpowers had tacitly cooperated to contain ethnic conflicts or to subordinate them to the requirements of the overall balance of power. The blood feuds in the Middle East and between India and Pakistan were conducted by states somewhat accessible to an international consensus, and they were restrained to some extent by the contestants' dependence on the superpowers for military equipment, economic assistance, and diplomatic support.

Cyprus proved to be a foretaste of a different kind of conflict, one that became increasingly common as the superpower rivalry receded. In ethnic conflicts, the contenders are not motivated by concern for stability, which, if anything, they identify with the status quo at the heart of their frustration. Harkening to some mythic Golden Age in which each of the contending groups believes itself to have been dominant, appeals to conciliation are treated as unforgivable appeasement of the hated rival. Resentments and grievances stored up for centuries leave no room for compromise, which, in any event, is interpreted as tantamount to historical defeat. The ideal national map of each group is incompatible with that of its adversary. None of the contestants will accept an outcome dependent on the good faith of the adversary presented to the children of each generation as the incarnation of evil. In these circumstances, power-sharing becomes a contradiction in terms.

Paradoxically, submitting to a more powerful outsider has often proved more tolerable than to the rule of a hated ethnic adversary occupying the same territory. This is why Bosnia was less violent under Austrian, Turkish, or Communist rule than when its constituent ethnic groups were asked to create a multi-ethnic state. The same was true of Cyprus under British rule.

For Gerald Ford, this meant that, from the first days of his presidency, he found himself enmeshed in a crisis for which there were few guideposts in the American experience. Indeed, what makes ethnic conflicts so difficult for Americans is that, in dealing with them, hallowed American principles almost inevitably clash.

The concept of majority rule is generally meaningful only where there exists some possibility for the minority to become a majority or where the legal tradition is so strong that appeals to the courts have a chance of overturning legislative acts. Neither condition existed in

Cyprus. The Turkish minority had preserved itself not through constitutional appeals in the courts but by means of illegally armed enclaves. In the absence of an overriding system of shared values, self-determination amounted to partition and majority rule to domination. Twenty years later, the same equation became operative in Bosnia.

It was Cyprus's geographic location at the intersection of Europe and the Middle East that dictated its strategic importance and its ethnic mix. Eight hundred years of Greek rule since the days of Byzantium had entrenched a Greek majority of some 80 percent. Three hundred years of Ottoman domination starting in 1571, reinforced by Turkey's geographic proximity, had ensconced a Turkish minority in the northern part of the island closest to Turkey (see map). In 1878, the Congress of Berlin awarded Cyprus to Great Britain as compensation for Russian gains in the Balkans and as a way of strengthening Great Britain's ability to protect the eastern Mediterranean against Russian incursions.

So long as an outside power dominated Cyprus, the ethnic animosities on the island only simmered. But once the worldwide thrust of decolonization reached its shores in the mid-twentieth century, civil conflict became inevitable, and the principles of majority rule and self-determination turned irreconcilable. For centuries, Greeks and Turks had nursed their mutual hatreds, periodically venting them in massacres and other atrocities. Each ethnic group could recite convincing evidence for why it must not entrust its fate to the goodwill of the other.

The Cold War calculus of deterrence and détente simply did not apply to Cyprus. Neither of the Cypriot parties cared particularly about superpower rivalry—except perhaps as a bargaining counter. Fearful of weakening the strategically crucial eastern flank of the Atlantic Alliance, the United States tried to do justice to the concerns of both sides and, in the process, often earned their opprobrium.

Because these concerns reflected the classic fault lines of ethnic conflicts, they were, in fact, unbridgeable. The Greek majority insisted on a unitary state, which, by turning the Turkish population into a permanent minority, in effect disenfranchised the Turks. The Turkish minority demanded a federal structure and multiple vetoes, which, given the ethnic animosities, amounted to partition.

In 1959, Britain brokered an arrangement which was doomed from the start because it sought to address the essentially irreconcilable demands of all the parties by agreeing to all of them simultaneously.

The so-called London-Zürich Agreements established an independent, sovereign, and unitary Cyprus in 1960 with a Greek Cypriot President and a Turkish Cypriot Vice President, each elected by his own community. The Turkish Cypriot Vice President had an absolute veto on defense and foreign policy issues and, provided he was supported by a majority of the Turkish Cypriot members of the legislature, a veto on fiscal matters as well.

This mélange of incompatibilities was guaranteed by Great Britain, Greece, and Turkey. In the event that concerted action by the Cypriot communities should prove impossible, each guarantor retained the unilateral right to intervene with "the sole aim of reestablishing the state of affairs created by the Treaty." To complete this witches' brew, both Greece and Turkey were permitted to station small military contingents on the island, and Great Britain to retain two air bases.

The idea seems to have been that an unworkable treaty could somehow be protected by a vague guarantee meant to be implemented by parties certain to disagree over what conditions they were expected to reestablish. The only comparable attempt to square the circle of ethnic conflict had been in Lebanon and, as we shall see, it would suffer the same fate as Cyprus at the end of the Ford presidency—a period in foreign policy framed as if between two bookends labeled "ethnic conflict."

## Makarios: The Wily Archbishop

The explosive potential of Cyprus was magnified by the extraordinary personality of its founding President, Archbishop Makarios. The son of a shepherd, he had risen to become the highest-ranking priest on Cyprus as well as its President—a legacy of the Greek Orthodox clergy's historic claim to both secular and religious leadership. Highly intelligent, unflappable, always well prepared, as complex in his tactics as he was single-minded in the pursuit of his objectives, Makarios exuded authority. His ecclesiastical garb and utter self-assurance were somewhat vitiated by his shrewd, watchful eyes, which seemed always to be calculating the possibilities of gaining the edge over an interlocutor—the only item open to question being the extent of that advantage, never the fact of it.

As a result, if one attribute eluded Makarios, it was the ability to inspire confidence—which happens to be the prerequisite for effective diplomacy. Displaying little concern (indeed, a certain disdain) for the point of view of the other party, he never understood that evoking trust is as much a practical as a moral imperative. True, a statesman's foremost responsibility is to look out for the interests of his own country. But the wisest of them—and, in the long run, the most successful—understand that only those agreements are destined to last in the maintenance of which the other side also develops an interest. For, in foreign policy, one meets the same people over and over again. The tricked or outsmarted will never again make reliable partners. And any international agreement has to be carried out by sovereign states, by the very definition of sovereignty in a position to renege on what they have come to regard as iniquitous.

Makarios rejected such thinking. Perhaps, like a star athlete, he felt obliged to practice to the fullest extent the skills God had vouchsafed to him. More likely he considered his own position too precarious to take into account the point of view of his interlocutors, most of whom were adversaries.

The archbishop found himself in an unusually complicated situation. Cyprus's war of independence had been conducted under the leadership of General George Grivas from mainland Greece. Grivas was a passionate advocate of *enosis,* or union with Greece. Makarios, however, preferred the presidency of an independent country to the governorship of a Greek province. For their part, the democratic political leaders of mainland Greece, though rhetorically committed to *enosis*—as was initially the majority of Cyprus's Greek population—were not eager to compete with Makarios's powerful personality for the leadership of all of Greece. But once the military junta took over in 1967, Makarios was perceived in Athens as an obstacle to fulfilling Greece's national mission.

Makarios was even more distrusted by Turkey, where he was considered to be the implacable defender of a unitary Cypriot state and a dedicated and effective opponent of rights for the Turkish minority. Nor did Great Britain, the third guaranteeing power, have any particular confidence in the archbishop.

To protect himself against interference from Greece and pressure from Turkey, Makarios tended to follow the path of Egypt's Gamal Abdel Nasser and Libya's Muammar Qaddafi by allying himself with the radical elements of the Nonaligned Movement. In addition, and especially after the military junta had seized power in Athens in 1967, Makarios relied increasingly on the Cypriot Communists for internal backing against machinations from the mainland. That same thinking prompted him to introduce Czech arms clandestinely into Cyprus to equip his presidential guard against a potential coup inspired from Athens and to increase his own freedom of action in Cyprus's ethnic conflicts.

My attitude toward Makarios reflected the general ambivalence. As a student of diplomatic history, I was quite familiar with the Byzantine tradition he represented and on which the master European diplomats such as Richelieu or Metternich had based their craft. I respected the dexterity and cold-bloodedness with which Makarios performed his high-wire act. At the same time, as the American Secretary of State, I was occasionally disquieted by the directions in which his conception of his self-interest took him; keeping the superpowers off balance was, after all, his negotiating leverage. But—and I ask his Cypriot acolytes to forgive me—I considered Makarios more of a nuisance than a menace. At no time during my period in office did we take any measure to reduce his hold on power. We maintained an aloof, respectful, and wary relationship with him.

On August 5, 1974, after the July 15 coup against Makarios and four days before Ford took office, I gave this assessment of Makarios to my senior colleagues in the State Department:

> We never for a moment thought that he was the "Castro of Cyprus," and in fact, if we had had our preferences, there would not have been the coup, and we could have coexisted with him very well. It wasn't a question of coexistence; we didn't consider him anti-American particularly. His major drawback, if he has any, is that his talents are too large for his island and, therefore, he could be subject to the temptation to play on a scale which is disquieting—not to us but to the other parties interested in the Cyprus question.

When all was said and done, Makarios, the proximate cause of most of Cyprus's tensions, was also the best hope for a long-term peaceful solution. For once he had exhausted all possible maneuvers, he could be eminently practical about his necessities.

The last time I met Makarios was in 1975 in Helsinki at the conclusion of the European Security Conference. By then Turkish troops were occupying about 35 percent of Cyprus. To get the stalled negotiations under way, Makarios belatedly agreed to a contiguous, self-governing Turkish area on the island, which, until then, he had always adamantly rejected. However, he argued that its size needed to be kept in proportion to the Turkish population, or some 20 percent of the territory. He added that he was prepared to compromise and would consider 25 percent, sketching a map that seemed to me edging toward 30 percent. When I pointed this out, Makarios was nonplussed and wearied by my obtuseness. "I define what constitutes 25 percent," he said.

The Helsinki conference was also the occasion of one of the archbishop's more skillful maneuvers. Ford and I, irritated by some statements of Makarios, had decided not to grant him a separate session with the President. When I informed the archbishop, he was nonplussed. "We shall see," he said in his customary imperturbable manner. One can imagine Ford's surprise when, at a coffee offered to the heads of delegations by the Finnish President, he found himself seated for nearly an hour next to Makarios. How the archbishop contrived this is lost to history. I have been able to find no Finnish official able to explain to me, as I was writing these pages, this piece of archbishopal legerdemain.

## Greek-Turkish Minuets

The London-Zürich Agreements collapsed within three years. Makarios would not grant any sort of meaningful autonomy to the Turkish minority for fear that it might secede; the Turkish minority continued to equate majority rule with disenfranchisement. Toward the end of 1963, Makarios broke the deadlock by imposing thirteen amendments to the constitution that effectively established a unitary state with majority rule.

Intercommunal violence was inevitable. It included a massacre in the Turkish quarter of Nicosia led by the thug Nikos Sampson, who was to play a key role in the 1974 events. In 1964, a conference of the parties was held in London (and later in Geneva). It failed, as did an American conciliation mission led by Under Secretary of State George Ball. Turkey threatened to invade to protect its compatriots and desisted only when a letter from President Lyndon Johnson warned that if the Soviet Union reacted, Turkey's allies might not recognize "an obligation to protect Turkey against the Soviet Union. . . ."[1] In other words, the Atlantic Alliance would not be invoked, and Turkey would be left at the Soviet Union's mercy.

Such language had never been directed at a NATO ally, nor would it be used again and for a very good reason: by definition, NATO protects its members not as a favor to the victim of potential aggression but for the sake of the national security interests of all members, including the United States. This is particularly the case with respect to a country like Turkey, situated in a geopolitically indispensable location. By casting doubt on these crucial premises, Johnson's letter transformed the NATO guarantee from a strategic necessity into a whim of American policy. And though Turkey recoiled from the brink, it did so at the price of resentments which mortgaged future Cyprus crises.

In the immediate aftermath of the 1964 crisis, Greece attempted to counteract the threat of Turkish invasion by infiltrating twelve thousand Greek troops into Cyprus. In 1967, after a communal clash that began with a Greek-Cypriot attack on Turkish villages, Turkey once again threatened invasion, and President Johnson sent another special emissary, Cyrus Vance, then at the beginning of his distinguished diplomatic career. Vance's mission was no more successful in resolving the communal conflict than the previous efforts, although the Greek junta did agree to withdraw some seven thousand of its troops from the island. The two Cyprus parties also undertook to begin intercommunal talks. All these frustrations heightened Turkey's resolve to vindicate its claims by force at the next opportunity.

When the Nixon Administration took office, the Greek military junta was a pariah within NATO; the Turkish parliamentary government was weak and the Turkish military restless; Makarios was, step by step, marginalizing the Turkish minority. In reaction, a series of de facto Turkish enclaves—illegally armed by Turkey—emerged in which the writ of the Cypriot central government no longer ran. If the cauldron boiled over, Turkish military intervention was probable. Saddled with quite enough intractable problems in Indochina, the Middle East, and India/Pakistan, we had little incentive to court trouble in a region that was, at least for the moment, quiescent.

Quiescence seemed, in any event, to be the best achievable outcome. Neither of the two Cypriot ethnic groups was prepared to compromise or to give its rival a voice in decisions affecting itself. Federalism was precluded by the Greek majority's refusal to grant significant autonomy to the Turkish minority. Majority rule was prevented by the Turkish minority's rejection of a permanently inferior status. Partitioning the island between Greece and Turkey was prevented by Makarios and the Nonaligned Movement. The Soviet Union opposed any increase in the influence of NATO members Greece and Turkey on Cyprus.

From time to time, the United States invoked sacramental language to the effect that anything acceptable to the Cypriot parties would be agreeable to us. But to the parties, these phrases sounded empty, if not cynical. No such formula has ever emerged in the eight American administrations obliged to deal with the problem since the London-Zürich Agreements. In the classic pattern of ethnic conflict as practiced from Lebanon to Bosnia, solutions are much more likely to emerge from the total victory of one side or from mutual exhaustion than from the contribution of mediators.

Cyprus remained quiet throughout almost all of Nixon's first term, even as relations between the ethnic groups steadily deteriorated. In January 1972, it was learned that, with Makarios's blessing, thousands of crates of Czech weapons had been received by Cypriot leftist elements. Makarios seemed to be heading down the same road as Egypt's Nasser two decades earlier except that Makarios was playing his game vis-à-vis an explosive mix of two powers—Greece and Turkey—both of which feared the Soviet Union, distrusted Makarios, and were guarantors of arrangements on Cyprus, hence had a legal right to intervene.

Makarios's acquisition of Czech arms provoked the Greek junta's rabid anti-Communism. On February 11, 1972, it delivered an ultimatum to Makarios demanding that the Czech arms be placed under United Nations control and that the Cyprus government be reconstituted on a broader basis. Further, a synod of three Cypriot Greek Orthodox bishops, no doubt spurred on by the junta, announced that spiritual and temporal power should be separated and that Makarios ought therefore to resign from the presidency—theologically quite an unconventional position for the Orthodox Church.

The Nixon Administration, whatever its reservations about Makarios, feared that his withdrawal from the scene might tempt Turkey to impose a contiguous Turkish enclave for which it had been pressing in the intercommunal talks and, if necessary, protect it with Turkish troops. That would surely be opposed by any new Cypriot government and, in the end, by Greece as well, generating a major crisis between NATO allies.

American Ambassador Henry J. Tasca was therefore instructed to warn the Greek junta against any "forcible change." The junta replied that Greece would not tolerate foreign intervention, a declaration explicitly "addressed also to our friends—to them more so than to others." Even as it rejected the principle of foreign intervention, the junta did accept our basic recommendation and, by March 4, 1972, renounced the use of force.

For his part, Makarios agreed to place the Czech arms under United Nations supervision and "reconstituted" his government by dismissing his foreign minister. Neither measure meant much. The three rebellious bishops were later summoned to a synod of Cypriot Greek Orthodox clergy and defrocked. The high-wire artist had won his gamble and survived once again with essentially enhanced power.

From then until the 1974 crisis, the pressure cooker of Cyprus simmered on, ever ready to explode but on the surface giving every appearance of quiescence. At the U.N. General Assembly in September 1972, neither the Greek nor the Turkish foreign ministers seemed sufficiently concerned to raise Cyprus in private talks with me. The same was true during the General Assembly of 1973. In April 1974, at a special session of the U.N. General Assembly, the foreign ministers of Greece and Turkey were indeed threatening military action against each other but not over Cyprus. The issue was oil exploration—specifically their respective rights to drill for oil in the Aegean. Despite these tensions, the Turkish foreign minister offered to resume the Cyprus intercommunal talks where they had broken off.

Nor did Makarios exhibit any anxiety when I called on him in Nicosia on May 7, 1974, where he was hosting a meeting between me and Soviet Foreign Minister Andrei Gromyko in the context of the Israeli-Syrian disengagement shuttle. Cyprus had been chosen as a "neutral" site that was not expected to present the superpowers with any special problem in the immediate future. Makarios, debonair as ever, presided at a lunch, during which he demonstrated his attention to detail by serving Wiener schnitzel—a special favorite of mine. Welcoming me, Makarios appeared relaxed:

> The problem of Cyprus is one of patience. We have not had many incidents between the two communities. Often we have intra-Greek and intra-Turk incidents. . . . We hope to resume the intercommunal talks. . . . In my view, if no formula can be agreed on in a short while, the Secretary General of the U.N. is coming here soon, and perhaps he can get the sides together.

There was no sense of imminent crisis nor any hint from Makarios that he was about to challenge the Greek position on the island.

A few weeks later, on June 18, 1974—less than a month before the coup against Makarios—during the semiannual NATO ministerial meeting in Ottawa, NATO Secretary General Joseph Luns wistfully appealed to the Greek and Turkish foreign ministers to place the interests of the Alliance above their dispute over oil exploration in the Aegean. Cyprus was not mentioned. The Greek and Turkish foreign ministers responded by professing their desire for peace. Neither referred to Cyprus.

On July 8–9, I stopped in London for a review of the international situation with British Foreign Secretary James Callaghan. Neither of us considered Cyprus—or even Greek-Turkish relations—sufficiently threatening to include on our agenda. On the same day, a week before the coup, the daily White House intelligence brief referred only to Greek-Turkish tensions in the Aegean; Cyprus was only peripherally mentioned.

After the coup in Cyprus, a cottage industry of investigative journalists claimed to have discovered intelligence warnings which were ignored by an administration driven by its dislike of Makarios and its obsession with geopolitics. What outside observers rarely understand is that, in a large bureaucratic government, it is almost always possible to discover some document or other predicting the event under investigation; it is a way for the bureaucracy to cover all bets. What really matters, however, is the context and to whose attention the warning was brought.

And the context was one of reassuring meetings with high Greek and Turkish officials, of soothing comments from Makarios, and, above all, of the preoccupations of our highest-ranking officials with other more pressing issues. I had been on a thirty-four-day Israeli-Syrian shuttle that ended on May 31, 1974, with a Syrian-Israeli disengagement agreement. From June 10 to 18, I accompanied Nixon to Egypt, Saudi Arabia, Syria, Israel, and Jordan. From June 27 to July 3, I went with him to his last summit in Moscow. I stayed on for a few days for consultations in Brussels, Paris, Rome, Munich, London, and Madrid and to watch the final match of the soccer World Cup on July 9—a certain indication that I did not believe a crisis was imminent. In the interval between these trips, an exorbitant amount of my time was taken by congressional investigations, especially a new and preposterous charge by Senator Henry Jackson that the Nixon White House had made some "secret deal" outside the SALT agreement with the Soviets on nuclear arms control.[2] As for Nixon, except for his final—basically ceremonial—foreign visits, he was consumed by Watergate.

The last thing he or I needed was to encourage a crisis in the eastern Mediterranean between two NATO allies.

The document most frequently cited in later congressional investigations of the Cyprus crisis was a prescient paper written in May 1974 by Thomas D. Boyatt, the State Department's desk officer for Cyprus. In it, he had correctly predicted the likely policy of Dimitrios Ioannides, the head of the Greek military police who had overthrown the previous Athens junta. The paper had been sent to me while I was on the Syrian-Israeli shuttle. During my absence from Washington, the acting secretary accepted Boyatt's recommendations that representations be made to Ioannides warning against the use of force or other actions which might upset the status quo in Cyprus, an exact replica of what we had done during the 1972 crisis.

Ambassador Tasca at first resisted these instructions on the ground that, given Ioannides's volatile temperament, they would inflame the junta leader rather than produce restraint. Moreover, Ioannides, though the strong man, did not have an official position; he operated from behind the facade of a President and foreign minister whom he controlled. Under pressure from Washington, Tasca did deliver the message to the Greek President, to the Greek foreign minister, and to Archbishop Seraphim, whom Tasca believed to be a close friend of Ioannides. Tasca was later accused of not having performed his task with adequate emphasis. No evidence to that effect was ever adduced, and the same ambassador had delivered a similar message effectively two years earlier.

What drove the situation on Cyprus out of control was not so much mistakes in Washington as actions by Makarios, who was once again testing his dexterity on the high wire—this time with disastrous results. On July 2, he informed the president of Greece that he was reducing the size of the National Guard, and he demanded the withdrawal of the Greek officers who controlled it. These two steps would greatly reduce, if not eliminate, Athens's influence in Cyprus and enable Makarios to rely even more on the local Communist Party internally and on the Nonaligned Movement internationally.

As was usual with Makarios, what appeared to be an impulsive move culminated a cold calculation. Ioannides had even less standing internationally—especially in the Atlantic Alliance—than his predecessor. Makarios was reasonably certain that the Western allies would thwart a move by Athens to implement its right as a guaranteeing power to enforce the London-Zürich Agreements. Surely Britain's Labour government, extremely hostile to the junta, would not enforce its treaty rights. As for Turkey, it was unlikely to object to a weakening of Greek influence on the island, and it would be further inhibited by an apparent political deadlock in Ankara, where a precarious coalition government had been formed between the socialist party of the new Prime Minister, Bulent Ecevit, and the right-wing, extremely national-ist National Salvation Party headed by the Islamic fundamentalist, Necmettin Erbakan. Ecevit, who had started out as a poet, Ioannides, who was basically a policeman, and Makarios, the Machiavellian in clerical garb, constituted an explosive mix amongst whom compromise surely did not count as one of life's blessings.

For fourteen years, the passions of the parties had been balanced by their inhibitions, at times reinforced by outside pressures. This delicate balance came unhinged in the summer of 1974. The historic balancers, the United States and Great Britain, were under the impres-sion that the crisis was of a kind with previous ones they had jointly contained several times over the previous decade. This expectation was reinforced by the apparent lack of any sense of urgency from Makarios, who had the most at stake. As late as July 12—three days before the coup—the archbishop told the newly appointed American ambassador, Rodger Davies—who was later assassinated in Nicosia—that he considered the situation "delicate" but not "critical." "He gave no indication," the ambassador reported, "[that] he was seeking any US intervention with Athens. . . ." All the judgments of all the parties turned out to be wrong.

Deterrence presumes calculability and rationality—qualities which, even in a bilateral relationship, are precarious. But Cyprus involved two ethnic rivals, three guaranteeing powers, and the United States. And all of them misjudged the situation more or less simultaneously. Makarios had undertaken one high-wire act too many.

Ioannides misunderstood the Turkish perception of the Cyprus problem—above all, that Turkey had never abandoned its demands for an autonomous Turkish region and had never forgiven the humiliations of 1964 and 1967. The United States, preoccupied with Watergate, did not believe the situation was approaching a critical point. Thus the explosion finally came when no one, not even Makarios, expected it, on the morning of July 15, 1974.

## Cyprus Erupts

In the early morning hours of that day, I was awakened with the news that, during the night, the Cyprus National Guard had staged a coup. Led by its Greek officers, it had preempted Makarios's own plan to strip it of power. Initial reports had it that Makarios had been killed, the presidential palace occupied, and a man with the (to me) unfamiliar name of Nikos Sampson had been declared President. Tom Boyatt briefed me that Sampson was a gunman who had allegedly killed twelve people during various ethnic clashes in Nicosia. Though Sampson proclaimed that he would continue the existing constitutional arrangements, he was known to be a passionate advocate of *enosis*—Cyprus's union with Greece.

At 10:15 that morning, the interagency Washington Special Actions Group (WSAG)—the crisis management group consisting of the deputy secretaries of state and defense, the National Security Adviser, the CIA Director, and the Chairman of the Joint Chiefs of Staff—convened in the Situation Room in the basement of the White House. Its imposing reputation notwithstanding, the Situation Room is small and cramped, furnished with only a medium-sized conference table and a row of chairs along walls which are covered with maps relevant to whatever crisis is on the agenda at the moment. It adjoins the White House Communications Center from which any part of the world can be reached almost instantaneously. Participants in Situation Room meetings often get up to use these facilities to check some fact or other.

As is nearly always the case at the onset of a crisis, the prevailing mood was confusion. No one present doubted, however, that the coup had been instigated by the Greek junta in Athens—more specifically, by General Ioannides—and that it marked the beginning of a major crisis.

Turkey would never accept *enosis*. If it considered domination by the Cypriot Greeks so unacceptable that, for a decade, it had teetered on the brink of launching an invasion to prevent it, Turkey would surely not acquiesce to the transformation of Cyprus into a province of mainland Greece. That Ankara had been thwarted from intervening in 1964 and 1967 would probably increase its determination to seek a pretext to settle accounts.

The overwhelming concern of the Washington Special Actions Group on the day of the coup was to prevent a war between two

NATO allies that would destroy the Alliance's eastern flank and open the way to Soviet penetration of the Mediterranean. Our first move, therefore, was to try to minimize pretexts for outside intervention by preserving as much of the existing constitutional structure as possible. Messages were sent to Ankara and to Athens, making clear that the United States rejected *enosis*. To Turkey, we added that we would oppose any curtailment of existing Turkish rights; to Athens, we stressed that the United States opposed "any change of the existing political status of the island or of the Turk Cypriot rights." Simultaneously, we rejected a Soviet mediating role between two NATO allies:

> A Soviet role will depend on the degree this stops being an internal Cyprus problem. . . . So we must keep this as an internal affair and keep it from becoming internationalized.

Even as we were drafting the cables, we knew that they were but opening moves for what was likely to turn into a very complex diplomacy. For a decade Makarios had been undermining the very constitutional arrangements to which we were now appealing while Turkey had been trying to supersede the London-Zürich Agreements, of which it was a guarantor. In 1964 and 1967, the United States had been preeminent; in 1974, on the verge of either impeachment or resignation, Nixon was in a very weak position either to threaten or to cajole. In 1964 and 1967, Makarios was in place to appeal to the Nonaligned Movement and to the United Nations; in 1974, what claimed to be the government of Cyprus was headed by Nikos Sampson, who was not recognized as President by *any* nation in the world. And the Greek government under Ioannides had no international standing and was approaching incoherence in its domestic arrangements.

Britain considered itself to have a special responsibility in dealing with the crisis. It had two air bases on the island, and the London-Zürich Agreements had been drafted under British auspices. On July 16, the day after the coup, Turkish Prime Minister Bulent Ecevit appealed to Great Britain for the consultations provided for in the London-Zürich Agreements.

We had every reason to welcome Callaghan's participation. There was no foreign leader with whom I enjoyed working more and very few I appreciated as much. Combining an avuncular personality with abundant good sense, Callaghan had rescued Anglo-American ties from the coolness into which Prime Minister Edward (Ted) Heath had plunged them in his attempt to demonstrate his commitment to Europe by dissociating, at least to some extent, from the "special relationship" with the United States (see Chapter 20). The drawback of Callaghan's leading role was that it was his first exposure to crisis diplomacy, and Cyprus was about as intractable and maddening a problem as could be wished on any diplomat. Three guaranteeing powers, two Cypriot ethnic communities, an unrecognized Cypriot government, Makarios in exile, and two superpowers were all jockeying for position.

Callaghan was an experienced political operator who, in the course of his rise to eminence, had been accused of occasionally using his elbows perhaps a shade too liberally—a tendency which, if it existed, he did not transfer to foreign policy and surely not to Anglo-American relations.[3] But there are ethical limits in British politics not generally observed in ethnic conflicts, let alone between Greeks and Turks. In personal relationships, Callaghan was more easygoing than I, but he tended to personalize foreign policy issues to a greater extent—especially where he held strong moral convictions, as he did with respect to the Greek junta and later on to Turkish intransigence. He could be more easily aroused to anger by the obstinacy and occasional duplicity of passionate interlocutors—perhaps because he expected more from them than I did.

With respect to Cyprus, the target of Callaghan's anger shifted with the changing situation: in the week following the coup, it was directed at the Athens junta, then at Ecevit for stalling on calls for a cease-fire, the next week at the new democratic Greek government when it dragged its feet in coming to the second round of negotiations (on July 24, Callaghan even threatened to start negotiations without it), until finally landing definitively on Ankara when the Turks resumed military operations.

Callaghan's principal experience had been in ministries concerned with domestic British problems where mediators are generally dealing with willing parties that start from the premise that a compromise will emerge sooner or later and whose statements of their objectives can be taken more or less at face value. By contrast, in ethnic conflicts, the mediator is on thin ice if he expects such criteria to guide parties whose mutual hatreds have been refined over the centuries. Unlike Callaghan, my experience in mediation came from Middle East diplomacy; hence I took the pronouncements of the parties less literally, and my expectations for rapid progress were correspondingly lower.

Differences in temperament and background aside, the spirit of our relationship is captured in my instructions to Ambassador William Buffum, assistant secretary of state for international organizations, on July 24, 1974, as he was leaving for Greek-Turkish negotiations chaired by Callaghan:

> Be cooperative and helpful to Callaghan but, on those things that affect our interests, we must make the decisions ourselves. . . . Tell him everything. We have no secret strategy. . . . It doesn't hurt us to have the British play a role in the Eastern Mediterranean. If Callaghan gets credit for the outcome we favor, that is just fine with me. The important thing is a favorable outcome.

Callaghan reciprocated though he could not forbear an occasional dig to remind me of Great Britain's presumed superior maturity: "You supply the muscle," he told me at the beginning of the Cyprus crisis, "and we will furnish the brains." No doubt some of his associates in the Foreign Office took that jibe literally.

As trusting as our relationship was, our initial approaches to the crisis differed—if only because of the perspective from which we viewed it. A practicing politician, Callaghan was at every step conscious of the prevailing view in the Labour Party, which, for purposes of the immediate crisis, meant being strongly anti–Greek junta. During the first week, my views were dominated by the desire not to add to Turkish incentives to invade, which an all-out dissociation from Athens might invite. I was as eager to get rid of Sampson as Callaghan and end the attempt to bring about *enosis*. But my tactics were tempered by the desire to keep Greece in the Alliance and provide Turkey no pretext for invasion.

In the meantime, Makarios reappeared and, by July 16, made his way to a British air base on Cyprus. While Makarios was being flown to London via Malta, Callaghan advanced three propositions: he refused to accept Sampson; he demanded the withdrawal of Greek officers serving with the Cyprus National Guard; and he insisted on the return of Makarios. By the morning of July 17—or forty-eight hours after the coup—Callaghan had enlisted the European Community behind his priorities:

> I'll tell you our position and this is basically the European position—all the countries in the Nine [the European Com-

munity] and NATO. We think the ideal solution would be to
get Makarios back. Whether we can do it by diplomatic
means remains to be seen. Makarios asked for diplomatic
activity to continue and the need for nonrecognition of the
new regime in Cyprus. When you look ahead for six months
—will the situation be more than or less tense? Our estima-
tion is more—that it would look to be more tense if we can't
get Makarios back—but the question is can we?

The Europeans now had declared objectives for the attainment of
which they had neither a strategy nor the means. The situation was
reminiscent of a World War II joke according to which someone proposed dealing with German submarines by heating the oceans and
boiling them to the surface. When asked how to accomplish this, he
was supposed to have replied: "I have given you the idea; the technical
implementation is up to you."

This was more or less Callaghan's reaction when I asked him how
we were going to bring Makarios back:

Well, hopefully you would exert your influence on the Greek
government about the National Guard officers. The Turks,
under our guarantee treaty, may say to us, what are you
going to do, and if action doesn't seem possible—any of the
three powers has the right to take action. I think we can take
it that we can talk about unilateral action and, if so, then
there has to be U.S. pressure on Greece.

That meant tolerating or at least threatening a Turkish invasion as a
last resort to restore Makarios if American pressure on Greece did not
work. Callaghan said he thought there was an "outside chance" (at
best three to one, probably five to one) that American pressure might
accomplish the return of Makarios and the removal of Greek officers.
He did not specify what pressure he had in mind.

Congressional thinking ran along the same lines. On July 19, Senate Majority Leader Mike Mansfield informed me that there was a lot
of "anti-Greek sentiment which is already evident in the Senate anyway" and that, if it got out of hand, "there'd be hell to pay." On the
other hand, Mansfield opposed the use of force: "If it comes to that
. . . then you are in great trouble, worse than Vietnam I would think."
Senator William Fulbright, chairman of the Foreign Relations Commit-

tee, made the same point, citing much the same conundrum: "I'm opposed to using force too, but I don't want to support the Greeks."

On July 17, I reported to Nixon that the Europeans were talking a tough game but wanted us to do the heavy lifting. While media, Congress, and our allies were clamoring for some kind of assault on the Greek junta, I was trying to navigate American policy to preserve the eastern flank of NATO and keep both Greece and Turkey in the Alliance. This, in my view, precluded an all-out identification of the United States with one of the parties—a view I maintained when the dominant mood took a 180-degree turn, and Turkey became the target. I therefore proposed to Nixon that the United States leave the sidelines and attempt to mediate. To this end, I would send Under Secretary of State Joseph Sisco first to London and then to Athens and Ankara to put forward our ideas. Four objectives needed to be reconciled: to undo the Athens-inspired coup in Nicosia; to prevent the growing danger of Turkish intervention or, if that could not be avoided, to mitigate its consequences; to stay in step with Britain as one of the guaranteeing powers; and to keep the Soviet Union out.

These objectives needed to be kept in balance; to overemphasize one of them had the potential to tear the entire delicate fabric. The aim of our strategy was to protect the junta's inevitable successors from Greek nationalists, both on the right and the left. Therefore, while working to prevent *enosis* and to remove Sampson, we resisted pressures from Congress, the media, and much of the bureaucracy to cut off military aid to Greece because, in our view, military aid to a NATO ally was an expression of the long-term interest of the Atlantic Alliance and not an expediency to be manipulated. To cast off Greece in the middle of an international crisis might accelerate Turkish intervention and Soviet meddling while Greek public opinion shifted the blame onto us for the near-certain—albeit self-inflicted—debacle in Cyprus. In the end, crisis management is about managing imperfections, not ideal solutions.

The critics accusing us of trying to protect the junta in Athens missed the point entirely. From the first, I was convinced that the coup would end in a debacle for its local sponsors as well as for the junta. On July 18, seventy-two hours after the coup, I told our crisis management team, the WSAG:

> I am not worried about Ioannides. If he falls, fine. . . . I don't think Ioannides is going to survive very long anyway.

On August 5, in a critique of our performance with the top staff of the State Department, I described the course we had adopted:

> We are professionals. We are here to serve the national inter-
> est. We are not here to . . . lead crusades before we know
> what is going on. Nor are we newspaper commentators. In
> the early stages of a crisis, it is our responsibility to deter-
> mine the balance of forces, assess the likely evolution and,
> above all, to shape these factors into a policy that serves the
> national and public good.[4]

And I defined the national interest as follows:

> . . . It must remain an objective of US policy that both
> Greece and Turkey remain members of the NATO structure,
> and those who make cynical comments about military bases
> in the Eastern Mediterranean should ask themselves what
> the United States would do in the foreseeable crisis in the
> Eastern Mediterranean if Greece and Turkey were not avail-
> able to us? . . . It makes a great deal of difference whether
> they are run by governments that feel betrayed by the United
> States and are built on a nationalism that edges toward
> hostility, or whether they are basically friendly to the United
> States and intend to cooperate with us.

That the problem was far more complex than the slogan of restoring Makarios became apparent as soon as Ecevit communicated Turkey's demands on July 17 first to our ambassador in Turkey, William
Macomber, and then to Callaghan in London. Ecevit put forward
the astonishing proposition that Turkey would invade Cyprus unless
Makarios was restored within twenty-four hours. The idea that Turkey
would use military force for the purpose of restoring its hereditary
enemy in a unitary state strained all credulity. Callaghan telephoned
me with the gist of Ecevit's proposals:

> I will tell you what Ecevit is saying. He wants a joint state-
> ment by the Turks and ourselves saying we don't recognize
> the new regime and the old regime should be restored and
> we can't wait on Makarios's replacement . . . Time is im-
> portant. NATO will break up . . . can't cooperate with

NATO or Greece any longer. We should now give, the Turks and ourselves, an ultimatum to Greece and the forces on the island should come under U.N. control and . . . more effective to the Turks, the United Kingdom should allow Turkish troops through our sovereign base on the island. And also that unilateral action is inevitable sooner or later because the Turks will regard themselves as hostages, and they will need to protect them. The force levels . . . will be open to the U.N., and they are willing to start dealing with Makarios.

In addition, Ecevit demanded widening the Turkish enclaves and providing them with access to the sea.

Every clause in that proposal was a land mine. Ecevit knew very well that no Greek government, mainland or Cypriot, could accede to these demands without war. Nor would Britain be able to permit Turkish troops to use British bases on Cyprus for an invasion without permanently rupturing its relationship with Greece. Much less onerous versions of Turkish views had been rejected for a decade. The most preposterous of the red herrings was the offer to hold immediate talks with Makarios, then en route to New York and difficult to produce within the deadline. Nor was there the slightest reason to believe that Makarios in exile would accede to demands that he, foremost among Cypriot leaders, had been rejecting for a decade. As I told Sisco: "Makarios won't be a Turkish satellite if he refuses to be a Greek satellite."

A week later, Ecevit's real views regarding Makarios could no longer be debated. On July 28, a week after the Turkish invasion of Cyprus, Ecevit—now on the verge of seizing his prize—adamantly rejected the return of Makarios under any conditions. The last thing Ecevit had in mind was to restore the status quo ante. Rather, Ecevit had seen an opportunity to bring about by force or pressure the goals for which Turkey had been striving for over a decade: a contiguous Turkish enclave with access to the sea. Nixon was on the verge of impeachment, the Cyprus regime was not recognized by any state, and the Greek junta was an international pariah. Ecevit found the temptation provided by this combination of circumstances impossible to resist.

## The Turkish Invasion

During the forty-eight hours in which Ecevit had been pressing his proposals, we sought to remove pretexts for military action by any of the parties. On July 16, the American ambassador in Athens was instructed to see Ioannides, who refused to receive Tasca on the ground that, since Ioannides held no official position, the ambassador should address himself to the Prime Minister. Tasca thereupon sent a trusted emissary to the junta leader, who warned Ioannides that the United States supported the independence of Cyprus and the existing constitutional arrangements—in other words, that we would oppose *enosis*. Ioannides's reaction as described in Ambassador Tasca's cable must be quoted in full, for no paraphrase could do it justice:

> After emissary completed message, the general literally blew up, jumped up, backed up, knocked over a table, broke empty glass and uttered a strong obscenity. He continued that one day Kissinger makes public statements regarding non-interference in Greek internal affairs and, a few weeks later, the USG [United States government] says "consistent with the above principles . . ." and threatens interference. No matter what happened in Cyprus, I [Ioannides] will be blamed. If I had pulled the troops out, the former politicians would have blamed me for turning the island over to the Communists. Some day USG will realize that on 15 July 1974 Cyprus was saved from falling into the hands of the Communists.

But after the explosion was over, Ioannides in effect accepted our view. He affirmed Greece's commitment to "noninterference in a free, independent, sovereign state of Cyprus"—in other words, he abandoned the quest for *enosis*.

We transmitted this assurance immediately to the Turkish government. Since Ecevit probably considered Ioannides even less credible than we did, we added that we intended to hold Ioannides to his word. On July 17, the Greek Prime Minister promised Ambassador Tasca not to increase the number of Greek troops on Cyprus or to use the periodic, authorized rotations to that end. We passed this assurance to Ankara as well. And to keep Moscow out of the evolving diplomacy, we sought to ease its concern that *enosis* implied expanding NATO to Cyprus. We therefore informed Brezhnev that we would do our utmost to bring about the restoration of constitutional rule. Contrary to the mythology that the United States encouraged the Turkish invasion— or even colluded with it—our strategy during the first week concentrated on removing Turkish pretexts for military action.

That same day, I sent Joe Sisco to London to work with Callaghan and Ecevit and to proceed from there to Athens and Ankara. Sisco, one of the stars of the State Department, had reached his position via the atypical route of having entered the Foreign Service at a middle level from the outside. Less polished than the stereotype and given to shouting down his interlocutors (including, if necessary, the Secretary of State), Sisco was living proof that, in the United States, careers are open to the talented from many different backgrounds provided they combine intelligence with determination and character. Adept at finding expedients with which to resolve the seemingly insoluble, occasionally supplying more answers than there had been questions, the energetic Sisco became my crisis manager par excellence, especially after he was promoted to under secretary of state, the third highest position in the State Department hierarchy.

Sisco was instructed to put forward a proposal we dubbed the "constitutional solution"—"constitutional" because it would elevate Glafkos Clerides, speaker of the Cypriot parliament under Makarios, to acting President for a period of six months. After this time, an election would be held in which Makarios would be free to run. In the interval, a new communal arrangement would be negotiated between the Greek and Turkish populations. Clerides had the reputation of being more moderate than Makarios and therefore provided a possible face-saving interim solution for both Athens and Ankara. The reasoning behind this proposal was that affirming the constitution ended the prospect of *enosis,* while making Clerides caretaker would avoid the need for Athens to deal with Makarios in the communal talks.

When I met with Makarios on July 22, a week after the coup, he seemed to go along with this approach ("seemed to" was the maximum commitment one could ever extract from the archbishop). He did not demand his own immediate restoration. Instead he recommended what we had already independently concluded: that any government installed in Nicosia be treated as a caretaker, thereby maintaining constitutional continuity.

Sisco spent July 18 in London, concerting policy with Callaghan, who agreed that Sisco should proceed to Athens and Ankara to explore the possibility of the Clerides compromise. On July 19, Sisco met in Athens with the Greek ministers, whose readiness to make concessions reflected the desperate straits into which the junta had maneuvered itself. For the first time, the junta implied that it might accept a single Turkish enclave in Cyprus, and it offered to replace all the Greek officers serving on Cyprus at the time the coup had occurred. It rejected Ecevit's demand of access to the sea for the Turkish enclave, the immediate return of Makarios, and the placing of Greek officers in Cyprus under United Nations command.

Sisco's next stop was Ankara, where he met with Prime Minister Ecevit. I had known Ecevit since 1957, when he was a student at the Harvard International Seminar. He had listed his profession as a writer; he had not yet entered full-time politics. Ecevit's political views then were conventional left-wing attitudes of mainstream European intellectuals taking their lead from Parisian literary circles. These views did not noticeably change after Ecevit made politics his career. Because his first passion had been poetry, I was hoping that he would prove more flexible and sensitive to nuance than the more traditional Turkish leaders who tended to favor trench warfare.

My conviction of the importance of Turkey to the American national interest had nothing to do with a personal relationship formed a decade earlier. I was prepared to use that relationship but not to rely on it, much less to subordinate American policy to it. I am certain that Ecevit was following the same principles in his relations with me.

This is evident from the sharp warning I asked Sisco to deliver upon arrival in Ankara. Having received ominous reports of Turkish military preparations for an invasion of Cyprus, I instructed the State Department from San Clemente, where I was with the President from July 18 to 20:

> I want a telegram to Sisco that as soon as he arrives he is to tell Ecevit that we are extremely concerned about unconfirmed reports we have about Turkish military moves. He is instructed to point out to the Turkish government that the US would take the gravest view of Turkish military moves before all diplomatic processes are exhausted. That is point one. That he must do immediately because I think we have been waffling and weeping around the place and we have not made clear that we are opposed to military intervention.

Secondly, he is to say we are doing this in the Turkish interests, that Turkish intervention will not be the last move, it will be the first of a whole sequence of moves. . . .

. . . Any government in Cyprus which would emerge at the end of this process would not better serve the Turkish interests because in order to attempt a counterbalance of Turkish dominance . . . government would inevitably look for support both internally and externally to Communism. You should give Ecevit an assurance that we are totally opposed to *enosis* whether direct or creeping. . . .

. . . Finally, you should tell Ecevit that as his friend and admirer, I must make clear my convictions that if he follows the course of military intervention, he will have started a process which will not only have serious adverse effects for Turkey in the long run, but will be extremely dangerous for the West as a whole.

Ecevit proved impervious both to American warnings and to Greek concessions. From the beginning of the crisis, Ecevit had been determined to avoid an extended negotiation that might freeze the constitutional status quo and deprive Turkey of the unique opportunity which Greek recklessness, the international situation, and America's domestic crisis presented to him. In the early morning of July 20, seventy-two hours after Ecevit put forward his proposals in London, Turkish forces began to land on Cyprus. On July 21, I urged a cease-fire on Ecevit, who told me:

We have followed the policy recommended by America in Cyprus for ten years, and where have we ended? We have different ideas about it. . . . But until now we have not been given a chance. . . . All the time we tried to do something about this. Now we took the initiative. . . . We want to make good use of it.

It was the terminal phase of Nixon's presidency. On July 19 at an acute point of the crisis, White House communications to San Clemente were jammed by the transmittal of the documentation of Nixon's appeal to the Supreme Court claiming executive privilege for his taping system.

Despite all the pressures, Nixon went about his customary daily routine without any visible alteration. An outsider would not have noticed any change in his insistence on reviewing the various options with a nearly compulsive repetitiveness. The few of us who continued to see him daily knew better. His glassy, faraway look told us that Nixon was already coming to terms with the emptiness that would soon be his. He kept up with the issues even while really bidding farewell to his life's work.

Once military operations had started, our principal goal was first to prevent an outbreak of war between two NATO allies; next to obtain a cease-fire on Cyprus; and, finally, to start negotiations between the parties. Sisco was instructed to call on Ecevit with the following message:

> I [Kissinger] take an extremely grave view of the Turkish military intervention on Cyprus which will have the most serious consequences, chief of which is the position it will place on free world security. We are deeply disappointed the Turkish government did not heed our pleas to exercise restraint.
>
> Now that the step has been taken, however, the most urgent means must be found to restore peace and stability in the area.
>
> While a conflict is easy to start, it is difficult to stop. Statesmanship of the highest order is required of all concerned.
>
> The United States, for its part, is prepared to support a constitutional solution and a level of forces which existed before the coup. The only way, in our view, to restore constitutional government is through the legitimate succession of Clerides. No other solution is possible or acceptable to the Greeks. . . .
>
> Prime Minister Ecevit has indicated that he has no special concern as to who the head of state should be, and therefore Sisco is on his way to Athens to propose to the Greeks the Clerides solution. We assume that, in light of what the prime minister told Sisco in their last meeting [in London], the GOT [government of Turkey] will agree. . . .
>
> We are proposing urgently to the UK that it call for immediate negotiations with the guarantor powers in London to seek the constitutional solution which will open the way for the restoration of stability in Cyprus and in the area.
>
> We urgently appeal to the Turkish government to weigh

most carefully the proposals we are making, for we are convinced that to do otherwise would be self-defeating in terms of Turkey's own interests.

And to make sure that our views reached Ecevit, I instructed Deputy Secretary of State Robert Ingersoll to deliver the same message to the Turkish ambassador in Washington. Sisco was instructed to return to Athens and to urge the same solution there, where the junta was reeling from the loss of prestige incurred by its increasingly obvious failure in Cyprus.

Evenhandedness in defense of America's national interest in the preservation of the eastern flank of NATO was inevitably rejected by the ethnic adversaries. Obsessed with their blood feud, neither Ankara nor Athens was ready to negotiate. Greece threatened to withdraw from military planning in NATO and mobilized its reserves. Turkey continued to reinforce its troops on Cyprus. In order to make clear to both parties that even our nearly sacrosanct commitment to NATO had its limits, I stressed at a press conference on July 20 that war between two NATO allies would lead to a cutoff of American aid:

> We have made it clear, I want to repeat here, that a war between Greece and Turkey will not be fought with American weapons. It may be fought with those weapons they have, but it will not be fought with an open supply line.[5]

Inside-the-Beltway maneuvering in Washington was slow to catch up to the emerging realities in the eastern Mediterranean. Though the Athens junta was teetering and the Nicosia coup collapsing, Congress, most of the media, and much of the bureaucracy continued to urge pressure on Athens. On July 21, the *Washington Post* led with a headline that the Defense Department favored cutting off all military aid to Greece. The *Post* was well informed; indeed, at a meeting of the Washington Special Actions Group that day, Secretary of Defense James Schlesinger had urged just that, together with the withdrawal of nuclear weapons from Greece.

I resisted. With Turkish troops fanning out across Cyprus, such a dissociation from the Greek authorities would surely whet Turkey's appetite. And short of war between Greece and Turkey, I would not go along with a cutoff of aid because I wanted to uphold the principle that the territorial integrity of the eastern flank was a vital and continuing

American interest. And once a cutoff is formally announced, it is very difficult to reverse. I agreed as a precautionary measure that all nuclear warheads be removed from their launchers and placed in safe storage. As it turned out, pressures for a cutoff of aid to Greece became moot within twenty-four hours when the Greek junta was overthrown.

Callaghan and I spent most of Sunday, July 21, on the telephone from our respective capitals, trying to induce parties whose principal ambition was to destroy each other to end hostilities.[6] Greece, the weaker, was the more ready, provided it could obtain the status quo ante. Ecevit too professed to be willing, provided he was handed what he wanted without war, which happened to be a drastic change of the status quo. Pending that, he refined procrastination into a high art. It took several hours to obtain Ecevit's agreement even to discuss the principle of a cease-fire; afterward he kept raising ingenuous technical objections. At one point, he claimed that any cease-fire would be unenforceable because, to shift the blame for any violations of a cease-fire onto Turkey, the devious Greeks were operating ships with person-nel that had learned to speak Turkish at NATO headquarters. Wearily I told Ecevit that no one would blame Turkey if it sank a Turkish-speaking ship. The actual transcript of the conversation gives a flavor:

> ECEVIT: We have a problem. We doubt the reliability of Greece. Ioannides's word of honor is a joke. We have now figured out what the joke is behind his words. He said we could fire on any ships bearing Greek flags. His ships are drawing Turkish flags!
>
> KISSINGER: Well, no one can blame you if you sink your own ships.
>
> ECEVIT: No, Dr. Kissinger, they are not our own ships. They are Greek ships. They are Greek ships drawing Turkish flags.
>
> KISSINGER: Yes, Mr. Prime Minister, but you can sink them if they are not your ships but are flying Turkish flags.
>
> ECEVIT: They are using two tricks. We are NATO allies, and the Turkish pilots know our codes. They speak Turkish. They call our pilots in Turkish using our code words. We can no longer rely on the words of Greece.
>
> KISSINGER: What exactly is it that you want? I know you are an intelligent man—I know that from the days of

> Harvard. With all due respect, I cannot take this. This
> can go on for six weeks on this basis.
>
> ECEVIT: They say that they want an armistice. It has be-
> come obvious that they want to exploit the cease-fire
> for massing troops on the islands. The Greeks must
> cease these methods.
>
> KISSINGER: What methods should they cease?
>
> ECEVIT: They say that they are ready for a cease-fire. They
> have already shown us the tricks that they will use to
> violate the cease-fire.
>
> KISSINGER: Are you telling me you will not accept a cease-
> fire?
>
> ECEVIT: We will accept a cease-fire.
>
> KISSINGER: Today?
>
> ECEVIT: We are in the middle of discussing the problem
> now.

In the end, as if to prove that America's words did carry some weight, the Turkish air force did sink a Turkish destroyer that very afternoon as the result of a pilot's error.

Together with our allies, we made every effort to keep the Soviet Union on the sidelines. A message from Nixon to Leonid Brezhnev emphasized that "we wish to cooperate with you in restoring peace and the previous constitutional arrangements in Cyprus." America, the message stated, did not support Turkish intervention or, more pointedly, any other military intervention:

> The United States does not support and has not supported
> external interference in the affairs of Cyprus. It opposes such
> interference whatever the source.

On the afternoon of July 21, Callaghan and I, backed by French Foreign Minister Jean Sauvagnargues, decided to insist on a cease-fire by issuing what was, in effect, an ultimatum: if a cease-fire was not agreed to within twelve hours, the United States would remove all of its nuclear weapons from both sides of the Greek-Turkish border in Thrace. Moreover, the three allies demanded that a cease-fire be fol-lowed immediately by a meeting under British auspices between its Greek and Turkish foreign ministers.

Ecevit reluctantly accepted the proposal an hour before the dead-line; Athens followed suit even more reluctantly some two hours later.

So great was the animosity between the two sides that neither party was prepared to accept a cease-fire originating with the other, or to make an offer of its own. When the July 22 cease-fire did finally come about, each party presented it not as an obligation to its adversary but as a unilateral acceptance of an American proposal.

The cease-fire proved to be the junta's final act. Some twenty-four hours later, it ceded power to a democratic government. Revolutions are rarely as dramatic in real life as in historical accounts of them. I learned of the return of democracy to Greece on the telephone from Ambassador Tasca at 5:00 P.M., July 22, or midnight Athens time:

> TASCA: I am in the office of [Phaidon] Gizikis, the President of Greece. All of the chiefs of the Greek military services are here as well as the new leadership of Greece, [Panayiotis] Kannellopoulos. They are very anxious to have a word with you. I have told them the efforts we have made and how much importance we attach to maintenance of peace in the area. They are very, very concerned about what is going on in Cyprus, and it has created an impossible problem for them politically to face as the first democratic government of Greece since 1967. They would like to have you speak to them and Kannellopoulos so they can explain this problem.
>
> KANNELLOPOULOS: Mr. K. speaking.
>
> KISSINGER: How nice to hear from you.
>
> KANNELLOPOULOS: We are all here very concerned, and we are in a dilemma. It is impossible for us to accept this continuation of such activities in Cyprus. The situation has become very critical. . . .
>
> KISSINGER: I have heard you very well.
>
> KANNELLOPOULOS: I have to tell you I am very glad to have this talk with you for the first time in my life.
>
> KISSINGER: I would like to tell you that our friendship for Greece is firm, and you can count on our friendship and our alliance. I will get immediately in touch with the Turkish Prime Minister and urge him to show the greatest restraint.

By the next morning, the last democratically elected Greek Prime Minister, Constantine Karamanlis, was recalled from his Paris exile, and the curtain fell on the first act of the Cyprus crisis.

## The Second Turkish Intervention

Our first reaction was euphoria at having navigated a crisis that could have torn the Alliance apart. Two sets of negotiations were scheduled to stabilize the situation, both under the aegis of Britain. The first—to firm up the cease-fire—starting two days hence, on July 24; the second, to achieve a political settlement, was to take place two weeks later, on August 8. A peace process similar to the one we had started in the Middle East seemed to be under way. Though we anticipated many ups and downs, we did not expect the outbreak of another round of fighting.

Not having any previous experience with ethnic conflict, we failed to understand that we had less influence on the parties in Cyprus than in the Middle East. The parties in the Middle East, though exploiting superpower rivalries, were at the same time constrained by them. In Cyprus, the adversaries accepted no such constraints. In fact, the new democratic government in Athens raised the Greek terms. Karamanlis and his colleagues saw no reason to pay any price to extricate Greece from dilemmas caused by the folly of their predecessors. Not prepared to expose themselves to the charge of having abandoned the Greek national interest, they persisted in the basic nationalist position of the junta. They rejected any federal solution for Cyprus and expected NATO and especially the United States to eject Turkey from the island in the name of Greek democracy. On the other hand, Turkey, having the edge militarily, insisted on partitioning Cyprus into Greek and Turkish political units.

For his part, Makarios had emerged as the linchpin of Cypriot nationalism. However, as Talleyrand said of the Bourbons after the French Revolution, he had neither learned nor forgotten anything. Makarios had called on me at the State Department on July 22, the day the cease-fire was signed, and again on July 29. While he accepted Glafkos Clerides as acting President, he made it clear that he would return to reclaim the presidency as soon as Cyprus calmed down. He urged American mediation but was not willing to contribute any element of flexibility to it. In his charmingly sardonic manner, Makarios rejected any cantonal, not to mention federal, arrangement as well as any return to the London-Zürich Agreements of 1960. What he suggested was a unitary state under Greek Cypriot control achieved by American military pressure on Turkey in the aftermath of a Greek defeat and without any Greek concessions.

Makarios felt the wind at his back because the domestic assault on the collapsing Nixon Administration had taken a 180-degree turn as soon as democracy was restored in Athens. For weeks we had been castigated for failing to pressure Greece, in effect, on behalf of Turkey. Suddenly within the space of a few days, we were being attacked for failing to pressure Turkey in order to help democratic Greece. The eastern flank of NATO was turning into a punching bag of American domestic politics.

My view remained what it had been when I was resisting excessive pressure on Greece. I told a staff meeting:

> The same people who wanted us to humiliate Greece now want us to move against Turkey. . . . In time we will be forced to oppose them [Turkey], but we will oppose them when we do so on some fundamental issue and for maximum effect and not for the editorial page of the *New York Times*. And until we do so, we are going to be in a position where they know that we have not just used every tactical opportunity to make their life more difficult.

I had rejected a policy of isolating and humiliating Greece—whatever my reservations about its government—because I considered it to be an essential pillar of our NATO strategy. From the geopolitical point of view, Turkey was, if anything, even more important. Bordering the Middle East, Central Asia, the Soviet Union, and Europe, Turkey was indispensable to American policy in each of these areas. Turkey had been a staunch and loyal ally in the entire Cold War period. Turkish troops had fought with distinction at our side in Korea. Twenty-six electronic stations were monitoring Soviet missile and space activities from Turkish territory. All this made me extremely reluctant to impose sanctions.

A provision of the Foreign Assistance Act prohibited the use of American weapons for purposes other than national self-defense, the aim being to preclude domestic repression or civil war being carried out with American assistance. But, to Turkey, Cyprus involved key issues of international security. I believed that Congress and the executive branch would, given the stakes involved, find some means of dealing with the legal ambiguities.

Clearly I had learned the wrong lesson from our successful resistance to pressures against Greece. No pressure group in the United States had urged the "punishment" of Greece. After democracy was restored in Athens, Greece did have a volatile and extraordinarily effective domestic constituency demanding sanctions against Turkey. Just as with the Jewish community regarding the Jackson-Vanik Amendment, the Greek-American community was so passionate that its leaders were deprived of any flexibility, and even the freedom of action of Greece's leaders was circumscribed by their American supporters. They insisted on outcomes which could be achieved only by American military action or by sanctions sufficient to break Turkey's back. Neither of these outcomes was in America's national interest or that of the Atlantic Alliance.

In this manner, our ability to manage the crisis deteriorated day by day. One difficulty was that the political negotiations had been scheduled too soon, especially in view of the fact that an entirely new political team had come to power in Greece that was finding it next to impossible to concert a position in the forty-eight hours before negotiations were to begin. Turkey, of course, was determined, in any event, on achieving major gains.

In retrospect, we probably should have played for time until the Greek government was more fully organized and Nixon's fate was settled. But on July 24, the day negotiations were scheduled to start, it was far from clear how long the terminal phase of Nixon's presidency might last. Callaghan, fearing a new outbreak of hostilities, was rightly impatient to proceed.

The Greek negotiators, preoccupied with forming a government, were slow to arrive in Geneva, and Callaghan threatened to start without them—a move we strongly opposed. When the parties finally did meet, on July 25, after a twenty-four-hour delay, they temporarily put aside the political issues in order to stabilize the cease-fire. On July 26, the new Greek prime minister, Constantine Karamanlis—eager to establish his credentials as defender of Greek interests—threatened to break up the talks over Turkish cease-fire violations. Not to be outdone, Ecevit delivered an ultimatum of his own on July 28, protesting what he described as Callaghan's peremptory conduct. Overcoming these passions, Callaghan achieved a cease-fire agreement on July 30 which provided for a cessation of offensive activities, a phased withdrawal of outside forces, and the establishment of a buffer zone between the adversaries.

On July 31, the State Department's Cyprus Task Force was dissolved. For a fleeting moment, we again wallowed in the illusion that the crisis was on its way to being defused.

It was not to be. Before the political phase of the peace process could start, Nixon's resignation knocked the props out from a significant role for us in Callaghan's efforts. The so carefully nurtured opportunity to contribute significantly to the political mediation scheduled to begin on August 8 collapsed.

Our strategy of acting as honest broker has been reflected in instructions to Arthur Hartman, assistant secretary of state for European Affairs, who had replaced Sisco as our emissary to the negotiations, the latter being needed in Washington to help prepare for the imminent arrival of Middle East foreign ministers. Hartman was to visit Athens and Ankara before the political talks began on August 8:

> Every effort must be made in the first few days to prevent emotional outbursts, ultimata or any other actions which tend to isolate any one of the parties.

There are some who argue that success in diplomacy reflects the ability to tell each party a different story. I believe the opposite to be true—especially in mediations. I therefore instructed Hartman:

> We should tell each party exactly what is possible with respect to the other party. . . . We must not permit any of the parties to be isolated, nor should we place ourselves in the position of appearing to support one party against the other.

But no time remained to implement a stately diplomatic minuet. Neither Callaghan nor I had expected a second Turkish military move and, during the crucial four days of the political negotiations, my days and—to an even greater degree—my emotions were focused on easing Nixon's travail and preparing for the transition to Ford.

It would probably have been wisest to request a postponement of the political negotiations scheduled for the precise day Nixon announced his resignation. Such a request would not have found smooth sailing. Callaghan might have objected to the implication of America's indispensability; Ecevit would almost surely have insisted on proceeding, since international pressures for Turkish restraints were growing, and the opportunity to impose a solution afforded by the turmoil in Washington might never recur. Nevertheless, postponement would have represented our best chance to develop a compromise proposal to prevent a second round of fighting. Failing such a scheme, we were unable to dominate the situation as we had when we insisted on the cease-fire three weeks earlier.

The presidential transition constrained our options even further because it prevented some such dramatic move as my joining the negotiations, which would, at a minimum, have slowed down the rush toward military action. Nor were we, in the first days in office of a nonelected President, in a position to consider military moves of our own. We therefore rejected Callaghan's request to support the threat of a British air strike against Turkish cease-fire violations. I cabled Hartman:

> [I]t is out of the question to be asking a president in the first 48 hours of his administration to consider supporting military action. . . . We will do everything we can to assist in keeping the talks going, but we will have little room for maneuver if he [Callaghan] continues to rattle the saber.

The parties started deadlocked and worked themselves into a deepening stalemate as the conference proceeded. They never deviated from their original positions. From the outset, the Turkish foreign minister insisted on a contiguous Turkish zone with access to the sea. The new Greek government was caught between a resurgent left appealing to Greek nationalism and a revanchist military unreconciled to its humiliation. With the first democratic election in nearly a decade approaching, it opted for intransigence and rejected all Turkish proposals while refusing to put forward any alternatives—as I urged in the hope of gaining time.

Karamanlis, who had just returned from exile in Paris, faced a fateful choice. When I had met him some years earlier at the Paris home of New York Times columnist C. L. Sulzberger, he struck me as intelligent, vain, and seized by that melancholy solitude characteristic of émigrés, living in a past which grows more irretrievable with every passing day, yet separated from their country's future by geography and nostalgia. Almost miraculously restored to office by the recklessness of the junta rather than by his own efforts, Karamanlis had lost the flair for heroism, if, in fact, he had ever had it, and he now hid his indecision behind a prickly vanity.

Once back in power, Karamanlis had the choice of either blaming his predecessors for the mess and, with our support, settling quickly for the best terms available or, in order to stave off nationalist criticism, seeking shelter behind the junta's traditional nationalist position. The former course might have enabled him to put Cyprus behind him at the risk of immediate political turmoil. Reliance on the nationalist card placated Karamanlis's potential critics for a brief time but, doomed as it was to failure, ultimately stultified his policy and made him appear ineffective. And, as usually happens when the quest for short-term popularity is equated with statesmanship, Karamanlis was, in the end, defeated by the very critics he had tried to appease. To be sure, he had not only the Greek opposition to worry about but also Makarios, equally insistent on a restoration of the precise status quo ante. That was beyond anyone's diplomatic capabilities; it could be achieved only by military force.

What I had in mind and believed to be attainable was two or three separate Turkish enclaves, which would have prevented partition. I explained this to President Ford on August 10, his first full day in office:

> KISSINGER: We are having some developments on Cyprus. Until I know how you want to work, I thought I should check with you on some of these actions. You know the Greeks and Turks are meeting under the British chairmanship in Geneva, and we have an assistant secretary there to be generally helpful.
>
> FORD: Sisco?
>
> KISSINGER: No. Art Hartman. . . . The Turks want a quick result leading to partition of the island into Greek and Turkish parts with sort of a general federal government, which would, however, be very weak. They have about 15 percent of the island and want 30 percent. They might try to grab it. I have talked to the Prime Minister of Turkey. He was a student of mine, and I have told him that we could not—really in the first forty-eight hours of your term of office—be very relaxed about unilateral military action.
>
> FORD: We sure cannot.
>
> KISSINGER: If that happens, we might have to dissociate from Turkey, which we have tried to avoid. Our danger is Turkey and why we must maneuver carefully. They might turn very nationalistic, and the Russians have

been trying to exploit that, but we cannot let them act unilaterally. I am writing a letter to Ecevit. He has promised to hold off for twenty-four hours. I am writing to Ecevit on my behalf outlining where I see the negotiations stand. The Turks propose two areas—one Turkish and one Greek. I think we can push the Greeks into a position where they would be willing to accept two or three autonomous Turkish areas but not one contiguous area. That would avoid a population transfer.

FORD: Right.

KISSINGER: This would give us an opportunity to stall military actions long enough to get it working on the foreign minister level to see if we can get a compromise. . . . [The general idea] is to take a position which is between the British and the Greek position and the Turkish one so we can ameliorate the Turkish demand but not let the Turks claim that we were the ones that thwarted them and at the same time be tough against unilateral Turkish military moves.

But compromise was precisely what George Mavros, Karamanlis's foreign minister, adamantly rejected. The practical consequence was that Ecevit was once more in a position to deploy his by now well-tested tactic of hinting at some nebulous flexibility just beyond the reach of being negotiable. It worked a second time because we were preoccupied with the presidential transition, and in an ethnic conflict, the weaker side frequently finds it easier to acquiesce in an imposed solution than to agree to a more favorable outcome by making a concession. Compromise implies a decision, while a fait accompli absolves the victim of any responsibility for the outcome.

Unable to proceed diplomatically with the concurrence of either party, I had the State Department issue a statement on August 13 that sketched the ideas I had put to Ford. It supported greater autonomy for the Turkish community in Cyprus—a hint that the United States favored a change to that effect in the London-Zürich Agreements. But signaling that we were not endorsing Turkey's insistence on a single contiguous area with access to the sea, we spoke of negotiations regarding one or more autonomous areas and said nothing about access to the sea. And we rejected any attempt at a military solution, clearly dissociating ourselves from renewed military operations by Turkey:

> The avenues of diplomacy have not been exhausted and therefore *the U.S. would consider a resort to military action unjustified.*[7]

The statement pleased no one. Greece would not accept the concept of autonomous areas; Turkey was determined not to become enmeshed in endless negotiations which would keep it from taking advantage of the unique opportunity afforded by the American presidential transition. At 7:00 A.M. local time on August 14, Turkey cut the Gordian knot by seizing the territory it had been demanding. Having reinforced its troops on the island all along, Ankara now swiftly expanded its area of control. Once he had conquered all the disputed areas, Ecevit on August 15 made another of his empty goodwill gestures. He authorized me to inform the Greek government and the U.N. Secretary General that Turkish military operations would cease at noon the following day. By that time, Turkish forces had occupied even more territory than what they had asked for originally and seized about 35 percent of the island, including the port city of Famagusta, which contained few Turkish inhabitants.

Unwilling to countenance a middle ground between total victory and total defeat, Greece and Turkey had worked themselves into deadlock. Turkey was in possession of the prize but lacked international recognition of its legitimacy; Greece had international support but lacked both the means to enforce its views and the domestic support to put forward a realistic compromise. America's attempt to trade American support and NATO legitimacy for a compromise requiring concessions by both parties had been vitiated by the second Turkish military attack and our preoccupation with the transition.

We remained ready to help find an outcome acceptable to both sides. But if mediation were to succeed, speed was of the essence; progress would have to be made before the Turkish control of the occupied territory could congeal. Domestic conditions in every capital —including in Washington—prevented such a course. Athens was seduced by its newfound congressional and media allies into believing that American pressures could achieve all its goals without any Greek concessions. In Ankara, Ecevit's fragile coalition was falling apart. At home, the new administration's energies were absorbed in trying to stave off congressional micromanagement of foreign policy and in the battles over East-West relations.

At the end of one of those long days of butting our heads against the obduracy of both parties, Callaghan and I found ourselves waxing melancholy about ethnic conflicts and what they might portend for the future of the world as we had come to know it:

> KISSINGER: You know, one respect in which all the humani-
> tarians and liberals and socialists were wrong in the last
> century was when they thought that mankind didn't
> like war.
> CALLAGHAN: Yes.
> KISSINGER: It's regrettable but . . .
> CALLAGHAN: I came to that conclusion a few years ago
> when I saw the position in Northern Ireland, Henry.
> KISSINGER: They love it.
> CALLAGHAN: There is only, mind you, a handful of people
> who do for a long period. Most of us like it for a day
> or two, but there is a handful who like it forever.
> KISSINGER: That's right. It doesn't mean that the humani-
> tarians were wrong; it just means life is harder than we
> thought.
> CALLAGHAN: Yes. And I think life is getting worse, Henry.
> KISSINGER: I think you are right.
> CALLAGHAN: I don't know what sort of age we're passing
> through or going to pass through, but historians like
> yourself ought really to give us a rundown on it some-
> time and tell us how you think this next half century is
> going to look.
> KISSINGER: I'll tell you. . . . I'm glad I'm not going to be
> running part of it. It's going to be brutal.

## Congress and Cyprus

As it turned out, congressional pressures did the Greek cause far more harm than good. From the moment Karamanlis was restored, the Greek-American community brought massive pressure to bear on Congress to legislate its preferred outcome. Ford inherited that whirlwind during his first weekend in office without having had any opportunity to shape the policies which had produced it or to alter radically the course of events. At first, he was quite relaxed about his old friends in Congress, assuring me that AHEPA—the Greek-

American lobbying organization—had never in his experience involved itself in foreign policy issues.

We soon learned better. Even at the height of the Vietnam protests, Congress had been reluctant to legislate specific courses of action; binding resolutions invariably failed and, instead, "sense of the Congress" resolutions emerged, recording Congress's point of view without assuming responsibility for the consequences. As Watergate gained momentum, Congress shed these restraints and prescribed the tactics of Cyprus policy. Turkish actions on Cyprus were held not to constitute self-defense under the provisions of the Foreign Assistance Act. At the end of September, House and Senate bills were introduced cutting off aid to Turkey, in the words of the House bill, "until the president certifies to Congress that substantial progress towards agreement" had been made.

The legislation set up a vicious circle. The Ford Administration had already committed itself to encouraging significant concessions from Turkey. But once Congress appointed itself as the arbiter of what constituted progress, its definition would go beyond the capacities of diplomacy. The issue was not who "controlled" foreign policy, as was often stated by the pundits and congressional leaders. In our system of separation of powers, neither branch can—or should—have total control. The American style of government works best when Congress concentrates on overall supervision of long-range policy without attempting to second-guess day-to-day tactics, a task for which it is not organized and for which it lacks perspective.

A congressional act is a blunt instrument. Passing it requires an agglomeration of constituencies united by the most general and often diverse purposes. An act of Congress can be changed only by assembling a similar consensus in reverse. Congressional mandates are therefore almost impossible to fine-tune in support of a fast-moving negotiation, especially between overwrought ethnic parties or where progress depends on inching forward from one nuance to the next. The protagonists become reluctant to show their hand: the side being supported by Congress will not want to jeopardize continued congressional pressures, while the side against which legislation is being directed fears that concessions will trigger new demands on the ground that the sanctions are working.

The difference between the congressional and executive branch perspectives became apparent when I showed a week's worth of cables to and from Ankara to the three congressional leaders most identified with the Greek cause. The purpose was to demonstrate to John Brade-mas, Benjamin Rosenthal, and Paul Sarbanes that they were risking a vital alliance without advancing the prospects of a Cyprus settlement. Though these were among our most able and responsible legislators, it proved a hopeless undertaking. The congressional mind-set was on justifying a single legislative act; mine was on managing a continuing process. The Congressmen were dealing with absolutes; I sought to accumulate nuances. My congressional interlocutors wanted me to challenge each point raised by the Turkish government; I thought it wiser to conserve whatever capital of trust we still had in Ankara for the negotiating process rather than squandering it on debating points.

Paradoxically, Karamanlis became the prisoner of his Greek-American supporters and of nationalists on both the left and the right inside Greece. American perfidy in having allegedly encouraged the Cyprus coup and then in failing to protect Greece from its conse-quences became a staple of Greek political oratory—the passion and eloquence was unfortunately not matched by a commensurate grasp of reality. There was not a shred of evidence for any of the calumnies. The Greek government never credited the United States for the many efforts of both the Nixon and Ford Administrations to delay Turkish moves, to produce a cease-fire, to accelerate the demise of both Samp-son in Nicosia and the junta in Athens, and then to negotiate an improved status for Cyprus.

By contrast, Anwar Sadat, when faced with a similar challenge, appealed to America's support in obtaining concessions from Israel. He did so by giving the United States a reputation for fairness we were then obliged to uphold. And he was prepared to modify Egypt's maximum demands. Karamanlis and his colleagues followed the oppo-site approach. When they were not themselves actively encouraging attacks on American motives, they offered no resistance when others vilified Washington.

Karamanlis welcomed American mediation privately even as his ministers were castigating our mediators publicly. The Greek govern-ment encouraged our efforts without committing itself to the enter-prise, much less to the results. It asked us to produce Turkish concessions without ever telling us how it would respond. In Septem-ber 1974, Foreign Minister Mavros told us that he would prefer to take no position on the negotiations until after the Greek election on November 17, wasting two months. In the interval, Ecevit—who as the organizer of the invasion of Cyprus had the greatest standing to make territorial concessions—resigned.

A year later, Greek policy was still being driven by domestic politics. On July 30, 1975, at the European Security Conference in Helsinki, Ford asked Karamanlis to tell him what complaints, if any, Greece had about current American policy and, above all, what recommendations he had for the immediate future. Karamanlis and Dimitrios Bitsios, his foreign minister, had no suggestions and vociferously denied charges by their Greek supporters in Congress that we might be colluding with the Turks: "That is gossip, and it is just not true." When Ford asked him to repeat this publicly, Karamanlis declined with the argument that such a statement would be "political suicide."

Greek procrastination played into Turkey's hands, for the longer the stalemate lasted, the more Turkey would be confirmed in possession of its prize. When, after the second Turkish military intervention, the Greek government rejected formal negotiations, I sent retired Ambassador William R. Tyler to Athens and Ambassador Wells Stabler to Ankara in early September on informal missions to determine whether any flexibility existed for American mediation. The emissaries were among our ablest Foreign Service officers, and Tyler had served with distinction as ambassador as well as assistant secretary of state for European affairs. They were instructed to put forward a concept for a bizonal federation of Cyprus and a significant reduction of the Turkish-controlled areas, as well as a phased withdrawal of Turkish forces. (These are still the American terms over twenty-five years later except that the reduction in size of the Turkish territory has been abandoned.)

Karamanlis was not prepared to accept an official emissary; Tyler had to concoct a pretext of visiting Athens in his private capacity as director of the Dumbarton Oaks Foundation. Karamanlis refused to put forward any Greek position until Turkey had made some undefined unilateral gestures—hardly a Turkish specialty. Nevertheless, I made the attempt, and Ecevit suggested some territorial gestures, including returning the city of Famagusta to Greek control. To explore whether Turkey might welcome some face-saving formula with which to jump-start the negotiating process, I offered to visit Ankara in early October.

We will never know what might have resulted, for, on October 17, 1974, Congress passed a cutoff of military aid to Turkey, including equipment already paid for. (In a bow to Ford's entreaties, a grace period of four months, to February 5, 1975, was granted if progress could be made in negotiations.)

This removed flexibility from both sides. For the Greek government, the congressional intervention was a deus ex machina that enabled it to sidestep the concessions which its more thoughtful members must have recognized to be necessary. For its part, Turkey greeted the aid cutoff with a combination of outrage and relief: outrage that its key ally should have turned the American-Turkish security alliance into a form of blackmail; relief because it also provided it with the pretext to ask me to postpone my trip to Ankara designed to discuss Turkish concessions.

With a nightmarish sense of déjà vu, I found myself employing arguments with the Greek foreign minister and the Greek-American community that, in the context of the Jackson-Vanik Amendment, had failed to persuade Israeli and American Jewish leaders. Then I had argued in vain—though, as it turned out, correctly—that the pending legislation would reduce rather than increase emigration from the Soviet Union. Now I stressed with equal futility that the proposed aid cutoff would hurt the Greek cause because it would delay, if not prevent, Turkish concessions while the situation was still fluid. Just as I had failed in convincing Israeli leaders that it was in their interest to moderate their demands, I now repeated the same process with Greek and Cypriot leaders. Indeed, Clerides, who had been installed with our assistance as acting President, claimed not even to know how to reach the head of the American lobbying effort, Eugene T. Rossides, and urged us to appeal to Britain to make the contact. On September 26, I told the congressional leadership that, while the *threat* of an aid cutoff might conceivably do some good, its implementation would prove disastrous:

> [T]he Greeks would expect concessions no one could get them. These restrictions would lose us the Turks without helping the Greeks and destroy this [negotiating] process I have been describing.

All the parties were on the verge of becoming prisoners of the American political process. The Ford Administration was prepared to do its utmost to improve the Greek position on Cyprus. Had we been able to move energetically in August and September 1974, there was a possibility to reduce the Turkish area of control to perhaps 25 percent of the island, to secure a Turkish withdrawal from the old city of Famagusta, and to achieve significant limitations on Turkish troop strength on the island. Our inability to explore seriously any Turkish hint of flexibility froze the Turkish occupation at its maximum extent and facilitated absolute

Turkish control. Twenty-five years later, Turkey still holds about 35 percent of Cyprus, the two parts of which are isolated from each other by a demarcation line policed by the United Nations.

By the fall of 1974, the opportunities for serious mediation were evaporating. On October 8, Karamanlis appointed a caretaker cabinet and scheduled elections for November 17, thereby enforcing a hiatus on diplomacy. Ecevit, attacked for intransigence by his NATO allies, found himself accused of being too accommodating by his nationalist coalition partner. In September, Ecevit too had resigned, hoping to use the popularity garnered by his Cyprus success to obtain a majority of his own in subsequent elections.

In this he miscalculated. Unlike the British Prime Minister, the head of government in Ankara does not have the power to dissolve parliament; only a parliamentary majority can make that decision. And the Turkish parliament was deadlocked. Unable to agree on a new coalition government, it also lacked a majority for dissolution because the majority that had defeated Ecevit was eager to prevent his return to office. Ecevit was out of office for a few years, but he has returned as premier three times since then.

An interim government was installed, headed by a nonpolitical professor from Istanbul University. He seemed to have no clear grasp even of the names of his colleagues, let alone those of his foreign visitors (including mine). Such a government—which remained in office for a crucial six months—was in no position to negotiate seriously on Cyprus, nor did it attempt to do so.

On December 7, 1974, Makarios returned to Cyprus, further restricting the freedom of action of all the parties. Month by month, the Cyprus issue slipped into the pattern which would later become increasingly familiar as ethnic conflicts grew more frequent in the post–Cold War period. Once an ethnic conflict breaks out, its outcome is much more apt to be either a massacre of the minority or the forcible separation of the ethnic groups than the restoration of political unity.

By the end of the Ford Administration, the territorial arrangement on Cyprus was much less favorable to the Greek side than what might have been attainable through negotiation. But it had the advantage vis-à-vis the Greek public of having been imposed upon Greece as a fait accompli rather than being the result of a compromise agreement. An equilibrium evolved in which Greek Cyprus achieved a thriving economy, and Turkish Cyprus—the agricultural northern third of the island—became a Turkish military base. The parent countries did not risk war over their Cypriot brethren, but neither were they prepared to restore normal relations.

The American embargo on aid to Turkey went into effect on February 5, 1975. By way of response, Turkey closed all American military installations except one air base. As the Cyprus situation turned into a stalemate, the cutoff gradually ran so counter to other American strategic objectives that both the Ford Administration and the Democratic congressional leadership wanted to end it. But congressional discipline had so broken down in the post-Watergate "reform" era that the embargo was not finally lifted until well into the Carter Administration.

Once Makarios returned to Cyprus, he played his usual complicated game, gradually edging, however, toward a settlement on terms he would have rejected indignantly two years earlier. When he died of a heart attack in 1977, I felt that with the by then somewhat chastened archbishop had also died the best hope for a rapid negotiated settlement of Cyprus. When all was said and done, Makarios more than any other Cypriot leader had the imagination to accept reality and the prestige to lead his compatriots in the direction of their necessities. I can imagine the sardonic gleam in the archbishop's eyes were he aware how many of his erstwhile critics missed him and his complicated, occasionally devious maneuvers. Makarios was, after all, a big man in a world not blessed with an excess of them.

## Conclusion

For Ford, Cyprus was a rough beginning and a foretaste of controversies ahead. The President was briefed daily at great length by Brent Scowcroft or me and played an active role, especially in relations with Congress. But the parameters of the issue had been established before Ford entered office, and the second Turkish military operation, as well as the congressional aid cutoff to Turkey, severely limited the diplomatic option.

In the end, the Ford Administration did achieve its most important objective: the eastern flank of NATO, though strained, remained intact. Despite Greek displeasure with the executive branch and Turkish outrage at Congress, both countries remained in NATO and on friendly terms with the United States. Throughout, the Soviet Union was kept at arm's length.

If success is measured by "solving" every problem, America's Cyprus policy failed in restoring a unitary Cypriot state. But not every problem has a definitive solution, and not every status quo ante can be restored. The communal conflict between Greeks and Turks on Cyprus has proved intractable for centuries. However, preserving the general peace and the structure of the Western Alliance on which peace depended were important objectives in their own right. And those objectives the Ford Administration did achieve in the Cyprus crisis of 1974.

# PART THREE

# EAST-WEST RELATIONS

# 8

# FORD INHERITS THE DEBATE
# OVER DÉTENTE

Testifying before Congress while Secretary of State, George Shultz once stated in response to congressional staff questioning: "[A]s you well know, or maybe you don't—you are not a Washingtonian—nothing ever gets settled in this town. . . ."[1] So it was in the nation's capital in the dramatic summer of 1974. The fact that a new President had just been inaugurated did not interrupt the rhythm established by Vietnam and Watergate; controversies roared on as if they had a life of their own.

When I testified on détente before the Senate Foreign Relations Committee, in the first weeks of the Ford Administration, all the familiar arguments of the Nixon period were recycled: the liberals, who were dominant on the committee, criticized the new Ford Administration as they had Nixon's for its insufficient commitment to arms control and human rights; conservatives and neoconservatives testifying before the committee took the opposite tack, condemning our allegedly excessive emphasis on East-West diplomacy and calling for an ideological crusade against Communism.

The philosophical debates were given impetus by the demands of the diplomatic calendar. The arms control negotiators were meeting in Geneva and waiting for instructions. A summit for the end of the year had been agreed upon by Nixon and Brezhnev when they had met in June. Ford intended to keep to that schedule to demonstrate continuity and also to become acquainted with his Soviet counterpart. In addition, unless the trade bill granting Most Favored Nation status to the Soviet Union was acted on immediately, the whole process would have to start all over again after a new Congress was elected in November and took office in January. This would impose a delay of at least a year, probably more. Thus the issues of arms control and Jewish emigration confronted Ford in his first weeks in office with familiar themes as if nothing unusual had happened when the President changed.

## Hearings on Détente

Symptomatic of the never-laid-to-rest national debates were the hearings on American-Soviet relations by the Senate Foreign Relations Committee, before which I had been scheduled to appear on August 8. That being the very day that Nixon announced his intention to resign, my testimony was postponed until the middle of September. Chairman J. William Fulbright had originally called the hearings in order to provide bipartisan support for the administration's East-West policy. The change in Presidents caused the first six weeks of the hearings to be dominated instead by conservative and neoconservative critics of both administrations.

In those days, the Senate Foreign Relations Committee was still the most prestigious of the congressional committees. Among its members were two defeated presidential candidates (Hubert Humphrey and George McGovern), at least two aspirants for the office (Edmund Muskie and Frank Church), and a number of Republican foreign policy heavyweights (most notably Charles Percy and Jacob Javits)—all led by the committee's redoubtable chairman, J. William Fulbright.

The dominant opinion in the committee was conventionally liberal, even among the Republicans. The committee supported détente, arms control, and foreign aid but, starting with Vietnam, it was uneasy about any military involvement by the United States or any display of American power. Its remedy for crises was negotiation; it liked summitry and strongly backed our China policy. Even when supportive of our policies, the committee was much less enthusiastic about our rationale for them. On the whole, its members did not believe in geopolitics or the balance of power; they were embarrassed by appeals to the national interest. They did not view East-West relations as we did in terms of managing an adversarial relationship so much as an opportunity for building friendships. They were Wilsonians to a man, committed to reshaping the world by emphasizing the legal basis for foreign policy. The committee was often our ally in calm times; it was much less steady during periods of stress.

The committee's gentlemanly, erudite chairman, Fulbright, had a quick mind and a high analytical ability. President Kennedy had once considered him a potential Secretary of State—or so Fulbright believed —but had rejected him for being too independent. Whether it was for that reason or not, Fulbright had since made querulousness toward incumbent administrations his stock-in-trade—and he treated Democratic administrations not much more gently than Republican ones. With a tutorial air which at times shaded into the condescending, the intellectual level of Fulbright's interventions was always high. My relationship with him was constructive but wary. I kept him fully informed, and he restrained his customary harassment to the absolute minimum needed to maintain his liberal standing—perhaps because he was on the verge of what would prove to be his last Senate campaign in basically conservative Arkansas.

During my period in office, Ed Muskie and Frank Church were the principal upholders of Democratic orthodoxy: Muskie in a somewhat ponderous, academic manner; Church in a quicksilver, oratorical style reminiscent of such legendary senators as William Borah from his own state of Idaho—though on the opposite side of the political spectrum.

Hubert Humphrey was my favorite Senator on the committee. His eloquence seemed to have no natural limit. It was said of him that he once spoke at a tree-planting ceremony and, by the time he finished, he was standing in the shade. Humphrey's volubility represented the overflow of his warmheartedness, and all the jokes about it could not obscure the fact that he was as intelligent as he was loquacious. When it came to analysis, Humphrey's was a tough-minded liberalism that had cut its teeth on resistance to Stalin's threats in the immediate postwar period. But, in the interval, his party had moved far to the left and had indeed abandoned Humphrey over Vietnam during the 1968 electoral campaign. The disappointment of it had broken his heart and quelled his willingness to do battle with the comrades of a lifetime. Hence Humphrey was more of a support to me and administration policy in private conversations (where we were often very close) than in the public arena.

I have Humphrey to thank for an idea that turned out to be my most effective means of rallying public support. In 1974, when systematic attacks on me began, he telephoned me with this message:

> Pay no attention to inside-the-Beltway chatter. Go out into
> the country where they believe in you. Give a speech in each
> state, meet opinion leaders and, while the East Coast media

will not cover it, the local media will give it saturation coverage, and the local Congressmen will notice. And when you
come to Minnesota, I will go around with you and introduce you.

Humphrey proved as good as his word. In March 1976, a presidential
election year, I stopped in Minnesota, and he did indeed accompany a
Republican Secretary of State and introduce him around.

At that time, there were no conservatives on the committee, hence
there was little difference between the Democratic and Republican
Senators. Senator Jacob Javits from New York, highly intelligent, articulate, and knowledgeable, was supportive so long as he could avoid
arousing the wrath of the *New York Times,* which meant that his
endorsement usually stopped well short of administration policy. He
navigated the passage between his liberal constituency and the administration with particular skill when the television lights were on.
Javits's voice would rise and a vein in his forehead throb as he barked
confrontational-sounding questions, creating the impression that he
was extracting reluctant testimony when, in fact, he was giving me the
opportunity to state something I was quite eager to put forward. We
were social friends—a relationship that briefly cooled when, in October 1974 at an Alfred E. Smith dinner in New York, I joked about a
trip Javits had taken to Cuba in violation of existing government
policy: "I did not mind his going. What bothered me was that he came
back."

This was the assemblage before which I appeared on September
19, 1974, to put forward the administration's view on détente. Ford
was anything but a liberal; during his entire political career, he had
argued for a strong national defense and resistance to Soviet expansionism. Though he had had no role in shaping Nixon's East-West
policy, he had loyally supported it and entered office with a strong bias
toward continuity. In our daily morning meetings, I introduced Ford to
the issues facing him. Early on, to familiarize him with the nature of
the Soviet system, I gave him a copy of Aleksandr Solzhenitsyn's *Gulag
Archipelago*—a somewhat ironic gesture in light of the controversy
regarding the great author that was to descend on Ford within the year
(see Chapter 21).

Having known Nixon for twenty-five years, Ford found the charge
that Nixon might be soft on Communism ridiculous, if not cynical. I
have explained in a previous chapter why the demands of conservatives

and neoconservatives to steer a deliberately confrontational course with the Soviet Union could not possibly be implemented by a non-elected President in the aftermath of Watergate and Vietnam and while Congress was eviscerating the defense budget (see Chapter 3). At the same time, no administration—not even Ronald Reagan's—was more determined to resist Soviet expansionism.

The most sensible testimony before the Senate Foreign Relations Committee should have been a simple paragraph along these lines: "President Ford considers himself the heir of a consistent bipartisan postwar foreign policy conducted for nearly three decades. We will resist Soviet expansionism rigorously—perhaps more rigorously than some of you may like. At the same time, we shall seek a relaxation of tensions as a moral obligation without risking national security and while enhancing the national interest—perhaps more intensively than some of our critics appreciate. The balance between these two approaches is not a partisan issue, and we should pursue it jointly on a national basis. Our nation has been too severely wounded by its domestic controversies. Let us turn foreign policy into an act of healing."

But the Secretary of State cannot afford such an epigrammatic approach before a Senate committee while television cameras are rolling. They expected that my statement of September 19 would respond to six weeks of conservative and neoconservative criticism that preceded it. Moreover, a group of distinguished American and British scholars had earlier produced an analysis, widely circulated by a subcommittee of the Senate Armed Services Committee headed by Senator Jackson, to the effect that détente was an illusion; Western statesmen might well be serious about it, but the Soviet Union considered it merely a tactic designed to undermine Western resolve. According to their published statement:

> In the present Soviet terminology, détente or "peaceful coexistence" denotes a strategic alternative to overtly militant antagonism against the so-called "capitalist countries." It does not imply abandonment by the Soviet Union and its allies of conflict with the liberal Western countries. It does not mean the cessation of the slogans about class warfare and about the "ideological" conflict between the two systems with the aim of replacing the capitalist (democratic) system by the Communist system. . . . Détente means a change of methods.[2]

Of course, détente must have served some Soviet purposes or else the Soviet leaders would not have engaged in it. The issue was whether, whatever the Soviet purposes, it also served our own goals.

Another group of critics argued that détente had not produced friendship at all, that a relaxation of tensions had been accompanied by continued Soviet attempts to achieve a strategic advantage. A good example was an article on the Middle East by George Will, then at the beginning of his distinguished career as a columnist. It was entitled "Détente Looks a Lot Like the Cold War" and ignored the fact that we had never claimed détente would result in friendship; for us, too, détente was a method for conducting the Cold War.[3]

Most surprisingly, Hans Morgenthau, the distinguished father in America of the theory of national interest–oriented foreign policy, put forward the proposition that the balance of power required the overthrow of the entire Soviet domestic structure. A Soviet domestic upheaval was a vital American interest, he wrote, because it would portend the return of the Soviet Union to a "system of arts, and laws and manners"; were the Soviet government to join such a system, "one would indeed not need to care on political grounds about how autocratic and despotic its government might be":

> Thus our interest in the totalitarian excesses of the Soviet government is not unwarranted meddling in the affairs of another sovereign nation in a misguided spirit of liberal re-form. Nor does it solely express a humanitarian concern or serve to placate public opinion at home. Foremost it is at the service of that basic interest which the United States and the Soviet Union have in common: survival in the nuclear age through a viable balance of power and genuine détente.[4]

Unlike the liberals, Morgenthau was not proclaiming that democracy in the Soviet Union would automatically produce peace but that *any* Russian government, however despotic, was acceptable, provided it followed a balance of power diplomacy. This, in Morgenthau's view, the Communist system was inherently incapable of doing.

The remarkable aspect of the critics' presentation was the extent to which it ignored the actual experience of the Nixon Administration. To be sure, the Kremlin continued the ideological and geopolitical competition and had sought to enhance the relative position of the Soviet Union. But the United States had managed to achieve its strategic aims in China, the Middle East, Cienfuegos, and Berlin, and had given up no strategic asset in the process.

The Middle East was perhaps the most striking example. The Soviet Union had indeed made the 1973 war possible by its supply of arms, but we had succeeded in thwarting every diplomatic initiative based on Soviet arms and had aided Israel during the war with a massive airlift. When the smoke cleared, the net beneficiary was the United States. Our de facto ally had won the military battles; we had excluded the Soviet Union from the subsequent peace process; and we had used the rewards and penalties of détente to encourage Soviet restraint even while the Kremlin was being consigned to the sidelines of Middle East diplomacy.

I have explained in previous chapters the strategy by which a non-elected President, saddled with a McGovernite Congress, trying to rebuild a discredited presidency, and dealing with ethnic conflict on Cyprus and the threat of war in the Middle East, sought to pursue the part adversarial, part cooperative relationship with the other nuclear superpower. In these pages, I will confine myself to the presentation made before the Senate.

The statement affirmed what our policy should long since have made clear: we were not basing our relationship with the Soviet Union on the assumption of an incipient friendship; rather, we viewed it as a strategy for controlling a relationship between adversaries:

> The United States cannot base its policy solely on Moscow's good intentions. But neither can we insist that all forward movement must await a convergence of American and Soviet purposes. We seek, regardless of Soviet intentions, to serve peace through a systematic resistance to pressure and conciliatory responses to moderate behavior.[5]

Aggressive action would be resisted as it had been in the Middle East, over the Soviet submarine base in Cienfuegos in Cuba, and over access to Berlin. But in the nuclear age, any administration had an obligation to the American people to conduct its foreign policy in a manner that took full account of the extent to which nuclear weapons had changed the calculation of risks:

> We must oppose aggressive actions and irresponsible behavior. But we must not seek confrontations lightly.

> We must maintain a strong national defense while recognizing that in the nuclear age the relationship between military strength and politically usable power is the most complex in all history.[6]

Finally, my statement touched on the neoconservative argument that we should seek not so much to coexist with the Soviet system as to overthrow it and that we should do so not by accelerating its historical erosion—as we believed we were doing—but by direct, if unspecified, confrontation:

> Where the age-old antagonism between freedom and tyranny is concerned, we are not neutral. But other imperatives impose limits on our ability to produce internal changes in foreign countries. Consciousness of our limits is recognition of the necessity of peace—not moral callousness. The preservation of human life and human society are moral values, too.[7]

The reaction of the Senate Foreign Relations Committee to my statement not only reflected its liberal bias but provided a taste of the Vietnam-era type of upheaval that would have been provoked had we pursued the confrontational course being urged on us by those who testified before me. For in the committee's view, the Ford Administration, far from being too conciliatory, was risking the peace by excessive concern with military security:

- Chairman Fulbright complained that the United States was spurring the arms race and that "we are always coming up with these new weapons."[8]
- Senator Muskie expressed his opposition to the new generation of missiles being developed under our aegis.
- Senator Church argued that détente, based as it was on pragmatic and geopolitical considerations, ran the risk of becoming "utterly unprincipled."[9] Since Church also opposed higher defense spending and geopolitical containment, he did not vouchsafe how a "principled" policy of opposition to Soviet expansionism should be carried out.
- Republican Senator Percy, supported by Democratic Senators Stuart Symington and Claiborne Pell, worried whether the Ford Adminis-

tration's acquisition of naval and air facilities on the island of Diego Garcia in the Indian Ocean "could in any way endanger détente." [10]

Not a single Senator put forward what later became the conservative position.

## The Debate on Arms Control Resumes

The Ford Administration in its first weeks inherited the Nixon legacy of being assaulted from two opposite directions: from the still dominant liberal end, for being too geopolitical and Cold War-ish; from the conservative side, for being too tactical and nonideological.

This is why Ford was obliged to turn almost immediately to two issues inherited from Nixon: arms control and Jewish emigration from the Soviet Union, both encrusted in long and complicated histories.

With respect to arms control, the actual debate concerned numbers which, in the process, grew more and more blurred amidst a cloud of esoterica; the real issue, however, was a change in the overall political and strategic environment.

There had been a powerful geopolitical rationale for SALT I: to calm the atmosphere during the difficult extrication from Vietnam and to give the Soviets an incentive for restraint on a whole complex of issues ranging from Berlin to the Middle East. But when Ford arrived on the scene, the retreat from Vietnam was complete, and access to Berlin was settled; the Soviet role in the Middle East was being systematically eroded; and East-West trade was under attack by Jackson and his legions. Other East-West initiatives were frozen as well. We were stonewalling Brezhnev's proposal for a superpower arrangement aimed at China (to be discussed in the next chapter) and dragging our feet on his initiative for an early European Security Conference at the head-of-state level.

In these circumstances, the geopolitical rationale for SALT II became increasingly the dialogue itself, the need to keep some kind of negotiation going. SALT having come to be fused in the public mind with détente, it now bore the full weight of the controversy regarding East-West relations. But so technically complex a negotiation was hardly the ideal surrogate for a fundamental national debate over East-West relations.

At the same time, the character of the arms race and of strategy was changing equally dramatically. Throughout nearly the entire

Nixon presidency, as described in Chapter 4, missiles carried only a single warhead. In these conditions, strategic assessments and arms control negotiations had concentrated on quantity. The strategic relationship could be determined fairly accurately from the number of strategic launchers on each side. But by the time Ford came into office, the United States had begun deploying multiple warheads for each launcher, and the Soviet Union was in the process of testing MIRVs. In addition, an entire new generation of weapons was being developed, comprising—on the American side—the Trident submarine, each carrying twenty-four new missiles with eight to ten much larger warheads; the Minuteman III with three warheads each; cruise missiles—in effect, pilotless airplanes; and the B-1 supersonic bomber. Technologically, the Soviets had been far less fertile. Nevertheless, Pentagon planners were concerned that MIRVs on the Soviet heavy missiles— the SS-18, for which there was no American counterpart—had the potential to render our land-based forces dangerously vulnerable.

High-flown theories about the moral significance of arms control notwithstanding, in the real world, the basic assignment of each side's negotiators became to protect those weapons which their planners were in the process of developing and eager to deploy. At the same time, each side's negotiators sought to constrain to the greatest extent possible those weapons of the adversary that worried them most. Thus the Soviets were pressing against America's missile defense while we were seeking to reduce Soviet heavy missiles.

In this sense, SALT I served as a kind of acceptance by each side of the unilateral plans of the other. Certainly on the American side, SALT I stopped no program, existing or planned. The numerical inequality in missiles it ratified were the voluntarily chosen existing programs for the foreseeable future. SALT II began the same way.

This state of affairs created a somewhat surreal situation. The programs of each side had been developed by differing criteria; each composed its weapons in different mixes. The Soviet Union had more and larger missiles, most of them based on land; ours were smaller and more accurate and based in a more diversified manner. The size of our program had been judged adequate by three administrations; for over a decade, Pentagon proposals to the White House had been to improve existing weapons, not to augment them. When Ford came into office, we were ahead in warheads and would be for about a decade; the Soviets had a larger number of delivery vehicles.

But once included in a SALT agreement, what had been a unilateral decision which each side had freely chosen became highly controversial. Quantitative equality turned into a slogan even as the real arms race depended less and less on numbers and more and more on quality. Given the different composition of the two forces, this created the following dilemma: if equal ceilings were established at the American level, the Soviet Union would have to undertake an essentially unilateral reduction of its forces. If they were set at the Soviet level, we would acquire the right to a buildup for which we had no program or strategic theory.

This became apparent when Ford met with the National Security Council for the first time on SALT matters on October 7. Because we had no program for augmenting our launchers beyond 2,000 and because a new program would require a decade to implement, I put forward the proposal which Nixon had made to Brezhnev two months earlier and which had been approved by the NSC, including Schlesinger. It called for maintaining the SALT I numbers for another five years (during which—given the long lead times—we could not have increased our totals anyway) in return for an advantage to the United States in the number of MIRVed warheads. Brezhnev had accepted the principle, but no agreement was reached because the edge on MIRVs Brezhnev was willing to concede was deemed inadequate by Nixon and his advisers.

Though the scheme of "offsetting asymmetries" had been put forward by Nixon, Schlesinger, backed by the Chairman of the Joint Chiefs of Staff, General George Brown, reversed his position as soon as Ford became President. Aware that Henry Jackson as perhaps the key member in the Senate Armed Services Committee was in a position to raise havoc with the defense budget, already under liberal assault, Schlesinger now argued in favor of equality across the board at levels of 2,500 launchers and 1,320 MIRVed vehicles. The American edge of some 300 MIRVed missiles or 1,000 warheads—which Nixon had proposed—would mean little, the Pentagon argued, once the Soviets had placed multiple warheads on 600 of their missiles because they would be able to cover every conceivable American target.

Ford was very knowledgeable about security issues from his service on the Defense Subcommittee of the House Appropriations Committee. He grew testy at the proposition that an American advantage of 300 MIRVed missiles with over 1,000 warheads should be deemed irrelevant, while a Soviet edge of 300 single-warhead missiles in the SALT I agreement had been denounced as a disaster. A strained dialogue ensued between Ford and his Secretary of Defense. With respect to Schlesinger's proposal of a ceiling of 2,500 for both sides, Ford pointed out that the modernization programs Congress had approved (prior to SALT) had provided for only 2,000 American delivery vehicles. Schlesinger replied that he would be able to bring the totals up to 2,250 at a cost of some $1 to $2 billion a year by retaining obsolescent Polaris submarines and B-52s scheduled for retirement. Ford resisted a scheme which would, in the name of arms control, augment our strategic forces with obsolescent weapons we had intended to retire. And he challenged Schlesinger's estimate on budgetary grounds. Congress, having cut the defense budget by $4.7 billion, would not go along:

> I don't share, Jim, your optimism with respect to the Congress. I remember the ABM fight where they beat us. And the recent 5 percent cuts across the board. And I am talking about our present Congress, and we will probably get a more unsupportive Congress in the next election. I am not optimistic that you can assume there will be increases in defense budgets, unless there is a crisis.

The bizarre aspect of the debate was that there was no objective reason for the palpable tension in the Cabinet Room. For there would be no difference in practice in the actual strategic forces of the two sides whether it was Schlesinger's scheme or Nixon's that was accepted. If Schlesinger prevailed, there would be formal equality, but the Soviet numerical edge in launchers would remain intact because we had no program or funds for building more. On the basis of Nixon's program, we would achieve a formal numerical advantage in MIRVs, though, in fact, the Soviet Union would not be technically in a position to exceed the permitted number of MIRVs until 1982 in any event. In other words, there was next to no practical difference between Schlesinger's position and Nixon's: Nixon had not recommended any cut in any existing American program; Schlesinger's new version implied no increase in any of the same programs.

Ford opted for the more easily comprehensible over the intellectually fastidious. Schlesinger's scheme had the political advantage of enshrining formal equality and of establishing a baseline for further agreements. Without disavowing Nixon's proposal, Ford urged me to give priority to what Schlesinger called his "rough-and-dirty option" and use Nixon's proposal only as a fallback position. Specifically I was to propose equal ceilings at the level of 2,500 delivery vehicles (requiring a Soviet reduction of some 150 delivery vehicles) and of some 1,320 MIRVs, the latter being precisely the numbers in our own MIRV program. These limits would reflect the existing strategic balance and, unless we spent several billion dollars retaining weapons we had declared to be obsolescent, would maintain the prevailing numerical gap in the Soviet favor. The benefit was that these ceilings would impose some—albeit limited—constraint on the Soviet Union, then still expanding its arsenal while the United States was concentrating on qualitative improvement. And they would preserve the only major East-West negotiation still intact.

As I prepared to leave for Moscow later in October, I was hopeful that the option Ford had selected would point the way to a breakthrough on the immediate issue before us. However, as the SALT process was turned into the centerpiece of East-West relations, it was growing increasingly fragile. For arms control would not by itself be able to carry the burden of a political relationship while tensions were escalating in other areas. One of these was the issue of Jewish emigration from the Soviet Union.

## Jewish Emigration from the Soviet Union

When Ford took office, the issue of Jewish emigration from the Soviet Union stood as follows. Henry Jackson had stated that a minimum rate of 100,000 emigrants a year was needed to meet the terms of the Jackson-Vanik Amendment. The Soviet government insisted that its emigration practices were a matter for domestic legislation and fell within the scope of its national sovereignty. In my quest to reconcile these positions, I had sought to elicit from Gromyko a description of actual Soviet emigration practices. I would then write a letter to the Senators reflecting my understanding of Soviet intentions as a basis for a presidential waiver of the Jackson-Vanik Amendment. In this manner, the Soviets could assert that I was describing their actual practice, not a new commitment; Jackson could claim progress on Jewish emigration.

Gromyko had grudgingly fallen in with this approach and, at meetings in Geneva and Moscow, had indicated that a number of 45,000 emigrants, or 25 percent above the highest previous level, might be achievable. Jackson had disdained this offer, continuing to insist on the 100,000 figure, finally terminating all discussions with the Nixon Administration at the end of June.

In July, Dobrynin had made Gromyko's numbers more realistic by informing me that the "normal" rejection rate for visa applicants had never exceeded 1.6 percent in the past and that the Soviet leaders did not intend to exceed that percentage in the future. Moreover, at his first meeting with Ford on August 14, Dobrynin volunteered that Brezhnev would personally stand behind all the assurances of recent months. Should any problems arise, Dobrynin said, Ford could appeal directly to Brezhnev.

On this basis, Ford decided to resume negotiations with the Senators. On August 15—or six days after his inauguration—he invited Henry Jackson, Jacob Javits, and Abe Ribicoff, the senatorial negotiating team, to meet with him in the Oval Office. Informing the Senators of his conversation with Dobrynin, Ford expressed the hope that, freed of the accumulated resentments of the Nixon era, we could now all work together to find a solution.

Jackson responded with his version of a conciliatory counteroffer. As a sign of his goodwill, he announced that he was reducing his target figure to 75,000 emigrants—as if the rate of Soviet emigration was somehow up to Ford to determine. He had arrived at this number— which doubled the highest previous figure—by claiming that there was a total of 300,000 applicants whose departures he had prorated over a four-year period. If the Kremlin stuck to its pledge of a rejection rate not exceeding 1.6 percent and if Jackson's guess of the number of applicants was accurate, the 75,000 figure might conceivably hold. But there was no basis in anything the Soviets had told us for putting it forward in writing; in fact, Gromyko had claimed the opposite—that, in the aftermath of the Middle East War, the number of Jews applying to emigrate to Israel had declined dramatically.

Nevertheless, to show our good intentions, I assigned Helmut ("Hal") Sonnenfeldt, then counselor of the State Department, to work with Jackson and his staff to draft a letter designed to summarize the assurances given to us by Moscow. I told Ford that the draft was more strident than I considered wise, but it might just barely fall within the outer limits of the tolerable. At this point, Jackson ratcheted matters up one more notch by proposing that the three Senators prepare an "interpretation" of my letter, thereby setting forth even more stringent technical definitions for every Soviet assurance. These would then be reviewed by Congress when Most Favored Nation status for the Soviet Union came up for renewal.

We were clearly negotiating with ourselves. I warned the three Senators at our next meeting on September 18:

I can fully justify my letter to Scoop from our talks with the Soviets—last April in Moscow and then confirmed in June in Moscow at the summit. I can also accept your interpretations as reasonable extrapolations of the points in my letter. But I can't apply this to the numbers. My view is that if they [the Soviets] live up to the understandings and there is a certain number of applicants, then the number of applicants should rise substantially over what it was before. But I can't say that the Soviets accept the number [in Jackson's interpretive letter]. And I can't be responsible for that number.

The entire exercise turned even more precarious when Jackson insisted that the presidential waiver of the Jackson-Vanik Amendment needed to be approved by Congress, with the first review eighteen months hence and annually thereafter. This placed the timing of the review into the middle of the primary campaign for the 1976 presidential nomination in which Jackson intended to be a candidate. It required no great acumen to determine that the Senator was quite likely to raise the stakes again at that time.

Finally, Jackson's staffers demanded a third document, a letter from me in effect confirming the Senators' interpretative statement. Jackson, they told us, would insist on publishing the entire exchange, including the target number.

All this was no doubt very impressive in senatorial back rooms where no one was obliged to negotiate any of it with Soviet leaders. The very people who were arguing that the Soviets were bent on world domination and considering a nuclear first strike were conducting themselves as if the Politburo would prove to be a total pushover with respect to American demands affecting its domestic legislation. Once again, I warned Jackson and his staff: "We can just get by with the [first] letter. The interpretative statements overload the circuit."

But Jackson was determined to prove how pliable the Soviets would be if really pressured (and therefore, by implication, how soft I was in dealing with them). Viewing a retreat from the outrageous to the impossible as a great concession, Jackson and his staff came up with another "compromise": a target figure of 60,000, which Jackson defined as the midpoint between Gromyko's figure of 45,000 and the Senators' figure of 75,000. We were arguing about numbers for which we had no basis and about assurances that had never been given to us.

In frustration, I appealed to Israeli Prime Minister Yitzhak Rabin

to intercede with the Senators. It was, of course, somewhat degrading
for a Secretary of State to have to ask a foreign leader, however friendly,
for help on what was essentially an American domestic issue. On
September 11, 1974, I told Rabin during a Washington visit:

> We can write letters until we're blue in the face. We can
> write a beautiful document, and they can still find adminis-
> trative ways to keep people in if that is what they want. We
> are willing to take it out of domestic politics. They [the
> Senators] can have the credit. If the Soviets prize détente,
> particularly with the new President, who may be in office for
> six years, they may do it. . . . They [the Senators] want us
> to write down a number—sixty thousand. If we want a
> demagogic game, we can do it.

But Rabin, who might need the Senators for the annual vote on Israeli
appropriations and as a safety net in the event of disagreement with
the administration, was too prudent to get involved.

When Gromyko called on Ford at the Oval Office on September
20, I had an opportunity to sum up for the President exactly where we
stood with respect to Soviet assurances. I summarized the exchanges
on the subject as I understood them:

> It is understood that, on the Soviet side, there will be no
> restrictions on applications for emigration; there will be no
> harassment, and there will be no restrictions on exit visas
> except for reasons of national security. If all these conditions
> are met, then everything will depend on the number of appli-
> cations. The Soviet Union has no responsibility to produce
> applicants. If 100,000 apply, then 99,000 will get out. If 9,000
> apply, then 8,000 will get out. We have made all of this clear
> to the Senators.
>
> You told me this, Mr. Foreign Minister, in Moscow and
> in Geneva. There have been no new concessions on your
> part. The Senators can think anything they want about num-
> bers, but this has not been discussed with them.

Gromyko again confirmed these understandings, especially that
the number of rejections would not exceed 1.6 percent. This provided
an occasion to explain to him, in Ford's presence, the various letters

and interpretative statements that were being planned. Gromyko made a sour face but acquiesced, however reluctantly, provided no target figures were used and no Soviet legal obligations were implied.

At this point, the wisest course would have been to hand the transcript of our conversations with Gromyko to the Senators and tell them that we could go no further; that any exchanges between the Senators and the White House would have to be consistent with this record, and that it was up to them whether to scuttle the trade bill along with Jewish emigration.

But Ford did not want to start his presidency with a clash with such key Senators and a key domestic constituency. That meant I was being sent back to the negotiating treadmill with the Senators on matters quite out of my control. Time and again, I explained that there was no basis for their emigration figure; to the extreme chagrin of Jackson, I refused to supply him with a third letter confirming the interpretative statement.

Finally, on October 18, Ford personally reached an agreement with Jackson that incorporated the essence of our exchanges with the Soviets, though in a needlessly strident form. Moreover, Jackson kept referring to the sixty-thousand figure as a "benchmark," strongly implying that he might seek an increase of it at the latest when MFN came up for renewal.

Unfortunately, Ford, in an excess of generosity, permitted Jackson to make the announcement and compounded the disaster by letting him do so in the White House Briefing Room. It not only conveyed the impression that Jackson was speaking for the executive branch but, above all, that his basic position had prevailed along the exact lines the Soviets had told us they would, under no circumstances, accept. Our understanding with the Soviets had depended on presenting the exchange of letters as an explanation of existing practice. Jackson did exactly the opposite. The Senator proclaimed that a great victory for human rights had been extorted from the Soviets, and he hinted as well that he had demonstrated the effectiveness of his method for negotiating with the Soviets. As to the number of emigrants, Jackson explicitly violated our injunction against specificity:

> We have identified as a benchmark and not as a quota 60,000 immigrants each year . . . and I anticipate that it should go beyond 60,000 based on the number of applications which we know exceed 130,000.[11]

The fat was now in the fire. The Soviets made no immediate response, probably because I was due to visit Moscow within the week to prepare for the summit at Vladivostok.

In the meantime, the White House did correct Jackson's statement and emphasized that my letter to the Senator had not mentioned any specific number.[12] The media, however, celebrated the great victory of Jackson's hardball tactics as a demonstration that the Soviets would yield when faced with tough American negotiators.

The "victory" proved short-lived. Less than two months later, the Soviets rejected MFN altogether and sharply curtailed emigration. But, in the interim, another round of talks with Soviet leaders supervened.

# 9

# A VISIT WITH BREZHNEV

## *Brezhnev and the Kremlin Leaders*

To visit Moscow during the Cold War was to experience a multitude of conflicting reactions and emotions. Anyone privy to intelligence reports was aware of the vast and ever-growing Soviet nuclear arsenal that had the capacity of destroying our country and, indeed, civilization itself. Nor could one forget that the Kremlin's governing ideology proclaimed the inevitable historical triumph of Communism or that its operational policy had generated most of the crises and confrontations of the postwar decades.

Despite these immutable realities, each meeting between senior officials of the two superpowers—and especially between their heads of state—renewed the widespread hope that half a century of conflict might be settled during a few days' exchange of views. Despite all the imprecations and confrontations of the period, no leader in the nuclear age could disregard the popular yearning for peace, or his own responsibility to the survival of civilization.

One was therefore struck with special force upon arrival in Moscow by the incongruity between the pretensions of the Communist state and its realities. Intelligence reports conveyed fearsome images of a vast military capacity in the service of an implacable resolve. But anyone who had ever been on an official visit to the Soviet Union— even as filtered through the meticulously orchestrated cocoon of VIP status—could not but gain the impression that the whole elaborately constructed stage set was precarious and might collapse at any moment. Just beneath the labored facade of hospitality flowed an undercurrent of incipient panic lest, in the end, the deadlocks and

bottlenecks that plagued Communism might derail the entire enterprise.

The strain on a society so inhospitable to spontaneity was bound
to take its toll. Despite Moscow's ostentatious military posturing and
its leaders' toughness and even brutality, to bear witness to this essentially moribund system was to feel in your bones how unlikely it was
to risk its survival on a single throw of the dice. Apocalyptic American scenarios that postulated Armageddon notwithstanding, creeping
expansionism seemed much more in keeping with Soviet history and
capabilities.

Firsthand encounters with Soviet leaders of the 1970s reinforced
these impressions. The governing triumvirate in the Kremlin during
the Nixon Administration resembled a cluster of semi-extinct volca-
nos: the voluble General Secretary Leonid Brezhnev, whose blustering
joviality was never quite sufficient to obscure his latent insecurity;
the intellectual, aloof, and sardonic bureaucratic manipulator, Premier
Alexei Kosygin; and President Nikolai Podgorny, the inside operator
uninterested in foreign policy and disinclined to contribute to our visits
much more than an occasional bow to the general atmosphere of
goodwill. As different as these three leaders were—and however com-
petitive with one another they turned out to be—their behavior lacked
inner dynamism and was more in keeping with actors playing assigned
roles. This was probably the long-term result of two seminal experiences which they all shared: Stalin's purges and the struggle against
Nazi Germany.

Though by the time I encountered this troika, Stalin had been dead
for nearly two decades, the inescapable impression was that the brutal
dictator had left them drained of initiative and intellectual energy. Each
had made his big step up the bureaucratic and party ladder during the
purges of the 1930s when Stalin killed off virtually every prominent
leader of his own generation. Having witnessed the extermination of
those who had made the revolution at the whim of the autocrat—and
on charges they knew better than anyone to have been grotesque—
Brezhnev and his associates were bound to have the essential precariousness of their own hold on power burned into their souls. They had
risen more rapidly than they could have dreamed possible, but they
paid for it with congenital doubts about their own legitimacy and
staying power. While Stalin was still alive, the survivors of the initial
purges had been the logical, indeed the designated, victims of his
unquenchable blood lusts and the targets for his inexhaustible need to

humiliate his entourage. None of them had ever witnessed a legitimate transfer of power; each previous Soviet leader had either died in office or, as in the case of Nikita Khrushchev, been overthrown by a conspiracy of his close associates—the very leaders I was, in fact, meeting regularly.

High office in the Soviet Union was not just a means of sating ambition; it was the prerequisite to surviving with any status at all. When a leader retired—which was very rare—or wound up as the loser in some internecine battle, the result was a precipitous decline, first in his status but soon in living standard as well. In the "classless" Soviet society, status depended, as it does in feudal societies, on having an official function, which provided access to personal luxuries that came—and went—with high office. Probably the hardest to bear was the social ostracism associated with the loss of official position.

During the May 1972 summit in Moscow, I witnessed a rather poignant demonstration of these realities. At a huge reception in the Kremlin's St. George's Hall, a section of that vast room was roped off for the Politburo and the senior members of the American delegation. One of the Americans noticed the aged Anastas Mikoyan—companion of Stalin and for decades member of the Politburo—in the crowd on the other side of the rope. His career had paralleled the history of Communism, but he had been in eclipse since Khrushchev's fall. Mikoyan was standing alone amidst a mob of low-ranking Soviet officials who were clearly shunning him and American journalists who did not recognize him or were uncharacteristically hesitant about approaching him. Feeling sympathy, the American invited the fallen Soviet leader to join the VIPs. Torn between prudence and vanity, Mikoyan allowed himself to be persuaded to enter the cordoned-off section which once had been his due. It proved to be a mistake. None of the Politburo members—all of whom had until recently worked with or under him—took the slightest notice of the erstwhile colleague of at least some of them. After a few painful minutes, he shrank back into the faces in the crowd and his own ostracism.

Every Soviet officeholder knew of similar cases. Whatever one's level, the motivating force in the Soviet system was to elevate political survival into a principal, at times obsessive, preoccupation. It was the Soviet officials' most finely honed skill, the subject about which they thought most creatively. By the same token, they paid for this obsession with a lack of imagination on matters of global strategy. The generation governing the Soviet Union in the 1970s accumulated military and geopolitical power less as an expression of long-range geopolitical aims than as a substitute for them. Inevitably the pursuit of strength for its own sake frightened most of the non-Communist world and brought about a tacit coalition of all industrial nations plus China against the Soviet Union, which made its ultimate collapse inevitable.

In my tens of hours of conversation with Brezhnev, I encountered a plethora of tactical expedients but never anything resembling a long-term political plan. Obsessed with China, Brezhnev kept putting forward transparent and rather clumsy proposals involving (as will be discussed) a Soviet-American global condominium aimed at his huge neighbor, though his entourage soon realized that we were evading the proposal or any variation of it. He usually grew bored with prolonged stalemates and would go on to another subject, displaying no particular ill will at having been thwarted.

Until the American executive authority disintegrated under the impact of Watergate, Brezhnev gave high priority to a relaxation of East-West tensions. He accepted—though not without some grumbling—the downgrading of Moscow's influence in the Middle East; he made no effort during Watergate to exploit Nixon's domestic weakness. Aside from his preoccupation with forging a nuclear condominium aimed at China, Brezhnev's principal concern was to obtain America's acceptance of a summit to conclude the European Security Conference. There was not a little pathos in this attempt by a superpower possessing thousands of nuclear weapons to achieve legitimacy for borders already guaranteed by a series of bilateral peace treaties and which no neighbor of the Soviet Union was in a position to challenge militarily. Yet Brezhnev was so eager to secure this recognition that he settled for a document which eventually made the case— and provided the mechanism—for dismantling the Soviet sphere of influence by providing a legal basis for German unification and establishing a forum which East European patriots used to vindicate their pursuit of human rights.

After détente collapsed, Brezhnev, by then increasingly debilitated by a series of strokes, began to project Soviet military capacities into Africa, South Yemen, and Afghanistan. It was an essentially opportunistic expansion that exploited situations the Soviets had not brought about. Dobrynin claims that Brezhnev was pressured into this course by the ideological wing of the Politburo. Yet, if unchecked, it threatened to merge with a quest for world domination.[1] In the event, the principal consequence of the new expansionism was to drain Soviet resources and to magnify the Soviet Union's long-term vulnerability, especially after the Reagan Administration launched a determined build-up of America's armed forces.

The experience of the generation of Soviet leaders who had survived the Second World War reinforced a preference for gradualism over apocalyptic confrontations. The outside world might view the Soviet Union as an implacable colossus, but its leaders could never forget how close-run the outcome had been. The Soviet Union had prevailed only after suffering 27 million casualties[2] and the total devastation of a third of the country. Proud as the Soviet leaders were of their ultimate victory, they had no desire to test their ability to survive an apocalyptic showdown a second time.

The generally boisterous and boastful Brezhnev never managed to achieve serenity or even to appear emotionally secure. His attitude toward the United States alternated between awe and envy. Equal status would have been treated by British, French, or Chinese leaders as owed to them by history and achievement. Brezhnev viewed it as a prize to be wrested from the very capitalist adversary whom Communist ideology had already consigned to the trash heap of history. His conduct, therefore, was not always consistent with his routine invocation of the superiority of the Communist system. In May 1973, Brezhnev invited me to the Politburo hunting lodge in Zavidovo (about ninety miles from Moscow) to prepare for his visit to the United States in June. Our lengthy daily meetings invariably began with a formal insistence by Brezhnev that he be treated on the basis of equality. After the first day, I started every session with the mantra that, in all his American encounters, Brezhnev would be meticulously treated as an equal. Seemingly oblivious to the condescension inherent in this repetitive certification of his status, Brezhnev would get up from his seat, walk around the table, and embrace me. For this reason, the issue of Most Favored Nation status for the Soviet Union was, for Brezhnev, not simply a commercial negotiation but a test case of America's basic attitude toward his country.

Brezhnev was reasonably well versed on military and economic matters, though rarely to the point of risking an independent view. When a technical issue arose, he seldom responded until there had been a huddle on the Soviet side of the table. When Brezhnev did act on his own, as during the initial SALT conversation with Nixon at the 1972 Moscow summit, he soon got himself into such difficulties that he had to be disavowed (a laborious process in the extremely hierarchical Soviet system).[3] On geopolitical subjects, he never offered penetrating insights and usually did little more than add the weight of his office to a Soviet position already well rehearsed by Gromyko—albeit in a less pedantic and more jovial manner. As General Secretary, Brezhnev had the authority to break diplomatic deadlocks and occasionally did so, most notably at the November 1974 Vladivostok summit with Ford when, according to Dobrynin, he overruled Defense Minister Andrei Grechko on the telephone to Moscow.[4] In contrast to the typical Soviet negotiator, Brezhnev would intersperse the discussions with anecdotes of various degrees of subtlety that might or might not be germane to the subject at hand.

Most formal negotiations took place in the Politburo meeting room in the Kremlin—a dark and cavernous hall, perhaps sixty feet in length, containing a long table, at the end of which stood a huge desk, presumably Brezhnev's working area. Microphones were built into the table before each seat, not only for the purpose of amplification but also for recording the conversations of Brezhnev's interlocutors. This became obvious when a Soviet technician pushed the wrong button and played back for all to hear some comment I had whispered to Helmut Sonnenfeldt, the State Department counselor, seated next to me.

Quite sensibly—but, in my experience, uniquely—Brezhnev considered it a waste of time to listen to presentations in a language he did not understand. Though my remarks were addressed to him, he would rise from the table as I spoke and wander about the room, signing papers, making phone calls, or joking with colleagues in loud stage whispers. When I completed my statement essentially to his empty seat, Brezhnev would return to the table and listen to the translation. After he gave his reply, the wanderings would resume while Viktor Sukhodrev, his brilliant interpreter, translated his observations into English.

Brezhnev did not have Gromyko's patience when it came to wearing down his interlocutor. Prolonged technical arguments made him visibly restless. He made certain to obtain Politburo support before offering concessions. Thus it was generally wise to schedule meetings aiming for a breakthrough for Moscow, and it is why these sessions were invariably punctuated by long interruptions while the Politburo met. But once Brezhnev had engaged his prestige, he grew palpably impatient to reach a conclusion. This was the case at the end of the May 1972 summit in Moscow, again at Vladivostok in November 1974, and finally in preparing the European Security Conference at Helsinki in the summer of 1975.

## The Kremlin's Perspective on Détente

My visit to Moscow from October 23 to 27, 1974, demonstrated the wide and still growing gulf that had opened up between conventional wisdom in Washington and perceptions in Moscow. The American media, much of Congress, and some members of the Ford Administration were more and more acquiescing in the critics' characterization of détente as a one-way street in which unreciprocated American concessions were being made in pursuit of Moscow's elusive and unreliable goodwill.

In Moscow, however, one heard the precise opposite. In hardly any area of East-West policy were Soviet leaders able to point to any benefit to them. The "settlement" of the MFN/emigration issue as announced by Senator Henry Jackson just before I left was considered insulting. The Soviet Union was being excluded from Middle East diplomacy. The European Security Conference was progressing at a glacial pace partly because we were trying to retain as long as possible what still remained of linkage. Brezhnev's proposal to Nixon of an American-Soviet nuclear condominium had received no response from Ford. Only SALT remained, and it was increasingly becoming a means by which to validate each side's unilateral strategic program.

Of my many visits to the Soviet Union, that October trip to prepare for the summit in Vladivostok stands out for its mellow, at times almost melancholy, character. Like an early frost, it heralded the onset of a winter chill, yet neither side was emotionally quite prepared for the approaching change of seasons. Each for its own reasons continued to pretend and, to some extent, to believe that it was witnessing a temporary aberration it was within its power to rectify. The American negotiators were only too well aware that domestic support for détente was slipping. But we also realized that a new President needed a period of tranquillity in which to establish himself, and we therefore sought to salvage what coherence we could via the SALT negotiations—the principal negotiation still taking place.

The Soviet case was more complex. According to the traditional rules of the Cold War, Watergate presented a rare opportunity for Soviet expansion. But no real challenge had as yet occurred. It was not until after the Soviet rejection of the trade bill as modified by the Jackson and Stevenson Amendments, the collapse of Indochina, and the congressional cutoff of aid to non-Communist forces in Angola that the Kremlin embarked on a more adventurous course.

Our objective was to prolong the Kremlin's quiescence as long as possible. We were all too conscious—more so, fortunately, than the Kremlin—that a restless liberal Congress, dominated by critics and facing a President just beginning to establish his authority, was unlikely to countenance prolonged confrontations, especially if the Kremlin justified challenges on the frustration of being a rejected suitor. Moscow certainly had the capacity to exacerbate tensions in the Middle East, and there were many opportunities for supporting radicals and guerrillas in the Third World.

In October 1974, however, none of these challenges had as yet materialized. Part of the reason was that the decline of American executive authority so worrisome to us was beyond the comprehension of the Soviet leaders. For the better part of two years, they seem to have expected a swift return to normality, which, to them, meant the thrusts and parries of the Nixon years. Critics of détente would, of course, argue that Soviet restraint reflected the enormous gains being made by the Kremlin—benefits I am still at a loss to discern even from the vantage of two decades. At that stage, Brezhnev's efforts still focused on a quest for status, in itself a sign of insecurity, since those who know themselves to be genuinely equals do not require constant certification of that fact.

Most importantly, Brezhnev's seemingly enduring commitment to détente may well have attested to a premonition of what would turn into the fatal dilemma of the Soviet state. For by then, the Kremlin's clumsy and bullying tactics toward all its neighbors had, as noted, driven all the world's major industrial powers plus China into coalitions against it. As Brezhnev's successors pointed out with enormous bitterness, this had been a historic blunder.[5] In these terms, Brezhnev's principal motive for sustaining détente was to break up or at least keep at bay the growing Sino-American strategic partnership.

Most of America's problems were temporary and likely to be overcome with the passage of time. But in the superpower competition, the Soviet Union held a fundamentally weak hand. With a stagnant economy and a GNP at best 40 percent of that of the United States, Moscow could only compete militarily by condemning its population to a standard of living which would sooner or later raise questions about the validity of the Communist system itself. And even at that level of civilian deprivation, the arms race strained the very limits of Soviet industrial capacity. Deep down, Soviet leaders must have been feeling the exact opposite of what the Ford Administration's domestic critics were alleging: less a sense of superiority than of vulnerability to the looming threat of all-out mobilization of American technology and industrial capacity. All the Soviet invocations of the historical inevitability of a Communist triumph notwithstanding and contrary to the doomsday scenarios of our critics, time was on America's side.

Obviously Brezhnev believed that he could relieve his dilemma by increased economic ties with the West and thereby perhaps avoid the need for structural reform. But the measures under consideration were not sufficient to alleviate significantly the basic weaknesses of his system. Sooner or later, the Soviets were bound to encounter what would become Mikhail Gorbachev's insoluble quandary: the Soviet system could not survive without reform yet it had become too arteriosclerotic to survive the reform process itself.

To be sure, if the Soviet Union were permitted to amass military power without a decisive American response or if the United States were to tolerate creeping expansionism, the Soviets might yet convert their disadvantageous position into a strategic gain by sheer brute power. But that was like speculating whether a chess player, down two pieces, might yet win the match; while theoretically possible, success against a competent adversary is decidedly unlikely. And the Ford Administration (like Nixon's before it) had no intention of permitting the requisite lapses.

## In the Politburo Chambers

In October 1974, both sides at the negotiating table in Moscow realized that the existing Soviet-American relationship was hanging by a thread. Whereas the American delegation understood what was happening at home without being able to do anything about it, the Soviet leaders, having no experience with democratic practices, seemed nonplussed and confused. With most issues—except arms control—either stymied or running on their own tracks, there was nothing precise to negotiate other than SALT. That is probably why the dialogue turned more philosophical than any of my encounters with Soviet leaders.

On Thursday morning, October 24, after a very jovial greeting, Brezhnev opened the talks in the Politburo meeting room with an extended statement of Soviet concerns. Putting the interlocutor on the defensive at the outset was, of course, a staple of the Soviet negotiating style. But normally the list of grievances was an introduction to some specific demands. On this occasion, Brezhnev advanced no proposals; his theme amounted to a plaintive request for an explanation of American conduct:

> What I would like to say first is that from our very first meeting and until today, I believe that the U.S. side has no grounds to reproach us for any lacking in good faith to fulfill our obligations. And, this is something I relate not only to our agreements but also to our general line of policy and the official statements made both by myself and my colleagues. We have never made any statements in any way interfering in internal U.S. affairs. Even when there have been some complicated events, we have never exploited them.

Brezhnev contrasted Soviet restraint on Watergate with America's provocative actions and statements. Avoiding any direct criticism of President Ford, he objected strongly to Jackson's presentation of the MFN/Jewish emigration compromise. The Soviets, he noted, had accepted Nixon's conditions for settling their Lend-Lease debt in return for MFN status. Yet after the terms of the agreement were completed, Jackson had introduced entirely new and unrelated conditions into the ratification process designed to humiliate the Soviet Union:

> The import of this is that Jackson has won a great victory over the White House and that he has managed to extract certain concessions from the Soviet Union.

Jackson's figures regarding Jewish emigration from the Soviet Union, Brezhnev went on, had no basis in fact; he would supply me with the correct statistics on the number of applications for emigration. The upshot was that the Soviet Union now found itself in the humiliating position of being the only country in the world to have conditions attached to its MFN status. Instead of according equality, the new trade agreement confirmed America's discrimination against the Soviet Union:

> Regarding the Soviet Union, MFN would be accorded only
> as a special favor and only for eighteen months. Let me say
> frankly that we cannot accept that "gift" [hits table with
> hand]. We see it as a discriminatory practice that we cannot
> agree to. I wish to emphasize that!

Brezhnev's complaints were not confined to Congress. Both Nixon
and I, he said, had paid inadequate attention to his warning at San
Clemente in June 1973 that a Middle East war was imminent. Afterward he had thought that an understanding had been reached on a
joint approach to the Middle East problem only to find that we were
going off on our own, splitting the Arabs (in his view):

> You began your travels. You played upon countries to dis-
> unite them. I believe you have now convinced yourself that
> nothing will come from such attempts.

Brezhnev's next complaint concerned the slow pace of negotiations regarding the European Security Conference. If the United States
really wanted to speed up matters, he argued, "your friends would
act." He had a point. We were indeed stalling to induce Soviet restraint
on other issues—especially on the Middle East. The irony was that,
as more and more deadlocks developed on trade and arms control,
our incentive to procrastinate at the European Security Conference
increased proportionally. It was after all one of our last rapidly
diminishing assets in what had started out as an active policy of
linkage.

The range of Brezhnev's complaints demonstrated the precariousness of the overall relationship. Some of the irritants—such as the
Jackson-Vanik Amendment—were an outgrowth of America's domestic politics; others—such as our Middle East policy—of the administration's pursuit of a geopolitical strategy; still others—such as the
European Security Conference—reflected negotiating tactics.

I replied at comparable length. With regard to the Jackson statements, I could only reaffirm the position that I had already summarized to Ford in Gromyko's presence. Our understanding concerned
the specific rejection rate of no more than 1.6 percent as first given to
us by Gromyko and then reaffirmed by Dobrynin on behalf of Brezhnev. The sixty-thousand figure was Jackson's, not ours:

The administration has no other position. If there are no
other interferences [than the normal rejection rate], the administration has no right to any objections [to this Soviet
position].

With respect to the Middle East, I blamed it all on Gromyko,
sitting to Brezhnev's right. Soviet policies were indistinguishable from
the radical Arab agenda, I argued, and we were being asked to do the
dirty work of imposing them on Israel:

> Since there was no difference between that plan [the Soviets']
> and the Arab plan, why shouldn't we deal directly with the
> Arabs? Since they were all asking us the same thing. So we
> have always had great difficulty understanding what it is
> that the Soviet Union was adding to the discussion. On the
> substance it supported every Arab position, and on the tac-
> tics we were forced to impose it unilaterally on Israel.

In other words, unless the Soviet Union separated to at least some
extent from its Arab clients, the American policy designed to reduce
Soviet influence in the Middle East would continue.

Only with respect to the European Security Conference could I
give Brezhnev some comfort. I offered to become more active in the
negotiations with a view to concluding them within a year, provided
the Soviet Union cooperated in settling two issues: the so-called Basket
III, which established human rights as a formal element of European
security, and inclusion of the principle that Europe's borders could be
changed by peaceful means—a prerequisite for German reunification
and now recognized as such (see Chapter 21).

Possibly it was Brezhnev's emerging realization of how precarious
East-West relations had become that accounted for the mellowness
with which he concluded the meetings of October 24. Before dinner,
he took me aside to assure me that the Soviet Union had not encouraged the 1973 Middle East War and had had only a very short advance
knowledge of it. Since Soviet advisers had been expelled from Egypt in
1972, Moscow had had less than three days' warning of an impending
war. They could not tell us, Brezhnev alleged, for fear that we would
pass the information on to the Israelis and trigger an Israeli preemptive
attack, which would have destroyed the Soviet position in the Middle
East. However, the Soviets had "taken other measures" to put us on

notice—presumably the withdrawal of Soviet dependents from Syria and Egypt forty-eight hours before the war started. If it had been intended as a signal, we surely misinterpreted it at the time—an illustration of how preconceived notions shape policy—for we had simply excluded in our deliberation the possibility of an Arab attack on Israel.[6]

Brezhnev's extraordinary revelation was primarily designed to create the mood for a set of questions he would pose after our advisers joined us regarding America's long-range intentions:

> What does it mean, and how should we react to statements emanating from various U.S. officials, including some government leaders, that the United States must be second to none in terms of strength and only then will peace in the world be secured? [Dobrynin corrects the translation: "samii silnyee" means "strongest of all."] How are we to understand such statements? . . . Don't look for information in your briefs; it is something I thought to bring up. It is something I wanted to bring up, taking the occasion of this personal meeting.
>
> My second question is, since tomorrow we will be taking up the question of strategic arms: do you believe or admit of the possibility of atomic war between our two nations? Or the possibility of atomic war anywhere in the world, for instance in Europe or elsewhere? Hearing my question, you would be entitled to ask me my view. On that thought, I wish you pleasant dreams.

Philosophical discussions with Soviet leaders were very rare indeed; usually they preferred slogging their way through an agenda essentially geared to specific negotiating documents. On this occasion, however —which was never repeated—Brezhnev had actually provided an opportunity for a serious explanation of American strategic doctrine.

I began the next day's meeting with a lengthy, essentially conceptual discussion. The debate over a military establishment "second to none," I said, was less about superiority than it was about equality. Such slogans, I added, were not, however, at the heart of the emerging deadlock on arms control negotiations. The real difficulty was that, over the years, two strategic forces had emerged, each designed on the basis of its own purposes, which were quite different from each other.

The American strategic force was primarily useful for retaliation while the evolving Soviet force was consistent with the design for a first strike:

> The General Secretary has often referred to the number of warheads we have, but the General Secretary also knows that the vast majority of these warheads—nearly two thirds of them—are on submarines. He knows that the size of the warheads on the submarines is relatively small. And very small compared to the Soviet warheads. And finally the General Secretary knows that to coordinate an attack from submarines dispersed all over the ocean—to coordinate a plausible attack—is so difficult as to be virtually impossible. In fact, I think the General Secretary should understand that even the number of warheads on the submarines was in reaction to the Soviet program; they were developed when we wanted to be able to penetrate antiballistic missile defenses and we wanted to have enough warheads on the submarines to survive these defenses.

By contrast, I argued, the Soviet buildup was generating the capability to threaten our land-based forces. When Brezhnev insisted volubly that "we have no intention of attacking you," I replied that his intention was irrelevant:

> I'm not saying you have the intention, but you clearly have the capability. . . .
> . . . When we look at the Soviet force, we observe some disquieting phenomena. Your missiles are larger than ours; the warheads of each missile are larger than ours.
> . . . The design of your strategic forces is such that they represent a very grave threat to our land-based forces, whether you plan to use them that way or not.
> In this generation, say until 1981 or '82, you still don't have as many warheads as we do. But that's essentially irrelevant, because beyond a certain point there is no conceivable use you could have for them. But after 1981 or '82, you can multiply your number of warheads because you have this great throw-weight [missile payload].

My analysis did not postulate parallel approaches to strategic analysis or extend soothing reassurances of American intentions in the way arms control experts of a liberal administration would have done; if anything, it most closely resembled the views of the neoconservatives. Where I diverged from the conservative and neoconservative camps was in the conclusion. The logic of Jackson's position was to use arms control negotiations to force the Soviets to redesign their forces in the American image. We in the Ford (and Nixon) Administrations judged this to be unattainable (nor was it ever achieved by any successor administrations). Instead, I sought to induce Soviet restraint by warning that if a strategic stability was not achieved, a massive American buildup was inevitable. I argued:

> If we're in a situation of essentially unrestrained competition, then we protect ourselves against the dangers I've described to you. This is not for purposes of superiority but for the purpose of defense. We will then build much larger missiles, and probably larger numbers. And you remember, if you look back to the late 1950s, Mr. General Secretary, your predecessor made certain threats growing out of his somewhat impetuous nature. When we perceived that we might be threatened by a possible missile gap, we began a very large program of missile production which produced several thousand missiles in a few years.

Brezhnev neither contradicted nor confirmed my analysis. Rather he protested that the Soviet Union would not, under any circumstances, initiate nuclear war. In truth, looking about me, it was difficult to believe that these damaged survivors of Stalin's terror would ever bring themselves to embrace the risks and uncertainties inherent in an all-out nuclear assault on the United States—of which, moreover, they were so clearly in awe. Such impressions could not, however, allay our concerns about how the Soviets might react to technological and numerical trends ten years hence when their deployment of multiple warheads would be complete and a more adventurous group of leaders might rule from the Kremlin. I told Brezhnev as much:

> Do I believe in the possibility of atomic war between us? I do not believe, with the present forces, that a leader can make a rational decision for an all-out attack on the other.

. . . After all, in every war, the military plans of one or the other side turn out to be wrong. And in a thermonuclear war, a military leader would have to convince a political leader that missiles that have never been fired, whose accuracy is untested against real targets, would have to be fired against targets whose hardness is unknown, and be assured that the targets would not be launched on warning—and I think this requires a degree of confidence that could hardly be achieved.

On the other hand, it is conceivable that if local tensions continue and if local conflict between the United States and the Soviet Union develops, given the arsenals on both sides, such a war could develop, even without the intention. Because presumably neither side will let itself be defeated.

Brezhnev passionately rejected the hypothesis that nuclear war was even remotely possible:

If you were to address my question back to me, whether I believe in the possibility of atomic war between us, I would reply I do not believe in such a possibility. I would say that regardless of who heads the American administration, because it depends not on who leads a country but the people of a country. Because there are many people, including scientists, who know what such a war would mean and how many would die. So I don't admit the possibility of either side taking a decision to launch such a war, of the possibility of such a war.

What a paradoxical reversal of roles! The representative of a pragmatic society lacking a geopolitical tradition and confident of its ability to transcend history was arguing that the momentum of technology and strategy might produce a catastrophe regardless of personal intentions unless some steps were taken now. On the other hand, the General Secretary of a Communist system based on the doctrine that historical inevitability and material factors always overcame personal convictions was resting his case on the proposition that, whatever the mistakes of omission and commission, in the end the horror of nuclear war would cause leaders to resist the pressures of material factors.

## A Step Toward a Breakthrough

When we finally turned to SALT on the evening of October 25, the third day of my visit, philosophy was quickly submerged in the usual nitpicking over the level of nuclear weapons required for "equal security." The overriding concern of both sides was the same as it had been all along: to protect its existing strategic programs, all of which had been designed before arms control negotiations had even begun. In this sense, the key purpose of SALT was to set some limits within which competition might continue at a more predictable—and hence, less threatening—pace.

Ford had authorized me to reaffirm the option of offsetting asymmetries—trading a Soviet edge in launchers for an American advantage in warheads—put forward by Nixon during the late June summit. But in order to avoid another domestic controversy over what constitutes equality, Ford had instructed me to shift the dialogue to equal aggregates at a level of 2,500 launchers and 1,320 MIRVed missiles, as the Pentagon had been urging.

Brezhnev expressed astonishment that we were switching from the approach which Nixon and I had been urging on him only four months earlier. Once needling over this reversal was out of the way, we ran into the standard Soviet contention that the British and French nuclear forces should be included in our totals and that the Soviets were entitled to some "compensation" for our overseas bases from which fighter-bombers could reach deep into Soviet territory. Brezhnev reinforced that last point by having one of his generals illustrate with arrows on a huge map the likely attack routes from our overseas bases.

We decided to set that issue aside and concentrate first on establishing agreed ceilings. I proposed a ceiling of 1,320 MIRVed vehicles within a total of 2,200 launchers, including airplanes. Though I was authorized to settle for 2,500, I chose the number of 2,200 because it was closer to our planned total of 2,000 and required a Soviet reduction of 450 from their existing total of 2,650. Odd as it was, the MIRV number—which reflected exactly our planned program with two extra Trident submarines thrown in for safety—was accepted immediately and without question. Was it possible that the Soviet military's own plans were identical with ours? Or did the Soviet generals believe that they would not be able to reach that total within the projected ten-year duration of the agreement?

With respect to the overall ceiling of 2,200, Georgi Korniyenko, then chief of the American division of the Soviet Foreign Ministry, who kept score on numbers for the Soviet delegation, wondered how we would arrive at such a total. Under SALT I, he argued, we had been permitted only 1,640 missiles, and we did not have enough bombers to fill out the proposed force of 2,200. He had a point—it was why, from a strictly intellectual point of view, I preferred the offsetting asymmetries approach. Were we using SALT to justify a buildup, Korniyenko wondered. In fact, it was worse than that. The Pentagon was planning no numerical buildup, nor did it propose one in any subsequent administration. What we were about was to placate troublesome domestic constituencies.

Since I could not admit to this, I invented an argument for how we would reach the total of 2,200. Explaining that the new B-1 strategic bomber would soon be introduced into our forces (airplanes were not counted under SALT I), I magnanimously offered to "limit" the total of B-1s to 250 as our contribution to SALT. It was one of those free-floating "restraints" that could be tossed around in the never-never land of SALT because I knew, but the Soviets did not, that we were planning to build only 240. (In fact, in the more than two decades since then—even including the "hawkish" Reagan Administration— only 100 have been built because of congressional, technical, and doctrinal constraints.) Brezhnev pointed out that if the ceiling were set at 2,200, the Soviet Union would have to dismantle 200 modern missiles in addition to the 210 obsolescent ones it was already dismantling under SALT I. In the arcane world of SALT, this was an encouraging intervention because Brezhnev objected only to the number and not to the principle of equal numbers for both sides. My hunch was reinforced when the meeting with Brezhnev scheduled for the following morning was canceled with the argument that the Politburo was deliberating a new proposal.

Brezhnev presented the new Soviet scheme late on October 26, about twelve hours before we were scheduled to leave Moscow. On one of the rare occasions when the Soviet leaders had been paying attention to the explanations of their interlocutors, Brezhnev proposed a ten-year agreement, which, assuming that he and Ford would reach a breakthrough at Vladivostok, would end in 1985. An overall ceiling of 2,400 launchers would be established. The United States would agree not to build more than 2,200 launchers until one year before the expiration of the agreement. British and French nuclear forces would be included in the American totals once the overall ceiling was reached but not as part of the 2,200 interim ceiling—which, of course, meant that the "interim" ceiling was permanent.

The two sides were closing in on a major breakthrough. As a question of principle, I rejected the proposition that we count the nuclear forces of France and Britain in our total. For the sake of domestic tranquillity, I turned down the two-stage approach to the final overall numbers even though it was well suited to our actual program.

Still, the mantra of equivalence was bound to carry the day, and I felt reasonably certain that, in the end, Brezhnev would agree to it. Since I was scheduled to leave for India in less than twelve hours and there would be no time for another Politburo meeting, I proposed deferring the remaining issues until Vladivostok. In the meantime, Dobrynin and I would try to narrow the differences. I would not have left it open unless I had been convinced that Brezhnev would, in the end, concede the point.

That Brezhnev meant to settle at Vladivostok on terms close to ours was evident from the way in which he phrased his agreement to my proposal:

> I agree with you on one condition: that whatever amend-
> ments you make will not be in the nature of fundamental
> new proposals or new in principle. Because I don't want
> this forthcoming—this first—meeting with the President to
> begin with a dispute.

It seemed for a moment that, despite our domestic ferment, we were on the verge of reaching an agreement on SALT, and a schedule for concluding the European Security Conference had been sketched. Still, I had the uneasy feeling that Jackson and his allies would some-how manage to refuse to take yes for an answer on arms control. Brezhnev too seemed seized by a premonition of troubles to come and warned me in a gentle way (by Soviet standards) that there was a limit to Soviet forbearance toward our domestic debate:

> Please do not forget not only the substance of this discussion
> on missiles but also what we discussed on the first day. I
> know you have not forgotten, and won't discuss it anymore.
> I endeavored to set out our position as clearly as possible.

## Nuclear Condominium

Two events before we left Moscow brought home just how precarious the relationship remained despite all the bonhomie and progress on SALT: the first was an American rebuff Brezhnev inflicted upon himself, the second an embarrassment imposed on the American visitors by their country's domestic politics.

The rebuff to Brezhnev resulted from the General Secretary's attempt to pick up the thread of a private meeting with Nixon four months earlier during the summit in June 1974. On that occasion, Brezhnev had proposed that the two superpowers establish what would amount to nuclear tutelage over the rest of the world. A few days later, at a dinner Nixon had hosted at Spaso House, the American Embassy residence, the President called me over and, with Brezhnev sitting beside him, described the Soviet leader's proposal. In effect, it was that the United States and the Soviet Union should cooperate to quell the nuclear ambitions of any other country by agreeing to act together militarily against any country using nuclear weapons. Nixon called it an "interesting idea" to be explored further between me and Dobrynin or Gromyko.[7] Brezhnev's overture for this Soviet-American nuclear condominium revealed the extent of his concern over Moscow's looming isolation and of his eagerness to turn the diplomatic tables on Beijing.

Those who knew Nixon well would have understood that the dramatic mandate over dinner meant little—being as compatible with his congenital inability to refuse an interlocutor face to face as with any desire to pursue the subject. We had no conceivable incentive to jeopardize our still fragile and incipient relationship with China by entering into a heavy-handed deal with Moscow. I took no action and waited for Nixon to clarify his intentions. A few weeks later, Nixon resigned without having mentioned the subject again (nor did he ever discuss it with me in the twenty years left to him). Dobrynin, too, never returned to the subject. When I briefed Ford about the incident, I indicated my hope that Brezhnev's proposal had lapsed with Nixon's resignation.

I had underestimated Brezhnev's tenacity (or perhaps his naïveté). For now, on my last night in Moscow, he invited me to a private meeting in his Kremlin office just prior to the SALT discussions and returned to the subject. Only Foreign Minister Gromyko on the Soviet

side and Hal Sonnenfeldt on ours attended, together with the ubiquitous Viktor Sukhodrev as interpreter. To convey the full flavor of
Brezhnev's design, I will quote his version of his earlier conversation
with Nixon:

> Could we not give thought to the possibility of our two
> powers who possess for the foreseeable future immense
> strength, especially in the military realm, achieving a treaty
> or an agreement in some form, in the interest of all mankind,
> and bearing in mind the threat of nuclear weapons to all
> peoples, to the effect that, in the event of an attack on either
> of us by any third power—we could even name it—each
> side, in the interest of keeping the peace, would use military
> power in support of the other. This would also apply to
> allies—say an attack on the FRG [West Germany] or Italy
> —we would also come to the assistance of them. Surely this
> would be a warning against those tempted to use nuclear
> weapons against us or our allies.
>
> At the time, President Nixon indicated he considered it
> a very interesting idea and seemed to support the general
> concept underlying it. He added that he took interest in the
> idea and in another couple of months would be in a position
> to give a reply to my propositions. We did not go into greater
> detail and what I have said is in effect a quotation of that
> talk. I give you my word, and Sukhodrev [Brezhnev's inter-
> preter] is responsible with his life, that I never showed the
> memorandum of the conversation to anyone.

Given the ponderous nature of Soviet bureaucratic procedures (not
to mention taping mechanisms), Sukhodrev's life might well have been
on the line on the basis of that last statement. But no matter how
widely the proposal might be known in the Soviet hierarchy, its meaning was that the United States and Soviet Union would be obliged to
come to each other's assistance if either of them was involved in a war
with another nuclear power. Specifically, not only would we have to
side with the Soviet Union if it became involved in a war with China,
we would even have to do so should one of our own close allies, such
as Great Britain or France, use nuclear weapons against it in response
to a Soviet conventional attack.

The dialogue was given a bizarre twist when Brezhnev interrupted

YEARS OF RENEWAL

his confidential and solemn presentation with periodic and very futile attempts at making a toy artillery piece fire off a small explosive charge. The following captures the flavor:

> KISSINGER: I have never been shot at by the General Secretary.
> [Brezhnev trains the gun at Sonnenfeldt.]
> GROMYKO: You should train it at your own foreign minister and not frighten the Americans.
> [Brezhnev inserts a shell into the gun and pulls the lanyard. Nothing happens.]
> BREZHNEV: I have to ask Sadat for spares.*

When Brezhnev finally did succeed in eliciting a loud explosion, he interrupted the meeting to strut about the room like a prizefighter who had just scored a knockout.

In this atmosphere, at once conspiratorial and buffoonish, I was obliged to frame some response to Brezhnev's proposal. We could not possibly entertain it without destroying the Atlantic Alliance, ending our opening to China, and isolating ourselves vis-à-vis the rest of the world. Indeed, if Brezhnev was taken seriously, the only way any country could escape Soviet-American tutelage was to sever its alliance with a superpower; it would have been the ultimate recruiting device for membership in the Nonaligned Movement. I therefore confined myself to posing clarifying questions about the circumstances in which the agreement would apply. At the same time, it is not recommended diplomatic practice to turn down the head of the Soviet Communist Party in the Politburo meeting room in front of a senior colleague. I therefore took refuge in stalling by saying that the subject needed to be referred to the President (which happened to be true since I had not had a full discussion with Ford about it before leaving):

> It is an extremely far-reaching and comprehensive approach. I had told President Ford generally that there were discussions between you and President Nixon. I will discuss it with the President when I return and of course well before your meeting at Vladivostok.

---

* The Soviets, wounded by the decline of their position in Egypt, often made sarcastic comments at Anwar Sadat's expense. On another occasion, Gromyko called him a "paper camel."

It was difficult to know what to make of Brezhnev's overture. Gromyko was experienced enough to have realized that nothing could ever come of it. Unlike the usual Soviet procedure whereby subordinates ceaselessly chip away at resistance to a General Secretary's preferences, neither Gromyko nor Dobrynin ever discussed the subject unless Brezhnev was present and had himself taken the lead. My glacial response left no doubt—surely among professionals—that nothing would come of the proposal at Vladivostok either, which, as we shall see, did not keep Brezhnev from raising it there again—not once but twice.

Which was the real Brezhnev? A seeker after détente and normalized relations? Or a sly manipulator proposing global Soviet-American tutelage in order to ruin America's alliances and our relationship with China? Probably both were real and, on the occasion of our meeting, Brezhnev himself almost surely did not yet know which would dominate. Would a continuation of the relaxation of tensions have lured him into emphasizing domestic reform, absorbing Soviet energies on domestic matters, and, as Mikhail Gorbachev was to learn, revealing the incompatibility of the Soviet system with a modern global economy? Or would it have provided the maneuvering room for more aggressive policies? We will never know, though I reflect with some melancholy about our failure to explore the prospect. In the end, détente was frustrated by American domestic controversies and by Brezhnev's inability to resist the temptation to seek to exploit our domestic problems after the trade bill failed and SALT ran into the sand.

So it happened that the session in which Brezhnev foreshadowed the breakthrough on SALT was sandwiched on both ends by discussions which would ultimately undermine the East-West relationship: preceded by an offer of superpower nuclear tutelage attesting to Soviet global aspirations and followed by another private discussion initiated by the General Secretary, this one on the subject of the Jackson-Vanik Amendment attesting to America's domestic incoherence.

After the official farewells, Brezhnev took me aside for one more private chat. I should not misunderstand, he said, how strongly the Politburo felt about Jackson's conduct. Of the over one hundred nations eligible for MFN, the Soviet Union alone was being singled out for discriminatory treatment, not only in the way MFN status was being tied to its domestic practices but in the proviso for an annual review. Jackson, Brezhnev continued, had announced figures on emigration for which there was no basis whatsoever in anything Soviet leaders had said to us. The fact that, based on Soviet domestic legislation, no more than 1.6 percent of applicants would be rejected did not, however, imply a commitment to guarantee a specific number of emigrants. Did Jackson want the Soviet Union to start expelling some of its citizens in order to meet targets set by the American Congress, Brezhnev asked. Was Jackson's purpose to demonstrate that he had bullied the Soviets into yielding on a subject universally recognized as a matter of a country's own domestic legislation?

The other shoe dropped the next morning, October 27. On the way to the airport, Gromyko handed me a letter dated the previous day. It was a strange document, written not on Foreign Ministry stationery but on plain brownish paper, almost as if it were a personal letter. In it, Gromyko formally rejected the substance of the exchange of correspondence with Jackson which had been released at the White House. Reminding me that the Soviet leadership had simply responded to my "wishes" to clarify practices related entirely to "the internal competence of our state," Gromyko "resolutely" rejected any interpretation that appeared as "some kind of assurance and almost pledge" and decried that "even some sort of figures are being mentioned regarding the supposed number. . . ."[8]

What I had been warning about for nearly two years had finally happened. When Ford took office, the trade bill was ready for approval, and a level of Jewish emigration of 45,000 had been promised by Gromyko and confirmed by Brezhnev. Now the Soviets were formally, and in writing, dissociating themselves from what could only have succeeded as a tacit understanding. Congressional pressures had obliged us to try to bridge the gap with a complex formula at the margin of the attainable. Jackson's determination to turn this already strained formula into a binding commitment and to demonstrate a method superior to the administration's for dealing with the Soviets was on the verge of wrecking the trade bill and stifling Jewish emigration.

Our departure from Moscow on the morning of October 27 may or may not have been symbolic. My wife, Nancy's, shoes had been packed by mistake and sent ahead with the luggage to the airplane. My executive assistant, L. Paul "Jerry" Bremer, gallantly stepped into the breach and let her use his shoes until we caught up with our luggage on the airplane. I can only imagine what our Soviet hosts at the airport made of the fact that my usually so elegant wife was wearing men's shoes and that one of my aides was in stocking feet. Our critics had fretted that we might lose our shirts in Moscow—but our shoes?

# 10

# VLADIVOSTOK AND THE CRISIS IN AMERICAN-SOVIET RELATIONS

## Arrival in Vladivostok

Ford set out for Vladivostok from Seoul on November 23. Because the Soviet Union did not then recognize South Korea, *Air Force One* had to double back to Tokyo, where we picked up our Soviet navigator. After the stately formality of Japan and the tumultuous reception in South Korea, the arrival in the Soviet Union seemed strikingly barren and even somewhat offhand.

*Air Force One* landed at a military air base some fifty miles from Vladivostok. The day before, a severe blizzard had raised doubts as to whether we would be able to land. We later learned that our hosts had considered shifting the venue to Khabarovsk—a mind-boggling prospect technically as well as politically: technically because improvising a summit in a Siberian city seven time zones from Moscow had the potential of turning chaotic; politically because, with the Chinese border literally at the outskirts of Khabarovsk along the Ussuri River, a Soviet-American summit there would surely have been interpreted in Beijing as a provocative flaunting of superpower collusion. Though we were spared this embarrassment, I learned in Beijing a few days later that the Chinese hardly considered the choice of Vladivostok much of an improvement (see Chapter 28).

With deep snow covering the reinforced shelters of the Soviet combat air base, nothing was visible across the white expanse except a few dark shapes standing at the edge of a wooden grandstand that turned out to be the Soviet welcoming party. Owing to the biting cold, the original plan of holding an arrival ceremony with a march-past of crack troops was abandoned. Brezhnev made up in boisterousness what was lacking in ceremony and hustled us off to a train bound for Okeanskaya, a resort town about ten miles from Vladivostok.

The train's extravagantly heavy appointment lent it the feel of some relic from the days of the tsars.[*1] One would not have been surprised had tea been served by some long-bearded figure clad in Russian folk dress and bearing a silver samovar. We chugged along the snow-covered plains, bounded on one side by a chain of low hills. When our Soviet hosts told us that the crest of some of these hills represented the border with China and that clashes between Soviet and Chinese forces had taken place there in 1969, it conferred on the journey some of the claustrophobic atmosphere I used to feel in pre-1967 Israel where one was also rarely out of sight of some contested border.

The feeling of vague paranoia inspired by the proximity of China's vastness surfaced again when, at the end of the visit, Brezhnev took our party on a tour of Vladivostok. It was then still closed to foreigners and, it being a Sunday, the town seemed more sedate than activist. Physically it resembled a Central European city plunked down at the edge of Asia. Populated almost entirely by Europeans, Vladivostok with its hills and water was attractive in the way San Francisco is and bore little resemblance to the teeming, hyperactive metropolises of Japan and Korea which Ford had just been visiting. The tsars' purpose in creating the city in the first place had been as a sally port for the Russian empire into Asia. For the Soviet Union, the danger was that outposts always run the risk of turning into besieged enclaves.

On the train, Ford and I were ushered into the dining car, where we sat around a table draped in a heavy white tablecloth: Brezhnev, Foreign Minister Andrei Gromyko, Ambassador Anatoly Dobrynin, and Viktor Sukhodrev, the Soviet crack interpreter, sat on one side; Ford, our ambassador to the Soviet Union, Walter Stoessel, and I on the other, together with our official interpreter, the extremely skillful Alex Akalovsky. Having an American interpreter present was a radical departure from the days of Nixon, who was convinced that State Department interpreters would leak his conversations.

Gerald Ford was face-to-face at last with Leonid Brezhnev, about

---

* I am indebted to William Hyland, my longtime associate both on the NSC and at the State Department on Soviet affairs, for his recollections of these and other trips on which he accompanied me.

whom he had read so voluminously. In my briefing memorandum for the summit, I had offered the following appraisal of Brezhnev:

> Basically, he is not very competent, is inclined to impatience with details, and is often poorly prepared (not to say misinformed). He covers these traits by various histrionics and diversions, though at bottom he is a tough, ruthless opponent, not given to paying off for mere good will.
>
> He will be wary of you because he does not know you, and also because he has a healthy, instinctive respect for the power of the US and of your office.
>
> Your best approach is to lay out frankly and soberly our position and let him absorb it.
>
> He may want to get you alone for an intimate chat, in which he will sincerely pledge himself to good relations; but there will be overtones of condominium; in effect, he will be testing to see whether you show any interest in such a relationship—which, in practice, is directed against China.

Ford had exhibited no insecurity while preparing for the trip, nor did he see now any need to depart from his natural style just because he found himself at the eastern limit of Siberia. Brezhnev opened the conversation in the joshing manner already quite familiar to me. He commented on Finnish President Urho Kekkonen's proclivity for coffee, a beverage Brezhnev purported to hate, and on the late Egyptian President Nasser's tendency to confuse publicity with diplomacy. As the pièce de résistance, he informed Ford that Gromyko, the usual butt of Brezhnev's jokes, had invented diplomatic protocol at the Congress of Vienna, where he had been present in his previous incarnation as tsar. Without missing a beat, Gromyko replied that Brezhnev had the title wrong and that he had been present at the Congress of Vienna as merely an observer. Still, Brezhnev had the last word: "as one of those nonaligned ones."

Ford's instinct, especially with people he was meeting for the first time, was to steer the conversation toward something practical. In this case, he inquired into the agricultural potential of the territory we were traversing. Brezhnev had not been prepared for this question and was not too well informed about agriculture in the Soviet Union's maritime provinces. After some desultory exchanges about the temperatures suitable for agriculture (Siberia's did not rank high), Ford came straight to the point and asked Brezhnev how he wished to proceed with respect to the agenda agreed in Moscow.

Accustomed to Nixon's elliptical approach, Brezhnev was at first thrown off stride but quickly recovered and put forward what he had clearly planned as his opening statement for the first plenary session. It turned out to be the standard Soviet recital of international issues such as arms control, the Middle East, and the European Security Conference. What his presentation lacked in specificity, Brezhnev made up in emotion:

> Let us not speak as diplomats but as human beings. Both you and I fought in World War II. That war was child's play as compared to nuclear war.

Ford briefly fell in with this theme, though, on the whole, somewhat perfunctorily. Concurring with his host that the consequences of a nuclear war would indeed be "unbelievable," Ford stated that his foreign policy would be basically a continuation of Nixon's.

Brezhnev made one more stab at a general discourse:

> Off the record, I am of the opinion that we have proceeded incorrectly, along a wrong course. We have not achieved any real limitation, and in fact we have been spurring the arms race further and further. That is wrong. Tomorrow science can present us with inventions we cannot even imagine today, and I just don't know how much farther we can go in building up so-called security. This does not mean that I am not prepared to discuss numbers or levels, but I do want to say that this arms race is fraught with great danger. . . . The people don't know all the details, otherwise they would really give us hell. We are spending billions on all these things, billions that would be much better spent for the benefit of the people.

It was a good point, in many ways at the heart of the Cold War dilemma: the arms race was insoluble without a measure of confidence, but the ideological gulf was so great that both sides were defining security only in technological terms which evoked as many perplexities as solutions, driving them back to protecting their basic strategic programs. It was a pity that we were not free to explore where

Brezhnev's ruminations might have led him and that soon after he became too disabled for creative diplomacy. In any event, on the train in Siberia en route to Okeanskaya, Ford felt that he had not come this far to discuss the general philosophy of arms control. Some agreement had to precede more sweeping measures:

> I am interested, Mr. General Secretary, in your statesmanlike approach to this problem and I think we could talk in this broader context at a later time. But I believe it important at this meeting to discuss these issues in specific terms and step by step. I think our proposal and your counterproposal could be a good basis for continuing the legacy of the 1972 agreement.

There being nothing further of substance to discuss until a plenary session, the Soviets reverted to joshing. Gromyko observed that Senator Walter Mondale had given up his presidential aspirations for 1976 because Brezhnev had refused to receive him in Moscow. Brezhnev shot back that he had done so because he preferred Henry Jackson. Using the Soviet dislike of Jackson as a pressure point, Ford made another stab at getting back to the subject at hand:

> In our system, people such as Senator Jackson have the right to disagree, but I believe the American people wish us to pursue our present course. If we can agree in this '75–'76 period, there will be better chances for continuing our policy until 1980.

Nixon had always emphasized his close personal relations with Brezhnev, not because he had any illusions about Soviet purposes but as a means of discomfiting his critics at home by demonstrating the respect felt for him abroad. Ford, being far more secure, felt no such compulsion to charm foreign leaders or to feign affection which he did not feel.

Our domicile in Okeanskaya for the next two days turned out to be a sanitorium for vacationing workers and servicemen (though some wags in our party speculated that it actually served as a lunatic asylum). It consisted of a park, the central feature of which was a large stone building surrounded by small cottages built of wood. One of these was assigned to me and, though far from elegant, it offered serviceable protection against the most penetrating cold I have ever experienced. An antediluvian potbellied stove threw off occasional sparks and inspired the concern that the entire structure might be made to go up in flames if one provoked our Soviet hosts. Ford, being housed in the sole stone building, was at least spared that particular anxiety.

## First Plenary Meeting

The plenary session was held in the winter garden of that austere stone building, the general grimness of which was relieved by the flowers which filled the glass-enclosed end of the large room. Dobrynin reports in his memoirs that Brezhnev had a "seizure" in his private compartment on the train after the introductory meeting with Ford and had been urged by his doctors to postpone negotiations set to begin that evening. If so, we saw no signs of flagging energy.[2]

It was the only time in Ford's presidency that he would be representing a united position of his government on SALT. Both Schlesinger and I had endorsed the concept of equal numbers for both sides, for which the technical term was "equal aggregates." In a memorandum written in my capacity as National Security Adviser, I nevertheless had warned Ford that, even should an agreement be reached, the domestic attack on SALT would continue: the conservatives would shift their pressures from equal aggregates to equal throw-weight, negotiable, if at all, only after a big American buildup, which the just elected McGovernite Congress would surely resist. And liberals would object to the principle of the increase in American forces implicit in the equal aggregates proposal. Despite these warnings, I had recommended that we proceed for the following reasons:

> (1) Politically, if we can achieve a breakthrough in SALT, it is insurance against a deterioration of the entire relationship, at a time when (a) we may face a possible confrontation in the Middle East, and (b) in a period when our bargaining leverage is not necessarily going to grow without massive budgetary increases.
>
> (2) With a new Congress, in a pre-election period, in the face of energy-related economic difficulties and inflationary pressures, our chances of appropriating and sustaining funds

for new systems beyond those already envisaged are not very good, particularly if the proposal seemed to offer a basis for agreement. . . .

(3) The prospective agreement has the advantage that it is premised on carrying out the Trident and B-1 programs, thus improving the chances for their survival in Congress. . . .

Arms control had come a long way from its original intention when it became a means to make possible new strategic programs rather than to limit them.

Schlesinger's support was more grudging and complicated, but the bottom line was that he would support an agreement with equal aggregates of 2,400 launchers and 1,320 MIRVs. There were enough technical caveats to provide the loophole by which to join our critics later but, for the moment, Ford had the necessary backing to fend off the domestic assaults.

The formal meetings began at 6:15 P.M. Brezhnev, plying his guests with sandwiches, cakes, and tea, repeated a shortened version of his philosophical presentation on the train, whereupon the discussion moved directly to arms control.

The resulting dialogue was somewhat like a Kabuki play—extremely stylized with a near-traditional script and a foreordained outcome, the chief difference being that the psychology of the actors was precarious, and they felt free to change the last act. The outcome was in a way predetermined because Brezhnev had conceded the principle of equal aggregates in Moscow and was unlikely to have the President come all the way to Vladivostok to let him fail over such issues as what was to be counted in the equal aggregates. On the other hand, Brezhnev might not be able to sell the necessary concessions to his Politburo because we were bringing no modification of our position with us. To see how a probable result is navigated through a summit while avoiding dangerous shoals, some discussion of the ebb and flow of the negotiation may be of interest.

Gerald Ford was a new experience for the Soviets and did not follow the script of his predecessor. Nixon, bored by details—especially the technical aspects of SALT—would have fallen in with Brezhnev's overall approach, put forward some general strategic and political propositions, and then waited until Brezhnev made a specific proposal. At that point, Nixon would have turned the details over to Gromyko and me. Ford, by contrast, came straight to the point and conducted much of the technical discussion himself. Major decisions were awaiting him, he noted not without an element of menace, with respect to the level of the defense budget, and these would be affected by whether the summit was successful.

The implicit threat was something of a bluff because the budget process for the next year was, for all practical purposes, nearly completed, and our overriding concern was that the new McGovernite Congress would cut our requests; raising them was a fantasy. Ford went on to emphasize the importance of basing any new agreement on "equivalence," which was his indirect way of rejecting Brezhnev's last proposal to me in Moscow that the Soviets be permitted to retain an edge of 200 missiles until the last eighteen months of the agreement. (It was an entirely theological argument, since the Joint Chiefs had no plan or means to reach the proposed totals of 2,400 at any point.)

Brezhnev responded by charging that we had stiffened our terms. Gromyko weighed in with the standard Soviet argument that American forward-based aircraft had to be counted as strategic weapons. Both Soviet leaders repeated their demand that the British and French nuclear forces be included in the proposed 2,400 total—in effect reinstating the original Soviet proposal that they be given a numerical advantage in launchers vis-à-vis the United States. Brezhnev returned to the charge by claiming—correctly—that, due to the Soviets' late start, the United States would have a numerical advantage in MIRVs until well into the 1980s no matter what numbers were written down.

The leaders next found themselves in the never-never land of what constituted strategic modernization. Heads of state rarely have the time or the technical expertise for so abstruse a topic. And Brezhnev raised an especially complex technical issue: SALT I had permitted existing silos to be enlarged by 15 percent and that, according to Brezhnev, gave the United States an advantage. Our Minuteman silos having been designed with more extra space than those of the Soviets, this additional volume, if added to the allowed 15 percent increase in missile volume, would give the United States some unspecified "advantage"—presumably that we could increase the size of our follow-on missiles by a larger percentage than what was granted to the Soviets. Brezhnev offered no specific proposal to remedy this presumed "inequality" and seemed content with having demonstrated his Job-like forbearance in the pursuit of peace.

The discussion soon trailed off, partly because Brezhnev simply did not know what he was talking about. Dobrynin and Georgi Korniyenko, the chief of the American division of the Soviet Foreign Ministry, kept trying to explain the facts to their somewhat baffled boss in whispers which could be overheard by the Russian speakers in our delegation. Finally, General Mikhail Kozlov of the Soviet General Staff drew a diagram for Brezhnev, showing that a 15 percent enlargement of silos was sufficient for Soviet modernization plans.

Actually Brezhnev had a point, though it was not the one he thought he was making. The modernization provisions of SALT did give the United States every opportunity to reduce the alleged Soviet advantage in throw-weight. They were no obstacle to placing a much larger missile than the Minuteman III in existing silos (and, had we increased the silos to the limits permitted by SALT I, we could have produced a truly heavy missile). Either course would enable us to multiply the number of warheads carried by each launcher or to enhance the destructive capability of each warhead; in fact, we had the capacity to do both simultaneously. In short, we had the unilateral capacity to close any throw-weight gap we considered strategically significant. Yet the Pentagon never requested a missile heavier than the MX, the follow-on to the Minuteman (which required no enlargement of the silo). Nor was I ever told of so much as a design for a heavy missile being put forward by the Defense Department in *any* successor administration. The Pentagon, whatever its rhetoric, in practice seemed content with the much maligned SALT I program.

Corrected by his own advisers, Brezhnev retreated to his pet scheme of nuclear condominium between the United States and the Soviet Union:

> I have another suggestion. You should convince Dr. Kissinger that we should become allies in the field of nuclear weapons, and then everything else would fall into place. Then we could make a concession and sign the agreement not here but in Washington. Then there would be no problem about nuclear weapons since we would be allies and our respective allies would also be reassured.

We, however, were determined to avoid any impression of a Soviet-American condominium, even one presented in utopian garb. Ford dodged Brezhnev's hint:

> Let's do it step by step. We are already cooperating in many areas and are doing so even in space. So we never know where we might go.

By now in full retreat toward equal aggregates, Brezhnev proposed a ceiling of 2,400 launchers for ten years, accompanied by an American side letter promising that we would not exceed 2,200 before 1983—in effect the same proposal he had made to me in Moscow except that the American limit would be secret and not public. Ford pointed out that public opinion would not stand for the disparity and that a side letter might not bind a successor. Brezhnev offered a simple solution: "President Ford should simply stay in office; why should he go?" That remark set off another flurry of whispers on the Soviet side as Gromyko explained to his chief that American Presidents are barred from serving more than two terms.

To provide an incentive for the Soviets' acceptance of equal aggregates and giving up on "compensation" for overseas bases, Ford offered to stop basing missile-carrying submarines at Rota, Spain, after 1983. Like many SALT provisions, this merely formalized existing American plans, since, by 1983, longer-range missiles on new Poseidon and Trident submarines would make forward bases for submarines unnecessary.

Brezhnev next raised a question—already put to me in Moscow by Korniyenko—that went to the heart of the gap between our defense planning and our SALT position, the latter heavily influenced by domestic politics: how could we possibly reach a level of 2,400 launchers without building new silos, which was barred by SALT I? I explained that Trident submarines carried twenty-four missiles instead of the sixteen on Polaris boats. This could produce over three hundred additional missiles, and we would build B-1 bombers to reach the agreed totals. (This was a negotiating argument; the actual program then and for the next twenty years was much lower.)

At this point, around 9:30 P.M., Brezhnev asked for a recess, which lasted quite some time. We subsequently learned that the reason for it had been a dispute on the telephone between Brezhnev and Soviet Defense Minister Andrei Grechko, who objected to conceding the issue of forward-based systems but was overruled by Brezhnev.[3] The moment for a breakthrough had arrived. In Brezhnev's own words:

> Well, Mr. President, what can we do? I fully appreciate the fact that your internal situation differs from ours, but I would also be asked questions, such as why there is no equal degree of security. So let's do it this way—we've had a tranquil discussion and obviously we can't settle everything in two days. What we should do, however, is attempt to

agree in principle on the following: 2,400 launchers for you
and 2,400 for us; 1,320 MIRVed missiles for you and 1,320
MIRVed missiles for us.

Both Ford and I asked Brezhnev to confirm that there would be no
side letters, no secret understandings, and that no allied forces would
be counted. Brezhnev replied:

Under this proposal, there would be no need for a letter,
because the ceiling could be reached at any time until 1985.
Both you and we will reach the levels of 2,400 and 1,320
during that period. So you can return and report to your
people that you have reached agreement on the basis of full
equality.

The scheduled formal dinner had long since been abandoned, and
talks had continued over sandwiches. Except for the occasional interruptions to enable Brezhnev to consult with Moscow, the meeting
lasted for six hours, until 12:35 A.M.

Ford and the American delegation were elated. Ford's first decision
regarding arms control had simplified the last proposal made by Nixon
to render it more compatible with the public mood in Washington.
Brezhnev had settled for the equal numbers across the board that the
Pentagon had been urging and at the very level proposed by Ford. We
had made no significant concession. Before giving his final approval,
Ford reviewed the bidding with his advisers. To frustrate Soviet listening devices, seven of us—the President, Helmut Sonnenfeldt, Brent
Scowcroft, William Hyland, Jan Lodal (our systems analyst), Ambassador Stoessel, and I—walked in circles around the garden in a cold
none of us had ever thought possible. Hyland argued that Brezhnev
having retreated relatively easily, we should attempt to extract one
more concession. In Moscow, Brezhnev had told me that the Soviet
Union intended to install MIRVs on only 180 of its 280 heavy missiles
(the SS-18s). Hyland argued that we should try to convert this unilateral assurance into a part of the SALT agreement.

In the sessions starting shortly after 10:00 A.M. the next morning,
Sunday, November 24, Ford attempted this. Gromyko, who undoubtedly thought that his chief had already gone quite far enough the night
before, took over the dialogue. He was hardly the ideal interlocutor
for achieving an essentially unilateral concession. Professional to the

core, Gromyko sought to extract an American concession in return. He would agree, he said, to a limit of 180 MIRVed missiles, provided we accepted a ceiling of 2,200 launchers for the United States until 1983.

The dialogue showed how essentially theological the SALT debate had become. Gromyko was offering to limit the MIRVing of Soviet missiles to a level the Soviet Union could probably not reach by 1985 in return for a limit on American missiles until 1983 for which we had no plan. We would have traded 200 missiles we never intended to build for 1,000 warheads (assuming that each SS-18 carried ten warheads) the Soviets never intended to deploy. This was confirmed when our sharp-eared Sovietologists heard Brezhnev whispering to Gromyko that our proposal, after all, reflected the existing Soviet program.

Arms control had taken so much time that there was very little opportunity to discuss other issues. Brezhnev repeated the standard Soviet line on the Middle East: that Israel should return to the 1967 borders, that the United States and the Soviet Union should guarantee these borders, and that the Geneva Conference should be reconvened as soon as possible to achieve those objectives. Ford's reply was equally familiar: he agreed to the desirability of ultimately reconvening the Geneva Conference and suggested that Dobrynin and I discuss the modalities. Brezhnev had to know that this amounted to a continuation of our stalling tactics and of our unilateral management of the peace process for at least one more round.

Ford proved more forthcoming with respect to the European Security Conference. In his approaching talks with German Chancellor Helmut Schmidt and French President Valéry Giscard d'Estaing in December, he said he would support a summit for later in 1975, provided he could hold out the prospect of progress on the clause allowing a peaceful change of European borders.

The issues of Jewish emigration and Most Favored Nation status for the Soviet Union were mentioned only in the context of repeating the existing understandings. Brezhnev never referred to Gromyko's letter that had been handed to me in Moscow during my October trip, reinforcing our belief that it had been essentially for the record. Ford summed up his understanding of where matters stood:

> Unfortunately, one of the members of the Senate mentioned some figure neither you nor I had agreed to. I want to assure you that I did not authorize any figures, because in our exchanges no figures had been mentioned. We only proceed

on the basis of three principles. One, that there will be no
limit on applications; two, that there will be no refusal except for security reasons; and three, that there will be no
prosecution of applicants. But we do not assume any specific
figure.

Brezhnev confirmed Ford's summary: "No one is being punished, detained, or harassed, and no tax is being levied." But he emphasized—
as he had in Moscow—that, since the 1973 Middle East War, the
number of applications for emigration to Israel had dropped significantly.

At a private meeting including Brezhnev, Gromyko, Dobrynin, and
a personal assistant to Brezhnev on the Soviet side and Ford, myself,
Brent Scowcroft, and Ambassador Stoessel on the American, Brezhnev
returned to his pet project of a nuclear condominium of the superpowers. Since my Moscow trip, Brezhnev had refined his proposal to include a pledge by the superpowers not to use nuclear weapons against
each other and to conclude a de facto alliance against any third country using nuclear weapons. Ford asked some clarifying questions and
then referred the subject to Dobrynin and me for further exploration.
Neither of us ever took it up again.

Our primary goal at Vladivostok had been to preserve East-West
relations in a period of severe American domestic turmoil and attacks
on détente. Neither side had any illusion that an agreement in principle
would do more than create a ceiling for an arms race which had
become essentially qualitative. Yet we told ourselves that it was an
important first step toward reductions and more sophisticated agreements. And it preserved a continuing dialogue, leaving open the possibility that a long period of peace might gradually alter Soviet purposes
and perhaps even the nature of the Soviet system. Each leader for
his own reason had striven to ensure a cooperative atmosphere.
When Ford and Brezhnev parted, both were confident that they had
achieved their objective of creating a new basis for American-Soviet
relations.[4]

## The Aftermath of Vladivostok: Détente Under Stress

On the way home, Ford's delegation was exuberant. The President
could rightly take credit for having developed an American position which—at least for the moment—seemed to have stemmed the

infighting between the State and Defense Departments. A comparison of the opening negotiating positions of the two sides showed that it was the Soviets who had made almost all the concessions. Brezhnev said no less on parting when he told Ford that he had done his utmost to enable the President to "return home with achievements no less important than those Mr. Nixon had brought back."

The jubilant mood on *Air Force One* was reflected in a boast by Ron Nessen, Ford's press secretary, that his President had negotiated in three months what Nixon had failed to achieve in five years. It was one of those silly statements of which press secretaries unburden themselves when they come to believe in their own pretense that their boss's standing in history is determined (or even affected) by their briefings. I was in no position to curb Nessen's exuberance because I was by then en route to Beijing to brief the Chinese leaders.

Our elation turned out to be misplaced. For the front lines of the détente debate in Washington were manned by dedicated men and women not about to modify their conviction that agreement with the Soviets was more dangerous than stalemate even after a successful summit. Determined to end détente, they opposed the fact of an agreement more than its content.

Once back in Washington, Ford was assailed by the same coalition which had been harassing East-West policy prior to the summit. Liberals derided Vladivostok as arms buildup rather than arms control. They objected to a ceiling higher than the existing program. The Arms Control Association criticized its "serious shortcomings";[5] a leading pioneer of arms control theory and practice, George Rathjens, told two of my associates that he would have preferred deadlock to the agreement reached at Vladivostok.[6] The *New York Times* produced a sour editorial on November 29 that there was "little reason to cheer about" the Vladivostok agreement and raising a whole host of questions that it claimed required close congressional scrutiny. An essentially time-wasting *Times* suggestion was that Congress should ask Ford to return "to the conference table to seek more meaningful arms control."[7] What the *Times* really wanted was to drag SALT into another presidential campaign. Writing in the *Times* a week later, the venerable James Reston suggested that the details of the accord were "still extremely vague" and that "the facts released so far raise some troubling questions."[8]

The *Washington Post,* which had started out on a less hostile note, fell in with the prevailing skepticism after a few days by echoing the conservative charge that the agreement "threatened" American strategic forces because it permitted the Soviets an excessive number of warheads.[9] The *Post* was silent, however, with respect to the analysis by which it had reached this incorrect conclusion. For a decade, we would possess more warheads than the Soviets while only a third of our strategic forces was land-based as against 90 percent of the Soviets'.

Paradoxically, Ford's success at Vladivostok shifted the arms control debate to the subject of reductions—heretofore a relatively minor theme. Jackson and his staff, as usual, took the lead. Now that the equal numbers so insistently demanded had been achieved, reductions became the new buzzword. This had two components: some of the traditional arms control advocates were pressing for lower numbers simply on the ground that any reduction of nuclear weapons decreased the threat to humanity. Strictly speaking, this was not necessarily true. For at the existing level of warheads, even reductions of 50 percent would not significantly affect the capacity of both sides to destroy the civilian life of the adversary and, unless coupled with many other restrictions, might actually enhance the capacity for a first strike by reducing the number of targets and making an attack more calculable.

Jackson appealed to this essentially liberal group by proposing that the Vladivostok ceiling be reduced to 1,700. He was asking the Soviet Union to reduce its strategic forces by a third in return for a less than 10 percent reduction of ours and at a time when he and his allies were eliminating trade and credit which could have served as Soviet incentives. Perhaps sensing the intellectual inadequacy of this approach, opponents of SALT now came up with a more sophisticated version of the reduction scheme which emphasized equal throw-weight.

This was conceptually better but nearly equally unachievable in the short term. Since Soviet missiles were larger than ours, albeit by our own choice, each of their weapons was able to carry a greater payload. Once equality was defined as a means to achieve equal throw-weight, a deadlock was certain. Of course, we could have closed the throw-weight gap by replacing the Minuteman III with MXs, which would have been quite permissible under Vladivostok ceilings, and, in the process, made the Soviet strategic forces far more vulnerable than ours. I had posed the challenge as follows at the October 7 NSC meeting:

> The only way we can get the Soviets to reduce significantly
> would be to stonewall the negotiations and kick off a big

U.S. program. They have to see we will go up and not just
hear us say it.

But Jackson and other critics knew that Congress would never agree
and, in fact, no administration ever made the attempt.

Thus, in practice, what the reduction proposal came down to was
to leave the Soviets with two choices, both of which they were bound
to reject. They could either reduce the number of their missiles, giving
us a huge numerical advantage, or they needed to redesign their entire
strategic force to mirror our own design. The essence of the bargain
being proposed was freedom for our existing American programs and
massive constraints on those of the Soviets. And even granting the
merits of the throw-weight argument, the critics failed to explain why
the Vladivostok agreement that had established an equal baseline
might not prove a useful first step in that direction. In the process, we
ran the risk of the worst of all worlds: no constraint on Soviet programs and no significant augmentation of our own.

The administration did not challenge the long-range importance
of throw-weight. Had Jackson shown even the slightest willingness to
cooperate, we would surely have built it into follow-on negotiations
once a baseline had been established. But it was not necessary to wreck
the Vladivostok agreement to achieve this end.

Procrastination became the critics' new strategy. One means of
stalling implementation of the Vladivostok agreement was the demand
that a Soviet medium-range supersonic bomber—which NATO called
the Backfire—be counted in the Soviet totals. Allegedly, if refueled, it
could reach the United States from Soviet territory (as could, of course,
almost any airplane if it was refueled often enough). As late as the
NSC meeting of October 7, Secretary of Defense James Schlesinger
and the Pentagon had described the Backfire as a marginal strategic
weapon, to be brought up only as a counter to the Soviet demand for
compensation for our overseas bases. As soon as the Soviets dropped
their demand for "compensation," however, appetites grew, and we
found ourselves being pressed to turn a bargaining ploy into a make-
or-break position.

Finding ourselves under attack by our familiar critics as well as by
those who, on the basis of their advocacy of arms control, we had
expected to be our allies, Ford and I watched with dismay as the
Vladivostok agreement dissolved before our eyes. Schlesinger had sent
a warm telegram to *Air Force One,* congratulating Ford on the negotia-

tions. But once Jackson entered the fray, Schlesinger fell silent. In the Senate, Edward Kennedy, Walter Mondale, and Charles Mathias sponsored a resolution supporting Vladivostok but coupled it with a proposal for early negotiated reductions. The only way to obtain additional reductions, however, would have been to threaten a buildup of our strategic forces—as Ford had done at Vladivostok and I at Moscow (and as Ronald Reagan later accomplished). In reply to a question at a press conference as to how I would react to pressure for further reductions, I replied: "The only way we could plausibly have achieved lower numbers is to begin building up our strategic forces dramatically in order to produce an incentive to reduce numbers on the other side."[10] The domestic dilemma faced by Ford was that the Senators supporting Vladivostok were generally in favor of cutting the defense budget, while those who favored an increase in the defense budget also opposed Vladivostok.

As the debate went on and on, its cumulative impact transformed Vladivostok from a spur to improving Soviet-American relations into a further obstacle to them. At Vladivostok, Ford had invited Brezhnev to visit the United States in 1975 for the purpose of signing the new agreement. It became clear almost immediately that this could not happen, indeed that the entire SALT process was floundering and might even collapse.

That realization must have been especially difficult for Brezhnev, who had made most of the concessions precisely to give impetus to Soviet-American relations. No doubt the various advisers in Moscow who had resisted his concessions at Vladivostok were now reminding him of their earlier misgivings. We did not learn until later that, at this very moment, Brezhnev was convalescing from another stroke he had suffered en route to Mongolia from Vladivostok, further impairing his ability to dominate the discussions inevitably taking place in Moscow.

## Jewish Emigration and the Collapse of the Trade Bill

With the opponents of our East-West policy approaching their goal of draining SALT of substance, trade became their next target. On December 3, I testified before the Senate Finance Committee on behalf of MFN. We had not yet made public the letter Gromyko had handed to me regarding the Jackson-Vanik Amendment.

Transmitting Gromyko's letter to Ford on October 27, I had

warned of the "not insubstantial danger" that Gromyko's letter might become public—though he had promised to make no use of it before I returned to Washington sometime around November 9. Therefore:

> We should plan to get the three senators in after my trip to discuss with them how we now proceed in light of the Soviet letter. We have two choices: (1) To stick by our exchange of letters and see how it works in practice; or (2) To cancel the whole effort.

The meeting with the Senators never took place, and the failure to arrange it was a serious mistake. Later on, there were all sorts of complicated analyses attributing this oversight to an inherent lack of candor or to some deliberate attempt to mislead Congress. A better explanation is to be found in the climate of the times.

When Gromyko handed me the letter, I was not due back in Washington for another two weeks, having stops scheduled for India, Bangladesh, Pakistan, Afghanistan, Iran, Romania, Yugoslavia, Italy, Egypt, Saudi Arabia, Jordan, Syria, Israel, and Tunisia, in that order. Ford was campaigning in the congressional elections only a week away, the result of which was a McGovernite Congress, spelling even more difficulty for the new President. There was only one week between my return and Ford's departure for Tokyo, Seoul, and Vladivostok.

There was as well a subconscious obstacle to disclosure. Congress was in recess; the Senators were out of town. Initial contact would have had to be with Jackson's staff—a prospect to which we looked forward with about as much enthusiasm as to an appointment with a dentist who did not use novocaine. Our lack of a sense of urgency was reinforced when, on November 5, Brezhnev wrote to Ford to thank him for sending me to Moscow, indicating flexibility on SALT, and never mentioning the MFN debate or Gromyko's letter.

Thus we opted to wait for the results of Vladivostok, where neither Brezhnev nor Gromyko would refer to the letter. Upon our return to Washington, we had our hands full defending the Vladivostok agreement against another Jackson onslaught. Ford decided that since Brezhnev had not brought up Gromyko's letter, it would be best to testify as to its substance without specifically mentioning it.

My statement on December 3 to the Senate Finance Committee in effect summed up Gromyko's letter:

It was consistently made clear to us that Soviet explanations
applied to the definition of criteria and did not represent a
commitment as to numbers. If any number was used in
regard to Soviet emigration this would be wholly our responsibility; that is, the Soviet Government could not be held
accountable for or bound by any such figure. This point has
been consistently made clear to Members of Congress with
whom we have dealt.[11]

To my amazement, Jackson hailed that statement as going beyond
"what had already been made public." Whether he intended this as a
gesture of conciliation or whether he was getting nervous about what
he might have wrought, no longer mattered. For the Jackson forces
had at last produced the straw that would break the camel's back.
Their vehicle for it was an amendment (introduced by Senator Adlai
Stevenson III) to the annual extension of the President's authority to
grant Export-Import Bank credits. It singled out the Soviet Union
by applying special restrictions to it. Export-Import Bank credits
were limited to a paltry $75 million a year, or $300 million over a
four-year period. Additional credits would require congressional approval; credits for mining and natural resources were prohibited altogether.

The Soviet Union was now worse off with respect to trade than it
had been before either détente or the trade bill. The sought after
equal status was transformed by Congress into a system of legalized
discrimination. MFN could only be granted via a presidential waiver
subject to annual renewal—making the Soviet Union the only country
subject to such restrictions. The first such renewal was slated for April
1976, chosen to give Jackson the maximum boost in the upcoming
presidential primaries.

For the Soviets, it was a no-win situation: if emigration increased,
Jackson would claim credit for having demonstrated that pressure
worked; if Jackson's quota was not met, the Soviet leaders would be
accused of violating assurances which they had, in fact, never given.
With even Export-Import Bank credits being for the first time placed
under restrictions, there now was no longer any aspect of American-
Soviet relations that was not under attack from this odd and passionate
coalition of liberal and conservative activists.

MFN, which had been intended as an incentive for responsible
Soviet *international* conduct and which Nixon had held up until there

was progress on Berlin access, Vietnam, SALT, and the payment of Lend-Lease debts—over incessant liberal protests—was now being made conditional on changes in Soviet *domestic* practices. The attempt to balance two strategic systems based on such different technical approaches as the Soviet and the American was being reduced to a demand for redesigning the entire Soviet arsenal in the image of ours while protecting every American weapons program. We were being urged to demand concessions but were simultaneously deprived of the ability to offer a quid pro quo. Agreement with the United States was to be its own reward.

On December 18, the Soviet leaders demonstrated the limits of this process. They published Gromyko's letter of October 26 on MFN together with a statement stressing that *any* new conditions ran counter to the 1972 trade agreement, which had made MFN conditional solely on the settlement of the Soviet Lend-Lease debt. Though it was now clear that Jackson's emigration figures were devoid of content, Congress nevertheless proceeded to pass the Trade Act of 1974. Jackson himself even managed to invoke cloture on the debate —that is, to place a limit on senatorial speeches.

It was too late to save MFN or Jewish emigration with parliamentary maneuvers, however. On December 25, Brezhnev addressed a personal letter to Ford, the first time he had done so since Vladivostok. At once blustering and melancholy, Brezhnev once more rejected congressional legislation linking East-West trade to Jewish emigration. The Soviet Union would not accept the waiver or any form of conditionality other than the settlement of the Lend-Lease debt. But Brezhnev was careful to stress that disagreement over trade need not affect other aspects of the basic East-West relationship:

> On our part, we shall do everything that is necessary to move further forward in our relations in the areas which so far have been the subject of our keen attention and to which both sides have devoted so many efforts. It applies both to bilateral Soviet-American relations and to the international problems touching upon the interests of our two States.

The letter concluded with a plaintive appeal, asking Ford to give the Soviet leaders the benefit of "your views with regard to improving the existing situation."

There was little Ford could say. The Trade Act would soon be dead;

SALT was mired in a haggle over insoluble technical issues, at the end of which beckoned a bitter controversy in Congress over its ratification. The sole remaining vestige of linkage was the European Security Conference, and the principal reason it had escaped assault was that our critics did not yet take it seriously—though as soon as its conclusion neared six months later, it too was savaged.

Ford postponed replying to Brezhnev until the trade bill had run the congressional gauntlet to the end. On January 3, 1975, he signed the Trade Act of 1974, hailing it as an "important part of our commercial and overall relations with Communist countries." At the same time, he expressed his "reservations about the wisdom of legislative language that can only be seen as objectionable and discriminatory by other sovereign nations." I attempted to persuade Dobrynin that the Soviet Union should defer the debate about conditionality until the first annual congressional review of MFN, scheduled for eighteen months hence.

The appeal proved futile. On January 10, Dobrynin delivered a note formally rejecting both credits and MFN on the terms set by Congress. Principal elements of our linkage strategy were now gone. But since East-West tensions had become correspondingly more likely, there was a need to unite the country. And so, despite all that had gone before, I extended an olive branch to Congress at a press conference on January 14, urging bipartisanship for the storms certain to be ahead:

> We want to make clear that there was no disagreement as to objectives. We differed with some of the Members of Congress about the methods to achieve these objectives—these disagreements are now part of a legislative history.
>
> As far as the administration is concerned, it will pursue the objectives that I have outlined in a spirit of cooperation with Congress.[12]

In this spirit, I warned the Soviets against using the rejection of the Trade Act as a pretext for intensifying international tensions:

> . . . the United States would resist with great determination and as a united people. We do not expect that to happen,

however, and as far as the United States is concerned, we
will continue to pursue the policy of relaxation of tensions
and of improving or seeking to improve relationships leading
toward a stable peace.[13]

But I knew better. American-Soviet relations were turning fragile
under the impact of an ideological crusade conducted without adequate regard for the long-term international consequences. Our critics
had a point when they stressed the need to ground our policies more
fully in the traditional beliefs of the American people. And we welcomed their pressures on behalf of strengthening American defenses.
But too many of them chose to assert their views as an ideological
challenge without understanding of or sympathy for the problems
before a nonelected President taking over in the aftermath of Watergate and facing a hostile McGovernite Congress. What made their
challenge to the Soviets particularly unfortunate was that it came at
the end of a period of considerable Soviet restraint, as I told Ford in
an Oval Office meeting on January 6:

> We bombed one of their allies to smithereens and they did
> nothing; we quieted Europe; they have been quiet in the
> Middle East—not cooperative, but quiet. We rebuffed the
> Soviets in the 1973 summit on the Middle East.
>
> We have de-fanged the left in Europe and their argument
> that friendship with the U.S. jeopardized the relaxation of
> tensions.
>
> The same in the U.S. The left is belligerent [toward
> Moscow] now, but let détente fail and they will swing to the
> left again.

On January 7, three days before the Soviet note rejecting the conditions of the Trade Act, I predicted to Ford:

> The Soviets have to keep détente going for political reasons,
> but our hold on them is gone. These economic projects
> would have gotten our hooks into them for ten years. The
> Chinese will be less scared now, and we will have a rockier
> time with the Soviet Union.

This is what happened. The Kremlin slowed Jewish emigration to a trickle. Relations with the Soviet Union moved into a gray area—not exactly confrontational but not cooperative either. The end of December saw the visit of a senior Soviet delegation to Vietnam and a significant step-up in Soviet military deliveries (see Chapter 15). A major Soviet arms program to Communist forces in Angola began about the same time (see Chapter 26). Had they always been planned, or were they at least partly induced by the impact of our domestic politics?

The Jackson-Vanik Amendment had performed a useful purpose when first put forward, eliciting from Moscow a more precise definition of emigration procedures than had existed previously. But once Congress went beyond these useful achievements to translating informal Soviet assurances into permanent legislation and an annual review, a blowup was foreordained.

Had the Senator and the administration found some way to cooperate, it would have been relatively easy to increase Jewish emigration for quite a few years, certainly to the annual level of 45,000 agreed to by Gromyko and perhaps to the 50,000 level Ford thought he heard Brezhnev mention at one point. By acting as if American legislators could impose a higher rate by fiat, however, Jackson and his colleagues became victims of their own rhetoric. And they removed incentives for Soviet restraint in other areas.

In the process, the Senator and his domestic constituency fell hostage to one another. Contemplating a presidential race in 1976, Jackson did not dare deviate from the course he had charted; his supporters in the Jewish community, many of whom were beginning to feel uneasy (and occasionally told me so), did not dare dissociate from their champion and likely protector should the American-led Middle East peace process get out of hand, at least from their point of view.

Even Jackson seems to have had second thoughts. If Dobrynin is to be believed, the Senator invited him to breakfast at his home in July 1975 and made a remarkable confession:

> Leaders of Congress, including himself, had developed a false impression that Moscow would eventually concede on Soviet emigration if they kept pressing. Eventually, their mistake became obvious, but by then the matter had become so clouded by emotion that it was too late to compromise. The resulting impasse did not benefit anybody.[14]

And if Dobrynin understood Jackson correctly, the Senator even granted what I have always maintained—that he and we were natural allies rather than adversaries:

> His approach toward the Soviet Union was not all that different from Presidents Nixon and Ford. But both presidents had to play at politics, while he was more candid in saying things with which both administrations would essentially agree, although their viewpoint would come out in actions rather than words. . . . He said he supported the improvement of Soviet-American relations, yet as a member of the opposition, he sometimes had to criticize the administration as a matter of tactics rather than strategy.[15]

What great tasks might have been accomplished had Jackson acted on this insight while there was still time.

## Final Note

I cannot end this chapter without a personal word about Scoop Jackson. In terms of the controversies described here, he was a kind of permanent adversary. But in terms of his overall contribution to the national security of the United States, I will always remember him as a seminal figure who helped preserve America's defenses during a desperate time. Seven years after the events described here, Jeane Kirkpatrick arranged a reconciliation between the Senator and me for which I shall always be grateful. Shortly before his untimely death, Jackson recommended to President Reagan that he appoint me chairman of the National Bipartisan Commission on Central America. And Vice President George Bush did me the great honor of taking me to Seattle in September 1983 as part of the official delegation to pay the nation's respects at the Senator's funeral.

# 11

# THE INTELLIGENCE INVESTIGATIONS

## Prelude to the Investigations

On December 22, 1974, four days after the Trade Act fiasco, Washington awoke to a new crisis when the *New York Times* headlined a story by its investigative reporter, Seymour M. "Sy" Hersh: "Huge CIA Operation Reported in U.S. Against Anti-War Forces, Other Dissidents in Nixon Years." The White House had had no warning, CIA Director William Colby having neglected to inform either the President or me of a long interview he had granted to Hersh two days earlier. Though the headline implied otherwise, the substance of the article, in fact, related to events which had taken place in previous administrations, primarily that of Lyndon Johnson. The initial revelations concerned investigations Johnson had ordered into charges that American Vietnam dissidents were being funded and supported from abroad. To the extent that the assignment involved domestic intelligence-gathering, it would have been prohibited by the Central Intelligence Agency's congressional charter.

The first Ford heard of the approaching scandal was the same day the article appeared. Colby placed a call to him on *Air Force One* en route to Vail, Colorado, where the President was to spend the Christmas holidays. Ford had no idea what the precise accusation was. Nor was I, back in Washington, much better off. Our confusion is evident from the following exchange with Chief of Staff Don Rumsfeld, whom I awoke the next morning in Vail where he was with the President:

KISSINGER: I want to talk to you about the Helms matter [Hersh's article blamed former CIA Director Richard Helms]. I don't know the facts remotely. I have no knowledge whatever to what body of fact it refers. If there were any such activities, they were not reported to the NSC office. . . . I think for a senior official to get vilified without opposition from the administration on the basis of such an article is dangerous business. There are no facts, just allegations. First, we should ask Colby to give us a report on the body of fact to which this refers, whatever it is. What could Hersh be referring to? If they conducted investigations of Americans—for what purpose? See what I mean? At least then we would know what we are talking about. I don't know now.

RUMSFELD: That is why I tried to reach you or Brent [Scowcroft], and I finally got [NSC staff deputy Dick] Kennedy. . . .

KISSINGER: . . . I don't know of any [CIA effort] where, in investigating foreign agents, they ran across Americans. If the files get constituted, it could be in this way. Perhaps they did investigations for Nixon. I don't know whom they report them to. They certainly never reported them to us and, if they reported them to Haldeman and Ehrlichman, why didn't that come out earlier?

After some more back-and-forth in the same vein, I suggested that:

I will ask Colby for a written report for the President's use. I do not know what body of fact this could be referring to. We will ask Schlesinger the same question. [Press Secretary] Nessen then can say the President has asked for a written report, and he will decide what to do after he has seen this report. That way we look disciplined and thoughtful. Obviously the CIA must operate within the law. I don't think we should express an opinion on an investigation at this point. I am saying at State that if any congressional committee wants Helms, of course, we will bring him back [Richard Helms, after leaving the CIA, had been serving as ambassador to Iran since 1973].

Ford approved this procedure. When, on December 23, I began exploring the subject with Colby, I realized we were in for a nightmare. Since the only record is a somewhat incoherent transcription from a scrambled telephone conversation, I will summarize it here in my own words (with the actual text contained in the Notes).[1]

In May 1973, when James Schlesinger was serving briefly as Director of Central Intelligence (DCI), he had found himself blindsided by the revelation that the CIA had given some assistance to E. Howard Hunt, who was investigating the leak of the Pentagon Papers for Nixon. On May 9—as it happened, one day before he was appointed Secretary of Defense—Schlesinger requested from each CIA department a report of any of its activities even remotely related to Watergate. When Colby succeeded Schlesinger, he extended that request to include any activity that might be construed as outside the CIA's charter or be otherwise questionable. In the Watergate atmosphere, such an inquiry was guaranteed to veer out of control. Accusations cascaded forth as frightened officials scrambled to protect themselves by pointing the finger at each other or, preferably, at their superiors regarding matters that, in retrospect, seemed contentious.

A grand total of 693 pages of alleged transgressions covering a quarter of a century was submitted to Colby's office. There they were distilled into a memorandum of some seventy pages labeled the "family jewels" by someone with a mordant sense of humor. The overwhelming majority referred to alleged transgressions prior to the Nixon Administration; Ford, of course, was not even in office when the list was put together. Such a compilation was dynamite. There was no possibility that it would not leak; the only open question was when. That the "family jewels" did not become public for fifteen months is far more astonishing than that they finally did.

Colby never informed the Presidents in office (Nixon and later Ford) nor me, the National Security Adviser, of the existence of the "family jewels," much less of their content. Colby's reticence toward his Presidents was particularly odd in light of the fact that he had briefed the chairmen of the congressional oversight committees a year earlier. They had maintained secrecy toward their colleagues in keeping with established procedures for especially sensitive information. They never mentioned them to the White House, presumably because they reasonably believed we were fully informed. In the telephone conversation on December 23, Colby described, but did not explain, his extraordinary conduct: "I bundled them together and briefed my two chairmen on it, and I let the skeletons sit quietly in the closet, hoping they would stay there."

I listened to Colby's account with a sinking feeling. Even in normal times, a memorandum such as the "family jewels" would have led to an investigation. But there would have been every prospect of conducting it with due regard to the sensitivity of the subject matter and with the intention of separating genuine abuses from policy disagreements masquerading as charges of malfeasance. Now, in the first months of the Ford presidency, a Kafkaesque pall had fallen over Washington. The credibility of government having been eroded by its own actions, media and congressional investigations abandoned all restraint. Accusation was equated with prima facie truth; denial was interpreted as cover-up. Government officials, witnessing careers ruined by "credibility gaps"—real or contrived—were bending over backward to avoid a similar fate. Leaking classified material turned into a way to preempt inquisitors. Once a "scandal" was authenticated by media attention, documents would gush forth, many of them as unfamiliar to the White House as they were to the public. The White House was obliged to conduct its own investigation before it could react to a burgeoning scandal.

It soon became clear that the charge of domestic intelligence-gathering had been merely the opening shot. The "family jewels" alleged as well assassination plots against foreign leaders during the Kennedy and Johnson Administrations and touched on every aspect of covert and paramilitary activities conducted by the American government over a twenty-five-year period. An investigation would find it difficult to insulate covert intelligence activities undertaken in support of the nation's foreign policy from transgressions in need of being remedied and punished.

After all the country had been through, a full-scale public investigation into the entire range of the nation's intelligence activities was a worrisome prospect in the existing morbid atmosphere. The public disclosure of what in every other government, including all the established democracies, is treated as the most sensitive of state secrets was bound to be profoundly damaging to America's standing in the world —partly because of misdeeds that might be revealed, above all because it would be interpreted by friend and foe alike as another example of the disintegration of America's domestic cohesion.

We already had some experience with the course the likely investigation would take. For Hersh's article had capped an assault on the intelligence community that had been building for months. CIA covert activities in Chile had precipitated a congressional inquiry headed by Senator Frank Church. Three administrations of both parties— Kennedy's, Johnson's, and Nixon's—convinced that Salvador Allende Gossens, the standard-bearer of the combined Socialists and Communists in the 1964 and 1970 elections, would establish a Cuba-style Communist dictatorship if elected, had approved covert support for democratic Chilean parties. The impact of an Allende victory on surrounding countries, each of which was facing various forms of radical pressures of its own, was judged to be extremely inimical to American national interests.

The American ambassador in Chile, Edward Korry—a lifelong Democrat and Johnson appointee whom Nixon had retained in office —had reported Allende's 1970 victory as follows:

> It is a sad fact that Chile has taken the path to Communism with only a little more than a third (36 percent) of the nation approving this choice, but it is an immutable fact. It will have the most profound effect on Latin America and beyond; we have suffered a grievous defeat; the consequences will be domestic and international; the repercussions will have immediate impact in some lands and delayed effect in others.[2]

By a retroactive imposition of the mood of the 1970s on the Cold War perceptions of the 1960s, these covert activities, designed to enable democratic parties and a free press to survive, were interpreted as gratuitous interference in Chile's democratic domestic affairs. In the September 1970 election, Allende had achieved a plurality because two traditional democratic candidates divided the large anti-Allende vote, which amounted to 64 percent of the total. The covert action was an attempt by the CIA, urged on by the White House, to encourage the Chilean congress (charged under its constitution to elect the President if no candidate achieved a majority) to order a runoff between the two leading candidates.[3] A victory for the democratic parties was likely once they combined in a single list. This effort, called Track I, failed, and Allende was installed as President by a vote of the Chilean congress.

A particular focus of congressional attention was the so-called Track II, which President Nixon ordered in the aftermath of the Chilean elections. In fact, no plan was ever implemented under it, and its origin was Nixon's reluctance to do combat with an obstreperous bureaucracy, described in Chapter 2. In the run-up to the Chilean elections, it became clear that the candidate with the best chance to defeat Allende was Jorge Alessandri, a conservative. The Christian Democratic candidate, Radomiro Tomic, was hovering at just over 20 percent in the polls. Nixon, passionately opposed to the emergence of another Castroite regime in the hemisphere, wanted to support Alessandri; the CIA and the State Department, accustomed to working with the Christian Democrats and gun-shy about backing a conservative in the climate of the Vietnam protest, opposed such an overt identification, arguing that Alessandri was so far ahead he needed no outside support. Upon White House urging, the CIA and the State Department agreed very late in the game to a contribution of $2 million, evenly divided between the democratic parties and thereby cancelling itself out.

When, against all predictions by State and CIA, Allende won, Nixon felt vindicated and was determined not to be thwarted a second time by the bureaucracy. He called in Helms, ordering him to find some way to prevent Allende's accession to power and not to feel constrained by budgetary considerations. Nixon offered no specific plan as to how to accomplish this.

As it happened, the chastened bureaucracy had, in regular channels at the 40 Committee-level, come up with its own idea for arranging a two-man presidential race, described above. Track II, in effect, turned into to an attempt to encourage the Chilean military to support the scenario of Track I. On October 15, I called off Track II before it had ever been implemented. (A week later, some of the plotters who had been involved in Track II and from whom we had disassociated attempted *on their own* to kidnap the chief of staff of the Chilean army, as a result of the bungling of which he was killed.) A thorough investigation by a hostile Senate committee absolved the Nixon Administration of having been involved in an assassination plot. Track I ended, of course, with the election of Allende by the Chilean congress.

As soon as he was in office, Allende systematically tried to throttle free expression, just as we had feared. He took over or suppressed the media, circumscribed free labor unions, and attempted wholesale constitutional and social changes. At that point, a covert program was resurrected in order to support free institutions in an effort to keep a democratic opposition alive.[4]

Though the charge at hand was misuse of the CIA, the real target of the attack was the substance of American foreign policy. Assaulting the CIA turned into a surrogate for reducing the country's international role. Senator Church described the Chilean operation, designed to preserve democracy in Chile, as a symbol of a runaway White House engaged in unnecessary foreign policy adventures. That three Presidents—two Democrats and one Republican—had agreed that an Allende victory threatened vital American interests was viewed as an aberration rather than as the expression of a bipartisan consensus.

On September 8, 1974, four weeks after Ford had taken the oath of office, an article in the *New York Times* accused the Nixon Administration of using covert activities to undermine the Allende government and of having "repeatedly and deliberately misled the public and Congress about the extent of U.S. involvement in the internal affairs of Chile. . . ."[5] This was untrue, since no covert action anywhere had ever been disclosed publicly, and Congress had been fully briefed according to the then existing procedures. Leading the charge was Senator Church, whose staff, on September 16, 1974, recommended perjury investigations against several administration witnesses, including former CIA Director Richard Helms, who had appeared before the subcommittee in 1973.[6]

Ford was well aware of the procedures by which CIA covert operations were reported to Congress. Oversight was restricted to the Appropriations and Armed Services Committees, two in each house. Other committees were not briefed, and any intelligence personnel appearing before them on unrelated matters evaded questions regarding covert operations. This was the origin of the perjury charge against Helms.

This system reflected an executive-congressional consensus in effect throughout the Cold War until it broke down at the end of the Nixon presidency. It had enabled the executive branch to consult with a handful of senior Senators and Members of Congress regarding the most sensitive issues of national policy and to take the pulse of Congress while minimizing the risk of leaks. Occasionally when the executive branch offered to provide more details, these were rejected by the oversight committees, which, in the climate of the Cold War, were only too willing to give the CIA maximum flexibility.

It was this consensus to which Ford appealed in a September 16 news conference which courageously defended the intelligence community in a way subsequent Presidents have not dared to do. For the first time, Ford confirmed the existence of a committee of the NSC—

then known as the "40 Committee"—which had for over two decades reviewed covert programs before they were submitted to the President for approval. Ford also disclosed that the relevant congressional committees had been kept informed of every covert program on the basis of procedures devised in cooperation with the congressional leadership:

> The 40 Committee was established in 1948. It has been in existence under presidents since that time. That committee reviews every covert operation undertaken by our government, and that information is relayed to the responsible congressional committees where it is reviewed by House and Senate committees.[7]

Ford acknowledged that the United States had assisted Chilean democratic parties and media:

> In a period of time, 3 or 4 years ago, there was an effort being made by the Allende government to destroy opposition news media, both the writing press as well as the electronic press, and to destroy opposition political parties.
>
> The effort that was made in this case was to help and assist the preservation of opposition newspapers and electronic media and to preserve opposition political parties.[8]

No major government had ever admitted that it was conducting covert operations, even less described the methods by which it reviewed them. But far from stemming the tide, the President's public acknowledgment of covert operations provided a new focal point for attacks on the intelligence services.

The generation of Representatives and Senators elected in the wake of Watergate was congenitally suspicious of the motives of the executive branch. The phrase, "CIA transgressions," masked their objections to the very concept of covert action and to the CIA as the symbol of America's Cold War role, which they were determined to end.

Even at this early stage, the CIA Director's conduct was ambiguous to say the least. Colby clearly fueled the fire by his inability—or unwillingness—to stem leaks from his agency. Before he became Director, leaks from the CIA had never been a major problem. Now they poured forth in profusion and were usually signaled by a call from Colby to the White House about some "inquiry" to which he said the CIA had already responded. At the same time, he appeared reluctant to provide the White House with adequate information with which to defend itself.

A good example was a *New York Times* article by Sy Hersh on September 20 accusing Ford and me of having lied when we said on September 16 that CIA funds had gone only to political parties and not to support political actions such as strikes.[9] The following telephone conversation on the same day between Colby and me provides a flavor of the atmosphere—of the difficulty the White House had in finding out what had happened and in extracting reliable information from the CIA director:

> KISSINGER: What is that Sy Hersh story today? Did we do it?
>
> COLBY: He called me yesterday.
>
> KISSINGER: I am not asking you what Sy Hersh did. Did we or did we not support the truckers' strike?
>
> COLBY: We did not. He refers to 1972.
>
> KISSINGER: The President has said publicly we only supported the political parties.
>
> COLBY: That is the point I made, on [ABC].
>
> KISSINGER: I am getting sick and tired of the way the intelligence community—If this keeps up, we'll have to talk to the President to see how to keep it under control. The President said, and I said, that we only supported the political parties. Now you say the [ABC] story.
>
> COLBY: No, I said we gave it to the political parties. We gave it to the parties to sustain them. They did not put it in the bank, but what they did with it, I don't know.
>
> KISSINGER: We did not give them money then?
>
> COLBY: Not to the truckers, no.
>
> KISSINGER: Did we know it would go to the truckers?
>
> COLBY: I don't know. I'll have to check.
>
> KISSINGER: Did we, did the 40 Committee know?
>
> COLBY: No, because the money was given to the parties.
>
> KISSINGER: It is incredible how the intelligence community can talk so much.
>
> COLBY: I don't know who the source is.
>
> KISSINGER: The 40 Committee has existed for years. . . . The leaders in this country know this is the case, and they are all letting us take it as though this is a scandal.

COLBY: We gave support. . . . I indicated yesterday that I did not use the word "destabilization," and it is not a fair representation of our policy, and I stick to it.

KISSINGER: My point is, if the President says something and I say it, and it is then made out to be a lie.

COLBY: But it isn't. We gave money to the political parties . . . but it is not destabilization.

KISSINGER: We did not know this?

COLBY: Let me check. I know we didn't do it in '73. I know that the idea was suggested and turned down. It alleges that, in the fall of '72, among the ones sustained were the organizers of the truckers' strike. I am sure we did not give. . . .

KISSINGER: Did it go before the 40 Committee?

COLBY: No, the 40 Committee approved giving it to the political parties.

KISSINGER: Thank you.

This was at 8:05 A.M. Around 4:40, Colby compounded the confusion with another opaque combination of implied threats and leakage:

COLBY: Just to let you know, Sy Hersh called our public affairs fellow and said he's in the course of writing a story that you only told about the propaganda funding and not about the other things we're funding. We didn't say a thing to him.

KISSINGER: What do you mean?

COLBY: Apparently he's trying to put together a story which implies you only told the people half the truth.

KISSINGER: On Chile?

COLBY: On Chile. At the Cabinet meeting or the briefing of the leadership.

KISSINGER: What else did you do?

COLBY: I sent you a little note telling you the whole story. I just sent it to you.

KISSINGER: What else did he have? You must know since he contacted the Agency.

COLBY: He has the . . .

KISSINGER: There's something very funny.

COLBY: He has the story he had this morning which is wrong, that we were supporting the truckers.

KISSINGER: Then what he's telling is not true.
COLBY: That's right.
KISSINGER: Or is there something else?
COLBY: No, it's all in the letter I sent you.
KISSINGER: Okay. Thank you.

## Ford Charts a Course

The Hersh article and the discovery of the "family jewels" had the effect of a burning match in a gasoline depot. In the aftermath of Nixon's resignation, civic leaders, former officials, and other pro-defense individuals who normally would have stood by the intelligence community hesitated to come forward lest some explosive new revelation make them appear as participants in a cover-up. And the involvement of some retired CIA personnel in various Watergate activities added to the discomfort of many traditional defenders of a strong foreign policy and intelligence service from the conservative camp.

The usual checks and balances monitoring attacks on security institutions broke down. In ordinary circumstances, the Director of Central Intelligence would have sounded the alarm against excessive disclosures inimical to national security. The President, in consultation with the Director and the Secretaries of State and Defense, would have sought to develop some criteria by which to define transgressions and confine investigations to these subjects. In consultation with the congressional leaders and together with them, he would have devised some procedure to prevent future abuses while preserving essential intelligence activities.

But these were not normal times. Triggered by the disclosure of the "family jewels," the traditional procedure failed its very first test, which was to develop a common position regarding the subject matter to be covered by the investigations. Ford had accepted my recommendation that Colby prepare a memorandum on the basis of which the President would take further decisions.

Yet from the moment I conveyed Ford's request, Colby made it clear that he had an altogether different view about how to proceed. He seemed less interested in devising a judicious inquiry than in getting out all the information on perceived CIA misdeeds without any further inquiry. On December 23, on behalf of the President, I asked Colby for a full report on the subjects covered by the Hersh article. The following conversation took place:

COLBY: You will have the full text. The problem is that, over the twenty-odd years of this Agency's history, there are a few things done that should not have been done so you cannot flatly deny that anything wrong was ever done.

KISSINGER: You are reporting this to the President?

COLBY: Yes. So you will know exactly what they are and the time bombs. I am trying to do it in an unclassified form.

KISSINGER: It is more important that the President know the exact facts. Let's not worry about the classification now.

COLBY: It will be both correct and . . .

KISSINGER: It should have everything he should know.

COLBY: Yes. And I will be able to cover the specific details later.

KISSINGER: If you do it unclassified, it will be leaked.

Ford rejected Colby's recommendation that the Director's report be released immediately because he said he wanted to conduct an investigation of his own. His first instinct was to create a bipartisan executive-congressional body analogous to the Warren Commission, which had investigated President Kennedy's assassination and on which Ford had served. But the congressional leadership balked at congressional participation. Therefore, on January 4, 1975, Ford announced the establishment of a bipartisan commission chaired by Vice President Nelson Rockefeller and composed of seven distinguished individuals drawn from private life.[10] It was to report within three months (later extended an additional two months) and would have the following responsibilities: to vet the "family jewels"; to determine what abuses—if any—had taken place; to propose remedies; and to winnow actual abuses from charges reflecting primarily disagreements on policy.

Testifying before the Senate Subcommittee on Intelligence Appropriations in closed session on January 15, 1975, Colby circumvented the President's order to keep the report to him classified by submitting an opening statement identical to the memorandum that he had submitted to Ford, without identifying it as such. Colby further agreed that his statement could be released by the committee—all this without consulting the White House, much less notifying it. In Colby's own words:

On my way down from the Hill that afternoon, I realized
that I had not told the White House what was coming in the
press next day, so I stopped there to give Brent Scowcroft
a copy of the statement the Committee had released; the
substance was well known to them, but the fact of its public
release was a new bombshell.[11]

It was an incitement to riot, severely limiting whatever restraint
the Rockefeller Commission might have provided. On January 27,
1975, the Senate voted 82–4 to establish a select committee composed
of six Democrats and five Republicans for the purpose of conducting
an investigation and study of American intelligence activities. The
committee, headed by Senator Frank Church, was to report by September 1, 1975, later extended to April 30, 1976.

Not to be outdone, on February 19, 1975, the House of Representatives passed Resolution 138, which established its own Select Committee on Intelligence. Ten members appointed by the Speaker would
"conduct an inquiry into the organization, operations, and oversight
of the intelligence community of the United States Government."[12]
After some internal strife, this committee came to be headed by Democratic Representative Otis G. Pike of New York.

There were now three intelligence investigations taking place simultaneously: Ford's Rockefeller Commission, the Senate's Church
Committee, and the House's Pike Committee. Moreover, the charters
of the two congressional committees were so sweeping as to cover
every aspect of America's intelligence activities. No criteria were
defined to distinguish between abuses and normal activities or even
to define what might constitute an abuse. Wholesale disclosure of
sources, methods and procedures—heretofore the most closely
guarded secrets—became inevitable, especially by the reckless Pike
Committee.

In normal circumstances, the CIA Director would have been expected to protect his sources and methods and, if pressed, to ask the
White House to intercede with the committees. Colby not only refused
to do this, he formally absolved his subordinates of the secrecy oaths
they had sworn upon entering the service. That made the disclosure of
national secrets depend almost entirely on the judgment of individual
CIA employees.[13]

Hiring an outside attorney as his principal adviser on the various
investigations, Colby kept his own counsel without reference to the

White House, which he generally informed only after the fact. He responded affirmatively to practically every congressional request for documents, be it a mere fishing expedition or a bona fide inquiry into some questionable CIA activity. As a result, a deluge of documents became public regarding even CIA activities about which no question had been raised.

Colby felt at liberty to supply Congress with documents it had not even requested, in his own words, "so as to place in proper context the documents selected by the investigators and to explain that they had another significance than guilt."[14] Finally, in September 1975, after massive leaks from the Pike Committee, which had insisted on the unilateral right to declassify all documents, Ford put his foot down and prohibited the release of any additional classified material to the committee until it had agreed to respect their classification. Colby managed to get around that order by "loaning" the disputed documents to the committee. The White House could do no more than register impotent chagrin when the Pike Committee's staff director, A. Searle Field, stated in open session that his staff had obtained the *names* and backgrounds of secret agents—a decision serving no conceivable investigative purpose, about which Ford or his National Security Adviser had never been consulted, and which put real people's lives at risk.

In his memoirs, Colby justified his conduct as a constitutional duty:

> My strategy quite simply had been to be guided by the Constitution and to apply its principles. That meant I had to cooperate with the investigations and educate the Congress, press, and public as well as I could . . .[15]

Until the Colby era, no CIA Director had ever advanced the proposition that he had the unilateral right to determine what intelligence information could be made public, even less that he had a responsibility to interpret constitutional principles on his own. Not even an independent department, the CIA was created under the National Security Act of 1947 as an advisory body to the National Security Council, which is headed by the President. The traditional approach would have been for Colby to leave the constitutional issue for the President and, in the event of conflict with Congress, to seek a final determination in the courts.

Ford was a new President, having been in office only five months. Determined to overcome the anger and bitterness of Watergate, he went the extra mile to avoid giving the impression that he was stonewalling a congressional inquiry. Ford's chief adviser on these issues was Phil Buchen, fresh out of Grand Rapids, by nature uncomfortable with confrontations and still somewhat shell-shocked from the reaction to the Nixon pardon.

The vaunted NSC machinery proved incapable of dealing simultaneously with a runaway Congress and a runaway CIA Director. Though I was still assistant for national security affairs for the greater part of the investigations, I spent most of my energies on three shuttles through the Middle East and on dealing with the collapse of Indochina. Thus Brent Scowcroft oversaw the intelligence investigations. He kept me scrupulously informed and handled the issues with impeccable skill and discretion. His problem—like that of the entire White House—was that, by the time issues reached him, Colby would have acted on his own. Scowcroft had neither the staff nor the time to evaluate what Colby had already released, nor was he even informed until after the event that congressional aides were rummaging through files at CIA headquarters that had not yet been turned over. Don Rumsfeld managed to prevent the official disclosure of the CIA's attempt to raise a Soviet submarine that had sunk in the Pacific's deep waters (see Chapter 1). The *Glomar Explorer* story was leaked anyway. On two occasions, Schlesinger and I—in an unusual display of harmony—met with Colby to voice our concern over the apparent destruction of our intelligence system. As Colby states in his memoirs, I expressed my mounting uneasiness in elliptical observations; Colby was proud of not permitting himself to be deflected.[16]

It was a dilemma worthy of being studied in political science seminars. On organization charts, the CIA Director is clearly and directly subordinate to the President. But in a situation in which the President has judged he cannot fire the Director, the organization chart becomes purely academic. Theoretically, Ford could have ordered that any documents released had to be approved by the White House. But aside from the fact that it would have placed the White House in the direct line of fire, how could he have made that order stick? The White House staff was in no position to review literally thousands of documents; the congressional staffs—especially that of the Pike Committee—were not prepared to show restraint either in their demands for documents or their determination to make them public.

Ironically, investigations purportedly undertaken to establish a more effective control over the intelligence agencies led—at least while they lasted—to a substantial loss of presidential control over the intelligence services.

Finally convinced by the Pike Committee's subpoenas that matters had gotten out of hand, Ford invoked executive privilege. He never challenged the necessity of turning over any documents or other information relevant to actual abuses. Ford was determined to end decisively any abuses that might be found. What he sought to prevent were fishing expeditions producing mountains of documents that would then be fed to the media. He offered to continue to supply the documents requested, provided the investigating committees agreed to safeguard their contents.

It was in vain. Ford did not believe the best interests of the country would be served by a series of court battles over the classification of documents, especially as the material that needed to be protected would have to be disclosed before the courts. Finally, with Watergate still lingering in the background, replacing Colby would have produced, in Ford's view, another massive clash between the executive and legislative branches—though, in the end, he did just that. Thus the hemorrhage continued for the better part of a year and a half until Congress, worried by the excesses of the Pike Committee, put an end to its depredations. By then, major damage, some of it irreparable, had been done.

I confess that I have never understood either Bill Colby's motivation or his conduct, especially why he insisted on acting on his own without consulting or even informing his President and the National Security Council apparatus. Or why he never explained his motives to his colleagues until after he had left office and published his memoirs.

I first met this most enigmatic of American officials in Saigon in 1965 when I served for a month as consultant to Ambassador Henry Cabot Lodge. Colby's probing gray eyes peered out from behind horn-rimmed glasses without revealing anything of the personality within. Though trim, he did not appear to be especially athletic and, if one had not known of his exceptionally courageous World War II military service (parachuting into France and Norway as a very young intelligence officer), one might have more easily taken him for a character straight out of a John le Carré spy novel: the epitome of discretion in thrall to anonymity.

As Senator Bob Kerrey noted in his moving eulogy at Colby's memorial service in May 1996, Colby represented the generation that had overcome the Depression, defeated one of the most heinous dictatorships in history, and won the battle against Communism without war. Colby had been a participant in most of the intelligence battles which helped to preserve the cause of freedom and, to his credit, never boasted about his extraordinary record of service.

In Saigon, he was put in charge of the so-called Phoenix Program, which sought to defeat the Communist guerrillas by turning some of their own methods against them. Colby was as upbeat about the assignment as he proved to be uncommunicative about its procedures.

After I became National Security Adviser and Colby returned to Washington, our paths would occasionally cross at White House meetings. Colby rarely spoke and never with any great fervor. In July 1973, Schlesinger moved from the CIA to the Defense Department, replacing Elliot Richardson, who became Attorney General. Al Haig, then Nixon's chief of staff, recommended Colby for CIA Director primarily because he thought that the Agency would function most efficiently and loyally when led by one of its own professionals. I made no formal recommendation but considered Colby a good choice.

Two explanations for Colby's conduct have been advanced. The first view has been put forth by General Vernon Walters, my trusted friend and Colby's deputy during this period. Walters argues that Colby came to believe that a fundamental shift in the Washington power balance had made Congress so dominant that the only way to preserve the CIA was to open its secrets to congressional committees, however unreasonable their requests or however reckless the attendant publicity. According to Walters's theory, Colby in effect threw the CIA on the mercy of Congress.

The second frequently heard explanation is that, somewhere along the way, Colby had developed second thoughts about his chosen profession. The way in which the Cold War was being pursued may have come to seem to him as weakening the moral fabric of American society. If that was indeed his premise, it may well be that Colby was seeking to purify his country by cooperating with the strategies of the protest movement. In these terms, weakening the very service entrusted to him became a necessary sacrifice which he pursued with the same single-mindedness that he had displayed as a combatant in World War II.

With this background, it is possible to address what the various committees actually produced.

## The Rockefeller Commission

The presidentially appointed Rockefeller Commission concentrated primarily on domestic CIA activities. Its report, issued on June 6, 1975, found ninety-six cases over a quarter century involving investigative techniques not authorized by law. The overwhelming majority occurred in the administrations preceding Nixon's and none in Ford's incumbency.

The initial finding of the Rockefeller Commission was that "the great majority of the CIA's domestic activities comply with its statutory authority" but that, during its twenty-eight-year history, the CIA had:

> . . . engaged in some activities that should be criticized and not permitted to happen again. . . . Some of these activities were initiated or ordered by Presidents, either directly or indirectly . . . [and] . . . some of them were plainly unlawful and constituted improper invasions upon the rights of Americans.[17]

Press coverage highlighted the "some" while ignoring the "great majority" aspect.

If the headline writers had examined the details, they might have been more charitable. Three fourths of the cases of so-called domestic spying involved security investigations of persons affiliated with the CIA.[18] Of the twenty-six investigations *not* involving persons connected with the CIA, eleven related to individuals who had had contact with present or former employees of the CIA. In the end, the Rockefeller Commission discovered only fifteen instances in which persons not connected directly or indirectly with the CIA were investigated over its history. The public at large had faced no danger from rogue CIA investigations.

The Rockefeller Commission made thirty specific recommendations requiring changes in legislation or in administrative and congressional procedures. Among these was a proposal to assign a larger role to the President's Foreign Intelligence Advisory Board (PFIAB).[19] Composed of distinguished citizens from various walks of life, the board was headed by a full-time chairman with a full-time staff and charged with monitoring the CIA's compliance with its statutory authority; with assessing the quality of its foreign intelligence collection, estimates, organization, and management; and with making recommendations to the President, the Director of Central Intelligence, and, where appropriate, the Attorney General. Ford accepted this recommendation.

## The Church Committee

Despite occasional lapses, such as Senator Walter Mondale's description of the CIA to the editors of Time as "those bastards down there in Washington,"[20] the Church Committee acted, on the whole, responsibly. It adopted a procedure for handling classified documents that gave the originating agency the right to excise particularly sensitive sentences or portions of documents. This eased, but did not solve, the problem, since foreign intelligence analysts would often be able to reconstruct the excised portion from the context or from other documents—especially since these documents had to be furnished to the committee in such haste as to inhibit a thoughtful review of their context.

What occasionally drove the committee into the sensational was not so much its disclosures as the natural affinity of Senators for publicity. A good example was staged on the very first day of public hearings on September 16, 1975. Senator Church asked Colby a loaded question: "Have you brought with you some of those devices which would have enabled the CIA to use this poison for killing people?"[21] Whereupon, and obviously by prearrangement, Colby produced what became known as the "CIA dart gun." Photos of Senator Church and his colleagues examining the device with grave expressions on their faces graced front pages and television screens and created the impression that CIA personnel were walking around with dart guns under their trench coats.

It was not until two days later that Charles Senseney, a Department of Defense employee, explained the true provenance of this frightening instrument: the dart gun was *not* a CIA device at all but a weapon developed by the Army. To spread the cost of development, the Army had tried to convince other government agencies to purchase the dart gun. In the event, the Army proved better at developing dart guns than at selling them, since the CIA neither purchased nor ever used the device.[22]

The Church Committee's investigation was conducted in a combination of closed executive sessions and televised testimony. The distinction between the two grew rather elastic because after nearly every executive committee session, Senator Church exercised his well-developed rhetorical skill, holding a briefing to summarize the proceedings.

Much of the committee's executive sessions was devoted to alleged assassination plots against foreign leaders. In late October 1975, the committee completed its investigation of this subject. President Ford, concerned that public discussion of the details would play into the hands of anti-American radicals around the world, particularly in countries where the plots had allegedly occurred, asked that the report not be released. He could make this appeal with an easy conscience because all the alleged assassination plots had taken place in Democratic administrations (though the committee, for reasons of partisan symmetry, had managed to drag into its hearings a bungled Chilean army coup attempt during the Nixon Administration as an American assassination plot, a charge its final report disavowed).

Senator Church rejected Ford's request on the ground that "the committee has voted to make the report public after first submitting it to a closed session of the Senate."[23] Unwilling to take any chance that his colleagues might prohibit publication, Church announced on the eve of the session on November 20 that the purpose of the closed session was not to approve publication but to give the other Senators an opportunity to ask questions. By then, the report had already been printed and a copy of it placed on every Senator's desk.

What Senator Church was so eager to share with the world came down to five alleged assassination plots, all except one during the Kennedy Administration: against Fidel Castro of Cuba, in 1961; Patrice Lumumba of Congo/Zaire, in 1961; Rafael Trujillo of the Dominican Republic, in 1961; Ngo Dinh Diem of South Vietnam, in 1963; and General René Schneider of Chile, in 1970. In only two cases—of Castro and Lumumba—did the report find that any actual steps to promote an assassination had been taken by American officials. The case of General Schneider was acknowledged as not having been an assassination plot at all. As for Lumumba, the report stated that the United States had not been involved in his death at the hands of domestic rivals in 1961.[24] For all the intense media attention, the facts had exonerated the CIA: in its entire history, it had assassinated no foreign leader, though, in the case of Castro, not for lack of trying (or presidential orders).

In its public hearings, the Church Committee's focus was on covert operations, where it found no current abuses. Rather all actions, except Nixon's so-called Track II in Chile, had been vetted by established policy procedures and briefed to the designated congressional oversight committees (and Track II lasted only a month and took no action, after which it merged with an identical program labeled "Track I" which had been vetted by the 40 Committee).[25] The problem was that the chairman and key members of the Senate majority were opposed to covert operations in principle and could justify themselves to their constituencies only by a policy of full disclosure of what they had investigated. Thus, while accurately describing the general purposes of the CIA covert action program, the Church Committee's final report included a detailed historical compendium of methods and sources and identified, with respect to Chile, many of the groups and individuals that had been of assistance to the CIA. Individuals who had supported American policy in good faith were severely compromised, and the CIA's capability to recruit for future operations was gravely weakened.

The Church Committee redeemed itself to a considerable extent by making a number of organizational proposals which have become the basis of contemporary intelligence organization (to be discussed below). And it had the grace to disavow its chairman in its final report when it stated that "the Central Intelligence Agency in broad terms is not 'out of control.'"[26]

## The Pike Committee

Up to this point, a degree of comity had been maintained between the executive and legislative branches. There had been excessive—and, in the administration's view, dangerous—disclosure of sensitive intelligence information. But in the Senate, we were dealing with responsible individuals who, even if they did not agree, would take into account the administration's view of the national interest.

It was different with the investigation in the House of Representatives. It had a late start. And behind the label of "intelligence investigations," it undertook to second-guess foreign policy decisions by pretending to examine the extent to which intelligence affected them.

The first act of the House committee was to depose its own chairman, Lucien Nedzi, because he had been briefed about the "family jewels" by Colby and never informed his committee. Nedzi was replaced by Representative Otis Pike for the purposes of the intelligence investigation.

The Pike Committee attempted to compensate for its tardy start by adopting a passionately adversarial attitude toward both the intelligence community and the Ford Administration. Its fifty-member staff, headed by thirty-year-old Searle Field, managed to outrage even Colby, who wrote about it as follows:

> He [Pike] accepted without change the ragtag, immature, and publicity-seeking committee staff that had been gathered for the investigation, a bunch of children who were out to seize the most sensational high ground they could and could not be interested in a serious review of what intelligence is really all about.[27]

The Pike Committee refused to abide by the very flexible rules worked out between the Church Committee and the executive branch. Staff members without experience in dealing with classified documents and with no background in security procedures were now handling some 75,000 classified documents made available to them by Colby.[28]

Matters were finally brought to a head when the Pike Committee began to deal with sensitive communications intercepts. Over the strenuous objections of both Colby and other senior members of the intelligence community, the committee threatened to release five different intelligence assessments regarding the imminence of the Arab-Israeli war in October 1973. Intelligence specialists argued these would reveal the extent of the American capability to monitor and analyze communications. There was no precedent for such conduct by a congressional committee.

When the Pike Committee nevertheless published the offending material on September 11, 1975, Ford finally had had enough. Assistant Attorney General Rex E. Lee appeared at an open hearing the next morning and, though frequently interrupted with scornful language by the chairman, threw down the gauntlet:

> The President's responsibilities for the national security and foreign relations of the United States leave him no alternative but to request the immediate return of all classified materials previously furnished to the committee. . . . And to direct all departments and agencies of the executive branch respect-

fully to decline to provide the select committee with classified materials.[29]

The recklessness of the Pike Committee raised the constitutional
issue whether committees of Congress had the right to release classified
information from the executive branch on their own authority. If the
committee's position prevailed, the most sensitive intelligence could
henceforth be subpoenaed and then published unilaterally.

Bent on a showdown, the Pike Committee continued to insist on
precisely this authority. It refused to return any of the classified material it had received and announced plans to hold public hearings regarding the Tet Offensive of 1968—which, of course, had occurred in
the Johnson Administration—for which it served Colby with subpoenas requesting additional communications intelligence. The White
House offered to furnish the disputed documents, provided classified
material was kept secret until the basic dispute was resolved. Pike
rejected this compromise (which I argued was going too far, but I was
overruled by Buchen).[30] As soon as the Pike Committee opened its
hearings on the Tet Offensive on September 18, 1975, it immediately
proceeded to declassify documents on its own, including material from
two "Secret Eyes Only" cables as well as the names of some CIA
agents serving abroad.[31]

Until then, I had been an observer of the unfolding drama—for
foreign policy reasons, uneasy about the flood of documents becoming
public but, like the rest of the White House, in no position to second-
guess the release of documents about which I usually learned only
after the event. It soon became clear that Chairman Pike had selected
me as a special target and had chosen a review of Cyprus policy as the
weapon. The issue had nothing to do with intelligence analysis or
collection. Rather Pike was seeking to impeach my handling of the
Cyprus crisis. He concentrated on my alleged tardiness in reacting to
warnings of an imminent coup by Thomas Boyatt, then head of the
State Department's Cyprus desk (see Chapter 7). Pike and his staff
also second-guessed the decision of our ambassador in Athens in June
1974 to communicate State Department concerns about a possible
coup to Archbishop Seraphim in Athens and to the junta foreign minister rather than to the strong man, Dimitrios Ioannides. None of this
had anything to do with the adequacy of our intelligence and everything with the conduct of our policy.

In pursuit of their Cyprus investigation, Pike and his egregious staff demanded all internal State Department documents on the subject, including every recommendation of every junior official up and down the line.

I had explained our Cyprus policy before congressional committees on many occasions, including the reason for how we responded to Boyatt's recommendations. I was willing, indeed eager, to do so again —even though the issue had nothing even remotely to do with the adequacy of our intelligence services. But I was also determined not to stand by while the State Department was being ripped apart as the CIA had been.

I offered to submit a detailed explanation of our policy, together with a description of all the options considered (by definition, including Boyatt's). I would as well assume full responsibility for our final conclusions. But I refused to tell the committee which officer had recommended a particular course of action. By doing so in the absence of any charge of malfeasance, the integrity, spontaneity, and confidentiality of the State Department's internal decision-making process would be destroyed. If every recommendation by every junior officer came to be written with an eye to having to be defended before a congressional committee, perhaps years after the event, those committees would, in effect, turn the day-to-day tactics of the State Department into a political football.

My concern was institutional, not personal. Boyatt's views were widely known in Washington; I felt certain that the Pike Committee was already in possession of his memo, as was later confirmed. Many journalists had read it. It was obvious that the committee was really seeking to establish the right to subpoena State Department working-level documents. Today the target was the Secretary of State, who, of course, has many means available with which to defend himself. Tomorrow, however, it might be some junior officer being hounded before congressional committees for having made recommendations which subsequently turned out to be "politically incorrect."

On October 14, 1975, I requested that the committee "work with me on alternate methods of putting before it the information relevant to its inquiry." I offered "to supply a summary of *all* contrary advice I received on the Cyprus crisis, so long as it is not necessary to disclose the source of this advice," and "personally to come before the committee to describe in detail the dissenting views put to me, and my reasons for rejecting them." I stressed that "the issue is not what information the committee should receive. . . . Rather, the issue is from whom the information should be sought, and the form in which it should be delivered."[32]

I therefore instructed Lawrence Eagleburger, then deputy under secretary of state for management, to issue the following guidelines for junior officers not holding presidential appointments:

> (a) Decline, by order of the president, to discuss classified material [this was pending the resolution of the issue whether the committee had the right to declassify documents on its own], and
>
> (b) Decline, by order of the Secretary of State, to give information which would disclose options considered by or recommended to more senior officers in the Department of State.

The distinction between what was being put forward by order of the President and what I ordered on my authority as Secretary of State was significant and, for me, potentially dangerous. Ford was withholding classified information because the committee refused to respect the classification system which was enshrined in a presidential executive order. His claim of executive privilege, backed by the Attorney General, would in all likelihood be upheld by the courts. I, on the other hand, was defending the integrity of the State Department's decision-making process and seeking to insulate junior officers from partisan pressures. The Attorney General, the distinguished Chicago Law School jurist and university president Edward Levi, doubted that executive privilege applied to the issue I had raised and declined to support such a claim. I persisted because the issue seemed to me a matter of principle over which I was prepared to resign and face a contempt citation.

For once, there was widespread public support over an issue of disclosure. In mid-October 1975, the governing board of the American Foreign Service Association endorsed my position in a vote of 7–0.[33] On October 19, a *New York Times* editorial described the attitude of the Pike Committee as "clearly contrary to the national interest."[34] George Kennan, arguably the country's most respected foreign service officer, weighed in with his own letter to the *Washington Post*:

> Secretary Kissinger stands on the firmest of ground in his uncompromising resistance to such demands—he has, in-

deed, no choice. He deserves vigorous public support in the position he has taken.[35]

To recount in detail the denouement of how the committee retreated from its position while issuing a blizzard of threats of contempt citations would go beyond the limits of this volume. In the end, Democratic Congressman Les Aspin prevented a major embarrassment when he abandoned his chairman and refused to vote for a contempt citation against me, thereby defeating the citation by one vote.

This setback magnified the determination of Pike and his staff to assert their power over sensitive documents in the files of the intelligence agencies. On November 6, the Pike Committee demanded the minutes of all NSC committees dealing with intelligence on a whole host of substantive issues.[36] Security considerations aside, such documentation would be impossible to assemble within the committee's deadline of a few days, let alone to analyze and incorporate in a thoughtful report in the ten weeks left to the committee by its charter.

Phil Buchen, ever reluctant to face confrontation, worked out a "compromise" by which the vast majority of the requested documents would be delivered to the committee (with the exception of the 40 Committee deliberations, which were to be briefed orally), with the proviso that the President could veto disclosure subject to judicial review. But the flood of leaks that quickly followed showed how utterly unconstrained the committee was even in the aftermath of its supposed arrangement with the White House.

The Pike Committee's recklessness reached a crescendo in the handling of its final report. On January 20, 1976, the *New York Times* and the *Washington Star* published stories allegedly based on portions of the draft report then in the process of being prepared by the Pike Committee and its staff. These dealt primarily with the Cyprus crisis of 1974, covert operations in Iraq, CIA arms supplies to Angola political factions, the collection of intelligence inside Soviet territorial waters using U.S. Navy submarines, and the failure of American intelligence to predict India's nuclear test explosion in 1974.[37]

On the following day, the *Washington Post,* claiming access to the Pike Committee draft report, published stories (appearing in the *New York Times* as well) about the alleged use of CIA funds to provide "kings with female companions."[38] When that same day some members of the committee voiced concern about the unilateral release of "certain classified information . . . in the staff's draft report,"[39] Chairman Pike replied "that the agreement [with the White House] is not binding" insofar as the committee report was concerned "and that the executive branch would not and does not have the right to edit or dictate what should go into the congressional report."[40]

This proved to be too much for the *Washington Post,* no special friend of the Ford Administration, which editorialized:

> Mr. Pike's position on the report of his House intelligence committee is, in brief, untenable. He agreed last September in accepting certain classified information from the executive branch that the White House would be the final arbiter of what part of it would be disclosed. To claim that his pledge applied to the receipt of information then but not to the reporting of it now is to make a mockery of his pledge and to undermine the basis on which any future intelligence oversight committee could ask for confidential information.[41]

By now the full House of Representatives was having second thoughts—perhaps under the impact of the assassination of Richard Welch, the CIA station chief in Athens, on December 23, 1975. His name had been disclosed during the intelligence investigations and had subsequently appeared in a variety of media. On January 29, 1976, the House of Representatives voted 264–124 to reinstate the agreement with President Ford and to block release of the Pike Committee report until the President could certify that it contained no information adversely affecting American intelligence activities.

Two weeks later, that decision collapsed. On February 16 and February 23, *The Village Voice* printed what it described as the Pike Report. CBS correspondent Daniel Schorr, who had started broadcasting excerpts as early as January 25, later confirmed that he had given his own bootleg copy of the report to *The Village Voice.*[42]

The House now turned to its own Committee of Official Conduct to undertake an investigation. As usual in Washington, the source of the leak was never found—though one may well reflect on the irony that Schorr's sources should have been more meticulously safeguarded than those of intelligence service professionals.

Throughout this turmoil, the Pike Committee continued drafting ever newer versions of its report. Soon there were so many versions floating about that it became impossible to make a specific response. I see no reason now to change my contemporary characterization of *The Village Voice* version as being "tendentious, misleading and totally irresponsible."[43]

In the event, the Pike Report never attained official status. Slapdash and distorted accounts of several covert operations circulated for a while, but only one of the Pike Committee's recommendations survived the controversy surrounding the leak of its final report: the creation of a House Standing Committee on Intelligence. It was not much to show for the avalanche of irresponsibility and hysteria which had gravely weakened America's intelligence capabilities and had for months distracted top policymakers from their primary duties.

## Was There an Intelligence Scandal and What Was the Outcome?

Ever since these intelligence investigations, conventional wisdom— at least conventional liberal wisdom—has propagated the view expressed by Senator Church at the start of his own inquiry to the effect that the CIA "was a rogue elephant out of control." To his credit, Church later recanted that statement in his committee's report. But it has since become a permanent feature of the proverbial folklore and of many films and television shows. If anything, the intelligence investigations proved the exact opposite, as becomes clear if the investigations are broken down into their components.

American intelligence activities have three elements. The analytical branch of the CIA supplies officials with reports and estimates ranging from personalities of foreign leaders to an evaluation of policy options. The operational branch of the CIA deals with the subjects upon which many movies have been made: the espionage, covert operations, and paramilitary actions that all major governments consider to be in their national interest but are reluctant to affirm. The third component consists of a plethora of organizations, many of them under the auspices of the Defense Department, charged with the collection of intelligence by technical means.

The CIA's analytical branch did not afford the congressional investigations much grist for their mills. While its reports sometimes exasperated me by their tendency to follow conventional liberal wisdom, it was indefatigable in calm periods and indispensable in crises. Given the scope of its assignments, occasional analytical shortcomings were inevitable and could have been remedied without taking documents out of context or quoting them selectively—the stock-in-trade of determined and clever critics. The Pike Committee tried hard to turn the Cyprus issue into an intelligence failure, but it was really challenging policy judgments rather than intelligence assessments.

The most pointless—and damaging—disclosures concerned technical intelligence. Of these, the revelation that American submarines were tapping Soviet underwater cables was the most outrageous. It destroyed the indispensable source which enabled our intelligence analysts to read the results of Soviet long-range missile tests, many of which were conducted off the Kamchatka Peninsula at the tip of Siberia and transmitted to the mainland by underwater cable. Other egregious examples of damaging technical disclosures concerned the *Glomar Explorer*—as mentioned previously, a ship specially designed to raise a sunken Soviet submarine from the ocean floor. Various communications intercepts, such as our ability to listen to some of the Soviet leaders' telephone conversations, were also pointlessly disclosed. These revelations involved intelligence successes, not failures, and carried not the slightest implication of abuse of authority.

The principal target of the investigations turned out to be covert operations. The Cold War had generated a gray area of superpower conflict not encompassed either in formal diplomacy nor by military action. A worldwide network of terrorists, guerrilla groups, and radical and Communist parties subsidized by Moscow threatened democratic societies, posing an unprecedented challenge to the global balance of power.

This is why every American President of the post–World War II era found America's covert capabilities indispensable—even when, like Carter and Clinton, they had originally been highly skeptical. The most frequent American covert operations were assistance to democratic parties or media in countries where radical or Communist groups, financed from abroad, threatened to become ascendant or sought to suppress free expression. On rarer occasions, covert operations financed paramilitary and even military resistance to takeovers by Communists or to forces considered to be a threat to our national security. During my service in government, this kind of covert operation encouraged autonomy for Kurds in Iraq and sought to prevent a Communist victory in Angola (to be discussed in later chapters). In my testimony before the Church Committee on February 5, 1976, I summed up what had led Ford to approve the covert operation in Angola:

> We helped black African countries at their request when
> substantial amounts of Soviet military equipment and
> Cuban military forces appeared in an adjoining country,
> when this [Soviet] military equipment was of a quantity that
> was larger than all of the military equipment previously sent
> to black Africa. And we did it in order to discourage similar
> actions in other parts of the world.[44]

Subsequent administrations have continued covert operations—often on a major scale—to this writing and in such far-flung places as Central America, the Caribbean, the Persian Gulf, and Bosnia, where the Clinton Administration trained and equipped one of the armies, essentially by covert means.

Covert operations are, of course, no more immune to human error than more traditional open policies, probably more so because of the ambiguities that give rise to them in the first place. That is why, in all administrations, they were vetted and controlled at the highest levels of government.

Occasional breakdowns were caused by misjudgments on the part of political leaders, not by excesses of the intelligence community. The driving force behind the investigations was not so much demonstrable abuses as the overriding convictions of the committees and their staffs that covert operations, in any form and no matter how they might be conducted or controlled, are inappropriate to American democracy. They were attacking the policies in the guise of criticizing the methods.

Oddly, the category of covert actions most in need of review was barely addressed by the committees. It is the military and paramilitary actions carried out in broad daylight in which the "covert" aspect concerns the method of financing rather than the secrecy of the operations—examples are the Laos operations in the Kennedy, Johnson, and Nixon Administrations, the Angola operation in the Ford Administration, and the various Bosnian operations in the Clinton Administration. Once such operations reach a certain scale, they should probably be shifted to some more open category and placed under the direction of personnel better qualified than intelligence specialists to supervise military operations.

The intelligence investigations of the 1970s concentrated on the more traditional covert intelligence activities. In the process, two elements were largely neglected. The first is that they occur in a shadowy and inherently precarious area involving a high possibility of failure; otherwise they would not have been handled in a covert manner in the first place. More importantly, the investigations took little or no account of the Cold War. In the context of Berlin blockades, the Cuban Missile Crisis, and Communist pressures around the Soviet periphery, the loss of countries such as Chile or Angola to Communism was considered irrevocable. Retroactive verdicts rendered a decade or two after the event were inherently unjust to the foot soldiers of silent battles along fronts which had been chosen for them by superiors who abandoned their troops when the public mood turned to looking for scapegoats.

Almost everyone with any experience in intelligence operations was appalled by the consequences. Then Secretary of Defense and former CIA Director James Schlesinger said in early August 1975:

> I think that we recognize that the sources of information coming into the CIA have been dramatically reduced in both liaison relationships and in relation to the willingness of foreigners to work with our intelligence people . . . [and that is] the inevitable effect of these kinds of revelations.[45]

Even President Carter, who had campaigned against the CIA and its alleged cult of secrecy, discovered early in his administration that matters had gone too far. In July 1978, he complained to congressional leaders that leaks of classified information were drying up America's intelligence sources and damaging national security. In March 1979, Senator Daniel Patrick Moynihan, a member of the Senate Select Committee on Intelligence, asserted: "There is no intelligence agency of any consequence left within the United States government."[46] In November 1979, Edward Heath, former Prime Minister of Great Britain, weighed in with his perspective: "What has happened to the American security services causes the greatest anxiety in the whole Western world."[47] Finally, James Schlesinger, who as CIA Director had started collecting the "family jewels" as they related to Watergate, summed up in February 1980:

> Since 1975, instead of strengthening what was a reasonably effective organization, the political process has tended to further weaken, cripple, hobble and destroy the intelligence-gathering services through legislation, through new procedures that preclude the necessarily secretive operations of an intelligence agency.[48]

Ford had taken the substance of all the charges very seriously. He waited until the Pike Committee had completed its work before issuing —on February 18, 1976—Executive Order 11905 reorganizing the intelligence community. Drawing on the recommendations of both the Rockefeller Commission and the Church Committee, the executive order: a) established a new foreign intelligence command structure providing the intelligence community with precise policy guidance; b) made public the guidelines for the responsibilities and duties of the intelligence community; c) provided a new set of procedures for vetting activities which raised issues of legality or propriety; and d) established new restraints—for example, prohibiting assassinations and creating new controls on electronic surveillance and the opening of mail.[49] The responsibilities and duties of the intelligence community were spelled out agency by agency. In some cases, the list of authorized functions recognized for the first time—publicly and specifically—activities that had for years been undertaken under classified directives.

These were useful steps. Ironically, as the next two decades would show, the real danger was not excesses of the intelligence community but the wisdom of orders issued by higher authorities, almost invariably the White House (with respect to Iran-contra in the Reagan Administration and the covert supply of Iranian arms to Bosnia in the Clinton Administration). It also became obvious that the requirement of consultation which was expanded to include eight congressional committees (finally reduced to two in 1980) before undertaking covert operations neither assured executive-congressional harmony nor safeguarded security. The earliest such case in point was the covert operation launched by the Ford Administration in Angola during 1975 to counter Soviet and Cuban domination of that part of Africa. After Ford had approved the operation, the three oversight committees in the House and the Senate plus the two intelligence committees were briefed meticulously and continuously. Each time a new decision was made with respect to Angola, these committees were informed in detail. Altogether eight congressional committees were briefed twenty-four different times. More than twenty Senators, one hundred Congressmen, and 150 staff members were briefed about the Angolan covert operation.[50] As it turned out, the widespread briefings gave an additional incentive to those viscerally opposed to covert operations to seek to thwart them by going public.

The question remains whether such vast upheaval was needed to bring about the improvements that were achieved. Though the various investigations claimed to aspire to improving intelligence activities, their efforts—especially in the case of the Pike Committee—coalesced into a powerful assault on established American foreign policy. Sensitive classified information was deliberately put into the public domain; intelligence officers were named, operational cables and internal memoranda were quoted, the identities of foreign agents were exposed by using transparent cover descriptions, and particular operational methods in specific countries were detailed. None of it was essential either to the ostensible purposes of the investigations or to the congressional oversight process.

The cumulative damage to the intelligence community lasted a long time. Having been so thoroughly dissected and occasionally ridiculed in the full glare of publicity, the CIA was stripped of its mystique of competence, reliability, and self-assurance so important to its mission. Created as an arm of the executive branch, the CIA suddenly found itself, in the words of a later Director, Robert M. Gates, at an anomalous equidistance between the President and Congress.[51] Buffeted by conflicting pressures and against the background of so many careers destroyed, CIA personnel discovered that even carrying out orders provided no protection against shifting public moods. As a result, cramped caution became their refuge. Each CIA employee in effect needed his own lawyer to check whether his orders or his response to them might not make him a victim of the next wave of purification. It became far easier and safer to bury oneself in bureaucratic paperwork than to stick one's neck out in a profession in which the risks at home sometimes exceeded those in the field.

Frequent internal organizational changes and drastic personnel reductions compounded the demoralization. Since these investigations, most (and perhaps all) covert operations have become public, defeating the very reason for their being covert. In the process, operational control has sometimes fallen into the hands of romantics, not strategists, as in the case of Iran-contra and of the green light given to the supply of Iranian arms to Bosnia.

The most poignant victims have been the CIA personnel who, during the Cold War, had been assigned to defend the front lines of freedom—which their superiors had defined for them—on behalf of a society not used to dealing with a global balance of power, much less with covert action. The men and women who undertook this thankless task in a secrecy which deprived them of either credit or, as it turned out, adequate protection were left naked before their enemies. Their traditional safeguards were suddenly stripped away, and their superiors either failed to come to their defense or simply fed them to the wolves. Their assigned tasks were suddenly vilified, often a decade or more after the event when few could recall the necessities that had given rise to them. Operating in a world with which few Americans have had any experience, they could be made to look foolish or incompetent by sharpshooters preoccupied with advancing their own ideological causes or their careers.

The most conspicuous casualty of this process was Richard Helms, one of the most distinguished public servants I have known. He was charged with having committed perjury while testifying in 1973 before the Senate Foreign Relations Committee during confirmation hearings for his appointment as ambassador to Iran. Technically, he had testified incompletely; substantively, it was a grave injustice. Following heretofore accepted procedures, Helms had denied covert operations before a committee not authorized to receive information about them, though he had already fully briefed the details to the four committees that were assigned the responsibility. What made the indictment which ruined Helms's public career and blighted his life particularly egregious was that the alleged perjury had been brought to the attention of the Attorney General by Helms's successor, William Colby, who had in turn been pressed to do so by a subordinate CIA official.

The intelligence investigations were but one act in the drama by which, starting with Vietnam, the United States struggled to come to grips with an imperfect world it could neither abandon nor dominate. Caught between those who, in the middle of the Cold War, insisted on an absolute standard for American conduct and others who were, above all, averse to all risk, the American intelligence community was torn apart in our nation's historic quest for moral purity. After the end of the Cold War, the United States has discovered—to our surprise— that our much abused intelligence service is sorely needed in an era of terrorism, proliferation of weapons of mass destruction, and economic competition. In a democracy, that service must, of course, be accountable. But there are ways to achieve this without institutionalizing paralysis and self-flagellation.

# PART FOUR

---

# BREAKTHROUGH
# IN THE
# MIDDLE EAST

# 12

# FORD AND MIDDLE EAST DIPLOMACY

It was the administration of Gerald Ford that helped Israel and its Arab neighbors across the critical dividing line from military disengagement agreements to the uncharted territory of a peace process. The disengagement agreements of 1974 in Nixon's term consolidated the cease-fires that had ended the 1973 Arab-Israeli war. The Sinai II Accord of 1975 in Ford's presidency was the decisive step on the path that culminated in a peace treaty between Israel and Egypt in March 1979, in the Oslo accords with the PLO in September 1993, and in a peace treaty between Israel and Jordan in October 1994.

Had Ford's succession been a normal transition, he would never have launched himself on such a complex and risky enterprise during his first week in office. But with the Middle East volatile and the industrial democracies panicked by the energy crisis, he had no choice. Invitations extended by Nixon to a number of Middle East leaders were coming due. During July 1974, Nixon's last full month in office, he had met with the Israeli deputy prime minister and foreign minister, Yigal Allon, and, in early August, with the Jordanian Prime Minister, Zaid Rifai. Visits by the Egyptian, Syrian, and Saudi foreign ministers as well as King Hussein had been scheduled at the rate of one a week for the month of August. In the morbidly suspicious and supercharged atmosphere of the Middle East, postponement of these visits risked being interpreted as a signal that the new administration was hesitant to pursue the peace process or, worse, that a change in policy was imminent, inflaming the area.

## The Cauldron

In the Middle East, the part of the world where mirages are natural phenomena, nothing is ever as it appears. When President Nixon left office, a "negotiating process" between Arab states and Israel had only just begun to clear away the vestiges of four wars in a twenty-five-year period. Even so, no Arab nation had recognized the state of Israel, nor had any Arab leader agreed to negotiate directly with an Israeli leader on political issues (except for King Hussein, who had done so surreptitiously and to no effect). The furthest the Arab states had gone was to permit technical military discussions regarding cease-fires, though only under third-party sponsorship—usually of the United States, occasionally of the United Nations.

In terms of traditional diplomacy, the peace process was a never-never land. Nations that did not recognize each other were talking about peace, and the formal program of some Arab leaders participating in the peace process still called for the eradication of the Jewish state. The near-sacramental language of U.N. Security Council Resolution 242—agreed in November 1967 and to this day one of the international legal foundations of negotiations—reflected these incongruities. It required Israel to withdraw to "secure and recognized boundaries" in the context of a contractual "just and lasting" peace without defining what these adjectives signified. The Arab states asked for the return of all conquered territories in exchange, they implied, for the recognition of Israel at the end of the process. Israel insisted on direct negotiations, implying recognition at the beginning of the process. Each side was demanding its ultimate goal as the entrance price into negotiations —an attitude which was to cause deadlocks in various forums for decades. The players have changed with the passage of time; the basic script has not.

Both Israel and the Arab states were driven by stereotypes of their respective histories. The Israelis, shunted into a de facto ghetto throughout their national history, endowed the peace process with a nearly metaphysical significance. They demanded of the peace treaty that it deliver relations with its neighbors as close as those between, say, Belgium and the Netherlands. Yet such a level of coexistence did not generally exist even between Arab states; between Israel and its neighbors, it could not possibly arise from a single formal document but only at the end of a lengthy period of peacefully living side by side.

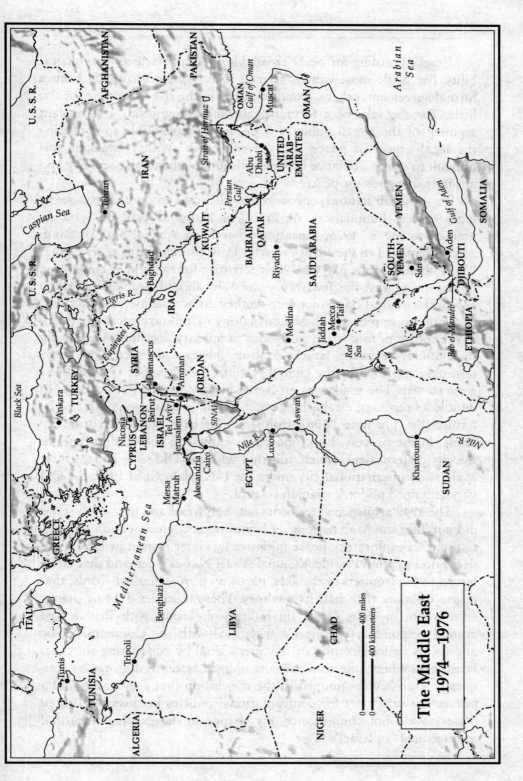

The Middle East
1974—1976

400 miles

400 kilometers

Israel's yearning for peace created both an obstacle and a vulnerability. For while most Israelis seemed to be asking too much from a formal agreement, others, paradoxically, ran the risk of settling for too little. For the sake of a formal peace and recognition, a significant segment of the Israeli public was becoming susceptible to confusing the legal aspect of peace with its substance. Within Israel, it was difficult to strike a balance between absolute demands for security and absolute demands for peace.

To the Arab nations, encounters with Israel amounted to a seemingly endless humiliation. As President Hafez al-Asad of Syria remarked to me in 1975, repeating what King Abd al-Aziz of Saudi Arabia had said to President Franklin D. Roosevelt thirty years earlier: "Why should Arabs pay with their territory for the crimes committed in Europe against the Jewish people? Why should Arabs be asked to accept the biblical claim of a religion they do not themselves practice?" Attempts to implement these convictions by military means had led, in the course of four wars, to a series of military disasters. Misjudging their military capacity, Israel's Arab neighbors had rejected the partition plan approved by the United Nations in November 1947 and had gone to war. The result was an Israeli victory which enabled Israel to double its territory, establishing what in later negotiations came to be termed the pre-June "1967 frontiers" (actually the 1949 armistice lines). In the process, Israel moved its capital to the modern part of the city of Jerusalem, which, together with the Old City, had been set aside as an international city under the U.N. plan. Until 1967, the Old City remained under Jordanian control.

The 1949 armistice agreements between Israel and four Arab states did not alter the Arab nations' policy of nonrecognition and nonnegotiation. An exploratory peace initiative by Great Britain in 1954 foundered on Egyptian President Gamal Abdel Nasser's demand that Israel return to the frontiers of the U.N. partition plan—in other words, that it give up more than half its territory. These attitudes did not change even when, in 1956, Israel (in military collusion with Britain and France) responded to Nasser's arms deal with the Communist bloc and to his nationalization of the Suez Canal by conquering the Sinai Peninsula. When American pressure obliged Israel to disgorge its conquests, Arab leaders jumped to the conclusion that they had found a permanent safety net for confrontational policies because the United States would not countenance any change in the existing territorial arrangements in Israel's favor.

The events of June 1967 taught them otherwise. In May of that year, Nasser peremptorily demanded the withdrawal of the United Nations Emergency Force (UNEF), which had been established as a buffer along the Egyptian-Israeli border in the aftermath of the Israeli withdrawal from the Sinai in 1956. He followed this by closing the Strait of Tiran, in effect blockading Israel's only Red Sea port at Eilat. When neither the U.N. nor the United States effectively challenged this abrogation of international agreements, Israel, in a sudden attack, achieved an overwhelming victory. Its troops once more reached the Suez Canal and occupied the Golan Heights and the West Bank of the Jordan River, together with the Old City of Jerusalem. Israel thereby doubled its territory a second time.

Suddenly the boundary lines of 1967, which no Arab state had ever recognized while they were in existence, took on a sacrosanct quality in Arab eyes and turned into the benchmark for negotiations for those countries prepared to negotiate at all. Even then some Arab leaders still found it difficult to bring themselves to utter the magic word "peace." In 1973, an Arab foreign minister told me that no one wanted to be the minister who would be cursed by posterity for having been the first to make peace with Israel.

Only one Arab leader had been completely unambiguous about his intentions before 1973: the doughty and chivalrous King Hussein of Jordan, who had ruled the West Bank and the Old City of Jerusalem until the 1967 war. A staunch friend of the West, he met frequently and clandestinely with Israeli leaders. But acting alone and in secret, Hussein was too weak either to threaten war or to conclude a separate peace. That Jordan would be the second, but could not be the first, Arab country to make peace developed into an axiom of American Middle East diplomacy—an epigram that did not really advance matters because it still left open the question of who would be the first and by what route.

Complicating that answer was the intra-Arab dispute over who should represent the Palestinians, whose fate was, after all, the origin of the crisis. The Palestine Liberation Organization (PLO) had been formed in 1964 to represent the claims of the Palestinian people, especially the 1.5 million refugees scattered across the Arab world when Nixon entered office (at this writing, the number has grown to over 5 million).

At that time, the PLO was far more extreme than the partially domesticated political organization that concluded the Oslo accords with Israel in September 1993. In those days, the PLO's principal weapon was terror against individuals or groups identified with peace negotiations. Its policies were radical and pro-Soviet, and its founding covenant called for the destruction of Israel.[1] In the 1970s, Israel returned the favor and refused to negotiate with the PLO.

The Arab states' attitude toward the PLO oscillated between unease and respect. The organization's capacity for assassination and producing civil turmoil was widely feared. At the same time, its assault on Israel was cast as part of the anti-colonial struggle so popular among Arab masses and the Nonaligned. By the time Nixon entered office in 1969, almost all Arab governments, except Jordan, were coming to treat the PLO as the true representative of the Palestinians—never mind that this destroyed any hope for negotiation with Israel.

To avoid this dilemma, some Arab leaders were willing to let Jordan do the negotiating—as it had at the Geneva conference of December 1973—on the grounds that it had governed the West Bank and the Old City of Jerusalem until the 1967 war.[2] They would generally do so with the caveat that any territory regained would have to be turned over to the PLO—guaranteeing Israeli stonewalling. It was a classic Middle East fantasy: Israel was to turn over territory by proxy to an organization whose charter provided for the destruction of Israel.

Over this cauldron hovered the Soviet Union. By the time of Nixon's inauguration, it had become the principal arms supplier for radical Arab governments, which, under Nasser, included Egypt. Moscow maintained close intelligence contact with the various terrorist groups, most of which received training in Soviet bloc camps or from Soviet bloc personnel. Soviet diplomacy gave all-out support to the maximum program of most Arab states: Israel's return to the 1967 borders and restoration of unspecified Palestinian rights in exchange for undefined international guarantees for Israel's borders. This would leave a corridor only nine miles wide between Israel's principal coastal cities of Tel Aviv and Haifa. The Soviet Union asked for no comparable sacrifices from its Arab clients.

It was a no-win proposition for the United States. We had no incentive to participate in a diplomacy—much less a multilateral conference—in which the Soviet Union would appear as the lawyer for the Arab side and maneuver us into a position where we would be either isolated at the side of Israel or obliged to deliver Israeli acquiescence to a program incompatible with its long-term survival. If Israel yielded to our pressures, we would have abandoned—and perhaps broken the back of—an ally, leaving the Soviets to garnish credit for the results; if we failed to deliver Israel, we would inflame even the moderate Arabs. I told Soviet Ambassador Anatoly Dobrynin repeatedly that we would cooperate with the Soviet Union in the Middle East only if Moscow separated itself from its radical clients to the same extent as Moscow was asking us to distinguish our position from Israel's. (Dobrynin has since indicated his regret that the Politburo had proved too rigid to follow such a course.)[3]

The nascent Nixon Administration looked at this impasse as a challenge to create incentives for Arab moderation, to reduce Soviet influence, and to encourage an Arab-Israeli negotiation on that basis. We had many assets for such a policy. So long as the United States kept Israel strong, our trump card would be that the Soviet Union—despite its capacity to raise the level of tensions diplomatically—had no means to bring about either a military conclusion or a diplomatic breakthrough on its terms. Whenever the Kremlin threatened to intervene, as it did in the wars of 1956 and 1973, it recoiled when faced with the risks of military confrontation with America.[4]

Assuming our analysis was correct and provided we played our cards carefully, either the United States would be in a position to oblige the Soviet Union to help shape a genuine compromise or, sooner or later, one of Moscow's Arab clients would break ranks and begin moving toward the United States to achieve at least part of its national goals. Early in Nixon's first term, I told journalists during a background briefing that the new administration would seek to "expel" the Soviet Union from the Middle East. It was an incautious and undiplomatic remark, and it created a furor at the time. But it accurately described the strategy of the Nixon White House.[5]

In pursuit of this goal, we adopted two complementary policies: we blocked every Arab move based on Soviet military support or involving a Soviet military threat, and we took charge of the peace process when frustration with the stalemate caused key Arab leaders to dissociate from the Soviet Union and turn to the United States.

The first indication that the strategy was working came in July 1972 after the Nixon-Brezhnev summit in May had made no progress on the Middle East. Sadat reacted by dismissing his Soviet military advisers and expelling Soviet technicians. In February 1973, Sadat initiated a diplomatic dialogue with the White House by sending his security adviser, Mohammed Hafiz Ismail, to Washington for a formal meeting with Nixon, followed by a secret meeting with me in New

York. Progress was slow because the United States was inhibited by the Watergate scandal, which was just beginning to gain momentum, and Sadat by his reluctance to antagonize either his Arab colleagues or Moscow so long as he needed their support for a military option.[6] As a result, Ismail presented what sounded to us like the standard Arab fare: total Israeli withdrawal to the 1967 borders with only vague assurances of Arab reciprocity.

We grossly underestimated Sadat. Based on the experiences of previous Arab-Israeli wars, we treated Sadat's threats to go to war unless there was diplomatic progress as so much operatic gesturing. Even his expulsion of Soviet advisers in July 1972 was interpreted with not a little condescension as one more symptom of congenital petulance, since Sadat had not tried to obtain any reciprocal gesture from us. It never occurred to us that he might be clearing the decks for military action and wanted to remove what he considered to be the Soviet obstacle to it. (Sadat was almost surely right in this analysis. The last thing the Soviet leaders wanted was a Middle East war involving its own forces.)

In October 1973, Egypt and Syria launched a surprise attack against Israel. The Arab armies fought more effectively than in any previous conflict but, even so, Israel managed to cross the Suez Canal and penetrate deep into Egypt, trapping the Egyptian Third Army in the process. And it also occupied Syrian territory to the very outskirts of Damascus.

A new element emerged when Sadat became the first Arab leader to make a decisive turn toward peace. Having demonstrated Egypt's military capacity, he proceeded to abandon Nasser's all-or-nothing approach to diplomacy and shifted Egypt's diplomatic priorities from Moscow to Washington. Sadat was also the first Arab leader to grasp that the Arab-Israeli conflict was as much psychological as it was political and military. The Arab posture of implacable hostility had given Israel no incentive to engage in diplomacy; with their country's existence permanently on the line, Israeli leaders clung to strategic positions of strength. And in the United States, the Arab cause had come to be identified with the actions of Arab terrorists.

Sadat set about to change both images. Two weeks after the end of the war, he agreed to hold direct talks between Egyptian and Israeli military representatives on the modalities of the cease-fire at a marker denoting Kilometer 101 on the Cairo–Suez road. A few weeks later, Sadat gave me a message for Israeli Prime Minister Golda Meir expressing his commitment to peace: "When I threatened war, I meant it. When I talk of peace now, I mean it." On January 18, 1974, I brought Golda Meir's reply to Sadat; in it, she stated that she "[would do her] best to establish trust and understanding between us. Both our peoples need and deserve peace."

A little later on that glorious January day, Sadat and I were talking in his study when an aide entered the room and whispered something in his ear. With tears in his eyes, Sadat walked over to me, kissed me on both cheeks, and said:

> They have just signed the agreement at Kilometer 101. I am today taking off my military uniform. I never expect to wear it again except for ceremonial occasions. Tell her [Prime Minister Meir] that is the answer to her letter.

Sadat kept his promise. When he was assassinated on October 6, 1981, he was wearing a uniform during the ceremonial occasion commemorating the beginning of the October 1973 war.

The January 1974 disengagement agreement between Egypt and Israel brought about Israel's withdrawal from the Suez Canal and pledged both sides to pursue the rest of their disagreements by peaceful means. A few months later, in May, even Syria's Asad, the more traditional Arab leader, concluded under American auspices a similar agreement—albeit with much more difficulty—for disengagement on the Golan Heights.

The two disengagement agreements—the first successful Arab-Israeli negotiations since 1949—liquidated the immediate consequences of the 1973 war. Israel withdrew from the Suez Canal and returned Quneitra, the largest city of the Golan Heights, to Syria.[7] When Gerald Ford entered office, no residue of the war remained to provide either incentive or pretext for continuing negotiations. Middle East diplomacy would have to be motivated by the ultimate goal of peace itself.

## Forging a New Strategy

At the start of the Ford Administration, our efforts in the Middle East began to run up against this conundrum: Arab leaders were proclaiming their indivisible unity, but their mutual suspicions made cooperation between them elusive. And since Israel refused to discuss the return to the 1967 frontiers with Syria on the Golan Heights or to negotiate with the PLO over the West Bank, attempting what was called a "comprehensive settlement"—that is, a negotiation covering all fronts and all issues—would guarantee prolonged stalemate or war.

Anwar Sadat, the most farsighted Arab leader, understood this dilemma and was prepared to inch ever closer to a separate arrangement with Israel. Distrustful of his Arab brethren's volatility and extremely dubious about their relations with Moscow, he was unwilling to submit Egypt's diplomatic opportunities to the scrutiny of the other Arab states. On the other hand, he was not yet sufficiently confident of America's staying power to risk a solitary course.

Sadat therefore adopted an extraordinarily subtle and ambiguous strategy. He paid his Arab dues by speaking out often and passionately on behalf of the Palestinians, and he urged us to negotiate with the PLO, which he knew from conversations with me would not happen so long as the PLO engaged in terrorism and maintained its charter calling for the destruction of Israel. Sadat spoke fervently about the importance of simultaneous progress on all fronts but with one crucial proviso: he gave us a deadline of three months for bringing about another Israeli withdrawal on some front, knowing this to be quite impossible on any front except the Egyptian. Indeed, that impossibility was his alibi for acting alone. Sadat left it to me to find a way through his Delphic pronouncements. He praised my diplomatic skills lavishly and publicly, which, though I like to think it was sincere, provided another alibi for his acting alone by shifting the onus for his solitary course onto my shoulders.

Only Syria's Asad, precluded by Israel from a separate partial solution, seemed genuinely interested in a comprehensive solution because he knew it to be his only chance of recovering Syrian territory. At a minimum, combining the negotiations on all fronts would give Asad a veto over the diplomacy of his Arab brothers and perhaps oblige them to add their pressures to his.

Trapped between Asad's insistence on a comprehensive solution and Sadat's preference for a solitary course, King Hussein became the odd man out—proof that life is not always just. He had crushed the PLO in Jordan in 1970, barred guerrilla attacks on Israeli-held territory from Jordanian soil, and conducted to no avail as many as five hundred hours of secret talks with Israeli leaders. Not having participated in the 1973 war, Hussein had no Israeli prisoners to exchange, and he was too weak to start a war by himself. Israel had little incentive to negotiate with Hussein, even as he was being kept at arm's length by the other Arab states which were cultivating the PLO sometimes from conviction, sometimes from fear.

Several Arab leaders had become quite skillful at manipulating pressures on us by industrial democracies afraid of another energy crisis. Some of the Arab leaders had drawn the ominous conclusion that Israel could not stand pain, as Asad said to me on more than one occasion. He had, in fact, identified Israel's neuralgic point. Given the country's small population and extraordinary concern with human life, relatively few casualties were needed to generate a searing shock.

The "comprehensive" approach was intellectually the most tempting and, indeed, had the support of most academic experts.[8] Until the 1973 war, it had been the State Department's preferred option. On the other hand, assembling all the parties at Geneva, as the Soviets and the hard-line Arabs urged and Sadat resisted, would have led to the amalgamation of all special claims. With the most radical groups having a veto over the more moderate elements and with the Soviet Union certain to assume the role of lawyer for the collective Arab position (backed as well by our European and Japanese allies), the result would be our isolation, a diplomatic stalemate, or war.

As for Israel, whatever the defiant bravado of the occasional leader in that war of all against all by which Israeli politicians conduct their internal battles, it was in no position to sustain a comprehensive negotiation. No Israeli leader had as yet agreed to accept for any price the 1967 frontiers on all fronts or, for that matter, on any front; to return the Old City of Jerusalem to Arab control; or to abandon the settlements established in conquered territories—all of which would be part of any joint Arab program.

For all these reasons, I recommended—and first Nixon and then Ford endorsed—what we called a "step-by-step" approach, which I described to the new Israeli Prime Minister, Yitzhak Rabin, during his inaugural visit to President Ford in September 1974, as follows:

> [The choice is] either [a] total settlement or a series of partial settlements. A total settlement would lump all the issues together, and its failure would lead to great pressures. Secondly, it would raise the issue of the 1967 borders prematurely. Thirdly, it would raise Jerusalem and the Palestinians. . . . [For all these reasons] there must be some alternative

framework to prevent the Palestinian issue from overwhelming all else. . . . It is essential that the Geneva conference
meet as late as possible and hopefully to ratify something
already done.

If foreign policy were as simple as the study of it in academic
seminars, Jordan would have been the logical candidate for a next step.
Hussein's conduct had been impeccably cooperative. A negotiation
with Jordan was Israel's best tactic for avoiding pressures to negotiate
with the PLO, which, according to its own charter, would be committed to the destruction of the Jewish state. If Jordan could be drawn
into a negotiation for the West Bank and persuaded to assume responsibility for a part of it, the explosive issue of Palestinian representation
would be removed from the agenda of a Geneva conference when and
if it reconvened. I had told the Senate Foreign Relations Committee in
an executive session on May 31, 1974:

> The best way to deal with the Palestinian question would be
> to draw the Jordanians into the West Bank and thereby
> turn the debate . . . into one between the Jordanians and the
> Palestinians.

In July, a week and a half before Nixon's resignation, I told Israeli
Foreign Minister Yigal Allon that Israel did not have the option of
freezing the status quo on the West Bank in expectation that a Jordanian negotiation would always remain available later on. If Israel did
not deal with Hussein now, PLO leader Yasser Arafat would be recognized as the spokesman for the West Bank within a year.

I elaborated on this theme with Rabin on his visit to Washington
in September 1974:

> With respect to Jordan, we agree that a Palestinian state is
> likely to have as its objective the destruction of both Jordan
> and Israel and is likely to have a high potential for disrupting
> the uneasy equilibrium in the area. Second, the Palestinians
> now are the elements with the greatest incentive for disrup-
> tion. Therefore the U.S. has no incentive to feature the
> Palestinians. . . .
> Therefore we think the best way to handle the Palestin-
> ian issue is through negotiations between Israel and Jordan.

That is what we've said publicly many times; that's our real policy. Therefore, we see a Jordanian negotiation as important.

A Jordan-first strategy faced formidable obstacles, however. Jordan might be the most responsible among Israel's neighbors, but it was also, as noted, the weakest. Since Hussein was in no position to start a war without allies, Israel would gain from progress on the Jordanian front only if other Arab states supported it. But during the fateful summer of 1974, the Arab leaders were extremely divided. When Zaid Rifai, then Jordan's Prime Minister, accompanied King Hussein to Washington in mid-August 1974 as part of the inaugural procession of Arab leaders, he described what had happened to an attempt to coordinate Arab positions:

> We decided that Egypt, Jordan, Syria, and the PLO would meet to coordinate a strategy on Geneva. The PLO would not go because Jordan was there. Syria would not go because Fahmy [the Egyptian foreign minister] was there, and they would not meet in Cairo. So it had to be Egypt, the PLO, and Jordan. And now we won't go.

Moreover, the few Arab states backing Jordan as the principal negotiator did so as a ploy to get as much of the West Bank as possible away from Israel, after which most of them would support turning the territory over to the PLO. But Israel had no incentive to encourage a negotiation of which the PLO would be the ultimate beneficiary.

These obstacles might have been overcome had Hussein's analysis of Sadat's necessities been closer to the mark. He argued for a Jordan-first strategy on the grounds that Sadat required a Jordanian "cover" for another move in the Sinai, which he was clearly determined to undertake. By then, our own strategy relied on Sadat as the key to Middle East peace. He was, after all, the most moderate leader and at the helm of the largest country in the region. We were therefore inclined to favor Hussein's analysis. But, as it turned out, Sadat had different views. He was not fond of kings and disliked Hussein. Nor did he believe that Hussein could provide him with the necessary cover for a separate move. In the end, Israeli procrastination and Sadat's opposition were to ruin the Jordanian option.

## The Jordanian Option

Israeli Foreign Minister Yigal Allon arrived in Washington on July 30, 1974, in the waning days of the Nixon Administration. Allon had been a personal friend since 1957 when he attended the Harvard International Seminar, a two-month summer program for promising younger foreign leaders which I directed. At that time, he and I had taken a trip through New England together during which he displayed his legendary courage by letting me do the driving. Allon, the first leading Israeli I had met, told me stories which at the time sounded romantic—how, during the war of 1948, his outnumbered, ragtag army, equipped with weapons scrounged from all across Europe, had defeated the British-trained and -equipped Egyptian army. Allon spoke about it not boastfully but with the humility reserved for having participated in a near-miracle.

In 1961, I visited Allon in Kibbutz Ginossar on the shores of the Sea of Galilee at the foot of the Golan Heights, where he lived in a small, spartan apartment. The environment conveyed that miracles do not happen to those who await them passively. Allon and his generation had wrested every inch of soil from unfriendly circumstances with their labor and often with their blood. In 1961, in the midst of what is now described as a period of peace, there were still bomb shelters all over Ginossar to protect the inhabitants against periodic shelling from the Syrian-held Golan Heights looming above them.

Even when he rose to high office, a part of Allon retained the almost childlike wonder that he should be now discussing such matters as high-performance aircraft and, even more miraculously, the disposition of Israel's conquests. This, however, did not necessarily make him a comfortable negotiating partner. Allon was imbued with the special brand of schizophrenia of the first generation of Israel's leaders. He had witnessed too many Israeli casualties to be at ease with the notion that confidence could be built by ceding territorial buffers. Yet that was precisely what the peace process was all about: to balance legitimacy and security, confidence and territory. Allon had an exceptionally sweet and gentle disposition; he was anything but a hard-liner. He recognized the importance of the peace process intellectually; what he recoiled from was its practical application.

This ambivalence defined as well the basic difference between how the United States and Israel viewed the Middle East peace process—a difference that continues to this day. For us, the step-by-step approach was a way of keeping the political initiative in American hands, of preventing the coalescence of radical Arab and Communist pressures, of forestalling Soviet mischief, and of deferring the most contentious and painful issues until a more propitious moment. Israel's leaders welcomed these benefits. But they were not emotionally—or institutionally—prepared for the decisions the peace process would impose on them. Had they been given truth serum, they would, that July of 1974, no doubt have expressed a deep yearning for a respite from all pressures—no matter how desirable the long-term goal of peace.

Yitzhak Rabin had just become Prime Minister, succeeding the legendary Golda Meir. He had been selected as leader of the Labor Party by a narrow majority over Shimon Peres, who now served in his cabinet as defense minister, and he governed with a parliamentary majority of one at the end of perhaps the most traumatic year in Israeli history. In the previous nine months, Israel had been the victim of a surprise attack and suffered over 2,800 dead, the equivalent of 200,000 American casualties. In addition, Israel had been the victim of continued radical Palestinian terrorist attacks. In the space of a month—at Kiryat Shmona near its northern border, on April 11, 1974, and at Ma'alot on May 15 (in the middle of my Syrian shuttle)—thirty-seven Israelis (mostly children) were brutally murdered. Israel had negotiated two disengagement agreements, in each of which it had retreated from the prewar cease-fire lines. Now, only three months after the draining Golan Heights negotiation, Israel was being asked to consider further withdrawals and on the West Bank, the most sensitive area geographically as well as psychologically—opening a domestic debate over whether Israel's leaders had a right to cede territory which to conservative Jews was a divine dispensation.

In its most fearful moments, the Israeli cabinet could see itself being pushed back step by fateful step toward the 1967 borders or worse by salami tactics whereby major changes result from the accumulating succession of seemingly marginal steps. And what appeared like small steps to Americans might be massive on a territory only fifty miles wide. Rabin was to point this out on September 11, 1974, while we were discussing the Jordanian option with him:

> KISSINGER: First, I recognize Israeli fears that the strategy
> I have outlined can be made to look like salami tactics.
> RABIN: It can produce the reality of salami tactics.

362   YEARS OF RENEWAL

KISSINGER: It can do both. I don't have any answer to that
except in a relationship of confidence.

No Israeli leader was emotionally more dedicated to peace in the
abstract than Allon. During the thirty-four-day Syrian shuttle, Allon,
then deputy prime minister and minister of labor, had escorted me on
many occasions on the one-hour drive from Jerusalem to Ben Gurion
Airport. In the course of frequent deadlocks, he would voice his
yearning for an agreement and his confidence in my ability to distill a
solution. Yet Allon never furnished any guidance as to how I might
realize his fervent wish; he simply built me into his unbounded faith
in Israel's future as another adventitious deus ex machina. In practice,
Allon's attitude was not all that different from that of the masseur at
the King David Hotel in Jerusalem who—in the act of proving that
massage is not the vocation for which Israelis will be remembered—
informed me that he was praying every night for the success of the
negotiations. When I asked him which part of the territory conquered
in 1973 (the 1967 conquest not being at issue) might be returned to
Syria, he became outraged: "Territory to the Syrians? You must be
crazy."

During Allon's visit to Washington, I invited him to Camp David
together with Israeli Ambassador Simcha Dinitz, Brent Scowcroft, and
my aide Peter Rodman for an evening of discussion over dinner. Allon's
message was as complicated as it was emotional. He said that Rabin,
having just entered office, had asked him to appeal to me to avoid any
move that might require an immediate Israeli election. This meant that
he did not want to proceed with the Jordanian option, since he had
promised to submit any territorial changes on the West Bank to Israel's
voters.

Speaking for himself, Allon did favor an Israeli withdrawal from
part of the West Bank. And he had devised an imaginative plan for
achieving it. Since the entire territory between the Jordan River and
the sea was only fifty miles deep, a straight-line withdrawal would
deprive Israel of the strategic depth needed to defend the coastal plain,
where most of its population was located, and to shelter it from Arab
armies that might enter Jordan after Hussein's death. In Allon's plan,
Israel would maintain a line of outposts along the Jordan River and
cede to Jordan a narrow corridor around Jericho into the center of the
West Bank, where the vast bulk (some 98 percent) of the Arab population lived (see map, page 363). In the areas returned to Arab control,

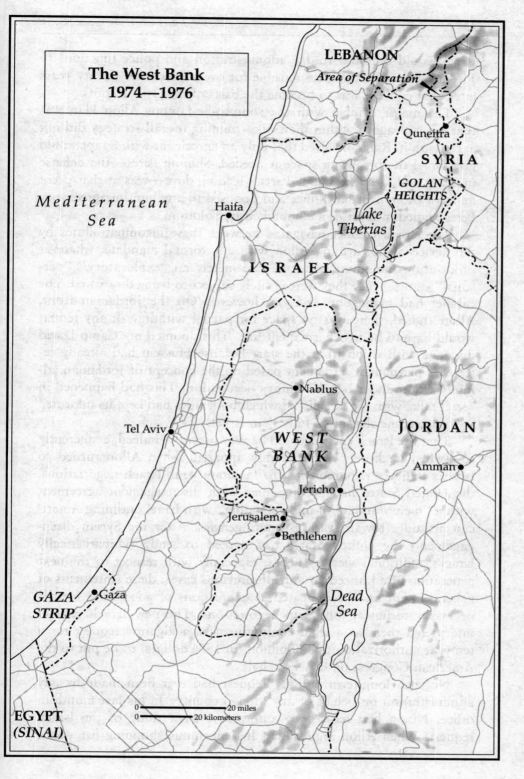

# The West Bank
# 1974—1976

*Mediterranean
Sea*

LEBANON
*Area of Separation*

Quneitra

SYRIA

*GOLAN
HEIGHTS*

Haifa

*Lake
Tiberias*

ISRAEL

Nablus

JORDAN

Tel Aviv

WEST
BANK

Amman

Jericho

Jerusalem

Bethlehem

*Dead
Sea*

GAZA
STRIP

Gaza

EGYPT
(SINAI)

| 0 | | 20 miles |
| 0 | | 20 kilometers |

Israel would cede day-to-day administration and police functions to Jordan while remaining responsible for overall security. Twenty years later, that concept was to become the basis of the Oslo accords.

The major trouble with the soon-to-be-famous Allon Plan was that his colleagues within the troika running overall strategy did not agree with it. Rabin believed that only an agreement with Egypt would give Israel the breathing space it needed. Shimon Peres—the defense minister and later the Labor Party's leading dove—was at that point its most prominent hard-liner and opposed to any interim agreement. Peres argued in favor of a comprehensive solution.

The Israeli cabinet navigated between these incompatibilities by the device of not arming Allon with any formal mandate; whatever propositions he advanced to me had merely an "exploratory," "personal" status, hence they were entirely subject to being disavowed. The cabinet had made one decision, however. On the Jordanian front, Allon argued, there was no space for partial withdrawal; any retreat would have to be to a permanent line. This doomed my Camp David dialogue with Allon from the start because Hussein had already rejected a permanent settlement based on the concept of Jordanian administration under Israeli military occupation. This had happened in secret talks with the Israelis, of which both sides had kept us informed —Jordan somewhat more fully than Israel.

That the Israeli cabinet could be very precise—indeed, exuberently so—when it chose became readily apparent when Allon turned to Israel's military requirements. To facilitate Arab-Israeli negotiations, the United States had accompanied each disengagement agreement with a "memorandum of understanding" with Israel outlining American attitudes toward various contingencies. After the Syrian disengagement, the United States had agreed to study sympathetically Israel's additional security needs, especially with respect to the next generation of advanced aircraft. In previous cases, these statements of general intent had been treated as expressions of good faith for the necessary technical follow-on negotiations. The new Israeli cabinet interpreted them as a legal commitment to a gigantic request for a ten-year authorization of $40 billion (in 1974 dollars) to be put to the American Congress on Israel's behalf.

No such long-term military request had ever been made by any administration on behalf of any foreign country. In his last month in office, Nixon had refused to authorize even a study of the Israeli request. When Allon argued that his enormous shopping list was a precondition for continuing the peace process, Nixon was so annoyed that, three days before the end of his presidency, he ordered a halt to the entire exercise. The transition to the new President rendered that decision moot.

How to deal with the Israeli aid request thus became the first decision on the Middle East to be put before Ford. Though still a novice in the intricacies of Middle East diplomacy, Ford was extremely well versed in the intricacies of the congressional budgetary processes. Twenty-four hours after Ford took the oath of office, Defense Secretary James Schlesinger used the first NSC meeting of the new presidency to ask for guidance regarding Israel's aid request.

The meeting went badly. Ford was unfamiliar with Israeli negotiating methods, which reject the biblical assurance that the meek shall inherit the earth, and he grew even more restless when he discovered that the Israeli request would draw down the reserve stocks of the American military and hence affect the readiness of American armed forces:

> SCHLESINGER: To the extent we provide some of the equip-
> ment that they have asked for, we must take it away
> from the U.S. forces with the result that those forces
> will be much less ready.
> FORD: Do they understand that that is the case?
> SCHLESINGER: Yes, sir, but they consider that their needs
> take priority.
> FORD: That certainly is an unselfish attitude.

Despite this uncharacteristically caustic remark, Ford two days later decided not to begin his presidency with a controversy with an old friend. He approved the NSC study memorandum Nixon had rejected, thereby launching the Israeli arms request into the bureaucratic machinery. It was also a skillful maneuver to delay any immediate decision, showing that Ford knew his way around Washington:

> I think we should hold them off until we see their attitude.
> That is a hole card we control. I am not sure Congress would
> jump at something like this with the current inflation.

## The Egyptian Option

Egypt's foreign minister, Ismail Fahmy, arrived in Washington on Sunday, August 11, two days after Ford's inauguration and two days before Turkey would resume military operations in Cyprus (see Chapter 7). I had first been introduced to Fahmy on October 29, 1973, when he arrived in Washington to replace Sadat's security adviser, Mohammed Hafiz Ismail, as our interlocutor.

"The President has sent me to make your acquaintance," he had announced then, "to report to him about you and to prepare your visit." It was Fahmy's way of saying that he had come—uninvited— not to negotiate but to size me up. And he gave me every opportunity to earn a passing grade, largely because he was sufficiently sophisticated to recognize that he had no other choice.

Debonair, clever, nimble—a professional's professional—Fahmy never lost sight of the fact that his principal task was to heal the psychological rift between Egypt and the West, especially the United States. In the initial stages of the as yet nonexistent peace process, this meant enlisting me as mediator.

The immediate issue at that first meeting had been the fate of the Egyptian Third Army in the Sinai, trapped by Israel when Ariel Sharon's armored column cut its last supply line (albeit after the United Nations–declared cease-fire had gone into effect). Fahmy behaved as if my assistance in extricating that army from a trap it had no means of escaping by itself was a special boon that was being conferred upon me by his President, whom at that point I had not met. Fahmy seemed to take for granted that Egypt and the United States would become partners in Middle East diplomacy, even though our two countries had still not restored the diplomatic relations broken off by Nasser in the aftermath of the 1967 Middle East War. Suave and vastly complicated, Fahmy was a master of the insinuating innuendo. His opening move was to elevate me to the status of master diplomat, in pursuit of which he would sometimes ascribe to me convoluted schemes of truly breathtaking complexity as his way of eliciting assurances regarding America's interest in good relations with Egypt. Ford, used to far less elliptical and complicated interlocutors, at first listened to Fahmy's presentations with amazement—unsure whether I might not have overlooked some item in my briefing—and later with the sort of appreciation one might reserve for a spectacular theatrical or athletic performance.

Among his Arab colleagues, Fahmy was sometimes accused of pro-Western leanings. The Syrian leaders in particular were wont to inquire sarcastically whether I intended to invite Fahmy to the next meeting of NATO foreign ministers. They used his obvious affinity for the Western lifestyle to score a debating point, and they knew it. For Fahmy was above all a passionate Egyptian nationalist who shared Sadat's view that America's diplomatic assistance was indispensable because no Arab nation was in a position to advance toward peace on its own and because attempts to forge a unified Arab front were likely to crumble beneath the weight of Arab individualism, innate competitiveness, and idiosyncrasy.

Fahmy, like his Arab colleagues, relied on volubility as a screen for secretiveness. Where he differed from them was in a talent for transforming oratory into diplomatic tactics and in the skillful dispensation of individual doses of carefully measured practicality which he distilled from Sadat's amalgam of epic poetry and prophetic vision. Maneuvering among the passions of the Arabs, the suspicions of the Israelis, the clumsy assertiveness of the Soviets, and the legalistic goodwill of the Americans, Fahmy adroitly edged ever closer to a separate agreement.

The summer of 1974 tested Fahmy's mettle. While bent on obtaining a separate agreement, Sadat (and Fahmy) needed to keep up the facade of Arab unity until they could be quite certain that an acceptable deal in the Sinai was indeed in the cards. The United States favored a next step with Jordan, which Sadat and Fahmy were convinced would delay an Egyptian agreement for many months, first during the run-up to the inevitable Israeli election and then for an indefinite period afterward while the conflicting claims of Jordan and the PLO over who should represent the Palestinians were being sorted out. The Egyptian leaders had no intention of miring their hope to recover at least part of the Sinai in the bottomless morass of West Bank haggling. Not yet in a position to relinquish Egypt's Soviet option, Fahmy was at the same time keenly aware of the absolute imperative that he preserve the confidence and goodwill of the United States.

Fahmy tiptoed through this maze exuding reasonableness and systematically foreclosing all options save a separate Egyptian-Israeli agreement. His jovial manner was a great hit with Ford and obscured the indirect threats he kept putting forward the way a doctor might present an unfavorable diagnosis—as events beyond his control. Absent some early progress in the Sinai—say, by November—he would claim, the Middle East would erupt again, probably triggered by Syria

(Fahmy did not explain why a separate Egyptian-Israeli agreement, which Asad passionately opposed, would restrain Syria). Fahmy informed us that he planned to accept an invitation to visit Moscow before too long, though he had no intention of making any "deal" there—which, of course, implied that he had the capacity to do precisely that. He welcomed our desire to make progress on the Palestinian front but insisted that this would require direct American contacts with the PLO, which, of course, precluded the Jordanian option and was certain to be rejected out of hand by Israel.

Fahmy ridiculed the proposition that Egypt needed Jordanian cover for its own independent diplomacy. Rather, the opposite was true:

> Jordan can't move without the solid support of President Sadat. No Arab leader can support King Hussein. As I told you, he is a very good man, a courageous man, but what happened in Black September [when Hussein's army defeated the PLO in Jordan in September 1970] . . . precludes him from acting without the support of Egypt.

From out of the welter of Fahmy's rhetoric and speculations, one unambiguous policy recommendation did emerge: Egypt would not wait for a Jordanian negotiation. "Any Jordanian disengagement is impossible to support if there is no further Egyptian withdrawal" (i.e., withdrawal by Israel on the Egyptian front). At times, Fahmy hinted that Sadat might go along with parallel negotiations with Egypt and Jordan, but it was more of a sop to our inexplicable preoccupation with a Jordanian initiative than a serious policy option. And, in truth, a simultaneous negotiation over both the West Bank and Sinai was beyond the emotional tolerance of both the United States and Israel. The upshot of Fahmy's visit was that a separate agreement between Israel and Egypt emerged as the most probable next step in the peace process.

## Hussein and the Peace Process

Two days after Fahmy's departure, on August 16—a week after Ford's inauguration—King Hussein landed in Washington to pursue the very Jordanian option which Israel and Egypt were ingenuously thwarting. As usual, the king's impeccable courtesy camouflaged a steely resolve to preserve his dynasty and to defend the dignity of his people.

Hussein was accompanied by Prime Minister Zaid Rifai, who had preceded him on a brief reconnaissance visit on August 6, forty-eight hours before Nixon announced his resignation. Middle East diplomacy had not been our top preoccupation in those frantic hours. The result was that Rifai was the only Middle East visitor whom I did not greet at the airport—a slight which, however understandable, was to burden our relationship for some time.

Rifai's importance did not stem from his ministerial rank, which was temporary, but from his close friendship with the King, which was permanent. A member of a small circle of confidants with whom Hussein felt at ease, Rifai would rotate in and out of office according to the requirements of Jordan's precarious position and the imperatives of the dynasty's survival. However dexterous Hussein's maneuvers within the maze of Arab internal politics might appear, he was no cynic, and he had great faith in the United States, never straying beyond the point that might jeopardize his American safety net.*

Rifai generally found himself in office when the King considered it safe to avow a pro-Western stance or considered it necessary to face down his Arab brothers. When the radical wind was blowing too fiercely, other associates from Hussein's entourage would be called to center stage—though Rifai never disappeared entirely from the inner circle.

Rifai was well suited to his role. Bluff and highly intelligent, he was a tough negotiator whose wicked sense of humor softened the vehemence and skill with which he defended the interests of his country and of the Hashemite dynasty. Of all our Arab interlocutors, Rifai was the least prone to the romanticism that occasionally caused even Sadat to bend reality to the rhythm of some epic poem.

Had the concept of an interim agreement found favor in Israel, Rifai would have settled for a very modest straight-line Israeli withdrawal of ten kilometers (about six miles) from the Jordan River on the ground that any further Jordanian advance would reach the Judean hills. And he was convinced that the "Israelis do not give up hilltops." Since a straight-line withdrawal all along the Jordan River had already

---

* The only time King Hussein came close to it was during the Gulf War of 1991 when he refused to join the anti-Saddam coalition, though I would make the argument that the survival of his dynasty was perhaps the most important service Hussein could have rendered to Middle East stability in that crisis.

been rejected by Israel, Rifai offered to examine the Allon Plan, provided it was in the context of an interim agreement and that Israeli military forces withdrew totally from any territory regained by Jordan.

As it turned out, he badly misjudged his bargaining position. Rifai was convinced that the Jordanian option was realistic because Sadat simply could not afford to antagonize his fellow Arabs by making another separate agreement. Rifai therefore urged either a strictly Jordanian-Israeli deal or a simultaneous Israeli negotiation with both Jordan and Egypt.

It was in this spirit that Hussein told Ford:

> We would like to know, sir, where we stand now. If we are not to be involved, we are prepared to turn over our responsibilities to the PLO and let them try to deal with the problem.

"We don't mind being used," Rifai interjected ominously, "but we want a piece of the cake." Hussein suggested that, after a West Bank agreement, he would offer the population a plebiscite under non-Arab U.N. supervision so that it might make its own free choice between joining Jordan or pursuing autonomy in a loose confederation with Jordan.

Had we been in a position to allow our sympathies to guide our policies, both Ford and I would have concurred eagerly. Unfortunately, we had learned enough from our contacts with Hussein's Arab "brothers" to realize that we were in no position to deliver a separate Jordanian negotiation. The best we could do, and even that without real conviction, was to promise to explore Fahmy's hint that simultaneous negotiations on two fronts might be conducted or at least to start Jordan's shortly after Egypt's.

## Two More Arab Visitors: Syria and Saudi Arabia

Two more Arab foreign ministers were on the agenda and had to be heard before Ford's initiation into the complexities and passions of the Arab side could be considered complete. Foreign Minister Abd al-Halim Khaddam of Syria arrived on Wednesday, August 21, and Omar Saqqaf of Saudi Arabia on Wednesday, August 28.

Khaddam had greeted me at the airport on the occasion of my first visit to Syria in December 1973 and had wasted no time informing me that Syria was not interested in any partial settlement and that it would judge any overall settlement by whether it restored Palestinian rights. Khaddam did not define these rights, nor did he give the impression that the survival of Israel ranked high among his priorities. The Syrian press reports of my visit reflected this attitude. And, on a subsequent trip to Damascus by way of Tel Aviv, it was rendered in the Syrian media as the American Secretary of State having arrived from "occupied territories."

The Syrian foreign minister distinguished himself from Fahmy immediately by pointing out that, in Syria, the civilians were if anything less conciliatory than the military. When I got to know Asad, I realized that this was Khaddam's way of warning me that whatever concessions were going to be made would have to be ordered by the President.

In the months to come, I saw a great deal of this passionate Syrian nationalist. Khaddam was brilliant and had a sardonic sense of humor. During the thirty-four-day shuttle, we shared a daily car ride from and to the Damascus airport, and we sat together through many endless meetings as Syria and Israel haggled their way to what, at this writing, remains the only formal Syrian-Israeli agreement. Since Khaddam did not then belong to Asad's inner circle, he was generally called in only after I had had a private discussion with his President, followed by a session with Syria's military chiefs. But when he did appear, his comments were trenchant and professional and his negotiating style ferociously tenacious.

Nevertheless, in the course of the shuttle, Khaddam moved gradually, if reluctantly, toward accepting some sort of peace process and a diplomacy based on the acceptance of the state of Israel—though probably with the arrière-pensée that, if the balance of power ever shifted to the Arab side, Syria reserved the option of settling accounts. But so long as that reversal remained illusory, the foreign minister carried out his diplomatic role with reluctant panache.

When he visited Washington, Khaddam was, of course, well aware from Israel's media that Israel would not consider another partial withdrawal on the Golan Heights and that, even in a final settlement, it proposed to retain a portion of that strategic area. If Israel maintained these positions, Syria would in effect be excluded from the step-by-step approach and had not much to gain even from a comprehensive settlement. Nevertheless, at the end of the day, the Syrian leadership concluded, as had Egypt's—albeit more grudgingly—that, if any progress was to be made, America's role was indispensable. As a result, the primary purpose of Khaddam's visit was to prevent Syria's exclusion from Middle East diplomacy. Thus he displayed none of the militant bravado in Washington that had characterized our earlier meetings in Damascus. He avoided even hinting at any threats of a unilateral Syrian military move, which was the standard warning in the repertoire of other Arab leaders—invoking Syrian threats as an indirect and safer surrogate for their own.

Khaddam's visit in August 1974 was in many ways the high point of the American-Syrian relationship. He joked that he would invite me to the next Arab summit since his colleagues were telling me everything anyway. To spite the despised Egyptians, Khaddam did not oppose a negotiation with Jordan over part of the West Bank "no matter how much, provided this is achieved [compatible] with the self-determination of the Palestinians." Unlike any other Arab leader, Syria's foreign minister did not equate self-determination for the Palestinians with the PLO. Asad did not much like the PLO, since he considered a separate Palestinian state an obstacle to the Greater Syria of his long-term strategy. He was always trying to develop a new Palestinian leadership under Syrian tutelage in opposition to Arafat.

In pursuit of that policy, Khaddam indicated that Syria might be prepared to work with Jordan on developing a special form of Palestinian self-determination not tied to the PLO. But we were aware as well of Hussein's abiding distrust of Syrian long-range goals, and we therefore did not expect that anything very practical would result from a Syrian-Jordanian collaboration over Palestine. The upshot of Khaddam's visit therefore was—inevitably—procrastination: we agreed that we would continue the dialogue in Damascus when I next visited the Middle East a few weeks hence.

Saudi Arabian Foreign Minister Omar Saqqaf was the next visitor. A traditional society based on fundamentalist Islamic principles (in the days before fundamentalism had become politicized), Saudi Arabia navigated between the pressures of Arab radicalism, Palestinian irredentism, its own fear of covetous neighbors, and Communist designs. Its leaders knew that, in the end, Saudi security—indeed, Saudi survival—depended on American support, but they had less confidence in our judgment and were concerned lest our impetuosity upset the subtle calculations by which they survived. Saudi Arabia was too experienced to feel secure in isolation and too weak to become a principal player in Middle East diplomacy. Unwilling to risk its domestic cohesion by injecting itself into the peace process, it adopted the role of a benevolent observer, encouraging the peace process without giving offense to the radicals in the tough neighborhood in which fate had forced them to live.

The rhetoric of Saudi diplomats on behalf of the Arab cause was impeccable and occasionally intransigent but, behind the scenes, Saudi policy was almost always helpful to American diplomacy. It had originated the oil embargo against the United States and the Netherlands to demonstrate solidarity with the Arab world during the October 1973 war. But the measure was more symbolic than substantive. Oil being fungible, the gesture had amounted to a reallocation of supplies —the United States obtained its oil from other oil producers whose traditional customers were now being supplied by Saudi Arabia. But the psychological impact of the oil embargo had shaken the industrialized world; a buying frenzy to increase oil reserves had swept the industrial democracies which persisted even after the embargo was lifted, driving prices up fourfold and causing inflation and recession— a subject I will discuss in Chapter 22.

Omar Saqqaf reflected all the Saudi complexities and ambivalences. For one thing, the Saudi foreign minister was an executor of policy, not a designer of it. Saudi strategy was established by the royal family—from the mid-1960s to mid-1970s by the subtle, skillful, and extremely secretive King Faisal. To underline the distinction, Saqqaf was seldom present at my audiences with the King and, on the rare occasions that he was invited, he sat so far down along the hierarchy of other advisers that he would have had to shout to get the King's attention. (Of course, the audiences did not encourage the participation of advisers no matter where they sat since the King and I would sit beside each other in the center of a vast room facing the interpreter while the advisers lined the walls at least ten feet away in each direction.)

In short, Saqqaf was an exalted messenger, transmitting and receiving messages on behalf of the royal family. He discharged that duty with extraordinary urbanity and sophistication. He knew the issues well and stated the Saudi case with an indirection that, while quite precise, nevertheless avoided drama or confrontation.

On his visit to Washington, Saqqaf was above all concerned with deflecting Western anger over the energy crisis from Saudi Arabia. I warned him that there was a limit to Western forbearance:

> My view is that current oil prices are going to create such
> an economic crisis in the West that other governments, what-
> ever their view, will be driven to drastic action.

In these circumstances, Saqqaf had every incentive not to magnify the strains in Arab-American relations by taking a hard line on Middle East negotiations. For the record, he sounded a formal warning against further separate moves. But he also left us convinced that Saudi Arabia would endorse any diplomatic progress so long as it did not have to assume responsibility for it.

## Rabin Visits Ford

A great deal would now depend on imminent meetings with Yitzhak Rabin, the new Israeli Prime Minister, who was arriving in Washington on September 10.

Unfortunately, Ford's relationship with Rabin never really prospered; their first encounter came as close to a disaster as the realities of domestic politics in either country would permit. It was a pity because, on the face of it, the two men should have gotten along well. Rabin had been an outstanding Israeli ambassador to Washington, where he had shown unusual understanding for the kind of moderate conservatism Ford represented. Ford had been a strong supporter of Israel throughout his congressional career. Yet the occasion of their first meeting ushered in a difficult period in American-Israeli relations.

Part of the problem was the psychological makeup of the two men. Rabin was cerebral and analytical, Ford instinctive and commonsensical. Rabin sought to persuade by aloof integrity, Ford by human warmth and goodwill. Ford had made his career in Congress, which operates by compromise; Rabin had earned his spurs as the chief of staff of the Israeli Defense Forces, which requires command skills. Ford had been in politics his entire life; Rabin was learning the art of politics in the premiership.

No greater contrast could be imagined than between Rabin and his predecessor, the formidable Golda Meir, with whom Washington had become familiar. Golda was, in fact, far more rigid on substance than Rabin, but she hid her inflexibility behind a behavior of exceptional bonhomie. As one of Israel's pioneers, she considered every square inch of Israeli soil to be sacrosanct, including—in effect—its conquests. Discussions of long-term political strategy made her restless. Golda's overriding fear was that some Soviet-American deal would be imposed at Israel's expense, though no such arrangement was ever discussed or contemplated.

Golda Meir had gone along with the disengagement agreements with Egypt and Syria without any great enthusiasm in large part to obtain the release of Israeli prisoners. On the occasion of Nixon's visit to Israel in June 1974 a few weeks after she had left office, Golda told the President that she would oppose any further partial Israeli withdrawal on *any* front for *any* reason. Henceforth, she argued, Israel should withdraw only in return for a final peace agreement. From this, however, she excluded the abandonment of *any* Israeli settlement wherever situated, in effect foreclosing the 1967 frontiers as a basis for a peace agreement even with Egypt, its most conciliatory neighbor.

Tough as Golda Meir could be in face-to-face negotiations, she never showed that side publicly when it came to Israel's relations with the United States. Ever conscious of the reality that, in the end, Israel's survival depended on American goodwill, she cultivated the relationship with charm and tenacity. On American television, Golda portrayed herself as the earth mother—compassionate, witty, critical only occasionally and then more in sorrow, never in anger. Toward me, she was somewhat less restrained, probably because she seemed to feel that my Jewish religion obliged me to extend unqualified support to Israel—though, even then, she made sure to voice her complaints with the demeanor of an elderly aunt toward an obstreperous nephew. When an American supporter of Israel complained to her that I seemed to place my duties to my office before the obligations of my religion, she replied: "I don't care. I read from right to left anyway."

By contrast, when he became Prime Minister in 1974, Rabin found himself far less at ease. As the first native-born Israeli to accede to that office, he did not share the aura of the pioneer generation of Israeli political leaders, most of them immigrants, who had founded and shaped the state. Their senior representatives remained on the scene, headed by Golda Meir and Rabin's former commander, Moshe Dayan, who was bitter that his failure to mobilize on the eve of the Yom Kippur War should have denied him the office to which his talents and accomplishments seemed at one time to be taking him.

At the same time, Rabin felt obliged to look over his shoulder at the rivals within his own cabinet. He was flanked by Yigal Allon and Shimon Peres. Rabin trusted Allon's character far more than his intelligence; his estimate of Peres was the precise opposite. Allon had been senior to him in the Israeli Defense Forces but, more interested in substance than in office, did not contest Rabin's preeminence either directly or even inwardly. What he did challenge was Rabin's strategy.

As a strong advocate of the Jordanian option, Allon was impatient with Rabin's careful strategizing; he would have preferred to make a deal over the West Bank and decide on the next move afterward.

Defense Minister Shimon Peres's rivalry with Rabin was to haunt the lives of both men for the next two decades. Peres had been the architect of the "French Connection," which had generated the weapons that won the Six Day War in 1967. He was instrumental in the acquisition or development of many of the weapons on which his country still depends. He was also perhaps the most erudite of that generation of Israel's leaders. Yet preeminence always just eluded him. Peres's combination of driven ambition and abstract intellectualism was not in keeping with the style of the Israeli public and contributed to his defeat in no fewer than five elections, including contests for Prime Minister.

Over the decades of their rivalry, Peres's thinking on relations with Israel's neighbors followed the same trajectory as Rabin's from "hawk" to at least "almost dove"—with Peres leaning somewhat more to extremes. He had been more of a hawk than Rabin, and he was to wind up as more of a dove. The difference was that Peres was intuitive where Rabin was analytical, intellectual where Rabin was practical. Peres's training had been in France, and he shared the trait of French academics, who tend to believe that the formulation of an idea is equivalent to its realization. In the end, this idealism provided the impetus for the Oslo accords with the PLO in 1993.

After that, and toward the end of Rabin's life, Rabin and Peres formed an almost ideal partnership. Peres had the soaring ideas from which Rabin would select those most useful to an overall strategy. When Rabin was murdered in November 1995, Peres lost his own dream for peace because, without Rabin, he could not sell it to the Israeli public.

When Rabin and Peres first appeared in the same cabinet in June 1974, they were already fierce competitors. Peres would assault Rabin on the ground that the Prime Minister was too accommodating to the United States. For all these reasons, Rabin treaded warily and gave higher priority to the cohesion of his cabinet than to the requirements of diplomacy. Nor did he particularly enjoy the political game. Withdrawn and shy, he lacked the capacity for small talk and was embarrassed by displays of emotion—which was all the more remarkable because, as his friends well knew, Rabin was at heart deeply sentimental. Once one had entered the circle of his friendship, Rabin's curmudgeonly integrity inspired affection. His daughter would say of him that he radiated his feelings rather than expressed them. But during his first term as Prime Minister, Rabin's apparent aloofness—his initial inability to reach the human dimension—compromised his effectiveness and surely complicated his relationship with the outgoing Gerald Ford.

It was a pity. For Rabin understood far better than Golda that, in the long run, diplomatic stalemate would isolate Israel diplomatically, to some extent even from the United States. His service as ambassador to Washington during the Vietnam War had taught him that there were limits to America's willingness to sustain the risk of war and economic costs on behalf of a geographically distant ally. On the basis of many private conversations, I never doubted that Rabin agreed with our underlying strategy. He summed it up during his meeting with Ford on September 11, as follows:

> The present situation cannot be freezed [sic]. We don't believe this situation can form a new status quo, because we think the Arab countries have learned that the combination of Israel's isolation in the international arena, the use of limited force—or rather the use of force for limited purposes—and the use of oil for blackmailing the United States, can be the means to prevent freezing the situation.
>
> Therefore there are two possibilities—either a move towards a settlement, or another war. We have no reason to assume the new status quo can be held any period of time. Maybe three months, maybe six months, but not for any length of time.

A military man, Rabin taught himself, step by reluctant step, the grammar of peace. In the course of a lifetime of military service, he became convinced that long-term security required Israel to go beyond the accumulation of military power. A people which had survived the tragedies of Jewish history is condemned to the constant premonition of disaster and cannot entrust its survival to the goodwill of other states. But a state of 5 million in a sea of several hundred million, perhaps the majority of whom consider the Jewish state somehow illegitimate, will consume its substance if it finds no way to transcend that mutual hostility. Rabin grew gradually convinced—and then deeply committed—to the proposition that his people owed it to themselves to attempt the peace of reconciliation, not merely the peace of strength.

Rabin had had to overcome his own instincts to reach that conclusion. Two weeks before his assassination, the then Australian Foreign Minister Gareth Evans, in trying to persuade him of some point regarding the peace process, said: "But I am preaching to the converted." Rabin replied: "Not to the converted, to the committed." He would have preferred to impose his preferences; he had understood that this required a tour de force beyond Israel's long-range emotional and physical capabilities.

It was not an easy journey. Like so many of his countrymen, Rabin hated the idea of trading the tangible benefits of territory for intangible gains in international recognition and mitigation of Arab hostility. From his military experience, he knew better than most that the concessions being urged on Israel were permanent while the contributions of its adversaries consisted of revocable declarations of peaceful intent and recognition.

At first, Rabin spoke in terms of "a piece of peace for a piece of land." But he was, in the end, too sophisticated to believe in the divisibility of peace. Thus he came to his ultimate insight: for Israel, peace is less a legal definition than the creation of a new reality for the Jewish people. Having lived in ghettos for nearly two millennia, Rabin would argue, they must not turn their national home into another ghetto, cut off from the rest of humanity by philosophical and political alienation. They cannot abandon their concern with security to that quest, but neither must they define their future entirely in military terms. The worldwide sense of loss generated by Rabin's death shows how close he came to realizing his goal.

Rabin never doubted that the process would be painful and therefore never resorted to describing peace as some fantasy nirvana in which all tensions would magically disappear. And though he was prepared for the possibility that his effort might not succeed, he was certain that Israel could face its ultimate adversity best for having made the effort. He was a sabra, his entire life consisting of variations of struggle. But if Rabin ever permitted himself a display of emotion, it was when he spoke of Israeli soldiers killed in battle and of families decimated by Israel's endless wars, as in this poignant speech during his second tour as Prime Minister:

> As a military man, as a commander, as a minister of defense,
> I ordered many military operations to be carried out. And
> together with the joy of victory and the grief of bereavement,

I shall always remember the moment just after taking such decisions: the hush as senior officers or cabinet ministers slowly rise from their seats, the sight of their receding backs, the sound of the closing door and then the silence in which I remain alone.

That is the moment you grasp that as a result of the decision just made, people might go to their deaths. People from my nation, people from other nations. And they still don't know it.

At that hour they are still laughing and weeping, still weaving plans and dreaming about love, still musing about planting a garden or building a house—and they have no idea these are their last hours on Earth. Which of them is fated to die? Whose picture will appear in the black frame in tomorrow's newspaper? Whose mother will soon be in mourning? Whose world will crumble under the weight of the loss?

As a former military man, I will also forever remember the silence of the moment before: the hush when the hands of the clock seem to be spinning forward, when time is running out and in another hour, another minute, the inferno will erupt.

In that moment of great tension just before the finger pulls the trigger, just before the fuse begins to burn—in the terrible quiet of the moment, there is still time to wonder, to wonder alone: Is it really imperative to act? Is there no other choice? No other way?[9]

It is no derogation of Rabin's ultimate stature to recall that, at the beginning of his diplomatic career, his steps toward greatness were halting. Relations with Ford got off to a bad start when the new Israeli Prime Minister dragged his feet about coming to the United States to meet the new President. He wanted to gain time in which to consolidate his domestic position. He also thought that Israel needed a period of respite from a process that had started with surprise attacks by Egypt and Syria and now threatened to enmesh him in decisions that never seemed to end and which was certain to embroil him with his cabinet.

The tug-of-war started when the State Department announced that Rabin had been invited to meet with the President in the first half of September, and he responded by complaining that it was a violation of protocol to publicize an invitation without first clearing it with the prospective visitor. Technically, Rabin was right. On the other hand, it had not occurred to anyone that an Israeli Prime Minister might be embarrassed by the publicity surrounding an invitation to visit the new President of Israel's closest ally—especially when Arab foreign ministers had been descending on Washington seriatim for over a month. Once he arrived, Rabin agreed to the step-by-step approach but subjected Ford to a tenacious haggle over its terms. Dogged rear-guard actions have been standard practice in any negotiation over Israeli withdrawals down to this writing. What made Rabin's unprecedented was that he did not flinch from frontally taking on the President of the United States.

However wary, Golda Meir would seek to avoid having to engage her prestige in a public debate with the President; she always concentrated her fire on some subordinate, often me. By contrast, Rabin sought to burnish his authority vis-à-vis his cabinet by posing direct challenges to the American President's management of negotiations. Perhaps it was his method of educating his divided and fractious colleagues as to the limits of American tolerance; perhaps he thought Ford would be easier to deal with than I. Whatever the reason, it conferred an unusual sharpness to the initial dialogue.

Rabin carried this approach over into his discussions regarding military assistance—the subject which Israeli Prime Ministers use to guarantee that they can return home from Washington with some achievement. (Indeed, settling some of Israel's military requests was almost standard operating procedure for a Prime Minister's visit.) As Allon had with Nixon, Rabin presented Israel's military requests as preconditions to its willingness to negotiate. The implication that Israel was engaging in the peace process as a favor to the United States irritated Ford to no small degree. His mood did not improve when Rabin insisted that his status as a former general entitled him to negotiate the details of the Israeli arms requests directly with the President. Ford, while more knowledgeable on the subject than Nixon had been, was not familiar with all the technical details and thought that the issue should be dealt with by the defense ministers. But given his rivalry with Peres, Rabin wanted the credit for success for himself. He kept insisting on Israel's unprecedented and mammoth ten-year request and belittled all partial measures. A painful silence followed when Ford, trying to make progress, told Rabin he was approving Israel's list of urgent priorities for the next two years. Israeli Ambassador Simcha Dinitz whispered something into Rabin's ear. But Rabin repeated the same argument which Allon had used with Nixon to the effect that some general statements made in a memorandum of understanding in the context of the Syrian disengagement agreement in May amounted to a specific commitment to a ten-year arms program. Rabin therefore was not prepared to concede that Ford had acted generously with respect to Israel's priority list: "My ambassador thinks I should thank you," he said. "But how many times are we supposed to express appreciation for the same thing?"

When the conversation turned to the principal subject on Ford's mind—the future of the peace process—Rabin endorsed our general strategy without committing himself to implement it. He put forward an acute analysis of the various choices:

> In my opinion it is better to start with Egypt. It is not a condition on our part. On the experience of the last twenty-six years, there has been no movement of any kind—war, or political arrangement—without Egypt leading. In '49 when Egypt decided on an armistice, all the others were queuing to do the same. In '56 it was a war between only Egypt and Israel. In '67 Egypt led. I don't believe the pattern can basically be changed.
>
> We know, for example, that the Jordanians think they can't do more than the other Arabs did, therefore a disengagement agreement. Therefore if we want to do more in a political arrangement, it has to be with Egypt. . . .
>
> . . . Then if Syria tries war, it will be much less serious.

The trouble was that, while Rabin did not foreclose any of the options, neither was he ready to embrace them. His presentation was theoretical and rather academic; it implied no action—indeed, the opposite. For his part, Ford, eager to reach a decision, interpreted Rabin's lengthy expositions as so much stalling. At intervals, he would interrupt by asking for a precise time frame. "A good strong commitment" was needed, he argued, because "we both have a strong interest to keep the momentum going." Rabin would venture no further than to promise to do his best to come up with concrete ideas by the time of a projected visit by me to the Middle East a month hence—thereby delaying the start of negotiations for at least that period of time.

As it turned out, even that shuttle—from October 9 to 15—failed to produce an agreement to open negotiations. I visited Egypt and Syria twice, as well as Israel, Jordan, Saudi Arabia, Algeria, and Morocco. All the parties repeated familiar themes. Sadat insisted that priority be given to negotiations regarding withdrawals on the Egyptian front. To speed its start, he agreed to concede to Israel many of the operational components of nonbelligerency, though without specifically using that label. Jordan remained eager to negotiate over the West Bank but was becoming increasingly frustrated and disillusioned. Asad, willing to share in the spoils of any progress, preferred an impasse to a separate Egyptian arrangement. All these incompatibilities were purely academic because the Israeli cabinet was still not prepared to approve a formal negotiating position or to open any specific negotiation. In frustration, I reported to Ford in a post-trip memo on October 15:

> Rabin and the other leaders are grappling with the dilemma of history and logic. The history has been one of pain, anguish, suspicion, suffering, and four costly wars. The logic is that the risks of standpatism are far greater than realistically facing up to necessary step-by-step compromises essential for progress towards a settlement because the choices they [Israel's leaders] will face a year from now if they let the situation drift will be much worse than those they face now. . . . We have an abiding interest to support Israel's security; but our interests in the area go beyond any one country. . . . Our strategy of segmenting the issues which divide Israel and its neighbors into negotiating units which are politically manageable . . . is based on the belief that a progressive series of limited agreements could create new situations which in turn will make further agreements possible.

## The Rabat Decision

At this point, the Arab heads of state foreclosed our options by demonstrating what Abba Eban once described as their proclivity "never to miss an opportunity to miss an opportunity." On October 28, they assembled at a summit in Rabat, Morocco, and unanimously endorsed the PLO as the "sole legitimate representative of the Palestinian people." Had we been able to put forward a plausible Jordanian negotiation, this might have been prevented. Now Hussein was out of the picture. Henceforth West Bank arrangements would have to be negotiated with the PLO with which Israel would refuse to deal. Hussein gallantly proclaimed that "when my tribe goes astray, I follow it." But given the PLO's vociferous rejection of Israel's right to exist and its active use of terrorism as an instrument of policy, the Rabat decision guaranteed a nineteen-year impasse on West Bank negotiations.

For a long time, I considered the collapse of the Jordanian option in 1974 as a major lost opportunity. And, in the abstract, it was. But negotiations are never conducted in a vacuum. It took Israel twenty years, a Palestinian uprising, and a more realistic Palestinian leadership to get used to the idea of coexistence with the PLO. Nor would our policy of drawing Hussein onto the West Bank have been as easy to implement as it appeared in theory. The acquisition by Hussein of any West Bank territory would have unleashed intense Arab pressures on behalf of turning over the regained territory to the PLO. A major crisis would have been inevitable; it was indeed the principal reason why Sadat was so adamant that Egypt go first.

Two decades later, in the summer of 1994, I sat next to Yasser Arafat at a dinner in Paris celebrating the presentation of the Félix Houphouët-Boigny Peace Prize to Rabin, Peres, and Arafat. Reminiscing in the way survivors of long-ago wars and half-forgotten battles are wont to do, we relived the summer of 1974. Arafat observed (correctly) that the interim territorial West Bank settlement which had been celebrated on the White House lawn in September 1993 seemed to him very similar to what I had been urging on the parties two decades earlier. I reminded that expert in political survival of one important difference: my purpose had been to keep the PLO out of the West Bank, not to turn the territory over to it. Arafat was not offended. Like a professor teaching elementary political science to a somewhat slow-witted student, he observed (perhaps whistling in the dark): "It would not have mattered. Hussein could not have held on to it by himself. We would have been established there by now."

History works in strange ways. The stalemate of the fall of 1974 proved to be the precondition for the breakthrough in Israeli-Egyptian negotiations which eventually led to a peace agreement. It was navigated into port by a slow meandering that eliminated all the other options, under the aegis of two men destined for greatness, Yitzhak Rabin and Anwar Sadat. Each had his own reasons for arranging a temporary diplomatic stalemate to pave the way for the next step toward peace: Rabin grudgingly, to solidify his domestic position and to teach his fractious cabinet the facts of international life; Sadat confidently, by navigating steadily toward a peace separate from his Arab brethren—even while signing joint affirmations of unity with them as at Rabat. After months of exploration, we thus reached a crossroads representing the amalgam of every participant's immediate goals, albeit at a heavy price.

At the cost of nineteen years of stalemate on Palestinian issues, Rabin had bought the time he needed to establish himself as Prime Minister and to set up a negotiation with Egypt, which he considered to be Israel's most desirable interlocutor.

At the cost of isolating himself in the Arab world, Sadat had turned the corner toward a separate Egyptian-Israeli negotiation and ultimate peace.

At the cost of excluding themselves from further West Bank negotiations, the other Arab leaders managed, in varying degrees, to satisfy their domestic political requirements by championing the PLO.

Throughout, the United States had held the ring against forces which, had they been permitted to coalesce, would have destroyed the peace process: the radical Arabs, the Soviet Union, and most of our European allies then trying to extricate from the energy crisis by championing radical Arab positions. The measure of America's achievement was that all parties took it for granted that the diplomatic framework we had established should continue and under American auspices.

# 13

# ONE SHUTTLE TOO MANY

## Post-Rabat Blues

Since Rabat had preempted the Jordanian option and Israel had rejected any partial settlement with Syria, an Egyptian-Israeli negotiation was the only alternative left, other than a resumption of the multilateral Geneva conference, which we wished to avoid. But abstract logic has rarely prevailed in Middle East diplomacy. Even as the parties seemed to be agreeing on the next step, they were pursuing very different objectives.

Sadat would abandon the united Arab front he had just helped forge at Rabat only if he could also demonstrate some major achievement. He therefore proclaimed as his minimum conditions for an interim agreement on the Sinai the Giddi and Mitla Passes about fifty miles from the Suez Canal and the Abu Rudeis oil fields on the southwestern coast of the peninsula because they were tangible landmarks in an essentially unpopulated sea of sand.

But if the withdrawal were really as significant as Sadat would claim, Israel was bound to demand a major political quid pro quo. It found it in the proclamation of an end to the formal state of belligerency between Israel and Egypt.

The ensuing minuet between Sadat and the Israelis was both stylized and shaped by each side's awareness that the ultimate significance of its demands was largely symbolic. Ending the state of belligerency was a revocable gesture short of peace, while the passes, which cut across a low range of hills, did not significantly affect the military situation. The latter was one of the few propositions on which the Egyptian and Israeli negotiating teams were in agreement, as can be seen from the following exchange with the Israeli cabinet in Jerusalem on March 18, 1975:

> KISSINGER: Then [Egyptian Defense Minister] Gamasy said it's total nonsense that this [the passes] will be used for offensive maneuvers; the only thing it's good for is infantry, and the decisive battles will be fought in the north. You will know whether he's right. . . .
> RABIN: Basically, he's right.

Since that issue grew into the very essence of the controversy, it is important to understand what in the context of the negotiations was meant by Israeli withdrawal from the passes. As the negotiations evolved, Israel was not being asked to cede the passes to Egyptian control but to a U.N. force that would be established between the two sides. Egyptian forces would be no closer than ten miles from the passes and would be kept in a zone of limited Egyptian armaments designed to preclude any offensive operation. The closest Egyptian force capable of offensive operations would be fifty miles away on the other side of the Suez Canal which, reopened to shipping, would pose yet another obstacle to surprise attacks.

It was also common knowledge that the Abu Rudeis oil fields were in the process of being depleted. The only real dispute was whether they would produce for another four years or six. What that issue boiled down to was how much compensation Israel should receive to replace Abu Rudeis oil on the international market. Nevertheless, it served the domestic interest of both sides to give the impression that the substantive importance of any agreement matched its symbolic significance: for Sadat, it was to justify a separate course; for Rabin, it was to cross the dividing line between agreements to stabilize a cease-fire and those which mark a step toward peace.

The biggest obstacle to rapid progress was psychological: the parties had still never met each other face-to-face and therefore tended to misjudge the impact of their demands on the other and to blame the mediator when their arguments did not prevail. Sadat thought the United States had the ability to command Israeli acquiescence in whatever plan we favored. As recent victims of an Egyptian surprise attack, the Israeli leaders found it difficult to credit my accounts of Sadat's moderation. At almost every meeting, the Israeli negotiators—Yigal Allon, in particular—warned that Sadat was about to go back to the

Soviet alliance (something I thought would only happen as a last resort) or was likely to break any agreement he might make (which I thought less and less probable the more Sadat separated himself from the Soviets and the Rabat decision).

Israel's flexibility was sharply circumscribed because of the divisions within its cabinet. Rabin preferred an agreement with Egypt, Allon with Jordan, and Peres urged stonewalling. Thus there was a majority within the Israeli negotiating team against any of the feasible interim steps.

Israeli negotiators can be unsettling in the best of circumstances. Because Israeli cabinets represent a coalition of competing personalities as well as parties, the opening Israeli position generally represents the sum of every key minister's preferences—especially when there is not a dominant Prime Minister, as was the case at the time of Rabin's first cabinet. Israeli negotiators modify their positions only after they have demonstrated to themselves and, above all, to their colleagues that there is no blood left to be squeezed out of the stone or, when there is a mediator—as there was during the shuttles—by saddling him with the blame for not having achieved their maximum position.

Veterans of this process would on occasion bring themselves to smile—albeit through clenched teeth—at its nervy tenacity and steel themselves to play out the role assigned to them by their interlocutors as the price of any final compromise. What gave the dialogue a particular edge in the negotiations over a Sinai interim agreement was the change in Israeli Prime Ministers. Whereas Golda Meir had conducted these almost inevitable disputes with sardonic humor and brought them to some end short of confrontation, Rabin's intellectual, almost professorial, approach tended to refine rather than mitigate disagreements.

Though friends of both leaders may consider the comparison nearly sacrilegious, there were striking similarities between the conduct of Rabin in his first tour in office and that of his later successor, Binyamin Netanyahu. Each had followed the first-generation leaders of their party. Each at first lacked the prestige and the aura that had surrounded these pioneers and felt a constant need to defend himself against other claimants to the mantle. Partly for this reason, both wanted a respite from the peace process and fought skillful rear-guard actions to reconcile their domestic and international imperatives. Both became embroiled with Washington.

But where Rabin always sought to educate his indispensable American allies in the subtleties and intangibles of his country's necessities,

Netanyahu has eschewed debates on substance and sought to slow the peace process by drawing it into the quagmire of Israeli domestic politics. Rabin's insistence on substantive clarity over time built a bridge across the gulf with Washington, leading to a real, even affectionate partnership; Netanyahu, at this writing, is still tempted by tests of strength which, even when there is an occasional agreement, have so far left the mutual incomprehension intact.

As for Ford, he had been in office only two months and lacked the necessary level of detachment. He interpreted the stalling tactics of the Israeli troika of Rabin, Peres, and Allon as reflecting their assessment that he was too weak to risk confrontation with Israel's supporters in Congress. I had warned Israeli Ambassador Simcha Dinitz and Rabin repeatedly against confusing Ford's goodwill with weakness. The President would surely pay thoughtful heed to their views, I would argue, but no responsible American leader could simply suspend Middle East diplomacy while the Israeli cabinet sorted out its internal conflicts.

My personal friendship with the Israeli leaders proved to be more of an obstacle than a spur to progress. Since Rabin, Allon, and I had been friends for many years, all three of us were convinced that an outright collision was impossible because, at the last moment, someone would veer away. Allon in particular had an almost mystical faith in my ability to bring off the most improbable negotiations and liked to console himself at every deadlock that these were but the prelude to some ultimate, though as yet unspecified, breakthrough. His faith in me, he would argue, had been rewarded in the Syrian negotiation and would be again. Allon proved deaf to my rejoinder that winning at roulette once does not make it a good idea to base one's annual budget on the spin of a wheel.

My friendship with Rabin and Allon remained constant through even the most painful deadlocks. But some of Israel's American supporters, especially in the intellectual community, turned on me. Their defense of Israel became fused with their critique of détente as they charged Ford and me with selling Israel out in order to placate the Soviet Union—never mind that a principal purpose of our diplomacy was to reduce and, wherever possible, to eliminate a significant Soviet role in the Middle East.

Jousting over détente could not, however, change the reality that the Ford Administration had only two options: either a step-by-step approach (which meant negotiating a new interim agreement with Egypt) or reconvening the multilateral Geneva conference in pursuit of an overall settlement (which meant involving the Soviet Union). At a Geneva conference, our deteriorating relations with the Soviets in the wake of the collapse of the trade agreement and the emerging deadlock over SALT would tempt the Kremlin to support the radical Arab program even more rigidly, and that would, in all probability, also be endorsed by our European allies and Japan. Though neither Allon nor Rabin contradicted this analysis, they seemed unwilling or unable to respond to Ford's and my repeated requests to develop a negotiating position and to start an alternative diplomacy.

Allon arrived in Washington on December 8, 1974, ostensibly to develop a joint strategy, but he brought no authority to go beyond Rabin's largely theoretical exposition of September. He put forward extremely precise ideas of what Israel would seek from Egypt but no cabinet position as to what Israel might concede in return. Since a formal Israeli proposal required a cabinet decision which had not been forthcoming, Allon put forward a list of actions described as "concepts" that would effectively eliminate any possibility of Egypt's resuming war with Israel. These included demilitarization of all areas vacated by Israeli forces; an Egyptian commitment not to join a war against Israel started by other Arab states; an end of economic warfare; an end to hostile propaganda or hostile diplomacy; a right of Israeli ships and crews to pass through the Suez Canal; and an understanding that Egypt would not resume a large-scale military supply relationship with the Soviet Union.

Cairo, we knew, would only consider such terms for a significant Israeli withdrawal. Yet Allon had not been given any authority whatever to put forward *any* new line. Instead, he offered a "concept" of a withdrawal which spoke vaguely of a distance of thirty to fifty kilometers and was otherwise specific only to the extent that it emphatically did *not* include the Giddi and Mitla Passes or the Abu Rudeis oil fields.

Allon's conversation with Ford on December 9 followed what were by now familiar lines. When Ford indicated that he would support the elements of nonbelligerency provided by Allon in the context of some concrete withdrawal scheme, Allon—lacking cabinet authority—turned the conversation to the Israeli request for a long-range military supply program. Ford, who had just approved a substantial increase in the annual aid package for Israel, balked at a long-range commitment with growing impatience: "I can't go for a long-term authorization for Israel if we don't get support for our foreign policy as a whole."

Nevertheless, we transmitted Allon's "concept" of a thirty- to fifty-kilometer withdrawal (excluding the passes) to Cairo and, as we had predicted, Sadat blew up. Ambassador Hermann Eilts reported Sadat's reaction:

> Concessions of the type demanded by Allon could not be made for 50-kilometer withdrawals without undermining his position. The Israelis were asking him to concede his territory and sovereignty. This he would not do.

To break the stalemate and determine whether some realistic position could be extracted from the parties, I came up with the idea of an "exploratory" shuttle. Israel accepted eagerly because it provided a further mechanism for delay; Sadat went along reluctantly as a way of starting a negotiating process even though he thought it highly improbable that the Israeli cabinet would commit itself to specifics during an "exploratory" trip.

Sadat was proved right. In an actual shuttle, the presence of a high-level American mediator supplies the deadline and hence a sense of urgency. The parties have an incentive to consider what cost a stalemate might exact in terms of their relationship with the United States. In an exploratory shuttle, however, there exists neither a deadline nor a penalty. The parties' incentive is to hold back their concessions in anticipation of the real thing. Stalemate is ingrained in such a process—as all succeeding administrations were to experience as well.

Another visit to the President by Allon on January 16, 1975, did not advance matters. Prior to that meeting, I summed up the state of play for Ford in a memorandum:

> Sadat has given us some general ideas about the concessions he is willing to make, including various aspects of nonbelligerency. The dilemma we face is that Sadat will not be more specific about the Egyptian concessions until he has a firm idea of the depth of the withdrawal Israel is prepared to make. . . .
>
> Israel, however, has stated privately and publicly its refusal to signal any meaningful territorial withdrawal unless and until Egypt makes known in some detail a broad range of political concessions.

Ford made another appeal to Allon, this one based on America's urgent need to gain time in which to recover from economic and political crises:

> I want Henry to go to Egypt. But he has to have something
> more tangible to bring there than what came from our previ-
> ous talk. I think we need another settlement by the end of
> February. We need stability for the next year and a half to
> two years, to recover our economy, our energy situation, and
> our position in the world. We need time, and a settlement
> will give that. But Henry has to have more for Sadat than
> you brought before.

Allon, however, simply did not have the authority to respond to the President. The exploratory shuttle was being launched into a vacuum.

## The Exploratory Shuttle

We began the February 1975 exploratory shuttle with feelings ranging from hope to premonition. On January 27, two weeks before my departure, I told Dinitz:

> It is not my intention to push Israel beyond what's bearable.
> . . . I'm trying to do what Rabin is doing by his compulsive
> arms acquisition—to regain some authority. Can we, by an
> act of statesmanship, make something which we'll know isn't
> that much, but we'll have bought some time?

Unfortunately, there was next to no compatibility between what we needed to reestablish executive authority in the United States and what the parties considered necessary for their own domestic consolidation. Our great test would be whether we could dominate Middle East diplomacy, ease the crisis in the Middle East, and prevent another outburst of violence which might drive the energy crisis out of control. Sadat needed to demonstrate to his colleagues that moderation produced tangible benefits. For the Israeli negotiating team, domestic consolidation depended on exactly the opposite: extracting concessions from Egypt and arms from the United States without having to pay any significant territorial price for either.

At the same time, American relations with the Soviet Union were deteriorating in the aftermath of the collapse of the Trade Act and the domestic assault on the Vladivostok agreement. On January 21, Ford wrote Brezhnev, informing him of the exploratory shuttle. It was the by now standard maneuver to keep the Soviet Union out of the diplomacy actually taking place by hinting at cooperation with it in the next phase. Ford's letter described the shuttle's purpose as an attempt to determine whether "preliminary steps" were possible "to moderate the tensions in the area," and he invited Brezhnev's views as to "possible cooperative action between us . . . once the steps the U.S. is presently engaged in have been completed."

Brezhnev could not have missed the point that Ford's offer of future cooperation was vague and without operational content. On January 27, he replied tartly that "the practical steps of the American side are in complete opposition to what has been agreed between us" and raised the not unreasonable question as to why cooperative measures should be explored *"after* but not *before* some steps are implemented." Nevertheless, Brezhnev agreed to a meeting between Gromyko and me, although he defined its purpose as fulfilling the Arab demand for a return to the 1967 borders and the establishment of a Palestinian entity. It was another example of Soviet rigidity, for it was precisely the impossibility of even starting negotiations on these perennial Soviet terms that excluded the Soviet Union from the Middle East peace process.

I set off on the exploratory shuttle leaving behind a Washington that was tense and divided. The assault on détente was gathering steam and increasingly being linked to our conduct of the Middle East negotiations. The intelligence investigations were getting under way, fed by a cascade of leaks and innuendos. Many of the controversies revolved around my own person. Ford, however, remained calm in the face of the storm and steadfast in support. The day before my departure, the President telephoned me:

> FORD: Henry, I have decided, and I would like your observa-
> tions. I want to come out to the airport tomorrow night.
> You and Nixon and I have done a first-class job, I think.
> . . . I want to come to the airport tomorrow night and
> see you off.
> KISSINGER: Let me think about it overnight as to whether
> it looks as if I asked you to prop me up. You know, I

have no feeling at all about our relationship. I don't
have any insecurity, and I could not have asked for better
support. . . .

FORD: Right. Henry, you be very strong over there. I am on
the same wavelength with you substantively.

KISSINGER: In terms of support and just the joy of working
together, I could not be more satisfied. So nothing I say
has anything to do with our relationship.

FORD: I agree, Henry, and if we ever disagree, you can tell
me, and I can tell you.

The exploratory shuttle began in Israel on Monday evening, February 10. As I had feared, the label "exploratory" tempted the Israeli negotiating team to confine itself to discussions of overall strategy with respect to which there was no significant difference of opinion between us. As before, the Israeli negotiators endorsed the step-by-step approach but stalled on defining terms. The next day, at a private session with Rabin, he left me with the impression that there was agreement regarding the ultimate outcome; his chief concern was to make sure that American economic assistance would be available for the changes in the Israeli military infrastructure made necessary by the proposed withdrawals. He was particularly emphatic about the cost of moving an airfield located just beyond the passes. From all this I assumed—as it turned out, incorrectly—that the principle having been accepted, the shuttle would be basically about price.

But when I met with the full negotiating team, it became clear that Rabin had not succeeded in convincing his colleagues. What produced, paradoxically, a sinking feeling was the absence of the tense, almost frenetic mood which had prevailed when actual withdrawals had been under discussion during the disengagement negotiations. Instead the Israeli negotiating team concentrated on a philosophical discussion of the relative merits of a step-by-step versus an overall approach without ever touching on the subject that had brought me to the Middle East: the specific terms for a Sinai interim agreement.

I did my best to convey the realities of our domestic situation: that executive discretion in managing crises had been eroded by Watergate; that it would make all the difference whether a Geneva conference took place after the United States had successfully managed a Middle East negotiation, or whether we would be dragged to Geneva as the result of a stalemate in the negotiations and at the mercy of an incipient Soviet-Arab-European coalition regarding Middle East issues; and that a successful step-by-step approach might even cause some Arab countries to proceed toward a peace agreement separately:

> In America, the situation is that, as a result of assassinations, Vietnam, and Watergate, executive authority is at an all-time low; and this is reflected in many things, but above all in the breakdown of discipline within the executive branch. . . .
>
> The Prime Minister remembers our management of the crisis in 1970; some of you may remember also 1973. This type of action is almost out of the question [today]. . . .
>
> Once the negotiation [in Geneva] starts, you will be on the total defensive. The Arab position will be totally supported by all the Europeans, the Japanese, and, of course, the Soviet Union. . . .
>
> For this reason, one advantage of the step-by-step approach is to get international opinion used to the idea that it is an extremely complex problem, and second, to get them used to the complexity of the solutions. And to create a mood in which, in order to get it all over with, some of the other [Arab] countries may want to settle rather than go into this year after year.

The Israeli negotiating team did not challenge this analysis, but its bearing conveyed that it saw no reason to cede territory because of it. Rabin concluded the otherwise abstract and theoretical dialogue with a helpful intervention:

> The point is we are still interested in step-by-step, not because of fear of Geneva, but because of the merits of this policy. And this policy can give the United States and Israel certain advantages if there is some return, and if we can get assurances that we won't be dragged to Geneva in a way we don't want.

An abstract statement of willingness to make an interim agreement with Egypt spelled progress in Jerusalem, but it was thin gruel for Sadat, trying to decide whether to run the risk of separating himself from his Arab brethren. Not surprisingly, I found him pensive and withdrawn when, on February 12 and 13, I visited him in Cairo. Sadat had been uneasy about the exploratory shuttle all along because he suspected that Israel would hold back its trump cards and, in the process, maneuver itself into a stalemate. My report, he added, raised the question whether the Israeli cabinet was too weak or too divided to undertake any major agreement, no matter what he might offer.

As he had been doing for months, Sadat warned that a formal pledge of nonbelligerency on his part while Egyptian territory remained in Israeli hands would be treated as treason throughout the Arab world. Nevertheless, while rejecting a formal commitment to nonbelligerency, Sadat agreed to include many of its elements in an interim agreement. But he refused to specify these elements; they would be leaked, he said, and be turned by Israel into the starting point for a new set of demands.

With each side waiting for the other to make the first move, or using the United States as a deus ex machina to extract concessions, Rabin seized the initiative during my second stop in Israel, February 13–14. In a background interview to the press traveling with me on February 14, he expressed his readiness to give up the passes and oil fields for an appropriate quid pro quo, which he defined as Egypt permanently renouncing any possibility of war with Israel, either to reclaim its own territory or to support the claims of other Arab states. It was the first time any Israeli leader had publicly gone this far. But Rabin's foray also underlined what we were up against. Though Sadat was headed in precisely that direction, his ability to follow through depended on the very ambiguity regarding the meaning of nonbelligerency that Rabin was now shredding.

Nevertheless, once Rabin had publicly agreed with the objectives of our diplomacy, I became quite hopeful that an agreement would emerge. Sadat would go far toward meeting Israeli needs on nonbelligerency, and Rabin had probably not yet spoken his last word. On that basis, I agreed with Rabin that the formal negotiating shuttle should start in about three weeks.

Golda Meir brought me back to the real world. Before leaving Israel—indeed, on the way to the airport on February 14—I called on her at her modest house in a suburb of Tel Aviv. She proved no less blunt in retirement than she had been while in office: "It will never work," she proclaimed. "The cabinet will never approve it." No Israeli minister had said or hinted as much. Indeed, Rabin had left me with the opposite impression. Later, on the plane, I told Under Secretary of

State Joseph Sisco what Golda Meir had said. "It is amazing," I remarked, "how quickly people get out of touch when they leave office."

Unfortunately, it was not Golda but I who was out of touch, at least as far as Israeli realities were concerned. I could not imagine that the Israeli cabinet would have allowed me to embark on a shuttle unless it was prepared to settle within the general framework Ford and I had repeatedly described to Rabin (we counted a total of twenty-four times). Israel, we thought, had too much at stake in a moderate Egypt to abort the negotiation, especially after having stonewalled the Jordanian option. What I had not calculated was that Israel might well drift into deadlock as a result of conflicts within its cabinet rather than from sober calculation.

To defuse objections to a separate agreement, I stopped in Damascus, Aqaba, and Riyadh before returning to Washington. It was a measure of American dominance over Middle East diplomacy that Syrian President Hafez al-Asad, though passionately opposed to a separate Egyptian move, was nevertheless interested in joining the peace process. He indicated his willingness to undertake another partial step on the Golan Heights, which he recognized was bound to be small, given the limited size of the territory. Even more significantly, he indicated that he would agree to formal nonbelligerency if Israel withdrew from the entire Golan Heights. Though I was certain Rabin would reject both proposals, they marked a big change from my first meeting with Asad almost a year and a half earlier.

In Aqaba, King Hussein, who had ambivalence imposed on him by circumstances beyond his control, resented that Sadat should benefit from having abandoned him at Rabat. But he preferred it to the Geneva conference, where his isolation would be generally visible.

In Riyadh, I met with King Faisal, that subtlest of diplomats who relied on the trappings of feudalism to navigate his country through the storms raging in his region. I greatly respected King Faisal and felt considerable affection for him. His demeanor might be remote, but he was trustworthy. As canny as he seemed exalted, the King used his singularity to ameliorate, balance, and shape the alien forces of modernity. Conscious that Saudi wealth might well prove a magnet for the covetousness of less well-endowed neighbors, Faisal maneuvered to combine support for Arab aspirations with recognition of the geopolitical realities he had observed over the many years he had been his country's foreign minister. Aware that the Arabs' romantic streak often led them to overextension, he also recognized that head-on opposition to these tendencies might unhinge the delicate balances of his kingdom. At the same time, despite his genuine friendship for the United States, Faisal was convinced that America's excessive pragmatism faced the kingdom with choices beyond its emotional capacities. He therefore maneuvered between the rhetoric of the Arabs and the practicalities of Washington. While he could not afford to endorse our policies formally, he found ways to support them so long as he could do so unobtrusively.

My first meeting with Faisal had reflected these tactics. The King spent hours eloquently endorsing the formal united Arab position, and I used the brief pauses in his discourse to explain the more limited realistic possibilities. After the notetaker had closed his book, Faisal escorted me to the door and said, in English: "We pray to Almighty God that He will continue to grant you success in all these noble efforts. I spoke very frankly to Your Excellency because I respect your proven ability and wisdom."

Though Faisal would not risk being publicly identified with our policies, he was prepared to facilitate them by means of subtle Saudi diplomacy and the more obvious temptation of Saudi cash. Once I understood this, I took to briefing Faisal regularly and outlining our problems without formally requesting Saudi assistance. Often we would discover later a Saudi footprint helping our negotiations along and removing obstacles to our policy.

On this visit, Faisal dutifully warned me against a separate agreement while urging me to use my best judgment to proceed toward peace. In other words, he defined the politically correct objective while supporting the only practical diplomacy.

The efforts dating back to the first days of the Ford Administration were finally culminating in a shuttle. All that was lacking was the cooperation of the parties.

## The Shuttle That Failed

When, on March 7, 1975, I headed to Egypt on what was expected to be the climactic shuttle, the disintegration of Vietnam was bringing American foreign policy to its nadir. Indochina was falling, and the global economic recession triggered by the energy crisis continued to rage.

But the Middle East parties were driven by entirely different concerns. Having served as ambassador in Washington, Rabin understood our necessities well enough, maybe better than he did the emotions of his public, which resisted the concept of trading territory for assurances. Sadat, while less constrained by Egyptian public opinion, had to maneuver against the background of having pledged himself to Arab unity in Rabat not five months previously.

All this caused the shuttle to be conducted in an atmosphere of extraordinary tension. We had to convince the Israeli negotiators that we were reliable partners even in the face of America's disintegrating effort in Indochina. And we needed to persuade Sadat that his bet on us remained valid even as so many other aspects of American foreign policy were under domestic assault.

The shuttles had a way of bringing home to the American team the vastness of the gulf between the national styles and perceptions of the Egyptian and Israeli leaders, obliging us to shift gears sometimes as often as three times in one day. Upon arriving in Israel, we would be taken directly by car or helicopter to the conference room adjoining the Prime Minister's office; our hosts never squandered precious time on such nonessentials as personal conversation or social meals. Upon arriving in Egypt, we would be enveloped, at Sadat's insistence, in a mandatory spell of relaxation—depending on the venue, at the beach or Sadat's garden at Alexandria, the presidential rest house near the pyramids in Cairo, or at some desert retreat near Aswan. Meetings in Jerusalem invariably alternated between the Prime Minister's residence, comparable to a middle executive's domicile in the suburb of some American metropolis, and the Prime Minister's austere conference room. There were few grace notes; our interlocutors went straight to the subject and never strayed far from it. Even the banter was strictly related to the issues at hand. When it concerned territorial adjustments, Israeli leaders were beyond frivolity. With survival at stake, the Israeli negotiating team was reluctant to interrupt the negotiation even for meals, most of which consisted of sandwiches while the talks continued.

It did not seem to matter that the United States had supplied Israel with almost all of its arms or that our backing was absolutely indispensable to the success of Israeli diplomacy. Treated with extraordinary wariness, the American negotiators were put on notice that any agreement would require monumental exertions. Israeli negotiators, steeped in the Talmudic tradition, parsed each document with supersophistication and subtlety, delighting in the discovery of abstruse shades of meaning that might have eluded us. Often grating on our emotional balance, their greatest fear seemed to be that they would be accused by their demanding and strident constituencies of having been taken in by their American allies. They had no intention of settling until they had absolved themselves of the slightest potential for blame by relentlessly imposing physical and emotional exhaustion on their American interlocutors.

There was something at once heroic and heartrending in such monumental intransigence: heroic because only unquenchable self-absorption could have transmuted total dependence into defiant insistence; heartrending because the defiance barely masked an undercurrent of panic lest this generation of Jews, through its own mistakes or—more likely—through the folly and shortsightedness of allies, be consigned to continue the tale of disasters that spell Jewish history. Israel's negotiators dared not avow what they feared the most: that the United States was being seduced by a newly moderate and charismatic Arab leader, and that, in the process, Israel would become a pawn in America's Cold War strategy and lose its traditional emotional anchor in the United States.

By contrast, Egypt's leaders seemed to have imbibed at least some of the rhythm of eternity implicit in the long history of their country. Egypt might have lost every war with Israel, but it was instinctively aware that its survival had never been at stake. Egyptian territory was too vast to be conquered by Israel; Cairo alone stood at nearly twice the population of all of Israel. All Egypt needed was a single victory, while Israel would be hazarding its very existence with a single defeat. Egypt could afford a margin for generosity; Israel, clinging to the very edge of survival, was bound to view any appeal to generosity as an invitation to disaster.

Egypt's leaders—in particular Sadat—were less preoccupied with semantic traps and legal loopholes and more willing to take gambles on the intangibles of personal relations and of historical evolution. For them, diplomacy was a balancing of emotional commitments. The Arabs' great weakness was the proclivity toward romanticism. It was not always easy to tell whether an interlocutor was putting forward epic poetry or a realistic appraisal of the situation at hand; at times, these blended imperceptibly. The Israeli obsession was legalistic exegesis; it led them to an odyssey in search of precision that occasionally lost touch with reality. The Arabs' quest was dignity and honor, the Israelis' security and survival.

While the negotiators concentrated on the discussions at the various venues, the task of the technical support teams proved unvaryingly backbreaking. Sometimes we shuttled twice in one day. Under Secretary of State Joseph Sisco, who was in charge of the backup; Assistant Secretary of State Alfred "Roy" Atherton; Harold "Hal" Saunders, who alternated between being Atherton's deputy and being responsible for Middle East staff work at the National Security Council; and Peter Rodman, my indispensable personal assistant, who was responsible inter alia for the documentation, serviced the shuttle.

A typical day for the backup team would begin in Jerusalem's King David Hotel, where it put together the checklists, texts, and maps likely to be required that day. Generally the American team would meet with its Israeli counterpart for a last-minute review before driving or flying by helicopter to the specially equipped U.S. Air Force plane waiting at Ben Gurion Airport. The ride to the airport and the flight to either a military airfield in the Nile delta or near Aswan was used for revising, retyping, and copying texts. After helicoptering to President Sadat's location, several hours with Sadat and his team produced by late afternoon both responses to the Israeli proposals as well as a new Egyptian proposal. Then it would be back to Jerusalem for another meeting with the Israeli negotiating team until the early hours of the morning, followed by further revision of checklists, texts, and maps.

Our flying office was a Boeing 707 which, in its better days, had served as President Johnson's presidential jet; by the early 1970s, it had been relegated to the status of presidential backup plane. It was divided into three compartments. The forward section—"headquarters" for me and two or three members of my personal staff—was furnished with a sofa, a conference table in the shape of an ellipse, and an oversized easy chair designed for—and perhaps by—President Johnson. The table and easy chair were unusual in that they could be raised and lowered by separate switches. Lack of technical facility once had me caught by the legs between an ascending easy chair and a descending table, from which more mechanically minded crew members extricated me.

Behind that section was a compartment of eight seats in four rows of two, together with some typewriters and a Xerox machine. There reigned Joe Sisco and his associates. And the third compartment contained seats three abreast for perhaps twenty-four people, housing the administrative staff and the accompanying press contingent.

Whenever we left one end of the shuttle, the backup team would be frantically preparing its analysis of the outstanding issues and their status, and fine-tuning the principals' generalities into negotiating language. As it took only an hour to fly from Cairo to Tel Aviv, accomplishing this in time required a major tour de force that frequently tapped all of Sisco's not inconsiderable histrionic abilities. On one occasion when the copying machine broke loose from its mooring, I heard a member of the backup team call out: "Retrieve it before Sisco falls into it because two Siscos would drive us crazy." Whenever Sadat moved the Egyptian venue to Aswan, he gained the backup team's undying gratitude for giving them an extra hour's flying time in which to finish their work.

On this occasion, Sadat had proposed that the shuttle start in Egypt. Convinced that the biggest obstacle to progress was psychological, he was in effect offering to make the first move so as to ease Rabin's task with his cabinet. With his usual sense of drama, Sadat received me in Aswan on the morning of Saturday, March 8, in the same room where, fourteen months earlier, he had conveyed his decision never to wear a uniform again except on ceremonial occasions.

Flanked by Foreign Minister Ismail Fahmy and Defense Minister General Mohammed Abdel Ghany el-Gamasy, Sadat began warmly but formally: "You are a dear friend. I hope your visit will be fruitful and decisive." With this, he dismissed his advisers. When we were alone, he began by making explicit his previous hints regarding the Israeli demand for nonbelligerency. He would not be able to agree to a formal statement of nonbelligerency while Israeli troops remained on Egyptian soil. He was, however, prepared to accept most of the constituent elements. He invited me to outline for him what such a list might contain.

I told Sadat that, in my judgment, the Israeli demand for a formal end of belligerency reflected four basic elements: an extended respite from war and the threat of war; assurances that Egypt would not join Syria in another war; creation of a demilitarized U.N. zone along the new lines for a fixed number of years not subject either to a U.N. Security Council veto or a unilateral Egyptian demand for its removal, as was the case with the disengagement agreements; and relaxation of Arab boycotts and blockades against Israeli cargos. Sadat promised his answer for the next day.

When we resumed the next morning, Sadat described his domestic situation. The Egyptian military, he said, was restive. Up to now, he had been able to pacify his soldiers with the argument that his strategy was recovering Egyptian territory. But if diplomacy stalemated, the army would surely remind him that going it alone had caused the Soviet Union to cut off military shipments and had isolated Egypt within the Arab world.

Nevertheless, in order to achieve a rapid breakthrough, Sadat was prepared to offer the following elements of nonbelligerency: a formal commitment to settle all future disputes by peaceful means; a pledge to abjure the use of force even if Syria reignited the war; significant limitations on Egyptian forces on the eastern side of the Suez Canal; a wide buffer zone between Israeli and Egyptian forces; freedom of passage for Israel-bound cargos through the Suez Canal; and an easing of the Arab boycott against American firms. The precise formulations were to be worked out by Fahmy and Sisco. In return, Sadat expected some significant withdrawals, at least vacating the Giddi and Mitla Passes and the Abu Rudeis oil fields.

Sadat's proposal was a big step forward, though its phraseology continued to be vague. At this early stage of the shuttle, I was still confident of success.

In this mood, I made a detour to Damascus on Sunday, March 9, so that I could brief Asad without the controversy an imminent separate Israeli-Egyptian agreement was bound to generate. It was also, I said only half facetiously to Sisco, a good rehearsal for what would be awaiting us in Jerusalem.

For, in truth, the negotiating styles of the Israelis and Syrians, who considered themselves to be implacable opponents, were fairly similar. At that point, neither of them really believed that a permanent peace was possible. They negotiated with each other out of necessity: Israel to legitimize its dealings with Egypt in Arab eyes, Syria to keep itself from being isolated. They were capable of making practical arrangements; the Golan Heights disengagement of 1974 has lasted at this writing nearly twenty-five years without charges of violations from either side. But they have never pretended that they were working toward qualitative change to endow the armistice between them with a moral foundation—as Sadat sought to do and as a succession of Israeli leaders, at first with disbelief but in time with conviction, learned to reciprocate.

The rulers in Cairo viewed themselves as heirs to an ancient civilization, the borders of which had been defined through the millennia. They participated in Arab politics more by choice than by vocation, for Egypt did not consider itself a purely Arab country. It looked as well toward Africa and the northern shores of the Mediterranean.

On the other hand, Syria's vocation—its very reason for existence —was Arab nationalism. Its borders were almost as arbitrary as Israel's, resulting from the division of Middle East spoils between Britain and France at the end of the First World War. Just as many in Israel sought fulfillment in extending Israeli control over biblical Palestine, so many Syrians saw themselves as the advance guard of an Arab nation which, in their dreams, included Lebanon, Jordan, Palestine, and, at exuberant moments, Iraq and Saudi Arabia. Thus Syrian leaders feel a responsibility not just for the entity which is today Syria but for the Arab cause as they interpret it. Asad explained this attitude during my second stop in Damascus on this shuttle:

> We cannot wait and we cannot stand still. Israel already accuses us of being expansionists just for wanting to take back Golan! We are being accused of all sorts of things just because we advocate Arab unity. To us Arab unity is sacred. Syria, historically, was quite a homeland for all peoples around here, so the Secretary should not be surprised if Syria would look with great favor upon uniting with our neighbors.

This was why, during the exploratory shuttle, Asad had offered only nonbelligerency in return for the Golan Heights. A peace agreement would have to wait for an overall settlement with *all* the Arabs, especially the Palestinians.

Asad reflected the conflicting tugs-of-war within the Syrian political system. He belonged to the Alawite sect, a minority that had become fully Muslim only in the last century. The requirements of political and even ethnic survival were therefore deeply ingrained in him. Though he has lasted far longer than his Israeli counterparts, Asad has survived domestically by pursuing the same balancing act among various factions in an ephemeral consensus. Unlike Israeli political leaders, he did not hesitate to call in the armed forces to sustain his rule—if necessary, with extreme brutality—and he therefore went to great lengths to assure the unity of the military.

When I negotiated with him, Asad usually followed a three-stage procedure which symbolized his power base. First he would meet with me and *my* interpreter alone, which enabled him to control what would be conveyed to his associates; then he would call in a group of military officers to hear a condensed version of the dialogue; finally, a civilian group would join us for an even more abbreviated version.

Asad presided over this process with aplomb and sardonic humor. Like Israeli negotiators, he neither believed in unilateral gestures nor was he in a position to implement them. Ruthless, intelligent, charming when he wanted to be, Asad was a specialist in pursuing every negotiation until he had convinced himself that he had extracted the last possible concession—even if that meant jeopardizing the entire negotiation and weakening Syria's overall standing. As far as he was concerned, peace had no abstract value, and he never pretended that it did. It registered, in Asad's view, an equilibrium of forces which would end when the equilibrium altered. Thus a formal agreement with Israel would only formalize an existing balance of power. A succession of American Secretaries of State have perceived their talks with him to be about moving him toward a breakthrough in his perception of the nature of peace. The effort was doomed to failure. Asad was never prepared to conclude more than an armistice no matter what heading might appear on top of the document being signed at the conclusion.

During the 1975 shuttle, Asad had two objectives: to prevent a separate Egyptian-Israeli agreement and, failing that, to participate in the negotiations in a way that would establish equal status with Sadat. But Israel would not negotiate on the Golan Heights, and Sadat would not let Syria determine the pace of his negotiations.

I knew Asad was quite aware of our strategy but too prudent to court a confrontation with the United States. I therefore kept him informed to retain the prospect of some future role for him and to confine his opposition to verbal objection. Asad went along because he had no better alternative. He would wait for opportunities either to scuttle the peace process or to benefit from it; the ultimate choice would be dictated by the balance of forces.

The dialogue with the Syrian President on March 9 turned out to be as inconclusive as we had expected (and, in a way, designed). I had nothing of any relevance to Syrian concerns to offer, and Asad did not believe in unreciprocated gestures.

We arrived in Israel that evening in an atmosphere inhospitable to negotiations. For Israel was mourning the murder of Israeli civilians and two soldiers in Tel Aviv by Arab terrorists who had landed in two small boats and had seized a beachfront hotel, which was then stormed by the Israeli army. Arab hostility, it was argued plausibly, was so ingrained that it was madness to risk the security afforded by a territorial buffer to achieve an illusory Arab goodwill.

As usual, we were taken straight from the airport to a meeting with the Israeli negotiating team. But, for the first time in our experience, Rabin had arranged a social dinner. To our astonishment, the Israeli negotiators did not subject my account of the conversation with Sadat at Aswan to the standard rigorous and skeptical cross-examination regarding Sadat's intentions. They concentrated instead on my brief and basically meaningless sojourn in Damascus. And since Rabin and his colleagues had no intention of negotiating with Syria, even that part of the conversation was comparatively jovial. It felt good for a change not to be subjected immediately to the grueling exegesis by which Israeli negotiators wear down their interlocutors.

At the same time, there was an ominous aspect to this unprecedentedly noncontentious atmosphere. The only possible explanation for the relaxed demeanor of the Israeli negotiating team was either that the cabinet had made its decision or, more likely, had once again failed to reach any decisions, so that the Israeli negotiators had nothing to tell us. Sisco, for one, was suspicious: "They are too friendly," he whispered to me. "We are getting too paranoid," I replied.

Rabin concluded the evening by handing me a memorandum containing seven principles which would guide the Israeli negotiating team —as if we were in an academic seminar and not the first stage of a shuttle. The language was conciliatory, but there was nothing to act on. The seven points were a generalized version of what we had been warning for months would not prove sufficient.

When finally on the morning of March 10, the third day of the shuttle, we got down to specifics, it became evident that, contrary to all our previous experience, Rabin had not used the delay he had imposed on us to move his cabinet toward compromise. To my astonishment, we were told that there would be no proposal to take back to Sadat, no map, not even a clarification of the concept of the thirty- to fifty-kilometer withdrawal Allon had described to Ford in December. Instead, Sadat's proposed elements of nonbelligerency were subjected to a withering legalistic critique based on the proposition that the concessions were either insufficient or meaningless because they could be revoked at any time.

The Israeli critique was both accurate and irrelevant. The same criticism could have been leveled had Sadat agreed to a formal pledge of nonbelligerency—or, for that matter, to formal peace. To be sure, the proposed Israeli concessions were territorial, while the proposed benefits were revocable. And yet it was irrelevant because, from the beginning, it was clear that this would have to be the structure of the negotiations. No matter what the heading of an agreement and what the formal provisions of duration might be, agreements between sovereign states—even peace agreements—can always be abrogated. What penalty has there ever been for revoking a peace agreement or for disregarding a proclamation of nonbelligerency other than going to war—precisely what the peace agreement or nonbelligerency pledge is supposed to prevent?

The ultimate decision before the Israeli negotiating team was whether weaning Sadat away from the Rabat consensus and his reliance on the Soviet Union by ceding territory which would leave the Egyptian lines still a hundred miles from Israel's borders was riskier than a return to a stalemate that risked if not war, then loss of the diplomacy of peace. The legalistic, taunting dissection of Sadat's offer ignored the crucial reality that the only alternative was to return to a multilateral forum at Geneva, where Israel would face a coalition of all its adversaries and the need to come to grips simultaneously with much more complex issues such as the future of Jerusalem and final borders. Some key members of the Israeli negotiating team—and surely Rabin—understood these choices well enough. But they sometimes left the impression that they were more afraid of each other than of a diplomatic explosion.

In the course of every negotiation, a point is reached when the parties either conclude that they will eventually come together or that they are hopelessly deadlocked. In the former case, the negotiation gathers steam; individual issues are reconsidered in the light of imminent consensus. In the latter instance, though the process may drag on for some time, the negotiation is doomed because, from then on, the parties concentrate on shifting the blame for failure to each other.

Though the shuttle continued for another ten days, it really ended after the first session with the Israeli negotiating team. This was not because Israel's demands were excessive. That was standard procedure for the initial session with Israeli negotiating teams, which are in the habit of aggregating the preferences of each of its members. But the change from Golda Meir to Rabin brought with it two differences in style which proved to be decisive. Golda was as tough in private as she was in the negotiating sessions; we knew where we stood. In his first tenure as Prime Minister, this was not the case with Rabin. In private conversations, he left us with the conviction that he agreed with not only our strategy but our basic terms; he seemed primarily concerned to mitigate costs for Israel in redesigning the military infrastructure supporting the new lines. But in the sessions of the negotiating team, Rabin adamantly insisted on his seven principles and would not countenance a gradual approach to them.

In retrospect, I believe this was due to a combination of a far more analytical cast of mind than Golda's and much greater fear of his cabinet. When the shuttles were effective, they were sustained because each party—including the Israelis—was prepared to make slight adjustments in its position at each visit of the mediating team. This eased the atmosphere and encouraged the other party to make adjustments of its own. In this manner, the two sides narrowed the gulf between them.

On this shuttle, the Israeli cabinet took the position that it would not modify its stance until I had achieved close to its maximum position from Sadat. I am sure that Rabin, like Allon, was hoping that somehow I would return from a shuttle having pulled the rabbit out of a hat. And Rabin would then have recommended significant Israeli concessions.

It was a misconception of shuttle diplomacy. For Sadat was bound to interpret what really constituted Israeli cabinet politics as an attack on his national dignity. With each shuttle, he became less amiable. And while he—playing by the old rules—kept modifying his stance, he no longer did so with the flair with which he had overridden all previous deadlocks.

Rabin understood the dilemma. Unable to move his cabinet toward compromise or even serious negotiation, he tried to bridge the chasm with a personal tour de force. He wrote an extraordinarily thoughtful letter to Sadat in which he attempted to substitute his own goodwill for the lack of consensus in the Israeli cabinet. The letter began with a tribute to Egypt's role in the region and a recognition of Sadat's moderate role:

> It has always been my firm conviction that Egypt, by virtue of its cultural heritage, its strength, its size and its influence, carries a leading voice with respect to the peace-making effort in our region. From what Dr. Kissinger has conveyed to me, as well as from your public statements, I feel assured

that you are determined to make strenuous efforts to achieve a settlement.

I, on my part, am determined to make all efforts to promote peace between us, and it is in this spirit that I express the aspiration that we shall yet succeed in reaching an agreement that will do honor to our two peoples.

Rabin expressed his willingness to make another withdrawal, but he could not do so without some demonstration that such a sacrifice represented a genuine turn toward peace. Sadat had often said to me, the letter continued, that the underlying problem between the Arabs and Israel was psychological. Rabin now set about defining that psychological challenge. He appealed to Sadat to include in the agreement some formal commitments to peaceful conduct; it was the almost identical request which his successor, Binyamin Netanyahu, took to the Wye plantation in less elevated language a quarter of a century later when the issue was Israeli withdrawal on the West Bank.

. . . [M]y people have to know that through the process of withdrawal to a new agreed line we have reached a turning point and that we are now entering an era in which we will be able to settle all our differences by peaceful means only. As Prime Minister, I must be able to convince both people and Government in Israel that in surrendering physical strategic positions we shall not be exposing ourselves to increased hardships created by lengthier and inferior lines in a resumed conflict. This can be possible only if it is visibly shown that the act of withdrawal marks the real beginning of progress towards peace by deeds and words that demonstrate the intention of peace.

I handed Rabin's letter to Sadat in Aswan on March 12 just before dinner. He was powerfully moved. Had the letter included any tangible Israeli concession, a breakthrough would almost surely have occurred.

Sadat puffed on his pipe for a few minutes before speaking: "It is very important for me to know who thought this up." I replied that it had been an Israeli idea, which was only partially correct because I had encouraged Rabin, who had responded eagerly. Sadat inquired: "Did they write it? That is even more important." I had not the slightest hesitation in affirming that it was an altogether Israeli draft, which I had not modified and had seen only after it was completed. Sadat folded the letter and put it in his pocket.

The next day, Sadat asked to see me alone and, with the letter in front of him, made the following oral reply, here reconstructed from my handwritten notes:

> What I want Yitzhak Rabin to know is the spirit behind the phrases of peaceful intent which we are negotiating. My attitude is that power will never again play a role in the relations of our two peoples. I will try to handle the Arab people if Rabin handles the Israeli people. My determination is to bring about the ultimate withdrawal to agreed lines by peaceful means only. If a Geneva conference is assembled after this agreement is signed, I will not touch this agreement or change anything between us at Geneva. Assure Rabin from my side I am not dreaming of solving this at Geneva. Whatever the problems, I will not use force. I would be ready to meet Rabin whenever the Israeli occupation of Egyptian territory is ended.

If Sadat's words had any meaning, Rabin had indeed achieved his most important political objective: Sadat had disavowed force in settling remaining disputes with Israel, even to bring about the return of the rest of Egyptian territory. He had agreed not to use the Geneva forum to harass Israel, and he had promised a then extraordinary face-to-face meeting. And if Sadat's words were not to be believed, formal provisions in an interim agreement would prove no more meaningful. In a curious way, the negotiation had become less about the details being addressed by the negotiating teams than about enabling the publics on both sides to catch up with their leaders' convictions.

A procedural change demonstrated that Sadat was reaching the limits of what he could achieve by himself. Until then, he and I had generally met privately to settle principles which experts—Sisco, Atherton, Saunders, and Ambassador Hermann Eilts on our side, Gamasy and Fahmy on the Egyptian—then transformed into treaty language. On this occasion, for the first time, at two meetings lasting three hours each on March 12 and 13, Sadat joined the drafting sessions—for which his patience quotient was severely limited. In all likelihood, he had understood that his associates would resist sweeping concessions they had not had a hand in shaping and were determined to make him assume responsibility for not only the general direction of the peace process but for its detailed provisions as well.

Sadat had given considerable thought to how he might invest an agreement with the political significance Rabin was demanding. He offered a clause describing the agreement as a step toward peace, including the formal declaration that Egypt would settle all remaining differences by peaceful means (including, by implication, territorial disputes concerning Egyptian territory). He proposed a clause by which the parties would renounce force for the duration of the agreement and, to alleviate Israeli fears over time limits and abrogation, added yet another clause to the effect that the agreement would remain in force until it was superseded by another agreement. Sadat agreed to the creation of mixed Egyptian-Israeli commissions to examine charges of violations and to open the Suez Canal as well as the Strait of Bab al-Mandeb (the entry to the Red Sea) to cargos which had Israel as a destination. Finally, he would reduce anti-Israel propaganda on Cairo radio and ease the economic boycott toward American firms on a case-by-case basis. Sadat concluded by saying only half in jest that if, with these concessions, I would be unable to obtain from Israel a description of the line to which it was willing to retreat, he and Fahmy might wind up getting arrested by Gamasy.

The pace of negotiations again turned glacial as, on March 14, the seventh day of the shuttle, I returned to Israel. The mood there was far from promising. The Israeli media were harping on purported American blackmail despite the fact that, up to that point, all the concessions had been made by Egypt. The negotiating team seemed unaffected by Sadat's reply to Rabin's letter and, since no cabinet meeting had taken place while I was in Aswan, the standard position was certain to have remained unchanged. The next cabinet meeting was scheduled for Sunday, March 16, delaying any new decision for two days at least.

At a tense three-hour meeting on March 14, the Israeli negotiators confined themselves to skeptical questions. They implied that Sadat's offers were not sufficient, if indeed they could be considered concessions at all—by which they meant that they continued to insist on a formal statement of nonbelligerency. They promised to deliver their reply to Sadat on the evening of March 16, or the ninth day of the shuttle.

The leisurely pace of Israeli decision-making with no Israeli contribution to resolving the deadlock was unprecedented. An Israeli backgrounder left little doubt as to the cabinet's likely decision when it called the Egyptian proposals "at first sight, insufficient and unsatisfactory" in many of its aspects.

During the hiatus, I traveled to Damascus and Amman on March 15 in an attempt to calm Israel's other increasingly restless and suspicious neighbors. Neither Asad nor Hussein would believe that the United States was unable to persuade Israel, and they interpreted the unprecedented delays as preludes to some sweeping deal which would exclude them.

Asad detested the prospect of a separate agreement between Egypt and Israel because it was bound to decrease his own leverage. He was well aware that we were the principal impetus behind a process likely to undermine the Syrian bargaining position. Nevertheless, my reception in Damascus was extraordinarily cordial because Asad also understood that his only options were deadlock or American mediation. This state of affairs was painful for the Syrian leader, especially as Israeli media never tired of trumpeting their government's rejection of any new interim agreement with Syria and its determination to keep most of the Golan Heights even in a final peace.

We met in Asad's office, where the velvet curtains were always drawn, creating a kind of sequestered, cocoon-like atmosphere. Seemingly unconstrained by any other schedule, Asad would spend a good deal of time on inter-Arab affairs and personalities, which provided many an opportunity for biting comments about Sadat's alleged treachery and Fahmy's duplicity. On this occasion, Asad conveyed his awareness—no doubt garnered from the Israeli media—that I had nothing new to report by letting me brief all his colleagues simultaneously. Afterward—reversing the usual procedure—we held our private meeting.

Asad professed his desire to improve relations with the United States, a pronouncement I interpreted less as a sign of goodwill than as a cold-blooded analysis of the balance of forces in the Middle East. Nor would Asad have been Asad had he failed to couple his statement of peaceful intent with a threat:

> I feel great pain when I see a child hurt. But when war is the
> only way out of a crisis or is the only method to regain one's
> honor and territory, then I don't count losses, human or

otherwise, because Syrian losses would then come under the heading of "sacrifices."

I replied that, in our estimate, Syria would suffer a crushing defeat. Asad countered that Syria, having learned that Israel "cannot stand pain," would pursue a strategy designed not so much to win as to inflict casualties in a protracted war. In contrast to my visit of the week before, Asad urged that a partial agreement on the Golan Heights be concluded simultaneously with an interim Egyptian negotiation.

Toward evening I proceeded to Amman, where a visit was always a respite from tensions. Though still smarting from having been excluded from the peace process in the wake of the Rabat decision, Hussein never lost sight of the fact that the United States was the indispensable guarantor of his dynasty's survival. The Jordanians cultivated American goodwill by impeccable manners and elaborate—though, on this occasion, restrained—hospitality. And because I, like they, believed in a community of interests, I solicited their opinions about the consequences should the shuttle they detested fail. How much longer should we press on?

Rising above their emotions, Hussein and Prime Minister Zaid Rifai urged me to go the extra mile. A failure in the negotiations, they said, might induce Sadat to reverse course or be overthrown, and that would "condemn the area to another war." Such an outcome would also be interpreted by all the countries of the region as a further proof of what they called "the United States giving up its friends and allies—Vietnam . . . Cambodia . . . and now Sadat and other moderates in the Middle East."

We met again with the Israeli negotiating team on Sunday evening, March 16, to receive the cabinet's formal position. The mood was, to say the least, wary. In my opening remarks, I referred to the hostile tone of the Israeli media, clearly fed by government briefings:

> First, I want to say I regret that in your public opinion the impression is created that the U.S. and Egypt are working in collusion to, by clever measures, extort things from Israel. This will be complicating, whatever short-term advantages it may give.

Rabin ignored the sally and at last delivered his cabinet's response to the Egyptian proposals we had brought two days earlier. It removed any doubt over whether the hostile media campaign had been an accident. For the cabinet had decided to nail itself to the position Ford and I had been warning against for six months. Further withdrawals in the Sinai would be made only in return for a "renunciation of acts of belligerency"; the Israeli quid pro quo would be either the passes or the oil fields but not both. The cabinet defined any Egyptian concession short of such a formal declaration as insufficient—including Sadat's valiant attempt to grant much of the substance of nonbelligerency without using the magic words. The cabinet refused to indicate a line to which it would be prepared to withdraw even in return for a formal pledge of nonbelligerency. Rabin's letter and Sadat's reply were yesterday's news.

An excerpt from the transcript of the meeting best describes its frosty atmosphere:

> RABIN: We have had a meeting. We have read what is put
> before us. You've done your utmost to put to the Egyptians our position. There are no doubts whatsoever.
> More than that, we really appreciate it. But when I try
> to sum it up, I see on the three main points crucial to
> us—the question of nonuse of force, the question of a
> real significant move toward peace, and the question of
> duration of the agreement—basically very little has
> been achieved.
>
> Israel will have to give something tangible, concrete,
> and we want to get something concrete even though it
> is to be expressed in words. . . .
>
> KISSINGER: I don't understand. They are prepared to use
> the phrase "not to resort to force."
>
> RABIN: But in the context of the peace process. Once the
> process stops. . . .
>
> KISSINGER: Then what do you want me to say to Sadat?
>
> RABIN: That unless he does move on these three key issues,
> I don't see what can be done.
>
> ALLON: And economic warfare.
>
> RABIN: I stuck to these three key points.
>
> KISSINGER: So I can give him no idea of lines or anything
> you would be prepared to do, assuming he comes up

with something satisfactory? You see, he suffers from
the illusion he's made a big effort. And the Syrians
believe he has too. We have two possibilities: if I go and
ask him to do better, or, I can go back with something
to show Gamasy, that he can get this if they are willing
to do more.

But the negotiating team did not have the authority to go beyond
what Rabin had put forward, neither with respect to what additional
aspect of nonbelligerency it wanted Sadat to concede, nor on a line of
withdrawal—not even if Sadat were miraculously to accept the Israeli
position. When I pointed out that the distinction between nonbelligerency and the nonuse of force was likely to prove elusive to the layman,
Rabin got down to the heart of the matter—which was cabinet paralysis:

> We are not entitled by the cabinet to discuss anything other
> than nonbelligerency. So we hoped you would bring some-
> thing closer to that. If so, we would discuss it with the
> cabinet.

Clearly the cabinet had decided that Sadat would have to deliver
Israel's maximum demands before it would reveal its quid pro quo. In
my view, the cabinet's position hazarded America's general credibility
as mediator:

> There is no sense fooling you. I can keep this going one more
> shuttle. Every shuttle increases the price to the United States.
> I do not think we're on anything like the same conceptual
> wavelength.
>     I think it will fail. It's a very serious question whether I
> should extract any more from Sadat if I think it will fail.
> Tell me the scenario of my first fifteen minutes with Sadat:
> "Israel may or may not give up the passes and fields. Please
> give more." Before Gamasy and Fahmy?

On Monday, March 17, as I was preparing to leave for Aswan, the
Israeli negotiating team, faced with the imminent breakup of the talks,
tried to shift the onus for failure on Sadat by slightly modifying its
position. Since there had been no additional cabinet meeting, the

changes could not be significant. The negotiating team offered to withdraw to the western edge (the Egyptian side) of the passes if Egypt agreed to forgo any hostile act, even in diplomacy. But it still refused to give us a map of what it understood as the "western edge" of the passes or to explain how it defined "hostile act," except that it included day-to-day diplomacy. Neither my colleagues nor I took that offer seriously. Not coupled with a map, the withdrawal offer meant little, for the passes were at least fifteen miles long and had no clear western edge. We therefore suspected that the offer was another way of putting forward the thirty- to fifty-kilometer withdrawal Allon had mentioned to Ford in December. With the demand for a renunciation of diplomatic pressure added to the already agreed stipulation not to use force, Sadat was, in effect, being asked to renounce what he considered Egyptian territory by forgoing even diplomacy to recover it.

In Egypt, a crisis of confidence was approaching. It was reflected in the increasing formality of the talks. When Sadat considered an agreement to be imminent, he would move to a conclusion in sudden and decisive leaps. But to sustain the looming stalemate, he needed wider backing. For the first time, Sadat introduced his new Vice President, Hosni Mubarak, wearing a blue air force uniform. Though Mubarak did not play a major role in the dialogue, he was a necessary guarantor of the military establishment's interests. Fahmy and Gamasy participated actively. Eilts and Sisco filled out our side.

Sadat's reaction to my account was somber: "They either cannot or do not want to settle." Having already renounced the use of force even while a large part of Egyptian territory remained in Israeli hands, how could he be asked to abandon diplomatic efforts as well—and all this in return for withdrawals Israel refused to specify?

Nevertheless, the next morning, March 18, Sadat and Fahmy came up with new formulations to meet Israel's concerns. These removed conditionality from the Egyptian pledge not to use force—specifically the link to the peace process to which Rabin had objected. In other words, Egypt's renunciation of force would remain in effect even were the peace process to falter. Sadat was prepared as well to pledge not to attack Israel, not only to Israel but also in a letter to the American President, provided Israel made the same pledge toward Egypt and in the same form. And he made explicit what I had always understood but about which Sadat had heretofore been ambiguous: that the passes were not to be handed over to Egypt but would be in a zone controlled by the U.N. I knew with a sinking feeling that, since all this still fell short of the formal proclamation of nonbelligerency on which the Israeli cabinet insisted, it would find no favor in Jerusalem.

Our only remaining means to keep the shuttle from collapsing was to make a formal American request to the Israeli cabinet to reconsider its position. This represented such a drastic departure from the easy informality with which American-Israeli discussions had previously been conducted that I cabled the President that day for his approval of the following formulation:

> The consequences of failure are so serious for both Israel and the US that it is essential that Israel reconsider its position in light of the latest concrete ideas which Egypt has asked me to convey to you. Failure to achieve a second-stage Egyptian-Israeli agreement after four months of arduous preparatory discussions in which the US has been so directly involved affects the vital interests of the US and of Israel.

I was reluctant to bring such formal pressure because, if it succeeded, it would demonstrate to Israel's adversaries the degree of its dependence on the United States, which might reduce their interest in moderation. And, if it failed, it would emphasize our impotence, which was hardly in our interest, especially in the months of Indochina's collapse. But it turned out that we had no other choice, since the Israeli cabinet had evidently misjudged our domestic situation. It seems to have believed that an unelected President whose party had just been routed in the congressional elections would not be in any position to insist on what Ford had put forward as our minimum program during his entire presidency. The Israeli cabinet may also have thought—or been told by American friends—that I was operating on my own without real presidential backing.

If so, this was a profound misreading of Ford's character and of our working relationship. Since literally his first week in the Oval Office, the President had been meeting with the key Middle East players; the premises on which the shuttle was based had his full backing. He had repeatedly and insistently urged them on both Rabin and Allon. Throughout the shuttle, I had been sending Ford detailed daily reports, supplemented with frequent phone calls to Brent Scowcroft, who briefed the President.

Ford's impatience with the looming stalemate was, if anything, stronger than mine because it was reinforced by a letter Sadat had sent without my knowledge after I left Egypt on Tuesday afternoon, March 18. Asking for Ford's personal intervention, Sadat expressed his indignation at Israel's proposals that demanded all the benefits of "a real and final peace" in return "for a very limited disengagement." An appeal to Ford over my head was unheard of and a clear signal that Sadat was losing patience both with the process and with the mediator.

Because he in effect shared Sadat's view, Ford's response to my proposed démarche to the Israeli government was blunt and unambiguous. Scowcroft cabled on the President's behalf:

> The President has read your latest report. He agrees with every word and would like you to impress upon the Prime Minister and the Cabinet that you are speaking with his full authority and total support. The President is totally and completely behind your current efforts and the strategy which they represent and feels deeply that these efforts have the overwhelming support of the American people.
>
> The President also said that we cannot be in a position to isolate ourselves from the rest of the world simply in order to stand behind the intransigence of Israel. He was not specific as to whether or not that particular comment was for attribution. I leave it to your judgment.

By now the Jerusalem end of the shuttle had settled into a routine. Since the cabinet never reviewed its position while we were in Egypt, I would have to wait at least a day after my return for its response or any new proposals. Given this schedule, the members of the Israeli negotiating team, divided among themselves and without new cabinet instructions, would devote the first evening of our return to Jerusalem to ask clarifying, usually heckling questions. To avoid having to brief their rampaging media or risk being accused of having made unauthorized concessions, they would not give an indication of their actual position. After reporting Sadat's reaction that Tuesday evening, there remained nothing more for me to do in Jerusalem until the cabinet had met. I therefore spent Wednesday, March 19, in Riyadh to brief King Faisal and Prince (and future King) Fahd. Despite Saudi Arabia's close ties to Syria and Asad's vocal opposition to a separate agreement, Faisal urged me to persevere. Remarkably enough, all the political prerequisites for a separate Israeli-Egyptian deal were in place except Israel's agreement.

It was at this point that the nature of shuttle diplomacy turned on itself. When shuttle diplomacy was initiated, both parties had been eager for agreement. Israel, exhausted from the October 1973 war, sought respite and a return of its prisoners. Sadat, aware of just how close to catastrophe he had come, was anxious to end the encirclement of his Third Army and to overcome the impasse which had led to war. The rapid changes of locale and the limited time I could devote to being away from Washington created their own deadlines and a sense of drama that made the parties cautious to cultivate their respective obstinacies.

Fourteen months later, the urgency was gone or at least was no longer felt symmetrically. And a stalled shuttle exaggerated any impasse, undermined the prestige of all the parties, especially of the United States, and threatened to transform drama into farce. Every concession we extracted from the parties without bringing us closer to a conclusion weakened America's ability to shape events not only on the immediate shuttle but in keeping the lid on the Middle East cauldron.

The March 1975 shuttle was rapidly reaching a point of self-stultification. The length of Israel's cabinet meetings grew in inverse proportion to the progress being made. Another ten-hour session on March 19 produced only token changes in the Israeli position. At a morning meeting on March 20, the negotiating team offered to withdraw to the middle of the passes, which, without a map, was nearly meaningless and which later was revealed to have been based on an eccentric definition of "middle." I was asked to take this to Sadat in return for extracting a last-minute formal pledge of nonbelligerency, including renunciation of unfriendly diplomacy—exactly what Sadat had explained he could not do. The Israeli negotiating team seemed unable to grasp that the process was ending. It was unmoved when I read out the formal request for reconsideration approved by Ford and remained adamant against producing a map or defining what was meant by the "middle" of the passes.

My last visit to Aswan late Thursday, March 20, was a sad occasion. Sadat had given up. Usually so ebullient, he now refined some of his positions morosely and without a show of conviction. And, as expected, he rejected the middle-of-the-passes offer as not serious in the absence of a map. We had reached the point where all hope for success having evaporated, additional changes would primarily weaken Sadat's domestic position without bringing an agreement closer. Indeed, pressing for modifications of the Egyptian position would undermine American prestige unless we could deliver Israel. Ambassador Eilts assessed Sadat's mood:

> There is considerable gloom, frustration and bitterness among the Egyptians. They profess [the] inability to understand how your mission could have been undertaken without a clearer idea about the correlation between Israeli demands and offers.

When, on my return to Israel midday on March 21, I told Rabin that we had reached the end of the line, he demurred, arguing that cabinet authorization would be required to break off negotiations—as if the parties had some legal right to demand that the United States continue its mediation. But it was really Rabin's own resigned way of giving his colleagues one last opportunity to change their minds.

Since March 22 was a Saturday, the Jewish Sabbath imposed another hiatus. I used the occasion to visit Masada, the site of a last-ditch Jewish resistance to Roman occupation. Our guide was the eminent archaeologist (and retired general) Yigael Yadin, who had excavated the site. On that windswept plateau overlooking the desert, a thousand diehard Jewish rebels against Roman rule had been besieged and then destroyed by four Roman legions, testimony to both Jewish faith and Roman implacability.

I met with the Israeli negotiating team for the last time on the evening of March 22 after the Sabbath had ended. The mood was melancholy. Even at this late stage, Allon and Peres thought it worthwhile to engage in a postmortem of how we had arrived at the impasse and insisted that Egypt had made no concessions. The review, however, would have to wait for another time. I summed up our view of what had happened:

> Mr. Prime Minister . . . We would not have conducted ourselves like this for the past seven months if we had known this would have been the final Israeli position.
>
> It is not accurate to say that Egypt made no concessions. The correct statement may be that both sides made the maximum concessions they were capable of making and that

was not enough. It is not a trivial matter for an Arab state for the first time to say that there will be no recourse to the use or threat of force, that all disputes henceforth between you will be settled by peaceful means, that the agreement will last until it is superseded by another agreement, together with an assurance to the United States that if Syria attacks Israel, Egypt will not join, and that the UN Emergency Force will be automatically extended indefinitely. There was also an assurance to the United States that no matter what happened at Geneva it would not affect the agreement. . . .

It was understood that the negotiations would be conducted in the interests of an overall strategy that would be overwhelmingly in Israel's interest. The quid pro quo would be enabling us to control the diplomacy. Ask yourselves what the position of the United States can be at Geneva without a plan, even for the most benevolent US President. That is my nightmare—what I now see marching toward you. Compared to that, 10 kilometers in the Sinai is trivial.[1]

Later that evening after another forlorn cabinet meeting, Rabin replied, without attempting to correct what I had said:

Mr. Secretary, I want to say how much we admire your efforts and how you conducted the talks.

All of us are, I would say, sad about how things have developed. I would say sad. We have no intention on our part but to praise the way you conducted these talks in very difficult circumstances. There is no doubt about your intentions, about what you sought to achieve, and we are very grateful to you.

As I walked down from the Prime Minister's office on the first floor, I was stopped at a landing by Defense Minister Shimon Peres, the leading hawk in the negotiations. With tears in his eyes, he assured me that what had transpired did not reflect his intentions. And I believed him. Peres had positioned himself to the right of Rabin in order to get credit for better terms, not to abort the peace process. (It was the last time he would use this tactic; Peres was to become his party's leading dove.)[2]

The next day, Rabin saw me off at Ben Gurion Airport—a gesture

of courtesy and friendship, for, according to protocol, it was the foreign minister's function to do these particular honors. We met alone
for perhaps fifteen minutes, and Rabin, usually so taciturn, said:

> I want you to know that the story will not end there. As you
> reflect on next steps, you should remember this: I feel about
> every soldier in the IDF [Israeli Defense Forces] as if he were
> my son. And my son is now in the IDF; my son-in-law is
> commanding a tank battalion in the Sinai.[3]

From Rabin this was the most emotional speech I had ever heard. And
I was powerfully moved. But I also knew, as I contemplated the wreckage of our design, much of it built side by side with Rabin, that a
rocky road lay ahead. We promised each other that we would do our
utmost to restore the traditional American-Israeli friendship, aware
that partisans on each side were only too eager to accuse the other of
bad faith. When Rabin and I embraced at the ramp of my plane, it
was with a sense of foreboding about what lay ahead.

# 14

# SINAI II AND
# THE ROAD TO PEACE

## *"Reassessment"*

March 1975 was a grim month for American foreign policy: relations with the Soviet Union were spiraling downward; Middle East diplomacy, heretofore a success story, stood deadlocked. Overshadowing everything was the collapse of two decades of American sacrifice and effort in Indochina. Even while our minds were on the Middle East, our hearts and our anguish were in Southeast Asia.

As if the gods wanted to emphasize just how angry they were, Saudi Arabia's King Faisal was assassinated on March 25, 1975, two days after I returned to Washington. It was another severe blow to American foreign policy. Faisal's death, just when the need for his understated wisdom and unobtrusive subtlety was greatest, was a tremendous setback.

The collapse of the March shuttle brought us face-to-face with our gravest Middle East crisis since the Yom Kippur War. On the one hand, America's fundamental national interest had not changed. We still needed to isolate the peace process from a combination of Soviet, European, and Arab pressures. Our support for moderate Arab leaders, especially for Anwar Sadat, remained crucial. If a Geneva conference proved unavoidable, we continued to want to shape it. If a separate step was still feasible, we would be open to it. The American national interest would continue to be served best by a diplomacy in which all the roads would lead to Washington, with Israel too strong

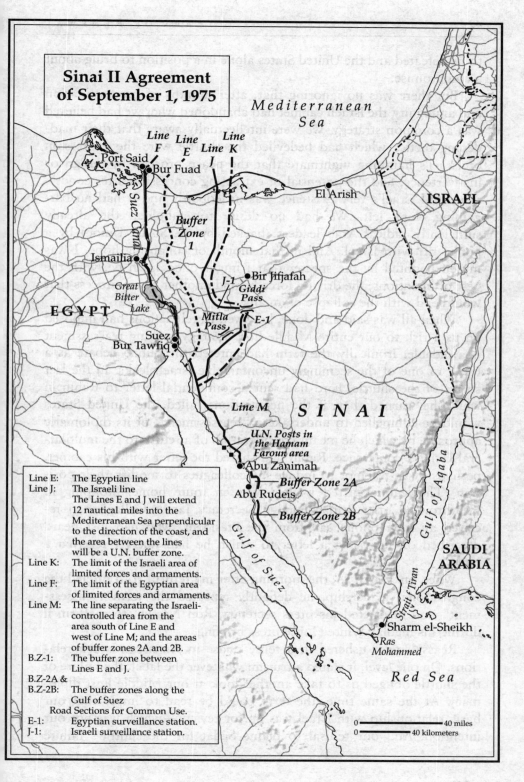

## Sinai II Agreement of September 1, 1975

*Mediterranean Sea*

Line F
Line E
Line J
Line K

Port Said
Bur Fuad
El Arish

**ISRAEL**

*Buffer Zone 1*

Suez Canal

Ismailia

J-1
Bir Jifjafah
Giddi Pass

*Great Bitter Lake*

**EGYPT**

Mitla Pass
E-1

Suez
Bur Tawfiq

Line M

**S I N A I**

U.N. Posts in the Hamam Faroun area
Abu Zanimah
Buffer Zone 2A
Abu Rudeis
Buffer Zone 2B

Gulf of Suez

Gulf of Aqaba

**SAUDI ARABIA**

Strait of Tiran

Sharm el-Sheikh
Ras Mohammed

*Red Sea*

| | |
|---|---|
| Line E: | The Egyptian line |
| Line J: | The Israeli line |
| | The Lines E and J will extend 12 nautical miles into the Mediterranean Sea perpendicular to the direction of the coast, and the area between the lines will be a U.N. buffer zone. |
| Line K: | The limit of the Israeli area of limited forces and armaments. |
| Line F: | The limit of the Egyptian area of limited forces and armaments. |
| Line M: | The line separating the Israeli-controlled area from the area south of Line E and west of Line M; and the areas of buffer zones 2A and 2B. |
| B.Z-1: | The buffer zone between Lines E and J. |
| B.Z-2A & B.Z-2B: | The buffer zones along the Gulf of Suez Road Sections for Common Use. |
| E-1: | Egyptian surveillance station. |
| J-1: | Israeli surveillance station. |

0 ———— 40 miles
0 ———— 40 kilometers

to be defeated and the United States alone in a position to bring about a compromise.

But there was no ignoring that, after months of procrastination and ambiguity, the Israeli cabinet had abandoned what we had believed was a common strategy. We were intellectually aware that their maddening tactics which had bedeviled the shuttle were the expression of Israel's haunting nightmare that the peace process, by design or inadvertence, had the potential of extracting concession after concession until Israel's very existence was in jeopardy and it had no bargaining chips left. We had no desire to embolden the already sufficiently radical Arab leaders (backed by the Soviet Union) by a public rift with Israel. And in that month of collapsing hope, I was myself haunted by the specter that I might once again be, with the best of intentions, the driving force behind another peace process that would end with the collapse of an ally.

When all was said and done, however, Israeli actions had imposed on us a risk to our entire Middle East strategy making reassessment unavoidable. Ironically, the term had entered the public debate as a result of one of the seemingly uncontainable Israeli leaks. In the last stages of the shuttle, Ford had sent a confidential letter to Rabin in which he warned that, if the negotiations failed, the United States would be compelled to undertake a "reassessment" of its diplomatic approach, by which he meant consideration of a return to the multilateral Geneva conference. Rabin had shared the letter with his cabinet, perhaps in an attempt to induce his colleagues to modify their position. The leak occurred while I was en route home. Stopping in Heathrow to brief British Foreign Secretary James Callaghan, I received an irate phone call from the President, who had just heard described on television a letter to which he had not yet received a reply.

When on March 24, the morning after my return, Ford briefed the congressional leadership, he defiantly repeated the term "reassessment" and instructed his press secretary, Ron Nessen, to reaffirm it during his regular White House press briefing.

Reassessment ushered in a tense phase in American-Israeli relations. On one level, it stated a truism: whatever the label, the failure of the shuttle obliged us to take another look at our Middle East diplomacy. At the same time, the term could be read to imply that our basic relationship with Israel was up for review—which was not our intention. And our refusal to blame Sadat for the shuttle's failure magnified Israeli concerns because it represented a departure from previous practice in which we had always automatically taken Israel's side.

To demonstrate his strong support of my conduct of the negotiations, Ford wanted to come to Andrews Air Force Base on Sunday evening, March 23, to welcome me back to Washington. I dissuaded him because Presidents should not, if avoidable, identify themselves publicly with failure, whatever its cause. Nothing, however, could keep Ford from greeting me on the South Lawn of the White House, where my helicopter touched down. Before a battery of television cameras, the President stated:

> I know that you made a maximum effort. Unfortunately, for reasons beyond our control, it did not turn out the way we wanted it. . . .
>
> . . . It is in the national, as well as in the international interest that we do everything we can with the emphasis on peace. Although we have—on a temporary basis, hopefully —not achieved all that we had desired, I continue to be an optimist, that the good judgment, the wise decisions of all parties will result in the ultimate objective of peace in the Middle East and its ramifications on a worldwide basis.[1]

A few days later, Ford told his old friend from Michigan, Max Fisher, who performed yeoman service as an informal liaison between the White House and the American Jewish leadership under both Nixon and Ford, that:

> I don't think I have ever been so disappointed as when I heard Henry was coming back without a settlement. It was as low as I have been in this office. The impression I had, after my meetings with Allon twice, with Rabin, with Golda, etc., was that we had been working so closely that when the chips were down they would see how deeply this would affect the prestige of the United States.

To Ford, the issue was not so much substantive disagreement as breaking faith with a friend. He explained to the National Security Council on March 28:

Since I have been in office, we have worked with Israel to try
and get a settlement. We acted in good faith and I assume
they did, also, but when the chips were down they showed a
lack of flexibility which was needed for an agreement. . . .

. . . I admire them [the Israelis] and respect them. And
I have never been so disappointed as to see people I respect
unable to see that we are trying to do something for their
interest as well as for our own. But in the final analysis our
commitment is to the United States.

Defense Secretary James Schlesinger, usually so ready to search for
flaws in my conduct of diplomacy, supported Ford at the same NSC
meeting:

We cannot allow Israel to continue its relationship with us
as if there were no problems. We cannot let them conclude
that they can upset the U.S. applecart but the administration
can do nothing about it. The military balance from the
Israeli standpoint is much better than the last time we met
[in the NSC] to discuss this problem. We overestimated
badly the amount of Soviet arms which Egypt had received.
So the balance for Israel is reasonably favorable and we need
not be concerned over our aloofness.

Years later, Ford was still chafing at the events of the spring of
1975. In his memoirs, he wrote:

The Israelis kept stalling. Their tactics frustrated the Egyptians and made me mad as hell. Both Henry and I had
received firm assurances from Rabin that a line could be
drawn that would be acceptable to Israel. But Rabin now
seemed afraid of his cabinet's response. He would not—or
could not—deliver on commitments he had made.[2]

The President's latent irritation was brought to the surface when
Israel protested a Ford statement actually intended to reassure Israel.
The United States, Ford had said, had always supported Israel's survival and would continue to do so. Heretofore the usual sacramental
statement had always endorsed Israel's "security"; this was deemed in
the Israeli protest to represent a higher threshold of significance than

mere "survival." Though the objection had semantic merit, the Israeli government had hardly selected the best moment to challenge the President head-on.

Ford's comment had, in fact, been made off-the-cuff and was not intended to imply any change in American policy. But the collapse of the shuttle had left him in no mood for what he considered arcane nitpicking. The Israeli protest therefore triggered an unusual outburst of anger from Ford at an NSC meeting of May 15:

> I have used survival and security interchangeably and synonymously. But they have now chosen to make a distinction, not I. I will therefore use *survival* and I do not want anyone else to paraphrase or explain away what I say.

The President remained adamant even after Schlesinger pointed out —correctly—that there was, in fact, a nuance of a difference. Ford replied:

> We want to stick with survival . . . they have made it an issue and we will not back down.

## The Resumption of Step-by-Step Policy

In this heartbreaking period when we had to manage simultaneously the collapse of Indochina and the salvaging of our Middle East effort, we came up against a core reality of American-Israeli relations: Americans considered trivial the territorial changes Israel was resisting; Israel, absorbed in a struggle for its very existence, had difficulty understanding the scale by which a superpower measures a requirement of survival (and this incongruity has not altered to this writing). The easy camaraderie and the frequent declarations of friendship could not obscure the fact that the two sides had a way of getting on each other's nerves: Israel resented the cavalier way Americans would dispose of territory perceived as part of its margin of survival; Israeli negotiating methods, which placed little faith in give-and-take and treated every concession as an extortion, often set American teeth on edge.

Until now, we had managed to overcome these tensions by sheer momentum. But with an impasse looming, it was becoming clear that the ultimate pressures each ally had available against the other were out of proportion to the issue before them. For the sake of a few miles in the desert a hundred miles from its borders, Israel was threatening to unravel an American stake in the Middle East painfully husbanded for nearly five years. To prevent this outcome, our last resort was to put forward our preferred solution and impose it on Israel by the threat of economic pressure and diplomatic isolation, thereby threatening its very existence.

Though several administrations have edged toward this strategy, they have, in the end, always recoiled. For when faced with such a course, America's leaders ultimately realized that publicly putting forward an overall U.S. position could turn into a trap. The Arab states might abandon diplomacy with Israel and concentrate all their pressures on the United States to extract ever better terms. And, in its isolation, Israel might either dig in or risk everything on one throw of the dice. We could be faced with war or the psychological disintegration of an ally.

In the weeks of Indochina's collapse, these considerations caused me to make a private pact with myself: if the step-by-step approach had to be abandoned and the United States was driven to state terms for a settlement, I would resign. The disparity between Israel's perception of its margin of survival and ours would become too difficult to bridge. If we prevailed, we would break Israel's back psychologically; if we failed, we would have doomed our role in the Middle East. Two years earlier, my colleagues and I had more or less imposed a settlement in Vietnam which, in all good faith and with high hopes, we had believed would bring peace to a tormented country. That settlement was now coming apart, and I had to manage the disaster. I would not be able to bear the responsibility for another such tragedy, especially vis-à-vis an ally so closely linked with my family's fate in the Holocaust.

As he was to do at all crucial points, Sadat gave us maneuvering room. Because confrontation with the United States would put him at the mercy of the Soviets and confrontation with Israel might, in the end, threaten his relationship with the United States, Sadat took three steps to reinforce Egypt's carefully built-up image of moderation. Within a week of the collapse of the shuttle, during a meeting on the occasion of King Faisal's funeral, Sadat told Vice President Nelson Rockefeller that, despite his disappointment, he continued to rely on the United States to navigate the road to peace. Shortly thereafter, in an address to his parliament on March 29, Sadat, speaking more in sorrow than in anger, announced the return to Israel of the bodies of thirty-nine missing Israeli soldiers whose remains Israel had been trying to retrieve since the end of the war. Simultaneously, he declared that, despite the suspension of negotiations, he would reopen the Suez Canal, closed since the 1967 war, on June 5. And to make his priorities quite clear, Sadat requested that the first foreign vessel to traverse the canal be a large American warship, which would be included in Egypt's inaugural procession. In the meantime, the six-month mandate of the U.N. forces separating Israeli and Egyptian forces in the Sinai had lapsed; by U.N. principles, Egypt's agreement was needed to renew it. Sadat proposed to extend it for three months—establishing a rough deadline for restarting negotiations.

We decided to leave it to the parties to make the first move toward restarting negotiations. So long as they assumed that we wanted agreement more than they did, both Egypt and Israel would maneuver to make the United States carry the burden of the necessary decisions. We needed to force the parties to commit themselves before we did. Reassessment became a strategy for doing that.

On March 29, we instructed the American ambassadors in Israel, Egypt, Syria, and Jordan to return to Washington for a policy review. Each was requested to pose three questions to the government to which he was accredited before departing: How did his interlocutor assess the state of play? Was an interim agreement still possible and, if so, on what terms? (In view of Israel's adamant opposition to another interim agreement on the Golan Heights, this question was omitted in the case of Syria.) If the preference was for a return to Geneva, how should it be organized? Similar queries were also sent to our ambassador in Moscow.

The answers showed that nobody, not even the Soviets, was eager to rush to Geneva. Though Ismail Fahmy formally asked the Soviet Union to hold exploratory talks on the subject, he proposed neither a date nor a procedure. At the same time, he turned our queries back on us by suggesting that we propose new ideas for restarting the negotiations.

As for Israel, its bravado in avowing eagerness to return to Geneva while the shuttle was going on turned into inertia when it came to proposing a way for doing so. Instead, the cabinet reaffirmed its strong preference for an interim agreement with Egypt and proposed that we restart the Egyptian negotiations where they had left off.

Syria's Asad claimed that he favored a return to Geneva (which he had refused to attend on the only occasion the parties had met there), but he added the familiar escape clause about the need for careful preparation. And the Soviets seemed hesitant; Gromyko called for prior consultations.

Each of the parties had its own reasons for not rushing to Geneva. Sadat, though gravely disappointed by the outcome of the shuttle, did not, in the end, consider a Geneva conference a preferable alternative. There he would encounter Syria, certain to press for a comprehensive settlement, and the Palestinians, more likely to produce deadlock or war than compromise. Nor was the inevitable Soviet co-chairman at Geneva a blessing for Egypt. In recent months, Sadat had taunted and embarrassed Soviet leaders too often to be able to count on meaningful support from them; they were more likely to try to block his separate initiatives toward Israel.

The most intriguing reaction was that of the Kremlin. A quick response to sudden and unexpected turns of events had never been Gromyko's strong suit; mordant suspiciousness was more in keeping with his style. When, after fifteen months of stonewalling, we suddenly declared our willingness to explore returning to the Geneva conference, Gromyko was wary of a trap. For all he knew, the treacherous Egyptians and the wily Americans were colluding to separate the Soviet Union from its remaining supporters in the region.

To mask its confusion, the Kremlin, in messages from Brezhnev to Ford and from Gromyko to me dated April 10 and 11, proposed consultations prior to convening the Geneva conference with a view toward achieving a common substantive Soviet-American position at the conference. Brezhnev suggested that the target date for reconvening the Geneva conference be sometime in June.

Yet no sooner had we started exploring what the Soviets might mean by a common position than we encountered the by now traditional liturgy. I formally asked Dobrynin for any ideas the Soviet Union wished to introduce, and Moscow fell silent. After some weeks, Gromyko did reply, but it was the standard fare. The opening Soviet position—nonnegotiable for the past six years—turned out to be its only position: return by Israel to the 1967 borders and international guarantees. The Kremlin would not separate from its radical allies in the Middle East. But we could have no conceivable interest in a joint position in Geneva—or even in assembling the conference—if it became a means of extracting unilateral concessions from Israel. If Geneva was to have any chance for success, the two co-chairmen, the

United States and the Soviet Union, would have to be prepared to ask their respective allies to make comparable sacrifices.

The most compelling reason for Soviet restraint was the sole remnant of the policy of linkage: the Soviets were eager to conclude the European Security Conference at a summit tentatively scheduled for Helsinki at the end of July. The Soviet leaders feared that, if they led the radical charge at a reassembled Geneva conference, the Helsinki summit might well become a casualty; but if they failed to back Syria and the PLO, the Soviet standing among its remaining Arab supporters would erode even further. Thus, in the critical months of our maximum domestic weakness while Indochina fell and Washington was divided, the Soviets procrastinated and gave us the opportunity to take charge of the peace process again.

Although somewhat battered by recent events, we remained the only party capable of dealing with all the others. For that reason, we were in no hurry, calculating that delay would emphasize our indispensability and encourage more accommodating policies. This was reflected in our instructions to Ambassador Kenneth Keating in Israel:

> You should not, repeat not, get into a post-mortem on why the negotiations reached an impasse or engage in discussion of the merits of any particular Israeli idea. Your posture should be one of seeking any new ideas the Israelis might have so you can report them when you return to Washington. While you should say that the USG [U.S. government], as has been said publicly, will treat any such ideas with an open mind, you have not come on instructions to press the Israelis. If Rabin puts forward any new ideas, you should ask him whether they are purely personal ideas or whether they are ideas which he feels the cabinet could support.

The last sentence was a reference to the gap between the views Rabin had expressed to us privately and what had emerged from his cabinet deliberations.

Ambassador Eilts in Cairo was instructed on April 1 to reply in the same vein to Fahmy's query about new American ideas:

> With respect to Fahmy's suggestion that we suggest some formulations for his and Sadat's consideration, you should tell Fahmy that I prefer to hold this idea in abeyance until

we can reach a judgment on the larger question of how best
to proceed in present circumstances.

During April, the parties repeated but also refined their positions.
Sadat went through the motions of preparing for at least diplomatic
confrontation, though he was careful to set no deadlines. On April 23,
he and Asad met in Riyadh and announced the formation of a committee to coordinate strategy toward Israel which, as far as I can determine, never convened. Fahmy visited Moscow and signed a joint
communiqué with Gromyko calling for "careful preparations" prior
to the assembling of a Geneva conference and insisted on the inclusion
of the PLO "enjoying equal rights with the other participants." Fahmy
was much too sophisticated not to have known that Israel would not
attend if the PLO did; he was proclaiming slogans for a prolonged
deadlock, not a call to action.

For his part, Ford, in the daily morning meetings with me, seemed
to favor a comprehensive solution without translating this preference
into a directive. He gave an interview to a team of CBS reporters on
April 21 and summed up the options for American policy:

> Now, there really are three options. You could resume the
> suspended negotiations without making a commitment to
> go to Geneva. You could go to Geneva and try to get an
> overall settlement, which is a very complicated matter—
> many people advocate it, however. But while you were going
> through this negotiation for an overall settlement, as a third
> option you might have an interim negotiated settlement be-
> tween two of the parties, such as Israel and Egypt.
>
> Now, those are basically the three options. We have not
> made any decision yet.[3]

On the Israeli side, Allon and Abba Eban journeyed to Washington, the latter in his private capacity, having been replaced by Allon
when Rabin succeeded Golda Meir a year earlier. Allon proposed
restarting the negotiations where they had been left off but clearly was
not authorized to propose any positions other than those that had
caused the deadlock. Eban, as always, put matters in an epigrammati-
cally elegant perspective: "The result of success wouldn't be peace; the
result of failure wouldn't be war."

By the middle of May, Ford decided that the time for an American initiative had come. He proposed to meet with President Sadat in Salzburg, Austria, on June 1–2 in connection with a European trip he was planning, and he invited Rabin to Washington for June 11–12.

## Ford and Sadat

By the time Ford invited the Middle East leaders to meet with him, he had reached his decision. Reassessment had brought us back to our original judgments: that an interim agreement between Egypt and Israel was the most desirable course, provided we could pursue it without becoming each party's alibi for their domestic deadlock. If that effort failed, we would reassemble the Geneva conference.

Ambassadors Eilts in Cairo and Keating in Tel Aviv were instructed to inform the host governments that the United States was willing to resume its mediating role but only if, at their forthcoming summits with Ford, their leaders could come up with some new ideas. While the parties were marking time, I summoned Ambassador Eilts and asked him to convey a personal message from me to Sadat. Sadat should not let himself be put off by Rabin's prickly behavior, I told him. While Rabin was indeed a difficult interlocutor, he was, paradoxically, also the Israeli leader most willing to make peace.

Since the option of reconvening the Geneva conference had to be kept in reserve, I met with Gromyko in Vienna on May 19–20. If ever, here was his opportunity to reinstate the Soviet Union as a key player in Middle East diplomacy. But Gromyko was not about to permit diplomatic opportunity to get in the way of legalistic and procedural pedantry. He proposed that the United States include the Soviet Union in all aspects of the Middle East peace process—indeed, that no meetings take place without Soviet participation. And he urged our two countries to invite the PLO immediately to a reconvened Geneva conference. Gromyko had to know that we would evade his first proposal and reject his second outright. In fact, the only unforeseeable aspect of my reaction was the sarcastic way in which I phrased it:

> KISSINGER: Do you want my honest reaction?
> GROMYKO: There are also possible nuances regarding the
> possible wording of the invitation. The Palestinians
> have their own views on the subject.
> Of course, I want an honest answer.

> KISSINGER: My honest reaction is that you asked it because
> your ambassadors can then go around the Middle East
> saying the Americans refused to give an invitation. So I
> give you that opportunity.

This turned out to be precisely what the Soviet ambassadors had been instructed to do—albeit rather ponderously. As it was, we pre-empted them by ourselves informing the Arab countries and Israel of our reaction.

In the meantime, Israel's supporters in the Senate were roiling tempers in the White House. On May 21, a week before Ford was scheduled to leave for his first NATO summit and thence for his meeting with Sadat, a letter was published in which seventy-six Senators, in effect, urged Ford to take Israel's side in the negotiations and to approve unconditionally its vast economic and military requests:

> Within the next several weeks, the Congress expects to receive
> your foreign aid requests for Fiscal Year 1976. We trust that
> your recommendations will be responsive to Israel's urgent
> military and economic needs. We urge you to make it clear,
> as we do, that the United States acting in its own national
> interests stands firmly with Israel in the search for peace in
> future negotiations, and that this premise is the basis of the
> current reassessment of US policy in the Middle East.

It was definitely not the way to deal with the President. To mistake Ford's affability for weakness was, for many, a great temptation and a permanent risk. "This kind of pressure is not the way to get decisions from me," he said. "They maybe can scare someone else, but that doesn't work with me."

Ford's visit to Salzburg began inauspiciously when he stumbled and fell as he was descending from the plane. He modestly included the incident with some dry wit in his briefing on June 6 of the congressional leaders, all of whom knew of his athletic prowess:

> We next went to Salzburg. I had a little trouble arriving
> there. I was coming down the steps of the airplane; it was
> raining like mad. I had Betty on one hand and was holding
> the umbrella with the other. Betty tripped me. I went flat on
> my face in the rain and she walked off with the umbrella.

The first meeting between Ford and Sadat took place on June 1 over lunch at Sadat's hotel on the shores of Lake Fuschl, where, in the Nazi period, Joachim von Ribbentrop had built a home to be close to Hitler in Berchtesgaden, just across the border in Germany.

Sadat greeted Ford warmly. For a few minutes, the two leaders strolled by themselves along the shore of the lake before sitting down to a table set for six: Under Secretary of State Joe Sisco and I were with Ford; Sadat was accompanied by Fahmy and Hosni Mubarak.

Ford, still smarting from the Senators' letter, opened the dialogue by insisting that it would not affect his conduct of foreign policy:

> I would like to make two points in particular. First, the importance of the letter signed by seventy-six Senators is being distorted out of proportion; half of them didn't read it and a quarter didn't understand the letter. Whereas the additional quarter knew very precisely what it was doing. The impact of the letter is negligible.

He then turned to the subject of the meeting:

> I was very disappointed in the position taken by Israel last March: the Israelis decided to go off in a direction different than we expected. I want to tell you that as far as we are concerned, stagnation is unacceptable. As you know, we are in the process of a reassessment. It would be helpful to me for you to tell me where you believe we are and any suggestions that you may have on how we can work together in the future toward peace in the Middle East.

Sadat was wise, a quality transcending intelligence. He expended no time on the aborted negotiations and analyzed instead the situation in their aftermath. Any other Middle East leader would at this point have introduced some element of blackmail by threatening us with his Soviet option. Sadat chose the precise opposite course; he informed Ford that he had broken irrevocably with the Soviet Union, whatever happened in the current round of diplomacy. Ever since he negotiated the first disengagement agreement in January 1974, Sadat said, the Soviets had been trying to undermine him by cutting off his arms supplies while modernizing the Syrian army. At a reconvened Geneva conference, Sadat continued, he would expect Moscow to embarrass him over procedure, over terms, and over the attendance of the Palestinians. Having thus relinquished what could have been his main bargaining chip, he placed his reliance on the United States by sketching the opportunity before us:

> I will be very disappointed if nothing can be achieved. Mr. President, we have gone beyond where any Arab has gone in the past. My people will be very disappointed if nothing can be achieved. I want us to make progress, to make a complete peace. And I want the United States only to achieve it, not the Soviet Union, not through a Geneva conference, where the U.S.S.R. is sitting.

Sadat's approach did not lack irony. His predecessor, Nasser, had tried to prevail by threatening the West with the Soviets; Sadat reversed Nasser's priorities by offering to turn Egypt into the chief bulwark against Soviet influence in the Arab world. A subtle element of blackmail was involved as well: failure risked a demonstration of America's impotence and therefore our entire position in the Middle East.

Not given to reflecting on history's ironies, Ford brought the discussions back to the current negotiations. He asked Sadat for "any key points . . . as to specifics for when I talk to Rabin. . . . I appreciate your suggestion that there has to be a framework for negotiation soon or we have to go to Geneva. Israel ought to be shrewd enough to see this."

Ford asked me to outline the principal obstacles to an agreement. The first was duration of the mandate for a U.N. force to separate the two parties—Israel was asking for at least three years in lieu of the standard six months for the existing U.N. force; the second was an easing of the Arab boycott against American firms doing business with Israel; and the third was a way to maintain Israel's large radar station overlooking the Suez Canal from the mountains near the Sinai passes, which Israel had declared essential to preventing a surprise attack. Sadat promised to give his reply at the next day's meeting.

The site of that session was the former seat of the archbishop in the days when Salzburg was still an independent ecclesiastical state. The so-called Residenz, a vast baroque structure located in the center of the city, is all that remains of the political influence of Salzburg when it was at the crossroads between Southern and Western Europe. Portraits of archbishops and Habsburg dukes observed our proceedings from the walls of the stately chambers with somber gazes born of their own experience with the transitoriness of human planning. In one of the vast, high-ceilinged drawing rooms overlooking a square surrounding a splendid fountain, the leaders of Egypt and the United States were discussing the fate of two low passes bisecting an inhospitable desert.

Sadat came straight to the point:

> I want you to have something to present to the Israelis despite the fact that they are occupying my lands and despite the fact that they are in a psychological state and confused. We are at a turning point. It seems to me that no one is able to work out peace in Israel. It is too weak a government. The world is waiting for results. I want to push the peace process. I want to move in the direction of agreement.

With this introduction, Sadat responded to each of the points I had raised at the end of the previous day's meeting. He noted that Israel's request for a three-year extension of the U.N. force's mandate might bring the peace process to an end. Relieved of concern over military pressures for at least three years, Israel would have no incentive to consider returning the remainder of Egyptian territory. Nevertheless, Sadat said he had decided to accept the demand and to entrust the recovery of Egypt's territory to the peace process and to the United States rather than to military pressure. In that spirit, he also conceded that Israel could maintain its warning stations behind Egypt's lines provided they were manned by Americans. Turning to Fahmy, Sadat said:

> We should work out the phraseology in this three-year thing, and on the veto question. There is also the question of the warning stations. We would propose that Americans man the warning stations. This is an important proposal. Americans would be witnesses. It would be a complete guarantee for the Israelis.

As the negotiations took shape, Sadat would endow the word "manned" with a most flexible interpretation: the actual operating personnel could be Israeli so long as there was some minimal American supervisory presence. In the course of the talks, the Egyptians also indicated some flexibility on the boycott issue.

Sadat's crucial contribution to the peace process was his recognition that breaking the cycle of suspicion and distrust was more important than the specific terms of any particular agreement. Israel was too beleaguered for an act of grace and the other Arab countries too weak, too radical, or too divided. Egypt alone was capable of rising above the prevailing suspicion and bitterness because, in Sadat's words, "Egypt is different from other Arabs. We have a background of patience, of civility and understanding."

Of course, Sadat was a far more complicated figure than the philosopher of peace that he presented at Salzburg. He had, after all, spent a lifetime and many years in prison as a revolutionary fighting for Egypt's independence and honor. And he had organized the Arab surprise attack on Israel not quite two years earlier. Sadat was therefore anything but a pacifist. But experience had taught him that Egypt would never regain its territory by military means even with Soviet help, and he was prepared to draw the obvious conclusion. A central role for the United States was the only realistic road to diplomatic progress, a fact that had eluded most of his Arab brethren.

When I first met Sadat, I was uncertain whether his moderation might not be a tactic to enlist us in restoring Egypt's borders, after which he might return to the vanguard of the Arab cause. And he himself probably did not know yet either. At Salzburg, we encountered Sadat midway to his final destination of a prophet for the cause of peace amidst the passions of his region. What had started as tactics was turning into his life's purpose.

By the time Ford returned from Salzburg, he was determined to push the peace process forward—if necessary, against congressional opposition. In briefing the congressional leaders on June 6, he took another swipe at the Senators' letter:

> Sadat and all the Arabs were very upset at the letter. I made it clear that the letter did not represent an official position of the United States; that it represented only the views of 76 Senators, some of whom later stated objections or clarifications of their views. It was a very disturbing influence on the talks. As much as I am confident about the situation, we cannot have a stalemate. If we don't get some movement, Geneva is where we are going and Geneva is not the best

forum. It will be an awful situation where everything will be fought over, but I want to be categorical about this; without any movement, this is where we are going.

It was a message Ford was certain would reach Rabin prior to his visit to Washington a few days hence.

## Ford and Rabin: Another Encounter

Rabin met with Ford and me on June 11 and 12 and separately with me before and after each of the meetings. In order to avoid another misunderstanding, I briefed Rabin on the points the President was likely to raise and, more importantly, summed up afterward what I believed had been agreed. Even that could not prevent another blowup because it proved impossible to synchronize the American and Israeli styles of decision-making. Ford was at every stage in a position to make decisions. Rabin was on a short leash; he had to clear every change, however minor, with his cabinet. Ford's private and official views were identical; in Rabin's case, the gulf was wide indeed.

On June 10, the day of Rabin's arrival, Marvin Kalb reported on CBS that the Prime Minister, disappointed by my refusal to support Israel's position unconditionally, would "be seeking to open a direct pipeline to President Ford." Rabin quickly discovered that, if anything, Ford was more insistent than his Secretary of State.

The following day in the Oval Office, Ford, as soon as the photographers had left the room, came straight to the point and, without any introductory social chitchat, launched into a lengthy, extemporaneous, and extremely blunt statement. It was his way, he said, to be frank, and he needed to get "what was bothering me off my chest":

> I want to say to you that I am disillusioned, I am disappointed and disturbed. I am disillusioned over the results of last March. I believe that Israel could have been more frank in the crunch. I was disillusioned over the inflexibility of Israel at the final testing point. I understand your political problems in trying to be more forthcoming, but I have to say to you that I was disappointed, disturbed, and disillusioned over the position taken.

While he was at it, Ford registered a strong complaint about the Israeli leak of his letter during the shuttle that had first used the term "reassessment." After the failure of the shuttle, he said, reassessment was his duty and not a threat against Israel. It was essential that Rabin understand just how serious Ford was about not tolerating a stalemate. Going beyond what the President and I had discussed before the meeting, Ford came close to making America's ultimate threat that he might propose his own comprehensive peace plan, including borders, and present it publicly within a few weeks:

> Where I come out, even though I have not made any final judgments, where I come out—and I want your assessment as well if I am wrong—I come out on the option of moving to an overall settlement to Geneva, to try to achieve a peace with guarantees, a peace with all of your neighbors that would include agreement on borders. Now, that is where I come out at the moment, and I would appreciate your views and assessment which would help me. My plan would be to make some kind of public announcement this summer, or earlier. However, I have an open mind and I would appreciate your frank assessment and recommendations. They will have a significant impact on what I decide.

I listened to this last point, which Ford had entirely improvised, with trepidation because no such plan as yet existed, not even in embryonic form—and I shuddered at the prospect of preparing one on such short notice, not to speak of the turmoil its presentation would cause. Moreover, as already noted, at that point American policy would cross my personal red line, not because Ford was unreasonable but because I would not be able to bear the responsibility for its execution.

Apologizing for the leak of the President's letter, Rabin avoided further references to the past. He put forward a brilliant and moving presentation of Israel's dilemmas—which, had he done so on his first visit nine months earlier, would have gone far toward preventing much of the later acrimony (see text in Notes).[4] Indeed, its basic philosophic premises, allowing for a change in the geography of the dividing lines, is applicable at this writing. Israel, Rabin noted, wanted peace; in the course of four wars, it had learned that "force will not bring a political settlement. . . . We have no interest in war but we have an interest in defending ourselves."

Israel, Rabin continued, would measure progress toward peace on the basis of three criteria and, with respect to each of them, the Arab and Israeli views were diametrically opposed. Whereas the Arabs defined peace as the absence of war, Israelis equated it with the normalization of relations and with exchanges in trade and travel. Arab leaders demanded restoration of the 1967 borders, while Israel considered these borders to be indefensible. The Arab leaders demanded a Palestinian state under a PLO which was championing terrorism and rejecting Israel's very existence; Israel thought such a state incompatible with its security: "As we see it, a return to the 1967 borders and the establishment of a Palestinian state means that Israel cannot survive." With Israel's very survival at stake, Rabin was, if anything, more eager than Ford to find some alternative to the endless warfare:

> In many realistic appraisals we have concluded that there is another way which is more practical, that is, especially an interim agreement with Egypt. Egypt is the key. I recall that Egypt on its own decided to sign the armistice agreement and the other Arabs then followed. Every war has stemmed from Egypt joining and every war has stopped when Egypt stopped. We hoped that through an interim agreement it can be a step toward peace, not just another military disengagement.

According to Rabin, the interim agreement with Egypt faced Israel with three dilemmas. If the passes were relinquished, where would the new Israeli defense line in the Sinai be located, and how long would it remain in place? Second, after a Sinai agreement, would the United States immediately press for a further step on the Golan Heights? Finally, if an interim Sinai settlement came about, what would be the timing of the Geneva conference, and what substantive proposals would the United States put forward there? In short, was it possible to avoid having a crisis with Washington every few months over some next step? For all these reasons, Israel needed guarantees regarding the duration of the agreement:

> There is no purpose served for Israel to go to an interim and lose one and a half of our three cards and then have a weaker situation for an overall. Why should we give up the passes

for nothing and end up negotiating an overall settlement in six months from a weaker position?

Rabin followed his thoughtful presentation with an equally astute analysis of Israel's position on all its other fronts, prompting me to pass a note to Sisco sitting next to me: "Why didn't they raise all this last year?" To which Sisco scribbled back that Rabin preferred to "buy time."

The impact of Rabin's presentation on Ford was all the greater because, for the first time, an Israeli explained to him Israel's subliminal worries instead of bickering over arms supplies or abstract lines in the desert. For Israel's dilemma was real enough: prolonged deadlock would lead to growing tension, if not war; undermine America's position in the Arab world and with the industrial democracies; and isolate Israel while it was being gradually drained psychologically and physically by escalating crises and conflicts. Yet to avoid deadlock by a series of retreats ultimately affecting Israeli security would not solve these problems, only compound and defer them. That Israel had a better historic than diplomatic case is shown by the fact that exactly the same dilemmas were put to President Clinton by Israeli Prime Minister Binyamin Netanyahu two decades later—the only difference being that the disputed line had moved from the Sinai to the center of Palestine and that the presentation was somewhat less philosophical and more geared to Israeli politics. It was not a choice between absolutes but a delicate balancing act between security conceived as a military balance and security including a political and psychological component. Ford cut to the heart of the matter from the American perspective by refining it into a set of practical decisions:

> The problem is how much longer can the status quo be maintained without political movement? It is a volatile situation. Either we have an interim settlement in a quick period of time—within two or three weeks—in which there would not be a lot of shuttle back and forth; it would be necessary to firm up things, to move fast, which would give us another span of time. Either we move in this way, or my choice—with all of its pitfalls as you suggest—is to move toward an overall settlement. The only way to bring about continued stability in the Middle East and keep all the parties reasonably satisfied, to give all the parties some hope of a perma-

nent settlement being possible, would be to move in this way. Your thoughts have been helpful. If we were to move in the direction of an interim agreement, we would have to do so rapidly, otherwise we lose that option and I would have no alternative but to go to an overall settlement.

The President concluded the meeting by suggesting that Rabin and I work out a concrete proposal together.

At breakfast the next morning, Rabin and I reached tentative agreements on how to proceed, which Rabin summarized for Ford immediately afterward—again brilliantly: Israel would move its defense line to the eastern end of the passes; it would ask for a guarantee that the U.N. force separating the Egyptian and Israeli armies in the Sinai remain in place preferably for four years (we already knew that Sadat was willing to concede three); the oil fields would be returned to Egypt with a strip of land, assuring uninterrupted access.

Rabin would not have been Rabin had he not coupled the proposed Israeli concessions with a vast shopping list for military and economic assistance from the United States. Nor did he let the occasion pass without asking for a veto over any proposals the United States might put forward if the Geneva conference were reassembled. Ford could not agree to a proposition which, if leaked—as it was certain to be— would destroy our mediating potential in the Arab world. The unscripted manner in which the President turned it aside shows that a straightforward and uncomplicated demeanor is not incompatible with subtlety:

> Time can pass quickly. We can be in a position to slow down the pressures toward a hard line which would affect your circumstances at home. I believe we have made headway in these talks. I am not going to push us if we get an interim agreement. We may have to use some rhetoric but not to pursue you into positions which make you isolate yourself.

In other words, what Israel ultimately had to gain from cooperating with the United States was not an exemption from our judgments but an atmosphere of trust that would reduce the intensity with which we would insist on them.

## Forging a New Initiative

When the Israeli negotiating team was subsequently asked to approve what Rabin and Ford had agreed, it turned the definition of what constiuted the eastern end of the passes into a life or death issue. Every American at that meeting with Rabin had taken the phrase literally. But when the Israeli cabinet was asked to ratify the decision, it defined the eastern end of the passes as a line barely east of the highest point of the mountain ridge. I asked Dinitz on June 20 how we were to explain to Sadat that, in return for his concessions at Salzburg—his agreement to a three-year extension for the U.N. force and the warning stations behind Egyptian lines—Israel proposed moving perhaps one hundred yards from the crest of the mountain.

Ford's reaction demonstrated that American-Israeli relations risked stormy weather if either side subordinated geopolitical necessities to domestic politics—a verity that would have to be relearned twenty years later during the Clinton-Netanyahu confrontations. The only road to consensus—which was tough enough given the differences in size and history—was for each side to put forward the most complete and frank statement of its real views and then work on reconciling differences. Verbal maneuvers based on ambiguous assertions are the most certain path to an explosion—particularly for Israel, so dependent on the United States for material, diplomatic, and psychological support. I had a great deal of sympathy for the basic Israeli security dilemma. But the verbal gymnastics about what constituted the end of the passes were more relevant to Israel's domestic politics than to objective dangers. And they played excessively with American chips.

This was definitely not the way to deal with Ford. When informed on June 15 how the Israeli negotiating team proposed to interpret the phrase "eastern end of the passes," Ford—entirely on his own—picked up the telephone and asked Rabin to reconsider his position. Rabin, who was still in New York, had no means to argue with his colleagues other than to hold a cabinet meeting, which could not take place until he returned to Israel. This only raised the temperature another notch.

The mood in the White House is best conveyed by an exchange I had with Ford that afternoon:

FORD: Let's say that I am very disappointed.

KISSINGER: We shouldn't say it yet.

FORD: You handle it, but if it comes to me, that is what I will say.

KISSINGER: We ought to get into it coolly and wait two or three days to see what they come back with. If we propose it now, Sadat won't accept it.

FORD: You handle that diplomatic maneuvering, but there is no question how I feel.

KISSINGER: The way in which they treated us I find outrageous.

FORD: The only way to handle it is to be mad about it. If you and Sisco want to moderate my feelings. . . .

KISSINGER: We don't want to. I would recommend, however, moderating your expressions for a couple of days.

FORD: I am telling you how I feel about it.

Sadat responded on June 25 as we had predicted. In a message to the President, he described the Israeli cabinet's propositions as "acrobatic" and America's conduct as "pampering" of Israel:

> I have responded positively to your efforts in such a manner that, if you take Egypt's position in March in Aswan and subsequently in Salzburg, I do not believe that you can ask me to do anything more than what I have done. I took that position because of my determination to work for peace . . . a genuine peace. Moreover, I wanted to extend to you a helping hand in your arduous efforts to achieve the same end. As you know, I have taken bold initiatives without hesitation and against all risks involved.

The time had come, Sadat insisted, for the United States "to propose an American map reflecting its proposals in order to avoid a complete and drastic deterioration of the situation." If that proved impossible, the Geneva conference should be reassembled and an invitation to attend it extended to the PLO.

We had steadfastly refused to put forward an American map because it would have obliged us to impose it on Israel. Such an act would have destroyed the possibility of further negotiations and required us to impose our solution at every subsequent impasse of the peace process. And that, I thought, would, in the long run, prove to be beyond our capacity to manage and Israel's capacity to survive.

Though not prepared to submit an American map, Ford, on June 27, sent an unusually explicit letter to Rabin. Summing up all the previous misunderstandings after personal talks with the prime minister and Allon, Ford formally asked that Israel reconsider its latest position before July 11 when I was scheduled to meet with Gromyko. On the basis of the Israeli reply, Ford said, he would decide whether we would continue to block a comprehensive approach or whether to reassemble the Geneva conference:

> With the formulation of your latest position and President Sadat's reply, we are now at a point where fundamental decisions must be made.
>
> I do not regard standing still a realistic choice. It runs an unacceptable risk of leading to another war and to a coalescence of the same international forces which Israel faced in 1973 and early 1974. Since such a situation would jeopardize fundamental U.S. interests—most of which are also of deep concern to Israel—the U.S. cannot be expected to underwrite such a course of action.

If Israel refused to reconsider, Ford threatened to go public with his own assessment of why the negotiations were stalemating:

> We must reserve our course on next steps, and explain to our people the administration's appraisal of our national interest in this matter.

Not since Eisenhower twenty years earlier had an American President addressed the Israeli government in so abrupt a manner.

The letter gave Rabin the ammunition he needed to convince his colleagues that Ford meant what he had been saying to Rabin and Allon for the past nine months. While I was on vacation on St. John Island in the Caribbean, I received word that Dinitz asked to see me immediately and secretly with a message from Rabin. Such a visit was not easy to arrange because Caneel Bay, where I was staying at a friend's house, has no airport. After much back-and-forth, Dinitz, accompanied by Deputy Under Secretary of State Lawrence Eagleburger, set off for St. Thomas in an Air Force Jetstar with its markings painted out and from there traveled by boat to Caneel Bay.

I had met Simcha Dinitz in 1970 when he was Golda Meir's chef de cabinet. In early 1973, just a few months before the Middle East War, he succeeded Rabin as ambassador to Washington. Because of Israel's extraordinary dependence on American aid and goodwill, the embassy in Washington is the most important post in Israeli diplomacy. By the standards of national power, the Israeli ambassador's role would have been comparatively insignificant because the normal diplomatic pressures available to Israel are minimal. The Israeli ambassador has, however, a unique weapon at his disposal: Israel's passionate and well-organized supporters. They are in a position to mount formidable pressures, as was shown during the debate over the Jackson-Vanik Amendment. The risk for any Israeli ambassador is that he will be torn hither and yon by America's often conflicting domestic crosscurrents from the administration, whose goodwill he needs for diplomacy; from the Congress, whose goodwill he needs for appropriations; and from clamoring supporters, whose enthusiasm sometimes outruns their judgment.

Dinitz navigated these riptides with charming effrontery, ever mitigated by his warmhearted sense of humor. He could be relentless in pursuit of his immediate priorities, and the implied threat from his battalions loomed ever menacingly behind his presentations. He was later criticized for being too close to the American administration, Israel being the only country in which such a statement could be advanced as criticism of its ambassador.

I liked Dinitz enormously. He was honest and honorable. He gave us unvarnished accounts of Israeli domestic maneuvering, and I had every confidence that he reported our views equally accurately to the Israeli cabinet. Dinitz's humor had a way of easing confrontations, and his professionalism often cut through the thorniest difficulties. In terms of service to his country, Dinitz deserves a monument in Israel for his role in helping to bring about the resupply of Israel's armed forces during the October war.

Upon landing at Caneel Bay on July 1, the first words from the irrepressible ambassador were "one has to be very rich to be willing to live so uncomfortably." (Should my host read these lines, Dinitz was not referring to the elegant accommodations but to the midsummer heat.) Next he informed me that Rabin was determined to proceed toward an interim agreement. However, since neither side could afford another failure, Rabin needed to assure himself of the administration's precise views on a number of issues: how Ford defined "the end of the passes" and the access routes to the oil fields, the duration of the U.N. peacekeepers' mandate, American intentions vis-à-vis Syria, and our goals at a reassembled Geneva conference.

Dinitz had brought along a topographical map. For the first time in the course of nine months of dialogue, the Israelis showed us their proposed line. It was an odd definition of the eastern end of the passes, since it turned out to be at an elevation of some 750 meters, barely short of the summit. I replied that Israel needed to withdraw clearly in the direction of what could plausibly be defined as the eastern end of the passes, one criterion for which would be some significantly lower elevation than the summit. If Rabin were to make a proposal along those lines, even if it were not exactly at sea level, "we would look at it with sympathy."

None of these issues had required a personal meeting, however, much less a secret one. What did—and constituted the main reason for Dinitz's visit—was to present a new idea originated by Israeli Defense Minister Shimon Peres: that four American sensor warning stations supervised by three American-manned outposts be placed on the roads leading to the passes. One did not have to be a military expert to recognize that the military significance of these outposts was negligible. The area they covered was unpopulated and included a zone of limited armaments supervised by an Israeli radar station in the hills behind it and garrisoned by a U.N. force backed by frequent reconnaissance overflights.

In terms of Israeli domestic politics, however, these proposed sensor stations signaled that Peres—then the most hawkish member of the Israeli negotiating team—was coming around to support an interim agreement. It was his way of saving face and putting himself in a position to claim credit for improving the outcome. I was in no position to accept or reject the scheme; it needed to be deferred until my return to Washington.

As too often happens with elaborate secret maneuvers, the veil of secrecy cloaking Dinitz's visit was blown away because no provision had been made for the most obvious contingency: that the airplane would need refueling. The handlers at St. Thomas airport adamantly refused to accept the government credit card of a pilot wearing civilian clothes and flying an unmarked plane. When we approached subordinate Air Force commanders, they reacted similarly. It took an appeal to the commanding officer of an Air Force base in Puerto Rico to vouch for the authenticity of our plane, which also blew our cover. In the end, it made absolutely no difference; not one journalist inquired into the purpose of the unusual Air Force sortie.

Ford reluctantly approved the concept of the warning stations because he rightly feared that they could create potential American hostages (which was, of course, in part why Peres wanted them). In the process of negotiating the Sinai II agreement, we successfully arranged for an American monitoring presence—the Sinai Support Mission—manned by civilians and a number of unmanned sensors.

To leave no room for further misunderstandings, Rabin and I met on July 12 at Schloss Gymnich, then the German state guest house near Bonn, where the Prime Minister was staying while on an official visit (I was in Europe for a meeting with Gromyko the day before in Geneva). The state guest house of a foreign country was not the ideal venue for a confidential dialogue. Neither Rabin nor I considered that good relations with our German hosts required us to leave on possible listening devices a verbatim record of our conversations (though we were willing enough to brief them in general terms).

Our discussions thus took place against the background noise of a "babbler," an electronic device emitting incoherent fragments of sentences designed to drown out or to override our voices. I had used the device on previous overseas visits, almost invariably in Moscow, though never, as now, during an actual negotiation. We had no idea whether it actually worked as advertised, since its target had no conceivable incentive to enlighten us or to admit that it had been listening in.

In that slightly bizarre setting—a German state guest house suffused with double-talk by the babbler—Rabin and I spent our time going over the various elevations in the passes, one hundred meters by one hundred meters, like mountain climbers setting out on a particularly difficult ascent. While we were at it, we also reviewed the access routes to the Abu Rudeis oil fields.

Finally, on July 18, Dinitz presented to me in Washington a map approved by the Israeli negotiating team and reflecting the Gymnich discussions. After nearly a year of trying to avoid the issue, the negotiating team was ready to vacate the passes—in a fashion. Its definition of entrance proved to be eccentric and quite a long way from how a layman would have understood the term. But it was close enough to enable me to tell Dinitz that I would submit the concept to Sadat with a favorable recommendation as being "as close to the best you can do."

In a Middle East negotiation, nothing can ever be considered completely settled. We needed to keep the Soviets from interfering, the Israelis committed to what had been agreed, and the Egyptians from having second thoughts. By this time, the Middle East peace process was following a choreography almost as stylized as a Kabuki play. Whenever we wanted to increase the level of diplomatic activity or when we had some reason to expect progress, we would contact the Soviets. We did so to blunt any attempt on their part to interfere with the negotiations and, at the same time, to preserve the option of reconvening the Geneva conference in the event of a last-minute deadlock in the step-by-step approach.

The Soviet response was equally stereotyped. Whenever they sensed an impasse in the American-sponsored negotiations, the Soviets would raise their terms for reassembling the Geneva conference, as Gromyko had done in Vienna on May 20 when he proposed issuing an invitation to the PLO—the biggest stumbling block to reconvening the Geneva conference. And whenever progress was being made on an interim agreement, Gromyko would lower his terms while our interest would flag correspondingly.

When I met Gromyko in Geneva on July 11, an interim agreement again seemed imminent, causing him to lower his terms. No longer insisting that the PLO be invited, Gromyko retreated to leaving it to the Arab participants at the conference to make that decision. To protect us against a last-minute deadlock, I began exploring procedures for a Geneva conference. To prevent the coalescence of maximum demands at the outset, I urged—and Gromyko agreed—that the parties at Geneva be required to engage in direct negotiation for a prolonged period before the superpowers interjected their own ideas, either separately or together.

Gromyko next attempted a little gentle blackmail in the guise of protesting Soviet goodwill. The Soviet Union, he said, had shown considerable restraint by reducing its arms sales to the Middle East, for it had the capacity to "paralyze" the peace process approach by increasing the flow of arms. I responded by stressing that, according to his own oft repeated assertions, we were both big boys and that unilateral steps had never been a Soviet specialty:

> This restraint isn't a favor you do to us but reflects common interests. Because the absence of restraint wouldn't solve the problem but would leave us in the same situation, only after another war. So I think both of us have an interest in exercising restraint.

Just when everything seemed to be heading toward resolution, there was another blowup. By now, Rabin seemed to be approaching cabinet approval for a new and more adequate proposal. We could deduce this from the fact that some of his cabinet colleagues were covering their flanks by claiming victory. Leaks coming out of Jerusalem alleged that the United States had rejected Egyptian proposals and was backing Israel's views. There was no basis whatever for these assertions, which seemed designed to humiliate Sadat. Matters became especially tense when Israeli diplomats began briefing European foreign ministries with a fairly accurate version of the state of the negotiations and urged our allies to appeal to Sadat for greater flexibility, as if Egypt were the principal obstacle to progress. (When Fahmy protested to us and we to Allon, we were told that no such démarches had been sent—in which case, as Eagleburger remarked, the Israelis were facing a European conspiracy of truly extraordinary proportions.) Finally, some unnamed senior source in Jerusalem asserted that, when all the maneuvering was over and done with, the Israeli armed forces would still be found well inside the passes.

This proved too much for Ford, who was still on his travels in the aftermath of the Helsinki conference. On August 4, he instructed me to send a blistering telegram to Rabin from *Air Force One:*

> The President has given the Egyptians his word, based on
> Israeli assurances, that the Israeli line is out of the passes.
> He will live up to that word and the Prime Minister should
> have no misapprehension about that.

Rabin reacted with great restraint. The last thing he wanted was a brawl over one kilometer of a pass which would, in any event, be in the U.N. zone and much closer to the Israeli than to the Egyptian lines. He suggested that we send a trusted aide to walk the two passes with Israeli officers and have them agree on a reasonable definition of the entrances.

We dispatched Samuel Hoskinson, a CIA expert and former NSC aide who had specialized in the Middle East, to help put an end to what was becoming an all but frivolous dispute. It was not clear what would mark the eastern end of the Giddi Pass. As Hoskinson reported, the Israeli line was east of the geographic divide but not out of that pass "by any stretch of the imagination." The Israelis were further out of the Mitla Pass, where Hoskinson proposed designating the "Parker Memorial" as the eastern end without, however, vouchsafing to us exactly what was being memorialized. Battle-weary, I mused: "I guess it is a fountain pen stuck in the sand, and they've called it the Parker Memorial!" Later we found out that the memorial was a stone slab in extreme disrepair commemorating a British engineer who had built roads in the Sinai during the last century. It turned out that even General Gamasy, who had spent much of his military service in the Sinai, had never heard of the Parker Memorial. Nevertheless, it did provide a tangible marker on which both sides could agree.

## Another Shuttle

Once more, the positions seemed close enough to risk another shuttle, which we proposed to start on Thursday, August 21. The mood in Jerusalem was ugly. Massive demonstrations against the United States—Israel's only major ally—were taking place in both Jerusalem and Tel Aviv.

Just before I left, Ford called to wish me well:

> FORD: It is ridiculous, Henry. I hate . . . to send you over there in that atmosphere.
>
> KISSINGER: I think it helps a little bit in this country. In this country, it makes it clear. In the Arab world, it helps. It shows the Arabs we have been extending ourselves. It will be a great help with Sadat.
>
> FORD: . . . Take care of yourself and Nancy. . . . Keep in touch. I have nothing but the highest faith that you will do what is in the best interest of the country.

On our first evening in Jerusalem, our motorcade was surrounded by an angry crowd attempting to tip over our cars. Quite a few of the placards were aimed at me personally: "Jewboy, go home," said one of the milder ones, paraphrasing an alleged Nixon remark; "Hitler spared you so you could finish the job" was more hurtful.

The Israeli negotiating team of Rabin, Allon, and Peres, embarrassed by these excesses, behaved courteously and professionally throughout. Still, even with many of the principles settled, they could not resist nitpicking at every clause if only to demonstrate their vigilance before cabinet colleagues.

Ultimately seven shuttles between Egypt and Israel took place, as well as side trips to Taif in Saudi Arabia, Jordan, and two to Syria. With the Israeli negotiating team defending each meter as if the passes were in downtown Tel Aviv rather than more than a hundred miles from Israel's borders, we finally had the CIA construct a table-sized, three-dimensional model to assist the deliberations. We carted it about on the plane from one stop to the next, greatly amusing—if not impressing—our Israeli and Egyptian friends.

In the end, the shuttle did succeed, though it was by then drained of the exhilaration accompanying previous successes. Egypt, Israel, and the United States were all equally reluctant to reassemble the Geneva conference and took turns blackmailing each other with that one agreed item. From it, they distilled an agreement which paved the way to peace between Israel and Egypt. In what seemed like never-ending sessions, the eastern entrance to the Giddi Pass was finally agreed, the American warning presence (the Sinai Support Mission) was put in place, and the Abu Rudeis oil fields were transferred to Egypt.

Though the Israeli negotiating team agreed that the passes were strategically irrelevant, it compensated for Israel's withdrawal eastward within the passes by moving the rest of its line *westward* just to the north and south, so that the passes would be effectively surrounded by the Israeli army even after it had vacated them (see map). Woe to the Egyptian soldier who, after crossing the U.N. zone, ventured into the passes from the western end. When I presented this latest wrinkle to Sadat, he simply threw up his hands in resignation.

The ebb and flow of the final negotiating process primarily demonstrated the incongruity between the mechanics of bargaining and the movement of history, between the passions of the moment and the ultimate fate of nations. Israel focused on legally binding assurances. It achieved some of these but gained, above all, Egypt's irrevocable turn toward a separate peace. Sadat insisted on some tangible territorial gains, but his major success was to commit the United States to treating Egypt as its principal partner in the region.

One episode is worth recounting because it shows that, in the Middle East, the improbable can sometimes supply the thread out of a diplomatic labyrinth.

Sadat had insisted on unimpeded Egyptian access to the Abu Rudeis oil fields on the southwest coast of the Sinai Peninsula, and Rabin had agreed to the principle of it with Ford. That was, however, before any of the chief actors had studied a map of the region. As soon as the negotiations turned to specifics, we discovered that there was only one road leading to Abu Rudeis, which Israel also needed for its own communications with the strategic base of Sharm al-Sheikh, guarding the entrance to the Gulf of Aqaba. Because there was only a relatively narrow strip of land between the sea and a range of mountains just behind it, it was impossible to build another road—not to mention the absurdity of it for just a few military convoys. The shuttle had only deepened the conundrum until I came up with a desperate proposal which I felt certain would be rejected but might at least tide us over until someone came up with a better idea. It was that both parties should use the same road but on alternate days, with one day a week set aside for U.N. traffic. To my astonishment, both parties accepted—and without the usual haggling. The road was used without incident on that basis for four years until the Camp David Accords returned the entire Sinai to Egypt starting in 1979.

The Sinai II agreement was finally initialed on September 1, 1975. Ford was elated. He had every right to take pride in the role he had played. Under his aegis, we had concluded the most significant Middle East agreement of both the Nixon and Ford Administrations. Ford's persistence had been a major factor in bringing about what became the decisive step toward Israeli peace agreements first with Egypt and later with Jordan. From the presidential retreat in Camp David, Maryland, he made televised phone calls to both Rabin and Sadat to congratulate them on their achievement. Each of the leaders spoke in a characteristic fashion, but they agreed on continuing the quest for peace. Rabin wryly called for direct negotiations in the future to save the United States a "lot of effort and time." And he added a touch of the Israeli yearning for peace:

> We really hope that it will be the beginning of something which we have not yet experienced in this area, and we hope that the other side, the Egyptian side, feels the same.

Sadat generously came close to agreeing with Israel's quest for formal nonbelligerency: "Let us create a new atmosphere . . . and let us reach the state of nonbelligerency *officially* and with guarantees [emphasis added]."

For the rest of us, exhaustion was the dominant sensation. This was especially true of the backup teams which had been obliged to redraft the final documents until the last second of the last day. I will let Harold Saunders, a key member of the American team, describe the final chaotic night in his own words:

> It had become a practice at the end of each shuttle for the Israelis to present proposals for American help to Israel to be written into a "memorandum of agreement." This night, those proposals ranged through sixteen paragraphs on subjects such as commitments to be sympathetic to Israel's military supply needs, to meet Israel's oil requirements if Israel could not buy what it needed, to consult if Egypt violated the agreement, to veto in the UN Security Council any measure adversely affecting the agreement, to "view with particular gravity threats to Israel's security or sovereignty by a world power," to make contingency plans for military supply to Israel in an emergency, and even to reassure Israel that the United States regards certain straits, including the Strait of Gibraltar, as international waterways.
>
> Beginning about 8:00 P.M., Israeli team members took individual members of our team into separate parts of the conference room and pressed their positions on each paragraph in the memorandum. This went on throughout the entire night.
>
> We returned to the hotel at sunrise to prepare three original copies of the agreement for initialing later that day. Meanwhile, we had cabled final provisions to Ambassador Hermann Eilts in Egypt for Foreign Minister Fahmy, who was sitting on the beach near Alexandria. Then we began receiving further changes from Fahmy's cabana. All these suggestions meant more telephone exchanges with the Israelis and, in a world without word processors, retyping all the documents.
>
> The Israelis finally initialed toward evening (September 1), and we flew back to Sadat's house. It was nearly midnight when Sadat initialed in the presence of the Egyptian and American teams. The room was oppressively hot, and the only escape was through a French door on to the beach where the damp air helped keep us awake.

The subject matter included a series of side letters to Ford from each of the signatories, making the American President the pivotal facilitator of the agreement. Sadat promised not to join a war if Syria attacked Israel; to maintain a formal symmetry, Rabin offered assurances that Israel would not attack Syria. Ford agreed to a commitment not to deal with the PLO until it recognized Israel's right to exist and accepted Security Council Resolutions 242 and 338 (which secured the cease-fire and called for negotiations between the parties at the end of the October 1973 war). In a letter to Rabin, Ford also indicated that, in any ultimate peace negotiation, he would give "great weight" to Israel's view that its security did not allow it to give up the Golan Heights. What we put in writing with respect to both the PLO and the Golan was not so much a new commitment as a formal statement of existing American policy.

That the remaining road to peace would be far from easy became immediately evident when, on my way back from the shuttle, I stopped in Damascus and Amman. Asad was icily contemptuous of Sadat, whom he accused of betraying the Arab cause. Syria would take no further initiative, he said. If I had a new proposal, he would examine it, but I should not expect the same eagerness to give up principle as I had experienced with Sadat: "What is the use of a few kilometers on the southern Syrian front? Are we kidding?" When I rejoined that, at the end of the day, he would have no other option than the one chosen by Sadat, Asad replied coldly: "You are selling out Vietnam; you will abandon Taiwan. And we will be here when you grow tired of Israel."

The reaction in Amman was ambivalent. For months, Hussein had been urging another interim agreement as the only hope of preventing a Middle East war. Yet when it happened, the King could not fail to note that he—arguably America's most constant friend—stood alone among Israel's neighbors in still having failed to achieve any territorial gain or other benefit with the assistance of the United States.

Hussein chose a symbolic way to show his displeasure. The band at the airport played only the American and not the Jordanian national anthem, there was no march-past of troops and no social event either at the palace or at the Crown Prince's residence as had been the unvarying custom on the night of my arrival. Courteous as ever, the King conducted the dialogue in his office seated across from me at a conference table—the only time I was received in this manner on any of my many visits to Amman before or after. I include these incidents to convey the mood but also to let my Jordanian friends know twenty years after the fact that we did understand the point they were making, though we saw no utility in commenting on it at the time.

## The Leaders and the Outcome

Objective factors determine the framework within which policies are conducted, but it is the leaders who must mold the clay. In the months following Indochina's collapse, Ford demonstrated America's continued relevance by taking charge of the Middle East peace process and steering it in a direction which prevented the coalescence of radical Middle East forces with Soviet strategy. De facto nonbelligerency emerged from a web of assurances, with the President serving as the pivot and backed up by his prestige and authority. Though he faced his own presidential election within fifteen months, Ford did not flinch when confronting volatile Middle East leaders or pressure groups at home capable of penalizing him in the forthcoming electoral contests. He proved indispensable in bridging the gulf between the suspicious parties by becoming the repository and moral guarantor of their assurances to each other.

Sadat's contribution was to take the decisive turn toward nonbelligerency that the Israeli negotiating team had been demanding for months and, even when it was achieved, did not dare to admit to itself. The agreement did place formidable physical and legal obstacles in the path of any Egyptian offensive move, but its larger significance was that Egypt had separated from both the united Arab front forged at Rabat as well as from the Soviet Union. Henceforth Sadat would either have to move forward toward peace or become a victim of the process he had started. In the end, both became his fate.

Anwar Sadat made all of his interlocutors look better than they sometimes deserved. At first, Israeli leaders suspected him of seeking a more advantageous starting point for the next Arab-Israeli war. After having overcome our own similar suspicions, those of us who had worked with Sadat came to understand that his true purpose was the precise opposite. He was tired of war; he knew that, at the end of another round of fighting, he would face exactly the same diplomatic challenge as now. Convinced that the issue was largely psychological, Sadat went to great lengths to ease Israel's suspicions. His generosity of spirit enabled the fractious members of the Israeli negotiating team to make peace with each other as they made peace with him by aggregating every negotiator's pet project into the final document. Sadat swallowed their escalating demands—the demand for assurances, warning stations, and deadlines—because he had staked everything on the gamble that, long before the interim agreement had run its course, he would have made another, this time conclusive, move toward peace.

Yitzhak Rabin had, in many ways, the most difficult role to play. In these pages, I have described the confrontational aspects of his tactics. Yet Rabin's careful, occasionally abrasive style reflected the central reality that he had far more at stake than Ford, was far less in control of his domestic situation than Sadat, and, above all, that his country's margin of survival was by far the narrowest of any of the participants in the peace process. Battered by his domestic opposition, assailed by competitors for leadership within his cabinet, pressed by his American allies to move faster, Rabin held to his determination to bring about some progress toward peace and not simply a new military arrangement. Had he moved too quickly, his cabinet would have fallen apart, and new elections would have had to be held; had he moved more slowly, he would have risked the American alliance.

Though Rabin basically agreed with our strategy, as he often told me, he had to adjust its pace to his own fragile political base and to what his beleaguered people could sustain. At the time he took office, Israel, having just concluded two disengagement agreements within five months, was being pressed into two more negotiations with Jordan and Egypt respectively. Though Rabin disrupted our preferred strategy, he was right from Israel's point of view to slow down the process and to seek a period of consolidation.

Rabin was a significant strategist. His gradualist approach moved his fractious cabinet and wary public to the breakthrough that made the Camp David Accords of 1978 possible. To Rabin's credit, he never mentioned his domestic difficulties to us, taking entirely upon himself the burdens of his cabinet's rivalries and the occasional outrage of his American friends. Our personal friendship made the periodic tensions painful for us both. It meant a great deal to me that, after a year of acrimony and months of reassessment, Rabin found it in his heart to say to me in Gymnich when we finally reconciled our policies:

> I have no doubt that you followed the strategy that was worked out in 1970–71, to deny the Arabs a military option and force them to a political option. We may have disagreements, but I never doubted you acted in the framework of the strategy.

The difference between Sadat and Rabin reflected, above all, the historical process which had brought them to this point. For Sadat, earning American goodwill was a strategic gain; for Rabin, American goodwill was a historic fact of life. Sadat made concessions in order to win America's confidence. Rabin and his colleagues believed that their people had already earned a claim on America's support by their suffering in the Holocaust and their democratic system of government. Sadat changed his strategic environment by gaining America's trust. Rabin worried lest Sadat's gains were at the expense of Israel's historic relationship with the United States. For Sadat, a mistake in negotiations would be a setback; for Rabin and his country, a mistake risked survival.

These two leaders who had edged so fitfully toward peace in the barren sands and desolate mountain passes of the Sinai went on to guide other major breakthroughs that resulted in two major peace treaties between Israelis and Arabs. Their efforts would also claim their lives. Each was murdered by fellow countrymen inured to war and violence and terrified of the new world that peace would bring.

# PART FIVE

# COLLAPSE IN INDOCHINA, TRAGEDY OF THE KURDS

# 15

# INDOCHINA TRAGEDY—
# THE BEGINNING OF THE END

## The Strangulation of Vietnam

Lawrence Durrell has written that every individual possesses a finite reservoir of courage or commitment which, however deep, is neither inexhaustible nor replenishable. This is what happened to the United States with respect to Indochina in 1975, two years after the Paris Agreement to end the war. Idealism had propelled America into Indochina, and exhaustion caused us to leave.

The United States devoted two decades of blood and treasure to help a group of newly independent, fledgling societies avoid conquest by their merciless and militarily more powerful Communist neighbor in North Vietnam. Yet, when the precarious peace wrought by the Paris Agreement was challenged, the United States, in the throes of physical and psychological abdication, cut off military and economic assistance to people whom we had given every encouragement to count on our protection. This consigned those we had made our wards to an implacable—and, in Cambodia, genocidal—Communist conqueror.

The passage of time has mercifully eased some of the pain of those somber months. Nevertheless, the way Indochina was brought to collapse in 1975 still evokes a sinking feeling in me, composed in equal parts of sadness for the victims that were abandoned and melancholy for what America did to itself. I will not review here the decisions which preceded the ultimate disaster; the literature regarding them covers shelves in libraries, and I have dealt with them at length elsewhere.[1] The particular heartbreak of the final ending is caused by the conviction that, by then, the debates of the Kennedy, Johnson, and Nixon years should have become irrelevant. Once the agreement to end the war was signed in January 1973, whatever the views regarding the wisdom of undertaking the war or of how it was conducted, we owed the peoples of South Vietnam and Cambodia who had stood with us the economic and military aid without which they had no chance of defending themselves.

Instead the United States, as if suddenly seized by a collective obsession to extrude a past which was, in fact, inescapable, seemed bent on extinguishing its witnesses, our former allies. Whether South Vietnam, Laos, and Cambodia could have survived by their own efforts indefinitely had they received the assistance promised to them will never be known. There is no doubt in my mind that, with anything close to an adequate level of American aid, they would not have collapsed in 1975. How this came about, how the ultimate fiasco presented itself to the policy level in Washington and how it was handled by the President who had inherited the problem are the subject of this chapter.

It is nearly impossible to re-create the mood of that period. For those who lived through it, any account must appear fragmentary; for those who were spared the turmoil of that time, the passions may well seem incomprehensible. The end came to Indochina as it does in a Greek tragedy where the principals are driven by their very natures to fulfill their destiny sometimes in full foreknowledge of the anguish that awaits them. In Indochina, the manner in which the chief actors had conducted themselves in the previous decade ultimately shaped their actions in 1975. The choices they made in the end were permutations of choices they had made years earlier. What had started as an almost philosophical controversy over what constitutes a nation's honor ended up as a technical debate about modalities of extrication. Even the new American President, really the only free agent among the principals, came to understand that there was no easy, heretofore undiscovered way out of this morass; given what had gone before, the tragedy had become simply inevitable.

In retrospect, it is clear that the curtain rose on the final act on the very day when, for a fleeting moment, it seemed that peace had come to Indochina. On January 24, 1973,* I concluded a White House

---

* The Paris Agreement was initialed by Le Duc Tho and me on January 23, 1973, and formally signed by foreign ministers in a public ceremony on January 27.

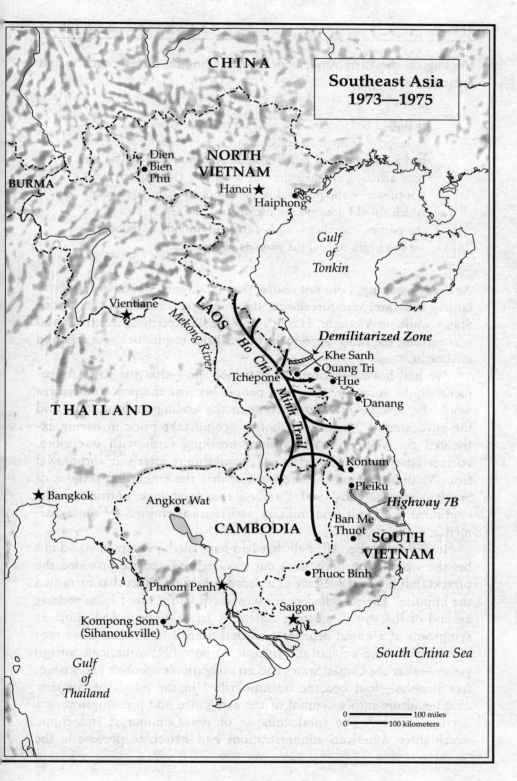

Southeast Asia
1973—1975

CHINA

BURMA

NORTH
VIETNAM

Dien
Bien
Phu

Hanoi ★

Haiphong

Gulf
of
Tonkin

Vientiane ★

LAOS

Mekong River

Ho Chi Minh Trail

Demilitarized Zone

Khe Sanh

Tchepone

Quang Tri

Hue

Danang

THAILAND

Bangkok ★

Angkor Wat

Kontum

Pleiku

Highway 7B

CAMBODIA

Ban Me
Thuot

SOUTH
VIETNAM

Phnom Penh ★

Phuoc Binh

Saigon ★

Kompong Som
(Sihanoukville)

Gulf
of
Thailand

South China Sea

0                100 miles
0                100 kilometers

briefing on the Paris Agreement by extending an olive branch to our critics:

> It should be clear by now that no one in this war has had a monopoly of anguish and that no one in these debates has had a monopoly of moral insight. And now that at last we have achieved an agreement in which the United States did not prescribe the political future to its allies, an agreement which should preserve the dignity and the self-respect of all the parties, together with healing the wounds in Indochina we can begin to heal the wounds in America.

As I was speaking, I did not realize that Watergate, of which I was still largely unaware, was foreclosing the hopes for healing in the United States while, in Vietnam, Hanoi's implacable determination to prevail was turning the peace agreement into a brief respite before a renewed onslaught.

We had hoped—naively, as it turned out—that the Paris Agreement would unite the American people because the peace movement would be able to find satisfaction in the ending of hostilities, and the advocates of "peace with honor" could take pride in having extricated the United States without breaking faith with our allies. Former adversaries, we had hoped, would unite after our withdrawal from Vietnam behind the proposition that the embattled peoples of South Vietnam, Laos, and Cambodia were at least entitled to the continued economic and military assistance permitted by the agreement.

It was not to be. After all that had happened, perhaps it could not be; the wounds on both sides cut too deep. Watergate provided the pretext, but it was the legacy of a decade of civil conflict that furnished the impulse. The so-called peace movement had evolved from seeking an end of the war to treating America's frustrations in Indochina as symptoms of a moral degeneration that needed to be eradicated root and branch. The animating principle of post-1945 American foreign policy—that the United States had an obligation to protect and sustain free peoples—had become transmogrified in the hands of the new counterculture into a symbol of the arrogance and presumption of a corrupt society.[2] The total collapse of non-Communist Indochina, which three American administrations had striven to prevent in the name of national security and honor, was, for this group, nothing less than a desirable national catharsis.

I had been introduced to Vietnam in the fall of 1965 when Ambassador Henry Cabot Lodge invited me to serve as a consultant to him. Though a confirmed Cold Warrior, I became convinced after a few weeks in the country that this war could not be won by rules of engagement permitting the guerrillas to choose the battlefield and determine the intensity of combat.[3] Since there were no front lines within South Vietnam and since the Johnson Administration refused to pursue the guerrillas into the sanctuaries just across the border in Laos and Cambodia, I advocated a negotiated outcome.

In late 1967, President Johnson entrusted me with an exploratory diplomatic mission, using as an intermediary a French acquaintance in whose house Ho Chi Minh had stayed in 1946 when negotiating with France. It ended as all American diplomatic initiatives toward the single-minded warriors from Hanoi were destined to end. Raymond Aubrac did go to Hanoi and was received by Ho Chi Minh, who made a few Delphic utterances interpreted in Washington as hints of a desire to negotiate but which we now know were designed to lull the United States prior to the Tet Offensive a few months later.

The strategy adopted by the Nixon Administration was foreshadowed in an article I had written for *Foreign Affairs* while still a professor at Harvard but which, owing to long lead time, was not published until shortly after my appointment as National Security Adviser. In it, I had urged that the military and political issues be treated separately. The military issues would be negotiated between the United States and the Vietnamese parties, leading to a cease-fire, withdrawal of outside troops, exchange of prisoners, and a limitation of armaments. The Vietnamese parties would then negotiate a political process by which the peoples of Indochina would be able to decide the future of their countries.[4]

Nixon adopted this approach, and it became the basis for the eventual settlement. For four painful years, however, Hanoi flatly rejected any outcome that did not foreordain a Communist victory. Until October 8, 1972, when the breakthrough finally occurred, Hanoi's terms never changed, no matter how much we might modify ours and while Hanoi kept persuading gullible protestors that only a bloodthirsty American administration stood in the way of an easily attainable settlement. Hanoi's unwavering terms were that the United States commit itself at the outset of any negotiation to a fixed deadline for the withdrawal of American forces. This schedule would, moreover, remain in effect regardless of what happened in the negotiations with respect to other issues or on the military front. Simultaneously, according to Hanoi's blueprint, the American "puppet government" in Saigon headed by President Nguyen Van Thieu would have to be replaced by a "coalition government" composed of Communists, representatives of a nebulous, supposedly neutral third force, and remnants of the Thieu administration. This effectively disarmed and decapitated, partially Communist coalition would then negotiate, in the absence of American forces, a final settlement with the heavily armed, all-Communist Provisional Revolutionary Government (PRG).* It was a crude prescription for surrender.

In the four years of negotiations, we never managed to extract from Le Duc Tho (Politburo member and the principal North Vietnamese negotiator) a single name from the panoply of known Vietnamese politicians that might prove acceptable to Hanoi for the "third force" elements of the proposed coalition. Stripped to their essence, Hanoi's terms amounted to the unconditional withdrawal of American forces accompanied by the overthrow—by us—of a government allied with the United States so that South Vietnam could be handed over to the Communists. Neither Nixon nor I was willing to end America's commitment to Vietnam, inherited from our predecessors, by betraying the millions who had placed their trust in our country.

When we could not achieve a negotiated withdrawal, we implemented as much of our program as was possible unilaterally, strengthening the Vietnamese forces, withdrawing well over half a million troops by the end of Nixon's first term, and reducing our known casualties from an average of 1,200 a month in 1968 to less than thirty in 1972. By the fall of 1972, only about thirty thousand American troops remained in Vietnam, and they were no longer engaged in ground combat. Every step along this road was passionately and occasionally violently opposed by the peace movement, whose only alternative to our policy was unilateral withdrawal in return for our prisoners.

* The Provisional Revolutionary Government of the Republic of South Vietnam (PRG) was the reincarnation of the National Liberation Front (NLF) or Vietcong—that is, the South Vietnamese Communists.

Thus our domestic debate, though obscured by clouds of self-righteous rhetoric, had come down to one relatively straightforward issue: the Nixon Administration thought it neither moral nor prudent for the leading nation of the democratic coalition simply to abdicate by overthrowing an allied government. The antiwar movement argued the exact opposite: that such an abdication purged the United States of its hubris and the American administration of its blood lust and that the latter, not Hanoi's intransigence, was the real obstacle to peace.

By October 1972, Hanoi gave up on imposing its terms by force and accepted the conditions Nixon had put forward publicly on January 25, 1972 (and privately in May 1971)—nine months before our presidential elections: continuation of the Saigon government, cease-fire, American withdrawal, end of North Vietnamese infiltration and reinforcements, return of prisoners, and a continuing political dialogue between the parties.

We had no illusions about what lay ahead. Neither Nixon nor I believed that Hanoi's dour, fanatical leaders had abandoned their lifetime struggle. I warned Nixon during the final phase of the negotiations in November 1972 that Hanoi would press against the edges of any agreement and that the peace could only be preserved by constant vigilance:

> As I have consistently told you since mid-September, this is a very high-risk operation. The eventual outcome of any settlement will essentially turn on the confidence and political performance of the two sides. Having seen the total hatred and pathological distrust between the Vietnamese parties, and knowing as well that Hanoi has no intention of giving up its strategic objectives, we must face the reality that this agreement may lack the foundation of minimum trust that may be needed. Thus it could well break down. It will certainly require from us a posture of constant readiness and willingness to intervene to keep Hanoi and its South Vietnamese allies from nibbling at the edges.[5]

In early 1973, we thought that we were in a position to fulfill these requirements. Provided Saigon received adequate military and economic assistance, the military balance would leave South Vietnam strong enough to resist Communist pressures—short of an all-out attack by the North Vietnamese regular army. Should North Vietnam betray the agreement and its prohibition against infiltration by launching an all-out invasion, we intended to defend with air- and seapower what over 55,000 Americans had died to achieve.

But no foreign policy is stronger than its domestic base. We took it for granted that the conclusion of the Paris accords implied the right to enforce them—as has been the case in every previous and subsequent conflict in which Americans have sacrificed their lives. But Watergate undermined the President's authority and altered the previous equilibrium between the executive and legislative branches. The Paris Agreement did not so much end the controversy as give it a new focus.

Throughout 1973 and 1974, enforcement of the agreement became as controversial as the war itself had been, and the arguments against it were identical. The antiwar movement would not accept the premise that we had achieved peace with honor, for to do so would contradict its basic theme that American power was itself a source of evil in the world.[6] The same groups that had opposed every measure that had enabled us to end the war now rejected any policy either to enforce the agreement or to sustain the peoples on behalf of whom the war had been fought.

They justified this post-agreement surrender with the specious proposition that there was no legal "obligation" to assist Vietnam or to uphold the Paris Agreement, only "secret" presidential letters expressing our intention of doing so. The accusation came with special bad grace from members of previous administrations who should have been well aware of presidential letters during their period in office which at least paralleled what Nixon had promised to President Thieu.[7]

Presidential letters are not legal commitments but expressions of the intent of the incumbent President with respect to foreseeable contingencies. They impose a moral, not a legal, obligation on his successors (which inevitably declines with the distance from the presidency). And, of course, no President is able to commit Congress by a unilateral declaration.

In the case of Vietnam, the President's letters were written in the interregnum between the election and inauguration. Thieu therefore had every reason to expect that Nixon would have four years to carry out statements of his intentions totally compatible with his previous record. Moreover, the President's associates repeatedly avowed the administration's determination to enforce the agreement publicly, as can be seen from the Nixon Administration public statements in the Notes.[8] These pronouncements repeated the substance of what was in the presidential letters to President Thieu.

In any event, the argument about the nature of America's obligation missed the central point. Neither the Ford nor the Nixon Administration ever invoked a legal obligation to assist Vietnam. What we insisted on was something deeper—a moral obligation. We owed such assistance to the peoples who had stood with us, to the casualties we had left, and to the common efforts in which we had been involved— in short, to ourselves.

When the United States concludes a peace agreement, the other party should be automatically on notice that we will not permit it to violate its terms with impunity. Without a penalty for violations, a cease-fire turns into a subterfuge for surrender. Every previous and subsequent administration has held that view; the outcome of the Gulf War of 1991 has been largely maintained because both Presidents Bush and especially Clinton have on occasion used force or threatened it to uphold the arrangements that ended the war with Iraq.

Within six months of the Paris accords, the traditional opponents of American involvement in Indochina legislated their preferred outcome by means of binding congressional acts—something they had never managed to accomplish while the war was raging. When, in June 1973, Congress prohibited the use of military force "in or over Indochina," the United States was effectively forbidden to enforce an agreement for which over 55,000 Americans and hundreds of thousands of Vietnamese had given their lives. At the same time, military assistance to Vietnam was slashed from $2.1 billion for Fiscal Year 1973 to $1 billion in FY 1974 and $700 million in FY 1975, despite the fact that oil prices were quadrupling and draining Saigon's scant reserves of hard currency.

In these circumstances, Hanoi infiltrated over 130,000 soldiers with tanks and heavy artillery into South Vietnam over the year and a half after the agreement and constructed a network of roads to shift its troops rapidly from sector to sector—all in flagrant violation of the agreement. The United States was throttling South Vietnam and paralyzing its own capacity to act. Not surprisingly, the tragedy ended with the entire North Vietnamese army invading South Vietnam while the United States stood by, paralyzed by its own divisions.

## Ford and Vietnam

When Ford became President, support for military or economic assistance to Indochina was visibly disintegrating. His first decision concerned how to react to a desperately inadequate military assistance budget wending its way through Congress. Appropriations for Vietnam had been reduced by 50 percent each year since the signing of the Paris Agreement. The Nixon Administration had requested $1.4 billion for military assistance for FY 1975. The Senate Armed Services Committee, headed by the venerable and conservative John Stennis from Mississippi, had reduced this to $1 billion. Now the Senate Appropriations Committee, headed by the equally conservative John McClellan from Arkansas, was slashing another $300 million from the military assistance program. At the same time, economic aid was being reduced from $650 million to $250 million. These cuts appear even more severe when measured in real dollars because the increase in oil prices and inflation reduced the effective value of the aid package to about one quarter of the 1973 amount.

The budgetary battles were surrogates for a fundamental challenge being pressed on the new President first by the Congress he had inherited from Nixon and even more insistently by the predominantly McGovernite Congress elected in 1974. The pressures to liquidate even American financial involvement in Indochina professed to be in the name of putting an end to the killing, oblivious to the massacre that a collapse of Indochina would engender. At the same time, some of Ford's associates from his congressional days, having seen career after career blighted by Vietnam, were urging him to avoid being drawn into the vortex, especially in what would clearly be a losing battle. In their more innocent moments, some of them entertained the illusion that their old friend might even garner public credit for ending America's involvement in Indochina.

Ford had no such misconceptions. He understood instinctively that the oath of office drew him into the fray, and it is to his credit that he recognized the fashionable slogan of ending American involvement for what it was: a euphemism for abandoning Indochina and for leaving it to our adversaries to finish off at will. American troops having long since left, our principal involvement now was by way of military and economic aid. Ending that would make us accomplices in the destruction of the institutions that we had put into place and of the men and women who had relied on us. Nevertheless, our opponents were gaining ground because no one was left to contest the field. The conservatives had lost heart with the bombing halt ordered by Johnson in 1968; the Nixon supporters were demoralized by Watergate; and the new White House staff had no stomach for the brutal fight they had heretofore watched from the sidelines. So Brent Scowcroft and I, always backed by Ford, soldiered on to sustain our ally and then, sick at heart, to at least save as many Vietnamese and Cambodian lives as possible before the final calamity which Congress and the media had imposed.

To symbolize his commitment to maintaining a free South Vietnam, Ford had made it a point to receive the South Vietnamese ambassador, Tran Kim Phuong, for a private meeting in the evening of his first day in office. The President assured Phuong that he was committed to Saigon's survival and would do his best to increase aid levels. On the same day, Ford reiterated this assurance in a letter to Thieu, adding to the NSC draft a paragraph of his own:

> Our legislative process is a complicated one and it is not yet completed. Although it may take a little time I do want to reassure you of my confidence that in the end our support will be adequate on both counts.

Neither Ford nor I had yet grasped the depth and scope of the emerging congressional opposition, or the letter would surely have been modified. Congressional support for aid to Vietnam had evaporated on both ends of the political spectrum. In June, while Nixon was still in office, Senator James Allen of Alabama, a conservative and master at legislative maneuvering, stated that he had supported the administration until the troops and the prisoners had come home but, once that task had been accomplished, "now, we should get out."[9] Senator Hubert Humphrey, the floor manager of the foreign aid bill, spoke to the same exhaustion in a liberal rhetoric: "We ignore the most important lesson, that political battles cannot be resolved by force of arms."[10] This is not a conclusion which most historians have reached. Even our own Civil War might have taught quite a different lesson to my good-hearted friend from Minnesota whose chances for the presidency had been destroyed by the Vietnam protest in 1968. And the neoconservatives, busy excoriating the Ford Administration for alleged softness toward Communist pressures, were nowhere to be found in the domestic debate over how to resist the only Communist military aggression actually taking place.

During the first few weeks of his presidency, in August 1974, Ford was preoccupied with the Cyprus crisis and staffing his administration, and deliberating over the Nixon pardon. It was not until September 5 that he was able to turn to the issue of aid for Indochina in a systematic way. During my daily meeting, I warned:

> Without massive effort on your part, we are in trouble on Vietnam. If we don't do enough, it doesn't matter how much too little you do. North Vietnam seems undecided. You might want to consider meeting with the congressional leaders next week. We are in trouble both with the restrictions and the dollar amounts. . . .
>
> . . . Others will see what happens to people who rely on the United States. First we make an undesirable settlement, but with the promise of unlimited aid—and then aid is cut off within two years.

For symmetry's sake, I presented the option of abandoning Vietnam:

> You do have an option as a new President. You could let it go—and not be blamed, at least through '76. I must say I think it is wrong. The liberals who would applaud it would fail you when the going was tough.

Ford never considered that option. He had been the ranking Republican member of the Defense Subcommittee of the House Appropriations Committee throughout the Vietnam War and had considerable knowledge of the significance of the aid levels. He needed no briefing to understand that the constantly declining levels of aid posed an ominous psychological and military danger. On September 12, I sent Ford a memorandum that described the impact of a $700 million level for military aid:

> —insufficient funds to replace damaged or lost equipment;
> —a 50 percent reduction in aircraft utilization on top of the 11 squadrons of aircraft already grounded;
> —reductions in operations by sea-going vessels by 30 percent and by riverine vessels by 82 percent;
> —medical supplies would be completely expended by the end of May 1975;
> —fuel for ground forces would be exhausted by late April 1975;
> —by the end of FY 75, the Army would have only one-quarter of the minimum ammunition reserve necessary to meet a major offensive;
> —unutilized aircraft and ground equipment will deteriorate rapidly.

South Vietnamese casualties were mounting in direct proportion to the above shortfalls and had reached 26,000 combat deaths since the signing of the Paris Agreement twenty months earlier. The congressional leaders were unmoved by these figures. The most Ford could extract from them was a promise by Senator Stennis to consider favorably a request for $300 million for a supplemental budget in January 1975. That did not help matters much because, as far as Saigon was concerned, funds would be disbursed at the rate implied by the $700 million budget until the supplemental budget could be passed, which, if it could be at all, would not be until well into 1975.

The supplemental request turned into a forum for another assault on funding for Indochina, the abandonment of which was being advocated more and more openly and with increasingly insistent alibis: did we have a legal commitment to extend aid to Vietnam; should we gear our assistance to the levels of Soviet and Chinese aid to Hanoi; should we not seek a political rather than a military solution? Every argument produced weeks of procrastination as new hearings were conducted by skeptical congressional committees. Finally the opponents of aid, now in a majority, abandoned their rearguard action and began to rally around the proposition that South Vietnam had to learn to stand on its own two feet and could expect at best a final lump sum grant as a sort of severance payment.

Within the administration, I was the principal advocate for meaningful aid levels. Having been the negotiator of the Paris accords, I felt a special responsibility. I would never have concluded the negotiation had I not been convinced that we would supply adequate assistance after our withdrawal. It never occurred to me that we might end up simply jettisoning an entire people to which we were allied. As Vietnam was collapsing, the thrust of my appeal was to such unfashionable concepts as "honor" and "moral obligation," not to realpolitik—as our critics had it. On March 22, 1974, I told a staff meeting:

> I do feel very strongly that having lost fifty thousand men,
> torn our country apart, staggered to a conclusion which was
> at least not dishonorable, to throw it all away now for $100
> million one way or the other is a disgrace. And I would
> much rather tell Congress what we think we need and let
> them take the responsibility for cutting it.

No country defended by the United States during the Cold War had ever been asked to stand entirely on its own without some continuing American protection afterward. American troops did not leave Europe at the end of the Second World War and have remained even after the collapse of the Soviet Union; several divisions have stayed in Korea for nearly half a century since the Korean War ended; a strong American presence has been retained in the Gulf since Iraq was expelled from Kuwait. Only in Vietnam did we insist that an ally defend itself entirely with its own forces and this against one of the most ruthless and determined adversaries faced by any of our allies. Did we not, at a minimum, owe Vietnam at least a reasonable opportunity to defend *itself* by supplying the wherewithal to do so? What would have happened in Europe, Korea, or the Gulf had the United States withdrawn its troops, cut off aid, and then legislated a prohibition against responding to aggression with American forces?

In 1971–73, when we were extricating ourselves from Vietnam, there had been many expressions of congressional support for the idea of giving substantial aid after an American troop withdrawal. Thus, on June 15, 1971, Senator Jacob Javits, a leading "dove," had advocated congressional appropriations on the order of $2 billion after an American withdrawal as an expression of "an obligation to the millions of

Vietnamese who have been drawn into the massive US operations within Vietnam."[11] On May 11, 1972, Senator Frank Church had been cited in the *Christian Science Monitor:*

> Senator Church and other doves go along with the intention of the Nixon Administration to give needed funds to the Saigon government. The Senator does point out that under a change of government that brought someone like Gen. Duong Van Minh (Big Minh) to the fore, there could be less reliance on US aid.[12]

On February 21, 1973, Senator Clifford Case of New Jersey, another "dove," had endorsed continued aid:

> Our aim in Indochina should be to make the countries, insofar as we can, what they were before all this trouble started. With that qualification I fully support the concept of foreign assistance and I do not think it [in] any way derogates from our ability to do what we properly should do at home.[13]

(A more comprehensive list can be found in the Notes.[14])

Suddenly collective amnesia set in. Once the Paris Agreement was concluded, Congress displayed an extraordinary penchant for disavowing what it had heretofore been proclaiming as articles of faith. One such argument was that our aid to Saigon should be no greater than Soviet and Chinese deliveries to Hanoi. But this compared the incommensurable. Saigon was obliged to defend a jungle frontier of nearly a thousand kilometers; the North Vietnamese could concentrate on any one point and, in flagrant violation of the Paris Agreement, were expanding and upgrading their logistics system to enable them to concentrate their forces rapidly and in superior numbers at decisive points. Until the summer of 1974, the South Vietnamese armed forces had been able to compensate with superior artillery and airpower; now congressional budget cuts were forcing the dramatic reductions in these activities described earlier.

Another alibi for the abandonment of South Vietnam invoked humane aims. Further American aid, it was said, would merely encourage Saigon to violate the political provisions of the agreement, such as holding free elections. No doubt Saigon dragged its feet in implementing some of the political provisions of the agreement, though Hanoi's conduct both before and after its victory gave no evidence of a burning desire for free elections (which, at this writing, have yet to be held anywhere in Vietnam under Communist control). But it was Hanoi's violation of the *military* provisions that undermined the Paris Agreement from the beginning—and American congressional opposition compounded by Watergate completed Saigon's doom.

In the spring of 1973, we were preparing to bomb the Ho Chi Minh Trail to deter or slow down Hanoi's buildup. In April, Nixon felt obliged to shelve the plan as the Watergate investigations gained momentum. In June 1973, Congress prohibited any military action "in or over Vietnam." This was followed in 1974 by the budget cuts already described. By 1975, Saigon's back was broken psychologically.

## Hanoi's Buildup

All the evidence at the time and even more since in the various accounts of the North Vietnamese commanders leaves no doubt that Hanoi was preparing for a military showdown from the day the peace accords were signed—regardless of Saigon's actions. Starting immediately, the North Vietnamese undertook a monumental effort to reequip and reorganize their forces in the South. They constructed a network of strategic roads totaling twenty thousand kilometers north and south, east and west, including an eight-meter wide, all-weather road suitable for trucks; they built five thousand kilometers of oil pipelines to fuel the tens of thousands of vehicles moving down the roads—all in flagrant violation of the Paris Agreement. As early as October 1973, the Twenty-first Plenum of the Central Committee of the North Vietnamese Communist Party decided to resume its program of "revolutionary violence." By March 1974, a Central Military Committee meeting was drawing up operational plans for resuming the "strategic offensive." The account of North Vietnamese General Van Tien Dung, who commanded the final assault, relates that, between April and October 1974, North Vietnamese units attacked the enemy "with no let-up, winning greater victories each day, at a greater pace," from which the general staff drew the conclusion that "the fighting capability of our mobile main-force units was superior to that of the enemy's."[15]

The reason, according to the same North Vietnamese general, was that great quantities of "tanks, armored cars, rockets, long-range artillery, and anti-aircraft guns" (all, of course, prohibited by the Paris Agreement) had been sent south. This was made possible by the extraordinary network of roads which, in the vivid words of Dung, were like "strong ropes inching gradually, day by day, around the neck, arms and legs of a demon, awaiting the order to jerk tight and bring the creature's life to an end."[16]

While South Vietnam was being gradually strangled, Washington was distracted by its divisions. Above all, Washington had grown tired of Vietnam.

New impetus came when the overwhelming Democratic victory in the 1974 election brought a group of congressional freshmen to Washington who, in the words of *The Almanac of American Politics, 1978,* represented a political realm "in which opposition to the Vietnam War was the most compelling source of motivation."[17] Only two years earlier, in the presidential election of 1972, George McGovern had been overwhelmed by the second largest landslide in American history over the issue of Vietnam. In the congressional elections of 1974, his erstwhile supporters prevailed on the issue of Watergate and emerged in a position to reverse the voters' earlier verdict on Vietnam.

So it happened that, as South Vietnam was approaching its final agony, Washington was debating by how much to cut aid and what pressure was needed to speed Saigon toward "democratization." Our intelligence agencies had no illusions. As early as May 23, 1974, a National Intelligence Estimate warned that if North Vietnam committed a substantial part of its strategic reserve:

> [The South Vietnamese forces] might be unable to regain the initiative, and it would be questionable whether the GVN [Saigon government] would be able to survive without combat participation by US Air Force and Navy units.
>
> At a minimum, large-scale US logistic support would be required to stop the Communist drive.

A report from the State Department Bureau of Intelligence and Research dated November 1, 1974, concluded that, if budgetary trends were not reversed, the Thieu government might well collapse:

> Its supplies are being drawn down to a point where emergency replenishment attempts, should they be needed to meet major NVA/VC [North Vietnamese army/Vietcong] attacks during 1975, could be too late to avert serious reverses. . . .
> . . . The Communists see the US as increasingly distracted by the overall world economic-energy-food crisis and reportedly view President Ford's ability to help the GVN as severely limited because of his need and desire to maintain good relations with Congress.

Hanoi's pitiless calculators had drawn the same conclusion. Closely analyzing the impact of every new reduction in American aid, the authoritative theoretical journal of the North Vietnamese Communist Party, *Hoc Tap*, spelled it out in January 1975:

> The intensity of firepower and the amount of mobile equipment of the puppet troops [Saigon] have markedly decreased. In the third quarter of 1974, the monthly number of artillery rounds fired by the puppet troops decreased approximately by three-fourths, compared with the monthly number in 1973. The number of daily tactical sorties of the puppet air force only equaled approximately one-fifth of those conducted in 1972. The present number of aircraft in the South, compared with the greatest number of aircraft on hand in the period of the limited war, has decreased by 70 percent, with the number of helicopters decreasing by 80 percent. . . . The bomb and ammunition reserves of the puppet troops have decreased and they are encountering great difficulties in fuel and in the maintenance, repair and use of various types of aircraft, tanks, combat vessels and heavy weapons.

Largely because of our neglect and indifference, the time for new Communist offensive operations had arrived.

Hanoi's determination to step up pressures received a boost from an apparent change in Soviet attitudes. In late December 1974, a high-ranking Soviet official visited Hanoi for the first time since the signing of the Paris Agreement. It turned out to be anything but a courtesy call. The chief of the Soviet General Staff, Viktor Kulikov, came to participate in the Politburo strategic discussions then under way (the last similar visit had been in 1971 prior to the 1972 offensive).

Memoirs have yet to recount the gist of the Soviet advice, but it seems clear that some previous restraints were lifted; Soviet shipments of military matériel increased fourfold in the months that followed. Until Soviet archives are opened, we cannot know the Soviet motive—whether it was aimed at China, was a reaction to the congressional attacks on the trade bill and Vladivostok, or whether it had been part of Soviet strategy all along. Whatever the answer, there is little doubt that Moscow was now encouraging Hanoi's bellicosity.

The only remaining element of uncertainty for Hanoi was the attitude of the United States. According to General Dung's account, Le Duan, the party's general secretary, concluded in October 1974 that "the internal contradictions within the United States administration and between the American political parties, too, were growing sharper. The Watergate affair had agitated the whole country. . . . American aid to the Saigon quisling administration was on the decline" to the point that the United States "cannot rescue the Saigon administration from its disastrous collapse." The 1975 offensives would test this judgment. While there are disagreements among the North Vietnamese military leaders who have written memoirs (largely over who gets credit for the winning strategy), they all agree on this central point: the offensives planned for 1975 were expected to be only a prelude to final victory in 1976 or even 1977. The American reaction to these offensives—or lack of it—would be a crucial test of how they would then proceed.[18]

The tone of communications from my longtime interlocutor, Le Duc Tho, was always a good indicator of the level of the confidence of Hanoi's Politburo. Nixon's resignation, coupled with congressional budget cuts for Vietnam, produced communications of an arrogance which suggested that Hanoi was feeling the wind at its back. On August 19, 1974, I used the occasion of Ford's recent inauguration to send a message warning against treating the transition as a military opportunity and expressing our desire for improved relations with Hanoi:

> President Ford, as you must be aware, has been a firm supporter of President Nixon's policy in Indochina for five and one-half years. In the spirit of mutual respect and candor which has always characterized our exchanges, Mr. Special Advisor, I must convey to you that President Ford is a man with a keen sense of American honor. He also shares the view, as we all do on the American side, that the DRV [North Vietnam] has a positive path open to it—of peaceful settlement, reconstruction, constructive ties with the United States and the western world, and a truly independent role in world affairs. The President is ready to engage with you on this path.

In an insolent reply on August 25, Le Duc Tho not only took credit for bringing about Nixon's resignation but threatened Ford with a similar fate:

> Mr. Nixon met with failure in the enterprise and had to leave the White House. Should Mr. Ford continue doing so, he would certainly and inevitably fail too.

After accusing me of betraying my "signature and my commitment" —a charge one makes in diplomacy only if one expects to prevail with no need for further negotiations—Le Duc Tho concluded on this ominous note:

> In case the US continues the implementation of the Nixon Doctrine without Nixon and the use of the Nguyen Van Thieu group to pursue the war and to undermine the Paris Agreement on Vietnam, then the Vietnamese people will resolutely carry on their struggle to defend peace and the Paris Agreement until complete victory.

While Hanoi opted for military victory, Washington was waffling over whether even the aid package of $700 million—which, as noted, in real terms amounted to a reduction by three quarters of the first peacetime year—might be too high. When Ford appealed to Senator Stennis for a restoration of the $300 million that had been cut from the military assistance budget, this staunch friend of the Pentagon and anything but a dove replied:

> I said if 700 million [for Vietnam] wasn't enough I would work for more. But I was getting information from some military people that we could cut down, and I wanted you to send someone out there to appraise it.

Thankfully there were a few, albeit at a relatively low level, who managed to rise above the prism of the Beltway. On December 20, 1974, James R. Bullington, the State Department's Vietnam desk officer, wrote a moving and extraordinarily prescient report after a visit to Saigon. He pointed out that even a supplemental of $300 million would only just barely cover expenditures for consumables and would leave no funds for replacements. A minimum of $1.3 billion would be needed for the same purpose in 1976. By then, the replacement of damaged and destroyed equipment could no longer be delayed, implying the need for an additional—and substantial—financial request. Interspersing his report with human interest vignettes of the growing despair among South Vietnamese, Bullington concluded that, without the supplemental, South Vietnam's position was hopeless. We had reached the point where, if the supplemental failed to materialize, only one option would be left to mitigate our country's dishonor—to save as many Vietnamese as possible:

> If the supplemental fails, we should also consider ways and means of saving as many anti-Communist South Vietnamese as possible. For example, do we not have a certain obligation to those many thousands of Vietnamese and their families who are present or former employees of the USG? To fail to help such people escape would, I believe, add considerable dishonor to our defeat in South Vietnam.

On December 30, 1974, in Vail, Colorado, Ford reluctantly signed the Foreign Assistance Act and coupled it with a strong objection to the deep cuts in aid for Vietnam it contained (made even more onerous by many legislative limitations on the use of the aid). The survival of Vietnam now depended on our ability to obtain the supplemental appropriation promised by the congressional leadership.

## Hanoi Resumes the Offensive

One of the nightmarish aspects of the Vietnam tragedy was that debates about it had the feel of religious rituals: they were their own end; they required no relationship to observable reality. Thus, in Washington, the fateful year began as if nothing extraordinary were happening in Indochina even though Hanoi had just run through a dress rehearsal of its options by launching the first of the limited offensives ordered by the Politburo. In mid-December, it initiated a series of sharp attacks throughout the southern provinces of South Vietnam. On January 7, 1975, Communist forces overran Phuoc Binh, capital of Phuoc Long province, the first provincial capital in the entire war to have been lost and never retaken by Saigon. While the offensive was under way, the Hanoi Politburo met to assess its results and chart its strategy. Phuoc Binh was the test case.[19] If the United States reacted, there was still a chance for Hanoi to withdraw from the brink.

But Washington was determined to withhold funds from an ally when the knife was at its throat even though the impact on other threatened countries associated with the United States was potentially demoralizing. I warned repeatedly at press conferences, before Congress, and to my staff of the danger to our national interest—for example, on January 3, to the top officials of the State Department:

> We have to defend the national interest. There is nothing else we can do. In this congressional session we are not going to go around wringing our hands. We are going to say what we think the national interest is. And if we take a little heat from the Congress, we will take it. Let the Congress go against it. If we start compromising and we start dancing around, we are already lost.

Congress was not ready to act quickly, to say the least. Thus the issue came down to whether other measures might be available to resist the Phuoc Long move. The previous pattern repeated itself. There had been little enough enthusiasm for a supplemental; there was now even less for other forms of assistance. Fortunately, there was at least one person in the executive branch who shared my basic view, and he happened to be the President of the United States. Under pressure from the media, urged by his immediate staff to dissociate from Vietnam (and me), disavowed by many of his former congressional colleagues, Ford remained steadfast and calm. Before every interdepartmental meeting, I would check with him to make sure I was reflecting his views, as I did on January 7 before the WSAG meeting to deal with the Phuoc Long offensive. The President's response was brief and decisive:

> KISSINGER: We are having a WSAG on Vietnam. I plan to
> take a tough line. I assume you are prepared to ask for
> a supplemental.
> FORD: By all means.

And again, on January 8, when I asked Ford about the military measures discussed at the WSAG meeting, he replied: "I think we should do it."

Unfortunately, the cupboard was bare indeed when the discussion turned to measures to show Hanoi that we viewed its actions with increasing gravity. The State Department checklist was far more likely to demonstrate our impotence than it was to give Hanoi pause. It included such frightening measures as appeals to Moscow, Beijing, and to the U.N. Security Council (in which, of course, both Beijing and Moscow had vetoes), and protesting to the eleven other parties and countries that had signed on as guarantors of the Paris Peace Agreement at the March 2, 1973, International Conference on Vietnam.*

None of these measures offered the slightest prospect of averting the looming North Vietnamese offensive and South Vietnamese debacle. We did send a circular dispatch to non-Vietnamese participants in the International Conference on Vietnam as well as to the four mem-

---

* There were twelve participants: United States, France, China, United Kingdom, Canada, Soviet Union, Hungary, Poland, Indonesia, Democratic Republic of Vietnam (DRV, i.e., North Vietnam), Republic of Vietnam (GVN, i.e., South Vietnam), and Provisional Revolutionary Government of the Republic of South Vietnam (PRG, i.e., the South Vietnamese Communists).

bers of the International Commission of Control and Supervision (Canada, Hungary, Poland, and Indonesia). This elicited a few evasive replies but mostly silence—which I would feel better about if I could describe it as embarrassed.

I had learned from experience that Hanoi would pay attention only to measures which, in its view, might affect the situation on the ground. We now know from memoirs how carefully its leaders were studying every American military and political move. The administration had no intention of violating the congressional prohibitions against direct American military involvement. But given Hanoi's near paranoid suspiciousness, there was a slight chance that moving some of our forces closer to Indochina might cause Hanoi to take a second look. The Defense Department provided a checklist of permitted possibilities:

- increasing reconnaissance activity over North Vietnam;
- having the aircraft carrier *Enterprise,* which was scheduled to move to the Indian Ocean from Subic Bay in the Philippines, detour slightly via the Gulf of Tonkin;
- redeploying F-4 fighter planes to the Philippines and Thailand and B-52s from the United States to Guam.

I favored all these proposals, arguing: "It has been my experience that when we move timidly, we lose. When we are bold, we are successful."

The WSAG accepted my recommendations, and Ford approved the entire checklist. But before any deployments could be implemented, the Defense Department recoiled in the face of the probable congressional and media assaults. The Pentagon's annual congressional budget battle was coming up—this time with a new McGovernite Congress—and the Pentagon was in no mood to expend any more capital on Vietnam. It either dragged its feet on implementing the WSAG recommendations or shifted the onus for them to the State Department. As expected, Hanoi protested the increase in reconnaissance flights as a violation of the Paris Agreement, every single provision of which it had been flagrantly violating for months. The media and Congress instantly clamored for clarification, whereupon the Pentagon announced that the State Department would do the briefing—thus passing the buck and implying that the Pentagon was washing its hands of the entire project. In the end, Schlesinger stepped up and, on January 14, 1975, undertook a strong defense of the reconnaissance flights. By then, Hanoi had learned what it needed to know: that our response was the maximum we were capable of doing and not the opening maneuver of determined resistance.

The deployment of a carrier group into the Gulf of Tonkin never took place. The *Enterprise* had barely left Subic Bay on the way to the Indian Ocean—and before the orders for diversion to the Gulf of Tonkin had even been received—when Hanoi started to beat the propaganda drums, claiming American provocation. By now we were quite familiar with the characteristic North Vietnamese tactic: Hanoi would blackmail us into reassuring them regarding measures they actually feared, then use the reassurance to demonstrate our impotence to the South Vietnamese. The Pentagon was so concerned about avoiding congressional wrath—and so reluctant to testify about its measures— that it ordered the *Enterprise* to proceed on its original course. Not until the *Enterprise* had traversed the Strait of Malacca did the White House learn that there had been a change of signals (not authorized by it). By then, of course, turning the carrier around would have magnified the firestorm.

The Defense Department offered to substitute another carrier— the *Coral Sea*—for the Gulf of Tonkin mission. But it was clear that we had lost the ability to move carriers in Southeast Asia without debilitating controversy. Deprived of serious military options even for diplomatic maneuver, I urged Ford on January 13 to reverse all other redeployments:

> I still think the moves in Southeast Asia are right, but Defense is so opposed to them that they would leak them and cause us an enormous problem with the Hill. Then you would have to say a thousand ways what you would *not* do. This is the worst way to deal with the North Vietnamese.

Even the White House staff was infected by the prevailing mood of abdication. Several of the new President's friends were urging two fantasies, already noted: that they could somehow get Ford credit for ending the Vietnam War; at a minimum, they sought to "protect" their

President from too close an association with the looming disaster. Neither option really existed. "Credit" for ending the Vietnam War was not to be gained by consigning those who had relied on us to a tragic end. Nor was there any way for Ford to avoid playing the hand which fate had dealt him, however unfairly. To the President's everlasting credit—in the way history and not contemporaries measures credit—he never succumbed to the temptation of believing that there was an easy way out; he remained firm in the refusal to dishonor his office by colluding with Hanoi in the destruction of our ally.

The attitude of the newly arrived White House staff was epitomized by Ron Nessen, who had been brought in as press secretary after Ford's first choice resigned over his pardon of Nixon. In his memoirs, Nessen describes a wonderful "fantasy" of his, according to which he would one day announce the end of the Vietnam War. He then proudly recounts his determination to *prevent* the White House from sending any message to the North Vietnamese by means of his daily briefings:

> He [the NSC staffer responsible for press guidance] wanted to scare the North Vietnamese a little, or at least leave them guessing about American intentions. I replied that I didn't think Hanoi devised its strategy according to my answers. . . .
>
> . . . I promised myself I would resist NSC efforts to use my press briefings to frighten North Vietnam, because such threats also could needlessly alarm the American people.[20]

With this attitude, it is not surprising that official Washington press briefings failed to exude determination or even recognition that a significant Communist assault was taking place. On January 7—the day the provincial capital of Phuoc Long fell—the Defense Department spokesman firmly denied that the increased level of Communist military activity constituted "the start of a major country-wide offensive." On the same day, Nessen emphatically disclaimed any intention on the part of the administration to circumvent the ban on American combat in Indochina.[21]

Despite Nessen's belief to the contrary, the North Vietnamese *were* watching. According to two North Vietnamese military sources, Premier Pham Van Dong wisecracked to a Politburo meeting at the end of 1974 that Washington was so paralyzed that "even if we offered the Americans a bribe to intervene again, they would not accept it." Thus he concluded that the campaign in the South should resume.[22] Another North Vietnamese source reports the similar conclusion of Hanoi Communist leader Le Duan, who persuaded the Politburo that, in view of the "weakening position of the enemy," Hanoi's original plan for a two-year campaign for 1975–76 should be modified to include another option: to seize "the opportune moment" to "win" and "immediately liberate the South in 1975."[23]

## *The End of the Road*

Our sole remaining card to prevent Saigon's collapse was the supplemental appropriation. Without it, everybody agreed, South Vietnam was doomed. But if the supplemental was delayed very much longer, it would be too late to reverse the slide toward disaster.

Of course, no one had any idea whether the figure of $300 million would be adequate.

A money bill has to pass through two stages in each house of Congress: authorization, followed by the actual appropriations. These decisions were handled by separate committees, required separate testimony, and were subject to separate votes. The Appropriations Committee could not exceed the authorized amount, only reduce it. It might later restore its cuts up to the authorized limit; that additional sum is called a supplemental appropriation. If the administration wanted a larger increase, it had to ask the Armed Services Committee for a new authorization.

The bureaucracy fastened on the $300 million figure primarily because it would avoid the authorization process. In fact, there was no reasonable basis for it. We had requested $1.4 billion (a reduction of $700 million from the level of the previous year); the Armed Services Committee had authorized $1 billion; and the Appropriations Committee had reduced the amount by another $300 million. It was this last cut we were now seeking to restore. Reluctant to start the entire authorization process over again, the Pentagon declared the $300 million to be precisely what was needed. I told a State Department staff meeting on January 20, 1975:

I simply call attention to the amazing coincidence that a figure that corresponds to nothing that anyone ever asked for, and that emerged by accident out of the authorization process at a quiet time should be exactly the figure you need at a period [of increased warfare].

Thieu, by now desperate, appealed to Ford in two letters dated January 24 and 25. He protested the capture of Phuoc Binh as "certainly the most massive and the most blatant violation of the Paris Agreement." He described the intensity of the North Vietnamese attacks, backed by the "massive application of fire power and armor." By contrast, the South Vietnamese troops "had to count every single shell they fired in order to make the ammunition last." Thieu pointedly reminded Ford of the assurances of continued American aid which had induced him to sign the Paris Agreement.

The letters triggered Ford's decision to overrule the White House staff, which had opposed the supplemental. He launched his effort in a televised interview with John Chancellor and Tom Brokaw on January 23, continued it at a meeting with congressional leaders on January 28, and culminated it with firm instructions to the Cabinet on January 29. The request to Congress provided grim details of the North Vietnamese buildup and the South Vietnamese shortfalls. Ford reminded Congress:

> We told the South Vietnamese, in effect, that we would not defend them with our military forces, but that we would provide them the means to defend themselves, as permitted by the Agreement. The South Vietnamese have performed effectively in accepting this challenge.

And he appealed to the Cabinet to close ranks:

> Yesterday I sent up an Indochina supplemental. I want it clearly understood that this Administration is clearly, firmly, unequivocally behind that. We want it, we are going to fight for it, and I want everyone behind it. I think it is vital and right, and I want no misunderstanding about that.

I weighed in with the congressional leadership on January 28:

The press is talking about new commitments; we are talking about keeping an old commitment. If we are not going to do enough, there is a question of whether we should do anything at all. No case can be made for giving less than adequate aid and aid that Congress has already authorized. Do we want to risk the failure of all that was done, at a sacrifice of 55,000 men and blood and treasure for want of enough money to enable them to defend themselves?

. . . The overwhelming objective of the national debate was to disengage our military forces and return our prisoners. There was no objection to the principle of supporting a government that was prepared to defend itself by its own efforts. They are now defending themselves. The South Vietnamese agreed to go it alone on the basis that we could give them the wherewithal to do it. They have a chance to defend themselves. That chance exists. That chance depends on American assistance.

It was to no avail; Congress was beyond being moved by such appeals. Senate Majority Leader Mike Mansfield explained that he would vote against the supplemental because "our friends are in this country, not in Southeast Asia or the Middle East." Speaker Carl Albert, usually a strong supporter of administration policy, did not even pretend that his decision had any substantive basis: "I won't say what I will do, but when all your fellows are against you, what can you do?" Senate Minority Leader Hugh Scott made a valiant effort to support the President, but the bulk of commentary ranged from hostile to fence-sitting.

The favorite theme of those who opposed the supplemental was that the administration should seek political rather than military solutions. But the aging revolutionaries in Hanoi had nothing but contempt for the proposition that diplomacy was somehow separable from strategy. They were not to be deprived of their ultimate victory by diplomatic sleights of hand or academic theories of conflict resolution. If we could not influence the situation on the ground, we stood no chance of making any impact on Hanoi via diplomacy.

Most of the domestic attacks came from by now familiar quarters. But to our immense surprise and huge disappointment, the cause of Vietnam was abandoned by Senator Henry Jackson, scourge of détente and Ford Administration critic for its alleged softness on Communism.

With his own presidential candidacy looming and primaries in New York and California on the horizon, Jackson decided to throw in the towel. Announcing his opposition to the supplemental, he stated:

> I voted to cut that $300 million last year and I am not going to vote to hand it back this year. There has to be a limit. There has to be a ceiling. There has to be an end. The problems of Southeast Asia are not going to be solved by $300 million more in ammunition.[24]

When even the traditional anti-Communist sentinels abandoned Indochina, the chasm between the views of the administration and Congress became too deep to be bridged. For the supplemental to have any impact on the ground in Vietnam, it needed to be passed by March so that the money for consumables could be made available immediately. The longer the delay, the more the South Vietnamese army, demoralized by shortages in fuel and ammunition and the mounting casualties, ran the risk of disintegration.

In these circumstances, the issue before Thieu was no longer how to defend his country but what he could afford to give up. Yet every redeployment into presumably more defensible areas only increased Hanoi's incentive to step up its attacks and to try for a knockout. In February, still waiting for the supplemental, Thieu decided to move his crack airborne units from the Central Highlands to Da Nang along the coast. That move settled the issue for Hanoi and triggered an all-out attack. The Army Chief of Staff, General Van Tien Dung, took over as its field commander in the South. According to Dung's memoirs, the plan was to fight in the Central Highlands through the dry season of 1975 and then move to the area near Saigon for the following year.[25]

Hanoi's burgeoning confidence produced a new political offer. It was hailed immediately as "moderate" by the peace movement but sounded all too familiar to us veterans of the negotiations. It was the old standby of an "end to United States involvement and interference and the formation in Saigon of a new administration that will implement the Paris Agreement." Three years earlier, I had asked Le Duc Tho what he meant by that sacramental phraseology. He had suggested a simple remedy: the assassination of Thieu. He seemed incapable of understanding why his proposal should have outraged me.

In the meantime, since Congress exhibited no urgency about re-

sponding to Ford's request for a supplemental, Hanoi became convinced that it did not need even the pretense of a political solution.
Indeed, South Vietnam's reverses, far from spurring Congress to action, set up another vicious cycle: the more Congress dissociated itself
from Vietnam, the more a demoralized Saigon retreated; the weaker
Saigon appeared, the more the congressional opposition insisted on
the need to "end the war"—its euphemism for strangling our allies.

Sir Robert Thompson, the British expert on counterinsurgency,
visited South Vietnam in February and reported to President Ford
that, if Hanoi became sufficiently emboldened to commit its reserve
divisions just north of the demarcation line (DMZ) dividing South
from North Vietnam:

> ARVN [the South Vietnamese army] would lose at least the
> airborne, marine, 1 and 3 divisions and would collapse. The
> war would be over. . . . The whole issue hinges on the re-
> straints and sanctions still operating on Hanoi. . . . The de-
> cision rests in part with the Congress and the American
> people. . . . It [Saigon] is ready to continue fighting and,
> given the minimum of support sufficient to encourage its
> people and to deter Hanoi, to hold out successfully so that
> the long American involvement can be ended. But, if the
> support is not forthcoming, South Vietnam will go down
> fighting to the eternal disgrace of the United States.

The trouble was that the most vocal groups within Congress and
the media—the ones setting the terms of the debate and fiercely denouncing an opposing view—thought the opposite: they saw disgrace
in having any association, even financial ties, with our allies in Saigon.
The protest movement reached its ultimate position: a campaign to
deprive non-Communist Vietnam (and Laos and Cambodia) of the
means of resistance. That point of view was epitomized in an editorial
in the *Los Angeles Times* of March 6, 1975, urging not only the
rejection of the proposed supplemental but drastic *cuts* in military
assistance to well below the $700 million level already approved:

> The key element must be to set the level of military aid to
> South Vietnam so that it serves as an incentive for political
> movement, compromise and concession by Nguyen Van

Thieu, and not as encouragement for him to consolidate his personal rule.[26]

Congress retreated into procrastination. Hearings consumed the better part of February, during which the North Vietnamese offensive rolled on. At that point, Senator Humphrey came up with the idea of a bipartisan congressional fact-finding mission to Vietnam on the theory that it would learn enough to support a responsible assistance program (and, in the process, waste some more time). Ford accepted Humphrey's proposal only reluctantly. He feared that none of the senior Senators Humphrey had proposed would be willing to identify themselves with so controversial a mission, while junior members would neither carry the necessary weight nor be prepared to risk the certain media assault.

Ford's misgivings were borne out by events. The Senate leadership refused to endorse the project, and senior Senators refused to go when the White House tried to organize the trip on its own. After weeks of discussion, only one Senator—Dewey Bartlett from Oklahoma, with a reputation as a maverick—and seven Representatives embarked on the trip, none from the leadership of either house. The Representatives included Bella Abzug, a protest movement activist; Paul McCloskey, long an opponent of an American role in Indochina; and Donald M. Fraser, former head of the liberal advocacy group Americans for Democratic Action. Not surprisingly, the congressional delegation accomplished nothing except to waste a few weeks during which Vietnam descended into catastrophe.

Senator Frank Church from Idaho, who had a long history of opposition to America's Indochina policy, took Ford up on a compromise suggestion the President had made in an interview with the *Chicago Tribune:* a terminal grant of two to three years, after which South Vietnam would be on its own. I did not like the idea of a terminal grant because it made it seem as if our assistance to Vietnam was an act of charity rather than of policy. I did not see how we could in good conscience ask of South Vietnam, under all-out attack, what we had never asked of far less threatened allies. And I feared the inevitable haggling over an appropriate amount and the reality that one Congress cannot bind its successor. But our ambassador in Saigon, Graham Martin, favored a terminal grant to gain time, and Ford had embraced the idea. In the end, I reluctantly supported a terminal grant in a press conference, as a "second-best choice."

As soon as we had accepted the principle, the terminal grant was turned into another device for cutting off Saigon from all aid. We were thinking in terms of several billion dollars; Church offered a one-time grant of at most $750 million—less than half of what we thought was needed for one year. And to obtain even that would require that the entire budgetary process start all over, which would take months. By then, it was the end of March, and events proceeded toward tragedy on their own momentum.

# 16

# THE COLLAPSE OF CAMBODIA

No country suffered more as a result of the Indochina conflict than the verdant land of the Khmer. Once the center of a great civilization radiating throughout all of Southeast Asia, the Khmer have been pushed back over centuries into their present borders. The grandiose ruins of their ancient capital, Angkor Wat, remain as a testament both to their ancient creativity and to the fragility of human aspirations.

We do not know precisely who governed in Angkor Wat or why and how the empire collapsed. Is it possible that this seemingly peaceful, almost pacifist society periodically lapses into self-destructive blood lusts? What we do know is that the Khmer Rouge ("Red Khmer") celebrated their victory in the Cambodian civil war by murdering between 1 and 2 million of their fellow citizens (between 15 and 30 percent of the population).

The United States became involved in Cambodia only reluctantly. For nearly a decade, successive American administrations had refused to recognize that, for Hanoi, all of Indochina represented a single battlefield. "Indochina is a strategic unit, a single theater of operations," General Vo Nguyen Giap declared as early as 1950. "Therefore we have the task of helping to liberate all of Indochina."[1] After the Laos settlement of 1962, the North Vietnamese ignored their pledge to respect Laos's neutrality and opened a supply line (the Ho Chi Minh Trail) through Laos and Cambodia to as far south as the Mekong Delta area of South Vietnam. When they introduced regular combat troops from North Vietnam, they occupied the part of Cambodia along the South Vietnamese border and turned it into a military base area, expelling the sparse local population. Four North Vietnamese divisions operated from there into South Vietnam. After killing scores of Americans each month and inflicting casualties and destruction, they would return to Cambodia, brazenly using the neutral status of their unwilling host to legitimize their sanctuaries. A flagrant violation of international law became the cover for invoking international law to protect the bases. Amazingly, the Kennedy and Johnson Administrations which committed us to ground warfare in Indochina fell in with the charade that the killers of thousands of Americans should be protected by the technicality of operating from the sovereign soil of a neutral country.

This background is essential to understanding the actions of the Nixon Administration with respect to Cambodia, beginning with the so-called "secret bombing." Literature on this has achieved a near-liturgical quality, not often related to the facts actually bearing on our decisions. I have dealt with the issues elsewhere in detail, but let me summarize them briefly here.[2]

The "secret bombing" was Nixon's reaction to a North Vietnamese offensive (the "mini-Tet"), launched two weeks after he assumed office. We were barely organized and had not yet taken any initiative on Vietnam policy for good or ill. Many of the attacks—if not the majority—were launched from Cambodian bases. After four weeks of this and over 1,000 American casualties, Nixon retaliated, starting in March 1969 by bombing a border zone 10 kilometers (six miles) wide where the sanctuaries were located. Prince Sihanouk, the Cambodian chief of state, had all but invited these American attacks the year before, both publicly and in remarks to Johnson Administration emissaries. He implied that he would ignore such attacks because the Cambodian population had been expelled by the North Vietnamese.

However one evaluates these decisions, to repeat the canard that they were unprovoked violations of Cambodian neutrality—as some critics have done—is a distortion of history.[3] We had originally planned to react to an expected Sihanouk protest by asking for a UN investigation of the sanctuaries, thereby admitting the bombings. But Sihanouk did not protest and even invited Nixon to Phnom Penh while the bombing was going on. Key members of Congress were briefed, including the chairmen of the Armed Services and Appropriations Committees, the Speaker—all of them Democrats—and other congressional leaders. I recall no objections nor any urging to widen the circle of those privy to the information.

Finally, the bombing was not even so secret. Journalists repeatedly asked Sihanouk to comment on reports of American attacks. His typical response was to repeat what he had said to the emissaries of our predecessors. For example, on May 13, 1969, two months after the "secret" bombings began, Sihanouk replied to a journalist by all but confirming the bombings and denying any loss of civilian life:

> Cambodia only protests against the destruction of the property and lives of Cambodians. All I can say is that I cannot make a protest as long as I am not informed. But I will protest if there is any destruction of Khmer [Cambodian] life and property.
> Here it is—the first report about several B-52 bombings. Yet I have not been informed about that at all, because I have not lost any houses, any countrymen, nothing, nothing. Nobody was caught in those barrages—nobody, no Cambodians.

And on August 22, 1969, Sihanouk told visiting Senator Mike Mansfield (according to a reporting cable):

> There were no Cambodian protests of bombings in his country when these hit only VCs [Vietcong] and not Cambodian villages or population. He declared that much of his information regarding US bombings of uninhabited regions of Cambodia came from US press and magazine statements. He strongly requested the avoidance of incidents involving Cambodian lives.

In March 1970, Sihanouk was deposed by the joint action of his own parliament and the very government he had appointed headed by Prime Minister Lon Nol. The reasons for the coup were largely connected with internal Cambodian politics. The United States had had no connection with it nor any foreknowledge (indeed, our first reaction was to interpret events in Phnom Penh as a complicated maneuver by Sihanouk). When the new government insisted on the withdrawal of all North Vietnamese troops from Cambodian territory, Hanoi reacted by increasing its blatant and menacing violations of Cambodian neutrality. Its forces left the sanctuaries, pushed deep into Cambodia, and threatened to take over the country.

To prevent Hanoi from opening South Vietnam's entire frontier to Communist infiltration and threatening American troops during our withdrawals, which had reached 150,000 a year, Nixon ordered American ground forces to destroy the North Vietnamese base areas. In an operation lasting two months, 20,000 tons of Communist weapons, vehicles, ammunition, facilities, and other supplies were destroyed, and the port of Sihanoukville, through which many supplies had reached the sanctuaries, was closed to North Vietnam. In the aftermath, the intensity of the war in the southern half of South Vietnam diminished dramatically; most importantly, American casualties immediately dropped by over 50 percent within two months and continued to decline for the remainder of the war.

Nixon limited the American operation to thirty kilometers and withdrew American troops from Cambodia after two months—perhaps the only time he blinked in the face of the radical protesters. In the aftermath, Hanoi stepped up arms to the indigenous Communists (the Khmer Rouge). By early 1973, a stalemate had developed in which the larger Communist ground forces were to some extent balanced by the superior firepower of the Cambodian army, equipped with American weapons and buttressed by American airpower. In June 1973, Congress destroyed this equilibrium by prohibiting American military support and, in March 1975, cut off all economic and military assistance to Cambodia.

I have already presented elsewhere in great detail my own role in the decisions summarized above.[4] Much later, perhaps because Cambodia was the one country in Indochina in which America's military involvement was not initiated by the Kennedy and Johnson Administrations, the so-called secret bombing, tacitly endorsed by its government, of an essentially uninhabited territory, and the later effort to buttress the successors to Sihanouk openly, were blamed for all the tragedies that befell Cambodia, including Pol Pot's genocide. This bizarre expression of self-hatred makes as much sense as blaming Hitler's Holocaust on the British bombing of Hamburg.

Whatever one's judgment as to the wisdom of individual American policies, the truth is that Cambodia was taken over by a homicidal clique primarily because Americans subordinated the country's survival to their own domestic drama. Once the war had spread to Cambodia by Hanoi's actions, our only honorable exit was either victory or, at worst, a compromise political settlement in which the non-Communist (probably anti-Communist) population would have the opportunity to determine its own political fate. Instead Cambodia became another victim of America's ideological civil war.

In a news conference on November 12, 1971, Nixon had called Cambodia "the Nixon Doctrine in its purest form." By this, he meant that it would be put in a position to defend itself with American financial assistance and military matériel but without American manpower. Nixon's opponents were determined to prevent this proposition from being proved valid, for they feared that the Nixon Doctrine would lure the United States into adventures which would tempt escalation and ultimately intervention. Thus they set about hemming in assistance to Cambodia with legislative restrictions which would render success impossible and make the ultimate collapse of Cambodia all but inevitable:

- The Fulbright Amendment to the Armed Forces Appropriation Authorization for FY 1971, passed on October 7, 1970, specified that South Vietnam and other allied countries could not use their funds for military support or assistance to Cambodia. It also prohibited South Vietnam and other allied countries such as Thailand from transferring military supplies furnished under the act to Cambodia. In other words, Cambodia's neighbors were prohibited from improving their own security by assisting Cambodia with American equipment, the only equipment they had.
- The Cooper-Church Amendment to the Supplementary Foreign Assistance Act of 1970, passed on January 5, 1971, prohibited the use of American funds for financing "the introduction of US ground combat troops into Cambodia, or to provide US advisers." Not only were American combat troops prohibited, but American advisers were barred from training or instructing Cambodian units on the use of the American equipment we were supplying.
- The Symington-Case Amendment to the Substitute Foreign Assistance Act and Related Assistance Act, passed on February 7, 1972, placed severe restrictions on civilians serving in Cambodia. It limited the total number of "civilian officers and employees of executive agencies of the US Government who are US citizens" to two hundred and the number of third-country nationals to eighty-five.
- The Second Supplemental Appropriations Act for FY 1973, signed reluctantly into law by President Nixon on July 1, 1973, prohibited the use of funds appropriated in the act to "support directly or indirectly combat activities in or over Cambodia, Laos, North Viet-

nam, and South Vietnam or off the shores of Cambodia, Laos, North Vietnam, South Vietnam."

- The Continuing Appropriations Act for FY 1974, likewise signed into law on July 1, 1973, prohibited the use of any funds to finance directly or indirectly combat activities by U.S. forces "in or over or from off the shores of North Vietnam, South Vietnam, Laos, or Cambodia."
- The Foreign Assistance Act of 1973, which became law on December 17, 1973, provided that no funds authorized or appropriated under any of its provisions would be available to finance military or paramilitary combat operations by foreign forces in Laos, Cambodia, North Vietnam, South Vietnam, or Thailand.

Congress, which had been voting yearly appropriations for Vietnam, acted as if successive American Presidents had sneaked into the country by subterfuge. And, by God, it was going to prevent this imaginary sequence being repeated in Cambodia, even by countries allied to the United States and even if it meant destroying Cambodia in the process. The effect of congressional restrictions was to impose an unbearable, almost vindictive constraint both on the scale of American assistance to impoverished Cambodia and on the flexibility with which Cambodia could use it, even to the extent of banning training and matériel aid from neighboring friendly countries.

By 1974, an overall ceiling of $377 million in aid to Cambodia had been established, and every individual expenditure was being counted against this total. As a result, food or economic aid could not be provided without reducing military expenditures and vice versa. Restrictions such as these had enabled the Khmer Rouge to survive when they were still embryonic and gradually turned the tide in their favor once they gained strength. Brigadier General William W. Palmer, chief of the Military Equipment Delivery Team in Cambodia (MEDTC), described in his final report how this led to the cumulative strangulation of the Cambodian military effort: restrictions on American training produced excessive reliance on American airpower; when this was banned by Congress, Cambodian artillery and tactical airpower became crucial, though we had not been permitted to train the Cambodians in the field on how to use them. In the end, even purely Cambodian defense efforts were choked off by escalating munitions costs due to inflation and reduced funding.

In the face of these restrictions, the Cambodian army did manage to resist the Khmer Rouge dry season offensive in 1973 (with the help of American airpower). It did so again in 1974, this time entirely with its own forces, in part due to Hanoi's ambivalent attitude toward the Khmer Rouge. Hanoi was willing to use the Khmer Rouge to expel the last vestige of American influence from Indochina. But it distrusted the movement's passionate nationalism, suspecting that it would be turned against Vietnam in the wake of a complete victory.

Hanoi therefore kept the Khmer Rouge on a short leash for the first eighteen months after the cease-fire. In the fall of 1974, however, it changed course and poured in weapons and ammunition—perhaps as part of its own general offensive, perhaps because it had decided that congressional shortfalls had doomed the Lon Nol government and there was no point in antagonizing the Khmer Rouge.

In a countrywide offensive beginning on January 1, 1975, the Khmer Rouge cut the Mekong River supply line to Phnom Penh. The combined result of increased combat activity and congressional ceilings was that the Cambodian army began to run out of ammunition. At the existing rate of expenditures, its stockpiles would not last beyond March. On January 28, Ford therefore asked Congress to lift the ceiling of $200 million for military assistance to Cambodia and to approve an additional $222 million. (I cannot determine at this remove how a figure of such precision was arrived at; perhaps some budget officer had a warped sense of humor.)

In addition to his formal request, Ford wrote a letter to House Speaker Carl Albert in which he eloquently stated the moral issue:

> Are we to deliberately abandon a small country in the midst of its life and death struggle? Is the United States, which so far has consistently stood by its friends through the most difficult of times, now to condemn, in effect a small Asian nation totally dependent upon us?[5]

I echoed this theme in many a press briefing. The voluminous records of State Department and White House staff meetings show that our private concerns for America's honor, self-respect, and credibility were identical with what we stated publicly; there was no hidden "geopolitical" agenda for the sake of which we continued the war. "Countries around the world," Ford wrote to Albert, "who depend on us for support—as well as their foes—will judge our performance." Cambodia was especially on our minds because, coinciding with its final agony, I was conducting shuttles meant to convince another small, friendly country—this time Israel—that it ought to put some of its physical security at risk by giving up territory at least partly on the basis of assurances of continued American support.

All appeals by Ford and me (there being few additional volunteers) met with the same reception as they had regarding Vietnam—even more so because the fate of Cambodia could be blamed entirely on the actions of Republican administrations. Media and congressional commentary paralleled the arguments against aid to Vietnam with the added twist that Cambodia's mounting agony was invoked as one more reason to withhold rather than extend aid. Expert sources, questioning whether Cambodia really needed additional aid, were quoted approvingly.[6] Conversely, it was said to be too late for extending aid since Cambodia was beyond saving.[7] Still others discerned no reason to extend aid because no binding commitment to Cambodia existed. Indeed, antiwar legislation from the early 1970s onward had specified that no "commitment" was implied. On February 13, 1975, the *Baltimore Sun* took the highly unusual step of clearing the administration of complicity in the overthrow of Sihanouk but only so that it could go on to the conclusion that, since we had not connived in his ouster, we had no obligation to Sihanouk's successors.[8] Aid would just prolong the killing and prevent the Cambodians from solving their own problems peacefully.[9] Since we really had nothing at stake, it was a mistake for the administration to create the impression that American credibility would be harmed if Cambodia fell.[10] Aid was pointless unless the administration could guarantee that a negotiated settlement would quickly follow.[11]

The smug (and disastrously wrong) theme that nothing could be worse for the Cambodian people than a continuation of American military aid was pervasive. That a cutoff of arms aid would end the suffering was treated as self-evident; the administration's warnings of a possible bloodbath were derided as baseless, insincere, outweighed by the presumed horror of the continuing battles, or rejected as a McCarthyesque ploy to blame Congress for the imminent loss of Indochina. In short, withholding assistance for Cambodia was declared to be the only humane and moral position.

The most one-sided coverage was in the *New York Times*. On March 13, in an article headed "The Enigmatic Cambodian Insurgents," its reporter disparaged the warnings of a bloodbath on a variety of grounds: the stories of deliberate Khmer Rouge atrocities in areas conquered by them were predictable examples of military indiscipline after hotly contested battles, or else they were the self-serving accounts of POWs and, as such, were probably "less than totally reliable." Once the Khmer Rouge had won, "some diplomats and other long-time observers" were quoted as saying that there would be "no need for random acts of terror." "Most Cambodians do not talk about a possible massacre and do not expect one," concluded the same reporter reassuringly. "Since all are Cambodians, an accommodation will be found." In any event, the Communist leadership was "more nationalist than Communist." The insurgent movement included some non-Communists and "possibly anti-Communists"; Communist leader Khieu Samphan was described as a "French-educated intellectual" who had joined the Communists in the 1960s "to fight against feudal privileges and social inequities." He was said to be highly regarded for his "integrity" and might be expected to "move somewhat to the right" once he came into power. The outcome would probably be "a more flexible nationalist socialism or Communism for Cambodia."[12]

Undoubtedly this grotesque account in the newspaper of record affected the congressional debate on whether to help Cambodia. But Congress needed little encouragement to throttle Cambodia. It did so less by any explicit decision to which blame might later be attached than by simply failing to act on the various administration requests. On March 12, the House Democratic caucus, by a vote of 189–49, rejected any further military aid to Cambodia. The administration was urged to accept a "compromise" put forward by a subcommittee of the House Foreign Affairs Committee chaired by Representative Lee Hamilton which would have given a terminal grant with a cutoff date of June 30. The administration was saved from the embarrassment of either vetoing or signing this stay of execution of three months because, on March 13, the full House Foreign Affairs Committee rejected the Hamilton compromise by an 18–15 vote for going too far—and, while it was at it, refused to consider any other compromise. Representative Donald Fraser was explicit about his objectives. He favored surrender, he said, "under controlled circumstances to minimize the loss of life."[13] That same day, the Senate Democratic caucus joined its House counterpart by voting 38–5 to oppose military aid to Cambodia and to reject the military aid supplemental for Vietnam by a vote of 34–6.

At this point, there occurred one of those "credibility gaps" by which Washington periodically flagellates itself and which, in the atmosphere of the time, was both nearly inevitable and a convenient excuse for avoiding decisions. It suddenly transpired that we had not run out of funds for Cambodia after all. On March 14, Secretary Schlesinger reported that the Defense Department had discovered that $21.5 million of funds from Fiscal Year 1974 had been set aside as a contingency for inflation and not been used. In other words, we had funds for two to three more weeks of ammunition deliveries than what we had told Congress.

In the near-hysteria of the time, this unexpected windfall enabling us to extend the life of besieged Phnom Penh by another few weeks was greeted not with relief or exultation but with dismay as a potential public relations catastrophe. Had we brought ourselves another terrifying "credibility gap"? Ford's reaction was to order that Congress be notified immediately—as if we were conveying some terrible discovery: "It never hurts to be honest, even in a tough spot like this." Mercifully, Congress adjourned for the Easter recess at this point, sparing the country for at least a few weeks the humiliation of a public debate on the best way to abandon a helpless ally totally dependent on us. By the time Congress returned in early April, Cambodia was beyond help, and Vietnam was unraveling.

## The Myth of the Failure to Negotiate on Cambodia

The standard alibi for the steps which made the catastrophe irreversible was to press the administration to bring about a negotiated end to the war in Cambodia. Indeed, cutting assistance off was increasingly put forward as the best means to facilitate a political solution by the simple device of eliminating Cambodia's ability to defend itself. Not all who used this argument were cynical—though hypocrisy was not in short supply. But for some, the quest for a pure diplomacy based solely on negotiating legerdemain, unsupported by any leverage, reflected a very American nostalgia. It is difficult to conceive a more sweeping misapprehension than that the ruthless Hanoi Politburo and the murderous Khmer Rouge could let themselves be persuaded to forgo total military victory by the brilliant verbal facility of an American negotiator.

Hanoi's aim was total victory. It would only compromise on

the basis of a balance of forces that it could not hope to alter; any other premise amounted to either an evasion or an abdication. In Cambodia, this balance of forces on the ground could only be achieved with the help of American airpower. In its absence, there were next to no diplomatic pressures available to alter the battlefield situation.

In the immediate aftermath of the Paris Agreement, a certain military balance seemed within reach. The Khmer Rouge were much weaker than the North Vietnamese and had very few outside sources of supply other than Hanoi, already stretched to the hilt in South Vietnam. A relatively small military effort, combined with a serious attempt to train the Cambodian army, could have achieved a military balance and possibly even military superiority. Had we been allowed to establish a military balance and—heaven forbid—perhaps even gain the upper hand, a negotiation seemed possible.

Many competing forces were involved in Cambodia. Until the very end, the Soviet Union recognized Lon Nol as the legitimate government. In China, ideology—or history, as Zhou Enlai once said to me —may have dictated a measure of Chinese support for North Vietnam (made riskless by the illusion that, in the end, the United States would not lose the war). But geopolitics made China wary of an outcome in which Hanoi dominated all of Indochina, thereby placing a major power on China's southern border. Thus Zhou Enlai confided to me in February 1973 that China did not consider a completely "red" Cambodia to be in its interest.[14]

Chinese suspicions toward Hanoi were reciprocated by the North Vietnamese. When I visited Hanoi in February 1973, Le Duc Tho took me to the historical museum where he made it a point to show me the exhibits celebrating Vietnam's centuries-old struggle against China (this being within weeks of ending the war as an ostensible ally of China). And I have already described Hanoi's extreme distrust of the Khmer Rouge.

Prince Sihanouk, living in exile in Beijing in what was arguably the most comfortable and elegant residence in that city, had no illusions about the Khmer Rouge: he had, after all, sentenced their leaders to death on charges of treason before he was overthrown. Sihanouk knew —and frequently admitted—that he would never play a significant role if the Khmer Rouge achieved complete victory.

Within Cambodia, the Lon Nol government was, in effect, Sihanouk's own government without Sihanouk. If any non-Communist forces participated in a negotiated outcome, they would have to be drawn from Lon Nol's entourage; there were no others. This is why Sihanouk always directed his venom against the person of Lon Nol, not against his associates, and why he never rejected the idea of some coalition structure in Phnom Penh under his leadership.

In China in February 1973, shortly after the Paris Agreement was signed, I asked Zhou Enlai to help mediate a diplomatic solution for Cambodia.[15] On May 27, we proposed the following framework to Zhou: militarily, an immediate cease-fire on the ground, including an end to American bombing; politically, Lon Nol's departure from the country after a suitable interval once a cease-fire was in place. The rest of Lon Nol's government would remain pending political negotiations which I would begin with Sihanouk in Beijing. Abandoning his usual pose that Cambodia was too distant for Beijing to know much about it, Zhou said he would submit the proposal to Sihanouk in early July when the Prince would return to Beijing from a trip to Africa. I scheduled a visit to Beijing for August 6 for consultations; discussions with Sihanouk were to play a prominent role.

The plan aborted when, at the end of June, Congress legislated an end to the American bombing effective August 15 and prohibited any American military action in Indochina. This knocked the props out from beneath both the Chinese and the American positions. The delicate compromise sought by both Beijing and Washington collapsed once Congress gave away the American side of the bargain unilaterally. Within three weeks of the congressional vote, Zhou informed us that he was no longer prepared to transmit our proposal to Sihanouk. He subtly hinted at the reason by moving the date of my visit to Beijing from August 6 to August 16, the day after the congressionally legislated bombing halt would go into effect. The legislation had not only managed to undermine both Phnom Penh and Sihanouk and derail American and Chinese diplomacy, it also, in my view, marked the beginning of Zhou's loss of influence.

We hardly needed instruction on the desirability of a diplomatic solution; what we lacked after the bombing halt was the objective conditions to achieve one. The more Congress reduced aid, the more certain became the victory of the Khmer Rouge; the more confident the Khmer Rouge were of success, the less open they were to a diplomatic outcome. No amount of negotiating skill could get us around this dilemma.

These realities eluded most of our critics in Congress and the media. We were being urged to abandon a military solution for a political one at the precise moment when the elements on which a political compromise might have been based were being systematically destroyed. In their absence, the demand for a political solution amounted to a discussion of the modalities of surrender.

As the end in Cambodia came more and more clearly into view, the same debate broke out within the administration. As our ambassadors in Saigon and Phnom Penh manned increasingly besieged battlements, they could not help contemplate their responsibilities or remain oblivious to their personal careers. Both found themselves in a heartbreaking situation. They were obliged to preside over the liquidation of their embassies and charged with rescuing all their employees and as many Cambodians and Vietnamese as possible—especially those who had cast their lot with the United States. Each ambassador faced an extremely fast-moving collapse, testing his initiative and his capacity to improvise because Washington was too far away and too unaware of the local intangibles to give meaningful day-to-day operational guidance. As a result, each ambassador developed proconsular attitudes and often felt free to disregard explicit instructions from Washington. Yet in their interpretation of the scope and purpose of their proconsular roles, the two men diverged dramatically.

In Saigon, Graham Martin acted as a senior Foreign Service officer of the old school; tough and self-assured, he was a classic Cold Warrior. Prepared to take great risks with his own career, he insisted on strict discipline within his embassy without applying the same strictures to his own conduct vis-à-vis Washington. In pursuit of his perception of his mission, Martin would take upon himself initiatives that more circumspect and less driven ambassadors would not have launched without first checking with Washington. And his style was sufficiently convoluted so that Washington could not always determine how he was interpreting its decisions.

Despite Martin's well-known idiosyncrasies, I had recommended his appointment to Saigon because, after the Paris Agreement, much would depend on the initiative and the determination of the ranking American. A strong ambassador capable of improvising was needed to hold together the American effort and to give Thieu the confidence to play the painfully difficult hand he had been dealt.

Once in Saigon, Martin performed heroically and upheld to the bitter end the American commitment to a free South Vietnam for which so many thousands, including—as it happened—his adopted son, had given their lives. To induce Washington to go along with his recommendations, Martin was not above shading his analysis to accord with his preconceptions. Philip Habib, the assistant secretary of state for East Asia who had served many years in Vietnam and leaned toward the dovish side, supplied the corrective.

Faced with imminent disaster, Martin decided to go down with his ship and battled for his convictions until the last second of the last day. Believing that the United States Congress had erred grievously in abandoning South Vietnam, he resisted conventional media and congressional wisdom and made no concessions to the illusory "compromises" with which they salved their consciences. I knew very well that Martin's many hortatory messages were designed in part to create a record which might later be published—perhaps even to my disadvantage. For Martin tended to consider anything less than 100 percent support as betrayal. But whatever the record, it would show Martin struggling to maintain America's moral commitments. I agreed with his objectives, if not always their feasibility, and I considered him an ally, albeit an occasionally aberrant one. In the meantime, my heart went out to Martin as I watched him mask his anguish with bravado.

The ambassador in Phnom Penh, John Gunther Dean, represented a different generation. Just as confident as Martin of the correctness of his views, Dean took great care to stay within the parameters of conventional wisdom. He always made sure that the media were aware of his commitment to the "politically correct" solution—labeled "political compromise"—even as whatever objective conditions might once have existed for it were evaporating.

Highly intelligent and well informed, Dean understood well enough that congressional restrictions on American funding and advisory activities were certain to doom the country to which he was accredited. And he made clear from the start that he would not go down with the sinking ship. Like the congressional doves, Dean advocated a "political" way out of the disaster he had been asked to administer. He therefore bent every effort to get a negotiation started, usually under his own auspices. A deluge of cables descended on Washington with a persistence that led me to the perhaps unworthy suspicion that, like Martin, Dean was building a record. But where Martin exhibited an excessive zeal in pursuing what was, after all, the approved strategy, Dean took it upon himself to alter national strategy from the improbable venue of Phnom Penh.

Dean's strategy was to urge negotiations now with the Khmer

Rouge, now with Sihanouk, at one moment through Indonesian President Suharto, at another via Prime Minister Lee Kuan Yew of Singapore. I will not review the stream of tactical suggestions, coupled with increasingly shrill demands for more rapid action, pouring forth from the Phnom Penh embassy. Dean's basic strategy was to replace the government to which he was accredited with a coalition structure of some kind as a prelude for negotiations with the Khmer Rouge.

Being obliged to deal with Congress on a daily basis, we hardly needed instruction on the precariousness of Cambodia's situation, and we shared with Dean the strong desire to ease Cambodia's fate. Whatever chances existed for a negotiated outcome—and, in light of the military situation and aid cutoff, we judged them to be minimal—we did not believe that the ambassador in Phnom Penh was the appropriate focal point for them. We had precious few bargaining chips, the two principal ones being the military establishment and the government structure headed by Lon Nol. Congress was dismantling the military, and the thrust of Dean's recommendations was to dismantle the Phnom Penh government at the beginning of some undefined diplomatic process.

We judged the key to whatever negotiation might develop to be Sihanouk, who was in Beijing. We were willing to explore that and other channels, including those suggested by Dean, such as using Suharto or Lee as intermediaries. Dean, however, was not well positioned with respect to any of these venues. Assuming a negotiation was even possible, his role in our strategy was to hold Phnom Penh together until we could find an interlocutor willing to negotiate.

On February 18, 1975, while I was on a shuttle in the Middle East, I instructed the State Department:

> Dean has now gone so far as to invite key Khmer military and civilian leaders to his home to discuss openly and with considerable enthusiasm the removal of the chief of state of [Cambodia].
>
> As far as I am concerned, if we are to leave Cambodia, we will leave with dignity. I am willing to listen to any recommendation that is consistent with that objective. But the frenzied approach which Dean seems to have adopted will solve nothing. I want him to adhere to a sober, deliberate policy that neither precludes positive action on our part nor rushes us into it headlong.

The subsequent careers of the two ambassadors are proof that it is far more dangerous to challenge conventional congressional and media wisdom than to harass the Secretary of State. Martin never received another ambassadorial post because he was henceforth considered impossible to confirm; Dean went on to serve as ambassador in Denmark and India before retiring.

Our strategy was to seek contacts preferably with Sihanouk either directly or through such trusted ambassadors as David Bruce and later George Bush in Beijing, or through capitals that had some influence on the Cambodian parties, such as those of Algeria or Indonesia. We far preferred Sihanouk as our interlocutor, for we judged the Khmer Rouge adamant against compromise and determined to disintegrate the Phnom Penh structure and make Sihanouk irrelevant. What we sought to avoid was the destruction of the Phnom Penh government as an entrance price into negotiations—as Dean was urging.

On several occasions throughout 1974, we had raised the basic formula of cease-fire, coalition government, and Lon Nol's departure with Chinese leaders (including Deng Xiaoping) and with Algerian Foreign Minister Abdelaziz Bouteflika, who represented the Nonaligned Movement that year. In addition, in the fall of 1974, we tried to organize an international conference on Cambodia but were unable to generate any interest. In February and March of 1975—partly at the urging of Dean—we approached Prime Minister Lee Kuan Yew and President Suharto to explore negotiating possibilities. They saw no chance so long as the government in Phnom Penh was facing imminent collapse.

Another attempt at negotiation occurred in December 1974. It was initiated when French President Valéry Giscard d'Estaing told Ford at their summit in Martinique of the conviction of his ambassador in Beijing, Etienne Manac'h, that a negotiated agreement with Sihanouk was attainable and would be supported by China. We had our doubts that, after Zhou's debacle, China would engage itself again or that, if it did, it would do so through French intermediaries. Despite our reservations, we authorized the French Foreign Ministry to proceed. We would go along with Sihanouk as head of government; to be able to govern independently, we argued, he would have to include strong non-Communist elements in his administration. In practice, this meant members of the Lon Nol structure, though not Lon Nol. Any other terms would have meant surrender and, to arrange this, we did not require a French intermediary. We stated our requirements in a formal paper on December 24:

We are prepared to accept Sihanouk as the leader of Cambodia,

—If Sihanouk returns to Phnom Penh as a genuine national leader and not figurehead.

—For Sihanouk to be a genuine national leader, he must have supporting him in his Government strong elements representing all important tendencies, including those of the present structure. How does he plan to bring this about? What is the structure and nature of the government envisaged by Sihanouk?

Discussions cannot be used to demoralize the existing government in Phnom Penh. If there is agreement in principle it should be implemented rapidly.

We favor that the new government would follow the principle of neutrality in foreign relations.

There must be assurance of durability in the compromise solution. We are not interested in a subterfuge for settlement which will be followed shortly thereafter by another upheaval.

Still smarting from its experience of the previous year, Beijing refused even to discuss the subject on the ground that foreign countries should not interfere in Cambodian affairs. Lest the point be missed and to shut off further discussions, Beijing denied a visa to the French emissary who was supposed to deliver the above message to Sihanouk.[16]

Years later, an ingenious investigative journalist ascribed the failure of the Manac'h mission to the final communiqué at Martinique, whose recommendation of negotiations between "the contending parties" was allegedly interpreted as implying a dialogue between Lon Nol and Sihanouk.[17] But diplomacy is not like a detective story in which one side tosses out vague clues and the other is supposed to guess the correct answer. Actual diplomacy is both simpler and more complex: it neither operates in a vacuum, nor does it typically depend on how a particular communication is phrased. Diplomacy is an expression of the balance of risks and incentives. Sihanouk had become marginalized because Lon Nol's military situation was collapsing, not by any particular language in a communiqué.

Far too late Sihanouk realized this. On March 25—after having rejected our overtures for nearly two years—he suddenly established contact in a manner that lent considerable credit to his subtlety, if not to his timing. In a letter to Ford via the French ambassador, the exiled Prince requested our assistance in returning to him his collection of Cambodian music and instruments which he had left behind on being deposed in 1970. On March 26, 1975, we instructed George Bush to seek a meeting with Sihanouk to inform him that we would do our utmost to respond to his request and to sketch for him one more time the outcome to the Cambodian tragedy we had been proposing for two years:

> As guidelines for this part of your meeting, you should open by advising him that we remain vitally interested in receiving his ideas for settling the war in Cambodia. We therefore invite him to use this opportunity to convey to us through you his latest thinking on how the war in Cambodia can be brought to a close in a manner which will preserve the integrity of his nation and enable him to exercise a personal leadership in unifying the Khmer people.
>
> You should also indicate that we continue to believe that it will be necessary to preserve a balance of forces between the opposing Khmer elements if a true peace settlement is to be achieved. Such a balance would serve as the indispensable basis not only for achieving a settlement, but also for assuring that Sihanouk will be able to realize the decisive leadership role we envisage.

On March 28, John Holdridge, our deputy chief of mission in Beijing, met with Phung Peng Chen, Sihanouk's chief of staff, at the French Embassy and delivered an invitation from Bush to Sihanouk for a discussion at a mutually agreed venue. Sihanouk rejected the proposal on March 29 via the same aide who used the excuse that the Prince did not wish to confuse "international opinion" by giving rise to rumors about the imminence of a political negotiation. We thereupon instructed Bush to inform Sihanouk that we had succeeded in safeguarding his cultural possessions and to use the occasion to deliver the political part of our message.

On April 1, Holdridge met with Phung Peng Chen and reported his response as follows:

> It would be very bad for Cambodia if the Red Khmer took over the entire government in Cambodia, since they were "very doctrinaire." It would be far better "for the free

world" if Prince Sihanouk, who had the support of the peasants and the people of Phnom Penh, could be brought back
to Cambodia and with the backing of the superpowers exercise some balance over the other forces. Phung indicated that
he hoped that the US could assist in bringing Sihanouk back.

We agreed with this analysis and had for several years. A "political"
solution could have been built on it. The trouble was that those who
had destroyed the possibility of a military balance had doomed a
political outcome as well.

## The Final Collapse

The Khmer Rouge offensive that began on January 1, 1975, closed
in on Phnom Penh at the beginning of April when Neak Luong,
the government's last foothold on the lower Mekong, was captured.
This freed at least six to seven thousand more Communist troops for
the final assault on Phnom Penh, now cut off from American supplies.

The remaining government troops fought until their ammunition
ran out and for nearly a week thereafter. That there was no dearth of
inefficiency and even corruption on the Cambodian side cannot be
denied. But it was also the case that, with American help and despite
stifling congressional restrictions, an essentially ceremonial force under
Sihanouk had been transformed into an army that, for two years,
fought the ferocious Khmer Rouge to a standstill.

By early April, reflections about what might have been had become
irrelevant. For, as the end approached, the American superpower had
already turned itself into an impotent spectator absorbed in a narcissistic pursuit of its own domestic controversy. There was nothing left
to do other than to watch in anguish, then with a growing sense of
horror as the Khmer Rouge turned the victory that American actions
had facilitated into genocide against their own people.

Ambassador Dean, now confined to his basic mission, conducted
the American withdrawal and attendant political transformations with
great skill and professionalism. Lon Nol left Phnom Penh on April 1,
ostensibly to go "on vacation." A number of changes in personnel at
the top were initiated to ease the transition and perhaps to retain a
foothold for the old order. Touchingly (and shamingly), the Cambodians still had so much confidence in the United States that they con-

sulted us at every step. Even at this late stage, the new acting President, Saukham Khoy, made a pathetic last-minute appeal to Ford on April 6:

> For [a] number of years now the Cambodian people have placed their trust in America. I cannot believe that this confidence was misplaced and that suddenly America will deny us the means which might give us a chance to find an acceptable solution to our conflict.

As everything was about to disintegrate, Sihanouk was suddenly heard from again. He had been punctuating the death throes of the Lon Nol government with intransigent statements in which he rejected any talk of a last-minute compromise as a "political plot." Labeling all the newly appointed ministers in Phnom Penh as traitors, Sihanouk asserted that:

> Under no circumstances, neither in the near future nor in the more remote future, will the Cambodian resistance agree to be reconciled with the traitors in the clique of Saukham Khoy, Pan Sothi and company.[18]

These bloodthirsty words were the now unavoidable tribute Sihanouk paid to his ostensible allies, the Khmer Rouge. What he thought privately was quite different and was conveyed to us in Beijing in his customary elliptical manner. Another meeting between Holdridge and Phung took place, this time on the pretext that Sihanouk wanted to send some Cambodian recordings to Ford in appreciation of our intercession in Phnom Penh on behalf of his cultural treasures. Holdridge had been instructed to convey the President's good wishes and to invite "any further messages Sihanouk might have for us." The meeting took place on April 10, forty-eight hours before the American evacuation. Phung, according to Holdridge, passed on the following observations:

> It is important that [a] solution be reached in Cambodia prior to the fall of Saigon; otherwise North Vietnamese and Red Khmer will take over all of Cambodia in same way Soviets took over Czechoslovakia. Phung stated that on this point he was expressing Sihanouk's personal views.
> Sihanouk is "helpless" in Peking to do anything about

situation in Cambodia. However, he does not want Red Khmer to take over the country completely.

It is a good thing to keep "the army" intact in Cambodia, since Sihanouk has the support of the soldiers and also of the Cambodian peasants. Phung made it very clear when questioned that by "the army" he meant the forces now defending Phnom Penh and not the Red Khmer forces.

Once again Sihanouk—if Phung was, in fact, speaking for him—had outlined the same strategy we had been attempting to implement for nearly two years. Sihanouk either had hoped that a military stalemate would occur in which he would be called back as the indispensable balancing factor, or else he had concluded that the Khmer Rouge were certain to prevail so that any diplomatic initiative on his part could only weaken his long-term influence. Probably he had pursued both convictions simultaneously. Now, at the last second when the counterweights to the Khmer Rouge were disintegrating, Sihanouk realized that his position was scarcely better than that of the remnants of the Lon Nol administration. Thus he finally engaged himself to achieve what might well have been possible had he been more forthright and America more united.

We undertook one last convulsive attempt to respond to Phung's message. Dean was instructed to suggest to Cambodia's acting President that he make an appeal to Sihanouk to return as the head of a government of national union. At the same time, Holdridge was instructed to contact Sihanouk to inform him of this overture and, if he agreed, to suggest that the Chinese fly him to Phnom Penh in a Chinese airplane.

The end of an era provides a kind of laboratory for studying how difficult it is to break established patterns of thought. By then, we had been dominant in Phnom Penh for so long that, though we were literally within hours of leaving, we were not emotionally prepared to accept the implications. We made this pathetic overture as the Cambodian army was collapsing and the American Embassy in Phnom Penh was packing to leave. By then, in a grim coincidence, the Cambodians had also totally run out of ammunition, and the situation had turned so perilous that Dean was instructed to proceed with evacuation whatever Sihanouk's reply. Had the scheme worked, Sihanouk, upon his return, would have found no Americans to assist him, only Cambodian military forces without ammunition.

Sihanouk spared us this embarrassment by replying with a message proving that he was either very subtle or totally out of touch. When, on April 11, Holdridge told Phung of our overture to Cambodia's acting President, he professed to be highly pleased but added that Sihanouk could not return on the basis of an appeal made by a leader he had only recently called a traitor. Phung therefore urged that Saukham Khoy buttress his request by appeals from "two chief Bonzes, other members of the priesthood, students, army men, Phnom Penh residents in general, and the peasants." We knew, even if Phung— seduced by a belief in America's invincibility—did not, that there was no longer any time left for such fancy maneuvers, since our embassy would be leaving April 12, the next day.

Incongruously, as the curtain fell on Cambodia, Washington returned to bureaucratic business as usual. Evacuation is heartrending for the victims; to those implementing it, it is above all a technical problem. In no time, Washington was consumed by the perennial discord between the Defense and State Departments. Stories were soon being leaked, rendering even Cambodia's death throes as yet another installment of a running turf battle between the Pentagon and the State Department.

These internal debates turned out to be a dress rehearsal for the much more complex evacuation of Saigon two weeks later. The dispute did not concern the necessity of evacuation, only its timing and modalities. The Defense Department, which would be responsible for implementation, wanted to start immediately, using fixed-wing aircraft. The State Department, backed by Dean, preferred to evacuate in a way that would reduce panic and enable as many Khmer who had worked with us as possible to flee. On April 3, there was a decision to evacuate with the actual timing left to the ambassador. Dean decided to delay a few days to avoid a panic and to better organize the departure. The ensuing tensions are illustrated by the following exchange at an 8:00 A.M. State Department staff meeting on April 11:

> HABIB: Defense—the Pentagon—is trying to tell us that if
> we don't do certain things fast enough, God help us. If
> they have an accident, they're going to blame us.
> KISSINGER: No doubt. The Pentagon has said, "It's your
> fault." I've heard it three times. . . .
> . . . Why was it delayed, as a matter of fact?
> HABIB: It was delayed because Dean came in with a mes-

sage saying, "I can't do it at this time," and all his
military advisers agreed. . . .

KISSINGER: . . . We've got a massive problem in the Middle
East; we've got a massive problem in Southeast Asia.
There's no way we can survive it by being tactical. I
know all these guys around town and I know their
position—that if one guy breaks a leg in the evacuation
it will be our fault. We'll just have to take that.

Yet we knew that all the quibbling was a dispute over arranging
the deck chairs on the *Titanic*. Dean told us on April 10 that both the
airport and the road leading to it were no longer safe and that evacuation by helicopter should start immediately. For technical reasons, the
airlift could not start until 8:00 A.M. local time on April 12. Eighty-two
Americans, 159 Cambodians, and thirty-five other nationals were evacuated in a little more than two hours.

Messages were sent to top-level Cambodians offering to evacuate
them as well. To our astonishment and shame, the vast majority refused, including Lon Nol's brother, Lon Non, and Premier Long Boret,
both of whom were on the Khmer Rouge's published death list. Ron
Nessen reacted perceptively: "In other words, the Cambodians are
telling us, 'Okay, you chickenshits, go ahead and bug out, but we are
going to stay and fight.'"[19]

Sirik Matak, former Prime Minister and the only leader of the
1970 coup still in Phnom Penh, expressed the attitude of the Khmer
leaders in more elevated language. Responding to Dean's offer to be
evacuated, he sent a note, handwritten in elegant French, on April 12
while the evacuation was in progress:

Dear Excellency and Friend:
    I thank you very sincerely for your letter and for your
offer to transport me towards freedom. I cannot, alas, leave
in such a cowardly fashion. As for you, and in particular for
your great country, I never believed for a moment that you
would have this sentiment of abandoning a people which has
chosen liberty. You have refused us your protection, and we
can do nothing about it.
    You leave, and my wish is that you and your country
will find happiness under this sky. But, mark it well, that if I
shall die here on the spot and in my country that I love, it is

no matter, because we all are born and must die. I have only committed this mistake of believing in you [the Americans].

Please accept, Excellency and dear friend, my faithful and friendly sentiments.

S/Sirik Matak.

On April 13, the *New York Times* correspondent reported the American departure under the headline, "Indochina Without Americans: For Most, a Better Life."[20]

The Khmer Rouge took Phnom Penh on April 17. Long Boret was executed immediately, as was every member of the previous government who had remained behind. All former government employees and their families were executed in the weeks that followed. The 2 million citizens of Phnom Penh were ordered to evacuate the city for the countryside ravaged by war and incapable of supporting urban dwellers unused to fending for themselves. Between 1 and 2 million Khmer were murdered by the Khmer Rouge until Hanoi occupied the country at the end of 1978, after which a civil war raged for another decade.

Sirik Matak was shot in the stomach and left without medical help. It took him three days to die.

# 17

# THE END OF VIETNAM

Those who thought that the agony of Cambodia might inure them to the pain of South Vietnam's unraveling soon learned better. The tragic end of two decades of American sacrifice, dedication, and national division proved beyond getting used to.

On March 10, the North Vietnamese, no longer even pretending to be bound by the Paris Agreement, launched a major offensive in the Central Highlands using divisions recently introduced from the North. They overran the strategic junction of Ban Me Thuot in two days, cutting all the roads from Saigon to the Central Highlands except for one very poor road constantly being harassed by Vietcong guerrillas.

While the Central Highlands were tottering, Tran Van Lam, a confidant of President Thieu, was sent to Washington to plead for the supplemental aid package. He reported to Saigon that there was no hope of obtaining any additional aid from the sitting Congress. Fear turned into certainty when, as noted in Chapter 16, the House and Senate Democratic caucuses (then the majority in Congress) voted overwhelmingly on March 12 and 13 against any further aid to South Vietnam.

Thieu understood that, with his shrinking resources, he would no longer be able to defend the entire territory of his besieged country and ordered a strategic withdrawal from the Central Highlands. At the same time, he redeployed the First Airborne Division from the northern border to the area around Da Nang—both moves to start a few days hence, on March 16. Thieu's intent was to create a defensible redoubt which might be held until a perhaps more sympathetic Congress was elected in 1976.

As a war college exercise, Thieu's move made good sense. In terms of Vietnamese realities, it ushered in catastrophe. Launched without preparation or detailed guidance from the Joint General Staff in Saigon, the "strategic withdrawal" had to be carried out over a single road—Route 7B—in bad repair and heavily mined. A major engineering job would have been required to make it usable, including the rebuilding of several collapsed bridges—tasks for which the South Vietnamese divisions were inadequately equipped. In addition to the combat units, Route 7B would have to accommodate a horde of fleeing civilians, for the dependents of the Army of the Republic of Vietnam (ARVN) divisions were always billeted close to the fighting units—in this case, in Pleiku, the capital of the Central Highlands. As soon as word of the withdrawal order filtered down, panic set in, and a mass exodus followed. To compound the chaos, the regional militias, composed mostly of local tribes called Montagnards, rioted upon hearing that they were to be left behind.

The lone escape route was soon clogged by an estimated 60,000 troops and 400,000 civilians. The system of food distribution broke down, and hungry soldiers started to pillage the villages along the way. South Vietnamese air force planes mistakenly bombed an ARVN armored unit, killing many troops and dependents. The North Vietnamese attacked this traveling conflagration. Only a small fraction of the fleeing soldiers and civilians made it to the coast; the Vietnamese divisions that had defended the Central Highlands evaporated.

Originally the North Vietnamese had intended to devote the 1975 campaigning season to the capture of the Central Highlands and to fight the decisive battles for Saigon in 1976. Within a matter of days, however, the North Vietnamese achieved their initial goal and without suffering any significant casualties or loss of equipment. The divisions aimed at the Central Highlands were now free to attack Da Nang and Hue along the coast, which they soon besieged. The flood of refugees from the Central Highlands engulfed the elite airborne division just transferred from the northern border, preventing any sustained defense of these major strategic bases. The North Vietnamese commander, General Van Tien Dung, later recounted:

> The matter had surpassed the bounds of this campaign and had reached strategic proportions. For the first time in the Indochina War, within the bounds of a campaign an enemy army corps with modern equipment had had to abandon an

important strategic area and flee. This situation would lead
to other important developments, and might lead to our
quickly and victoriously concluding the war.[1]

The Middle East deadlock overlapped precisely the period of the
Central Highlands debacle, the full extent of which did not become
apparent until I returned to Washington on March 23. Both crises had
to be dealt with simultaneously. Then, amidst all this heartache, another friendly people, the Kurds, whom we had supported covertly,
were overrun by the Iraqi army, newly reequipped by the Soviets.

Fortunately, high office absorbs self-pity or even second thoughts
in the need to deal with a crisis. Starting March 24, daily WSAG and
staff meetings tried to master the concurrent crises in Indochina and
the Middle East. The news from Vietnam recorded an endless stream
of disasters. The old imperial city of Hue fell on March 25 (two days
after my return from the aborted shuttle), Da Nang on March 30.
With a million refugees in Da Nang and food supplies running out,
the key issue in the northern part of the country was humanitarian,
not defense.

Nevertheless, at WSAG meetings, we found ourselves at times addressing problems driven into the bizarre by legalistic wrangling. For
example, some of us wanted to use American Landing Ship/Tanks
(LSTs) to help evacuate refugees. Our congressional experts were fret-
ting whether this would violate Article 7 of the Paris Agreement prohibiting the introduction of military equipment except to replace losses
—an article never observed for one day by the North Vietnamese. The
next issue was whether we could evacuate any of the frantic refugees
by whatever means before notifying Congress under the War Powers
Act. The matter was judged sufficiently important to require a presidential decision. Ford ruled: "I think we ought to do it, notify them,
and make a public announcement." I interpreted the ruling to mean
that we were to do so in that order.

Movies depict turning points in portentous terms, with decision-
makers agonizing over long-term consequences and dilemmas of
choice. In real life, however, even the fall of a nation tends to compart-
mentalize itself into a series of nearly pedestrian decisions. To the
WSAG, I estimated South Vietnam's ability to survive at a maximum
of three months.

The collapse was somber, tragic, and poignant. But for those of us
making the decisions, the overwhelming challenge was how to manage

the by now nearly inevitable evacuation of the remaining six thousand Americans as well as those Vietnamese who were in jeopardy by virtue of their association with the United States. "I want the list of categories of people," I said at a State Department staff meeting of April 8, "how they're going to be moved to a place from which they can be evacuated, in what order, and with what prior consultation with the government." (This was because the State Department, via the American ambassador, was responsible for evacuations.)

Surrealistically, evacuation planning was taking place side by side with an internal debate about whether to request military aid for South Vietnam at this late stage and how much. Ford and I were the principal advocates of continuing with the request to Congress for additional aid until the last moment. How to reconcile that seeming inconsistency between my estimate of Saigon's chances for survival, insistence on evacuation planning, and continued advocacy of aid appropriations for South Vietnam?

The overwhelming majority of the media (I can think of no significant exception) clamored for the dismantling of Saigon, for the replacement of Thieu, and for an immediate complete withdrawal from Vietnam. Congress was not far behind. Within the administration, CIA Director William Colby favored offering a deal whereby we would jettison Thieu for unimpeded evacuation of Americans. Ford's White House staff was eager to liquidate Vietnam to avoid tarnishing his presidency with further Vietnam controversies.

But those of us who were meeting daily in the White House Situation Room faced real, not theoretical, choices. We would need to withdraw the six thousand Americans still remaining in Vietnam and try to help the tens of thousands of Vietnamese, who had jeopardized their lives by working with us, to leave the country. But we would not be able to evacuate any of our South Vietnamese friends unless we prolonged the withdrawal of Americans, for Congress would surely pull the plug with the departure of the last American.

Whatever course we adopted required maintaining our request for assistance to Vietnam. The moment we abandoned it, panic would sweep the disintegrating country. At that point, the battered South Vietnamese army might turn on our remnants in despair and rage over what it was bound to consider our betrayal. In early April, I told Colby that, though Thieu would probably fall soon, if we offered him up in any bargain, Hanoi would immediately demand the head of his successor as well until it had destroyed the entire South Vietnamese political structure (which is essentially what happened). On April 3, a document of a provincial committee of the South Vietnamese Communist Provisional Revolutionary Government (PRG) confirmed this prediction. It described the various offers of tripartite government—the sole goal of Hanoi's struggle, according to the American peace movement—as "merely stratagems to isolate the GVN [Government of South Vietnam]."

We needed time to synchronize the evacuations of both Americans and Vietnamese to whom we had incurred a moral obligation. Maintaining the request for aid was the only way to preserve the morale of those Vietnamese still prepared to fight for a decent outcome—now unhappily to be defined in terms of people rescued.

But what level of assistance should be requested? My recommendation was to propose a figure relevant to South Vietnam's actual needs. On January 28, we had requested a supplemental of $300 million which Senator John Stennis had promised us. Even then the figure bore no relationship to the need, but at least Vietnam had been relatively calm. That sum was no longer adequate to deal with the catastrophe all around us. Ford agreed and sent General Fred C. Weyand, the Army chief of staff who had commanded the First Cavalry Division in Vietnam, to Saigon to come up with a realistic estimate.

Throughout this controversy, Ford stood tall; he quite simply could not imagine abandoning those who had risked their lives for decades by cooperating with what five Presidents of both American parties had declared essential for the security of the free world. I did my best to ensure that this courageous and decent man would have the widest range of choices available and took great care to give Ford a way out. On March 27, as the extent of the military debacle was becoming apparent, I concluded an Oval Office briefing on Saigon's military requests as follows:

> I say this with a bleeding heart—but maybe you must put
> Vietnam behind you and not tear the country apart again.
> The Vietnam agreements were based on two things: our
> threat of military support and the continuation of aid. In
> July '73 we stopped our support, and we also cut the aid
> below the minimum they needed. Now we are faced with a
> desperate situation.

Ford would not hear of it because, he said, it would go "against my grain." His reply was much the same on April 3 when I reminded him that he had the option of doing nothing. On April 9, the day before Ford formally requested additional funds for Vietnam, I called to his attention Ron Nessen's view that the President should lead America out of Vietnam, not into it. Ford replied: "That is not the way I am. . . . I couldn't do it."

At a press conference on April 3, Ford stood by his request for both economic and military aid for South Vietnam. He accused the North Vietnamese of blatant violations of the Paris Agreement, criticized Congress for reducing our requests for assistance to South Vietnam, and ordered an emergency airlift for two thousand Vietnamese orphans. Ford refused the journalists' needling that he jettison Thieu because "I don't believe that it is my prerogative to tell the head of state elected by the people to leave office:"[2]

> We will stand by our allies, and I specifically warn any adversaries they should not, under any circumstances, feel that the tragedy of Vietnam is an indication that the American people have lost their will or their desire to stand up for freedom anyplace in the world.[3]

These were highly unpopular positions, and Ford put them forward calmly, almost soothingly, as if no other approach to the national interest was conceivable.

Media reaction was predictable. Ford was accused by the *New York Times* of being confused[4] and by the *Washington Post* of engaging in a shell game.[5] Somewhat more charitably, the *Los Angeles Times* demanded a "new direction," which it defined as a cutoff of military aid for Indochina.[6] When I repeated Ford's arguments at a press conference on April 5, I encountered the same reception, reflected in questions such as these: How could we expect congressional cooperation while we were blaming Congress for what was happening? What made us think that any more money would do any good? Wasn't it all Thieu's fault? How could we have signed the Paris Agreement expecting any other outcome? And, most insistently, just what was the nature of our commitment to South Vietnam?

I reiterated what I had been saying for months. Our request was based on a moral, not a legal, obligation:

> It is a very important moral question for the United States whether when people who, with its encouragement, have fought for many years should in their hour of extremity be

told by the United States that while they want to continue
fighting that the United States would no longer help them.[7]

I ended with this appeal:

> Many of you have heard me brief on this subject now for six
> years, and I think none of you have ever heard me question
> the travail and concern of those who have opposed the war.
> All we can ask is that those of you who have been critical
> ought to keep in mind that there is a great human tragedy
> that those in the administration are viewing and they are
> trying to deal with it in the best interest of the United States
> and in the best interests of world peace.[8]

It was to no avail. To our immense regret, Senator Henry Jackson
once again joined the assault. Despite our disagreements over East-
West policy, we had continued to regard him as an ally in the geopolitical battle with Communism. But on April 8, he repeated his earlier
opposition to additional aid for Vietnam on the ground that the request was based on "secret agreements, accords, understandings in
writing" which he implied I had somehow kept from President Ford.[9]
The charge was demonstrably false. Beyond the immediate issue, it
illuminated the bitterness with which our national debate has become
suffused. The proposition that a Secretary of State would keep agreements secret from his President was as novel as it was absurd and
marked a new low in our domestic controversy.

Neither Ford nor I ever based our appeal on the existence of formal
commitments. All we claimed with Vietnam under assault was an
underlying moral obligation. Not the least irony of the death throes of
Vietnam was that those who were usually being attacked for realpolitik
insisted on honor and moral obligations while their critics, usually so
free with moral claims, were acting like lawyers looking for escape
clauses in a contract.

General Weyand reported to President Ford in Palm Springs on
April 5. The military situation, he said, was deteriorating, and he
described the choices before us as follows: the $300 million supplemen-
tal would only partially replace consumables. It would not make up
for the vast amount of equipment lost in the disasters of the past few
weeks. The South Vietnamese army had, in fact, received no replacement equipment for two years. Therefore, Weyand argued, the original

supplemental was no longer adequate. Instead he submitted a list of what would be needed to reconstitute some of the units destroyed in recent battles. The minimum amount that made sense was $722 million.

On one level, it was preposterous. Vietnam was likely to collapse before any equipment could arrive there. At the same time, if we were going to submit any figure, we might as well pick one associated with a program that had some intellectual basis. It was the minimum amount with which something might still be salvaged, the one most likely to give the South Vietnamese the shot in the arm with which to gain time for evacuation. And if Vietnam collapsed before any aid could reach it, we would at least have discharged our moral obligations. Ford accepted Weyand's number.

A National Security Council meeting on April 9 went through essentially the same intellectual evolution. Ford was presented with three options: requesting no funds; sticking with the $300 million request of three months earlier; or backing Weyand's recommendation for $722 million. The discussion followed well-established lines. Everyone agreed that cutting off funds would guarantee the loss of any influence over events. Schlesinger recommended sticking with the $300 million figure, since, in view of Vietnam's imminent military collapse, it was not worth fighting with Congress over the difference. I supported Weyand's figure because the $300 million, by ignoring the debacles of recent months, would be so patently inadequate as to amount to an elegant throwing in of the towel. Given South Vietnam's progressive disintegration, it might not make any practical difference which figure was chosen; what mattered was how we ourselves would feel about our conduct afterward.

Ford announced his decision to the NSC at the end of the meeting with a longer and more eloquent explanation than was his custom:

> I will ask for $722 million because we can justify it. At least the record will be clear. I will ask that it be done by a date certain, perhaps May 1, though we still have to decide that.
>
> I will ask for humanitarian aid but not through the United Nations. Third, I will ask for authority, which I think is needed, to evacuate the Americans and others to whom we have an obligation.
>
> I do not rule out at some point letting the North Vietnamese know that any interference with our humanitarian

efforts will be met with strong measures. That is why I want flexibility.

It will be a strong speech in my own way, not perhaps in Churchill's. It will not be a phony.

I gather, Jim [Schlesinger], that you have reservations. But this is the decision. This will be the only group that knows it. I have spent a lot of time on this, now and even earlier, going back to 1952. I think our policy, going back to Presidents Truman and Eisenhower, was the right policy. We did not always implement it well, and we may have made many mistakes. But it was the right policy. . . .

On April 10, the President addressed a joint session of Congress. In a firm and unapologetic speech, he endorsed the purposes which had caused his predecessors to involve the United States in Indochina; traced the evolution of the Paris Agreement; and stressed that the United States had neither supplied adequate aid to its ally nor enforced the agreement. Ford concluded by warning Congress about some of its other assaults on our foreign policy:

That the national interests of the United States and the cause of world stability require that we continue to give both military and humanitarian assistance to the South Vietnamese. . . . We cannot in the meantime abandon our friends while our adversaries support and encourage theirs. We cannot dismantle our defenses, our diplomacy, or our intelligence capability while others increase and strengthen theirs.[10]

The next day, I summed up my view of what was at stake in a pep talk to the senior staff of the State Department:

If the President last night had said what so many congressmen say he should have said—namely, "We've done enough; we can no longer give military aid," I think Phil Habib [assistant secretary for East Asia] will agree there will be total uncontrollable, chaotic collapse in Saigon starting this morning. Once the President decided he was not going to do nothing, he might just as well ask for what is right on this because the opposition on the Hill is not hinged on a figure; it's hinged on the principle. . . .

This thing is now going to go its course; its course is reasonably predictable. And what we are trying to do is to manage it with dignity and to preserve a basis for which we can conduct the foreign policy, in which people can have some confidence in us. . . .

We're not going to accuse anybody of having been wrong. I have no intention, when this thing is over, of turning it into a vendetta and going around the country. I think people are going to feel badly when it's over. I don't think there are going to be many heroes left in this. But this department . . . is going to stand for what's right. We have no other choice in the world.

## The Debate over Evacuation

This was far from conventional wisdom in either Congress or the media. In their vast majority, they asked us to administer the coup de grâce to a country with which we had been associated for over two decades.

Within the administration, the President's speech shifted the controversies from whether to request aid to how to deal with the increasingly likely collapse of South Vietnam. In practice, this reduced itself to the question of how quickly to evacuate and with what concern for the Vietnamese who had worked with us.

The Pentagon wanted to evacuate as fast as possible. As in Cambodia, it made daily representations to speed up the process. It was willing enough to evacuate some Vietnamese so long as this did not slow down getting all Americans out at the fastest pace possible. The Pentagon saw no point in risking casualties, congressional inquiries, or accidents by prolonging evacuation. Proficient in bureaucratic infighting, the Pentagon built a record meant to demonstrate that, for what it considered strictly political reasons, Americans were not being evacuated at a rate the existing airlift capacity would have allowed. Daily warning memos or phone calls to that effect were sent to my office. C-141 transports were leaving Saigon each day with well-documented empty seats to prove that, if there were any casualties, it would be someone else's fault—Ambassador Martin's or mine.

Graham Martin stood at the other extreme. The management of evacuations is traditionally the responsibility of the State Department, with the ambassador acting as field commander. Martin was a born generalissimo—the Foreign Service's equivalent of Douglas MacArthur. He had his own very definite views on the optimum rate of evacuation and not exactly excessive regard for directives from faraway Washington. Passionately committed to the people we would soon be obliged to abandon, Martin considered it his duty to space the American withdrawal over the longest period of time possible in order to leave enough of an American presence to justify rescuing Vietnamese. Believing that, in the short term, panic in Saigon was a greater worry than Hanoi's capabilities, Martin strove for a much slower pace of evacuation than even Ford, Scowcroft, or I—the administration "hawks"—thought appropriate. He flooded us with cables, the gist of which was that I would be the one held responsible if any potential refugees were needlessly left behind. With the State Department being harassed by the Pentagon because we were evacuating too slowly and by Martin because we were leaving too fast, the mean emerged as far more precarious than golden.

My position was, in fact, much closer to Martin's than to the Pentagon's. Where I parted company with the ambassador was in our respective assessments of South Vietnam's prospects for survival— hence of the time available for evacuation. Even after the collapse of the Central Highlands, Martin was arguing that a viable redoubt could be constructed around Nha Trang, Saigon, and the Delta—a proposition vehemently disputed by the irrepressible Phil Habib, who was no shrinking violet either. When Saigon's collapse became too obvious to be wished away, Martin argued that we could manage the transfer of power in Saigon by means of a coalition government gradually enough to maintain a refugee airlift for many more weeks than I considered feasible. Having sat across from Le Duc Tho for all these years, I was certain that he would never acquiesce in a gradual transfer of authority or any autonomous political structure in Saigon, however temporary —not even an autonomous Communist one. Hanoi would take no chances on the emergence of Titoism in South Vietnam.

Much as I sympathized with Martin's objectives, our policy had to take account of the increasingly ominous intelligence assessments that South Vietnam would be able to hold out only for a matter of weeks.

With the approval of the President, I therefore adopted the following plan. First we determined our helicopter lift capacity for one day, which turned out to be around 1,250. On that basis, on April 18 (a week after the President's address), I ordered Martin to reduce the American personnel to that level by April 22. This last group of Americans, together with as many remaining Vietnamese employees as possible, would be evacuated from the embassy grounds at the point when the Saigon airport (Tan Son Nhut) was threatened. During the intervening period, a maximum effort would be made to evacuate Vietnamese, with preference given to those who had exposed themselves on our behalf.

Senatorial pressures for a speedy retreat from Vietnam were mounting daily. On April 14, the entire Senate Foreign Relations Committee called on the President in the Cabinet Room, the first time this had happened since Woodrow Wilson. Schlesinger and I delivered grim, nearly identical briefings about the military situation and Saigon's prospects. The distinguished Senators replied that they had not come to discuss Vietnam strategy but to speed the evacuation of Americans and to make sure we were not delaying it in order to rescue Vietnamese. Giving priority to saving South Vietnamese, they held, would get us involved militarily all over again. Ford tells the story in his memoirs:

> The message was clear: get out, *fast*. "I will give you large sums for evacuation," New York's Jacob Javits said, "but not one nickel for military aid." Idaho's Frank Church saw grave problems which "could involve us in a very large war" if we attempted to evacuate all the South Vietnamese who had been loyal to us. Delaware's Joseph Biden echoed a similar refrain. "I will vote for any amount for getting the Americans out," he said; "I don't want it mixed with getting the Vietnamese out."[11]

The President's reply was polite and unyielding:

> Believe me, we need to buy time, even a few days. Thank you for coming down. We've had a good discussion but the decision is my responsibility and I'll accept the consequences.[12]

## The Search for a Political Solution

Commentators and Congress, of course, had another alternative: their cherished "political solution." But the side facing total defeat has nothing to offer to the adversary and little more than risk to possible intermediaries. France showed a keen interest in becoming active. But even while we politely discussed various French schemes for partitioning South Vietnam, we judged their démarches—as on Cambodia—to be more a reflection of nostalgia for lost colonial influence than a realistic assessment of how to conclude the Vietnam tragedy.

The only "political" move we could think of was to approach Moscow, which, despite the collapse of the trade bill, continued to have a stake in the American relationship. Brezhnev still pined after the summit conference on European security he had been pursuing for three years and which was now tentatively planned to be held in late July. I told my daily State Department senior staff meeting on April 18 that we would approach the Soviet Union even though I rated the chances of its doing something constructive on the order of one in a thousand. We were in the humiliating position summed up by British historian Edward Gibbon: that persuasion is the resource of the feeble and the feeble can seldom persuade. What made our situation so especially harrowing was that we had been made feeble by choice, not by necessity.

On April 19, I delivered an "oral note" from Ford to Brezhnev via Dobrynin. (An oral note is a written document having the same status as an oral conversation but put in writing for precision and emphasis.) The note stated that a cease-fire in Vietnam was needed to accomplish the "evacuation of American citizens and those South Vietnamese to whom we have a direct and special obligation." We were approaching Moscow, we said not without a touch of menace, because "it is in our long-term mutual interest that the situation be brought to its conclusion in a manner that does not jeopardize Soviet-American relations, or affect the attitude of the American people toward other international problems."

To give a more realistic cast to this essentially threadbare appeal, we stressed our willingness "to discuss the special political circumstances that could make this [a cease-fire] possible"—in other words, a change in the political situation in Saigon. We bluffed about the dangerous consequences of an attack on airfields and passenger planes —though so expert an observer of American congressional debates as Dobrynin was unlikely to take that threat very seriously.

While awaiting the Soviet reply, Martin, on April 20, hinted to Thieu that the South Vietnamese President might consider resigning. Martin purported to speak in his personal capacity, though in fact the démarche had been approved by Ford and coordinated with my White House office. I had no illusions about what the North Vietnamese response would be to such a step, but I acquiesced on the slim hope that our approach might lead to a negotiation, giving us a few extra days for evacuating our friends. Rather icily, Thieu replied to Martin that he would do what was best for his country. Martin ended his report to Washington on this poignant note: "I went home, read the daily news digests from Washington, took a shower, scrubbed very hard with the strongest soap I could find. It didn't help very much." Ford, Scowcroft, and I felt the same way.

The White House sense of urgency about evacuating the maximum number of Vietnamese had not yet engaged the Justice Department, which refused to waive visa requirements. It may seem strange to those unfamiliar with Washington that a President can be in a position to be obliged to fight bitter battles with a Cabinet agency about its willingness to "extend parole"—the technical term for waiving visa requirements—which was within the executive branch's authority. At last, on April 22, the Justice Department—with the approval of the Senate Judiciary Committee—agreed to waive restrictions for up to 130,000 refugees from Indochina, including fifty thousand in the high-risk category. The last such exception had been made in 1960 on behalf of Cuban refugees.

While many of their seniors in Washington were engaged in passing the buck, two junior Foreign Service officers—Lionel Rosenblatt and Craig Johnstone—who had served earlier in Vietnam, did something on their own to ease the suffering there. On April 20, they left their Washington posts without permission. Traveling at their own expense and with regular (not diplomatic) passports, they arrived in Saigon and helped some of the Vietnamese who had worked with them escape. It was an egregious breach of Foreign Service discipline and who knows how many State Department regulations. The State Department bureaucracy was outraged and recommended penalties ranging from dismissal to a severe reprimand, which would have blighted Rosenblatt's and Johnstone's careers. When they returned to Washington two weeks later, I told Larry Eagleburger, then deputy under secretary of state for administration, to read them the riot act and then bring them to my office. After making some formal noises of disapproval, I said: "There has been little of which we can be proud these last months. But you have brought credit to your country and to the Foreign Service." No disciplinary action was taken. A year later, I saw to it that each received the State Department Superior Honor Award. Johnstone remained in the Foreign Service, later becoming ambassador to Algeria; Rosenblatt has devoted his life and career to nongovernmental organizations for helping refugees.

On the evening of April 21, Nguyen Van Thieu resigned with a bitter speech castigating the United States for failing either to enforce the Paris Agreement or to extend the promised material assistance to South Vietnam. The media hailed his departure. A "negotiated agreement" in accordance with the Paris Agreement was now possible at last, argued the *Washington Post* and *New York Times,* as if Thieu had been the obstacle to a negotiated outcome. Thieu's complaints against the United States were dismissed as the rantings of a "discredited and embittered Vietnamese politician"; for once, the liberal media were happy to defend the administration.[13]

Thieu had every reason to resent America's conduct. Though he hated me as few people ever have because he held me responsible for the negotiations that had ended the American military role, I respect him as a patriot who served his country with courage and honor. Thieu had never been the obstacle to peace that antiwar critics alleged. Both he and his country deserved a better fate. Had I thought it possible that Congress would, in effect, cut off aid to a beleaguered ally, I would not have pressed as I did in the final negotiations in 1972.

Hopes for a "political solution" proved to be every bit as fragile as all our experience had indicated they would be. Radio Hanoi attacked Thieu's successor, Tran Van Huong, as viciously as it had the departed President. No sooner had Thieu resigned than Hanoi escalated its demands, insisting on the immediate departure of all American personnel, both civilian and military.

Twenty years of hope, frustration, and discord over Vietnam had now been reduced to a single objective: to save the maximum number of potential Vietnamese victims from the consequences of America's abandonment. We in the White House clung to every refugee flight as if it could somehow redeem the accumulated anguish of America's war with itself. Starting on April 21, a round-the-clock airlift from Saigon was begun with C-141s flying in the daytime and C-130s at night. Over the next ten days, this helped to save close to fifty thousand Vietnamese (another eighty thousand escaped by other means). The only meaningful debate within our government was how long to keep the airlift going.

The Communist incentive to grant us that crucial time diminished when White House staffers masterminded a typical inside-the-Beltway bureaucratic victory. They inserted into a presidential speech at Tulane University in New Orleans on April 23 a phrase to the effect that, as far as Ford was concerned, the war was over. The relevant passage reads as follows:

> Today, America can regain the sense of pride that existed before Vietnam. But it cannot be achieved by refighting a war that is finished as far as America is concerned. As I see it, the time has come to look forward to an agenda for the future, to unify, to bind up the Nation's wounds, and to restore its health and its optimistic self-confidence.[14]

Background briefings by White House staffers stressed that neither Scowcroft nor I had been consulted about the wording and described the speech as a presidential "declaration of independence" from his Secretary of State.

What the gloaters over the paragraph in question failed to understand was that the war *was* over, with or without the paragraph; the only remaining issue was how many Vietnamese we could save and how much longer we would be permitted to carry on this essentially humanitarian activity. Some ambiguity about how far we were willing to go to achieve our objective was desirable. I described this strategy to the House Appropriations Committee on April 21:

> Our difficulty, our problem, in the last ten days has been to conduct ourselves in such a manner that we can save the maximum number of lives without at the same time creating a panic which would prevent the saving of any lives. If you understand this is the basic principle of our policy over the last ten days, it will be a key to many things that have been done.

In practice, the Tulane speech did not alter Ford's conduct of affairs. Later that day, he instructed Ron Nessen to inform the media that he stood by his request for $722 million in aid to Vietnam. In the midst of the heartbreaking turmoil all around us, I saw no point in debating speechwriting prerogatives with the President. I never raised the issue, and Ford never volunteered an explanation. Apparently he did not consider the Tulane speech as significant as some of his entourage did, for he makes no mention of it in his memoirs.

## The Evacuation

For a few days after the Tulane speech, all was quiet, though the Communists had advanced to within artillery range of Tan Son Nhut airport. Were they regrouping for a final assault, or had they opened up a window for evacuation?

Actually they were doing both. On April 24, Dobrynin telephoned at 4:00 P.M. and read me the Soviet reply to our note of April 19. It sounded like an explicit green light to evacuate Americans, and it claimed that Hanoi would seek a political outcome guided by the Paris Agreement. The North Vietnamese allegedly told Moscow that they "do not intend to damage the prestige of the United States." This emboldened Brezhnev to try to restrain nonexisting American adventurousness by expressing his hope that we would take no action "fraught with a new exacerbation of the situation in Indochina."

If the Soviet note meant what it seemed to say, there might be some breathing room for evacuation. Though the note confined itself to the evacuation of Americans, its practical effect was to help extricate Vietnamese as well, since we were evacuating both groups simultaneously, usually on the same planes. And if Hanoi really intended to bring about the political change by the procedures envisaged in the Paris Agreement, some more time might be gained.

The outcome, of course, would be the same: the total Communist takeover we had resisted so strenuously for two decades. Yet, for the sake of saving more Vietnamese lives, we were prepared to grit our teeth and play along. Brezhnev's desire to salvage the European Security Conference gave us a little leverage—though every congressional hearing undercut the last flicker of threat that we might come back in at the last moment.

A State Department staff meeting assessing Brezhnev's message agreed that we should use it to gain a little time, though Bill Hyland, head of the Bureau of Intelligence and Research, estimated "a little" to be at most one week. I therefore instructed Martin to reduce the number of Americans to below eight hundred (the number that could be lifted in two and a half hours, according to the estimate of the Joint Chiefs), and thereafter to "trickle out" the remainder so that an airlift could be kept going to rescue the maximum number of Vietnamese.

In the afternoon of April 24, Ford held an NSC meeting to review the final evacuation plans. Schlesinger continued to advocate immediate evacuation of the remaining Americans, which would, of course, end the evacuation of Vietnamese as well. Ford put an end to the argument as he had at the meeting on April 9:

> FORD: I understand the risk. It is mine and I am doing it.
>     But let's make sure we carry out the orders.
> ROCKEFELLER: You can't insure the interests of America
>     without risks.
> FORD: With God's help.

Grasping for every last possible extension, we replied to the Soviets at 8:25 P.M. on April 24. In our message, we posed a number of questions in the hope that the refugee airlift might continue while the Soviets prepared their answers. In our message, we noted that, in view of the "constructive [Soviet] reply . . . the US side is proceeding with the evacuation of Americans under the assumption that conditions will remain favorable." We invited Hanoi's views on how to implement the provisions of the Paris Agreement "relative to the achievement of a political settlement." The President reassured Brezhnev that we would desist from what the Congress was, in any event, prohibiting. So long as there was no interference with the evacuation, our note continued, the United States would "take no steps which might exacerbate the situation."

It was thin gruel but, as I said to the State Department staff meeting, all we had left to us now was a show of nerve. There is, however, a limit to what can be accomplished by diplomatic maneuvering, especially when dealing with the steely-eyed calculators from Hanoi.

On the evening of April 28 Washington time (April 29 in Vietnam), the final collapse of Saigon began with a rocket attack on Tan Son Nhut airport. Eight thousand particularly endangered Vietnamese and four hundred Americans had been assembled there in order to enable the evacuation planes to be filled and turned around without delay.

Though the firing soon ceased, the refugees' very peril became their undoing. Panicked, they swarmed over the runways, and in effect stopped the airlift. At 10:45 P.M. Washington time on April 28, Ford very reluctantly ordered the final evacuation. Shortly before, we had talked not in the apocalyptic terms in which the occasion may appear in history books. Rather it had about it the feel of mourning for the unfortunate victims we were about to leave behind:

> KISSINGER: They have the authority to call for the emergency airlift anytime tonight—our night—and they must call for it before the end of the day out there.
>
> FORD: By the end of the day out there or by tomorrow morning here?
>
> KISSINGER: By tomorrow morning here if the C-130s haven't taken them off, then the helicopters will.
>
> FORD: That's a real shame! Twenty-four more hours—or twelve more hours?
>
> KISSINGER: Twelve more hours and we would have saved eight thousand lives.
>
> FORD: Henry, we did the best we could.
>
> KISSINGER: Mr. President, you carried it single-handedly against all the advice and we played it out as far as it would play.
>
> FORD: Well, I just hope [General] Smith and [Graham] Martin now understand where we are and will not hesitate to act.
>
> KISSINGER: Well, we checked with Martin. I talked with him fifteen minutes ago. I can't say that he's doing it willingly but he's going to do it. He wants to stay behind with two people to take care of Americans that might come out of the woodwork. But I just don't think we can justify it.
>
> FORD: I don't think so either, Henry.
>
> KISSINGER: We can't give them any hostages.

(To give a sense of the strange mixture of banality and sadness of these final hours, I am attaching the relevant conversations in the Notes.[15])

At 11:00 P.M., I called Graham Martin and told him to pull the plug: all Americans must come out together with as many Vietnamese as could be loaded on the helicopters in what would irrevocably be the final day of the airlift. Martin agreed to the evacuation but proposed staying behind with two volunteers to supervise its orderly transfer, confirming my suspicion that he planned to go down like General George "Chinese" Gordon—the famed British commander who was killed in Khartoum by the Mahdi in 1885 after refusing to leave. We needed few things less than to have our ambassador in Saigon taken hostage by the North Vietnamese on the day our effort there collapsed. So I ordered Martin to leave: "We need our heroes back in Washington; there aren't too many of them here."

The record is unclear as to whether Hanoi accelerated the final assault on Saigon at the last moment or whether the North Vietnamese were following a plan for which their reply to the Soviets had been their final deception. At the time, I believed that Ford's Tulane speech had advanced Hanoi's timetable because, in effect, it removed the last danger of American reintervention—though actually it would have required a truly extraordinary level of North Vietnamese paranoia to take such a threat seriously. The memoirs of General Van Tien Dung, the commander, do not refer to Ford's speech, as they do to almost every other milestone in the American domestic debate.[16] According to Dung, what seems to have hastened Hanoi's decision-making, however, were the "cunning diplomatic plans" of the "United States and its puppets":

> The Americans' and puppets' cunning diplomatic plans coming one on top of the other, coupled with threatening hints to us, were aimed at blocking our troops' general offensive on Saigon, and showed all the more that we must fight more urgently, attack more quickly, and make the best use of each hour, each minute for total victory.[17]

Hanoi's idea of "cunning diplomatic plans" was that Saigon tried to implement the steps which the American protest movement had been demanding for a decade: Thieu's removal and broadening of the government. Thieu had already left and, on April 24, his successor, President Tran Van Huong, broadened the government by inviting General Duong Van Minh to take over as Prime Minister. "Big Minh," as he was nicknamed, had been the great hope of the anti-Vietnam protesters since 1967 when he had lost out in a power struggle with Thieu. Alleged to be a neutralist, Minh was deemed to be acceptable to the Communists, though Le Duc Tho had given me quite the opposite impression.

In the final struggle over who would be captain of the sinking ship, Minh refused to serve as Prime Minister because he said the offer came from the old power structure, now overthrown. Instead, he asked that the National Assembly appoint him President with the charge to end the war and to create a transitional administration. Two days were spent accomplishing this maneuver, and Big Minh was finally installed as President on April 27. He remained in office less than seventy-two hours, only long enough to undertake two significant acts: he asked Hanoi for a cease-fire and political negotiations—which were rejected —and, on April 29, he demanded that all Americans leave within twenty-four hours. Since this coincided precisely with our withdrawal schedule, it in fact helped our extrication by avoiding the charge that we were abandoning our friends. Simultaneously, the French Foreign Office attempted to establish diplomatic contact between the PRG representative in Paris and American diplomats—for which the PRG envoys were allegedly eager.

But Hanoi's leaders had not fought for three decades to tolerate a transitional government in Saigon, much less an independent—even if Communist—state. Paradoxically, the installation of Minh may well have speeded up Hanoi's timetable. It might have been more prepared to grant Thieu a period of grace than to his increasingly abject successors. Thieu's regime was collapsing, and a few extra days would not resuscitate it. But if an internationally recognized government emerged in Saigon capable of negotiating a cease-fire and dealing with the United States, it might lead to a kind of independence for South Vietnam—albeit a Communist one. This Hanoi would not countenance. So it happened that Hanoi's last battle in Saigon was ironically aimed at the South Vietnamese Communists whose guerrilla movement had started the entire tragedy all those years earlier.

Not surprisingly, the contact with the PRG in Paris never materialized.

## The Last Day

After hounding the White House for three weeks to speed up the final evacuation, the Pentagon's plans for implementing it turned out to be far from precise. There was a glitch in communications between the helicopters on the aircraft carriers and the tactical air cover for them based in Thailand, leading to a disagreement among the various commands about when the operation should start, whether it was Greenwich Mean Time or local time. A new schedule had to be established, and the operation started in earnest with a few hours' delay.

As Americans were being lifted from the roof of the American

Embassy during the morning of April 29 (Washington time), Ford, Schlesinger, and I briefed the congressional leadership. Continuing to fight yesterday's battles, the legislators kept harping on a "political" solution, oblivious to the fact that the evacuation we were describing ended America's ability to influence the political outcome.

After that, all was silence. I sat alone in the National Security Adviser's corner office in the West Wing of the White House, enveloped by the eerie solitude that sometimes attends momentous events. The White House NSC office was the Washington command center for the evacuation of Vietnam even though the actual airlift was being conducted by the Pentagon. The careful record established by the Pentagon of its repeated requests for a speedy evacuation guaranteed that Ford and I would be held accountable should anything go wrong at this last moment. On the other hand, neither Ford nor I could any longer influence the outcome; we had become spectators of the final act. So we each sat in our offices, freed of other duties yet unable to affect the ongoing tragedy, with a serenity rarely experienced in high office.

Ours was, in fact, a command post with essentially nothing to do. Ford and I received regular reports on the progress of the evacuation. My deputy, Brent Scowcroft, kept track of the myriad details; without his selfless dedication and efficiency, we would never have come this close to an honorable extrication, if an extrication under these conditions could ever be described as honorable. Robert C. "Bud" McFarlane, later Ronald Reagan's National Security Adviser, was in charge of the administration of my office. He had served in Vietnam and now, with tears in his eyes, had to tend to the mechanics of the collapse. Many of his fellow Marines had died to keep this tragedy from happening. Bud was deeply moved, though he made a valiant and nearly successful effort to try not to burden the rest of us with his sorrow.

In that almost mystical stillness, Vietnam played back in my mind as if in slow motion. I felt too drained to analyze the various decisions that had led to this moment of dashed hopes. Had I done so, I would probably have concluded, as I still believe, that no real alternative existed short of surrender to the strategy we pursued. But what did torment me in these hours was my own role in the next-to-last act: the acceleration of negotiations after Le Duc Tho's breakthrough offer of October 8, 1972. No doubt had I stalled, the North Vietnamese would have gone public even earlier than they did. Thieu would have dug in his heels anyway; the diplomatic outcome (if any) would have been even less favorable. Congress would have forced a conclusion by cutting off funds.

What has torn at me ever since is whether such an outcome might not have been better. Did the demoralizations of the Saigon structure which led to its collapse in 1975 start with the pace of negotiations we imposed back in 1972? Did Nixon and I assume too much when we tried to carry the full weight of our concept of national honor? Was there a basis for the elation of my negotiating team and me on October 8, 1972, when Le Duc Tho, in effect, accepted our terms, and we thought ourselves on the verge of both an honorable end of the war and national reconciliation?

My colleagues and I believed that it was our duty to struggle for an outcome other than abdication. Protesters could speak of Vietnam in terms of the excesses of an aberrant society, but when my colleagues and I thought of Vietnam, it was in terms of dedicated men and women—soldiers and Foreign Service officers—who had struggled and suffered there and of our Vietnamese associates now condemned to face an uncertain but surely painful fate. These Americans had honestly believed that they were defending the cause of freedom against a brutal enemy in treacherous jungles and distant rice paddies. Vilified by the media, assailed in Congress, and ridiculed by the protest movement, they had sustained America's idealistic tradition, risking their lives and expending their youth on a struggle that American leadership groups had initiated, then abandoned, and finally disdained. It was they and not the few bad apples, their goals and not their ultimate failures, American responsibility for the safety of the free world and not the frustrations associated with it that formed my thoughts as I sat at my desk and Vietnam wound down.

My reveries were interrupted by one telephone call I received that day not related to the helicopter lift. It was from Lew Wasserman, then head of MCA, the Hollywood communications giant, and a recent friend: "The purpose of the call is to tell you that with all the problems you're having there are a lot of your friends out here who are thinking about you." He hung up before I could reply. Lew Wasserman was a devout Democrat, a constant critic of our Vietnam policies, and I could not be of any conceivable use to his business. It was a genuine act of grace, and I have never forgotten it.

Then, in its very death throes, Vietnam swept me back into its frustrations and tragedy. By now it was early afternoon in Washington, well after midnight in Saigon. Despite his original inclination to end the airlift at dusk in Vietnam, Ford had ordered it to continue all night so that the largest number of Vietnamese might be rescued—especially those still inside the embassy compound. Around 2:00 P.M., I learned that there were still 760 people there and that, for whatever reason, only one helicopter had landed in the previous two hours. I called Schlesinger to discuss how we could evacuate this group and at the same time establish a deadline by which the evacuation would be completed. For it was clear that the North Vietnamese would occupy Saigon at daybreak. For once, Schlesinger and I were in complete harmony. We computed that thirteen helicopters would do the trick. But to throw in a safety factor, we agreed on a total of nineteen. Martin was to be on the last helicopter.

The conversation between Schlesinger and me during which this decision was reached conveys the atmosphere of those hours better than any narrative could:

> KISSINGER: Jim.
>
> SCHLESINGER: Yeah, Henry. We are sending a message to them because of the 46s as well as the 53s [types of helicopters]—that the 19 choppers, which should handle 760 people—[are] all that he gets, and we expect them—him—out on the 19th chopper at the latest at the pace to terminate around 3:30.
>
> KISSINGER: All right. Now, you tell him, Jim; if you don't add that this is a presidential order, he won't come out.
>
> SCHLESINGER: Right. We shall do that.
>
> KISSINGER: That's what I wanted to make sure that you add.
>
> SCHLESINGER: Shall do. He is a man with a mission.
>
> KISSINGER: Well, he lost a son there.
>
> SCHLESINGER: Yes. You have got to admire that man.
>
> KISSINGER: Look, his thoughts are in the right direction.
>
> SCHLESINGER: That's right. Dedication and energy.
>
> KISSINGER: And I think . . .
>
> SCHLESINGER: You weep.
>
> KISSINGER: I think you and I will be glad we went this way.

I mention this episode because, twenty years later, I was watching a cable television program in which a very impressive colonel expressed his outrage that four hundred Vietnamese friends of the United States should have been left behind inside the embassy compound where he had helped supervise the evacuation. I was stunned and tracked down the colonel at the Army War College and confirmed his statements on the program. No one had told me any such thing, nor is there any record of such abandonment in the many staff meetings surrounding the event. I still do not understand what happened. I know that nineteen helicopters left—because I was receiving a report on each departure—and that Martin was on the last one. I have no explanation as to why anyone was left behind unless the gates of the embassy had been reopened to let in another group beyond the original 760.

Shortly after 4:00 P.M., I was able to reassure George Meany, president of the AFL-CIO, that Vietnamese labor leaders had just been rescued. His was one of many requests we had received to rescue some Vietnamese with special ties to the United States. At 4:58 P.M. Washington time (4:58 the next morning in Saigon), Martin left with the nineteenth or last helicopter—or what we thought was the last. He had done an extraordinary job. Imperious, occasionally insubordinate, he was as dedicated and courageous as he had been contentious. Over a two-week period, Martin had orchestrated the evacuation of over fifty thousand South Vietnamese and six thousand Americans with only four casualties. He had kept the situation sufficiently calm to allow another eighty thousand refugees to get out on their own. The accolade I sent him on the rescue ship came from the heart:

> I am sure you know how deeply I feel about your performance under the most trying circumstances. My heartfelt thanks. Warm regards.

Brent Scowcroft, who had had to bear the brunt of the nearly daily exchanges with Martin, added his own postscript: "Graham: You were superb. Brent." For the taciturn Brent, this was the equivalent of decorating Martin with the Scowcroft Medal of Honor.

As soon as I thought the last helicopter had left, I crossed the passageway between the White House and Old Executive Office Building to brief the press. Summarizing the day's events, I responded to questions, the overwhelming thrust of which was to get me to confirm the journalists' established view that everything that had ever happened had been an unforgivable mistake. Awed by the tragedy taking place halfway around the globe, I refused to take the bait:

I think this is not the occasion, when the last American has barely left Saigon, to make an assessment of a decade and a half of American foreign policy, because it could equally well be argued that if five administrations that were staffed, after all, by serious people dedicated to the welfare of their country came to certain conclusions, that maybe there was something in their assessment, even if for a variety of reasons the effort did not succeed.

As I have already pointed out, special factors have operated in recent years. But I would think that what we need now in this country, for some weeks at least, and hopefully for some months, is to heal the wounds and to put Vietnam behind us and to concentrate on the problems of the future.[18]

Returning to my office, I found that Vietnam still would not let go easily. While Graham Martin and the remnants of the embassy staff had indeed departed at 4:58 A.M. Saigon time, elements of the 9th Marine Amphibious Brigade protecting the evacuation—comprising 129 Marines—had been left behind for some inexplicable reason. Huge credibility gaps had been manufactured from far less than this, but those of us in the White House Situation Room had no time to worry about public relations. The helicopter lift was resumed. It was 7:53 P.M. Washington time (and already daylight in Saigon) when the helicopter carrying the last Marines left the embassy roof.

Two hours later, North Vietnamese tanks rolled into Saigon. One of the first smashed through the gates of the presidential palace. There was no turnover of authority because that would have implied the existence of an independent, or at least autonomous, South Vietnam. Instead, Big Minh and his entire cabinet were arrested and disappeared from public view.

The Provisional Revolutionary Government (PRG), the reincarnation of the National Liberation Front (NLF)—advertised in the West for a decade as the putative centerpiece of a South Vietnamese democratic coalition government—disappeared with Big Minh. Within a year, the two Vietnams were unified along the traditional Communist pattern. Not a shred of autonomy remained for the South. Hundreds of thousands of South Vietnamese, including all those who had been in the government or armed forces, were herded into so-called reeducation camps—a euphemism for concentration camps—where they stayed for the better part of a decade. Tens of thousands fled as boat people. The Buddhist monks, whose quest for autonomy from the Saigon authorities had contributed to inducing the Kennedy Administration to overthrow the former South Vietnamese President Ngo Dinh Diem government, were imprisoned under the most brutal conditions.

In Washington, not much changed as a result of the tragedy of Vietnam. On May 1, 1975, the day after Saigon fell, the House of Representatives refused to approve a request by Ford for $327 million for the care and transportation of Indochinese refugees. Congressional leaders for weeks had argued against efforts to save Vietnamese, and now the House turned down refugee relief for those who had already been saved. Second thoughts have been few and far between.[19]

For the sake of our long-term peace of mind, we must some day undertake an assessment of why good men on all sides found no way to avoid this disaster and why our domestic drama first paralyzed and then overwhelmed us. But, on the day the last helicopter left the roof of the embassy, only a feeling of emptiness remained. Those of us who had fought the battles to avoid the final disaster were too close to the tragedy to review the history of twenty years of American involvement. And now it was too late to alter the course of events.

# 18

# ANATOMY OF A CRISIS: THE *MAYAGUEZ*

We thought we were at last free to turn to healing the nation's wounds when Indochina suddenly reached out and, like a drowning man, dragged us back into the vortex. The entire episode lasted only three days and, unlike most of our experiences in the region, had a positive outcome. Because it was relatively clear-cut, it permits an examination of the genre of crisis management and of the confusion, the bureaucratic role-playing, and the inherent uncertainties involved in the process.

During my tenure as Secretary of State, whenever I was in Washington, I generally held meetings with my senior staff twice a week. These took place in a nondescript, oblong conference room across the hall from the Secretary of State's more elegant suite. Since then, the State Department's entire seventh-floor complex, housing its most senior officials, has been remodeled and upgraded under the guidance of its brilliant and relentless curator, Clement Conger. In my day, Conger had just begun the process, starting with the deputy secretary's suite.

Usually some twenty to twenty-five people attended: the assistant and under secretaries, along with a few top staff aides. The purpose of these meetings was not to design policy—they were much too large for that—but to keep key officials informed of major trends. Actual crises and negotiations were handled by much smaller special groups. Almost the last thing one expected to address at a staff meeting was a sudden, fast-breaking crisis.

The May 12, 1975, meeting began routinely enough at 8:00 A.M. Going around the table, I asked the head of each regional or functional bureau to describe to his colleagues the key issues facing his office. When I came to J. Owen Zurhellen, Jr., the deputy assistant secretary of state for East Asia, who was sitting in for the traveling Philip Habib, he reported:

> [A]n American merchant ship has been captured by Cambo-
> dians about a hundred miles off the coast and is proceeding
> into Sihanoukville under Cambodian troop guard.

He was unable to enlighten me when I asked incredulously: "How can that be?"—addressed as much to the event as to the fact that I should be learning of it in such an offhand fashion. The hapless Zurhellen, having himself been informed only two minutes before the meeting, replied truthfully: "It's beyond me."

Zurhellen was then subjected to a barrage of questions from an increasingly testy Secretary of State—from "how long did the report of the capture sit on various desks before it reached the top levels?" to "what are we doing about it?" No one had an answer to either query, whereupon I asked that a call be placed to Brent Scowcroft at the White House to find out whether he had received any information from the Pentagon. Donning my National Security Adviser's hat, I requested a quick survey of what American forces in the area might be capable of intercepting the ship, reportedly still a hundred miles at sea. I closed the meeting by saying: "I know you damned well cannot let Cambodia capture a ship a hundred miles at sea and do nothing."

The ship in question was the *Mayaguez*. Built in 1944, she was redesigned in 1960 as America's first fully containerized ship. Her past had been anything but glorious. On her maiden voyage to Venezuela, local stevedores, fearing that containerization would threaten their livelihood, refused to unload the ship. Returned to Baltimore, the *Mayaguez* lay idle for two years before she resumed the delivery of cargo, mostly to Asia.[1] There was nothing to distinguish her from hundreds of similar ships plying their trade until, quite by accident, the *Mayaguez* emerged as the centerpiece of an international crisis. Three dramatic days later, she was rescued and relapsed into anonymity.

It took a few hours to piece together the sequence of events that had propelled us into this crisis. In the early afternoon (local time) of the same Monday, May 12, 1975 (early morning in Washington), the *Mayaguez* had been crossing the Gulf of Thailand on a northwesterly

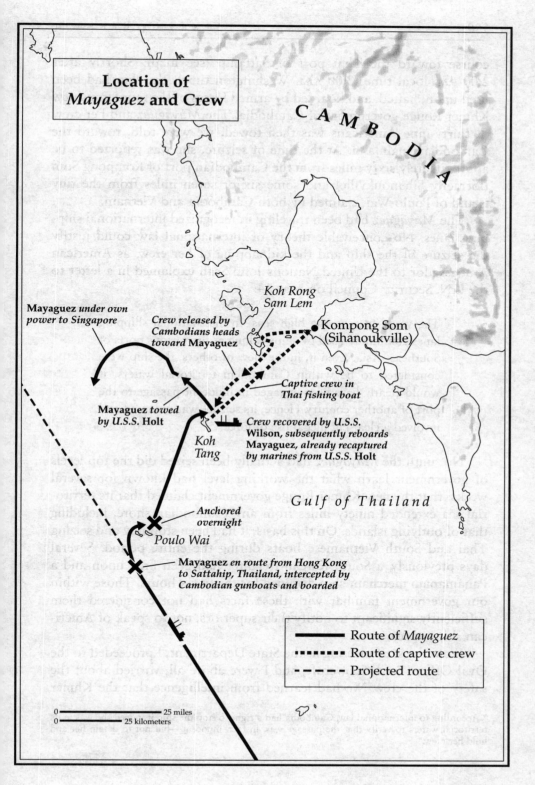

## Location of *Mayaguez* and Crew

C A M B O D I A

*Koh Rong*
*Sam Lem*

Kompong Som
(Sihanoukville)

**Mayaguez *under own***
**power to Singapore**

*Crew released by*
*Cambodians heads*
*toward* **Mayaguez**

*Captive crew in*
*Thai fishing boat*

**Mayaguez *towed***
**by U.S.S. Holt**

*Crew recovered by U.S.S.*
**Wilson,** *subsequently reboards*
**Mayaguez,** *already recaptured*
*by marines from U.S.S. Holt*

*Koh*
*Tang*

*Gulf of Thailand*

*Anchored*
*overnight*

*Poulo Wai*

**Mayaguez *en route from Hong Kong***
**to Sattahip, Thailand, intercepted by**
**Cambodian gunboats and boarded**

———— Route of *Mayaguez*
·········· Route of captive crew
– – – – Projected route

0 ———— 25 miles
0 ———— 25 kilometers

549

course toward the Thai port of Sattahip (see map). Shortly after 2:00 P.M. local time (3:00 A.M. Washington time), the ship had been fired upon, halted, and boarded by armed forces of the murderous new Khmer Rouge government of Cambodia. The *Mayaguez* and her crew of thirty-nine Americans was then towed, we were told, toward the Cambodian mainland. At the time of seizure, she was reported to be approximately sixty miles from the Cambodian port of Kompong Som (formerly Sihanoukville) and some six or seven miles from the tiny island of Poulo Wai, claimed by both Cambodia and Vietnam.

The *Mayaguez* had been traveling in recognized international shipping lanes. No conceivable theory of international law could justify the seizure of the ship and the kidnapping of her crew, as American Ambassador to the United Nations John Scali explained in a letter to the U.N. Security Council on May 14:

> The vessel was on the high seas, in international shipping lanes commonly used by ships calling at the various ports of Southeast Asia. Even if, in the view of others, the ship were considered to be within Cambodian territorial waters, it would clearly have been engaged in innocent passage to the port of another country. Hence, its seizure was unlawful and involved a clear-cut illegal use of force.[2]*

Not until the *Mayaguez* had actually been seized did the top levels of government learn what the working level had known for several weeks: that the new Khmer Rouge government claimed that its territorial sea extended ninety miles from any Cambodian shore, including that of outlying islands. On this basis, it had been stopping and seizing Thai and South Vietnamese boats during the entire period. Several days previously, a South Korean freighter had been fired upon and a Panamanian merchant ship detained for thirty-six hours. Those within our government familiar with these facts had not considered them sufficiently significant to notify their superiors, not to speak of American ships at sea.

From the staff meeting at the State Department, I proceeded to the Oval Office. Ford, Scowcroft, and I were above all worried about the safety of the crew. We had learned from intelligence that the Khmer

---

* According to international law, Cambodia had a right to stop the ship if indeed she was in its territorial waters to verify that the passage was, in fact, innocent—but not to detain her and hold her crew.

Rouge had ordered the killing of all officials of the Lon Nol government as well as their families, including children. And these orders were in the process of being expanded to include all individuals with "bourgeois" education. Though our media ignored attempts to publicize the massacre, we knew the facts and feared for the Americans' lives.

Foreign policy considerations weighed heavily as well. Especially in the aftermath of Indochina's collapse, the United States needed to demonstrate that there were limits to what it would tolerate. Allies in the region—Japan and the Republic of Korea, in particular—would scrutinize our conduct to determine whether the fall of Saigon marked an aberration or America's permanent retreat from international responsibility. Even China, though friendly to the Khmer Rouge, would analyze our actions in terms of our ability or willingness to assert our national interest—a matter of some relevance to its own overriding concern with Soviet hegemonic aspirations.

Every decision-maker views events through the prism of his own experience. Ford was in Congress when the *Pueblo,* an electronic surveillance ship, was seized by North Korea during the Johnson Administration. Her crew had been held hostage for eleven months and released only after a near-apology from the United States for violating North Korea's territorial waters, which Pyongyang trumpeted all over Asia as "another great victory of the Korean people who have crushed the myth of the mightiness of United States imperialism to smithereens."[3] From the outset, Ford was determined not to permit a repetition of such a sequence of events.

The trouble was that we had no idea of the location of the *Mayaguez,* where she was being taken, or what American forces might be available for countermeasures. While this intelligence was being gathered, Ford ordered intensive reconnaissance pending a special National Security Council meeting which he called for noon in the Cabinet Room.

Crises frequently corner the policymaker into acting on more or less informed guesses—especially at the outset. That was surely the case during the first NSC meeting on the subject of the *Mayaguez.* In addition to myself, it was attended by President Ford; Vice President Rockefeller; Defense Secretary James Schlesinger and Deputy Defense Secretary William Clements; Acting Chairman of the Joint Chiefs of Staff (JCS) General David Jones (Chairman General George Brown being in Europe); Director of Central Intelligence William Colby; Deputy National Security Adviser General Brent Scowcroft; Deputy Secretary of State Robert Ingersoll; the NSC staff member responsible for

East Asia, W. Richard Smyser; and White House Chief of Staff Donald Rumsfeld. We were treated to a detailed intelligence briefing by Colby which turned out to be wrong in every detail. He reported that the *Mayaguez* was proceeding under her own power to the port of Kompong Som (Sihanoukville) at a speed of ten nautical miles an hour. That would have placed her near port by the time of the NSC meeting —a judgment confirmed by Schlesinger: "When I left the Pentagon, the ship was already only about ten miles out."

Twelve hours later, we discovered that the *Mayaguez* had never moved at all and was still anchored exactly where she had been captured. Some uncertainty as to the location of the ship was unavoidable given the short time available for analysis and the fact that, because it was nighttime in Southeast Asia, our reconnaissance had to rely on infrared sensors. But the NSC was not told of any limitations, which would have been understood; the information we received sounded meticulously precise. Some confusion was expected; totally inaccurate precision is harder to explain—indeed, I do not understand to this day what the basis for it was.

The briefing deflected our discussion from how to intercept the ship to what pressures might force the Khmer Rouge to release her. For if the *Mayaguez* was to be found in a mainland harbor by the time the NSC meeting ended, we would, in fact, be facing a challenge nearly identical to the *Pueblo* crisis and exactly the scenario Ford was so determined to avoid.

Colby proved more accurate with respect to Cambodian motivations. He argued that Khmer Rouge occupation of the islands (and attendant claim to a new territorial sea) was meant to forestall North Vietnamese designs on the same territory. Clements supported Colby's analysis by pointing to the conflicting claims of the two Communist states for oil exploration rights in the offshore area. Ford cut the discussion short:

> That is interesting, but it does not solve our problem. I think we should have a strong public statement and a strong note. We should also issue orders to get the carrier [the U.S.S. *Coral Sea*] turned around.*

The President then asked me, in my capacity as National Security Adviser, to outline the options. Laboring under the misapprehension

---

* At the time, the *Coral Sea* was en route to a courtesy visit to Australia.

that the *Mayaguez* had already reached port, I focused on a strategy that might force the Khmer Rouge to release the ship. I recommended against any negotiation because that would accept the principle of the hijacking and put a premium on American hostages. To bring about an unconditional release of the ship, I recommended a strong public statement, a forceful note via Beijing to Cambodia (since we had no diplomatic relations with Phnom Penh), and a rapid, ominous concentration of military forces. Ford recalls that I concluded my presentation with these words:

> At some point, the United States must draw the line. This is not our idea of the best such situation. It is not our choice. But we must act upon it now and firmly.[4]

Our inventory of the forces available for rescue included the *Coral Sea,* perhaps two to three days away, and an auxiliary carrier, the U.S.S. *Hancock,* under repair in Subic Bay in the Philippines, available within a similar time frame. The destroyer U.S.S. *Holt* had the capacity to reach the area twenty-four hours earlier (by Wednesday morning Washington time). U.S. Marines could be moved from Okinawa to Thailand.

But the legacy of Indochina's collapse saddled us with a number of obstacles as well: Thailand had already asked us to vacate our bases, and the Philippines would refuse permission to use American bases for a rescue operation—at least with respect to ground and air forces. If we went ahead without permission, the already strong pressures to kick us out immediately would mount. In this manner, the B-52s based in Guam entered into the catalogue of options; they were ready, and they could be used without the permission of any other country.

Ford made no decision about what military action he planned to take, but he left no doubt that he would not acquiesce in prolonged captivity for the hostages:

> Within an hour or so, there will be a public statement. Let us make an announcement ahead of time, and a tough one so that we get the initiative. Let us not tell Congress that we will do anything militarily since we have not decided. I think that it is important to make a strong statement publicly before the news gets out otherwise.

He ordered the Pentagon to submit a list of military options by the end of the afternoon and, anticipating foot-dragging, added: "I can assure you that, irrespective of the Congress, we will move." As commander-in-chief, Ford argued, the President has inherent rights to rescue American citizens—especially when they were endangered by as murderous a group as the Khmer Rouge were known to be.

At 1:50 P.M., Press Secretary Ron Nessen issued the following statement from the White House briefing room:

> We have been informed that a Cambodian naval vessel has seized an American merchant ship on the high seas and forced it to the port of Kompong Som. The President has met with the NSC. He considers this seizure an act of piracy. He has instructed the State Department to demand the immediate release of the ship. Failure to do so would have the most serious consequences.[5]

The odd timing of the release was due to the fact that, by the time the NSC meeting ended, the reporters had concluded that nothing worthy of delaying lunch had transpired. Nessen took the unusual step of calling as many journalistic haunts as he could think of, and he distributed the statement as soon as he had assembled a quorum, thereby heightening the ominous tone of the announcement.[6]

By then, I was on an airplane heading for St. Louis, so that the first stages of the crisis were being managed by Brent Scowcroft. My visit to St. Louis and Kansas City had been arranged as part of an effort to try to build a new consensus behind America's international role in the wake of Indochina. In each city, I had scheduled a formal speech, a press conference, a meeting with local leaders, and local television interviews. The theme was that American leadership remained the key to both peace and progress, and expressed—without recrimination—Ford's and my confidence that, despite setbacks, we would master the tasks before us.

If I canceled the first such visit because of yet another crisis in Indochina, it might convey that the Southeast Asian nightmare would never end. And given the time needed to concentrate our forces and await a Chinese reply, the point of decision would not be reached before my return thirty-six hours hence.

At 4:30 P.M., Deputy and, in my absence, Acting Secretary of State Ingersoll conveyed a message to Huang Zhen, chief of the Chinese

Liaison Office (the de facto Beijing Embassy), demanding the immediate release of the *Mayaguez* and her crew. Huang Zhen refused to accept the message, insisting that the new Khmer Rouge government was independent, sovereign, and beyond the reach of Chinese diplomacy. It did not surprise me that a Washington-based Chinese diplomat would steer clear of the responsibility associated with passing a message on so delicate an issue and with respect to which he could not as yet have received instructions. But he was bound to report the attempt, putting Beijing on notice that a crisis was brewing on its doorstep.

Anticipating Huang Zhen's reaction, I had already asked George Bush, head of the U.S. Liaison Office in Beijing, to deliver the same message in Beijing, both to the Chinese Foreign Ministry and to the Cambodian Embassy there. Bush was instructed to escalate the rhetoric another notch by adding, as an unsigned "oral note":

> The government of the United States demands the immediate
> release of the vessel and of the full crew. If that release does
> not immediately take place, the authorities in Phnom Penh
> will be responsible for the consequences.

In diplomatese, assigning responsibility for the consequences means that military action is likely; it is the nearest thing to an ultimatum.

In St. Louis and Kansas City, I confined myself to general statements about the *Mayaguez* to the effect that we were giving diplomacy a chance but that its failure would have serious consequences. Washington was quiescent, awaiting daylight in Asia—still a few hours off —and reports from our reconnaissance aircraft.

During that hiatus, on the evening of May 12, I addressed the World Affairs Council of St. Louis. It proved to be one of the most sustaining experiences of the period. I had left a capital still fashionably rehearsing the familiar Vietnam debates. In the heartland in St. Louis, it was clear that bitterness had not spread beyond the Beltway. In what is often described as the epicenter of American isolationism, the audience had evidently not lost faith in our country's purposes. It reacted supportively when I reaffirmed American commitments and called for national unity:

> . . . Let us never forget that by any measurement, we
> have given more in the last 30 years than any other nation in

history. We have successfully resisted serious threats to world order from those who wished to change it in ways that would have involved unacceptable consequences for democratic governments. We have provided more economic assistance to others than any other country. We have contributed more food, educated more people from other lands, and welcomed more immigrants. We have done so not only out of a generous spirit—though we should not apologize for this trait—but above all because the American people, after more than a century of isolation, had learned that assistance to others is not a gift to be given, but a service to be rendered for international stability and our own self-interest.

For our own sake and that of the rest of mankind let us now make sure that this lesson does not have to be learned again.[7]

Local dignitaries in attendance were generous to someone so publicly identified with the Indochina tragedy. Indeed, they turned the tables on me. I had come to bring a message of hope; instead it was I who left with renewed confidence.

## How to Liberate a Ship

Meanwhile Washington was having a harder time finding out what was going on with the *Mayaguez* than in defining a course of action—or, more precisely, in the absence of accurate intelligence, no meaningful course of action could be formulated. On May 12, at 9:16 P.M. Washington time—or 8:16 A.M. May 13 in Cambodia—Scowcroft had been informed that a P-3 Navy reconnaissance plane flying low enough to read the name had spotted the *Mayaguez* and had been fired on, sustaining slight damage. It turned out that the *Mayaguez* was not at Kompong Som—as Ford had been told nine hours earlier—but was precisely where she had been captured, off Poulo Wai Island. An hour later, Scowcroft had received a report to the effect that the *Mayaguez* had raised her anchor. The intelligence community, being generally loath to abandon its preconceptions, repeated its original—and erroneous—judgment of the previous day: the ship was once again said to be heading for Kompong Som and would reach there within six hours.

Scowcroft had requested that he be notified as soon as the ship actually started moving. At 2:23, having heard nothing for nearly four hours, he inquired and was told that the ship was now fifteen minutes to an hour out of Kompong Som harbor—exactly the same assessment with which the crisis had started. At this news, Scowcroft lost his temper—an unprecedented event—and was soon joined by Ford, equally irate that several precious hours should have been lost during which the airplanes based in Thailand might have intercepted the *Mayaguez*. Ford ordered that fighter planes attempt to stop the ship even at this late hour.

But the ship's captors again managed to foil the predictions of the intelligence analysts. After hours of searching, the *Mayaguez* was finally located anchored off Koh Tang, an island some thirty-four miles southwest of Kompong Som. At each new report, Scowcroft had awakened the President; I received a summary of the night's events the following morning, May 13, in St. Louis.

At 10:20 A.M. on Tuesday, May 13, the second day of the crisis, Ford summoned the NSC back into session. The Khmer Rouge had not made any statement despite having held the ship for thirty-one hours, nor had they responded to our message. The same group as on the previous day attended the meeting except that Joseph Sisco, under secretary of state for political affairs, was representing the State Department in my absence, and Ford's aides, Jack Marsh and Bob Hartmann, joined. After Colby's briefing, Rockefeller complained about the conflicting and inaccurate intelligence reports, and Ford raised questions about the delays in reporting at every stage of the crisis. In everyone's mind, the chief goal remained not to repeat the *Pueblo* incident. But that could happen only if the Khmer Rouge could be prevented from turning the ship's crew into hostages. Rockefeller urged that, at a minimum, we isolate Koh Tang:

> I think we need to respond quickly. The longer we wait, the
> more time they have to get ready. Why not sink their boats
> until they move? Once they have got hostages, they can twist
> our tails for months to come, and if you go ashore, we may
> lose more Marines trying to land than the Americans who
> were on the boat originally. Why not just sink their ships
> until they respond?

Schlesinger, so stern when it came to arms control issues, balked at military action. He favored using force to keep the *Mayaguez* from leaving the island and being taken into port. But he opposed sinking

Cambodian boats because it might injure the crew and because the Khmer Rouge might scuttle the *Mayaguez* in retaliation. Ford's decisions were crisp:

> —First, we use the aircraft to stop any boats leaving the island. You do not sink them, necessarily, but can you take some preventive action? . . .
> —Second, I think you should stop all boats coming to the island.
> —Third, I think we should be prepared to land on the ship tomorrow morning.

Ford next ordered a battalion landing team of Marines to be air-lifted from Okinawa to Utapao, Thailand, and the aircraft carrier *Hancock* to be moved from Subic Bay to off the coast of Cambodia.

I recount these exchanges because they triggered—in my absence—a new crisis of confidence between the President and his Secretary of Defense which would culminate in Schlesinger's dismissal five months later. One of the most painful casualties of the Vietnam War was the morale of the Pentagon. The idea of reengaging in Indochina only two weeks after the evacuation of Saigon evoked revulsion. When the Pentagon is less than enthusiastic, it does not reinterpret orders—as the Foreign Service is wont to do—but fulfills them literally without any additional initiative on its part. Given the complexity of military deployments, the practical effect is the same as procrastination. Throughout the *Mayaguez* crisis, the Pentagon dutifully assembled the forces as it was ordered to do. But it was clearly reluctant, offered no ideas of its own, left it to the civilians to prod it into action, and—remembering the outcry after the B-52 bombing of the Hanoi area—reflexively opposed the use of the strategic bombers.

Most of the communication mix-ups and sloppy intelligence reporting that plagued the *Mayaguez* crisis happened because the doubts of the Secretary of Defense compounded the trauma of the military. Clements excepted, the Pentagon seemed above all determined never again to be cast in the role of villain. The absence of the Chairman of the JCS, who was away on a trip to Europe, magnified the problem because his stand-ins were reluctant to use the direct access to the President which is the Chairman's prerogative by law. In this case, the only channel of the White House to the Pentagon was via a Secretary of Defense who was extremely ambivalent about the President's strategy.

By the second day of the crisis and while I was still in Kansas City, Ford's restlessness mounted as it became apparent that the order to prevent all departures and arrivals at Koh Tang was not being implemented. Possibly due to the fact that it was already nighttime in Asia when the President ordered the blockade, there was no report of any action resulting from it for nearly ten hours. Or it may have been because written orders were not sent out from the Pentagon until over four hours after the presidential directive. The Pentagon claimed later that oral orders had been issued straightaway.

Whatever the reason for the delay, Scowcroft did not receive the first action report until 8:10 P.M. on Tuesday, May 13, ten hours after the NSC meeting. Three small boats had left Koh Tang and were heading for the mainland. One had been sunk, the second had returned to the island, and the third was proceeding at full speed. Schlesinger's military aide, Major General John A. Wickham (later army chief of staff), requested instructions as to what to do about that vessel. In light of the President's explicit orders to sink every ship approaching or leaving the island, the query was inexplicable except as a maneuver to avoid being blamed should anything go wrong. Scowcroft, meticulous as always, checked with the President, who confirmed his original directive, saying pointedly: "If we don't do it, it is an indication of considerable weakness."

An hour and a half later, at 9:48 P.M. Washington time, Wickham was back with a new query. Another small ship had been observed moving from the island toward Kompong Som. When one of our pilots tried to stop it with cannon fire, he noticed during a low pass that a group of Caucasians was huddled in the bow. The pilot, asking for instructions, thought—as it turned out correctly—that they might be at least part of the crew of the *Mayaguez*. Ford, realizing the merit of the Pentagon's concerns, ordered the NSC assembled at 10:40 P.M. to review where matters stood.

During the day, despite the increasingly ominous tone of our public statements, there had been little pressure on us from other countries to desist. Our allies were silent, if somewhat pained, as they balanced their restless domestic public opinion against their dependence on American protection. As it happened, the most helpful commentary came from China. When Deng Xiaoping, on a visit to Paris, was asked to comment on American threats, he burst into laughter: "If they intervene, there is nothing we can do." Pressed by journalists, Deng would not be drawn into so much as a hint that China might support the Khmer Rouge even diplomatically. "You are journalists," Deng responded jovially. "You have more recent information than I do."[8] In other words, China was washing its hands of the problem. And Prince Norodom Sihanouk, just reappointed Cambodian head of state but still residing in Beijing, remained uncharacteristically silent throughout the crisis.

I had returned from the Midwest barely in time for this third NSC meeting of the crisis. The attendees included participants of the previous meetings plus Philip Buchen, Ford's counselor. Ford began by criticizing the slow communications from the Pentagon; he called the delay in transmitting his orders in writing to sink all ships approaching or leaving Koh Tang "inexcusable." Only extreme frustration accounts for the usually so equable Ford lashing out at the military establishment, an institution he truly revered and in which he was so proud to have served as a naval officer.

The first order of business was what to do about the boat carrying the Caucasians. By the time the NSC assembled, it was reported to be six miles from Kompong Som or less than an hour away—which seemed to have become the standard time measurement for reporting all ship movements near Kompong Som. That did not leave much time for decision, whereupon Ford ordered that the boat possibly carrying the *Mayaguez* crew be disabled with riot control agents and the accompanying speedboats sunk.

The NSC deliberations were shaped by the impression that the boat approaching Kompong Som carried only part of the crew (if any) and that the remainder (probably the majority) were still on Koh Tang. We were sliding into a position in which much of the President's time and the NSC's was taken up with decisions about the movement of individual small boats eight thousand miles away. To avoid this, Ford ordered the destruction of all the boats near Koh Tang, squelching attempts to return to a case-by-case consideration.

With this, the NSC could at last turn to how to generate pressures to compel the Khmer Rouge to free the crew and the ship. General Jones presented a chart showing that the Marines and the destroyer *Holt* would be in place within fourteen hours and the aircraft carriers *Coral Sea* and *Hancock* within twenty-eight hours, or by late afternoon of Wednesday, May 14, Washington time. Jones therefore recommended delaying any military action for forty-eight hours —or until Thursday afternoon—so that everything could be coordinated.

Ford's first instinct was to seize the *Mayaguez* and the island immediately via helicopter landings by Marines from the American base in Utapao, Thailand. The consensus in the NSC was that it was best not to consult the Thai government about this plan, since, as noted, in the wake of the fall of Saigon, the Thai government had already asked us to leave our bases within the year. A formal request would surely be refused, and unilateral action would at worst speed up that timetable. We were convinced that, whatever later Thai protests or reactions, the Thai leadership—and especially the military leadership—would welcome a strong American stand.

Devising a strategy for rescuing the *Mayaguez* crew proved more controversial. Everyone agreed that we should seize the ship and occupy Koh Tang, where we (erroneously) believed most of the crew was being held. Ford, with only Schlesinger dissenting, also favored air strikes against the port of Kompong Som. One reason was to prevent interference from the mainland with our planned seizure of the *Mayaguez* and Koh Tang. Another consideration was to exact a penalty from the Khmer Rouge for having taken American hostages. Schlesinger argued for restricting our military operations to those directly relevant to freeing the *Mayaguez* and her crew.

This was a valid argument, and Schlesinger presented it trenchantly. Unfortunately, his spokesman, Joseph Laitin, missed no opportunity to transform honest disagreements into aspects of a feud between the Secretaries of State and Defense. Newspaper columns kept describing our deliberations in terms of "Dr. Strangelove" restrained by the humanistic Secretary of Defense. I was alleged to have advocated indiscriminate B-52 bombings in contrast to Schlesinger, who stood for a more precise "tit-for-tat" retaliation.[9]

That had never been the issue. The real debate concerned the timing of American retaliation. The Pentagon had left us with the impression that the *Coral Sea* would be ready for action only after forty-eight hours, which all of us, except Schlesinger, judged too risky for the safety of the hostages and the long-term prospects of extricating them. Thus, if there was to be a coordinated attack within twenty-four hours, B-52s would have to be used for the attack on Kompong Som. That was the extent of the NSC discussion regarding the use of B-52s. I include the verbatim transcript to permit the reader to assess the gap between actual policy discussions and public relations presentation of them:

> KISSINGER: I think that when we move, we should hit the mainland as well as the island. We should hit targets at Kompong Som and the airfield and say that we are doing it to suppress any supporting action against our operations to regain the ship and seize the island.
>
> If the B-52s can do it, I would like to do it tomorrow night. Forty-eight hours are better militarily. But so much can happen, domestically and internationally. We have to be ready to take the island and the ship and to hit Kompong Som.
>
> FORD: I think we should be ready to go in twenty-four hours. We may, however, want to wait.
>
> SCHLESINGER: We will be prepared to go on the morning of the fifteenth. We will see if we can get the Marines on the *Holt*. At first light, we will have plans to go to the island. Simultaneously, we will go for the ship.
>
> We will have the B-52s at Guam ready to go for Kompong Som. But I think there are political advantages to using the aircraft from the *Coral Sea*. You will have more problems on the Hill with the B-52s from Guam.
>
> ROCKEFELLER: Why?
>
> SCHLESINGER: The B-52s are a red flag on the Hill. Moreover, they bomb a very large box and they are not so accurate. They might generate a lot of casualties outside the exact areas that we would want to hit.
>
> FORD: Let's see what the Chiefs say is better, the aircraft from the carrier or the B-52s. It should be their judgment.

In short, the key difference was not the choice of weapons but the urgency of undertaking military action within twenty-four hours.

At this point, Don Rumsfeld (a former naval aviator) cut the Gordian knot by asking a question no one had bothered to raise: "Is it not possible that the *Coral Sea* aircraft could strike Cambodia even when the *Coral Sea* is still hours away?" Amazingly enough, during a day of debate over the timing of an attack, this question had never been raised. Schlesinger said he would check and found that the *Coral Sea* would indeed be within range in the next few hours. Nobody from the Defense Department had volunteered this information.

Rumsfeld's query produced a presidential decision and an NSC consensus. When the meeting ended at 12:30 A.M. on Wednesday, May 14, Ford deferred seizing the *Mayaguez* for twenty-four hours. But he would accept no delay beyond that; at the end of the twenty-four hours, the ship would be boarded, Koh Tang captured, and the mainland attacked from the air. The President left open only the method of the strike against the port of Kompong Som—whether it would be B-52s or aircraft from the *Coral Sea*—until the following morning. After the meeting, Ford proved that, in his less than ten months in office, he had learned a great deal about the bureaucracy. He told me that he preferred to use the carrier planes but had kept open the B-52 option to give the Pentagon every incentive to make sure the *Coral Sea* arrived on time.

Ford was still of the same mind when I met with him at 11:45 A.M. on May 14 to prepare for the afternoon NSC meeting at which the final decision between the *Coral Sea* and the B-52s would be made. He said that he would use the *Coral Sea* if the Pentagon could convince him that it indeed had the capacity to launch a serious attack from the carrier.

> FORD: I am disturbed at the lack of carrying out orders. I
> can give all the orders, but if they don't carry them out
> . . . I was mad yesterday.
> KISSINGER: This is your first crisis. You should establish a
> reputation for being too tough to tackle. . . . I see the
> argument against the B-52s.
> FORD: I think I should say I favor the B-52s unless they can
> show they can do as much with tacair [tactical aircraft].
> KISSINGER: That is a good way to get at the problem. The
> price will be the same. If you use force it should be
> ferociously.

Whenever military action is imminent, the State Department accompanies it with a diplomatic scenario. During the interval before the NSC meeting, Ambassador Scali was instructed to deliver a letter to U.N. Secretary-General Kurt Waldheim calling the seizure of the *Mayaguez* illegal and a threat to international peace—a clear warning of an impending resort to force. We were still pursuing the release of the ship and crew through diplomatic channels, the letter said; we would welcome Waldheim's assistance. If diplomacy failed, however, the United States reserved the right to take appropriate steps, including measures of self-defense under Article 51 of the U.N. Charter.

The diplomatic environment remained reassuring; it was becoming clearer by the hour that the Khmer Rouge would receive no support from any country—least of all from China. On the morning of May 14, we received a report that a Chinese diplomat in Teheran had predicted the release of the ship and crew "soon." "Embarrassed" by the *Mayaguez* seizure, China was—according to the unnamed diplomat—using its influence to secure the ship's release. This alleged Chinese view—perhaps a subtle hint that military action would not be necessary—proved perhaps too subtle. It was not communicated directly to the United States but came to us via a junior Pakistani diplomat in Teheran, who passed the information to an American Embassy officer. The Pakistani did not name his source. Tantalizing as it was, this information seemed to us too fragmentary to affect our decisions. And had we acted on the hint, "soon" might have turned into a very long time.

Later in the day, we received an opaquely helpful message directly from Beijing. During the afternoon of May 14, the Chinese Foreign Ministry returned our note of the day before, stating that it was not in a position to pass it on to the Cambodian government. That the Chinese had held the message for over thirty hours (in contrast to the country's Washington representative, who had flatly refused to accept it) implied that the message had been studied. That China did not take formal exception to its content and especially to the threat to use force suggested, together with Deng's nonchalant comments in Paris the previous day, that the Khmer Rouge were on their own.

The fourth NSC meeting in two days lasted from 3:52 P.M. to 5:42 P.M. on May 14 and was confined to making final decisions on military options. Colby led off with an intelligence briefing, stating that some crew members had been transported to the mainland—though the majority were still believed to be held on Koh Tang. The Thai government, we were told, was formally aloof, though the Thai army commander had told us privately that he was "extremely pleased" that we were acting decisively.

General Jones put forward the JCS recommendation: a boarding party was to seize the *Mayaguez;* Marines were to land on Koh Tang to rescue the crew members believed to be held there; carrier-based planes from the *Coral Sea* were to attack mainland targets, especially the airfields and port facilities at Kompong Som. To meet the schedule for landings, the order to "execute" would be required within twenty-four hours—a subtle hint that the Pentagon still preferred to wait.

Bureaucratic maneuvering aside, the Pentagon's technical performance had been impressive. Within forty-eight hours, an aircraft carrier, two destroyers, and one thousand Marines had already been deployed; an auxiliary carrier was scheduled to arrive a day later in a region where we had previously had no thought of taking any military action. B-52s were on alert, and tactical aircraft were blanketing the area. No other country would have been capable of undertaking so rapid and relevant a deployment.

Ford overruled Jones's request for a delay and ordered that all three operations be set in motion immediately and that four air strikes against mainland targets be conducted from the *Coral Sea*. Reflecting his unease about Pentagon resolve, Ford added that the air strikes "should not stop until we tell them." Admiral James L. Holloway III, chief of naval operations, periodically left the room to transmit decisions as they were being made.

At 6:30 P.M., Ford, accompanied by Schlesinger and me, briefed the congressional leaders. He presented a detailed account of the reasons for military action. No word having been received for over sixty hours from the Khmer Rouge or from anyone speaking on their behalf, he could not justify the risk of permitting the crew to become hostages.

The congressional leaders were unenthusiastic. Senator Mike Mansfield wanted to know "why are we again going into the mainland of Asia, especially at a time when we almost have the boat in our custody once again?" Even the usually stalwart Senator John McClellan expressed his uneasiness about the attack on the mainland. Speaker Thomas P. "Tip" O'Neill implied that the boat was a "Pentagon charter," as if this changed the reality of its having been hijacked in international waters; he continued low-key grumbling even after Schlesinger assured him that his suspicion was unfounded. Senator Robert Byrd complained about inadequate consultation. An exchange between Ford and Byrd, in which Ford in effect accused the congressional leaders of being prone to leak, illustrates that the President's conciliatory nature did not preclude firmness:

> SENATOR BYRD: Let me respectfully press this. I know you
> are doing what you think best and I certainly don't
> question your authority to do it, but I want to know

why the leaders were not brought in in advance of your
decision?

FORD: We have a government of separation of powers. The
President has the authority to act. I have an obligation
to act. We have lived within the law of the War Powers
Act. We may have differences over judgments and decisions, but I would never forgive myself if I had let our
Marines be attacked by the 2,400 Cambodian soldiers
[our intelligence estimate of the Khmer Rouge troop
strength in Kompong Som].

## The Freeing of the Mayaguez

The end of the congressional briefing ushered in one of the most
bizarre and tense evenings of my experience in government. A
working dinner for the Dutch Prime Minister, Johannes den Uyl, had
been scheduled that evening for many weeks. Not wishing to embarrass his guest, Ford decided to go ahead with the dinner even though
military operations were starting half a world away.

It turned out to be a case of carrying personal delicacy too far.
The dinner, inexplicably arranged as a black tie affair, had to be
delayed by half an hour. Of the American invitees, Scowcroft and
Rumsfeld made only token appearances; I came for one course; and
Schlesinger arrived late but stayed until dessert had been served. Ford
kept leaving the room to receive reports from the military operations
in the usher's office adjoining the state dining room.

Den Uyl was not the ideal guest with whom American policymakers involved with monitoring a military operation might have wished
to share that evening. Since he was from the pacifist wing of the Dutch
Labor Party, den Uyl's enthusiasm for any Indochina-related military
activity was muted, to say the least. He had obviously been briefed to
avoid being provocative, a feat he never quite managed. At intervals,
den Uyl could not restrain himself from stressing in a professorial
manner that he was not passing judgment on any particular military
operation but, in principle, he did not consider military force the
appropriate way to solve political problems. It was an odd comment
from the representative of a NATO ally whose country we had pledged
to defend. Nor was it consistent with Dutch history. Den Uyl never
vouchsafed to us by what other means we might induce the Khmer
Rouge to release the hostages.

Den Uyl's interlocutors were not exactly receptive to his uplifting pronouncements, preoccupied as they were with monitoring military operations on three different fronts: the recapture of the *Mayaguez,* the landing on Koh Tang, and the air attacks on the mainland. The information of each operation arrived in Washington through different channels: from the Marines for Koh Tang; from the Air Force for tactical support; and from the Navy for Kompong Som.

The seizure of the *Mayaguez* went well. A landing party of Marines aboard the destroyer *Holt* pulled up alongside the *Mayaguez,* and the Marines seized the ship. No crew members were found.

But the Marines on Koh Tang were running into trouble. We had expected only about two dozen Cambodians to be on the island. In fact, our helicopters flew into a heavy fire from several hundred troops equipped with rockets, mortars, and automatic weapons that had been placed on the island to prevent its seizure by the Vietnamese. Because we believed the *Mayaguez* crewmen to be there, no preparatory bombardment had taken place. And the Air Force gunship made available for the operation proved unable to communicate with the ground. Fifteen Marines out of the original party of 175 were killed; eight of the nine helicopters participating in the first wave were shot down or disabled.

Illustrating the so-called fog of battle, just as our military operations were beginning, the Khmer Rouge were implying in a broadcast that the *Mayaguez* would be released, though Washington did not learn of the statement for nearly another hour and a quarter. The sequence of events was as follows:

At 7:07 P.M. Washington time on May 14, Phnom Penh domestic radio began broadcasting a long statement in Cambodian by Hu Nim, the Khmer Rouge information and propaganda minister. Not until toward the end of the nineteen-minute statement did he get to the point, which seemed to be that the ship was being "expelled." Given the time needed for translation, its essence was not communicated to the White House until almost an hour later (see below).

At 7:09 P.M., before Hu Nim had reached the operative portion of his statement, our helicopter assault on Koh Tang got under way.

At 7:20 P.M., unknown to Washington, the Khmer Rouge authorities on the island of Koh Rong Sam Lem, near Kompong Som, released the *Mayaguez* crew and deposited them on a Thai fishing boat.

At 8:05 P.M.—still before the text of Hu Nim's statement had reached the White House—the first aircraft were being launched from the *Coral Sea.* It would take them less than an hour to reach their targets on the mainland.

At 8:06 P.M., the first summary of the Hu Nim statement came over the Foreign Broadcast Information Service (FBIS) ticker.[10]

At approximately 8:15 P.M., Scowcroft and I received the summary of Hu Nim's statement.

At 8:25 P.M., the *Holt* pulled alongside the empty *Mayaguez* and seized her.

At 8:29 P.M., the President was informed of the radio broadcast.

Hu Nim's statement justified the seizure of the ship by citing Khmer Rouge fears of "espionage" activities from "U.S. imperialist" spy ships. He also claimed that the *Mayaguez* had entered Cambodia's territorial waters. The operative portion of Hu Nim's tirade came at the very end: "We have no intention of detaining it [the ship] permanently. . . . Wishing to provoke no one or to make trouble, adhering to the stand of peace and neutrality, we will release this ship." There was no reference to the crew.

When this first—indirect and ambiguous—communication was received in the White House Situation Room after two and a half days of ominous silence, our military operations were already under way. We could not stop the military action on Koh Tang without risking the remaining one hundred Marines there becoming Khmer Rouge prisoners. The *Mayaguez* was likely to be retaken within minutes of the receipt of the broadcast.

A decision had to be made whether to go through with air strikes against the mainland. The planes from the *Coral Sea* were under way but would not reach their targets for another fifteen to thirty minutes. The problem was whether to cancel the bombing. It was a tricky decision. After two and a half days of detention—by a regime whose murderous tendencies had already become abundantly evident—the lack of precision regarding the crew appeared ominous. The Khmer Rouge leaders had had many means of communicating their decision hours or days earlier; they could have informed us officially through the Chinese or the United Nations but made no attempt to do so.

On the other hand, if the Khmer Rouge had intended to release the crew and then refused to do so because bombing continued after the broadcast, the congressional reaction would be violent. I therefore asked Scowcroft to instruct the National Military Command Center that I would be seeking presidential guidance and that I also intended to consult Secretary Schlesinger. Since there was little time left, I suggested that the planes from the *Coral Sea* proceed on course but drop no ordnance until the President had made his decision.

Ford proved skeptical when I called him at 8:30 P.M., just as he prepared to greet the Dutch Prime Minister. He would not alter any of his directives, he said, until he was sure of the crew's release.

Schlesinger shared the President's view. For all we knew, he argued, the Khmer Rouge statement was pure propaganda. When I called Ford again at 8:50 P.M. to inform him of Schlesinger's views, the *Mayaguez* had been retaken, and the planes from the *Coral Sea* were still en route. Ford made his decision: "Tell them to go ahead, right now."

At the same time, we decided to end the air attacks as soon as we knew that the crew had, in fact, been released. But how to communicate this decision to the Khmer Rouge? In the age of instantaneous communication and multiple channels, we were remarkably at a loss as to how to convey that assurance. Except for those of China and Vietnam, there were no foreign embassies in Cambodia and no Cambodian embassies abroad through which we might contact Phnom Penh.

After toying with the idea of breaking into Cambodian communications, we decided that the most expeditious way would be to release a statement to the news services. Scowcroft asked Ron Nessen to come to my office so that I could give him a draft statement to read to the press. Nessen refused; he stood on the prerogative that I could not order him to come to see me. In the process of announcing the beginning of military operations, he took the reasonable position that, if he offered to end military operations about which the American public as yet knew nothing, he would only create confusion. He was right, but that did not solve our problem. Scowcroft finally had to drag Nessen almost physically to my office to help put the finishing touches on the following statement, issued at 9:15 P.M.:

> We have heard [a] radio broadcast that you are prepared to release the S.S. *Mayaguez*. We welcome this development, if true.
>
> As you know, we have seized the ship. As soon as you issue a statement that you are prepared to release the crew members you hold unconditionally and immediately, we will promptly cease military operations.

No reply ever reached us. At 10:49, the recently arrived destroyer U.S.S. *Wilson* picked up the crew of the *Mayaguez* after their captors had deposited them on a Thai fishing vessel equipped with white sheets on long poles to attract the attention of American planes or ships. The President learned about it minutes later in the Oval Office, where his close associates had assembled after the den Uyl fiasco.

In my experience, even when a crisis ends amidst elation—as this one surely did—a letdown nearly inevitably follows. First, because the moment of triumph reminds us that foreign policy knows no resting place and that its every success is usually an admission ticket to a new set of decisions. More importantly, the postmortem often reveals some previously unsuspected problems in need of attention. In the case of the *Mayaguez,* amidst pride in what had been accomplished, there was the nagging feeling that we must not again face a crisis with the procedures and bureaucratic confusion that had beset our conduct in this case.

Indeed, even as those of us assembled in the Oval Office were celebrating came a reminder of the absence of rapport between the Defense Secretary and the President. Schlesinger's spokesman, Joseph Laitin, took it upon himself to announce that the crew was safe rather than leaving the announcement of the good news to the President. Ford, whose leadership had steered us toward this outcome, was thereby obliged—not without a gnashing of teeth—to announce the end of the crisis almost as an afterthought after quickly changing from his tuxedo into a business suit. That done, he returned to the Oval Office and simply announced: "I'm going home and going to bed." That was the end of the *Mayaguez* crisis.[11]

## Postmortems

It was not the end of the postmortems, however. While there was pride in the outcome and in the ability of the Defense Department to bring American power to bear quickly, nagging questions remained. Intelligence had been poor throughout. At too many stages, starting with the very first NSC meeting, decisions were made on the basis of information that had turned out to be almost totally wrong. The crisis concluded with an inaccurate assessment of the situation on Koh Tang, where we were told some of the crew were being held by only a very few Khmer Rouge guards. In fairness, it was difficult to acquire intelligence in an area which was normally of only marginal interest to Washington and where, as a result, intelligence collection had to start from scratch. But this limitation was never made clear to the officials deliberating in the Cabinet Room.

What caused the greatest and most lingering unease was the evident communication gap between the White House and the Pentagon, starting with leaks from NSC deliberations and concluding with the conduct of the military operations. This time the friction was not between Schlesinger and me. It was President Ford, the commander-in-chief, who felt that he had not been kept adequately informed. He learned of some key decisions only at the final wrap-up NSC meetings and then only by accident. The President had agreed to use planes from the *Coral Sea* rather than the B-52s on the condition that a maximum effort be made, that at least *four* separate strikes be undertaken, and that they not end until he issued a direct order to that effect. At the postmortem NSC meeting on Thursday, May 15, 1975, General Jones briefed on what had happened and spoke of the four waves of planes that had been launched from the *Coral Sea.* But, describing the first wave, he said: "The first was armed reconnaissance. They did not expend ordnance." I could see Ford's face reddening. He did not say anything until the following exchange exhausted his patience:

> KISSINGER: How many aircraft were used altogether?
> JONES: About thirty-two to forty.
> SCHLESINGER: Not the eighty-one that had been on the
> carrier.

When it became clear that the *Coral Sea* had made far from the maximum effort he had ordered, Ford interrupted the meeting and invited me to step out of the Cabinet Room with him for a moment. He asked me to summarize my understanding of the orders he had given. After I did so, he returned to the NSC meeting without another word. Addressing Schlesinger, he said coldly:

> Jim, I would like a full factual report giving a summary
> and chronology of what happened. It should include orders,
> summary results, photographs, etc., and indications of what
> we did when.

With this, the President terminated discussions on the *Mayaguez* and turned to another subject.

At our daily morning meeting the next day, Ford was still irate that the first wave had not used its ordnance. He recognized that there could have been some confusion due to the pause ordered to discuss the Khmer Rouge statement; what rankled him was that he had never been told of the "armed reconnaissance"—whatever that meant—and that, in fact, Schlesinger had left him with the opposite impression when he had reported "first strike completed" after the first wave. Above all, Ford could not forgive cancellation of the fourth strike:

> FORD: My recollection is I told [Chief of Naval Operations Admiral James] Holloway to continue the strikes until I said to stop.
>
> SCOWCROFT: That is my recollection. And you told Schlesinger.
>
> FORD: I want a detailed summary of the orders which went out and any changes which were made. I want an assessment of the operation—including the time sequence of takeoffs and what happened.
>
> KISSINGER: You should ask for all the orders that were issued from the beginning of the operation.
>
> FORD: That should include the orders from the Pentagon to CINCPAC [the United States Pacific Command] and from there to commanders on the scene. I want the DOD submission compared with the orders issued in the NSC. . . . Include what happened in the first wave, the second wave, and the other waves after that. It seems to me that what happens in the Situation Room is being bypassed by what goes on in the NMCC [the Pentagon's National Military Command Center].

A review did not clear up all these mysteries. Some confusion undoubtedly resulted from our initial hesitation, in light of the Cambodian statement, about whether to proceed with the strikes on the mainland. Ford had explicitly reaffirmed his original order at 8:51, however, and it had been transmitted to Schlesinger and the National Military Command Center at 8:52. As for a fourth wave of strikes, during Jones's briefing, we learned that it had never been launched and that none of the others contained the full complement Ford had ordered. In fairness to Schlesinger, he might have acted on the basis of the Nessen statement of earlier in the evening, in reply to the Khmer broadcast, that military actions would cease once the prisoners were released.

In retrospect—though I did not think so at the time—these events demonstrate the risk of planning military operations in the National Security Council without any preparatory work by a subordinate group and without some official short of the President being made responsible for the hour-by-hour coordination. The NSC is better designed for over-all decisions than for micromanagement. The President had ordered all-out strikes at the NSC meeting and, in the absence of the Chairman of the Joint Chiefs of Staff, there was no military officer sufficiently close to him to transmit the orders unambiguously through the chain of command. This gave the Secretary of Defense—who is actually, in our system, not directly in the chain of command—what turned out to be a decisive voice. To those of us in hourly contact with the President, it was inconceivable that he could have meant that the first wave be confined to armed reconnaissance in which no ordnance would be expended. How various NSC members in less frequent contact with Ford perceived his directives should not have been left to their subjective interpretations.

The NSC is too unwieldy to supervise operations in that much detail. This is why President Kennedy created the so-called Ex-Comm (Executive Committee of the NSC) in the Cuban Missile Crisis and why the Nixon and Ford Administrations generally backed up the NSC with the Washington Special Actions Group (WSAG) at the deputy secretary level. In this case, senior officials at the NSC meeting were dealing directly with the President on tactical questions or created the impression with their subordinates that they were doing so. That made it hard to trace the responsibility for individual acts.

A review of the various orders emanating from the Pentagon failed to clear up the mystery of why the first wave of planes dropped no bombs, why the President had been told by Schlesinger that the first strike had been "completed," and how the fourth wave of strikes never occurred. In his memoirs, Ford states that the Pentagon explanations were "not satisfactory" but that he "let the matter drop" because the operation had succeeded.[12] Although no heads rolled then, Ford never recovered confidence in his Secretary of Defense.

All that was now left was to clean up some of the residue insepara-ble from crises. The reaction of most nations outside the Communist bloc ranged from relief to indifference. China tried to make up for its permissive attitude during the crisis by having Vice Premier Li Xiannian assert at a reception that American conduct had amounted to "acts of piracy." The remark was prominently featured in the *People's Daily*. Though this and similar comments stopped short of being put forward as official statements, I instructed Winston Lord (head of the Policy Planning Staff) and William Gleysteen (assistant secretary for

East Asia, Habib having been promoted to under secretary) on May 23 to protest to Han Xu, the head of Beijing's Liaison Office in Washington:

> Such statements as have been made by the Chinese side can have a serious impact on our public opinion. These kinds of statements, if they continue, can only be unhelpful for our relations.

The other loose end needing attention was the reaction of Thailand. We had used Thai bases without permission—indeed, without even informing the government. In the wake of the collapse of Indochina, Thailand had, as noted, already requested that we withdraw from these bases within a year. It now demanded our immediate withdrawal, in what turned out to be an entirely symbolic gesture. On May 19, we sent a note both expressing regret "for the misunderstandings that have arisen between Thailand and the United States" and our determination to work "in harmony and friendship with the Royal Thai government." Relations soon returned to normal. The Thai ambassador, having been recalled, came back to Washington, and American military personnel were withdrawn from Thailand according to the original schedule of one year.

Crises in Washington end only when the media say so, and the ritual is never complete without the liturgical closing news conference. This one took place on May 16 at the State Department. The queries from the press were perhaps best described by John Osborne when he called them "a disgrace to journalism and to the journalists concerned."[13] The opening question set the tone by referring to the entire operation as "this caper." All subsequent questions were tacit accusations in one form or another: that we had infringed on Thai sovereignty; that our aircraft might have killed the crewmen instead of saving them; that the United States government was at fault because it should have warned all ships beforehand that incidents were occurring in the area; that the entire action had been undertaken as a morale-booster for the American public; that we had not given diplomacy a chance to work.

By now a veteran of this kind of assault, I replied that:

- We could not risk another *Pueblo*-type situation, leaving innocent crewmen to be held as hostages while we were teased with the prospect of negotiations over a long period of time;
- "We never received a communication, [or] proposition, that would

have enabled us to explore a diplomatic solution." By the time the Khmer Rouge's altogether too ambiguous radio broadcast was received, the operation had already begun;

• We were not looking for opportunities to prove our manhood, only that it was essential for America's global role in the wake of the fall of Saigon to establish that there were limits beyond which the United States could not be pushed.

On May 17, the *Mayaguez* sailed into Singapore where a mob of journalists was waiting. A news conference was held at pierside. It soon became apparent that the ship's master, Captain Charles T. Miller, refused to follow the politically correct script preferred by the journalists. In reply to cynical questions, he praised President Ford and the United States Marines for rescuing his ship and crew. Had it not been for the military rescue efforts, the captain declared emphatically, the crew "would be in prison or dead now." Miller was visibly moved as he recounted how, aboard the naval vessels that rescued them, the crew discovered that Marines had died and been wounded in the military operations which saved them.

Captain Miller asserted that the American military action played a major part in the Khmer Rouge's decision to release the boat and crew. In fact, the captain had used the American military moves as a bargaining counter, telling his Khmer Rouge captors that, if the crew were let go, he would intercede with the American government not to take further military action.

On May 23, Ford summed up the *Mayaguez* episode in his understated manner in an interview with European journalists taped for the British Broadcasting Corporation:

> I am sure that both domestically in the United States, as well
> as worldwide, the handling of the *Mayaguez* incident should
> be a firm assurance that the United States is capable and has
> the will to act in emergencies, in challenges. I think this is a
> clear, clear indication that we are not only strong but we
> have the will and the capability of moving.[14]

With this, Indochina disappeared from the American agenda. What Ford had said was true, but it could not alter the reality that we had entered Indochina to save a country, and that we had ended by rescuing a ship.

# 19

# TRAGEDY OF THE KURDS

## *Origins of the Program*

The gods did not smile on America's friends in the spring of 1975. At the very time when Congress relinquished the people of Indochina to the Communist yoke, the Shah of Iran left the Kurds of Iraq defenseless in the face of the radical regime in Baghdad, even then controlled, if not yet formally headed, by Saddam Hussein.

The United States had been assisting the Kurds since 1972, though our involvement was negligible compared to the effort we had made in Indochina. But while Indochina could have been kept from falling—at least during 1975—by extending assistance our allies had every reason to expect, saving the Kurds would have required the opening of a new front in inhospitable mountains close to the Soviet border. An open commitment of considerable magnitude and unpredictable consequences would have had to be undertaken while Indochina was disintegrating, East-West relations were weakening, and Middle East negotiations stood deadlocked. And all this to sustain a "covert operation," and while congressional assaults on the very concept of such activities were gaining momentum.

Within a few months, however, the fate of the Kurds was to become another of those episodes in self-flagellation by which the narcissistic 1970s sought to atone for the exuberant optimism of the early 1960s. Congressional committees attacked the Nixon Administration for its role in attempting to help the Kurds achieve autonomy and the Ford Administration for not having prevented the Shah from abandoning this joint effort. It was one way by which some of those

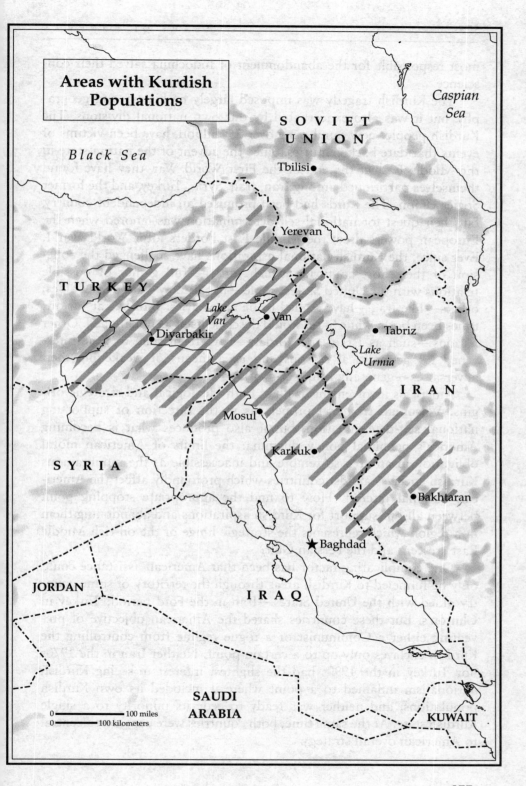

# Areas with Kurdish Populations

Black Sea

Caspian Sea

S O V I E T
U N I O N

Tbilisi ●

Yerevan ●

T U R K E Y

Lake Van

● Van

Diyarbakir ●

● Tabriz

Lake Urmia

I R A N

Mosul ●

Karkuk ●

S Y R I A

● Bakhtaran

★ Baghdad

JORDAN

I R A Q

0 ———— 100 miles
0 ———— 100 kilometers

SAUDI
ARABIA

KUWAIT

most responsible for the abandonment of Indochina salved their conscience.

The Kurdish tragedy was imposed largely by history and geography, but it was also exacerbated by our own national divisions. The Kurdish people, now numbering over 25 million, have been victims of events that date back centuries. Since the advent of the nation-state in the Middle East at the end of the First World War, they have found themselves partitioned among Iran, Iraq, Syria, Turkey, and the former Soviet Union. The Kurds had been promised an independent country, but their quest for national self-determination was ignored when the European powers drew the Middle East borders after World War I. Ever since, the Kurdish national aspirations have challenged the cohesion of their host countries, which ran the full gamut of possible relations with the United States: some—like Turkey—have been allies; others—like Iraq—have tended to be adversaries; Iran has at various times been both; while Syria would describe itself as nonaligned. Other nations—such as Israel and Jordan—have from time to time intervened for geopolitical reasons and as a means of weakening their adversaries—generally Iraq (see map).

America's involvement has had both ideological and strategic origins. Wilsonian tradition propels us in the direction of supporting national self-determination, but it also produces what is becoming America's perennial policy dilemma: the limits of American moral obligation in an area so remote and inaccessible as the mountainous Kurdish enclaves amidst countries which profoundly affect the American national interest. How to find the appropriate stopping point between all-out support for Kurdish aspirations and abandoning them in a region which represents the strategic hinge of the oil-rich Middle East crescent and the Persian Gulf?

One complicating factor has been that American assistance could only be funneled to Kurdish areas through the territory of some country allied with the United States—Iran in the Ford period, Turkey in Clinton's. But these countries shared the American objective of preventing either a Communist or a rogue regime from controlling the Kurdish enclaves only up to a certain point. Neither Iran in the 1970s nor Turkey in the 1990s had the slightest interest in seeing Kurdish nationalism inflamed to a point where it included its own Kurdish populations, and neither was ready to cede its minority to a single Kurdish state. At the same time, both countries were considered central to American overall strategy.

Inevitably, ambivalence has characterized and finally overwhelmed American efforts in the Kurdish regions of Iraq. Neighboring states such as Turkey or Iran would support the Kurds to deflect Iraqi pressures from their own territory. But they were at no point prepared to embrace the creation of a Kurdish national state. By the same token, neither the Nixon, nor the Ford, Bush, or Clinton Administrations ever supported independence for the Iraqi Kurds, much less for those in the neighboring countries. All sought to combine Kurdish autonomy with preserving Iraq's territorial integrity, fearing that Iraq's disintegration would trigger decades of turmoil as its neighbors fought over the spoils. Especially after Iran turned into a hostile fundamentalist state under Ayatollah Khomeini, Iraq's territorial integrity was perceived as a counterbalance to Iranian ambitions.

The interaction of these conflicting objectives was bound to bring disappointment and even tragedy to the Kurds. That was what happened in March 1975 when Iran and Iraq reached an agreement in which Kurdish autonomy was overwhelmed by the national interests of their two neighbors. It was repeated in 1996 when Kurdish autonomy established under the American aegis after the Gulf War in 1991 was substantially reduced by Saddam Hussein when one Kurdish faction sided with him to defeat their American-backed Kurdish rivals. In my view, the Ford Administration had better grounds for not extending its commitment than Clinton's—but both instances illustrate the limits and the perplexities of our interest in the distant land of the Kurds.

The Nixon and Ford Administrations did not invent outside support for the Kurdish aspirations to autonomy as is usually claimed, but they were the first to put American resources behind them directly. Because we were supporting an ethnic group against its legal government and because other countries, especially Iran and Israel, were involved, the operation had to be "covert"—in that gray area between overt force and diplomacy.

Our direct involvement with the Kurds had its origin in Nixon's visit to the Shah in Tehran in May 1972, following his summit with Brezhnev in Moscow. A week of Kremlin hospitality in celebration of détente had not altered Nixon's strategic priorities. In promoting détente, he never abandoned his quest for maximum maneuvering room in the global political competition with the Soviet Union.

One of these competitions was taking place in Iraq, at the Shah's doorstep. At issue was the future political orientation of a country second only to Saudi Arabia in its reserves of oil, hence with resources to threaten the equilibrium in the Middle East and especially in the Gulf. In 1968, the Ba'ath party, committed domestically to a radical socialist program and avowing militant hostility to the West, had returned to power in Baghdad. Not surprisingly, Iraq under Saddam Hussein was edging ever closer to the Soviet Union and this at a moment when the presence of fifteen thousand Soviet troops in Egypt underlined the danger that the entire Middle East might succumb to Soviet strategic influence. Whatever the status of détente, reducing Soviet influence was a central objective of our strategy. Indeed, we viewed détente as a means for hedging the risks of that strategy.

The countries that considered themselves most threatened by the new Iraqi direction were Jordan and Iran, both sharing a long border with Iraq, and Israel, ever wary of new radical Arab regimes propped up by Soviet arms. All three countries were friends of the United States. All three were extending covert aid to the Kurds. They treated the latter's quest for autonomy in the inhospitable, mountainous north of Iraq as a card to be played to divert the Ba'athist regime's energies and resources away from their own borders. Though we did not actually participate in this covert assistance, our intelligence agencies were briefed on it by their counterparts in each of the countries involved. And, of course, all these countries were receiving economic and military aid from the United States.

For a fleeting moment, it looked as if the Iraqis and Kurds might settle their differences. On March 11, 1970, an agreement was reached between Baghdad and Kurdish leader Mustafa Barzani.[1] The Ba'athist government agreed to transform Iraq into a multiethnic state composed of two main nationalities, Arab and Kurd. It provided for a Kurdish vice president; for Kurdish to become an official language; and for proportional Kurdish representation in a newly established Iraqi parliament.

In the months that followed, the agreement frayed over the definition of autonomy, as usually happens when an attempt is made to allocate power between hostile ethnic groups. To Barzani, autonomy meant nudging ever closer to de facto independence, while Saddam Hussein treated the agreement as a tactical step along the road of implementing the Ba'athist ideal of a unitary state.

By the fall of 1971, relations between the Kurds and Baghdad were once again at the breaking point. The Kurds blamed an attempt on Barzani's life on Saddam Hussein, who only magnified their suspicions by moving toward a national unity government that included the Communist Party. This isolated the Kurds, whereupon they resumed guerrilla activity, supported by Iran and Israel. In November 1971 and again in March 1972, the Shah appealed to Nixon to cooperate with him in assisting Barzani. On March 28, the King of Jordan acted as intermediary for a direct appeal from Barzani to Nixon. And Israel, though it never made a direct request for funds, kept us informed of its concerns over the direction of Iraqi policy and its interest in autonomy for the Kurdish areas.

We had turned away the approaches for direct aid because we did not want to provoke a further influx of Soviet arms and influence. Joseph Farland, the American ambassador in Iran, weighed in with a warning that, once launched, a Kurdish covert operation would risk becoming open-ended and, if stopped, would be vulnerable to "unfortunate misinterpretations."

A visit by Soviet Premier Alexei Kosygin to Baghdad in April 1972 caused us to reconsider our hands-off policy. On April 9, he signed a Friendship Treaty with Iraq that, even in the absence of American intervention on the side of the Kurds, included provisions for large-scale supply of Soviet arms. Iraq was thereby transforming itself into a geopolitical challenge and was on the way to becoming the principal Soviet ally in the area. Emboldened by the additional arms, Iraqi forces stepped up their attacks on the Kurds beyond a level that could be balanced by covert Iranian and Israeli assistance. Clashes between Iraqi and Iranian troops along their common border followed.

This was the setting for Nixon's visit to the Shah in Tehran on May 30–31, 1972. All of us were drained by the emotional and physical toll of the Moscow summit, which Nixon had brought off despite the bombing and blockading of North Vietnam, a Soviet ally—two weeks before his scheduled visit and six months before a presidential election.

The overwhelming Iranian hospitality magnified the exhaustion of the traveling party and of the press corps. One fallout of that exhaustion was Nixon's toast at the extravagant welcoming dinner offered by the Shah. The television lights were too bright for the President to read his prepared script, especially as he was unwilling to wear eyeglasses on television. Thus Nixon decided to speak extemporaneously, which he did ably enough except that a fitting peroration seemed to elude him. He went around the track a few times, finally hitting upon a capital idea. Looking directly at the Shah, Nixon reminded the King

of Kings of President Eisenhower's view that all the Senators he knew
had married above themselves. In that spirit, Nixon concluded trium-
phantly, and he proposed a toast to His Majesty and the lovely Em-
press at his side. The applause from the Iranian side was tepid at best.

All lightheartedness ceased, however, as soon as Nixon and the
Shah began reviewing the international situation. Fresh from exchanges of fulsome toasts at the Kremlin, Nixon demonstrated that he
was the American President least likely to be seduced by personal
relations with the leader of the Communist superpower. In his opening
remarks, he reiterated his determination to stand by America's friends
and to prevent Soviet adventures in the Middle East. Though we would
seek to keep regional conflicts from escalating into international confrontations, we would also not permit changes either in the global or
the Middle East balance of power. Indeed, in the Middle East, we
would strive to tip the balance in our favor by demonstrating that
neither Arab radicalism nor Soviet arms could achieve Arab aims. I
interjected that we would not accept "selective détente," which I defined as "settlements on some matters with some adversaries in order
to isolate others. . . . We had sought to bring this home to the Soviets."
I summed up the essence of our design a year later, in July 1973, on
the occasion of the return visit by the Shah to Washington:

> We are trying to checkmate Soviet influence wherever it ap-
> pears and to exhaust them in any adventures they may pur-
> sue. We want to create a frame of mind in the Politburo that
> is tired of costly activities in the Middle East which do not
> produce results.

The Shah therefore found Nixon a receptive listener when he expressed
his worry that "the Soviets would establish a coalition of the Kurds,
the Ba'athists, and the Communists; the Kurdish problem, instead of
being a thorn in their side, could become an asset to the Communists."

Nixon made two decisions as a result of his dialogue with the
Shah. To counteract the Kosygin-Saddam arms deal, he approved the
sale of high-performance aircraft which had been ordered by the Shah
but held up by bureaucratic disputes within the Pentagon over whether
to deliver the Air Force F-15 or the Navy F-14. Nixon resolved the
issue by approving both versions and leaving the ultimate choice between them to the Shah. (This is the origin of the canard that Nixon

ordered the Pentagon to give the Shah what he wanted. The order applied only to the choice between F-14s and F-15s.)

At the same time, Nixon concluded that, without American support, the existing Kurdish uprising against the Baghdad government would collapse. American participation in some form was needed to maintain the morale of such key allies as Iran and Jordan, disparate as their motives were, and as a contribution to the regional balance of power.

Our purpose was to raise the cost to the Iraqis of imposing their regime, to increase the Kurds' bargaining power, and thereby to induce Baghdad to conduct a policy more respectful of the security concerns of Iraq's neighbors and the autonomy of the Kurdish minority. American participation was believed to be the key: it would bring about coherence among the occasionally conflicting purposes of the other financial contributors, each of which attached great importance to its relations with the United States, and to inhibit them from abandoning the Kurds—a judgment which, as we shall see, proved too optimistic.

## Internal Controversies

Ever since the intelligence investigations of the Church and Pike Committees popularized the theme in television, films, and print, the American intelligence services have been portrayed as fanatical Cold Warriors not amenable to political control and ever eager to risk American assets in pursuit of their frequently maniacal schemes. If such a CIA ever existed, it was in hiding throughout the Nixon and Ford periods. All the major covert operations of that era—Chile, the Kurds, and Angola—were ordered by the White House and conducted as covert operations mainly because no appropriate overt diplomatic category existed for them. The Kurdish uprising took place on the sovereign territory of a recognized state allied to the Soviet Union, and it was already being covertly supported by a group of countries allied with the United States and financially supported by us. There was a risk of escalation but also one of permitting Saddam Hussein to consolidate his rule, transforming the Kurdish region of Iraq into a base for subversion of Kurdish areas in all the neighboring countries. In time, this subversion, backed by the rapidly growing Iraqi armed forces, had the potential to become a powerful weapon against the Gulf States, Iran, and even Turkey.

In retrospect, the pros and cons of the decision to support the Kurdish uprisings seem more evenly balanced than they did at the time. We probably should have analyzed more carefully the disparate motives of the anti-Iraqi coalition together with the consequences of one of the partners jumping ship. Above all, we should have understood better that the Kurds might prove to be volatile partners, difficult to fit into any overall strategy. Whatever the professions of their leaders, their principal goal was bound to be independence or at least complete autonomy, and they would always resist attempts to calibrate their priorities in relation to outside powers' conception of geopolitical equilibrium. Heroes, we were learning, are more pleasant to read about than to deal with; the very qualities that inspire their courage also meld their inflexibility.

Yet even the benefit of hindsight would have left us with a Hobson's choice which has not changed much in the quarter century since: failure to act might cause the existing anti-Iraq coalition to come apart, leave the Kurds at the mercy of Saddam Hussein, and demoralize the Gulf; while commitment might saddle us with the same painful dilemma down the road if the Soviets increased their supply of arms substantially beyond existing levels. In a choice between the certain and the conjectural danger, the far-off risk tends to appear more attractive. And this, in effect, was our decision in 1972. On August 1, 1972, Nixon signed a directive ordering the covert program.* The United States allocated $250,000 a month in direct support for Fiscal Year 1973 plus another $2 million for ammunition, or some $5 million a year. The Shah contributed a larger sum. The total, together with Israeli, British, and Iranian assistance for the Kurds, amounted to almost $1 million a month. By Cold War standards, it was not a major effort.

While we were deliberating the wisdom of American participation, Soviet troops and advisers were expelled from Egypt in July 1972. This enhanced Iraq's importance to Soviet Middle East strategy and gave Moscow a new incentive to strengthen its ties with the Baghdad regime. In late August, Mikhail Suslov, a member of the Politburo, urged Barzani to join a new unity government being offered by Saddam

---

* There was no formal 40 Committee meeting. For reasons of security, the recommendation was hand-carried to the principals: the under secretary of state, the deputy secretary of defense, and the Chairman of the Joint Chiefs of Staff, in addition to the CIA Director. Each had the opportunity to object but did not. The Pike Committee was to make much of the absence of a formal meeting, though it would surely not have produced a different outcome.

Hussein. According to Barzani, Suslov warned that, after having been expelled from Egypt, the Soviet Union attached even greater importance to its relations with Iraq and would increase its support for the Baghdad government. The stakes were obviously being raised.

On our side, the Shah and King Hussein had met at the Shah's palace on the Caspian Sea from July 31 to August 2, 1972. They welcomed American aid and sought to lay down ground rules for the common effort. They warned Barzani to avoid dramatic moves that might trigger an all-out Iraqi assault, such as declaring a separate Kurdish state. Their emphasis was on strengthening Kurdish defensive capabilities to preserve the greatest measure of autonomy.

Throughout 1973, the fighting escalated, and so did the Kurds' financial requests. On March 29, 1973, I supported a CIA request signed by Jim Schlesinger during his brief tenure as CIA director for additional resources, which Nixon approved soon afterward. My memorandum argued that Iraq had become the principal Soviet client in the Middle East; that the Ba'ath government under Saddam Hussein continued to finance terrorist organizations as far afield as Pakistan; and that it was the driving force in the "rejection front" seeking to block Arab-Israeli peace initiatives. For all these reasons, I recommended increasing our support beyond $5 million a year. The Shah added a much larger financial commitment, closer to $30 million, and, in addition, continued his logistics and artillery support which consisted of Iranian long-range artillery providing cover for the Kurds from Iran. Nevertheless, I warned Nixon of the risks if the Kurds escalated beyond a defensive posture:

> We may wish to try to avoid the impression of a long-term escalating commitment by telling Barzani that we will provide these additional funds for this year on a monthly basis but, in any event, would emphasize that we share the Shah's view regarding maintenance of the defensive posture of the Kurds.

In its first year, the Kurdish covert effort seemed to be achieving its objective. On October 5, 1972, I transmitted to Nixon a report from CIA Director Richard Helms, later to become ambassador to Iran, informing us that the Kurds were tying down two-thirds of the Ba'athist army:

> All is not well with the Ba'athist regime. . . . Barzani's main-
> tenance of a secure redoubt will continue to pin down two-
> thirds of the Iraqi army and deprive the Ba'athists of a secure
> base from which to launch sabotage and assassination teams
> against Iran.

When the Middle East War broke out in 1973, it presented us with a new array of problems. These concerned whether we should use the opportunity to encourage a Kurdish offensive into the Iraqi-held areas to topple the Saddam regime. We turned down a proposal to that effect from Israeli liaison officers—a decision which became controversial in subsequent years.[2]

The criticism was a classic example of retroactive heroism. When the Arab-Israeli war broke out, the covert program was a little more than a year old. The Kurds possessed very few heavy weapons; such artillery as they had was manned by Iranians who never ventured far from the Iranian border. The Kurds were capable of defending their mountainous homeland where Iraqi tanks and aircraft found it difficult to operate. But their lightly armed forces did not stand a chance in the flat terrain beyond their homeland against a large Iraqi army equipped with advanced Soviet heavy weapons and hundreds of tanks. An offensive beyond the redoubt would have guaranteed the complete destruction of Kurdish military forces.

This was particularly the case because, contrary to the retroactive folklore, the Iraqis did not divert substantial forces to help the Arab side in the Middle East War. The Kurds continued to tie down two-thirds of the Iraqi army, as Helms had informed us a year earlier. Not surprisingly, given the tense state of Iraqi relations with Syria—the sole front Iraq was geographically in a position to affect—only one Iraqi brigade was dispatched to fight Israel. "Fight" is a courtesy word, for the Iraqi brigade set no speed records getting to the front. It took nearly ten days to reach the general vicinity of the battle zone and even then kept well back from the front lines. The only casualties it incurred were an accidental firefight with a Saudi brigade which had likewise managed to spend ten days getting within earshot of hostile gunfire. The reluctant combatants ran into each other in the final days of the Middle East War. Unaware of the other's presence, the two Arab units thought they had unexpectedly come upon Israeli forces and commenced firing.

The very idea of the guerrillas launching an offensive came up rather late in the war when the tide of battle on the Egyptian-Israeli front had already turned. On October 15, the ninth day of the war, the very day Israel had decisively repulsed an Egyptian thrust into the Sinai, we received an urgent message from Barzani asking our opinion as to whether he should take the advice of an Israeli liaison officer to launch an attack into the flat Iraqi terrain. It was the sort of proposal liaison officers eager to burnish their credentials at home are apt to make. No such request ever reached us from Tel Aviv.

The message had, as usual, come through CIA channels, and William Colby, the new CIA Director, wasted no time opposing any expansion of the war. When we consulted the Shah, who was supplying most of the matériel and advisers for the Kurds, he supported Colby's view. The Kurds, he argued, were not armed for offensive operations, especially in the plains. The Israeli proposal risked the total loss of the "Kurdish card."

I agreed. In addition, I considered it unwise to tie the Kurds too explicitly to Israel's tactical preferences and thereby bring down on the already beleaguered Kurds the wrath of other Arab states. With Nixon's approval, I therefore sent the following message to Barzani on October 16:

> We do not—repeat, not—consider it advisable for you to undertake the offensive military action that the Israelis have suggested to you.

Any other decision would have risked the destruction of the Kurds without helping Israel. Barzani received my message on the same day General Ariel Sharon was crossing the Suez Canal with his armored forces. Six days later, there was a cease-fire in the Middle East War.

## The End of Kurdish Autonomy

As Anwar Sadat inched ever more explicitly toward the United States in the aftermath of the Middle East War, Soviet emphasis on Iraq increased commensurably. For the first time, Moscow began to supply Saddam Hussein with heavy artillery, which revolutionized Iraqi strategy against the Kurds. Until 1973, the Iraqi army had conducted a campaign in the mountains each summer and withdrawn into the plains at the onset of winter. In the winter of 1973–74, for the first time, the Iraqi army remained in the positions it had seized during the summer offensive and fortified them. That meant that the next summer's campaign would start from much deeper within Kurdish territory; clearly Iraq was seeking to wear down the Kurdish redoubt by attrition. This strategy became all the more worrisome because Soviet heavy artillery enabled the Iraqi army to undertake sieges against hitherto impregnable Kurdish strong points.

On March 11, 1974, exactly four years to the day after his original offer of autonomy, the Iraqis announced a new plan for the governance of the Kurdish region. While continuing to pay lip service to autonomy, it in fact proposed to tighten Iraqi political control. Since Barzani's rejection was foreordained, Baghdad's proposal amounted to an ultimatum. As military activity resumed, all the previous debates over Kurdish policy were rekindled in Washington:

• The Shah warned that a defeat of the Kurds would remove one of the balance wheels within Iraq and increase radical and Soviet influence in the region, magnifying the threat to the Gulf and to Iran.
• Israel weighed in with its own appeals for additional support for the Kurds; Golda Meir specifically raised the issue with me on a number of occasions during the shuttle that produced the disengagement agreement on the Golan Heights in May 1974.
• Barzani was only too ready to pick up the gauntlet. He interpreted the breakdown of talks with Baghdad as an opportunity to loosen the restraints of his allies and to establish his authority in a way that he would still describe as autonomy but which was essentially indistinguishable from separate statehood. On March 16, 1974, Barzani presented us with two options for his proposed strategy: $180 million for full autonomy; $360 million to establish what he called a "proper" infrastructure for independence.

Barzani was driven by the single-mindedness without which few independence struggles would ever be undertaken. Initially always conducted against superior forces, these struggles are sustained by extraordinary faith and a kind of obliviousness to the normal calculation of the balance of forces. Though inspiration is often able to substitute for material resources, there is an objective limit which no amount of dedication can alter. Barzani's version of Kurdish autonomy would never have been supported by the Shah (or by Turkey for that matter). And the United States was in no position to generate by itself the funds he requested. Even Barzani's minimum figure would exceed the total budget allotted to all covert operations being undertaken by the United States. But the Congress of 1974 systematically gutting Indochina appropriations at the height of Watergate would surely have rejected a request for overt funds for large-scale guerrilla warfare in the mountains of Iraq near the Soviet border. And it would have been reckless to try to induce the Shah, whose country shared a long frontier with the Soviet Union, to intervene overtly on the soil of a Soviet near-ally.

Barzani's request triggered a flood of communications from Colby warning against *any* increase in American aid. Colby's reluctance was as unrealistic as Barzani's enthusiasm. All observers agreed that, in view of the new Iraqi strategy, the existing program was inadequate even for defense. In my capacity as National Security Adviser, I pushed for increased assistance to the Kurds and asked Dick Helms and Brent Scowcroft to submit a proposal.

In early April 1974, Helms and Scowcroft presented their conclusions. These amounted to nearly a doubling of the existing resources; the American covert contribution was increased from $5 to $8 million. Overt sources provided another $1 million for refugee relief. The Shah agreed to increase his share of the program from $30 to $75 million a year; Britain and Israel maintained their assistance at prevailing levels.

To help forge a common strategy, if not a common purpose, I instructed Helms to tell both the Shah and Barzani that:

> As we see them, US interests are (a) to give Kurds capacity to maintain a reasonable base for negotiating recognition of rights by Baghdad Government; (b) to keep present Iraqi government tied down, but (c) not to divide Iraq permanently because an independent Kurdish area would not be economically viable and US and Iran have no interest in closing door on good relations with Iraq under moderate leadership.

Similar instructions were conveyed to Colby.

Everyone professed to agree with the objectives, yet the interpretations of the various players came to differ wildly throughout 1974. The CIA, charged with implementation on the American side, dragged its feet in carrying out the new program; the Shah aimed for a defensive stalemate; and Barzani sought victory with resources barely adequate to defend his redoubt.

The trouble with Colby's strategy was that it was more geared to avoiding harassment by congressional committees than to the situation on the ground; the trouble with Barzani's strategy was that it could be accomplished only by regular warfare, not by guerrillas; the trouble with the White House and Iranian strategy was that Kurdish autonomy required a near permanent stalemate, and stalemates against a determined opponent are difficult to sustain by means of unavowed covert operations.

Throughout, the conduct of the Kurds made it difficult to assess their actual needs. Sometimes they sounded desperate, other times exultant. For example, on July 27, 1974, the Shah forwarded an urgent plea from Barzani for assistance and attached to it a warning of his own regarding the grave consequences—for Iran and the entire Gulf —should Kurdish resistance collapse.

Yet only a few weeks later, in early September, Barzani proposed offensive Kurdish operations against the Kirkuk oil fields. We rejected the proposal on September 18 because we did not want to compound the already grave energy crisis by triggering a cycle of violence against Middle East oil installations. But Barzani's periodic push for Kurdish offensives strengthened the argument of the opponents of additional aid by allowing them to claim that the Kurds must be possessing sufficient resources to defend their redoubt, if they were pressing for additional weapons so that they could conduct a major offensive.

In the abstract, the summer of 1974 was an ideal time to review the situation. There were two obstacles, however. Only outsiders are in a position to reflect on events freed of the constraints of time. The summer of 1974 was replete with crises, many crying out for our attention: in May, the Syrian shuttle; in June, presidential trips to the Middle East and to the Soviet Union; in July, the Cyprus crisis; in August, the unraveling of Nixon's presidency; afterward, the transition, Cyprus, détente, the collapse of the trade bill, a developing diplomatic stalemate in the Middle East, and finally the culminating tragedy in Indochina. There was very little time available for any systematic review of the options in faraway Kurdish areas.

Yet even if the policymakers had faced no other challenge, I doubt that they would have discovered better options than continuing the program. Had we never embarked on the covert program in 1972, the Kurds would have been defeated quite rapidly. The intervening two decades having given us an opportunity to become more familiar with Saddam Hussein's methods leave no doubt that the Kurds would not have eased their fate by surrendering. By the summer of 1974, our options had not improved. Had we accepted the CIA's advice and provided no additional resources, the Kurds would surely have collapsed. We did not have the option of overt support in a war so logistically difficult, so remote, and so incomprehensible to the American public. For the victory Barzani sought required overt Iranian intervention backed by the United States. But to open another front with Vietnam tottering, the Middle East precarious, and détente under assault would have recklessly staked the fate of yet another ally and would surely have been rejected by Congress.

When I briefed the new President about the Kurdish operation on August 26, 1974, I informed him that the Shah was considering sending regular forces (he already had auxiliaries there, dressed in Kurdish garb). But I warned that, however tempting, such an action would be too open-ended and too dangerous. Unless I was instructed to the contrary by Ford, my inclination was to drop the subject. The President did not pursue it.

Caught in the crosscurrents, I came up with two stopgap expedients. We allocated regular overt economic assistance funds to the Kurds for refugee relief. And on August 26, Ford approved a scheme that Israeli Ambassador Simcha Dinitz and I had been developing for several weeks. It provided for the transfer of Soviet equipment captured by Israel in the 1973 war to the Kurds. We would make Israel whole with equivalent American weapons. (This turned into another bureaucratic nightmare requiring months of interagency negotiations.) In the end, some $28 million worth of Soviet equipment was transferred until the Israelis ran out of Soviet weapons suitable for warfare in the Kurdish terrain.

By the fall of 1974, as the Iraqi offensive against the Kurds gained momentum, we received increasingly urgent Kurdish appeals for additional assistance, often endorsed by the Shah. All these requests were opposed by the CIA. For example, on October 22, 1974, Colby reported that Barzani's most efficient supply line to Iran and his headquarters were being threatened. Nevertheless, he recommended "against increasing the level of our support" because it would risk jeopardizing secrecy, as if secrecy were more important than the plight of the Kurds: "Our assistance to Barzani for FY 1973, 1974 and 1975 totals almost $20 million and has included over 1,250 tons of ordnance. . . . The Iranians are able to give all of the assistance the Kurds need, and the Agency recommends that further increases in aid to the Kurds be left up to the Iranians." But if the Shah went much beyond the $75 million in assistance he was already supplying, he would face the same problem as Israel. Unless we supplied replacement weapons, he would be weakening his own armed forces. But if we did so, we would find ourselves in a hopeless congressional battle.

## The Collapse of Kurdish Resistance

It was at this point, with Iraq making slow but steady progress, that the Shah, without warning, suddenly decided to throw in his hand. He had witnessed two years of steadily declining executive authority in the United States. He had never objected to any of our various decisions regarding aid to the Kurds, perhaps because he feared that expressing doubts about our steadfastness would undermine the relationship on which he had based the security of his country. But the cutoff of funds to Indochina at precisely this moment could hardly have encouraged the Shah to risk his country in open warfare with Iraq, which was his only remaining option, or to disregard his long frontier with the Soviet Union without ironclad assurances from the United States which we were in no position to give.

The Shah therefore decided to clothe retreat in the mantle of statesmanship. At a meeting with me in Zürich on February 18, 1975, at the end of my "exploratory" shuttle to the Middle East, he informed me without any prior warning that he was exploring a negotiation with Saddam Hussein. I reported to Ford:

> In response to an Iraqi overture, he is planning on meeting with its strongman, Saddam Hussein. The Shah said he cannot accept an autonomous Kurdish state which would be under the dominance of a Communist Iraqi central government. He is suspicious that the Iraqis will stimulate some incidents along the Iraqi-Iranian border which could lead to an internationalization of the Kurdish question and its being brought before the United Nations Security Council which he would consider most unhelpful. In short, he seems tempted to try to move in the direction of some understanding with Iraq regarding the Kurds, but is understandably

skeptical that much is possible. In the meantime, he intends
to continue his support for the Kurds.

I reminded the Shah of his own repeated warnings that the collapse
of the Kurds would destabilize the entire area. Any assurances by
Saddam regarding the governance of the Kurdish area, I cautioned,
would be worthless. And since the Soviets would view Iran's retreat as
symptomatic of the growing weakness of the West, their adventurism
was likely to increase even on that front.

My strictures proved academic. Since the Kurds could no longer be
sustained by a covert program, continuation of the struggle required
some overt Iranian intervention backed up by the United States. The
estimate for this enterprise was two Iranian divisions and an annual
budget of $300 million. And the Iranians needed only to glance at our
media on Indochina to know that there was no domestic support
whatsoever for such a policy.

On February 22, shortly after my meeting with the Shah, I informed Dinitz:

> He's afraid the Kurds have had it. He may begin a negotia-
> tion with the Iraqis if they meet at OPEC, in exchange for a
> veto over whom they put in if Barzani gets driven out. I
> warned him strongly against it.

On March 9, I elaborated to Rabin after the agreement between
the Shah and Saddam Hussein was announced:

> In Zürich, he told me about it in a hypothetical way. He said,
> "If I meet Saddam at Algiers [at the OPEC meeting] . . ." He
> put it as an idea, what turned up in the agreement. I told
> him strongly that it was a bad idea—particularly the idea
> that he believed the [Iraqi] assurances that no Communist
> would be put in [in an autonomous Kurdish zone].

The Shah had not mentioned that a deal was imminent or that he
would acquiesce in total Iraqi control of the Kurdish area. As a result,
I still continued to encourage Barzani. On February 20, I replied to a
letter from him suggesting a personal meeting:

> I was most pleased to receive your message of January 22. I
> want you to know of our admiration for you and your people

and for the valiant effort you are making. The difficulties
you have faced are formidable. I very much appreciated reading your assessment of the military and political situation.
You can be assured that your messages receive the most
serious attention at the highest levels of the United States
Government because of the importance we attach to them.

If you would like to send a trusted emissary to Washington to give the US Government further information about
the situation, we would be honored and pleased to receive
him.

A little more than two weeks later, on March 6, as I was preparing
to embark on the Middle East shuttle that deadlocked, the Shah
stunned us with the announcement that he had reached an agreement
with Saddam Hussein in which he in effect abandoned the Kurds. The
Shah closed his border and stopped all assistance to the Kurds in
return for Iraqi concessions on the Shatt-al-Arab River, the waterway
demarcating the Iranian-Iraqi frontier.

On the human level, the Shah's actions were brutal and indefensible. But in terms of a cold-blooded assessment of Iran's security, the
Shah's decision was as understandable as it was painful. Only overt
Iranian intervention could now save the Kurds, the costs of which
would surely exceed the $360 million Barzani had requested in 1974.
The United States, absorbed with liquidating Indochina, could not
even consider opening another military front and, given congressional
attitudes, even political support was doubtful.

I did not care for the Shah's actions and even less for his deceptive
methods. On March 10, I sent a frosty telegram in which I stopped
well short of endorsing his actions and implied that I had doubts
about the benefits the Shah seemed to hold in store for himself:

> With respect to the Kurdish question, there is little I can add
> to what I have already said to you personally during our
> recent meeting. This is obviously a matter for Your Majesty
> to decide in the best interests of your nation. Our policy
> remains as always to support Iran as a close and staunch
> friend of the United States. I will, of course, follow with
> great interest the evolution of Iraqi-Iranian relations and of
> Iraqi policy in your area generally and toward the Soviet
> Union in particular.

When it was all over, heroes of retroactive confrontation savaged the Ford Administration—and me in particular—for having "abandoned" the Kurds. But the Shah had made the decision, and we had neither plausible arguments nor strategies to dissuade him. The remedy suggested by some of our critics—that we should have threatened the Shah with a cutoff of assistance—made no sense. How could we urge a key ally to begin military operations on his own—the only alternative—when Congress was cutting off allies who had the knife at their throats?

Events since the fall of the Shah have underlined the validity of our judgment that a friendly Iran was nearly indispensable to both the regional and global equilibrium. It would have been frivolous and irresponsible to unhinge another key ally by launching a political assault on the Shah or cutting off aid to Iran. Our commitment to the defense of Iran had not been a favor to be withdrawn when we were displeased but an expression of our own geopolitical interest. I thus had to bear witness to the enslavement of yet another friendly people, aware that, while the Shah's conduct could be used as an alibi, our paralyzing internal crisis had been a contributing cause.

As Kurdish resistance collapsed, the usual stylized Washington maneuvering began for how to apportion the blame. Colby was the first to be heard from. On March 13, he used the occasion of a frantic Barzani request for *direct* American aid to propose dissociating the CIA from the entire enterprise. Because American policy had been to channel aid through Iran, wrote Colby, any *direct* aid to the Kurds now that resistance was crumbling would be even less defensible than it had been in the past. He doubted that the Shah—having ended his own aid to Barzani—would be willing to continue to serve as a conduit for American funds. To gain time, Colby insisted that the Kurdish request would need to be studied on my return from the Middle East shuttle, by which time he knew very well from his own intelligence reports that it would be too late. Meanwhile, Colby recommended that, since the Kurds were so emotional and indiscreet, the CIA subsidy for March be paid—a pitiful Band-Aid considering the tragedy about to descend on the Kurds.

As it happened, Colby's representatives in the field could not bring themselves to take so nonchalant an attitude. Up to this point, they had without exception opposed giving any additional aid to the Kurds —at least that was what Colby had been communicating to the White House.

But as Saddam Hussein launched an all-out offensive, the local CIA representatives were suddenly overwhelmed by the tragedy unfolding around them. While I was on the Mideast shuttle, they transmitted desperate pleas for help from the Kurdish leaders and followed up with many a chiding note when these went unanswered. As on Indochina, passing the buck was the name of the game, and my office had been selected as the place where this buck would stop. For a year, what increased American aid had gone to the Kurds had been as the result of my pressures overcoming CIA opposition. The reason I did not reply now to the desperate pleas for help was because there was nothing I could say, and the authors knew very well that, with the Iranian border closed to us, no emergency assistance was possible.

The Kurdish crisis ended sadly, as it would do again over twenty years later for less valid reasons: forbidding geography, ambivalent motives on the part of neighboring countries, and incompatible motivations within the Kurdish community itself. Those who afterward spoke so righteously about "cynicism" and "betrayal"—having remained silent, or worse, about the far vaster tragedy taking place in Indochina—never put forward an alternative course we could, in fact, have pursued.

As a case study, the Kurdish tragedy provides material for a variety of conclusions: the need to clarify objectives at the outset; the importance of relating goals to available means; the need to review an operation periodically; and the importance of coherence among allies. All these maxims were, in fact, addressed at one time or another, though perhaps not with the requisite care. But their application to the situation at hand proved elusive.

For a variety of reasons, we were unable to generate the resources needed to prevail, and yet we remained unwilling to face the consequences of abdication. We strove, therefore, for a military stalemate and the gradual exhaustion of our adversary. What we could not have known when the Kurdish program was launched was the degree to which our own domestic upheavals would undermine our staying power. Even from the perspective of two decades, I like the alternatives to the course we pursued even less. Had we refused to undertake the Kurdish operation in 1972 and left the Iraqis free to concentrate their efforts on the Gulf, the subsequent course of Middle East diplomacy might have been quite different, especially during and after the October 1973 Middle East War. For the Kurdish people, perennial victims of history, this is, of course, no consolation.

# PART SIX

# THE ATLANTIC RELATIONSHIP

# 20

# THE RESTORATION OF
# WESTERN UNITY

Gerald Ford was of the generation of Republicans who had guided their party's transition in the 1940s from isolationism to support of the Marshall Plan and the North Atlantic Alliance. Ford felt a deep commitment to Atlantic partnership; close ties with Western Europe were second nature to him. A Midwesterner, his attitude in this respect was akin to Harry Truman's, who, when I once asked him of what achievement he was most proud, had replied: "We completely defeated our enemies and made them surrender. And then we helped them to recover, to become democratic, and to rejoin the community of nations."

By the time Ford entered the White House, America's relations with Europe were in unexpected crisis, however. On the one hand, the objectives of the Marshall Plan of twenty years earlier had been substantially achieved. The countries of Western Europe had rebuilt their economies and, despite the vast growth of Soviet power, they were no longer nearly so afraid of Soviet invasion. This was especially the case because the last outstanding issue with the potential to lead to war in Europe had been settled under our aegis in 1971, when a four-power agreement guaranteed access to West Berlin. Simultaneously, Europe began moving from economic to political integration.

Yet there had been no initiative in Atlantic relations since President Kennedy's assassination. European attitudes toward the Vietnam War ranged from embarrassment to outright hostility; Europe was both afraid that the United States might lose interest in world leadership and uneasy about our definition of a world role.

With the end of the Vietnam War, Nixon (and I) thought the time had come to revitalize the Atlantic Alliance. On behalf of the President, I put forward an initiative. Naming it the "Year of Europe"[1] was perhaps too grandiloquent but, in retrospect, I would not alter the analysis with which, in a speech in New York on April 23, 1973, I defined its objectives, many of which remain to be fulfilled:

> In Europe, a new generation to whom war and its dislocations are not personal experiences takes stability for granted. But it is less committed to the unity that made peace possible and to the effort required to maintain it. In the United States, decades of global burdens have fostered, and the frustrations of the war in Southeast Asia have accentuated, a reluctance to sustain global involvements on the basis of preponderant American responsibility.

I had called for a summit of the leaders of the Atlantic Alliance to define the objectives of the Alliance for the last quarter of the century and the political relations between the United States and the European Community, which was expanding from six to nine members on January 1, 1973, and taking its first steps toward coordinating its foreign policy.

The initiative turned out to be far off the mark. With new Watergate revelations shaking Washington almost daily, no European leader was eager to risk his domestic standing on a summit with an embattled American President whose capacity to undertake long-term commitments was visibly eroding.

The Year of Europe initiative immediately ran up against the reality that, in the early 1970s, our European allies were far more preoccupied with European integration than with Atlantic cohesion. And Europe—especially the old established nations such as Britain and France—found the transition to supranationalism traumatic. The more complicated the process of European integration became, the less its supporters were willing to brook any interruption or dilution of it by American schemes promoting broader Atlantic cooperation, however well intentioned.

In this context, our initiative for enhanced consultations between the European Community and the United States came to be viewed—mostly in France, but not only there—as an American stratagem to thwart the reemergence of a specifically European identity and institu-

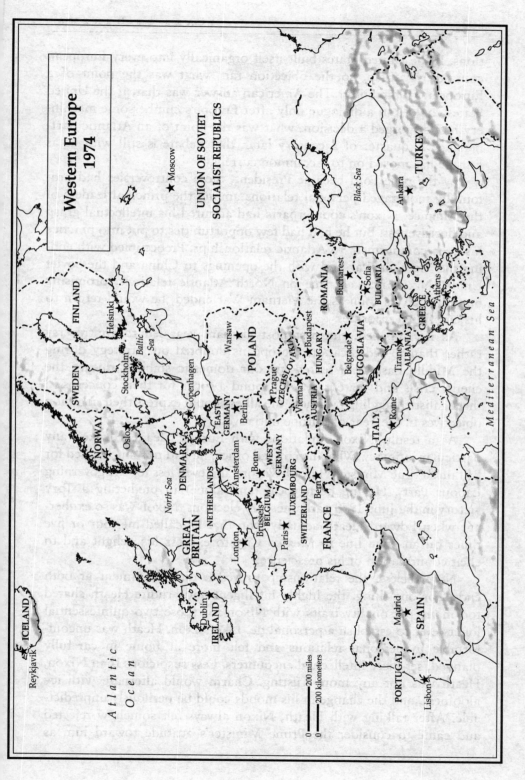

Western Europe
1974

ICELAND
Reykjavik

Atlantic
Ocean

IRELAND
Dublin

GREAT
BRITAIN
London

NORWAY
Oslo

SWEDEN
Stockholm

DENMARK
Copenhagen

North Sea

Baltic
Sea

FINLAND
Helsinki

UNION OF SOVIET
SOCIALIST REPUBLICS

Moscow

NETHERLANDS
Amsterdam

BELGIUM
Brussels

LUXEMBOURG

FRANCE
Paris

EAST
GERMANY
Berlin

WEST
GERMANY
Bonn

SWITZERLAND
Bern

POLAND
Warsaw

CZECHOSLOVAKIA
Prague

AUSTRIA
Vienna

HUNGARY
Budapest

ITALY
Rome

SPAIN
Madrid

PORTUGAL
Lisbon

YUGOSLAVIA
Belgrade

ALBANIA
Tirane

ROMANIA
Bucharest

BULGARIA
Sofia

GREECE
Athens

TURKEY
Ankara

Black Sea

Mediterranean Sea

0        200 miles
0    200 kilometers

tions. If the United States built itself organically into every European consultative organ, so the objection ran, what was the point of a European Community? The American answer was that, if the United States could join a dialogue only after Europe's cumbersome machinery had disgorged a decision, what was the point of an Atlantic partnership? A quarter of a century later, that debate is still with us as Europe has moved on to a common currency.

By the time Ford became President, these controversies had profoundly mortgaged personal relations among the principal leaders of the Alliance. Nixon's counterparts had admired his intellectual grasp and decisiveness. But he had had few opportunities to put into practice his deep commitment to Atlantic relationships. Preoccupied with ending the Vietnam War and with the openings to China and the Soviet Union, Nixon marked time on North Atlantic relations, promising himself that, as soon as the Vietnam War ended, he would return to his emotional priorities.

As it happened, the first post-Vietnam year led to controversy rather than to rededication. Europeans doubted our strategy during the Middle East War, feared for our domestic stability due to the energy crisis and Watergate, and found a focus for their concerns in the legalistic haggling over how the allies should express their common objectives in the Year of Europe initiative.

As a result, Nixon's relations with Europe's leaders lacked any particular intimacy. When he entered office, he had not much cared for Britain's Prime Minister Harold Wilson, and even less for the governing Labour Party. Having been vocal (and alone) in predicting a Tory victory in the June 1970 parliamentary elections, Nixon was so exuberant when Edward Heath actually won that he called me four or five times on an open line in Mexico City to express his delight and to elicit confirmation of his prescience.

Nevertheless, the relationship proved a disappointment at both ends. For one thing, the highly intelligent and erudite Heath shared too many personality traits with Nixon for those two quintessential loners ever to establish a personal tie. Like Nixon, Heath was uncomfortable in personal relations and felt more at home in carefully planned, set-piece intellectual encounters. Less suspicious than Nixon, Heath was not any more trusting. Charm would alternate with icy aloofness, and the change in his moods could be perilously unpredictable. After talking with Heath, Nixon always felt somehow rejected and came to consider the Prime Minister's attitude toward him as verging on condescension (recognizing that Nixon's threshold for feeling that way was quite low).

Personalities aside, Heath's passionate Eurocentrism was bound to produce a certain amount of coolness in someone like Nixon whose political maturation had coincided with the growth of the Atlantic Alliance. In 1962, Heath had been the principal negotiator for Britain's entry into the European Community. In the interim, he had convinced himself that French President Charles de Gaulle's veto in 1963 of British entry into Europe had been caused by France's exclusion from the Nassau agreement on nuclear cooperation between President Kennedy and Prime Minister Harold Macmillan. Heath was determined not to give France any further pretext to accuse Britain of being subordinate to the United States. He was the only British leader I encountered who not only failed to cultivate the "special relationship" with the United States but actively sought to downgrade it and to give Europe pride of place in British policy. All of this made for an unprecedented period of strain in Anglo-American relations.

Nixon's relationship with Willy Brandt, the German Chancellor from 1969 to 1974, was no more made in heaven. Brandt, one of the seminal figures of the postwar period, almost single-handedly reversed German policy toward Eastern Europe and the Soviet Union. When he took office in 1969, the Federal Republic was still pursuing the so-called Hallstein Doctrine, whereby Germany refused to maintain diplomatic relations with any country that recognized the East German satellite. As that regime consolidated itself, the Hallstein Doctrine produced a self-isolation which cut the Federal Republic off from an ever-growing number of countries, especially in the developing world.

Brandt was determined to increase Germany's diplomatic options. More intuitive than analytical, more emotional than calculating, he had been a courageous spokesman on behalf of Berlin's freedom during Stalin's blockade in 1948–49. Brandt was a passionate advocate of German unification, for only unification could end Berlin's peril— surrounded as it was by Communist East German territory. Throughout the 1950s, as mayor of Berlin, he sought to achieve this goal in concert with Germany's allies. The building of the Berlin Wall in 1961, essentially unopposed by the allies, shook his faith in the prevalent view that allied cohesion would translate automatically into German unification. From that time on, Brandt advocated an at least partially distinct national German approach to the Soviet Union. And when he became Chancellor in 1969, he implemented it, concluding a bilateral treaty with the Soviets which, in effect, accepted the division of Germany while aspiring to some easing of the barriers between the German states.

For leaders such as Nixon brought up on the Cold War—and for Europeans like Wilson and French President Georges Pompidou who feared a revival of nationalism in Germany—a separate German diplomacy was cause for suspicion. They feared that Brandt's so-called *Ostpolitik* (Eastern policy) might metamorphose into German nationalism, separate the Federal Republic from the Atlantic Alliance, and entrench the Soviet Union in Central Europe. I liked Brandt, and Nixon respected him. Though uneasy about the nationalist potential of *Ostpolitik,* we tried to draw its sting by cooperating in its implementation. The White House–Bonn–Kremlin backchannel made possible the conclusion of the four-power negotiation on access to Berlin.[2]

Though Brandt was grateful for our effort in facilitating *Ostpolitik,* the relationship between the Nixon White House and Brandt was never warm. Brandt's eloquence was reserved for public occasions. On the personal level, he was given to brooding silences—at least with Nixon—and he was almost exclusively preoccupied with German issues. With Brandt concentrating on Germany and Nixon on Asia, there were few opportunities for a probing dialogue between them on the emerging international order.

Nixon's relations with French president Georges Pompidou started out very well. Nixon had admired Charles de Gaulle, and Pompidou appreciated that Nixon was the first head of state to announce he would attend a memorial service for de Gaulle in Notre Dame on November 12, 1970, thereby guaranteeing an avalanche of acceptances by other heads of state.

Both Nixon and I had sympathized with de Gaulle's quest for an autonomous French voice in defense and foreign policy. Our first encounters with his successor, Pompidou, were therefore warm and productive. Wise, erudite, and balanced, Pompidou pursued de Gaulle's policies without the great man's aloof condescension. Moreover, Pompidou's general analysis of international affairs was quite similar to Nixon's. He was extremely helpful in facilitating my secret visits to Paris for the Vietnam peace negotiations—without ever asking for, or even hinting at, a quid pro quo. Pompidou was given to witty epigrams. When I briefed him somewhat despondently on an impasse in Vietnam negotiations, he consoled me by presciently stating that my long-term problem was not failure but success: "Vous êtes condamné à réussir"

("You are condemned to succeed"). And when, at Reykjavik in 1973, Nixon pressed him to speed up French consideration of the Year of Europe initiative, Pompidou rejoined: "Conception is more fun than giving birth."

A number of incidents—accidents, even—conspired against the Franco-American relationship. During Pompidou's state visit in February 1970, Madame Pompidou was roughed up in Chicago by Jewish activists protesting the sale of French military aircraft to Libya. Though Nixon tried his best to mitigate the damage by attending a civic dinner in New York in honor of the French President, Pompidou could not overcome a certain anti-American resentment thereafter.

In 1972, Pompidou fell ill with cancer. The combination of pain, medication, and perhaps even rage at having to work against the ultimate deadline at a relatively early age caused his heretofore so characteristic balance to give way to unprecedented irritability.

This coincided with a strategic disagreement over Middle East policy during the 1973 war, in the course of which Pompidou assumed the role of defender of Europe's interests against America's alleged one-sided pro-Israeli policy and provocative handling of the energy crisis. Another bone of contention was the Year of Europe initiative itself, which the French President had, in fact, urged on us in theory but came to interpret—when he saw its reality—as a challenge to French leadership on the continent. The new French foreign minister, Michel Jobert, emerging from an obscure staff job into a mother lode of publicity, stoked the Gaullist fires so that, at the time of Pompidou's death, Franco-American relations were at an all-time low.

At this point when the democracies seemed to be returning to the dark side of a history so filled with fratricidal strife, two events brought about a reversal: the first was the coincidence that, even before Nixon resigned, the heads of government of Britain, France, and Germany were replaced as well. In March 1974, the government of British Prime Minister Edward Heath was defeated by Harold Wilson in an election triggered by a coal miners' strike. In France, Pompidou died on April 2, and a two-stage election in May brought Valéry Giscard d'Estaing to the Élysée. In Germany, Chancellor Willy Brandt resigned on May 6, taking responsibility for a scandal involving the arrest of one of his assistants as an East German spy; on May 16, he was succeeded as Chancellor by Helmut Schmidt.

This new and far more compatible group of leaders was immediately obliged to deal with the energy crisis which urgently required joint action, for the cartel's quadrupling of the price of oil in the fall of 1973 threatened the social and political stability of the Western democracies.

Unlike the Soviet challenge, the energy crisis put at risk not physical survival but the democracies' internal cohesion, based on their public's faith in uninterrupted social and economic progress. As a result, Communist parties were making a serious bid for power in several West European countries—especially Italy and Portugal. Nor would any industrial democracy be able to deal with the crisis by itself; none had either the energy reserves or the financial system to withstand the oil cartel's assault.

A strategy was needed for rallying the industrial democracies to conserve energy, work out a system of mutual support to withstand (or deter) a new oil embargo, and protect the global financial system against the consequences of the massive transfer of wealth being generated by the explosion in oil prices. The Ford Administration responded together with its allies, as will be described in Chapter 22. The legacy of that spirit of cooperation includes the International Energy Agency, the World Food Program, and the Group of Seven (G-7), the summit meetings of which symbolize the unity and frequently the success of the industrial democracies.

This progress owes a great deal to the key leaders who took power in 1974. A sketch of their personalities is therefore in order.

## Harold Wilson and James Callaghan: The Operation of the Special Relationship

Rededication to a new era of Atlantic cooperation came most easily to the leaders of Great Britain. Staving off world domination by Nazi Germany had turned out to be Britain's last great solitary service in pursuit of its traditional role as upholder of the global balance of power. While this effort had drained the material substance of Britain's historic world role, its leaders displayed extraordinary moral stamina by insisting on a sustaining role in shaping the global equilibrium. What Britain could no longer achieve by throwing its power into the scales alone, it now sought to extract by fashioning a special relationship with the world's strongest democracy.

Twice in this century, the United States had been the decisive force in winning, at Britain's side, a war that had started in Europe. Sober calculation buttressed emotional ties when Britain, at a moment that coupled victory with relative decline, decided to tie its policies to America rather than Europe. And to indicate that more than an alliance was involved, it called the choice a "special relationship."

Only a morally strong and cohesive society could have undertaken this tour de force of preserving its identity through an act of ostensible subordination. Tenaciously and skillfully, Britain's leaders wove a network of transatlantic cooperation and consultations on diplomacy, strategy, intelligence, and (to a lesser extent) economics that substituted influence for power. Traditional diplomacy achieves its goals by rewards and penalties. The special relationship had available neither of these tools. Instead, Britain based its claim to special consideration on performance and a persistent, subtle, and pervasive discipline unobtrusively conveyed through growing habits of familiarity.

The special relationship could not have lasted so long—or persisted even to this writing (albeit in somewhat attenuated form)—but for joint efforts to meld British and American interests. Had Britain passively acceded to America's preferences, the special relationship would have soon degenerated into demoralizing dependence and fallen into disrepair. A succession of British governments of both parties continued the close ties as American leaders, also of both parties, came to appreciate the combination of dignity and competence with which Britain contributed to the common enterprise, both in the sophistication of British diplomacy and the seriousness of the British military effort. Nearly two decades after the events being described here, the British contingent in the 1991 Gulf War was the largest and most effective among the allies; similarly, Britain was the first NATO country to dispatch land forces to Bosnia in 1993.

Withal when Ford came into office, the special relationship was facing severe strains for the reasons described earlier in this chapter. Ironically, it was the return of a Labour government in March 1974—philosophically remote from a Republican administration—that put an end to mutual frustrations.

When Harold Wilson succeeded Heath, he wasted no time in restoring the special relationship. He had been described to us as excessively influenced by the left wing of the Labour Party and somewhat of an opportunist. It is a measure of Wilson's commitment to the special relationship that these qualities—attested by many reputable observers—never surfaced in his dealings with the two administrations in which I served. He proved to be a staunch supporter of the Atlantic

Alliance and of Britain's friendship with the United States. We had no reason to complain of lack of straightforwardness. Wilson did not hide his doubts regarding America's involvement in Vietnam, but then we were not exactly overwhelmed by expressions of support from other European leaders.

Wilson prided himself on having an extraordinary memory which enabled him to recall the exact position of sentences on a page. Though one might not consider this to be a skill easily introduced into casual conversation, Wilson possessed an enormous flair for constructing occasions that would enable him to demonstrate his gift. Alas, the gods are wont to punish spiritual pride: in his final years, Wilson suffered from an almost complete loss of memory.

When Wilson returned to office in 1974 as unexpectedly as he had been defeated in 1970, it was almost as if his ambitions had become sated by the very act of reversing his previous loss. The enthusiasm and vigor of his first period in office were lacking. Intelligent and precise when he engaged himself, Wilson left the day-to-day chores of dealing with the United States to his foreign secretary (and soon-to-be successor), James Callaghan.

Thus when, in early 1974, I stopped off in London to establish a working relationship with the new British government, Callaghan was my principal interlocutor. We met in the foreign secretary's spacious, high-ceilinged office in Whitehall, furnished in the understated elegance that bespoke a time when Great Britain's preeminence required no emphasis.

The British civil service is an extraordinary instrument. Whenever a new party takes over, only the ministers change while all other officials remain in place. Moreover, in order to avoid partisan temptations, the records of the previous cabinet are sealed, making the cabinet secretary—who is the senior civil servant—both the executor and the memory bank of the new cabinet. When the new Prime Minister unintentionally violates some secret international understanding, it is the cabinet secretary's responsibility to caution the incumbent and to negotiate with the deposed Prime Minister on how the records in question are to be made available.

If my personal experience is any indication, the British system handles transitions with extraordinary aplomb. When Callaghan entered the Foreign Office, he used exactly the same entourage as his Conservative predecessor. At our first meeting, my associates and I were therefore initially exposed to much of the same ever-so-polite needling familiar from the Heath period which had been designed to underscore the new priority of Europe in British policy. Callaghan quickly called a halt: "Henry and I are going to work together. If there are any disagreements, bring them to me, and Henry and I will solve them."

Callaghan combined an avuncular personality with abundant good sense. He and Ford resembled one another in many ways, though Callaghan had served in national office much longer as a member of the previous Labour cabinet. Both shared a calm and jovial disposition and were more self-confident than egotistical. It is no accident that the two have remained close friends in the two decades since they left office.

Coming to the Foreign Office relatively late in life, Callaghan had developed a shrewd sense of his own capabilities. He was neither a strategist nor a geopolitician, and he knew it. Nor did he need to be, since, in his mind, the basic lines of British policy were already settled. Thus Callaghan was content to leave the broad design of strategy to us, when necessary leavening our approach with doses of common sense. When it came to tactical disagreements, Callaghan could be relentless, enveloping us in joviality while his skillful experts bombarded us with briefs designed to move us in the direction of British preferences.

Trust does not come to me spontaneously. But Callaghan managed to gain my confidence by the solidity of his judgment, his calm in crisis, and his practicality. He never specifically invoked the special relationship; rather he brought it to life by his conduct. I came to rely heavily on Callaghan's judgment, especially on tactics, not because of any abstract theory of Anglo-American relations but because it frequently sustained American policy.

I also benefited personally from his wisdom. After the so-called Halloween Massacre of October 31 and early November 1975, during the course of which Ford dismissed James Schlesinger as Secretary of Defense, relieved William Colby as head of the CIA, and abolished my dual position as National Security Adviser and Secretary of State, Callaghan telephoned me (see Chapter 27). He knew that Ford's decision was reasonable but that, in Washington, the appearance of the loss of power can quickly transmute itself into the reality of it. I must be thinking of resigning, he said, but "one does not resign on an issue of status. If you do, you will ruin what you stand for. Resignations can only be done for principle." Upon reflection, I came to agree.

The spirit of our relationship echoes through my instructions to

Assistant Secretary of State for International Organizations William Buffum on July 24, 1974, as he was about to attend Greek-Turkish negotiations on the Cyprus crisis chaired by Callaghan. I told Buffum, as previously quoted, to share all our information and to support Callaghan to the maximum: "It doesn't hurt us to have the British play a role in the Eastern Mediterranean."

## Helmut Schmidt and Hans-Dietrich Genscher: Alliance and Unification

History played a dirty trick on Helmut Schmidt. With his interest in architecture, music, and political economy, Schmidt was the most erudite of Germany's postwar leaders. In addition, he had that special quality marking the great leader of being able to grow with the challenge. But, to achieve greatness, a statesman must possess not only knowledge and character; he needs also to be blessed with the opportunity for a heroic response. Schmidt had the intrinsic attributes, but history did not vouchsafe him the opportunity to fulfill ultimate tasks. Among his predecessors, Konrad Adenauer will be remembered for having brought a defeated Germany from unconditional surrender into full membership in the Western Alliance; Willy Brandt for reconciling it with the countries to the east; Helmut Kohl for bringing about German unification. Schmidt never had comparable opportunities. He conducted the affairs of his country with intelligence and skill, even flair. But it was not given to him to repeat the drama of Brandt or to carry out the fulfillment of Kohl.

Schmidt was destined to be a transitional figure on many different levels: between Germany's past as an occupied and divided country and its future as the strongest European nation; between its obsession with security and the need to participate in building a global economic world order; between his Social Democratic Party's belated commitment to the Atlantic Alliance and the reappearance of some of its earlier nationalist, even neutralist, tendencies. Schmidt navigated these shoals with wisdom and skill. He was the European leader with the best comprehension of the political and social implications of the energy crisis. Because of his service as defense minister, he had an unusual grasp of the political dangers implicit in Soviet nuclear predominance in Europe.

But energy is one of those subjects more conducive to demonstrations of competence than of greatness and, in the aftermath of Vietnam, defense ceased to be a fashionable subject. Schmidt pursued wise policies with respect to all of these subjects. But he was brought down in 1982—ironically a little more than a year after winning an election —because his own party was no longer prepared to support American missile deployment in Europe and because his coalition partner, the liberal Free Democratic Party, sensing Schmidt's declining base, abandoned the joint government.

Helmut Schmidt had entered politics almost as an afterthought, his first love having been architecture and city planning. Had he possessed sufficient funds at the end of the Second World War to pursue time-consuming studies, he probably would have devoted his extraordinary energy and intelligence to rebuilding Germany's war-ravaged cities. As it was, Schmidt chose political economy, the least expensive course of study—something his interlocutors in later years have occasionally had cause to regret when subjected to thoughtful but insistent and lengthy disquisitions.

That Schmidt had wound up in the Social Democratic Party was dictated above all by his birthplace. Since Hamburg had been a Social Democratic stronghold for the better part of a century, membership in another party would have consigned him to commentator or observer roles incompatible with his activist temperament. Later on, it often came to be said that Schmidt would have been happier (and perhaps been able to stay in office longer) as a member of the more conservative Christian Democratic Union. There is some merit in that view, given his free-market orientation, advocacy of a strong defense, and devotion to the Atlantic Alliance (at least during his period in office).

Ever questing for the truth in dealing with the vast array of problems that attracted his attention, Schmidt would defend his conclusions against all comers, including those in his own party. This did not always make him a welcome interlocutor and, in the end, it contributed to his downfall. But it was comforting as well, for one could be sure that Schmidt's views never were related to personal advancement or parochial national interests.

In conversation, Schmidt oscillated between the taciturn and the voluble: taciturn with respect to personal matters, voluble on political or intellectual issues. He had no gift for small talk and no patience with it. Even a carefully prepared conceptual presentation might encounter brooding silence. But Schmidt was just as likely to come back to the subject at the next meeting and in a manner demonstrating that he had given it careful thought. Though he could be abrupt, even abrasive, he was deeply sentimental and loyal—often touchingly so—to his friends. Well aware that posterity judges statesmen by their accomplishments, Schmidt nevertheless insisted that moral conviction was the prerequisite to meaningful political achievement: "Politics without a conscience tends towards criminality," he said on one occasion. "I understand politics as pragmatic action for moral purposes."[3]

Through it all, the Federal Republic remained a special case within the Western Alliance. Conscious of the division of Germany, of the latent distrust of its neighbors, of Soviet power, and of the precarious position of Berlin, the Federal Republic of the 1970s was meticulous about limiting its risks and defining carefully the horizons of its policy. The free western half of Berlin, the former capital of Germany, was located deep inside the territory of a Soviet satellite state, the German Democratic Republic. NATO and the Warsaw Pact faced off along the dividing line between the two German states. A war between them was certain to devastate Germany and decimate its population.

Any German Chancellor was obliged to navigate with great care. The Federal Republic required special expressions and acts of reassurance: from the United States against the threat of Soviet invasion, and from France against political isolation in Europe. Any Chancellor was driven by public opinion to avow the goal of German unification, though none of his allies—and even less the countries to the east—shared a similar preoccupation. Indeed, most of them preferred that Germany remain divided. The German Chancellor therefore had to calibrate his moves carefully so as to maintain public support without risking the self-inflicted isolation that had brought about so many of Germany's twentieth-century tragedies.

Schmidt carried out this balancing act with great skill and humanity and with due consideration for Atlantic concerns. Though, like all outcomes, German unification appears inevitable in retrospect, this was not even remotely self-evident to the statesmen of the 1970s (nor, for that matter, of the 1980s until the reality was nearly upon them). Much as Brandt is admired today, most European leaders at the time found Schmidt's sober style more reassuring, especially his reluctance to sacrifice Germany's Atlantic and European ties to national goals which depended on an evolution in the Soviet Union that the Federal Republic could only marginally influence, if at all. Schmidt formed close ties with Giscard d'Estaing and was an avid supporter of European unification, an advocacy which, in later years, grew more pronounced as he became increasingly disillusioned with the United States. During the Ford Administration, he kept his European and American vocations in balance.

Because he had served as defense minister, the growth of nuclear weapons on both sides of the Iron Curtain was never far from Schmidt's mind. He detested these weapons but never questioned Germany's dependence on them for its defense. This ambivalence was to torment Schmidt for the rest of his tenure in office.

In 1977, a German commando unit undertook a daring raid to rescue German hostages being held captive on an airplane that had been hijacked by Arab terrorists to Mogadishu in Somalia. A few weeks later, Schmidt recounted to me his anguish in the hours before he knew that the raid had been successful and no one had been killed. If he could feel so deeply about the survival of eighty-six hostages and the lives of the commando unit, he mused, how would he ever be able to bring himself to implement the NATO strategy involving nuclear weapons? And yet, when the time came to decide on the deployment of medium-range nuclear missiles in Germany, Schmidt overcame his emotions to carry out what intellectually he considered to be his duty toward the West—in opposition to the majority of his party. It turned into the proximate cause of his downfall.

During the Ford Administration, Schmidt's principal concern was not nuclear strategy but the impact of the oil crisis on the social and political well-being of the West. Convinced that only collective action by the industrial democracies could avert a collapse of the postwar social order, Schmidt had, as finance minister, been instrumental in bringing the Washington Energy Conference to a successful conclusion in 1974—the first step toward creating the International Energy Agency as the coordinating body for the industrial democracies' reaction to the oil crisis. For this, Schmidt was accused by then French Foreign Minister Michel Jobert of betraying European unity—a painful dig for someone with Schmidt's passionate convictions on this subject. During the Ford Administration, as we shall see, Schmidt's staunch support of American efforts to rally the principal consumer nations to common measures vis-à-vis the oil cartel continued even more strongly.

At the time, Schmidt viewed cooperation with the United States as indispensable for both political and moral reasons. During his first visit to Washington as Chancellor, he subjected Ford to a lengthy discourse, not on any conceivable American-European agenda, but rather on the fiscal crisis then gripping New York City. Schmidt argued that New York, the world's financial center, could not—at a moment of general disquietude about American trends—be permitted to slide into bankruptcy. This, he argued, would accelerate the drift toward panic and declining confidence in the United States. Ford accepted Schmidt's advice—or, more likely, came to the same conclusions independently. It was the beginning of a lasting friendship.

While Ford was in office, Schmidt never missed an opportunity to demonstrate his confidence in the United States. When the President and I were briefing Schmidt about the Vladivostok agreement, Schmidt asked probing and knowledgeable questions. But when we attempted to rebut Senator Jackson's charges that we had neglected American and allied security interests, Schmidt interrupted: "You do not need to reassure us. We have no doubts."

For Schmidt, the central importance of the United States was, at that time, a moral issue. Once while he and I were exchanging rather melancholy reflections as friends and former academics about the governability of Western democracies, Schmidt interrupted: "Whatever we say here, we must never repeat except to our closest friends. Too much depends on America to question its ability to solve its problems."

Later on, Schmidt's clashes with Ford's successor soured him to the point that he violated his own injunction never to question America's ability to master its problems. He became increasingly critical of American policy and institutions. After the collapse of the Soviet Union removed the military threat to Germany, Schmidt, now in private life, came to treat friendship with France as a higher priority than the American relationship. While in office, however, Schmidt was a mainstay of close Atlantic ties, and the free peoples owe a great deal to his substantive and moral contributions.

The qualities of Schmidt's foreign minister, the redoubtable Hans-Dietrich Genscher, complemented his own. Schmidt's approach was conceptual, Genscher's tactical. Schmidt was reflective, Genscher eminently practical. Schmidt subordinated specifically German issues to global and European challenges. Genscher tended to reverse these priorities.

My first encounter with Genscher took place in June 1974, a month after he became foreign minister; previously he had served as interior minister. We met in Bad Reichenhall at the southern tip of Bavaria, chosen because Nixon had arranged for a one-day rest stop in Schloss Klessheim near Salzburg en route to the Middle East.

Though, in those early days of his long tenure, Genscher's grasp of foreign policy could most charitably be described as incomplete, he conducted himself with extraordinary aplomb. At a news conference that very morning, June 11, I had reacted to Watergate-related wiretap accusations by demanding an investigation by the Senate Foreign Relations Committee and offering to resign if I was not cleared.[4] Genscher made no reference to either the press conference or to Watergate, treating these events—as did most Europeans—as if they were some incomprehensible, strictly American epidemic. Rather he focused on removing the vestigial remains of the tensions over the Year of Europe initiative.[5]

Over the next three years, Genscher and I worked closely together. His command of foreign policy waxed at an astonishing pace. After I left office, he evolved into the dominant foreign minister in Europe, partly as a result of Germany's power but also due significantly to his own abilities. I developed considerable respect for this clever, dedicated, vulnerable man—passionate in his convictions yet wary of frontal battles, sensitive to aspersions on his motives yet prone to maneuvers inviting them. I did not always agree with Genscher's tactics, but I respected his objectives, and I appreciated the loyalty, even sentimentality, with which he cultivated his personal friendships.

Genscher approached his goals so obliquely that his complicated moves occasionally obscured the purpose animating them, and that may well have been his design. There was the danger that, in less subtle hands, the Genscher style might have evolved into maneuvering between two sides, had the collapse of the Soviet Union not removed that opportunity at least for a time. That such an impact could be generated by a solitary individual who represented a small third party is a tribute to Genscher's powerful personality.

Genscher became foreign minister because his tiny Free Democratic Party (it rarely had more than 8 percent of the vote) had become indispensable for whichever of the large parties (the Christian Democrats or the Social Democrats) tried to form a government. This is why Genscher served as foreign minister under both Schmidt and Helmut Kohl. Indeed, Kohl would not have become Chancellor when he did had not Genscher switched sides in the middle of a parliamentary term to which his party had been elected as coalition partner with Schmidt.

The way he did so tells a lot about Genscher's tactical skill. About a year after the election in which he had fought at the side of Schmidt, Genscher told me that, unless the Free Democrats switched, the public would conclude that Genscher's party, having conducted three successive elections as allies of the Social Democrats, was, in fact, a faction of the Socialists and that there was therefore no reason for a separate line on the ballot. To forestall irrelevance, a coalition with the Christian Democrats had become necessary. Yet such a switch would present a major dilemma: if it occurred too close to the last election, it would appear cynical; if it took place too close to the next election, the turmoil attendant on a change of sides might mortally wound the Free Democrats. In the event, Genscher chose precisely the right moment— or was receptive to the pressures of his colleague, Otto Lambsdorff— to save his party at least for the next decade.

The price Germany has had to pay for its relatively late emergence as a national state has been the lack of a tradition defining the national interest. Only twice in modern history has this problem been solved— by Otto von Bismarck after having forged a unified Germany between 1871 and 1890, and by Konrad Adenauer and his successors in the wake of World War II. Bordering more neighbors than any other European state, Germany has had a correspondingly smaller margin for error. It was stronger than any single neighbor but weaker than a coalition of all of them. The threat of having to face hostile coalitions was therefore congenital and turned into a nightmare of German foreign policy. Ironically, Germany's attempt to break up these incipient coalitions by threats or blackmail before the First World War became a self-fulfilling prophecy that rendered the emergence of hostile coalitions almost inevitable.

Bismarck had chosen dexterity as his way out of this conundrum. To forestall the emergence of hostile coalitions, he maneuvered to arrange a series of alliances and undertakings so that Germany would always have more options than any potential rival. Adenauer and his successors opted for reliability. Adenauer reasoned that Germany's conduct in the Nazi period had fomented too much distrust for the Bismarckian style of amoral flexibility to be tolerated and that the Romantic tendencies of the German psyche were, in any event, inimical to the sense of proportion essential to Bismarck's freewheeling approach. Adenauer's solution was to dissolve Germany's Bismarckian temptations in a rigid commitment to Atlantic and, later, European cohesion.

When Genscher came on the scene, he sought to liberate the Federal Republic from what he considered the rigidities of Adenauer's approach. During the crucial period leading up to German unification, prudence might well have suggested that Germany wait passively at the side of its allies for the eventual collapse of the Soviet empire. But such a course would have meant that German unification disappeared from the international agenda because none of Germany's allies perceived unification to be a dominant national interest. No German foreign minister could pursue so passive a policy, least of all a native of East Germany such as Genscher, whose emotions never migrated very far from his birthplace of Halle.

Genscher's tactical aptitude was, in fact, sustained by a passionate commitment to the eventual liberation of his East German homeland. His colleagues might sometimes wonder how such a seemingly practical minister could be so imbued by a goal many of us avowed only as a challenge for a distant future. Yet Genscher would make us promise to accompany him to his hometown after Germany was unified. And I owe to this pledge a moving visit to Halle, together with Mikhail Gorbachev and Genscher, a year after unification. My promise had been made without the expectation of its being redeemed anytime soon. Gorbachev must have agreed because he was convinced that he was in a position to prevent the pledge from ever being implemented. Yet there we were in Halle together because, in the end, Genscher's faith reflected a deeper reality than our practical assessments.[6]

History will surely give high marks to the tour de force of achieving the unification of Germany while remaining anchored in its Atlantic relationships. Much of this was due to Kohl's stalwart strategy. But Genscher's contribution was indispensable. He was obliged to steer the narrowest of passages among the superpowers and a host of suspicious neighbors. He never lost sight of the reality that, if German policy were too passive, it ran the risk of being engulfed by the storms swirling around the center of the continent. But if German policy became too active, it might magnify those storms. If the Federal Republic pressed too insistently for unification, it might resurrect the fear of German nationalism. But if it completely geared its policy to that of its allies, unification might never take place. Genscher navigated these crosscurrents with extraordinary dexterity, achieving for his country influence and prestige which transcended the calculations of relative power.

## Valéry Giscard d'Estaing—France: Ally or Gadfly?

When Valéry Giscard d'Estaing became President of France in May 1974, he inherited a long agenda of Franco-American disagreements. Both sides had their grievances. We objected to French unilateral tactics on Europe, the Middle East, and energy policy. The

French accused us of insensitivity to their national concerns, interference in the fragile process of European unification, and a general impulse to dominate.

The disputes were less over policy than over the deeper and essentially philosophical issue of how nations cooperate. Heirs of the Wilsonian tradition, American statesmen generally proclaim that, since the interests of democracies are inherently harmonious, alliances amount to a mechanism for burden-sharing. Each ally is assigned a portion of the overall task, and allied consultation becomes a kind of shareholders' meeting in a publicly held company in which influence reflects the amount of capital invested. America's leaders have been wont to proclaim that transatlantic tensions result primarily from the inequality of power and will disappear once Europe gains strength and cohesion—hence the American inclination to view European unity as a vehicle for increased cooperation among the nations of the North Atlantic.

Nothing in France's centuries-long diplomatic history supports such an approach. At least since Richelieu in the seventeenth century, French diplomacy has been guided by a calculation of rewards and penalties. France is traditionally less concerned with the consultation machinery than with each side's options at every stage of a diplomatic process. In the French view, a permanent minority position in the political world is tantamount to abdication. It is the ability to refuse cooperation which determines a country's influence. Thus French diplomacy reacts in an almost Pavlovian way when asked to cooperate with a power of greater strength. Rather than being accorded a leadership role, the strongest ally becomes the target of a systematic effort to reduce its preeminence and hence its capacity to impose its solution, an attitude pithily summed up by de Gaulle:

> Man "limited by his nature" is "infinite in his desires." The world is thus full of opposing forces. Of course, human wisdom has often succeeded in preventing these rivalries from degenerating into murderous conflicts. But the competition of efforts is the condition of life. . . . In the last analysis and as always, it is only in equilibrium that the world will find peace.[7]

In the French view, nations do not make joint sacrifices in order to share burdens (especially those already being assumed by others);

rather they share burdens in order to achieve a specific common political purpose. A united Europe is conceived as an instrument for achieving discrete European purposes and for reducing America's international influence.

The Nixon Administration, open to a policy based on national interest, was prepared to cooperate with a France insistent on making its own national decisions. But by the time Ford came on the scene, an ailing Pompidou, egged on by Jobert and irritated by some American tactics, had more and more identified autonomy with confrontation. France had ostentatiously dissociated from the United States during the Middle East War; it had refused to join the other industrial democracies in cooperating on energy; it had tried to mobilize Europe behind a Middle East diplomacy we considered inimical to the peace process under way; and it had blocked our various initiatives on the Year of Europe.

French diplomacy was, in fact, oscillating between seeking recognition for France as America's equal in some kind of great-power Directorate, first put forward by de Gaulle, or else organizing a united Europe as a counterweight to America. German Foreign Minister Walter Scheel said to me in March 1974: "He [Jobert] thinks what you want is for the United States to envelop Europe in an overall structure which you will dominate." According to Scheel, French policy was therefore aimed at thwarting alleged American designs for predominance. Similarly, when we proposed that common policies on energy include Japan, the French foreign minister interpreted that, too, as an expression of the same American design: "They feel," reported Scheel, "that a trilateral with Japan and the U.S. would encompass the whole world and make clear U.S. predominance."

Even while they professed to speak on behalf of Europe, French leaders were frequently disparaging about their European partners: Germany was a "U.S. protectorate"; in Britain, Heath was "the only European," and anyway Britain "looked out to the sea"; Italy was "disorganized and weak."[8] In part to create a German incentive for closer relations with France, French diplomats in the last year of Pompidou's presidency lost few opportunities to dwell on the alleged—and allegedly imminent—danger of a Soviet-American condominium. At the same time, they cultivated Moscow on their own, taking care to leave the impression that, for some purposes, Paris represented a better option for Moscow than Washington.

The dilemma of French foreign policy was that France no longer possessed the resources to implement by itself the very rational tradition it had been espousing for centuries. In the eighteenth and much of the nineteenth centuries, France was the strongest nation on the European continent; in the twentieth century, it lacked a comparable power base to challenge the United States. Within the Atlantic Alliance, when obliged to choose between France and the United States, most European leaders—but especially Germany's, who were the real targets of French policy—would opt for America, especially during the Cold War. Their approach to international relations made French leaders supersensitive to any potential shifts in either the European equilibrium or the balance between the superpowers. But that sensitivity often led to frustration because the French refused to accept that France simply was no longer in a position to shape the outcome decisively by itself.

Nevertheless, French leaders struggled mightily and not ineffectively to earn recognition for the independent course they had charted for their country. The basic ingredients of this tour de force were: insistence on a strong national defense, including an independent nuclear deterrent; recognition of the importance of American military strength to balance the Soviet threat despite claims to French self-reliance (but since America's defense of Europe was perceived to be in America's *own* self-interest, it hardly constituted an obligation for reciprocity on France); a preoccupation with, and fear of, a resurgent Germany; sensitivity to any changes in the global balance, including China's reentry onto the world stage; and the necessity of détente with the Soviet Union, if only to reassure domestic opinion and to balance both the United States and Germany.

We agreed with many of the components of Gaullist foreign policy. Despite its challenging and at times irritating tone, we viewed French policy as a healthy assertion of a sense of responsibility which was needed for a serious contribution to establishing a new international system.

In many respects, Franco-American tensions were more the result of a cultural gap than of policy disagreement. British diplomats stressed partnership and practical solutions. French leaders emphasized theory and adopted an instructional, superior, often hectoring manner. Britain sought cooperation; France maneuvered to create the impression that Paris had somehow exacted what we might have been quite willing to offer. The occasionally grating impact of the French style of diplomacy had already been aptly described by British diplomat Sir Harold Nicolson in the 1930s:

> The French diplomatic service . . . is staffed by men of remarkable intelligence, wide experience and great social charm. The French combine with acuteness of observation a special gift of lucid persuasiveness. They are honourable and precise. Yet they lack tolerance. So convinced is the average Frenchman of his own intellectual pre-eminence, so conscious is he of the superiority of his own culture, that he finds it difficult at times to conceal his impatience with the barbarians who inhabit other countries. . . . Their superb intellectual integrity tempts them to regard as insincere the confused fumblings of less lucid minds and to feel irritated, dry contempt, when what is necessary is a little lubricating indulgence.[9]

At the same time, while French leaders might be condescending, American officials were frequently insensitive to French emotional needs. Britain had won the war at our side. France had been defeated and occupied. Britain was in a position to build the special relationship on the basis of shared culture and wartime experience. France was tempted to compensate for its wartime humiliations and decades of colonial wars by an occasionally strident assertiveness. Britain, whose policy reflected continuity, could emphasize substance over status; to France, seeking to redefine a national role, status was a form of substance.

A wise American policy would have bristled less at France's assertions of self-will and treated them as inevitable stages of national regeneration. But while many American leaders—myself included—recognized this in principle, we too often overreacted to the sometimes patronizing style of French policy without taking adequate account of its underlying necessities.

When Valéry Giscard d'Estaing assumed office some three months before Gerald Ford, Franco-American relations had deteriorated from irritation into near-confrontation. Giscard's presidency transformed them to a close approximation of genuine partnership. It was his contribution to separate the symbolic from the substantive and to steer relations between the two countries to the cooperation required by their real interests.

Not having participated in the disasters of the 1930s and 1940s or the frustrations of the Algerian war, Giscard felt less driven than his predecessors to score prestige points. He was also the first French President who spoke English fluently and was not reluctant to do so. Giscard kept himself informed of the public debates in the Anglo-Saxon countries and was occasionally prepared to participate in them personally. Having defeated the orthodox Gaullist and Socialist candidates in the election (he was a founder and member of the pro-Gaullist Republican Party), he set out to wean the French presidency from both Marxist doctrine and heroic posturing.

A graduate of the École Polytechnique, one of France's elite institutions, Giscard had the most well-rounded formal education of any Western leader. He could be as charming as he was intelligent. Once one was admitted past the aloof exterior, one encountered a warm and articulate personality. The distinguishing characteristic of most heads of state is ruthlessness; Giscard's was analytical ability. By far the most cosmopolitan of the Presidents of the Fifth Republic, Giscard was an extraordinarily perceptive student of global trends, and he saw the challenges faced by the West in ways that paralleled our own, even when tactical differences would crop up from time to time.

Giscard achieved by intellectual eminence and skillful diplomacy what had been wrongly rejected when de Gaulle first proposed it in 1958 and later when he failed to bring it about by pressure: a de facto Directorate of the United States, Britain, France, and the Federal Republic of Germany in which France did not have to yield pride of place to any country, including Britain. During the Ford Administration, the leaders of these countries brought about a joint global strategy. The range of their common policies expanded in direct proportion to the growing mutual confidence, moving from the familiar Cold War and Atlantic issues to energy and the challenge of Eurocommunism—the threat of Communist participation in the governments of Portugal and Italy, and the succession to Francisco Franco in Spain. Giscard made a special contribution to our understanding of Africa which proved valuable after the Cuban expeditionary corps appeared in Angola (see Chapter 26).

Valéry Giscard d'Estaing was a significant President. He was also the only President of the Fifth Republic to be defeated for reelection (all the others having retired or died in office). Eloquent and elegant, Giscard was a shade too aloof, too much the aristocrat to strike that particular balance which the French people so appreciate: to conduct the presidency as bourgeois in substance and monarchical in style. Relatively anonymous achievement proved to be insufficient nourishment for a French public accustomed to *la gloire*—especially in foreign policy. The dramatic and relatively riskless confrontations with the United States which flattered the French sense for the dramatic were discarded by Giscard as part of his effort to enhance France's real influence.

Curiously, the foppish aspect of Giscard's personality which put off the French reflected a certain social insecurity quite the opposite of the arrogance to which it was ascribed. Of more serious consequence for Giscard's political fate was the nature of his political base. He was caught between the Gaullist right, which distrusted his internationalism, and the Marxist left, which questioned his bias for market economics. As different as Giscard and Ford were as personalities, they shared a similar domestic problem: each represented a moderate center being crushed by irreconcilables from both the conservative right and the doctrinaire left.

Pompidou once said to me that Giscard's weakness as a politician was that he gave a greater priority to placating his adversaries than to solidifying his base: "That type of politician usually loses." Pompidou took Giscard's special circumstances too lightly. For as leader of the non-Gaullist right, Giscard had already committed the ineradicable sin in Gaullist eyes of remaining outside the Gaullist structure. Aroused conservatives are notoriously difficult to placate. The only chance Giscard had of winning them over was to abandon his party and join the Gaullists and, even then, they would almost certainly have preferred one of their own.

Giscard told me on one occasion that reelection to a second term would enable him to lure the moderate wing of the Socialists into a government of the center. The strategy failed narrowly because the election fell into an unfortunate period essentially outside of Giscard's control. A second energy crisis, triggered by the collapse of the Shah of Iran in 1979, caused simultaneous inflation, recession, and financial instability in Western Europe, undermining the political base of every democratic leader in Western Europe. In every change of government between 1979 and 1982, the incumbent was ousted regardless of ideology. In Germany and Britain, conservative leaders replaced the Social Democratic ones but, in France, the Socialist leader François Mitterrand overcame the moderate conservative Giscard d'Estaing.

Despite his shaky domestic base, Giscard turned energetically to the restoration of Franco-American relations—a policy about which neither Socialists nor conservatives felt really comfortable. At a NATO meeting in Ottawa in June 1974, his new foreign minister, Jean Sauvagnargues, settled the residual controversies of the Year of Europe initiative by way of a joint declaration affirming NATO's long-range purposes. Though the initiative had long since failed in its objective of giving a new moral and psychological impetus to Atlantic relations, concluding the exercise in a cooperative manner at least removed the element of discord and served as an augury of a new era.

For the first few months of Ford's and Giscard's incumbency, there was some fencing about energy policy, as will be described in a subsequent chapter. But the new relationship became firmly established as soon as Ford and Giscard met in December 1974. Deciding on the site of the summit involved one of the peripheral matters of prestige that had so bedeviled the Franco-American relationship for a decade. Giscard could not come to Washington before Ford had visited Paris since the last state visit in the series had been Pompidou's trip to the United States in 1970. A return visit had not taken place earlier because Pompidou would not accept a state visit which was part of a broader European tour, while Nixon feared that a special trip to Paris would offend our other European allies.

As a result, Nixon and Pompidou had met twice on islands in the Atlantic which did not represent the soil of either country: the Azores in 1971 and Iceland in 1973. The Giscard-Ford meeting was arranged for Martinique in December 1974, technically a French province, which meant that Ford could be said to have paid a visit to France.

Giscard skillfully used the occasion to signal a new approach. The meetings were held in a comfortable but deliberately unostentatious and somewhat out-of-the-way resort. Discussion was conducted by the Presidents and the foreign ministers in sports clothes. Giscard scheduled one session for the swimming pool, where he, Ford, Sauvagnargues, and I reviewed the European Security Conference while paddling about in the water.

The formal subjects were familiar Atlantic agenda items: NATO strategy, East-West relations, and, above all, energy. Giscard introduced a subject close to French hearts: the future of Cambodia. He had been persuaded by Etienne Manac'h, his ambassador to China, that it was possible for France to mediate an end to the conflict and that Manac'h was the diplomat to do it. Ford and I agreed to let him try, as has been described in an earlier chapter. But it was far too late. The Khmer

Rouge, on the verge of victory, were not about to negotiate, especially when Congress dealt our Cambodian allies the coup de grâce by cutting off their funds.

The subjects were familiar enough, but the atmosphere was unprecedented. As was his custom, Ford got straight to the point. He had cast one of his first votes in Congress in favor of the North Atlantic Treaty, he said. That made it hard for him to understand "French actions and statements which seem to undercut U.S. positions and disparage the United States. We think this is not healthy." That disagreements would arise from time to time was inevitable, but "we would hope for a better understanding."

Giscard replied eloquently. He did not catalogue American failures or provocations—as French diplomats had a habit of doing. Instead, he tried to explain France's psychological challenge:

> To understand our relationship, we have to realize our relative size. France was humiliated by the travails of its political system after World War II. When de Gaulle came in, he wanted to restore French dignity. That required antagonizing the major powers. For example: in the 1960s, our ministers had to have visas to come to the United States, while American dignitaries came to Paris in American planes, and were met by cars, et cetera. When Kennedy was President, the United States press announced a new head of NATO, without any consultation. There was a de facto situation of inequality. French political life is especially sensitive to U.S.-French relations. The Communists play on this issue. . . . So we have this compulsion for independence and self-esteem.

Ford responded by suggesting regular consultations at every level to find common positions on outstanding issues.

If a professional diplomat had uttered such assurances, they would have been dismissed as so many diplomatic platitudes. But Ford always meant what he said, and Giscard fell in with his goodwill. For the rest of Ford's term, theological disputes regarding America's relations with a unifying Europe were set aside. The two Presidents agreed that the United States would continue to deal bilaterally with individual European countries—there was indeed no other option—and France would stop harassing its European partners on that subject. France would continue to pursue European integration, and the United States would place no obstacles in its path. France and the United States would stop undercutting each other; each would keep the other informed of planned initiatives.

With the Martinique meeting, an inner group to conduct the affairs of the Alliance evolved that was very similar to the Directorate de Gaulle had proposed. Ford, Wilson/Callaghan, Schmidt, and Giscard trusted each other; they enjoyed each other's company and suffered from no complexes. In many ways, Ford's role was central. He was wise enough to recognize instinctively that America's power required no special affirmation and that we could achieve more on the basis of mutual respect than by throwing our weight around. He added the human cement that made the system work.

Together they shaped four dramatic summits in one year which gave a new direction to the industrial democracies—the kind of impetus, in fact, that we had sought to achieve in vain with the Year of Europe initiative: a NATO summit in May 1975, the European Security Conference in July, the Rambouillet summit of industrial democracies in November, and, nine months later, its successor in Puerto Rico. These economic summits have since become annual fixtures on the international calendar.

## Eurocommunism and the Atlantic Alliance

Allied cohesion was being challenged not only by the energy crisis but by domestic changes in three key countries: in Italy and Portugal, it appeared that the Communist Party might join the government, and, in Spain, the allies needed to deal with the imminent end of Francisco Franco's rule.

The challenge of Eurocommunism appeared first in Italy, where parliamentary deadlock made entry of the Communist Party into a normal governmental coalition seem inevitable. Concurrently in Portugal, Eurocommunism took the even more dramatic form of a potential Communist coup.

The situation in Italy was difficult to deal with because the Communist Party seemed to be on the march through the regular operation of the electoral system. In the regional elections of 1975, it increased its share of the vote to 33.5 percent, only 2 percent behind the governing Christian Democrats. In the national elections of 1976, the Communists did even better, capturing 34.4 percent of the popular vote, compared to 38.7 percent for the Christian Democrats. The Communists increased their representation in parliament, winning the presidency of the lower house and the chairmanship of four of its committees as well as of three in the senate. Together with the Fascists on the right, they now controlled over 40 percent of the parliamentary seats.

It was a situation analogous to that of the Weimar Republic of the early 1930s which had led to the collapse of democracy in Germany. When the democratic parties are reduced to barely more than a majority, it is impossible for the normal democratic process to operate. Either all the democratic parties form a coalition, which spells the end of any democratic opposition, or they split, in which case the nondemocratic parties are enabled to bring down any government by combining with the democratic opposition.

Not surprisingly, some Italian leaders with impeccably anti-Communist records came to the conclusion that long-term stability could best be served by transforming the Communists' tacit toleration into active cooperation. According to the advocates of such an "opening to the left," it would introduce the Italian Communists to democratic processes and transform them into long-term partners. This school of thought found many adherents in the United States, particularly in liberal circles. If we were able to cooperate with the Communists in Moscow, so the argument went, why not with the seemingly much more flexible Communist Party in Rome?

I was strongly opposed to any American encouragement of Communist participation in the government of a NATO country. I rejected the analogy to the détente policy. There was a crucial difference between managing a conflict with adversaries and including representatives of the adversary in an alliance of democracies. The key issue was not the degree of independence of the European Communist Parties from Moscow but their Communist ideology and organization. Neither the internal dynamics nor the electoral programs of the Communist Parties seemed to me compatible with democracy or the established purposes of the Atlantic Alliance. No European Communist Party—not even Italy's—had supported the Atlantic Alliance. Whatever difficulties their supposed independence might pose for Moscow, a common strategy for the defense of Western democracies was not on their agendas. The system of close allied consultations based on shared goals and compatible philosophies would weaken, if not disintegrate altogether. The exchange of highly classified information and the integrated military planning would both be at risk. Many of the same factors would weaken the movement toward European integration as well.[10]

Of course, there was very little we could do directly to affect the domestic decisions of political leaders of a country so central to the Atlantic community as Italy and one historically so friendly to the United States. But the American attitude was bound to be of some importance to many Italian leaders—as it certainly would be if we seemed to acquiesce in a Communist role in government.

An important principle was involved. As leader of the democratic nations, the United States had a special responsibility to maintain the moral cohesion of the Alliance. If we weakened on that issue, a rush to expediency would soon follow. I stated my views during a closed-door meeting of American ambassadors in Europe in London on December 13, 1975:

> The intellectual community in the United States is trying to resolve a paradox. We are accused of being soft on Communism and hard on Communist parties. We are asked to be tough with Moscow but to have a dialogue with Communist parties in the West.
>
> One thing is clear, however, the dominance of Communist parties in the West is unacceptable. This has nothing to do with the reasonableness of these parties or with the degree of their independence from Russia. It is hard to imagine that, if one or the other of these parties takes control of a Western government, it will permit the democratic process to operate and thereby face the possibility that it may itself be removed from office. . . . We must do our utmost to assure the survival of democratic processes and to preserve the Western political orientation of Western European countries. . . .
>
> . . . It is difficult to see how we could continue to have NATO discussions if these various Communist parties did achieve control of Western European governments. We could, as with China, perhaps have parallel policies. But the alliance, as it is now, could not survive. The Western alliance has always had an importance beyond military security. The United States would be alone and isolated in a world in which we had no relations by values to other countries.[11]

Ford spoke in the same sense to Italian Prime Minister Aldo Moro in Helsinki when he warned in strong words about the proposed "historic compromise" in Italy under the pretext of expressing his reluctance to "tolerate" a Marxist government in Portugal or to permit extensive NATO consultations with it:

> We do not see how it is possible to tolerate a Marxist government in NATO. . . . With the liberal, leftist leanings of these people, you are sure to end up with a Communist government, and such a situation would be completely unacceptable to us if they were in NATO.

The danger of Communist participation in the Portuguese government was serious indeed. On April 25, 1974, Portugal's conservative authoritarian government was overthrown by General António de Spinola and a group of officers disenchanted with the wars Portugal was waging to retain its African colonies. We knew next to nothing about any of the personalities involved, only that they concentrated initially on the decolonization of Portugal's African empire. Between September 1974 and November 1976, Guinea-Bissau, Mozambique, Cape Verde, São Tomé and Príncipe, and Angola achieved independence under left-wing governments. We quickly established normal diplomatic relations with all of them except Angola because of the Soviet and Cuban military presence there (on Angola, see Chapter 26).

Over the months that followed, the Communist influence increased in Portugal itself. Many of the leaders of the so-called Armed Forces Movement had served in Africa where they had adopted the liberation philosophies of radical guerrillas very close to Communist ideology. Moreover, the Portuguese Communist Party had retained its Stalinist structure and honed its militancy in the underground during five decades of authoritarian rule when all parties were banned. It now emerged as the best organized political force in the country. Between May 1974 and July 1976, six provisional governments held what passed for power in Lisbon, and all of them moved progressively to the left. The President, Francisco da Costa Gomes, was later described by our extremely astute Ambassador Frank Carlucci as being

> very far to the left. The Prime Minister, the leadership of the army, the labor unions, and a number of the ministers

were all either communists or very close to the Communist
Party. . . .
. . . [T]he PCP [Portuguese Communist Party] had a
very clear sense of direction. They followed a classic policy
of going for the ministry of labor, the ministry of education,
and the propaganda division of the military so that with
relatively few people they were able to penetrate.[12]

When the Western leaders met at the NATO summit in Brussels in
May 1975 and then again at the European Security Conference in
Helsinki in July, the Armed Forces Movement, the radical left, and the
Communist Party seemed to be well on the way to turning Portugal
into a Communist-style "people's democracy."

The state of mind of many of the new leaders was exemplified by
Colonel Vasco dos Santos Gonçalves, who served as Prime Minister
from mid-1974 to August 1975, and who, if not an outright Communist, only refrained from membership in order to save paying his party
dues. At the NATO summit of May 1975, he told Ford that the democratic non-Communist parties were not really democratic because, by
definition, each of them represented the viewpoint of only a segment
of the electorate. Gonçalves claimed that he represented a more inclu-
sive view of politics above party—a concept straight out of Lenin,
though Lenin would not have been so naive as to speak that way to an
American President.

It was this Leninist tendency that had led me to make the not-so-
tactful comment to Mario Soares, the head of the Socialist Party, that
the democratic leaders risked ending up like Aleksandr Kerensky—the
last democratic Russian leader before Lenin's coup.* It was no reflection on Soares's good intentions; after the Communists were defeated,
he was to make major contributions as Prime Minister and later as
President. But in 1975–76, I was alarmed at the democratic politicians'
lack of a strategy to halt the Communist trend. In the end, it was
the moderate officers within the Armed Forces Movement, not the
politicians, who turned the tide and then gave power back to the
democratic politicians.

No NATO country had faced the prospect of an internal Communist takeover since the early days of the Cold War. The danger in
Portugal was magnified by the fact that simultaneously the Italian

* I made this comment to Soares at a lunch I hosted for him at the State Department in October
1974.

Christian Democrats under Aldo Moro were playing with the idea of forming a coalition with the Italian Communist Party—the so-called historic compromise noted earlier. If the Communists gained a hold over the government in either country, it would create a sense of inevitability, facilitating inclusion of Communists in other NATO governments. With the Western world reeling from the energy crisis, the American leadership under a cloud because of Watergate and the Vietnam protests, and Soviet leaders emphasizing a shift in the "correlation of forces,"[13] the phenomenon of Eurocommunism in Western Europe could become a dangerous trend.

The issue before the NATO allies was how to respond to a request by the increasingly leftist government in Lisbon for economic assistance. After the conservative authoritarian government was overthrown in April 1974, I recommended an aid program of $20 million in loan guarantees as a gesture on behalf of democracy. As each succeeding government veered further to the left, the question was whether to continue, let alone increase, this assistance. Ambassador Carlucci favored helping the radical government on the theory that the moderates would somehow benefit from our demonstration of goodwill.

I had urged Carlucci's appointment and took his views very seriously. Still I initially differed with him. I did not see how moderates could be strengthened by aid for radicals, and I favored keeping aid at modest levels until the radicals had been squeezed out of the government so that the democratic political leaders could get the credit for increases in assistance.

Similar differences of opinion existed among the allies. Schmidt favored increased aid; Giscard supported Ford's harder line; Callaghan urged a compromise: aid coupled with increased covert support to the regime's opponents. Though tactics differed, there was no disagreement on the objective of trying to force the Communists out of the Portuguese government. Finally, it was decided that each ally should play its own hand while keeping the others closely informed. Ford and Giscard took on the role of the "bad cops," Schmidt the good one, and Callaghan the mediating father figure trying to meld both policies.

The resolution of the dispute within the United States government has been accurately described by Carlucci:

> Certainly we had differences in views, but they were overblown. He [Kissinger] had a worldwide perspective; I had a particular problem to deal with. We had some sharp

exchanges but eventually came to an agreement that the policy I was recommending would be given a chance. Once we reached that agreement, he couldn't have been more supportive. So we were able to pull together an effective policy on such things as Azorian separatism (a key issue that was being pushed by the right wing), the context of our aid programs, and how we would approach what was a very serious security issue for NATO. I had no problem telling the Portuguese that they couldn't be accommodated in NATO if they were a security risk, as long as at the same time we could hold out some hope for support and we could deal with the right elements in Portuguese society.[14]

A little later, the Western Alliance was confronted with another imminent political change, this time at the other end of the political spectrum, requiring delicacy and unity: the management of the post-Franco transition in Spain. When Ford entered office, it was already becoming evident that he would in all likelihood have to deal with the consequences of Franco's death during his term. We were hopeful about the prospects of a democratic evolution, since Franco had made unusually thoughtful preparations for succession by reestablishing the monarchy and initiating the beginnings of democratic procedures. Our principal concern was whether a society still riven by the memory of the civil war could transcend its rancorous past and learn to coexist with political opponents in a pluralistic system. There was no precedent in recent Spanish history for such self-restraint.

While Franco was still in office though obviously failing, we took the first steps to bring Spain closer to the democracies. The occasion was the lapsing of the bilateral agreement for American bases in Spain first negotiated during the Eisenhower Administration in 1955. Among our allies, those with left-of-center governments—which was practically every country except France—concurred that there was a sound military reason for renewing the base agreement. But they could not bring themselves to be seen cooperating with Spain while Franco was still in power. The Ford Administration thus had the delicate task of helping Spain move toward the West on behalf of the Alliance without causing indispensable allies to bolt.

In a speech at the NATO summit on May 29, 1975, Ford expressed the American view:

> [We] should begin now to consider how to relate Spain with
> Western defense. Spain has already made, and continues to
> make, an important contribution to Western military secu-
> rity as a result of its bilateral relationship with the United
> States.[15]

The proposition was greeted as premature, to put it mildly. Dutch
Prime Minister Johannes den Uyl, who had last had an opportunity to
instruct us during the *Mayaguez* crisis (see Chapter 18), did not miss
this occasion to deliver a new lecture. Any military gain from a gesture
toward the Spanish regime, he told Ford, "would be offset by the loss
of political credibility that the Alliance would incur."[16]

Even the staunch Helmut Schmidt warned about the impact on
German public opinion of too ardent a pursuit of relations with Spain:

> SCHMIDT: The Franco era is obviously coming to an end
> [Francisco Franco died on November 20, 1975]. It is
> still not clear who will take the helm. We should be
> encouraging those we hope will govern after Franco.
> That means we must deal not only with those who are
> in power now.
>
> FORD: We are now negotiating a treaty for a military base,
> and we assign a high priority to it. Should these negotia-
> tions fail, the alliance would suffer appreciable disad-
> vantages. So we have to walk a tightrope.
>
> SCHMIDT: Yes, certainly. But so that you can be sure of
> your bases and your special strategic ties with Spain
> beyond today, you should talk about it with tomorrow's
> rulers as well. What is also at stake is the United States'
> standing in Europe. No one should be able to say of the
> United States that it was supporting the wrong regime.[17]

In the end, the Alliance reached all its objectives; after Franco's
death in November 1975, Spain became a vital democracy and joined
NATO in 1982. In Italy, the participation of Communists in government was delayed for over twenty years until well after Communism
had collapsed in the Soviet Union. In 1976, moderates in the Portuguese military gained the upper hand, a left-wing rebellion in the
armed forces was suppressed, and a civilian democratic government
took office in Lisbon.

The renewed sense of allied cohesion contributed above all to re-dressing the political and psychological balance between East and West. Henceforth it was the Soviet Union which, with few interruptions, was on the ideological defensive. The thirty-five-nation Helsinki summit, designed to ratify the consensus document of the European Security Conference, was the next milestone in this process.

# 21

# THE EUROPEAN
# SECURITY CONFERENCE

Turning points often pass unrecognized by contemporaries. Many events perceived as seminal when they occur are diminished by the perspective of history to little more than sensational incidents. Others that were either controversial or ignored by contemporaries are elevated by posterity into turning points.

The latter was the case with the European Security Conference, which culminated in Helsinki in July 1975 in a summit meeting of thirty-five heads of state or government. Proposed by the Soviets in 1954 and intended as a maneuver to undermine the Atlantic Alliance, it was hesitantly accepted by the democracies and concluded amidst bitter controversy. Yet, with the passage of time, it came to be appreciated as a political and moral landmark that contributed to the progressive decline and eventual collapse of the Soviet system over the next decade and a half.

Rarely has a diplomatic process so illuminated the limitations of human foresight. The Soviets sought the conference to achieve recognition of their postwar dominion over Central and Eastern Europe; they also hoped to replace the Atlantic Alliance with a pan-European collective security system, thereby undermining Western cohesion. For whereas an alliance defines the territory to be defended and lays down a dividing line between the allies and the potential aggressor, a collective security system represents a legal concept which prejudges no potential threat to the peace—hence all nations in the envisaged system, including the potential aggressor, participate.

The challenge to an alliance is unambiguous; it is triggered by a violation of the dividing line. A system of collective security, on the other hand, proceeds from a quasi-legal act, a determination as to whether an aggression has, in fact, taken place. An alliance generally has military forces designated to defend its territory; a system of collective security must assemble military force from case to case. Because the judgment as to what constitutes a threat is left until the occasion arises, collective security arrangements such as the League of Nations, the United Nations, or the Locarno Treaty rarely work in practice. In the European Security Conference, the Soviet Union, treated by NATO as a potential threat to the peace, participated as a founding member, thus threatening to subsume NATO in a system of collective security which would have ended the Atlantic Alliance as the postwar world has known it.

Through much of the negotiations leading up to Helsinki, the democracies considered themselves to be on the defensive and sought to ward off the dangers to their cohesion without raising the level of tensions with the Soviet Union. That the real balance of forces was quite different—that, in fact, the democracies held the upper hand psychologically and materially—emerged only gradually in the course of the process. At the beginning, few perceived the opportunity; at the end, the Ford Administration achieved what turned out to be a strategic victory, albeit it saw its success blighted by widespread accusations within the United States that it had sold out to the Soviets.

An all-European security conference had originally been proposed in 1954 by Soviet Foreign Minister Vyacheslav Molotov. Because it specifically excluded the United States, it was rejected out of hand as a transparent ploy to prevent the consolidation of NATO, then in its infancy. But Soviet (and, for that matter, Russian) policy makes up in persistence what it lacks in imagination. There were (and are) no quality journals in Moscow criticizing Kremlin leaders for advancing variations of the same proposals over and over again. When dealing with restless democracies eager to demonstrate their flexibility to their publics, Soviet (and Russian) diplomats can be as inexorable as drops of water on a stone and with the same eroding effect. Thus the Soviets revived their idea for a conference in July 1966, when the Warsaw Pact nations issued a "Declaration on Strengthening Peace and Security in Europe." In April 1967 a conference of European Communist parties followed suit.

In December of that year, NATO reacted. A report on the future of NATO drafted by Belgian Foreign Minister Pierre Harmel gave priority to the search for a stable "détente" with the Communist East, second only to deterring aggression.

As part of a campaign to defuse the uproar over the Soviet occupation of Czechoslovakia and perhaps to limit the freedom of action of the new American President, whom Moscow suspected of being hardline, a Warsaw Pact meeting on March 17, 1969, put forward the project again, this time as a formal diplomatic proposal requiring a response. It called for the convening of a European security conference, the stated goal of which was to be the improvement of East-West relations, recognition of the inviolability of Europe's frontiers, and mutual recognition by East and West Germany of the inter-German dividing line (this was before Brandt had become Chancellor and accepted the dividing line as a German decision).

On April 3, Soviet Ambassador Anatoly Dobrynin emphasized the importance the Soviet leadership attached to the proposal by delivering it personally to the White House, garnished with two so-called concessions: that the Soviet Union would withdraw its objection to United States participation and that it no longer required that the dissolution of NATO be part of the conference agenda.

Dobrynin's note was a symptom of the growing—if only just emerging—dilemmas of Soviet foreign policy. On the one hand, it was a classic Soviet maneuver, treating the withdrawal of two preposterous and one-sided conditions as a concession requiring Western reciprocity. At the same time, the "concessions," however meaningless, did reflect some of the new realities encroaching on Soviet freedom of maneuver. Once the European Security Conference was no longer designed to replace the Atlantic Alliance and confirmed the United States as a European power, Soviet policy found itself on the defensive. The goal of stabilizing relationships between two blocs—however voluntary the one and however coercive the other—symbolized that, at least as far as Europe was concerned, Moscow henceforth would be on the defensive, attempting to hold on to what it had acquired.

Neither Nixon nor I felt obliged to reward the Soviet Union for what reality had imposed on it. In a memorandum to the President, I wrote that "we should not make the Soviets think that they are doing us a favor if they agree to such an obvious fact of life."

Our NATO allies were more willing to go along with the Soviet proposal. Eager to appeal to constituencies radicalized in part by the anti-Vietnam protest spilling over from the United States, they urged us to accept at least the "principle" of the European Security Conference—the familiar opening wedge from which detailed negotiations inevitably follow. Willy Brandt did so to achieve allied cover for his *Ostpolitik*, which was about to recognize the inter-German dividing line; Georges Pompidou urged it as a way of keeping *Ostpolitik* from turning into a purely national German enterprise; and Harold Wilson, with an election approaching, saw it as an opportunity to demonstrate his moderating influence on Nixon.

Unwilling to be dragged into an open-ended multilateral negotiation which lacked a meaningful agenda and was ultimately designed to undermine allied cohesion, the Nixon Administration responded by invoking linkage. The conference, we argued, could not possibly succeed unless concrete issues producing tensions were settled first—specifically, the permanent threat to free access to beleaguered West Berlin. We also insisted on opening a negotiation to limit conventional forces in Europe (in which the Soviets enjoyed a significant superiority). Because no conference could be assembled without us, we managed to use the European Security Conference as a wedge to extract progress on other issues as well and to moderate Soviet conduct for four years, until July 1973. By then, a negotiation on Mutual and Balanced Force Reductions (MBFR) had been assembled, starting in January 1973, and access to Berlin had been guaranteed by a 1971 agreement so effectively that the issue never came up again until the collapse of the East German regime in 1989.

By the time the conference assembled in July 1973 it had been given its formal name: the Conference on Security and Cooperation in Europe (CSCE).* Months passed in exploratory discussions until, in January 1974, the stage of drafting an actual document was reached. It soon became apparent that the debates over the purpose of the conference paled before the squabbles arising over the content of what later became known as the Helsinki Final Act.

For the Soviet Union, a principal aim of the document was to be a declaration of principles implying general acceptance of the territorial status quo in Europe. To endow this with the maximum solemnity, the Soviets proposed that the final meeting and signing of the document take place at the summit level.

As it turned out, the negotiations did not evolve into the one-way

---

* In 1995, this body—which continued in existence after the Helsinki summit—was renamed the Organization for Security and Cooperation in Europe (OSCE).

street the Kremlin had envisaged. For the democracies came to understand that they could do better than avoid a setback, which was their initial goal; as the conference ground on, they gradually transformed it into a strategic opportunity for the West. It was hardly a sign of self-confidence that the superpower with the largest conventional forces in the world and a nuclear arsenal rivaling that of the United States should be asking for an assurance that its borders were inviolable from countries some of which it occupied and none of which except the United States was in a position to challenge the Soviet Union militarily. Such a pledge, if it had any operational meaning at all, would duplicate clauses in peace agreements already signed by the wartime allies with all the nations of Eastern Europe between 1945 and 1948 and in a series of bilateral agreements between the nations of Western and Eastern Europe. The most recent of these were the treaties by which the Federal Republic of Germany under Willy Brandt had accepted the territorial status quo, including the dividing line in Germany.

What was novel about the European Security Conference was that it enabled the Federal Republic to raise the issue of peaceful change of frontiers, which in time would provide the legal and political authority for German unification. In the bilateral treaty negotiated between Brandt and Brezhnev in 1970–71, the Federal Republic had accepted existing European boundaries as "inviolable" without conditions. But at the European Security Conference, where the Federal Republic was backed by its allies—especially the United States—it was able to extract a provision stating that "frontiers can be changed, in accordance with international law, by peaceful means and by agreement."[1] And German leaders have given the principal credit for this clause to the United States.[2]

Equally important were the provisions for the free movement of peoples and ideas and for the protection of "human rights and fundamental freedoms," which the democracies insisted on including in the Final Act. Our purpose was to inhibit, through international agreement, Soviet repression of upheavals and long-standing protests, such as had happened in Hungary in 1956 and Czechoslovakia in 1968. Visionary and courageous activists like Václav Havel and Lech Walesa turned these clauses of the Final Act into rallying cries for resisting totalitarianism in the Communist world and thereby ultimately brought about the liberation of Eastern Europe.

In addition, the Western powers insisted on obtaining some improvement in military security notwithstanding the fact the principal forum for this subject was the negotiations on troop reductions (MBFR) that had just opened in Vienna. But the democracies, as well as some of the East European Soviet satellites, wanted to bring about additional inhibitions on troop deployments in Europe. These so-called confidence-building measures (CBMs) involved such procedures as prior notification of maneuvers of a given size and within a certain distance from the boundaries of any of the participants. And that meant a restraint on Soviet troop movement within European Russia.

At first, the American strategy was to create no obstacles to progress but to do little to accelerate it either. The passage of time was serving Western interests by gradually draining the exercise of its original rationale of consolidating Soviet power. As this goal was being achieved, we intervened on key issues, such as the confidence-building measures, the human rights provisions, and the German quest for the "peaceful change of frontiers" clause. In this manner, the balance of benefits shifted inexorably to the side of the democracies. At the beginning of 1974, it was obvious that the Soviets were not achieving the symbolic outcome they had sought. The drafting process was long, tedious, and esoteric. The Soviets tried to draw the sting from the human rights clauses by inserting a preamble that none of the provisions of the Final Act could be used to interfere in the internal affairs of signatories. This, of course, would have vitiated the entire purpose of the provisions on human rights, and the Soviet maneuver eventually failed.

The clause permitting peaceful change of borders generated a comparable controversy. The Soviets might consider the concept, they said, so long as it was in a preamble detached from the principle on "inviolability of frontiers." They seemed to reason that this would confer on the recognition of existing borders a higher status than on the idea of changing them peacefully. The Germans, of course, saw through this maneuver and called on the United States for assistance. The final "compromise" was a free-standing article that affirmed not only the principle of peaceful change but also the right of each signatory to join or leave alliances.

As a result, where actual negotiations wandered more and more into committees of experts, terminology grew increasingly esoteric: Dutch "compromises," Finnish "plans," and German "proposals"— each labeled as such—were flung about. This diplomatic witches' brew had been ingeniously organized by the British into "baskets." Basket I dealt with security issues, Basket II with economics, and Basket III with human rights, free movements, and related issues.

Senior negotiators sufficiently courageous to participate in the drafting process quickly found themselves overwhelmed by arcana. Gromyko seemed to be well informed about the issues concerning the Soviet Union, but even this remarkable professional grew vague when it came to some of the more exotic propositions. I prided myself on being on top of the details of negotiations conducted under my direction, but CSCE defeated me. I was clear about what we were trying to accomplish and defended the thrust of the provisions we were urging. But the precise formulations often eluded my comprehension. I never fully grasped the distinction between "equal applicability" versus "equal validity" of principles, about which bitter battles were fought; why commas around a clause changed its operational significance, another bone of contention; or why the significance of a phrase located in one paragraph changed if moved to another. As Gromyko seemed to be in the same predicament, he tended to base Soviet opposition to Basket III on a defense of Soviet puritanical morality by claiming that the clause about free movement of peoples was a Trojan horse designed to permit scantily clad Dutch cabaret performers to contaminate the motherland of the proletariat.

The military confidence-building measures led to similar haggling. The Western powers sought to secure a commitment of sixty days' prior notification of movements of brigades; the Soviets countered with an offer of five days for maneuvers of army corps. The compromise wound up being thirty days for the deployment of divisions. The heads of state quickly passed issues as these to their foreign ministers, who just as rapidly turned them over to their experts. Fortunately our principal working-level negotiator, Assistant Secretary Arthur Hartman, somehow mastered all the details and skillfully navigated them to a successful conclusion.

Basically, the various controversies marked stages of a Soviet retreat on the issues of peaceful change, confidence-building measures, and human rights. By May 1974 agreement seemed sufficiently imminent that exchanges began on the subject of concluding at the summit level. But by that stage the withdrawal from office in rapid succession of Heath, Pompidou, Brandt, and Nixon imposed a new hiatus and widened the gap in knowledge between the top leaders and their experts even further. It began to seem as if the drafting process would become an end in itself, comprehensible only to a select group of diplomats involved as they toiled away like so many cloistered medieval monks elaborating sacred texts.

In some respects, it was a case of multilateral diplomacy run amok. As one of the impulses behind the conference had been to give the smaller European states greater freedom of maneuver, the major powers had to be careful not to ride roughshod over their preferences or even their self-will. A particular transgressor in this last regard was Dom Mintoff, the Prime Minister of Malta. As the conference was nearing its conclusion and only the date for the summit remained to be set, Mintoff held up proceedings for the better part of three days. Our Finnish hosts grew frantic because they could not make preparations for the summit until a final decision had been reached. For one entire day, Mintoff was unreachable; the Maltese ambassador alleged that he was horseback-riding—though on a relatively small island, the task of finding him should not have proved insuperable. For two more days, Mintoff held out, trying to extort some further gains. Finally, our Finnish hosts, who throughout the conference had been models of integrity combined with diplomatic competence, surmounted the impasse, the exact nature of which I have since forgotten and by means of some formula that is now even more elusive in my memory and about which I failed to keep any records.

Even Ford succumbed to a rare demonstration of self-will when he insisted on a delay of one week for the opening of the conference in retaliation for some Gromyko nitpick.

At this point, with the Final Act nearly complete and a summit approaching, domestic critics attacked the Helsinki conference as a dangerous idea sprung spontaneously from the heads of two détente-obsessed leaders, Ford and me (and, by implication, Nixon as well), bulldozed by the Soviets into making one-sided concessions such as abandoning Eastern Europe to eternal Soviet domination.

The *New York Times* wrote in its lead editorial on July 21, 1975:

> The 35-nation Conference on Security and Cooperation in Europe, now nearing its climax after 32 months of semantic quibbling, should not have happened. Never have so many struggled for so long over so little as the conference's 100-page declaration of good intentions in East-West relations. So little, and yet so much.
>
> So little, because after hundreds of diplomats drafted this document, they specified that it will not be legally bind-

ing on anyone. So much, because it commits the United States, Canada and 33 nations of Europe to the "inviolability of frontiers," symbolically ratifying the territorial status quo, including the division of Germany and Europe and the Soviet Union's huge annexations of East European territory, including all three independent Baltic states plus large chunks of Poland, Czechoslovakia and Rumania.[3]

*The Wall Street Journal* on July 23 argued that the conference "is purely symbolic, and the symbol is one of Soviet hegemony in Eastern Europe. . . . [T]he agreement to be signed there will be a formal version of Yalta, without Yalta's redeeming features."[4]

And Osvalds Akmentins, the vice president of the Latvian Press Society, had this to say:

> President Ford will sign his name on a miserable and un-American treaty—a treaty which buries the hopes of millions of Eastern European peoples in ever securing freedom and independence, a treaty which buries the principles of the Atlantic Charter, the ideals of which kept hope in the hearts of the Latvians, Lithuanians, Estonians, Ukrainians, Poles, etc.[5]

All this was a grotesque distortion of reality. When Ford became President, the conference had already been in session for a year. Thirty-five nations were committed to it, including the Vatican in its role as a European city-state. All our NATO allies were eager to conclude the conference and to do so at a summit. Major portions of the final communiqué had been drafted. And every week it became clearer that the democracies were getting the better of the negotiations. For the United States to withdraw at this point would have achieved the extraordinary feat of antagonizing all the nations of Europe and the Soviet Union for no definable gain; indeed, we would have sacrificed the considerable gain we had already made.

Had the public debate not been overwhelmed by passions oblivious of the real issues, it would have become apparent that a pledge of inviolability of frontiers posed a much greater restraint on the power possessing the largest land army—and of which every neighbor was afraid—than on the democracies, which possessed neither the arms nor the public support for an aggressive war. After all, the only borders

that had been violated during the Cold War were those of the Soviet
Union's neighbors at the hands of the Red Army. The captive nations
of Eastern Europe understood this much better than some in the Western democracies, prone as they were to periodic bouts of self-
flagellation. Callaghan reminded us of the realities of Eastern Europe
over breakfast with Ford, Wilson, and me in Helsinki on July 30:

> CALLAGHAN: [Hungarian leader Janos] Kadar told us yes-
>   terday that they regarded it as a moral and political
>   commitment.
> KISSINGER: Even inviolability of frontiers has proved more
>   helpful to others than to the Soviet Union.
> CALLAGHAN: No Soviet government can ever justify inva-
>   sion again.
> KISSINGER: CSCE will not prevent it, but it can never be
>   explained again.

The states described by our critics as principal victims of the Final
Act were its strongest supporters. As noted, the Federal Republic considered the peaceful change clause a great success and repeatedly credited the United States for alone being able to achieve it. Fifteen years
later, it provided the legal basis for German unification, and, as already
noted, the same paragraph regarding peaceful change included language implicitly rejecting the Soviet Union's rationale for invading
Hungary and Czechoslovakia. In final form, it read:

> They [the signatories] consider that their frontiers can be
> changed, in accordance with international law, by peaceful
> means and by agreement. *They also have the right to belong*
> *or not to belong to international organizations, to be or not*
> *to be a party to bilateral or multilateral treaties including*
> *the right to be or not to be a party to treaties of alliance;*
> *they also have the right to neutrality* [italics added].[6]

If the clause had any operational meaning, it vitiated the Brezhnev
Doctrine of 1968, whereby Moscow justified its use of force against
Czechoslovakia as a means to maintain the unity of the socialist camp,
and Khrushchev's pretext for suppressing the Hungarian revolution in
1956 because it tried to leave the Warsaw Pact.

The East European satellites were telling us privately that the Final

Act would increase Soviet inhibitions against military intervention and thereby enhance their capacity to conduct a national foreign policy. Some of our critics, on the other hand, described the statements of East European leaders as choreographed by their diabolically cunning masters in the Kremlin. Those of us who had been on the anti-Communist barricades throughout and dealt with the satellites on a daily basis knew better. To be sure, on some of the subsidiary drafting points, the East Europeans did go along with the power occupying their territory. But the principal purpose of such countries as Poland, Hungary, and Romania, as they made clear to us, was to increase their margin of maneuver in the face of the Soviet Union. In varying degrees, they had all come to believe that Communist ideology had run out of steam. After all, the only popular upheavals in industrial countries had occurred on their soil, not in the bastions of capitalism, as Marxism had predicted. Because they realized that their future depended on their ability to appeal to their countries' historic nationalism, the leaders of Poland, Hungary, Czechoslovakia, and Romania considered the principles of the European Security Conference to be important, above all, in inhibiting Soviet invasion or interference. Tito's nonaligned Yugoslavia made the same point even more strongly.

For all these reasons, Ford judged a concluding CSCE summit to be in the national interest, provided we could achieve our purposes on the key issues of peaceful change, human rights, and confidence-building measures. As in all critical decisions, the President was calm and understated. On May 5 in the Oval Office, as the conclusion of the conference and a summit were fast approaching, I warned him:

> KISSINGER: Jackson and the others will start to hit you about the CSCE summit as a fraud that isn't worthy of a summit. They will mobilize the Baltics and the East European emigrants. It doesn't change the situation of the Baltic states. . . .
>
> FORD: . . . I think if we didn't participate, it would appear we were sulking and going back to Cold War. I don't think the American people would understand.

But Ford would not proceed unless American goals were achieved. On May 26, 1975, I briefed him on the Soviet formulations with respect to confidence-building measures and the human rights provisions of Basket III:

> I think your position must [be] hard-line. . . . If they [the
> Soviets] want a conference, let them concede. . . . I would
> listen and not get engaged. Say if we can get a decent settle-
> ment, fine; if not, wait a few months.

Ford agreed: "I think we should hang back," he said.

The extraordinary solidarity that had developed among the leaders
of the Atlantic Alliance after Ford came on the scene greatly facilitated
a favorable outcome. While the conference was meandering to a conclusion, the allied leaders met periodically to plan common strategy.
To find their way through the maze, one of the allies generally took
the lead on a particular issue with the others in support. Thus France
conducted much of the negotiations on Basket III (human rights),
Britain on Basket II (military confidence-building measures), and the
United States on Basket I, which included the "peaceful change" provisions. The unusual camaraderie is evident from this letter by French
Foreign Minister Jean Sauvagnargues of mid-June:

> Dear Henry:
>     Thank you for having informed me on June 8 [1975]
> about the new Soviet inclinations on advance notification of
> large-scale military maneuvers envisioned by the CSCE and
> more precisely the extension of the geographical area con-
> cerned for the USSR.
>     As you know, confidence-building measures do not rep-
> resent, for France, one of the essential points of the Confer-
> ence. . . .
>     Nonetheless, I share your viewpoint that a zone 250-
> kilometers deep in Soviet territory represents, for the USSR,
> a substantial concession capable of promoting the basis of a
> satisfactory compromise which I am hopeful can possibly be
> reached soon.
>     I am giving the necessary instructions to our delegation
> in Geneva so that it will act in this spirit in liaison with your
> delegation as well as those of the European Community.
>     With warm regards.

One of the curious patterns of Soviet decision-making—so at variance with the public image of implacable determination which the
Soviet negotiators sought to foster was the sudden shifts from rigid

persistence during the process of negotiations to almost frantic haste to conclude once a deadline (often self-imposed) was approaching. It was as if the Politburo could achieve unanimity during the course of a negotiation only by mutual displays of toughness. But once the leaders had committed themselves to a deadline, the Soviet negotiators seemed suddenly overwhelmed by the reverse side of the previous truculence —an anxiety that all the months of disciplined negotiations might go for naught and might even supply ammunition to potential rivals.

In my experience, the closing days of a negotiation with the Soviets usually produced more concessions than did the preceding months and sometimes years. This was what happened at the end of the SALT I negotiations in 1972 and again at Vladivostok in 1974. And the pattern recurred as the deadline for a summit to conclude the European Security Conference approached. By mid-June 1975 the outstanding issues were being resolved. The Soviet Union had moved very close to the position of the democracies on all disputed issues regarding peaceful change, human rights, and confidence-building measures. The road to a Helsinki summit now lay open.

With the approach of the summit, the political debate in the United States broke out in earnest. Conservatives feared that any summit with Soviet leaders would confuse the democracies; neoconservatives— newly arrived on the anti-Communist battlefront—wanted ideological combat, not diplomatic maneuver. Leaders like Ronald Reagan and Henry Jackson were preparing to make détente an issue in the 1976 presidential campaign, the primaries of which were less than a year away. Reagan, making his first public criticism of Ford, said: "I am against it, and I think all Americans should be against it."[7] Senator Jackson weighed in with similar comments. Liberals dismissed the Final Act's attention to human rights as inadequate. As we shall see, all these still disparate strands were to coalesce after a dramatic visit of Aleksandr Solzhenitsyn to Washington a month before the Helsinki summit.

Within the White House staff, the pattern of the collapse of Indochina repeated itself. Several of the new arrivals thought they could pull the teeth of the onslaught by somehow dissociating Ford from the policy he was espousing. Others tried to belittle the result by claiming that it had no legal significance—an extraordinary proposition to make about a document the President was about to sign. But partial dissociation—or blaming me for it, which was another favorite tactic —achieved no diplomatic purpose and only weakened Ford domestically. There was no middle ground between stopping the process and concluding it.

Drawing up a balance sheet of the Final Act, the "inviolability of frontiers" provisions did no more than reaffirm clauses already contained in the postwar allied peace treaties between 1946 and 1949, which included the United States, and in Willy Brandt's more recent *Ostpolitik* treaties. The West had never threatened force as a means of changing European frontiers and, indeed, no democracy except the United States had the capability to make such a threat. Finally, the essential problem of Eastern Europe had nothing to do with the location of frontiers but everything with the Communist dictatorships that had been imposed by Soviet power and were still being sustained by Soviet coercion.

The price the Soviet Union paid for its desperate quest for legitimacy was agreeing to the clause endorsing peaceful change of frontiers, which played a significant role in the negotiations on German unification and to the extensive human rights language of Basket III, which took on an extraordinary life of its own. "Helsinki monitoring groups" sprang up in several East bloc countries, the most famous of which was Charter 77 in Czechoslovakia. They interpreted the Helsinki Final Act as enshrining human rights in international law—a view we fully supported.

Any major agreement between adversaries represents a bet on the future. Undoubtedly, the Soviet leaders sought CSCE because they hoped to demoralize the democracies by freezing the European status quo. The Western democracies pushed Basket III and peaceful change to exploit what we had come to recognize as the latent vulnerabilities of the Soviet empire.

## Aleksandr Solzhenitsyn

Aleksandr Solzhenitsyn is a remarkable writer and a sustaining moral force of our age. His political convictions, though they can hardly be described as passionately devoted to pluralistic democracy or Western culture, lent a powerful impetus to the fight against Communist tyranny. I had long admired his novels; his three-volume *Gulag Archipelago*—a history of the Soviet prison labor camps—moved me as few political books have. When Ford became President, I gave him a copy of the first volume and urged him to read it so that he would better understand the nature of the Soviet challenge.

Fearing for this dauntless fighter as the Soviets ratcheted up pressures on him, I repeatedly appealed to Dobrynin to permit Solzhenitsyn to leave the Soviet Union. I stressed that the appeal was on humanitarian grounds and that the American administration would not exploit Solzhenitsyn's exile for political purposes. My admiration for the author's historic contributions to the cause of fighting Communist totalitarianism and to the ultimate triumph of the human spirit has not lessened in the intervening decades—which is more than can be said for many who were his acolytes in 1975.

Solzhenitsyn was expelled from the Soviet Union on February 13, 1974, and came to the United States some months later. The AFL-CIO, under the leadership of its strongly anti-Communist president, George Meany, invited him to address a dinner in Washington on June 30, 1975, not long before Ford's departure to sign the Final Act of the European Security Conference. The date had been carefully chosen; if Solzhenitsyn expressed anything like his well-known views, he would supply plenty of material for the opponents of CSCE.

Solzhenitsyn did not disappoint his sponsors. His speech passionately castigated the Soviet political regime and called on the democracies to wage a policy of confrontation against it. He urged an end to what he described as unilateral concessions, in which he included every Western negotiation with the Soviet Union, starting with Roosevelt's recognition of the U.S.S.R. and even Lend-Lease. Solzhenitsyn urged the United States to lead a crusade against Communism even inside the Soviet Union and disdained the argument that such a course represented interference in Soviet domestic affairs: "Interfere more and more," Solzhenitsyn implored. "Interfere as much as you can. We beg you to come and interfere."[8]

A distinguished audience had come to hear the speech, including Secretary of Defense James Schlesinger, who sat on the dais, surely aware that the purpose of the event was to undermine the policy of the administration in which he served.

On July 2, Senators Jesse Helms and Strom Thurmond contacted Ford's counselor, Jack Marsh, to request an appointment for Solzhenitsyn with the President before July 5, when Solzhenitsyn was scheduled to leave Washington. Ford was due to depart for Cincinnati and Cleveland the next day, July 3. Thus, the Senators' request amounted to asking for a meeting on July 4, the national holiday, with next to no notice. Viewing this discourtesy as an ultimatum to embarrass him with the Republican right wing, Ford decided not to receive Solzhenitsyn and had Marsh cite scheduling difficulties as the reason. At that point, the decision was not directly related to East-West relations; its driving force was the domestic side of the White House (though the NSC staff could surely have reversed the decision had it appealed to the President).[9]

I was on vacation in St. John in the Virgin Islands when all this occurred. Scowcroft knew my views and informed me after the decision had been made. I concurred. This did not stop the media and Ford's anti-détente critics from making me the villain of the piece. Perhaps, had I been in town, I would have been wise enough to propose a low-key meeting with either the President or me, both of which were offered after the outcry arose. Both were rejected by Solzhenitsyn. Heroes are rarely a joy to deal with on the personal level. Had I been consulted, I would in all likelihood have advised against holding a formal, televised meeting, since Ford was about to travel to Helsinki, where he would meet Leonid Brezhnev, who had released Solzhenitsyn on compassionate grounds only a few months earlier—at least in part in response to personal White House appeals.

The Senators now had their cause célèbre. And the anti-détente critics made me the villain.

At a press conference on July 16, I pointed out that the original decision had been made on the basis of scheduling considerations and not on foreign policy grounds. Nevertheless, I emphasized that I supported Ford's decision for reasons of foreign policy. I made a distinction between the substance of Solzhenitsyn's speech, which I welcomed, and meetings on the presidential level:

> I consider Solzhenitsyn one of the greatest writers of this period. In my present position, I seem to read only classified papers. Solzhenitsyn is one of the few unclassified documents that I have been reading. So I have enormous respect and admiration for Solzhenitsyn as a writer.
>
> Secondly, I think this country can well afford to listen to a man of his distinction without worrying about what effect it will have on the foreign policy interests of the United States.
>
> As for seeing senior officials, this can be considered from the foreign policy aspect. From the point of view of foreign policy the symbolic effect of that can be disadvantageous—which has nothing to do with a respect either for the man or for his message.[10]

All hell broke loose. Jackson issued a statement that it was a sad day for the country when the chief spokesman of American foreign policy sided with the Soviets instead of with freedom of speech. *The Wall Street Journal* took a swipe at me:

> President Ford, in the most unworthy decision of his tenure, gave heed to certain advisers who warned that a White House invitation for Mr. Solzhenitsyn might offend the Kremlin.[11]

The *New York Times* accused Ford of crossing the line from détente to appeasement—undeterred by the fact that, less than three months earlier, the same newspaper had urged the cutoff of aid to Indochina, where an actual battle against Communism was being fought. Distinguished scholars such as Harvard University's Adam Ulam wrote protesting letters to leading journals.[12]

What rendered the charge that Ford and I were being soft on Communism so ironic was that it was being directed against an administration that was at that very moment trying to organize resistance to the Communist military buildup in Angola and was under attack by many of the same critics for its strong stand against any form of participation by Communist parties in NATO governments.

As I said publicly, I agreed almost totally with Solzhenitsyn's analysis of the Soviet system—far more so than did many of those criticizing us over Helsinki. In particular, I shared his view on the injustice of our abdication in Indochina as expressed in a lengthy portion of his AFL-CIO speech, which the overwhelming majority of the media chose not to cover.[13]

In retrospect, I believe we would have been wise to ignore the Senators' flagrant discourtesy and schedule a meeting with the President on July 4 in as unobtrusive and dignified a manner as possible—even if Solzhenitsyn and his sponsors had moved heaven and earth to prevent a low-key approach. As it was, our ability to conduct a balanced Soviet policy was far more damaged than it would have been had we found some way to meet with this great and courageous champion of freedom.

By turning Solzhenitsyn's visit into a political football, his sponsors were, in effect, pressing a nonelected President, in his eleventh month in office, to announce a crusade against a nuclear superpower two months after the collapse of Indochina, in the midst of a delicate negotiation in the still-explosive Middle East, and while Angola was erupting, investigations were paralyzing our intelligence services, and Congress was urging reduction of our forces overseas and legislating a military embargo against Turkey, an indispensable NATO ally—all this while Ford was preparing to meet with Brezhnev a few weeks later. Our critics seemed above all interested in adding CSCE to such trophies as the collapsed trade bill and the stagnating arms control negotiations.

The Ford Administration's overriding obligation was to devise a policy that enabled the United States to recover from the traumas of Vietnam and Watergate and advance the values and security of the democracies over the long term. I outlined these considerations in an interview later published in *Time* magazine:

> We have to consider what this country has gone through with Vietnam, Watergate, and the attendant congressional restrictions. For us to run the risks of a confrontation that will be considered by our people as unnecessary is to invite massive foreign policy defeats.
>
> I believe that the policy we are carrying out with the Soviet Union has put us in the best position to resist Soviet pressures and in the best position to exploit possibilities of positive development in Soviet policies.[14]

And we could proceed with conviction, I indicated, because we were convinced that the European Security Conference would represent a significant marker in the advance of freedom. As Ford said in his modest way on the day before his departure:

> If it all fails, Europe will be no worse off than it is now. If even a part of it succeeds, the lot of the people in Eastern Europe will be that much better, and the cause of freedom will advance at least that far.[15]

Far more than part of the agreement succeeded and, at the end of the process, the peoples of Eastern Europe were indeed demonstrably better off.

## Prelude to Helsinki

As Ford set off on his trip to Helsinki on July 26, he left a cheerless country. Aleksandr Solzhenitsyn had helped trigger the onslaught when, in his speech to the AFL-CIO, he dismissed the Soviets' human rights concessions as "one one-thousandth of what natural law should provide—things which people should be able to do even before such negotiations are undertaken." Going the next step, he denounced the entire Helsinki process:

> What sort of agreement will this be? The proposed agreement is the funeral of Eastern Europe. It means that Western Europe will finally, once and for all, sign away from Eastern Europe, stating that it is perfectly willing to see Eastern Europe oppressed, only please don't bother us.[16]

Solzhenitsyn found eager supporters. Reagan and Jackson, and the *New York Times* and *The Wall Street Journal,* in rare agreement kept up the drumfire. Former Under Secretary of State George Ball called the Final Act a "capitulation." Americans of East European descent organized a protest vigil outside the White House. *The Wall Street Journal* headlined its July 23 editorial, "Jerry, Don't Go."

Demonstrations of national disunity were not confined to Soviet issues. Two days before Ford's departure for the conference, at which he would be meeting Turkish Prime Minister Suliman Demirel, the House of Representatives undercut him by refusing to lift its arms embargo against Turkey. In retaliation, Ankara asked us to close our bases, which were essential to monitor Soviet missile tests and to sustain military operations in the Middle East.

Ford's journey to Helsinki had been planned to symbolize American priorities, with stops in Germany and Poland scheduled on the way to Helsinki, and in Romania and Yugoslavia on the return trip. Bonn was selected because it had much at stake in the successful outcome of the conference. No country had a stronger reason than the Federal Republic to oppose acceptance of the status quo, which American critics alleged to be inherent in the Final Act. But the German leaders regarded the Helsinki Final Act as a major achievement. Schmidt and Genscher saw in the clause allowing peaceful change of frontiers an international endorsement of the only road open to Germany to fulfill its national aspirations.

Warsaw, Bucharest, and Belgrade had been selected for presidential visits because they were the Communist capitals with the strongest record of seeking freedom of action vis-à-vis the Soviet Union. Warsaw was purchasing domestic maneuvering room by following Soviet foreign policy in a perfunctory manner (stopping well short of confrontation with the United States). Romania was the exact opposite: there a Stalinist economy and method of government was coupled with a nationalist foreign policy verging on neutralism. And Tito had kept his country free of Soviet tutelage in both domestic and foreign policy for over a quarter of a century. The presidential itinerary was designed to put the Soviet Union on notice of Ford's commitment to the Atlantic Alliance and German unification, and his resolve to magnify any cracks in the apparent Communist monolith.

In this atmosphere of hope and progress, Helmut Schmidt greeted Ford as near to exuberantly as his reserved Hanseatic nature permitted. Convinced that German national concerns had been fostered by the Final Act and that American support had been decisive in bringing this about, Schmidt saw no reason to devote much time to East-West relations. He had organized a cruise on the Rhine and a small dinner with only a handful of each side's closest advisers.

Schmidt's overwhelming preoccupation remained the energy crisis. German and French industrial production, he pointed out, had fallen to a mere 65 percent of capacity, and he suspected Britain's to be even lower. The overwhelming threat to the democracies was not Soviet military pressure or Eurocommunism, he maintained, but flagging economic vitality:

> If it were a political or military crisis, leaders would get
> together and act. Since it is economic, we leave it to our
> finance ministers. If we leave it this way for five years, there
> will be a political disaster.

In a "private" memorandum handed to Ford at Helsinki a few days later (meaning that it had not been submitted to the cabinet), Schmidt supported a proposal first advanced by Giscard that, before the end of the year, a summit conference of the world's leading industrial democracies should be convened to discuss prospects of the world economy and monetary system. The participants would be the United

States, Great Britain, France, Japan, the Federal Republic, and possibly Italy. It was to be the first of the annual economic summits that, since 1975, have become a regular feature of the diplomatic calendar.

Poland's response was equally warm. One could not visit that heroic country—even under Communist rule—without being moved by the dedication and faith that have shaped and preserved it. For centuries a great state at the frontiers of Western Christianity, Poland after Russia's rise in the eighteenth century was wedged between a colossus to the east and an increasingly assertive German nation to the west. The wildly individualist style of the Polish governing class proved incompatible with Polish survival in so vulnerable a situation. At the end of the eighteenth century Poland was partitioned among Prussia, Russia, and Austria. It yearned for national renewal and strove for it by means of an extraordinary, indeed exalted, perception: that Polish freedom could best be restored if its patriots merged their struggles with the struggle for independence of other enslaved peoples. Hence the independence struggles of the nineteenth century—including our own earlier—were generally ennobled by the shedding of some Polish blood.

No people has suffered more for its convictions or has been more consistently assaulted by its neighbors. In the Second World War its leaders were massacred first by the Nazis, then by the Communists. Its capital was razed by the Nazis while the Red Army looked on from a few hundred yards away across the Vistula River. And no Pole can ever forget the massacre in the Katyn Forest of the Polish officers taken prisoner by the Red Army in 1939.

At the end of the Second World War, Poland's borders were bodily moved—almost in the way a chair might be across a room—some two hundred miles west when the Soviet Union annexed eastern Poland and compensated Poland with a slice of historically German territory up to the Oder River. By creating the potential for permanent German-Polish irredentism, this move supplied, in Moscow's eyes, insurance against German-Polish rapprochement.

A people with such a history was not likely to be an enthusiastic Soviet satellite. So strong was the Polish sense of national identity that even the country's Communist rulers felt obliged to rebuild the medieval old city of Warsaw from ancient plans while confining the heavy Stalinist architecture from Moscow to one building. The Poles rebelled in 1956 and then again in the late 1970s via the Solidarity movement. From the revolt of 1956, the Communist rulers learned the need to pursue a national policy, especially in international relations. Hence they welcomed the European Security Conference as a step toward loosening the Soviet grip on the country.

Against this background, a presidential visit to Warsaw always turned into an opportunity for Poles to reaffirm their commitment to freedom—so much so that Polish passions affected the American presidential election the following year, probably decisively. Ford correctly interpreted the exuberance of the Polish population as a rejection of Communism and of Soviet dominance. But it also tempted him into stating in his television debate with Jimmy Carter on October 6, 1976, that he did not consider Poland to be under Soviet domination. Ford was accurately depicting Polish sentiments, though not the de facto status of a country still cruelly occupied by Soviet forces. Most observers agree that the resulting controversy cost Ford the narrow election.

Ford's accommodations in Warsaw were in the only baroque palace to have miraculously survived both German and Soviet depredations. One meeting with Edward Gierek, the Polish Communist Party secretary, took place there, the other in the drab and heavy government building that had served as the headquarters of the Russian garrison prior to World War I.

Gierek was of the second generation of party leaders. Although his career had been forged entirely within the Communist Party, his bent was managerial and technocratic rather than ideological. While a market economy remained beyond his imagination, he did understand that Poland could best achieve a breathing space under conditions of a relaxation of East-West tensions. He was careful, therefore, to leave a record that could be read with approval in Moscow, stressing his country's "unbreakable" alliance with the Soviet Union. However, he praised that alliance ambiguously, not for its own sake but because it made *Polish-American* relations "less sensitive to inadvisable moments on the international scene"—a complex way of saying that Poland would do what it could to extend the limits imposed by its dominant neighbor on its relations with the United States.

Gierek went on to praise America for its "role . . . in the world, in Europe, and in the relations between our two nations." It was an odd compliment considering that a permanent aim of Soviet policy had been—and still was—to reduce our role in the world, that the European Security Conference had been proposed in the first place to push the United States out of Europe, and that the obvious thrust of American policy was to loosen Poland's dependence on the Soviet Union.

Gierek spoke highly of America's contribution to CSCE, noting particularly "the position of the United States . . . on cultural exchanges and exchanges of persons, seeing in them a contribution to rapprochement among nations." In other words, Poland saw in Basket III the same potential for increasing its political flexibility that we did. Gierek concluded his opening presentation by thanking Ford: "These are our feelings. It is your contribution, and the contribution of your close collaborators which we value very highly." Clearly the Polish leaders felt to some extent liberated and not imprisoned by the Final Act, which Ford was about to sign.

## Helsinki

Ford had left Washington on the defensive, but in Helsinki, where he arrived on July 29, he was the central figure. Any open-minded observer would have had a hard time reconciling the conventional wisdom of our domestic debate—that the United States was in retreat, being hornswoggled by the devilishly clever Soviet strategists—with the stature Ford was accorded as the head of the principal superpower, which European leaders, West and East, wanted to enlist on behalf of their various causes. All the leaders of Eastern Europe—many more than could be accommodated—were seeking private meetings with him. Ford's schedule was becoming exceptionally tight because, characteristically, he felt that he owed it, especially to the smaller countries, to be present at the speech of every last one of the leaders. This meant sitting through thirty-four speeches in the three days of the conference—not to mention the obligatory toasts and speeches at official meals. Ford's presence had the effect of freezing me to my seat as well, although I managed to sneak out for two brief bilateral meetings.

With the drafting of the Final Act already completed, the only significant diplomacy took place in bilateral meetings, for which the time available was short. Ford's most important meetings were with Brezhnev and a four-power lunch with his colleagues from France, Germany, and Britain.

The plenary sessions took place in the vast, modernistic Finlandia Hall. Our Finnish hosts had arranged the seating in a curious way. Supposedly alphabetical in English, the arrangement located the United States delegation toward the front and the Union of Soviet Socialist Republics' delegation at the rear of the room. Whether this was the revenge of Finnish protocol for decades of Soviet pressure (courageously and skillfully resisted by the Finns) or whether it followed some more elusive criterion, the upshot was that it captured the dominant role of the United States at the conference.

Ford conducted nearly a dozen bilateral meetings and delivered a powerful speech on August 1. One of its key passages was an eloquent affirmation that the United States was serious about all the clauses of the agreement and meant to see them implemented, especially the human rights provisions of Basket III:

> The United States considers that the principles on which this conference has agreed are a part of the great heritage of European civilization, which we hold in trust for all mankind. To my country, they are not clichés or empty phrases. We take this work and these words very seriously. . . . It is important that you recognize the deep devotion of the American people and their government to human rights and fundamental freedoms.[17]

Its concluding section was especially strong:

> History will judge this Conference not by what we say here today, but by what we do tomorrow—not by the promises we make, but by the promises we keep.[18]

In his memoirs, Ford contends that he looked directly at Leonid Brezhnev while delivering these lines, and this was surely his intention.[19] Given the distance between the rostrum and Brezhnev's seat at the rear of the room, however, there were undoubtedly many other leaders who had reason to believe that the President was looking directly at them.

The leader of the other superpower, Leonid Brezhnev, neither looked nor conducted himself as representative of the wave of the future. The stroke he had suffered on the way back from Vladivostok eight months earlier had taken its toll. Inside the conference hall, he seemed bored and at no point attracted the sort of attention showered on Ford, not even among East European leaders. Indeed, Brezhnev did not even seem to desire it.

He looked tired, and his attention span was brief. In two meetings with Ford, one could almost set one's watch by the limitation of his tolerance for sustained dialogue. Two hours seemed to be the maximum. Toward the end of that interval his concentration would begin to flag and his speech become slurred, and Gromyko would take over. Gromyko, however, had not survived as foreign minister for two decades by being a risk-taker; hence his part of the negotiation tended toward stalemate pending Brezhnev's reasserting control at a subsequent meeting.

Brezhnev's physical decline produced a number of bizarre exchanges. When the Middle East came up at the end of the two-hour period, he was palpably eager to be done with the subject. At one point he sounded almost as if he was endorsing our strategy of cutting the Soviet Union out of Middle East diplomacy—apparently just so the meeting might draw to a close. Turning to Gromyko, he said in a stage whisper that he did not understand why the issue under discussion was not already settled; it was all a question of people playing politics—to which I interjected:

> KISSINGER: Is this a private conversation here, or is it directed to us?
>
> SUKHODREV [INTERPRETER]: Private.
>
> GROMYKO: Private but not secret. [laughter]
>
> KISSINGER: If it is a private fight, can anybody join? [laughter]
>
> BREZHNEV: This problem is very complicated. It is very complicated for you, for us, and for the Arabs.
>
> FORD: It's almost unbelievable that some of those nations can't talk as you and I do, Mr. Secretary. I am sure if they had the same understanding of the need for discussions and the same willingness that we do, then there would be progress toward a solution by them in that area.
>
> BREZHNEV: When things get difficult, the best way is to instruct Kissinger to go into the matter.
>
> GROMYKO: But only together with us!

What a change this resigned near-abdication was from Brezhnev's position at Vladivostok, where he had insisted that the Soviet Union participate at every step of Middle East diplomacy. And what a difference between the drained figure sitting before us and the description our critics delighted in sketching of Brezhnev maneuvering to seize global leadership from a weakening and incompetent United States.

At the end of the first meeting, Ford proposed a deal exchanging American agricultural products for Soviet oil at a discount. Our purpose was to bring more oil on the market and to spook the oil cartel. The proposition (discussed in the Chapter 22) intrigued Brezhnev, but he was bored by the resulting haggle between Gromyko and me over prices. He did not perk up until he heard Gromyko note sarcastically: "Kissinger, the farmer." This thought struck Brezhnev as extremely funny, and he kept chuckling to himself, "Kissinger, the farmer," while Gromyko and I continued to haggle.

All of the Atlantic Alliance leaders looked to Ford on Middle East issues and Cyprus and on the future of economic cooperation in the West. The four-power lunch with Giscard, Wilson, Schmidt, and their foreign ministers symbolized Western unity, and their cordiality emphasized that, for once, symbolism approached reality. Indeed, the democracies were united as they had not been since the early days of the Cold War.

Thus what had started out twenty years earlier as a Soviet initiative to expel the United States from Europe culminated in Helsinki in the cementing of America's presence in Europe and the reaffirmation of Western values even for Communist-dominated Eastern Europe. The validation of America's permanent role in Europe, the enshrinement of human rights in Basket III in a major international agreement signed by the Soviet Union, the possibility that frontiers could be changed legally, and the Soviet acquiescence in all these terms were far more significant than the qualified (and double-edged) endorsement of the inviolability of frontiers. At Helsinki, all the East European countries increased their maneuvering room and felt encouraged by Ford's demonstrative visit to the most independent of them. (These countries had, of course, invited the President precisely to make that point.)

## Aftermath

The return trip via Bucharest and Belgrade August 2–4 represented a further reaffirmation of these achievements. A visit to the Romanian capital under Nicolae Ceaușescu was an extraordinary experience. Nowhere else in Eastern Europe was the gap between the professed egalitarianism of Communist ideology and the imperial style of the rulers so pronounced. Accordingly, state guests were housed in a vast residence in which each suite had its own swimming pool, as part of the bathroom; indeed, one could measure one's status in Romanian eyes by the size of the pool.

Nowhere as well was the political precariousness of the Communist hold on Eastern Europe so trenchantly evident as in Ceauşescu's Bucharest. On the one hand, the Romanian ruler ran the closest approximation to a Stalinist dictatorship in the entire Soviet orbit. Yet he felt obliged to strive for domestic support by pursuing a highly nationalistic foreign policy independent of the Soviet Union. (In 1969 he had postponed a scheduled visit by Brezhnev on one week's notice to enable Nixon to come instead and had even had the welcoming posters for Brezhnev, already hanging at the airport, painted over.) Romania's principal objective was to reduce the scope for Soviet intervention in its domestic affairs, as Ceauşescu had told me on a preparatory visit in November 1974.

For Ceauşescu, constricting the superpowers' freedom of maneuver had a specific meaning. The countries of Eastern Europe, he argued, felt threatened by their impotence, by the provisional nature of the European settlement, which amounted to an armistice signed at Potsdam more than thirty years earlier, and—most importantly—by the right granted to the World War II victors to intervene against former enemy states. This concern led to the following exchange:

> KISSINGER: Tell me, are you an enemy state of the U.S.S.R.? . . .
>
> CEAUŞESCU: Legally no, but Article 53 [of the U.N. Charter] allows for intervention in the affairs of former enemy states and any interpretation could be given to this article.

For Ceauşescu, the only problem with the inviolability clause was that it did not make his frontiers sufficiently inviolable vis-à-vis the Soviet Union.

What Gierek had conveyed elliptically in Warsaw, Ceauşescu made explicit. Like Gierek, Ceauşescu was eager to increase his own public support by parading the American President before as many Romanians as possible. His device was a train ride to an erstwhile royal castle during which the leaders exchanged ideas—when they were not meeting crowds assembled at the various stops. Ceauşescu welcomed

Ford's statement that he had seen more leaders from Eastern Europe at Helsinki than he had from the West:

> This means that you have an advantageous position in the East. In any case, it's no reason for *you* to be annoyed when people start talking in an anti-imperialist way since these are questions which have a larger applicability.

In other words, the standard anti-imperialist slogans of East European leaders should be understood as so much Aesopian language aimed at Moscow.

Ceauşescu's major concern was that CSCE did not go far enough. With respect to such countries as Yugoslavia, he was confident that "what was signed at Helsinki will exclude any type of intervention." But repeating his earlier observations, he said he was doubtful whether it would adequately safeguard countries which had been enemy states of the superpowers during the Second World War; these states, protected only by the Potsdam Treaty, remained in a legally highly vulnerable position. What Ceauşescu seemed to have in mind was that the reunification of Germany, by ending the state of war, could also end the legal basis for Soviet intervention in Eastern Europe.

For reasons that escape me at this remove, I replied that I expected Germany to be reunified within fifteen years. What led me to this accurate prediction I cannot now reconstruct. I *was* convinced that Germany would inevitably be reunified, but I had no precise deadline in mind. I make note of it here primarily to keep future researchers working with these documents from ascribing an undeserved prescience to me.

In any event, Ceauşescu's basic point was the exact opposite of what the critics of CSCE were asserting: not only had the Soviet Union not acquired additional rights in the Final Act; new obstacles to Soviet intervention had been created. Romania's only concern was whether they were sufficient to protect those countries of Eastern Europe that could be classified by the Soviet Union as former enemy states.

But this was not how the conference was perceived in the United States. The *New York Times,* as previously mentioned, dismissed it editorially as a waste of time at best. *Newsweek* magazine sneered at Helsinki as "considerable ceremony, little substance."[20] Ronald Reagan, gearing up for his political campaign, argued: "Mr. Ford flew halfway around the world to sign an agreement at Helsinki which placed the American seal of approval on the Soviet empire in Eastern Europe." And a year later, Ford, having narrowly defeated Reagan for the nomination, was obliged to accept this humiliating plank into the Republican platform: "Agreements that are negotiated, such as the one signed in Helsinki, must not take from those who do not have freedom the hope of one day gaining it."

At this remove, it is best to leave the charges of "Super Yalta" and "sellout" in our media and public debate in the dusty drawers of time. For the convictions of the Ford Administration have been vindicated by events, as I predicted in a speech in Birmingham, Alabama, on August 14, 1975:

> It is not we who were on the defensive at Helsinki; it is not we who were being challenged by all the delegations to live up to the principles being signed. At Helsinki, for the first time in the postwar period, human rights and fundamental freedoms became recognized subjects of East-West discourse and negotiation. The conference put forward *our* standards of humane conduct, which have been—and still are—a beacon of hope to millions.[21]

And the democracies won their bet. After fifteen years, Germany was unified; the satellite orbit collapsed; the Baltic states regained their independence; and the USSR dissolved peacefully—the exact opposite of what the critics of Helsinki had predicted.

The Ford Administration was not clairvoyant; statesmen act on the basis of tendencies, not certainties. We did not foresee all the consequences of our policies, and I for one was initially skeptical about the possibilities of Basket III. We did not expect the Soviet empire to collapse so quickly; we were content to loosen its bonds wherever possible and to push the right of peaceful change while awaiting the conditions that would enable the democracies to pursue it. We had supported Basket III on human rights to promote some amelioration of Communist rule as well as to establish international criteria to inhibit Soviet suppression of revolts, such as had occurred in Hungary and Czechoslovakia. We can rest on what was achieved without taking credit away from great men like Havel, Walesa, and their contemporaries who transformed a diplomatic enterprise into a triumph of the human spirit.

# 22

# THE ENERGY CRISIS

No crisis of the second half of the twentieth century fell on a world less prepared for it than the one triggered by the quadrupling of oil prices in the fall of 1973.[1] Within the space of three months the global political and economic system found itself faced with a series of stark challenges threatening its very foundations.

A hemorrhage of capital from the industrial to the oil-producing nations led to an unprecedented *additional* annual trade deficit of $40 billion of the Organization for Economic Cooperation and Development nations (equal to nearly $125 billion in 1997 dollars). The oil price shock caused a deadly combination of severe recession and high inflation which, in the United States, reached 14 percent a year at its height. The energy crisis was even more disastrous for the non-oil-producing nations of the developing world. They were immediately saddled with an *additional* collective annual deficit more than double the *total* annual influx of foreign aid.

Six months earlier such a crisis would have been unimaginable as the industrial democracies were living in a fool's paradise of plentiful and cheap oil. Now, they suddenly confronted a grave challenge to the expectations of constantly rising levels of well-being on which their political stability had been based. Faced with an accelerating spiral of inflation and recession, President Ford and the leaders of the industrial democracies had no more compelling task than to rescue the cohesion of their societies and, less explicitly, their own political survival, from the sudden onslaught.*

---

* At this writing, when oil is again plentiful and relatively cheap, the events described here may seem remote. It is to be hoped that this state of affairs persists. But that is unlikely. New

The leaders of the democracies had come to understand the geo-politics of the Cold War through many challenges they had overcome together. They had grown increasingly confident of their ability to resist the Communist political and military threat and were substantially united on the means to do so. Consultations on these subjects took place regularly through many tested institutions.

No comparable consensus existed with respect to the causes of the energy crisis or the means to overcome it. Many of the oil-consuming nations were reluctant to undertake joint countermeasures lest these trigger more severe exactions from the oil producers, whose newfound strength tempted them to press our allies to break ranks with us on Middle East policy and not without some success.

The industrial democracies slid into these dilemmas because too few policymakers understood that the conditions which had provided plentiful oil at cheap prices for two generations were evaporating.

Until 1972 the United States had been in a position to control the world price of oil because it was producing well below full capacity. Thus America was, in effect, able to set the price by increasing or withholding production. As late as 1950 the country supplied almost all of its energy needs from its own production; in 1960 we were importing 16 percent of our requirements while still having significant unused capacity; by 1970 we were approaching full production and importing 35 percent of what we consumed.

In early 1972 the Texas Railroad Commission, the organization that established the ceilings on American production, felt compelled to make a fateful decision, although it went essentially unnoticed. With demand having risen to a point where it threatened an explosion of prices, the commission authorized full production. And that seemingly technical decision signaled the end of America's ability to set the world oil price.

In the meantime, at the beginning of the 1970s, the governments of the oil-producing countries had begun nationalizing production facilities, ending the dominance of the major (Western-owned) international oil companies. For more than a decade thereafter these governments were able to set the oil price provided they agreed on production

---

technologies are improving the process of oil discovery and production and increasing the efficiency of energy use. That helps keep prices low. But oil supplies continue to depend on perhaps the most volatile regions of the world. Another crisis remains a distinct possibility. And if it occurs, the earlier experiences will prove relevant.

ceilings among themselves. Hence, setting the price of oil moved from the Texas Railroad Commission to the meeting place of OPEC—the Organization of Petroleum Exporting Countries.

The significance of this revolutionary upheaval did not sink in immediately. Throughout this period, energy was dealt with by the domestic side of the Nixon Administration with no participation by the NSC process. Though prices rose by 40 percent in 1972, they did so from a very low base, and they remained compatible with the financial and economic stability of industrial democracies.

It was the Middle East War of 1973 that gave the oil-producing countries the pretext for unleashing their new bargaining power to its full extent. On October 16, 1973, OPEC raised the price of oil by 70 percent, from $3.01 a barrel to $5.12. On October 17 the Arab OPEC oil ministers met in Kuwait and agreed to reduce OPEC production by 5 percent in order to sustain the higher oil price. On October 18, Saudi Arabia, as a sign of solidarity with the Arab cause, cut its production by 10 percent. On October 20, to protest the American airlift to Israel, Saudi Arabia announced a total embargo of oil exports to the United States and also to the Netherlands, which was deemed too supportive of Israel.

The combined impact of these decisions precipitated an energy crisis lasting well over a decade. Because the principal Western policymakers lacked sufficient understanding of the oil market, their initial reaction made matters worse. Regulatory blunders at home exacerbated short-term shortages. In addition, the urgency and frequency of Nixon Administration appeals to remove the embargoes probably convinced the oil producers that they had discovered a marvelous new lever for extorting concessions.

In fact, because oil is fungible and was being distributed from a common pool, what Saudi Arabia refused to deliver was being replaced by non-Arab producers such as Venezuela, Nigeria, and Iran (still friendly), whose customers then received Arab oil. What brought about the rise in prices was not the embargoes or even primarily the cutbacks in production. It was pure and simple panic. Oil consumers began to build up inventories to levels far exceeding what had previously been considered adequate, with the result that the shortages they had hoped to avoid became more severe, and far more destabilizing.

On December 22–23, 1973, in Tehran, two months after the Middle East War had ended, the Gulf members of OPEC dropped the other shoe and more than doubled the price of oil again, to $11.65 a barrel—an increase of 387 percent in eight weeks. For some months thereafer the oil producers seemed in a position to blackmail the industrial democracies in return for cheaper oil prices, for access to mushrooming OPEC funds, or for special export arrangements.

Soon other dangers loomed. Spurred by OPEC's success, producers of other commodities began exploring the prospects of organizing cartels of their own and then linking these with OPEC. For a few years the oil producers even threatened the stability of the world financial system by accumulating enormous surpluses, which they could move from the financial institutions of the industrial democracies to those of more accommodating states.

Never before had nations so weak militarily—and in some cases politically—been able to impose such strains on the international system. A century earlier the consuming nations would have responded by seizing the oil fields. From time to time, as will be seen, the United States threatened to do just that but never received any support from the other industrial democracies.

## An Emerging Strategy

For the actual and potential victims of the oil shock, the first order of business was recovering control over their own destiny. A sustained, long-term program was needed to restore their bargaining power. At a closed-door meeting of American Middle East ambassadors in Riyadh on February 15, 1975, during the shuttle described in Chapter 13, I defined that goal as follows:

> We are trying to reduce the power of OPEC. We are trying to decrease our dependence on OPEC and to restore the West's freedom to act. Without this a sense of impotence will seize Western Europe and Japan until vague fears about what the oil producers will do will create unmanageable abuse.

We were not without assets. Two of the key nations sustaining OPEC's production ceiling—Iran and Saudi Arabia—were dependent on American political support for their domestic stability and on American protection for their external security. They could not afford to push confrontation with the United States beyond a certain point lest they be left at the mercy of internal or external enemies.

Moreover, though the oil producers did not yet realize it, their greed was preparing major latent crises for them. Where the funds were retained by the ruling families, the gap between mind-boggling affluence and shocking poverty was sowing the seeds of revolution. Where the funds were used for development, a technocratic middle class hostile to traditional rulers emerged. If the producers spent their tribute too lavishly, they risked seismic domestic upheavals. If their demands on the oil-consuming nations grew too exorbitant, they risked destroying the entire international financial system and, with it, the very institutions on which the preservation of their hoard depended.

Both the Nixon and Ford Administrations had no higher priority than to bring about a reduction of oil prices by breaking the power of OPEC. The strategy reflected not only economic analysis but—even more—political, indeed moral, conviction. The industrial democracies could not permit themselves to be turned into panicked, paralyzed bystanders while the oil producers played fast and loose with the internal cohesion of their societies.

For the power of OPEC to be broken, solidarity among the industrial democracies had to be established across a wide front, both political and economic. For this task, American leadership was as indispensable as in the early days of the Cold War. It was also more complicated. Failure to meet the Soviet threat would have immediate consequences while the penalties for failure on energy would take some time to become apparent.

Convinced that, without consumer solidarity, a financial crisis and major recession were inevitable, we threw ourselves into the task of restoring to the democracies the sense that they still shaped their future. The United States was in a stronger position than most of our allies. Though no longer self-sufficient, we remained substantial oil producers while most of the other industrial democracies imported virtually all of their energy. Thus we would be able to withstand pressures from the producers, including the threat of a new embargo —even to the point of offering to share some of our own increasingly scarce supplies of oil in case of an emergency.

The instrument for developing a coherent strategy had been created at the Washington Energy Conference called by Nixon a few months earlier, in February 1974. Despite French opposition, that conference had spawned the so-called Energy Coordinating Group (ECG), composed of twelve nations. Once Valéry Giscard d'Estaing became President later that year, even France joined the ECG's programs, via its membership in the European Community.

We devoted the summer of 1974 to transforming the Energy Coordinating Group into a permanent institution and to devising a detailed program for it. When Ford came into office, the diplomacy leading to the creation of the International Energy Agency was nearing completion, and a detailed operational program awaited the President's approval.

On August 17, 1974, a little more than a week after his swearing-in, I briefed Ford:

> We have to find a way to break the cartel. We can't do it without cooperation with the other consumers. It is intolerable that countries of 40 million can blackmail 800 million people in the industrial world.
>
> We have to get into position carefully so we don't get out ahead and our allies don't move in to pick up the pieces and get an economic advantage. That was the purpose of the Washington Energy Conference. . . .
>
> . . . We won't be in a position to confront the producers before the middle of 1975.

I outlined our program: consumer solidarity, including a program of emergency sharing; energy conservation; active development of alternative energy sources; creation of a financial safety net. Although somewhat surprised by the program's scope, Ford endorsed it immediately. When I described one item as providing us with a good diplomatic issue even if it was not accepted, he reacted characteristically: "I am not interested in issues, but in results."

The sweeping energy program approved by the President laid the basis not only for surmounting the energy crisis but also ultimately for redressing the bargaining imbalance between the consuming and producing nations. For once, the many American agencies responsible for the different portions of the complex problem worked in harness. An energy coordinator for domestic programs was appointed at the White House—first John Sawhill and then Frank Zarb—and charged with reducing our oil imports. The Treasury Department was responsible for international financial aspects. And the State Department's task was to create the political framework. As National Security Adviser, I coordinated the various strands of policy.

An energy program of such scope could never have been mounted but for the affectionate comradeship existing between Secretary of the Treasury William Simon and me. It was all the more remarkable because we had serious differences about strategy and were both experienced defenders of our bureaucratic turf.

Simon's background had been in investment banking. He believed the oil crisis was caused by political interference with the market, and he advocated massive American pressure on the country he—in my view, incorrectly—held most responsible: Iran. Simon urged a cutoff of arms to Tehran and the threat of withholding military protection unless the Shah agreed to reduce the price of oil. Buoyant, infinitely energetic, and charming, Simon took his case to the Gulf States on a visit in July 1974. He persuaded—or thought he had—the Saudi oil minister, Sheikh Ahmed Zaki Yamani, to promise that the Saudis would auction oil beyond the OPEC production ceilings, thereby tilting the balance between supply and demand and thus leading to lower prices.

Unaccustomed to the subtle indirections of Gulf diplomacy, Simon came away believing that oil prices were about to fall by 30 percent below the official OPEC price and oblige the other OPEC nations to follow suit at their next meeting, scheduled several months hence.

Carried away by these heady prospects, Simon urged all-out pressure on the Shah and, to create the appropriate atmosphere, even called him a "nut" in public—not a form of address standard textbooks on diplomacy would have recommended toward the autocratic head of an indispensable ally producing 6 million barrels of oil a day. Simon later tried to make amends by letting it be known that he had been quoted out of context. The Shah professed to be pacified—though Simon never revealed in what context the King of Kings could be called a nut without offense.

Even before the wisdom of applying pressure on a vital link in Soviet containment could be brought to the new President for decision, the Saudis informed us—as I had expected—that the auction promised to Simon had turned out not to be practical because opposition from the radical Arab states proved too great. Nevertheless, Simon continued to wage his campaign for pressure on Iran. I opposed it on a number of grounds.

Foremost was my conviction that the Shah was the wrong target for a policy of pressure. To be sure, he and his ministers had sounded like "price hawks" at various OPEC meetings. But the price of oil was not determined by rhetoric. The markets had been driven out of control by specific actions, particularly the production cutbacks sustained primarily by the Arab producers. Compounded by the Saudi embargo against the United States and the Netherlands and the threat of new embargoes, this had produced panic among the consumers. The Shah, ruler of a non-Arab country, had reduced his production by only half that of the Gulf States, had refused to join the Arab embargo, and had made it clear that he would refuse to join any new one. His impact on market forces had therefore been relatively limited—except to the extent that his hawkish rhetoric had stiffened the backs of some of his fellow producers.

No doubt the Shah had welcomed the rise in prices because, unlike most of his neighbors, he had an ambitious strategy for domestic development that was in need of funds. His tough rhetoric was compounded by greed and vanity as well as by his desire to refurbish relations with his Arab neighbors after his refusal to support them during the Middle East War of 1973. But the only way the Shah could have driven up prices in practice would have been to decrease his oil production and, for this, he had no inclination whatsoever.

The geopolitical rationale for rejecting Simon's strategy was even greater. Events since the Shah's fall have demonstrated most pointedly Iran's crucial importance for the peace and stability of the region. The cornerstone of our Gulf strategy, Iran had stood by us during the 1973 Middle East War when it had been the *only* neighbor of the Soviet Union to refuse permission for Soviet planes to overfly its territory. Iran had refueled our fleet (we were so confident of the Shah's willingness to do so that we had moved the Seventh Fleet from Asia into the Indian Ocean even before we had received his formal agreement). During the negotiation of the Paris Agreement on Vietnam when a great deal depended on our ability to augment Saigon's inventory of combat planes *before* the agreement was signed (since afterward only replacements would be permitted), the Shah made available a substantial number of Iran's inventory of fighters on very short notice. I told Simon at a Senior Review Group meeting on August 3, 1974, in the very week of Nixon's resignation:

> I am reluctant to get into a confrontation with Iran for three
> reasons: (1) we will need their oil in an emergency; (2) I

don't want to force them into the anti-Israel coalition; and
(3) I don't think it would work unless we are ready to go the
limit.

What "go the limit" meant in practice was that we would break the
back of the strongest ally in the region—indeed, the only one with a
significant capacity to resist Soviet pressures. This made no strategic
sense at all and would probably have compounded the oil crisis. When
the Shah fell five years later, oil prices again doubled because the
market quite reasonably feared for the long-term stability of the entire
region.

The same considerations applied even more strongly to Saudi Arabia. If we adopted Simon's recommendations to pressure the country
in the best position to lower the oil price, Saudi Arabia would have
been the logical target. For it was technically able to increase its oil
production by at least 50 percent, which would have had a decisive
impact on the price of oil.

However, I was convinced that Saudi Arabia would not dare to
undertake so demonstrative a dissociation from its OPEC brethren or
even the auction envisaged by Simon. The Saudi ruling family had,
after all, navigated the shoals of Middle East and Gulf tensions by
exercising its extraordinary skill at never putting itself into the front
line of a confrontation. Dependent on the West for military and diplomatic support yet fearful of the radical Arab regimes' capacity to
threaten Saudi domestic stability, the Saudi royal family maneuvered
with consummate prudence. Carefully modulating conservative foreign and domestic policies with occasional radical rhetoric, it professed sympathy for America's concern with the price of oil. Yet
whenever American importuning on the subject turned practical, we
were shunted off, in the politest way possible, to some other address,
usually Tehran.

Simon's dialogue with Sheikh Yamani provides a good illustration
of Saudi tactics. Smartly dressed in the latest Western garb whenever
he traveled outside Saudi Arabia, highly intelligent and articulate, Yamani was easy to mistake for a Western oil company executive. His
phenomenal mastery of the subtleties of the oil market invited the
expectation that he had a comparable influence on strategy. This was
not the case, however. The royal family treated Yamani as an important technical expert, not as a high-ranking policymaker. He was,
in fact, a transitional figure between the Saudi feudal past and the
inexorable technocratic future. On one occasion, I told Yamani that

one minister of his training and capacities would greatly buttress the existing Saudi institutions, but ten thousand like him would probably destroy them.

At my meetings with King Faisal, Yamani—if he was invited at all —sat so far toward the end of the wall along which the royal advisers were lined up that he would have had difficulty being heard even if he had been asked to intervene, which he never was. His low rank at court left no doubt—at least in my mind—that he was unlikely to have a significant voice on an issue as fraught with long-term political consequences as whether Saudi Arabia should break publicly with the oil cartel.

Nor were Yamani's own attitudes comparable to those of a Western oil executive. Not to put too fine a point on it, his reasoning was never free of the convoluted tendencies of the Middle East. Much later, in 1991 over breakfast at the state guest house in Bonn, Yamani told me that he held me responsible for the outbreak of the Gulf War. The war had not been over Kuwait, he stated, but over sustaining the price of oil by taking Iraq's production off the market. Saddam Hussein had been led into a trap by the wily Americans, from which he had been too clumsy to extricate himself. Since no one in the Bush Administration was clever enough to hatch such a design, even less to implement it, the finger of suspicion, according to Yamani, pointed at me. There was no sense replying that I was not smart enough either to conceive such a scheme or implement it, especially as I had not been in government for fourteen years—a fact which would undoubtedly have convinced Yamani of my complicity even more.

I had predicted the collapse of Simon's auction scheme all along. At the Senior Review Group meeting of August 3, 1974, mentioned previously, I told Simon:

> In a confrontation over oil supply, Algeria would go into massive political opposition to us. Syria would follow. The Saudis would then be the only Arab country holding out from solidarity in a confrontation with the imperialists, and the politics of that are unworkable. I don't mean to say that the Saudis were out to fool you [Secretary Simon] during your trip, but only that no matter what they say or mean that it would be wrong to count on them in a confrontation.

I made the same point to Ford when I briefed him on the oil crisis on August 17:

Simon wants a confrontation with the Shah. He thinks the Saudis would reduce prices if the Shah would go along. I doubt the Saudis want to get out in front. . . . They have maneuvered skillfully. I think they are trying to tell us—they said they would have an auction—it will never come off. They tell us they can live with lower prices, but they won't fight for them. They would be jumped on by the radicals if they got in front.

I repeated publicly what I had advised internally in an interview with *Business Week,* which was conducted on December 23, 1974, and published in the January 13, 1975, issue:

> The only chance to bring oil prices down immediately would be massive political warfare against countries like Saudi Arabia and Iran to make them risk their political stability and maybe their security if they did not cooperate. That is too high a price to pay even for an immediate reduction in oil prices.
>
> If you bring about an overthrow of the existing system in Saudi Arabia and a Qaddafi takes over, or if you break Iran's image of being capable of resisting outside pressures, you're going to open up political trends which could defeat your economic objectives. Economic pressures or incentives, on the other hand, take time to organize and cannot be effective without consumer solidarity. Moreover, if we had created the political crisis that I described, we would almost certainly have had to do it against the opposition of Europe, Japan, and the Soviet Union.[2]

## A Long-Term Strategy

After the debates of July and August 1974, Simon and I came together on a long-term strategy and had an extremely amicable working relationship. He relished playing the bad cop role while I played the good cop in pursuit of an agreed strategy. Arthur Burns, Chairman of the Federal Reserve Board, became our balance wheel. As head of an independent agency, he neither needed to be consulted nor had the right to insist that his views be heard. On the other hand, a wise Secretary of the Treasury (or of State) will always discuss with the Fed Chairman those measures with respect to which some Federal Reserve action may at some point be needed. In Burns's case, bureaucratic prudence was reinforced by the admiration both Simon and I felt for his intellectual and human qualities. In my capacity as National Security Adviser, I therefore set up a steering group under my chairmanship composed of Simon, Burns, and Frank Zarb, with George Shultz (former Secretary of the Treasury, then president of the Bechtel Corporation) serving as an unofficial—and invaluable—outside adviser. An interdepartmental working group under Assistant Secretary of State for Economic Affairs Thomas O. Enders was given responsibility for developing recommendations.

It was a fortunate choice. Tom Enders had come to my attention in October 1972 when, with the Vietnam War expected to end, I visited Phnom Penh to discuss Cambodia's prospects. Suspended between hope and premonition, Enders, serving as deputy chief of mission, made a brilliant and compassionate presentation, free of the cant characteristic of the period. I decided on the spot that I would bring him to Washington at the earliest opportunity, which arose when I became Secretary of State in September 1973.

I needed a lot of help on economic analysis for the energy program I sought for strategic and geopolitical reasons. I made Enders assistant secretary of state for economic affairs, a position he would not have reached for several years in the normal course of a diplomatic career.

Being junior to his colleagues did not crimp Enders's style, for humility was not one of his distinguishing characteristics. Larry Eagleburger was wont to say that Tom was the only six foot seven inch man who suffered from a Napoleonic complex. Enders would live up to his reputation by tossing out the occasional epigram—for instance, that he had gotten more good work out of me than out of any other Secretary of State he had served. In the Washington pecking order, assistant secretary is a mid-level position on the lowest rung of presidential appointments. Yet, on energy issues, Enders managed to enlist such genuine heavyweights as Bill Simon and Arthur Burns, who vastly outranked him, behind a program of great scope and vision.

Enders did not shrink from waging epic battles with other departments. I have lost count of the occasions when Cabinet members would complain to me, not so much about Enders's ideas as about his disrespect for bureaucratic prerogative. Invariably, I would promise to rein Tom in and then call him to my office to cheer him on in the great job he was doing. Bill Simon, quite pugnacious in his own right, often had to smile—albeit through clenched teeth—at the end of the day because, however unhierarchical Tom's bureaucratic methods, they helped shape a program that restored the strategic initiative to the industrial democracies.

First on the steering group's agenda was a program of energy conservation. The producers were maintaining high prices by reducing their production by about 7 million barrels per day and allocating the cuts among themselves. An effective conservation program would, we estimated, exert intolerable pressure for the poorer oil producers to break ranks. Under Secretary of the Treasury Jack F. Bennett, who had come to government from the oil industry, put the case as follows at a Senior Review Group meeting on September 21, 1974:

> An effective conservation program would make them [the producers] about 30 percent shut in [not produced]. That would mean that some of them would be producing at only 60 percent. At that point, Libya, Algeria, and some of the others would crack.

(Ten percent was already shut in by OPEC's production quotas.)

Second, to enhance the consumers' ability to resist blackmail by the cartel, we proposed that each consuming nation establish a ninety-day reserve stock of oil. In an emergency, consumer nations would then share available stocks according to preestablished criteria.

Third, we strove to blunt the producers' newfound financial power by creating a financial facility to smooth out flows of the producers' surplus funds and to provide financial assistance to consumer nations in the event of a crisis.

Finally, we pressed for a joint program to spur the development of alternative energy sources. By combining conservation with new production, we hoped to shift the bargaining balance from the producers to the consumers.

The Energy Coordinating Group established by the Washington Energy Conference formally adopted all these proposals in September 1974 at a meeting held in Brussels and transformed itself into a permanent institution, the International Energy Agency (IEA), which has performed a great service to the industrial democracies ever since. The Energy Coordinating Group was composed of sub-cabinet officials;

hence the agreement was *ad referendum,* meaning that it needed to be approved by the governments involved.

Organizing the consumers was not the only string to our bow. Though some ultimate confrontation with the producers was clearly implicit in our quest for consumer solidarity, it was a last recourse. Our primary goal was to create incentives for the producing nations to become responsible participants in the international economy. To do so, we sought to elaborate clear distinctions between the moderates and more radical members of OPEC. A year later, in November 1975, I told the Rambouillet summit:

> We agree on the need for cooperation with producers. With cooperation we can separate the moderates from the radicals within OPEC, the LDCs [less developed countries] from the OPEC countries, and prevent a lot of other "PECs."

In this spirit, Ford had written in a personal note to King Faisal on August 29, 1974:

> It is my hope that, with Your Majesty's leadership as an example, the principal oil-producing countries will adopt a statesmanlike posture that will lead to a pricing structure more in accord with the capabilities of the world economy.

The oil producers did have a case when they complained that for nearly twenty years, the price of oil had risen far more slowly than that of the manufactured goods they were obliged to purchase from the industrialized democracies. What made the new oil price intolerable was that it had been raised within three months by 400 percent while, in the preceding fifteen years, the price of manufactured goods had risen by little more than 50 percent.

To encourage cooperative solutions, we created bilateral economic development commissions at the cabinet level initially with Iran and Saudi Arabia, though the offer remained open to the other oil producers. The purpose of these commissions was to weaken OPEC solidarity, to encourage the use of surplus dollars for development projects, to reduce the producers' free funds for waging economic warfare or blackmail against the industrial democracies, and to return some of the extorted funds to our economy.

Comparably complex motives were at the heart of our approach toward the poorer non-oil-producing developing nations. To keep their grievances from coalescing with OPEC, we sought to create alternatives to policies of extortion. We put forward sweeping proposals for stabilizing raw material prices and enhancing food security for the world's poorest nations. Our strategy was to give the nonoil commodity producers a stake they would be jeopardizing by following in the footsteps of OPEC or supporting it.

At Rambouillet, I outlined our strategy to the heads of state at Ford's request:

> We should try to break what the Chancellor [Helmut Schmidt] correctly called the unholy alliance between the LDCs and OPEC. This can happen, and we can achieve our results, if they know that their disruptive actions could stop discussions on commodities or that they will pay a price in terms of cooperation, or military exports. In this way we can combat our dependence with a coherent strategy.

## The Implementation of the Energy Program

On September 18, 1974, Ford delivered his maiden speech before the United Nations General Assembly. Addressed primarily to the Third World, it sought to split the least developed nations from their oil-producing brethren. To this end, Ford described food and oil as commodities with global implications. He spoke of the unprecedented stress that was being placed on the world economy by shortages in both commodities.[3] He also promised that I would officially put forward a generous American food initiative at the World Food Conference in Rome six weeks hence. For the moment, we were content to contrast the conduct of the near-monopolists on oil and the near-monopolists on food. While Ford formally rejected the idea of using food as a political weapon, many world leaders surely did not overlook the existence of that option if we were pushed too far.

Lest his U.N. speech be considered one-shot rhetoric, Ford reiterated the connection between food and energy less than a week later, on September 23, before the Ninth World Energy Conference in Detroit. This time he was more explicit:

> Sovereign nations cannot allow their policies to be dictated
> or their fate decided by artificial rigging and distortion of

world commodity markets. No one can foresee the extent of damage, nor the end of the disastrous consequences if nations refuse to share nature's gifts for the benefit of all mankind.[4]

Ford deliberately left open whether the disastrous consequences he foresaw were likely to be brought about by economic breakdowns caused by OPEC or by the angry reaction of OPEC's victims.

That same day, in the annual address of the Secretary of State to the United Nations General Assembly, I described in even starker terms than Ford had the impact of the energy crisis on every consuming nation, and I blamed the distress it caused on deliberate, hence avoidable, political decisions:

> The early warning signs of an economic crisis are evident.
> . . . Unlike food prices, the high cost of oil is not the result
> of economic factors—of an actual shortage of capacity or
> of the free play of supply and demand. Rather it is caused
> by deliberate decisions to restrict production and maintain
> an artificial price level.[5]

As Ford had done, I put forward an alternative approach based on cooperation. I elaborated on the President's speech by calling for an increase in world food production and for ways to enable the poorest nations to share in it. I also left no doubt about what we were demanding: "What has gone up by political decision can be reduced by political decision."[6]

The oil producers reacted to these speeches as if the industrial democracies had no right to resist an assault on their economies and ways of life. Some OPEC members accused the United States—accurately enough—of waging a "war of nerves." The Shah, demonstrating that he understood what we were about, warned that the industrial nations were bound to lose in any showdown with the oil producers, the standard posture when worried statesmen are trying to bluff an interlocutor out of a course of action they fear. In the same vein, in early October, radical President Houari Boumedienne of Algeria sent a message to U.N. Secretary General Kurt Waldheim charging that "certain large industrial countries" were mounting an economic and political offensive against the oil exporters. Were they really prepared, he asked, to take mankind "to the brink of the abyss" in order to bring about a lowering of oil prices?[7] On September 25, in a public letter to President Ford (which appeared as an advertisement in the *New York Times*), Venezuelan President Carlos Andrés Pérez had replied to Ford's criticism by arguing for a "just" price for his country's oil, which, not surprisingly, he identified as the prevailing one.[8]

Unfortunately, growing skittishness among the oil producers was matched by escalating timidity among the consumers. The day after my speech to the U.N. General Assembly, French Foreign Minister Jean Sauvagnargues, at a U.N. Correspondents Association luncheon, expressed a view dominant among our allies. He agreed with my assessment of the energy situation but warned against confrontation with the producers because he could discern no practical policy by which the consuming nations could bring about a reduction of oil prices. In other words, the victims had no choice but to await the dictates of the cartel. It was a proposition we totally rejected lest extortion turn into strangulation.

The speeches and warnings achieved at least some of their purpose. Though refusing to lower oil prices, OPEC announced at its September 1974 meeting that prices would not be raised for the next six months. Due to the inflation prevailing in the industrial countries, this amounted to a hidden price reduction. And for the remainder of the Ford Administration, energy price increases continued to lag behind inflation, translating into a de facto reduction in real prices between 1974 and 1978. But we meant to end the vicious cycle of near-permanent price increases, not manipulate it, and to bring about a reduction in actual prices. For this, continued and visibly increasing cooperation among the consumers was imperative.

The world's finance ministers and central bankers are assembled annually by the World Bank and the International Monetary Fund in late September, every two out of three years in Washington. At generally the same time, the foreign ministers meet in New York for the opening session of the United Nations General Assembly. I used the occasion to invite the foreign and finance ministers of the United Kingdom, the Federal Republic of Germany, France, and Japan to meet "privately" with Secretary Simon and me at Camp David on September 28–29. The intention was to foster and give symbolic expression to consumer solidarity. The fact that we labeled the meeting "private" was a bow to the fainthearted in the group, providing a fig leaf for the oil cartel that no formal decisions were being taken.

Most of our allies would not have been heartbroken had the invitation never been issued. The industrial democracies were torn between their desire for American financial and diplomatic support and their recurring nightmare that consumer solidarity might trigger a crisis with the oil cartel. Case studies in ambivalence, they at no time challenged our analysis, but neither were they eager to countenance its implication.

Perhaps symbolically, the so-called Camp David group never reached its destination. Heavy rains prevented the helicopter trip to the presidential retreat, and the entire enterprise had to be moved to the State Department. The initial reaction of our guests mirrored the weather. Several of them were clearly nervous lest any appearance of coordinated action trigger a confrontation: "We have already taken risks by holding this meeting," cautioned Denis Healey, Britain's chancellor of the exchequer. "We should limit the scope of our activities."

Undeterred, I presented the rationale for the working group's program of energy cooperation:

> The energy problem is soluble only on a cooperative basis. The stakes go beyond oil prices and economics and involve the whole framework of future political relations. If producers continue to manipulate prices and consumers fail to develop an effective response, a major power shift is inevitable. The producers will be able to shake the world banking system by virtue of their ability to manipulate their assets. Oil revenues will become the source of ever-spiraling arms races threatening the world peace. Western unity will disintegrate if the industrial democracies do not regain both the sense and the actuality that they control their destinies.

Bill Simon followed up with specific recommendations in three areas: conservation, financial solidarity, and coordination of economic policies.

The response was less than electric. Although our guests purported to agree with our analysis and offered to "study" our program (much of which had, in fact, already been approved in the sub-cabinet allied working group), they resisted our proposal that the consumers announce a single forum of their own—a consumer counterpart to OPEC, so to speak. Fearful of OPEC's reaction, the allied ministers insisted as well that the final communiqué state that they had merely met to "review" the situation.

It was not our allies' most heroic moment. But clever drafting can only obscure reality; it cannot change it. And the reality was that even the most timid consumers were, in the end, more afraid of isolation than of producer ill will. A "working group" to study the American proposals was therefore established under American chairmanship. It was our allies' way of deferring their moment of decision. At the same time, whoever controls the agenda of an international effort is in a strong position to shape the outcome—particularly when there is no disagreement regarding the underlying analysis and a man like Tom Enders is in the chair. And before much time had passed, the mounting economic crisis in all the industrial democracies generated a sense of urgency transcending the fears of confrontation. By late fall the various programs proposed at the State Department meeting were moving toward implementation.

Just as the program of consumer solidarity was falling into place, one of the key players came up with an alternative approach. While a few months earlier Simon had urged the shortcut of all-out confrontation, French President Giscard d'Estaing suddenly espoused a strategy of all-out conciliation. On October 24, 1974, he publicly proposed convening a conference composed of energy producers, industrialized consumers, and non-oil-producing developing countries. Europe would be represented as a single entity. To make his initiative more palatable to the cartel, Giscard also announced that France would not sign the oil-sharing agreement among the twelve consuming nations in the process of being reviewed. Though the oil-sharing scheme was an entirely defensive emergency arrangement to be implemented only in case of an Arab embargo, Giscard described it as too much of an embryo confrontation to be risked. In the process, he took a crack at countries aiming at "domination" (presumably the United States) and left a loophole for future OPEC price increases, seemingly approving indexing—that is, relating oil prices to inflation.

Not a little paranoid after a year of nonstop confrontation with France, we interpreted Giscard's proposal as yet another challenge, seemingly belying the conciliatory tone of his earlier communications with us. We did not oppose a conference with the producers. But we wanted to make our support contingent on the prior establishment of consumer solidarity. In its absence, a dialogue would leave the consumers too divided and vulnerable. What made the French initiative appear all the more gratuitous was that the producers had not even asked for a meeting with the consumers.

Away on a shuttle in the Middle East, I summarized my reaction in a blistering cable to Ford:

Giscard has invited selected producers, consumers and less-developed countries to discuss the energy problem. Giscard also proposes a system of indexing which, because of continued inflation in consuming countries, will certainly lead to higher oil prices. Such a meeting is contrary to our strategy —and the strategy agreed by most of France's partners— that the consumers must first develop a common program before they will have anything to talk to producers about. This France rejects by refusing to join the energy coordinating group.

While this initiative may cause a certain amount of confusion, it cannot really get anywhere. A meeting with producers without a common consumer position is an invitation to confrontation or surrender. Giscard invites the EC-9 [European Community] to act as a unit. This gives the Europeans a dilemma which may cause the FRG [Federal Republic of Germany], UK and Italy to waffle in dealing with us without being able to work with France for, in the end, these countries will have to cooperate with us because that is the only way to meet the financial crisis.

We did not accept Giscard's definition of the alternatives as a choice between dialogue and confrontation. The real choice concerned the nature of the dialogue. Our pressures had already brought about a nine-month standstill in oil prices, and our threats of military action provided the principal counterweight against another embargo. We were not about to see these assets dissipated in a multilateral forum in which the producers would be in a position to play off the most irresolute and fearful of the consumers against the United States.

Instead we decided to use Giscard's proposal as a form of leverage, agreeing in principle to an eventual consumer/producer conference but making it conditional on prior agreement to a concrete program of consumer cooperation. At a NATO meeting on December 12, 1974, I told French Foreign Minister Sauvagnargues that we would not agree even to a preparatory meeting with the producers until a program of consumer solidarity was firmly in place.

This gave France an incentive to go along. Even when it did not formally join them, it no longer sought to obstruct the various programs for consumer cooperation. The emergency sharing program proposed in September had been accepted by the IEA (International Energy Agency) in November. In an emergency, all the major consuming nations, France excepted, would share oil stocks according to an agreed formula. The major consuming countries were also beginning to implement conservation programs, albeit at uneven speeds.

The time had come to put forward the next component of our energy strategy: a facility to help recycle the vast financial resources being generated by the high oil prices. Exploding oil prices were producing growing surpluses for the producers amounting to $75 billion a year or nearly $235 billion in 1997 dollars. These represented a vulnerability for the industrialized world because the investments of the cartel tended to be short-term while the banks recycled them in the form of long-term loans. Thus the oil producers had the capacity, by means of massive withdrawals, to threaten the banking system even in the normal course of doing business. And if the producers shifted their funds according to a political strategy, their financial resources could turn into a formidable political weapon.

To demonstrate the importance we attached to overcoming this danger, I wedged a major speech into the ten days between the Middle East shuttle described above and the Vladivostok summit. On November 14, 1974, in Chicago, I said:

> Producer revenues will inevitably be reinvested in the industrialized world; there is no other outlet. But they will not necessarily flow back to the countries whose balance-of-payments problems are most acute. Thus many countries will remain unable to finance their deficits and all will be vulnerable to massive sudden withdrawals.
>
> The industrialized nations, acting together, can correct this imbalance and reduce their vulnerability. Just as producers are free to choose where they place their funds, so the consumers must be free to redistribute these funds to meet their own needs and those of the developing countries.[9]

We proposed to create a facility for recycling $25 billion in 1975 and an equal sum the following year from the funds being invested in the consuming nations by the oil producers. Such an institution would reduce the ability of the producers to exert political pressure by the manner in which they invested their vast financial resources and would discourage weaker consumers from imposing trade restrictions on non-oil imports to reduce their oil-related trade deficits. That program was in place by the end of January 1975.

In early February we presented the final component of our consumer solidarity initiative. The proposal for a so called floor price for oil would turn out to be our most controversial initiative. It was designed to create incentives for the development of alternative sources of energy, which would be needed even if all conservation goals were met. For if conservation worked as intended, the economic recovery it would spawn was bound to rekindle the demand for oil, thereby restoring to some extent the cartel's ability to set prices.

On the other hand, development of alternative sources of energy would prove costly—an estimated $500 billion over a ten-year period. The cartel might therefore be in a position to ruin our strategy by a tactical reduction of its prices, rendering the new sources noncompetitive.

In a speech to the National Press Club on February 3, addressing these dangers, I proposed the creation of two consortiums within the IEA: one would be concerned with the development of synthetic fuels and the other with general energy research and development. Predatory price-cutting by OPEC would be resisted through import fees designed to bring about a protected price for synthetic fuels "well below the current world oil prices" but still high enough to encourage the development of alternative energy sources. We estimated that an appropriate level for the floor price would be around $7 a barrel in 1974 prices, or about 60 percent of the then posted price. Our goal was to leave the producers with these choices:

> They can accept a significant price reduction now in return
> for stability over a longer period; or they can run the risk of
> a dramatic break in prices when the program of alternative
> sources begins to pay off. The longer OPEC waits, the
> stronger our bargaining position becomes.[10]

On February 5, the United States submitted the floor price concept to the IEA.

For all its ingenuity, the floor price plan turned out to be the only element of our strategy that was never implemented. Helmut Schmidt was right when he pointed out at Rambouillet in November 1975 that the theory was impeccable, but we would never find adequate political support because its perspective was too long-range; the political leaders who paid the price for it would in all likelihood not be around to garner the benefits. Another obstacle was that the industrial democracies were unenthusiastic about protecting alternative sources of energy, which would be largely under American control. In the end, the IEA accepted the concept of a floor price, but none of the members (nor our Congress) passed the necessary enabling legislation. The idea's principal utility turned out to be as a symbol of America's determination to challenge fundamentally the existing oil arrangements.

## Consumer Solidarity: Meeting with Giscard at Martinique

Ford's introductory meetings with the heads of state of Germany, Britain, and France concentrated on how to restore economic vitality and coordinate the economic policies of the industrial democracies —even as the traditional agendas of East-West relations or the Middle East were dominating the headlines.

From the perspective of several decades, the record of these summit talks demonstrates the ephemeral nature of economic orthodoxies. In 1974–75, all European heads of government were urging on Ford the precise opposite of what was to become conventional wisdom ten years later. Fearing inflation far less than recession, they argued— often passionately—against what is, at this writing, considered the only road to sustainable long-term growth. None of them had great confidence in the market. All urged American deficits to grow the way out of recession.

Schmidt was the first German Chancellor who, in talking to an American President, stressed economics more than security. Above all concerned with preventing inflation, Germany's perennial nightmare ever since its middle class had been wiped out by the inflation of the 1920s, he wanted to ensure that the United States not seek to navigate the crisis alone, possibly at the expense of America's allies.

Ford understood instinctively that this challenge was above all psychological. With great sensitivity, he disarmed Schmidt on his first visit to Washington, on December 5–6, 1974, by inviting him to meet alone with Ford's economic team and give a critique of its views afterward. This was well geared to Schmidt's psyche because it was an expression of trust and an indication that Ford considered the economic destinies of the democracies linked. Schmidt responded with extended comments on the global economic situation, mostly on the theme that a significant American deficit was needed for global recovery.

While explaining his own opposing view regarding the deficit, Ford focused on consumer solidarity. He would refuse to participate in Giscard's proposed consumer/producer conference, he said, until a common consumer program existed. Lacking solidarity, the industrial democracies would compound their problems by rehearsing disagreements in front of the producers, who had caused the crisis in the first place. Schmidt agreed to Ford's approach and offered to help persuade Giscard to adopt it. The informal agreement reflected the reality that Schmidt needed Ford's support in reviving the German economy more urgently than he needed France's general political support on Europe.

The close relations between Ford and Schmidt made it possible for the meeting between Ford and Giscard at Martinique a week later, on December 14–16, to take place in an unusually conciliatory atmosphere. Once economic recovery had become the principal item on the agenda, there was no incentive for France to pursue the legalistic and bureaucratic disputes that had bedeviled the Year of Europe initiative.

In a private meeting with Ford, Giscard made the unprecedented statement that American and French interests in the energy field had become inseparable:

> We can't make an agreement without the support—not just the consent—of the United States. To go one step further, our view is there might be, at the end, some confrontation that is unavoidable. If the producers cartel is unyielding, we will not accept it. But this should come after the attempt to have discussions and cooperation. What is important is to show our desire to make agreement; and if this fails, we would be tough.

Put this way, the dispute over the consumer/producer conference was largely tactical: whether pressure on the producers should be preceded by dialogue with them, the failure of which would then justify confrontation, or whether it might be preferable to establish consumer solidarity first and, from that basis, proceed toward a dialogue with the producers. Though it sounded like a controversy among pedantic political scientists, the dispute over that nuance, in the American view, involved the key to a successful energy policy.

This was the point Ford made in his reply to Giscard:

> We don't plan to go to a producer meeting for a confrontation, but we have to go to the meeting with a consumer

position and an agenda. We do have to have substantive consumer solidarity. We need a high degree of solidarity before we sit down with the producers. Otherwise, some of our friends would be picked off individually—they have weaker positions and could be susceptible to producer suggestions which would undercut the positions of the U.S. and France and destroy the effort to resolve the problem. We don't need a document, but a consumer idea which gives us our strength to meet with the producers, who are well organized. How can they complain when they themselves meet every three months, or more often? They are forcing down our throats higher and higher prices while offering no solution to anything.

Less than a year earlier, Georges Pompidou had refused to endorse the concept of an International Energy Agency at the Washington Energy Conference. Giscard, dependent on the support of the Gaullist Party, which was his coalition partner, could not risk reversing that decision formally. But he agreed not to oppose the IEA's efforts to complete the program of conservation and emergency sharing and promised to support these policies by parallel French efforts.

Giscard kept his word. In fact, French efforts at conservation and the development of alternative sources of energy (especially nuclear) exceeded those of the other industrial democracies by a considerable margin. Giscard indicated as well that France would support the emergency financial facility to help recycle producer funds on deposit in the West. The deadline for all these steps was set as the end of January 1975.

Consumer solidarity was turning into a reality. Both sides "won," which is why their cooperation lasted. Giscard gained America's commitment in principle to his consumer/producer dialogue. Ford elicited French cooperation in the prior completion of the three key elements of existing American strategy: conservation, emergency sharing, and financial solidarity.

Perhaps the most important result of the Martinique meeting was the decision to constitute an informal and unofficial group of trusted advisers of the key industrial democracies. These personal representatives of the heads of government were instructed to meet regularly to plan joint policies regarding the oil crisis and economic recovery. We again called on George Shultz, still a private citizen, foreshadowing his later distinguished service as Secretary of State; Schmidt appointed Wilfried

Guth, chairman of Deutsche Bank, Germany's most influential financial institution; Giscard sent Raymond Barre, who later became French Prime Minister; Wilson appointed banker Eric Roll; and Japan's representative was Nobuhiko Ushiba, retired ambassador to Washington.

The "unofficial" group, which met for the remainder of Ford's term, facilitated intensive consultation among the principal industrial democracies, free of bureaucratic and political pressures and with immediate access to the heads of government. Out of this grew a year later the first annual economic summit of the industrialized democracies.

On the return trip from Martinique, Ford wrote to Schmidt and I to Jim Callaghan. We described what had been agreed and the need to put the consumer program into place before proceeding with the consumer/producer dialogue. Callaghan replied that he would instruct the British representative who was chairing the IEA group dealing with consumer/producer relations to proceed on the basis of these priorities. Schmidt applauded the plan for establishing a group of trusted nongovernmental advisers.

Amidst all the preoccupations with arms control negotiations, the Jackson-Vanik Amendment, Cyprus, intelligence investigations, and Middle East shuttles, the Ford Administration was, by the end of 1974, the catalyst of a comprehensive international energy policy. Consumer cooperation—so controversial at the beginning of the year—had been embedded in agreed specific programs and new institutions.

On January 13, 1975, Ford put forward the domestic counterpart to our international efforts, focusing on the conservation program.[11] In the end, he was more successful with his international energy policy than with the domestic variant. Afraid of windfall profits for domestic producers, Congress maintained a two-tier price system that in practice subsidized the consumption of imported oil and discouraged the development of new domestic supplies.

By this time we were sufficiently confident of consumer cohesion to warn the cartel that we might well react to another embargo by force. Schlesinger foreshadowed the possible use of force in September 1974. I followed suit in the interview with *Business Week* in December cited earlier:

> I am not saying that there's no circumstance where we would not use force. But it is one thing to use it in the case of a dispute over price; it's another where there is some actual strangulation of the industrialized world.[12]

Even such a highly qualified threat of force—embedded as it was in a double negative—caused allies as well as the Nonaligned to demand a "clarification" that would have amounted to a retraction. But we stuck to our guns. On January 5, 1975, presidential spokesman Ron Nessen, responding to undoubtedly accurate press reports claiming that unnamed White House aides were dismayed by my rhetoric, declared that my observations reflected the President's views. And I maintained that position in a television interview with Bill Moyers on January 15:

> I was speaking hypothetically about an extreme situation. It would have to be provoked by other countries. I think it is self-evident that the United States cannot permit itself to be strangled. But I also do not believe that this will really be attempted.[13]

Even our critical allies in the end benefited from the caution which our strong rhetoric imposed on the oil producers. I said as much at the Rambouillet summit in November 1975:

> After the initial outburst and after all our friends had dissociated themselves from us, the oil-producing countries came to us to ask what was needed to prevent such a course of action [military intervention]. . . .
> . . . The oil prices are being maintained by moderate countries in OPEC—those who are most psychologically dependent on the U.S. We can do a lot if we are not immediately disassociated [disavowed] by our colleagues. We expect a cry of outrage from the producers. We can take that if we are not disavowed by our friends.

The producers did not repeat the threat of an embargo for the remainder of the Ford Administration.

## Separate Oil Deals

The cooperative consumer measures were obliging the producers to keep an increasing percentage of their production shut down in order to sustain the high oil price. We were convinced that sooner or later someone would break ranks.

The first tremors of it occurred in the summer of 1975 when the Shah offered to sell us some oil beyond the OPEC quota at a hidden discount. The sale would be to our strategic reserve and be paid for by Treasury bonds; the reduction would occur by providing for a six-month grace period in interest payments. The amount of the discount was, in fact, less important than the flow of additional oil to the market, automatically magnifying the pressure on prices.

The transaction was never consummated because Simon balked at the idea of the Shah—whom he still blamed for the oil crisis—getting any additional benefits and because the major oil companies, not averse to the high OPEC oil price, were reluctant to cooperate. But we considered Iran's overture to be an augury of things to come. OPEC discipline was beginning to crack—a process that would have accelerated had not the fall of the Shah in 1978 created another unexpected shortfall in supply and thus resurrected widespread panic.

We persisted in seeking to induce some non-OPEC nations to bring additional oil on the market as one way of reversing market forces. In 1975 when the Soviet Union faced a food shortage, we perceived such an opportunity. We tried to make the sale of 15 million additional tons of grain conditional on obtaining oil from the Soviet Union. Ford raised the issue with Brezhnev at Helsinki in 1975, and the Soviet leader agreed in principle. But to avoid the charge of "softness" on the Soviet Union, Ford felt that he could justify oil purchases only if he could demonstrate a significant price reduction. At this, Brezhnev balked.

It turned out to be another case in which a possibly significant political and economic gain was aborted by our frozen domestic debate. For the benefit to the United States of oil purchases from the Soviet Union and the penalty for OPEC were, in fact, identical whatever the price: additional oil on the market would force the cartel to reduce production proportionally, thereby magnifying its internal stresses. Then, too, there would have been some humor in having our strategic reserve filled in part by Soviet supplies.

Consumer solidarity having been largely achieved by early 1975, we agreed to a preparatory consumer/producer conference, which opened in Paris on April 7 at the sub-cabinet level. Under Secretary of State Charles Robinson represented the United States. Almost immediately, the conference deadlocked over its agenda. The producers insisted on discussing *all* raw materials, implying that OPEC cartel methods should be applied to other commodities. We were strongly opposed. The last thing we wanted was to have to deal with a supercartel encompassing all the raw material producers. And the deadlock proved that our strategy of isolating OPEC was bearing fruit. For both the industrial democracies as well as the principal raw material producers rejected the proposals for a comprehensive agenda.

## The Rambouillet Summit

Step by step, what had started out mired in controversy over whether to deal with the oil cartel by dialogue or by confrontation had turned into a joint enterprise to chart a common economic future for the industrial democracies. The informal group of nonofficial advisers proposed by Giscard and accepted by Ford at Martinique was making significant progress, leading Giscard on August 1 at Helsinki to propose that the heads of government undertake a similar dialogue among themselves with just a few advisers and a minimum of publicity.

Within our government, some saw the proposal as a French (and German) maneuver to blame the United States for the slow pace of economic recovery. And the Treasury Department worried that Giscard would try to use the summit to convince Ford to return to the system of fixed exchange rates that had been abandoned in 1971.

Ford disagreed. We had been insisting, he argued, on charting a common destiny for the industrial democracies in our diplomacy and in our public pronouncements, and he would not turn his back on the opportunity to give it additional meaning. In early September, Ford and I met with George Shultz, our indispensable troubleshooter, and asked him to work on an agenda. Shultz first met with Schmidt, Giscard, and Wilson separately. Out of those meetings grew a preparatory group composed of Shultz; Raymond Barre; Karl-Otto Pöhl, a close associate of Schmidt's; and Sir John Hunt, British cabinet secretary.[14]

It turned out that what caused the greatest controversy was not the agenda, on which agreement was reached fairly quickly, but the composition of the conference. Giscard and Schmidt favored limiting participation to the five countries represented at the meeting of foreign and finance ministers in Washington the previous September—the United States, Britain, France, Germany, and Japan. Ford, supported by Wilson, argued on behalf of including Italy and—more passionately —Canada. Finally Giscard, who as the host was by diplomatic protocol entitled to extend the formal invitations, agreed on Italy's attendance.

Giscard remained adamantly opposed to the inclusion of Canada, however. His principal motive was to exclude middle-sized European countries such as the Benelux—a position somewhat at odds with France's public claim to act as spokesman for Europe (or perhaps an expression of how France understood that role). Ford was irate because he thought Giscard was abusing the technical advantage of being the host and because Canada was our principal trading partner. At first he considered refusing to attend the summit but eventually relented, though not without vowing to behave coldly toward Giscard—a threat that did not survive the first half-hour of the next private meeting between the two Presidents. (Ford finally got even by inviting Canada to the next economic summit meeting eight months later in Puerto Rico, where he served as the host.)

Though labeled a summit of the principal economic powers to deflect the objections of those left out, the conference provided a kind of political *directoire* of the industrial democracies, and that was its greatest contribution. In a speech on November 11, a few days before the summit, I stressed that the unity of the democracies (and not détente with the Soviet Union) was the centerpiece of Ford Administration foreign policy:

> The immediate task of the summit is to deal with economic
> questions. But in a more fundamental sense, it is a step to
> confirm and consolidate allied cooperation in every sphere
> at a crucial moment in history. It will not resolve all prob-
> lems, but it can set goals for common policies and chart a
> direction for common action.[15]

The deepest challenge, I argued, was not economic but "the erosion of people's confidence in their society's future and a resulting loss of faith in democratic means." The goal of the summit leaders was "to give their peoples the sense that they are masters of their destiny, that they are not subject to blind forces beyond their control."

Rambouillet is a smallish castle—at least by French standards—ennobled by intricate tapestries adorning many of its walls. We convened there from November 15–17, 1975, in a meeting room long and relatively narrow, creating an intimate atmosphere. Only the head of each government and two of his cabinet members were seated at the oblong table; each principal was permitted to have one adviser (who doubled as note taker) seated behind him. Bill Simon and I were at the table on each side of the President; Robert Hormats sat behind us, occasionally rotating with other White House aides—often William Seidman—when their specific advice was needed.

Only some twenty people were in the room at any one time, rendering the discussions as close to being personal as is possible among heads of government. The presentations were much more spontaneous than is customary at high-level meetings and, because the texts were not to be made public, participants could address their interlocutors rather than domestic constituencies. All of this changed a few years later when the meetings became institutionalized and reverted to the more familiar priority of public relations.

The Rambouillet agenda consisted of four topics: the international economic situation, trade, monetary issues, and energy. Each topic was introduced by a different head of government. Schmidt led off on the world economy; Japanese Prime Minister Takeo Miki on trade; Giscard on monetary matters; and Ford on energy. During the aborted Year of Europe initiative, our proposal to hold regular meetings of economic and finance ministers had been rejected by France as outside the scope of Atlantic relations. Yet when Ford invoked the importance for the rest of the world of close cooperation among democratic societies, he elicited an unprecedented response from Giscard: "It is important to make it known that if moderate growth is not achieved, we will face up to it together. . . . That message given by Rambouillet to the rest of the world will be very important."

When Ford led off the session on energy by describing the American domestic energy program and I explained our international strategy, the comments of the other leaders showed how far we had come in forging an allied consensus. As previously mentioned, Schmidt spoke of the unholy alliance between OPEC and other developing countries, and he praised our efforts to loosen these ties. Wilson followed suit:

> We have won ourselves a breathing space. The initiative on these issues has, at least partially, been transferred to the sort of people sitting around this table. But we cannot rest on what we have achieved so far. The conditions of the developing countries have worsened while the expectations have increased.

A lot of water had gone down the Seine for a French President to lament, as Giscard did, that "we have not had more coordination in our energy programs":

[W]e must, therefore, limit the amount of money we spend on oil imports and decide what steps could be taken to avoid further balance of payments problems resulting from new oil price increases.

The one possible exception to the general cooperative mood was Japanese Prime Minister Miki. Except for his opening statement on trade, which had concentrated on Japan's national problems rather than the global economic system, Miki was not heard from. He seemed to be dozing through most of the presentations, which was a polite way of avoiding participation in the dialogue being, however, carefully transcribed by a note taker. This caused Simon to send me an irreverent note—"I think Miki has just died"—which I had framed as a reminder that not every moment of high-level meetings is equally portentous.

The origin of Miki's conduct was both cultural and political. Decisions in Japan reflect consensus, not—as they do in the West—acts of will. A Japanese Prime Minister is therefore not in a position to engage in a dialogue, which implies that he has the authority to adapt his view to what he might be hearing from his interlocutors. He is authorized to explain the Japanese position but not to adjust it to the views of others without the approval of the group which formed the position in the first place.

Secondly, Japanese leaders—certainly those of Miki's generation, whose formative experiences had been before the Second World War —found it difficult to relate to concepts of a global world order or of international organization. Their society had survived by cultivating its uniqueness on islands poor in resources. It had done so by extraordinary self-discipline, which enabled Japan to retain its cultural essence even while adopting the techniques and even some of the institutions of the West. But its motive was the very opposite of what is today called globalization. Japan joined the world trading system to protect its unique characteristics, not to dissolve them in a universal culture or economy. Despite an unfailing politeness, the Japanese delegation seemed more comfortable with pursuing the Japanese national interest than a general theory of world order. This did not mean that Miki balked at specific proposals or hesitated in signing the final declaration —only that his actions were justified by the necessities of his own country rather than some global consensus—hardly the worst thing one can say about a Prime Minister.

The jaded press corps accompanying the President to Rambouillet filed the same kind of skeptical reports they had issued from Helsinki three months earlier. Not much had been achieved, they said. Some of the goals announced before the conference had not been attained—for example, institutionalizing regular meetings of ministers responsible for economic affairs, which in fact is exactly what did occur.

Yet just as in Helsinki, skepticism missed the point. Just as Helsinki had marked a turning point in East-West relations, Rambouillet a few months later launched a new era of institutionalized economic and political cooperation among the democracies—proving that media deadlines do not necessarily correspond to the rhythms of history.

The energy crisis had burst upon the world unexpectedly in the midst of the Cold War. The Soviet Union had not caused it, nor was our chief adversary in a position to affect the outcome significantly— foreshadowing its emerging irrelevance in all but the military sphere.* The process of surmounting the energy crisis had many of the attributes that marked the West's victory in the Cold War. In both cases there were two dominant schools of thought on how best to prevail: some considered resistance too dangerous or too futile; others wanted to end the crisis in one fell swoop by confrontation. As at the beginning of the Cold War, reality at first permitted nothing more dramatic than containment: a policy of taking the sting out of the challenge and permitting the underlying forces to chip away at it. Once that was achieved, the industrial democracies would be in a position to turn the tables, provided they were willing to pursue vigorously their growing advantage.

I expressed our satisfaction with that prospect to the Economic Club of Detroit on November 24, in the aftermath of Rambouillet:

> We will never forget that our most important relationships are with those nations which share our principles, our way of life, and our future.
>
> We strongly support the words of the Declaration of Rambouillet signed by President Ford together with the leaders of Britain, France, Italy, Japan, and Germany: "We came together because of shared beliefs and shared responsibili-

---

* The U.S.S.R., as a major energy producer, profited from the boost in prices but then suffered in the 1980s when prices fell.

ties. We are each responsible for the government of an open, democratic society, dedicated to individual liberty and social advancement. Our success will strengthen, indeed is essential to democratic societies everywhere." [16]

## The Consumer/Producer Dialogue

With the core element of our strategy—the solidarity of the democracies—demonstrated by Rambouillet, we were ready to undertake the consumer/producer conference envisaged by Giscard. When it met in Paris in December 1975, it became part of our strategy to split off the non-oil-producing developing countries from their OPEC brethren. We had set the stage for this by putting forward, during the preceding twelve months, a series of initiatives designed to give the developing countries an opportunity to throw in their lot with the industrial democracies rather than with OPEC.

Foremost was the initiative on food promised by Ford to the U.N. General Assembly in the fall of 1974. As noted, the President had drawn a distinction between America's treatment of food exports, which we dominated, and OPEC's handling of its monopoly position on oil. In a follow-up speech, I had proposed a World Food Conference to implement Ford's principles. Soon thereafter, the President removed domestic restrictions on food production.

The World Food Conference convened in Rome in November 1974. Though such a conference constituted a highly unusual forum for a Secretary of State, I interrupted a Middle East shuttle to address it and to submit a five-point proposal in marked contrast to OPEC's restricted production and high prices. Our proposal called for an increase in exports by the food surplus nations; accelerated food production in developing countries with American assistance; improved means of financing food imports; and better ways to protect against food emergencies by means of an internationally coordinated but nationally held system of food reserves.

The next item on our agenda was to assist the least developed countries in dealing with the financial exactions of OPEC. For that purpose, we proposed the establishment of a Special Oil Facility (SOF) at the International Monetary Fund, which came to be almost exclusively used by developing countries, although Italy also had occasion to appeal to it. To assist the poorest developing nations that could not afford the interest rates of the special facility, I proposed on November 14, 1974, a second financing facility. Contributions would come from the oil producers, from other countries in a strong foreign exchange reserve position, and from the proceeds of the sale of IMF gold.

Finally, on September 1, 1975, we put the various strands of our plans toward the developed world before the United Nations, which had scheduled a special session of the General Assembly devoted to economic development. I had intended to deliver this blueprint in person. But, because I was still enmeshed in the shuttle that produced the Sinai II interim agreement, I at the last minute asked our ambassador to the United Nations, Pat Moynihan, to present it in my behalf. My staff and I had been working on these proposals for months, together with Bill Simon, Arthur Burns, and helpful advice from George Shultz. Bob Hormats, Peter Rodman, and Win Lord refined them at every stop of our travels in the Middle East, further cutting into the already limited number of hours of sleep my associates were getting.

With Moynihan flourishes, it took over two hours to deliver the speech. Its essence was contained in this concluding section:

—We have proposed steps to improve basic economic security—to safeguard the world economy, and particularly the developing countries, against the cruel cycles that undermine their export earnings.

—We have proposed measures to improve developing countries' access to capital, new technology, and management skills to lift themselves from stagnation onto the path of accelerating growth.

—We have proposed structural improvements in the world trading system, to be addressed in the ongoing multilateral trade negotiations, to enhance developing countries' opportunities to earn their own way through trade.

—We have proposed a new approach to improving market conditions in food and other basic commodities, on which the economies and indeed the lives of hundreds of millions of people depend.

—We have proposed specific ways of giving special help to the development needs of the poorest countries.

My government does not offer these proposals as an act of charity, nor should they be received as if due. We know that the world economy nourishes us all; we know that we live on a shrinking planet. Materially as well as morally, our destinies are intertwined.[17]

During the shaping of these proposals, critics occasionally attacked them as if they were some abstract academic program for reform. No doubt we were convinced of the importance of adapting the global economic system to the new realities. But we also had a very immediate imperative: we needed to isolate OPEC lest the resentments of the least developed countries and the panic of the consumers produce a global catastrophe. By the time Giscard's consumer/producer conference—officially labeled the Conference on International Economic Cooperation—met in Paris some three months later on December 16, 1975, we had succeeded in shaping its content and confining its dimensions. We felt sufficiently confident so that, in my opening speech, I went on the offensive by highlighting the unfortunate impact of OPEC's policies on the world's poorest nations:

> Our deliberations here must address the plight of the one-quarter of mankind whose lives are overwhelmed by poverty and hunger and numbed by insecurity and despair. This group has suffered immeasurably from high prices of food and fuel. Their export revenues have been seriously undermined by global recession.
>
> In these regions less than one person in five is literate; one baby in 10 dies in childhood, and in some areas closer to one out of two; life expectancy is less than 50 years; and birth rates continue to be intolerably high. . . . Alongside the Third World with its increasing power and assertiveness, there has come into being a fourth world, where human beings still struggle for bare existence.
>
> In one international conference after another, we have all pointed to the fourth world with sincere intentions of giving immediate help, providing long-term assistance, and devising special arrangements. We have agreed that this is a major test of a just international structure. It is time for all of us here to act on our words.[18]

The address indicated the extent to which we had recast the dialogue with the developing nations away from the confrontational course of OPEC and toward the concept of interdependence and world order.

The term "world order" has been reduced to a platitude in more recent times. Yet it implies not so much a destination as a process, one that each generation is obliged to master anew. The members of an international system will either find it possible to bring about an arrangement most of them consider sufficiently just to allow for the peaceful and constructive settlement of disputes and adjustment to inevitable changes, or a series of upheavals will occur until such an arrangement is, in fact, achieved. Fortunate generations live in a world order so taken for granted that they do not even use that term in reference to the rules they live by and consider eternal. Less blessed ages struggle over the rules of the game and, while they inevitably experience greater tumult, in its wake arrives the possibility of enhanced creativity and greater fulfillment. No generation can choose its challenge, but it can try to achieve to the fullest the possibilities presented to it. That was the test the oil crisis posed for the industrial democracies, which I summed up in my speech at the Paris conference:

> The challenge of our time is to build a stable and just international structure. This task has two principal dimensions. There is the imperative of peace—the more traditional problems of building security, resolving conflicts, easing tensions. These issues dominate the agenda of relations between East and West. No less urgent is the imperative of justice—the compelling requirements of global economic progress and social advance. These are now the major issues in the relationship between North and South. They too carry the potential for either conflict or order. Neither the goal of peace nor that of social justice can be achieved in isolation. We must succeed in both quests or we will succeed in neither.[19]

# PART SEVEN

# LATIN AMERICA

# 23

# PANAMA, MEXICO, AND THE "NEW DIALOGUE"

Before the Cold War, the closest the United States had ever come to a permanent foreign policy was in our relationship with the nations of the Western Hemisphere. In 1823 the Monroe Doctrine proclaimed our determination to insulate the Western Hemisphere from the contests over the European balance of power, by force if necessary. And for nearly a century afterward, the causes of America's wars were to be found in the Western Hemisphere: in the wars against Mexico and Spain, and in threats to use force to end Napoleon III's effort to install a European dynasty in Mexico.

Throughout, the Western Hemisphere was treated as *sui generis*— in the nineteenth century, less as an arena for foreign policy in the traditional sense than as an expression of our quasi-domestic "manifest destiny." But, in the end, reciprocity is the foundation of a permanent foreign policy, and that challenge was not easy to meet when, south of the border, the actions of the United States were often viewed as uninvited paternalism.

Ambivalence was thus built into the relationship, a situation that persisted even when, under Franklin Delano Roosevelt, the United States shifted its approach to dealing with the region as a unit rather than country by country. The "good neighbor" policy was the only time prior to the Cold War that a geographic region was singled out in peacetime for special treatment. In the end it led to few practical measures beyond the withdrawal of the remaining marine occupation forces in Haiti. After World War II, the United States sought to modernize its relationship with the Western Hemisphere. The new Organization of American States (OAS) was, under Chapter VIII of the U.N. Charter, designed to be a system of dispute settlement and collective security for the Americas.

These measures did not alter the Latin American perception of the United States as the colossus of the north—partly because that perception reflected economic and military reality. Flattered by our interest, our neighbors have also been made uneasy by it; they have welcomed our assistance while fearing our intervention; they have been willing to explore closer hemisphere security ties for their safety, but they also have embraced them as a device to tie our hands. Thus, the price the Latin Americans exacted for the new collective security commitments of the 1948 charter of the OAS was a promise of nonintervention by the United States "directly or indirectly, for any reason whatever, in the internal or external affairs of any other State"—or even to "use or encourage the use of coercive measures of an economic or political character in order to force the sovereign will of another State." The paradox of U.S. relations with Latin America has been the difficulty of defining truly cooperative measures even while the importance of Western Hemispheric ties was being ritualistically affirmed.

The major program of the Cold War period specifically tailored to Latin America was the Kennedy Administration's "Alliance for Progress," announced in 1961. Although it was the first time the United States had given economic and social development equal pride of place with security, the "Alliance" was soon beset with tensions inherent in the hemispheric relationship. Its programs for social and economic improvement were both welcomed and resented. Intense American involvement in attempts to reform domestic social and political institutions were accepted when they brought foreign aid and economic development, but attacked as a form of "gringo imperialism" when they sought social and political reform. The programs were both lauded as a new sign of United States interest and criticized for having been "made in the United States."

During the 1960s, obstacles to genuine cooperation multiplied as nationalism, radicalism, and social unrest spread throughout Latin America. By 1968, Argentina, Brazil, Paraguay, Bolivia, Peru, and Panama had military governments, and in Haiti, Nicaragua, and Cuba civilian dictatorships ruled. In many countries, foreign investment was restricted, foreign companies nationalized, markets closed, and tariffs raised. The doctrine of import substitution, first put forward by the

Latin America
1976

UNITED
STATES

*Gulf of*
*Mexico*

BAHAMAS

MEXICO

★Mexico City

CUBA          HAITI     DOMINICAN
                        REPUBLIC

BR. HONDÚRAS                  PUERTO RICO
(BELIZE)
Guatemala          JAMAICA    Santo
City ★  HONDÚRAS              Domingo

GUATEMALA    NICARAGUA    *Caribbean Sea*
EL SALVADOR
COSTA RICA   Panama
             City ★     Caracas
San                                   GUYANA
Jos                    VENEZUELA      SURINAME
PANAMA                                FRENCH GUIANA

             ★Bogot
             COLOMBIA

*Atlantic*
*Ocean*

ECUADOR

BRAZIL

PERU
★Lima                    Bras lia ★

             BOLIVIA

                PARAGUAY

CHILE

*Pacific*
*Ocean*
             Santiago ★    Buenos    URUGUAY
                           Aires ★
                    ARGENTINA

Falkland/Malvinas
Islands

0 ——— 400 miles
0 ——— 400 kilometers

Chilean economist Raúl Prebisch, dominated. It opposed foreign private investment and advocated public funds to finance domestic industry and commerce. The region's economic ills were blamed on excessive "dependence" on the United States. Reaction against President Johnson's move into the Dominican Republic in 1965 reinforced Latin American fears of United States interventions.

Nationalist trends in Latin America were paralleled by the growth of neoisolationism in the United States. In 1968 the Johnson Administration secured funds for the Alliance of Progress only after a major fight—and what Congress gave with one reluctant hand, it took away with the other. As Johnson's presidency neared its end, Congress passed a number of retaliatory measures to punish Latin American expropriations and seizures of United States fishing boats.


## Nixon and the "Mature Partnership"

On being named National Security Adviser in 1968, I had had little direct involvement with Latin America. The focus of my academic interests had been on the Cold War and its battlefronts, which were located primarily in Europe and Asia. Like many of my contemporaries, I suffered from a distorted geographic perspective: London, Paris, Rome, and Bonn seemed close; Mexico City seemed far away, Rio de Janeiro or Buenos Aires beyond reach. I would think nothing of traveling to Europe for a weekend conference. A visit to Mexico City presented itself as a complex enterprise.

Until I entered government, the only Latin American country I had visited was Brazil at the time of the presidency of João Belchoir Marques Goulart, head of the extreme leftist Labor Party. He had just succeeded Jânio da Silva Quadros, following the latter's bizarre resignation; Goulart's advent accelerated Brazil's drift toward radicalism. Left-wing students had fortified their headquarters in downtown Rio de Janeiro, making the trend toward leftist Marxism and statism palpable. But not even this nascent radicalism could lessen the charm of the country or the spontaneity of its people. My visit coincided with Brazil's winning the 1962 World Cup in soccer, unleashing a carnival that taught me much about the country's national pride, and even more about its capacity for joy.

My early views about Latin America were profoundly shaped by my association with Nelson Rockefeller. He had served as coordinator of inter-American affairs and assistant secretary of state for Latin America under President Franklin D. Roosevelt. Convinced that the United States was destined to play an ever larger role in world affairs, Rockefeller believed that we should engage in this enterprise on the basis of close cooperation with the nations of the Western Hemisphere —pioneer societies that had been engaged as we had in taming a complex environment and affirming their dedication to the promotion of human dignity. What message did the United States have for the developing world, Rockefeller would ask, if we could not make it work with nations of comparable histories and values?

Even though I was not prepared to concede Europe's pride of place, I sympathized with these views. It is no derogation of Rockefeller's vision to emphasize the difficulty of translating it into an action program. Beyond proposing that the assistant secretary for Latin America be elevated to under secretary level and after proclaiming the importance of the subject, Rockefeller faced the same difficulty in defining reciprocity that had bedeviled the relationship from the beginning.

Before appointing me as his National Security Adviser, Nixon had visited virtually all the countries of South and Central America and the Caribbean. He experienced their growing nationalism and radicalism at first hand when, as Vice President in 1958, his motorcade in Venezuela was engulfed by a riot of such magnitude that President Eisenhower alerted airborne troops to assist in Nixon's rescue if needed. During the presidential campaign of 1968, Nixon had proposed a new policy for Latin America with emphasis on trade instead of aid, and on stimulating private investment. On his first full day in office, Nixon invited Galo Plaza Lasso, Secretary General of the Organization of American States, to the Oval Office and requested that he sound out the hemisphere leaders about their recommendations for a new policy. Galo Plaza suggested that Nelson Rockefeller be entrusted with this mission; that same day Nixon asked me to call Rockefeller to undertake it (and perhaps also to demonstrate to Rockefeller that I now had a new boss).

Rockefeller put together a high-level group that made three fact-finding missions to Latin America. His longtime commitment to the region did not, however, ensure that his reception would be friendly. Anti-American demonstrations in several countries blighted Rockefeller's mission. Riots in Chile and fishing disputes with Peru forced him to cancel visits to those countries. In the end, Rockefeller proposed a

series of measures designed to reestablish the "special relationship"*
between the countries of the Western Hemisphere, culminating in the
evocation of a statement of intent that would move toward a true
partnership within a community of independent, self-reliant nations.[1]

Still, the problem of what these unexceptionable goals meant in
terms of concrete cooperative policies remained unsolved. In response
to Nixon's invitation soliciting their views, the Latin American nations
organized themselves into a Special Latin American Coordinating
Committee (CECLA, from its Spanish acronym), from which the
United States was by definition excluded. In May 1969, CECLA met in
Viña del Mar, Chile, and drew up a document typical of the way the
inter-American dialogue had evolved: it called for a change in United
States policies and for a greater emphasis on trade. What it failed to
indicate was what changes the Latin Americans would be willing to
make if these wishes were fulfilled.

The Viña del Mar declaration foreshadowed the difficulties that
seemed to arise almost inevitably when we dealt with the hemisphere
as a unit. Since the nations were seriously divided when it came to
their national objectives, they could agree when they spoke collegially
only on a series of demands directed toward the United States, not on
a strategy of cooperation with it.

On the United States side, there was a comparable ambivalence.
Much has been written about the domination of foreign policy by the
Nixon White House. With respect to East-West relations, Vietnam,
and China policy, this was true. It was not the case with Latin America,
however, in which Nixon at first left the initiative largely to the State
Department. But, in the absence of an impetus from a determined
Secretary of State or from the White House, the State Department is
better at dealing with day-to-day problems than at developing long-
range designs. Preoccupied with the hundreds of cables that pour in
daily from posts all around the world, the department bureaucracy,
unless jolted out of its routine, is likely to pay attention to immediate
grievances or to short-term goals.

When the State Department fails to recommend a policy, Presidents
are likely to attempt to fill the void with a major speech that can serve
as a signal from the White House about its intentions. This is what

* The term "special relationship" has become most familiar in denoting the post–World War
II Anglo-American relationship. In fact, it has a longer history in the Western Hemisphere,
dating back to the late nineteenth century and the beginning of the inter-American system.

Nixon did on October 31, 1969, when he addressed the annual meeting of the Inter American Press Association in a speech largely drafted by the NSC's Latin American experts, Viron P. "Pete" Vaky, a Foreign Service officer, and Arnold Nachmanoff. In the first speech to be beamed by satellite throughout the hemisphere, Nixon called for a new, more balanced, and "more mature partnership in which all voices are heard and none is predominant."[2] He implied a greater readiness to accept independent policies by the Latin American nations; he specifically committed himself to involve them in defining common interests. Nixon hinted that he was ready to consider a system of special trade preferences for Latin America and expanding the role of multilateral organizations in disbursing aid. The purpose was to reduce Latin fears of American pressure and to foster a Latin American regional identity.

It was an idea that was ahead of its time. Instead of rallying the bureaucracy, Nixon's speech brought its divisions to the surface. A doctrinal debate developed between the drafters of the Nixon approach and advocates of a global multilateral trading system in the various departments who rejected any kind of special treatment for Latin America. After he became Secretary of the Treasury in 1971, John Connally transformed Treasury Department foot dragging into open resistance. He strongly opposed *any* formal American commitment to the hemisphere's development effort and urged delay in submitting legislation for a system of Latin American preferential tariffs. Nearly two years after Nixon's speech, legislation for such a system had not yet been submitted to Congress. And Congress proved reluctant to channel its appropriations through multilateral agencies; in 1970, it had even reduced support for the Inter-American Development Bank.

The global economic crisis of August 1971 put an end to any further multilateral effort in the Western Hemisphere for the remainder of Nixon's first term. When the President proclaimed a new economic policy that provided for a 10 percent reduction in foreign aid and a 10 percent surcharge on imports, our neighbors felt deeply aggrieved. They called attention to the large United States trade surplus with the Western Hemisphere nations and considered the unilateral announcement of the new economic policy to be a breach of the promise to consult on policy matters that would affect them. So emotional was their reaction that they overlooked the President's gesture to exempt Latin America from the 10 percent aid reduction. The dispatch of presidential counselor Robert Finch to Latin America did little to soothe their outrage. For the remainder of Nixon's first term, our main preoccupations in Latin America were to contain the consequences of Salvador Allende's electoral victory in Chile in 1970 and to manage the negotiations over a new status for the Panama Canal.

But at the beginning of Nixon's second term, two events brought home the need for closer Western Hemisphere ties. One was the growing insistence of developing countries on bringing about a redistribution of the world's wealth by votes in international forums. The Charter of Economic Rights and Duties of States put forward by Mexican President Luis Echeverría Alvarez was a good illustration of a series of these unilateral demands on the industrial world coupled with a catalogue of its sins. This problem grew more grave when, within a month of my having become Secretary of State, the outbreak of the Middle East War and the energy crisis conferred a particular urgency on relations between the industrial and the developing worlds. We had no intention of yielding to one-sided propositions. And, as described in Chapter 22, we were determined to prevent other commodity producers from repeating OPEC's success in quadrupling oil prices, by means of forming similar monopolies. Isolating the oil producers through a variety of measures was a particular challenge in the Western Hemisphere, where many of the nations relied on the export of commodities. Some were members of OPEC, and others—such as Mexico—were favorable to the OPEC approach.

At the same time, we preferred to pursue our strategy in the name of some system of genuine cooperation rather than by confrontation with the developing world. In that context, we were prepared to give our neighbors to the south a special status. This quest for cooperative solutions was given special impetus by the end of the war in Vietnam. After the Paris agreements of 1973, we intended to turn our attention toward tightening our relations with nations sharing much of our history and our values in Europe and the Americas.

It was thus with a mix of high-mindedness and practicality that two days after having been sworn in as Secretary of State, I addressed the U.N. General Assembly on September 24, 1973, to pledge a new vigor to the policy of partnership in the Western Hemisphere.[3] A little more than a week later—on October 5, 1973, the very eve of the Middle East War—at a lunch for the heads of Western Hemisphere U.N. delegations (mostly foreign ministers), I called for "a new dialogue" to deepen "a friendship based on equality and on respect for mutual dignity." I invited my guests to contribute their views and suggestions:

> We in this room with all the ups and downs in our relation-
> ships, share a common history and similar values and many
> similar experiences. . . . So if the technically advanced na-
> tions can ever cooperate with the developing nations, if peo-
> ple with similar aspirations can ever achieve common goals,
> then it must start here in the Western Hemisphere.[4]

The response of the Western Hemisphere nations was positive, at least as far as procedure was concerned. Colombian foreign minister Alfredo Vásquez Carrizosa convened a meeting of sixteen Latin American foreign ministers and seven special representatives from the hemisphere in Bogotá to draw up an agenda for the "New Dialogue" with the United States. As was by now customary, the participants were divided between those seeking an opportunity for cooperation (Brazil, Colombia, most of the Central America countries, Chile, Bolivia, Uruguay, and Paraguay) and those trying to use the occasion to constrain the United States (Venezuela, Argentina, Peru, and, to some extent, Panama). Mexico and Jamaica wanted to do both. The meeting finally settled on a compromise and issued a statement of principles that avoided the controversial issue of Cuba while expressing solidarity with Panama's demand for sovereignty over the Canal Zone. And on economic matters, it reflected the standard Latin American ambivalence. The key theme was a call for the United States to end its intervention in Latin American affairs while, at the same time, demanding a United States commitment to a system of special preferences for Latin American trade. As Talleyrand is alleged to have said: "Intervention is a curious word meaning approximately the same as nonintervention."

In late November 1973, the Bogotá declaration was transmitted to me by the Colombian foreign minister. I agreed to discuss it at a meeting of the foreign ministers of the hemisphere in Mexico City scheduled for February 1974.

## Panama Canal Negotiations: First Phase

The Panama Canal negotiations were another time bomb left for Nixon by the Johnson Administration. In 1964, violent riots in Panama left twenty-nine dead and destroyed American projects valued at $2 million. This convinced President Johnson to open negotiations for a modification of the existing arrangements, according to which the country of Panama was bisected by an extraterritorial zone five miles wide on each side of the canal under United States control and administration and described in the original treaty to be the functional equivalent of "sovereignty."

Three new treaties were agreed in 1967. But when they were leaked to the *Chicago Tribune* before the signing ceremony in the Rose Garden, an outburst of congressional opposition caused Johnson to defer ratification of the treaties until after the elections. Thus the new Nixon Administration was saddled with a situation in which the principle of modifying the existing status had already been conceded by our predecessors, with the terms remaining extremely controversial.

It is not easy to conclude a treaty that turns out to be unacceptable to both sides. But this was the situation in 1967. In Panama, opposition was even more passionate and vocal than in the United States. Arnulfo Arias, running for President in 1968, was actively fomenting nationalist demonstrations. President Marco Robles dared not submit the drafts to the National Assembly. When Arias, age sixty-seven, won the election and assumed office on October 1, 1968, he demanded the immediate return of the Zone to Panamanian jurisdiction. His agitation turned somewhat ironic when, within weeks, a coup by the National Guard obliged him to seek American protection in the Canal Zone. From there, Arias fled to Florida, whence, throughout the Nixon and Ford Administrations, he continued to agitate to return to power in Panama and opposed the thrust of the negotiations we were conducting. By mid-1969, the new Panamanian authorities, led by General Omar Torrijos Herrera, indicated that they would request new negotiations.

As with Vietnam, our predecessors had left us difficult choices. In an age of global anti-colonialism, it would prove too costly to insist on the status quo of extraterritorial rights bisecting a sovereign country— especially when the principle of a changed status had already been conceded. Demonstrations, pressure, terrorism, even guerrilla warfare would, over time, rally all of Latin America against us, and isolate us in every international forum.

While we were prepared, largely for geopolitical reasons, to start negotiations over the status of the Canal Zone, we were determined not to give up America's ultimate capability to defend the canal or our legal right to do so. On September 3, 1969, Nixon began to move toward a resumption of negotiations by authorizing a study of diplomatic options. But he also decided that these should be geared to Defense Department studies of what would be required to ensure the canal's defense. Nixon was determined to proceed only on the basis of congressional consensus and a united government because, if domestic inhibitions aborted another negotiation, the blow to our position in the Western Hemisphere could be grave.

A personality issue arose that forced a hiatus. The United States negotiator and special presidential emissary on Panama, Robert B. Anderson, was a holdover from the Johnson Administration. Nixon had kept him in office partly to provide continuity and partly because he did not want to dismiss one of his colleagues from the days of the Eisenhower Administration, in which Anderson had served as deputy secretary of defense and Secretary of the Treasury. But Nixon also held a grudge against Anderson, to which, characteristically, he would admit only to a few close associates. In 1956, Eisenhower had briefly considered Anderson as a possible vice presidential candidate to replace Nixon. As a result, in 1969, Nixon neither replaced Anderson nor encouraged any contact with him, thereby substantially achieving the objective of moving the negotiations with deliberate speed. Exploratory talks with the Panamanians did not begin until July 1970, and formal negotiations did not start until June 1971. By then it was too close to the United States presidential election to present a treaty— especially as the Vietnam War was reaching a climax.

By early 1973, Torrijos, under heavy pressure in Panama, sought to generate international pressure to speed up the negotiations. With Latin American backing, he convinced the U.N. Security Council to call a special session in Panama under the pretext of discussing peace and security in Latin America.

The session, held on March 15–21, inflamed passions surrounding the canal issue in both countries and was therefore unhelpful, to put it mildly. Torrijos opened the meeting with a polemical broadside, accusing the United States of having created a "colony" in the middle of his country. The atmosphere did not improve when Panama's demands were warmly supported by Cuban foreign minister Raúl Roa, who was permitted to address the Security Council, despite the fact that Cuba was not a member. A resolution sponsored by Panama and Peru endorsed the Panamanian position without making any reference to United States interests or to residual defense rights. It was unanimously approved, except for the United Kingdom, which abstained, and the United States, which vetoed it. Our U.N. ambassador, John Scali, was

instructed to warn that the procedure taken threatened the integrity of
the U.N. Security Council:

> Finally, I would respectfully suggest that we all assess with
> great care the nature and outcome of this meeting so as to
> avoid any repetition of a course of action that could prove
> damaging to the role and reputation of the Security Council.
> It would be most unfortunate if the Security Council were to
> be transformed into a small replica of the General Assembly,
> thereby impairing its capacity to deal effectively with specific
> issues affecting peace and security.[5]

As it turned out, the long-term impact of the meeting was better
than its rhetoric deserved. In the United States, it provided added
impetus to the argument that insisting on the status quo would increasingly isolate us, and not only in the Western Hemisphere. At the
same time the aftermath of the meeting brought home to Torrijos the
difference between a U.N. resolution and actual diplomatic progress.
Far more practical than his rhetoric indicated, the Panamanian leader
came up with a scheme to defuse the tension and demonstrate some
progress without exceeding the limits of what was possible. He proposed that discussions proceed in two stages: a declaration of principles, followed by negotiations over the text of a treaty.

As for Nixon, though he had trod warily on Panama in his first
term, he was determined to make major progress in his second. The
problem would not become any easier; the pressures would grow more
difficult to control. And having decided to give priority to Panama
negotiations in his second term, Nixon finally replaced Anderson as
chief negotiator with Ellsworth Bunker. There were few public servants
for whom we had higher regard than this tall, angular New Englander.
He had served as ambassador in Saigon, as our representative to the
stillborn Middle East conference in Geneva, and, at the age of seventy-
nine, had accompanied me on a series of exhausting Middle East
shuttles. Ellsworth Bunker was the quintessence of integrity. Always
precise, never promoting a personal agenda, Bunker considered service
to the nation his principal vocation, no matter what the inconvenience
or what party was in office. A balm for Secretaries of State and a safe
harbor for Presidents, he enjoyed comparable prestige in Congress and
among the military, whose support would be essential.

By the time Bunker made his first visit to Panama, in late November 1973, I had become Secretary of State, and Nixon had approved Torrijos's suggested approach. By the end of his visit, Bunker reported that substantial agreement had been reached on a statement of principles. The eight principles stipulated a joint commitment to reach a treaty that would return jurisdiction over the Zone to Panama and assure Panama of an equitable share of the canal's tolls. Panama would participate in the operation and defense of the canal and give the United States the right to use the land and water areas and airspace necessary for the canal's defense. From the United States perspective, the Joint Statement of Principles helped to calm the growing impatience and unrest in Panama. And we could use this step forward as a symbol for a more cooperative and less confrontational Western Hemisphere relationship.

Having crossed our Rubicon, Nixon and I felt that it would be symbolically useful for me to go to Panama in February 1974 to sign the Joint Statement of Principles on behalf of the United States. To begin building the necessary domestic consensus, I invited four leaders from the congressional subcommittees dealing with Panama to accompany me.

We were greeted by a tumultuous and friendly public demonstration, though we had no illusion about the fact that Torrijos could have just as easily produced a crowd equally passionate in the opposite direction. In my remarks upon arrival, I sought to move the Panama negotiations from the technical level to the symbolic, as an illustration of our new approach to Western Hemisphere relations:

> I have come here today to tell you on behalf of our President that we are fully committed to a major effort to build a vital Western Hemisphere community. . . .
> —In short, can the countries of Latin America, the Caribbean and the United States, each conscious of its own identity, fashion a common vision of the world and of this hemisphere . . .[6]

Afterward I met with Torrijos. Tough, cynical, and passionate, he was a nationalist who tended to play with fire but knew at every step exactly where the fire brigade could be found. When it came to the role of truth in advancing negotiations, he had his own relativity theory: "I always speak the truth, but it is important to realize that what is true today may not be true tomorrow as situations change." Torrijos claimed that his nationalist rhetoric and his negotiations with rioting students during the Johnson Administration had bought five years of peace. As practical men, we described to each other the respective domestic limitations we were facing:

> TORRIJOS: Your visit will pay dividends in peace. My ministers and I believe that your visit will cool the hotheads for two to four weeks. There is a large group of people, however, whose mission it is to see to it that there is no agreement. They live off this problem.
>
> KISSINGER: There are many Americans who don't want an agreement. The basic problem is that most Americans don't give a damn. A small minority is violently opposed to the agreement, but no group is really for it.

The requirements of the two sides, in fact, ran in diametrically opposite directions: Torrijos needed to convey to his people that he was insisting on more than he knew was attainable; the United States negotiators were obliged to gear progress to our electoral cycle. Everyone understood that the final debate in the United States had to take place in an electoral off-year. Thus, if the negotiations were not completed by the fall of 1975, which was unlikely, they could not be completed until after our presidential election in 1976—a challenge both to diplomatic skill and to Panamanian patience.

## Mexico and the New Dialogue

We had gone along with Mexican foreign minister Emilio Rabasa's proposal that the first meeting of the New Dialogue take place in Mexico City. Mexico, perhaps because of its proximity, exhibited in innumerable ways an even greater ambivalence toward us than other countries in the hemisphere. It had no choice about the intimacy of its relationship with the United States; geography, economics, and history imposed it. Yet Mexico's memory of past interaction was anything but happy. Mexicans could not forget that their country had been coerced into ceding over one third of its historic territory to the United States during the nineteenth century, and had been subjected to American military incursions as recently as 1916. At the heart of Mexico's occasional petulance is its resentment of injustices suffered at the hands of the United States. Standing as a reminder is the monument at Chapultepec in the center of the capital to the "boy heroes" *(niños heroes)* who died defending Mexico City against American troops under Winfield Scott in 1847.

Though Mexico's well-being is fundamentally affected by the American economy, its input in American economic decisions has been negligible. And Mexican immigration to the United States—much of it illegal—has been a source of tension on both sides of the border.

Through the greater part of the relationship, the commonplace assertion that the United States and Mexico share a comparable history and similar aspirations was more courtesy than fact. The United States was settled in a largely empty region, in the subsequent history of which the indigenous population played only a marginal role. Mexico's history began with the conquest of a functioning empire, which, except in military technology, was comparable in sophistication to the European societies of the day. Although decimated, the Indian population remained a major factor while the European settlers and their descendants comprised the upper classes. Mexican society remained far more stratified than its United States counterpart; the population did not identify its history with the conquest of a territory but rather with the subjugation of a people.

While invoking the principles of the French Revolution, Mexican politics has not been democratic in the North American sense. Over the centuries, Mexico has witnessed extremes of political quiescence that have alternated with conflicts of extraordinary violence. As the twentieth century dawned, the heroic impulses of Mexico's people—the reverse of its extraordinary capacity for suffering—caused, in the course of a savage civil war, casualties amounting to over 10 percent of the population.

For the next three quarters of a century, the memory of that bloodletting produced an overwhelming desire to avoid the risks of a domestic upheaval. The formal expression of this is the PRI, the Spanish acronym for the Institutional Revolutionary Party, which has dominated Mexico's local and national politics for four generations.

The PRI represented an attempt to navigate between dictatorship and chaos by retaining some democratic elements without risking the practice of North American pluralism. Although in absolute control, the PRI differed from totalitarian parties by striving to forge and express a national consensus within its own ranks. Periodic elections provided some means of popular expression even though the outcome was basically foreordained. Every Mexican President has emerged from a system of cooptation as mysterious as was the ancient Aztec procedures for electing kings. While the new leader was publicly introduced as the explicit choice of his predecessor, it is highly unlikely that the reigning President acted alone. Various constituencies undoubtedly had significant input and, in some cases, perhaps even a veto. (This system is now in the process of being changed to a primary election.)

However they were selected, Mexican Presidents have governed by trying to achieve consensus among the major groups supporting the PRI. The ultimate limit to the power of Mexican Presidents has been that their near-absolute position during their six-year term has always been coupled with being consigned to oblivion at its end—thus preventing the rise of personal dictatorships.

In practice, these various balances have translated into a conservative domestic policy that exists side by side with a foreign policy that appeals to nationalist and left-leaning elements. Given the history of American interventions, no Mexican President could afford to appear too accommodating to the United States. By the time of the Nixon presidency, Mexico was ostentatiously friendly to Cuba; it tended to support radical Third World positions in international forums and occasionally a confrontational approach to the United States in the Organization of American States.

During most of my time in office, Luis Echeverría served as Mexico's President. As interior minister, he had bloodily suppressed a student uprising in 1968 and was therefore believed to belong to the right wing of the PRI. As is often the case with Mexican Presidents, Echeverría defied expectations. Whether to compensate for his earlier ruthlessness or because of a long-held conviction, he was more passionately oriented toward the Third World than were any of his predecessors, and he was generally to be found on the side of the radicals in inter-American disputes.

At a staff meeting on January 10, 1975, I voiced the exasperation that we sometimes felt with some of the public positions of the Echeverría administration:

> Mexico—there is a yearly left-wing cause that Echeverría uses to appeal to his left wing. If it is not Cuba, it is the Charter [of Economic Rights and Responsibilities]. And it always has an anti-American twist to it. So we could recog-

nize Castro tomorrow, I could meet him in Cozumel, and
that would get us exactly three weeks from Echeverría. And
then they would have another left-wing cause. He needs it.
At any rate, he thinks he needs it.

But having paid their dues to the left, Mexican Presidents—including Echeverría—rarely insisted on their rhetoric. When it came to bilateral issues they were generally practical and conciliatory. The many meetings between Mexican Presidents and high-level Americans in the Nixon and Ford Administrations were conducted in a friendly atmosphere.

Despite occasional irritations on both sides, United States–Mexican bilateral relations during the Nixon and Ford Administrations were remarkably constructive. Perhaps it was because a number of dramatic breakthroughs with which Nixon and I had been associated tempted our Mexican interlocutors to hope that we might pull a few stellar rabbits out of our hat with respect to Mexico's problems—without necessarily being able to define what the rabbit should look like.

Above all, the cordial personal relationship between Mexico's leaders and ours reflected Echeverría's instinct for the requirements of Mexico's long-run interest and progress. Whatever their rhetoric, Mexico's leaders knew that the destinies of our two countries were intertwined. They were, of course, influenced by historical memories and sensitive to the disparities in American and Mexican wealth and power. I might exclaim to my staff: "Whenever Rabasa announces himself for a visit, you can be sure that he or his President has just done something outrageous." But these pinpricks were rarely, if ever, pushed to the point of confrontation. Even when pride and circumstances kept them from avowing it, my Mexican interlocutors knew the limits of rhetoric and the imperatives of the practical.

It was different in inter-American or U.N. forums. Mexico's U.N. vote in 1975 supporting the resolution declaring Zionism to be a form of racism was inspired less by intellectual conviction than by a desire to demonstrate that the Echeverría administration was not in Washington's pocket. And the Mexican President spent a major share of his considerable energies sponsoring and promoting another mischievous United Nations initiative, the so-called Charter of Economic Rights and Duties of States, which proclaimed the justice of massive redistribution of the world's resources. While he was aware of our objections and our alternative program, Echeverría forced it to a vote, which also forced us to vote against it, at the General Assembly meeting in late 1974, suggesting that a demonstration of Mexico's political independence was a higher priority for him than the technical subject of economic cooperation.

Strangely enough, Echeverría appeared impervious to the impact his conduct in those institutions had had on us. As his six-year term neared its end, he stunned me by seeking United States support for his candidacy as Secretary General of the United Nations, his argument being that he would be a good spokesman for the Third World. That he could have expected us to ignore the extensive record of Mexican criticisms at the U.N. and other multilateral forums says a great deal about the true significance of these gestures in Mexican eyes. It was not an easy plea to deal with, coming from the President of a neighbor we considered central to Western Hemisphere ties, so we delayed the answer until Echeverría left office, after which the various balances in the United Nations—as well as the rhythm of Mexican politics, including a raging financial crisis—resolved matters without the need for any action by the United States.

Complex impulses governed our own attitudes. Any serious student of international politics and economics knew that for the United States, Mexico could never be just another foreign country. It was against our national interest to encourage chaos or resentment in a nation at our border with a population approaching 100 million by the end of the century, and with millions of its peoples constituting a growing segment of our own population. Any United States President would feel obliged to establish the closest possible relations and to avoid unnecessary confrontations.

In the late summer of 1976, when Mexico faced a financial crisis and Under Secretary of Treasury Ed Yeo departed on an exploratory mission to Echeverría, I sent him off with this injunction: "Remember to deal with him as a friend." The domestic necessities of the two countries did not alter the imperatives of Mexican-American interdependence nor the importance of maintaining cordiality in bilateral relations. But this mutual dependence was difficult to express in action programs. A network of consultative arrangements covered a broad range of bilateral concerns that ranged from salinity to emigration. But it was only in the administrations of George Bush in the United States and Carlos Salinas de Gortari in Mexico that the North American Free Trade Agreement (NAFTA) provided a project that was both feasible and equally compelling for both sides.*

Echeverría's foreign minister, Emilio Rabasa—a lawyer and professor, highly intelligent, somewhat abrasive, and well acquainted with the United States—sought to bridge the gap between his chief's rhetoric and his own knowledge of the limits of American tolerance. To that end, Rabasa cultivated a cordial relationship with me which, however initially motivated by tactics, subsequently evolved into mutual affection.

We had met in 1972 when Rabasa called on me while I was vacationing in Acapulco. He had come to put forward the Mexican case on the excessive salinity in the Colorado River waters delivered from the United States and used for irrigation in northern Mexico. According to Rabasa, this contravened a treaty signed during the Roosevelt Administration in 1944. I knew nothing of the subject but promised to look into it and to support a solution if Rabasa's analysis was confirmed by our experts. After my return, I recommended that Herbert Brownell, Attorney General during the Eisenhower Administration, be asked to work out an agreement with Mexico that was also acceptable to our domestic interests. Brownell skillfully resolved the issue in 1974.

Rabasa was eager to host the New Dialogue in Mexico City as a means of burnishing his President's inter-American credentials. Because I calculated that Rabasa would be more restrained as host than he would have been as a simple participant, I agreed, and since the purpose of the New Dialogue was to determine whether it was possible to break through encrusted rhetoric and to find a basis for a common hemispheric approach, Mexico was symbolic of the challenge, providing an interesting test for the possibility of its solution.

## The Conference of Tlatelolco

Mexico's Foreign Ministry is located in a district of Mexico City still known by its Aztec name of Tlatelolco. Ruins of the period can be seen from a veranda of the dining room—a not-so-subtle reminder to diplomats of the ephemeral nature of their efforts. To underscore the importance we attached to this meeting and to charting a

---

* The idea of a Western Hemisphere free trade area had originated with Ronald Reagan.

new approach, I had a few weeks earlier invited a senior congressional delegation: Speaker Carl Albert; Chairman of the House Subcommittee on Latin American Affairs Dante Fascell; its ranking minority member, William Mailliard, later our ambassador to the OAS; Senate Majority Leader Mike Mansfield; Minority Leader Hugh Scott; and Gale McGee, chairman of the Latin American Subcommittee of the Foreign Relations Committee.

Our Mexican hosts did not exactly promote the United States idea of community. Everything was arranged to create the impression that the conference was not a dialogue but rather a kind of confrontation between all of Latin America and the United States. At the opening session, two Latin American foreign ministers escorted Echeverría into the room. After the President's opening statement, the Colombian foreign minister presented the conclusions of the Bogotá meeting, the conciliatory tone of which could not obscure that they represented a series of unilateral demands on the United States.

I responded by stressing—as I had already done in Panama—the concept of a Western Hemisphere community:

> In the nineteenth and early twentieth centuries, the United States declared what those outside this hemisphere should not do within it. In the 1930s, we stipulated what the United States would not do. . . .
> . . . [O]ur fundamental task at this meeting—more important even than the specifics of our agenda—is to set a common direction and infuse our efforts with new purpose. Let us therefore avoid both condescension and confrontation. If the United States is not to presume to supply all the answers, neither should it be asked to bear all the responsibilities. Let us together bring about a new commitment to the inter-American community.[7]

I then put forth the United States program, which had emerged from a quasi-philosophical debate within our government. I had proposed the New Dialogue to establish a new special relationship within the Western Hemisphere. In conception, the motive was at the same time defensive and constructive. It was defensive because we were seeking to prevent a coalition of commodity producers whose objective would be a general rise of commodity prices; it was constructive in the sense that the special relationship was designed to create an alternative to the confrontational policy urged in Third World forums. At a meeting of State and Treasury Department officials developing a program for the Tlatelolco conference, I had outlined the proposed strategy:

> What I fear is a tendency for the Latin Americans more and more to side with the nonaligned countries. This could have profound political significance. . . . I want to give the Latin Americans a feeling of a special relationship with us. . . . I want to be able to say something in Mexico that shows our special concern for the Latin Americans.

Neither the State Department's Latin American bureau nor the Treasury Department had found this approach compelling.

Unlike the State Department's African bureau, which did not come into its own until the end of European imperialism, the Bureau of Inter-American Affairs had had a long tradition and a consistent policy. ARA (so called from the days when the bureau was designated American Republic Affairs) was comprised of outstanding personnel who were heirs to a paternalistic tradition in which the United States took an active part in shaping the governments of Latin America. Habits proved hard to break even when, as was the case with the good neighbor policy, emphasis was placed on consultation instead. The Latin American bureau was willing enough to inform the Latin American nations of our intent in principle, but not to the point of constricting our own freedom of action. And the economic bureau, as well as the Policy Planning Staff, objected to singling out any region for special consideration.

The real issue was American policy in the international forums that the energy crisis and the emerging world had made inevitable. Was it better to organize support issue by issue ad hoc, or was it wiser to seek to organize a special grouping? The answer depended in part on one's conception of the emerging international order. The Treasury Department, represented on these issues by its under secretary Paul Volcker—who went on to perform even more distinguished public service as chairman of the Federal Reserve Board—preferred global multilateral arrangements. This approach treats states as economic units, not as political entities, and expects that a balancing of economic interests will more or less automatically harmonize political ones. My view was that regional groupings were inevitable and that we were risking isolation:

> I know a policy of building a bloc runs against what we have been doing. The Europeans are forming blocs. They have special relations with many countries. We asked for compensation for injury to our trade interests, but that's a rear guard, defensive action. We are the only multilateralists left and that plays into the hands of the countries that are forming blocs.

Volcker was correct when he pointed out: "More substance does not come easily. We have been at this for many years, and it is difficult to develop new substantive, concrete proposals." Nevertheless, in response to my pressure, a series of specific proposals was put together in four areas: trade policy, energy, methods for settling investment disputes, and an effort to define principles of interdependence. It was more than could have been generated by normal procedures and in the absence of the deadline for the foreign ministers meeting, even if it did not represent the conceptual breakthrough for which I was groping.

After Echeverría provided lunch to the delegations at his official residence at Chapultepec Castle, replete with mournful mariachis, the foreign ministers assembled around a square table at the Foreign Ministry. The agenda was a series of questions by my fellow foreign ministers regarding the meaning of my speech.

It cannot be said that the reaction of my Latin American colleagues was electric. They were benevolent toward most of the concrete proposals, although some balked at the idea of a mechanism that would settle investment disputes as potential interference in their domestic jurisdictions. What troubled them was the concept of "community": in the words of Venezuela's foreign minister, was it a proposal for a new institution or was it a new word for existing arrangements? Clearly they feared that the United States had found a new formula for its traditional hegemonic aspirations. And they objected to my evocation of the need for reciprocity.

I had perhaps used a too grandiloquent phrase for what was really a system of closer Western Hemisphere consultation, especially for international forums on subjects like trade and energy. But I did insist on the concept of reciprocity:

> For as long as I have been connected with government, my friends from Latin America have complained about the neglect of them by the United States and, for as long as I have been in government, my friends from Latin America have told me that the United States had some special obligations toward Latin America. . . . [But] we cannot both claim special concerns and no special relationship. . . .
>
> . . . When we talk of reciprocity in the United States delegation, we do not mean that we must get an equivalent quid pro quo for everything we do. It does mean that we believe a healthy relationship requires some commitment on the other party. I think it is the only basis for a dignified relationship.

The next morning, my Latin American colleagues presented me with their response, which, if accepted, they proposed to publish as the official communiqué. It did not define a new relationship so much as it delineated the least common denominator; it was, in effect, the traditional Latin American "wish list," consisting of a series of unilateral demands for modifications of United States policies.

My reaction, however, was anything but traditional. I took the unprecedented step of refusing even to discuss the draft. I insisted that there either be an agreement reflecting some degree of Western Hemisphere solidarity or a simple communiqué that we had met and would continue the dialogue in Washington in April. At its first meeting, the New Dialogue threatened to deadlock.

Foreign Minister Mario Gibson Barbosa helped resolve the looming stalemate. As the representative of Brazil, which considered itself an incipient superpower, he saw no great benefit in diluting his country's foreign policy influence by a series of parochial propositions. Brazil's foreign minister would participate in the New Dialogue, but his principal objective would be to avoid both grandiloquent declarations as well as confrontation with the United States. Earlier in the session, Gibson Barbosa had responded to one of my comments to the effect that the Arab oil producers respected only strength with a skeptical phrase: "Yes, especially in the strong."

The Brazilian foreign minister came up with a Solomonic proposal. My objections to the Latin American draft, he said, were occasioned by the fact that it had been written in Spanish—a heroic language more suitable for confrontation than for consensus. Gibson Barbosa

proposed that the English-speaking members of the conference try
their hand at a counterdraft and that foreign minister "Sonny" Ramphal of Guyana and I serve as the drafting committee.

It was an extraordinary proposition. Guyana was invariably on the
side of the radicals in Third World forums. Like all the successor states
of Europe's Caribbean possessions, it was not part of the historic
inter-American system and was not even a member of the OAS. Tlatelolco was, in fact, the first meeting of Western Hemisphere foreign
ministers to which Ramphal had been invited. On the other hand,
Guyana had border disputes with Venezuela, with respect to which
United States goodwill might prove useful. Above all, Ramphal, whose
command of English was awe-inspiring and who was as charming as
he was eloquent, hugely enjoyed his pivotal role. In the end, he and I
managed to produce a draft more compatible with the original intentions of the New Dialogue.

Ramphal and I were still in the midst of the drafting process
when the time arrived for the conference's closing session. The same
formidable assemblage that had gathered for the opening session had
been invited; satellite airtime had been booked. Our Mexican hosts
and Latin American colleagues did not allow the absence of a communiqué to stand in the way of a solemn commemoration of its as-yet-
undisclosed content. The Venezuelan foreign minister celebrated the
results of the conference with an eloquence that belied Gibson Barbosa's comments that Spanish was not the language of conciliation.

Afterward all the foreign ministers met to consolidate the various
drafts into a final document worthy of the oratory with which it had
just been celebrated. Luigi Einaudi, from our Policy Planning Staff,
called the final product an "American program and Peruvian principles
set into a Mexican framework." The communiqué changed the phrase
"Western Hemisphere community" to "inter-American solidarity," but
on the whole it reflected the philosophy of our approach:

> The conference took place in an atmosphere of cordiality,
> free from the old rigidities which have so often obstructed
> our dialogues in more traditional forums. The participants
> met as equals, conscious that the policy initiated here may
> be of deep historical significance. But for it to be so we must
> recognize that we are at a turning point and be prepared to
> dedicate ourselves to new horizons of understanding and
> cooperation.

> The foreign ministers agreed . . . that interdependence
> has become a physical and moral imperative, and that a
> new, vigorous spirit of inter-American solidarity is therefore
> essential.[8]

The communiqué endorsed most of our program, albeit some of it in the form of nonbinding recommendations for study; it also spoke favorably of the various schemes for some concept of global economic security. The issue of Cuban sanctions, which would have proved highly contentious, was kept off the agenda and was not mentioned in the communiqué. None of this would have been possible without the cooperation of the radical group of countries and especially of the host foreign minister, Emilio Rabasa—a dividend for the conciliatoriness we had shown on bilateral problems, including the salinity issue.

Senate Majority Leader Mansfield reported as follows to his colleagues:

> The spirit of community engendered at the conference, in
> my judgment, was genuine and substantial, if not necessarily
> universal. From the point of view of the United States, the
> conference served the highly useful purpose of checking what
> had been a growing aversion to aspects of this nation's poli-
> cies and practices. The durability of the new spirit, of course,
> is another matter.

## The End of the New Dialogue

Less than two months later, on April 17–18, the New Dialogue continued in Washington, where a meeting of foreign ministers agreed to set up working groups on investment and the transfer of technology. Nixon invited the foreign ministers for dinner at the White House and addressed them with a strong endorsement of the concepts and program I had put forward at Tlatelolco.

However, we did not succeed in avoiding a discussion of the Cuban issue, as we had at Tlatelolco. A large majority of the Latin Americans made no secret of their restlessness over the hemisphere-wide OAS ban on commerce with the island, and particularly over their opposition to prohibition of trade with Cuba by American companies domiciled in Latin American countries and Canada. We managed to avoid a formal vote, but it was clear that the OAS policy of collective sanctions against Cuba would not survive many more multilateral meetings—either OAS or New Dialogue—and that an overwhelming majority of the delegates (even if perhaps not yet the two-thirds majority required by the OAS Charter) wanted each country to be free to set its own sanctions policy. The strength of Latin American feeling was shown when Argentine foreign minister Alberto J. Vignes announced that, in his capacity as host of the next meeting, he would invite Cuba to the next session of the New Dialogue, scheduled for Buenos Aires in March 1975. I warned him that we would not attend if the New Dialogue became a forum for pressure regarding Cuba and that we would walk out if it were sprung on us in Buenos Aires.

In order to prevent the OAS sanctions from simply being ignored, we agreed to a special OAS meeting to debate leaving each country free to follow its own interests. But we made it clear that even if the OAS sanctions were lifted, the United States would maintain its own national sanctions until a fundamental change had occurred in Cuba's policy of support for subversion abroad and its military ties to the Soviet Union. At the special meeting of the OAS in Quito, Ecuador, in November 1974, the proposal to lift OAS sanctions failed to achieve the necessary two-thirds majority by two votes, after which we were blamed by many of the Latin American countries for not having solved their problem by pressing others to end sanctions that we intended to continue.

This kept the Cuban issue on the inter-American agenda, and it continued to absorb far too much diplomatic energy. Finally, at the next OAS meeting in May 1975, a special session of the OAS was called to discuss changes in the OAS Charter. One of the proposed changes would be to permit ending OAS sanctions—not specifically Cuba's- -by a majority vote. If that provision, which would not mention Cuba, would pass by a two-thirds vote, Cuba sanctions would then be lifted by a majority vote, which was clearly available. This procedure finally removed the issue of Cuba sanctions from the inter-American agenda (see Chapter 25). But by then, I had developed increasing doubts as to whether multilateral forums were the best venue for achieving a special Western Hemisphere relationship.

The Policy Planning Staff of the State Department, headed by Winston Lord, submitted a number of thoughtful memoranda on the subject. Luigi Einaudi stressed the contradictory impulses that continued to divide the Latin Americans. Countries such as Mexico, Peru, and Argentina embraced the New Dialogue as a forum to ease the reintegration of Cuba into hemispheric deliberations. Brazil, which considered its basic Western Hemisphere relationship to be with the United States, was skeptical of any entanglements that might limit its freedom of action. As for the smaller Latin American countries, they preferred the prevailing OAS system as a protection against both their larger neighbors and against the United States. A State Department report succinctly stated the case:

> The dominant political fact is that the United States remains the one country in the hemisphere able to evoke regional unity—against itself.

At this point, actions driven by American domestic politics spared us the embarrassment of acting on our own growing doubts. A series of countervailing duty investigations initiated by the Treasury Department, required by law, offset much of the positive impact of our pledges to avoid new trade restrictions. Brazil was particularly infuriated about restrictions on footwear imports because it rightly regarded our action as contrary to a promise I had made to Gibson Barbosa that the United States would avoid any retaliatory step until the new government under General Ernesto Geisel had taken office. Secretary of Treasury George Shultz—in one of our rare disagreements—took the position that the executive branch's broader interest in trade legislation required meticulous application of the existing law. This did not explain why our economic agencies had given little or no advance notice to the governments involved.

The individual countries' irritations engulfed the entire hemisphere when, in the Trade Act of 1974, Congress voted to exclude from the system of preferences *all* members of OPEC (whether or not they had participated in the oil boycott); members of any cartel-like arrangement withholding vital supplies or raising prices to unreasonable levels; and countries expropriating property of United States citizens without adequate compensation.

While the trade legislation gave the executive authority to negotiate further reductions in trade barriers and to work toward improvement of the world trading system, its retaliatory provisions were perceived throughout the hemisphere as so much backtracking on liberalized trade, the single most important American economic commitment to Latin America. It also reawakened long-standing sensitivities to "intervention," sensitivities that were magnified by continuing revelations of past CIA activities in Latin America. Trade, which had been proclaimed as the centerpiece of American initiative to the region, had become its greatest liability. (It was the same Trade Act that severely strained our relations with the Soviet Union; it is not often that Congress had thus managed to legislate simultaneous crises in two major United States relationships on opposite sides of the world.)

The Latin American outcry, predictably shrill from the beginning, gathered force throughout the early months of 1975. The most vocal were OPEC members Venezuela and Ecuador. President Pérez of Venezuela termed the law "offensive," an act of "economic aggression and political pressure," and charged that the law violated basic principles of the OAS Charter. Ecuador threatened to boycott the foreign ministers meeting scheduled for March in Buenos Aires. Peru's left-leaning military ruler, General Juan Velasco Alvarado, suggested excluding the United States from the New Dialogue in order to demonstrate disapproval of the legislation. While he was at it, Velasco also wrongly accused the CIA of having been involved in domestic riots protesting his economic policies. Brazil threatened retaliatory action over the protectionist aspects of the legislation, especially the footwear issue. Mexico and Panama also were highly critical. Venezuela and Ecuador called for a special meeting of the OAS Permanent Council to discuss United States trade legislation. Ironically, the Trade Act had managed to unify Latin America to a far greater degree than the New Dialogue.

The Latin American countries vented their outrage in a 20–0 vote in the OAS Permanent Council (with the United States abstaining) that termed the Trade Act "discriminatory and coercive" and "counter to the fundamental provision of the OAS." Almost simultaneously, Ecuador and Venezuela announced that they would boycott the New Dialogue foreign ministers meeting in Buenos Aires. The President of Mexico announced—from Havana no less—that his foreign minister would also not attend, because of Cuba's exclusion. Chile made clear it would not come if Cuba were invited.

With its conference in shambles, the Argentine government at the end of January 1975 canceled the meeting, and in order to get at least some political benefit from its own leftists, claimed that the cancellation was in protest of the Trade Act. To underline the point, Argentina announced that the dialogue could resume as soon as the United States revoked the act's discriminatory provisions that were damaging to Latin American interests and unity.

For a year, Latin American policy had been the principal focus of that part of our foreign policy not driven by immediate crises. I had met my colleagues from the Western Hemisphere five times as a group and many more times for individual discussions. In March 1974, Mrs. Nixon headed the American delegation to the presidential inaugurations of Carlos Andrés Pérez in Venezuela and Ernesto Geisel in Brazil. Secretary of the Treasury George Shultz visited the same countries, as well as Chile, to consult on a number of economic and trade initiatives. Ambassador William Eberle, the United States trade representative, traveled to eleven Latin American countries to fulfill our commitment to solicit Latin American views on the Multilateral Trade Negotiations. (These were the global negotiations that led to the so-called Uruguay round of multilateral trade liberalization.)

Still, after all these United States initiatives, the only unified position our neighbors in the hemisphere had been able to muster was opposition to the Trade Act and solidarity with Panamanian pressure for a canal settlement.

At the end of the process, Assistant Secretary of State William Rogers summed up what had happened:

> You urged us to search for something more—something beyond a concrete United States response to Latin American proposals, something which would unite the hemisphere in a new and common purpose. We looked hard. But we could not find an action proposal of this sort which we could honestly say to you is ripe for presentation to the hemisphere and which the hemisphere is ready for the United States to propose.

It is now apparent that our search for common ground and an agenda the Latin American and Caribbean nations could embrace—an agenda that went beyond rhetorical exercises and challenges to our policies—was premature. Because many Latin American economies were statist, most governments were autocratic, and Marxist parties were influential in key countries, the concept of a Western Hemisphere community was impossible to implement. The collective undertaking to defend democracy throughout the region, as well as the agreement to a free trade area for the entire hemisphere by 2005, would both have to wait for two elements: until the Organization of American States could build a new collective security program in the course of the Bush presidency, and until President Clinton's Miami summit with the regional leaders in December 1994. The New Dialogue was the forerunner of an idea whose time had not quite come.

# 24

# BRAZIL, CHILE, AND WESTERN HEMISPHERE UNITY

During the last two years of the Ford Administration, the gap between appearance and reality was unusually wide in Western Hemisphere relationships. The public dialogue was replete with re-crimination: on the Latin American side, against the Trade Act of 1974, the disclosures of covert CIA activities in Latin America, and each country's bilateral list of grievances against the United States; on our side, there was unhappiness with the membership of Venezuela and Ecuador in OPEC and resentment over Latin American votes on the "Zionism as a form of racism" U.N. General Assembly resolution of 1975.

At the same time, the official discussions that were actually taking place between the United States and the hemisphere's other nations were warmer and more substantive than with any other group of developing countries—and, indeed, even with many of our NATO allies. On April 1, 1976, I mentioned this anomaly to a group of Senators after my first trip through South America:

> They get domestic rewards for posturing against the U.S.
> And yet there is a depository of goodwill toward the U.S.
> Warmth and affection I don't get any place else—including
> Europe. This is a paradox. We can't get actions we want,
> but we have a community. And it's interesting. The Caribbe-
> ans come to the OAS meetings and act like foreigners, but
> with the Latin Americans . . . we have a sense of family—

even in Peru [at that time, governed by a radical military junta].

During the Ford presidency, I devoted an enormous amount of time and effort to the Western Hemisphere, though in terms of our immediate challenges the Latin American nations could do very little for us. Occasionally they participated in international conferences between industrialized and developing nations dealing with the so-called New Economic Order. But their role was rarely decisive because rhetoric aside they were not major players among the nonaligned nations. The New Dialogue had shown that a single all-embracing concept for Western Hemisphere relations was still out of reach. Nevertheless, as we reflected on the long-term role of the United States in the world, relations in the Western Hemisphere took on a different meaning. I had frequently criticized the applicability of all-purpose Wilsonianism for conducting foreign policy. I had emphasized the need for a consistent view of the national interest and recognition of the importance of the balance of power. At the same time, it was wrong to treat Wilsonianism as the idiosyncrasy of a few American intellectuals. Instead it was the instinctive expression of a society founded and shaped by immigrants who had affirmed universal principles of liberty and justice to distinguish their society from the values and practices of the Old World. An international order based entirely upon national self-interest would not be sustained by a people who thought of their country as the "shining city on a hill."

In many parts of the world, we had no choice but to pursue the diplomacy of the Old World, with its careful calculations of rewards and penalties. But in our relations with Western Europe and the Western Hemisphere, a sophisticated version of Wilsonian idealism was in many ways the best cement for a permanent relationship. In both regions, war between the major countries was nearly inconceivable. Even when these allies or neighbors disagreed with us, the solution would generally emerge from persuasion and consensus rather than from traditional calculations of incentives based on raw power. Of course, the dividing line between the two approaches is not absolute, and the overwhelming power of the United States is unavoidable, but with Western Europe and in the Western Hemisphere, our relationships are more based on consensus than elsewhere.

In the aftermath of the Indochina tragedy, we sought—perhaps too anxiously—to find some symbolic expression for this moral consensus with Western Europe and Latin America. Because the attempt to treat the two regions as units turned out to be premature, the Year of Europe and the New Dialogue foundered. In the aftermath, we shifted in Europe from an overall approach to an effort to build confidence via a common energy strategy and annual economic summits. By the same token, after the interruption in the New Dialogue, we moved in the Western Hemisphere toward building consensus through bilateral dialogue.

In the end, whatever the criticism of the United States, no Latin American country—except Cuba—rejected the idea that some sort of special relationship *did* exist in the Western Hemisphere. On our part, we were prepared to accept some unique obligations as our contribution to a sense of common purpose.

A global forum in which we regularly met with our neighbors to the south was the so-called North-South dialogue between industrial and developing nations, beginning in April 1975, and held in Paris. Under the benevolent eye of our French hosts, the "South" proffered a series of insistent demands to the "North" that would alter the functioning of the international marketplace in their favor. It was a program of state intervention on a global scale. Mexican President Luis Echeverría's Charter of Economic Rights and Duties of States provided a rhetorical and theoretical foundation, while the adroit Venezuelan delegation was in the forefront of the day-to-day diplomacy on its behalf.

Determined to resist the attempt to reorder the world market, we nevertheless wanted to do so in the name of an alternative concept of international cooperation. We had attempted this via the New Dialogue described in the previous chapter. We now sought the same aim on a country-by-country basis. My position was that if we did nothing but challenge the New Economic Order head-on, we would eventually face a united front of *all* developing countries, which were bound to be joined by the Latin American states, and in the end by many of the industrial democracies, eager to appeal to left-leaning public opinion. To avoid this prospect, I pressed for an American agenda of cooperation by offering the key developing countries bilateral commissions on science, technology, and trade. My strategy, I said to the President on May 24, 1975, was "to project an image of the United States which is progressive. . . . but I want to fuzz it up . . . I don't want to accept a New Economic Order."

This strategy clashed with the views of my good friend Bill Simon, the Secretary of the Treasury, who was determined to dig in for an uncompromising defensive battle. Since we were friends, our dialogue was carried out behind closed White House doors. The more combative Simon argued that slogans are in effect reality; he wanted to extirpate the concept of a New Economic Order root and branch. Lukewarm about country-by-country commissions, he was also wary of my rhetoric about cooperation. His position brought the issue before the President, to whom, on May 26, 1975, I elaborated my proposed strategy along the following lines:

> Our job will be to discuss the particular issues and divide the LDCs [less developed countries]. We can't do this on a theological basis. The LDCs will unite and the developed countries will split up. We are much better off doing this on a concrete basis in which there are some who have something to gain. We should appear forthcoming so that we are not outside of the process. We should not put them in the position where they can unite by defending a few platitudes.

Simon eloquently defended his alternative of turning the multilateral forum into an ideological confrontation: "There are many who look to us for defense of the system. They would be surprised if we did not defend the system strongly."

In my mind, the issue was not whether to defend our principles, but the choice of battlefield. Fighting the entire developing world simultaneously was neither consistent with our values nor with a wise strategy. Far better, I argued, to break up the issues posed by the demand for a New Economic Order in such a way that we could appeal to the more moderate developing countries through a process in which they would risk possible gains for their country if they joined a united front against the industrial democracies.

On May 10, 1975, I expressed what I had in mind in a conversation with Venezuelan foreign minister Ramón Escovar Salóm. I coupled a stern warning about the consequences of a confrontational policy with the offer of working cooperatively through bilateral United States–Venezuelan commissions:

> At Paris [the North-South conference], Venezuela was closer to Algeria than to us. If relations between the developed and developing world are to become those of bloc confrontations, then, sooner or later, the rule of power will prevail.

This would be a disaster for the developing countries. It is not logical to presume that the developed nations will remain paralyzed forever. . . . One idea which has occurred to me is that we should discuss scientific, technological, and, occasionally, political themes. This could be through a bilateral joint commission as in the Middle East. It could allow a more natural informal contact. We cannot do this with every country, but we thought that it could be done with Venezuela, which is in a crucial position between the developed and the Third World.

In his commonsensical way, Ford settled the issue of strategy in the North-South dialogue:

I strongly believe in the free enterprise system. I have always been in favor of it, and I see no reason for changing. On the other hand, I believe strongly in pragmatism. Sometimes I think it is important to solve problems rather than to be too concerned about phraseology. . . . You may have to give a little on words in order to achieve something necessary to solve problems. I don't believe that you get practical solutions by being too sticky on phraseology. But we are obviously not going to compromise on our basic philosophy.

Unlike the typical Washington internal debate, which is rarely—if ever—finally settled, Simon took his bureaucratic setback with notable good grace, and became an effective partner in pursuit of a common strategy. Together, we put a sweeping set of concrete proposals before the Seventh Special Session of the U.N. General Assembly on September 1, 1975 (see Chapter 22). On each topic, we offered to form separate commissions with key countries, specifically Saudi Arabia, Iran, Brazil, and Venezuela, enabling us to tailor programs to specific national needs. The offer was open-ended. So long as our partners benefitted from these commissions, they were unlikely to drift into general confrontation either in the hemisphere or in broader international forums.*

The shift from the multilateral to the bilateral approach coincided roughly with the transition from the Nixon to the Ford Administra-

---

* In the transition paper which the State Department prepared for the incoming Carter Administration in late 1976, I listed thirty-five initiatives we had taken to fulfill the program outlined before the Seventh Special Session.

tion. The new President met with the Latin American ambassadors in Washington during his first day in office, but for the next few months he found himself engulfed by the crises described in previous chapters. Ford objected to the indiscriminate penalties levied against Latin American OPEC members in the Trade Act, but he did not veto the bill because it contained other vital measures, such as fast-track trade negotiating authority.

I used the transition to make a change in the leadership of the State Department's Latin American bureau. The incumbent, Jack Kubisch, was a distinguished Foreign Service officer who had performed effectively as assistant secretary. But his replacement, William D. Rogers, a well-known Washington lawyer with a sensitive and subtle intellect, had made Latin American policy his vocation.* Rogers's politics were on the liberal side; he had chaired a Latin American task force for McGovern in the 1972 presidential campaign. A number of unusually perceptive articles from his pen had brought Rogers to my attention. I was attracted both by his potential contributions and by the symbolism of the nonpartisan nature of Western Hemisphere policy. Ford approved my recommendation for the same reasons. Rogers—who was the only head of a regional State Department bureau not drawn from the Foreign Service—earned my gratitude by providing creative leadership toward a purposeful Western Hemisphere policy. We have remained friends ever since.

## First Visit to Latin America: Venezuela, Peru, Colombia, and Brazil

As soon as Rogers joined the State Department, we mapped out a visit to Latin America for February 1975. The scheduled itinerary —Venezuela, Argentina, Chile, Brazil, Peru, Colombia, and Costa Rica—was designed to dramatize the shift to the bilateral approach. At the last moment, the trip had to be postponed so that I could undertake the "exploratory shuttle" (described in Chapter 13) to keep the Sinai negotiations between Israel and Egypt alive. Rescheduled for April, fate intervened again. The collapse of Indochina kept me in Washington, and the Middle East diplomatic stalemate prolonged my stay. In July, the European Security Conference demanded my presence;

---

* Not to be confused with William P. Rogers, who had served as Eisenhower's Attorney General and as my predecessor as President Nixon's Secretary of State.

in August, the conclusion of the Middle East negotiations diverted me; and from September onward, the Angola crisis, SALT negotiations, presidential trips to China, Indonesia, and the Philippines, and the Rambouillet summit all intervened. This caused two more postponements; the trip was delayed for a year, and even then it had to occur in two segments. There had been compelling reasons for each postponement, but the cumulative impact was bound to raise valid questions about the priority we attached to Latin America. Basically, it was a case of the urgent driving out the important.

To fill the gap, I met frequently with Latin American foreign ministers—especially those of Venezuela, Argentina, Mexico, Brazil, and Peru. In addition I made a number of major speeches on the subject.

My first visit as Secretary of State to Latin America included Caracas, Venezuela; Lima, Peru; Brasilia, Brazil; Bogotá, Colombia; and San José, Costa Rica. From the point of view of our long-range policy, Brazil was the most important stop of my journey. For it was in Brazil that I planned to establish a special relationship meant to serve as a pattern for the dealings of the United States with the other nations of the hemisphere. While it is a part of Latin America, Brazil is distinguished from its Spanish-speaking neighbors by the Portuguese language and a more peaceful and evolutionary history. Its dimensions are continental, and its history as the onetime seat of the Portuguese empire (while Napoleon's army occupied Portugal) is partly global. Hence, Brazil has a self-assurance that other South American states do not always manage—except possibly Argentina, whose pretensions until recently found less of an echo among its neighbors. And Brazil has few complexes about being dominated by the United States and no experience with the direct exercise of American power.

Brazil has the resources, the population, and the scale to become one of the world's leading powers. Although its progress toward that status has been fitful, Brazil's perception of itself is that it is indeed a world power—and not without cause. The Brazilian civil service, especially its Foreign Ministry, is world-class, subtle, intelligent, and persistent. Brazilian diplomats pursue their objectives so tenaciously, charmingly, and almost anonymously that their interlocutors are ever in danger of being tranquilized into forgetting that they are face-to-face with the long-range and tough pursuit of national interest.

For Brazil, this national interest has expressed itself in a quest to be recognized, especially by the United States, as Latin America's principal country. In the back of Brazilian minds, a kind of dumbbell theory has prevailed for most of the country's history. According to this approach, the United States and Brazil are destined to cooperate in organizing the hemisphere—the United States in the north and Brazil in the south. Until the 1960s, this attitude was expressed in Brazil's efforts to present itself as America's most loyal ally in the Western Hemisphere—much as Britain after the end of World War II conducted itself in Europe. Once its then President, Getulio Vargas, overcame a brief flirtation with neutrality, Brazil entered the Second World War at the side of the United States, and a Brazilian division fought in Italy. Similarly, Brazil supported the United States's intervention in the Dominican Republic in 1965. In Santo Domingo, Brazilian military units stood beside our troops, and the OAS's second-in-command was a Brazilian general. As in the case of Britain, the quid pro quo was a special status in Washington, all the more important for never being explicit.

By the time I encountered Brazilian diplomats a decade later, the center of gravity of the country's foreign policy had shifted slightly. The military takeover in 1964 had caused the Johnson Administration to loosen Washington's ties with Brazil, and even Nixon did not succeed in convincing our bureaucracy to return to the traditional level of cordiality.

Relations had cooled also on the part of Brazil. As a result of America's domestic crisis over Vietnam, Watergate, the intelligence investigations, and Angola, Brazil, ever practical, was cautiously exploring to see just how much its margin of maneuver might have increased. It was not enthusiastic about the New Dialogue, because it feared that the multilateralization of inter-American relations would dilute Brazil's status. But in true Brazilian fashion, its diplomats went along with it and did what they could to limit the damage without exerting themselves to turn it into a success. The collapse of the New Dialogue enabled Brazil to reassert a formal claim to a special relationship with the United States. This fact dominated my dealings with Foreign Minister Antonio Azeredo da Silveira and his President, Ernesto Geisel.

In 1976, Brazil had a military government. The takeover had occurred a decade earlier in a typically Brazilian bloodless coup. The military had ousted the incumbent President João Goulart, who had come into office in a bizarre episode when the incumbent President, Jânio Quadros, resigned in a conflict with his congress. Quadros had expected that the congress would be so afraid of then Vice President Goulart's radical tendencies that it would call him back with enhanced powers. While Quadros was correct about Goulart's left-wing views, he did not realize that the congress feared his own erratic behavior more than Goulart's radicalism. As a result, Quadros lost his gamble and found himself out of power. Goulart moved the country steadily left until the military ousted him in 1964.

By Latin American standards of the day, Brazil's military rule was remarkably benign. Intent on a market-oriented program of rapid economic growth under the brilliant planning minister Roberto Campos, the Brazilians did not base their rule primarily on violence. The opposition went into exile, rather than to prison or to death.

In the United States, Brazil's military government suffered the condemnation customarily reserved by the media and the McGovernite Congress for regimes perceived to be right-wing. The attack focused less on human rights abuses than on the country's slow return to democracy. The treatment of the far more brutal and authoritarian, but leftist, Peruvian military regime was much more restrained.

Brazil's military regime made no claim to permanence. As I reported to Ford: "There is no feeling here that the military are the Jesuits of a new order but that they are part of a total national effort." No one wore a uniform to the office; below the President and his chief of staff, General Golbery do Couta e Silva, the government was run by civilian ministers and officials—especially the Foreign Ministry. Golbery, whom I described to Ford as looking like a grade-school mathematics teacher, spoke like a speculative philosopher, and was responsible for political reform. He told me that Brazil had successfully navigated the passage from dictatorship to autocracy and was now engaged in "political decompression" in moving toward democracy. He said that the only issue was "how fast, not whether."

My attitude toward Brazil was summed up in my report to Ford:

> They take a world view. Furthermore, the interest of Brazil
> in world affairs—SALT, the opening to China, détente, the
> Middle East—is the interest of serious men, not dilettantes,
> for they think that they have a world role to play.

Brazilian foreign minister Silveira did his utmost to justify that judgment. A product of the Brazilian Foreign Service, he had served as ambassador in Germany and Argentina, and was later to head the Brazilian mission in Washington. Garrulous, clever, he was, like almost all Brazilian diplomats, in perfect command of the English language.

His style was at substantial variance from that of his Latin American colleagues, who felt obliged to accompany occasional agreement with the United States with defiant gestures to demonstrate that they were impervious to United States attempts to dominate. Silveira felt under no comparable pressure. He insisted on being heard because, alone among the nations of Latin America, Brazil was conducting a global policy. It had no need to be defiant, but it did insist on a voice. "Brazil is not Honduras," Silveira said at a meeting in September 1975. "We are becoming a country that must be counted."

Silveira saw his role in accelerating this process. When I told him at the OAS meeting in Santiago that he did not need to press so hard for status because Brazil was destined to become a significant country, he replied: "Foreign policy puts a country ahead of its time." In Silveira's view, Brazilian self-assertion was all the more important because our domestic divisions made our conduct too unpredictable:

> We will have to count on ourselves. With the election of a new President, your government will have more authority. Today it is difficult. Your friends are considered enemies. You know the Soviets; they come giving arms first. The U.S. does the opposite. We need serenity. Otherwise we would be left alone.

Serenity meant that Brazil would move at its own pace and not follow fashionable slogans. But it also implied the strategy of a great power. Brazil used its Third World ties not to weaken the United States but to achieve great-power status for itself.

> SILVEIRA: Brazil must emphasize its role as a developing country so that it is able to contribute something to the overall scheme of things; otherwise it will lose its possibilities for exercising pressure.
>
> KISSINGER: On whom do you want to exercise pressure? The United States?
>
> SILVEIRA: No. But I want Brazil to have its place in the world. I am not a dreamer.

Eager to burnish their Third World credentials, most nations of the Western Hemisphere defined independence as an avoidance of a joint position with the United States. Brazil adopted the opposite course: it used its Third World links to *insist* on a common policy with the United States. In Silveira's words: "You need a new dimension in your relations with Brazil. We can help the United States have a more constructive dialogue with other countries." When I inquired what countries he had in mind, Silveira mentioned Paraguay, Bolivia, and Uruguay. In the nineteenth century, this would have been called a sphere of influence. As of this writing, they are the core of what goes under the name of Mercosur, an incipient South American bloc under Brazilian leadership.

Silveira's concept was more sweeping than merely dividing the hemisphere into spheres of influence; he sought to participate in the United States's global role. At a crucial point in the Angola crisis when I complained about Brazil's recognition of the MPLA (the Communist-supported faction in Angola), Silveira reminded me of Brazil's national interest in all of Portugal's former possessions in Africa. It was a continuity claimed by no other former colony. Brazil felt free to consult its own interests and history because we had neither sought its advice nor informed it of our intentions:

> The United States and Brazil cannot be half-allies. The United States cannot hide certain information from Brazil. We did not know you were intervening in Angola. We would have taken this into consideration. You said nothing to me. We have special responsibilities in Angola. We understand your efforts to stop the Soviets. You may think we recognized them for other reasons—to project ourselves in the Third World. No! We did it because we have interests in that part of Africa.

Silveira's idea of a relationship with Brazil that would imply prior consultation coincided with our idea of hemispheric cooperation. What had not worked on a hemisphere-wide basis might succeed in association with the most populous and highly developed of the Latin American countries. Silveira and I therefore signed a memorandum of understanding at the end of my visit to Brazil on February 21. This provided for biannual consultations by the foreign ministers, who would be empowered, and indeed expected, to create other groups on a wide range of political, economic, and scientific subjects. This special relationship would reduce Brazilian temptations to lead a Third World or Latin American bloc in opposition to the United States. At the same time, it would oblige *us* to take into account Brazil's interests in international forums and in other key aspects of our overall foreign policy. It also had the potential to become the beginning of a new hemispheric partnership.

To be sure, Silveira, personal friend that he became, would not abandon Brazil's national interest, as he saw it, simply for the privilege of meeting with me periodically. Sooner or later, Brazil would exercise the leadership role in South America that its resources, population, and skill made appear highly probable. By the time that point was reached, I hoped that the cooperation foreseen in the memorandum of understanding would provide the institutional framework by which the two largest nations in the hemisphere would transform their bilateral cooperation into a hemisphere-wide project. The jury is still out on whether this goal—even more important at this writing—can in fact be accomplished.

The immediate reaction of the other hemispheric countries was partly negative, but largely encouraging: negative because they objected to our giving Brazil a special status; encouraging because they were, in effect, asking for the same intimacy that was being accorded Brazil. It was a pleasant problem for a United States Secretary of State to have Latin American countries seek *closer* ties, rather than voice complaints regarding United States domination. I was particularly gratified when Argentine foreign minister Vignes, who had canceled the Buenos Aires New Dialogue meeting with such anti-American gusto a year earlier, telephoned Assistant Secretary Rogers to complain that we had established a special relationship with Argentina's rival for hemispheric leadership. He then proceeded to suggest that all would be well if the United States did the same for Argentina.

In general, the request for closer institutionalized ties for other countries was easy to satisfy; it was, after all, what we had proposed a year earlier on a multilateral basis in the New Dialogue. At both of my next stops—in Bogotá and San José—I used the Brazilian precedent to stress our willingness to strengthen both bilateral and hemispheric ties. At a press conference in San José on February 24, 1976, I said in response to a question:

> The United States will not or cannot appoint any one country as the leader of Latin America. The United States is prepared to have special consultative arrangements with any

nation of the Western Hemisphere where our relationships have reached a level of complexity or intensity where such relationships are necessary. But even when we have these special consultative arrangements, they are not meant to the exclusion of hemispheric ties . . .[1]

In the United States, the chairman of the House Foreign Relations Committee, Thomas "Doc" Morgan, suggested that Brazil was using the United States as leverage for world-power status. I replied:

> Mr. Chairman, this agreement does not make Brazil a world power. Brazil has a population of 100 million, vast economic resources, a very rapid rate of economic development. Brazil is becoming a world power, and it does not need our approval to become one, and it is our obligation in the conduct of foreign policy to deal with the realities that exist.

In the end, the arrangement did not have the long-term impact we had envisioned. During the Ford Administration, the provisions of the Trade Act and the perspective of our economic agencies, eager to placate domestic interest groups, made it difficult to hold up our end of the consultative bargain. Even before I returned from my Latin American journey, countervailing duties on Brazilian shoe exports were imposed without advance warning.

These problems would surely have been overcome had Ford won the presidential election. The Carter Administration, pressing Brazil to return to elected government, gave democratization a higher priority than the consultative process, which gradually atrophied, not without regrets on the Brazilian side. A hiatus in intimacy followed that lasted nearly ten years, a period during which patterns of partnership and consultation languished.

When progress resumed, it was in a different context. Brazilian-American relations remain close; given the importance of Brazil's role in the world, they could hardly be otherwise. But there is, as of this writing, a certain wariness on the Brazilian side mitigated by the need for assistance in financial crises. On our side there is a preoccupation with domestic politics. This combination might, in time, turn into a contest between a United States–dominated NAFTA and a Brazilian-led Mercosur—a competition all the more potentially real for being vociferously denied. For both our countries and for the evolution of the Western Hemisphere, this would be a tragedy.

Among my other stops, Caracas was chosen because of Venezuela's energy resources and its gyrations between international radicalism and closer ties with the United States. Lima was included because of the need to contain Peru's odd mixture of military autocracy and Nasserite semisocialist aspirations, which tempted both Soviet and Cuban overtures. The stop in Bogotá was meant to strengthen the relationship with a country that symbolized most of Latin America's challenges: a moderate elected government undermined by guerrilla groups, a drug culture, and a national mood alternating between responsibility and panic. San José was selected as the capital of the longest-functioning democracy in Latin America, and as the country whose conciliatory style of democratic domestic politics, we hoped, would become a model for the rest of Central America.

Publicly, and not undeservedly, Venezuela was viewed as one of the leaders of the radical group within the Nonaligned Movement. In fact, Venezuela's leaders were less interested in a major Third World role than in increasing their own standing within their country's volatile and passionate domestic politics. But Venezuela's leaders understood very well that, at the end of the day, geography and the nature of their resources oblige them to seek close ties with us.

President Carlos Andrés Pérez was a charismatic figure. His bearing radiated a kind of authority akin to that of a Spanish *caudillo*. He might have railed against the Trade Act or American economic imperialism and offer to place some of Venezuela's oil revenues into a trust fund to combat American economic domination, but when I finally arrived in Caracas, Pérez treated me with great courtesy and was eager to talk about cooperation.

The reason was twofold. Even while nationalizing Venezuela's petroleum resources, Pérez sought our technical help and the participation of United States oil companies in developing and exploiting the huge reservoirs of heavy oil in Venezuela's interior and in bringing Venezuelan production to market. In addition, Pérez had a powerful political motive to maintain, behind the smoke screen of bloodcurdling Third World rhetoric, a friendly attitude toward the United States. Earlier in his political career when he was interior minister, he had countered a violent Communist Party takeover attempt without excessive regard for judicial process. Pérez harbored no illusions about Castro. As was the case with several other Latin American countries that had been pressing us to lift OAS sanctions, the fall of Indochina and Angola nudged Pérez's memory about the extent to which he was counting on the U.S. to defend Venezuela against Cuban encroachments. Bill Rogers summed up Pérez's reactions upon returning from Caracas, where he had advanced my trip:

> The general attitude, if a generalization about Latin America is possible, was best expressed by Pérez, the President of Venezuela, when I saw him, who, as you know, has few equals as a militant Third Worlder in terms of the redistribution questions. [He] expressed his serious concern at the same time about the effects of the recession of U.S. power around the world and the consequences that might have here in Washington.

So it happened that during my visit to Caracas Pérez went along with the key element of our overall strategy by agreeing to form United States–Venezuelan commissions to deal with scientific cooperation, transfer of technology, and energy research. By their very existence, the commissions suggested that on the issues which formed their subject matter, Venezuela and the United States would rely on their bilateral relationship, and not on multilateral forums.

By his second presidency a decade later, Carlos Andrés Pérez had transformed himself into a staunch advocate of free market reforms, privatization of state enterprises, and prudent financial policies. This remarkable reincarnation—and it was mimicked by other Latin American leaders during this same period—could not have been entirely unrelated to the constructive way in which we dampened Latin America's economic radicalism in the 1970s.

In contrast, my visit to Lima was largely damage-limiting. Peru's military leadership considered itself the vanguard of a new type of Latin American revolution. Heretofore closely linked to the financial and commercial oligarchies, Peru's military authoritarians had by now cast themselves firmly in a Nasserite mode. They identified with the social and economic aspirations of Third World radicalism—acquiring Soviet military equipment, welcoming Cuban advisers, and occasionally rattling their sabers against Chile. Nevertheless, at home they were staunchly anti-Communist. The fact that Peru was a military dictatorship soured its relations with democratic Venezuela, but on the substance of the North-South disputes, its rhetoric paralleled and went beyond that of Pérez. For example, when Vietnam fell, Peru and Mexico were the only countries to express gratification over the triumph of what its President Velasco described as the forces arrayed against imperialism.

United States–Peruvian relations were further burdened by a number of expropriations of American companies—particularly Marcona Mining and the International Petroleum Company—and by the seizure of American fishing boats in disputes over the extent of territorial seas. Rather than fight the principle, we focused on assuring prompt and fair compensation, thereby preventing demagogic hemispheric battles over the right to nationalize.[2]

I maintained a working relationship with Peru's foreign minister, Miguel Angel de la Flor Valle (described, in his ever-present uniform, in one of our internal papers as looking like a Pat Oliphant cartoon). I was confident that middle-aged leaders who had spent their entire lives in the military would, in the end, stress the nationalist over the socialist aspects of Peruvian policies. One result was that, despite Peru's ideological posturing, it generally adopted a constructive role in hemispheric forums, except on Cuba. When some of the participants at the Tlatelolco conference wanted to insist on the original and confrontational draft, de la Flor supported the conciliatory declaration drafted by the Guyanese foreign minister and me. And at various OAS meetings, he did not push his radical agenda.

Bogotá, where I arrived on February 22, was a study in ambivalence. Colombia had a functioning democracy and a generally moderate government that was friendly toward the United States. But it was also the seat of a savage civil war made nearly ineradicable by the cooperation between the guerrillas and a drug culture that possessed larger resources than the government. All this afforded radical groups a greater influence on the conduct of internal politics than their numbers would have warranted.

The difference between Caracas and Bogotá was akin to that between Houston and Boston. The Venezuelan establishment was largely self-made, and its style was that of the raucous self-assurance of the frontier. Bogotá was more sedate; the legal part of the county was run by established families who alternated in government by time-honored procedures. But they had not been able to suppress the guerrillas, nor overcome the drug traffic.

As a result, there were few places in the Western Hemisphere that exhibited greater contradictions between their leaders' convictions and their pronouncements. Colombia's President at the time, Alfonso López Michelsen, might have passed for an English gentleman, conducting himself like a member of the landed gentry, of which he was, in fact, a part. The foreign minister, Indalécio Lievano, had the manner of a thoughtful, slightly pedantic professor. Both expressed—and I am sure this reflected their real conviction—a hope for the kind of Western Hemisphere structure that I had been advancing ever since the beginning of Nixon's second term. Lievano urged the creation of a Western Hemisphere system of trade preferences that was staunchly opposed in Washington by the combined exertions of the Treasury and State Department bureaucracies (and which, had it surmounted these hurdles, would probably have been defeated in Congress).

But the appearance of staid middle-class respectability was belied by my hosts' reluctance to permit me to spend the night in Bogotá for fear of sparking uncontrollable demonstrations. President López Michelsen invited me to his country retreat some twenty miles outside of the city, where, in a tranquil and verdant surrounding, he described his abiding concern over the long-term implications of Cuba's victory in Angola. Since most Cuban troops overseas were black, he feared that when they returned home they might become shock troops for Cuban intervention in South American regions with comparable ethnic compositions. The coastal areas of Colombia were described by López Michelsen as racially distinct from the predominantly white interior highlands and were therefore, in his view, especially vulnerable to Cuban influence.

But the next morning, at a press conference, López Michelsen showed that he was already so concerned by Castro's influence in Colombia that he would not repeat publicly what only hours before he had affirmed privately. He refused to condemn Cuban intervention in Angola. Indeed, he compared it with America's actions in Vietnam: "This is not the first time that a country of this hemisphere has intervened outside the hemisphere." *

---

* In these pages, there is little reference to Argentina, one of the most dramatic and potentially rich countries in the world. The reason is not a lack of appreciation for the importance of that very special nation—very special because culturally it often feels itself to be more European than American, while politically and economically it cannot escape being part of a region from which it has historically believed itself somewhat distinct. But during the period described here, Argentina was hors de combat for domestic reasons. Exiled former President Juan Perón returned in 1973 in a big electoral victory; he died within a year and was succeeded by his third wife, Maria Estella (Isabelle) Perón. She, in turn, was overthrown by a military coup a year later. There were three Argentine foreign ministers within eighteen months while Argentina descended into near–civil war. Civilian rule and democratic elections were restored only after Argentina's disastrous invasion of the Falkland/Malvinas Islands in 1982. Though I met the foreign ministers frequently, it was not until I left government and Argentina had emerged from the Perón/military era that I became personally acquainted with Argentina and grew to love that exciting and sophisticated nation.

## Chile, Human Rights, and the Organization of American States*

Whatever priority we might give to bilateral ties needed to be related to the parallel demands of Western Hemisphere multilateral relations. For the nations of the Western Hemisphere meet regularly as a group, either at meetings of the Organization of American States, or on special occasions to discuss problems of common concern. Unlike the regular NATO meetings, their substance was not based on the premise of a common danger. Very frequently, the United States was the focus of Latin American criticism. The different cultural backgrounds involved produced a greater tendency toward theory and rhetoric than was true of comparable Atlantic meetings.

But in the end these encounters had the character of a family gathering. Whether obstreperous or benign, our partners treated the Western Hemisphere relationship as essentially collegial. They might reject the legal concept of a hemispheric community, as they had at the Tlatelolco conference, but they acted as though we indeed shared a common destiny—a sense so strong that the weaker siblings felt free, without serious penalty, to denounce the United States, even while looking to us for security and economic progress.

In view of the increased priority we had given Latin America, I therefore looked forward to the next scheduled meeting of the Organization of American States in June 1976. As fate would have it, the meeting was planned to be held in Santiago, the capital of Chile. Our attitude at the meeting would be particularly delicate, since one of the principal items on the agenda would be a report by the Inter-American Commission on Human Rights (IACHR) criticizing Chile's human rights practices, despite the fact that many of the other Latin American countries were at the time themselves authoritarian.

Neither Ford nor I considered it desirable to run from the challenge. On the contrary, with the approach of our national election, I thought it essential to stake out a clear United States position, especially on the sensitive issue of human rights. I told the Secretary General of the OAS, Alejandro Orfila, beforehand:

---

* This section was written to explain the attitudes of the Ford Administration toward human rights and Chile from the perspective of a full twenty-five years before the arrest of General Augusto Pinochet reopened many of these issues. I have not changed the text in light of more recent events.

What I'm trying to do is to keep the pride of the American
people in our foreign policy, this summer and throughout
the fall. That's why I'm going to all these meetings and
making all these speeches. I want to assure that whoever is
President next year, we will still have a foreign policy.

I was acutely aware that Chile had become a sore point in our
domestic debate and also in some foreign countries. Salvador Allende
was increasingly being described as a democratic martyr arbitrarily
overthrown by a quasi-fascist military junta in collusion with a Cold
War–obsessed Nixon Administration. The left wing of the Democratic
Party and the protest movement of the European left did not perceive
the same degree of danger in a Communist state on the mainland
that we did at the height of the Cold War, after painful experiences
with Castro's Cuba, including the Missile Crisis, and with terrorist
guerrilla activities in many Latin American countries, especially Chile's
neighbors.

Nor were they prepared to admit that Allende was heading in that
direction. Yet all the available evidence indicated that he was determined to establish a government like Castro's and sponsor hemispheric
revolution. "Cuba in the Caribbean and a socialist Chile in the Southern Cone," Allende had announced in his 1970 campaign, "will make
the revolution in Latin America." After he had been sworn in as
President, Allende was asked by the radical French journalist Régis
Debray—an admirer and companion of Che Guevara—who was using
whom: Allende the democratic structure, or vice versa. Allende replied:
"The answer is the proletariat. If it wasn't so, I wouldn't be here." At
another point in the conversation, Allende said: "As for the bourgeois
state, at the present moment, we are seeking to overcome it. To overthrow it."[3] And in an unprecedented gesture in November 1971, Fidel
Castro spent almost a month in Chile.

After Allende's overthrow, the myth was propagated that the
United States had organized the coup or had at least made it possible
by a systematic program of "destabilization." In fact, after Allende
entered office on November 3, 1970, the covert programs seeking to
block his inauguration were terminated (see Chapter 11). For budgetary reasons, President Johnson had already phased out formal grant
aid during Eduardo Frei Montalva's presidency. But a host of other
programs continued under Allende, from loan guarantees to humanitarian projects, including assistance to Chilean universities. In total,

the Allende government received $17 million in United States humanitarian aid; $82.5 million from the IMF, in favor of which the United States voted; $42 million in military aid; and $250 million in rescheduled loans, for a total of over $350 million (or $1.2 billion in current dollars). In contrast, Congress later progressively cut off the government headed by General Augusto Pinochet from *all* United States funds.

What our opponents called destabilization was in fact an effort to help the institutions of civil democratic society survive Allende's pressures to destroy them. Covert financial support was extended to democratic parties, labor unions, and newspapers, which were being systematically throttled. Our objective at that stage was not to overthrow Allende, but to keep both a democratic opposition and democratic organizations alive for the scheduled elections in 1976 and to ensure that these elections be held.[4] The absence of a United States role in the coup was confirmed by the Senate's Church Committee (see Chapter 11) and by Pinochet himself in 1975, when he told *New York Times* columnist C. L. Sulzberger: "I can swear to you as a Christian that I never had any kind of contact with anyone from the CIA or with any ambassador, U.S. or otherwise. I wanted to be free of any obligation to anyone."[5]

In September 1973, matters came to a head, brought about not by the United States, but by the resistance of Chile's democratic institutions, which perceived Allende—who had been elected by a bare 36 percent of the votes cast—as leading his country inexorably toward a dictatorship.[6] Thousands of extralegal militia had been armed with Cuban weapons, some of them smuggled into the presidential palace labeled as artworks. Strikes were widespread. On May 15, the National Assembly of the Christian Democratic Party accused Allende of "seeking the totality of power, which meant Communist tyranny disguised as the dictatorship of the proletariat." A series of Allende's totalitarian-style decrees had been declared unconstitutional and outside the law by the Chilean Supreme Court on May 26, 1973, by the comptroller general on July 2, 1973, and by the Chamber of Deputies on August 22, 1973. The parliament went so far as to demand the inclusion of military officers in the government. And the army's intervention which followed was welcomed by Chile's democratic parties. So unquestioned a democrat as former President Frei greeted Pinochet's military coup with these words, viewing many of Allende's supporters as anything but the peaceful democrats they were later portrayed as being:

The military have saved Chile and all of us whose lives are certainly not as important as Chile's, but they are human lives, and many, and all of them are not yet safe because the armed forces continue discovering hideouts and arsenals. A civil war was being well prepared by the Marxists. And that is what the world does not know, refuses to know.[7]

And Patricio Aylwin, leader of the Christian Democratic Party until the coup, who became President of Chile as Pinochet's successor from 1990 to 1994, said in an interview on October 19, 1973:

The truth is that the action of the Armed Forces and the Police Force turned out to be nothing more than a preventive measure, anticipating an official coup d'état which the Government was planning with the assistance of an armed militia of enormous military power, which the Government had at its disposal, and with the collaboration of the no fewer than ten thousand foreigners, which there were in the country, in order to establish a Communist dictatorship.[8]

Nevertheless, within weeks of Allende's overthrow, the incompetence, corruption, and violation of democratic rights characteristic of his regime—which had been widely acknowledged while he was alive—were virtually expunged from the public discourse. Allende was invariably referred to as a "democratically elected leader," with nary a mention of his totalitarian-style assault on Chile's institutional order or his radical threat to hemispheric security.

The question was never asked about what had triggered the Chilean army, previously noted for its meticulous observance of constitutional norms, into a coup. Nor was there any acknowledgment that the brutalities in Chile were those of a continuing civil war, launched in the first instance by the radical left, as Frei's statement makes clear. No doubt Pinochet and his associates exceeded acceptable moral norms once they were in power. Such measures as the "disappearance" of suspected opponents cannot be justified by the terrorism practiced by the junta's opponents. But an honest assessment of the forces at work is necessary if the events in question are ever to be properly understood.

In the United States, the media both reflected and shaped the congressional mood. Senators Edward Kennedy and Frank Church and

Representatives Donald Fraser and Michael Harrington were increasingly hostile to the military junta and its actions. When it became apparent that the previous democratic system would not immediately be restored, Chile's political parties joined the chorus. By the time I was preparing to go to the OAS meeting, Congress was in the process of cutting Chile off from United States aid, even from programs that had been provided to Allende.

Given this institutionalized amnesia, I will attempt to describe how the situation appeared to those at the helm in the critical period, which, it must be remembered, occurred at the height of the Cold War and while we were dealing with Watergate, a presidential transition, the Middle East War, and the Cuban challenge.

At the time, the so-called Southern Cone of South America was under violent attack from radical, antidemocratic, and antimarket forces. In Argentina, the collapse of democracy ultimately ran full circle and brought back Juan Perón after twenty years of exile, with his history of hostility toward the United States and market economies. He was being challenged by even more radical forces dedicated to violence who, with assassinations and kidnappings, were seeking to drive Argentina to ungovernability as a prelude to their takeover. Similar conditions existed in Uruguay. Peru, of course, was already dominated by leftist, authoritarian, antimarket military leaders, as described earlier.

Of all the leaders of the region, we considered Allende the most inimical to our interests. He was vocally pro-Castro and opposed to the United States. His internal policies were a threat to Chilean democratic liberties and human rights—as the Chilean congress and other democratic institutions had certified for well over a year. Though we had had no hand in the military coup, we thought it saved Chile from totalitarianism and the Southern Cone from collapse into radicalism. We did not approve of Pinochet's methods, and I warned Chile's foreign minister, Ismael Huerta, within weeks of the coup that, while we wanted his government to succeed, I would feel free to call its attention to actions that might weaken its international acceptability. I told Huerta that "we would take the liberty from time to time to make our views known." We used our influence to bring about the safe passage of well over a thousand individuals who had sought asylum in various embassies. And we arranged for the trade of Chile's Communist leader for a Soviet dissident into our custody.

There was, however, an important difference between our approach to the Pinochet government and that of the congressional and media critics. They were determined to bring Pinochet down; we sought to moderate and democratize his conduct. We were prepared to press the junta to maintain Chile's democratic institutions and to improve its human rights performance, but we did so from the position of recognizing that the forces of radical upheaval in South America posed a greater threat. All subsequent administrations—even those more vocal on human rights than ours—stayed within this matrix until Pinochet relinquished power after a plebiscite in 1989.

We were also highly conscious of the double standard that was being applied to post-coup Chile. No radical anti-American revolution suffered the vituperation launched against the clumsy authoritarians in Santiago. The European left's venomous hatred of Pinochet was not matched by any comparable condemnation of Castro, or of the truly brutal regime in Vietnam. Sweden's socialist government cut off aid to Chile within forty-eight hours of the coup, before any human rights violations were apparent, but it had shown no such fastidiousness vis-à-vis the repressive leaders in Hanoi, whom, in fact, Sweden had been supporting politically and economically for nearly a decade. Why were we being urged to moderate left-wing autocrats by showering them with economic aid while the remedy for Chile's right-wing abuses was to be total ostracism?

Whatever our view as to the hypocrisy of some of Chile's critics, we did make the fostering of democratic institutions a significant element in our Latin American policy. Cold War reality impelled us to maintain a constructive relationship with authoritarian regimes of South America, but we exercised our influence to advance the cause of democratic institutions so long as we could do so without damaging fundamental United States interests or unleashing the radical violent left. We did so through engagement with regimes compatible with or supportive of our national security interests, rather than through confrontation, as we were being urged.

The debate over whether engagement or pressure is the better method has become a sterile controversy. In fact, there is no clear-cut dividing line; ideally both methods should come into play together. Progress is most likely whenever Congress and the executive branch cooperate in playing the roles for which they are best suited. Congress is the appropriate vehicle for demonstrating America's concern; the executive branch is then able to adapt the threat of legislative pressure to what is compatible with our national security at any one moment (allowing for the fact that some kinds of human rights violations, such as genocide, cannot become part of a tactical calculation).

Such a division of roles requires a balanced coordination between Congress and the executive branch. That degree of mutual confidence did not exist with respect to Chile (or human rights in general) in the mid-1970s. Human rights advocates in Congress accused the administration of moving on human rights only in response to pressure. We, in turn, believed that Congress was reflecting single-issue ideological and political agendas, pushed to a point that the administration considered inimical to broader United States strategic or geopolitical interests, or oblivious to them. There was a measure of merit in both views. True, I felt obliged to translate abstract democratic ideas into the concrete objectives of diplomacy; I was, after all, Secretary of State, obliged in that capacity to put any particular American interest into the broader context of an overall strategy. But I was also convinced that the concept of human dignity was the ultimate cement of our relationships within the Western Hemisphere and with Europe. This is why I maintained respectful relations throughout with Senator Kennedy and Representative Fraser, the leading congressional proponents of sanctions policy.

My trip to the OAS meetings in Santiago represented a balance between these considerations. Earlier, an Inter-American Commission on Human Rights team had been denied permission to visit Chile. Its report to the Santiago meeting was highly critical of Chile's human rights record, though it dealt with traditional violations and not charges of genocide of later vintage. And it gave Chile credit for some improvement in its human rights record. Before my departure, I had told the Chilean ambassador that the United States would support a full discussion of the report at Santiago and that I would be expressing traditional American views on the subject. We also urged progress toward human rights in Chile prior to my arrival.

The Chilean government responded by announcing that three hundred political prisoners would be freed. The first forty-nine were released in May on the eve of the arrival of Treasury Secretary Bill Simon for two days of economic talks with Chilean officials. Another forty-nine were released before he left.

I chose the occasion of a stopover in Santo Domingo, the capital of the Dominican Republic, to leave no doubt about our priorities. At a lunch offered me by President Joaquín Balaguer on June 6, I stressed the importance we would attach to the human rights issue in Santiago:

> The origins of our hemispheric traditions and the values of our civilization tell us . . . that material progress is not sufficient for the human personality. We of the Americas have a special obligation to ourselves and the world to maintain and advance international standards of justice and freedom. . . .
>
> . . . During this trip, I shall stress that the struggle for human dignity is central, both to national development and to international cooperation, and I shall propose a strengthened role for the Inter-American Human Rights Commission.[9]

Pinochet's opening speech to the OAS General Assembly on June 4, which was delivered prior to my arrival, defended Chile's human rights record. He asserted that Chile had defeated an imminent Communist coup and had begun to build a new democracy "through the creation of a new juridical institutionality." He announced that the Chilean government would soon propose a series of provisions on human rights that would make its constitution "one of the most advanced and complete documents in the world." Seeking to undercut the IACHR, Pinochet proposed that the OAS create a new unit on human rights that would have "precisely defined" scope and limited independence of action. (This proposal was later rejected by the General Assembly; we voted with the majority.)

In an effort to improve Chile's image, Pinochet invited OAS Secretary General Orfila to visit the notorious Tres Alamos detention camp, and he announced the release of another sixty-nine prisoners. During the General Assembly, he allowed publication of the text of the entire IACHR report criticizing Chile's human rights record. *El Mercurio*, Chile's most respected daily newspaper, printed the report, accompanied with the Chilean government's long rebuttal.

Without doubt, congressional pressure greatly added to Chile's incentive to improve its conduct on human rights. But our strategy offered the occasion and enabled us to raise the human rights issue bilaterally with the Chilean authorities as a test of good relations with the United States. On the subject of Chile, the fundamental difference between the Ford Administration and its critics was that if forced to choose, *they* would have preferred the radical Allende forces over Pinochet, whatever the long-term cost to American geopolitical or democratic interests. Indeed, many of them considered the violence of the radicals a necessary, perhaps regrettable, prerequisite to the emergence of their ideal world. The Ford Administration, on the other hand, would not pursue a policy so blatantly inimical to our national interest.

Short of seeking to overthrow Pinochet, we made it clear as to where we stood on human rights. I did so emphatically in my address at the OAS in Santiago on June 8:

> [B]asic human rights must be preserved, cherished, and defended if peace and prosperity are to be more than hollow technical achievements. For technological progress without social justice mocks humanity; national unity without freedom is sterile; nationalism without a consciousness of human community—which means a shared concern for human rights—refines instruments of oppression.

Turning to Chile, I acknowledged that progress was being made. Nevertheless:

> [T]he commission has asserted that violations continue to occur, and this is a matter of bilateral as well as international attention. In the United States, concern is widespread in the executive branch, in the press, and in the Congress, which has taken the extraordinary step of enacting specific statutory limits on U.S. military and economic aid to Chile.
>
> The condition of human rights as assessed by the OAS Human Rights Commission has impaired our relationship with Chile and will continue to do so. We wish this relationship to be close, and all friends of Chile hope that obstacles raised by conditions alleged in the report will soon be removed.

But I would have been untrue to our convictions had I failed to stress the double standard that was being practiced by many of Chile's critics:

> The cause of human dignity is not served by those who hypocritically manipulate concerns with human rights to further their political preferences, nor by those who single

out for human rights condemnation only those countries
with whose political views they disagree.[10]

Before I delivered this speech, Pinochet received me in the Spanish-
style building that housed his office. No observer would have judged
the relationship to have the intimacy alleged by those of our critics
who viewed him as an American tool. Courtly, aloof, courteous, and
to the point, Pinochet exhibited no special warmth either toward the
United States or its representative. He went through the agenda, referring only in passing to the anomaly that, although a proclaimed friend
of the United States, he was subject to far more intense American
pressures than had been Allende, who had missed no opportunity to
undermine United States interests and its position in the hemisphere.

In the end, it was obvious that Pinochet and I were struggling with
quite different objective conditions: for me, Chile's human rights
record was mortgaging our Latin American strategy and domestic
support for our overall foreign policy; Pinochet was preoccupied with
a violent brand of domestic radicalism and the threatening stance of
Peru, armed by the Soviets and with a Cuban-trained army.

Inevitably, a considerable amount of time in my dialogue with
Pinochet was devoted to human rights, which were, in fact, the principal obstacle to close United States relations with Chile. I outlined the
main points of my speech to the OAS which I would deliver the next
day. Pinochet made no comment. For the rest, I stressed that we were
"sympathetic" to Chile's goals of stability, market economics, and
resistance to Communism, and that we were not urging human rights
improvements to undermine Chile's government. But Pinochet needed
to understand that:

> [T]his [human rights] is a problem which complicates our
> relationships and the efforts of those who are friends of
> Chile. I am going to speak about human rights this after-
> noon in the General Assembly. I delayed my statement until
> I could talk to you. I wanted you to understand my position.
> We want to deal in moral persuasion, not by legal sanctions.

I acknowledged that many of Pinochet's critics attacked him for
having overthrown a government that was going Communist. Nevertheless:

> [W]e have a practical problem we have to take into account,
> without bringing about pressures incompatible with your
> dignity, and at the same time which does not lead to U.S.
> laws which will undermine our relationship. It would really
> help if you would let us know the measures you are taking
> in the human rights field.

Advocates of human rights, espousing the single-minded stance appropriate to their vocation, would have stated our objectives in more absolute terms. As Secretary of State, I felt I had the responsibility to encourage the Chilean government in the direction of greater democracy through a policy of understanding Pinochet's concerns, without unleashing the forces on which Allende had relied for his revolution.

In any event, understanding was all I was in a position to offer. Chilean concerns about internal subversion and pressures from Peru, now equipped with Soviet long-range artillery and tanks and poised on disputed borders, were real enough. Pinochet reminded me that "Russia supports their people 100 percent. We are behind you. You are the leader. But you have a punitive system for your friends." I returned to my underlying theme that any major help from us would realistically depend on progress on human rights.

On June 18, the General Assembly, with our active support, passed a resolution that urged Chile to "continue adopting measures to assure the observance of human rights" and to "give the Inter-American Commission on Human Rights the cooperation it needs to carry out its work." The resolution passed by a vote of 19–1. Jamaica was the only country voting against the resolution; Chile and Brazil abstained.

Within Chile, human rights abuses subsided, especially after Pinochet disbanded the counterterrorist intelligence agency responsible for most of them in 1978. In 1988, Pinochet turned over a functioning market economy to a democratic government in response to a narrow defeat in a plebiscite.

The visit to the OAS meeting also served the long-range strategic purpose of creating a forum for a multilateral Western Hemisphere dialogue on Western Hemisphere economic issues within the framework of the OAS. In a separate speech on June 9, I pledged that the Ford Administration would begin "now":

• "to give special attention to the economic concerns of Latin America in *every* area in which our executive branch possesses the power of discretionary decision";

- "to coordinate our positions on *all* economic issues of concern to the hemisphere prior to consideration of those issues in major international forums";
- "to consider special arrangements in the hemisphere in economic areas . . . such as the transfer and development of technology"; and
- to make "every effort to bring about the amendment of the U.S. Trade Act."[11]

I proposed a Special Session of the General Assembly of the OAS for March 1977 in order to deal with the problems of the middle-income developing countries so representative of much of Latin America. In that spirit, I told Uruguayan foreign minister Juan Carlos Blanco:

> I have no objection to giving money to the poorest countries, but we should make a distinction between assistance and relief. We have to find a way to prevent the alienation of a total bloc of middle income countries because they do not have access to outside capital. . . . It is a mistake for us to force the Latin American countries such as yours into the position where, if they are to get what they need, they must join the Third World. ·

I knew that the implementation of these proposals would unleash a bitter struggle in Washington over the issue of a special status for Latin America. But I was convinced that a newly elected President would be in a good position to insist on the concept.

At the conclusion of the OAS meeting, I reported to Ford:

> The success of this meeting reflects the distance we have come in our Latin American policy from four years ago. . . . Today, on every important Latin American issue we have expressed a forthright position which is listened to and respected by the Latins. We have played a leading role in bringing balance and respectability to consideration of human rights; practicality to the discussion of reform of the OAS; and hope and fairness to trade and development issues.

## Panama

One reason for our success in managing the hemispheric relationship in Santiago was the growing confidence that negotiations on the Panama Canal treaty were moving toward a successful conclusion. Without exception, the Latin American countries were advocating a change in conditions which they considered the last vestiges of colonialism in the hemisphere, and a revised treaty served our interest by heading off a permanent crisis with Latin America.

By the end of the Santiago meeting, the nations of Latin America understood that we were moving toward a conclusion that would embody these principles: the 1903 treaty would be abrogated; our presence in Panama would have a fixed termination date; we would cede the Zone as well as the operation of the canal to Panama and recognize its full sovereignty, but we would maintain the ultimate defense responsibility.

It was clear that the remaining issues would not prevent a successful end of the negotiations, but the problem of when and precisely how to conclude the treaty remained. Also, we had to convince the other foreign ministers that we were both sincere about concluding an agreement and obliged to be dilatory. It was an expression of their confidence that they accepted our assurance that the conclusion would have to be deferred until after our elections when a new administration might well be in office. On June 11 in Santiago, I met with Panamanian foreign minister Aquilino Boyd and told him as much:

> You have to remember that, for us to continue the formal consideration process during a campaign, is something. We have no discipline now. People don't care if they're fired. If the Democrats win, they will pursue our policy. If Ford wins, you know what we would do. The thing is to get through the next few months without it becoming an issue.

Boyd and I issued a bland joint statement expressing our desire to continue negotiations and our commitment to seeing that progress was being made. This was unanimously endorsed by the OAS General Assembly.

The reaction in the United States was not nearly so benign. During his term in office, Ford took many courageous decisions, several of them—such as support for majority rule in Africa—of no conceivable political benefit to him. None was more courageous, or potentially more damaging to him politically, than his willingness to negotiate a revised Panama Canal treaty. Barely a constituency existed in the United States on its behalf, while the opponents were passionate, well financed, and well organized.

In his first months as President, Ford was too preoccupied with the crises he had inherited to deal in detail with the Panama negotiations. But he endorsed the principle of a new fixed-term treaty and gave Ellsworth Bunker authority to pursue that objective. Bunker's character was a guarantee of good faith to all parties. He was especially helpful in calming disputes arising between the Defense and State Departments. Initially, the Defense Department preferred to face the complexities of the status quo rather than the uncertainties of a new arrangement. The State Department (before, during, and after my tenure as Secretary of State) argued that insistence on the status quo would ultimately isolate us politically within the hemisphere, disrupt our strategy toward the Third World, and in time inhibit the operation and perhaps the defense of the canal.

Bunker threaded his way with characteristic skill and imperturbability through the plethora of technical issues. The key items remaining for Ford's term concerned "duration"—the length of time the United States would continue to operate the canal and the longer period during which it would be authorized to defend it unilaterally. Gradually our internal deliberations produced a consensus that the terms should be twenty years for operation and forty years for defense —partly because, after forty years, the canal was judged to be obsolescent and would need to be replaced by a new one, on new terms, or at least upgraded substantially.

The matter came before the NSC for the first time under Ford on May 15, 1975, and I described the issues to the President as follows:

> First, whether you are willing to go along with the concept
> of separating operation from defense. The agencies all agree
> on this approach. Though not on the numbers—what is
> going to happen in forty years is so hard to predict. Two, if
> you are willing to go that route, then what is the minimum
> we can accept? Three, if you don't want a treaty now, you
> have to decide whether there are some unilateral steps we
> can take which ease the situation for Panama—steps which

give up some of the lands but do not change the relationship. It is my strong impression from the OAS sessions which have just been taking place, in which I talked to most of the Latin ministers, that we will get no help from them, but, on the contrary, they will not hesitate to contribute to our problems. On the other hand, I have been hammered by [Senator Strom] Thurmond and [Senator James] Buckley on this and am fully aware of the problems raised from that side.

Schlesinger eloquently stated the case for standing pat: "When the United States shows strength and determination, it receives respect. When it recedes from its position, it whets appetites." As a theoretical statement his point was valid, but the judgment of all those familiar with the issue (including, in the end, Schlesinger's closest associates in the Pentagon) was that the price for standing pat was too high, especially since we could protect our essential interests through the arrangements being negotiated.

The President asked for another study that would analyze the costs and benefits domestically, as well as internationally, of concluding versus delaying a treaty. The study should focus on the national interest, he said, and not on the interests of the small but vocal group of Canal Zone employees, who, in his view, had enjoyed a disproportionate amount of influence on Capitol Hill.

On July 23, Ford assembled another NSC meeting at which I presented the emerging consensus before the President. It was to accept the twenty-year limit for operations and the forty-year deadline for defense, while retaining residual defense responsibilities indefinitely. Another key decision before the President concerned tactics: to conduct the negotiations with Panama in such a way that progress would be made throughout the electoral period, but the treaty would not be concluded until afterward:

> It will not be easy to do, but we think we can. If you want to go that route, it would be a mistake to give away anything just to keep the lid on things. The instructions have to be changed. As they now stand, Bunker is required to negotiate fifty years for both operation and defense. We recommend a substantial reduction for operations to twenty-five years and defense to forty-five; then, as a fallback, to go no lower than forty years for defense and twenty years for operation. We're

not insisting on exact details. The questions are, first, do you want a treaty? And do you want the negotiations to go forward? Second, will you agree to change the instructions? Then, third, what is the minimum beyond which we should not go?

Schlesinger maintained the opposition he had displayed in the previous meeting, though less insistently. He confined himself to the argument that, once sovereignty was given up, the length of time for which we could exercise various rights would become highly vulnerable to new pressures. But Deputy Secretary of Defense Bill Clements, who as a Texan considered himself something of an expert on Latin America, dissociated from his Secretary—an almost unprecedented occurrence at an NSC meeting and an indication of the strained relations between the two men:

> If we want to maintain our relationships with South America, and they are important, we need to have a more enlightened view than that of trying to maintain our sovereignty over the Panama Canal. If we work at it, and the Army will do so, if we give them the right framework to work in, we can maintain the right relationship.

The Chairman of the Joint Chiefs of Staff, George Brown, demonstrated that top generals' rise to eminence is not unrelated to their political skills, for he managed to take a position equidistant between his two civilian superiors. Brown concurred with Schlesinger's philosophy and with Clements's practical proposals. He preferred Schlesinger's basic views, Brown averred, but since our claim to sovereignty had been abandoned by President Johnson a decade earlier, he would now support the course recommended by Bunker, Clements, and me.

On this basis, Ford approved the recommendations for the various time limits and for delaying the conclusion of the agreement until after the election. He sent Bunker off with this injunction: show good faith and act in a sophisticated way. Each attribute would be needed for a diplomacy implying both progress and foot-dragging without making either too obvious.

Before Bunker resumed negotiations, he undertook in September 1975 an "orientation" visit to Panama, traveling together with Deputy Secretary of Defense Clements, General Brown, and Assistant Secretary of State Bill Rogers. The trip's primary purpose was to arrange matters with General Torrijos. They met the general privately. It was a delicate moment, and Bill Clements chose to be candid: we would not be able to conclude the negotiations before the election, although the unresolved issues could be quickly settled afterward. Torrijos acquiesced, and assured the American delegation that Panama would cause no trouble over the delay.

General Brown made the perhaps decisive contribution when he read a statement to the press after the meeting in which he put the military on record in favor of a new treaty: "I assured General Torrijos that the Joint Chiefs and the Department of Defense were committed to working out a new treaty and that we fully support Ambassador Bunker's efforts." [12]

The last substantive talks took place in February 1976. Public opinion, both in Panama and in the United States, became the chief concern. On the occasion of my trip to Latin America that month, I urged Venezuelan President Pérez and Colombian President López Michelsen to encourage Panamanian and Latin American restraint during our electoral period. At my meeting with Central American foreign ministers on February 24, 1976, in San José at trip's end, I summed up our intentions once again:

> As long as there is no publicity, we can work. We can complete an agreement conceptually by the end of the year. There will be some drafting, but we can begin the campaign for ratification even while the drafting is going on. By January or February next year, it will become an American domestic problem and not yours. This is the schedule we are working on.

The position was not cynical. We were convinced that the leading Democratic candidates would support our basic position, no matter how they might hedge their views during the campaign season.

The hope of keeping the negotiations from turning into a political football proved to be in vain. By the fall of 1975, presidential hopefuls were staking out their positions on the Panama issue. Ronald Reagan attacked the entire concept. In December 1975, he met in Miami with former Panamanian President Arnulfo Arias, as always scheming a return to power, on the basis of joint opposition to the Canal treaty negotiations. The fact that Arias opposed the negotiations from a diametrically different position—because they did *not* immediately return the Canal—did not disturb the prevailing harmony. John Connally announced that he would fight to retain American ownership of the canal.

At nearly every campaign stop, Ford was greeted with questions about a Panama treaty, and his replies became more muscular in keeping with his audiences' expectations. In February 1976, while I was in Latin America, Reagan accused the administration of planning to "give away the canal," charging that the President was not being fully informed by the State Department and that the American people were being deceived. Reagan next called for an end to the negotiations: "[W]e bought it, we paid for it, it's ours, and we should tell Torrijos and company that we are going to keep it." [13]

The issue proved particularly intense in the Texas primary. On April 10, Ford, carried away by the prevailing mood, said that "the United States will *never* give up its defense rights to the Panama Canal and will *never* give up its operation rights as far as Panama is concerned." [14]

Since this statement was quite different from what we were actually negotiating, the White House was obliged to issue "clarifications" on April 14 and 15, which more or less reflected the actual state of play. Finally Ford went on the offensive, charging Reagan with being irresponsible in his attempt to terminate the negotiations. The President also began to talk about the canal's having a "useful economic lifetime" that coincided with the length of time during which the United States would retain undisputed control. His statement did not calm the storm, either in the United States or in Panama. Foreign Minister Boyd described Torrijos's reaction to the President's words: "He was very upset. He said, 'What do they want to give us, a piece of junk?' "

Senator Barry Goldwater eased matters when a trip to Panama turned him into a supporter of a revised treaty arrangement. Ford "accepted" the "endorsement" of this icon among conservatives with relish, but he nevertheless lost the Texas primary disastrously. Some in the Republican leadership attributed the loss to the issue of Panama, citing particularly Bunker's return to Panama in May to continue talks with the Panamanians. I was criticized for leaving Ford in an exposed position, although the criticism was less harsh than that I had received over Africa (see Chapter 32).

After Ford secured the Republican nomination by a narrow margin, the debate continued. The Democratic nominee, Jimmy Carter, unexpectedly began to stake out an ambiguously conservative position. In an address in June, he pledged to retain American control over the canal while at the same time offering continued negotiations and "sharing" of sovereignty.

He did not explain how he would accomplish this feat or how it differed from the administration's position. In his foreign policy debate with Ford, Carter reiterated that he favored continued negotiations with Panama but said he would not give up "practical control" of the canal. In his response, Ford focused on the need to retain "complete access" to the canal and a defense capability, further adding that we must "maintain our national security interests in the canal." Both Carter, who had been briefed on the negotiations, and Ford remained at the outer limits of truth by fudging the definitions of "control," "access," and "defense."[15]

After Carter was elected on November 2, the leaders of Panama pushed for some signal of the new administration's intentions, expressing the hope that the talks could resume immediately. Bunker supported the plea for informal talks during the transition. I believed that the new administration should be given the opportunity to set its own policy first. In general terms I sought to reassure Boyd, telling him that my "impression" was that Carter had a "realistic" attitude toward Panama and that there was "no incompatibility between his views and those of this administration." After clearing it with my successor, Cyrus Vance, I agreed to send the negotiators to Panama as a symbolic gesture of America's continuing commitment to the negotiation.

In February 1977, formal negotiations resumed with Sol Linowitz named as co-negotiator with Bunker. Linowitz was a distinguished lawyer and businessman who later served as Ambassador to the Organization of American States (OAS). Agreement "in principle" on the basic elements of a new treaty was announced in August. The treaty provided for transfer of the canal and the Canal Zone to Panamanian control by the year 2000. It embodied the main terms approved by Ford: twenty years for American operation and forty years for defense. A crucial separate treaty spelled out a right for the United States to defend the canal's "permanent neutrality." All these terms had in their essence been negotiated by the Ford Administration. This is not to take away from the Carter Administration's courage in taking on so controversial an issue at the very beginning of its term or the determination with which Carter brought it to a conclusion.

General Torrijos came to Washington for the September 7, 1977, initialing of the texts. The battleground moved to the Senate, where Senators Thurmond and Helms—supported by Orrin Hatch and others—sought to portray the treaty as a "giveaway" of America's vital interests.

In late 1977, Gerald Ford and I testified before the Senate Foreign Relations Committee in support of the treaty. The most difficult issue during the hearings arose over interpretations of the parallel treaty that gave the United States a continuing right to defend the canal's permanent neutrality. Following another White House meeting in mid-October, President Carter and Torrijos issued a clarifying statement to the effect that the United States would have the right to act against *any* aggression or threat directed against the canal, even against Panamanian opposition if necessary. The joint statement added that this did not mean the United States had the right to intervene in the internal affairs of Panama.

Contentious as they were, the committee hearings and floor debates were a model of conscientious legislative deliberation on a historic foreign policy issue. Panama did its part to help. On October 23, 1977, the Panamanian people voted two to one in favor of the treaties in a national plebiscite. In November, Torrijos offered to resign if the United States Senators considered him an obstacle to securing American ratification. While he was widely popular at home as a nationalist, Torrijos's questionable human rights practices were another club that opponents used against the treaties.

The Senate finally approved the two treaties on March 16 and April 18, 1978, by a vote of 68–32.[16] The tally, which included sixteen Republicans, was exactly one vote over the two thirds required for ratification. A major rearrangement of vital American interests had been negotiated by a united Republican administration, carried to completion by the succeeding Democratic administration and, in the end, ratified by the Senate on a bipartisan basis. Republican Leader Howard Baker had courageously joined the majority and, in the process, severely damaged his presidential prospects.

Painful as it was, revising the canal arrangements was the right decision. It defused an explosive issue and, as the year 2000 approached, did not prevent both sides from exploring in a much better atmosphere the possibilities of further revision that might restore some United States role in canal management.

## Conclusion

In 1958, Vice President Nixon's trip through Latin America had provoked massive hostile demonstrations, which, in Caracas, had even threatened his life. In 1969, presidential emissary Nelson Rockefeller had been kept from visiting Chile and Peru by anti–United States sentiments and had encountered demonstrations almost everywhere. By the end of the Ford Administration, my visits to key Latin American countries were warmly received—the conservative administration I represented notwithstanding—in keeping with the increasingly cooperative relationship that had developed. Long-standing grievances with Peru and Mexico had been removed; the Panama Canal issue had disappeared from the inter-American and international agendas; Cuban sanctions by the OAS had found an agreed upon solution. A special relationship had been established with Brazil, one that all other major nations of Latin America were seeking to join.

The Western Hemisphere structure that would develop a common approach to the international order had not yet fully emerged. But we contributed to an evolution from which, in the fullness of time, grew the vision of NAFTA and a Western Hemisphere free trade area.

# 25

# CUBAN INTERLUDE

Since the seizure of power by Fidel Castro in 1959, Cuban-American relations have been frozen in a pattern of hostility. But in 1975, the Ford Administration, to harmonize relations within the Western Hemisphere, undertook an effort at normalization. We offered to end the quarantine if Castro stopped the support of revolutions, reduced Cuba's military ties to the Soviet Union, and undertook specified humanitarian measures. Castro rebuffed this overture and instead sent a large expeditionary force numbering over 40,000 at its height to Angola to help install and then to sustain a Communist-dominated government.

For almost sixty years after its independence, Cuba experienced indifference from the United States—some of it benevolent, some less so. Then, after Castro appeared on the scene, Cuba turned into a focus of nearly obsessive attention. A Caribbean island known to the American public mostly for its beaches, casinos, and a corrupt tyranny was transformed within the space of a few years into a major preoccupation of American strategists, diplomats, and journalists. The advent of a Soviet ally ninety miles from America's shores was perceived as a challenge to our nation's historic leadership in the Western Hemisphere as well as to our own national security.

Castro's rule generated a flood of refugees to the United States whose growing numbers and implacable hostility to the Castro regime became a factor in our domestic politics, especially in Florida. In the rest of the Western Hemisphere, Castro's defiance of the American giant, his survival of the Bay of Pigs of 1961 (a United States–backed invasion plan to topple him) and of the Cuban Missile Crisis of 1962, and his military ties to the Soviet Union made him an object of both dread and admiration: dread because of his potential for fostering civil unrest, perhaps even revolution; admiration for his daring in pulling the eagle's feathers.

In 1962, the United States imposed a total economic embargo on Cuba that extended even to American companies based in foreign countries and to ships seeking to bunker at American ports after calling at Cuba. In 1964, the Organization of American States (OAS) —which had excluded Cuba in 1962—imposed sanctions under the Rio Treaty binding on all members of the inter-American system.

The Nixon Administration spent little time on Cuba, treating mutual hostility as a fact of life. Nixon disliked Castro intensely. He held the Cuban leader responsible for his defeat in the presidential campaign of 1960 when Nixon's inside knowledge of the then supersecret Bay of Pigs project had caused him to deny the existence of any plans to overthrow Castro, while Kennedy, though briefed on such a plan as a presidential candidate, was scoring heavily by urging an invasion of Cuba.[1] Nixon was also convinced that it had been the Cuban Missile Crisis in 1962 that had caused him to lose the gubernatorial race in California by deflecting voter attention from state issues.[2] Nevertheless, despite his intense feelings, Nixon initiated no significant anti-Castro measures or diplomacy once he took office.

In September 1970, we suddenly became aware that the Soviets were building a base suitable for servicing nuclear missile-carrying submarines in the Cuban port of Cienfuegos. Nixon asked me to notify the Soviets that such a deployment ran directly counter to the 1962 Khrushchev-Kennedy agreement that ended the Cuban Missile Crisis. Under its terms, the Soviet Union had agreed to withdraw its missiles from Cuba and to abstain from reintroducing them. In a press conference, I stressed that, in our view, this agreement applied as well to missiles on submarines.[3] After Nixon had ordered naval concentrations off Cuba and after several messages had been exchanged, the Soviet Union confirmed that the Khrushchev-Kennedy agreement applied to missile-carrying submarines. These the Kremlin promised would never be serviced in Cuba or call there in an operational capacity.

Following that confrontation, Cuban-American relations relapsed into the familiar torpor. A gradual decline in the Latin American perception of a Cuban threat set in, as well as a corresponding impatience with the mandatory ban on trade. The chorus of demands that the OAS ban be scrapped was growing with each year; the nations of the Western Hemisphere demanded the right to decide for themselves how to manage their relations with Cuba. In November 1974 as already noted, at a meeting of the Organization of American States in Quito, Ecuador, its members, led by Costa Rica and Mexico, were within two votes of the two thirds required to drop the mandatory sanctions.

An executive order dating back to the Kennedy Administration which imposed penalties on American subsidiaries trading with Cuba while domiciled in foreign countries was even more controversial. Canada and Argentina were threatening reprisals against the attempt to extend American jurisdiction to companies operating under their laws. Increasingly our sanctions policy was damaging relations with traditional friends. We decided to develop a coherent sanctions policy, the essence of which left each Western Hemisphere nation free to pursue its own national interest and, in the process, to redefine the American strategy toward Cuba. As I told Ford on February 25, 1975: "The danger is we will fritter it [our sanctions policy] away piece by piece under pressure."

We had begun that reexamination toward the end of the Nixon presidency in January 1974 as part of a new emphasis we intended to give to Latin America via the "New Dialogue." On January 10, I stated at a press conference:

> Our position is that our objection to Cuban policy has concerned its attempt to export its revolution to subvert existing governments in the Western Hemisphere. Our attitude would be subject to change if Cuba pursued a more restrained international course.[4]

As a signal of an openness to a dialogue, we validated the passport of the principal staffer of the Senate Foreign Relations Committee for Latin America for a visit to Cuba, where he would meet Castro.

But we had no direct contact with Castro. Cuba had no diplomats in Washington; we were unsure about the status of Cuba's diplomats at the United Nations, and we did not want Castro to make capital out of a rebuffed overture. Thus we were looking for some nonofficial, disavowable intermediary. These are rarely in short supply. High officials are deluged with self-appointed intermediaries eager to be helpful, either because they have some sort of special access or because they think that they have developed an original approach. Generally these volunteers overestimate what an outsider can contribute, and their eagerness makes it difficult to control them.

But there are rare occasions when intermediaries can be used to signal a new approach and to elicit a response—especially in seemingly intractable situations. We had taken this approach with China, relying on communications and gestures that, insignificant in themselves, might signal a desire for a serious dialogue.

In June, a possible—if implausible—intermediary did present himself. Then a freelance journalist, Frank Mankiewicz was sufficiently remote politically from the Nixon Administration that disavowing him would be easy. Actually "remote" is an egregious understatement, for Mankiewicz happened to be a special phobia of Nixon's. As spokesman for Robert Kennedy and an acerbic liberal critic, he was a representative of what Nixon dismissed as "the Kennedy crowd." I had met him when I served briefly as a consultant in the Kennedy White House, and we had remained in friendly, if cursory, social contact since. His anguished professionalism at the time of Robert Kennedy's assassination had moved me deeply.

Mankiewicz advised me that he would be interviewing Castro for a book and was prepared to pass on any message from the administration to the Cuban Premier. Mankiewicz's distance from the administration made him an ideal emissary. He could convey a message, but he could not drag us into anything irrevocable. I trusted him as a person, and he did not let me down.

Nixon was not enthusiastic about the emissary and would not have felt unfulfilled had the initiative never been undertaken, but he approved the following indirect statement, which Mankiewicz was to put forward as his own interpretation of our views: America was in principle prepared to improve relations on the basis of reciprocal measures agreed in confidential discussions; and we were willing to show our goodwill by making symbolic first moves. However, any substantive progress would depend on the strictest reciprocity on the part of Cuba.

In late August, Mankiewicz returned from Cuba and brought me a box of cigars allegedly as a gift from Castro (which had little impact on me since I am a nonsmoker). He also conveyed a cryptic oral message that Castro was ready to explore a relaxation of tensions. The message contained no substance and no specific response to our overture. Larry Eagleburger received the message and agreed with Mankiewicz that he would serve as the contact point if either side wished to go further.

For months, nothing more happened. The new Ford Administration was preoccupied with the transition and the plethora of domestic and international crises which it had inherited. Castro was biding his time.

I briefed Ford about our initiative on August 15, less than a week after he had taken the oath of office. Unenthusiastic because of the impact on domestic politics prior to congressional elections, the new President asked for a definition of our objectives. I listed release of prisoners, open emigration, the settlement of some claims, Cuban nonintervention in the Western Hemisphere, reduction of Soviet military presence. Ford indicated that free emigration would do most to defuse domestic opposition.

On September 13, 1974, Ford returned to the subject of Cuba:

> FORD: Speaking of Rogers and Cuba, where are we?
>
> KISSINGER: I planned to talk to you soon. There are two aspects: bilateral and in the OAS. State is preparing a paper with these guidelines: we are being moved into relations with Cuba, but it should not appear to the American people as if it is being forced on us. So I would hold tough in the OAS, using the Brazilians. But we should start with low-level talks with the Cubans to see what we can get for it. If we don't, we may be driven by majority votes from one position to another.
>
> FORD: Let me look at the paper. What price would we want?
>
> KISSINGER: Some promise against subversion. Some principle on expropriation of assets; some foreign policy moves.
>
> FORD: What would be the Soviet attitude?
>
> KISSINGER: It is costing them a lot. We have little to gain from Cuba. There is nothing Castro can do for us. A little embarrassment in Third World meetings. We should move slowly.

In late September, Senators Javits and Pell visited Cuba and had a meeting with Castro which they interpreted as conciliatory, as they had been disposed to find before they left home. When Senator Barry Goldwater wrote the President asking what the visit meant, Ford replied on November 15:

> With regard to this Administration's attitude toward Cuba, as you know I have stated on several occasions, including my recent press conference on October 21 in Tubac [Arizona], that our policy toward Cuba is based in part on the sanctions voted by the Organization of American States. I have also said that as Cuba changes its policy toward us and our Latin American partners, we would, of course, consider exercising the option, depending on what the changes are, to change our own policy. We have, however, seen no evidence of a significant change in Cuba's policies or attitude toward us.

In January 1975, Ramón Sánchez-Parodi, a senior official of the Cuban Communist Party, approached Mankiewicz and asked him to arrange a meeting with some senior American diplomat. I designated Eagleburger. The meeting took place at La Guardia Airport on January 11 in a crowded cafeteria. Eagleburger would have preferred a quieter airport restaurant, but the wait for a table proved too long. Paradoxically, public places often prove the most secure, especially when they are at improbable locations. Mankiewicz, whose conduct throughout and since these episodes was impeccable, introduced the participants in the dialogue, who, on the Cuban side, were Sánchez-Parodi and Nestor García, first secretary of Cuba's U.N. Mission. Eagleburger gave the Cubans written "talking points," which means that they do not quite rise to the status of a formal note but are put in writing to achieve precision. These put forward a conceptual approach to American-Cuban relations and a method for improving them:

> The ideological differences between us are wide. But the fact that such talks will not bridge the ideological differences does not mean that they cannot be useful in addressing concrete issues which it is in the interest of both countries to resolve.[5]

We proposed that this first meeting identify issues which might be discussed and the sequence in which we might best deal with them.

But the Cuban delegation, it became obvious, had gone to school with Hanoi. Sánchez-Parodi and García had come "to listen and report to their authorities in Havana," they said. They had no specific issues to put on the table except one: they conveyed their "personal" opinion that Castro would not authorize negotiations unless the United States first lifted the embargo. Such a move would create "favorable" conditions for the solution of other issues which they would be graciously prepared to list in exploratory conversations but not to negotiate about. The formula of personal opinion was probably used to enable Castro to deny even the slim menu being offered.

To us, it sounded like a replay of the negotiations with Hanoi. Castro was demanding a major unilateral American concession as an entrance price for further negotiations: we were being asked to give up our most comprehensive weapon in order to "facilitate" unspecified negotiations on other undefined issues. What incentive there would remain for Castro to alter his policies after gaining such one-sided concessions was not explained.

Eagleburger rejected the Cuban proposal out of hand. Progress could only be made on the basis of reciprocal steps; lifting of the embargo would occur at the end of the process, not at the beginning, though a step-by-step approach was possible. The two parties finally settled on the standard formula of a diplomatic stalemate: when they had something more to say to each other, they would be in touch.

A month later, in mid-February 1975, we undertook a technical measure to facilitate the dialogue with Cuba: permission for diplomats at the Cuban U.N. Mission in New York to travel a distance of 250 miles instead of the twenty-five-mile radius to which they had been confined heretofore. It was to enable a Cuban diplomat to come to Washington to pursue the dialogue. As it happened, it was used for that purpose only once, after which the dialogue collapsed. Ford approved the gesture unenthusiastically: "The people [in Congress] who welcome it won't help us, and the ones who help us, it will hurt."

While waiting for some Cuban response, Ford and I made one of the symbolic gestures we had foreshadowed to the Cubans. Each of us put forward America's openness to a dialogue with Cuba using a "good cop/bad cop" approach. As the "bad cop," Ford indicated a grudging willingness to take another look at our Cuban policy at a press conference on February 26, 1975:

> Very frequently in my daily meetings with Secretary of State
> Kissinger we discuss Latin American policy, including our
> policy toward Cuba. The policy today is the same as it has

been, which is that if Cuba will reevaluate and give us some indication of a change of its policy toward the United States, then we certainly would take another look.

But thus far there's no sign of Mr. Castro's change of heart, and so we think it's in our best interest to continue the policies that are in effect at the present time.[6]

As the "good cop," I restated Ford's comments in a speech in Houston on March 1 with a somewhat more positive spin. As part of this omnibus presentation, I put forward the administration's thinking on Cuba. It was a restatement of both our willingness to explore a step-by-step approach and our insistence on reciprocity:

We see no virtue in perpetual antagonism between the United States and Cuba. Our concerns relate above all to Cuba's external policies and military relationships with countries outside the hemisphere. We have taken some symbolic steps to indicate that we are prepared to move in a new direction if Cuba will. Fundamental change cannot come, however, unless Cuba demonstrates a readiness to assume the mutuality of obligation and regard upon which a new relationship must be founded.[7]

In Congress, calls for change in the American sanctions policy were gaining momentum. In an interview with Mexican television, Senator Edward Kennedy on February 9 stressed that the trade embargo had been a mistake and called for the United States to normalize relations with Cuba. Senator John Sparkman, chairman of the Foreign Relations Committee, branded American efforts to isolate Cuba as a "failure" and urged us to examine a change in the policy.[8] On March 4, Kennedy introduced legislation aimed at removing the prohibitions against trade with and travel to Cuba and at ending punitive measures against other countries that dealt with Cuba. A senior Republican joined a senior Democrat on the Foreign Relations Committee when Senators Jacob Javits and Claiborne Pell introduced a resolution urging President Ford to improve relations with Cuba. And outside Congress, baseball commissioner Bowie Kuhn was promoting "baseball diplomacy" by pressing with considerable publicity for a visit of a major league team to Cuba. In the absence of any reciprocity by Castro, we rejected Kuhn's proposal as premature.

In May 1975, Castro responded to these various overtures by taking another page from Hanoi's playbook. Faced with responding either to the administration or to Congress, he undertook the reciprocal step we had suggested but in a way that gave the credit to Cuba's friends in Congress. Senator George McGovern and television personality Barbara Walters were invited to Cuba, where they were informed that Cuba was returning $2 million of a ransom paid to three hijackers of a Southern Airways plane that had been diverted to Havana. This gesture also provided Castro with an opportunity to repeat on American television his demand for lifting of the embargo.

Castro must have felt the wind at his back because all these moves coincided with the by now unavoidable lifting of the unpopular OAS sanctions. The next meeting of the Organization of American States was scheduled for Washington in May, and the lifting of sanctions in the American capital would undoubtedly have been touted as a major victory by Castro. We maneuvered to prevent that this decision be taken in Washington.

As described in Chapter 23, the OAS called a special meeting for San José, Costa Rica, in July to review the Rio Treaty. That meeting, in a two-step process, recommended by a two-thirds vote that henceforth OAS sanctions could be lifted by a majority vote. After that, each state was free to consult its own interests in deciding whether to continue sanctions on its own—thus ratifying what was taking place in any event. America's own sanctions remained in place.

## The Dialogue

Concurrently, the direct channel with Havana sprung to life, though not without a glitch, proving once again that clandestine action is not an American specialty. It had been left that if the Cubans wanted to talk, they should call Larry Eagleburger's private number and ask for the code name, "Mr. Henderson." Larry had forewarned his wife Marlene, but she had forgotten. Several Cuban phone calls one evening asking for "Mr. Henderson" were rebuffed by the annoyed Mrs. Eagleburger as the wrong number until finally, giving up on our ability to handle secret codes, they asked for Larry by name, thereby establishing the connection.

A meeting was scheduled for July 9 at the Pierre Hotel in New York. Eagleburger and Assistant Secretary of State for Latin America

William D. Rogers attended on our side and faced the same Cuban delegation that had met in the airport cafeteria in January. I instructed our emissaries as follows:

> Behave chivalrously; do it like a big guy, not like a shyster.
> Let him know: we are moving in a new direction.

They carried out their instructions to the letter and even arranged a lunch, which Rogers described years later as follows:

> We made the appropriate diplomatic effort to establish a congenial atmosphere. The hotel, quite in the dark as to the weighty purposes of the meeting, set aside an immodest banquet room and spread before the four diplomats a luncheon which should have stirred some reservations among the Cuban team about the material advantages of Communism. But they proved to be beyond temptation.

Rogers began with a long presentation. He pointed out that we had already taken measures on our own to facilitate a dialogue, such as modifying the travel restrictions for Cuban diplomats accredited to the UN. He repeated what we had already said publicly: that we were prepared for a step-by-step easing of the embargo and other measures leading to normalization of relations by a reciprocal process; and that we would not impede the OAS decision to lift the mandatory inter-American sanctions. As to the future, we were prepared to lift the American embargo progressively in tandem with the following steps by Cuba:

1. the release of eight American nationals held in Cuban prisons;

2. exit permits for some eight hundred American citizens holding dual citizenship;

3. easing the strain on divided families by permitting family visits in each direction (we suggested one hundred a week);

4. restrictions on Cuban military relations with the Soviet Union. Had a negotiation developed on this point, we would have proposed an end to Soviet reconnaissance flights along our East Coast emanating in the Soviet Union and using Cuban bases, and for restrictions on Soviet fleet visits to Cuba;

5. Cuban restraint in promoting Puerto Rican independence;

6. nonintervention in the Western Hemisphere, specifically an end

to the transfer of Soviet weapons and training of guerrillas around the world but especially in the Western Hemisphere;

7. movement toward the settlement of American citizens' claims to property expropriated by Cuba.

We did not ask Cuba to undertake all these steps simultaneously. Rather they could be linked to a step-by-step easing of the embargo, provided only that normalization of relations between Cuba and the United States was treated as a two-way street and would occur at the end of the process, not as a precondition for it.

The response of the Cuban emissaries brought home to us that the Chinese precedent of cumulative reciprocal concessions would not be repeated with respect to Cuba. China had a strong self-interest in the normalization of relations with the United States and a strategy for it. Castro had neither. Such reciprocal steps as he was prepared to consider were not designed to lead to normalization. Rather they were a safety valve to control the tensions which Cuba's provocative conduct in the developing world would likely generate.

Thus Rogers's presentation found no favor with the Cuban interlocutors. Though personally a great deal more conciliatory than the Vietnamese, they not only rejected our step-by-step approach but declared any negotiation impossible until the American embargo was totally lifted. While describing the ongoing process as positive, they unequivocally rejected actual negotiations:

> We cannot negotiate under the blockade. We are willing to discuss issues related to easing the blockade but until the embargo is lifted, Cuba and the United States cannot deal with each other as equals and consequently cannot negotiate.

In any event, according to Sánchez-Parodi, there was little to talk about because Cuba would not accept any point on our list except possibly a few family visits. Cuba, he stressed, did not recognize the principle of dual citizenship. With respect to Cuba's military ties to the Soviet Union, Sánchez-Parodi denied any aggressive intent while insisting that Cuba would "always reserve our right to take those measures which we find convenient." And he implied that the extent of Cuba's ties to the Soviet Union depended on the magnitude of the American threat, which, given the disparity of power, was impossible to reduce decisively without Soviet help.

Sánchez-Parodi responded with similar abruptness to our proposal that Cuba pledge not to intervene in the domestic affairs of the countries of the Western Hemisphere. Cuba, he said, was quite willing to proclaim respect for the principle of nonintervention. However:

> In this context we must discuss U.S. attitudes toward other countries in the hemisphere. For example, Chile and the Dominican Republic. We must have assurances that what has happened in the past will not happen again.

In other words, the United States had to confess to guilty conduct in Chile and the Dominican Republic and pledge not to repeat it. Cuba's price for normalization of relations was to be accepted by Washington as Latin America's spokesman against "gringo" imperialist tendencies. It also meant that the American commitments against intervention contained in existing OAS documents needed to be countersigned, as it were, by Havana. Cuba's claim that the United States certify its revolutionary credentials did not sit well when Ford was briefed on the subject, especially in the context of Sánchez-Parodi's rejection of our request for Cuban restraint on Puerto Rico:

> The history and the struggles of Cuba and Puerto Rico are very closely related. The essential difference is that we won our struggle for independence and the Puerto Ricans did not. It must be recognized that we believe Puerto Rico is a distinct and independent nationality. Puerto Rico is in fact a colonial matter. This explains our attitude in the U.N. We believe that Puerto Rico has a need for independence and self-determination. . . . We do not believe that the current situation in Puerto Rico is a reflection of the will of the people of Puerto Rico.

For good measure, Sánchez-Parodi insisted that CIA activities against Cuba and the status of the American base at Guantánamo be placed on the agenda of future discussions.

The sole element of flexibility offered by Sánchez-Parodi concerned family visits and these only "in principle." An actual proposal was deferred to a future meeting. There remained in the Cuban response a vague distinction between negotiations for which the lifting of the embargo was the precondition and "discussions" which could be begun immediately. Possible loopholes aside, Sánchez-Parodi's had been a bravura performance in the classic Communist negotiating style—no concessions, innumerable attempts to turn proposals back against the proposer as an indictment of his country's behavior, constant *tu quoque* point-making.

Rogers had been authorized to offer one more round of the secret talks at the foreign minister level provided Cuba had something constructive to say in response to our various proposals. In that case, I would be prepared to meet with the Cuban foreign minister if he requested it during the U.N. General Assembly in September. When the Organ of Consultation of the OAS applied the newly approved majority vote formula for lifting sanctions, the State Department spokesman on July 30 repeated our basic approach:

> The Cubans know that there are established channels to get in touch with us. We have said publicly—the President has and the Secretary—that we are prepared to enter into serious exchanges. I repeated that today.[9]

On August 21, the State Department announced the lifting of punitive sanctions against subsidiaries of American corporations domiciled abroad. It was to be the last conciliatory gesture of the dialogue, and the timing was unfortunate. In August, a special session of the U.N. Committee on Colonialism had convened. Cuba insisted on including the issue of Puerto Rican independence on the agenda despite our warning at the Pierre Hotel meeting that we objected to Cuban initiatives on the subject. To rub salt into the wound, Castro convoked a "private" international conference on Puerto Rican independence to take place in Cuba in early September.

Owing to a bureaucratic glitch, the State Department announced the lifting of punitive sanctions against subsidiaries domiciled abroad on the very day Cuba was inciting the U.N. against us on Puerto Rico. Our U.N. ambassador, Daniel "Pat" Moynihan, whose skill in battling the Cuban onslaught matched his eloquence, was justifiably furious. What had happened was that the sanctions decision had been made at the State Department in July before the controversy over Puerto Rico broke out. It was then submitted to the White House for approval, came back routinely by the middle of August, and was announced just as routinely.

The mood in Washington is reflected in a telephone conversation I had with Moynihan on August 14 which shows that, at this point, we were far closer personally than some (including Moynihan) may remember:

MOYNIHAN: The Committee on 24 [Committee on Colonialism] is meeting now and will be for the next couple of days to consider the Cuban resolution on Puerto Rico, which is horrible.

KISSINGER: Just be brutal.

MOYNIHAN: We are not on the committee. The State Department is preparing a cable to go to the capitals. If I may say in your personal interest as well as in the interest of the United States, I think that cable should say to these countries that we would regard it as an unfriendly act.

KISSINGER: Oh, yes.

MOYNIHAN: Can I say that?

KISSINGER: Certainly.

MOYNIHAN: To which we will have to consider the consequences.

KISSINGER: Just say it would be an unfriendly act, and we will act accordingly.

MOYNIHAN: All right. I have been terrifying the IO [State Department bureau dealing with the U.N.] by asking that they get a list of the countries involved because we will probably want to bombard them.

KISSINGER: Call [Assistant Secretary William] Buffum and tell him to put it on my desk in the morning.

Moynihan was referring to one of his more original contributions: to compile a roster of countries opposing us on sensitive U.N. votes. The implication was that we would use the roster to take retaliatory action against especially recalcitrant countries. The State Department bureaucracy was strongly opposed on the ground that it would needlessly undermine our relations with developing countries. I favored it then and do so now. I ordered the list compiled, though the bureaucracy broke no speed records in implementing that directive. Whatever penalties we did impose resulted from Moynihan's pressures and, less frequently, from my own.

Ford shared the general feeling of outrage. In early September, he told Scowcroft that if Castro continued to behave this way, "Cuba might as well forget about an improvement of bilateral relations." The last vestige of conciliation disappeared when the Cuban foreign minister made no attempt to contact us when he was in New York for the U.N. session of the General Assembly in September 1975. Instead, Cuban combat troops began arriving in Angola.

On November 24, in a speech in Detroit, I warned that the United States would not accept Cuban military activities in Angola,[10] a point I repeated in even sharper language at a press conference: "The United States . . . will not accept Cuban meddling in Puerto Rico or Cuban intervention in the affairs of other countries."[11] On December 20 at a press conference, Ford put relations with Cuba into a deep freeze:

> The action of the Cuban Government in the effort that they made to get Puerto Rico free and clear from the United States and the action of the Cuban Government to involve itself in a massive military way in Angola with combat troops ends, as far as I am concerned, any efforts at all to have friendlier relations with the Government of Cuba.[12]

Two more meetings laid the aborted overture to rest. On January 12, 1976, Nestor García was invited to continue his tour of coffee shops initiated at La Guardia Airport when he was asked to meet with Bill Rogers at Washington's National Airport. Rogers put García on notice that Cuba's "dispatch of combat troops to take part in an internal conflict between Africans in Angola is a fundamental obstacle to any far-reaching effort to resolve the basic issues between us at this time." García replied that he had nothing to add to Castro's comments on Angola. Since he could not have come to Washington without instructions on the subject, it was clearly a deliberate rebuff.

In early February, the Cubans requested another meeting. Eagleburger met Nestor García on February 7 in New York. Rather than reply to our note on Angola, García picked up the request for family visits made by Rogers during the July 9, 1975, meeting at the Pierre seven months previously. The Cuban response was snide. We had proposed a hundred visits a week in both directions; Castro offered ten visits on a one-time basis and only from the United States to Cuba, not in the other direction. García's commentary regarding this offer was made all the more insolent by mimicking our own formulations over the past year:

> It [the family visits] constitutes a gesture which indicates
> that, on the part of Cuba, there is not an attitude of perma-
> nent hostility toward the United States.

Whereupon the curtain fell on meetings between Cuban and American officials for the remainder of the Ford Administration.

## Sources of Cuban Conduct

How is one to explain Castro's rejection of a serious opportunity to bring about a fundamental change in his relations with the United States? The Ford Administration had outlined a clear step-by-step route toward ultimate normalization. The liberal Congress was receptive. The conditions we put forward were heavily weighted in favor of easing the human burden on Cuban-American relations; what we asked of Cuba primarily was to cease being an outpost for revolution in the Western Hemisphere and a base for the projection of Soviet power there or elsewhere.

Castro rejected these propositions because he considered a normal relationship with the United States incompatible with his self-appointed role as leader of the revolutionary struggle. He was probably the most genuine revolutionary leader then in power. Mao was preoccupied with the Soviet threat, the obduracy of a millennial society, and his failing health. The Soviet Union was being run by its third generation of leaders. Survivors of Stalin's purges, they were no longer interested in sustained ideological crusades. By contrast, Castro, driven by ideological zeal, had come through exile and guerrilla war, overcome the Bay of Pigs, and survived the Missile Crisis sustained by his Communist faith.

Castro had emerged as a leader of the Nonaligned Movement, as the inspiration of radicals throughout Latin America (and to some in the United States as well), and as a focal point of attention even for the superpowers. For over a decade since the end of the Cuban Missile Crisis, Castro had grown increasingly quiescent. Support for radical subversion had declined markedly. We learned in Angola that this had been due to the absence of opportunity, not to the banking of the revolutionary fire. Castro's priority remained the overthrow of the existing order rather than its stabilization. He had no interest in a step-by-step approach for the privilege of trading in his international role for our embargo, which was the essence of our proposal. He did not hesitate to sacrifice improvement of relations with the United States for appeals for Puerto Rican independence and military intervention in Africa.

Castro despised the advocates of détente in the Kremlin for having sacrificed ideology to expediency, and he had begun criticizing the leaders in Beijing for abandoning ideology in favor of geopolitics. His motive was not only ideological but also strategic; if détente became real, the superpowers might sacrifice Castro on its altar. And this reasoning set limits as well to Castro's own dealings with the United States. If he permitted himself to be drawn into the kind of negotiations we proposed, he might accelerate Soviet temptations for accommodation and destroy Moscow's incentive for supporting him. He might become vulnerable to a change of course in America. And Castro would be giving up his distinctive quality and the motivating force of his life for the privilege of joining a category of bourgeois statesmen whom, deep down, he disdained.

At that point, Castro needed the United States as an enemy to justify his totalitarian grip on the country and to maintain military support from the Soviet Union. So long as he could claim that Cuba was threatened, he could insist that his island could not afford the luxuries of a more open system, politically or economically. Normalization of relations with the United States would have been difficult to reconcile with continued Communist rule.

When the opportunity to assist the Angolan Marxists presented itself in the summer of 1975, Castro did not hesitate to sacrifice his dialogue with the United States. He probably did not even think he was making a difficult choice. At the time, the majority view in Washington was that Castro had acted as a Soviet surrogate, that he was paying back the Soviets for their military and economic support. Moynihan referred to the Cubans in Angola as Moscow's "Gurkhas" (British auxiliaries from Nepal). Documents of the period prove this judgment to have been mistaken.

Originally Moscow's efforts in Angola were modeled on its conduct in the Congo fifteen years earlier—the supply of weapons and advisers to an indigenous movement—if on a larger scale. These we thought could be dealt with by the American covert program described earlier.

But starting in August 1975, it was Castro who gave the Angolan crisis a new dimension. Quite on his own initiative, he sent a few hundred instructors to Angola in May and followed them in the fall with several thousand combat troops (and by February 1976 as many as eleven thousand and still climbing), many on Soviet planes commandeered in Cuba. Once Cuban forces were in place and winning, Moscow opportunistically stepped up its own airlift and military support. It was Castro who engineered the collapse not only of his own dialogue with the United States but of the last vestiges of détente by forcing Brezhnev's hand on Angola (see next chapter).

No doubt Castro's intransigence in 1975 was given impetus by circumstance. The year that Indochina collapsed and Congress was dismantling the intelligence services was not the ideal time to wean Castro away from ideological confrontation and revolutionary opportunity. In light of America's visible divisions, why not apply the method of conciliatory statements without practical significance and negotiations demanding unilateral American renunciations? The edge could be taken off these tactics by inviting congressional leaders and prominent journalists who would provide public pressure for unilateral American concessions.

On January 15, 1976, Castro gave his version of the breakup of the talks with the United States:

> It is not that Cuba reject[s] the ideal of improving relations with the United States—we are in favor of peace, of the policy of détente, of coexistence between states with different social systems. What we do not accept are humiliating conditions—the absurd price which the United States apparently would have us pay for an improvement of relations.[13]

What defined the unbridgeable chasm was precisely that Castro considered absurd an offer the essence of which was noninterference by the United States in Cuba's domestic arrangements in return for Cuban nonintervention abroad, and that, indeed, he launched himself into Angola at the very moment the offer was being made.

# PART EIGHT

# RELATIONS WITH THE COMMUNIST WORLD

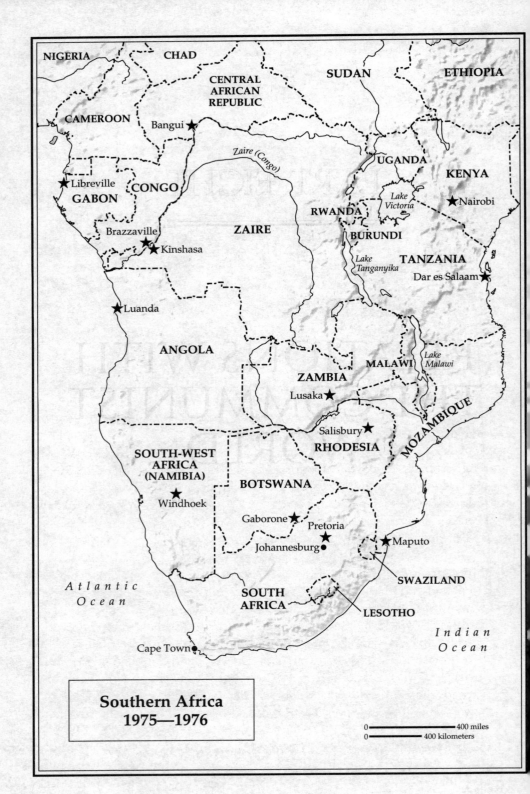

NIGERIA

CHAD

CENTRAL
AFRICAN
REPUBLIC

SUDAN

ETHIOPIA

CAMEROON

★ Bangui

★ Libreville
CONGO
GABON

*Zaire (Congo)*

UGANDA

KENYA

★ Nairobi

Brazzaville
★ Kinshasa

ZAIRE

RWANDA

*Lake Victoria*

BURUNDI

★ Luanda

ANGOLA

*Lake Tanganyika*

TANZANIA

Dar es Salaam ★

ZAMBIA

MALAWI

*Lake Malawi*

Lusaka ★

Salisbury ★

SOUTH-WEST
AFRICA
(NAMIBIA)

RHODESIA

MOZAMBIQUE

★ Windhoek

BOTSWANA

Gaborone ★

Pretoria
★

Johannesburg ●

★ Maputo

*Atlantic Ocean*

SWAZILAND

SOUTH
AFRICA

LESOTHO

Cape Town ●

*Indian Ocean*

## Southern Africa
## 1975—1976

0 ————— 400 miles

0 ————— 400 kilometers

# 26

# CIVIL WAR IN ANGOLA

## *Gathering Storm Clouds*

Only on the rarest occasions does a single state visit change American national policy. Yet President Kenneth Kaunda of Zambia managed to accomplish precisely that feat when he came to Washington on April 19, 1975. On that occasion, he convinced President Ford and me that the Soviet Union was intervening in Angola with military advisers and weapons and that we should oppose this intrusion for the sake of Angola's neighbors.

For our part, there was nothing we needed or desired less than another crisis in a distant continent heretofore largely insulated from the Cold War and one likely to lead to another domestic controversy. Indochina was collapsing that very month, Kurdish autonomy had just been destroyed, the Portuguese revolution was tilting ever further left, and Middle East diplomacy stood stalemated.

Kaunda's visit had been scheduled months earlier as a sign of respect for one of the pioneers in Africa's struggle for independence. No major initiatives were anticipated to result from it. Yet a new policy grew quite unexpectedly out of the meeting. Kaunda persuaded Ford that Soviet arms deliveries were threatening to help the Angolan Marxist MPLA (Popular Movement for the Liberation of Angola) seize power and that American assistance was essential to frustrate Soviet designs. His argument was given added force by our just having learned that radical officers of the departing Portuguese colonial power were turning over their weapons depots in Angola to the MPLA.

If foreign policy were purely a calculus of power, our task should have been relatively simple. Angola was far from Soviet territory and adjoined countries, such as Zaire, closely associated with the West. Precisely this constellation had defeated Soviet intervention in the former Belgian Congo fifteen years earlier.

But this was 1975, and the United States was no longer so pristine. Vietnam had created in many Americans' minds a reluctance to fight Communism on remote battlefields or even to permit international relations to be defined in such terms. The intelligence investigations were stigmatizing covert operations—the only means to resist a Communist-sponsored takeover of Angola. Liberals were eager to insulate Africa from the Cold War, even as the Soviet and soon Cuban buildup made this objective increasingly a dream. Conservatives about to enter the imminent primaries against Ford with their new standard-bearer, Ronald Reagan, would not let themselves be deflected from their crusade against the Ford Administration's alleged softness by joining it in a geopolitical struggle to keep the Soviet Union out of Africa. And the largely McGovernite Congress was hostile to any foreign adventures, especially when conducted by intelligence agencies.

But the challenge brought to our attention by Kaunda was real enough. A few months later, on October 16, 1975, I expressed it as follows to a Foreign Service officer stationed in Kinshasa, Zaire, who had filed a cable in the so-called dissent channel, which enables Foreign Service personnel to express objections outside regular channels. I summoned him to Washington to explain our policy in a personal conversation:

> My assessment was if the Soviet Union can interfere eight thousand miles from home in an undisputed way and control Zaire's and Zambia's access to the sea, then the Southern African countries must conclude that the U.S. has abdicated in Southern Africa. Maybe for the best of reasons in the world. They will then have two choices as to where to turn —to China or to the U.S.S.R. While I am going to China tomorrow, I don't think they are doing us any good in Africa. This tendency will then spread. It would shift Tanzania and others further left, and have a major effect in Africa. Therefore, I thought we had a major obligation perhaps not to reverse the situation for which it was too late, but at least to balance the power so that we were not faced at

independence with an undisputed claim by the Communists in Luanda [Angola].

I continue to believe this analysis was, in its essence, correct.

## The Beginning of the Involvement

Eloquent, exuding dignity and inward strength, Zambia's President, Kenneth Kaunda, epitomized the generation of African leaders who had wrested independence from colonialism. Inspired by Western anti-colonial ideals—and, in Kaunda's case, those of America's Founding Fathers—they were often treated by Western intellectuals as embodiments of liberal progressivism. Yet they were the survivors of a far more rigorous school. Resistance to colonial authority was painful and often dangerous. It is not the sort of career likely to attract men and women seeking a predictable life, even less those who treasure a contemplative one. A certain hardness and manipulativeness always go with that territory.

The pioneers of African independence had overcome a far more complex challenge than the nation-builders of Europe and the Americas. The nations of Europe had, on the whole, represented cultural, ethnic, and—above all—linguistic units, whereas the African nations were the liberated vestige of colonies carved out of the continent by European colonialists in their struggles with one another. Borders had been drawn for the convenience of colonial administrators or to register an African version of the European balance of power. To discourage unified resistance and to ensure that the language of the imperial power became the lingua franca, frontiers often deliberately cut across tribal divisions.

Nevertheless, African leaders have embarked on the overwhelming task of creating nations out of the mélange of tribes and, occasionally, languages they inherited rather than to risk the free-for-all that a redrawing of colonial borders along ethnic or linguistic lines would have generated. Survivors of that process, however elevated their rhetoric, never lost sight of the practicalities of the simultaneous struggles they had to conduct against both the colonialists and rival claimants to power within their own territories or movements.

In that context, Kaunda's position was unusually delicate. When he called on Ford on April 19, 1975, his country had been independent for over ten years (since October 24, 1964, to be precise). But colonialism still survived all around him, challenged by various struggles for independence. Zambia bordered on almost every type of European colonialism: to the east, Mozambique, under a Marxist liberation movement, FRELIMO (Front for the Liberation of Mozambique), had just won independence from Portugal; to the south, Rhodesia, formerly under British rule, was now governed by a white minority bitterly assailed by the African indigenous majority and all independent African states; Namibia was under South African control; Zaire, a Belgian legacy, was governed by the erratic and autocratic Mobutu Sese Seko; and to the west, Portuguese-ruled Angola had proclaimed independence for November and was heading toward civil war.

During his visit to Washington, Angola was Kaunda's dominant concern. The problem was not so much Marxism as the projection of Soviet military power into Africa. When the vocally Marxist FRELIMO took over Mozambique from Portugal, we had immediately recognized it and began the process of establishing diplomatic relations despite its ideological coloration. We had reacted in the same manner when the postindependence movement in formerly Portuguese Guinea-Bissau veered sharply to the left.

In Angola, however, there were three competing liberation factions struggling for dominance as Angola approached the magic date of November 11, 1975, for its independence. The FNLA (National Front for the Liberation of Angola) was strong in the north because its leader, Holden Roberto, came from the Bakongo tribe and was supported by his brother-in-law, Zaire's President Mobutu. In the south, where the Ovimbundu tribe was the most powerful, its liberation movement, UNITA (National Union for the Total Independence of Angola), was headed by Jonas Savimbi. Like many African leaders, he had accepted support from wherever it was available, which, in his case, for a long time was China and, to a lesser extent, admirers from Scandinavia, mostly from Sweden. The Marxist MPLA, led by Agostinho Neto, a medical doctor, was less tribally based and was strongest in the capital city of Luanda and the surrounding area. And since control of the capital where the foreign embassies were located was symbolically important in the race for foreign recognition, the MPLA had an edge.

The United States had no official representatives in Angola and was only episodically informed about the maneuvers of the various factions. The CIA had been supporting Holden Roberto with a stipend of $100,000 a year almost exclusively to establish a claim for information and access to the group our intelligence agencies judged to be the most likely to succeed—if only because of Roberto's family ties to Mobutu, the head of the most powerful state in the region. As Angola was heating up, it surely attested to our detachment from the fray when I asked, on the occasion of a State Department briefing on January 6, 1975, which of the contending groups was most compatible with the American national interest.

On January 10, the three Angolan factions met with Portuguese leaders in Alvor in southern Portugal. An accord was reached providing for the withdrawal of Portuguese troops by April 30, to be replaced by an integrated armed force drawn from all three factions which would also form a transitional government. The *New York Times* hailed the Alvor agreement editorially as a precedent "certain to have profound impact on developments in Rhodesia and South Africa."[1] Yet its correspondent on the ground proved closer to the Angolan reality when he quoted one observer who had seen Roberto, Neto, and Savimbi together: "I wondered to myself who among them would be alive a year from now."[2]

In the aftermath of Alvor, the CIA on January 22, 1975, asked the 40 Committee for authority to increase its support for Roberto to $300,000 a year. That same 40 Committee meeting refused to authorize support for Savimbi. Later it was charged that the modest increase in the political subsidy to Roberto triggered all subsequent escalations. This is an absurdity. We know now from Soviet documents that the Soviet plan to arm the MPLA in a major way had been decided in December 1974, two months before, and that Cubans had been training the MPLA for years.[3] Soviet weapons and equipment began to arrive through the port of Brazzaville in Congo after the pipeline had been established in early spring, and Cuba stepped up its military training of the MPLA.

While ideologically strongly opposed to militant Marxism, the Ford Administration had never sought to prevent Marxist or quasi-Marxist governments from coming to power in Africa so long as their roots were indigenous. We maintained working contacts with left-wing African countries such as Algeria and Tanzania, and, as noted, we recognized successor Marxist regimes in other Portuguese colonies. Our red line was intervention from outside the continent and domination from Moscow.

The message Kaunda was bringing us on April 19, 1975, was that, in Angola, this red line had been crossed. Kaunda claimed—as it turned out, in an excess of exuberance—that he spoke on behalf of all the Presidents of Zambia's neighbors (he mentioned specifically Julius Nyerere of Tanzania, Mobutu of Zaire, and Samora Machel of Mozambique). He argued that the incipient conflict in Angola was no longer purely indigenous. The MPLA was not simply a Marxist group like FRELIMO in Mozambique but a tool of Moscow:

> FORD: Are there substantial ideological differences in the area?
> KAUNDA: MPLA and its leader Neto follow the Moscow line.
> KISSINGER: And they are financed by Moscow?
> KAUNDA: MPLA is financed by Moscow.

For all these reasons, Kaunda, allegedly on behalf of the other Presidents, urged Ford to support Savimbi as head of the emerging Angolan state (I say "allegedly" because, as the crisis evolved, the unanimity between the four Presidents either dissolved or had been exaggerated by Kaunda to begin with):

> Our colleagues had ignored Savimbi in the past, but this time he emerged as someone who could save the situation. Mobutu said that Neto of MPLA would not accept Roberto as President of a free Angola. Holden Roberto of FLNA would not accept Neto. The only chance we had of putting someone forward to the OAU [Organization of African Unity] with the possibility of acceptance was to suggest that Neto and Roberto should each lead his party and Savimbi would be the compromise leader of all three.

Kaunda elaborated on his proposal and indicated that such a strategy would be supported as well by Samora Machel, the President of newly independent Mozambique:

> We had ignored Savimbi while he was fighting in the bush, although he had made pleas to Zambia to recognize him. He said if Zambia did not recognize him, the OAU would not recognize him either. He came out of Angola last year and we changed our minds. We concluded that if we did not

bring him into the picture, he could cause trouble. Therefore, Zambia sponsored his membership in the OAU and then we asked him to come and talk with us. All of us in UNIP [United National Independence Party] were impressed with Savimbi's sincerity and his honesty of purpose. This changed us overnight. We asked President Nyerere to see him and also Mobutu. Both were impressed. . . .

. . . Savimbi is a man of humility and good qualities. All of us in Southern Africa, including Machel, are impressed with him. This is our finding.

Finally, Kaunda also claimed the support of Colonel Ernesto Augusto de Melo Antunes, the new and moderate Portuguese foreign minister:

I first met Melo Antunes when he was minister without portfolio. When I recently met with him as the new foreign minister I asked how he looked at Savimbi. Melo Antunes said he was worried about Neto, who was supported by the Communist Party in Portugal, and because of this he could not support him. Melo Antunes further said the Portuguese could not support Neto because he had repeatedly embarrassed them. He said he would tell us he approved certain issues only to change his mind and follow the Communist line. For this reason, Melo Antunes said he would rather support Savimbi. I told Melo Antunes that we Zambians had the same problem with Neto.

I asked whether, if the OAU supported Savimbi, this would "eliminate the other two groups in the election." Kaunda, mustering as much restraint as such a flagrant demonstration of naïveté permitted, replied: "Regardless of the outcome of the elections, Savimbi would be the President." He did not vouchsafe how this maneuver would be accomplished but showed not the slightest doubt as to its feasibility.

## Angola Strategy Discussions: The African Bureau

Kaunda's presentation persuaded Ford and me that what was at stake in Angola was not the advent of a Marxist government in

Luanda but its victory by means of a substantial infusion of Soviet arms. We were receiving intelligence reports of a Soviet airlift of arms to Brazzaville, from whence they were transshipped to Luanda. Soviet seaborne deliveries were said to involve two dozen ships, and Yugoslav vessels delivered sixteen truckloads of arms to Luanda. By the time of Kaunda's visit, it was estimated that between seven thousand and ten thousand MPLA fighters were being equipped and trained by Soviets and Cubans—a large number for Africa. This changed the balance of power, especially in Luanda. Soon this was translated into MPLA attacks on the other members of the transition government. Roberto's and Savimbi's forces were expelled from the capital and its surroundings. The victor of the fight over Luanda would have a prima facie claim to international recognition.

When I became more familiar with the intricacies of African politics, I learned that Kaunda's motivation was more complex than he had presented and the unanimity of the regional Presidents much more dubious. Kaunda had been involved in the internal politics of the MPLA, having supported a splinter group under Daniel Chipenda, which had been defeated by Neto. It soon became apparent that Nyerere's support of Savimbi was less firm than Kaunda seemed to believe (Nyerere would support the MPLA in the final phase), and Machel seems never to have backed Savimbi at all.

None of this changed the basic challenge, which was the intensity of Soviet intervention on a scale not seen in Africa for fifteen years. If not countered, a whole series of fragile governments might adapt to the emerging dominant trends. Following Kaunda's visit, I therefore asked the State Department's Bureau of African Affairs to propose United States policy options in the event that the Zambian President's judgments turned out to be valid, and I requested that the CIA develop a program of assistance to Savimbi, both to be submitted to the President.

This triggered a confrontation with the governing ethos of the State Department's African bureau. A brief word about the organization of the department is needed to explain what followed.

The indispensable advisers to the Secretary of State are the assistant secretaries, especially those in charge of the various regions of the world, located on the sixth floor of the State Department. They monitor events in their region, develop ideas for American policy, represent the State Department in interagency deliberations, and draft most outgoing telegrams of instructions to ambassadors in the field. They also have the responsibility of winnowing from the flood of incoming cables what is brought to the attention of the Secretary of State, located on the seventh floor. Since even the most diligent and best-informed Secretary cannot possibly absorb all the details, the assistant secretaries and their staffs have, in fact, substantial discretionary latitude in shaping the direction of American policy.

In a large bureaucracy, the danger of being submerged in detail, of emphasizing the urgent over the important, is ever present. It is the assistant secretary implementing the guidance of the President and the Secretary of State who must ensure that American policy in his or her region is coherent, purposeful, and consistent with settled policy. When he disagrees with the Secretary of State, he has the obligation to say so explicitly and, if he is overruled, he must still see to it that national policy is implemented. If he feels this to be incompatible with his convictions, he should resign.

Because the position of assistant secretary is so important in forming policy and so decisive in implementation, I assigned the ablest professional Foreign Service officers I could find to these posts (the only outsider being William Rogers, who served as assistant secretary for inter-American affairs). There has never been a more able, dedicated, and, at the same time, independent group of assistant secretaries than Philip Habib in Asia, Walter Stoessel and then Arthur Hartman in Europe, Joseph Sisco and then Roy Atherton in the Middle East, William Büffum in international organization affairs, and Thomas Enders in economic affairs. Insistent on stating their own views forcefully if they felt I was the one in need of guidance, they were at the same time guarantors of efficient execution once a decision had been made.

The one bureau that went its own way was African affairs. Until I became Secretary, the majority of Foreign Service officers spent their entire careers in the bureau to which they had been assigned early on. Thus they tended to reflect the point of view of the regions with which they had been associated most of their professional lives as well as the conventional wisdom of academicians and other savants in their areas of responsibility. For officers dealing with Europe or Asia or the Middle East, this regional perspective was inevitably related to America's broad Cold War strategy; since each of these regions contained major powers and was affected by Soviet policies, they were obliged to consider their problems from a global outlook. But the backwaters of policy—Latin America to some extent and Africa in very large measure—did not encourage geopolitical perspectives. (I tried to overcome this parochialism by ordering a rotation of 20 percent out of each regional bureau every year. Unfortunately this did not work, since each bureau removed its least effective officers in this manner and, before a full rotation could be accomplished, the program was abandoned by my successors.)

Until well into the 1970s, a special kind of officer seemed to find the African bureau congenial. Insulated as the bureau was from the Cold War, it provided the ideal sort of environment for the promulgation of a rather inflexible version of Wilsonianism: one basing stability on economic progress, peace on democratic institutions, and international relations on multilateral diplomacy and international law. Since they were not part of the mainstream of policymaking, many officers in the African bureau evolved a kind of siege mentality in which they transmuted their isolation into a claim to moral superiority, casting themselves as the defenders of American idealism. Determined to keep the Cold War out of their region and to protect Africa from the depredations of power politics, they became passionate apostles of the view that African issues had a special character requiring a unique kind of "African" solution: not weapons but economic aid, not alignments but a mystical African skill of maneuvering among contending forces without ever blighting the effort by a relationship to historic elements of power.

I had not challenged the bureau's point of view prior to the Angola crisis because, so long as all major powers stayed aloof from Africa, it had considerable merit. But in Angola in 1975, the problem was precisely that the Cold War *was* intruding. It was all very well to speak of the desirability of African solutions. But there was no way the non-Communist majority in Angola—or in Africa as a whole—could prevail against an MPLA heavily armed by the Soviet Union and trained by Cubans. The issue therefore became whether America's interest in Angola or in Africa was sufficient to justify resistance to a forcible takeover engineered by Moscow. This in turn translated into the very question I had put to the African bureau: "Forget for a moment how important Angola itself may be. I am concerned about the impact on Nyerere and Kaunda and Mobutu when they see we have done nothing."

Ideally the assistant secretary would have come up with an options paper explaining what was needed to resist, the costs, risks, and, if that was his view, the case for staying aloof. But the officer I had chosen to head the bureau was not prepared to do more than reaffirm traditional African bureau verities without reference to the circum-

stances actually before us. Nathaniel Davis had served ably and courageously as ambassador in Chile from 1971 to 1973, including the
period of the military coup against Salvador Allende. He had had
nothing to do with it because the United States had had no direct role
in Allende's overthrow.[4] Davis had nevertheless taken a fearful battering before the Church Committee and in the media.

I had recommended Davis's appointment as assistant secretary for
Africa. I respected his character and ability, thought he had been unfairly treated, and feared for his career if he were not given a major
assignment. A career diplomat must not be hounded out of the service
for having performed honorably in a thankless and difficult post; to
countenance such a sacrifice would destroy the professional service.

With Chairman William Fulbright in the vanguard, the liberal senators on the Foreign Relations Committee took strong exception to
Davis's appointment. The Organization of African Unity made a formal protest. But Ford and I stood by Davis, letting it be known that
there was no fallback position: if Davis went down, there would be no
other appointment to assistant secretary for African affairs for the
remainder of Ford's term; an acting assistant secretary would perform
the responsibilities. After a battle lasting three months, Davis was
finally confirmed, aided in no small part by Fulbright's defeat in the
1974 election and his replacement as chairman by John Sparkman
from Alabama. Davis was sworn in on April 2, 1975, two weeks before
the Kaunda visit and just in time to be propelled into the Angola
vortex.*

Davis turned out to be willing, indeed eager, to implement conventional wisdom, which meant nonintervention. But he clearly had no
stomach for covert operations or, in the wake of his experience before
the Church Committee, for a new confrontation with Congress. By his

---

* In light of my later controversies with Davis, the reader may be interested in the passion with
which I defended him on February 22, 1975, in a telephone conversation with Meg Greenfield,
who had written a hostile editorial against him in the *Washington Post*. I asked her: "What did
Nat Davis do? . . . If you want qualifications, name me five FSOs [Foreign Service officers]
better qualified. Here is a man who was in the Peace Corps where he traveled around Africa.
He has taught at Howard University, has been a minister in a black church. Here is a man with
deep compassion for the blacks. Why should he be the victim?" Greenfield asked if I thought
he was the right choice. I told her to look over my appointments "and find me one case where
I have not killed myself to put the best man in the job. I thought so highly of him that it was
between him and [Joseph] Sisco for under secretary of political affairs." I continued that, if
Sisco had accepted a university presidency, "I would have made Davis that. I made him director
general of the Foreign Service instead. . . . I say it is McCarthyism. At least when John Service
[the Chinese expert in the McCarthy era] was crossed off, it was for views he held. He [Nat
Davis] is attacked for having been ambassador to Chile. On that basis, no ambassador feels
presently he can get another post. . . . It is our sickness expressed abroad."

own published account, Davis was dismayed at the modest covert financial support for Holden Roberto approved in January: "I had not been aware that such programs were still being approved in the wake of congressional investigations and interest in US covert activities abroad."[5] In other words, Davis had serious qualms about covert operations in principle.

Unfortunately there was no conceivable way to interject ourselves in a post-colonial civil war in Africa except by means of a covert operation. Announcing formal intervention in the Angolan civil war would have been opposed by all African states, including those seeking our help. They might implore our assistance but were not prepared to avow it for fear of legitimizing a whole series of outside interventions. Nor was the intervention to be all that covert. Eight congressional committees would have to be briefed—and were indeed briefed a total of forty times over a period of six months. Davis's opposition to a covert operation in principle meant that the issue the President wanted most to address could not be dealt with: whether the national interest obliged the United States to resist the projection of Soviet power into Southern Africa by the only practical means, which were of necessity covert.

Angola belonged to the category of covert military operations such as Guatemala, the Bay of Pigs, the war in Laos, and the Kurdish operation which differed from classical covert intelligence operations in that they were not really secret. Since all of them involved military actions of some kind, there was no way to pretend that they were not taking place. Their covert aspect was twofold: since their expenditures did not go through the normal congressional budgetary process, Congress had an opportunity to acquiesce in what it would not endorse. Second, the covert operations were not officially avowed by the American government. This enabled other governments to adopt a low-key posture as well.* The key players on all sides were, in fact, well aware what was occurring in Angola. Open avowal by the United States would only have forced other governments to react more openly— making a diplomatic solution that much harder to achieve.

An additional reason for the African bureau's foot-dragging was that any covert program for Angola had to be based in Zaire and

---

* The U-2 overflights of the Soviet Union, started in the Eisenhower Administration, are a good example. The Soviet leaders obviously knew these were taking place, but they reacted violently only after a plane was shot down and Eisenhower publicly acknowledged that these flights had taken place.

involve the assistance of its President, Mobutu, whose conduct even then was approaching the egregious. I will deal with Mobutu in Chapter 30; for present purposes, it is enough to point out that he was sustained by successive American and European administrations because they feared chaos in Zaire more than they objected to Mobutu's conduct. For nearly forty years, every American administration supported both Zaire's independence and Mobutu's rule. Presidents Kennedy, Ford, Carter, and Reagan maneuvered to maintain Zaire's territorial integrity against assaults from radical neighbors. And the Clinton Administration, which cooperated in the overthrow of Mobutu, has pursued essentially the same policy toward his Stalinist successor, Laurent Kabila, who rules in as absolute a fashion as Mobutu and whose human rights record is even more deplorable.

Zaire's longest frontier was with Angola. Because the borders separated tribes living in both countries, they participated in each other's civil wars. In 1975, Mobutu intervened in Angola's civil wars and, in 1997, Angola reciprocated by helping to bring Mobutu's rule to an end.

In 1975, any American involvement in Angola had to be based logistically in Zaire. I told my staff meeting that I preferred other dinner companions to Mobutu, but he was the "only game in town." The alternative was to acquiesce in a Soviet scheme to tilt the African equilibrium. Mobutu would be far easier to deal with than a Moscow-dominated government in Luanda.

When the State Department bureaucracy chooses not to oppose frontally a policy with which it disagrees, it deploys its masterful skills in evasion. The options paper I had requested quite simply was never produced. Instead I received homilies irrelevant to our problem. Thus, on May 7, an African bureau memo signed by Davis recommended against "any direct, over-involvement in Angola's pre-independence political struggle. . . . US influence in Angola can be most effectively extended by means of extending aid at the time of independence." But what if, on the day of independence, a civil war was raging? What if, before then, the MPLA had taken over with Soviet help? What would constitute "over-involvement"? Did the recommendation mean that the bureau saw no difference in terms of American interests between the various factions? Did his memo mean the United States should extend economic assistance to any Angolan government even if it were a Communist dictatorship put in power by a Soviet airlift and Soviet and Cuban advisers?

Davis did not address these questions; instead he went off to Africa to introduce himself as the new assistant secretary of state, returning on May 24, when he delivered the following recommendation:

> We do not believe that US interests in Angola are strong enough to warrant a high level of US involvement or a significant commitment of US resources, particularly in providing arms.

Once again, there was no reference to broader implications of Soviet arms tilting the balance in an African quarrel; it was the bureau's traditional position for purely African conflicts. And it begged the question of what these American interests were or why, in the face of the sustained Soviet arms supply to the Marxist faction, helping the non-Communist group with American arms was so objectionable.

The different perspectives at the heart of these deliberations are reflected in a lapidary exchange between Davis and me on July 16:

> DAVIS: If we take the choice of not doing something, we can be very effective with that in the African community.
>
> KISSINGER: Where? Zaire? Zambia?
>
> DAVIS: The OAU meeting is on the 28th.
>
> KISSINGER: But what specific countries will be impressed? Will Zaire be impressed by our nonparticipation?
>
> DAVIS: No. . . .
>
> KISSINGER: . . . What about Zambia?
>
> DAVIS: Yes, I think so.
>
> KISSINGER: I doubt it. What about Nyerere [of Tanzania]?
>
> DAVIS: Yes.
>
> KISSINGER: Being impressed, what conclusions do they draw?
>
> DAVIS: The Africans should begin to realize that they are responsible for their own destiny.
>
> KISSINGER: Suppose they realize that their destiny is with the Eastern Europeans and then use the Chinese to balance it off?
>
> DAVIS: They've been surprisingly successful in the past decade.

> KISSINGER: That was before the Soviets made one of
> them win.

The African bureau had much to teach me about Africa. I was not familiar with the internal relationships among key leaders. I would have benefited from a detailed analysis of risks and of why the bureau was so relaxed about the emergence of a Communist government in Angola installed by Soviet arms and Cuban trainers. Instead I received repetitions of the standard litany which did not deign to address the specific crisis we were seeking to overcome.

After delivering his memorandum of May 24, Davis again traveled to Africa for another round of introductory visits. Given the pressures in Angola and the various deadlines for action, his sojourns had the practical consequence of taking the chief of the African bureau out of Washington decision-making. With Davis avoiding the issues, the President and I tried to deal with them. On June 18, we sent two senior Foreign Service officers to Zaire to take stock of the situation on the ground. They were Sheldon Vance, a former ambassador to Zaire, and Walter Cutler, country director for Zaire (and later ambassador there). They were instructed to obtain Mobutu's recommendation and to have an "unvarnished dialogue" with him about the likely consequences. My experience with Mobutu had been that, however grotesque his public conduct, he was a sharp analyst of the requirements of his own survival.

On June 27, Vance and Cutler reported to me, accompanied by Edward Mulcahy, Davis's deputy (Davis was again on one of his introductory trips). They advised that Mobutu, not wanting a Communist-dominated government along his border, requested American assistance to defeat the MPLA. He would be willing to back up an American effort with his own forces. The following is an extract from my conversation with Vance and Mulcahy:

> KISSINGER: If we do it, we should not do it halfheartedly.
> Can we win?
> VANCE: They think it can be done.
> KISSINGER: What's your view?
> VANCE: It would take a lot of direct advice. I gathered that
> our minimum requirement is to avoid having Neto take
> over.

KISSINGER: My disposition is, if we do it at all, we should
try to win. Can the Soviets escalate?

VANCE: Not as fast as we can. We have a contiguous territory through which we can supply and they don't.

KISSINGER: Should we try to involve Kaunda?

VANCE: I don't know enough about Kaunda and Mobutu's
relations. Kaunda and Nyerere are supporting Savimbi.

MULCAHY: They urged us to support Savimbi. I think we
should let them know we're helping—but not in detail.

While Washington was dithering, Soviet arms kept arriving in Angola in increasing quantities. MPLA attacks on Roberto's forces continued and succeeded in expelling them from most of Luanda.
According to a press interview given by Cuba's deputy prime minister,
Carlos Rafael Rodríguez, on January 10, 1976, 230 Cuban combat
advisers had arrived in Angola in the late spring of the previous year.

On our side, the CIA had not been breaking any speed records in
responding to my request for a program of assistance to Kaunda and
Savimbi. Finally, the agency recommended expenditures of about $6
million for such an effort—a paltry sum compared to the Soviet undertaking.

On July 16, I brought matters to a head after Davis told me that it
had become too late to act because Neto had achieved a dominant
position. This was only three months after the African bureau and the
CIA had reported that Holden Roberto was by far the strongest among
the contenders and therefore needed little, if any, help:

> During the past year, I asked repeatedly for an analysis of
> the situation, but AF [African bureau] said that no one
> would win so we should not be involved. Then they said if
> anyone would win, Roberto would. . . .
> . . . It's hard to understand such a change of view. It is
> the same group which sabotaged my requests for answers by
> giving no answers or my requests for papers by sending me
> nonpapers. How can they now come to me with the argu-
> ment that it's over—leaving aside the question of judgment.
> You may be right or wrong, but a group of professionals
> owed it to their leadership to put flags—warnings—of dan-
> ger. If we do anything, I'll be the one in the hot seat.

I put Davis on notice that I would recommend covert assistance to the non-Communist forces in Angola and told him that I would be prepared to take a memorandum by him opposing the project to the President:

> If Angola goes Communist, it will have an effect in Angola, in Zaire, and in Zambia, etc. These countries can only conclude that the U.S. is no longer a factor in Southern Africa. We will pay for it for decades. It will affect their orientation. They will conclude that if the Soviets can put in massive aid and we cannot, it will mean the Soviets are the power factor that they have to deal with. But I cannot see how professionals could not bring to the attention of their leaders that there was a problem. It predates you, Nat, by many months, but coupled with Indochina, it is not a trivial thing which is happening in Southern Africa. . . .
>
> . . . On Angola, we will be giving the paper to the President tomorrow. I am almost certain that he'll approve the $6 million. The State view will be given to him unchanged and not summarized, and he will get your papers on top, too. He will get the State view and the individual views, too. My judgment is that he'll go ahead.

Washington in July 1975 was in a surreal mood. We were being battered by Aleksandr Solzhenitsyn and the conservatives for not being tough enough on Communism and criticized by the liberals (and the African bureau of the State Department) for being far too obsessed with Communism. Congressional harassment was guaranteed if we went ahead and might involve a replay of the Vietnam debate concluded only a few months earlier.

And yet there was no way of getting around the challenge we faced, which I described to Ford on July 17 when I recommended approval of the covert program proposed by the CIA:

> KISSINGER: I favor action. If the U.S. does nothing when the Soviet-supported group gains dominance, I think all the movements will draw the conclusion that they must accommodate to the Soviet Union and China. I think reluctantly we must do something. But you must know

> that we have massive problems within the State Depart-
> ment. They are passionately opposed and it will leak.
>
> FORD: How about Davis?
>
> KISSINGER: He will resign and take some with him.
>
> FORD: After what you and I did for him.

I handed Ford Davis's memorandum containing his objections and urged him to study it before reaching a final decision.

The CIA program made available $6 million to be spent mostly for Holden Roberto's forces and would be conducted from Zaire. My preferred strategy was to win, as I told the two emissaries on June 27. But the eight committees of the McGovernite Congress that still had to be consulted would never have approved what they would have castigated as a military approach. So we adopted—unwisely—a strategy to achieve a stalemate on the ground by arming Savimbi and Roberto and then going public with pressure on the Soviet Union to stop its arms supply. At that point, with the factions in equilibrium and the non-Communist side gaining, we would support an OAU appeal for an end to outside military support, thereby returning the issue to an African dimension. I say "unwisely" because an equilibrium is difficult to calibrate. And while I would have sought to nudge equilibrium toward victory, CIA Director William Colby used it as an excuse to confine our effort to a dimension which would minimize controversy and thereby risked defeat.

The next morning, July 18, at our regular Oval Office meeting, Ford announced his decision:

> FORD: I have decided on Angola. I think we should go.
>
> KISSINGER: You will have to certify it.
>
> FORD: I am willing to do it.
>
> KISSINGER: We'll send [Sheldon] Vance to Mobutu with
> $1 million, and take a CIA guy with him. We'll tell him
> we have $6 million, and more if needed, and ask him to
> come up with a program. It may be too late because
> Luanda is lost. Unless we can seize it back, it is pretty
> hopeless. We'll have a resignation from Davis, then I'll
> clean out the AF bureau.
>
> FORD: But if we do nothing, we will lose Southern Africa.
> I think we have an understandable position. I think we

can defend it to the public. I won't let someone in Foggy
Bottom deter me.

The President and I briefly discussed the relationship of our actions
to our détente policy. I argued that détente enabled us to be tough on
issues involving important national interests because it gave the Soviet
Union an incentive "to keep its head down" when challenged. Whatever the theory, however, the die was now cast, and we set our program
into motion.

Sheldon Vance and Walter Cutler were dispatched again to inform
Mobutu. A few other African leaders, notably Kaunda, were briefed
by CIA personnel. Selected African newspapers were given details of
the Soviet supply effort in Africa in order to build a backfire at an
OAU conference scheduled for Nairobi on July 28. Representations
were made to no avail to the leftward-tilting Portuguese government
to encourage it to instruct its personnel in Angola—especially the
military officers—to adopt a more evenhanded attitude and to halt its
distribution of arms to the MPLA. Funds for the Angolan program
were increased to $20 million.

As soon as the covert program was approved by the President,
Davis resigned. He had been in office for just a little more than three
months and had spent most of that time on introductory visits to
Africa. To avoid public controversy and because we respected Davis's
past service, we appointed him ambassador to Switzerland.

Initial reactions in Africa were encouraging. Mobutu was enthusiastic; Kaunda, the warnings of the African bureau notwithstanding,
was very positive. He described our briefing as "very reassuring" and
agreed to cooperate in support of Savimbi through Zambia. Intelligence liaison was established via his trusted adviser, Mark Chona, who
had previously been used by Kaunda as his representative on sensitive
diplomatic missions.

## The Angolan Strategy

Considering how it ended, I have often asked myself—most recently in the course of writing these pages—whether the enterprise should ever have been undertaken. We surely did not enter into
it lightly. It was highly uncharacteristic for us to spend three months
analyzing our choices. Conscious as we were of the near certainty of

having to face intense congressional opposition, we were hardly looking for pretexts to undertake African adventures.

But we simply could not bring ourselves to abdicate in the face of
so brazen a challenge, and we hoped that, if we assumed the initial
responsibility, Congress would see it the same way in the end. Not
since the Belgian Congo became independent fifteen years earlier had
there been a serious Soviet effort to tilt the political balance of Africa
by means of military deliveries and advisers. If the Soviet Union could
prevail so far from its borders in the face of such logistic difficulties
and our command of the seas, to what measures might it be tempted
in areas closer to Russian historical national interests—such as the
Middle East? What conclusions would the other nations of Africa
draw if we implemented the African bureau's recommendation, which
had evolved from not importing the Cold War to Africa to refusing to
resist Cold War adventures by the Soviet Union? Leaving the field to
Soviet military operations would doom us to irrelevance in the upheavals in Southern Africa looming on the horizon and probably in other
regions as well. The issue, in short, was not the intrinsic importance
of Angola but the implications for Soviet foreign policy and long-term
East-West relations.

Ford and I had few doubts about what was in store for us domestically. At the very moment that we were asking the CIA to organize
resistance to a Soviet takeover in Angola, our intelligence agencies
were being dismantled by a McGovernite Congress and the CIA Director was in a state of shock. The conservatives were assaulting the Ford
Administration over the Helsinki Final Act of the European Security
Conference, and the neoconservatives were tooling up criticisms on the
esoterics of SALT. Decades later, heroes of retroactive confrontation
wrote disquisitions on the Ford Administration's lack of ideological
resolve in resisting Communist expansion. They were rarely found on
the battlefields such as Angola where the confrontation was actually
occurring.

Ford and I were aware of our isolation but also of our duty to the
country as we saw it. It involved a philosophical question yet to be
answered conclusively: what is the responsibility of those charged with
conducting national policy when the imperatives of the national interest and domestic politics clash? Ford and I held the view that a country
as strong and vital as the United States and on which so much depends
has no right to abdicate what its leaders recognize as a vital national
interest to domestic politics. If the leaders fight for what is necessary,

even if they fail, they will have kept their bargain with our people, which is to help shape a better and safer future. If the leaders refuse to pursue the national interest as they perceive it, the people will have no criteria for dealing with the inevitable debacle. And they do not forgive debacles even if they arise from leaders carrying out the people's ostensible wishes.

We erred not in paying too little attention to domestic concerns but in paying too much. The actual strategy we pursued was so concerned with congressional and departmental objections that it left little margin for the unpredictable. Had Davis made himself more a part of the discussion, his prescient comment in his memorandum of disagreement which I had submitted to the President would have had a greater impact: "So far as the CIA draft Action Plan is concerned, my view—which I have expressed—is that the measures proposed are inadequate to accomplish the purposes outlined." It was not clear whether Davis meant that no military intervention could succeed (the African bureau orthodoxy) or that the means actually proposed were inadequate to achieve an otherwise attainable objective. If Davis implied that the means proposed were inadequate to the objective, he was right on the mark. Policymakers usually pay a price when they express their doubts by hedging the implementation.

The basic mistake was not the decision to prevent a Communist takeover in Angola but the manner in which we executed the policy. One problem was that Ford, Scowcroft, and I, the chief proponents of the program, were spread too thin. A few days after the Angola decision, Ford and his principal advisers left for Helsinki and other European stops. I spent most of August preoccupied with the shuttle that led to an interim agreement between Egypt and Israel. In October, I traveled to China to prepare Ford's visit there. And in November, the President and his key advisers journeyed to the Rambouillet summit and afterward to China, Indonesia, and the Philippines. And the African bureau, normally charged with holding such an operation together, was paralyzed by the resignation of its assistant secretary and the inevitable hiatus while his successor was being confirmed by the Senate.

This would have mattered less had the chain of command below the top level been clearer and more highly motivated. The President and Secretary of State do not normally supervise day-to-day operations and never the covert ones. In the case of Angola, there was, however, a wide gap in attitudes between the top level and those who actually conducted the operation. Historically, covert programs, after having been approved by the 40 Committee, had been run on a day-by-day basis by the CIA. This was appropriate so long as covert operations were traditional intelligence efforts, focused on political action. But it made no sense with respect to military operations on the scale now unfolding.

Funding from the CIA budget should not have required that the actual operations be conducted by CIA personnel. They were not trained to command military units and therefore resorted to foreign mercenaries who were not familiar with our overall design. When CIA operatives ran military operations, they often lacked a sense of tactical feasibility and were attracted to dramatic ploys rather than to a coherent long-term strategy. What was lacking was a commander on the ground with a professionally staffed headquarters collating all available information and purposefully pulling together into a coherent strategy the various indigenous Angolan forces we were supporting.

As a result, William Colby emerged by default as the de facto commander of the Angolan operation. He was the official through whom communications from and to the field went. A Working Group from all agencies was technically in charge under Colby's chairmanship. But, in practice, such groups tend to magnify inhibitions rather than pursue opportunities; since few careers have been ruined for failure to foresee an opportunity, their consensus is more likely to represent a sum of fears than a strategic direction.

Colby's interpretation of 40 Committee decisions in effect became the operational Washington guidance. In retrospect, we should have appointed someone at the White House—someone with real conviction about what we were doing—to coordinate the operation. Colby spent much, if not most, of his time defending his agency before congressional investigative committees. Given his growing aversion to covert operations, he had little predisposition to give impetus to the Angola operation and even less to add to the seemingly endless congressional exactions on him. He sought to achieve this by clearing every tactical directive on Angola with the appropriate committees, transforming congressional review from general supervision to day-to-day monitoring.

While the formal 40 Committee ruling had been to establish a balance of power in Angola as a prelude to negotiations, no one attending the 40 Committee meeting could doubt that—speaking on behalf of Ford—I favored the most liberal interpretation of that term.

I had specifically warned against repeating the experience in Indochina and stressed that there "are no rewards for losing with moderation." But Colby's instructions to the field insisted on an interpretation of equilibrium that amounted at best to stalemate and constrained any major initiatives. The best strategy would have been to spend as much of the allocated funds as early as possible in order to bring about a rapid and significant change in the situation on the ground and to intimidate Soviet escalation. But Colby prorated the funds made available by the 40 Committee over a year and doled them out on a monthly basis. In this manner, we wasted the crucial two months before Cuban forces arrived in large numbers.

All kinds of other restrictions confined operational flexibility, one being that CIA personnel were not permitted to enter Angola (except those stationed in Luanda, whose number was not increased). As a result, mercenaries were recruited in Brazil, Portugal, or African states to act as the desperately needed advisers to the Angolan forces. Wherever possible, the CIA urged Roberto and Savimbi to buy their weapons on the open market, albeit with funds we had generated, rather than have us supply them, causing me to remark that "the difference in virginity eludes me."

In the face of these restrictions, our program was very slow in evolving while the Soviet air- and sealift continued and Cuban combat troops began to arrive. In exasperation, I told my staff on September 15:

> There is something absurd about the Soviets being able to project their power at the farthest distance from the U.S.S.R., while the U.S. with enormous sea- and airpower cannot be active. It is really almost inconceivable.

This attitude not only inhibited strategic purposefulness but also kept information from the field urging a more muscular approach from reaching the White House. A case in point was the experience of John Stockwell, a CIA operative stationed in Zaire, who, violating orders, visited the Angolan battlefronts and reached the conclusion that the war was winnable. He summarized his views in a book, *In Search of Enemies*:

> We had two viable options in Angola. We could give the FNLA and UNITA enough support to win—by going in

quickly with tactical air support and advisors we could take Luanda and put the MPLA out of business before the Soviets could react. Otherwise, if we weren't willing to do that, we would further US interests by staying out of the conflict. The middle ground, feeling our way along with small amounts of aid, would only escalate the war and get the United States far out on a fragile limb.[6]

This—minus American air support—was precisely my view (though I have never met Stockwell). This approach would surely have been supported had it been submitted to the White House or the 40 Committee.

In fairness to Colby, it must be kept in mind that he was reflecting the inside-the-Beltway mood. To the White House, the Soviet move into Angola was an urgent geopolitical challenge. To Colby, the overriding reality was his almost daily testimony before hostile congressional groups. The White House wanted to change the situation on the ground in Angola as rapidly as possible and well before Angolan independence day, November 11. Colby's incentive was exactly the opposite. Since he was obliged to brief eight congressional committees on every escalation, he thought it prudent—and perhaps even protective of the operation—to keep every new step as small and as unobtrusive as possible. Even with all these restrictions, we came heartbreakingly close to success.

As independence day approached, the CIA estimated that UNITA and the FNLA controlled two thirds of the Angolan population (out of 6 million). A CIA report on November 5 to the 40 Committee shows that success was within reach:

As November 11, 1975, approaches, we can report a marked improvement in the net military balance in Angola in favor of the FNLA and UNITA. Despite a heavy commitment of Soviet weapons, armor, trainers, battlefield advisors and more recently Cuban combat troops, the FNLA has kept up the pressure on Luanda, and the UNITA and FNLA have captured four provincial capitals, including the key ports of Lobito and Benguela.

The weapons from our program have been a key factor —as has the participation of small combat units of the Zairois and later the South African army. The MPLA holds the capital but only six of 15 provincial centers. The MPLA has been denied a quick victory and the FNLA and UNITA have maintained their claims to participate in an Angolan government to succeed the Portuguese regime. The immediate aim of the United States covert action program has been achieved.

## The Diplomatic Framework

In early November, with Roberto's forces advancing on Luanda from the north and Savimbi's forces gaining ground in the south, the time for a political move had arrived to return the conflict to African dimensions. At this point, five developments prevented the culmination of our strategy: 1) a massive step-up in the Soviet airlift; 2) the commitment of Cuban forces to actual combat; 3) the appearance of South African forces in Angola; 4) the leak of the details of the covert operation to the media, transforming Angola from a covert operation into a political issue; and 5) the resulting congressional vote cutting off any further funds for Angola.

On November 18, the CIA reported that thirteen An-22s, a heavy-cargo plane, and seven An-12 medium-cargo planes had delivered equipment via Brazzaville or directly to Luanda since October 31. The Soviet Union was estimated to have delivered two hundred armored vehicles, including up to fifty tanks, air defense weapons, rocket launchers, heavy artillery, including 122mm field guns, and over twenty thousand rifles of various kinds, dwarfing the American supply effort, which consisted mostly of light weapons. Simultaneously, some eight hundred Cuban combat troops were being airlifted into Angola.

The scale of the Soviet effort was unexpected, and the intervention of Cuban combat forces came as a total surprise. The Soviet Union never having intervened massively so far from its borders and historic interests, we interpreted its effort at first as a harassing move rather than a strategic decision. We therefore judged that Moscow would recoil once the United States asserted an important national interest by introducing arms and trained personnel. Even were the Soviets to persist, our logistic advantage should enable us to prevail—as both Ambassador Vance and I emphasized in the conversation quoted previously.

These judgments proved accurate enough in the initial phase of our intervention. Had we moved more rapidly, a decisive victory would have been within reach. But preoccupied with our domestic rifts and preconceptions, our leisurely deployment was overtaken by an escalation nobody had foreseen: the arrival of well-trained Cuban combat troops with equipment superior to anything possessed by the essentially guerrilla armies that we were backing.

That the Soviet Union should have staked so much in an area, on the face of it, so unpromising as Angola had not been predicted by any of our intelligence agencies—nor, in fairness, could it have been, because it made no strategic sense. A United States less riven internally could have overcome the challenge—as we nearly did even after the arrival of the Cubans—had Congress not stopped us.

In his memoirs, Soviet Ambassador Anatoly Dobrynin suggests that Brezhnev was propelled into Africa by ideologues in the Politburo who placed support of liberation movements above détente.[7] Georgii Arbatov ascribes it to temptation and opportunism.[8] These important factors were magnified by the weakening of American-Soviet relations. The collapse of the trade bill, the Jackson and Stevenson Amendments, the growing stalemate over arms control issues assumed to have been settled at Vladivostok, and the cacophony over the Final Act of the European Security Conference all contributed to the erosion of Soviet restraint. Similarly, our Middle East diplomacy, gearing up for another Egyptian-Israeli interim agreement, was surely unwelcome in Moscow and created the temptation to outmaneuver us in at least one geographic region—even one as unlikely as Southern Africa.

The Soviet phobia about China was probably another contributing factor: the ideological faction of the Politburo was concerned about growing Chinese influence in African liberation movements and thought it could not pass up an opportunity to reduce it.[9] And Angola was also a potential occasion to bring home to the Chinese leaders the limits of American capacities and resolution, thus knocking the props out from under our triangular policy.

Finally, there was the wild card represented by Fidel Castro. At the time, we thought he was operating as a Soviet surrogate. We could not imagine that he would act so provocatively so far from home unless he was pressured by Moscow to repay the Soviet Union for its military and economic support. Evidence now available suggests that the opposite was the case. In 1975, Castro was on an ideological high. He seems to have interpreted the collapse of Indochina as a demonstration of a perhaps fatal weakening of American authority and as an opportunity to establish himself as the ideological leader of the wave of the future. Filled with hubris, Castro rebuffed American efforts to explore the normalization of relations and sent an expeditionary corps to Angola initially largely on his own. Georgi Korniyenko, then Soviet deputy foreign minister, later recalled in an interview:

> I read a cable from our ambassador in Conakry [Guinea] which said, among many other things, that the Cuban ambassador had told him that the next day some planes with Cuban troops will land in Conakry for refueling on the way to Angola. I asked Gromyko, do you know anything? He called [KGB chief Yuri] Andropov, he called [Soviet Defense Minister] Grechko. Nobody knew anything. All of them were against it and reported it immediately to the Politburo and suggested that we stop Castro. It took some hours to write the report, to get the decision, and to send the message to Castro. By this time the planes were in the air. You could rightly ask: How could it be—Soviet planes, stationed on Cuba, but it was Soviet planes and we had quite a few military people there. . . . I checked. Well, technically, our people were involved, our planes were there for Cuban use, our advisers were involved, but they were completely convinced that a political decision had been taken [in Moscow].[10]

A similar version was told to Secretary of State Alexander Haig in the fall of 1981 at a clandestine meeting in Mexico City with Cuban official Carlos Rafael Rodríguez. Rodríguez used the occasion to deny that Moscow had been pulling the strings; Castro, not Brezhnev, had been the driving force behind sending military forces to revolutionary leaders in Africa.[11]

Even at this relatively late stage, the Cuban intervention could have been overcome—especially in its early phase—had we pursued the Angola program with the energy and coherence that the stakes warranted and had Congress not jettisoned the enterprise when a political solution was on the horizon.

By the middle of November, it was clear that the balance of forces

would soon shift against Roberto and Savimbi. We therefore undertook four countermeasures: (1) on November 14, the CIA called for,
and the Working Group approved, a request for additional funds to
compensate for the Communist buildup; (2) we challenged Soviet actions in Angola both diplomatically and publicly; (3) we began a
campaign to induce the OAU to refuse to recognize the MPLA and to
call for a withdrawal of all foreign forces; (4) we began discussions
with France to enlist its help in French-speaking African countries
diplomatically and in reversing the tide of battle.

We initiated the diplomacy toward Moscow on November 20. The
two superpowers had been maneuvering against each other by proxy
for three months without either side raising the subject officially. Ford
had not mentioned Angola to Brezhnev when they met in Helsinki in
July because he had just approved the covert program, and we wanted
to restore the balance before turning to diplomacy. Brezhnev had not
raised it presumably because he thought the MPLA was winning. Now
an unsigned note—officially more than a conversation, less than a
letter—was handed to Dobrynin at the State Department warning that
Soviet actions in Angola were passing all "reasonable bounds." We
objected to the Soviet Union's recognition of the MPLA, which, in fact,
represented only "a minority of the population and controlled less
than one-third of Angolan territory" and that only because of massive
Soviet military supplies. We urged the Soviet Union to discontinue the
airlift, which could only escalate the fighting (a veiled threat that we
were determined to maintain the African balance of power). We expressed our support of OAU efforts to obtain a negotiated solution
and asked the Soviet Union to join an OAU appeal to all nations to
cease their intervention in Angola's internal affairs. The note concluded that we were seeking no unilateral advantage and were willing
to play a "helpful" diplomatic role.

On November 22, the Soviets replied with uncharacteristic alacrity.
A long and polemical message demonstrated the growing influence of
the Politburo's ideological faction. Blaming the tense situation in Angola on "foreign monopolies," the note called our charges of military
intervention "groundless" and rejected the claim that it was inconsis-
tent with existing Soviet-American understandings. But once the obligatory bluster was out of the way, the Soviet note turned more
cooperative. Moscow favored the consolidation of all Angolan patriotic forces, it said, free of any outside interference; it was prepared to
make a statement to that effect and invited us to make a similar

declaration. What was meant by "patriotic forces" was not defined, and no reference was made to the massive supply effort. We therefore decided to increase the pressure.

In a speech in Detroit on November 24, I repeated the charges we had made in our note—a clear warning to the Soviets that the limits of our restraint were being reached:

> The United States cannot be indifferent while an outside power embarks upon an interventionist policy—so distant from its homeland and so removed from traditional Russian interests. The Soviet Union still has an opportunity for a policy of restraint which permits Angolans to resolve their own differences without outside intervention. We would be glad to cooperate in such a course. But time is running out; continuation of an interventionist policy must inevitably threaten other relationships.[12]

Ford followed up by endorsing my speech in even blunter language at a subsequent press conference:

> I agree with the speech made by Secretary Kissinger in Detroit . . . the Soviet Union is not helping the cause of détente by what they are doing. And I hope the message comes across.[13]

Both the President and I picked up on the Soviet note of November 22 by reiterating America's willingness to contribute to an African solution through the OAU and negotiations among the three Angolan parties.

A presidential trip to China, Indonesia, and the Philippines lasting from December 1 to 7 brought about a hiatus in American-Soviet exchanges. In China, Ford stressed, especially to Mao, our determination to resist a Soviet-sponsored takeover of Angola and urged China to use its influence in the same direction. In his elliptical style, Mao indicated that he would explore China's possibilities, especially via Zaire. The exchange did not do much for Sino-American relations, which, from the Chinese perspective, were largely based on America's ability to maintain the global balance of power and indirectly the security of China's own long frontier with the Soviet Union. Asking for Chinese support against Soviet depredations so far from both Chinese and Soviet sources of strength was no great demonstration of either American strength or determination.

In the interval, Soviet policy seemed to turn more conciliatory. On December 7, the head of the Soviet Foreign Ministry's African bureau spoke to the Zairian ambassador in Moscow in a manner Mobutu interpreted as an indication that the Soviet Union might want to "disengage" from its all-out support of the MPLA. At the same time, we accelerated our diplomacy toward the African states. An OAU summit had been scheduled for mid-January in Addis Ababa. Our strategy was to bring about a negotiation that removed foreign forces and produced an agreement among the Angolan factions.

By then the demand for the removal of foreign forces applied as well to those of South Africa, which had entered Angola from Namibia (then still in practice South African territory). In August, South African forces had moved troops just across the border to protect the Cunene River hydroelectric power project, which had been jointly financed by Portugal and South Africa. By October 31, the CIA reported that 100 to 150 South African advisers were with Savimbi's rear-echelon units. In the absence of American personnel on the ground, it was difficult to verify these estimates. Based on information now available, the number was almost certainly larger and their role less anonymous than the CIA report claimed.

South Africa had opted for intervention without prior consultation with the United States. We learned of it no later than the CIA report of October 31, and local CIA personnel may well have known about it earlier. With Cuban troops pouring in, we decided to treat the South African forces as one of the outside elements to be removed by a settlement. I told a congressional committee on January 29, 1976, that it would surely prove a great deal easier to get rid of the South African than the Cuban forces.

At the time, it was widely claimed that Cuban intervention had been triggered by South African moves. What we know now about the actual sequence of events belies that conjecture. Cuban intervention began in May, accelerated in July when the MPLA was, in fact, gaining ground, and turned massive in September and October. The first Cuban contingents—over 200 advisers—arrived by late spring or early summer (before the appearance of the South Africans) and were intended to train MPLA forces in Soviet tactics and the use of Soviet equipment.[14] In mid-August, Castro proposed a major expansion of intervention to Brezhnev and, when the Soviet leader stalled, went ahead on his own. Regular Cuban combat troops began to arrive in late September and early October and eventually reached levels twenty times that of the maximum South African deployments.

To us, the South African intervention represented both a political embarrassment and a bargaining chip. It was not a significant element in our strategy, which, as will be seen, relied above all on our efforts in enlisting some African forces generated by France. And despite the South African move, our diplomacy was making headway on the continent. We had been urging African countries not to recognize the MPLA. On November 21, I had written to the OAU's Secretary General, William Eteki, supporting the OAU's call for a cease-fire, for negotiations among the parties, and for withholding exclusive recognition from one of the factions:

> For our part, the United States is pursuing no unilateral interests in Angola. As I have stated publicly, the United States has no other interests there but the territorial integrity and independence of Angola. We believe the people of Angola have a right to a government of their own choosing and to live in peaceful independence and well-being.

By the end of November, only twelve of twenty-nine African governments had recognized the MPLA regime in Luanda, and very few states from outside the continent had done so.

Against this background, we judged the time ripe to bring matters to a head with the Soviets. On December 9, Ford called Soviet Ambassador Dobrynin to the Oval Office. I attended. The President avoided small talk and came straight to the point: the Angolan situation was "not a healthy situation"; committed as Ford was to détente, the President found it difficult to understand Soviet actions so far from any previous Soviet or Russian security interest. Ever the professional, Dobrynin asked whether we meant to make a specific proposal. I suggested withdrawal of all foreign forces and an end to resupply. Dobrynin replied that a political solution probably would have to come first—the usual position of those who want to use their superior military position to shape the political outcome. Ford insisted that the presence of Cuban troops would inevitably raise serious questions about overall American-Soviet relations. On parting, Dobrynin again invited an American proposal:

> Angola is a long way away. I will convey this to my government. If you had some proposal other than "you just shouldn't do this" . . .

The next day, Dobrynin demonstrated that, at least in meetings with the President, he never spoke without instructions. He telephoned me to review our "proposals": the content of a joint American-Soviet appeal to the OAU for the withdrawal of foreign forces, and how a ban on weapons deliveries might be constructed and enforced.

On December 10, the Soviet airlift to Angola ceased and was not resumed until after Congress had legislated the end of the American program for Angola. On December 16, Soviet President Nikolai Podgorny commented to the British ambassador paying a departure visit that a coalition government built around the MPLA might solve the Angolan crisis. We would not accept the MPLA as the main element of a coalition but interpreted Podgorny's comment as an initial move toward our position.

While waiting for a formal Soviet response, we looked for some new elements with which to restore the balance against the Cuban interventions. On December 16, during the consumer/producer conference in Paris (see Chapter 22), I reviewed the situation in Angola over dinner with French President Giscard d'Estaing. France had a special interest in French-speaking Africa, with whose governments it maintained closer relations and whose internal security it protected more assiduously than any other former colonial power did its former wards. And Zaire, though a former Belgian colony, was French-speaking.

The heirs of Richelieu's statecraft had no confidence in pious declarations of goodwill or of "keeping Africa out of the Cold War." Giscard shared our view that the combination of Soviet supplies and Cuban troops could undermine stability in all French-speaking territories and not only in Zaire. Throughout the Angolan enterprise, the French government had displayed a benevolent interest, and its daring and imaginative chief of intelligence, Count Alexandre de Marenches, had given invaluable advice and, on occasion, technical assistance. On November 19, Giscard had written a thoughtful letter to Ford calling his attention to the new reality that "the Soviet Union for the last several days is no longer holding back an open and massive aid for the MPLA of Mr. Neto." He posed the strategic issues as follows:

> Are the Soviets trying to give their protégés the means to regain the initiative and to eliminate their adversaries militarily, or are they simply trying to avoid the annihilation of the MPLA and leave the MPLA in a position to negotiate?
>
> As far as the United States is concerned, will the massive Soviet intervention have an effect on American relations with the two other Angolan movements regarding the level of aid supplied and the public character of this aid? Or rather, does the United States believe that it would be preferable to work for the conclusion of a ceasefire and the installation of a tripartite coalition government?
>
> These are questions about which I would be interested in knowing your views. They are also the subject of questions I am receiving from certain worried African chiefs of state, and this is why I am taking the liberty of sending you this message.

Would that our own deliberations in Washington had crystallized the issues so incisively and concisely. In his reply on November 25, Ford summed up our policy. The Soviets, he argued, were seeking to maneuver the MPLA into a dominant position. Indeed, having recognized the MPLA as the sole legitimate government, "the Soviets have publicly staked their prestige on the outcome." Ford also argued that there was a substantial anti-Chinese element in the Soviet move. They hoped to demonstrate to militant Third World leaders that they could pursue their revolutionary ambitions only with Soviet aid and to the Chinese that the United States could not stop Soviet aggressiveness even in distant Africa, much less at the Siberian border. Ford concluded that the United States could not remain aloof from a Soviet power play of such dimensions. Nevertheless, we were prepared to settle for what the OAU was urging: a withdrawal of foreign forces, an end to outside supply, and an interim coalition government under OAU auspices.

Over dinner in Paris, Giscard addressed himself to this exchange of letters. He was at his best in such a setting—charming, warm, and brilliant. He was explicit about the implications of his letter. Defeating the Soviet moves in Angola was in the interest of both France and its African friends, and Giscard was therefore prepared to act on this conviction. He would assist by making available auxiliary (French African or Moroccan) troops and a number of Alouette helicopters armed with S-11 missiles as a counter to the Soviet 122mm rockets, which so demoralized the forces of Roberto and Savimbi. He would station Mirage fighters in Zaire and help us obtain diplomatic support from French-speaking African countries. Count de Marenches would elaborate on these measures through Vernon Walters, our deputy director of intelligence.

On December 18, we received the Soviet reply to Ford's conversation with Dobrynin. Conciliatory in tone, it acknowledged that we had a common task to keep Angola from undermining American-Soviet relations:

> [T]he President cannot, of course, be but concerned by the attempts of certain circles within and outside the United States to use the events in this African country for bringing complications into the Soviet-American relations. Since there is no real foundation, as we are convinced, for such a turn of events, the task consequently is not to give the upper hand to these attempts.

Addressing the President's specific proposals, Moscow strenuously denied that it could ever be "a champion of unleashing a civil war in that country." It dodged Ford's proposal for a joint American-Soviet appeal for a cease-fire but agreed to make an appeal for the removal of foreign forces:

> What should be pursued now is the end of foreign military intervention in that country so that its people could in reality be ensured the right to decide by themselves the questions of building a new life in conditions of independence and freedom without any interference from outside.

Going further, the Soviet note suggested issuing a joint American-Soviet statement to that effect:

> We would welcome such a statement also on the part of the United States, as well as its practical actions leading towards the above goal.

If the Soviet Union was prepared to make a joint appeal for the removal of all foreign forces, we might be on the way to a diplomatic solution, provided it was accompanied by a cease-fire. And we were confident that we could arrange for the OAU meeting to call with our support for a cease-fire among the African belligerents. Of course, there were many loose ends: the Soviet Union might have labeled some of the black Cuban troops as indigenous or stalled implementation until its matériel buildup was complete, whereupon the Cuban forces could sweep the field.

On the other hand, the final paragraph of the Soviet note intimated that Moscow was eager to avoid a confrontation with the United States over Angola:

> In conclusion, we would like to underline once again that the President can rest assured that the Soviet side is in no way interested in having the events in Angola viewed from the angle of "confrontation between Moscow and Washington" and as "a test of the policy of relaxation of tension."

The pieces of our strategy were falling into place. A modest increase in our own military support coupled with French assistance would, at a minimum, prevent a Soviet-Cuban victory and create the basis for a diplomacy to bring about the withdrawal of foreign forces. French support in the French-speaking countries, led by President Leopold Senghor of Senegal, and our own diplomacy should generate an OAU resolution supporting the political outcome favored by us. The OAU summit was scheduled for mid-January 1976 in Addis Ababa. And in the aftermath of such a solution, the Western powers would be holding all the cards of propinquity, of African experience and logistics.

At this point, Congress exploded our design.

## The Tunney and Clark Amendments

Giscard had requested two C-130 transport planes to fly French helicopters with French crews to counteract the Cuban 122mm rockets to Angola. Though the Soviet equipment and Cuban forces had not yet been decisive except around Luanda, an infusion of additional matériel was urgently needed to keep the Communist side from a decisive victory. This could not be accomplished within the funds approved by the 40 Committee.

The Working Group therefore examined three levels of additional assistance: $28 million, $60 million, and $100 million. Gun-shy from years of battering, the CIA opted for the smallest increment; Colby had since been dismissed but had graciously stayed until his successor, George Bush, was confirmed by the Senate. Understandably, Colby's desire to expand the program was lower than ever. I recommended the $60 million tranche. No agency recommended the highest number.

At the urging of his congressional advisers, Ford approved the smallest option, or $28 million. This amount could be allocated to the covert Angola program by "reprogramming"—a budgetary device no longer available by which amounts of less than $50 million could be switched from one category to another within the overall budget of a department with the approval of the chairmen of the House and Senate Appropriations Committees (the other options would have to go through the entire appropriations process). Since Representative George Mahon from Texas and Senator John McClellan from Arkansas were from the conservative wing of the Democratic Party and good friends of Ford, the President felt reasonably certain that the approval of the modest request for reprogramming would prove to be routine.

But Congress had changed dramatically since Ford left it only two years earlier. The Congress elected in the McGovernite landslide of the previous year represented the high point of the radical protest. It was violently opposed to intervention abroad, especially in the developing world, ever suspicious of the CIA, deeply hostile to covert operations, and distrustful of the veracity of the executive branch. In the first flush of victory, the new Congress had abrogated the tradition by which the chairmanship of committees went to the most senior members of the majority party. Though, in practice, the seniority system remained in place in the vast majority of the committees, the chairmen were gun-shy about exercising the discretionary authority they had previously enjoyed.

This proved especially true with respect to Angola because the covert program had suddenly become passionately controversial. The opposition had nothing to do with its covert character because Congress had been well aware of the program all along. Between July and December, State Department and CIA officers had briefed congressional committees, subcommittees, and individual members and staff on a constant basis. Forty briefings had taken place in that six-month period. Some of the committees had designated only two members (one from each party) to receive the briefings; others had sent as many as thirteen. The choice had been up to them. Altogether more than two dozen senators, 150 congressmen, and one hundred staff members of both houses had been briefed (a chronicle of the briefings is attached in the Notes).[15] Each escalation was duly reported.

Congress had proved responsible and vigilant in safeguarding information; very few, if any, leaks could be traced to congressional sources. In the year of Indochina's collapse, Congress was not anxious to assume responsibility for consigning yet another country to Communism—especially in the face of overwhelming evidence of Soviet and Cuban complicity.

I had expected leaks to occur earlier but, in order to protect Davis's nomination as ambassador to Switzerland, the dissidents in the State Department and CIA had maintained discipline. Within days of Davis's confirmation by the Senate Foreign Relations Committee on November 19, however, the floodgates opened. By then, the African bureau was run by Ed Mulcahy in a professional and disciplined manner, so that the leaks probably came either from Congress or from some of the supporters of Davis's point of view in the CIA. As usual, it proved impossible to pinpoint the source. Be that as it may, Davis's opposition and the doubts of his friends were documented in the media and received massive editorial support.[16]

This public outcry ended Congress's acquiescence in the covert program because few of those briefed were prepared to face the onslaught if they publicly endorsed what they had secretly approved. Despite the many briefings, they would not even abandon their time-honored alibi that there had been inadequate consultation. Thus Senator Dick Clark of Iowa, who, as chairman of the Subcommittee on African Affairs of the Senate Foreign Relations Committee, had been briefed more than any other senator, felt at liberty to talk about Angola on December 5 as if he had just learned of the Angolan civil war from news accounts:

> Press reports over the last few weeks have described an apparent surge of Soviet activity in support of the Angolan MPLA. Other reports have disclosed the presence of units of the Zairian and South African Armies and white mercenaries fighting with the two Angolan groups which opposed the MPLA.

Two days ago *Newsday* reported significant American armament shipments to Angola. Obviously, these reports are unconfirmed.[17]

Since that position was unsustainable, Senator Clark a few weeks later, on January 29, 1976, developed the extraordinary theory that congressional briefings did not necessarily constitute consultation:

My question is whether the people who were being briefed were advised that their consultation was being sought. It seems to me that it leaves these people who were being briefed in a very difficult position if they are expected to give a yes or a no or some indication on every single covert activity that is presented to them or in the event that if they do not do that they can later be quoted as having said that they did not oppose it. That puts them in a difficult position if they are not previously advised that their opposition is going to make a difference.[18]

What exactly the senator thought the purpose of these briefings might have been other than to invite congressional approval, he failed to explain.

The flight from responsibility became bipartisan. Republican Senator Clifford Case insisted that congressional silence could not be interpreted as acquiescence and that, even if it had been, it ought not to have been expected to last:

A failure to make overt objection, particularly when we are under the restriction of secrecy to what was proposed in July, I never felt, and do not still feel that it stopped us from objecting in December.[19]

And he added that any opposition to a foreign country "that involves money, I think, should be done in the open"—a doctrine that would take the United States out of the intelligence business.

Senator Joseph Biden, Democrat of Delaware, put forward—with disarming frankness—an explanation for why senators objected in December to what they had approved in July:

From one member's viewpoint, that is how it looked . . . that there was no way it would be found out, so there would be

> no domestic embarrassment, or they did not see the possibil-
> ity of it because of the amounts and the manner in which
> they were being shipped in.[20]

In other words, senators would acquiesce in the program so long as the public did not know of it; they would run for cover once it became public and they were needed to defend their previous positions. What then was the purpose of the newly established congressional vetting of covert activities which had been meticulously followed?

In this atmosphere, the outcome of the debate was foreordained. Like actors in a well-rehearsed classic, the representatives and senators kept repeating a catechism on behalf of American abdication already finely honed in the Vietnam debate nine months earlier. Senator Clark argued on January 29 that the United States had no significant strategic military or economic stake in Angola—begging the question of whether we (and all of Africa) did not have an interest in preventing Soviet military power from emerging as the arbiter of Africa's struggles.

Republican Senator Charles Percy of Illinois answered this question in hearings on Angola a few days later by invoking Vietnam:

> Just because the Soviets are in there, do we have to go in?
> That was our problem in Vietnam. Our vital interests were
> not at stake, really. It is a long way away logistically, extraor-
> dinarily hard to back it up and we were backing a side that
> did not have the moral strength, did not have the necessary
> resolve or sense of unity.[21]

Percy did not vouchsafe how resolve could overcome the massive Soviet assistance and the large Cuban combat contingent without American help.

Senator Jacob Javits argued that the United States ought to forswear the role of global policeman—a theme echoed by Senator Biden. This was of a piece with the argument that African nationalism, not American covert support, was the most effective counterweight to a Soviet foothold in Southern Africa. But how would African nationalism be able to prevail when the fighting forces on the MPLA side were largely Cuban and their equipment of all forces the result of a massive Soviet airlift, which, in a three-month period, had already delivered more arms to Angola than had previously existed in all of sub-Saharan black Africa put together?

While the dialogue was polite, the chasm between the President and Congress proved unbridgeable. The opponents were seeking to vindicate a theory of international politics abjuring geopolitics and equilibrium, a watered-down version of Wilsonianism in which the forces of good would prevail by dint of their intrinsic virtue, not by strategy and especially not by power. The attack on covert operations was therefore a surrogate for a fundamental assault on the way in which postwar American foreign policy had been conducted for over a generation.

All the standard Vietnam arguments were repeated. But while the argument over Vietnam nine months earlier had been about the implications of national honor in the face of incipient defeat, in Angola a totally unnecessary strategic setback was being imposed by our divisions where success was quite achievable.

On December 18, the night before the crucial vote, I met with the Senate leadership in Majority Leader Mike Mansfield's office and laid out our strategy for them, including the hopeful Soviet reply of that day and the French option (in guarded terms). As I was to testify before the Senate Foreign Relations Committee over a month later, I explained the reason our program had been covert:

> We chose covert means because we wanted to keep our visibility to a minimum. We wanted the greatest possible opportunity for an African solution. We felt that overt assistance would elaborate a formal doctrine justifying great power intervention.[22]

I repeated our motive for resisting Soviet interventions in Angola:

> Do we really want the world to conclude that if the Soviet Union chooses to intervene in a massive way, and if Cuban or other troops are used as an expeditionary force, the United States will not be able to muster the unity or resolve to provide even financial assistance? Can those faced with such a threat without hope of assistance from us be expected to resist? Do we want our potential adversaries to conclude that in the event of future challenges America's internal divisions are likely to deprive us of even minimal leverage over

developments of global significance? . . . And what conclusion will an unopposed superpower draw when the next
opportunity for intervention beckons?[23]

I stated our objectives: a cease-fire, ending the tragic bloodshed in
that country; withdrawal of outside forces: Soviet, Cuban, and South
African; cessation of foreign military involvement; and negotiations
among the Angolan factions.[24]

The senators seemed reflective. Senator Hubert Humphrey, my
greatly respected friend, said: "I think we should give the Secretary a
chance."

But by the next morning, the mood of the Senate was too overwhelming. Humphrey called to say that the sentiment was too strong
and that he could not bring himself to split with his liberal friends and
constituents a second time: "I don't want them to break my heart
again."

In this manner, not only the arguments of the Indochina debate of
nine months earlier were repeated but so was the anguish. And the
reason was very similar. The traditional liberal opposition had not
been unexpected; what was missing was a conservative balance. Very
few of the gladiators of the Solzhenitsyn, Helsinki, and SALT controversies joined us on the parapets when an actual Soviet geopolitical
challenge arose, and those who did were very restrained.

While the conservatives and especially the neoconservatives battered us on esoteric subjects such as the precise range of a Soviet
medium bomber and various types of cruise missiles, we were struggling to avoid a debacle in which, for the first time in the Cold War,
the United States would capitulate to a Soviet-sponsored military adventure. While the liberal abdication at least extrapolated a consistent
position, the conservative opposition was more painful and more worrisome. Not even a geopolitical Soviet challenge could bring the neoconservative critics to join forces with the administration. Having
defined the ideological conflict with Communism and implacable opposition to the existing version of arms control as the only meaningful
agenda, they would not take time out from these pursuits even if the
issue was the projection of Soviet and Cuban military power to Africa.

There was another less philosophical reason for the neoconservatives' silence. In the primary campaign, they had staked their case
against Ford on his administration's alleged softness in the face of the
Communist challenge. Had they supported the administration, they

would have been obliged to concede what the reality was: that the difference between their position and ours was a question of tactics, not of principle. They could not afford to join a battle which should have been theirs because they could not psychologically ally themselves with those who were already on the front lines of the struggle they were so shrilly defining. The civil war in the conservative camp left the field to their liberal opposition.

This confluence of forces brought about America's abdication in Angola. On December 19, 1975, the Senate passed the Tunney Amendment to the Defense Appropriations bill, banning *any* use of funds for Angola unless specifically appropriated in the budget. This meant the end of our covert program, for any overt assistance would have to await the legislative process in the next session of Congress extending over months—long after the issue would be decided. Nor could we have any illusions about the outcome of open legislation. The supporters of the Tunney Amendment would surely vote down overt assistance to the fighting in Angola. In June 1976, the Clark Amendment made the Tunney Amendment permanent.

Such conservative stalwarts as Paul Laxalt, Barry Goldwater, James Eastland, and Herman Talmadge went unrecorded. Jesse Helms voted for the amendments; Henry Jackson split the difference, voting against the President on one vote and pairing against Tunney on another.

On December 19 after the Senate vote, President Ford lashed out:

> This abdication of responsibility by a majority of the Senate
> will have the gravest consequences for the long-term position
> of the United States and for international order in general.
> A great nation cannot escape its responsibilities. Responsi-
> bilities abandoned today will return as more acute crises
> tomorrow.
>     I therefore call upon the Senate to reverse its position
> before it adjourns. Failure to do so will, in my judgment,
> seriously damage the national interest of the United States.[25]

In fact, it was all over. On December 24, the Soviet airlift resumed at an accelerated pace. In the next month, Cuban forces in Angola doubled. Even then, twenty-two African nations refused to recognize the MPLA government at the OAU summit at Addis Ababa in January; imagine what diplomatic support we would have achieved had we maintained a military equilibrium. The Soviet Union rejected any further discussion of Angola. Cuban troops remained there for another fifteen years and spread into Ethiopia, Somalia, and South Yemen in the Carter Administration. They were not driven out until the Reagan Administration brought about the repeal of the Clark Amendment and resurrected the very covert program Gerald Ford had been obliged to abandon on the verge of success.[26]

# 27

# LAST VISIT TO MOSCOW

### The Halloween Massacre

The winter of 1975–76 was a painful and difficult time for Gerald Ford. By the fall of 1975, his prospects for election in his own right the following year began to dim. In early January 1976, his approval rating in the polls plunged below 50 percent. And with Ronald Reagan gearing up to challenge him for the Republican nomination, Ford was leading an increasingly divided party. As a result, the administration run by the most conciliatory of leaders found itself engulfed in simultaneous controversies, both with the Democratic Congress on his left and the President's own Republican rivals on his right.

Executive-congressional tensions are often blamed on inadequate consultation. In the Ford Administration, this cliché was clearly off the mark. Congress was closely and frequently consulted, as could be expected from a President who had spent all of his prior political career in the House of Representatives. But Ford was to learn the painful lesson that goodwill has its limits when it comes to eliciting congressional restraint; the capacity of the President to influence legislators' electoral prospects plays a crucial role as well. A nonelected President perceived to have no coattails to help carry marginal seats is in a weak position with Congress. In more tranquil times, or had a presidential election been less imminent, the personal affection most members of Congress—including those in the Democratic majority—felt for Ford might have overcome these handicaps.

But Vietnam and Watergate had skewed every aspect of personal relations. Three months after Ford took the oath of office, a new extremely liberal Congress was elected in the wake of the Watergate scandal. Its composition reversed the results of a presidential election fought two years earlier essentially on foreign policy issues in which Nixon had prevailed by the second largest margin in history. Due to internal upheavals within the Democratic Party, this new Congress turned out to be militantly hostile to the policies of Nixon and Ford and closer to those of George McGovern, who had been decisively defeated by the voters just two years before. Though foreign policy had not been an issue in the 1974 congressional election, the new McGovernite Congress cut off military aid to Turkey, Vietnam, and Cambodia, legislated an end to the attempt to stop Cuban and Soviet interventions in Angola, eviscerated the intelligence services, and harassed East-West policy with amendments and hearings designed to destroy presidential flexibility.

At the same time, the Republican Party was deeply divided. Its right wing, strengthened by the same domestic crises, perceived an opportunity to win the presidential nomination of 1976 for its standard-bearer Ronald Reagan. Many in the country who rejected the liberal critique of the United States as the source of evil in the world reacted to the Indochina humiliation with a patriotic resurgence. Ironically, this was directed—not a little abetted by the neoconservatives recently recruited from the liberal camp—less against the liberals than against the conservative Gerald Ford, who, to his amazement, found himself accused as insufficiently vigilant against Communism.

All this cumulatively contributed to a totally false image of presidential weakness. Discipline within the administration began to erode. Inevitable bureaucratic contests turned intractable in the face of the gnawing sensation that the President's authority was slipping away. Some senior officials began positioning themselves in the first year of the Ford presidency for the *post-Ford* period. In this kind of political maneuvering, which usually occurs only at the end of a second presidential term, officials became reluctant to face additional criticisms from the growing conservative and neoconservative wing.

For a while, Ford observed the conflicts between Schlesinger and me, and between Rumsfeld and Nelson Rockefeller and Bill Simon, with no visible reaction. He did not encourage the internal fighting, as Nixon had been wont to do, nor did he countenance discussions of it. Convinced that the country needed stability above all, Ford tried to draw the poison from the maneuvering whirling all around him by participating in no cliques, by never badmouthing his associates, and by keeping his actions relentlessly focused on substance—which, in truth, was all-consuming. In 1975 alone, the President had to deal with the Soviet rejection of Congress's terms for a trade agreement, the growing deadlock over arms control, the collapse of Indochina, the *Mayaguez* incident, the uproar over Aleksandr Solzhenitsyn, the turbulent negotiation of a second-stage Egyptian-Israeli agreement, the European Security Conference and its controversies, the intelligence investigations, and Angola. Few peacetime Presidents have been obliged to face such an array of challenges in their first full year in office.

By October 1975, fourteen months after he had taken the oath of office, Ford no longer had any choice but to turn to politics. The election was barely a year away, and he concluded that he needed a more coherent team. He asked Rockefeller to take himself off the ticket as the vice presidential candidate for the 1976 election. And he shook up his Cabinet, replacing Schlesinger with White House Chief of Staff Donald Rumsfeld, Bill Colby with George Bush (then chief of the U.S. Liaison Office in Beijing), and appointing our ambassador in London Elliot Richardson to the position of Secretary of Commerce, from which Rogers Morton had resigned some weeks earlier for personal reasons. In the process, Ford asked me to relinquish the National Security Adviser's hat, which I had continued to wear after Nixon appointed me Secretary of State in the fall of 1973.* Altogether, five major Cabinet-level changes marked the dramatic shake-up.

Ford came to these decisions while I was on a trip to Asia from October 17 to 24 to prepare the President's summit with Chinese leaders four weeks hence. I had not been consulted about the changes, nor had Ford ever mentioned before my departure or during my trip that he was considering a realignment of his administration. On Saturday afternoon, October 25, after my return from Asia, Ford called Rumsfeld and me to the Oval Office to inform us of his decision, providing little explanation.

A classic Washington scene followed. Rumsfeld and I sat on the two sofas which framed the President's easy chair in front of the fireplace. I do not know whether Rumsfeld had had any advance warn-

---

* The Assistant to the President for National Security Affairs, often informally referred to as the National Security Adviser, is a White House staff aide who advises the President on national security issues and manages the interagency committee process of the National Security Council.

ing; I was too surprised to react to the substance of what Ford was saying. In truth, there was not much to say, since the President did not invite any discussion. Both Rumsfeld and I had been around Washington long enough to know that the appointments were not the end of the process but the start of a whole series of adjustments. Since all new appointees were political heavyweights and potential presidential candidates (at least in their own perception) and I was by far the best known and most controversial holdover, a new turf battle was inevitable. We pledged to cooperate with each other, no doubt in good faith, but the pledge would only be tested when the process of decision-making resumed.

There was a brief crossing of swords over who should replace me as National Security Adviser. Rumsfeld recommended Arthur Hartman, then serving as assistant secretary of state for Europe, who had been a friend of Rumsfeld's since Rumsfeld served as ambassador to NATO. I had very high regard for Hartman. But I did not relish the idea of a current subordinate in a position so decisive for my relationship with the President. So I recommended Brent Scowcroft, believing him to be the best qualified and also the person most comfortable with existing procedures. Ford reserved making a decision at this meeting and then selected Scowcroft shortly afterward.

The President paid a heavy price for trying to solve the political challenge to him in one fell swoop. Political advisers who had been chafing at the bit for fourteen months had prevailed with the sort of recommendation that looks better in theory than in practice. Thunderstruck, I wondered who could have convinced Ford to undertake such a major upheaval as Rockefeller's removal from the ticket less than six months before the primaries. Some of Ford's associates told me of their hope that sacrificing Rockefeller, the bête noire of the conservatives, might defuse the right-wing challenge and even persuade Reagan to withdraw as well. Though no political expert, I thought the opposite more likely. Reagan and his advisers would interpret Ford's decision as a sign of panic; they sought the presidency, not sacrificial offerings. Eliminating Nelson Rockefeller, their old adversary, would whet the conservatives' appetites while depriving Ford of the services of a well-known, seasoned campaigner. No doubt my reaction was influenced by my affection for Rockefeller, a friend and mentor for two decades. But even from the perspective of two more decades, dropping Rockefeller still strikes me as the single worst decision of Ford's presidency.

Ford obtained no benefit from replacing Rockefeller. The decision appeared inexplicable to the public—though Rockefeller gallantly pretended that he had himself chosen to withdraw. He had been nominated as Vice President in August 1974. The Democratic Congress, not keen on having this dynamic figure participate in the fall elections, delayed his confirmation until early December and, in the process, subjected Rockefeller to an excruciatingly detailed disclosure of his finances. Rockefeller was sworn in on December 19, 1974, and now, after serving ten months as Vice President, he was said to be "withdrawing." It was not credible, and the public did not believe it.

Rockefeller did his utmost to mitigate the damage. As close a friend as I was, I never heard a word of complaint from him about the shabby treatment he had received; he simply refused to discuss the subject of his withdrawal. Rockefeller behaved toward Ford with courtesy and goodwill and gave the President full support within the government and in public. The next summer, he led the New York State delegation at the Republican convention that helped assure Ford's nomination by a narrow margin. And he remained Ford's good friend after they both left office. On the human level, it was one of Rockefeller's finest hours.

The other aspects of what the media came to call the "Halloween Massacre" had a better rationale. If Ford was to realign his administration, it was best to do it all at once and as much before the primary season as possible. He had concluded months earlier that the intelligence community needed a new chief and was waiting only for the congressional investigations to be completed. Ford had been as disappointed as I by Colby's conduct throughout the investigations, but he did not believe it fair for a new Director to begin his tour of duty amidst total turmoil.

The impetus for the "massacre," however, was Ford's decision to fire Schlesinger. Not being consulted, I do not know what caused the President to move at that particular juncture. The venerable Republican political consultant Bryce Harlow informed me after the event that he had been telling Ford for months that it was too dangerous to enter an electoral year with the Defense Secretary taking potshots at the President's foreign policy. I had my own tensions with Schlesinger, but these had, in fact, ameliorated in the weeks before his dismissal to a point where I thought we would come together on the final phase of the SALT negotiations.

Later it was said that I had undermined Schlesinger in my daily briefings with the President. The transcripts will show that my contro-versies with Schlesinger came up very rarely indeed. Ford did not need me to tell him of tensions about which he could read in the newspapers or hear from his staff. In his memoirs, Ford has described at length why he never felt at ease with his Secretary of Defense, one of the few people who made him uncomfortable.[1] The final straw seems to have been Schlesinger's sharp criticism of Ford's old friend, George Mahon, chairman of the House Appropriations Committee, over cuts in the defense budget. Ford agreed with Schlesinger's attempt to protect our defense program, but he considered the personal nature of the criticism unwarranted; the episode reminded him that his repeated urgings that Schlesinger soften his treatment of Congress were being ignored.

The decision to ask me to relinquish my NSC hat made sense whatever the blow to my feelings. The jobs of Secretary of State and Assistant to the President for National Security Affairs are each in themselves almost too demanding; combining them is bound to slight one or the other. There is, moreover, an inherent conflict of interest between the two positions. The Secretary of State has an obligation to put forward his best judgment of foreign policy objectives and implications; in presenting the options to the President, the National Security Adviser needs to be an honest broker, ensuring that the President hears all agencies' views in an impartial fashion. Whether it is possible for one person to be sufficiently objective to represent both the convictions of his department and the President's need for options is an interesting subject for academic debate. Whatever the conclusion, in a town such as Washington where appearance comes close to defin-ing reality, appearances are definitely against it.

From a bureaucratic point of view, it should have been a relief to be freed of the anomalous position in which, as National Security Adviser, I chaired meetings in the Situation Room with the deputy secretary of state representing the State Department, fresh from a meeting with me on the seventh floor of the department. But the capacity to conduct policy in Washington and to be effective abroad does not depend on organization charts alone or even primarily. It is largely a question of who is perceived to enjoy the confidence of the President. Though the shake-up did not affect this intangible relation-ship, it was certain to unleash a wave of speculation, both in Washing-ton and in foreign capitals, about whether it signified a reduction in my standing with the President. Precious time would have to be spent on demeaning media inquiries and reassurances, the very need for which undermined their purpose. And all this would take place in a contentious atmosphere, since I was convinced that the Cabinet changes would focus the attacks from the Reagan forces onto me.

But these issues of perception paled in the face of the real challenge certain to emerge from the transition at the Defense Department. Given the context of the shake-up and its political fallout, I was convinced that Rumsfeld would prove a far more difficult colleague than Schlesinger. Schlesinger had no obvious political ambition except for status within the administration. Though he and the right wing of the Republican Party, as well as Henry Jackson, used each other, Schlesinger had no real political base or genuine political interests. But with SALT negotiations looming, I feared that Rumsfeld would not want to risk Ford's standing (nor his own) with the Reagan wing by entering the lists on behalf of our East-West policy. Rumsfeld was not unfriendly to me personally, but he would run no risks and seek to delay decisions until after the election. And this is more or less what happened.

The original plan had been for Nelson Rockefeller to announce his withdrawal from the ticket on November 3, a Monday. The Cabinet and other changes would be made public a week later, on November 10. But the plan misfired. Since the Washington calendar never stops whatever the internal problems of the administration in office, Ford made these decisions just before Anwar Sadat arrived on his first state visit to the United States. One stop of this trip was to be in Jacksonville, Florida, where Ford and Sadat planned to review the next stage of Middle East strategy in a relaxed atmosphere on an estate belonging to a friend of the President's.

On Saturday, November 1, as Ford and I were preparing to leave for Jacksonville, I received a phone call from Bruce Van Voorst, then a correspondent for Newsweek. He had heard, he said, that I was about to be relieved of the post of National Security Adviser. The President was said to be displeased with the result of my preparatory trip to China, with the progress of SALT, and with the disagreements between Schlesinger and me. The phrasing of the journalistic query left me in the typical Washington Catch-22 situation. If I only denied that I had lost the President's confidence, I would be acknowledging that I was giving up my NSC hat; if I denied both, I would create a permanent credibility gap. I evaded the question about losing the position and denied the White House displeasure with my performance as "a pack of lies." Van Voorst was too experienced to be put off and asked point-blank whether I was giving up my NSC hat. On this, I waffled.

I immediately called Ford to tell him what had happened. If Van Voorst had the story, it was only a matter of hours before others did, too. Ford decided that he would have to announce the changes at once; indeed, it needed to be done on the weekend before *Newsweek* came out on Monday, November 3.

Schlesinger and Colby were called to the Oval Office on Sunday morning, November 2, and dismissed. Rockefeller's withdrawal was announced as scheduled the next day. The improvisation prevented Ford from nominating the replacements and enabled some in the media to link his decision with the pardon of Nixon, which had also occurred on a Sunday.

The reaction was explosive and venomous. Ford was accused of blundering, I of being the driving force behind what was quickly dubbed a "massacre." "The last vestige of dissent may be wiped out," said Senator Henry Jackson. "Dissent to Dr. Kissinger, I mean." Senator John McClellan concurred: "I think they are giving Kissinger too much power at the White House," said the chairman of the Senate Appropriations Committee on the very day I was losing my White House position.[2] George Will expressed his views in his customary pithy way: "There is every reason to believe that Kissinger wanted Schlesinger out, and there is no reason to believe that Mr. Ford has independent views—independent of Kissinger—about matters touching foreign policy."[3] A *Washington Post* editorial of November 5 aimed its fire at Ford: "The President with this drastic and summary treatment of his problem managed to confirm both the degree of disarray that he has allowed to set in and his own inability to deal with it except by the most abrupt and heavy-handed manner."[4] Ronald Reagan described the treatment of Rockefeller as shabby and attacked détente as "a one-way street."[5]

As a matter of fact, I was highly ambivalent about the replacement of Schlesinger. But there can be no doubt of the President's conviction on this matter. When informed that I was preparing a chapter for this volume on the subject, Ford wrote me on October 14, 1997: "I believe the White House changes with the firing of Schlesinger and Colby were affirmative. For them to continue in office would have been intolerable." They had both lost his confidence.

But Ford paid a heavy price. Détente became even more controversial. I had always believed—perhaps it was an illusion—that, at the

end of the day, Schlesinger and I would resolve our essentially bureaucratic turf battles and close ranks behind an agreed East-West and
arms control policy. We would have been an ideal "good cop/bad cop"
team. In a painful but cordial conversation shortly after his dismissal,
Schlesinger told me that he shared this assessment and graciously
dissociated from attacks on me:

> KISSINGER: It is a pity our relationship developed as it did
> because I think you and I could have held this thing
> together . . . perhaps only you and I.
> SCHLESINGER: I am afraid there may be something in that,
> Henry. Someone today said Henry has the best mind,
> but we have to be careful. I myself will be careful in the
> sense of protective—there is a lot of unfair stuff about
> you going around.

For the immediate future, the challenge for Ford was to manage the
aftermath of the dismissals. Schlesinger left immediately, and Rumsfeld was quickly confirmed by the Senate. Colby stayed on until his
successor, George Bush, was confirmed by the Senate, which took until
well into the new year. Bush brought a touch of class to an otherwise
dismal period of maneuvering. Ford had asked me to find out whether
Bush would accept the position of CIA Director. I will let him speak
for himself by excerpting below a cable he addressed to me from
Beijing:

> Here are my heartfelt views.
> First, I wish I had some time to talk to one or two close
> friends about this matter.
> Second, I do not have politics out of my system entirely,
> and I see this as the total end of any political future.
> Third, I cannot from out here, halfway around the
> world, measure the mood on the Hill as to my nomination
> for this new job.
> Fourth, I sure wish I had time to think and sort things
> out. Henry, you did not know my father. The President did.
> My dad inculcated into his sons a set of values that have
> served me well in my own short public life. One of these
> values quite simply is that one should serve his country and
> his President.

And so if this is what the President wants me to do, the answer is a firm "yes."

In all candor, I would not have selected this controversial position if the decision had been mine, but I serve at the pleasure of our President, and I do not believe in complicating his already enormously difficult job. . . . I will work my heart out.

And so he did, serving with great distinction and with no harm to his presidential prospects.

The premature announcements prevented the leisurely conversation Sadat and Ford had planned regarding the next stage of the Middle East peace process. Instead there was a desultory exchange in an atmosphere overhung by domestic preoccupations. Sadat showed no reaction and made no comment when Ford explained what he had done. But in the evening, as I escorted the Egyptian President to the airport, he was even more pensive than usual, and we barely spoke. When we were already on the tarmac, he said: "I know you are thinking of resigning. Don't do it. Ford is a good man. And we need you for a while longer in the Middle East."

I was indeed thinking of resigning. Henceforth I would be the principal target of Ford's opposition. Rumsfeld, in the end, had a learning period before him, and he would likely be tempted to avoid the looming controversies; the President, my safety net, would soon be preoccupied with primary campaigns.

I could do nothing in reaction to the immediate situation because of Ford's imminent travels to China, Indonesia, and the Philippines. After we returned to Washington a month later, I met three or four times with close friends and advisers, including Larry Eagleburger, Winston Lord, and David Bruce. I asked Dean Rusk to join us for a day.

In the end, I took to heart Jim Callaghan's advice not to resign over a question of status. My only concern, Callaghan said, should be if my capacity to shape events had been impaired. There was only one way to find out. I drafted a letter of resignation and brought it unsigned to Ford. I said: "If it helps you, or if it diffuses the criticism, I will sign it." Ford replied: "Don't leave. I need you. I believe in what we are doing."[6] And that settled it.

I was to pay an extremely painful personal price for Schlesinger's dismissal in quite a different way. No person had had a greater impact on my intellectual and human development than Dr. Fritz G. A. Kraemer, also a refugee from Germany but, unlike me, a refugee by choice. The son of a Prussian official, Kraemer was as learned as he was dramatic, as dedicated as he was eloquent. Wearing a monocle and affirming strong conservative values, he seemed an unlikely recruit for the American army. But this was where I encountered him during the Second World War when I was a private in Company G of the 84th Infantry Division. The commanding general had discovered Kraemer and assigned him to the G-2 (intelligence) section, from which, chauffeured by a second lieutenant, he sallied forth to give dramatic speeches about Germany and Europe to infantry trainees astounded by the tailored uniform and monocle of a fellow enlisted man. An inspiring speaker and a man of high and rigid principles, he moved me to write him a letter about how much one of his talks had affected me. Kraemer took an interest in me. Once the division reached Europe, he arranged eventually to have me transferred to the G-2 section as well. Our division was in combat most of the time. Somewhat incongruously a few miles behind the front, Kraemer would lecture me, then barely twenty-one, on his view of history and of current events during long evenings at various combat headquarters and on walks through the shells of conquered towns. He was a father figure to me then and for nearly three decades afterward.

My service in Washington ended that friendship. As my mentor, Kraemer taught in terms of absolute verities. But as a policymaker, I was obliged to deal in terms of contingencies, an approach Kraemer was bound to consider too accommodating. We began to see less of one another, largely because I found the gap between his expectations and what I could deliver increasingly painful. I agreed with Kraemer's analysis of the danger of Communism. But in the midst of often violent demonstrations for peace in Vietnam, I did not think the country would stand for another crusade. I have explained the reasoning behind our policies—our strategy resisting Communism from a platform of peace—in previous chapters, especially in Chapters 3 and 4. But Kraemer was opposed to the Vietnam settlement and negotiations with the Soviet Union. By then an analyst in the Pentagon, he had come to Schlesinger's attention, and Schlesinger persuaded Kraemer that he was in sympathy with his approach. Kraemer took Schlesinger's dismissal as a personal insult instigated by me and resolved never to speak to me again. He has kept to this resolution—and no doubt will until our respective ends. The loss of that friendship became the most painful and permanent wound of my service in high office.

## The New Team in Action

At the time of the Halloween Massacre, Soviet-American relations reflected the spectrum of ambiguities besetting two ideological adversaries engaged in global competition but condemned to coexistence by their mutual capacity to destroy mankind. We were in the process of seeking to defeat, or at least to stalemate, a Soviet move into Africa not witnessed since a similar intervention in the Congo fifteen years earlier. We were also seeking to complete the strategic arms control negotiations agreed at Vladivostok a year before. Determined as we were to prevent any expansion of the Soviet sphere, we also felt that, in a world of tens of thousands of nuclear weapons, we owed it to our people and to our allies to demonstrate that any military confrontation was a last resort and not a preferred strategy—an especially grave obligation in the year Indochina collapsed and with the wounds of Watergate still fresh.

A policy of simultaneous confrontation and cooperation with the arch-adversary was a daunting challenge for a democratic society that found the apparent relativism of such a policy hard to assimilate into its historic way of looking at international relations as a morality play.

In the month of the Halloween Massacre, both the complexity and scope of this diplomacy were, in fact, demonstrated. On November 8, Dobrynin delivered an "oral message" from Brezhnev to Ford saying that he was prepared to break the SALT deadlock on the basis of concessions by both sides and suggesting that I meet with him in December in Moscow for that purpose. Ford replied on November 10, proposing that I visit Moscow on December 18–19. Brezhnev accepted the dates on November 13.

While these exchanges were taking place, Cuban troops and Soviet forces were arriving in Angola. Was Brezhnev sincere in his SALT offer, or was he trying to tranquilize us in anticipation of a political and military offensive in Africa? Almost certainly he was doing both. Like chess players, statesmen tend to develop options and wait for the reaction of the adversary before they decide the ultimate course.

On December 9, while we were exploring with Giscard d'Estaing the introduction of outside forces to counter the Cubans, we warned Dobrynin that Soviet actions in Angola were incompatible with existing American-Soviet relations and proposed joint measures to end the Angolan crisis. Two days later, the Soviet airlift to Angola ceased and was not resumed until two days after the Tunney Amendment passed the Senate and abandoned the battlefield to the Cubans. But in the same meeting with Dobrynin, the American side showed that it could not arrive at an internally agreed SALT position, since once again we asked for a month's postponement of my trip to the Soviet Union.

Would the Soviets have launched themselves into the Angolan adventure had the negotiations to complete the Vladivostok agreement proceeded on schedule and the Jackson and Stevenson Amendments not killed the trade agreement? Would they have persisted had we not been prevented by our domestic divisions from carrying out our planned resistance? Would they have cooperated in a solution after the Cubans arrived had we carried out the requirement of any balance of power policy, which is to uphold your own end of the balance with determination?

It is never possible to reinvent history in retrospect. Obviously I believed that our capacity to shape an acceptable Angolan outcome was related to the overall diplomacy of East-West relations. Our critics on the left—who controlled Congress—were determined to thwart our efforts in Angola while reducing our defenses and to spur SALT in isolation from all other issues. Our opponents on the right rejected both confrontation in Africa and negotiation on arms control. They wanted an anti-Soviet crusade, never mind that it would have had to be sustained by a McGovernite Congress. They kept demanding that détente should induce Soviet restraint. But by depriving us of both the carrot and the stick, Congress deprived our policy of any content save rhetorical.

The Soviet leaders were not that sentimental. As the Angolan situation disintegrated, we were preparing for what would clearly be the climactic negotiation on SALT for the rest of the Ford Administration. Perhaps, under the doctrine of linkage, we should have abandoned the attempt when the debacle in Angola became inevitable. But it would have been a fateful admission of paralysis to stop a negotiation to implement a summit agreement barely a year old in which Brezhnev had accepted our basic SALT framework.

Moreover, in the immediate aftermath of the personnel changes, the administration seemed to come together behind an agreed position. On November 6, Deputy Secretary of Defense William Clements and Chairman of the Joint Chiefs of Staff George Brown called on me with a proposal to break the deadlock within our government. Interpreting the dismissal of Schlesinger as a sign of presidential determination to impose progress on SALT, they proposed to complete the Vladivostok accords as a ten-year agreement of ceilings at 2,400 delivery vehicles and 1,320 MIRVed weapons as had been agreed and to place the systems about which disputes had developed into a separate five-year accord.

To show my determination to take account of one of Schlesinger's justified complaints, I invited James Wade, the Defense Department representative on the interagency working group, to accompany me to Moscow. I also proposed immediate close cooperation between Wade and Hal Sonnenfeldt and Bill Hyland on my staff so that formal NSC meetings would lose their confrontational character.

The major issues have been explained in a previous chapter insofar as this is possible with arguments both esoteric and, in the perspective of time, mind-boggling. I shall try to summarize them here, though the reader might do himself a favor by skipping ahead to where the narrative resumes.

One of the issues concerned the Soviet bomber that NATO called the Backfire, a supersonic plane with a normal range of 3,700 kilometers (just over 2,000 miles), a little over one third that of our intercontinental bomber, the B-52. Before the Vladivostok agreement, the Pentagon had never raised the issue internally, nor had it ever been put to the Soviets. Moreover, the Backfire had never been deployed in a way that suggested it was intended for intercontinental missions.

Nevertheless, shortly after the Vladivostok agreement, the domestic cry went up to include the Backfire in the Soviet totals for strategic (that is, long-range) bombers. It was argued that, if refueled, the plane could reach the United States (which was, of course, true of any airplane if refueled often enough) or, under certain assumptions, that it might fly to Cuba on one-way missions, attacking the United States en route. Since the Soviets were expected to produce about 400 Backfire bombers, the demand for counting them would have had the practical effect of reducing the rest of the Soviet strategic forces discussed at Vladivostok by 16 percent. The Soviets interpreted this new proposition as a device for scuttling the agreement. They argued—not without merit—that, at Vladivostok, they had given up their previous demands to include the strategic forces of France and Britain in our totals as well as the American forward-based systems (missiles and bombers)— all of which had a far greater potential for strategic missions than the Backfire.

I considered the Backfire issue essentially contrived to thwart a negotiation for other, deeper reasons. But there were real issues as well. The Vladivostok agreement included a provision limiting the Soviet "heavy" missiles to 300. A definition of what constituted a heavy ballistic missile needed to be established to prevent the Soviets from upgrading their medium-range missiles, each new version of which was getting larger.

In addition, technology generated new weapons at a faster pace than that of the arms control negotiations. One of these new technologies was the cruise missile—in essence, a pilotless plane. In 1973, the Pentagon had wanted to drop these missiles from the defense budget lest they compete for scarce funds with the Air Force's then priority project—the B-1 bomber—and the Navy's Trident submarines. I had recommended to Nixon that he overrule the Pentagon to preserve a strategic option and a bargaining chip. But the cruise missiles raised a whole new set of problems for arms control negotiators. Their range was essentially unverifiable because all that was needed to extend it was to add another fuel tank to the missile or to use a lighter warhead. Moreover, they could be launched from ships, from planes, or from land.

Finally, each of the provisions of the basic accord required detailed verification procedures.

These issues were to be dealt with by an NSC subcommittee called the Verification Panel, on which the interested agencies were represented at the deputy secretary level. For important issues, the heads of the department attended.

But it soon became evident that though the petty wrangling had eased after the Halloween Massacre, the substance of the positions had hardened. The reason was that the ultimate objection to SALT was not technical. The technical issues were frequently the pretext for a more complex set of objectives: the conviction that the SALT process might tranquilize the democracies and become a means by which the Soviet Union would gradually accumulate a decisive strategic superiority, perhaps even a first-strike capability.

Critics holding such views had a vested interest in undermining the credibility of the negotiations. Richard Perle, Jackson's staff aide, was especially fecund in alleging Soviet violations or raising issues so complicated and abstruse that responses to them contributed to the general unease.

One method for fighting arms control was to set up criteria for success inherently impossible to fulfill. One such scheme was that

SALT should be judged on its ability by itself to solve any strategic problems that the United States faced, including those that had been produced by our own unilateral decisions. The various proposals for "equal throw-weight" were in that category. Since the Soviet missiles were large and ours small by choices each side had made on its own, there were only three ways to achieve this objective: (1) by tripling our force while the Soviets' remained unchanged; (2) by the Soviets cutting their forces to one third while ours remained unchanged; (3) by the Soviets redesigning their forces to mirror our own.

Key officials in the Pentagon, demoralized by the controversies raging in Congress and aware that any agreement would be subjected to the most minute scrutiny, maneuvered to get out of the line of fire. The concept of balanced concessions fell victim to this process. Increasingly, Congress and the media demanded that all our weapons programs be preserved while those of the Soviets be severely curtailed.

These difficulties were magnified by a major mistake made by Nixon in staffing his second administration. At the end of his first term, Nixon went along with a proposal by Henry Jackson, then still considered an ally, to appoint undisputed hawks to head the United States Arms Control and Disarmament Agency. Thus Fred C. Iklé became the director, and later brought in John F. Lehman as deputy director and General Ed Rowny as principal negotiator.

I had known and respected the new appointees for a long time. John Lehman had worked on my NSC staff for several years. Their view of the Soviet danger was close to mine, but they were far better suited for service in the Pentagon, where, indeed, they subsequently served with great distinction in the Reagan Administration. They strongly sympathized with the point of view of the neoconservatives; they advocated positions amounting to a demand for the Soviets to redesign their forces and to abandon or count the Backfire without significant reciprocity from our side.

The Washington bureaucratic process thrives on adversarial procedures; the President can operate best if he takes a middle position between conflicting points of view. Otherwise he is either obliged to ratify a consensus or, when he disagrees with it, he is publicly isolated without safety nets.

This is what happened at the end of the Nixon Administration and during Ford's presidency with respect to arms control. In all bureaucratic discussions, the Arms Control and Disarmament Agency placed itself to the right of the Pentagon; the State Department and the NSC staff became the lone advocates of the arms control process, justifying it on geopolitical grounds, but they did not have a public standing on military strategy. In these circumstances, the military stuck to existing planning. NSC meetings turned into a series of bureaucratic dares to the President.

This deadlock could have been overcome only by a firm presidential decision to drive toward agreement, backed by the strong and unblinking support of the Secretary of Defense. This Rumsfeld was not prepared to give. Whether he disagreed with the substance of the evolving negotiations or whether he thought it unwise to take such a controversial step in an election year (a perfectly honorable point of view), he in effect permitted and indeed encouraged the bureaucratic process to run into the sand.

The Verification Panel meetings never reached a point of decision. A flood of options was put before the Verification Panel with one peculiar characteristic in common: none except the one requiring the counting of the Backfire without a quid pro quo from our side had the approval of the Defense Department. The President was being asked to preside over a procedure more like an arms control seminar at an academic institution. There were plenty of ideas, but no policies. If Ford wanted any option other than to count the Backfire, he would have to impose it.

To break the deadlock, I suggested on November 26 that the Verification Panel review all the options by December 9 and make a recommendation. Rumsfeld agreed to the procedure but pointed out that he would be in Europe for a meeting of NATO's Defense Policy Group. I suggested moving the Verification Panel meeting to Europe for December 11, since all the relevant officials would be there anyway for the semiannual NATO meetings. Rumsfeld agreed at first, then insisted that all meetings take place in Washington, to which he would not return before December 14. Since after the Verification Panel there would have to be an NSC meeting, this meant that negotiations in Moscow could not start before December 21, assuming there was any expectation of bringing the process to a conclusion at one meeting in each group. I thought it unwise to rely on so tight a schedule or to negotiate in Moscow with a Christmas deadline hanging over our heads. The result was that, at the December 9 meeting with Dobrynin at which Ford warned the Soviet leaders that their conduct in Angola was threatening détente, the President was unable to combine stick and carrot and found himself obliged to request a delay of a month for my visit to Moscow.

It turned out to be a fateful decision. Had my trip remained on schedule, it would have preceded the votes on the Tunney Amendment. I intended to ask Brezhnev for a permanent end to the Soviet airlift to Angola (which was in abeyance after Ford's meeting with Dobrynin) and for a joint appeal to the OAU for the withdrawal of all foreign troops, including—and especially—Cuban forces. Moscow would have had to evaluate the impact of stonewalling on the simultaneous SALT negotiations. Given the conciliatory Soviet note on Angola of December 18, there was at least a chance of consummating such an outcome.

Alas, history does not allow for multiple endings. Might-have-beens provide interesting subjects of speculation, but it is never possible to play out the alternative scenario very far. What did happen was that, at the very time I was planning to be in Moscow, the Tunney Amendment legislating a Cuban victory in Angola passed Congress. (I am bound to believe that even the McGovernite Congress would not have done this with the Secretary of State in Moscow.) Henceforth there would be nothing to talk about with the Soviets on that subject. And with victory for the Cuban and Soviet forces in Angola, the geopolitical context for SALT was gone. The Tunney Amendment not only doomed Angola, it also marked a victory for those wanting to dismantle our East-West policy. By creating such a moment of geopolitical weakness, they destroyed the psychological environment for a negotiation with the Kremlin.

Nor did the delay serve to improve our internal discussions concerning SALT. Two NSC meetings in January did little but add more complexities to the existing options. The very morning of my departure for Moscow, a two-hour NSC meeting was needed to produce a formal position. Ford left little doubt about his own priorities when he addressed me in front of our colleagues:

> You are going there, not for a stalemate, but for the purpose
> of getting an agreement. . . . The trip is needed and desir-
> able. There isn't any question about it; no agreement is the
> worst possibility.

These presidential priorities were not reflected in the discussions of the National Security Council, which regurgitated familiar views.

The Pentagon put forth as Option IV its familiar position of counting the Backfire as a strategic bomber. To demonstrate flexibility, it also proposed a modified Option IV, which allowed the Soviets (for some inscrutable reason lost in the mists of time) to avoid counting whatever Backfires had been produced by the time the SALT interim agreement ended in 1977, perhaps 100 to 120 bombers. Finally, there emerged an Option III which, in a five-year agreement ending in 1982, balanced 300 Backfires against the right to have 15 cruise missiles of a range up to 2,500 kilometers on each of 25 surface ships, or a total of 375.

Ford decided to put forward every option before him. I was instructed to try Option IV first, followed by the modified Option IV and, if these were turned down—as I believed certain—to put forward Option III but only *after* consulting Washington. Ford framed the decision this way:

> After Henry negotiates on Wednesday on the basis of Modi-
> fied IV and Variant IV, and gets a feel for their attitudes and
> reactions, under our agreed procedures, he will communi-
> cate with me Wednesday evening our time. From those com-
> ments I will get Bill Clements, Admiral Holloway, Fred Iklé,
> and Bill Colby together to discuss the content of Henry's
> communication. Following that meeting, we expect to go to
> Option III.

He added that it would be "particularly helpful" if we could convince Brezhnev to reduce the ceiling for strategic forces to 2,300. According to the President, General Brown—who was present and did not demur —had agreed that a balance between 300 and 400 Backfires and an equal number of cruise missiles on surface ships would make "a good trade-off."

It was a humiliating experience. I had been negotiating on behalf of the United States for seven years, and I had always had latitude to use my judgment within parameters laid down by the President after consulting the NSC. In addition, to retreat from position to position violated every negotiating principle I believed in; such a salami tactic almost guarantees deadlock because it tempts the interlocutor at each slice to stonewall to see what the next slice might hold. Nor had I ever been asked to report back before putting forward an option already approved by the President and the NSC. It left me looking isolated in Washington and weak in Moscow: isolated in Washington because, however unrealistic Option IV, as had been demonstrated for over fifteen months, failure to achieve it could be blamed on my lack of determination, and weak in Moscow because the Politburo had never seen me on a leash so short, rendering my role that of a messenger.

The whole exercise was a beautiful example of inside-the-Beltway maneuvering. Instead of giving an impetus for the negotiations, the NSC process had been turned into a straitjacket. My only choice was to resign or to proceed.

Having only a few days earlier promised Ford to serve out the rest of his term, I set out for Moscow on the evening of January 19, 1976, with grave misgivings. Neither the international nor the domestic circumstances could have been much worse.

## The End of East-West Negotiations

By this time, visits in Moscow followed a standard protocol. The veteran Andrei Gromyko would greet my party at the airport and escort us to the state guest house on the western side of the city near Moscow University. On the way, we would exchange last-minute ideas to help shape the negotiations about to begin. On this occasion, Gromyko mentioned that the Backfire had become a big issue in the Politburo because Brezhnev at Vladivostok had let our forward-based missiles and bombers run free without asking for comparable concessions from our side. He promised that Brezhnev nevertheless would have something new to say and that a serious effort would be made to break the deadlock.

On the morning of January 21, Brezhnev greeted us in his cavernous office in the Kremlin. Newsmen were admitted first, whereupon Brezhnev appeared with his negotiating team, including General Mikhail Kozlov, deputy chief of the general staff. Brezhnev wore a natty blue suit, blue shirt, a red-patterned tie, and four medals, which he proceeded to identify to us as Hero of the Soviet Union, Hero of Socialist Labor, the Lenin Peace Prize, and the Joliot-Curie Prize.

As the American delegation entered, Brezhnev tried to establish a jovial mood: "This is a link-up of Soviet and American journalists like Soyuz and Apollo." Matters might have rested there had a journalist not managed to breach the ground rules for a photo opportunity by asking a question. The following exchange was to mortgage Soviet-American relations for the remainder of Ford's term:

> REPORTER: Will Angola be among the subjects?
> BREZHNEV: I have no questions about Angola. Angola is not my country.
> KISSINGER: It will certainly be discussed.
> GROMYKO: The agenda is always adopted by mutual agreement.
> KISSINGER: Then I will discuss it.
> BREZHNEV: You'll discuss it with Sonnenfeldt. That will insure complete agreement. I've never seen him have a disagreement with Sonnenfeldt.

By thus publicly rubbing our noses in our defeat in Angola, however self-inflicted, Brezhnev destroyed whatever sentiment was left in the United States for agreements with the Kremlin. It was also quite unnecessary, for Brezhnev, if he answered at all, could have used the conventional retort that each side was free to raise any subject it wished.

Once the photographers had left, Brezhnev, apparently oblivious to what he had done, opened with a somewhat plaintive discussion on "the hitch that had developed" in American-Soviet relations:

> I, Dr. Kissinger, would not be mistaken to say that you know full well that the Soviet Union—the Soviet Government and the entire Party, and I myself—are in favor of truly business-like relations with the United States on a broad range of questions. And I don't know what the reasons are why objections are raised and proposals are put forth that are overly complicated.

With this, Brezhnev pulled back from what he had said to the journalist:

> Dr. Kissinger, this is by no means our first meeting. We have had others. There is a good tradition that has been established in the past, and it is one of a frank exchange of views on whatever questions arise. And I'd like to suggest

we discuss today whatever questions we have in the same spirit.

It would have been far better for the mood in Washington had Brezhnev been able to bring himself to say this in front of the media. I responded by affirming the importance Ford attached to concluding the SALT agreement but, before turning to strategic arms, I concluded with a strong warning on Angola:

> It is intolerable to us that a country in the Western Hemisphere should launch a virtual invasion of Africa. Moreover, the support of the Soviet Union to this Cuban force creates a precedent that the United States must resist. We have made it a cardinal principle of our relations that one great power must exercise restraint and not strive for unilateral advantage. If that principle is now abandoned, the prospect is for a chain of action and reaction with the potential for disastrous results.

Again Brezhnev volubly protested that the Soviet Union had done no more than supply arms to a friendly liberation movement. That was no reason to treat the Vladivostok agreement as a scrap of paper. I ended the discussion with another warning about adventurism:

> I must tell you frankly, the introduction into Angola of a Cuban expeditionary force backed by Soviet arms is a matter that we must take extremely seriously. I agree also that we should be prepared to work on strategic arms. We have worked almost five years on this. If we do not complete it, our successors will have to. We will work with all seriousness to conclude the agreement we achieved at Vladivostok, which we do not consider a scrap of paper.

With this, we turned to the negotiation that had brought me to Moscow. As instructed, I put forward Option IV and, as predicted, Brezhnev turned it down. Since there were many provisions and a great deal of clarification was needed, the process took nearly three hours, lasting from 11:00 A.M. to about 2:00 P.M. With respect to the Backfire, Brezhnev asserted it had a radius of 2,200 kilometers, or about 1,400 miles. He offered to agree not to change the characteristics of the plane nor its range during the term of the agreement (the Brezhnev figure was later hotly disputed in Washington). Good progress was made on the weapons systems we had specifically discussed at Vladivostok. The definition of what constituted a heavy missile was agreed, and a number of verification issues were settled.

At the end of the first day, we finally reached the point at which we should have started, for we could have easily determined the Soviet reaction to Option IV and its variations—as I, in fact, proposed—by submitting it at the formal negotiation in Geneva or giving it to Dobrynin in advance.

The time had come to take the next step as envisaged at the NSC meeting and ask for authority to put forward Option III—that is, a balance of 300 Backfires against 375 cruise missiles. On no previous visit to Moscow had I been obliged to tell the Soviets that I needed to consult with Washington before proceeding, especially when the basic concept of Option III implied no ambiguity, and we had been negotiating for only about six hours.

The response from Washington indicated that a new bureaucratic lineup had emerged in the forty-eight hours since I had left. I received not instructions but a bombshell. Instead of the pro forma endorsement of Option III that Ford had expected, he encountered a JCS volte-face with respect to positions adopted barely forty-eight hours earlier in his presence. The essence of Option III was to balance 300 Backfires against 375 cruise missile platforms on 25 surface ships in a five-year interim agreement starting in 1977. This would have barely constrained us, since we did not intend to deploy cruise missiles before 1980.

What the cable from Washington indicated, however, was that the Pentagon abandoned its previously passionately avowed interest in ship-launched cruise missiles (SLCMs). At the January 19 meeting, General Brown, Chairman of the Joint Chiefs of Staff, had given this answer to a direct question posed by Ford:

> FORD: As a practical matter, how many surface ships do
> we now have in mind would be deployed with cruise
> missiles?
> BROWN: There are no more than 200 ships today that could
> take such cruise missiles.

Now, only forty-eight hours later, there was a total reversal. Chief of Naval Operations (CNO) Admiral James Holloway, acting as Chairman of the Joint Chiefs for General Brown (who, together with Rumsfeld, was traveling), disclaimed any American interest in surface-launched cruise missiles. The Navy, Holloway seemed to be saying, was against any agreement limiting it to 375 surface-launched missiles because it was not planning to build that many, if any. Hence Option III gave the Soviets 300 Backfires for nothing. Scowcroft reported:

> I have just come from a two-hour NSC meeting which I can only describe as surreal. The President opened with a good summary of where we stand, stressing the Soviet concessions and the advantages of your approach for dealing with Backfire and cruise missiles in a separate agreement with a five-year limitation. He then asked Admiral Holloway what the Navy program was for the number of SLCM launchers per ship.
>
> Holloway thereupon launched into an incredible commentary on the unacceptability of the proposed Backfire–surface ship SLCM trade-off. He stated that there is no U.S. surface ship SLCM program; that the Navy has always envisioned using submarines as the platform for cruise missiles; that the first money for developing a surface ship cruise missile capability isn't programmed until 1978 and that the maximum deployment by 1982 would be limited to six ships (nuclear strike cruisers). Under heavy prodding from [Deputy Defense Secretary William] Clements, he later acknowledged that it might be possible to reach as many as 15 ships, if the Spruance class frigates were reconfigured, but bad-mouthed that approach as seriously degrading the Spruance class for other missions. He said almost in as many words that he was not sure the surface ship cruise missile concept had any merit at all. . . .
>
> . . . After the meeting, the President was angrier than I have ever seen him. He ranted about the total inconsistency with previous Defense positions, said that Rumsfeld and Brown could damn well try themselves to get the extra money necessary when we failed to get a SALT agreement, and stormed out to go to the Kennedy Center. It was a complete debacle, and I really don't know where we stand now.

I knew where *I* stood. I would have to face Brezhnev in a few hours' time with no instructions on Option III and a reversal even of

Option IV, which had included a ban—put forward by the JCS—on cruise missiles with a range of more than 600 kilometers on submarines.

The cable I sent back was calmer than I actually felt:

> Have just now read your report on the NSC meeting. There are several points I want to emphasize strongly to the President. First, we have had two Verification Panels and four NSC meetings at which agreed options were developed.
>
> Second, the President approved, at DOD urging, Option IV which includes a ban on submarine-launched SLCMs beyond 600 km, and this was submitted to the Soviets in writing. Thus, we cannot simply repudiate it.
>
> Third, the President approved as a fallback Option III including the numbers for a Backfire/surface ship trade-off.

Sonnenfeldt and Hyland, then deputy to Scowcroft, sent back, without my knowledge, a more passionate message, which I include in the Notes to give a flavor of the mood of the American delegation in Moscow.[7]

In these circumstances, my meeting with Brezhnev on January 22, 1976, lasting from 6:00 to 9:30 P.M., was one of the most difficult of my service in government. With no proposal to put forward at all, I had to concentrate on completing the basic parameters of the Vladivostok agreement, leaving aside only the Backfire issue. We achieved what, in less frenzied times, would have been celebrated as a significant breakthrough:

- The problem of cruise missiles on heavy bombers was solved by counting each plane with cruise missiles in the MIRV total of 1,320 no matter how many cruise missiles of more than 600-kilometer range it carried.
- Cruise missiles of more than a 600-kilometer range were banned from planes other than heavy bombers, thus banning them from the Backfire.
- An agreement was reached on the definition of heavy missiles.
- A definition was reached on the permissible expansion of silos for modernization.

- The Soviets agreed to counting rules according to which every ICBM, once tested with a MIRV, would be counted as a MIRV even if it carried only a single warhead.
- Brezhnev was more specific on the characteristics of the Backfire.

Above all, Brezhnev agreed to reduce the Vladivostok totals to "2,300 or below," by which I was sure he meant 2,200. I reported all these results to Ford, concluding:

> I could probably have wrapped up the agreement under normal conditions. In light of the discussions in Washington that Brent has reported, I could not go further than to say this was a constructive initiative on Brezhnev's part, but that I would have to report it, and we would reply within two or three weeks. Given the massive confusions reflected in the NSC meeting, I had no choice but to let the opportunity to exploit this breakthrough go by.

Essentially what was left was whether the Soviets would agree to limit the Backfire in return for some limits on ship-launched cruise missiles (Option III). And the verification schemes for all these agreements would require technical discussions.

There was an extended discussion with Gromyko about political matters during which I summed up our view on Angola once again:

> When there are twenty flights a week from Cuba to Angola with Soviet planes, with two hundred troops a day from Cuba to Angola, it isn't something the Soviet government can simply say doesn't concern the Soviet Union. . . .
> . . . It wouldn't be the first time in history that events that no one can explain afterwards give rise to consequences out of proportion to their intrinsic significance.

Thus the long-anticipated Moscow visit ended in a paradox: success regarding the provisions of a possible agreement, paralysis in actually consummating it. Ideological blinders tempted the Soviet leaders to give precedence to the opportunities before them in Angola, however far removed these might be from any historic definition of Russian national interest and even though they put at risk the long-term American-Soviet relationship.

When I left Moscow on January 23, I promised Brezhnev an answer within two to three weeks, but I knew the balance of bureaucratic forces in Washington would prevent a SALT agreement before the election. The JCS, Defense Department, and Arms Control and Disarmament Agency had dug in on terms the Soviets would not accept. As soon as I returned, the options game started all over again. Whenever some concept was nailed down, another loophole would be conceived. For example, the limits on cruise missiles on bombers agreed with Brezhnev were suddenly declared to apply only to nuclear-armed cruise missiles. The only reason this proposal had any plausibility was that the Soviets did not yet have cruise missiles. Since there was no way to verify what kind of warhead a missile carried and since a conventional warhead is much lighter than a nuclear one, it meant that bombers would be able to carry conventional cruise missiles with a range at least double the agreed figure. The Pentagon would never have lived with such a limit in a serious negotiation once the Soviets developed cruise missiles of their own.

On February 15, 1976, at a meeting between Rumsfeld, Ford, and me, Rumsfeld stated that he would testify on behalf of a SALT agreement if Ford decided to proceed on the basis of Option III. But he carefully avoided the word "support." After the meeting, I recommended that the President abandon the quest for a SALT agreement before the election because it was too divisive to conclude an agreement while conducting a primary and then a presidential campaign against the hands-off position adopted by his Secretary of Defense and the fervent opposition of a wing of his own party. Reluctantly Ford went along with my suggestion that the only option was to accept the latest Pentagon proposal: to complete the agreement as it stood and leave the Backfire and long-range cruise missiles (except for those carried on aircraft) for later negotiations. Operational testing and production would be permitted throughout the period. This proposal had been rejected twice during the course of the current negotiations. It was certain to be rejected again. The Pentagon position was a backhanded acknowledgment that the Backfire was of no great concern. For it amounted to letting it run free for the sake of maintaining an unlimited right to deploy SLCMs.

Ford wrote Brezhnev on February 16, proposing that compromise. Brezhnev turned it down on March 17. There were no further arms control negotiations in the Ford Administration.

Paradoxically, the impact of the deadlock on both defense programs and arms control was minimal. Though SALT I technically lapsed in 1977, our successors did not increase the total numbers of strategic vehicles about which they had complained so strenuously, nor did the later stalemate on SALT II cause them to accelerate the Ford Administration's cruise missile programs. The Carter Administration experimented with various different approaches until it finally produced a SALT II agreement not easily distinguishable from where matters stood at the end of my last visit to Moscow—except that, as a result of cuts the Carter Administration had made in the Ford Administration strategic program, the strategic balance was slightly less favorable to us.[8] The Soviet invasion of Afghanistan prevented that agreement from being put to a Senate vote for advice and consent to ratification. Revealing once again the bizarre ambivalence characteristic of the rhetorical hard-liners on arms control, the Reagan Administration later announced that it would abide by the agreement's provisions so long as the Soviets did. Since SALT I, the critics have accepted de facto arrangements they vociferously opposed as part of the diplomatic process. It may have salved their conscience, but it did not change America's strategic situation. In 1987, after fifteen years of anti-SALT rhetoric, the composition of our forces under START (the new name for strategic arms control) was essentially the same as it had been in 1976. Nothing was heard of "strategic inferiority" from specialists on that subject. (Reagan had conducted a vigorous buildup, but within SALT limits strongly supported by Ford and me.)

## The Doctrine That Never Was: Sonnenfeldt and Eastern Europe

The collapse of SALT did not end the controversies over East-West relations. By now, both parties had split into radical and moderate wings. With the extremes of each party in effect cooperating with each other, East-West relations became fair game for attacks from both directions. The administration, which had tried to rally aid for Indochina, organized opposition to a Communist victory in Angola, vocally opposed Eurocommunism, kept the Soviet Union out of Middle East diplomacy, threatened to use force against a new oil embargo, and played a major role in the Helsinki accords (which challenged Soviet hegemony in Eastern Europe), found itself being accused of being "soft," "defeatist," and "pessimistic."

The underlying issue was not policy but attitude: our critics sought an ideological crusade against the Soviet Union of the kind being urged by Solzhenitsyn. The yearning for ideological purity surely reflects one of the strengths of the American character. But when Vietnam was falling and the wounds of Watergate were still fresh, the overriding need was to restore confidence and strength and, above all, not to allow our domestic ideological disputes to drive us from the geopolitical battlefields on which the cause of freedom was actually being fought. In a speech before the Boston World Affairs Council on March 11, 1976, I warned about self-induced paralysis:

> If one group of critics undermines arms control negotiations and cuts off the prospect of more constructive ties with the Soviet Union, while another group cuts away at our defense budgets and intelligence services and thwarts American resistance to Soviet adventurism, both combined will— whether they have intended it or not—end by wrecking the nation's ability to conduct a strong, creative, moderate and prudent foreign policy.[9]

The debate was soon overwhelmed by a violent controversy over remarks before a meeting of American ambassadors in December 1975 by a close collaborator of mine, Hal Sonnenfeldt, counselor of the State Department. What made the debate so maddening was that I read these remarks for the first time after a wildly distorted version appeared in the media.[10]

Hal Sonnenfeldt is my friend. He is also one of the most able public servants I have known. A thoughtful student of the Soviet Union, both his published record and his service to our country over the course of three decades would mark him as an unsentimental hard-liner.

At the time, Sonnenfeldt's primary responsibility was Soviet relationships and European policy. Friends as we were, ours was nevertheless a complex relationship. Sonnenfeldt had the same background as I: born in Germany, educated in the United States, service in the U.S. Army. We even shared the same mentor in Fritz Kraemer, though Hal —despite the so-called Sonnenfeldt Doctrine (described below)—did not draw on his head the interdict I suffered. Hal interpreted his charter to deal with Soviet affairs in such expansive terms that he claimed a role in everything even remotely affecting, or being affected by, the Soviet Union. The Soviet Union being a superpower, that, of course, covered about the same subject matter as my job description. In pursuit of that goal, Hal was indefatigable in checking on my schedule to make sure that I did not overlook his jurisdictional prerogative as he saw it. "Hal has the best intelligence system in town," said an exasperated aide. "Unfortunately, it is aimed at you."

I tended to indulge Hal because of my genuine affection for him and because the service he rendered exceeded by many orders of magnitude whatever occasional aggravation he caused. The ambassadorial conference at which Hal spoke in December 1975 was one of the periodic opportunities for the American ambassadors of a geographic region to exchange ideas and experiences with each other and with the Secretary of State and his staff. They also enable the Secretary to give guidance in the form of a coherent presentation of his views.

All this had been accomplished in the London meeting of American ambassadors in December 1975, which I had concluded with a speech on Europe, East-West relations, and, above all, Eurocommunism. (I have quoted from that speech in Chapter 20.) The normal work of the ambassadorial conference being completed, Hal, as usual, found a gap in my presentation. He felt I had neglected Eastern Europe, and he offered to hold an informal session with the ambassadors the next morning, a Sunday.

I saw some good in Hal's proposal and no prospect for a monumental event, much less the emergence of a new "doctrine." I did not attend the session—in itself a sign of its informal status—nor did any member of my immediate staff. But if Hal had said anything the assembled ambassadors considered new or outrageous, I would certainly have heard about it.

Matters would have rested there had Hal not decided—two months after the event—to memorialize his extemporaneous remarks for the benefit not only of the ambassadors present but also their staffs. To this end, a summary—not a transcript—was prepared by a staff aide.[11] At this point, some sharpshooter discovered a paragraph in the document that could be twisted into tacit American collusion with Soviet hegemony in Eastern Europe and went to work.

The offending paragraph read as follows:

> With regard to Eastern Europe, it must be in our long term interest to influence events in this area—because of the present unnatural relationship with the Soviet Union—so that

they will not sooner or later explode, causing World War III. This inorganic, unnatural relationship is a far greater danger to world peace than the conflict between East and West. . . .

. . . So it must be our policy to strive for an evolution that makes the relationship between the Eastern Europeans and the Soviet Union an organic one. Any excess of zeal on our part is bound to produce results that could reverse the desired process for a period of time, even though the process would remain inevitable within the next 100 years. But, of course, for us that is too long a time to wait.[12]

Had Hal asked for my views, I might have called his attention to infelicitous phrasing but, being familiar with his thinking, I would have understood what he meant: that we should seek to eliminate to the extent possible the "unnatural" military domination of the Soviet Union over Eastern Europe and insist that the relationship become more normal (what Hal, in an unfortunate turn of phrase, called "organic"). Deprived of its military domination, the Soviet Union would not be able to control the increasingly visible pressures for autonomy in East European countries. Indeed, Sonnenfeldt specifically mentioned Poland and Hungary as examples of what he had in mind: to achieve for the countries of Eastern Europe at the very least a status similar to that of Finland, cramped by Soviet proximity but carving out a wide area of internal freedom and a relatively independent foreign policy not inimical to the West. In that period of history, this would have been seen as a political and moral breakthrough.

This is what I would have expected, whatever the phraseology, from one of my chief advisers on presidential trips by both Nixon and Ford to Poland, Romania, and Yugoslavia to show the flag in Eastern Europe—trips designed to reward the countries which had demonstrated independence from the Soviet Union while ostracizing others such as Czechoslovakia and Bulgaria which we thought too subservient to the Soviet Union. It was an exact precursor of Reagan's policy of "differentiation" in America's relations with Warsaw Pact countries in the 1980s.

Our policy in Eastern Europe had never been controversial until the so-called Sonnenfeldt Doctrine was invented as the 1976 political scandal of the month. With Soviet military forces based all over the region, we did not encourage revolutions. Two uprisings—in Hungary in 1956 and in Czechoslovakia in 1968—had been bloodily suppressed while the democracies had stood aside. The policies of both the Nixon and Ford Administrations were designed to give the East European satellites the widest possible margin of maneuver short of violent upheaval.

In September 1975, I described our attitude toward Eastern Europe to Chinese Foreign Minister Qiao Guanhua at the U.N. as follows: "We are trying to weaken Soviet influence in Central Europe by presidential visits and by developing military relations with the Yugoslavs. . . . Our strategy is to weaken the Soviet Union." A Japanese observer described our policy as appearing to "acquiesce in the status quo in order to change the status quo."[13] Against the background of our actual policy, Sonnenfeldt's was a reasonable statement of an intermediate objective representing a vast improvement over the existing situation.

All this the critics could have determined for themselves by reading a carefully prepared speech on Soviet relations that I had delivered in San Francisco two months after the London conference and before the controversy broke.[14] The *New York Times,* however, declined to cover my speech while lavishing attention on the "Sonnenfeldt Doctrine." It was an election year, and the issue was too juicy to pass up. The "Sonnenfeldt Doctrine," it was alleged, conceded to the Soviet Union a sphere of influence in Eastern Europe. It became a symbol of the alleged softness inherent in détente and an expression of my alleged secret worldview. "The idea sent shivers up the spine," wrote C. L. Sulzberger in the *New York Times.*[15] It put "the U.S. on record for stabilization of the Soviet empire," wrote columnists Rowland Evans and Robert Novak.[16] Ronald Reagan exploited the "Sonnenfeldt Doctrine" mercilessly, claiming it meant that "slaves should accept their fate."[17]

There was no such policy. Nor did the attacks disappear when I stated the obvious: "If there were truly a new doctrine of this administration, it would not be named after Hal Sonnenfeldt."

I reiterated our formal position at the Alastair Buchan Memorial Lecture on June 25, 1976, in London:

> —The benefits of relaxation of tensions must extend to Eastern as well as Western Europe. There should be no room for misconceptions about US policy:
>> —We are determined to deal with Eastern Europe on the basis of the sovereignty and independence of each of

its countries. We recognize no spheres of influence and no pretensions to hegemony. . . .

—For the same reason, we will persist in our efforts to improve our contacts and develop our concrete bilateral relations in economic and other fields with the countries of Eastern Europe. . . .

—We will continue to pursue measures to improve the lives of the people in Eastern Europe in basic human terms —such as freer emigration, the unification of families, greater flow of information, increased economic interchange, and more opportunities for travel. . . .

—Rhetoric is no substitute for patient and realistic actions. We will raise no expectations that we cannot fulfill. But we will never cease to assert our traditional principles of human liberty and national self-determination. . . .[18]

But with the presidential nominations approaching, reasoned debate was at an end. During the campaign, liberal Democrats picked up the arguments of the conservative Republicans without improving them. The "Sonnenfeldt Doctrine" became a staple of campaign rhetoric and passed into mythology. Part of the damage it did was in the Carter-Ford debate on October 6 when Ford, briefed to the gills on the "Sonnenfeldt Doctrine," was primed to deny vociferously that any such thing existed. Unfortunately, the question came to him in a different form—about Soviet domination of Eastern Europe—and his reflexive denial of that contributed to his losing the election.

The civil war between essentially like-minded groups on the conservative side produced a paralysis, the consequences of which are difficult to assess.

Though some of his former associates differ, I now believe Ford was right not to push for the attainable SALT agreement in 1976. The ensuing political controversy would have split the country too deeply.

Strangely enough, the practical result of the stalemate was far less than the passions it had engendered. As noted, through the Reagan Administration the SALT critics in fact accepted the limits they had decried and refused to ratify. In a second Ford term, an evolution of the process in which we were engaged and which increasingly stressed reductions was likely to have moved the Ford group in the same direction as the START treaty later negotiated by the Reagan Administration.

I am convinced that Brezhnev *did* want serious improvement in relations with the United States in the early 1970s. Was Brezhnev's quest for improved relations with the United States a trap, as our critics argued, to lure us to our destruction? Or was it a reflection of an instinctive, inchoate sense that the Soviet system needed fixing? If, preoccupied with the country's economic problems, Brezhnev had agreed to a respite in the international environment, would a turning inward have unleashed earlier the forces which later produced Mikhail Gorbachev? We will never know and, in the event, the collapse of détente meant another round of U.S.-Soviet confrontation before the climactic events of the Reagan-Gorbachev period. Whichever side had the better of the argument in the early 1970s, it ended well when the Soviet Union collapsed. Whether the road to victory was unnecessarily circuitous is not a subject that will tear historians apart.

# 28

# PRESERVING THE
# SINO-AMERICAN RELATIONSHIP

In the spring of 1974, Deng Xiaoping replaced Zhou Enlai as our
principal interlocutor in China. Having grown accustomed to Mao
Zedong's cryptic philosophical allusions and to Zhou's smooth professionalism, I needed some time to adjust to Deng's acerbic, no-nonsense
style, his sarcastic interjections, and his disdain of the philosophical in
favor of the eminently practical. Compact and wiry, he entered a room
ready for business. A spittoon ever before him—which he frequently
used as if to punctuate his remarks—Deng rarely wasted time on
pleasantries. Nor did he feel it necessary to soften his remarks by
swaddling them in parables. He did not envelop one with solicitude as
Zhou was wont to do, nor did he treat me, as Mao had, as a fellow
philosopher worthy of his personal attention. Deng's attitude was that
we were both there to do our nations' business and adult enough to
handle the rough patches without taking matters personally.

Deng's position on Sino-American relations was closely related to
his views regarding China's internal evolution. Mao and Zhou had
conducted rapprochement with the United States largely on foreign
policy and security grounds. Deng always treated close relations with
America as a necessary component of Chinese modernization. Like his
predecessors, he held that, in a world composed of a menacing Russia,
a resurgent Japan, an increasingly assertive India, and a North Vietnam in the process of achieving hegemony over Indochina, China's
best strategic option was to improve relations with the United States.

But Deng thought friendly relations with America were needed for
the sake of China's domestic evolution as well. By the time I met him,

he had had enough of political turmoil. In pursuit of economic progress Deng strove for a significant improvement in the well-being of the Chinese people. American technology and economic cooperation were essential for the economic and social reform to which he was committed.

## A Visit to Beijing

My first formal negotiation with Deng occurred when I visited Beijing from November 25 to 29, 1974, to brief the Chinese leadership immediately after Ford's summit with Brezhnev at Vladivostok. It was not the most propitious moment for an inaugural meeting.

The Soviet maritime provinces, of which Vladivostok was now the capital, had been wrested from China in the nineteenth century, and Vladivostok had been created as a naval base for sallies into Korea and the Pacific. To a leadership like the Chinese, which considers every act purposeful and every event symbolic, the locale of the summit served to confirm Mao's suspicion (as he had told me in February 1973) that American strategy was to cause the "ill water [to] flow toward China." These feelings were no doubt reinforced by the fact that Brezhnev himself had never previously visited Vladivostok or the Maritime Provinces—a fact we learned too late to affect the decision to meet there.

Vladivostok had been selected for a host of technical reasons, each of which seemed plausible at the time. None had anything to do with directing the Soviet Union's attention to the Pacific, as some Chinese eaders—perhaps including Mao—clearly believed. On taking the oath of office, Ford was eager to meet Brezhnev. We rejected a European site because the President, wanting to revitalize Atlantic ties, thought that meeting his European colleagues in the shadow of a summit with Brezhnev might give the appearance of downgrading Europe. And when Dobrynin pointed out that Vladivostok would fit nicely into a presidential trip scheduled for Japan and Korea in November, we made the convenient choice. A Brezhnev summit in Asia was logistically easy, and it was unprecedented, therefore both exciting and newsworthy. No expert in any agency warned against the implications for China, though I should have known better on my own.

Deng wasted no time voicing Chinese displeasure. During welcoming chitchat at the Great Hall of the People on Monday, November 25, he asked how I had found Vladivostok. I replied that I had never been so cold in my life as at Vladivostok and, somewhat addled from a week of presidential trips and the long sessions at the summit, added: "Now I know why the Chinese never settled in that territory." By implying that Vladivostok had always been Russian, I had, of course, poured fuel onto an already raging fire of resentment. Deng immediately set me straight: "There have been many Chinese in that area. In the past, the inhabitants were mainly Chinese." The different name given to the city by the Chinese and the Russians reflected their respective purposes, according to Deng. For the Chinese name translated into "sea slug," while the Russian name meant "rule of the east." "I don't think it has any other meaning except what it means at face value," Deng added. Nor should we have any illusions that a Russian eastward thrust could be confined to China. "East also includes the part of the Pacific you are in," warned Deng.

To demonstrate that two could play at triangles, Deng set about doing so within our government by conveying, on Mao's behalf, an invitation for Secretary of Defense James Schlesinger to visit China. His itinerary, Deng suggested innocently, might include Xinjiang and Inner Mongolia, both of which were military regions along the Soviet border. Since one could never be certain that Westerners got the point, Deng stressed that the fact of the visit would be its own meaning. Mao and Deng could not have been unaware of the backbiting going on between Schlesinger and me; it was a guaranteed space filler for Washington columnists. Weighing in on the side of the ostensible anti-détente forces in the United States was undoubtedly a tempting riposte to our faux pas in going to Vladivostok.

The invitation also served a strategic purpose. A visit by the American Secretary of Defense to China—especially when highlighted by stops in the regions bordering the Soviet Union—would be received as an overt challenge in Moscow—especially since no Secretary of Defense had ever visited Moscow. With the trade bill teetering on the brink of collapse and the Vladivostok agreement under attack, we neither needed nor wanted such a taunt at that stage.

I replied that we welcomed visits to China of Cabinet members but that a visit by the Secretary of Defense was premature. I softened the rejection by offering to accept an invitation for President Ford to visit China in 1975. Deng extended the invitation immediately without even pretending to check with Mao. For all I know—though I doubt it—the sole purpose of the Schlesinger invitation may have been to get me to volunteer a presidential visit.

The Chinese side had other means to show its displeasure. The visit to Beijing on the heels of the summit at Vladivostok was the only time since my secret visit that I was not received by Mao. Our triangular diplomacy had clearly become too transparent for these experts of realpolitik. Allowing high American policymakers to confer with Brezhnev and Mao within a few days of each other was too much.

Nevertheless, our hosts would not dissociate the visit entirely from the leaders who had restored the Sino-American relationship. On arrival, and before the meeting with Deng, my children, Nancy, and I were taken for a brief meeting with Zhou Enlai in what was said to be a hospital but appeared to be a normal state guest house. Zhou was charming while insisting that his doctors had prescribed a cure preventing him from discussing political subjects that might strain him (see Chapter 5).

Once the Chinese point had been made about the strategic triangle, Deng saw to it that the actual discussions proceeded in an extremely cordial manner. He set the tone within hearing of the press when he greeted me at the Great Hall of the People:

> People are saying in the world that now relations between our two nations are chilling a bit. This is the seventh visit of the Doctor and this can be taken as the third exchange of views between our nations this year. So this opinion circulating in some places cannot be taken as accurate.

I confirmed that relations were proceeding well, whereupon Deng reiterated the importance China attached to its ties with Washington: "I don't think the signing of the Shanghai Communiqué on either side was taken as an expedient move." To underscore the affable atmosphere, Deng attended as a guest the welcoming dinner for my party, which for reasons of protocol was hosted by the foreign minister. Several hundred officials and diplomats had been invited, and a military band interspersed Chinese songs with popular American tunes, much as it had during Nixon's visit. The next evening, Deng invited my delegation to share a Mongolian hot pot meal with him in the private room of a public restaurant—another unusual courtesy.

Throughout all subsequent meetings, Deng insisted on calling me "the Doctor"—an honorific tribute to my academic background and one which was also adopted by Mao. Under Deng, the pace of the conversations was far less leisurely and discursive than it had been with Zhou. Meetings were scheduled for fixed periods of time and followed an agenda agreed in advance. There were generally three meetings a day lasting one and a half hours each and, as under Zhou, they alternated between the state guest house and the Great Hall of the People.

At first, the discussions followed familiar lines. Deng, if anything more anti-Soviet than Zhou, discussed the Sino-American relationship as if containment of the Soviet Union was a joint enterprise—as if, in fact, we were members of the same alliance. He pledged Chinese cooperation in strengthening America's relations with Europe as essential parts of the strategy for thwarting Soviet expansionism. To facilitate this strategy, Deng said he was encouraging us to maintain close relations with Japan, heretofore a source of great Chinese concern:

> It is our wish that the U.S. keep its good relations with Europe and Japan. . . . Because now the Soviet Union is determined to seek hegemony in the world, if they wish to launch a world war and don't get Europe first, they won't succeed in achieving hegemony in other parts of the world, because Europe is so important politically, economically, and militarily . . . We feel with respect to the U.S. that when the U.S. deals with the *polar bear*, it is also necessary for the U.S. to have strong allies in Europe and Japan.

He hoped the United States, Europe, and Japan would "be in a position of partnership based on equality. It is only on the basis of equality that you can establish real partnership." No wonder that I remarked to Deng that China was turning into one of our better NATO allies.

But if we agreed on strategy, serious differences existed as to tactics. Deng and his associates rejected détente with a passion that would have pleased the neoconservatives at *Commentary*. He asserted that Soviet goals were unchanging:

> To try to divide the U.S. from its allies . . . they will never give up this goal, whether in the past, present, or future. And the third purpose will be to maintain the monopolistic status of your two countries in the field of nuclear weapons [and thus] intimidate countries with only a few nuclear weapons and thus reach their aim of hegemony.

Any treaties the Soviets signed were mere way stations of that strategy. Hence:

> On our side, we don't believe it is possible to reach détente
> —still less maintain ten years of détente. And we don't think
> there is any agreement that can bind the hands of Russia.

I agreed with Deng's analysis of Soviet objectives and the imperative of thwarting them. But America's tactical needs were different. Having just surmounted Watergate, we needed a more complex strategy. So long as the United States could be portrayed as embarked on a needlessly belligerent policy, the various peace movements would reappear, coalescing under the banner of restraining a warlike America, and European governments would be under pressure to dissociate from us. In our view, being identified with the pursuit of peace was the precondition of an adequate defense policy and a strong alliance.

I cannot report that our Chinese interlocutors were swept off their feet by my arguments. They did not contest them. But since détente gave us more options than they had, it was not a condition statesmen tend to celebrate. Foreign Minister Qiao Guanhua pointed out why tactics had to be subordinate to strategy: "The decisive fact is not any treaty but a policy, the principles and the lines." In the end, Deng declared a truce. He hoped that the United States would maintain military superiority:

> As for the strategic emphasis of the Soviet Union, we see it
> as "a feint toward the East to attack in the West"—to attack
> in Europe. It doesn't matter if we have different views, we
> can see what happens.

What happened next was that America's capacity to act internationally was reduced even further by domestic paralysis. The spring and summer of 1975, as we have seen, witnessed a stalemate in SALT, the collapse of the American-Soviet trade agreement, the fall of Indochina, and the culmination of the intelligence investigations. Beijing surely welcomed the cooling of American-Soviet relations, though not when it was imposed by American domestic weakness. But the increasing stalemate between the President and Congress clearly devalued the United States as a strategic partner in Chinese eyes. All this found expression in a *People's Daily* editorial of May 9 that described the United States as "increasingly vulnerable and strategically passive."

For Beijing, the nightmare that China might confront a dreaded isolation reappeared as a result of Washington's creeping internal paralysis. This was a matter of great domestic import as well. For if the United States was becoming incapable of protecting the equilibrium, China would have to rally its people to a new round of nationalism and sacrifice. But that, in turn, would lead to an exacerbation of the Taiwan issue, jeopardizing the American relationship even more. As Chinese confidence in America's ability to supply a counterweight to Soviet expansionism declined, Beijing began to withdraw into a Third World posture of blaming both superpowers, though the Soviet Union was still receiving the brunt of the criticism.

At the same time, China's domestic situation was also becoming more complicated. Mao was growing feebler; Zhou was ill (physically and probably politically); Deng was still establishing himself. In the meantime, increasingly assertive domestic opposition to Deng's reformist policies was festering around what later came to be known as the Gang of Four, led by Mao's wife, Jiang Qing. For all these reasons, China's foreign policy lacked the clear sense of direction which usually distinguishes it. Some of China's leaders and media throughout 1975 and the better part of 1976 involved themselves in our domestic politics by joining the attack on détente.

## Dialogue with Deng and Mao

It was a strange state of affairs. No allied leaders received fuller briefings regarding our policy and intentions than the Chinese. Since there was little economic interaction and few explicitly cooperative political projects, the best way to coordinate policies was by means of an accurate understanding of each other's strategy. And the Chinese leaders, following the same principle, reciprocated by providing considerable detail about their own approach.

This had two consequences. In normal diplomacy, high officials discuss specific steps their countries can take together or try to induce action from their interlocutor by offering some quid pro quo. Nothing like that occurred in the first years of Sino-American relations. My discussions with Mao, Zhou, or Deng were conceptual, almost theoretical. The one attempt at tactical collaboration—China's mediation on Cambodia in June 1973—was not repeated; Zhou and later Deng did not again risk their standing on the mysteries of American domestic politics.[1]

Regarding long-term strategy, our policies, though parallel, were never formally coordinated and continued to depend on conceptual discussions, which, in 1975–76, had to address Chinese concerns about America's decreasing capacity to shape events and about our strategy. The Chinese leaders argued that détente might weaken the vigilance of potential victims of Soviet expansionism without rallying American public opinion. In actuality, they were worried lest our assessment turn out to be on the mark and lay the predicate to more effective opposition to Soviet moves in the West. For then the practical result might be to cause the "ill water [to] flow toward China," as Mao had said, and thus enhance the danger of Soviet pressure on China. To explain to these practitioners of realpolitik that such a strategy was beyond the ken of American policymakers would have run up against Chinese experiences accumulated over five thousand years of shifting alliances.

In essence the debate was not about the specific arguments being advanced but about the nature of flexibility. It was natural for Chinese leaders to seek to reduce our options to the fewest number and preferably to the one most compatible with China's long-term security, which was an explicitly confrontational course toward the Soviet Union, for that would reduce their uncertainty as well as our bargaining power. It was equally in our interest to maintain options that gave us the possibility to adjust specific policies to our strategic requirements as well as imperatives of gaining public support.

This was particularly the case because, at that moment, Chinese policy was beginning to veer toward ideological rigidity. The so-called Gang of Four, which included, in addition to Mao's wife, Zhang Chunqiao, Yao Wenyuan, and Wang Hongwen, played a dominant role during the last six months of Mao's life. Far more ideological and radical than Deng, they denounced his reform policies as a return to the "capitalist road" and also adopted an increasingly belligerent attitude toward America's relations with Taiwan. Clearly they were appealing to Mao's ideological proclivities, which the aged Chairman himself had only muted in the face of extreme danger from the Soviet Union.

Thus my next trip to Beijing, starting on October 19, 1975, proved to be the most difficult of all my encounters with Chinese leaders. The purpose was to prepare Ford's summit with Mao and Deng planned for early December. As the visit progressed, it became clear that Chinese Foreign Minister Qiao Guanhua was pursuing a harder line than Deng without the latter seeming able to rein in his subordinate. Years later, we learned that Qiao had thrown in his lot with the Gang of Four, who, within six months, were to succeed in overthrowing Deng.

Qiao Guanhua was not a natural recruit for this quartet. A disciple of Zhou Enlai, he had been my counterpart in drafting the Shanghai Communiqué in 1972. He had impressed me as subtle, extremely erudite, and very charming when it suited him. Qiao came from the bourgeoisie, had studied in Germany, and prided himself on his knowledge of Hegel. Why he took up with the Gang of Four must remain conjectural since he never explained it in the years that remained to him after Deng returned from exile a second time and Qiao was dismissed. Was it conviction, opportunism, or the influence of his young wife, a close friend of Mao's wife? Whatever the reason, Qiao displayed a convert's zeal and with good reason. For he was a classic type of Chinese politician-bureaucrat whom the ideologists identified as "Confucian" and to whom Mao occasionally referred sarcastically as "Lord Qiao."

A few weeks earlier, at the United Nations, Qiao had made a blistering attack on our détente policies, and now he resisted the drafting of a communiqué without which the Ford summit might appear anticlimactic. Part of the problem was inherent in the evolution of the relationship. Richard Nixon's historic 1972 trip had produced the Shanghai Communiqué, which had laid down a basic charter of restored Sino-American relations; there was no need to repeat its maxims. The next step would be to recognize Beijing as the government of China, for which we were not ready, and the Chinese leaders were reluctant for their own domestic reasons to agree to a communiqué that did not mention Taiwan. Still, the Chinese leaders, especially Deng, attached great importance to Ford's visit and to a demonstration that Sino-American relations were still close, for this was one of their key international assets.

So it happened that, in October 1975, I represented a divided United States in a Chinese capital beset by its own divisions. Deng welcomed me at the Great Hall of the People and sought to ease the tension associated with the foreign minister's U.N. speech. Even when we differed, he said, "we meet as familiar friends." I observed half jokingly that the foreign minister was trying to intimidate me: "He fires so many cannons." "They are empty," replied Deng. Yet Qiao seemed strong enough domestically to ignore the rebuke. At the opening banquet which followed and which Deng also attended, Qiao turned his toast into an attack on détente drawn verbatim from his U.N. speech, about which I had already indicated my displeasure:

> The stark reality is not that détente has developed to a new
> stage but that the danger of a new world war is mounting.

> We do not believe there is any lasting peace. Things develop according to objective laws independently of man's will. The only way to deal with hegemonism is to wage a tit-for-tat struggle against it. To base oneself on illusions, to mistake hopes or wishes for reality and act accordingly, will only abet the ambitions of expansionism and lead to grave consequences.[2]

I replied sharply and extemporaneously, ignoring my prepared remarks. Our country was pursuing the policy most suited to its particular circumstances, I said. We would resist hegemony wherever it was attempted. But we would not seek confrontations for their own sake, and we alone would determine when to engage in them. In any event, our firm actions had contributed more to thwarting Soviet expansionism than the tough-sounding rhetoric of "others" (a crack at Qiao). While I was speaking, the television lights were suddenly extinguished, and American viewers therefore never witnessed the tense exchange.

The next morning, Deng tried to remove the sting from the previous evening's events. He was looking forward to the President's visit, he said. And the fact of the visit was far more important than whatever disagreements might exist: "It will be all right if our minds meet, or if they do not. We will welcome him."

After some discussion on the technicalities of the President's trip, I presented our international strategy in some detail:

> The strategic necessity which we both face is that of the Soviet threat. I think it is important to understand that here we face three problems: one, the overall strategy; second, the tactics that we have to pursue; and third, our relationship as it relates to the overall international situation.

The Soviet Union, I continued, was becoming stronger militarily but as a result of the evolution of technology, not of our détente policies. I was agnostic as to whether the Soviet strategic focus was toward the West or toward the East:

> Since the Soviet Union is both a European and an Asian country, it is important to prevent it from achieving hegemony in either place. And since we are the principal element

of defense against the Soviet Union, we have to be strong in both places. As I have said to your foreign minister, I do not know which theory is correct—whether they are feinting in the East to attack in the West or feinting in the West to attack in the East. I do not think it makes any difference, because if they attack in the West and succeed, the East will eventually face a much more massive force; and if they attack in the East, then the West will eventually face a much more massive force. So, as far as the United States is concerned, the problem is not significantly different.

Where we differed, I argued, was over tactics and, with respect to these, we faced a paradox. The Chinese public stance was extremely intransigent, though, in most parts of the world, China's day-to-day policy was, in fact, quite passive. The American public stance was more flexible in part because we were to be found on all the battlefronts, wherever "the Soviet Union stretches out its hands." And we could sustain these battles only by convincing our public of our essentially peaceful purposes:

> Therefore, in the Middle East, in Angola, in Portugal, and in other places, we have been quite active in order to prevent Soviet expansion, even when we had to do it alone and even when we were criticized for doing it.
>
> In order to pursue this policy after the domestic upheavals we have had in America as a result of Vietnam and Watergate, it is absolutely essential for us that we are in a public posture at home that we are being provoked rather than causing the tension.

But the fine points of how we achieved domestic support for a containment policy were not China's concern—still less so because the ability of the American chief executive to manage his public opinion had been thrown into question by a series of, in Chinese eyes, nearly inexplicable upheavals of which Watergate was the most prominent. Therefore, Deng's response began with a number of eminently practical debating points: How much grain was the United States selling to the Soviet Union? How much technology were we transferring? And did the Helsinki Final Act constitute a recognition of a Soviet sphere of influence? These extremely sensible questions culminated in a general proposition:

> We do not understand why the United States and the West have used their strong points to make up for the Soviet weakness. If the United States and Europe have taken advantage of the weaknesses of the Soviet Union, you might have been in a stronger negotiating position.

During the next session, Deng advanced a rebuttal to my presentation. The Soviet Union needed to be confronted. Its nuclear arsenal was growing even as ever more agreements to restrain it were being signed, and its real target was the West; the buildup in the East was basically a feint. The trouble was that Deng was claiming a voice in the strategy of the West without offering a quid pro quo other than preserving China's own independence. This it did, as I pointed out to Deng, for its own necessities and not as a favor to us. The strategic partnership between China and the United States resulted from the parallelism imposed by geopolitical necessities: even when we differed on tactics, Sino-U.S. cooperation would curb Soviet expansionism in practice.

With this, we turned to the subject on which a communiqué during Ford's visit depended: whether progress could be made on the issue of Taiwan. I had suggested that the American liaison office maintained in Beijing and the embassy located in Taipei reverse their formal status. The American mission in Beijing would be upgraded to an embassy while the one in Taiwan would become a liaison office.

Deng rejected the proposal because an American liaison office in Taipei and a Taiwanese office in Washington would leave Taiwan too much political status. In Beijing's eyes, Taiwan was a province of China and could not be accorded any diplomatic representation. Deng articulated three principles for the future of Taiwan:

> The first principle is that we insist—that we should insist on the Shanghai Communiqué. That is, we refuse any method which will lead to the solution of "two Chinas," or "one China, one Taiwan," or any variation of these two.
>
> The idea of setting up an embassy here in Beijing and a liaison office in Taiwan is a variation on "one China-one Taiwan," which we cannot accept.

The second principle is that the solution of the Taiwan question is an internal issue of the Chinese people, and it can only be left to the Chinese people themselves to solve. As to what means we will use to finally solve the Taiwan question—whether peaceful methods or nonpeaceful methods—it is a matter, an internal affair, which should be left to the Chinese people to decide.

The third point, which is also a principle to us, is that we do not admit that there can be another country which will take part in the solution of the Taiwan question, including the United States.

Deng's three principles are central to understanding Beijing's basic attitude—then as now—toward the future of Taiwan. To Chinese of whatever political views, Taiwan is a part of China so recognized internationally for centuries and reaffirmed at the Cairo Conference of November 1943 as well as in all postwar settlements. In China's eyes, Taiwan was where the alienation of its provinces began when Japan annexed the island in 1895. To Beijing, Taiwan is not a foreign country; its claim to independence is perceived as a challenge to national cohesion by legitimizing national aspirations in other geographically remote provinces close to predatory powers. China will go to war rather than give up this principle.

At the same time, the United States through six administrations has declared its insistence on a peaceful solution. Whatever the legal status of that commitment—and Deng clearly challenged its validity in his response quoted above—any Chinese government runs great risk in testing its applicability. Until the Taiwan issue finds a negotiated solution, the two sides must navigate with great restraint between their respective necessities. If China seeks a solution by force, it will hazard an American response; if the United States permits itself to be drawn into becoming a party in the Chinese civil war by recognizing or colluding with the recognition of a sovereign Taiwan, it will risk a conflict in which it will find China a tenacious and relentless adversary.

Deng, who well understood these two poles, therefore immediately softened his remarks by reminding me of Mao's statement to Nixon about being prepared to wait one hundred years for reunification with Taiwan. But the improvement in Sino-American relations did not have to wait, he said, and should proceed immediately.

To symbolize the importance the Chinese leadership attached to American relations, Deng altered the next day's schedule to arrange an elaborate picnic for the American delegation in the Fragrant Hills near Beijing, a resort area for the Communist elite. And that same theme was pursued by Mao when he received me that afternoon.

## Conversation with Mao

The interview with Mao came about in the by now customary manner. On October 21, Deng and I were discussing the southern flank of NATO—an example of how wide-ranging the practical discussions were—when Assistant Minister of Foreign Affairs Wang Hairong (whom we believed to be Mao's niece) entered around 6:00 and handed Deng a slip of paper. "The Chairman will be prepared to meet you at 6:30," Deng announced. The Chinese indicated that Mao would also like to meet my wife, who, alas, had gone shopping. Chinese communications proved to be better than one would have inferred from the then still primitive telephone system. Within fifteen minutes, Nancy was almost physically extricated from a shop and brought to the Chairman's residence.

I was shocked by Mao's appearance. He stood, as customary, before the semicircle of easy chairs in the middle of his study. But he had declined so alarmingly since I had last seen him two years earlier that two nurses were required to hold him up. Saliva dripped from his chin. He had had several strokes and could barely articulate words. Chinese being a tonal language, the interpreter had great difficulty understanding Mao and was obliged first to repeat back to him what she believed the Chairman was saying, and if she failed to understand him after several tries, he would write it out by hand.

The Chairman seemed so diminished that I feared I might prove to be the cause of his demise if the conversation lasted more than fifteen minutes. He devoted the first few minutes to Nancy: "She towers over you," he croaked.

After Nancy had left and we turned to substance, Mao seemed to gain strength. The meeting lasted over an hour and a half and turned out to be the most interesting and also the most tense of my five meetings with him.

Mao opened the conversations with his familiar bantering:

> MAO: You know I have various ailments all over me. I am going to heaven soon.
> KISSINGER: Not soon.

MAO: Soon. I've already received an invitation from God.
KISSINGER: I hope you won't accept it for a long while.
MAO: I accept the orders of the Doctor.
KISSINGER: Thank you. The President is looking forward
     very much to a visit to China and the opportunity to
     meet the Chairman.
MAO: He will be very welcome.

Mao quickly demonstrated that his mind and sardonic analytical ability were intact. The abstract, verging on academic, debate about tactics for dealing with the Soviet Union of the day before were not for Mao:

> Yesterday, during your quarrel with the vice premier, you said the U.S. asked nothing of China and China asked nothing of the U.S. As I see it, this is partially right and partially wrong. The small issue is Taiwan, the big issue is the world. [He begins coughing, and the nurse comes in to help him.] If neither side had anything to ask from the other, why would you be coming to Beijing? If neither side had anything to ask, then why did you want to come to Beijing, and why would we want to receive you and the President?

When I responded that my reason for coming was that "we have some common opponents," Mao said "yes" in English. For emphasis, he wrote "yes" on a slip of paper and handed it to me—making me probably the only person possessing a scrap of paper in English from the Chairman. My next comment, that another reason for coming to Beijing had been to benefit from China's clear perception of world affairs, found less favor: "Those words are not reliable because according to your priorities the first is the Soviet Union, the second is Europe, and the third is Japan." Mao explained how he had come to this conclusion:

> [Gesturing with his fingers] You are this [wide space between two fingers], and we are this [small space]. Because you have the atom bombs, and we don't.

And when I rejected this definition of our priorities, Mao translated his analysis of power into an interpretation of American strategy:

> There are only two superpowers in the world [counting on
> his fingers]. We are backward [counting on his fingers].
> America, the Soviet Union, Europe, Japan, China. We come
> last. America, Soviet Union, Europe, Japan, China. . . .
> . . . We see that what you are doing is leaping to Mos-
> cow by way of our shoulders, and these shoulders are now
> useless. You see, we are the fifth. We are the small finger.

So that was it. The real dispute was not over tactics against a
common opponent or over the design of détente policies; it was
whether the United States still considered the Soviet Union an adversary in the first place. Had the opening to China been just a tactical
maneuver to open the road to Moscow for a deal to divide the world
between the superpowers? Was China being led by the nose to facilitate
the carving out of American and Soviet spheres of influence which, in
time, might include China?

Mao answered my argument that such a course would be suicidal
by describing a strategy within which it might make sense. Perhaps we
were seeking to get rid of Communism once and for all by embroiling
the two Communist giants with each other and then turning on the
victor. After encouraging a Soviet attack on China, Mao explained, we
would next finish off an exhausted Soviet Union. He described this
strategy as follows:

> Let them get bogged down in China. . . . And then you can
> poke your finger at the Soviet back. And your slogan then
> will be peace, that is you must bring down socialist imperial-
> ism for the sake of peace.

The aged revolutionary who had never known a period without
struggle—and who had become emotionally so dependent on it that
he was ever contriving upheavals even after victory—would not have
believed (or would have lost respect for us had he come to believe)
that the post-Vietnam and post-Watergate America had its hands full
mobilizing the American people in defense of the global equilibrium.
To have encouraged a Soviet attack on a China with which we were
ostensibly seeking to improve relations as a prelude to an American
showdown against the Soviet rear was too Machiavellian for the United
States of the 1970s and, I dare say, of any other period. And therefore,
after my indignant rejoinder, Mao dropped the subject.

The increasing paranoia of Mao's later years surely played a role in producing this theory, which was at once brilliant and inherently frustrating for its originator. For if Mao believed what he was saying, there was no point in the conversation. If Washington and Moscow were indeed colluding, nothing I said would make any difference. And thus Mao returned to the only realistic theme, the only one which justified such a combination of defiance and plaintiveness: the attempt to coordinate Chinese and American policies in pursuit of the common objective of preventing Soviet aggression or defeating it if it occurred.

In resisting potential aggression, there are always at least two options: to try to force a showdown, or to play for time. The first course is indicated if the adversary is deemed to be implacable and if the position of the potential victim is likely to deteriorate with the passage of time. This was Britain's situation in the 1930s. Adolf Hitler was implacable, and Britain's position was bound to deteriorate as Germany rearmed.

A different strategy is called for when time is judged to be on the side of the country (or countries) on the defensive or if the threatened country is undergoing a period of temporary weakness from which it needs to recover. As indicated in earlier chapters, we thought the Soviet Union on the strategic decline, especially after the United States recovered from Vietnam and Watergate. I reminded Mao of the conversations nearly two years earlier during the course of which we had agreed to prevent or to thwart any Soviet move against the balance of power. Our strategic objective had not changed, but "we've had a difficult period because of the resignation of President Nixon, and we've had to do more maneuvering than we would have liked." That was an argument the Chairman understood; he had done plenty of maneuvering in his time. "I think that can be done," he said. "Maneuvering is allowable."

Once the dialogue had returned to the design of a common strategy, Mao raised a further challenge. Granting that there was a common objective, how was that design to be accomplished? We obviously had no confidence in our army, he said; otherwise why was it so small and so inferior to that of the Soviets? And there were apparently many Americans who doubted that nuclear weapons would ever be used to defend Europe; Mao cited a speech by Senator Barry Goldwater and a book by the military correspondent of the *New York Times* (we suspected he meant Drew Middleton) to that effect. And though he did not say so, the implication was clear: how would we defend China with a small army and inhibitions about using nuclear weapons? Was ours what Mao called a "Dunkirk strategy," even for Europe? In other words, were we preparing to evacuate the Eurasian landmass and trying to wear down the Soviet Union with a long-range strategy?

Mao had raised the central moral and strategic dilemma of the Cold War from which we escaped due to the collapse of the Soviet Union: we would not be able to prevail in a conventional war, at least initially the period of most concern to potential victims such as China, and civilization would not be able to survive a nuclear one. I replied more confidently than accurately:

> If there's a substantial attack in Western Europe, we'll certainly use nuclear weapons. We have seven thousand weapons in Europe, and they are not there to be captured. That is in Europe. In the U.S., we have many more. . . .
> . . . Mr. Chairman, finally we have to have a minimum confidence in each other's statements. There will be no Dunkirk strategy, either in the West or in the East. And if there is an attack, once we have stopped the attack, after we have mobilized, we are certain to win a war against the Soviet Union.

This response caused the Chairman to ruminate over what he called the "softness" of Europe and to throw out a parting sally. Mao pointed out that France feared the unification of Germany. I responded that we supported it, though "Soviet power in Europe must be weakened before it can happen." Mao shot back: "Without a fight, the Soviet Union cannot be weakened." (In this, Mao proved wrong.) In the Chairman's view, it was Watergate which impeded that effort. "And it seems it was not necessary to conduct the Watergate affair in that manner," he said, still mystified by the disintegration of the Nixon presidency.

Mao concluded the meeting by reiterating Deng's invitation to Schlesinger of the previous year. The Secretary of Defense would be welcome in China either as part of the President's party or separately. The purpose of the visit would be for its potential impact on the Soviet Union. And if Schlesinger came, Mao (as Deng) hoped that he would visit Xinjiang and Inner Mongolia—right at the Soviet border.

It was a performance as spectacular physically as it had been intellectually because of the scope, subtlety, and passion of the presentation. The transcript cannot reflect the extraordinary tour de force speaking represented for the ailing Chairman. Words tore themselves loose like gasps for breath, followed by exhaustion before another burst of energy produced another gust from Mao's decaying frame.

To make sure that nothing deflected the United States and China from the central challenge, Mao in effect shelved the principles with respect to Taiwan put forward by Deng the day before. He reiterated with whimsical irony his comment to Nixon that the issue of Taiwan could wait a hundred years:

> A hundred years hence we will want it and fight for it. . . .
> And when I go to heaven to see God, I will tell him that for
> the present it is better to have Taiwan under the care of the
> United States.

Afterward the Chinese released a statement which said that Mao "had a conversation in a friendly atmosphere with Dr. Kissinger"—in diplomat-speak, a very positive comment. This was slightly mitigated by a photo of Mao standing next to my wife and me in which he was smiling but wagging a finger, implying (since we had learned that these pictures were treated as signals by the population) that I (or the United States) was in need of some friendly tutoring.

## Ford and Mao: The 1975 Summit

Despite the upbeat ending of the conversation with Mao, I developed growing doubts about the President's visit. Though Mao's words were less contentious than Deng's and much less so than Qiao's, they did contain an undertone of hectoring which might, during a presidential visit, turn threatening. The Chinese leaders could have no interest in demonstrating a cooling of relations with the United States. But if they were reaching the conclusion that we were becoming irrelevant because of our domestic travails—or if the Chinese internal situation grew more embattled—ideological proclivities might prevail. And whatever the explanation for the obvious Chinese reluctance to agree to a communiqué, it signified, at a minimum, that the top leaders either did not expect significant new developments in American-Chinese relations or believed that any attempt to go beyond the

Shanghai Communiqué would raise insuperable obstacles in either Washington or Beijing, or both.

We therefore took three steps: we notified Beijing that it was best to stop further work on a communiqué and that a press statement at the end of the visit would suffice; we curtailed the itinerary by eliminating the provincial stops and limiting Ford's trip to a series of working meetings in Beijing; and we decided to add brief visits to Indonesia and the Philippines in place of the sightseeing tour of China's provinces. This would reduce the weight that the China visit would carry in American public opinion, and it was a gesture Beijing was sure to understand: that the United States would not make its policy in Asia hostage to any country however important.

When Ford dismissed Schlesinger a week after I returned from Beijing, it was no doubt perceived in China in the same manner. The two events were in no way connected. Ford had made the decision while I was traveling on grounds not having the remotest connection with my visit to Beijing or the Chinese invitation to Schlesinger. In China, however, it was undoubtedly regarded—at least initially—as a response to the attempt to manipulate the tensions between members of the Ford Administration and between the administration and Congress.

The Chinese did react sharply. On November 4, a little less than forty-eight hours after Schlesinger's dismissal, Qiao called in George Bush, then head of our liaison office, and requested that the announcement of the President's trip be delayed. He told Bush that China based its policy on self-reliance and that China "neither fears intimidation nor seeks protection." At the same time, Qiao conspicuously repeated that China was in no hurry with respect to Taiwan, removing the most contentious issue from the immediate agenda. The United States owed China a debt, he said, but further delay in establishing full American-Chinese relations would not "cause the sky to fall." On November 13, the trip was finally announced.

The mood in Washington was shown in my final briefing memo to Ford just before his departure. If he were hectored about détente, I wrote, he should "ask who has been doing the talking and who has been doing the acting. . . . I would not accept any criticism. If they attack détente, tell them it is our business. Don't reassure them. But be extremely courteous."

As it turned out, Ford was received on December 1, 1975, with impeccable courtesy. Deng greeted us at the airport with an impressive entourage of leaders (notably excluding Madame Mao) and escorted us to the state guest house, where, in one of China's subtle touches, Zhou Enlai's wife, Deng Yingchao, was waiting to convey her husband's welcome (though incapacitated, Zhou retained the title of Premier). Vice Premier Deng set the tone during the social chitchat: "Your visit should reflect the relations between our countries and our friendship."

Deng continued in this vein at the welcoming banquet. Mao's wife made a token appearance during the photo session, exchanged the minimum number of words with the President, and then disappeared, oozing dissociation. For the rest of the evening, the festive air was marred only by the fact that the superb army band, confused as to Ford's alma mater, was playing Michigan State instead of Michigan songs, proving that even the normally impeccable Chinese protocol is capable of a lapse.

Deng's welcoming toast had none of the fire and brimstone of Qiao's earlier greeting to me. He described the President's visit as a major event; called Americans a great people; lauded the Shanghai Communiqué as "famous" and "unique"; reaffirmed the common objective of opposing hegemony; and noted that, "on the whole," there had been "an increase in the contacts and friendship between our two countries." Deng concluded with some exalted Maoisms about "there is turmoil under the heavens," attacks on "hegemony," and an evocation of the Chinese mission to dispel illusions of peace— a by now almost obligatory dig at détente.

Ford replied in a dignified manner, affirming the importance we attached to friendship with China but holding firm on the basic lines of our policy:

> The United States will strive both to reduce the dangers and to explore new opportunities for peace without illusion. The current situation requires strength, vigilance, and firmness. But we will also continue our efforts to achieve a more peaceful world, even as we remain determined to resist any actions that threaten the independence and well-being of others.[3]

The next day, Ford and Deng elaborated on the themes of the banquet. Deng set the stage by welcoming the President and affirming the significance of the meeting:

> We believe in having deep exchanges on matters. It does not matter if we have different views or even if we quarrel sometimes. And perhaps the Secretary will remember that Chairman Mao once told him: small quarrels can lead to big unity.

I did not recall Mao making any such remark. But I was happy enough to go along with Deng's effort to confer Mao's blessing on the effort to improve American-Chinese relations. Deng took the occasion to distinguish himself from his foreign minister when he agreed to Ford's suggestion that Qiao and I be assigned the task of looking into the feasibility of a public statement: "Yes, we can leave that to those two who have always specialized in that work, including quarreling."

Ford then took over the floor for an extensive tour d'horizon. Long, formal pronouncements were not his favorite means of communication. But he had prepared himself carefully, having distilled the bulky briefing books into notes from which he spoke. His presentation was thoughtful and subtle. Ford rebutted some of the arguments Mao had made to me. He rejected the Chairman's proposition that China had become our fifth priority and that we would never use nuclear weapons in defense of the balance of power in Eurasia:

> We, of course, do feel that our relations with other nations are important, but we attach a special significance to the relationship that we have with the People's Republic of China. . . .
>
> . . . We do not disguise or hide the fact that we are negotiating with the Soviet Union to stabilize the international system and to improve our bilateral relations. This is in our best interest in a context where in a conflict it might be very, very difficult to contain the resort to nuclear weapons. If we can reduce tensions, it enables us in the United States to mobilize the support necessary to be a vital force in resisting Soviet expansionism.
>
> Even though we make this effort to relax tensions with the Soviet Union, and even though we seek to stabilize the international scene, let me assure you that we will resist expansion in either the East or West—any military expansion by the Soviet Union—and with our nuclear capability.

When Deng repeated his historical analogy to Western weakness in the face of Fascism in the 1930s, Ford retorted:

> We agree with you that the Soviet Union in many respects is comparable to Hitler in the 1930s. But I think there is somewhat a different situation today. Under no circumstances will you find the United States in the 1970s adopting a similar position [to Britain's in the 1930s] now or in the future. . . .
> . . . Our military budgets will continue to grow, and we will maintain the strength to meet aggressors. . . .

In concluding, Ford put an end to the history lessons by reminding Deng that Communist Russia had made war with Nazi Germany inevitable by its own appeasement of Hitler, which, in fact, had had more far-reaching consequences than Britain's:

> We have been talking about history, Mr. Vice Premier. It is true that the West made some mistakes against Hitler, but it is fair to say when Poland was invaded, the West did respond. History also shows that in the East the response came only after the invasion [of the Soviet Union] began: so we all made mistakes.

All of us—including Deng—understood that the official Chinese line would emerge from the President's meeting with Mao. As usual, it was scheduled on short notice and, as four weeks earlier, some of my assistants were whisked away from wherever they happened to be (Joe Sisco, for example, whom I wanted to give an opportunity to shake Mao's hand, was retrieved from the Ming Tombs fifty kilometers from Beijing).

Mao seemed in slightly better shape physically than he had been four weeks earlier; he could stand somewhat more easily, though his speech showed no improvement. Perhaps out of deference to his visitor, Mao made no fiery revolutionary assertions, but his joshing style was intact. He opened the substantive part of the conversation by asking Ford what he had discussed with Deng in the morning. The President replied:

> FORD: We discussed the problems we have with the Soviet Union and the need to have parallel actions as we look at the overall circumstances internationally, the need for

> your country and mine to work in parallel to achieve
> what is good for both of us.
>
> MAO: We do not have much ability. We can only fire such
> empty cannons.
>
> FORD: I do not believe that, Mr. Chairman.
>
> MAO: With regard to cursing, we have some ability in that
> respect.

While Mao's disabilities appeared to have somewhat improved, he conveyed his preoccupations about them in his usual sardonic manner:

> MAO: Your Secretary of State has been interfering in my
> internal affairs.
>
> FORD: Tell me about it.
>
> MAO: He does not allow me to go and meet God. He even
> tells me to disobey the order that God has given to
> me. God has sent me an invitation, yet he [Secretary
> Kissinger] says, don't go.
>
> KISSINGER: That would be too powerful a combination if
> he went there.
>
> MAO: He is an atheist [Secretary Kissinger]. He is opposed
> to God. And he is also undermining my relations with
> God. He is a very ferocious man, and I have no other
> recourse than to obey his orders.
>
> KISSINGER: We are very glad.
>
> MAO: Yes, indeed. I have no other way out, no way at all.
> He [Secretary Kissinger] gave an order.
>
> FORD: To God?
>
> MAO: No, to me.

For Mao, the potential divisions within his country were an even graver preoccupation. He referred to this elliptically when he informed Ford that the head of the People's Republic's liaison office in Washington, Huang Zhen (who was present), had been asked to extend his tour of duty for two years. But that was not the real purpose of Mao's observation; it was, rather, to hint at domestic tensions within China, the full import of which we did not understand for some months:

> There are some young people who have some criticism about
> him [Ambassador Huang]. And these two [Wang Hairong,

his niece, and Nancy Tang, the interpreter] also have some criticism of Lord Qiao. And these people are not to be trifled with. Otherwise, you will suffer at their hands—that is, a civil war. There are now many big character posters out. And you perhaps can go to Qinghua University and Beijing University to have a look at them.

Was the octogenarian revolutionary afraid of a revolution by his own disciples as the end approached? Or was he generating one of his periodic assaults on whatever Establishment was in place? Did Mao fear that China's ultimate danger was internal instability? Or was he encouraging turmoil to keep the revolutionary fires burning? Was he warning the older generation that his ideological disciples—which Wang and Tang certainly were—were about to sweep it away? Or was Mao unfolding a design that ended with the overthrow of Deng four months later? Did he know what outcome he preferred at this stage? Or had he finally understood that the tensions between an ancient civilization's quest for stability and his dream of a permanent revolution were beyond his capacity to control, leaving it to the waves to determine the ultimate impact of the storm he had unleashed?

These preoccupations also explain why Mao spoke to Ford about Sino-American relations more with a sense of resignation than with any particular sense of direction:

> It seems to me at present there is nothing very much between our two countries, your country and mine. Probably this year, next year, and the year after there will not be anything great happening between our two countries. Perhaps afterwards the situation might become better.

Yet even at this moment of relative passivity, there was more to Mao's statement than the stagnation it seemed to foreshadow. Since neither side was in a position to undertake dramatic departures on Taiwan, Mao was basically repeating in operational terms his earlier statement that China could wait a hundred years for the solution of the Taiwan problem. It was a kind of assurance that China would be patient and that it would not press the subject for the immediate future.

When Ford raised a series of concrete issues in various regions of the world, Mao made characteristically cryptic comments on the

President's explanation of American policy. With respect to Yugoslavia, Mao said—presciently as events proved—that he had his doubts about the cohesion of the country after Tito because "it is made up of so many former states." Mao favored Spain's membership in the European Community because Europe was far too divided as it was. The mood of the conversation was free of the innuendos to which I had been subjected four weeks earlier.

The subject of Angola took up a significant part of the conversation and was to mortgage American-Chinese relations for some time to come. Just as the attempt to secure Chinese mediation on Cambodia two years earlier had been aborted by the congressional ban on military action there, so Chinese efforts to cooperate on Angola failed when the Tunney and Clark Amendments destroyed the possibility of American assistance to the anti-MPLA forces. When Ford outlined our effort to stop the Soviet-Cuban enterprise, Mao interjected somewhat embarrassingly: "You don't seem to have many means."

The President explained that he had just approved another $35 million in support funds—the small amount of which tended to support rather than contradict Mao's implied criticism—and asked the Chairman to help out. For Mao, whose relationship with the United States was importantly based on the expectation of American support against the Soviet Union on its borders, it could not have been exactly confidence-inspiring to be asked to assist in stopping Soviet moves in Africa, thousands of miles from Soviet territory and much more accessible to American power.

Mao went along with Ford's request. This led to some desultory talk about which African country might allow transit for Chinese equipment. Because Tanzania's Julius Nyerere, China's traditional friend in Africa, had thrown in his lot with the MPLA, Mao urged using Zaire (three months later, when I was shuttling around Africa, I found that Mao had, in fact, kept his promise and delivered some thirty tanks). Ford urged Mao to use his influence to keep Mozambique neutral on Angola, and Mao, while skeptical, indicated that "we can make a try."

Two weeks later, Congress stopped the disbursement of the funds Ford had mentioned to Mao and ended our Angolan involvement. But at that moment in the Chairman's study, the mood was still upbeat: "We have not had," said Mao, putting his imprimatur on Ford's visit, "discussions, conversations with the Soviet Union like the ones we have had with you. I went to Moscow twice and Khrushchev came three times to Beijing. On none of these occasions did the talks go really well."

To demonstrate his good feelings, Mao escorted Ford to the front door of his residence—a signal courtesy that had not been vouchsafed to Nixon. Given his infirmity, it was particularly noteworthy, for Mao could barely stand, and walking—even when supported by two aides —must have been excruciatingly difficult. This atmosphere of bonhomie inspired a Ford effort to add a light touch by reverting to the beginning of the conversation: "I will tell Henry to stop interfering in your domestic affairs." Realizing that he had just told Mao to drop dead, the President corrected himself by saying that he hoped Mao, even without orders from me, would not follow God's invitation. Just to play it safe, I added that I would stand by my orders, whereupon Mao indicated that he would obey.

By the end of Ford's visit to China in December 1975, the glow of the courtship period of Sino-American relations was waning; the complexities inherent in the relationship—which Soviet Ambassador Anatoly Dobrynin facetiously called "trying to pick up caviar with chopsticks"—were becoming apparent. But, as in lasting marriages, this meant that the two sides were learning to live with each other's sometimes differing needs. The Chinese were beginning to understand that we would do our utmost to prevent Soviet expansionism even when they questioned our method. And we recognized that China's foreign policy was dictated by its perception of its national interest and thus depended on the Chinese assessment of our ability to preserve the global balance of power.

## Domestic Distractions

Before American-Chinese relations could settle down, however, domestic upheavals in both countries produced an interval of uncertainty lasting a little more than two years. On December 19, seventeen days after Ford's conversation with Mao, Congress passed the Tunney Amendment proscribing further assistance to Angola and thwarting, for the second time in two years, an attempt to collaborate with China. Afterward, Chinese journals began to criticize America's strategic paralysis, and the head of China's liaison office in Washington blamed it all on American policy: "United States policy abetted Soviet efforts." If we were unwilling or unable to prevent Soviet domination in the

Third World, he argued, China might have to reassess its relations with the United States and the Soviet Union.

At the end of December 1975, the Chinese publicly released a Soviet helicopter and crew that they had been holding since March 1974 on suspicion of espionage; they even gave a dinner for the crew just prior to its release. The CIA interpreted this as a signal of displeasure at our abdication and described the Chinese gesture as the most conciliatory move Beijing had made toward Moscow since 1969 when Premier Alexei Kosygin was invited to stop briefly in China on the way home from Ho Chi Minh's funeral.

China was clearly toying with playing its Soviet card. But the objective conditions for it did not exist. Displeasure with American policy did not lessen Chinese concern about Soviet expansionism or make rapprochement with Moscow less risky. And therefore, during the course of 1976, Beijing resumed its harsh anti-Soviet line, lashing out at Soviet imperialism and hegemony, which, because of America's weaker position, made Moscow "the main source" (in Chinese news agency Xinhua's words) "of the peril of war."

On February 6, 1976, it was announced that Richard Nixon would soon be visiting China as a private citizen. On the human level, it was a thoughtful gesture to honor a friend in exile and in great human distress. On the political level, however, the implications were more ambiguous. Was it a signal to the Ford Administration to return to the policies of the Nixon period? During my visits in the fall, there had been hints contrasting Nixon and Ford which I had vigorously rebutted. Or was it an attempt to affect our domestic politics because the New Hampshire primary, in which Reagan was opposing Ford, would be taking place the same week as Nixon's visit to China? Whatever the explanation for the timing of the invitation, it raised hackles, especially on the political side of the Ford White House.

For the remainder of 1976, our election campaign imposed a hiatus on major American foreign policy initiatives toward the Communist world. It made little difference because China was undergoing an even more severe internal trauma. On January 8, 1976, Zhou Enlai died, and his funeral was the occasion for a spontaneous display of grief in Tiananmen Square commemorating the man whom the Chinese public considered the most humane of its Communist leaders.

It had been widely expected that Deng would succeed Zhou as Premier. Instead, it was announced on February 7 that a heretofore obscure leader from Hunan province, Hua Guofeng, had been appointed acting Premier. In early April, apparently spontaneous mass demonstrations took place in Tiananmen Square involving a dispute over laying wreaths in Zhou's honor at the same memorial that was to become the focal point of even more massive antigovernment demonstrations a decade and a half later. These were answered by carefully staged counterdemonstrations from ministries and other official organs. Foreign Minister Qiao Guanhua led his ministry's march through Tiananmen Square, surely a painful—and almost certainly involuntary—task for this disciple of Zhou whose style and conduct were far closer to that of the deceased Premier than to that of any of China's other leaders.

Shortly thereafter, on April 6, 1976, Deng was dismissed from all his posts but permitted to keep his party membership "so as to see how he will behave himself in the future." Hua Guofeng was made first vice chairman of the party—that is, successor to Mao—and Premier. Overnight, posters denouncing Deng appeared on the streets and anti-Deng demonstrations were organized.

In May, the astute China expert on the NSC staff, Richard Solomon, described the situation as follows:

> One month after the purging of Vice Premier Deng . . . Beijing's political scene shows no signs of returning to "normal." Anomalies in the public appearance pattern of senior leaders suggest continuing tensions and uncertainties of role among the central elite. Cadres are grumbling privately—and to foreigners—about Chairman Mao's willful behavior in purging Deng; and the military has been put on heightened alert against "counterrevolutionary" acts. In sum, China's domestic politics show every sign of suffering from a serious dissipation of central authority, continuing factional tension within the Politburo, and the prospect for further trouble.

The new Premier did not receive Tom Gates, the new head of our liaison office, for four months, though, when he did in June, he repeated the main lines of what we had heard from Deng and Mao. Except for needling Gates about the "Sonnenfeldt Doctrine," the rest of what Hua Guofeng told him was familiar enough: international issues took precedence over bilateral problems (such as Taiwan); ASEAN was useful for keeping "the tiger [Vietnam] from entering the back door while the wolf was being driven out the front"; Japan's top priority should be good relations with the United States.

But a month later, in mid-July, Vice Premier Zhang Chunqiao, generally regarded as the strongest man in the leadership and a key member of the Gang of Four, took the occasion of a visit by Senate Minority Leader Hugh Scott to put forward an extremely bellicose position regarding Taiwan:

> We are very clear on Taiwan. Since the issue of Taiwan has arisen, this is a noose around the neck of the U.S. It is in the interests of the American people to take it off. If you don't, the PLA [People's Liberation Army] will cut it off. This will be good both for the American and Chinese peoples—we are generous—we are ready to help the U.S. solve the problem by our bayonets—perhaps that doesn't sound pleasant, but that is the way it is.

On September 9, 1976, Mao's death was announced and, four weeks later, the Gang of Four was overthrown. Within a few months, Deng returned from exile and was to dominate China's life for the next two decades while instituting the most fundamental reform in his country's modern history.

Tensions with China dissipated with Deng's return. His priority was reform; his foreign policy was based on cooperative relations with the United States. Lectures on the philosophy for dealing with the Soviet Union ceased. Rather, Deng concentrated on specific policies, avoiding arguments about the nature of East-West relations—even during the Carter Administration, whose policies toward Moscow would surely have evoked hard criticisms had Mao still been at the helm. To be sure, Deng's definition of friendship was quintessentially Chinese—that is, without a trace of sentimentality. It reflected his assessment of the requirements of Chinese security and the conviction that China could progress economically only in a relaxed international atmosphere for which good relations with the United States were the essential precondition.

In 1979, President Carter normalized relations with China substantially on the basis of the three principles Deng had outlined in November 1975. In 1982, the Reagan Administration agreed in a communiqué to limit American military supplies to Taiwan. Thereafter, Taiwan disappeared from the Sino-American agenda for well over a decade—

until Taiwan evolved in a democratic direction and an independence movement emerged.

On Taiwan, a tacit bargain emerged, already foreshadowed during the Nixon visit, which was solidified and then maintained by all subsequent administrations. This understanding—going beyond the formal communiqué—had the following components: first, the United States endorsed a one-China policy, including abjuring a two-China or a one-China, one-Taiwan outcome; second, Mao's comment to Ford, "We can wait one hundred years," which was endorsed by Deng, meant—at least in our interpretation—that Beijing would not press the Taiwan issue to the point of using force; and third, Taiwan would foster its autonomy without challenging the ultimate unity of China.[4]

The dialogues described in this chapter provide an insight into the Chinese approach to statecraft: the precise calculation of rewards and penalties; the emphasis on considerations of equilibrium; the absence of ideology in the goals or analysis of foreign policy—a tendency even stronger in the wake of Deng's reforms than it was at their beginning; the desire for cooperative relations with the United States.

All of these represent a marked contrast from the Soviet approach. The Soviet leaders were no strangers to balance of power calculations, and they, too, could assess rewards and punishment—often quite well. But they also considered themselves the leaders of a world Communist ideology. A Brezhnev Doctrine—the right to intervene in maintaining in power Communist governments threatened by domestic upheavals —would have been improbable under Mao and unthinkable under Deng (or Deng's successors). Nor would Chinese leaders have permitted a dependent Communist regime or its own ideological factions to drag them into adventures such as Angola.

Has the Sino-American relationship changed after the collapse of the Soviet Union? Might China itself become the principal threat to America's security? The United States must make clear that it will defend the Asia-Pacific equilibrium and maintain both its alliances and its military strength in the region; this will have only a steadying influence on U.S.-China relations over the long term. But from the point of view of the balance of power, China's situation differs substantially from that of the Soviet Union during the Cold War. The Soviet nuclear arsenal represented a potential mortal threat to the United States; China will not have any comparable capability for a generation at least. The Soviet Union bordered on weak countries which it could blackmail with its overwhelming conventional forces.

China's neighbors are anything but weak, and a coalition of them would represent a significant threat to China. To forestall such a coalition is likely for the next generation to be the basis for Chinese foreign policy, together with close economic ties with the West. This is the objective basis for China's continuing need for a relationship with the United States.

As for the United States, it must navigate between an ideological hostility to China which would strain all its other Asian relationships and a reflexive sentimentality which would prevent a realistic analysis of shifting elements of Asian power. To adjust to this new reality of a Sino-American relationship in a world absent a Soviet threat was to be the challenge of Ford's (and Deng's) successors.

# PART NINE

# SOUTHERN AFRICA

# 29

# AN AFRICAN STRATEGY

## *The Challenge*

**B**efore the event, it would not have been predicted by any observer of American politics that a Republican administration would take the lead in bringing about the breakthrough to majority rule in Southern Africa. Majority rule had been a liberal cause, never translated into an operational policy. At the beginning of Nixon's first term, NSDM 38 (National Security Decision Memorandum 38) had consigned Africa to a low priority for a variety of reasons: the administration's preoccupation with Southeast Asia and the triangular relationship with China and the Soviet Union; concern about the Middle East; a reluctance to expose the white African minorities to precarious futures and to risk access to Southern Africa's strategic minerals.[1] It was therefore no small irony that the presidency of Gerald Ford should have achieved the breakthrough to majority rule in Rhodesia and accelerated the diplomacy that brought independence to Namibia, and that it did so in the name of the American national interest.

The Ford Administration had espoused the principle of majority rule even before we decided to place the full weight of American power and diplomacy behind it. At what point in the normal course of events our moral preference would have turned into policy is difficult to determine in retrospect; the need for some initiative arose from the collapse of the Portuguese empire. But surely the Angolan crisis in 1975 conferred a sense of urgency. It convinced us that to resist future depredations of outside powers, we needed to identify ourselves with African aspirations and to persuade South Africa to abandon its historic support for white minority rule in the neighboring countries.

However influenced by geopolitical considerations, we embarked with conviction and determination on the evolution to majority rule. A policy based on national interest cannot succeed unless it is geared to the convictions of those whom it is seeking to persuade, nor can those who practice it be persuasive unless they believe in what they are doing. For us, reducing the Soviet and Cuban capacity to turn Africa into a front in the Cold War was certainly a major objective. But we could only achieve it as part of a broad policy enlisting the support of the countries of the region in terms of their own sense of priorities and values.

Thus the Ford Administration's contribution to African policy was less its endorsement of the principle of majority rule than the mobilization of the elements needed for success. Our strategy achieved the support of the apartheid regime in South Africa for the principle of majority rule in Rhodesia and Namibia; won the endorsement of the African front-line states (the countries bordering Rhodesia and Namibia) of an evolutionary, rather than a confrontational, policy; and backed up the front-line states with moderate English- and French-speaking African countries. As a result, we found substantial support within the Organization of African Unity (OAU); defined a role for Britain to provide the political framework for the transition to majority rule in Rhodesia; and involved, for the first time, the African-American leadership in a consistent dialogue on Africa with top American policymakers. This enabled us to build a congressional base which sustained America's policy on the continent.

As it turned out, our practical and basically strategic approach to Africa proved to be an asset in our dealings with its leaders. Unlike many of their intellectual supporters in the United States, they did not ask a great power such as America to conduct its foreign policy solely on the basis of altruistic principle. Moral convictions may have given them the impetus to begin the struggle for independence and sustained them through its perils and sacrifices. But they had survived and prevailed by learning to be finely attuned to the nuances of the power relationships on at least three levels: vis-à-vis the erstwhile colonial power, the American-Soviet competition, and the struggles for preeminence within their own movements. They had to be, and were, realists.

Very few leaders in other continents faced the challenges inherent in the governance of Africa's nations. In Africa, leaders did not so much express a national consensus as they were obliged to create it, day after day. In Europe and the Americas, a ruler's legitimacy was

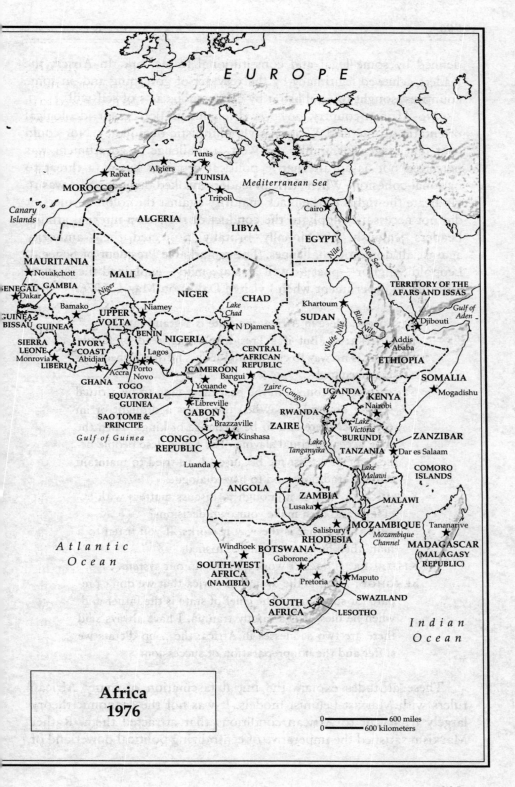

EUROPE

Mediterranean Sea

**MOROCCO**
Rabat ★
Algiers ★
Tunis ★
**TUNISIA**
Tripoli ★

*Canary Islands*

**ALGERIA**

**LIBYA**

Cairo ★

**EGYPT**

*Nile*

*Red Sea*

**MAURITANIA**
Nouakchott ★

**MALI**

Bamako ★

**NIGER**
Niamey ★

**CHAD**
*Lake Chad*

Khartoum ★

**SUDAN**

*Blue Nile*

*White Nile*

**TERRITORY OF THE AFARS AND ISSAS**
Djibouti ★

*Gulf of Aden*

SENEGAL
Dakar ★
**GAMBIA**
*Niger*

GUINEA BISSAU
**GUINEA**

**UPPER VOLTA**

**SIERRA LEONE**
Monrovia ★
**LIBERIA**

**IVORY COAST**
Abidjan ★

**BENIN**
Lagos ★
**NIGERIA**

Accra ★
**GHANA**
Porto Novo ★
**TOGO**

**CENTRAL AFRICAN REPUBLIC**

Addis Ababa ★

**ETHIOPIA**

**EQUATORIAL GUINEA**

**CAMEROON**
Youande ★
Bangui ★

*Zaire (Congo)*

**UGANDA**

**KENYA**
Nairobi ★

**SOMALIA**
Mogadishu ★

Libreville ★
**GABON**

**RWANDA**

**SAO TOME & PRINCIPE**

Brazzaville ★
**ZAIRE**
Kinshasa ★

**BURUNDI**
*Lake Victoria*

**ZANZIBAR**

*Gulf of Guinea*

**CONGO REPUBLIC**

*Lake Tanganyika*

**TANZANIA**
Dar es Salaam ★

Luanda ★

*Lake Malawi*

**COMORO ISLANDS**

*Atlantic Ocean*

**ANGOLA**

**ZAMBIA**
Lusaka ★

**MALAWI**

Salisbury ★
**RHODESIA**

**MOZAMBIQUE**

*Mozambique Channel*

Tananarive ★

**MADAGASCAR (MALAGASY REPUBLIC)**

Windhoek ★
**SOUTH-WEST AFRICA (NAMIBIA)**

**BOTSWANA**
Gaborone ★

Pretoria ★
Maputo ★

**SWAZILAND**

**SOUTH AFRICA**
**LESOTHO**

*Indian Ocean*

**Africa 1976**

0 — 600 miles
0 — 600 kilometers

defined by some legal and constitutional framework. In Africa, the leaders achieved legitimacy by the very act of governing and, in some countries, sought to establish it by conspicuous acts of self-will.

No African country, however divergent its policies or ideological orientation, practiced Western-style pluralistic democracy. Nor could it at that stage. For, unlike the West, a challenge to government was perceived not as an alternative political program but as a threat to national cohesion. When African leaders invoked democracy, it was to vindicate the rights of the black majority against the colonial rulers; it did not necessarily apply to the conduct of their own internal affairs. Leaders jealously, occasionally brutally, protected their authority against all domestic challenges. The remarkable President of Senegal, Leopold Senghor—poet as well as statesman—explained the African attitudes to government when I visited Dakar on May 1, 1976:

> SENGHOR: Here in Africa, the state is a grand family. . . .
>
> KISSINGER: . . . But if a President is the head of family, there is no way to change him unless he dies or becomes incapacitated.
>
> SENGHOR: Of course, in the past there used to be a ritual slaying of the king. When there was a drought or an epidemic, there had to be a change of kings. Then the king accepted ritual slaying. The Senegalese people believe me and trust me because I have tried to maintain African traditions and to have dialogue.
>
> KISSINGER: Well, is it enough to discuss matters with everyone and then make your own decisions?
>
> SENGHOR: Yes, that is the way it works. If you listen to a man, then he is at least half-satisfied.
>
> KISSINGER: It doesn't work that way in our system. . . .
>
> SENGHOR: . . . It is the drama of Africa that we don't prepare for succession. The chief of state is the father and, when he dies, it is a family trauma. I have always said there are two sadnesses in Africa: the coup d'etats we suffer and the nonpreparation of succession.

These attitudes explain the initial fascination of many African rulers with Marxist-Leninist models. It was not the economic theory largely irrelevant to African conditions that attracted them. Rather Marxism satisfied the imperative of centralizing political power and of providing political continuity. And it served the subsidiary purpose of not so subtly pressuring the West to open is coffers.

Given their biographies and domestic experiences, African leaders did not expect a great power to act out of altruistic motives. My relations with them did not suffer—in fact, I believe they were enhanced—by my insistence that they had to be based on reciprocal common interests. Thus, in a dinner speech to the African foreign ministers attending the United Nations General Assembly on September 23, 1975, I stated:

> We do not expect you to be in concert with us on all international issues. We ask only that as we respect your interests, are mindful of your rights, and sympathize with your concerns, you give us the same consideration.[2]

On April 21, 1976, two days before I left for Africa to launch the diplomacy that would lead to majority rule in Rhodesia, I met with the African ambassadors stationed in Washington and told them:

> We think that the future of Africa can best be achieved by Africans, and for this we believe that African unity is essential. We have no peculiar American interest that we want to serve in Africa, in the sense that we have no interest in achieving a predominant position for the United States.
>
> We believe, of course, that the development of Africa, the progress of Africa, is also in our interest. As you would have to expect, no nation does something that is not also in its own interest.

On this basis, my African opposite numbers and I established warm personal relations. They had common sense, outgoing personalities, and, quite often, a wicked sense of humor. They had no illusions about the grammar of staying in power; politics, in their view, was not a profession for weaklings. In private conversations, they rarely used the anti-Western rhetoric with which they established their credentials within the Nonaligned Movement. What they asked from the United States was understanding for their special problems, economic aid, and cooperation with their liberation movements. To end colonial rule, they were prepared to accept assistance from any quarter. This did not make them satellites of their patrons, who, they correctly believed, were serving interests of their own. To the extent that there existed a specifically African approach insulating the new African nations from the Cold War—as so many intellectuals, members of the media, and State Department officials were claiming—it was a heroic self-centeredness and a conviction that gratitude, while relevant to personal relationships, plays no role in politics.

For a long time, the Soviets gained little by their open support of African liberation movements, and we lost little by our preoccupations elsewhere. But Angola changed things. There, for the first time, an African liberation movement prevailed first through massive (at least by African standards) military deliveries from the Soviet Union, including a significant Soviet airlift, and then by the intervention of Cuban combat forces equipped by the Soviet Union. For a considerable period, there was no MPLA army to speak of; the decisive fighting was done almost exclusively by Cubans, assisted by Soviet combat advisers.

In these conditions, it was no longer possible to speak plausibly of special African "solutions." If the Soviet Union and its auxiliaries were not stopped, they would emerge as the potentially decisive factor in the affairs of the continent. The most practical and least ideological African leaders would be driven by the emerging power relationships to throw in their lot with Moscow. If they wished to avoid Moscow's (or Cuba's) embrace, they could—if the United States stood aside—at best turn to China, which was willing enough to compete with Moscow but did not possess the reach nor the resources to deal with the Soviet-Cuban thrust. Once a Soviet-Cuban base was established, it would take a major military operation to dislodge it (Cuban troops were to remain in Angola for more than fifteen years and were induced to withdraw only when—belatedly—significant military counterpressures were brought to bear by the Reagan Administration).

The most vulnerable target for the next crisis appeared to be the former Southern Rhodesia (now Zimbabwe), where a European minority of 270,000 governed some 6 million Africans. As a British colony that had unilaterally declared itself independent in 1965, Rhodesia's international legal status was anomalous. At the beginning, Britain had sought American cooperation in bringing the new regime headed by Ian Smith to heel. The Johnson Administration had demurred, and Smith had continued as Prime Minister for another full decade. Since it was not recognized by any other state, Rhodesia was technically still a British colony. Conventional wisdom had it that a solution would require Rhodesia to revoke its claim to independence, after which a new constitution providing for majority rule would be drafted under British auspices as the last act of its colonial rule.

The trouble was that Britain no longer had the power to achieve this goal by itself. Several meetings between Ian Smith and British Prime Minister Harold Wilson failed to achieve a breakthrough in the early 1970s. And international sanctions could not be effective so long as South Africa and the Portuguese colony of Mozambique were offering transit to Rhodesian trade.

By 1974, Portuguese decolonization had revolutionized the geopolitical context. The new Marxist government of Mozambique closed its border with Rhodesia and became a base for guerrillas. Of all of Rhodesia's neighbors, it was considered ideologically most disposed to inviting Cuban intervention. Faced with these potential pressures, South Africa, long a supporter of Ian Smith, began to have second thoughts about sustaining Rhodesia and withdrew the police units it had sent to the Zambian-Rhodesian frontier. South Africa's foreign minister met in Lusaka with the foreign ministers of Tanzania, Botswana, and Zambia and arranged a meeting between Smith and the leaders of the African National Council (the umbrella organization for the Rhodesian African independence movement). They gathered in a railway car at Victoria Falls, the picturesque border between Zambia and Rhodesia, under the watchful eyes of Zambia's Kenneth Kaunda and South African Prime Minister Johannes Vorster as guaranteeing powers. That extraordinary meeting, too, ended in deadlock.

The stalemate created increasing risks of outside involvement. If the guerrilla war escalated, the resistance fighters might begin to destabilize the states where they were based, especially Zambia, much as the PLO was doing to the legitimate government in Lebanon (see Chapter 33). Cuban troops might appear. And South African intervention would then be likely.

This was the geopolitical problem with which the Ford Administration sought to deal as it focused on developing a program with which African leaders could identify and a platform from which we could resist further Cuban and Soviet depredations.

## The World Looks at Angola

On September 5, 1975, four and a half months after Kenneth Kaunda's visit to Washington, I met with his foreign minister, Rupiah

Banda, in New York during the Seventh Special Session of the U.N. General Assembly. Neither of us mentioned Angola. On our side, it was because our covert program had just begun, and we expected it to succeed despite all hesitations and delays. And Banda did not raise the subject, probably because of the sensitivity of the advice his President had given us but also because no African leader could think it possible that we might fail, even less that we would be forced into failure by our own Congress.

Instead, Banda and I talked about Rhodesia. With no special sense of urgency, he put forward a practical proposal, suggesting that both the United States and Zambia should urge South African Prime Minister Vorster to use his good offices with Ian Smith: "This is where you and we come in. We should talk to Vorster and urge him to exert his influence on Smith." It was my first experience with the fact that, for many of Africa's leaders, hatred for apartheid was no insurmountable obstacle to practical cooperation with South Africa on Africa's problems. Banda extended an invitation to come to Zambia, and I accepted in principle for the following spring.

In the meantime, I sought to create the appropriate public framework for greater involvement in Africa's concerns. Both in the Secretary of State's annual speech to the United Nations General Assembly on September 22 and at the dinner I offered to African foreign ministers and their permanent representatives on September 23, I stressed America's backing for Africa's goals of economic progress, racial justice, and aloofness from great-power rivalry.[3]

I met Banda again on December 17 during the consumer-producer conference in Paris. Angola had become a public issue in which the OAU was beginning to involve itself. Banda supported our position, which was to refuse recognition to the Soviet-Cuban–backed MPLA, and I was still optimistic that the combination of French assistance, reprogrammed Defense Department funds, and American-Soviet diplomacy would bring about our objectives of cease-fire, withdrawal of foreign forces, and coalition government. Again Rhodesia was the principal subject of the conversation, and again Banda urged a joint approach to South Africa (despite the by now visible role of South African forces in Angola).

Within days, our Angolan strategy was ended by the Tunney and, later, Clark Amendments. The MPLA gained the upper hand, and the challenge of preventing Soviet-armed Cuban expeditionary forces from emerging as the arbiters of Southern Africa had become urgent. In the immediate aftermath of the unraveling of our Angolan effort, four African nations appealed to us to prevent such an outcome.

On February 5, 1976, Mark Chona, Kaunda's confidant, visited Washington and delivered a letter from his chief to Ford. Its thrust was that the only way to break the Rhodesian deadlock was a message from me to Ian Smith urging negotiations. Otherwise the guerrillas poised in Zambia and Mozambique would undoubtedly step up the war and, once armed struggle was under way, the guerrillas would accept assistance from any quarter, certainly including Cuba. I replied sharply that the threat was inappropriate and that we would not toler- ate another Cuban move into Southern Africa. Chona stressed that he was not threatening us but appealing to the United States to take measures to preclude further Cuban and Soviet actions in Southern Africa. He and Kaunda considered current trends to pose a serious danger to the security and independence of the entire region.

On February 11, Foreign Minister Nguza Karl-I-Bond of Zaire and Ambassador André Coulbary of Senegal called on Ford to express the views of the French-speaking countries. Geographically more remote, they were less concerned about majority rule in Rhodesia and far more unsettled by Soviet successes and the apparent American decision to "back out." Ford replied that "we will do everything within our power to assure that no repetition of this can take place. We are determined, and I think the mood is changing." It was an insight into congressional thinking which, on my frequent appearances before congressional committees, had thus far eluded me.

Egypt was heard from next. Minister of State Mohamed Riad visited a number of African countries in mid-February and afterward shared with American Ambassador Hermann Eilts his deep concern over the growing Soviet role on the continent and the decline of Ameri- can influence. Under the impact of the debacle in Angola, he reported, countries such as Morocco, Ethiopia, and Kenya considered themselves in serious danger; even leftist leaders like Julius Nyerere of Tanzania, who had supported the MPLA, were said to be disturbed at the magni- tude of the Soviet presence and the degree of American abdication. Riad made an impassioned plea, as a friend of the United States, that a "more active and responsive" American African policy was urgently needed. He concluded with the observation that most African leaders he had met in his journeys questioned whether the United States had any African policy at all.

During a trip through Latin America in the latter half of February,

I heard the same analysis from the leaders of the Western Hemisphere. I reported to Ford on the attitude of Venezuelan President Carlos Andrés Pérez, whose affection for Republican administrations had heretofore been distinctly muted:

> In Venezuela, it has hardly escaped President Pérez's attention that the new government in Luanda came to power on the bayonets of a Latin American state (or rather a Caribbean country, since Venezuela deeply fears that Cuba can create a black Caribbean bloc). . . .
>
> . . . In this sense, Angola, for Latin America, is more important than Vietnam. Now as then, they are interested in what is happening in Washington, not Saigon or Luanda. They know that a Latin American nation—for the first time in history—has launched an overseas invasion of military force with considerable firepower into an internal conflict in another nation with absolutely decisive results—and we tried to do something about it and failed, by our own internal division, to stop Cuba.
>
> The Venezuelans were as explicit about our failure as courtesy would permit them to be. The Peruvians were a little less willing to show anxiety, probably since Peru treasures its credentials as a nonaligned state. But there was no doubt at either Caracas or Lima that our response to the Cubans in Angola has altered the Latin view of the United States—and not for the better.

On February 23, I reported to Ford from Colombia on the views of President Alfonso López Michelsen:

> He is as concerned now about Cuba as President Pérez of Venezuela is, but . . . he sees the danger as a new Cuban strategy to exploit the racial dimension in the troubled geopolitics of the region [Latin America]. He thinks Castro will just not go to his grave before he has tried for some role in the world beyond Cuba.

I had used the occasion of my Latin American trip to stress that we would not tolerate another Cuban military move in Africa. The audience was largely skeptical. Brazilian Foreign Minister Antonio da

Silveira expressed bluntly what his colleagues in Peru, Venezuela, and Colombia had been saying more delicately. When he expressed concern that Cuban forces might show up to support Guyana in its border dispute with Brazil, I said that we would surely not tolerate such a Cuban adventure. Da Silveira shot back: "We are not sure we can rely on the United States any longer."

## Shaping of an Angolan Strategy

On March 4, 1976, the United Kingdom's ambassador, Peter Ramsbotham, conveyed to me the observations of a senior British group which had visited Rhodesia at Prime Minister James Callaghan's behest:

> The situation has marched on for the worse. The situation for the West is more serious. As David Ennals [head of the Foreign Office's Rhodesia department] said yesterday, there has been massive Communist infiltration. We are concerned about a racial war, too. Now with Rhodesia, there is a special UK situation—the constitutional problem. Jim Callaghan will not have responsibility with no power.

I told Ramsbotham that we would be "sympathetic to whatever Callaghan decides." But I warned him that we would not accept failure to achieve majority rule as an alibi for standing still for another Cuban military incursion into Africa:

> I can tell you that, in spite of the possible outcry here, we will not accept any more Cuban intervention. The consequences for Africa—and I can say from my Latin American trip—for the South Americans, for the Caribbeans—including Britain's black Caribbean possessions—of a victorious Cuban army having won will be extremely serious. We can't have a Cuban army marching all over Africa.

Ramsbotham was too disciplined and too polite to express his disagreement. But clearly he was more enthusiastic about borrowing American power to support Callaghan's quest for majority rule than about joining us in resisting further Cuban adventures. The difference in emphasis was illustrated when Mozambique closed its border with Rhodesia on March 3. Our European allies encouraged this measure by making available an aid program to Mozambique without any conditions regarding Cuban intervention. The United States refused to join the stampede; we made clear that our small contribution would lapse if Mozambique permitted outside military forces to participate in the Rhodesian struggle.

On February 12 I had conveyed our determination to resist further Cuban-Soviet interventions to Guyana's foreign minister, Fred Wills, who was visiting Washington. As a known friend and admirer of Castro's, he was certain to pass on our warning that Castro was playing with fire, that "sooner or later we will stop him," and that we would choose where to resist:

> If Cuba does not watch itself, there is going to be a military confrontation more likely in Cuba, and not in Angola. We have done everything to improve relations, but Castro can no longer get away with sending troops all over the globe.

On March 12, Ford said the same thing publicly: the United States will "strongly oppose" any further action by the Soviet Union or Cuban forces as "pure international adventurism."[4]

We did not propose to rest our policy on strategic considerations alone. On March 13, Ford for the first time committed the United States to unequivocal support for majority rule in Southern Africa: "The United States is totally dedicated to seeing to it that the majority becomes the ruling power in Rhodesia."[5]

In the best tradition of the Anglo-American special relationship, Callaghan did not explicitly argue with my comment to Ramsbotham that we would resist further Cuban adventures whether or not majority rule had been achieved in Rhodesia. Rather, pretending that resistance to new Cuban moves was largely a political problem, Callaghan unveiled a new British proposal on March 22 to "preempt" the Soviets. Its principal feature was a precise timetable for majority rule within eighteen to twenty-four months.

I supported Callaghan's proposal in a speech in Dallas the same day, calling it "most constructive." And I coupled it with a warning to Castro:

> Our cooperation is not available to those who rely on Cuban troops. The United States cannot acquiesce indefinitely in

the presence of Cuban expeditionary forces in distant lands
for the purpose of pressure and to determine the political
evolution by force of arms.[6]

Within twenty-four hours, Ian Smith turned down Callaghan's initiative. Clearly, diplomatic proposals could not by themselves change the balance of incentives which had enabled Smith to stonewall for ten years. Britain did not have the power to subdue him and could add little to what the front-line states were doing—rather ineffectively—on their own. Announcing one futile plan after another ran the risk of frustrating the African parties and providing a pretext for Soviet and Cuban intervention. As the only power capable of affecting the calculations of the parties, the United States needed to take charge of developing a strategy for Southern Africa.

"Take charge" as a slogan is as empty as it is impressive unless it generates actions which alter the circumstances that produced the crisis in the first place. A deadline is needed to galvanize action, either imposed from the outside or by a more or less arbitrary decision.

Ford decided that the best way to establish such a deadline would be to schedule a trip by me to Africa to demonstrate our interest and to put forward a coherent American position in a major speech before an African audience. If we wanted to make progress toward a political settlement before things got out of control and Ford would be absorbed in the election campaign, we needed to start as soon as possible.

When the decision was made in early February that I should go to Africa, the primary season was just about to begin. Amazingly by the standards of politics at this writing, the primaries were never discussed when the trip was set for the end of April. Part of the reason may have been that there was no practical way to take account of them. From the end of February to the end of June, there would be a primary in some state or other every two or three weeks. These would be followed by the nominating conventions and the elections.

As he had shown during the Cyprus crisis, the debate over the Jackson Amendment, and the "reassessment" of Middle East policy, Ford would not suspend foreign policy to help his electoral prospects. When I returned from my first African trip to widespread critical clamor, he told a National Security Council meeting on May 11:

> Henry has now gone to Africa, and he has carried out a
> good, responsible policy. We got a little political flak out of

the trip, but it was totally without merit. If we are going to hold our position in the world, we cannot have a foreign policy in limbo in an election year. We will continue to do what is right regardless of the primaries. This will sometimes be tough, but it is right.

We selected Lusaka to put forward our program for majority rule because, of all the front-line states, Zambia was the most directly affected by the Rhodesian issue. In 1969, the front-line states had issued the so-called Lusaka Manifesto, which, in eloquent language, had pronounced the right and duty of "all men to participate as equal members of the society in their own government." A call for majority rule, it could also be read as an assurance of the European minority to an honorable existence after it ceded power. We chose the latter half of April as the target date to enable me, during the same trip, to deliver a speech to a U.N. development conference in Nairobi outlining a program relevant to the rest of Africa. It turned out that the trip bracketed the Texas primary and that my speech was widely blamed for Ford's disastrous defeat. Ford chose to give priority to his conception of what was needed to defend the national interest over his political prospects.

## Components of a Strategy

Before launching ourselves into Africa, we needed to distill a strategy from the partially overlapping, partially incompatible objectives of the various parties. Our principal asset was that the African states themselves were urging us to become involved while the white minority governments trusted us more than any other country or, for that matter, any alternative leadership group in the United States. As for the other parties or potential parties:

• The front-line states of Mozambique, Zambia, Tanzania, and Botswana, on whose territory the guerrillas were organizing, were the conduit for arms from outside the continent and for foreign advisers or Cuban troops. But their leaders also knew that the Rhodesian forces were well armed and tough. A war would be costly and might well end with the guerrilla forces ceasing to be guests and instead dominating the host country.

- The other African states, less immediately engaged, supported majority rule in principle but were prepared to cooperate in preventing the continent from becoming a battleground of the Cold War.
- South Africa feared that armed struggle in Rhodesia might turn into the prelude to an assault against South Africa itself. At the same time, all the front-line states recognized that South African assistance was indispensable to a Rhodesian solution, for, without it, the transition would be bloody, the outcome uncertain, and the radicalization of the whole region inevitable.
- For Britain, Rhodesia represented a painful reminder of the diminution of its international status. Britain's inability to force Rhodesia into submission weakened its effort to develop a new African role based on cooperation with its former colonies. It explains as well the personal hatred many British leaders felt for Ian Smith, which complicated and often frustrated British dealings with him.
- As for the Rhodesian authorities, they had the least to gain from the processes unfolding all around them. Whatever guarantees of minority rights might be associated with majority rule, the position of the European population would inevitably atrophy. When, on April 24, I asked Sir Anthony Duff, whose specific responsibility in the British Foreign Office was Africa and the Middle East, about the Europeans' prospects after majority rule, he replied: "They could keep their businesses, but their children probably wouldn't have a future." The Ian Smith authorities could be induced to settle only by having it brought home to them that the policy we were fashioning was the least distasteful of the painful choices before them.

This maze of incommensurables—that those with power had no legitimacy and those with legitimacy no power, that the passions of the parties were matched by their distrust of each other—defined both the limits of our African strategy and its prospects.

Our first and most fundamental decision was to commit the United States unambiguously and urgently to the principle of majority rule. That decision was bitterly attacked and became an issue in the presidential campaign. But it was the simplest of the choices before us. We could not take a stand in Africa by giving lessons on geopolitics or by basing ourselves on minority governments. If we wanted to resist future Soviet and Cuban adventures in Southern Africa and to reduce and

expel Soviet and Cuban influence there—as we had in the Middle East
—our policy would have to reflect the aspirations of the vast majority
of the continent. What the defenders of the white minorities in our
domestic politics did not understand was that our course was the only
means to preserve some chance of a decent life for the settlers—albeit
in reduced circumstances.

Previous efforts had failed because they could not generate the
balance of rewards and penalties to reconcile the conflicting motivations comprising the cauldron of Southern Africa. We proposed to
develop a coherent strategy for breaking the deadlock once and for all:

- We offered the front-line states a shortcut to majority rule by throwing the weight of American diplomacy behind their goals. They
  would be spared the destruction attendant on a prolonged struggle
  and the risk to their domestic stability of establishing large guerrilla
  units on their soil. In return, we insisted that they keep foreign
  forces out of the conflict, assume responsibility for the negotiating
  positions of the Rhodesian liberation movements, and guarantee
  minority rights.
- We worked closely with moderate African leaders, especially in
  Kenya, Zaire, Senegal, and the Ivory Coast, to help shape a consensus in the OAU supportive of our policies and to protect the front-
  line Presidents from radical African and international pressures.
  (Nigeria generally supported a radical course.)
- We counted on Britain to reenter the diplomacy in Southern Africa
  and to play an important role in the constitutional conference that
  would be the culmination of the breakthrough we hoped to achieve.
  In the meantime, we would draw heavily on British expertise and
  advice.
- To South Africa's leaders, we conveyed that they would be given a
  responsible role in helping shape an Africa of peace, stability, and
  racial justice. South Africa would be treated as a valuable interlocutor and given a breathing space in dealing with its own problems
  provided it helped move Southern Africa toward a new political
  dispensation. But we made it very clear that our support of majority
  rule did not stop at the borders of South Africa.
- The odd man out was Ian Smith. All previous efforts had failed
  because they had started with negotiations with this representative
  of a white minority that had no conceivable incentive to abandon its
  dominance. We therefore proposed to deal with Smith only after the

other parties' commitments had been agreed. We could do nothing about the reality that Smith and his European minority had little to gain from our diplomacy. But we proposed to ease the transition by treating him with respect. I had no record with him either for good or ill and considered him a problem to be dealt with rather than an enemy to be overcome. And even as I was seeking to change the way of life of the Rhodesian minority, I, as a former refugee, had sympathy for the anguish with which it faced the imminent collapse of its way of life.

## African Policy and the Domestic Consensus

In our daily meetings, Ford took an active interest in the evolution of African policy and urged us to give it the most sweeping formulation, including the development of military options to back up our political goals. For it was clear that resisting the Soviet-Cuban drive to make Cuba the military vanguard of Communism required more than a political manifesto.

On March 24, 1976, I assembled our WSAG crisis management group in the Situation Room in the White House basement. Because of the importance and sensitivity of the subject, it was, in effect, an NSC meeting without the President. Because I was already coordinating African policy in preparation for my trip, Ford asked me to chair the meeting, though, since the so-called Halloween Massacre described earlier, the responsibility for the NSC machinery had become Scowcroft's. I outlined the task ahead:

> We want to get planning started in the political, economic, and military fields so that we can see what we can do if we want to move against Cuba. We should get a range of options. Later there will be an NSC meeting to discuss our objectives. Now we have to look at our capabilities so that the President can make a political decision of what to do, and how to plan it. . . .

Next I defined the strategic objective:

> . . . We must get it into the heads of the leaders of African countries that they can't have it both ways. They can't have

both the Cubans in Africa and our support. . . . We have to know what we want to do. We should consider two or three likely courses of action and go into them in detail and see what problems would result.

Deputy CIA Chief Vernon Walters prepared the following assessment for the meeting:

Although the insurgency will continue to grow, the guerrillas will remain too weak to achieve a military victory, so long as their support is limited to *moderate* amounts of matériel assistance and Cuban and Soviet *advisory* personnel.

In this situation, they will be under mounting pressure to accept Soviet and Cuban aid on a larger scale, plus Cuban *combat* personnel. It will be increasingly difficult for the very African leaders who now are seeking to *limit* Soviet and Cuban involvement to resist such pressures.

Ford told a group of senators that same day that he was determined to take firm action against such an eventuality.

The Agency's sense of urgency was not shared by all. Donald Rumsfeld, the new Secretary of Defense, reflected the Pentagon's traditional caution. Contrary to popular myth, the military likes to acquire weapons; it is reluctant to use them except in the face of the most direct challenge to American security. Limited political goals make the military nervous—especially since the Vietnam War.

When the Pentagon is reluctant, it digs in by insisting on a full consideration of options so vast and complex that the President finds himself embroiled in an almost scholarly exercise, magnifying his perplexities Rumsfeld expressed agreement with our strategy; what troubled him, he said, were the specifics of implementation. He could think of at least 150 military options, Rumsfeld averred, each related to a series of political assumptions. Before military action could be planned, each military and political permutation would have to be considered, separately as well as in relation to all the others.

Such a task was likely to consume the remainder of Ford's term, if not of the decade, and it could hardly be finished in a time frame relevant to the perils we were seeking to counter.

Much shrewder about the proclivities of his associates than he let on, Ford remained calm. The Pentagon, he ruled on March 29, need not come up with a final recommendation before my Africa trip at the end of April, only with a preliminary set of conclusions to help the President in an emergency:

> I don't think we need to say what we will do, but I think we should be prepared to take affirmative action. I don't want the Communists to get the idea that we would not take drastic action.

In the meantime, press leaks for once rendered a useful service by putting Castro on notice that things were getting serious. On March 26, a headline in the *Washington Post* read: "White House, Pentagon Weigh Military Action Against Cuba."[7] A story like that might get drowned out in the general background noise of Washington, but it was sure to catch Havana's attention.

On April 22, before I left for Africa, the WSAG reviewed the contingency planning of the past four weeks. Again principals attended. Much of the meeting was devoted to a comprehensive intelligence briefing by new CIA Director George Bush. The essence of his presentation—backed by much supporting detail—was summed up in this pithy sentence: "It is the intelligence community's prediction that Cuban troops will be involved in Rhodesia before the end of 1976."

Though Ford did not succeed in extracting a specific recommendation from the Pentagon, Rumsfeld did supply the WSAG with a competent and comprehensive set of options in six graduated steps. These plans listed the forces required and the risks involved at each stage. In a crisis, it would provide a useful compendium of the available choices, though the President would surely face bitter disagreements before taking a final decision.

As we ventured into heretofore uncharted territory, we made a major effort to build domestic support. Between March and September 1976, I met four times with groups of African-American leaders, about thirty in number. Secretary of Transportation William T. Coleman, a distinguished African-American lawyer, helped identify participants to ensure that every significant segment of opinion was represented and took part in the meetings. Dr. Leon Sullivan, who was a pioneer in working with American corporations to establish rules designed to break down apartheid in South Africa, provided much useful advice in helping to bridge the gap with the African-American community.

The meetings themselves were quite emotional because it was the first time that leaders of the African-American community had been systematically consulted by a Secretary of State. Even such a longtime critic of the administrations in which I served as Rev. Jesse Jackson pledged his support:

> We appreciate that you have accorded us respect. No other Secretary of State has accorded such respect to the black American community. . . .
>     . . . We support the African policy that you have enunciated. You have our support on this. Other Secretaries of State would not have met with us as you have.

Though there were diverse views as to tactics, the leaders of the African-American community were extremely supportive of our general strategy.

Congress proved less receptive. On March 18, I met with six members of the Senate Foreign Relations Committee—mostly from the liberal side whence we judged most of our difficulties would originate if we stood up to another Cuban military move: Hubert Humphrey, Gale McGee, Dick Clark, Clifford Case, Jacob Javits, and Charles Percy. I pulled no punches about our intentions. We planned to put the United States squarely behind majority rule in Southern Africa, and we would work to achieve breakthroughs on Rhodesia and possibly Namibia that summer. But if Cuban troops intervened, I said, "We would not do something in Rhodesia, but we might have to do something, including military pressure against Cuba."

Senator Clark, author of the amendment which had proscribed further resistance to Cuban moves in Angola, claimed to agree with the strategy in principle. But he argued that Rhodesia was not the appropriate place to take that stand because it would ally us with the white minority government under Ian Smith.

Avoiding this dilemma was, of course, the reason for putting forward America's support of majority rule. I pointed out that, if we were forbidden to oppose Cuban and Soviet military moves while we were in the process of implementing our political program, it would "lead to the permanent presence of Cubans in Southern Africa" because they were bound to intervene where resistance was politically difficult.

Humphrey summed up the senators' conclusion:

> The American people are very concerned about Cuba. They care a lot more about this hemisphere. There is anger in the

country about what the Cubans are doing in Africa. I think whatever you do in this hemisphere would get support, and from the Congress. We think intervention in Africa is a lost cause.

I spent the next weeks briefing congressional committees and received roughly the same response: desire for a more active policy, concern about Cuban intervention, reluctance to resist it by force. Thus Southern Africa placed into sharp relief once again our national divisions whenever an attempt was made to relate power to policy. The liberals quested after a nirvana combining principle and low risk. Unfortunately, as I told Senator Humphrey, since the Soviets and Cubans had the initiative, they were unlikely to attack in places convenient to us. At the same time, the conservatives, as I noted in the speech in Dallas on March 22, were preaching "strategic superiority while practicing regional retreat." And the neoconservatives were more concerned with honing their ideological assault on Ford and his associates than with joining the anti-Communist struggle where it was actually being contested.

Time was of the essence. Armed conflict was starting in Rhodesia via Mozambique and Zambia, and the CIA was predicting imminent Cuban intervention. An out-of-control race war seemed on the verge of erupting in Southern Africa. A dominant Soviet-Cuban role in liberation struggles in Africa had the potential of magnifying instability throughout the continent (this in fact happened after Ford left office). And, once Cuban troops returned to their homeland, they might turn into a destabilizing element in the racial politics of all of Latin America, as the presidents of Venezuela and Colombia had pointed out.

My mission to Africa was to determine whether we could promote an evolution consistent with both our values and our security. Afterward the President was accused of political obtuseness for having done so and perhaps of having not understood exactly what we were undertaking. He also faced the standard alibi for congressional abdication that he had not consulted adequately.

No one should have been surprised by our Africa policy. We had been talking about majority rule for Southern Africa within our government, to Congress, and to foreign leaders for months. We had also made clear our intention to safeguard white minority rights in any new constitutional arrangement growing out of our African initiative.

The President never even discussed the primary campaign with me; I was the one who raised the political cost of what I was about to

undertake in an Oval Office meeting of April 12. Ford's response was
to urge me to act on principle and not be too tactical:

> KISSINGER: I am going to Africa. I plan to take a strong
> stand for the blacks with respect to South Africa.
> FORD: That is okay with me.
> KISSINGER: You will get some flak from the South on it. I
> will support repeal of the Byrd Amendment [exempting
> Rhodesian chrome from U.N. sanctions].
> FORD: That is our position—but it should be on its merits,
> not as an amendment on another bill.

What caused the shock was that Ford, even in an election year, did
not alter his idea of service. The presidency having been thrust on him
by destiny, Ford dedicated himself to be worthy of the responsibilities
of the office. He was too humble to believe that he had a right to
subordinate the national interest to his prospects for reelection. Modern politics disdains such attitudes. History, however, is bound to be
far more charitable.

# 30

# FIRST VISIT TO AFRICA

The principal purpose of my first visit to Africa was to deliver a speech in Lusaka, Zambia, that would place the United States squarely behind majority rule in Southern Africa. I would be offering not only a declaration of principle, but a program for achieving it. The cooperation of the front-line states, especially Tanzania and Zambia, was a prerequisite for an eventual independence that would protect the rights of European minorities, and the support of the Organization of African Unity (OAU) would be needed in order to insulate the emerging process from pressures or blackmail by non-African states. For this reason, I included a variety of English- and French-speaking countries on the itinerary—specifically Kenya, Tanzania, Zambia, Zaire, Liberia, and Senegal.

## Anthony Crosland and the Role of Britain

The journey began on April 24, 1976, in Britain, upon whose expertise we were counting and whose participation was essential for a smooth transition to majority rule in Rhodesia. Since no nation recognized the Rhodesian authorities headed by Ian Smith, Britain continued to be the legal ruler and would have to preside, albeit temporarily, over the transfer to majority rule.

Because Harold Wilson had suddenly resigned as Prime Minister without offering an explanation, then or later, a new foreign secretary was awaiting us. James Callaghan had replaced Wilson at Number 10 Downing Street, and Anthony Crosland was now foreign secretary. We knew Callaghan well and trusted him; Crosland was quite unfamiliar to us.

Tony Crosland was one of the Labour Party's leading intellectuals. Mostly concerned with domestic or economic issues, he had contested the party leadership with Callaghan and Denis Healey, who remained Chancellor of the Exchequer. Crosland's attitude toward Callaghan was not unlike Adlai Stevenson's toward John F. Kennedy—at heart, he could not understand why the party should prefer the politician to the intellectual. Nor was he happy that Callaghan had denied him the one post other than Prime Minister he really craved—that of Chancellor of the Exchequer. I suspect that Callaghan, faced with two brilliant and talented intellectuals who were inclined to insist on their own views, placed Crosland in the unfamiliar landscape of the Foreign Office and kept Healey, whose real passion was foreign policy, in the Exchequer, to curb their temptation to journey beyond the outer limits of orthodoxy.

It turned out to be an effective way of dealing with his potential rivals. Without challenging conventional wisdom, which tended to be his style in foreign policy, Healey continued his solid performance at the Exchequer. Crosland, who was sullen and somewhat resentful when he was first appointed foreign secretary, discovered that he had a remarkable aptitude for the job. After a few weeks in office, his pleasure in immersing himself in an unfamiliar field diluted his disappointment over having been defeated for the leadership.

At the outset, however, Crosland's articulate petulance—combined with a languid, offhand manner—served to turn him into the *enfant terrible* of diplomacy. He made no secret of the fact that the routine of international diplomacy bored him. Among the more hallowed diplomatic rituals is the tradition that any international meeting—especially one with few participants—fill the time allotted for it. If not, the media will claim failure, and those in the meeting are obliged to come up with explanations for the seemingly premature breakup. Crosland had no patience with this and would end a meeting as soon as the agenda had been exhausted. In so doing, he foreclosed the leisurely exchanges that usually follow the official discussion. These informal discussions serve as a way to build confidence for those moments when decisions may have to be made under the pressure of events.

Crosland's somewhat supercilious behavior continued until he received a deservedly warm reception from his colleagues on the North

Atlantic Council for a brilliant report on a visit to Beijing. The ice was broken, and cooperation on Africa provided the occasion. Crosland and I worked closely together, and on the subject of Rhodesia our staffs operated, in effect, as a single team.

I benefited greatly from Crosland's unique analytical ability that enabled him to come up with many thoughtful contributions to our common initiatives. He also turned out to have a bizarre sense of humor. To keep ourselves from drifting into the pomposity often associated with the diplomatic craft, Crosland invented a game in which each side scored points whenever the other committed some absurdity. Since he both made the rules and kept the score, I was doomed to defeat. For instance, I discovered that I had been assessed 800 points when, at a White House dinner for Queen Elizabeth on July 7, 1976, Prince Philip's dinner partner (who shall remain nameless) asked him what part of Germany he was from. But when Crosland showed up at a white-tie dinner wearing a tuxedo and black tie, I earned only 200 points.

In preparation for my departure from the scene after the approaching American election, Crosland would describe 1976 as his tutorial year on foreign policy. Once I left office, he would announce, he intended to emerge as the major force in shaping Atlantic foreign policy—combining subtle flattery regarding my alleged preeminence with intimations of my dispensability. Sadly, just a few weeks after I left office, he was felled by a fatal stroke. It was a personal tragedy; England lost an able political leader, and I a valued friend.

All this still lay ahead, however, when Crosland and I met on the morning of April 24 at Waddington Royal Air Force station in the north of England, near his constituency at Grimsby. He had chosen this location to avoid the criticism to which his predecessor had been subjected: that I would allegedly summon Callaghan to Heathrow Airport to brief him during fuel stops. Accompanied by the permanent head of the Foreign Office and the under secretary responsible for Africa, Crosland undertook the undoubtedly painful task of ceding to the United States—at least for an interim period—Britain's traditional role of leadership in Southern Africa.

The British advice was to avoid stressing the Cold War aspect of my mission because Africa's leaders were concerned almost exclusively with African problems. The Cold War, argued Crosland, might be of interest to our African opposite numbers, if at all, primarily as an opportunity to blackmail us and to play us off against the Soviets.

According to Crosland, Callaghan's initiative of March 22 on majority rule for Rhodesia had been rejected by Ian Smith because the proposal had not sufficiently taken the concerns of the white minority into account. I thought the biggest problem was that Britain no longer had the resources to balance the necessary rewards and penalties. If my trip was going to succeed in moving Smith toward majority rule, some guarantees for the European population would have to be included in the final package. I told Crosland that we hoped Britain would draft the appropriate constitutional documents and preside over any eventual constitutional assembly.

## Jomo Kenyatta: The Extinct Volcano

We had chosen Kenya as our first stop in Africa because in those days, it seemed to be a model for how majority rule might be combined with guaranteed rights for the white minorities. (Since then, Kenya's internal policies have evolved in a far more repressive direction, although the principal victims have been African opponents of the incumbent President.) And we were hoping that Kenya's legendary President, Jomo Kenyatta, would support our policy within the OAU.

The meeting with Kenyatta took place at his country residence in Nakuru (he rarely ventured into Nairobi). We had to fly there in a small, twin-engine piston plane—not my favorite means of transportation. When the pilot made a sudden dive to avoid a flock of birds, it became less so.

With his chiseled ebony features and gray beard, Kenyatta cut an imposing figure as he greeted us at his pink stucco villa. Much of his early life had been spent abroad. In the 1930s, he had studied in England, then had studied two years at Moscow University, finally earning a postgraduate degree in anthropology at the London School of Economics. Returning to Kenya in 1946, Kenyatta became active in liberation politics and organized the Mau Mau guerrillas. From 1953 to 1961, he had been imprisoned by Britain until, like many other guerrilla leaders, he graduated from the jail cell to the leadership of his country.

It was difficult to envision the Kenyatta we met, clad in a double-breasted suit and with a bearing of regal dignity, as the commander of a tough guerrilla movement that had forced Britain to abandon its imperial role in Kenya. But the image of the London banker evaporated when Kenyatta flicked the giraffe-hair fly whisk he carried and shouted the Kenyan national slogan—"harambee!" (pronounced "hara-aaaaam-bey")—meaning "let us all work together."

One of the extraordinary aspects of the African struggle for independence is the inverse nature of the relationship that often develops between the suffering during the struggle and the readiness for conciliation afterward. Kenyatta was clearly at peace with himself. He was determined to live in harmony with the former targets of his often brutal guerrilla struggle, much like Nelson Mandela, a more significant figure, would turn out to be twenty years later. The following dialogue shows Kenyatta's attitude:

> KISSINGER: You proved you had the spirit of reconciliation and human dignity.
> KENYATTA: I hated to be a slave. I wanted to be free—we didn't hate Britain.
> KISSINGER: Now you're admired in Britain.
> KENYATTA: Some said Kenyatta would be cutting their throats. All I wanted was to be free.

When we turned to substance, it became apparent that at this stage of his life Kenyatta had reached the limit of his ambitions. Southern Africa's conflicts interested him only for symbolic reasons. When I gave him an outline of the speech on majority rule I intended to give in Lusaka, his response was tepid. No dialogue ensued. In addition, as our memorandum of conversation reported: "It was obvious that Kenyatta did not wish to allow Foreign Minister [Munyua] Waiyaki to speak [on Southern Africa issues]."

Kenyatta behaved as though his contribution to African solidarity required no more than moral support for the prevailing liberation struggles that were taking place on the continent. Having conducted his own battle without foreign help, he seemed to feel that the force of his own example was enough. For his part, Kenyatta would concentrate on preserving what he had created. And to that end, he did not consider the struggles in faraway Southern Africa to be especially relevant. For him, the greatest threat to his country came from neighbors armed by the Soviets, such as Somalia.

American economic and military aid were Kenyatta's primary concerns. "Once I looked on America as something horrid," Kenyatta said, but having become acquainted with the country, he appreciated "very, very much what you have been doing for our people. We have many Kenyans in America in your schools and elsewhere. They come home with a very good report of what they have seen. Unfortunately for us, some have refused to return home." There was no question that in African forums Kenyatta would support our policy for Southern Africa because of Kenya's strategic necessities as he interpreted them.

As the meeting turned to the details of economic and military assistance, Kenyatta grew visibly impatient, especially once a not-so-distant sound of drums reached the conference room. At that point, he put an end to the proceedings by proclaiming that "too many words are useless." Since no Kenyan would be prepared to speak after such a command from his chief, conversation languished. Kenyatta obviously thought the time had come to fulfill a promise he had announced at the beginning of the meeting. "Some of the people have asked me if I would allow them to come and dance for you," he had said, "and when we finish here I will take you to see the people themselves and their dances."

Kenyatta brought me to a semicircular arena, three sides of which were enclosed by bleachers, and then led the way to two throne-like chairs positioned beneath a canopy at the open end. Here, despite his Western suit, he was every bit the tribal chieftain, flicking his whisk and shouting "harambee." Scores of dancers and several thousand spectators were assembled. Kenyatta delivered a booming speech and invited me to follow him. "The audience won't understand me," I protested. "There are some tribes here who don't understand me either," Kenyatta replied, "but they expect a chief to make a speech in a loud voice." I cannot recall at this remove what I said. Surely my remarks made no lasting contribution to political thought.

Afterward I watched women with shaved heads and elaborate jewelry dance. Masai warriors brandishing spears made my security detail nervous. Finally, scores of children attired in the Kenyan national colors sang "Red River Valley" in Swahili. After a while, Kenyatta insisted I join him with the dancers. He was at home, graceful and yet full of dignity. I, on the other hand, felt, and no doubt acted, like an elephant trapped among a group of gazelles.

## Julius Nyerere and Tanzania:
## The Ambivalent Intellectual

D ar es Salaam, the capital of Tanzania and our next stop, permitted no such pleasantries. Situated at an altitude of five thousand feet, market-oriented Nairobi had been cool, bustling, and semimodern. Socialist Dar es Salaam, at sea level, was hot, grimy, and poor. In Kenya, where progress was sought through friendship with the United States, the welcoming party at the airport had included the country's vice president and three cabinet members. In Dar es Salaam, the capital of a country committed to nonalignment, the American party was greeted by a deputy foreign minister and a rather bedraggled group of demonstrators chanting anti-American Third World slogans.

Having dutifully paid obeisance to his socialist convictions and his radical Third World friends, Tanzanian President Julius Nyerere proceeded to arrange an official reception that could not have been more cordial. The motive, however, was altogether different from Kenyatta's. Nyerere, an austere believer in socialism, was, at heart, deeply suspicious of American society and American intentions.

In international forums, Tanzania's ministers frequently castigated us. Nyerere would not have described friendship with the United States as a national priority; instead, he tended to think of relations with us as a necessary evil. Kenyatta had sought our assistance to protect his country and to help it prosper. Nyerere wanted to "borrow our power," as he expressed it to me some months later, to help bring majority rule to Southern Africa and to expel the white minority's influence in the aftermath. Kenyatta, in his eighties, wanted to preserve the fruit of his struggles; Nyerere, at the height of his powers, saw himself in mid-struggle. "We didn't fight a guerrilla war," he said in his self-mocking way. "We agitated a little—very British." To Nyerere, the United States was a weapon to be employed to accelerate the liberation struggle. For this, he was prepared to pay some price in moderating his colleagues. More reluctantly, he was prepared to grant some rights to the white minorities, and, even more reluctantly, to exclude Cuban participation in the struggle. But none of this altered Nyerere's basic wariness toward the United States and toward the very idea of market economics.

Brilliant and charming, Nyerere had an influence in Africa out of proportion to the resources of his country, proof that power cannot be measured in physical terms alone. Tanzania was a front-line state in the struggle with Rhodesia, together with Zambia, Botswana, and Mozambique, recently independent. Because Tanzania was involved in the armed struggle that was taking place in Rhodesia, and because of Nyerere's intellectual dominance, Nyerere would be a key to any solution.

But Nyerere's perception of what constituted a desirable outcome coincided with ours only partially. We sought an evolution toward majority rule that excluded the Soviet Union and Cuba and provided some guarantees for the white minorities. Nyerere welcomed our pressures to dismantle the white regimes, but he also wanted to reduce our role in the aftermath to a minimum. Our strategy required that if this visit to the front-line states succeeded, a negotiation with the white regimes would follow—if we wanted to avoid a fight to the finish, the discussion would have to include some guarantees for the European minorities. Nyerere was willing enough to discuss the principle, although he interpreted it as paying compensation for the eventual departure of the Europeans. Since protection of political minorities could hardly be called a special concern of Tanzanian politics, it was not surprising that he was neither creative nor enthusiastic on the subject of protecting white minorities that remained.

Many of Nyerere's American admirers thought that he and his colleagues were the embodiment of American values and liberal traditions. By contrast, his American critics viewed Nyerere as a spokesman for Communist ideology. Neither view was accurate. Nyerere was his own man. His idiosyncratic blend of Western liberal rhetoric, socialist practice, nonaligned righteousness, and African tribalism was driven, above all, by a passionate desire to free his continent from Western categories of thought, of which Marxism happens to be one. His ideas were emphatically his own. I got along with the front-line Presidents, including and especially Nyerere, because I took them seriously. I met them on their own terms and did not treat them—as did so many of their admirers in the West—as extensions of Western preconceptions.

For our first meeting, Nyerere, a slight, wiry man, invited me to his modest private residence. It was a signal honor, and he introduced me to his mother and several members of his family. He was graceful and elegant, his eyes sparkling, his gestures fluid. With an awesome command of the English language (he had translated *Julius Caesar* into Swahili), Nyerere could be a seductive interlocutor. But he was also capable of steely hostility. I had the opportunity to see both these sides during my three visits to Dar es Salaam. He took pride in his chosen role as "Mwalimu" (the "teacher") of his people. The distinguishing characteristic of a teacher, of course, is that he knows more than his students. Among his students, Nyerere often included us Americans. His sense of mission magnified the African reasons for a one-party government as described earlier. And he saw no reason to apologize for it:

> They're very democratic in that hemisphere [Latin America]. They have to say different things in public and in private. Here we're not so democratic. We say the same thing publicly as we say privately.

The democracy he was defending was the freedom of Africans from white minority rule, not the democracy of a pluralistic, multiparty government.

Our first conversation took place in a small, stifling sitting room, where we talked for seventy-five minutes with only one aide on each side. (I brought Peter Rodman.) Nyerere used the occasion to summarize his approach:

> NYERERE: Mr. Secretary, we are very, very grateful to have this opportunity to meet with you. We will meet again tonight, and I will have an opportunity to say it formally with my friends. We very much welcome the opportunity to discuss with you privately our problems.
>
> We have problems. Liberation on the continent. You are celebrating your two hundredth year; we are in the process of liberation. We are celebrating our fourteenth year—Tanzania and Zanzibar. It will be fifteen years in October. So really the continent is in the process of liberation.
>
> The problem is classical colonialism as in Rhodesia, or with our friend [South African Prime Minister] Vorster, racialism. It is our big headache. We live with it. We try to solve it. We can't do it without the assistance or at least the understanding of the big powers. And for a continent like Africa, liberation isn't enough; we need economic development. I think we in Tanzania are really the Fourth World when they put us into categories! . . .
>
> KISSINGER: . . . What help do you have in mind?

NYERERE: In Southern Africa. We will explain our view. Things are changing. What was needed in '75 might not be needed now. We want pressure on the regime in Rhodesia; we want pressure on Vorster regarding Namibia, and ultimately for change in South Africa. We can't live with South Africa as it is.

As to what you can do, sometimes the things we ask are extravagant for you within the limits of the old system. You might not be able to give us arms, but what can you give us? We hope you will answer that question, within the limits not of your power, but of your system.

It was a measure of Nyerere's subtlety that he defined the inhibition of our policy not in terms of limited power but in terms of domestic restraints.

In response, I described the strategy we proposed to follow along the lines outlined in the previous chapter. This meant, I stressed, that we needed South Africa's help and therefore while we would condemn apartheid publicly and explicitly, we would separate the solution of South Africa's problems from those of Namibia's and Rhodesia's. Nyerere replied thoughtfully:

South Africa is harder. I am not sure personally that Africa has given itself much thinking. Africa understands the colonial issue; but it has not fully understood the problem of South Africa and fully thought about how to solve it.

Regardless of the difference in South African conditions and however delayed, the goal must be majority rule:

Some say it is not the same as Rhodesia, but it is. Smith may say to Vorster: "You fortunately declared your independence in 1905 [1910], and we did it in 1965. It is an accident that your independence is recognized and ours isn't." Maybe he hasn't said it. But I'm sure Smith at least thinks of saying this to Vorster.

Recognizing that South Africa is a tougher nut to crack, we would still be saying the objective in South Africa, as in Rhodesia, is majority rule.

I told Nyerere that I would deliver a speech in Lusaka that would not only support majority rule in principle but would lay out a program for achieving it. Our cooperation, however, was absolutely conditional on an agreement that no Cuban forces or Soviet advisers would be permitted in the armed struggle against Rhodesia. Another condition was that no guerrilla units outside the control of the front-line states would be established on their territory where they might then turn on the central authorities—such as the PLO in Lebanon or the North Vietnamese in the border regions of Cambodia. Nyerere replied that he did not want any of the big powers to entrench themselves in Africa under any guise: "When one does, the other will." He deferred further discussion to the next day when his key ministers would be joining us for another meeting.

That day, April 26, began with a parade in the sports stadium celebrating the twelfth anniversary of the event that formed Tanzania, namely Tanganyika's union with Zanzibar, an island just off the coast that historically had been a base for Arab traders and raiders and which still maintains a large Arab population. Students of Africa have doubted the spontaneity of this union or its adherence to the principles of majority rule. But on that muggy morning, unity was the prevailing word of the day.

I sat beside Nyerere in the presidential box. He looked cool and elegant in a light gray bush suit. I felt clumsy and uncomfortable in my blue pinstriped diplomat's uniform. The parade reflected some of the training the Tanzanian army had received in Communist East Germany. Its precision was somewhat handicapped, however. The army's instruction in goose-stepping had obviously taken place when the soldiers wore Prussian-style boots. Now the marchers were shod in indigenous African sandals. The result was that periodically a shoe would come off and fly into the air, forcing the hapless soldier to continue unshod for the rest of the way.

After the parade, Nyerere assembled a larger group over lunch. In beautifully cadenced English, he elaborated for the benefit of his associates the points he had made the previous evening at his home, with particular emphasis on my concern over Cuban and Soviet intervention. Nyerere said he would do his utmost to prevent Cuban troops from spreading to Mozambique—the only country in Southern Africa that in his view might conceivably receive them. He said he would bring about their withdrawal from Angola. Great-power presence, from whatever quarter, was unwelcome in Southern Africa.

In truth Nyerere feared great-power collusion almost as much as he feared great-power conflict. The OAU summit in January 1976 had been a case in point. Formally, the issue had been whether to recognize the MPLA government in Luanda, backed by Cuba and the Soviet Union, a month after the Tunney Amendment had prevented American assistance to its opponents. The result had been a twenty-three to twenty-three tie. "These were not African votes," said Nyerere, "but were twenty-three votes for the United States and twenty-three votes for the Soviet Union. . . . Not one country voted for Africa."

In summary, Nyerere stated that he would support constitutional guarantees for those Europeans choosing to remain and relocation assistance for those wishing to leave. He made it clear that he favored relocation. Once Smith had accepted the principle of majority rule, Nyerere would deliver the "liberation movement" to a conference and support a cease-fire. He would see to it that supplies to the liberation movement passed through agencies of the front-line states and not directly to various guerrilla units, thereby reducing the scope for outside intervention. As a sign of good faith, Nyerere offered to have the foreign ministers of the front-line states, including Mozambique, meet with me for a review and a discussion of possible parallel strategies. This would take place at the end of my Africa trip, ten days hence, when I would be returning to Nairobi to address the United Nations Conference on Trade and Development (UNCTAD).

Nyerere was the key to the front-line states. He was the bridge between such moderates as Zambia's Kenneth Kaunda and Botswana's President Seretse Khama on one side, and the radicals Samora Machel and Agostinho Neto in the former Portuguese colonies of Mozambique and Angola on the other. I reported to Ford:

> I have no illusions: he will remain ideologically opposed and watch our future actions very strictly. On the other hand, he certainly has a better comprehension of our motives and intentions; sees the opportunity for parallel actions; is smart enough to take my points about American public opinion; understands that it is in his own self-interest to ease matters for us; and should use his considerable influence with others on Southern African issues.

## Kenneth Kaunda: The Closet Moderate

Zambia has a long frontier with Rhodesia and the two countries' economies were closely linked. Indeed, before independence, Zambia had been called Northern Rhodesia. Copper mining, Zambia's main industry, was held hostage to the whims of its neighbor because its main shipping routes and communications with the outside world ran through Rhodesia. If the armed struggle intensified, Zambia would find growing guerrilla armies on its territory. Nyerere's good-faith assurances notwithstanding, neither he nor Kaunda would, in the end, be able to control these guests, whose strength could in the future easily exceed that of the Zambian and Tanzanian armies.

Moreover, Kaunda did not want the so-called external forces (led eventually by Robert Mugabe) to prevail in Rhodesia. He feared the impact of their radicalism on Zambia and their possible ties to Communist countries. In 1975, only considerable pressure from his neighbors had persuaded him to agree to a step-up of the armed struggle. Though adept at playing the superpowers against each other, Kaunda —in contrast to Nyerere—clearly felt more comfortable with the West. Eagerness to burnish his Third World credentials could lead Kaunda to exaggerated verbal confrontation with the United States. But at the end of the day, we knew that his occasional outbursts had more to do with his quest for a leadership role than with ideological convictions.

Tall and solidly built, Kenneth Kaunda was a striking figure. With his white hair, flashing eyes, and ready smile, he exuded authority. With only the equivalent of a secondary school education, Kaunda, though highly intelligent, could not compete with the rhetorical flights of Julius Nyerere. Kaunda's strengths were practicality and common sense. He was the first African leader to negotiate with Ian Smith and, later on, with South African Prime Minister Vorster.

Kaunda counted on the United States to dominate the Southern African crisis and, in particular, to maneuver his friend Joshua Nkomo into the leadership role in Rhodesia under moderate rule. The trouble was that Mugabe's "external resistance" held most of the arms. Moreover, Nkomo was handicapped by his tribal origins. As a Ndebele, a Zulu offshoot, Nkomo had a constituency that comprised one third of the Rhodesian population at most; the "external resistance" was primarily made up of the dominant Shona tribe.

These complexities drew Kaunda into complicated maneuvers in which the United States was assigned the role of deus ex machina. Kaunda wanted us to produce his preferred outcome, without obliging him to put it forward himself and occasionally permitting him to disavow what he had himself recommended. He kept in touch with us through a number of emissaries, the principal among them Mark Chona, whom I have already mentioned. The drawback was that if the proposed scheme did not, in the end, convince the other front-line presidents, Kaunda was quite likely to join the African consensus and leave us high and dry. It was a price we were usually willing to risk in return for Kaunda's moderation, common sense, and continued goodwill.

With so many practical problems facing Kaunda, he steered our meeting to the operational issues, among them the question of how to bring pressure on Rhodesia and how to enlist Vorster's support. Many of the suggestions Kaunda made were already contained in the speech that was scheduled for lunchtime. He proved far less grudging about European minority rights than Nyerere:

> African leaders have never said they were chasing away any-body. We are all Africans, and the whites in South Africa have their own right to live in their own country. But the issue of Southern Africa is a question of life and death. For you, Mr. Secretary, the question for your decision is what you want to do to make life more meaningful for all. Your decision to come here shows that you want to find solutions to the Southern African problems.

One of Kaunda's major concerns was that I talk to Joshua Nkomo, thereby conveying American support for the leader Kaunda was eager to see take over the Rhodesian government. But Kaunda did not want to be perceived as having arranged the meeting. I therefore invited Nkomo to visit me in my hotel, but I also sent invitations to the other leaders of the Rhodesian resistance. Because they did not want Kaunda to be seen as the sponsor of the entire Rhodesian liberation movement, however, they refused to come to Lusaka and offered to meet me in Washington.

A mountain of a man, tall and extremely heavy, Nkomo had a bulk that seemed to expand when encountering political frustrations. On this occasion, his circumference, while substantial, seemed reasonably under control. Perhaps this was because we were meeting at the high point of his prospects. With the United States engaged, Kaunda well disposed, and the external resistance not yet fully organized, Nkomo could hope to inherit power—provided the transition to majority rule occurred fairly rapidly. If a real guerrilla war developed, the "boys with the guns," as Nyerere called them, were likely to become dominant. I briefed Nkomo on my forthcoming speech; he reassured me that there was a secure place for whites in Zimbabwe under a negotiated settlement.

Long-anticipated events, especially when focused on such a single act as a speech, often turn out to be anticlimactic. This was not the case as regards my Lusaka address. The impact of the United States, in the person of its Secretary of State, putting its full diplomatic weight behind a specific program of majority rule in Southern Africa was dramatic.

The setting for the speech did not match its intended reach. It took place at a nearly private lunch organized by Kaunda and was attended by no more than fifty people seated around a very long table. Kaunda had obviously arranged it so that he would not lose too much face if I did not deliver what we had promised. A podium had been set up at one end of the room. The media, both American and local, easily outnumbered the regular guests. Though Kaunda introduced me politely, the words he used conveyed the standard vernacular of the Third World, replete with criticism of great-power evils. As I began to speak, however, his demeanor underwent a dramatic change. He followed my words attentively, and then tears began to roll down his cheeks. When I finished, Kaunda rose to embrace me: "Some of us," he said, "were emotionally charged when you were speaking. We could not believe this was a Secretary of State from Washington, D.C."

I had put forward a ten-point program for immediate commitment to majority rule for Rhodesia. I had urged South Africa to establish a firm, early deadline for granting self-determination to Namibia, its former trust territory. Condemning South African apartheid, I called for a "clear" evolution within a "reasonable" period of time toward equality and basic human rights. But I indicated as well America's readiness to grant South Africa time to achieve these momentous transformations so long as it showed "its dedication to Africa" by helping to bring about majority rule for Rhodesia. That, in plain language, meant putting pressure on Ian Smith's regime. "This we are sure," I added, "would be viewed positively by the community of nations as well as by the rest of Africa." Finally, I proposed guarantees for the protection of minority rights after independence and offered to devote some of the promised American economic assistance for Southern Africa to this end.[1]

The new American attitude was captured in the concluding paragraphs:

> What Africa needs now from the United States is not exuberant promises or emotional expressions of good will. What it needs is a concrete program, which I have sought to offer today. So let us get down to business. Let us direct our eyes toward our great goals—national independence, economic development, racial justice, goals that can be achieved by common action. . . .
>
> . . . So let it be said that black people and white people working together achieved on this continent, which has suffered so much and seen so much injustice, a new era of peace, well-being, and human dignity.[2]

As it turned out, the Lusaka speech had an immediate dramatic impact in the United States. I had left Washington on April 23; the Lusaka speech was delivered on April 27. On May 1, Ford, in the middle of a bitter primary campaign against Ronald Reagan, was catastrophically defeated in the Texas Republican primary. Some political experts subsequently claimed that it was our support of majority rule—interpreted as abandonment of the white populations of Southern Africa—that had transformed Ford's probable setback into a debacle. Blame was divided between my alleged recklessness and Ford's political obtuseness.

At a meeting with the President, the assistant Republican leader in the Senate, Senator Robert P. Griffin of Michigan, mentioned that a Republican leader had "suggested that Secretary Kissinger ought to go." The House Republican leader, John Rhodes of Arizona, found the Africa trip ill-timed and added that "in my opinion Henry Kissinger has been and is a fine Secretary of State." He further stated that "one of the real signs of his greatness is that he will know when he has gathered enough barnacles and scars so he can no longer be an effective Secretary of State." (A spokesman later said that Rhodes had not meant that last remark to indicate that he was recommending such a course—thereby repeating the nudge a second time.) Rather less elliptically, Rep. Robert H. Michel of Illinois, the assistant House Republican leader, suggested that I ought to be "muzzled."[3]

Our Africa policy should have come as no surprise to our domestic critics. We had been talking about it within our government, to Congress, to foreign leaders, and at press conferences at least since the collapse of Angola in December, as I have outlined in earlier chapters. We had also made clear our intention to safeguard white minority rights in any new constitutional arrangement that emerged from our African initiative. Nevertheless, the sweep and decisiveness of the actual policy caused surprise.

In a report to Scowcroft, I summed up our strategy for the benefit of restive conservatives:

> We are trading our diplomatic support for a refusal to let Cubans and Soviets get involved (see my Zambia report to the President). By emphasizing African unity, we can resist Soviet and Cuban intervention or supporting factions. The approach in the speech in short gives us a platform to prevent future Angolas—the only one possible under current conditions.

The next day, my critics nearly got their wish when my party and I went to Livingston to view the splendor of Victoria Falls, the world's highest waterfall. This was followed by a boat ride on the Zambezi River, arranged in part because William Scranton, our U.N. ambassador, had reported seeing nineteen hippopotamuses on a recent visit. When we arrived at the landing, we found that the usual—and presumably spacious—excursion boat had broken down. The substitute boat could seat only seventeen, woefully inadequate for a Secretary of State's party on a foreign trip. By the time Zambian officials, embassy and security personnel, and other individuals who considered themselves to be indispensable had crowded onto the boat, there was a total of twenty-five people aboard.

Soon after casting off, we began taking on water. The level rose rather alarmingly because the small flotilla of security and press boats buzzing around us had produced rather large waves. At one point, the engine began to sputter, raising two prospects. Either we might end up drifting toward the scenic falls we had just been admiring from the safety of dry land, or possibly we would be braving the crocodile-infested Zambezi. Fortunately, neither disaster occurred, but then neither did we see any hippopotamuses. One journalist helpfully offered to put a positive spin on the story by suggesting he report that I had seen nineteen fewer hippopotamuses than Ambassador Scranton.

Moscow's reaction to my Africa trip proved that the Soviets understood our strategy far better than did our domestic critics. According to *Pravda,* the main purpose of my trip had been "to try to hinder the strengthening in Africa of the authority of the Soviet Union and Cuba." A Moscow radio commentator condemned my proposal that the liberation movements "rely on their own efforts and not seek assistance from other countries" as being "in full contradiction to the principles of backing the freedom and independence of all nations."

With the Lusaka speech, our African strategy was falling into place: first, agreement with front-line states on an overall strategy for Southern Africa; next, a visit to some Central and West African countries to reassure them about America's staying power and to enlist their support in African forums; and, finally, a return to the Nairobi UNCTAD meeting to place African economic growth into a global context and to put forward a program for development for all of Africa which transcended the immediate crisis.

## Mobutu: The Controversial Ally

While every stop of the journey made eminent sense, beyond Lusaka, I was torn by qualms whether I should return home to help the beleaguered President fight the domestic battle which had been rendered that much more difficult by my Lusaka speech. Ford's political advisers were just as happy that I remained in Africa for another week, since I had become the Reagan campaign's main foreign policy target. No matter that one of the principal purposes of the trip was to create a platform from which to resist the spread of Communism in Africa.

Thus, with my mind on Washington, I found myself on the evening of April 28, 1976, at the airport in Kinshasa. Surrounded by scores of undulating dancers chanting in my honor, I listened to giant tom-toms beating a rhythm that must have reverberated twenty miles away to the capital. Greeting me was Foreign Minister Nguza Karl-I-Bond, whom I had already met two months earlier in Washington when he had called on Ford to express Zairian concerns about the outcome of the Angolan crisis.

Nguza's career spanned the entire spectrum of the vagaries that defined Zairian politics. Highly intelligent and extremely tough, he described himself over breakfast on April 29 as being a member of a tribe spread across Zaire, Zambia, and Angola. The chief of the tribe was, in fact, his uncle. Whether a foreign minister with such a broad power base was too dangerous for Mobutu or whether there was some other reason, two years after the events described here Nguza was accused of treason. He was sentenced to death and thrown into a prison—actually a hole in the ground—to await execution. The intercession of Schmidt, Giscard, Callaghan, myself, and others who had worked with Nguza prompted Mobutu to pardon his foreign minister. Another possibility was that the entire exercise had been planned all along for the sole purpose of teaching Nguza who was boss in Zaire.

After two more years, Nguza was reinstalled by Mobutu as foreign minister. When the newly reconciled pair visited New York, I had breakfast with them in an atmosphere of demonstrative mutual affection. But after another three years, Nguza was again out of office and once more sentenced to death. This time he was prudent and chose exile in Brussels, where he headed an anti-Mobutu opposition group.

Nguza escorted me to the guest house usually reserved for heads of state. As a special courtesy, Mobutu was making the house available to me and my party. It was a vast marble edifice decorated with colorful, vivid murals that never managed to cross the line from the ostentatious to the attractive. I was assigned a large suite, the distinguishing feature of which was an octagonal room containing only a swivel chair and an imposing console with several switches. "This will enable you to look through one-way mirrors into the rooms of your associates," the protocol officer announced. Since I never tested the console, I still do not know whether he was serious or was pulling my leg while showing me the television room.

Standard to academic and media discussions of American Africa policy is the notion that American "support" of Mobutu for his thirty-seven-year rule evidenced the American preference for authoritarian supporters of Cold War policies over genuine democratic leaders. This argument was publicly put forward by President Clinton on his African journey in 1998. It reflected far more the mind-set of the generation coming of age in the early 1970s rather than the reality of the African situation. The overwhelming majority of African leaders during the first decades of independence had been their countries' leaders in the independence struggles. There were no visible alternatives, democratic or otherwise. Except for Zaire, I cannot think of a single African leader who owed his rule to the conspicuous or even covert support of the United States. And in Zaire the alternative was not a democrat, but an autocratic paladin of the radical world.

The issue of American support arose exclusively in countries such as Zaire and later Angola, where the departing colonial power had left a political vacuum, a vacuum that various authoritarian and totalitarian movements were vying to fill. In these situations, American Presidents of both parties tended to support movements that opposed leaders dominated or backed by the Soviet Union. Policy decisions that allow no real choice are not that difficult.

Zaire is vast—as large as Western Europe—and became a single national state only because Belgium had chosen to govern it as a single territory. It did so because until 1908 Zaire had been the personal property of the King of Belgium. Another reason was that when African territory was divided among the European powers, only a very small coastline had been left for what later became Zaire. Thus unity was imposed partly for logistical reasons.

As a result, the various tribes—speaking different languages—developed even less of a national feeling than tribes did in other parts of Africa. In addition, the Belgian colonial power neither prepared nor cultivated an indigenous group of educated leaders. Partly ideological and largely tribal, a civil war developed in which the Western allies—for once united—opposed those leaders and movements supported by the Soviet Union. The United States, France, Belgium, and, to some extent, Britain considered support for Mobutu as the least of the existing evils. Mobutu defeated the radicals, put an end to tribal warfare, and did not govern all that differently from most of his neighbors until the last ten years of his rule. None of the problems the democracies faced in Southern Africa in 1975 and 1976 would have been eased by overthrowing Mobutu. In fact, many of them would have been aggravated by destabilizing Zaire.

Presidents as diverse as Kennedy, Johnson, Nixon, Ford, Carter, Reagan, and Bush came to the same conclusion: the risks of overthrowing Mobutu outweighed the supposed benefits. It was not until well after the end of the Cold War that the Clinton Administration finally moved against him, first by dissociation and then by colluding in his overthrow. And even then, Mobutu was not brought down by indigenous elements, much less by democratic ones. What toppled him were forces from the neighboring states of Uganda, Rwanda, and Angola moving against him in the aftermath of their own civil wars. They were led not by some more democratic figure but by Laurent Kabila, a disciple of Patrice Lumumba and Che Guevara, who, a generation earlier, all Western countries had considered too radical. As of this writing, it remains to be seen whether Mobutu's overthrow improves the human rights situation in the Congo, the political stability of the region, or the American position on the continent. What *is* known is that Kabila's accession to power was accompanied by a degree of mass murder that far overshadowed the excesses of Mobutu, whose besetting sin had been greed rather than blood lust.

A succession of American administrations maintained a working relationship with Mobutu because none of them wanted to add turmoil in Central Africa to an already excessive list of foreign crises. Mobutu's African colleagues shared this attitude. Those who had fought their own independence battles might sneer at him as an upstart; others might snicker at his imperial style. But they treated him as a respectable member of their club—perhaps overexuberant in his lavish trappings of power, which several of them might well have imitated, nevertheless, had they possessed the resources of Zaire. And they innately understood that Mobutu—precisely because he had *not* been anointed by the act of waging his own struggle for national independence—needed the ostentation he so clearly enjoyed to establish for himself an aura of overwhelming power and majesty.

Bordering on thirteen states, Zaire had an awesome potential to generate turmoil, either by pursuing radical policies or by simply collapsing into a vacuum. This is why the Kennedy Administration supported Mobutu against Lumumba in the 1960s. In 1978, the human rights–oriented Jimmy Carter cooperated in foiling an invasion from Angola into the Zairian province of Katanga by the deployment of French auxiliaries. He probably used the plan Giscard had suggested to me in 1975 regarding Angola, which had been thwarted by the Tunney and Clark Amendments. And, as previously described, during 1975 and 1976 the Ford Administration considered Zaire an essential counterweight to Angola. The administration also considered Zaire to be a safety net for Zambia, which—without a moderate Zairian neighbor—would have been entirely surrounded by radical states. In addition, Zaire was a vital bridge to the French-speaking states of West Africa.

My conversations with Mobutu took place before and after lunch during a four-hour journey down the Congo River on his extravagant, triple-deckered riverboat, complete with a helicopter platform. A shrewd observer of his African colleagues, Mobutu devoted some time to explaining his view of their internal politics. He claimed that, prior to Kaunda's visit to Washington, the various leaders had agreed on the following division of labor: Mobutu would take the lead on Angola, Kaunda on Rhodesia, and Nyerere on Mozambique. He and Kaunda had concurred on the danger of an MPLA victory in Angola, and Nyerere had seemed to go along with them, albeit hesitantly. But after Portuguese rule in Mozambique collapsed more rapidly than expected and the radical Samora Machel took over, Nyerere—according to Mobutu—grew more ambitious and, giving vent to his radical preferences, began to support Neto, the MPLA, and the Cubans. Whatever he might be saying now, Mobutu warned, Nyerere would wind up on the radical side on Rhodesia, though he would probably stop short of involving foreign forces. It was an analysis that fit the facts as I had observed them and proved prescient for the future of diplomacy regarding Rhodesia.

Given the fact that three hundred tanks and sixty helicopter gunships were in the possession of the Angolan armed forces, Mobutu was primarily concerned with the security of his country. With some justification, he complained about the Pentagon's reluctance to let Zaire purchase advanced weapons. Indeed, largely due to congressional pressures, American assistance to Zaire was marginal relative to the problems the country faced. Mobutu added that he had been sent thirty light and twenty-four medium tanks by China where "they have a special sense of the Soviet danger"—a consequence of the Ford-Mao conversation described earlier. He urged a joint program with such well-disposed European countries as France, the goal of which would be to transform Zaire into an economic showplace displaying benefits of Western cooperation.

I was sympathetic, as was Giscard when I briefed him in Paris on the way back from Africa. But it was not to be. Mobutu was not prepared to govern with the discipline needed to turn the diverse tribes of his country into the modern nation its resources would have made possible. And he felt too insecure domestically—perhaps because of how he came to power—to forgo the accumulation of personal wealth for his eventual exile, draining the coffers of his country. In turn, the democracies, beset by economic crises and multiple claims on their resources, fell into their habitual posture of pushing their problems ahead of them. They would generate enough assistance to stave off immediate disasters, but it was never sufficient to bring about fundamental change. Over the decades, Mobutu's rule gradually transformed Zaire into a caricature of Africa's ills—until he fell beneath the combined weight of his own extravagant conduct and the imperialist designs of his country's neighbors.

## Liberia: History Without a Point

Our next stop was in Liberia, another dramatization of an African tragedy for which, as a nation, we bore a more direct responsibility. Founded in 1822 as a haven for African-Americans seeking to return to their ancestral home, it is Africa's oldest independent nation and the recipient of one fifth of all American investment in the continent. It should have been a showplace for democracy and market economics. It was neither. Its capital, Monrovia, was a poverty-stricken amalgam of shacks interspersed with a few monumental government buildings. The country was being governed by a self-perpetuating oligarchy that was ingeniously diverting the bulk of foreign investment for its own benefit.

We used the stop in Liberia as the occasion for another major speech, this one on African economic development and America's role in it. It was a bow to a historical legacy. There was, however, something rather incongruous about choosing this dilapidated outpost of America's early attempt to escape the blight of slavery as the site of a speech that would affirm the importance of the United States to the growth of Africa's economies.

In Liberia, I was reunited with Ambassador Beverly Carter, one of the first African-Americans to have achieved ambassadorial rank. An imposing, towering man possessed of high intelligence and a charming manner, he had run afoul of me a year earlier while he was serving the last few months of his tour as ambassador to Tanzania. The eastern part of Zaire that adjoins Tanzania was in the hands of a small, anti-Mobutu, radical dissident group headed by the same Kabila who later took over the country. The group controlled its enclave and financed its revolt with the proceeds from a small gold mine and from occasional kidnappings. In one of these "fund-raising" expeditions, a roving band had entered Tanzania, kidnapped five American college students, and held them for ransom.

The understandably frantic parents descended on our embassy in

Dar es Salaam and asked for assistance in freeing their children. They were prepared to pay ransom, thereby violating a policy about which I felt very strongly. I held firmly to the view that the best method for ending terrorism, other than attacking terrorist bases militarily, was to deprive such acts of any possible benefit. This meant that I absolutely forbade negotiations and was firmly against any kind of ransom payment.

Of course, I was not the one on the firing line with the desperate relatives, and Ambassador Carter, in the last months of his tour of duty, was. Yielding to their entreaties, Carter went to the Zairian enclave and negotiated with the hostage-takers. Afterward, he was involved in the payment of the ransom. I believed that our policy of nonnegotiation obliged me to take a hard, even ferocious, line or else we would be nibbled to death with one "special case" after another. To show we meant business, I withdrew my recommendation to the President that Carter's next appointment be as ambassador to Denmark.

All hell broke loose. The Congressional Black Caucus and a segment of the media rallied to Carter's defense. I stood my ground. Some months later, on Christmas Eve 1975, believing that my point had been made, I approached Carter at a reception and offered him the ambassadorship to Liberia. The visual disparities between Monrovia and Copenhagen were stark, to say the least. Nevertheless, by State Department standards, I was promoting Carter: as the Foreign Service measures these things, Monrovia was rated a Class 2 post, while Copenhagen was a Class 4. The difference connotes distinctions in staffing, resources, and perks. In fact, Monrovia was then, for inexplicable reasons, our largest post in Africa.

Carter proved he was a big man in more than size when he accepted. To demonstrate that nothing personal had been involved, I conducted his swearing-in myself. I told the audience that I had persuaded Carter to go to Africa once more by threatening him with the alternative of being assigned to my staff. Carter gave as good as he got. After thanking me for swearing him in personally, he remarked: "As you know, the Secretary does not always have the time to swear in ambassadors. Swear them out, yes, but not in."

By the time we reached Liberia, our nerves were rather frayed from the battering in Congress and the media. We were exhausted after a week of nonstop conferences. In this atmosphere, a cable from Scowcroft suggesting that we make our daily reports to the President more factual and less "florid" fed the mounting paranoia, especially that of

Winston Lord, the principal drafter of the offending reports. Lord retaliated by adding an abbreviated summary to his typically voluminous and eloquent submission. I sent both to Scowcroft, suggesting that he pass on to the President whichever he felt best met his literary standards. The summary began with the sentence: "Today we are in Liberia. It is hot." It went on to report the meeting with President William Tolbert, Jr., in the following sarcastic fashion:

> He said Liberia would like more money. I said we would see what we can do, but he had to understand that OMB [Office of Management and Budget] had the final word and that we intended to lose the world in a fully coordinated way.

Reacting to Scowcroft's stricture that we spare the President our descriptions of local color, Lord reported thus on a cultural event held in our honor:

> Next we went to see a cultural performance. It was interesting; since this is a poor country, some of the girls only had half a costume, but I don't want to bore you with color or tell you which half was missing since this would needlessly excite you.

Fortunately, Scowcroft, who had been right in the first place, has a good sense of humor and spiked the abbreviated version.

## Leopold Senghor: The Philosopher-King

Our last stop in West Africa was Dakar, the capital of Senegal, an elegant and modern city—at least the part I saw. Independent since 1960, Senegal was governed by Leopold Senghor, one of Africa's more remarkable personalities. A poet and a statesman, he belonged to several cultures at once. Though avowing an intellectual debt to European culture, Senghor proclaimed the philosophy of *négritude*. This somewhat soggy concept sought to move the idea of black culture away from ethnic exclusivity into an integral relationship with the Mediterranean and southern European countries, which, according to Senghor, were related to Africa in some fashion.

The two most impressive leaders I encountered on this trip, Nyerere and Senghor, were at opposite ends of the African spectrum. In a sense, they represented metaphors for the varying approaches to African identity. Nyerere was a militant who used ideology as a weapon; Senghor was an intellectual who had taught himself the grammar of power. Nyerere considered himself as leader of an Africa that should evolve in a unique way, separate from the currents in the rest of the world which Africa would use without permitting them to contaminate its essence. Senghor saw himself as a participant in an international order in which Africa and *négritude* would play a significant, but not isolated, role. When all was said and done, Nyerere strove for the victory of black Africa while Senghor sought a reconciliation of cultures within the context of self-determination.

The difference between the two leaders also demonstrated the contrast in African reactions to British and French colonialism. Britain had awed its subjects; France had seduced them. Britain's subjects copied its constitutional forms and judicial procedures, but they knew in their hearts that they could never become British. They adopted British institutions as a means of freeing themselves from Britain's domination and of elaborating a political identity as distinct from the colonial rulers as possible.

France, on the other hand, dazzled its colonial subjects with its culture, and even its language, rather than with its institutions. Even as they made themselves politically independent, most French colonies retained close intellectual ties to France and looked to it for their internal and external security. The President of the Ivory Coast, Félix Houphouët-Boigny, had been a French senator; Leopold Senghor had served in the cabinet of French Prime Minister Edgar Faure. Both were Africans by birth and conviction, but they continued to perceive themselves as belonging as well to the intellectual and political life of the colonial power.

Major French-speaking countries such as Senegal and the Ivory Coast viewed the struggles of Southern Africa from a perspective that was quite similar to our own. They supported the quest for majority rule and approved my Lusaka speech. At the same time, they placed the evolution of Southern Africa into a geopolitical context. Unless the battle against African radicalism was won—and especially if the Soviet Union and Cuba were permitted to become major players—the cooperative world they envisaged would never come into being. Thus, Senghor interpreted what had happened in Angola as a defeat for all of moderate Africa:

The United States did not pay sufficient attention to Africa. Angola was a disaster for the whole West, not just the United States. I have said it was a disaster not only for the capitalist West but for social democracy. . . .

. . . The Africans are terrorized by this. The French minister told me, "The Africans all want arms now." This doesn't mean numbers of troops, but armaments—tanks, missiles, planes. Mali, Guinea—can they have arms to resist the Soviets and the Cubans? It is not a question of intervention but Western help. . . .

You've said the essential thing—that there will not be a second Angola.

He was contemptuous of the West African military regimes, especially in the former British colonies:

Nigeria now reflects the malady of the West. The military regime is a regime of instability. To hold power, it takes leftist positions. . . . Nigeria and Algeria try to introduce Arabs into Africa to destroy *négritude,* to impose Arab imperialism. Senegal will resist.

To this student of French statecraft, the obvious riposte to the disturbance in the balance of power was to build a pro-Western bloc in Africa. Yet our domestic situation proscribed it, and American conventional wisdom regarding African attitudes warned against it. Except in a few French-speaking countries, such a policy would not be understood and would be passionately opposed by many, particularly the former British colonies. Our best strategy was to affirm the unity and nonalignment of Africa. Should the Soviets attempt to create a bloc of their own or continue pouring arms into the continent, we would then resist in the name of these principles.

Whatever the strategy for resisting the further spread of Communist influence by military means, one of the key objectives of my trip revolved around a question that would become a key issue in the United States, one that I now put to Senghor:

KISSINGER: If we resist the Cubans somewhere, can we get enough African support so it's not [seen as] an imperialist move? . . .

SENGHOR: . . . I think if you resist, you will have the approval of the moderates. We will not hide. On Angola,
we said we opposed Soviet intervention. We think the
majority of African states will approve. . . . Because
strength counts. If you appear strong, the majority of
Africans will support you.

"Strength counts"—anyone who had seen African leaders in action would only affirm this aphorism. Yet many of Africa's advocates
in the United States were claiming that Africa was somehow immune
to the lessons of history, and that it possessed a special recipe for
standing apart from them. Senghor did not succumb to this nostalgic
thinking. He favored me with a lengthy discussion of how his aphorism
applied to the international situation, covering Soviet trends, Chinese
policies, the Middle East, Eurocommunism, and such regional issues
as the future of the Maghreb. Deeply impressed, I told Senghor:

If you feel strongly about something—if you feel we're
wrong, or if you feel we can do something better—get in
touch with me or directly with President Ford. I'll see it.
And get it to us in a way that we can be assured it won't
leak.

In Dakar, too, I made a speech avowing our readiness to participate
in an international effort to reverse the drought afflicting the Sahel
area, of which Senegal was a major part. It was part of our determination to show that America's African policy had its own positive purposes which were not driven by fear of Cuba or the Soviet Union.
But in the supercharged atmosphere of election-year Washington, this
essentially token program was denounced as another example of a
hopeless application of a "do-good" attitude toward Africa.

Just before my departure, I visited Gorée Island, where newly captured slaves had been held before being shipped to North America,
sometimes chained in dingy cells for months. I was powerfully moved
by this reminder of the emotional torture inflicted upon those who
had been wrenched from their native soil—compounded, in the African case, by unspeakable physical suffering. And I referred to it in my
departure statement on May 2:

This morning we had the opportunity to visit Gorée Island,
which is a symbol of the inhumanity that man has histori-

cally inflicted upon each other and which should call all of us to our duty to build on this continent a period in which all human beings—black as well as white—can work together, in which all Africans can achieve dignity and human progress, and in which the foreign intervention that has been the tragedy of Africa for centuries will at last be banished forever from this continent.[4]

## Nairobi: Meeting with Front-Line Ministers

Late in the evening of May 2, I was back in Nairobi after having flown across the continent for eight hours to present the American position at UNCTAD, a quadrennial meeting of economic and development ministers to discuss programs for the Third World. At past UNCTAD meetings, we had been represented by a Cabinet member dealing with economic development; those advanced industrial countries that sent ministers at all were being represented at that level. At the end of my journey through Africa, a tour that had focused on strategic and political topics, I chose to speak on behalf of the United States in order to symbolize the political importance we attached to the need for new cooperative international economic arrangements. (The subject of the speech has been dealt with in Chapter 22.)

Eight days had elapsed since my previous stay in Nairobi. I had visited five African countries; put forward a program for majority rule in Southern Africa; demonstrated American concern for the economic development of the continent in a long toast in Monrovia. I had sketched ideas for dealing with the problems of the Sahel in Dakar, and had capped the series at UNCTAD with a proposal to smooth out the impact of excessive market fluctuations for developing countries with economies dependent on a single commodity.

Nyerere had promised that he would encourage key ministers of the front-line states to review the situation with me before I returned home. And he kept his word. The foreign ministers of Zambia and Mozambique attended, as did the minister of commerce and industry from Botswana (the foreign minister was on a trip to the United States with his President). Nyerere sent the minister of state from the President's office whom he had designated as our contact. It was the first meeting between a senior member of the American administration and a high official from Mozambique—the most radical and Marxist of the front-line states, the one most vulnerable to Soviet overtures, and the one most likely to cooperate with Cuban auxiliary forces.

Foreign Minister Joaquim Chissano of Mozambique (as of this writing, his country's President) was on his best behavior. When I got to know him later, I learned that he was both fiercely independent and reasonable. Chissano urged me to meet President Samora Machel on my next trip to Africa. He agreed that the front-line states would act as a unit, lending some credence to Nyerere's promise to channel arms from abroad to the liberation forces through a central agency rather than to each guerrilla group separately, thereby reducing the opportunities for Cuban involvement.

I used the occasion of the meeting with Southern African ministers to warn once again that our cooperation would cease if Cuban or Soviet forces participated in the armed struggle. Responding to a comment from Nyerere's representative, Peter Siyovelwa, I also outlined the limits of our assistance:

> I don't want to mislead you. We can't associate ourselves with an armed struggle. We can associate ourselves with diplomatic and economic steps. Your President [Nyerere] said to our press that he didn't need help for an armed struggle but he needed understanding. . . .
>
> . . . While I don't ask your help, it would be helpful if you at least don't ascribe the worst motives, and if the American people see that the Africans give us the benefit of the doubt. So we both have to be understanding of the other's necessities.

Since our strategy was based on gaining the support of South Africa, I previewed my intention to conduct high-level talks with South Africa's leaders. More precisely, I asked the representatives of the front-line states how they would react to such an effort. Siyovelwa replied:

> We believed it was impossible to work with South Africa. But if there are any quarters, like the United States, that could pressurize them enough, to really impose sanctions [on Rhodesia] . . .

We agreed that we would meet again during the U.N. General Assembly in September to review where matters stood.

## Return to Washington

My African trip had begun with consultations in Britain, a NATO country with a major historical role in Africa. It would end with consultations in France, the European country with perhaps the strongest continuing involvement in Africa. It was an expression of the close cooperation that had developed between Giscard and the Ford Administration. The French President strongly supported our policy— not the most frequent occurrence in our past dealings with Gaullist France. The task of relating Africa to the West, Giscard argued, was too great for the United States acting alone; there should be a division of labor. The United States should handle the diplomacy leading toward majority rule in Southern Africa; Britain should make itself responsible for the actual negotiations; and he, Giscard, was prepared to put forward a joint Western program for the economic development designed to rally the moderate states, the program's principal beneficiaries.

But Washington was in no mood for global strategies. It was an election year, and politics was king. The prospect of a President being unseated by a challenger within his own party caused blood to course in the veins of the inhabitants inside the Beltway, turning the Ford-Reagan primary campaign into a national obsession. Conservatives who might have been sympathetic to the attempt to reverse the Cuban tide in Africa turned deaf ears to a policy that might reduce the advantage seemingly enjoyed by their hero, Ronald Reagan, in his campaign against the alleged softness of Ford and his administration. There was also a less attractive aspect to their criticism: the wave of resentment that the United States should be taking sides against a white minority was a kind of reflexive prejudice. It displayed an inability to understand that, in the face of mounting radicalism in Southern Africa, this was the only strategy to hold out any hope of achieving some degree of coexistence for the white minorities.

Our critics began to apply to Africa the methods that had debilitated the policy of détente with the Soviet Union, mounting an attack on some issue that lent itself to being viewed as a symbol of our allegedly weak-kneed approach. With respect to détente, it had been SALT and Jewish emigration from the Soviet Union; on African policy, it was aid to Mozambique. Since only $12.5 million was being requested, it was hardly a question of the amount which we needed

primarily to establish some relationship with Machel as the leader—
by everyone's assessment—most prone to invite Cuban troops. Instead, the attack's purpose was the gradual wearing down of administration policies, demonstrating our impotence in achieving even the
most limited objectives. The prevailing mood among many Republicans was expressed by James A. Baker III, then an official in the Ford
campaign and later Secretary of State under George Bush, when he
publicly urged me to resign for the good of the President.

But this time the attack did not succeed in wearing down the administration. Senator Hubert Humphrey and eight moderate Republicans
came forward and offered a resolution commending our "more moral
foreign policy," which promised "a new realism in United States policy
toward Africa."[5] Above all, the President had decided to fight.

It was one of Ford's noble moments. When a Cabinet member is
under violent attack, all too frequently the White House procedure is
to issue a token statement of support, then withdraw from the battlefield until the smoke clears, thereby limiting damage to the President.

Ford would have none of it. While I was still in Africa, he ordered
Ron Nessen to issue a statement: "The President makes foreign policy,
and Dr. Kissinger carries out and enunciates that foreign policy, and
that is what he has done on the African trip."[6] From the moment I
returned, Ford put himself conspicuously behind our African policy.
He organized two publicized meetings with me (one on a Sunday) to
receive my report. On May 11, he held a National Security Council
meeting (again announced to the press) to permit me to report to the
administration's key policymaking group. He summed up his view of
the results of the trip:

> I think that from what Henry has already told me and will
> expand on further here, we have halted the radicalization
> in Africa and opened the door for movement in a positive
> direction.

The next morning, Ford called a bipartisan leadership meeting at
the White House. He opened the meeting with these words:

> Following the Angolan tragedy, the situation in Southern
> Africa began to accelerate to the point of potential disaster
> for the moderate African states. They were beginning to get
> very apprehensive, while the radical states became increas-

ingly active in fomenting violence in that region. We thought that something had to be done and that we should come up with some proposals to attempt to stabilize the situation. Our first efforts were designed to thwart the Soviets and the Cubans because it was our belief that if we didn't do something, all of the area would soon be ripe for Soviet picking.

I know there was some criticism at the timing of the Secretary's trip, but it was my assessment that we couldn't hold foreign policy in limbo every four years. The United States cannot tell the world it will let things drift for six months during our elections, and I am willing to proceed with what needs to be done and take the lumps if necessary.

Upon hearing that John Osborne of *The New Republic* was writing an article about my African trip, an assistant of the President telephoned, as described by Osborne: "One of the few heartening features was the assurance conveyed to me that the president is determined to stick with Kissinger." In a later compilation, Osborne added: "The 'assurance' mentioned at the end of this report was conveyed by a White House assistant at the direction of Mr. Ford."[7]

Ford's backing both obliged and inspired me to carry on. But the furious uproar had obscured the very real fact that we had only taken a first step. We had organized those who would benefit from our new policy and induced them to take the political risk of negotiation. Those who would have to make the sacrifices—the European populations of Southern Africa and, of course, South Africa itself—had yet to be heard from.

# 31

# TOWARD MAJORITY RULE IN SOUTHERN AFRICA

## *South Africa and the United States*

Convincing the white minorities in Southern Africa that they needed to adapt to the winds of change—in Harold Macmillan's phrase—was even more a psychological than a diplomatic challenge. For at the end of the road we were charting, the European populations of Rhodesia and Namibia would at best have a limited veto; they would no longer be able to shape their political—nor probably, in the long run, their economic—future. In undertaking this task, we had two possible assets: South African support for change in Rhodesia and Namibia, if we could bring it about, and the Ford Administration's attitude toward the rights of the white minorities, on which South African cooperation and American domestic support depended.

Rhodesia and Namibia had turned into liabilities for South Africa internationally and a drain on its resources. The South Africans had no wish to deepen their international isolation by supporting a Rhodesian white regime not recognized by any country in the world. And they were prepared for similar reasons to abandon Namibia, albeit more slowly. What South Africa's leaders sought to avoid was to be obliged to stand by while the white minority in Rhodesia was being overrun militarily by black guerrillas. And no doubt they hoped to create successor regimes in both Rhodesia and Namibia which, though black, would stem the radical tide before it could reach South Africa's borders.

In their heart of hearts, the more thoughtful South Africans knew that the transformation would not stop there. Though they instinctively sensed the inevitability of the coming upheaval, they had no clear idea of how to manage it or in which direction to move. They had been isolated for decades, trapped—indeed, paralyzed—by their unique history and lack of imagination.

It was a measure of both their isolation and sense of foreboding that the South Africans should have accepted so readily the only quid pro quo I could offer in exchange for their cooperation on Rhodesia and Namibia: time in which to solve their problems. In every conversation with South African officials, including with Prime Minister Vorster, I stressed that the principles I had put forward publicly in Lusaka applied to South Africa as well. "I think history is against you," I informed South African Ambassador Roelof "Pik" Botha on May 14, 1976, shortly after I returned from Africa, "but we want to buy time at least. . . . If we can separate the South African issue from Rhodesia, it will give more time to deal with South Africa—unless Rhodesia is settled in a way that accelerates the problem."

Thin gruel though it was, it proved sufficient to forge a dialogue because the South African leaders—and, once we met them, those in Rhodesia as well—realized that the Ford Administration was not waging a crusade against them as individuals; indeed, that we had compassion for the agonizing dilemmas bequeathed them by preceding generations. The qualities to which our critics objected in our conduct of foreign policy as a balancing of interests rather than as crusades now served to reassure our opposite numbers among the white minorities. We were not out to punish them for their fathers' sins or even their own—as were so many of their critics in the West. Rather, our goal was to bring them face-to-face with their realities and lead them as gently as possible to the acceptance of the fact that these dictated change both on moral and on political grounds. Without a political solution, they might manage to hold on a few extra years at the price of forfeiting any possibility of remaining in Africa. If they wanted to remain in Africa, they had to be made to realize that an understanding with the black majority was imperative. When Ford and I spoke of guaranteeing some minority rights, we thought more of a political than a judicial process. We were not doing so primarily in response to conservative domestic pressures but as an expression of our convictions; despite grave doubts about the permanence of constitutional guarantees, we would do our best to make them meaningful.

Once we began to deal with Southern Africa, Namibia joined

Rhodesia as a key issue. Formerly German South-West Africa, it is located on an arid plateau between two deserts. Its sparse population of 850,000 then (under 2 million today) nevertheless contains the usual potpourri concocted by the arbitrary drawing of borders by the colonial powers: approximately 45 percent belong to the Ovambo tribe located on both sides of the border with Angola; the remainder are members of some nine other tribes scattered across the rest of the country. The entire territory had been assigned to South Africa at the end of the First World War as a League of Nations mandate.

In 1946, following the Second World War, South Africa informed the United Nations that it wished to annex the territory. When the request was refused, a tug-of-war between South Africa and the United Nations developed, lasting for nearly four decades. Between 1966 and 1968, the U.N. voted a series of resolutions to terminate South Africa's mandate and established an eleven-nation Council for Namibia as the lawful authority. South Africa's response was, in effect, to annex the territory and give it the status of a South African province.

In 1971, the International Court of Justice terminated South Africa's mandate and, in 1972, the U.N. Security Council voted sanctions against South Africa. These were vetoed by the United States, Britain, and France. In the late 1960s, a guerrilla movement had emerged based largely within the Ovambo tribe in the north. SWAPO (South-West Africa People's Organization) engaged in armed resistance which, while not threatening South African control militarily, undermined it politically by gaining increasing support from the Third World nations and gradually from the industrial democracies as well.

The diplomatic process which followed conformed to the script typical of every other struggle for independence: the dominant power's step-by-step dilution of colonial rule in the vain hope of thus being able to avoid the ultimate yielding of power; a proposed negotiation that excluded the guerrilla movement, culminating in the ultimate acquiescence of the colonial power to the side conducting armed struggle. By the early 1970s, South Africa had agreed to the principle of Namibian self-determination but refused to deal with SWAPO because of its alleged terrorist activities or to recognize any jurisdiction for the U.N. It convoked a conference in Windhoek, the capital of Namibia, to draft a constitution and invited the various tribes to send representatives. Neither SWAPO nor the U.N. was asked to participate.

In the spring of 1976, when I first dealt in depth with the Namibian issue, Cuban forces stood poised across the Angolan border. The front-line states, especially Zambia, Mozambique, and Tanzania, while giving strong political support to SWAPO, were geographically more remote than they were from Rhodesia and therefore felt less pressure from unwanted guerrilla forces on their soil. A deadline of August 31 had been established by the U.N. Security Council for South Africa to end its administration of Namibia. If it did not, sanctions were likely. If we vetoed them, we would endanger the support of black African countries for our Southern Africa policy; if we did not, we would jeopardize South Africa's cooperation on the problems of the region. In my trip through Africa, I therefore gave Namibia a high priority and, in Lusaka, called on South Africa to set an early date for independence.

Incongruously, pariah South Africa, the citadel of apartheid, was emerging as the key to progress toward majority rule in Southern Africa. All black African leaders castigated it, and all of them urged us into a dialogue with South Africa's leaders. Condemned as archenemy of African freedom, South Africa nevertheless provided the immediate hope for a rapid breakthrough toward majority rule, which would, at the end of the process, leave it alone without any buffer to face an Africa united in its demand for an end to apartheid. Though sooner or later such demands were bound to become irresistible, South Africa's leaders allowed us to guide them onto a course which, whatever their intransigent pronouncements to the contrary, would eventually overwhelm the barriers they had so systematically erected.

That they were prepared to do so showed just how African its population—at least the Afrikaner part—had become in the three centuries since these Dutch Calvinists had first landed in the then nearly empty Cape of Good Hope to begin a life unconstrained by the religious wars and persecutions of seventeenth-century Europe. They brought with them a stern fundamentalism which turned its back on all the subsequent movements of intellectual change in Europe. The Boers, or Afrikaners as they came to call themselves, developed an identity unique in the history of European colonialism. Cut off from the mother country, they remained unaffected by the rationalistic heritage of the Enlightenment or by the democratic dispensation of the French Revolution.

So distinct was their sense of identity that when Britain annexed the Cape Province during the Napoleonic wars, the Afrikaners packed up and moved nearly a thousand miles to the north. They did this not as individual settlers but as an entire people, taking with them their governmental institutions, churches, schools, and prejudices. In their new home, the Afrikaners encountered large black populations whom they treated with a condescension derived from their special sense of religious mission. Theirs was less the sin of colonialism than a kind of spiritual pride which, in the process, absorbed from the stark soil of that beautiful and brooding land a very special, almost mystical devotion to Africa.

The Afrikaners' isolation did not last long. The discovery of gold lured British prospectors and merchants to their new territory. But the Boers, being only slightly less exclusive toward their fellow Europeans than they were toward Africans, resisted this influx, an impulse culminating in the Boer War in which the tiny Boer republics fought the British Empire, at the height of its power, nearly to a standstill. Defeat put an end to the Afrikaners' physical separateness; it could not overcome their spiritual isolation. The two white communities, coexisting amidst an ever growing black majority, lived essentially separated from each other: the English, paradoxically both more liberal and more distant from Africa, remained ever the colonialists, adhering to the values and mores of the mother country; the Afrikaners, marooned in what, for better or worse, they had forged as a homeland for themselves, had become so disconnected from the Old World that they quite literally had no place else to go.

By 1948, demographics within the white population, which alone had the vote, favored the Afrikaners. While segregation in the American sense existed at all times, the now dominant Boers set about separating the races with a degrading legalism. The 3 million Cape Coloured—descendants of the aboriginal Hottentot population— were deprived of the franchise, as was the Indian community of 1 million. The black community had, of course, never had the vote. Strict laws were passed prohibiting intermarriage and defining separate living arrangements, working conditions, and restricting the freedom of movement of the nonwhite population. Apartheid meant exclusion. Blacks had to live in strictly segregated communities on the least desirable land and received the lowest priority in health care, welfare benefits, and education. While the level of these services was higher than almost anywhere else in Africa, the violation of human dignity implicit in apartheid outweighed all material benefits.

Apartheid offended nearly every Western democratic principle. Because it obliged the white population to hold down a growing majority of all the other races by brute force, it proved as incompatible with common decency as with the processes of industrialization and education.

And yet, when as a professor I first visited South Africa in 1962 to speak at workshops organized by European Lutheran churches, I became convinced that, when all was said and done, this beautiful and melancholy land would not end in the catastrophe that reason and history predicted. Even more oddly, I began to believe that it would ultimately be the Afrikaners, ostensibly the more repressive element of the white population, and not the seemingly more liberal English community, which would lead the way. Somehow through some hidden instinct I could not describe and which the Afrikaners vociferously denied, it seemed predestined that they would find a way, albeit after much turmoil, whereby the very depth of the common suffering—the fear giving rise to oppression and the strength required to survive it—would be distilled into some new form of South African identity, and that it would come about not by way of Western liberalism but by an arrangement brokered between South Africa's white and black tribes.

On the issue of apartheid, I never wavered. At no stage of my negotiations with the South African leaders did I leave them in any doubt about America's opposition to it; I never went further than to try to give them a limited amount of time in which to seek their own solution. On August 2, 1976, at the height of our Southern Africa diplomacy and when the outcome depended crucially on South African cooperation, I expressed in a speech to the national convention of the Urban League what I was at the same time saying privately to South Africa's leaders:

> No one—including the responsible leaders of black Africa —challenges the right of white South Africans to live in their country. They are not colonialists; historically they are an African people; they have lived on African soil for 300 years. But South Africa's internal structure is explosive and incompatible with any concept of human dignity.
>
> Racial discrimination is a blight which afflicts many nations of the world. But South Africa is unique in institutionalizing discrimination in an all-pervasive enforced separation of the races which mocks any definition of human equality. . . .
>
> . . . The United States, true to its own beliefs, will use all its influence to encourage peaceful change, an end to

institutionalized inequality, and equality of opportunity and
basic human rights in South Africa.[1]

That precisely was the theme with which I approached South African Ambassador Pik Botha on May 14, 1976, to initiate the second phase of our African strategy. Within a week of my return from Africa, I offered to meet with either South Africa's Prime Minister or its foreign minister—preferably in Europe. I left open the possibility of a subsequent visit to South Africa. No American Secretary of State had been prepared to meet South African leaders in over thirty years, much less to negotiate with them—even in world forums like the U.N. I was, in effect, offering South Africa a role in shaping the future of Southern Africa in return for a commitment to majority rule in the neighboring countries and ultimately in their own. This prospect alone proved a powerful incentive to at least explore the possibility of a solution for Rhodesia and Namibia. President Ford spoke to the same effect in a television interview preceding the May 18 Michigan primary.

> I see that that is a possibility as we move ahead . . . [I]f that
> at some point would seem wise to meet with the two heads
> of Rhodesia and South Africa, I certainly would.[2]

Referring to Ian Smith, leader of unrecognized Rhodesia, as a head of state was an inadvertence—at least in terms of conventional wisdom —that did not do much for us in black Africa. But, as was so often the case with Ford, it also reflected a psychological sensitivity. For any sign of human respect would go a long way toward softening the rigidity of Ian Smith and his colleagues, which was the reverse side of their fear of a hostile outside world and an uncertain future within Rhodesia. Ford added a reassurance about rights for the white minority:

> Anything that we can do to avoid violence, anything we can
> do to go ahead with self-determination, with full guarantee
> of rights of the minority, including the white minority, I think
> is in the best interests of the world as a whole.[3]

Ambassador Pik Botha had already told me on May 14 that the South African response would probably be revealed in a public speech either by the foreign minister or the Prime Minister. I replied, partly in jest: "If he could say something which would show that you are not a totally reactionary, racist state."

Prime Minister Vorster decided to give his response in a conciliatory speech before the Cape Town Press Club on May 18. Expressing appreciation for Ford's openness to dialogue, he agreed to promote solutions in Rhodesia and Namibia based on self-determination. That allowed us to take the next step of scheduling a meeting in Germany at the end of June.

## Meeting South Africa's Prime Minister

In the interim, we sought to coordinate our policies with our European allies, especially Great Britain. On May 21, during a meeting with my British, French, and German colleagues at the margins of a NATO foreign ministers' meeting, I supported Giscard d'Estaing's proposal to create an African development fund: "The attraction of the French proposal is it gives a political framework. We need something so we can group countries together without seeming to." But the allies were cautious. To the experienced observer of NATO affairs, the setting up of a group at the under secretary level to "study" the French proposal meant that most allies preferred to avoid the appearance of a unified Western political position for Africa, at least for the time being, to enable them to keep open their option of pursuing their own national interest. In the end, Giscard's proposal for a unified Western program disappeared from the NATO agenda after the change of American administrations.

On May 26, I met with Callaghan and Crosland at 10 Downing Street to discuss how to pursue the Southern Africa diplomacy during my meeting with Vorster and in its aftermath. The British ministers, still finding it hard to accept that the United States might succeed where Britain had failed, were skeptical of our ability to obtain Vorster's cooperation and seemed to draw some comfort from predicting deadlock. They had no great enthusiasm to participate in negotiations including Smith or to play the transitional role we envisaged if the Rhodesians did accept majority rule. Nevertheless, only Britain possessed the experience and the legal basis for devising guarantees for the minorities or to provide a transitional government in the interval before majority rule would go into effect. Therefore, I urged Callaghan to play the role he himself had outlined in his proposal of March 22 and offered to "put additional weight in the scale behind you." But Callaghan answered coyly: "I don't want to duck out, but you're coming fresh to it, and someone coming fresh to it has more influence."

Callaghan's hesitation was, in no small measure, caused by his reluctance to risk either Britain's remaining standing in its former colonies or the cohesion of the Labour Party until a breakthrough had been achieved. The left of the party, led by Michael Foot, was passionately opposed to Ian Smith and to South Africa on moral grounds. It would not be tolerant of the give-and-take of a negotiation on what it considered a moral issue—especially if Smith and South Africa were involved—and would be reluctant to press its African friends toward moderation, without which any attempt at negotiation was doomed. Caught between Michael Foot and Ian Smith, Callaghan opted for asking me to undertake at least one more shuttle as a purely American effort. Nevertheless, he and Crosland agreed to the creation of a working group of high-level British and American officials that would alternate meetings between Washington and London and be charged with keeping African policy under constant review.

On the eve of my meeting with Vorster scheduled for June 23, events in South Africa threatened to doom any major diplomatic role for that country. On June 16, riots broke out in the black township of Soweto near Johannesburg. Tension had been building for some months over the government's insistence that black children learn the Afrikaans language and be taught in it. The riots quickly turned into the opening phase of months of civil unrest which ultimately claimed four hundred lives, including those of many schoolchildren. The ever steadfast Ford urged that I proceed with our plans: "I think this makes it more important that you go. What we are trying to do is overcome things like this." We voted for a strong U.N. Security Council resolution condemning South African practices but not without criticizing the blind eye the U.N. was turning to human rights violations in countries shielded from international scrutiny by their leftist orientations. U.S. Representative Albert W. Sherer, Jr., told the Council on June 19:

> South Africa in its policy of apartheid represents a flagrant violation of human rights. But it would be wrong, indeed it would be hypocritical, were it not said to this Council that South Africa is not the only government which pursues delib-

erate policies which result in flagrant violations of human rights.[4]

Before leaving for the dialogue with South Africa's leaders, I met with all the ambassadors from the African states in Washington and with the House International Affairs Committee. Both groups endorsed my meeting with Vorster. On June 22, the day before the scheduled meeting, I briefed the foreign ministers of Britain, France, and the Federal Republic of Germany in Paris. Zambia had for the first time permitted guerrilla bases to be established on its territory, opening another six-hundred-mile stretch of Rhodesian border to guerrilla infiltration. More importantly, if the war dragged on, the presence of armed guerrilla camps could undermine the moderate orientation of Kaunda and, in time, perhaps even his authority. The various competing guerrilla groups might then seek help from abroad, as had happened in Angola. Our allies expressed their goodwill and avowed their readiness to make a financial contribution for reconstruction and transition costs for the European minorities should a breakthrough to majority rule actually be achieved.

When Vorster had proposed that we meet in Germany, both Chancellor Schmidt and Foreign Minister Genscher had accepted enthusiastically and, thinking it a political asset, even suggested Hamburg, Schmidt's hometown, as the site. They soon learned better. When plans for massive demonstrations were announced in this Social Democrat bastion, the German leaders panicked and moved the meeting without consulting us to a vacation resort in conservative Bavaria, not far from the Czech border at the edge of the Bohemian forest—a region presumably inaccessible to demonstrators. It was a breach of protocol to do so without consulting the parties but, in the end, we accepted our exile. Two hotels with adequate accommodations could not be found in any of the towns in the remote region. Thus Vorster and I wound up about thirty miles apart. Each of our hotels was surrounded by scores of green-clad police to keep the protesters, who, overcoming geography and inconvenience, had managed to arrive en masse, although kept out of shouting range.

The American delegation helicoptered on June 23 to the South Africans' hotel in Bodenmais for the first meeting. As Prime Minister, Vorster outranked me and, in any event, I thought it best to put the South African delegation at ease.

Vorster's record in the South African government stamped him as a hard-liner. As minister of justice for ten years, he had been responsible for the tough crackdown on "subversives"—a term to which he gave a sweeping interpretation. Despite (or perhaps because of) this reputation, Vorster had turned out to be more flexible as Prime Minister than his predecessors, easing some aspects of apartheid and opening a dialogue with neighboring African states.

The bluff and genial Vorster greeted me with his advisers—among them the foreign minister, the permanent head of the Foreign Ministry, the security adviser, and South Africa's ambassadors to the United States and Germany. Both sides, eager to demonstrate that they had not yielded to the other, eschewed the customary banter that accompanies meetings between friendly delegations during the photo sessions.

I invited Vorster to a private session while our delegations began exploring some technical issues, particularly with respect to providing a definition of what would constitute economic security for the European minority in Rhodesia. Over tea and cakes in a smallish sitting room, I began—as was my habit in almost all negotiations—with a philosophical discussion of what we were trying to achieve. I was addressing Vorster, I said, as the leader responsible for the future of his society, which had come a long way to find itself face-to-face with a fundamental decision. If Vorster identified the future of his country with the fate of Rhodesia and Namibia, the outcome would be complicated and surely considerably delayed. But in the end, majority rule was unavoidable in Rhodesia, and South Africa had already granted the principle of it for Namibia. Violence would increase; radicals would gain control of the armed struggle, aided probably by foreign forces, at which point South Africa would face the dilemma of holding still while the European populations of Rhodesia and Namibia were expelled or joining the conflict. But internationalizing the struggle would unite the world against South Africa, and the United States would be obliged to fulfill its tradition of supporting democratic solutions and self-determination.

On the other hand, I argued, Vorster could draw a distinction between his northern neighbors and South Africa based on the reality that South Africa was considered even in Africa as an African, not a colonial, country—however resented its domestic institutions were. This point had been stressed by every African leader I had encountered. Working with us and the front-line states to solve the issues of Rhodesia and Namibia would enhance South Africa's standing as an African society. The opportunity I was offering Vorster was to achieve a certain breathing space in which his country might solve its problems peacefully, not a means for escaping them.

I presented these views more in sorrow than in anger, not as a debate over South Africa's past so much as an option for its future. Highly intelligent, Vorster could not have missed that I was describing a process that could not possibly stop at South Africa's borders. Undoubtedly he was hoping that the time he might gain would somehow permit an outcome for South Africa other than undiluted majority rule or perhaps the emergence of some kind of *cordon sanitaire* at his northern border. But, if he did, it was wishful thinking.

Vorster opened his reply with an exposition of what he and his colleagues understood by self-determination for South Africa: a series of self-governing black homelands united with one or two white homelands which would be clearly dominant. I said that apartheid would never be accepted in the United States, nor would we recognize the so-called black homelands. However, if time could be gained now, it might well lead to a continuing dialogue in the course of which to seek an outcome acceptable to all parties.

Vorster's entire bearing suggested that, faced with a superpower which treated them with some consideration, the Afrikaners were not circling their wagons as they had been obliged to do too often in their difficult history. Provided he was not being asked to abandon Rhodesia's European population without any rights, he would support our efforts to produce majority rule in Rhodesia. He agreed that a moderate outcome in Rhodesia was possible only if the armed struggle was brought to an early end. Joshua Nkomo was, in his view, the most suitable leader for a moderate evolution because he represented a minority tribe that had an interest in guarantees for all minorities, including the European one. Such guarantees, Vorster argued, were needed to persuade South African public opinion. Vorster estimated that there was a window of at most one year for bringing about such an outcome. I told him we would support guarantees for the minorities but that it was premature to make the outcome depend on an individual about whom we in the United States knew so little.

At that point, Vorster and I joined the delegations for dinner. He asked permission to say grace and a moment of silent prayer for the success of what we, each in our own way, were trying to accomplish. With that, somewhat incongruously, Vorster turned the floor over to his military adviser.

General Hendrik Johannes Van den Berg described the military situation. If a military solution were sought, he said, Rhodesia might hold out for quite some time. Rhodesian casualties were low and confined almost entirely to the black militia. The Rhodesian armed forces were capable of defending the country unless troops from overseas entered the war. According to the South African delegation, the guerrillas were losing support because they were concentrating their attacks on civilian populations. This was partly true and partly a negotiating ploy to weaken the American argument about the urgency of the crisis. I replied that the analysis was, in effect, irrelevant:

> Leaving aside the moral question, the example of Algeria —where they [the French population] were there longer— guerrillas started by attacking the local population. At first they're outraged, then they're intimidated. The government has to intensify measures. If they make reprisals, they lose their international position; if they don't, they lose the war.

General Van den Berg did not argue the case.

The next day, the two delegations met at our hotel in Grafenau and concentrated on Namibia. As before, Vorster and I met alone in my suite while our colleagues worked on a guarantee plan for Rhodesia. I used essentially the same arguments I had put before Vorster with respect to Rhodesia. The world community would never recognize a government emerging out of the Windhoek conference as now constituted, and that meant that South Africa would never be able to achieve its objective of abandoning direct control of Namibia by that device. Whatever South African views regarding SWAPO's methods, the history of independence struggles was replete with instances in which today's terrorists are tomorrow's national leaders. And since the whole exercise had been triggered by a series of U.N. resolutions, U.N. participation was essential.

To break the deadlock, I proposed three steps: that the Windhoek conference be moved to Geneva, that a representative of the U.N. Secretary General be invited as observer (establishing the indispensable link to the world organization), and that the conference invite SWAPO as a participant.

Vorster must have understood that I was proposing a face-saving process, at the end of which SWAPO would become the principal spokesman for Namibian independence. That was because of a crucial difference between anti-colonial armed struggles and the maxims of

Western liberalism. If the will of the majority had been the principal issue, the controversies would have been about election procedures; the armed forces would stand neutral, and constitutional provisions would determine the nature of the electoral contest. Instead, in almost all African countries which emerged from armed struggle, control of the armed forces determined the outcome of the election. Nkomo might well be the best-known and most moderate leader inside Rhodesia— as both Kaunda and Vorster, in rare agreement, were arguing—but he possessed no military forces with which to compete with the guerrillas assembling in the neighboring countries. Whatever strength he had would have to emerge at elections, and their result would be largely determined by the military outcome.

The same applied to Namibia. It might well be true, as the South Africans claimed, that SWAPO's following outside the Ovambo area was minuscule. But if the purpose of the slogan "majority rule" was to end the armed struggle, then the "boys with the guns" would prove decisive if only because they were the only group in a position to end the war. They would wind up forming the transition government, making the electoral rules, and winning the election. This is why majority rule typically has been a euphemism for the advent to power by the group that led the armed struggle. They had, after all, suffered and sacrificed to gain power and not to make themselves dispensable.

High-level meetings are not the occasion for reflections on political theory. And this first one between South African and American leaders was fully occupied with finding a practical way out of the Rhodesian and Namibian difficulties. I summed up the emerging cooperation on Rhodesia on June 24 as follows:

> KISSINGER: The Prime Minister and I—if I may sum up our discussion—reviewed the situation with respect to Rhodesia, along the lines of our discussion yesterday and at dinner, too. That is, whether we can put together a package that reasonable people might consider just and honorable with respect to the economic prospects of the white community in Rhodesia; and if we can do this, the Prime Minister might be prepared to use his influence with the Rhodesian government to see what can be achieved. We will work with the black African governments. We will also see if we can have an international meeting for considering the question of guaran-

tees, in which the South African government could participate, at least at the preliminary stage.

This is where the Rhodesia matter stands.

VORSTER: That is right.

On Namibia, I was more cautious. I outlined the proposal to move the conference out of Windhoek, and I was keeping the issue of participation at the conference open, which was a wedge for SWAPO joining it:

> KISSINGER: On South-West Africa [the South African term for Namibia], I have suggested to the Prime Minister that the constitutional convention be moved to somewhere else from Windhoek. The participants will be decided later, but the site should be moved. My impression is this was a proposition the Prime Minister did not reject.
>
> VORSTER: Yes.

Vorster added that he would accept participation of a personal representative of the U.N. Secretary General and that the conference would determine its own composition, which would make it possible to invite SWAPO. Though I was quite convinced that, as in all analogous situations, the guerrillas would insist on being designated as the sole legitimate interlocutor, we had come a long way.

## Great Britain and the Front-Line States

Of all the negotiations I conducted, by far the most complex was the one over majority rule in Southern Africa. There were five front-line states, each with its own emphasis; internal groups competing with one another inside Rhodesia and Namibia; the government of South Africa; the authorities in Rhodesia; and the special position of Great Britain. Their purposes were partly overlapping, partly adversarial. A change in the position of one party could send shock waves through the entire system and threaten to unravel what was being so painfully constructed. Before formal positions could be advanced, it was necessary to reconnoiter the ground with all the parties and, even then, one had to be careful never to discuss the position of one side before committing the others—at least to some extent—lest concessions be pocketed and generate a new round of demands.

We had advanced two steps: the front-line states had welcomed our initiative and were offering various levels of support; South Africa would cooperate on Rhodesia if we were able to develop a package of guarantees for the white minority and, on Namibia, if a way could be found for it to save the South Africans' face. But to translate these general commitments into permanent progress, the assistance and political support of Britain would be essential.

If Ian Smith did agree to revoke his 1965 unilateral declaration of independence and accept majority rule, there would be no legitimate authority in Rhodesia at all unless Britain agreed to return, however reluctantly, for an interim period in the role of governing authority while a new constitution was being drafted. But Britain would never agree to undertake the task unless requested to do so by the black front-line states, if then. It fell on us, therefore, to embark on the ironic dual mission of persuading reluctant Britain to reassume for a brief period the imperial mantle it had been shedding for three decades and to convince its former colonial subjects to invite their erstwhile rulers to return so that imperial rule could be abandoned properly and legitimately.

I returned to London from my meetings with Vorster to consult with Callaghan on June 25. With its narrow passageways and twisting stairs, 10 Downing Street registers its impact by understatement. On the way to the Prime Minister's quarters on the second floor, I encountered John Hunt, the cabinet secretary. We chatted about the "nonofficial" group on global economics at which we were represented by George Shultz (see Chapter 22) and about the Puerto Rico G-7 economic summit about to take place when the Prime Minister shouted welcomingly: "I hear that voice."

In 10 Downing Street's dowdy living room, I outlined the three objectives to the attainment of which a British role was essential: (1) a rapid evolution toward majority rule; (2) helping to work out guarantees for the white minority; (3) reassuming colonial administration to encourage the successor regime to evolve in the direction of moderate Kenya rather than radical Mozambique (an ironic request in light of developments since then).

Callaghan was professional and sympathetic. Britain was willing to assume responsibility for the transition, he affirmed, but was "reluctant to get drawn in militarily and be stuck with maintaining law and order. . . . Do we put in British troops? And if so, how do they get out?" Practical as ever, he put his finger on the central point: the nature of the Rhodesian governing authority. Nkomo was the best guarantee for a moderate evolution, but he had no military force:

> The problem is how we deal with the other Africans regarding Nkomo. He is a father figure and a tailor-made Kenyatta, but he has been losing ground lately. . . .
>    . . . So how do we deal with the guerrillas on the border, if they don't accept Nkomo? Who keeps Nkomo in power? That is the question.

We agreed that the prospects of Nkomo or some other moderate leader inside Rhodesia would be enhanced if the war ended quickly and the guerrillas were deprived of a base within Zambia.

To assess these prospects, I offered to send William Schaufele, assistant secretary of state for Africa, to discuss our plans with Kaunda and Nyerere. In the meantime, a joint British-American task force would develop a formal proposal on Rhodesia to be put before the front-line states and Vorster. The meeting ended on a warm, if slightly wary, note which turned out to be prescient:

> CALLAGHAN: I think you should tell Nyerere and Kaunda: "Isn't it time you put pressure on the British to do something like this?"
> KISSINGER: We would appreciate it if you tell us what you tell them. And we will tell you.
> CALLAGHAN: It is natural if you go around and say "the situation is critical. You should get the British moving."
> KISSINGER: I think this is a good idea.
> CALLAGHAN: Tell us how you blacken our names so we can defend ourselves. . . . [laughter]
> KISSINGER: . . . At the end you will say the incompetent Americans had to be rescued by the British after we hashed it up. [laughter]

When the banter was over, a formal announcement disclosed Britain's willingness to participate in Rhodesian diplomacy:

> The Secretary [of State] gave the Prime Minister an account of his conversations with Prime Minister Vorster.

The Secretary expressed the view that the UK had a central role to play in Southern Africa, especially in helping to achieve a solution to the Rhodesian question.

The Prime Minister indicated to the Secretary that the UK accepts her full responsibility in this regard.[5]

## Another Sortie to Africa

Schaufele left on his mission on July 5. In order to elicit the maximum incentive for flexibility on the part of Nyerere and Kaunda, I instructed him to describe the South African cooperation as being somewhat less assured than I believed it to be. On July 13, I spoke to South African Ambassador Pik Botha in that sense:

I do not tell anybody I have South African agreement on anything. I say: "If I can get your support, I can try for this. If I get South African agreement, will you support it?"

If the front-line Presidents agreed to our strategy, including a transitional role for Britain, Schaufele was to pledge our intention to make a major effort to induce South Africa to help bring majority rule to Rhodesia and independence to Namibia (a fairly safe promise after the Vorster meeting).

That last promise, it was meanwhile becoming clear, was growing difficult to honor because Britain's leaders were developing second thoughts. A meeting with Tony Crosland in Washington on July 8 showed that agreement on a desirable outcome did not guarantee agreement on tactics. The British did not trust Vorster and were less convinced than we that he would carry out what he had promised. And they detested Ian Smith, believing he had deceived and embarrassed them, first by declaring independence and then in the course of a number of stalemated negotiations. Because he did not want to deal with Smith as head, or even as a member, of an interim government, Crosland occasionally spent more time discussing plans to overthrow Smith than on the complex diplomacy that was in train.

I disagreed. Having never met Smith or any other Rhodesian leader, I had no preconceived notions about them. If our policy succeeded, Smith and his colleagues would be replaced by majority rule. Hence I saw no point in diverting energies to overthrowing them or humiliating them and risk a political vacuum with unpredictable consequences—one of which might well be to derail the entire initiative. I told Crosland:

> Smith is an obstacle, but [he] is also a bargaining chip. If they [the front-line leaders] think he's hard to dislodge, they have an incentive to agree. If he's replaced by someone who has no stomach for fighting, they may decide to keep the war going.

In the process, a perhaps unworthy suspicion grew in the American group that London might be seeking to maneuver the United States into becoming identified with the white regimes while Britain would conduct itself as principal spokesman for black Africa—a division of responsibilities I told Crosland we would not accept. Nor did Crosland's sardonic wit go over as well with my colleagues as it did with me. Thus the Treasury representative in our working group was not amused when, in reply to my question of how much Britain would contribute to a guarantee fund, Crosland quipped: "Whatever we can't persuade you and the Germans to assume."

Occasional disagreements reflected differing domestic circumstances: the pressures on Callaghan came from the left; the pressures on Ford and me came from the right. The difference was illustrated in this exchange:

> KISSINGER: It would be easier domestically for us with Smith.
> CROSLAND: It would be easier for us the other way.

When I warned Crosland that a coup against Smith might well unhinge everything in the middle of a negotiation, especially inside Rhodesia, Crosland replied: "The appearance of a coup will have enormous advantages in Britain—and would change the political atmosphere."

The deeper issue concerned who would assume responsibility for the negotiations. We would have preferred British participation from the outset and, in order to give the negotiations a focus, we urged London to put forward a proposal for a transition government. But Callaghan and Crosland were in no hurry. It is always difficult to accept that another country might succeed where one has failed—even if the failure was caused by a historic evolution long antedating the current British government. But this was precisely Britain's position with respect to Rhodesia. Since the United States had designed the strategy and its power would be needed for the actual negotiating, Callaghan was reluctant to pay the political price either at home or in Africa for what Britain no longer had the means to carry through by itself. As for transitional rule, Callaghan feared that Britain, forced back reluctantly into its colonial role, might be isolated if the guerrillas refused to stop fighting. Less than confident that we would be able to deliver Vorster and Smith, Callaghan and Crosland sought to cross every "t" and dot every "i" before moving forward—a time-consuming procedure. By contrast, I believed that speed was of the essence lest the accelerating guerrilla war soon destroy the possibility for negotiations.

Despite these differences in emphasis, American-British cooperation represented a perhaps late full flowering of the special relationship. Our disagreements were more debates between strong-minded individuals within a common enterprise than disputes between sovereign entities with their attendant pressures and initiatives.

## African Complexities

On my first trip through Africa in April, all the front-line Presidents had been so eager to enlist American pressure on their behalf that they had gone out of their way to downplay potential obstacles. Now they encountered the practical consequences: whether our strategy succeeded or failed, they faced risks and needed to protect their position and the interests of their country. This brought their differing approaches into the open.

Nyerere had not been nicknamed "the teacher" for nothing. He saw himself as the philosopher of the African independence movement —especially in Southern Africa. Since Tanzania did not have a common border with either Rhodesia or Namibia, Nyerere was less concerned with the practical implementation of majority rule than with the impact of how it came about on the rest of Africa. So long as he was trying to seduce the United States into involving itself in the diplomacy for Southern Africa, he had found it prudent to go along with such American concerns as protection for white minority rights. But with the diplomacy now concentrating on specific terms, Nyerere felt obliged to assess the outcome in relation to his influence on what he called the "boys with the guns" and his relationship with the more radical Samora Machel of Mozambique, his neighbor. Once majority rule had been agreed, Nyerere would be in no hurry to see it implemented, for he realized that delay would enhance the prospects of the radical fighters he considered his natural allies.

The opposite was true of Kaunda. Zambia shared a long border with Rhodesia; most of its exports passed through that country, and Rhodesia was a significant customer for Zambia's products. Kaunda wanted majority rule for Rhodesia quickly as a way of guaranteeing stability to Zambia. He feared that a prolonged civil war in Rhodesia would enable its guerrillas to entrench themselves on Zambia's territory and undermine his own authority and, to some extent, Zambia's independence. He preferred that Nkomo and a largely civilian government rule in Rhodesia (to be called Zimbabwe after independence). Kaunda also wanted the Europeans to stay on because a strong Rhodesian economy would help Zambia's exports and because the white minorities were likely to support Nkomo or other moderate elements.

In a sense, Kaunda and Nyerere each had a veto over the other, for neither could afford an open rift. Kaunda, less ideological, nevertheless wanted to remain on good terms with the radical camp. And Nyerere, though his preference lay with the radical camp, was much too sophisticated to maneuver himself into isolation from the West. I assessed the front-line Presidents to Crosland on September 4:

> I have the impression, which may be wrong, that they are scarcely less terrified we won't deliver Smith than that we will deliver Smith.
>
> Secondly, these leaders—again except for Machel—are uncertain what they can deliver. Nyerere and Kaunda, if alone, would be fairly responsive to the kind of plan we have, and willing to take two risks—that Smith will not accept, or that Smith will accept and they will be accused by Machel of selling out the others. So they are torn between fear of failure and fear of success.

With Kaunda and Nyerere tilting in opposite directions, our management of the negotiations grew at times nerve-racking. American and British emissaries took turns touring through Africa to determine the prospects for a settlement. The first off the mark was Assistant Secretary Schaufele, sent to report to the front-line Presidents on the meeting with Vorster. He saw Kaunda on July 8 and again on July 10, and met with Nyerere on July 11. Kaunda agreed to the general concept of our program (majority rule, transitional government for up to two years, minority guarantees) and indicated that he would be willing "to stick his neck out for it" if Vorster and Smith went along. Worried about the guerrillas and Nkomo's prospects, Kaunda considered a two-year transition period too long.

Nyerere was complimentary about the Vorster meeting but used the occasion to express a practical reservation which defined what the struggle was about for Africans. If the transitional government were backed by the "freedom fighters," things would evolve smoothly. However, if an attempt were made to establish some alternative government —obviously implying Nkomo—the "boys with the guns" might decide to continue fighting. Nevertheless, Nyerere urged us "to push on." He was forthcoming on Namibia:

> If it appeared possible to achieve objectives under reasonable terms, SWAPO should not be setting up conditions aimed more at strengthening itself than establishing Namibian independence.

But ten days later, on July 22, Nyerere had developed second thoughts. In a conversation with the American ambassador, James Spain, he rejected a transitional role for Britain in Rhodesia because, he said, Britain lacked the power to enforce its views on reluctant parties. Perhaps reflecting opposition from Machel and the guerrillas, he argued that it might be best to leave Rhodesia alone until more military pressures built up.

Nyerere concluded that he would stay in touch with us as the situation developed. Was he trying to avoid responsibility for the outcome, at least before the event? Or was he warning us off? Did he seek to improve the African bargaining position by pretending great confidence in a military outcome, or had he given up on American mediation altogether?

The temptation to abandon the negotiation at this point was overwhelming. Our effort was highly divisive in the United States; the Republicans on the whole would have been relieved if we had desisted. The front-line states, while urging us on, were unable to develop a common position. We were not short of alibis for ending the process.

But we were also convinced that, if we stopped now, we might trigger events which quite possibly would get out of control. Above all, I thought that, appearances to the contrary, we were tantalizingly close to success. The original strategy had been to work out a common position with the front-line states, take it to Vorster, and then impose it on Smith. Nyerere's evasions (which continued through August) convinced me that we would never be able to extract a workable program from the front-line states. Their rivalries, ambivalence about Britain's constitutional role, and psychological block against offering colonialists compensation for ending colonialism made it unlikely that a comprehensive proposal could emerge from their deliberations. So I decided to reverse the procedure. I would try to work out a detailed proposal with Callaghan, obtain Vorster's support, clear the principles of it with the front-line Presidents, convince Smith with Vorster's help, and then bring it back to the front-line Presidents for their final approval.

It was a complicated scenario depending crucially on our stage-managing it in such a way as to have the final breakthrough emerge as Smith's acceptance of terms proposed by Britain and the United States to which the front-line states were invited to respond, and not as African concessions to Smith. That scenario could, in any case, not evolve until the British-American discussions were completed. On August 5, over a long breakfast with Callaghan and Crosland at 10 Downing Street, we put the finishing touches on the joint economic program for Rhodesia. After it was put into final form, an American team headed by Under Secretary of State for Economic Affairs William Rogers and a separate British team headed by Edward "Ted" Rowlands and Sir Anthony Duff would go to Africa and present it to the front-line Presidents. While each team had its own talking points—informal instructions of what to put forward—they were approved in advance by the other, and both sides agreed not to go beyond these instructions.

During the breakfast, I learned for the first time that Callaghan had made a decision not to have Britain reassume its colonial rule, however temporarily. It would be turning the clock back ten years, he argued; under the constitution, the British governor would be responsible for security, and thus British forces would run the risk of finding themselves involved in a guerrilla war. Instead, Britain would work out a plan for a transitional government that would incorporate institutions for carrying out essentially the same functions as those of a colonial governor, albeit without that title. Callaghan would also be prepared to send a senior British civil servant in an advisory role. I thought the American approach simpler (and it was, in fact, later implemented by Prime Minister Margaret Thatcher).

The start of the mission was delayed until after the Republican convention, due to open on August 16. On the same date, a conference of the Nonaligned Movement was scheduled in Sri Lanka and claimed the presence of the front-line Presidents, who, under the impact of Third World rhetoric, were not likely to return from the conference in a conciliatory mood. Throughout this period, Ford was preoccupied with holding on to his slim margin for the presidential nomination against the challenge of Ronald Reagan, who was redoubling his efforts to topple the incumbent President at the Republican convention.

I briefed Ford daily, either personally or, when either of us was traveling, by long reports. On August 13, on the eve of the convention, I warned the President that, if given half a chance, the British would settle for overthrowing Smith and let the rest take care of itself. This would produce a nearly precise analogy to Angola with various African factions competing for control while outside forces were choosing sides. Ford asked about guarantees for the white minorities and, assured that they were part of our plan, remained steady: "That was our plan before, and I think we should stick with it."

The mission headed by Under Secretary Rogers in late August, which presented the economic program for Rhodesia to the front-line states, encountered the same divisions Schaufele had faced a few weeks earlier. Kaunda and Nyerere urged majority rule, were suspicious of South Africa's role, could think of no better way to make progress, and encouraged us to proceed while expressing doubt about our ability to prevail. There was always some statement or tidbit which we could interpret as a token of their support but, equally, there was no shortage of statements making it seem foolhardy for us to proceed.

Kaunda was positive on Rhodesia and hard-line on Namibia. He maneuvered Rogers and Schaufele into meeting with Sam Nujoma, president of SWAPO, by the simple device of opening the door into the next room where Nujoma stood waiting—a gesture certain to cause trouble, as Pretoria was unlikely to believe that we were surprised. Nujoma took no chances risking the goodwill of my emissaries by understating their importance. He addressed Rogers as "Your Excellentness." His political proposals were similarly extravagant. Nujoma wanted the proposed conference on the future of Namibia to install SWAPO as the principal Namibian authority, perhaps legitimized later by a referendum. He rejected the participation of other

Namibian groups in the negotiation except as part of the SWAPO delegation. Kaunda, who had paid his dues to the radicals by arranging the meeting, urged us to proceed on the established course, though he had to have known that what Nujoma was asking for was not in the cards: "We will give you all our blessings while we fight. We will continue to be as helpful as possible." There was no Zambian fighting in Namibia.

Nyerere proved clever and elusive as always. On August 26, two days before meeting Rogers and Schaufele, he had sent me a brilliant analysis of the situation in Southern Africa. He reiterated his belief that further efforts on Rhodesia would prove futile and outlined conditions for progress in Namibia which were moving ever closer to Nujoma's hard-line position. But when our emissaries met him face-to-face on August 28, Nyerere modified his position once again. He welcomed another visit by me to Africa, which made sense only if he wanted our initiative to continue. He still thought progress on Namibia would be easier; on Rhodesia, he remained pessimistic. But the main reason for Nyerere's skepticism was not disagreement with our program but the division among the Rhodesian nationalists. The political leadership inside the country, he averred, was not yet in tune with the guerrillas. In other words, Nyerere, more sympathetic to the radicals, was not eager for rapid progress in Rhodesia if it redounded to the benefit of Nkomo, Kaunda's protégé. However, so that the "major opportunity" of the American initiative not be lost, he offered to try to unify the nationalist leaders. At a second meeting that day, Nyerere informed Schaufele that he was calling a meeting of front-line Presidents and nationalist leaders in Dar es Salaam on September 5–6 to try to achieve unity, urging it especially on the freedom fighters. In Schaufele's words: "He [Nyerere] concluded by stating that he agrees with your strategy, and his job is to convince them on the basis of our consultations."

Since Nyerere had not vouchsafed to Schaufele what he understood by our strategy, I sent him a letter warning that the opportunity was limited and might not recur:

> I am sure you understand the South African domestic situation well enough to realize that if we do not move rapidly, Vorster will find it increasingly difficult to cooperate. I am frank to tell you that if the present modest hopes for a solution fade even further and violence in Rhodesia in-

creases, our ability to make a positive contribution will deteriorate as well. Such are the political realities, especially during an election year, in our country. Indeed, events in America could well produce a hiatus after October until well into the new year, making a peaceful solution that much more difficult.

## A Political Program for Rhodesia

Throughout this period, public opinion in the United States seemed violently opposed to any settlement that could be construed as at the expense of the white communities. After my Lusaka speech, the State Department received 1,700 negative letters and only twenty-three supporting majority rule. By now, Ford had squeaked through the convention but only at the humiliating price of having to accept a plank in the Republican platform all but disavowing our Soviet policy and containing a number of unelevating digs at me personally. During the morning briefing of August 30, I gave Ford another chance to pull back from our African policy: "We need to think about . . . your political situation. . . . I don't want another Texas situation." I described the chances on Rhodesia as slightly better than 50 percent and, on Namibia, somewhat higher. "I can't say we can't wait until November 15, but if it goes beyond January we will be beyond the point of combatting it." Ford did not waver:

> I think if South Africa is involved in the solution, the perception would be different. I think if it is right, we should do it, and the political consequences will come out all right.

That was my goal when I stopped in London to settle on a political program which we could take to Vorster. The British had prepared a blueprint for a transitional government for a maximum period of two years—the famous Annex C. Instead of a British governor, it called for a Council of State in which the Rhodesian whites would have a majority and the blacks a blocking veto, and a Council of Ministers with a black chief minister and a white blocking minority (the white majority in the Council of State was later modified at Callaghan's request to even numbers on both sides and a white chairman who would have no vote). The Council of State would be responsible for implementing majority rule, for defense and internal security. Britain would handle foreign relations. The cabinet would oversee day-to-day administration. The purpose was to accomplish a gradual shift to full majority rule over at most two years without panicking the white population or exacerbating tensions within the black community.

Annex C was a subtle document drawn entirely from British constitutional practice. It sounded reasonable to my associates and me. In truth, we had no basis for objecting to the details nor enough experience to go beyond them. After the transitional period, the new constitution for Rhodesia—to be prepared at a constitutional conference—would govern the future. We accepted the British draft and used it as the basic document in all our political negotiations in Africa.

Because the chief actors on both sides worked smoothly and comfortably together, a true division of labor emerged. Americans conducted the negotiations leading to the breakthrough but on the basis of programs deserving the label "Made in Britain." Economic guarantees for the white minorities were largely drafted in the State Department with some British input. The proposed political guarantees and institutions for the transitional period contained in the controversial Annex C (basically an expansion of Callaghan's proposal of March 22) were so entirely of British origin that British spelling was retained. Later there would be a brief flurry about the official status of Annex C—whether it was a working document or had formal cabinet approval—an issue Callaghan resolved by inviting me to a cabinet meeting which put its formal imprimatur on the document (discussed in the following chapter). Whatever the temporary and occasional confusions of a diplomacy which had no precedent, it did bring about the breakthrough on the basis of American strategy, muscle, and energy combined with British ideas—all that can be asked of an alliance and far more than most have achieved.

# 32

# BREAKTHROUGH TO MAJORITY RULE

## Second Meeting with Vorster

As we were approaching the climax, success would depend on whether we could convince Vorster to bring pressure on Smith, whether Smith would then agree to the essence of Annex C, and whether we would be able to persuade the front-line Presidents to accept an actual agreement rather than an exhortation to majority rule.

On Saturday, September 4, 1976, I met with South African Prime Minister Johannes Vorster for the second time in two months—in itself, a major event for the South Africans, for whom it spelled a symbolic end to their isolation. The venue was the Dolder Grand Hotel, situated in a vast park on a hill overlooking Zürich. The Swiss had insisted on this site over some less elaborate hotel in town because it was easier to protect from demonstrators.

I followed the procedure of the previous meeting by first paying a brief courtesy call on Vorster at his hotel, the somewhat less elegant Dolder Waldhaus about a half mile down the road, overruling associates who wanted to avoid a press photo for fear of a negative impact in Africa and within the African-American community. I felt confident that the African-American groups would judge us by the ultimate outcome, and the African leaders had urged the dialogue with Vorster as the key to progress with Smith.

The South African leader did not waste time on the details of Annex C. Accepting majority rule for Rhodesia in principle, he agreed to cut Smith off if he rejected Annex C; he also modified the position on Namibia they had put forward during our meeting in Germany. These were seminal decisions. For whether or not Vorster and his delegation had fully analyzed the implications of their decisions, they were, in fact, launching a process which would inexorably lead to majority rule in their own country as well.

The decision to support majority rule in Rhodesia having been made, the drama of the previous meeting was absent. There were three sessions: a working dinner on Saturday at the Dolder Grand lasting four hours and hosted by Vorster; a working lunch hosted by me the next day dealing largely with Namibia, which the South Africans, in deference to the Dutch Reformed injunction against working on the Sabbath, announced as a social occasion; and a third meeting on Monday, September 6, involving no meals and lasting four hours.

With respect to Rhodesia, the discussions focused on measures to implement documents I had brought from London: Annex C, dealing with the transitional government, and the joint Anglo-American plan on constitutional guarantees and economic incentives for the white minority. Agreement was reached quite rapidly. The only modification made by the South Africans reflected their distrust of the British: it was that the members of the Council of State would be chosen by each Rhodesian community rather than by the British government. Callaghan and Crosland went along with this change when I returned to London.

With respect to Namibia, the Zürich meeting marked a full-scale retreat by Vorster from South Africa's previous position. In Germany, he had proposed that the constitution for Namibia's independence be drafted by the various Namibian tribes under South African tutelage but without formal South African participation in Windhoek, the capital of Namibia. SWAPO was to be excluded from the process.

The plan emerging from the Zürich meeting proposed moving the conference from Windhoek to Geneva, arranged for U.N. participation and a South African "presence," provided a mechanism for including SWAPO, and set December 31, 1978, as the target date for independence. (The exact progression of the discussions is contained in the drafts exchanged between the delegations, in the Notes.)[1]

Reporting the results to Ford on September 6, I described the next steps:

> I do not—repeat, not—plan to surface these papers with anyone at this stage, because it is essential that we not reveal

South Africa's forthcoming position until the black Africans commit themselves more concretely. In my press conference at the end of my talks, I gave an upbeat presentation but no details.

When I go to Africa next week, I will go to Tanzania and Zambia to nail down the positions of the black leaders, and then go to South Africa to reach final agreement with Vorster. (In the meantime, I am sending Bill Schaufele there Tuesday to get a read-out on the black leaders' conclave in Dar es Salaam and to give them a rough characterization of the Vorster talks.)

On the way back to Washington, I stopped in London for a few hours to fine-tune the agreed documents with Callaghan and Crosland. At Callaghan's request, I sent Bill Rogers to brief the new Conservative Party leader, Margaret Thatcher, on our plans and on the agreed documents. Callaghan had feared that she might join our American critics in attacking majority rule. Thatcher did no such thing. She approved our program, even though her heart was not in it. Three years later when she came into office, she and her foreign secretary, Peter Carrington, ended British ambivalence about reassuming colonial jurisdiction and adopted the procedure we had originally recommended of appointing a British governor to guide Rhodesia toward majority rule.

On the eve of my return to Africa, I felt encouraged not only by the results of the Zürich meeting but even more by the attitude of Julius Nyerere—de facto spokesman of the radical side. His complicated tactics notwithstanding, Nyerere was clearly navigating toward support for the evolving design. On September 7, Bernard Muganda of the Tanzanian Foreign Office told our ambassador that Nyerere urged me to come "the sooner . . . the better." On September 8, Nyerere spoke in the same sense to Assistant Secretary William Schaufele, who had been sent to brief him about the meeting with Vorster. Reporting on the conclave of the front-line Presidents with the resistance leaders, Nyerere informed us that, unfortunately, unity still eluded them. The antagonistic attitude of the resistance leaders toward each other made him wary of how they might react to a breakthrough to majority rule. It was quite possible that they would not agree on how to assume power—a truly "shameful" prospect. Nevertheless, Nyerere told Schaufele the conference had convinced him that Anglo-American pressures might lead to success. He had disclosed his thinking to some of Rhodesia's leaders whom he trusted, including the "boys with the guns," but had not said too much to too many lest they "blow" the initiative.

In Washington, Ford and I briefed Senators and Representatives extensively. Between us, we called forty-seven members of Congress, most of whom played it safe by reserving judgment until some agreement had been concluded.

Jimmy Carter had, in the meanwhile, been chosen as the Democratic presidential candidate, and Ford sought to establish contact with him regarding the pending negotiations. Because the President resented a number of disparaging comments Carter had made about him and did not want to provide a platform to his opponent, he invited former Secretary of State Dean Rusk, an occasional adviser of Carter, for a briefing on our African policy. Rusk was one of America's distinguished public servants. A staff officer under General George Marshall, he had imbibed something of that remarkable man's sense of duty. As Secretary of State for eight years, he had found himself in office when the nation was slithering step by step into Vietnam. Less originator than executor of that tragedy, Rusk had a deep respect for the presidency that made him stay the course even after some of those who had urged our involvement far more passionately turned against it.

Rusk persevered without great designs but with a high sense of honor. In the frenzied atmosphere of the time, he paid for his loyalty to his Presidents by becoming a pariah when he left office. To the shame of the so-called Establishment, no prestigious directorships nor highly paid lectures awaited him; he probably would not have accepted them anyway. It was his home state of Georgia that came to the rescue with the offer of a professorship at the state university in Athens. There Dean Rusk lived out the remaining twenty-five years of his life in obscurity—never complaining, never participating in public controversies, ever available for advice to Presidents and Secretaries of State without obtruding himself. Both the Presidents I served offered him major ambassadorships. He refused all honors, considering his public service completed.

When I was appointed Secretary of State, Rusk's was the first phone call I received, and his congratulations were characteristic. They were addressed to the office, not the person: "Congratulations, Number 56," he said, reminding me that as the fifty-sixth Secretary of State, I had an obligation of continuity and also of living up to the standards of great predecessors. I would call him frequently, especially when I had a close decision to make. Rusk was always available, and I could count on his complete discretion.

Rusk's reaction to Ford's overture for help in insulating African policy from partisan politics was characteristically gallant: "I am here in no other role than as a former Secretary of State. As such, I have a stake in every President." He said he would speak to Carter to that effect, but his call for bipartisanship would be most effective if Ford could bring himself to appeal personally to his adversary.

Rusk called back two days later with a carefully hedged reply from Carter:

> I am not a spokesman for Jimmy Carter. I did talk with him, and I can tell you that I think there is a good chance things could work out if things develop favorably in Africa. The importance as I see it [is] of having some representative African leaders on board, and also you keeping in close touch with some of the congressional leaders.

However qualified, bipartisanship was not completely dead.

## Another Round with Nyerere and Kaunda

Late on the evening of Tuesday, September 14, I was welcomed to Dar es Salaam by a noisy crowd of some two hundred student demonstrators, several of whom seemed familiar to me from my previous visit. Apparently there was one standard reception committee for Western leaders arriving in this nonaligned metropolis, the French foreign minister being treated to a comparable welcome on a later visit. Nyerere saw nothing inappropriate in arranging an inhospitable greeting for the principal negotiator on behalf of majority rule in Southern Africa. It was a convenient way for him to burnish radical credentials even while in fact encouraging a moderate policy. To protect his flanks, Nyerere had to make success appear to have been extracted from the colonialists and put the blame for any inadequacies of the outcome on the democracies.

I managed to ignore the demonstrators at the airport. But they became a nuisance when they followed me to the hotel, where their chanting threatened to keep me awake all night. As it happened, at the height of the demonstration, Nyerere telephoned to welcome me to Dar es Salaam. In the process, he expressed regret for any inconvenience, adding that, in a democracy, demonstrations were regrettably not controllable—an explanation I would have found more convincing had I not seen the government vehicles which transported the group from the airport. I replied that, if the demonstration did not end soon, I would spend the night in Nairobi and rejoin him in the morning. Fifteen minutes later, the crowd miraculously disappeared in the same dilapidated government buses which had brought them.

The next day's meetings with Nyerere and his associates lacked the warmth of my first visit. The goal of luring me into committing the United States to the principle of majority rule having been achieved, Nyerere was now engrossed in its modalities. Of necessity, this involved inter-African relationships and hence his own standing. Over a period of six hours, there were two private meetings, a plenary session with staffs, and a formal lunch. Nyerere followed his by now well-established tactic, which I described to Ford as giving us "the green light on most of our proposals for both Rhodesia and Namibia while beating us over the head publicly."

The private meeting took place in Nyerere's cluttered office, the walls of which were covered with large maps of the districts into which Tanzania was subdivided. Nyerere opened with a welcome promise:

> Let me give you one assurance, so you can stop worrying. We will not allow foreign troops in Zimbabwe or in Namibia. I can speak with more confidence regarding Zimbabwe than Namibia—because President Samora [Machel] and I are closer. And armed struggle has moved further. We have absolutely no intention of involving foreign troops.

On one level, this removed the immediate concern which had triggered our diplomacy. But except for possibly Samora Machel, the President of Mozambique, we had never considered the front-line Presidents as being likely to invite foreign troops. Our bigger worry was that they might lose control over their own territories to the guerrillas. And there was an even more complicated little secret which the front-line Presidents shared but were not eager to publicize: if Rhodesia collapsed, in the way the Portuguese colonies had, the various internal factions presently at each other's throats in Dar es Salaam were likely to decide to back up their verbal recriminations with force. All bets would then be off. Whatever restraints had existed so long as the armed struggle had been supervised by the front-line Presidents would disappear. At this point, the various factions might invite foreign troops, as had occurred in Angola. It was because Nyerere knew this better than we that he had assembled all the front-line Presidents and resistance groups in Dar es Salaam in an attempt to forge unity among them. It was also why he continued to cooperate with the American initiatives whatever formal misgivings he might be voicing for the benefit of his African colleagues.

In the plenary session in the cavernous high-ceilinged main room of the State House, Nyerere therefore coupled his pessimistic restatements regarding the prospects for our Rhodesian initiative with a detailed discussion of the proposals of Annex C and the economic program. He suggested that the arrangements for a transitional government (the subject of Annex C) were less important than those for drafting a final constitution:

> Supposing a miracle took place—I really think of it as a miracle—and Vorster gets Smith to say "Majority rule must come; it's better that it come peacefully, so I accept Mr. Callaghan's position." He might not say "Callaghan's position." At that point, the best thing to happen is that the British call a constitutional conference, and all the Rhodesians concerned go to London. Two things would emerge: immediate establishment of a provisional government . . . and then they work out a constitution. I'd be happy if it's Smith, or someone else, and the British call a constitutional conference.

I already knew from Crosland that Britain would agree to call such a conference. And I knew from Vorster—though Nyerere did not—that the "miracle" of Smith's acceptance of majority rule was awaiting me in Pretoria.

It turned out that Nyerere had changed his position on Namibia since Rogers and Schaufele had talked to him four weeks earlier. Then he had argued that SWAPO should not be permitted to make conditions once the principle of its participation in the modified Windhoek conference had been agreed. Now being personally involved in the complex discussions on Rhodesia, Nyerere had no wish to quarrel with another radical associate, Sam Nujoma, the head of SWAPO.

Moreover, Namibia represented less of an immediate threat to the stability of the front-line states than Rhodesia. It was therefore politically safer to hold out for maximum terms.

I had brought with me from Zürich the agreed program of phased negotiations in which SWAPO and South Africa would participate together with the original members of the Windhoek conference. The record of other similar negotiations left little doubt that, at the end of the day, South Africa and SWAPO would emerge as the principal interlocutors. Perhaps for that very reason, Nyerere and Kaunda insisted on shortcutting the process and, from the outset, confining the negotiations to South Africa and SWAPO. Kaunda and Nyerere were primarily concerned with Rhodesia, which imposed specific decisions on them affecting their own relative positions. Since they had no borders with Namibia—except for a tiny strip of Zambia—and no physical means to influence the outcome, they could afford a pristinely radical position on Namibia while exploring compromise on Rhodesia. (Nyerere's thoughtful analysis of the Namibian problem at the plenary session is included in the Notes.)[2]

I left Dar es Salaam on September 16 both encouraged and put on notice: encouraged because we had, in fact, achieved what we had come for—a go-ahead to settle Rhodesia on the terms of Annex C and a road map for Namibia, though it would take longer to implement than we had hoped; I was put on notice because, just before my departure, Nyerere in a press conference presented himself as "less hopeful" than he had been before my first visit and sniped at my forthcoming meeting with Vorster in Pretoria. When pressed, however, he did admit that he had made no effort to discourage it. Nyerere's expectations for that mission were modest and slightly condescending; it would accomplish little other than "clarifying" the issues and educating the United States in the realities of Africa's struggle. It would be a "miracle," he said, if Smith agreed to majority rule. While he was at it, Nyerere ridiculed the American "obsession" with Cuba and reiterated his earlier view that the purpose of an economic package should be to encourage the whites to leave Rhodesia, not to give them an incentive to stay.

By this time, I had grown sufficiently familiar with Nyerere's methods to understand that I was watching a virtuoso performance, which, in effect, endorsed our diplomacy while hedging against its failure. The possibility of a "miracle" was explicitly left open, and it was defined in much the same terms we had outlined to Nyerere and to which Vorster had essentially agreed. Nevertheless, I did not want Nyerere's declarations to panic Kaunda and thus, at my own press conference, I responded by reminding the journalists that I had come at Nyerere's urgent invitation: "Nothing has changed from what was known a week ago, and therefore I cannot make judgments based on fluctuating moods."[3]

## *Another Visit to Lusaka*

Kaunda's welcome in Zambia on September 16 was free of Nyerere's subtle ambivalence. His situation was more precarious, since an upsurge of fighting in Rhodesia was certain to spread to Zambia. To him, my mission was not an occasion for philosophical speculation about appropriate constitutional forms to transfer power but a means to avoid armed struggle, which—unlike Nyerere—he treated as a last resort, close to an act of desperation if all else failed. Unlike Nyerere, Kaunda did not disparage my mission in public but treated it—almost pleadingly—as a last chance to save Southern Africa from disaster. He sensed that anti-American demonstrations and public sarcasm (even when the private dialogue was positive) would jeopardize public support in the United States. Or perhaps Kaunda's conduct simply reflected his own generous nature. Whatever the reason, he welcomed me at the State House with a moving, at times desperate speech in which he endorsed my visit to Pretoria by reminding his audience that even he, an African leader, had considered majority rule a prize worth negotiating with Vorster. So he publicly wished me Godspeed on my journey to Pretoria:

> Mr. Secretary of State, may I say first of all welcome to Zambia again. We welcome you in the name of the party, government, and people of Zambia because we like to believe Mr. Secretary that your President, you yourself, and your administration are interested in helping the peoples of Southern Africa to find a peaceful solution to their problems. Indeed we pray very hard that you should succeed because if you don't succeed I can only use Mr. Vorster's own words, "the alternative will be too ghastly to contemplate." . . .
>
> . . . This document [the Lusaka Manifesto of 1969] states very clearly that Africa, black Africa, accepts men and women of all races. We want them to make their homes here

because, not so much because of their skills as that they are fellow human beings, made by the same Creator as the one who made us. This document states very clearly that we accept South Africa as independent, but abhor and indeed we will fight apartheid in any shape or form. I would have thought, Mr. Secretary, that Mr. Vorster would help us all by accepting the sincerity, the honest purpose behind this document and help you because, by the accident of your birth, you happen to be white and where we failed because we carried the wrong color, you have the right passport and therefore I hope that he will be able to see sense and accept the importance of your mission. . . .

. . . Who knew that I would ever meet Mr. Vorster, shake his hand. All in the course of the [Lusaka] manifesto on Southern Africa I had to do that. Literally I went to Cape Town. I did not go there physically but I met Mr. Vorster here on Zambian soil. I had never dreamt of doing that. But I knew well that failure to negotiate with him . . . I can't do more on behalf of the Zambian people to their party, other than to impress upon you Mr. Secretary that your mission is very important. You only have a few days, not weeks, to succeed. If you fail, we shall reach a point of no return. May God help you in your mission.

It was one of those moments that compensate for the frustrations, competitiveness, and self-seeking that are so much a part of public life.

The mood Kaunda set in his welcoming remarks shaped the substantive talks. He displayed even less eagerness than Nyerere to discuss the specific provisions of Annex C or the constitutional guarantees. Since the actual terms of the transitional rule would involve major political interests of many parties, no African leader was prepared to tie his hands in too much detail with respect to them. Kaunda voiced no objections to the general outline and agreed to have it raised with Vorster and Smith, implying that it was substantially acceptable. As a hardy survivor of African politics, he knew only too well that the nature of an independent government in Rhodesia would be determined by who held the reins of power rather than by constitutional provisions. Therefore Kaunda's principal concern was that a transitional government be established rapidly, for the prospects of his client Nkomo depended on it. Though he claimed that Nyerere was also backing Nkomo, the State Department African experts seriously doubted it. They believed that Nyerere might be willing to accept Nkomo if he had no other choice but that he preferred Mugabe ideologically and would do what he could to advance his prospects.

Kaunda and Chona were dismissive of Mugabe, claiming that he had no support whatsoever inside Rhodesia. That may have been true. But Mugabe had the military muscle, as he increasingly controlled the "boys with the guns."

Kaunda and Nyerere were at one in the desire for American pressure to achieve the breakthrough toward majority rule. But they differed about the pace of implementing it once the principle was established. Kaunda wanted the speedy establishment of a transitional government under Nkomo. Nyerere preferred to keep matters fluid because every passing month would strengthen the guerrillas' and therefore Mugabe's hands.

When I met Joshua Nkomo on Friday, September 17, he seemed oblivious to these tendencies or, more likely, he had decided that he could help his cause best by presenting his aspirations as if they were already the existing reality. He delivered an assessment of the situation that did not coincide with anything I had heard or seen on my journeys through Africa. He described himself as "the leader of Zimbabwe"— a judgment that had not been voiced by any other African leader, not even by Kaunda. Nkomo rejected Nyerere's idea of a constitutional conference—which both Britain and the United States had already accepted—on the ground that the transitional government should be the sole arbiter of appropriate procedures for drafting a constitution. Assuming that he would prevail, this, of course, greatly enhanced Nkomo's role. Neither the front-line Presidents nor the "boys with the guns" seemed to enter into the calculations of this huge, essentially moderate individual whose boastfulness struck me as a desperate reaction to the dawning realization that events were beginning to pass him by.

## Breakthrough with Vorster and Smith

On the evening of Friday, September 17, we reached Pretoria for negotiations with Vorster and with Smith which would determine the fate of our initiative. Conscious of the domestic pressures, we did not announce the meeting with Smith in advance; he came to Pretoria on the pretext of attending a rugby match. I also requested that the traditional arrival ceremony be dispensed with.

Ambassador John E. Reinhardt, an African-American serving as assistant secretary of state for public affairs, had recently joined my negotiating team. I had always admired his analytical skill and enjoyed his epigrammatic sense of humor. When I became Secretary of State, Reinhardt had turned down my offer to serve as assistant secretary for Africa because, as he put it tactfully afterward, "you had never been to Africa"—meaning that, in his judgment, I was not yet sufficiently committed to enable him to serve effectively. That lacuna now having been remedied with a vengeance, Reinhardt became a key member of my team for African diplomacy, participating in staff meetings and the final negotiations of the Rhodesian and Namibian initiatives. From time to time I asked him to head teams to brief other African countries on our various dialogues.

In Pretoria, I saw to it that Reinhardt attended every meeting with South African leaders in order to give my South African interlocutors a demonstration of our rejection of apartheid. Our hosts treated Reinhardt with impeccable—if distant—correctness, marred only when Vorster got carried away in explaining black African psychology to the American delegation over dinner at Libertas, the Prime Minister's residence, which combined the ubiquitous British imperial style and the innate frugality of the Afrikaner way of life. Vorster made two principal points. The first was that black Africans were more interested in rhetoric than in substance. Hence, in trials, defendants did not want to be acquitted on technicalities; they craved rhetorical flourishes. Vorster's second point was that black Africans were poor farmers. Before the Boers arrived, they had been essentially nomads, unable to understand the importance of building reservoirs to store the region's sporadic rainfall or to learn the principles of irrigation. And, according to Vorster, they remained uncomfortable farmers. Reinhardt did not bat an eye during this disquisition, though afterward he would occasionally remind me that he was making good progress irrigating his garden at home.

The reason for the leisurely pace in Pretoria was that I could not meet Smith until he had attended the rugby match which was his pretext for being in Pretoria. Also, to prevent the ante from being raised in Dar es Salaam or Lusaka, I had created the impression that I would seek to extract from Vorster what he had already conceded in Zürich. The next morning, September 18, we breakfasted at the American Embassy with Vorster and his colleagues, basically to review agreed documents.

Vorster was reassuring about our forthcoming meeting with Ian

Smith, scheduled for Sunday, September 19. At a meeting on September 13, Vorster said he had, in effect, given Smith an ultimatum to accept the principles contained in the Anglo-American memoranda. He would repeat these strictures to Smith after breakfast.

I spent the rest of the day at the American Embassy with two groups of South Africans: first, leaders of the black and Asian communities, and then with white opponents of the South African administration (the African National Congress was banned, and its leader, Nelson Mandela, was still in prison).

My report to Ford summed up their reactions:

> The first session was with ten representatives of the black and Asian communities of South Africa, ranging from tribal chiefs to union leaders to university teachers. All were passionate opponents of apartheid. They were articulate, intelligent, and impressive. All were basically moderates; all wanted a humane multiracial society in which no race dominated any other. Their frightening message was that they were the last generation to be interested in moderate solutions, and that already their young people had renounced moderation and embraced the politics of violence. . . .
>
> . . . The second group I met was composed mainly of white moderates—liberal opposition leaders, newspaper editors, university heads, and businessmen. They all hoped for an early move by their government to announce a program of ending apartheid. They had varying emphases—a federal system, equal economic opportunity, etc. There was no consensus on methods, and none of them had a coherent program. The disarray of the moderate whites is one of the most tragic features of the South African situation.

Zulu Chief Mangosuthu Gatsha Buthelezi was the most impressive of my interlocutors. He made a strong plea on behalf of Mandela and warned against settlements for Rhodesia and Namibia on terms that strengthened apartheid—a warning I took very much to heart. I reported to Ford:

> Any settlement of the Zimbabwe and Namibian political ills which strengthens the apartheid hand of Mr. Vorster will

most certainly herald a new wave of despair that will make
violent options the only options for political realists.

Diplomatic climaxes are rarely dramatic, often consisting of either
technical documents or of formal statements, the implications of which
elude the layman. My meeting with Ian Smith and seven of his advisers
on Sunday, September 19, fell into neither of these categories. No
senior American official had ever met with Smith. British leaders detested him, and the front-line African Presidents resented him. Yet the
eight Rhodesian leaders who appeared at the American Embassy
looked more like British provincial middle-class businessmen or farmers than practicing Machiavellians. For its own and—to the Rhodesians—incomprehensible reasons, fate had propelled them into the
presence of the representative of a superpower determined to end the
political structure which represented their way of life. Smith had
earned a reputation for heroism as a Royal Air Force fighter pilot
during World War II, during which he had suffered injuries resulting
in partial facial paralysis that gave him the appearance of being impas-
sive or even insensitive. Smith and his associates were neither antagonistic nor deferential. They would do their duty to their people as they
saw it without recrimination directed at the spokesman of a world
order that excluded them.

I had not been looking forward to this encounter for which I bore
the major responsibility. Matters would surely not have reached this
stage so rapidly had the American government not insisted emphatically on majority rule or failed to persuade South Africa's leaders to
support us. Convinced as I was of the moral and political necessity of
our course, I had pushed the policy through a Washington that would
have been only too happy to be spared the resulting controversy. Even
though it had been my diplomacy which had closed off Smith's every
escape route, I nevertheless did not relish having to tell my interlocutors that their way of life was coming to an end.

In dealing with Ian Smith and his colleagues, I saw no point in
compounding pain with humiliation and addressed him as "Prime
Minister." The irony was that the only time Smith would be so addressed by an American (or British) official was in the process of
agreeing to a document that would abolish his position. I treated him
as a fellow statesman rather than as a pariah, which made it possible
for him to accept his necessities without being blinded by resentments.

I began our meeting, held at the residence of American Ambassador William Bowdler, with an analysis of the international situation to make clear that what I was proposing was also in the long-term interest of Rhodesia's European population:

> The collapse of Angola, imposed on us by our Congress, and the presence of seventeen thousand Cuban troops, have created a situation in which events can be determined by outside intervention, and there cannot be American support. . . .
>
> . . . Our intelligence is that the attrition on you, absent foreign assistance, will make it more and more unmanageable. I don't see where foreign assistance could come from. There is no domestic support for it in America.
>
> There are many conservatives in America who are heroic in speeches until they have to vote for military aid for someone. For example, Jesse Helms, who accuses me of being a Communist agent, voted against aid to Angola, while I am the one who fought for it.

Smith replied that he was prepared to do things "no one expected we would do." But he had an obligation to tell me what was possible and that a constitutional change required a two-thirds majority of his own (white-run) parliament. With this, we launched into a detailed discussion of the provisions of the various Anglo-American memoranda. Smith calmly analyzed the practical implications of each of the provisions, pointing out the difficulties of some and asking for an interpretation of others. I warned him that going beyond what we had agreed with Britain would jeopardize what had been achieved because it would enable the front-line Presidents to raise new demands of their own:

> If the British indicate, even by only a passive attitude to the black Presidents, that what we agree here is only the starting point for a negotiation, we will not have served you or ourselves. So we have been very careful in recent weeks to keep the British with us.

After three hours of exploring what was on offer, I brought matters to a head. Smith had only three realistic choices, I said: to accept the key provisions of Annex C, to give an evasive reply, or to reject our terms. "But if you fight it out, a year from now you will face the same situation in more tragic circumstances. . . . If you turn us down, we can do no more than let nature take its course." With this, I handed him a memorandum amounting to an ultimatum. Its five points summed up the main provisions of Annex C. These I thought would be supported by Britain and would be, in the end, accepted by the African Presidents (see Notes).[4]

Smith asked for an opportunity to discuss the memorandum with his colleagues. We agreed to meet in three hours' time, at 5:00 P.M., in Vorster's official residence. We parted without either of us referring to the fact that white rule in Rhodesia was ending; our exchange was more as if a difficult business deal was being concluded:

> SMITH: I'm eternally grateful for the time you have devoted
> to this little dot on the map.
> KISSINGER: I want to express my appreciation for the way
> you and your colleagues have conducted yourselves,
> under the most trying circumstances.

I had done what was necessary, but my heart went out to the forlorn group that tried so hard, and nearly successfully, to hide their dejection and their tears.

The meeting with the Rhodesian delegation at Libertas was attended by Vorster and his foreign minister. They would be our unofficial guarantors that Smith would carry out his side of the bargain. Smith had come personally to accept the five-point program:

> When I put these proposals to my colleagues, they were
> horrified. They expected me to go here and convince you
> they were unacceptable. But after hearing the evidence, I and
> my colleagues have decided we have to go back and convince
> them. We have to hedge against my not convincing them.

With this, the question of Rhodesia's future was turned into a series of drafting issues over the distribution of power in the transitional government. To prevent a stampede of the white population, Smith asked that the defense and internal security portfolio be placed into the hands of white ministers during the two years of the transition under a black Prime Minister. I promised to put the idea forward but warned that I thought Britain would be unsympathetic and that the African Presidents would refuse to go along, although a white minister in one of the security posts might prove acceptable. Smith also urged that sanctions be lifted and guerrilla warfare cease as soon as a transitional government was established. When he asked for assurances of American support if the guerrillas continued their attacks even after a transitional government was established, I was obliged to give him a candid assessment of the American domestic realities:

> If a Republican government is in office, and there is a guerrilla attack [after the establishment of a transitional government], we would at least give you diplomatic support and look favorably on others who give military support. If there is Communist intervention, we might even be able to do it.
>
> If there is a Democratic administration, and it happens early in the administration, I have to say it won't be. . . .
>
> . . . Whether in fact it is possible to convince our Congress to do something, I don't know.

We left it that Smith would report to his colleagues, and I would consult Nyerere and Kaunda. I would let Smith know within seventy-two hours whether the front-line Presidents approved the five points. And he should let me know within the same time frame whether he would be announcing his acceptance of them.

At this point, Smith allowed himself his only personal comments. I had stressed the importance of convincing his colleagues because, if our efforts were to fail after I had briefed Kaunda and Nyerere, it would prove "damaging to the prestige of the United States." Smith replied:

> I am conscious this is the first time I have dealt with you. I know my image in the world, that I'm a crook—due to the vindictiveness of the British press. My friends say to me I'm too honest.

Whatever Ian Smith's record in other negotiations, he kept his word and behaved correctly and honorably in his dealings with the United States.

After three hours of this kind of discussion, I met the media with a formulation, the careful pedantry of which obscured the emotions of the day:

> I reported to Mr. Smith the propositions developed jointly by the United States and the United Kingdom in close consultation with the Presidents of black Africa. Mr. Smith and

his colleagues considered these propositions, and they have now returned to Salisbury. I am satisfied that Mr. Smith and his three close collaborators will report favorably to their other colleagues. After consultation with their colleagues, they will have to present these propositions to their party caucus. While the Rhodesian institutional processes are taking place, I will seek certain clarifications from the Presidents of black Africa, particularly President Kaunda and President Nyerere. We expect that this process of clarification and consultation will be concluded toward the end of this week.[5]

Each step forward on the issue of Rhodesia imposed the need for a comparable step on Namibia. Therefore, after making the announcement regarding Rhodesia, I met with Vorster to take account of Nyerere's objections with respect to what we had agreed on Namibia in Zürich. We modified some of the provisions. For example, the proposed conference on Namibia was described not as a continuation of the Windhoek conference but as a new and separate effort; the South African representative was elevated from "contact" to having full powers to negotiate all "issues affecting South Africa"; the composition of the conference was kept open, meaning that SWAPO no longer needed a special invitation. Namibian independence was reaffirmed to take place no later than December 31, 1978.

It was by now nearly midnight. After eleven hours of negotiation, we had achieved the goals we had set for ourselves. It had taken five months from the Lusaka speech to break through to majority rule in Rhodesia; on the basis of what I had seen, I did not share the suspicions of many—especially the British—that Smith would wriggle out of his promise at the last moment. It was one thing to reject initiatives of Britain, whose capacity for retaliation was limited; it was quite another to defy joint pressures from the United States and South Africa, especially after having accepted the American proposal. And on Namibia, we had established a negotiating framework that would surely lead to a comparable breakthrough as soon as the front-line states were ready for it.

## Reaction of Kaunda and Nyerere

The most frequent companion of diplomatic success is exhaustion rather than elation because of the realization that diplomatic breakthroughs usually generate a whole new set of problems, beginning with the implementation of what had been achieved.

This was certainly the case as our African diplomacy was moving to a climax. I would now be returning to Lusaka and Dar es Salaam to inform the Zambian and Tanzanian leaders that the proposals they had approved in general terms three days earlier had been accepted in detail. How would they react to achieving what they had been demanding for over a decade? Would I be in a position to notify Smith by Wednesday (three days later) that the African Presidents would go along with the five-point plan? Or would they evade a clear-cut commitment? No African leader would want to be in the position of having agreed to a solution disavowed by Smith at the last moment. None would want to take responsibility for having thwarted a breakthrough; none dared to court criticisms that they had settled for too little.

On the flight from Pretoria to Lusaka, John Reinhardt had warned me that it was unlikely that the front-line Presidents would simply accept Smith's word. To satisfy their constituencies, they would need to find some way to distance themselves to a degree so that they could extract additional concessions. Reinhardt turned out to be prescient.

The reaction of Zambia's leaders typified this ambivalence. In a three-hour meeting over lunch on September 20, Kaunda—usually more given to exhortation than precision—proved that one does not become the leader of a victorious independence movement without a fine sense of the realities of power. He asked penetrating questions about the five-point program and was careful to stress the need to consult his Zambian colleagues as well as Nyerere and representatives of the external resistance. For all that, Kaunda exuded satisfaction. He supported the outcome regarding Namibia without qualifications. Toward the end of the meal, he abandoned his initial reserve about Rhodesia: "We want to express satisfaction for what you have done. We can see light here. There is a chance of succeeding." Mark Chona added that a "tremendous advance" had been made that no one had thought possible.

By dinnertime, Kaunda had convinced himself that the basic plan was sound, even in its details, and stressed the need for speed in implementing it. He would urge Nyerere to facilitate a transitional government even before I reached Dar es Salaam toward noon the next day. Moving quickly was critical if Kaunda's friend Nkomo was to have any chance of achieving power. At the end of dinner, Nkomo joined the group, and Kaunda tactfully left, though Chona remained. The more realistic Nkomo warned that Nyerere would make every effort to prevent him from taking power. The next day just before I left, my Zambian hosts summed up their goals. Nkomo told me: "Your job has been to move Smith, and this is what you have done." And Kaunda's parting words were: "The main thing is to get the interim government formed. The main thing is the backing of the U.S. and U.K."

The more Kaunda reflected on the outcome at Pretoria, the more enthusiastic he became. Two days later, in a conversation with Schaufele on September 23, the day before Smith's speech was due, he expressed his "pleasure and satisfaction" with the agreed paper on Namibia. He assured Schaufele that he had "no problem" with it. On Rhodesia, Kaunda was equally positive. If Smith accepted the American proposal, Kaunda assured us of his support and promised to "move everything" forward.

As I had expected, the formidable Julius Nyerere did not share Kaunda's sense of urgency. Now that the breakthrough had been achieved, he wanted to reduce, not enhance, our role. For Nyerere, the real battle was only now beginning. Kaunda saw in what had been achieved a means to stabilize the region, safeguard his country, and secure majority rule under a moderate government for his neighbors. Nyerere, believing himself to be the ideological leader of Southern Africa's nonalignment and anti-colonial struggles, viewed Rhodesia as part of a continuing contest. He did not want it to appear as having emerged from some bargain with the imperialists (especially the United States) but as a moral victory extracted by radical Africa. Nyerere kept urging a constitutional conference under British chairmanship (surely not discouraged in London), the practical result of which would be a delay of many months in the formation of the transitional government.

As a result, in our meeting on September 21, Nyerere spent very little time exploring the five-point plan for Rhodesia. When I told him about the proposed procedure and Vorster's threat to cut off oil for Rhodesia if Smith went back on his assurances, Nyerere said: "I am

happy. I am completely happy on this basis." After some further explanation, he added: "That looks fine to me. Frankly, I think you have
done it. . . . I for one will give it a chance."

But Nyerere's agreement amounted to a careful preparation of the
next battlefield. He was urging a constitutional conference under British chairmanship and wanted it to appoint the transitional government
only *after* the basic constitutional principles had been agreed, thus
adding two levels of delay: first for assembling the conference and then
for agreeing on principles. During the likely protracted negotiations,
the issue of who governed in Rhodesia would remain open, the guerrillas would stay in place, sanctions would continue, the "boys with the
guns" would gain influence, and Nkomo's prospects would plummet.

Nyerere's desire to enhance his radical credentials also shaped his
response to the modified proposals on Namibia. He admitted that
there had been "great movement" in Pretoria. But, in sharp contrast
to Kaunda, he was adamant that he would not cooperate in any
formula designed to permit a South African retreat over a period of
two years. Pretoria would have to accept SWAPO as the only legitimate
interlocutor from the outset; if South Africa wanted any Namibians
other than SWAPO to participate in the conference, they should join
the South African delegation—a certain kiss of death for them. On
Namibia, step-by-step progress was not enough; Nyerere insisted on
South African surrender as an entrance price into negotiations.

Just before I left Dar es Salaam, Nyerere held another press conference, a bit more upbeat than his previous one. He agreed that progress
had been made and directed his sarcasm at the press rather than at the
United States: if Smith accepted the American plan, Nyerere said, there
would be a basis for negotiations, and he would urge the various
Rhodesian factions—including the guerrillas—to join. What Nyerere
seemed to be endorsing was the opening of negotiations instead of the
details of the five-point plan as he had done privately. On the other
hand, his circuitous tactics no doubt reflected his concern that the
guerrillas would not accept a provisional government imposed by a
conference of the front-line Presidents (as Kaunda seemed to prefer).
The result might be an Angolan situation with various black factions
lining up outside support. No doubt, to Nyerere, procrastination
seemed the most prudent course.

## Blow-up with London

While I was trying to sort out the differences between Lusaka and Dar es Salaam, tempers between London and our party snapped as they had been threatening to do throughout the shuttle. At the beginning of the exercise, we had suggested that Crosland assign a senior official to our party to participate in the talks and to help modify the agreed texts if this proved necessary. Crosland had evaded the request and instead assigned a middle-level diplomat from the Washington embassy to join the shuttle. British insistence that London alone could approve modifications of the agreed text further strengthened our conviction that we were proceeding on the basis of a document having government approval. The young British diplomat, Richard Samuel, was affable, intelligent, and helpful, and he quickly became a full-fledged member of our negotiating team; he was thoroughly briefed by Schaufele and Rogers and participated in our internal meetings, to which he made several useful contributions. Yet he seemed to be no better informed of London's reservations, if any, than we were; he surely never raised any objections during the shuttle.

In order to make absolutely certain that we were proceeding in complete harmony with London, I briefed British ambassadors or high commissioners at each stop and sent every proposed modification of our joint papers to London. In light of the close coordination that had preceded my mission and the fact that Annex C was a British paper down to its spelling, the reaction of these British representatives was mystifying. The ambassadors (or high commissioners) claimed to be without instructions and kept asking clarifying questions as if they were seeing the relevant documents for the first time.

Finally, upon my return to Lusaka, I received a message from London objecting to my public statement that Smith was considering proposals formulated by the British and American governments. Whatever Smith said in the end should be put forward as a Rhodesian "offer," not as the acceptance of an Anglo-American document. But it was clear to all of us on the shuttle that the front-line Presidents would never agree to a program coming ostensibly from Smith with the implication that they were somehow yielding to the white Rhodesians. It was equally doubtful that Smith would be prepared to offer the five-point program as a voluntary action or be able to obtain the support of his parliamentary caucus on that basis.

The British media seemed to reflect the official wariness. Anne Armstrong, the splendid American ambassador to London, reported on September 21:

> The British press has reacted with skepticism to reports of "considerable progress" resulting from American shuttle diplomacy in Southern Africa. Three themes run through the September 21 reports and comments of London's leading papers: (1) Smith is up to his old tricks; he is playing out Kissinger the same way he played out Wilson. Timely majority rule is too miraculous to believe; (2) Even if there is agreement to the broad outlines of a settlement, there are too many other obstacles in the way, and any optimism is premature. . . . (3) The pessimism, caution and wariness in the press reflects the atmosphere in Whitehall and the private speculation of Foreign Office officials.

Not a little put out, I called in the British high commissioner in Lusaka and the hapless British diplomat assigned to me. We could not move without the approval of the black Presidents, I said, and they were already under pressure from the most extreme among them:

> If you say that all sides enter the agreement with a free hand, both the five Presidents and Smith will impose impossible conditions. . . .
>
> . . . I don't want abstract support. I want tactical and strategic support. Either support me or stay out.

Crosland replied by message that same day, restating the British position in a very conciliatory fashion. He invoked a distinction between a "discussion paper" and proposals put forward with cabinet approval—a position I had never encountered from any British cabinet before the Rhodesia shuttle or since. As for the proposals we had put forward, "we support them strongly but have no powers to enforce them on either side, only to endorse them as constructive proposals." Enforcement had never been requested; we would have preferred endorsement to be less academic and more direct. Crosland closed with a generous sentence which, at the same time, showed why the British found our mediation in the heart of their former African colonies—named after one of Britain's pioneers in the region—so painful: "If you can pull this off where we have so often failed, it will be a major coup."

On September 22, I replied to Crosland from Kinshasa. I argued that it was important to adhere as close as possible to Annex C. There could be no question whatsoever of any pride of authorship, since Annex C was entirely a British draft. But if there were no parameters for the negotiation regarding a transitional government, each side would put forward its maximum position and "the argument over the balances of authority between the races would have been endless." The resulting chaos would jeopardize our ability to resist African radicals and Soviet-Cuban intervention, the principal goal of the entire enterprise.

I will digress to explain the origin of the misunderstanding, if such it was. Annex C was entirely British right down to the official paper on which it was typed. There was no American precedent for it and, indeed, it was we Americans who had urged the British to appoint a governor instead of the complex procedures of Annex C. While the British after the event tended to refer to Annex C as a discussion paper, our imagination did not extend to the concept of a written document handed to us by the foreign secretary and the Prime Minister in the cabinet room as having no official standing—especially since the same British leaders knew full well we would be showing it to Vorster, as the following exchange on September 4 demonstrates:

> CROSLAND: You will be back here Monday to talk to the Prime Minister. Of course, we're not committed formally to anything as a government. If the omens are good on Monday. . . .
>
> KISSINGER: I'm, of course, assuming you're prepared to proceed on a jointly prepared paper.
>
> CROSLAND: It is virtually certain. But I can't tell what the Prime Minister will do.
>
> KISSINGER: The paper is the same.
>
> DUFF: The new Annex C deals with the interim government.
>
> KISSINGER: Can you give us Annex C? If we agree with it, we can give it to the South Africans.
>
> DUFF: Yes.

On September 6, in a meeting with advisers at 10 Downing Street during which I briefed Callaghan about the meeting with Vorster, the following exchange regarding Annex C took place, again showing that the British were aware the document had been handed over:

> KISSINGER: Are you satisfied with the information being exchanged?
>
> CROSLAND: Absolutely. The last week has been an absolute model.
>
> KISSINGER: On Rhodesia: Britain, we know, considered it an important sign of good faith that Ian Smith be removed. And we gave him [Vorster] the paper.
>
> CROSLAND: Our paper. The revised Annex C.
>
> KISSINGER: We handed them the revised Annex C. And there are a number of questions they've asked about that, but they think it is a reasonable basis for discussion.

After the meeting, Callaghan and Crosland took me to the cabinet room and wished me luck, stressing that they were standing behind me. I took that to be the prime ministerial endorsement Crosland had indicated as being almost certain two days earlier.

I recount the dialogues in such detail because some accounts of the period, including one by Crosland's widow—who was not privy to the conversations—have indulged in preposterous fantasies of the Americans charging about spreading chaos with a mixture of enthusiasm and naïveté, until they were rescued at the last moment by their more mature British allies.[6]

Nothing could be less accurate. We moved in synchronized steps with the British government: I saw Callaghan and Crosland before and immediately after every trip. Between April and September, I met with Crosland another eight times, and subordinate officials were meeting even more frequently. Rogers and Schaufele presented the British economic plan to the front-line Presidents. I reviewed the principles of Annex C with the front-line Presidents before my visit to Pretoria—all with explicit British approval. On the shuttle, I briefed British ambassadors a total of ten times.

When it all blew up, Crosland wrote to me that I needed a better understanding of the nature of cabinet government. As a former professor of political science, I understood cabinet government well enough. What I did not understand was how a document which I had been handed at 10 Downing Street, with which I was traveling all over Africa, and which had been turned over to other governments with full British knowledge could fail to be backed by its originating authorities.

The mystery was solved on September 23 when I arrived in London from Kinshasa at 9:00 P.M. The drama of the African stops followed me. Crosland and Ambassador Armstrong greeted me at the airport. Normal protocol would have had Crosland take his leave and the ambassador accompany me to my hotel. But Crosland had other ideas. The key members of the cabinet, he informed me, were waiting in the cabinet room at 10 Downing Street. He would accompany me there, but he first needed to talk to me alone.

The extremely able Ambassador Armstrong was in tears of rage, only slightly assuaged by Crosland inviting her to the cabinet meeting. In the car, Crosland revealed why he wanted no witnesses to our conversation. Annex C, he told me, had not only never been approved by the cabinet, it had never even been shown to the cabinet. It would be mortifying for the Prime Minister if I were to repeat before the cabinet my conviction that I had been presenting a joint Anglo-American proposal all along. I could speak of a joint concept and even stretch it to a joint plan so long as I assumed responsibility for the actual conduct and substance of the negotiations.

Crosland did not explain why Callaghan had chosen such a complicated method. Perhaps, based on British experiences, he thought I would fail and did not want to risk controversy within the Labour Party over a debacle involving both Vorster and Smith. Perhaps he wanted to maintain the greatest degree of freedom of action for the follow-up negotiations if the shuttle succeeded. Whatever the reason, I did not forget the staunch support we had received from Callaghan over the years or the friendship he had shown me. I therefore went along with the somewhat surreal proposition that I persuade the British cabinet to endorse a negotiation based on a document which had, in fact, originated with the British foreign secretary and Prime Minister.

Callaghan made things as easy as possible by greeting me outside 10 Downing Street. He informed the waiting press that I had been operating "within the personal framework of a common plan" based on his own proposal of March 22. It was a formulation of which the drafters could be proud. It gave away little while stressing the magic word "common" and qualifying it with the equally sacramental "personal." Leaving the media to unravel his Delphic utterance—of a "common" plan negotiated as a "personal" effort—Callaghan ushered me into the cabinet room, where I briefed his cabinet on the negotiations without ever mentioning Annex C. When I finished, Callaghan brought appearance and reality back into harmony by addressing me in front of his cabinet:

> I hope to speak with you in all candor, Henry. In our cabinet, there is marked reluctance to get involved because we have been caught before. For us, the Rhodesian problem is a debt of honor. There is no interest for us except to settle the issue.
>
> You can imagine, in our present economic situation and lots of other problems, there is no great rush in the cabinet to get into the process again. The great difference now is Smith will have made a declaration, and you will be willing to help. On that basis, I will be glad to recommend to the cabinet to go along.

And that is what the cabinet did, with the invaluable assistance of Michael Foot about whose possible defection Callaghan had been most concerned when the whole process began.

The next day, Crosland and I held a joint press conference in which we affirmed that we had proceeded on a common plan and expected to continue to do so.

On Friday evening, September 24, Ian Smith accepted the five points in a dignified and unemotional broadcast. He made it clear that he had yielded to pressure:

> As you are all aware, I have recently had a series of meetings in Pretoria, firstly with the South African Prime Minister, then with Dr. Kissinger, and finally with Dr. Kissinger and Mr. Vorster together.
>
> At these meetings, the position of Rhodesia in relation to the rest of Southern Africa, and indeed to the Western nations, was discussed in great detail. It was made abundantly clear to me, and to my colleagues who accompanied me, that as long as the present circumstances in Rhodesia prevailed, we could expect no help or support of any kind from the free world. On the contrary, the pressures on us from the free world would continue to mount. Dr. Kissinger

has been working in close consultation with the British government, and he has the full support of the other major Western powers.

The British government issued a statement expressing its satisfaction that Smith had accepted proposals representing an amalgam of ideas put forward by British and American leaders as well as by the front-line Presidents. And it made up for the tensions at the end of the shuttle by concluding with this generous tribute to my role:

> HMG [Her Majesty's Government] extends its warmest congratulations to the United States Secretary of State, Dr. Henry Kissinger, for having brought matters to such a pass. Men of goodwill everywhere owe him, and others who have contributed to his success, a debt of profound gratitude. It could not have been achieved without his skill and enthusiasm.

## Return to Washington

The reaction of my own government was less generous. President Ford read a brief statement in the White House press room on September 24. It called on the parties to establish rapidly conditions for majority rule under which all the peoples of Rhodesia would be able to live in harmony. The statement praised Callaghan, Vorster, the African front-line Presidents, and even (by implication) Ian Smith. It omitted only the U.S. Secretary of State. What had obviously happened was that a statement drafted by my staff and including a brief reference to my role had been edited by the political advisers and turned over to Ford as having been approved by the NSC. It being the middle of the presidential campaign, Ford's advisers had concluded that mentioning my name would inflame some voters Ford was obliged to court. I had become a political liability. Because I understood the reasoning, I decided that this would be my last shuttle. Should Ford win the election, the time had come for me to leave office.

On September 26, the five front-line Presidents responded to Smith's broadcast with a fighting statement. Hailing the "collapse" of the illegal racist minority regime in Southern Rhodesia, it gave full credit to the freedom fighters for the achievement. The statement called for the immediate formation of an interim government and the convening of a constitutional conference, and denounced Smith's proposals as "tantamount to legalizing the colonialist and racist structures of power." Details of the transitional government would be left to the conference. There was no mention of the role of the United States and Britain. The front-line Presidents wanted to proclaim a victory, not the success of diplomacy; majority rule needed to be perceived as having been imposed on the colonialists, not as a deal facilitated with their cooperation.

The fighting rhetoric obscured the reality that the front-line Presidents had, in fact, accepted the basic structure of our proposal: a transitional government followed by a constituent assembly based on a Council of State appointed by Britain. All they were explicitly rejecting was the provision for two European security ministers, which I had already warned Smith had not been endorsed either by Britain or the front-line Presidents.

By this time, we were sufficiently familiar with local customs to know that soothing explanations would almost invariably follow the belligerent rhetoric of the front-line Presidents. And sure enough, on September 27, Nyerere called in the American and British ambassadors in Dar es Salaam and expressed his gratification at the positive American and British reactions to their Lusaka statement. He said that our interpretation of the Presidents' statement was indeed correct: it was not intended as a rejection. Professing flexibility, he stressed that the Africans would go to a conference with no preconditions of their own. Nyerere added that he would not object to the two white security ministers if all the Rhodesian factions wished to accept them, though personally he disapproved of the idea.

The Zambian leaders sounded even more positive. According to Mark Chona, Kaunda's mood was one of "exhilaration." All the front-line Presidents regarded the Smith announcement as a "real breakthrough." Kaunda added his own gloss. The front-line Presidents had accepted the basic framework, even to the point of separating the problem of forming the transitional government from the drafting of the constitution.

Nyerere, collaborator on the breakthrough and frequent adversary on its implementation, in a letter to me of October 5 eloquently put his finger on the different perspectives involved:

> You and I, Dr. Kissinger, have very different "political constituencies" to take account of, and inevitably there is a

danger that in dealing with them we shall each appear insensitive to the problems of the other. Indeed, we may truly complicate the problems of the other, although I hope that through frank and friendly contact we can reduce misunderstandings between us to the minimum.

And certainly nothing will reduce the respect for you as a person which I have developed during our meetings, or the pleasure they gave me. I hope that some time in the future we shall be able to meet again, at greater leisure, with the freedom to exchange ideas on subjects other than Zimbabwe and Namibia!

On October 28, the negotiations on Rhodesia started in Geneva. On November 2, Gerald Ford lost the election to Jimmy Carter.

We had always expected that Britain would carry the laboring oar in the follow-up negotiations. But with Ford's defeat, the difference between the British approach and ours—which had been at the heart of the flap over Annex C—resurfaced. The Americans felt a moral obligation to the Rhodesians and South Africa to carry out the terms under which we had pressed Ian Smith to accept majority rule. Britain's distrust of Ian Smith was total; its leaders were viscerally opposed to backing him on any aspect of the follow-up negotiations, including minority rights. Both we and the British shared a high opinion of Nyerere's abilities. But London could never bring itself to oppose his frequent forays into promoting his radical friends among the Rhodesian guerrillas. By contrast, I believed that precisely because Nyerere was so committed to playing a major role in the radical camp, it was necessary to give him some alibi for making concessions by a policy of polite firmness. Otherwise he might well become the prisoner of forces that would, in the end, overwhelm him as well.

In the follow-up negotiations, the balances which had brought the breakthrough began to disintegrate. Crosland refused to chair the constitutional conference called for Geneva. Ivor Richards, who was appointed to do so, was new to African problems and without the political backing which might have given pause to the passions of the parties. I had become a lame duck. For some weeks, we conducted diplomacy as if the election results were just another obstacle to be faced down. But inevitably—and correctly—world leaders were waiting for the new administration to take office and therefore were simply marking time.

When the Carter Administration took over, it sought to distinguish itself from Ford's by a more explicit human rights policy toward South Africa. In the process, it destroyed Vorster's incentives to be helpful on Rhodesia and Namibia. The Geneva conference ran into the sand shortly after the new administration took office.

Nevertheless Rhodesia was now irrevocably on the road to majority rule. Smith tried to negotiate it directly with various leaders of the "internal" resistance, but they could not handle the "boys with the guns." In the end, Margaret Thatcher, on becoming Prime Minister, called a conference on Rhodesian majority rule at Lancaster House. She grasped the nettle and appointed a British governor and a Council of State, implementing the basic concepts of Annex C. The price paid for the delay was that the radical factions of the guerrillas headed by Robert Mugabe assumed power under majority rule. The delay worked much as Nyerere had hoped and Kaunda had feared—though Nyerere was to derive little joy from the ascendance of Mugabe, who proved to be an intractable partner. It took even longer—until 1990—for Namibia to emerge into independence on the basis of the procedures worked out in the 1976 shuttle.

From the geopolitical perspective, we had achieved the purpose of our African diplomacy. Six months after the debacle of Angola, the United States was demonstrating a continuing capacity to shape events in Africa. The erosion of faith in Western relevance had been arrested. Rhodesia and Namibia became independent, implementing principles and procedures agreed during the African shuttles—though more slowly and with the emergence of more radical governments, especially in Rhodesia, than we would have liked. International war in Southern Africa was avoided; armed struggle there did not bring in outside forces; there were to be no other Cuban adventures in the independence struggles of Southern Africa (though they appeared in our successor's administration in the Horn of Africa—a move we would surely have resisted). The white minority in Rhodesia, on whose status under majority rule we had expended so much effort, is still, twenty years after the events described here, living in the new country of Zimbabwe —even Ian Smith and most of his cabinet stayed on under black rule (only a quarter has left, mostly civil servants of the old regime). Smith retired to his farm.

In the melancholy interregnum between administrations, Nyerere provided one of the more uplifting moments. Throughout this hectic period, our relationship had been both warm and ambivalent. I greatly respected him and liked him. Evidently the feeling was mutual as each of us tried to utilize but also to contain the other's influence.

Now, as my term of office was drawing to a close, these battles, both the joint and the adversarial, were behind us. On December 9, 1976, Nyerere wrote me a letter which meant a great deal to me even while—and perhaps because—all that was left to us was mutual sympathy:

> Dr. Kissinger: Our letters inevitably concentrate on difficulties and disagreements because it is they which require our thought, and perhaps action. But I do want to emphasize my very great appreciation of the efforts you have made this year to get a settlement on the basis of majority rule in Zimbabwe and Namibia. That there has been movement on the non-military front in Southern Africa during 1976 is due in very large part to the initiatives you have taken, and these have demanded a great amount of time and travelling and negotiation (perhaps not always easy or pleasant) on your part. We do not yet know whether, when this vortex of negotiation has settled, we shall have reached the objective; we are dealing with questions of long standing which have become even more difficult as time has passed. But whatever happens I want to stress that I do appreciate your efforts, and I do hope that you will not allow any disappointments (temporary or otherwise) to lead to doubt either about the validity of this attempt, or about the cause of majority rule in Southern Africa for which we have been working.
>
> This letter therefore comes to you with my very warm personal good wishes once again. I am sure we shall have further contact in the future—after January as well as possibly again before the change in the American Government.

# PART TEN

# END OF THE FORD PRESIDENCY

# 33

# CIVIL WAR IN LEBANON AND MIDDLE EAST PEACE

Duration negotiations for the interim agreement of September 1975, President Ford had promised Israeli Prime Minister Yitzhak Rabin that the United States would not ask Israel to make further major decisions until after the presidential inauguration of January 1977. Egyptian President Anwar Sadat had agreed to such a hiatus a few months earlier when he met Ford at Salzburg in June 1975. After two years of war and the tensions surrounding the negotiations for three major agreements, the Middle East parties as well as the United States needed a breathing space for reflection on next steps. How fast to travel on the road to peace and how far, and in what sequence when the peace process resumed, were to be subjects for exploration during this breathing space.

But amidst the passions of the Middle East, pauses are not simple to bring about. Ford, Rabin, and Sadat were not in a position to arrange it by themselves. Syria and the PLO (Palestine Liberation Organization), excluded as they were from the Sinai II interim agreement, had no interest in a respite before another round of diplomacy that likely would again exclude them. All the other parties would position themselves in light of their own priorities, among which delay did not rank high. Paradoxically, the diplomacy needed to bring about a pause turned out to be almost as complex as the actual peace process itself.

Suddenly an explosion occurred, long in preparation and yet—as so often happens in the Middle East—quite unexpected in its extent and violence. It abated the pressures for a resumption of the peace process. Starting in the spring of 1975, Lebanon was convulsed by ethnic and religious violence over the distribution of power between the historic Christian and Muslim communities that rapidly degenerated into a murderous civil war. All the Middle East parties and much of the rest of the Arab world soon found themselves involved on behalf of one of the many Lebanese factions, while the United States emerged as the only country in contact with all the factions.

In its first days, the Ford presidency had been drawn into the vortex of an ethnic crisis in Cyprus (see Chapter 7), and now, toward its end, it was hurled into another one, in Lebanon. Each crisis demanded a complicated diplomacy to enable the United States to protect its national interest amidst the primal passions. Because these were rooted in feuds and religious conflicts going back over centuries, the Arab-Israeli peace played only an indirect role—if any—in the calculations of the many parties, to whom, in addition, the imperatives of global stability meant nothing.

The complexity of the ethnic and religious conflict in Lebanon stood in the same relationship to that in Cyprus as advanced calculus does to elementary algebra. Cyprus had involved two ethnic groups and three outside powers; Lebanon drew into its conflicts a plethora of groups on each side of two major communities—at least four on the Muslim side and three on the Christian, each of which was supported by an Arab or other outside power. Israel and Syria undertook periodic forays into Lebanon; France considered itself to be heir of interests dating back to the League of Nations Mandate it had exercised between the two world wars and to its earlier interventions in the nineteenth century. The Soviet Union claimed a role as a superpower; the United States was active to protect the peace process and to prevent a radical outcome.

This chaos erupted at the precise moment when the participants of the 1973 Middle East War were beginning to feel their way—however fitfully—toward peace among themselves and consumed a small nation heretofore considered the oasis of reason and piously invoked as a model of the possibility of pluralism wrought from the emotions of the Middle East.

## The Lebanon Crisis Unfolds

In *Years of Upheaval*, the second volume of my memoirs, I concluded a description of my visit to Lebanon on December 16, 1973, to meet with President Suleiman Frangieh with this reflection:

## Lebanon

Tripoli

Mediterranean
Sea

**LEBANON**

Baalbek

Beirut ★

Zahle ●

B E K A A   V A L L E Y

Beirut—Damascus
Highway

Awali R.

Sidon ●

★ Damascus

Litani R.

Tyre ●

**SYRIA**

*Area of Separation*

*GOLAN
HEIGHTS*

------- Autonomous
province of
Lebanon,
1861—1915

*Sea of Galilee
(Lake Tiberias)*

**ISRAEL**

Haifa ●

—·—·— Modern
boundaries

| 0 | 10 miles |
| 0 | 10 kilometers |

**JORDAN**

I think with sadness of these civilized men who in a turbulent part of the world had fashioned a democratic society based on genuine mutual respect of religion. Their achievement did not survive. The passions sweeping the area were too powerful to be contained by subtle constitutional arrangements. As it had attempted in Jordan, the Palestinian movement wrecked the delicate balance of Lebanon's stability. Before the peace process could run its course, Lebanon was torn apart. Over its prostrate body at this writing all the factions and forces of the Middle East still chase their eternal dreams and act out their perennial nightmares.[1]

Less than a year and a half after that visit, Lebanon was on the brink of civil war. Sparring between the Palestinians (Yasser Arafat was then in his radical heyday) and the Maronite Christians degenerated into open warfare on April 13, 1975. The hostilities intensified over the next eighteen months, punctuated by at least sixty attempted cease-fires. As the Lebanese central government and military authority broke down, next-door neighbor Syria, considering itself the inheritor of historic claims, became the principal mediator among the factions. In late May 1976, it overtly joined the fray with its own military forces, triggering intense Israeli concern and, in 1982, direct Israeli intervention.

The underlying causes of the crisis were manifold: the subtle equilibrium on which the stability of Lebanon had been based for over half a century had disintegrated because the population balance between Christians and Muslims had changed since a 1943 arrangement which allocated power between the Christian and Muslim communities. This was compounded when the PLO, after its expulsion from Jordan in 1970, began using Lebanon as its principal base, drawing Lebanon into the Arab-Israeli conflict. And each of the factions was able to enlist some outside power on its behalf. All this turned Lebanon into a miniature model of all the Middle East conflicts rather than, as it had been historically, a symbol of their resolution.

On Mount Lebanon, along the rugged coast where the ancient Phoenicians had plied their trade, the remnants of the crusaders and other Christians attracted to the Holy Land had established a kind of autonomy under Turkish rule. Over the centuries, the Maronites, an offshoot of the Catholic religion, were joined by other groups—some Greek Orthodox, some fringe groups of the Muslim world such as the Druzes, and the Shiites. This autonomous Lebanese emirate, in which a Christian majority shared political power with minority Muslim communities, was an anomaly in the Ottoman empire.

In a revolution in 1860, a Muslim victory was prevented only by a French expeditionary force which saved the Maronite Christians and preserved an autonomous province of Lebanon with reduced borders but a clear Christian majority. Nevertheless, many in the Maronite leadership continued to advocate the restoration of the original emirate, which had been about twice the size of the post-revolutionary one (see map). The Maronites achieved their aim in 1920. When France acquired a League of Nations Mandate, it added the largely Muslim cities of Tripoli, Sidon, Baalbek, and Tyre from Syria. In order to expand their role, the Maronites had laid the seeds for a growing threat to their identity. The French colonial power went along because it believed that a more even ethnic balance would discourage any Christian quest for independence and establish France as the permanent protector of Maronites. The French decision also stimulated a permanent irredentism in Syria to regain, if not the territories lost, at least a permanent influence over them and to prevent the creation of a Christian state which might turn into a beachhead for future Western colonialism. In short, the existence of Lebanon in the 1970s had been mortgaged by decisions taken in completely different circumstances fifty years earlier when few had expected the swift rise of Arab nationalism.

The internal arrangements of Lebanon were tolerant and wise. Despite the growth of the Muslim population, the National Pact of 1943 established a division of power which retained Christian dominance while giving the Muslims a significant role. The presidency, the most powerful office, was held by a Christian; the Prime Minister, appointed by the President, was a Sunni Muslim; the speaker of parliament was a Shiite Muslim. Offices of state were apportioned in favor of the Christians in a ratio of 6 to 5. The small army of fourteen thousand men was, in the main, officered by Christians.

This arrangement could not withstand the impact of a Muslim population growing much faster than the Christian, and the emergence of the PLO after its ejection from Jordan in 1970. The writ of the central government did not run in the PLO camps; indeed, Lebanese security forces or police were not permitted to enter them. The militia of the various factions (without counting the PLO), which were estimated to number at least forty thousand, were stronger by far than the armed forces of the central government.

Fighting broke out in April 1975 while the United States was preoccupied with the fall of Saigon and the stalemated Israeli-Egyptian diplomacy. Initially between radical Palestinians and the Christian militia (called the Phalange), the battle was soon joined by multitudes of groups and leaders on both sides. In addition to the PLO and other even more radical Palestinian groups eager to establish Lebanon as a guerrilla base against Israel, there was the Druze leftist leader Kamal Jumblatt, determined to establish a purely Muslim state; moderate Muslims desirous of changing the balance of power with the Christians; and Maronites split into three groups: one favoring the partition of Lebanon into Christian and Muslim states, another wanting to retain Christian predominance in a united Lebanon, and, finally, moderates willing to face the fact that the Muslim population now outnumbered the Christian and prepared to adjust internal arrangements to reflect this reality.

Each of these groups had outside sponsors. The radical Muslims looked to Libya, Iraq, and Algeria for assistance. The PLO could count for financial support on Saudi Arabia and for political support on Egypt—both of which used the PLO to demonstrate at low risk their loyalty to the Arab cause. Sadat in particular, for reasons of the internal Arab equilibrium, opposed the increase of Syrian prestige and influence that would occur if its President, Hafez al-Asad, emerged as the dominant factor in Lebanon. Between these forces, the Lebanese moderates were ground down.

The Maronite Christians had no ideological or political backing in the Muslim world. They were supported more rhetorically than effectively by France; the United States opposed assaults on their autonomy diplomatically, though, in the year of the collapse of Vietnam and the abdication in Angola, direct military support was out of the question. Two unlikely tacit partners emerged which were prepared to help the Christians: Israel and, at various stages, Syria.

Israel opposed the emergence of a radical Islamic country at its northern border—especially if the PLO should gain the decisive influence. But neither did Syria favor such an outcome. However counter this attitude ran to general preconception, Asad did not relish finding himself squeezed between a radical Lebanon and a militant Iraq, jointly defining the Arab cause in the northern crescent. And he saw in Arafat and the PLO an obstacle to the creation of the "Greater Syria" embracing Lebanon, Jordan, and Palestine, which, even if he could not achieve it in his lifetime, he hoped to leave as a mission to his successors. Finally, Asad, while willing to pre-serve the territorial integrity of Lebanon, did not desire a strong and centralized government in Beirut—not even an initially pro-Syrian one —lest over time it seek to reduce Syrian influence. To achieve all these aims, Asad was prepared to bolster the Maronite community and its institutions against the Muslim majority. In this manner, he found himself in an unlikely, uneasy, and spasmodic cooperation with the Israelis.

It was our challenge to navigate these complexities. We did not want the PLO to dominate Lebanon, open another front against Israel, and either disrupt the peace process or force itself prematurely into it. We had a traditional policy of supporting the Christian community; opposed Syrian hegemony in Lebanon; saw a role for Syria in balanc-ing the radical Muslim groups so long as this did not cause Israel to preempt and start a Middle East war. We admired Sadat, but Egypt's support of the PLO in Lebanon ran counter to our priorities in Leba-non. Above all, in this whirlpool of suspicion and hatreds, we sought to preserve the Arab-Israeli peace process. We opposed foreign inter-vention while seeking to balance the various forces so that none would gain a decisive advantage. In a press conference of January 14, 1976, I stated:

> We support the independence and sovereignty of Leb-anon. . . . Any outside military intervention, from whatever quarter, would involve the gravest threat to peace and stabil-ity in the Middle East; and we have left the parties concerned in no doubt that the United States would oppose any mili-tary intervention from whatever quarter.[2]

In this atmosphere, some Maronite groups were discussing parti-tion into separate Muslim and Christian states. On November 16, 1975, Syrian foreign minister Abd al-Halim Khaddam warned that Syria would view partition of Lebanon as a "most serious plot"— implying the threat of opposing it by force.[3] Twelve days later, Saudi Crown Prince Fahd warned that partition would have "the most seri-ous consequences" on Lebanese-Saudi relations.[4] No sooner did one Arab party proclaim its views than all the others felt obliged to issue countervailing statements, compounding the general din. As fighting raged in Beirut and its suburbs, the French government on November

19 sent former Premier Maurice Couve de Murville to Lebanon on a fact-finding mission.[5]

Late in December, Saudi King Khalid announced his support for Syrian mediation efforts. Rabin replied that Israel would not tolerate outside intervention in Lebanon.[6] Cairo countered on January 12 to the effect that Egypt would "not stand by handcuffed" if Israel moved into Lebanon.[7] And Arab League Secretary General Mahmoud Riad called for an Arab summit conference on the Lebanese crisis.[8] On January 20, 1976, at a press conference, I reiterated my previous warning against outside intervention:

> The United States has warned all the interested parties—
> and I want to repeat it here—against any unilateral act that
> could lead to an expansion of the conflict in Lebanon to
> wider areas, and the United States will oppose any unilateral
> act by any country that would lead to an expansion of
> hostilities. . . . The international community has an obliga-
> tion to end the killing that is going on . . . and to use its
> mediating efforts to permit both communities to coexist in
> peace as they have for so many decades and to put an end to
> the civil strife that now goes on.[9]

There were grounds for concern about Syrian intentions. Units of the Palestine Liberation Army (PLA)—formally an armed component of the PLO but, in practice, a Palestinian branch of the Syrian army—began infiltrating into Lebanon, causing Rabin to warn Ford on the occasion of an Oval Office meeting on January 28 that, if organized units of the Syrian army followed, Israeli forces would move into Lebanon up to the Litani River (some twenty miles north of the border).

I instructed Ambassador Richard Murphy in Damascus to convey our hope to Brigadier General Hikmat al-Shihabi, the Syrian army chief of staff, that the Syrians "will do whatever they can to secure a cease-fire and to lay the groundwork for a compromise political settlement." I noted that the flow of reinforcements to the Palestinian guerrillas was increasing and "some of these reinforcements may be in the form of Syrian-backed PLA units," which the Israelis would surely oppose. To demonstrate evenhandedness, I added that Shihabi should understand that, in voicing our opposition to outside intervention from any quarter, "we have been addressing the Israelis as well as the Syrians."

As it turned out, the warning had been overtaken by events. For on January 22, Syrian mediation brought about a cease-fire and a proposal for political reform which was finally elaborated during a visit by President Frangieh to Damascus and announced by him on February 14. As had all previous "settlements," it reduced but did not totally eliminate Christian supremacy. The President remained Christian, but his power vis-à-vis the Sunni Prime Minister was reduced, and the number of Christian and Muslim deputies in parliament was equalized. (We called this the "Syrian solution" in our later internal discussions.)

The first phase of the Lebanese crisis was over. The tacit cooperation of Israel, Syria, and the United States had induced the Lebanese parties to redefine a new equilibrium. But it was precarious. For the outcome was vulnerable to the actions of any one of the multitude of factions contesting for preeminence. And we had experienced in Cyprus two years earlier that a balance of power produces stability only if the various parties desire peace or if they are too exhausted to continue their struggles. Neither condition as yet obtained in Lebanon.

In these circumstances, returning to the tasks of the Arab-Israeli peace process was almost a relief.

## Back to the Peace Process

The civil war in Lebanon added a new dimension to Arab-Israeli diplomacy. Its potential for transforming itself into a general Middle East war made progress toward an overall settlement more urgent. But it also produced an odd reversal of fronts. Sadat was indispensable for our overall strategy but, in Lebanon, Egyptian support for the PLO strengthened the radicals. Asad was the most difficult interlocutor for the general negotiations but, in Lebanon, his distrust of a radical outcome coincided with our interests. We would have to conduct an active Arab-Israeli diplomacy even though we had agreed with Rabin and Sadat that we would not bring it to fruition immediately, and we had to do so while contending with the passions and intricacies of Lebanon.

The trouble was that the parties resisted passivity, but they also recoiled before the prospects opened up by any available diplomatic option. Israel was not prepared to return to the 1967 borders or to negotiate with the PLO—the two basic Arab demands. But Rabin knew that Israel required some diplomatic cover to prevent the coalescence of all hostile pressures. Sadat, under attack especially from Syria for having made two separate agreements with Israel, was seeking to demonstrate that other Arabs might benefit from the same kind of diplomacy—all the while keeping open the options of proceeding alone.

Asad was maneuvering between finding a way to participate in an interim agreement of his own or, failing that, to block another separate initiative by anyone else—all the while manipulating events in Lebanon. King Hussein of Jordan was warily watching the maneuvers of the Palestinians and the acrobatics of Sadat. Since over half of Jordan's population was Palestinian, he was afraid that establishing the PLO on the West Bank might threaten Hashemite rule. But he was prevented by the October 1974 Rabat Arab summit from pursuing a diplomacy of his own. The divided Arab leaders—suspicious of each other, and yet all proclaiming Arab unity—were demanding some proof that the peace process was not frozen.

We therefore decided to use 1976 to prepare a strategy to be implemented after the presidential election. To prevent a hiatus from increasing tensions, we were obliged to deal with all parties simultaneously. An actual negotiation on one front alone might be brought off by momentum and legitimized by success. But if no negotiation could take place for at least a year, all the parties with nothing to gain would have an incentive to gang up on the leader most likely to proceed on his own, which was Sadat.

We had learned in 1975 that the very emotions that made a peace process so important militated against "exploratory" talks. Concessions difficult enough to sell to passionate publics on behalf of an actual deal became nearly unmanageable when part of a hypothetical agreement more than a year away. This was a particular problem in democratic Israel. But while Arab negotiators did not face quite the same restive constituencies, they generally had domestic rivals who might use abstract concessions—or even the delay in reaching an agreement—against them. They were also so suspicious of their fellow Arab rulers that they were reluctant to share their long-term views with them—or even to elaborate long-term views in the first place.

Sadat's policy held the most promise, but it was most effective when he was in a position to undertake sudden dramatic moves. The Egyptian President therefore tried to traverse the hiatus of 1976 behind a screen of voluble assertiveness. Aware that another separate step might isolate him and cut off the subventions he was receiving from the oil-producing Arab states, Sadat championed the Arab cause by urging American overtures toward the PLO. Some of our "Arabists" took this at face value; my assessment was different. In my view, Sadat wanted few things less than a Palestinian negotiation before Egypt had recovered its national territories. To introduce the PLO into the negotiations would guarantee a prolonged deadlock, for it would raise such life-or-death issues for Israel that all other initiatives would have to be deferred. I stated my assessment in a meeting with America's ambassadors to the Arab countries in Paris on June 22:

> [H]e is using Arafat now to end his own isolation. He's enjoying himself now. A year from now, when we're in the middle of the peace process . . . and the PLO starts scream- ing, "what about the Palestinians," Sadat will close all the PLO offices and kick them out.

When Sadat urged progress on all fronts, I invariably viewed it as a cover for an eventual separate Egyptian diplomacy and as a device to justify what he had already done on his own. I summed up the challenge faced by Sadat in a memorandum to Ford in late January 1976:

> Sadat has had to prove his basic loyalty to the Arab cause while remaining faithful to the commitments he had made to Israel in Sinai II. The touchstone of loyalty to the Arab cause has become support for the Palestinians, and Sadat has done what he could to establish his credentials in this respect and not leave the field entirely to Syria. Here again he faced a dilemma of sorts, however, since to promote the cause of the PLO as Asad was doing tended to deadlock the negotiations and, for Sadat, the only really satisfactory way out of his isolation was to have the negotiations proceed and draw in the other Arab parties.

Asad's strategy was similarly complex; though, since he had little to gain, he was above all concerned with blocking Sadat. During the negotiation of the interim agreement and in its immediate aftermath, Asad had been willing to explore a similar arrangement for Syria on the Golan Heights. Yet an interim arrangement with Syria was much more difficult because the entire territory in question was at most fifty kilometers deep. A partial Israeli withdrawal combined the dual disadvantage of being less dramatic in the public eye than Egypt's advance in the large Sinai, yet strategically more threatening to Israel because of its proximity to Israeli population centers. Moreover, Asad could read in every Israeli newspaper that the Israeli cabinet rejected any interim agreement for the Golan and that it would, under no circumstances, give up all of the Golan Heights even for a final peace.

Thus Asad increasingly cast himself in the role of spokesman for the overall Arab cause. He summarized his objection to Sadat's policy in a letter of October 30, 1975, to French President Giscard d'Estaing. Sadat's approach, Asad argued, transformed what was a general Arab-Israeli conflict into a dispute between individual Arab nations and Israel, contravening resolutions of a series of Arab summits. The provision in the Sinai II accord that it would remain valid "until superseded by another agreement" deprived even Egypt—not to mention the other Arab states—of leverage to regain the remaining territories occupied by Israel in 1967. The massive supply of arms by the United States to induce Israel to make the agreement "contradicted" the American-sponsored peace process. All of this had placed Egypt more firmly in the American camp than Asad deemed wise:

> We have thought, and we will always think, that it is neces-
> sary to deal with the two great powers without falling in the
> political wake of one of them. Strong by this conception, we
> have made serious efforts to prevent the polarization on the
> part of the two great powers in the region, whereas the Sinai
> Accord contradicts these efforts.

Nevertheless, Asad did not preclude an interim step, though not an isolated Syrian one. He proposed that the U.N. Security Council seize the issue and, within that framework, Syria would consider an interim agreement so long as it also included the Palestinians. This we opposed for the same reason that we evaded a convening of the Geneva Conference: it was a forum stacked against us.

The tension between Egypt and Syria enhanced the role of the PLO both in the peace process and in Lebanon. But since no direct Israeli negotiation with the PLO was possible, a potential role for King Hussein as a spokesman for the Palestinians was emerging. Bruised by his experience during the 1974 negotiations, Hussein was cautious. He indicated that, in principle, he would be willing to bypass the Rabat

Arab summit decision if Israel would make a "worthwhile" territorial offer, which he defined as a straight line some eight to ten kilometers beyond the Jordan River. In that case, Hussein would seek Syrian, Saudi, and Egyptian authorization to assume the role of negotiator. As with almost every initial proposal in the Middle East peace process, there was less to this offer than met the eye, since a straight-line withdrawal from the river had always been rejected by Israel, whose only concept for a solution on the West Bank was the so-called Allon Plan described in Chapter 11.

Of all the parties, Israel was faced with the most difficult psychological challenge. For two years—since the Arab surprise attack of October 1973—it had had no respite from wrenching decisions: first the war and now seemingly endless negotiations, each of which implied the giving up of some of Israel's tangible security for the intangibles of a peace process. Each separate negotiation always seemed to leave some Arab party unsatisfied and hence capable of starting the confrontation all over again. Finally, though the step-by-step approach shielded Israel from having to face the most difficult decisions all at once, it also offered no dramatic conclusion. Rabin had a point when he said to Ford: "This is what worries some in Israel. Rather than exhausting the Arabs, America will be exhausted."

## Sadat and Rabin Visit Washington

Sadat was the first Egyptian head of state to visit the United States. My briefing memorandum for the trip, which lasted from October 26 to November 5, 1975, reminded Ford:

> [This visit] dramatizes the extraordinary change which has taken place over the past two years. . . . We have a tactical interest in reinforcing Sadat's conviction that the United States is the only world power able to bring about a resolution of the Middle East conflict on terms satisfactory to Egypt and the Arabs.

As for the longer term:

> [The United States] has a strategic interest in seeing Egypt's current course in the world and in the Middle East main-

tained [and to] begin to develop a relationship with Egypt
that will endure beyond Sadat. . . . In order to maintain the
viability of our Salzburg strategy, and keep the USSR and
Arab radicals from making a resurgence at our and Sadat's
expense, we need to develop together with Sadat some specific ideas for further progress which will add something—
even if very limited—for Syria and indicate some flexibility
in our attitude toward the Palestinians.

We did not start in a vacuum. At the end of the shuttle leading to
the interim agreement in September, I had met with Sadat and Egyptian defense minister Mohammed Abdel Ghany el-Gamasy in Aswan
to discuss next steps. We had, I had argued, the same two choices as all
along: to reassemble a comprehensive forum at Geneva, or to develop
another interim step. Geneva guaranteed deadlock. The Soviet Union
and Syria would insist on the full participation of the PLO, which
Israel would refuse to accept. Once the conference was assembled after
months of controversy, the next issue would be united Arab and Soviet
pressure for the 1967 borders. While this outcome was barely conceivable on the Egyptian front, there was no possibility of Israel accepting
these borders on the Golan Heights or on the West Bank.

It was therefore preferable to avoid debates over procedure and
turn straight to substance. But for an interim agreement to work, the
step must be truly significant. To avoid the charge that the purpose
was to divide the Arabs, it would be necessary to offer the same
concept on all fronts. What was needed was a withdrawal by Israel
sufficiently substantial to justify an end to the state of war (or belligerency). If everyone received the same basic proposal, the further evolution of the peace process was then up to each party. In other words,
once the concept existed, each party would be free to consult its own
interests in elaborating it.

Sadat had been pensive but did not reject the general approach. He
would let me have his answer when he visited Washington in two
months. But in the complex minuet of the Middle East, nonrejection
of another partial move came close to acceptance.

In Washington, Sadat's conversations with American policymakers
were divided into two parts. He discussed the basic concept with Ford
and the elaborations of the Aswan conversations with me.

The Egyptian President made it easy for Ford. Having geared his
policy—and, in many ways, the Arab cause—to gaining the confi-

dence of the United States, he wisely chose neither to threaten nor to blackmail us. Instead, in his first meeting with the President in the Oval Office on October 27, Sadat thanked Ford profusely for the efforts he had made to bring about the Sinai II agreement and thereby established a claim for future support:

> Without these efforts, we could not have achieved this Sinai agreement. I must congratulate you. For the first time, the Israelis hear logic and firmness. It is for the benefit of the Israelis as well as of my Arab colleagues—even if neither of them understand it now.

Sadat had chosen exactly the right method to enlist the President from Grand Rapids. Ford was always much more amenable to demonstrations of good faith than to pressure and more responsive to arguments on behalf of the general interest than to assertions of self-will. In his reply, Ford therefore pledged his support to a peace process which Sadat and I were to discuss, leaving open only the question of timing:

> You must work with us on the timing. But I can assure you I will be as firm in the future as I have been in the past. There is no sense in taking a number of little steps when we can take a big step.

Sadat reiterated that he was not pressing: we have "a long road ahead of us. . . . For this visit, I have nothing special." In this manner, he achieved his objective of inducing Ford to offer a major American role in the next phase of Middle Eastern strategy. Ford promised Sadat:

> I want to fill the void. The question is how quickly we can do it. But we will do so. The next question is how we can work together on a common strategy for the Middle East.

For the rest, Sadat spoke as an ally, not as a supplicant. He made his usual appeal for the United States to open talks with the PLO, though he urged it less for its contribution to the peace process than as a means to reduce Soviet influence among the Arabs. Unlike his Arab brethren, Sadat did not take seriously the danger that Syria, unless satisfied, might initiate another Middle Eastern war:

I do not think that Syria will go to war. They are doing this
mostly for domestic reasons to show how tough they are.
Maybe Lebanon is the cause.

Even then, in October 1975, Sadat was already concerned about the
impact of Lebanon on the general prospects for peace:

> Please make sure, Mr. President, that the Israelis do not
> intervene. Nobody in the Arab world will believe that there
> is no coordination [with the United States].

Next came Sadat's attack on King Hussein, a Sadat trademark in
the way that film director Alfred Hitchcock made fleeting appearances
in all his movies. He described the King as "a nice man" advised by an
"unreliable Prime Minister" (Zaid Rifai) and embarked on a "suicidal
course" of confrontation with both the PLO and Syria, from which
the United States should dissuade him. When all was said and done,
this meant that Sadat was urging talks with the PLO, with which Israel
would not negotiate, and rejecting a role for Jordan, with which Israel
might be prepared to talk. It was a clear prescription for stalemate on
the Palestinian front and a basis for yet another separate Egyptian
move as the peace process unfolded.

As Ford had suggested, Sadat and I held several meetings in Washington and a final one in Jacksonville, Florida, to develop a common
strategy for 1976 and 1977. My associates (Hal Saunders, Roy Atherton, and Peter Rodman) and I had elaborated on the approach which I
had outlined to Sadat in Aswan. Since distances meant little in the
trackless expanse of the Sinai desert, the negotiator's mind inevitably
turns to some landmark around which to anchor any negotiation that
might develop. We therefore proposed for study a line south from
beyond the Mediterranean coastal town of El-Arish, about thirty-
five kilometers from the Israeli frontier. This would require an Israeli
withdrawal of one hundred kilometers and returning four fifths of the
Sinai to Egypt in exchange for Egypt's ending the state of belligerency
with Israel.

Sadat demonstrated that he had given considerable thought to our
ideas. He asked whether the State Department had ever examined the
difference between ending the state of belligerency and achieving final
peace. I had no idea but promised to give such a study to Foreign
Minister Ismail Fahmy if it existed. Sadat then asked Fahmy to form a

working group to examine the idea. And then suddenly, as was his custom, came a near-breakthrough. Sadat said he would be able to "consider" the concept of land for peace only for an Israeli withdrawal to a line no more than twenty-five kilometers from the Israeli border. (This was asking for ten kilometers more than I had suggested—which was within negotiating range.)

We had gone as far as we could. I told Sadat that we would explore the subject with Rabin and also with Asad and Hussein and report back to him afterward.

The rest of Sadat's American visit went far toward achieving his goal of presenting a humane and conciliatory Arab face to the American public. In New York, there were protests by various groups on the ground that Sadat had as yet not demonstrated adequate dedication to the cause of peace. But Sadat was treated to warm civic receptions in Chicago and Houston and gave urbane interviews to a series of, on the whole, friendly commentators.

There is bound to be some mix-up in the course of any long-planned trip. Ford was so carried away at the return dinner offered by Sadat that he ended up toasting the great people of Israel, who were, of course, much more frequent guests at White House dinners than the Egyptians, who were on their first state visit. The President corrected the slip immediately, and it would have gone unnoticed had not his press secretary, Ron Nessen, decided he would create a credibility gap if he edited the stenographic transcript. Even this pedantic punctiliousness, however, did no noticeable damage.*

By now Middle East diplomacy had taken on an almost operatic character, the gratification from which results less from the discovery of the new than from refinement of familiar nuances. Sadat played the role of the grand seigneur while Rabin—who visited the United States from January 26 to February 5—was cast as a wary small landholder struggling for survival. These attitudes reflected not so much differing personalities as the different situations in which the countries found themselves. When you rule a country that extends from the Mediterranean to the heart of Africa, as Sadat did, you possess the geography for grand gestures. When the national territory can be traversed by car in one hour, the scope for dramatic initiatives is minimal. A concession by Sadat meant that he would receive something less than he had

---

* The only discordant note was an internal American matter, the so-called Halloween Massacre which occurred on the next to last day of Sadat's stay in the United States (see Chapter 27).

sought; for Rabin, even the most generous deal implied a loss of territory and a complicated calculus between security and legitimacy. These calculations were made even more difficult by a narrow parliamentary majority, a divided cabinet, and the still essentially abstract and theoretical nature of the "hiatus" diplomacy.

Rabin had learned a great deal from his experiences the previous year. He had come to understand that Washington found it difficult to distinguish between what he put forward as a personal opinion and what his cabinet would support. This time around, Rabin made sure before each of his three meetings in the Oval Office to review with me what he was going to say to the President and to explain how it would be interpreted in the struggles of all against all which constitute Israeli cabinet politics—especially during Rabin's first term. Because of my affection for Rabin, my confidence in his intentions, and because I was as anxious as he to avoid the misunderstandings of the previous year, I would after each meeting sum up for him—again one on one—how Ford and I would interpret what had been discussed or agreed.

At their first meeting in the Oval Office on January 28, 1976, Ford stressed that stalling was not an option:

> Whatever we decide, our approach must be a positive one and must reflect movement in some form. You, Mr. Prime Minister, and the Secretary should devise a strategy for 1976 and 1977 aimed at this objective. This may require tough decisions by both of our countries—decisions that may have difficult repercussions both domestically and with regard to other relationships—for example, with the Soviet Union. We must convince the world that our strategy involves, and is designed, to promote forward movement. We must keep the momentum going. In this process, Israel and the United States must stay together.

I briefed Rabin on Sadat's apparent willingness to consider an end to belligerency if Israel withdrew to around twenty-five kilometers from its border. Ever the strategist, Rabin immediately translated this into a line south from the vicinity of El-Arish.

When the discussion turned to West Bank issues, I summed up for Ford, in Rabin's presence, the status of our discussions:

> I have always felt that we must have some program permitting us to dominate the debate and the negotiations, and this

would include agreement on possible gains in advance of Geneva so that the other side would have some reason for attending the conference without the PLO. My impression from our discussions at breakfast was that the Prime Minister thought this concept was worth exploring. He feels that it would work well with Egypt and Syria; concerning the latter, the removal of some settlements in exchange for non-belligerency would be conceivable. Regarding Jordan, however, the approach would give rise to serious domestic problems in Israel. This question therefore remains unresolved, but we agreed that, during the Prime Minister's stay in the United States, we would meet again in order to pursue the issue further.

In other words, Rabin agreed that an offer of substantial withdrawals on all fronts (short of the 1967 border) in return for an agreement to end the state of war with Israel would represent the best strategy for 1976 and 1977. Every Arab country could justify its decision by a significant territorial gain and, if the comprehensive offer failed, Sadat would have the justification for proceeding on his own. Rabin reserved his position on negotiating with Jordan.

Rabin and I met again in Los Angeles on February 3 to review the strategy after a "Salute to Israel" dinner at the Beverly Hills Hotel during which leading representatives of the film industry proclaimed their support for Israel. During the entertainment, Rabin was invited by Diana Ross to lead a sing-along—a prospect that filled the taciturn Prime Minister with more open discomfort than I had ever seen him display, even on West Bank issues. When we finally reached an upstairs room to review the common strategy, he informed me that he would recommend a negotiation with Jordan to his cabinet. Anything to avoid another sing-along.

On February 25, Ambassador Simcha Dinitz informed me that Rabin had achieved cabinet approval for a major withdrawal in return for nonbelligerency, including Jordan. The cabinet defined the line for Egypt as going from El-Arish to Ras Mohammed, which would have left a third of the Sinai in Israeli hands. Sadat would probably reject this definition but, at this stage, agreement to the concept was more significant than the application of it. Opening Israeli proposals are never modest and yet, after harrowing negotiations, usually subject to adaptation.

By early March, we felt confident enough to convey Israel's reaction to Sadat and to ask his permission to transmit our formal proposal to Asad and Hussein. The instructions to our ambassador in Cairo, Hermann Eilts, gave us an opportunity to sum up the advantages of the strategy and to place the alternatives before Sadat:

> If President Sadat considers it a useful approach, we would want to have his judgment about how to proceed. How should the effort be organized, and how should the other Arab governments be involved in it? We will await Sadat's response before making a further move.
>
> If President Sadat does not agree, there is no point in our developing the proposal further with the Israelis. Instead, we would have to look for some procedural route to reconvene Geneva, with all the difficulties that lie in this direction.

On March 11, Eilts put our new formal proposal to Sadat, who deferred a formal reply until he could consult his advisers. As I had expected, Sadat pointed out the shortcoming of the El-Arish to Ras Mohammed line, but he did not use it to reject the concept. He also described the absence of a role for the PLO as a "serious problem," which, in diplomatese, meant that excluding Arafat was not an insuperable obstacle. When all was said and done, despite his reservations, Sadat—according to Eilts—"repeatedly stressed that his position has always been to look seriously at any opportunity to get back 'any inch' of territory and that he has frequently urged Arafat and his Arab colleagues to do the same." He thought U.S. efforts to get Israel to even talk about the West Bank were terrific—"bravo." He thought it might be useful to try out the concept (but not the Sinai details) on Asad, and "if Asad reacted positively, then one could explore broader modalities."

On March 18, Fahmy repeated Sadat's critique but, in the end (in Eilts's words), "ultimately agreed to our broaching the concept to the Syrians and the Jordanians, provided we do not—repeat not—speak about the Egyptian front," which we interpreted to mean that Sadat did not want to be second-guessed about a deal he was obviously contemplating.

The road was thus clear to put forward our general concept to Asad and Hussein. We did just that but, before our explorations could get very far, the attention of the parties was diverted to Lebanon. For at that precise moment, the simmering Lebanese volcano erupted.

## Syrian Intervention in Lebanon

On March 8, dissident Muslim soldiers of the Lebanese army deserted and joined a so-called Lebanese Arab Army. On March 11, the Sunni commander of the Beirut area proclaimed himself governor of Lebanon and demanded the immediate resignation of the President of Lebanon, Suleiman Frangieh. Heavy fighting immediately broke out, mostly between Muslims and Christians but also between the various Muslim factions. The general confusion was demonstrated when units of the combined rebellious Muslim forces, advancing on the palace of the Christian President, were stopped by Palestinian guerrillas of the PLA (which—as noted—while technically belonging to the PLO, was in fact an auxiliary of the Syrian army).

When the PLA proved inadequate, Syria began to consider overt intervention—a prospect which had concerned us since the beginning of the crisis. On March 14, Syrian army chief Shihabi told our ambassador, Richard Murphy, that he despaired of solving the Lebanese situation short of introducing regular Syrian forces; he talked about having the Syrian army "enter and take up positions to ensure [that] Lebanon's border remained calm." Murphy warned that the Israelis would never accept this. "Perhaps not," Shihabi replied. "[The] Israelis might understand 'with or without a formal agreement'; it was simply a peacekeeping force"—in other words, it would not be of a nature to represent a strategic threat to Israel. When Murphy asked for an elaboration of the sensitive issue of introducing Syrian regulars, Shihabi turned evasive. "He was not 'proposing' this," reported Murphy, "nor was he suggesting that I report his thinking to Washington, but as one surveyed the Lebanese scene, what alternative was there?"

It was a strange conversation. Shihabi had to know that his views would be reported to Washington; why else would he seek out Murphy? Was Shihabi—whom we considered a relative moderate—informing us, or was he asking our opinion? Was he hinting at working out an agreement on spheres of interest with Israel in Lebanon via American mediation? Since it was impossible that Shihabi was acting on his own, the likelihood was that Asad was testing our reactions via his trusted associate. The conversation certainly demonstrated our central role in the area. We alone were in touch with all the parties.

Shihabi's overture placed us in a delicate situation. As I told a staff meeting on March 28, our preferred outcome was the "Syrian solution" of January 22 achieved without the presence of Syrian troops. This agreement had preserved a balance between the religious groups, slightly weighted toward the Christians, as well as the traditional political and social framework of Lebanon. We supported it because it had the best prospect of removing Lebanon as a potential flashpoint of a general Middle East conflagration. Syria promoted it because it averted partition of Lebanon between Christians and Muslims, which had three drawbacks for Asad: it would create another state in the area which would be obliged to rely on the West; it would set a precedent for other ethnic or religious groups to split off from existing states; and the Muslim part would in all likelihood be dominated by factions tied to radical Arab states. As for us, we were uneasy about partition because it would unite the Arab world against us and could not be sustained without massive military intervention.

The anomaly was that the January 22 compromise was inherently shaky unless buttressed by outside military forces, which, if they were Syrian, would raise the specter of Syrian hegemony and involve the risk of Israeli intervention. And, if they were an Arab force as Egypt proposed, it would tilt toward the PLO, and Syria (and probably Israel) would surely resist. I briefed congressional leaders on April 7:

> In this crisis, we are facing a strange reversal of roles, with Syria supporting the Christians and fighting the PLO. Syrians are also supporting the moderate wing of the PLO, while cutting supplies to Jumblatt leftists and protecting the Christian areas. The Egyptians, on the other hand, are supporting the radicals because of their hatred for the Syrians. The United States would prefer the same political outcome as the Syrians do, and so do the Israelis. But the United States and Israel do not want Syrian military intervention. The paradox is that, without Syrian intervention, the PLO may, in fact, win. Our policy is designed to prevent a Syrian intervention, but to support their political mediation efforts along the lines of the January 22 settlement.

There was no possibility of involving American forces, though, in early April, Senator Henry Jackson blamed us for not sending in the Marines, as President Eisenhower had done in 1958. Less than a year after our withdrawal from Saigon and three months after Congress voted us out of Angola, the American public would not stand for the massive and continuing effort required. Except for Jackson's single sally, the idea received short shrift both in the primaries and in the election campaign. Nor did any member of the NSC advocate it. For it was hard to conceive of a meaningful military mission. Had we inserted ourselves between the warring parties, significant casualties would have been unavoidable. I told a WSAG meeting on April 22:

> If U.S. troops move in as a buffer to separate opposing forces,
> it could well embroil us with the Syrians. The Syrians might
> then move massively into Lebanon. We might then be faced
> with protecting the PLO from the Syrians. Once we move in,
> there is no easy way to get out. . . . We must ask ourselves
> what national interests we have there which would lead us
> to put in our forces.

And our aims in Lebanon were far more complicated than simply separating the opposing forces. It was a lesson the Reagan Administration would learn the hard way in 1983–84 when it proved unwilling to pay the price for sustaining a much smaller force and for much more limited objectives in a much more benign American domestic environment.

On March 30, on my recommendation, Ford recalled Dean Brown, a distinguished Foreign Service officer, to serve as special emissary to Lebanon. Recently retired, Brown had served with great panache and skill as ambassador during the critical September 1970 days in Jordan when a PLO uprising and an invasion from Syria threatened the survival of the Hashemite dynasty.[10]

At a staff meeting on March 30, I gave Brown the following instructions:

> What we need precisely is, first, an exact assessment of the
> situation. Second, we want to be helpful to encourage a
> cease-fire. Third, we want to see an outcome something like
> the Syrian solution at the end of January. Fourth, we want
> to get in some contact with the PLO. . . . We've got to try to
> split off Jumblatt from the PLO. They've got to be made to
> understand that the PLO will be the principal victim of
> Israeli intervention. Fifth, we cannot break the back of the
> Christians. They must not collapse on us. Sixth, we've got
> to keep the Syrians out. Seven, the Syrians must get the

impression that we're working like hell to find a solution
along their lines. . . . I'm in favor of support for the Christians. You know I'm doing nothing to prevent the Israelis
helping the Christians. The stronger they are, the better.

The reference to the PLO requires some explanation. We had
agreed with Israel not to negotiate with the PLO unless the latter
accepted Israel's right to exist and forswore terrorism. But we considered Lebanon a special case. In pursuit of the strategy we had concerted with Israel, we wanted to isolate the radical Lebanese faction
under Jumblatt in order to prevent the emergence of another radical
state, possibly associated with Iraq and Libya and surely with the
Soviet Union, along Israel's northern border. We briefly toyed with the
idea of discussing Lebanon with the PLO. Brown was instructed to
obtain Washington's approval before undertaking any such dialogue.

At an NSC meeting on April 7, I told Ford:

> To get a solution, we may have to ask for your authorization
> to deal with the PLO, Mr. President. There would be no
> change in our position toward the PLO on the Middle East
> question, but we have no commitment to Israel not to talk
> to the PLO exclusively about the situation in Lebanon.

In the event, we never asked for the authority even when evacuating
Americans through the PLO-controlled areas of Beirut. For that occasion, Egypt acted as our intermediary to the PLO for political issues;
lower-level security personnel may have had contacts with PLO func-
tionaries to facilitate technical aspects of the evacuation. But there
were no substantive exchanges.

The relationship with the Christian community was equally complex. We clearly wanted to strengthen it. But overt arms shipments
would turn all the Muslim states of the region against us—it was one
of the few points on which Syria, Egypt, and Saudi Arabia were in
agreement. And without cooperative relations with these countries, the
overall peace process would collapse. Thus we encouraged Israel to
serve as arms supplier of the Christians even while Syria was acting—
at least temporarily—as their protector.

In this manner, the already intricate Middle East situation reached
a point of complexity that made it difficult to identify all the players,
much less the games they were playing at any particular moment.
Israel had some parallel interests with Syria in preventing predomi-

nance of the radicals—essentially Jumblatt and the PLO—and preserving the Maronites as a counterweight to them. But if either sought to further that interest by military means, the other was likely to seek to counter it. Neither Syria nor Israel was prepared for war—Syria because it was too weak, Israel because it had not yet recovered from the shock of the last war two years earlier. But they might drift into confrontation through misunderstanding. Egypt supported the radicals but primarily as a counterweight to Syria in overall Arab politics; it surely did not wish an increase in overall tensions. Saudi Arabia generally backed Syria short of encouraging the destruction of the PLO. The Soviet Union, observing its Arab policy in shambles as two of its clients—Syria and the PLO—were at each other's throats, navigated confusedly in the name of opposing foreign intervention, though, in the end, Moscow came down against Syria in support of the radicals. France wanted to preserve some of its historic role in Lebanon, but it was torn between its tradition of supporting the Maronites and the desire to play a continuing role in the Arab world.

Our asset in managing this maelstrom was that none of the parties could achieve its objectives without our support. Israel wanted us to restrain Syria; Syria was seeking our support in preventing an Israeli move into Lebanon. Egypt knew that we were the key to rapid progress when the peace process resumed. The Soviet Union was paralyzed by its perplexities. We emerged as the indispensable balance wheel of diplomacy in Lebanon because all the players had a stake in good relations with us.

This was not a one-time assignment with a foreseeable end in mind; it needed to be reinvented every day for the better part of a year —while we were simultaneously conducting the Latin American and Southern African diplomacy described in previous chapters. It was almost a caricature of classic balance-of-power diplomacy, and yet there was no alternative to it.

Our central role was symbolized by our first communication to Asad after Shihabi's overture to us on March 14. On March 15, I instructed Murphy to see Asad:

> [A]sk him what he is up to and, if we agree with him, we will
> do our best to help him. But warn him what he does must be
> done without the use of Syrian regular forces. In that event, we
> will guarantee that the Israelis do not interfere.

On the same day, I instructed Assistant Secretary Atherton to inform the Israeli ambassador that we had no confirmation of Syrian troop movements into Lebanon and warned against acting on the basis of fragmentary information: "We have to be informed in advance." I urged Dinitz to "tell him [Rabin] to move with great circumspection."

On March 18, Asad received Murphy and pointed out that Christian President Frangieh had asked for Syrian intervention and that "we would not be Arabs if we did not extend the helping hand to our brothers." Asad stressed that Syria's sole goal was to keep the peace and that it was urging all parties to "stop fighting, talk it out, and find a common political denominator. . . . Violence will not solve the problem." Syria would continue its mediation efforts based on the January agreement. Although Asad conveyed sensitivity to the security of Israel's northern border, he added, "I cannot guarantee anything" —meaning that he did not want to be accused of reassuring a country which he did not recognize even though this was exactly what he was doing. He hoped the United States would urge Israel to understand that "they have nothing to do with this internal Arab affair." After the meeting, Asad, in an uncharacteristically conciliatory mood, phoned Murphy to say he hoped the United States would communicate any new ideas it had to help solve the Lebanese problem.

In Washington that same day, Atherton reported to me that Arafat was negotiating with Egypt to back him and the rebellious Muslim forces against the Syrians and that Egypt was inclined to be responsive.

All this diplomatic maneuvering was punctuated by intense fighting among the Lebanese factions. Typical of the chaos, on March 19, a Syrian air force plane with Prime Minister Rashid Karami and other Lebanese leaders on board was set afire at Beirut airport shortly before it planned to depart for Damascus. Partisans of President Frangieh were shelling Druze positions in areas north of the Lebanese President's residence.[11] The American University of Beirut was forced to close on March 17;[12] Reuters and al-Nahar press offices were evacuated on March 21;[13] Phalangists and Muslims were battling around the Beirut Holiday Inn.[14] On March 22, Karami met with Frangieh, who refused to resign. The Lebanese cabinet thereupon assembled in emergency session to consider a proposed constitutional amendment to permit the immediate selection of a new President.[15] *

---

* As noted further on, the issue of a constitutional change to permit election of a new President was resolved in April. Elias Sarkis was ultimately elected President of Lebanon on May 8 (after much maneuvering by Frangieh). He was supported by Syria, but he could not take office until September 23.

Nervousness regarding Syria's intervention produced a classic case of war jitters. On March 25, Deputy Secretary of Defense William Clements telephoned to inform me that a Syrian armored division was on the move, in all likelihood toward Lebanon. Fifteen minutes later, he confirmed it. I informed both Dinitz and British Ambassador Peter Ramsbotham, who told me that British intelligence had not reported any such activity. A few hours later, I was obliged to call Ramsbotham back: "Our intelligence service does not know the difference between Damascus and Cairo. The armored brigade is from Cairo, not Damascus" (and obviously not heading toward Lebanon).

Rabin replied to my queries on March 23. In case of Syrian intervention, Israeli forces would occupy "as quietly as they can" strategic positions in southern Lebanon. The next day, an Israeli memorandum specified in some detail the types of weapons and forces the cabinet would consider unacceptable Syrian intervention. Specifically mentioned was the entrance of Syrian infantry forces above brigade size (including those forces already in Lebanon), which, of course, signified that a certain degree of Syrian infiltration was already being tolerated. This was reinforced when the memorandum specified the maximum extent of permissible Syrian intervention. Israel would not tolerate movement of Syrian forces beyond an area of ten kilometers south of the Damascus–Beirut axis. This was the famous "red line," which, in effect, defined the Israeli and Syrian accord on spheres of influence and which, however tacit, is still intact.

A careful minuet was taking place in which Israel and Syria, two countries technically still at war, were defining to each other their risks and commitments amidst the vacuum that had suddenly opened up in Lebanon. And because the arrangement reflected tacit understandings requiring an element of deniability, Dinitz and I read formal statements to one another quite out of keeping with the informal, almost bantering style of our usual encounters. Their purpose was to avoid the possibility that tacit understandings might be misunderstood or be interpreted as legal obligations and turn into domestic political issues. Each side used the occasion to restate its principal concerns. Rejecting Syrian intervention in principle while defining its modalities in practice, Dinitz said:

> I want to emphasize that all the information . . . is a reply
> to questions asked and should by no means imply any acqui-
> escence whatsoever by Israel to any Syrian penetration. In
> fact, our position for this [opposition to intervention in prin-

ciple] remains as clearly stated in the past and is repeated today.

My response reversed the procedure. Implying acquiescence in an Israeli reaction under some circumstances, I insisted on prior consultation even in case of Syrian intervention. Receiving the Israeli answers in no way constituted American "acquiescence in an Israeli move, nor does it mean there should not be a discussion with us before an Israeli move, if there is a Syrian move."

The exchange was so stylized because inhibitions and objectives were being balanced by the methods of traditional diplomacy, not by lawyers drafting formal commitments, as I explained to the NSC on April 7:

> We know that the Syrians are scared of the Israelis so the idea of a Syrian attack can be pretty much ruled out. We exaggerate Israel's eagerness to enter Lebanon, but Syria is not about to start a war if it can be avoided. Only if they have to go into Lebanon and Israel also goes in. We have also learned that the Soviets are not eager for a war. They are supporting the Lebanese Communist Party and other local elements, including the PLO, but overall they are a factor of restraint. The Lebanese Communist Party is most helpful, but the Soviets seem to be counseling the Syrians against moving. They want to have their cake and eat it, too. The Soviets are not looking for trouble, but they will be forced to move rather than lose all their assets in the Middle East, should another war come.

For the rest of the spring, the pattern thus established continued. Syrian forces edged forward, tolerated by Israel, in almost every case at the request of Christian leaders—either of the local or, more usually, of the central government, such as it was. Israel grumbled at each move but acquiesced so long as Syria did not establish a major military presence and stayed well clear of the red line.

A complex balance was emerging. Syria controlled the Bekaa Valley while the cities were no-man's-lands, divided among Jumblatt, the PLO, Christians, and Syrians, especially in Beirut where each area was sealed off from the other. In Lebanon, Syria faced the reverse of our situation in Vietnam. There we had controlled the cities, and it was the countryside which was contested. In Lebanon, Syria controlled much of the countryside while the civil war was fought out in the cities. Despite its superior forces, Syria was no more able to establish firm control over all of Lebanon than we had been able to do in Vietnam—though Syria proved more tenacious. Its freedom of action was further circumscribed when the Arab League sent a force composed of Sudanese, Saudi, and Libyan contingents to take over some of the police functions in Beirut. It was not a terrifying military deployment, but it symbolized the constraints on Syrian policy not only from Israel but also from its Arab brethren.

The political process went on fitfully but inexorably. On April 10, the Lebanese National Assembly adopted a constitutional amendment permitting an early change of the presidency. On May 8, Elias Sarkis, Syria's candidate, was chosen to be President. But because President Frangieh refused to resign, Sarkis did not take office until September 23.

After that, fighting gradually died down, though never below the level of an armed truce and frequently interrupted by flare-ups. Beirut remained divided into fortified enclaves.

One of the most painful events for the United States was the assassination of Ambassador Francis E. Meloy, Jr., along with his Economic Counselor, Robert O. Waring, on June 16. Having arrived in Beirut to replace Dean Brown only a few weeks earlier, Meloy was killed on the way to his first official appointment. I had asked Meloy to show the flag by calling on the recently elected Sarkis. Sarkis's office was located in the Christian part of Beirut, the embassy in the Muslim sector. In accordance with standard procedure, the follow-up security car left the ambassador at the checkpoint leaving the Muslim sector; the Christians would take over security at the other side. Meloy was abducted in the no-man's-land before entering the Christian area by a Palestinian terrorist splinter group. He was executed shortly afterward.

Meloy's death hit me hard. Not only had I sent him on the mission that cost him his life, I also felt personally responsible for assigning him to Lebanon in the first place. Meloy had come to my attention only a few months earlier when I visited Guatemala in February 1976 after a terrible earthquake. Then our ambassador, Meloy had shown the enormous courage to scrap on his own authority the entire program laid out for me by my staff because he thought it inappropriate to the situation. When, a few weeks later, Dean Brown's family demanded that he set a time limit for his mission in Lebanon (he had come out of retirement to serve), I immediately thought of Meloy. As I told the Lebanese ambassador, Ghassan Tueini, after the event:

> He [Meloy] was superb in Guatemala in tackling related problems. . . . He was a good man. I didn't like him until I saw him in Guatemala after a great earthquake there. It was a crisis. He disobeyed virtually every order I sent him. But he demonstrated that he was right, and I was wrong. . . . God knows, there are not many ambassadors that have been so impressive. I feel a deep sense of responsibility for having sent him to Lebanon.

Meloy's assassination triggered a crisis over those Americans remaining in Beirut. We offered to evacuate them, in the process launching a debate over the best means to accomplish this. The easiest way out of Lebanon was by air, but Syria warned us that the airport, surrounded by Palestinian refugee camps, was not secure; a single missile might kill a planeload of evacuees. The most efficient route was by sea, but the port area was controlled by the PLO, whose standing we preferred not to enhance. On the other hand, the overland route to Damascus was controlled by so many different militias that only a major U.S. military deployment could have guaranteed the Americans' safety. In the end, we chose sea evacuation in two installments.

By this time, the astonishing reversal of fronts was nearly complete. Syria, which had been the principal sponsor of PLO participation in the peace process, was either fighting the PLO on the ground in Lebanon or standing aside while Christian militias laid siege to PLO camps. In order to thwart Syria's emergence as a rival in the Arab world, Egypt, our closest Arab friend, was encouraging the radical forces in Lebanon that were bound to oppose Egypt as our joint Middle East diplomacy evolved. The Soviet Union, heretofore Syria's most reliable ally, turned on it over Syrian military and political pressure against the Palestinians. On July 20, the French newspaper *Le Monde* published a letter allegedly written by Brezhnev and distributed to Jumblatt and the PLO (it was, in fact, never denied by Moscow). In it, Brezhnev exhorted Asad to stop operations "against the resistance and the Lebanese national movement" and coupled his advice with a threat: "Our country's friendship toward you is assured and stable. Unless Syria behaves in such a way as to cause rifts in the relations between our countries." King Hussein confirmed these Soviet communications to Asad and added that the Soviets had threatened to cancel deliveries of spare parts for the Syrian armed forces.

That all was not well in Soviet-Syrian relations was apparent from a long speech of Asad's on July 20. He vowed that Syria would never bow to any ultimatum, praised Ambassador Brown's mission, and indicated that any outside endeavors to end the fighting would be welcome "even if they come from America." In the course of a three-hour discourse, Asad never mentioned the Soviet Union. And he left no doubt where he stood with respect to the Palestinians in Lebanon: Syria would "never bow to any demand by any Palestinian to withdraw from Lebanon"—only the Lebanese could request that (a safe enough offer since the Christian President had originally invited Syria in).

The degree to which the situation in Lebanon had changed the international landscape was reflected in my instructions to Murphy about the speech, which Murphy was to take up with Asad: "The message is that we support an independent foreign policy, and for this reason, we don't want to embarrass him." Murphy was asked to express "the hope that if he felt this [independent foreign policy] was threatened at any time, he would inform the United States so that we could examine together what steps could be taken to relieve the threat . . . we are prepared to be forthcoming."

To emphasize the seriousness with which we took Syrian views, I authorized Murphy to brief Asad about what we knew of Soviet shipments to the PLO: "Tell him what quantities are going directly and our estimate of what is going through Libya. And contacts. Don't mention Egypt." A diplomatic revolution had taken place when the American Secretary of State could offer Syria diplomatic assistance against Russia and intelligence information regarding Lebanon.

On August 7, Asad expressed his appreciation and professed a parallelism of interests with the United States with respect to the defeat of radical forces not only in Lebanon but throughout the Middle East. Murphy reported Asad's comments as follows:

> Lebanon had become the target of elements (unspecified) in the Arab world which could uproot the whole structure of society and bring about a total revolution. Lebanese Communists were effectively exploiting the current in local public opinion which sought a change in the old Lebanon. The US government and other countries interested in bringing about

[a] peaceful evolution of the area should be aware of that danger in the Lebanese crisis. It was not just a question of keeping Lebanon from becoming the spark for an area-wide conflagration (i.e., in the Arab-Israel context), nor was it simply a civil war whose lack of solution would inhibit future peace efforts. The problem was more basic; it directly bore on the future evolution of the Arab world. Saudi Arabia and the Gulf states, to mention but two, had a vital stake in insuring that elements dedicated to revolution did not succeed.

As a theoretical statement, we agreed with many of Asad's points, though our interpretations would diverge as the Lebanese crisis evolved and surely with respect to the overall Middle East diplomacy after our presidential election. But so long as Asad was at loggerheads with the Soviet Union and preoccupied with Lebanon, the intensity with which he would be able to oppose our planned initiative would be sharply reduced.

By the summer of 1976, we had navigated the worst dangers of the Lebanese explosion and were well advanced to creating conditions for a new Middle East peace initiative. Not only had our initial concern of a general conflagration been overcome, the radical coalition against the peace process was in tatters. Syria was preoccupied with Lebanon, the PLO with Syria. The radical factions in Lebanon were under pressure from the Syrians and Christians, but Syria was not strong enough —or was too afraid of Israel's reaction—to dominate Lebanon completely and add it to its strategic territory. The Christians had lost their traditional dominance as much as a consequence of the changed population balance as of the actions of their adversaries. In any event, armed by the Israelis and encouraged by Washington, they remained an essential obstacle to a radical victory or total Syrian domination.

Our policy had not produced all these results, but they would not have taken place in its absence. Had we stood aside, the careful calibration between Syria and Israel would almost surely have broken down and resulted in a war. Had we scared off Asad temporarily as Fahmy kept urging—which, if possible at all, would have required mobilizing an Israeli threat—it would probably have led to a radical PLO victory and almost certainly later Syrian or Israeli intervention under much more dangerous circumstances. Syria and Israel were bound to be the major players in the Lebanese evolution; diplomacy cannot abolish geography and geopolitical reality.

The delicate equilibrium which emerged in 1976 preserved the prospects for overall peace in the area. To be sure, the historic pattern of coexistence between the religions which had characterized Lebanon for most of the century became the victim of these events. This was due not so much to the machinations of outside powers as to the changed population balance and, above all, to the explosive mix that had assembled on Lebanese soil—the principal new element of that balance being the PLO. Most of the outside powers were primarily concerned to prevent Lebanon's troubles from exacerbating their own situation and getting in the way of goals they had developed independent of the crisis in Lebanon. By the end of that summer, even the people of Lebanon were better off than at the beginning of the year because the murderous intensity of the civil war had abated and some vestige of civil government was being restored which was to last for a period of nearly four years until Israel attempted to help impose a Maronite-dominated settlement starting in late 1980.

## Return to the Peace Process

Once Sadat had approved the across-the-board end of belligerency approach outlined above in March, instructions were drafted for Ambassadors Richard Murphy in Damascus and Thomas Pickering in Jordan to present the concept to their host governments. But since this coincided with the climax of the controversy over Syria's role in Lebanon, we urged Murphy on April 9 not to press Asad: "The important thing is to pick a time when he will be most receptive." The occasion did not, in fact, arise until May 9, when Asad, demonstrating the low priority he attached to the peace process, asked Murphy to present the talking points to his principal personal assistant, Adib Daoudi. Murphy did see Daoudi on May 15 and reiterated Rabin's offer that Israel was prepared to consider relinquishing some settlements on the Golan in exchange for an end to the state of belligerency —an unprecedented and generous proposition. Murphy's instructions outlined the basic concept:

> They [the Israelis] have now authorized us to explore an end of the state of war between Israel and Egypt, Syria and Jordan. . . . In essence an end to the state of war would be an interim stage, short of the state of peace which would have to be part of a final settlement. By definition, therefore,

the lines [to which Israel would withdraw under any "end to
the state of war" agreements] could not represent final Israeli
borders.

Asad never formally responded to the proposal but made two speeches
which warned against unspecified attempts to split Arabs, which, in
the atmosphere generated by Lebanon, could mean anything.

In the tense Middle East, reading tea leaves sometimes substitutes
for analysis. We took Asad's official silence as an indication that he
intended to keep his options open. We were not excessively concerned
by his speeches, for we did not expect him to approve our approach
openly, especially at a time when he needed all the Arab support he
could gather for his actions in Lebanon. Asad surely would not tip his
hand until he could learn more precisely what territorial adjustments
Israel was, in fact, willing to make. Even were Asad to persist in the
vein of his speeches, Syria's increasing isolation would reduce Asad's
capacity to oppose American initiatives. If the joint approach failed,
Sadat was gaining maneuvering room to proceed with a separate Egyptian move—which I thought the likely outcome.

King Hussein was similarly inscrutable when Ford presented our
concept to him on March 25. Like all his colleagues, Hussein was
primarily concerned with Lebanon. As for the West Bank, he told Ford
that he would be prepared to approach his Arab brethren on behalf of
a meaningful territorial offer from Israel and ask for authority to
negotiate despite the Rabat summit decision. But he was no more
willing than Asad to put himself on the line on behalf of a concept
that would not be implemented for another year. What Hussein authorized us to convey to the Syrian President was evasive opaqueness:

> While King Hussein expressed skepticism that Israel would
> be willing to make sufficient territorial concessions, no de-
> finitive conclusions were reached in our talks with him. . . .
> It was our impression that King Hussein prefers to defer a
> judgment until we have had a chance to discuss this idea
> with President Asad and to learn his reaction.

On June 22, I assembled our ambassadors to Arab countries at the
American Embassy in Paris to review the status of Lebanon and the
Middle East peace process. We met in the "tank," a soundproof room
designed to overcome potential listening devices. Free standing inside

a large room and encased by translucent walls, the tank created a
claustrophobic atmosphere that discouraged loquaciousness. Nevertheless, even with oratory reduced to a minimum, the subject matter
required a meeting of three hours. The participants were Roy Atherton, the assistant secretary, Ambassadors Hermann Eilts (Egypt), Richard Murphy (Syria), Thomas Pickering (Jordan), William Porter (Saudi
Arabia), and Talcott Seelye (recently appointed to replace Meloy in
Lebanon). The United States has never been represented by a better
team in the Middle East, and its professionalism is shown by the fact
that most of them went on to distinguished service in other administrations of both our major political parties.

I warned that, in Lebanon, "there is a danger that we will be
everyone's fall guy; but if we play it right we can continue to play an
important role." I added that I was getting tired of being accused by
every Arab state of colluding with the others:

> The Egyptians accuse us of colluding with the Syrians, and
> the Jordanians blame us for Syrian setbacks because we
> didn't encourage Syria to invade.

The consensus of the group was that these charges in fact showed that
our strategy of preventing the domination of Lebanon by any one of
the competing outside powers was working.

The ambassadors and I next reviewed the Arab-Israeli peace process. I explained why I preferred to concentrate on dealing with the
existing Arab states in the next stage rather than involve the PLO
(Seelye especially was urging this, supported—if less passionately—by
the other ambassadors):

> Once they [the PLO] are in the peace process, they can
> radicalize all the others. They'll raise all the issues the Israe-
> lis can't handle, and no other Arab can raise any other issues
> once the PLO is raised. So I felt the PLO issue couldn't be
> the first, not because I didn't favor the PLO but for this
> reason. Because the Egyptians and the Syrians have more
> flexibility than the PLO. As for the PLO as such, at some
> point some Palestinian entity will emerge, perhaps in confed-
> eration with Jordan.
>
> So I wouldn't have wept any great tears if the PLO had
> been weakened at the end of March.

All of us recognized that not much could be done before the November elections. In the meantime, I gave the ambassadors special messages for Sadat and Asad. Eilts was instructed:

> Tell Sadat the possibility that we will switch to Syria is absolutely impossible. We've put our chips on Egypt. All these allusions of Fahmy are absurd. On the other hand, we want his judgment about avoiding a situation where Asad is either overthrown or ties up with the Iraqis. This is more divisive for anything we could do. While we won't switch to Syria, we do feel we need Asad in the next phase for our common strategy.

Murphy's instructions for Asad said essentially the same:

> Tell him we need Syria in the next phase. He'll ask about the Palestinians. Tell him we need his help to bring them in somehow. If he has the statesmanship to bring the Palestinians and the Jordanians together, we can make progress. Lebanon blocks everything.
>
> I don't mind if Sadat tells him we told him Egypt was the key. We've told Sadat Syria has to have a role.

So much for the proposition that the essence of our diplomacy was to tell a different version to each side.

On August 7, I assembled our Middle East ambassadors (minus Murphy, who was meeting with Asad) once again. I was in Tehran for a meeting of the U.S.-Iran joint commission, and I knew there was some restiveness in the ranks about my attitude toward the PLO. I was aware that most of the ambassadors would have preferred including the PLO in the peace process and to begin negotiating with them. I therefore met separately with Talcott Seelye, our ambassador to Lebanon and the principal advocate of the PLO-first strategy in the State Department, to explain why I disagreed:

> You and I have a philosophical disagreement, but we knew that before you went out. You stated your views, and we disagreed with them a number of times, which is all within the normal way of doing business. . . .
>
> My view—and I could be wrong—is that the PLO

should be left to the end of the process. Once we recognize the PLO, we have lost all our leverage over them—we have lost all that we can sell to them. Of course, it is also possible that, after recognition, they would be more serious negotiators, but I think they would probably just be more cocky and arrogant.

And to the ambassadors as a group, I repeated the strategy I proposed to follow in 1977:

> Our strategy is to bring the PLO into negotiations at the end, keeping them a step behind Egypt, Syria, and Jordan so that they will be manageable. Otherwise, the PLO will disrupt the negotiations by demanding more than the Arab governments want or can meet. They will have the support of the Soviets. The Israelis will reject the demand, and the negotiations will collapse. We have no illusion about Asad, but we want to keep Syria split from Libya and Iraq and the USSR. If a radical crescent involving Iraq, Syria, a PLO-controlled Lebanon, and Libya comes into being—following the overthrow of Asad—it will be very bad for Egypt.

I reemphasized to Eilts the decisive role of Egypt for our strategy:

> KISSINGER: You should see Sadat alone—can you see him alone?
>
> EILTS: Yes, particularly since Fahmy will be away when I get back.
>
> KISSINGER: And give him my analysis of the situation. As an old and trusted friend, I would like him to know what I think, and I would like him to tell me where it is wrong. Egypt is still the key element in our policy, but I want his comments on my analysis.

On August 11, Eilts met alone with Sadat for an interview that culminated our strategy. Sadat stressed that the situation in the Middle East was "chaotic." He had no confidence in the ability of either Asad or Hussein to carry out an agreed strategy. Nevertheless, Sadat said, if the United States put forward a comprehensive plan in 1977 involving movement on all three fronts, there was just a chance that the Arab leaders would subordinate their interests in Lebanon to the possibilities of overall peace. Lebanon might still be unresolved but could become more manageable.

If, however, the Arab situation was not yet stable in 1977, Sadat asked that I consider an idea that he had been turning over in his mind. While he had not yet worked out details, it would involve urging the Israelis to "put all cards on the table" and begin a new round of negotiations between Egypt and Israel. Such negotiations should be conducted "openly" so that if "a certain solution" could be reached, Egypt would be in a position to point out to the Arab world, either at a summit conference or through some other way, that the other Arab states also needed to face up to their responsibilities. Sadat asked me to begin thinking with him about what might be done in 1977 to prevent the Palestinians, Syrians, or Hussein from hindering further peace efforts. They had no strategy, but we must think of the future. We should prepare ourselves for the next round. In 1977, he repeatedly reiterated, there must be movement.

We had achieved what we had set out to accomplish: we would begin with an attempt to move on all fronts and, failing that, support a major step in a separate Egyptian-Israeli negotiation—though it was beyond my imagination that Sadat included a trip to Jerusalem in his definition of "putting all cards on the table." In the event, all this was to unfold after we left office, yet these talks clearly prepared the ground for the next phase of the peace process.

After these meetings, Middle East policy subsided into pre-election doldrums. As for Lebanon, an Arab summit in Riyadh from October 17 to 18 established an Arab Deterrent Force largely manned by Syria which gradually imposed an end to the immediate fighting. But the end of the bloodshed could not restore the old order any more than the cease-fire in Bosnia twenty years later would enable the various ethnic groups to form a common government. The political situation in the Lebanon of 1976 was described as follows by a thoughtful Israeli observer:

> The authority of Lebanon's president, government, parliament, and central bureaucracy was limited to a small part of Beirut. Lebanon's territory was in fact divided among external forces and local baronies. Syria controlled and administered directly large parts of eastern and northern Lebanon; an autonomous Christian entity developed north of

Beirut, with its capital in Jounieh; a comparable protostate dominated by the Palestinians and their Lebanese allies existed south of Beirut; in the southernmost part of Lebanon, along the Israeli border, Major Sa'd Haddad and his pro-Israeli militia vied with the PLO and leftist militias for control; in the far north, the Faranjiyya [Frangieh] family and the Sunni political bosses and militia leaders maintained their respective fiefs.[16]

The fate of the vast majority of the people of Lebanon who were not participants in the battles and maneuvers of the various militias and outside forces called to mind a story told me by Julius Nyerere, the President of Tanzania. At one Nonaligned meeting or another, Nyerere had justified his mistrust of the great powers to pro-Western Lee Kuan Yew, the Prime Minister of Singapore, by saying: "When elephants fight, the grass gets trampled." Lee had replied: "When elephants make love, the grass gets trampled too."

By then, the strategy for the peace process was clearly set. We had Sadat's assurance that Egypt would fall in with our strategy; Jordan would go along if Israel would make a territorial offer the King could justify to his Arab brethren. Asad would clearly wait to see what the other Arab states would do and also what line the Israelis might suggest for the Golan. This was further than he had ever gone before. Still, the road from concept to completed negotiation on even one front would be nerve-racking. And the thought of proceeding on all three fronts simultaneously was sufficiently nightmarish to make me almost hope for an electoral outcome that would place the implementation of our policy in other hands.

The Carter Administration adopted our general concept of moving forward on all fronts. But eager for new departures, it did so not on behalf of a move toward nonbelligerency but in quest of a final comprehensive peace. Sadat, who had thought the "end of belligerency" concept represented the absolute maximum achievable, knew that such an approach guaranteed a prolonged deadlock. Making a return to the Geneva conference a centerpiece, as the Carter Administration proposed, raised for Sadat the specter of a Syrian and Soviet veto over his actions. So he threw into motion the unilateral alternative which he had outlined to Eilts in August 1976. Alone among the statesmen of the time, Sadat understood that the Middle East process required a transcendent act of generosity. We helped him by putting forward a new approach. But the ultimate step was his journey to Jerusalem in 1977—which no participant or observer, including myself, had thought possible. Thereby he returned diplomacy to the bilateral Egyptian-Israeli negotiation, but on a level which guaranteed the breakthrough we had been seeking.

In preparation for the "end of belligerency" strategy, my staff, especially Hal Saunders and Roy Atherton, prepared voluminous studies of various territorial options and definitions of peace which I believe were of some use to our successors after Sadat opened the door for the last step. For two decades, four administrations from both parties have brought about two peace treaties and are at this writing engaged in attempting to end the core dispute between Israel and the Palestinians. It is an honorable task, one of the too rare examples of bipartisanship and continuity of American principles and foreign policy goals. Those of us in the Nixon and Ford Administrations who had the honor to make the first steps take some pride in having laid down some of the markers on the road still being traveled.

# 34

# REFLECTIONS

## *The End of the Ford Administration*

Then, as suddenly as I had been catapulted into public service, it was over. The "big ticket" items had been on hold for the better part of 1976: relations with the Soviet Union, China diplomacy, and the Atlantic Alliance. In February, Ford had decided not to proceed with strategic arms control negotiations until after the election. The deaths of Zhou Enlai and Mao Zedong within nine months of each other, followed by the overthrow of the radical Gang of Four, imposed a pause in the dialogue with Beijing. Atlantic relations had reached a level of intimacy at which they could be sustained by regular meetings between the heads of government and the foreign ministers without the need for a special agenda.

As it happened, the lull turned into an opportunity to broaden the scope of our diplomacy by freeing us to attend to subjects that had previously been pushed aside by crises: the initiative for majority rule in Southern Africa and recasting Western Hemisphere relations. All the while, the civil war in Lebanon kept the passions of the Middle East before America's policymakers.

In the course of that long electoral year, my stewardship of foreign policy came under increasing attack from the two opposite camps of American idealism. In the Republican primaries, Ronald Reagan criticized our foreign policy for being too accommodating toward the Soviet Union; during the national election, Jimmy Carter attacked it for being too power-oriented and too insensitive to human rights.

For both camps, I had become the lightning rod. Ironically, this was largely a consequence of Watergate, during the course of which, by tacit consensus, I had been endowed with quasi-presidential authority in order to insulate national security from our domestic upheavals. Gerald Ford had continued my role partly for the same reasons but largely because of the close bonds of mutual respect and friendship that had developed between us. Though with the advent of a normal presidency my dominant role diminished somewhat, the American political process almost instinctively compensates for excessive concentration of power. As a result, I turned into a surrogate target for partisan attacks that normally would have been aimed at a President.

This position at the vortex of events went beyond any ambition—indeed, any fantasy—I had had with respect to government service. As a university professor, I was certainly attracted to the prospect of service in Washington, especially during and after the Kennedy presidency. But the highest position I considered within reach was as head of the Policy Planning Staff in the State Department or assistant secretary of defense for international security affairs (ISA). So modest was my view of my prospects that when President-elect Nixon, in his characteristic elliptical manner, offered me the White House National Security Adviser's post, I thought he was talking about the directorship of the Policy Planning Staff of the State Department.

I had met Nixon only once, in 1967, for a brief handshake in the New York apartment of Clare Boothe Luce. For over a decade, I had been a faculty member at Harvard, where opposition to Nixon was almost part of the curriculum. Since the mid-1950s, I had been foreign policy adviser to Nelson Rockefeller, whose political opposition to Nixon was reinforced by his personal dislike of him and whom Nixon had defeated twice for the presidential nomination. And for a year, in 1961, I served as a consultant to the Kennedy White House.

I demonstrated that I was not driven by an unquenchable yearning to serve in the new administration when, three days after our initial conversation, Nixon offered me the White House position in an unambiguous manner. Rather than jump at the opportunity, I displayed my academic provincialism by making the impudent request that I be given a week to reflect and to consult with friends as to whether I would jeopardize my relationship with them by serving in a Nixon Administration. Instead of showing me the door, Nixon not only gave me the week's grace but, in a touching gesture, even supplied a reference by suggesting that I talk about him to Harvard Law School professor Lon Fuller, who had taught him at Duke.

Nelson Rockefeller, who had been on his ranch in Venezuela during my meeting with Nixon and out of telephonic reach, put an end to the travesty of having the President of the United States give personal references to a prospective assistant. When he returned forty-eight hours later, he proved less than taken by my conduct. "Nixon is taking a much bigger chance on you than you on him," he said, adding what should have been obvious: "Pick up the phone and accept unconditionally." And so I did.

That after this rather unpromising start I should have gained the influence I ultimately did could not have been predicted when Nixon was inaugurated. I was initially not part of the White House inner circle. My role evolved gradually due to a confluence of factors: Nixon's personality, as already described; the Establishment's disdain of him; the near–civil war conditions growing out of the Vietnam protest; the reluctance of the bureaucracy to take Nixon's views on foreign policy at face value; and the manner in which Nixon constituted his Cabinet. All these factors magnified his already highly developed sense of isolation and reinforced his tendency to operate from the White House via a very small number of personal assistants.

The members of Nixon's Cabinet involved in foreign policy were either associates of long standing or recruits from the political world. None of them had shown any sustained interest in foreign policy; they lacked Nixon's strategic grasp or much sympathy for it. Most had been traumatized by the Vietnam protest. They acquiesced in Nixon's sober worldview without feeling really comfortable. As a result, I wound up—partly by default—as principal negotiator and executor of Nixon's foreign policy. I became the spokesman for it, even though I had no experience with press conferences. Until October 1972, my briefings were always on "background"—that is, not for attribution to me or for broadcast—because Nixon feared, in his words, that my accent would disturb the good citizens of Peoria. (The background restriction was only lifted in the last months of Nixon's first term.)

By the end of the Ford Administration, the shock of having become a political issue had worn off; the attacks had become part of the permanent political landscape for me. The disputes had many causes, some of which were undoubtedly rooted in my personality and style of conducting foreign policy. But their ultimate source was America's need to adjust to a world which had no final answers, in which every solution was the beginning of another challenge—in other words, coming to terms with the end of America's hitherto unique relationship to history. It marked a rebellion, to be discussed later in this chapter, against the world of permanent complexity—a yearning for the sort of definitive remedies which had served traditionally as the central themes of American history: the quest for permanent peace brought about by the crusading triumph of American values or the dominance of American power.

Jimmy Carter's defeat of Gerald Ford on November 2, 1976, moved these debates from the policy to the philosophical level; so far as I was concerned, it marked the end of my role in the direct shaping of American foreign policy. This did not happen overnight. For a month after the elections, day-to-day policymaking continued unchanged as if on autopilot; the chief difference was that long-range planning more or less ceased. But once Cyrus Vance was designated as the next Secretary of State on December 10, power shifted palpably and with my strong encouragement. With every passing week, my role became more and more that of caretaker. Our influence on the negotiations over majority rule in Rhodesia declined precipitously. The major diplomatic efforts—arms control, the Middle East, China, and the Atlantic Alliance—awaited the new administration. Mercifully the vestiges of our Lebanon diplomacy held; the civil war subsided during the interregnum, though more due to the dynamics previously put in place than to our occasional, now almost ritualistic, strictures to observe the cease-fire.

There are two aspects to presidential transitions: the passing of power, and the emergence of a new approach to policy. New administrations almost invariably start by overestimating the range of flexibility open to them. Aware above all of ideas they have been able to refine while unencumbered by decision-making, the new arrivals usually initiate a wholesale review of existing policy, unsettling routine but also bringing fresh air into the musty corridors of bureaucratic ritual.

The transition period is at once one of the heartaches and the glories of the American system of government. It is a heartache because there is no more important and personally fulfilling role than public service, especially in high office. Every action, however buffeted by bureaucratic and media storms, has the potential of making a difference. No tasks on the outside can compare in significance. Someone once told me that Dean Acheson compared leaving the office of Secretary of State to the end of a great love affair. Certainly, for me, one of the most moving experiences was my last day in office when I held an open house for anyone wishing to say goodbye, and hundreds from all levels of the department lined up for hours of leave-taking. A part of me stayed behind with these dedicated men and women who had sustained me through so many crises and hopes.

As it happened, the passage of formal power turned out to be easier to adjust to than the recognition that it was inevitably coupled with a change of policy. This took some weeks to sink in. Vance was too much the gentleman to make a point of it. And when I met for a day in Plains, Georgia, with Jimmy Carter and Vice President–elect Walter Mondale, they were very patient and courteous when I presented foreign policy as a straight-line projection of what existed— after all, it was official policy because we had concluded that it represented the best course. It was different when, close to the inauguration, I briefed Andrew Young, Zbigniew Brzezinski, and a few of their associates in my State Department office on African policy. Though meticulously polite, Young and Brzezinski conveyed in their bearing and sparse commentary that they had come for a ritual—not for guidance, not to perpetuate what they found but to modify it. Painful as it proved after all the efforts we had made, it was also inevitable. The new administration had, after all, promised to change things.

Their personal impact on the departing administration aside, presidential transitions demonstrate the vitality of the American system. No other democracy dares to risk its stability on a wholesale shake-up of its top personnel at regular intervals. Several thousand jobs are changed, many going to individuals with no prior experience in their new fields or even in high office. While the transition involves a gross interruption of continuity, it insures against the danger of fatigue or conducting policy by rote. Above all, it is a celebration of the cohesiveness of our society. The transitions that I have observed were characterized by extraordinary demonstrations of goodwill even when the electoral campaigns preceding them had been bitter. In both 1968–69 and 1976–77, no partisan or personal acrimony affected the cooperation of the outgoing administrations with their successors.

Surely no transition could have gone more smoothly than that of Gerald Ford to Jimmy Carter. This was no accident. Ford was proud to have restored, in the wake of Watergate, a large measure of calm and equilibrium to our government and society. This process needed to be culminated by a transfer of power expressing national reconciliation.

Ford gave all his Cabinet members to understand that they had a duty to ease the tasks of their successors. For me, this proved an easy assignment. Cyrus Vance was a friend of long standing whose opinion I had often sought. A lawyer by profession, solid, decent, and well informed, Vance held views well on the liberal side of mine, but he knew the State Department and was a guarantor of thoughtful policy. I assigned Philip Habib, my undersecretary for political affairs and a distinguished career diplomat, as liaison. Habib was instructed to make certain that Vance received any and all documentation available on current problems (including all backchannel negotiations) and all outgoing cables that went beyond housekeeping functions. Vance and I met at least twice a week to review where we stood and to see to it that, in the performance of day-to-day functions prior to January 20, I did not unintentionally cut across the designs of the new administration.

As for Gerald Ford, he displayed neither the bitterness nor the regrets frequently associated with electoral defeat. Never in my presence—and I doubt in anyone else's—did he complain about Ronald Reagan's relentless attacks in the primaries or about Reagan's refusal to extend more than token support—if that—during the general election campaign, both major factors in Ford's defeat. Ford also never commented on the irony that the Congress he genuinely loved and respected had harassed his presidency unmercifully from the beginning and encumbered it with unprecedented restrictions, crippling many aspects of his foreign policy. Ford bore no grudges against those who had thwarted some of his policies, did not insist on exclusive personal credit for his accomplishments, and never sought to shift blame for setbacks to his associates. In the more than twenty years since Gerald Ford left office, his Cabinet and key sub-Cabinet officials and their wives—close to two hundred of them—have been meeting for dinner every June to celebrate their work together and, above all, to express their gratification over having had the privilege of serving under a strong, honorable, and genuinely decent man.

They could take pride in a long list of foreign policy accomplishments. The Ford Administration had managed the collapse of Indochina with decency and honor; it navigated the United States through two bitter ethnic conflicts—in Cyprus and Lebanon—preventing a wider conflagration; in the Arab-Israeli conflict, it had maintained America's central diplomatic role, and advanced from removing the residue of war to initiating first decisive steps toward peace. In East-West relations, it had conducted a policy of strength in the face of congressional depredations against the defense budget and intelligence establishment. It had resisted the Kremlin's attempts to expand the Soviet sphere while keeping open the possibility of improving relations with the Soviet adversary should it moderate its ideology and conduct foreign policy as a state rather than a cause.

Over strong opposition, Ford had signed the Helsinki Final Act of the European Security Conference, generally considered by posterity as a landmark in the West's victory over Communism. Prompted by the energy crisis, he had brought about an unprecedented level of cooperation among the industrial democracies and institutionalized it in what are today's G-7 economic summits. To this day, Helmut Schmidt, Valéry Giscard d'Estaing, and James Callaghan still spend a weekend in Vail, Colorado, each year together with their erstwhile American counterpart. Finally, the constraints of the election year notwithstanding, Ford achieved the breakthrough to majority rule in Rhodesia and to a new Panama Canal treaty—all this during only thirty months in office.

Most important, in a period when passions still ran deep, Ford rescued a cohesive American foreign policy from the carnage of Vietnam and Watergate. He made this contribution despite the handicap that, facing our only unelected President, Congress and the media felt freed of some of the shackles that normally place a limit on excessive self-will.

Ford achieved all this without histrionics and visible emotional strain largely because he was so unlike the political leaders now brought into prominence by our normal electoral processes. In perhaps no other period has the importance of leadership been more insistently proclaimed. Yet very rarely has it been so difficult to match aspiration with performance. The ultimate task of a leader is to take his society from where it is to where it has never been. But this requires a willingness to travel on the difficult road between a nation's experience and its destiny. He is bound to be alone at least part of the way until his society's experience catches up with its possibilities. A leader who travels too much of that journey entirely on his own loses touch with his people and the capacity to shape events—as happened to Woodrow Wilson. A leader unwilling to risk solitary acts will doom himself and his society to stagnation—witness the democratic leaders of Europe between the two world wars. This is why courage is probably the most important single attribute of a successful leader.

Modern leaders crave the renown of being strong without being willing to pay the price for it. Congenitally fearful of standing alone, wanting their courage certified by the anchorman of the evening news, they alternate between paralysis and frantic maneuvering to satisfy pollsters or focus groups. Glibness rather than profundity, adeptness rather than analytical skill constitute their dominant traits.

A redeeming result of Watergate was that it gave the United States a leader from out of a different mold. Whereas in the age of mass media, highly developed verbal skills are among the distinctive attributes of national leaders, in Ford's congressional district in small-town, Midwestern America, a far higher premium was placed on sincerity and on substance than on facileness. Since Ford had never developed a capacity for quick repartee and sound bites, he was dismissed by many in the media as inadequate. In fact, Ford, a Yale Law School graduate, had a first-class analytical mind. Since television rewards glibness rather than substance, the media delighted in making Ford squirm as he tried to distance himself from clumsy formulations, even when journalists knew quite well this did not reflect his real competence.

In time, Ford's relative lack of verbal agility turned into an asset. Unlike more mediagenic politicians, he was not tempted to reduce complex problems to slogans; he worked on issues to grasp their essence. No great conceptualizer, Ford was eminently practical and always open to ideas that advanced a solution. And once he committed himself to a course of action, he pursued it regardless of political or popular consequences—as he proved with respect to the Helsinki Final Act of the European Security Conference, the Sinai interim agreement, the Panama negotiations, and the policy that achieved the breakthrough to majority rule in Southern Africa.

Despite his reverence for Congress, Ford steeled himself to defend executive authority. He wound up vetoing an unprecedented number of congressional acts and proceeded with his foreign policy in the face of considerable congressional opposition. As his administration evolved, Ford's lack of guile became a part of the healing process. For the battle-scarred survivors of the Vietnam and Watergate periods inside the government, Ford's understated serenity had a hugely calming effect. He carried off one of the most complex assumptions of authority with such apparent ease, and he established his brand of leadership at home and abroad with such remarkable speed, that it came to be forgotten how close to chaos Watergate had brought us.

Ford understood that to achieve his objective of national reconciliation, he had to begin by replacing the idiosyncratic style of the Nixon era with a more transparent, less personal method of government. Decisions had to emerge—and be seen to emerge—from a clearly defined process, not from executive fiat. Ford's more collegial decision-making did not guarantee substantive agreement, but it did help to drain the bitterness from policy disputes and permitted the establishment of a framework enabling the major trends of Ford Administration policy to be continued by his successors.

Because our Constitution confers extraordinary powers on the President, there can be no absolute rules as to how policy should be formulated or conducted; some scope must be left for the chief executive's personality and psychological makeup. Nevertheless, I would distill certain general principles from what I have observed or studied.

First, an effective decision-making process must not squander the President's time on secondary issues. Instead it should focus his attention on those issues that he alone is in a position to decide. These, however, *must* be brought to the President, not avoided in the hope that time will somehow resolve them or keep bureaucratic disputes from surfacing.

Second, the President has to be given every opportunity to overcome the root dilemma of high office that decisions must often be made while information is still incomplete and invariably while the consequences of the action are unclear. But if a President waits on events too long, he loses the ability to shape them. Therefore issues must not only be correctly defined, they must be dealt with while there still remains scope for creative action.

Third, decisions should prescribe a specific course of action, not a general theory or the least common bureaucratic denominator.

Fourth, the decision-making process should involve the greatest possible number of those who will be obliged to carry out the decisions, thus giving them a stake both in their execution and presentation to the public. Solitary action often offers many advantages in terms of speed, decisiveness, coherence, and flexibility, as the early Nixon period proved. But as a permanent feature of foreign policy, it risks coherence and continuity.[1]

Fifth, decisions must reflect well-thought-out policy choices—that is, they must answer these questions: What are we trying to achieve, or what are we trying to prevent? What consequences do we expect from this decision, and what steps do we have in mind for dealing with them? What is the cost of the proposed action? Are we willing to pay that price, and for what length of time?

Finally, there must be a procedure to monitor that the President's decisions are carried out faithfully in all their nuances.

No procedure will work unless the President knows his purposes, unless these purposes coincide with the national and global interest, and unless he has the courage to pursue his convictions in the face of adversity and the political skill to mobilize sufficient public support to stay the course. This is not the same as gearing foreign policy to public opinion polls. For the public does not forgive its leaders for disasters even if these followed its ostensible preferences—witness the fate of Neville Chamberlain after Munich.

Ford followed most of these principles to a remarkable degree, not because he had read textbooks on political science but because they grew out of his psychological makeup.* This enabled him to steer his country safely through dangerous rapids into calmer waters and is a fundamental reason why his presidency represents a period of renewal.

## Morality and Pragmatism

Gerald Ford became President at a time when American foreign policy had to come to terms with its limits. He presided over the final collapse of Indochina, which resulted from decisions long antedating his presidency. But Vietnam was a symbol, not a cause, of the national trauma of the 1970s, which arose from the gap that had opened between historic convictions regarding America's mission and the practical challenges of a new international environment. For the greatest part of our history, the United States had been sufficiently powerful and remote from the rest of the world to sustain the assumption that, alone among the major nations of the world, we had the choice of whether or not to commit ourselves to an international role and that, if we chose to, we would be able to overcome in a definite time frame whatever challenge had elicited our involvement.

As the Cold War progressed, both assumptions were proved largely wrong. We found ourselves involved in conflicts in parts of the world most Americans could not locate in their atlases for causes which either were ambiguous or which seemed to require enormous exertions with no end in sight. In that sense, the upheavals of the late 1960s and 1970s marked a rebellion for which the war in Vietnam became a symbol of a world that no longer permitted final answers or escape from its imperatives.

---

* In the last stages of SALT in 1976, the administration fell short. But Ford understood it and bowed for once to domestic political necessity.

The form of this rebellion was in a classically American mold: not as a quest to understand better the emerging new world but as an effort to oblige it to conform to our maxims or to our power. Rejecting limits, both poles of the American domestic debate put forward an increasingly assertive and militant Wilsonianism. One group charged that the inconclusive nature—as it seemed to them—of our international role was due to having strayed from Wilsonian idealism. In their view, our frustrations could be ended by a rededication to the spread of democracy around the world by conversion if possible, by pressure if necessary. We were failing in Vietnam, that group argued, and were embroiled in difficulties elsewhere because we had chosen means incompatible with our moral values in support of leaders unable or unwilling to act on our principles. It was a demand for moral cleansing—if necessary, by means of a temporary period of withdrawal—as a prelude to creating a new world order reflecting America's version of order.

The opposite criticism held that what frustrated us was not moral shortcomings but our inhibitions against the full deployment of our power in pursuit of our existing values. The Cold War was winnable and universal peace could be achieved, it was argued, not just by attrition—as official policy held—but by ideological mobilization and deliberate confrontation.

As a result, one wing of the national debate over foreign policy focused on reducing reliance on power by cutting the defense budget and unhinging many of the instruments—such as the intelligence agencies—with which the Cold War was being fought. Simultaneously, the opposite wing urged policies that would intensify the Cold War, thereby making these traditional instruments that much more indispensable.

When Ford took office, he found himself whipsawed by these partly complementary, partly contradictory impulses and their attendant pressures. Congress and the media generally supported the view of the liberal community that American policy had been too Cold War–oriented, inadequately attentive to human rights, and neglectful of the developing nations. But the public reaction to the collapse of Vietnam ran in the opposite direction. The new neoconservative philosophy of strenuous ideological confrontation based on the aggressive support of human rights was gaining ground. Reagan's eventual ascendancy was the American people's delayed reaction to the largely self-imposed humiliation in Vietnam.

This philosophical debate masquerading as a political contest buffeted the entire period of the Ford Administration. The real issues were rarely those dominating the headlines but invariably resulted from conflicting assumptions about the nature of American foreign policy. Based on our improving relations with our allies, the triangular diplomacy with Moscow and Beijing in which we were in the driver's seat, our domination of Middle East diplomacy, and our blunting of Third World radicalism, we thought we had demonstrated that a wise foreign policy would blend morality and power rather than risk everything on pursuing one or the other. Our message of balance ran up against the Wilsonian sense of American mission; we affirmed gradualism, the critics urged fulfillment.

The difficulty of achieving a sense of proportion was magnified during the Ford presidency because the intellectual community, which might have provided perspective and ballast, was itself in the process of transforming into another political interest group. When I started in academic life in the early 1950s, professors did not view themselves as participants in the policy process. To have an impact on policy, they were generally obliged to advance a mid- or long-term view. This, it turned out, was also most helpful to policymakers ever in danger of succumbing to the urgent at the expense of the important, to the expedient over the long-range.

John F. Kennedy's presidency changed all that. Never had so many intellectuals attained policymaking positions, automatically raising the expectation in the minds of those not yet summoned that they were potential policymakers as well. (The New Deal brought in a few intellectuals as advisers but not, as under Kennedy, into policymaking positions.) It was not an unmixed blessing. For it foreshortened the perspective of intellectuals on the outside but ambitious to participate by focusing them on the immediate and the tactical. It also subjected those in office to the kind of jealous backbiting characteristic of university faculties.

The shock and disappointment following Kennedy's assassination were compounded by the frustrations of the Vietnam War tinged with feelings of guilt. The policy-oriented element of the intellectual community became divided into two warring camps: aspirants to Washington office, usually enlisted in the service of political candidates and the writing of policy papers, and perennial radicals questioning American institutions and philosophies. In effect, the radicals were also aspirants for office should their point of view ever prevail—as it did in parts of the Clinton Administration. Both groups essentially abandoned the historical and intellectual role of their calling in favor of servicing the ongoing political struggle.

It took me a long time to understand just how deep this chasm had become. At the beginning of the Nixon Administration, I believed with what now strikes me as incredible naïveté that the national divisions over Vietnam could be overcome once the new administration demonstrated an unambiguous desire to end the Vietnam War on honorable terms. I soon found that the real debate was not over the practical question of appropriate terms for ending the war but over the definition of national honor.

Similarly, during the Ford and well into the Reagan period, I ascribed the conservative and especially the neoconservative critique to a misunderstanding. For I shared their distrust of Communism and their apparent determination to thwart its aims. I thought once they realized that our goal was not to placate but to outmaneuver the Soviet Union, we would be able to join forces in a common cause. But there was no misunderstanding. Our neoconservative critics wanted to prevail in the name of ideology, not superior tactics—indeed, they saw no other way for America to prevail.

Ironically I went along with some of the objectives of both sides of the debate. I agreed with the liberals' desire to end the war in Vietnam, but I became increasingly convinced that the one-sidedness of their commitment took the United States in directions incompatible with our honor. I shared almost all the long-range objectives of the conservatives. But I thought they did not correctly estimate the circumstances in which these had to be implemented.

As for Vietnam, I had become convinced on a visit in 1965 that the war could not be won by the methods to which we had been committed and that an honorable exit must be sought. But the radical protest, which eventually became the liberal position, assailed America's involvement as the inevitable product of our society's latent capacity for violence and imperialism; its definition of honor was a humiliating outcome that would put an end to these proclivities once and for all.

This was the real issue between me and much of the academic community at the time. Having found a haven from Nazi tyranny in the United States, I had personally experienced what our nation meant to the rest of the world, especially to the persecuted and disadvantaged. Therefore I viewed the Vietnam experience as the consequence of an American idealism which, in its exuberance for global reform, had strayed into regions where the relationship between ends and means had been lost.[2] The radicals were railing against the alleged flaws of "Amerika" and interpreted them as symptoms of an incipient totalitarianism. I saw in the honorable extrication from Vietnam a challenge from which our country could learn the complexities of a world in which our desire for peace was limited by our commitment to the nation's honor. But the liberal critics would not tolerate this equation. For them, there was only one route to national redemption, which was to make peace on any terms—if necessary, by jettisoning everything for which we had fought. The debate was not over policy but over America's worthiness to conduct any foreign policy at all.

With the emergence of the neoconservative challenge, the roles were reversed. To the radicals of the Vietnam protest, our policy was much too hard-line; to the conservative and especially the neoconservative critics, it appeared far too accommodating. They insisted on two propositions: that the challenges to peace invariably arose from non-democratic governments, and that therefore the United States had an obligation to advance the cause of democracy in all countries simultaneously and by use of sanctions, at the very least; and that human rights was our most effective weapon with which to undermine and defeat our Communist adversaries.

I agreed with the goal but considered the conclusions too simplified. In the West, democracy did not result from a single decision but rather from an evolution extending over centuries. The unique features of the Western pluralistic evolution began with the Catholic Church, which, while hardly democratic in its internal organization, did create the basis for it by insisting on its own distinct governance and by defining the moral order as having a claim superior to that of the state.

This separation of authority between God and Caesar amounted to the first step toward political pluralism and the limitation of state power. Centuries later, pluralism became institutionalized when the Reformation broke up the Universal Church by emphasizing the role of the individual conscience. These trends were accelerated by the Enlightenment, which stressed the dominance of reason; by the Age of Discovery, which stretched intellectual horizons; and by capitalism, which rewarded individual autonomy and initiative and enlarged the middle class.

No other culture has produced a similar evolution. In Islamic societies, the separation of mosque and state is complicated because, for the true believers, the words of the Koran must permeate every aspect even of secular life. Inevitably secularization leads to tensions with religion. In most Confucian societies, neither religion nor nongovernmental groups have had the organization, the autonomy, or the doctrine to encourage the emergence of an alternative center of political authority.

For these reasons, I was generally uneasy about making the transition to constitutional principles that took centuries to evolve in the West the preeminent goal of American foreign policy, to be pursued by overt pressures regardless of the history and the social conditions of other societies. Of course, systematic violations of human rights cannot be condoned by invoking stages of historical evolution. And the United States, to be true to itself, has a duty to stand for human rights and democracy.

Activists perform a service in recalling us to first principles. But policymakers need to show some humility in translating these appeals into day-to-day actions. In many countries, pluralistic democracy is likely to evolve only gradually, obliging us in the meantime to deal with governments occasionally falling short of our norms on human rights because other important interests are involved. If we treat all these issues as resolvable only by the overthrow of the offending government—or by its public surrender to American pressures—we will turn every problem into a life-or-death struggle, actually inhibiting progress on human rights. Our foreign policy must leave room for measures to influence the practices of other societies without being perceived as trying to undermine them.

Much of the anguish of foreign policy results from the need to establish priorities among competing, sometimes conflicting, necessities. This requires relating American idealism to the pragmatic imperatives of a given situation. The refusal to accept this dualism tends to conflate foreign policy and domestic politics as competing groups seek to impose their passionate views of justice on particular concerns to them. Oversimplification tempts the United States into simultaneous overextension and abdication, into seeking to impose its views of appropriate domestic structures by sanctions and pressure or else to invoke the alleged moral shortcomings of potential partners as an alibi for isolationism.

The philosophical struggle that rent the United States during my government service could have been overcome by strong presidential moral leadership of the kind Franklin Delano Roosevelt had demonstrated, in which he guided his isolationist country into the Second

World War. But the two Presidents I served did not play this role. Richard Nixon had the background in international affairs and the record. He often gave thoughtful speeches but, as I have explained, he was more comfortable outmaneuvering than persuading his critics. And Gerald Ford, coming into office unelected, had neither the experience nor the formal background to lead a conceptual debate—though I believe that, had he been granted a second term, his combination of integrity, common sense, and courage might have enabled him to rebuild the necessary consensus.

As it was, after Watergate began, I found myself carrying out the President's normal role of articulating foreign policy. It was a function no Secretary of State is in a position to fill. My skills were strategic analysis and diplomacy, not the essentially political task of mobilizing popular constituencies for a long-range, mature, and complex foreign policy.

American idealism, the underlying cause of the national debate on both sides of the argument, is, of course, a symptom of America's strength—an expression of faith that our society is eternally able to renew itself, transcend history, and reshape reality. But we must take care that rebellion against the very concept of limits does not become the permanent feature of the American response to international politics. For the recognition of some constraints is an attribute, perhaps the price, of maturing in societies as well as in people. The test of a society is not the denial but the proper understanding of its constraints. Mediocre societies and statesmen limit themselves to the easily attainable. Great societies and statesmen strive at the outer reaches of their possibilities. But the denial of any limits leads to exhaustion or disaster.

Vietnam was once thought to have taught us those limits—in my view, far too well. Ironically, the healing initiated by Ford and culminated by Reagan has been so extraordinary as to tempt the United States again into a missionary version of Wilsonian enthusiasm that threatens anew to involve us in every one of the world's upheavals in the name of a global mission, this time justified by our position as the sole superpower. Having defeated our ideological adversary in the sundry battles of the Cold War, too many seem eager to conduct foreign policy as a permanent crusade for apocalyptic outcomes against all regimes that offend our sensibilities. But if the United States is to remain the principal force for freedom and progress, it must temper its missionary spirit with a concept of the national interest and rely on its head as well as its heart in defining its duty to the world.

The attempt to reduce foreign policy to a single formula runs counter as well to the reality of the present world. In America's relations to Europe and Latin America—regions where democratic institutions thrive and wars between major countries are next to unthinkable—Wilsonian principles should indeed be dominant. But in Asia the nations think of each other as strategic rivals; it is impossible to conceive policy there without understanding principles of equilibrium. And in other parts—for example, with respect to Islamic fundamentalism—even more basic, essentially revolutionary, motives govern.

The crucial lesson of my service in government has been the need to understand these different thrusts and to strike a balance. It remains the single most important task before our nation.

For any student of history, change is the law of life. Any attempt to contain it guarantees an explosion down the road; the more rigid the adherence to the status quo, the more violent the ultimate outcome will be. But it is also one of the lessons of history that the more abrupt the change, the greater needs to be the violence to bring it into being. Fortunate is the society or the international order which can evolve organically without violence—or at least excessive violence—and without stunting growth. In such circumstances, a sense of shared obligations replaces force, and progress is achieved by consensus. The United States—with the single exception of the Civil War—has found itself in such a situation. And so have international orders which witnessed long periods without major war.

But the more abrupt the upheaval, the less reliance there can be on consensus. Force must replace a sense of obligation. Victory is prized over continuity; opponents are eradicated, not persuaded. The great symbols of this attitude are the conqueror and the prophet. The conqueror makes no secret of his design; his mission is to impose his will, though if his conquests last, he must sooner or later transform dominance into a sense of obligation. This is how empires achieve legitimacy.

The prophet's role is more subtle. Though his cause is based on proclaimed values, his claims are for this reason even more universal and insistent. Righteousness is the parent of fanaticism and intolerance. Opponents are extirpated—often, it is alleged, for their own good. Reigns of terror become necessities, not aberrations. The symbol of such a period is the commissar who kills millions without love and without hatred in the pursuit of an abstract duty. This is why crusades have often created as much havoc and suffering as conquests.

The totalitarian horrors of the twentieth century should have brought home to us the fragility of the restraints that embody civilization. The domestic experience of the United States, peaceful, stable, and content, inhibits our capacity to understand the vulnerabilities of other societies or international orders. Blessed by history and a benign environment, we are tempted to view our power as a dispensation and to use it to impose our preferences. Such an attitude runs the risk of being viewed as hegemonic by the rest of the world and will gradually be opposed by it. Excessive reliance on power and excessive insistence on our virtue may wind up corroding the very values in the name of which our policy is being conducted.

For this reason, I am made uneasy by foreign policies largely shaped by ideologues. For ideologues have a tendency to drive societies as well as international systems beyond their capacities. The alleged dichotomy of pragmatism and morality seems to me a misleading choice. Pragmatism without a moral element leads to random activism, brutality, or stagnation; moral conviction not tempered by a sense of reality leads to self-righteousness, fanaticism, and the erosion of all restraint. We must always be pragmatic about our national security. We cannot abandon national security in pursuit of virtue. But beyond this bedrock of all policy, our challenge is to advance our principles in a way that does not isolate us in the long run.

Each generation must discover that sense of proportion for itself. In that regard, the present generation, and even more its successors, encounter a special challenge. For we are living through not only an exceptional period of fluidity in international relations but through an even more profound upheaval in how publics and leaders view the world around them. In its scope and eventual impact, this intellectual change is comparable to, and probably exceeds, the consequences of the invention of the printing press five centuries ago.

Before printing, knowledge had to be based largely on memory. To establish any unified knowledge, it was necessary to concentrate on texts on which everyone could agree—essentially religious texts and epic poems. The medieval period was therefore inherently a religious age.

The printing press dramatically enlarged the range of available knowledge. No longer limited to the religious or the epic, human awareness exploded into the secular world. Science explored heretofore unimaginable areas; political legitimacy came to be increasingly based on secular criteria, on principles of reason rather than divine right. The range of knowledge grew exponentially.

Withal, knowledge from books had its limits. Reading is relatively difficult and time-consuming; to ease the process, style is important, increasing the appreciation of aesthetics. Since it is not possible to read all books on a given subject, much less the totality of all books, or to organize easily everything one has read, learning from books placed a premium on conceptual thinking—the ability to recognize comparable data and events and project them into the future. In this manner, the prevalent state of technology conferred a premium on learning dependent on perspective—in politics and foreign affairs, via a sense of history.

The computer has, to a considerable extent, solved the problem of acquiring, preserving, and retrieving knowledge. Data can be stored in unlimited quantities and in manageable form. The push of a button retrieves it; there is no need to store it in one's memory or to undertake complex research to compile it. The mind can therefore be trained for other purposes. The computer makes available a range of data inconceivable in the age of books. It packages it effectively; style is no longer needed to make it accessible, thus destroying one element of aesthetics. The operator of the computer has a vast array of facts immediately at his disposal. In dealing with a single decision separated from its context, the computer supplies tools unimaginable even a decade ago.

But it also shrinks perspective. Because knowledge is so accessible and communication so instantaneous, there is a lack of training in its significance. Policymakers are forever tempted to wait for a case to arise before dealing with it; manipulation replaces reflection as the principal policy tool. But the dilemmas of foreign policy are not only —or perhaps even primarily—the by-product of contemporary events; rather they are the end product of the historical process that shaped them. Modern decision-making is overwhelmed not only by contemporary facts but by the immediate echo which overwhelms perspective. Instant punditry and the egalitarian conception that any view is as valid as any other combine with a cascade of immediate symptoms to crush a sense of perspective.

However different the great statesmen of history, they had in common a sense of the past and a vision of the future. The contemporary statesman is constantly seduced by tactics. The irony is that mastery of facts may lead to loss of understanding of the subject matter and, indeed, control over it. Foreign policy is in danger of turning into a subdivision of domestic politics instead of an adventure in shaping the future.

The problem of most previous periods was that purposes outran knowledge. The challenge of our period is the opposite: knowledge is far outrunning purposes. The task for the United States therefore is not only to reconcile its power and its morality but to temper its faith with wisdom.

## A Personal Note

As a policymaker it fell to me to help define the relationship between the pragmatic and the moral in American foreign policy. And, as is inevitable in turbulent times, these judgments were often controversial. Some commentators have asserted that my emphasis on a sense of proportion in foreign policy springs from a preference for order over justice, which they ascribe to the experience of having grown up in Nazi Germany. But the Germany of my youth had a great deal of order and very little justice; it was not the sort of place likely to inspire devotion to order in the abstract.

Through the prism of segregation, delegitimization, and emigration, my childhood views were shaped much more by my family than by reflections on politics in the abstract. In retrospect, my parents epitomize the two aspects of human conduct—the practical and the ethical—without either of which life grows precarious and politics loses its meaning. My mother—practical, vital, courageous—saw to the necessities; my father—thoughtful, sensitive, gentle—defined the family's moral compass.

In 1946, while I was serving with the United States Army in Europe, my father entered a hospital in New York for an operation from which he was not expected to recover. He left a letter for my brother, Walter, (then in the United States Army in Korea) and me. It was our father's single most demonstrative gesture toward his sons. Others will have to judge the degree to which I have lived up to my father's personal precepts. I cite his letter here because it helps to explain the gratitude I have always felt for having been permitted to serve the country that gave my family refuge in America's traditional quest for a world in which the weak are secure and the just free.

After a few personal remarks, the letter (written in English) read as follows:

> Your grandfather Falk, this fine and honest man, used to say: "Der Mensch muß seine Schuldigkeit tun" (a human being must always fulfill his moral obligation). These simple words shall become a principle in your life. Do always your duty toward your mother in the first line, to your relatives, to the Jewish community, to this great country, to yourselves.
>
> I know the different conditions in this country which gave a man of my age so little hope for future life made it impossible for me to be a guide for you both as I would have been in normal times. But I subordinated all my personal decisions to your future.
>
> In all the hard times of the war, the confidence lived in me that God will protect you. I am grateful to Him that He was with you. I am confident that you both will always go the right way. I am proud of you and am convinced that your future life will confirm my pride.
>
> Always keep in mind that we find real satisfaction only in what we are doing for others. Try always to be good, faithful, helpful, reliable, selfless.
>
> I would have liked to see you grown up and to be witness of your success and happiness. God bless you.

My father recovered and lived until 1982 through all the events described in these memoirs.

# NOTES

## 1: A FORD, NOT A LINCOLN

1. Henry Kissinger, *Years of Upheaval* (Boston: Little, Brown, 1982), pp. 1193–1214.
2. Gerald R. Ford, *A Time to Heal* (New York: Harper & Row and The Reader's Digest Association, 1979), p. 21.
3. Anatoly Dobrynin claims in his memoirs (*In Confidence: Moscow's Ambassador to America's Six Cold War Presidents* [New York: Times Books, 1995], p. 319) that I took him to see the new President within hours of his inauguration. I probably would have, had he been in town. Dobrynin happened to be in the Soviet Union at the time, however, on vacation.
4. Kissinger, *Years of Upheaval,* p. 1213; Richard Nixon, Remarks on Departure from the White House, August 9, 1974, in Richard Nixon, *Public Papers of the Presidents of the United States, 1974* (Washington, D.C.: U.S. Government Printing Office, 1975), pp. 630–33.
5. Gerald R. Ford, Remarks on Taking the Oath of Office, August 9, 1974, in Gerald R. Ford, *Public Papers of the Presidents of the United States, 1974* (Washington, D.C.: U.S. Government Printing Office, 1975), p. 2.
6. Richard Reeves, "I'm Sorry, Mr. President," *American Heritage,* December 1996, pp. 52–55.
7. See Henry Kissinger, *Diplomacy* (New York: Simon & Schuster, 1994), Chapters 25, 26, 27.
8. Ford, *A Time to Heal.*

## 2: THE MAN AND THE ORGANIZATION

1. Henry Kissinger, *White House Years* (Boston: Little, Brown, 1979), p. 1086.
2. Ibid., p. 1476.
3. See, e.g., ibid., pp. 288–303.
4. Richard M. Nixon, *Six Crises* (New York: Doubleday, 1962).
5. H. R. Haldeman, *The Haldeman Diaries: Inside the Nixon White House* (New York: G. P. Putnam's Sons, 1994).
6. If some journalists are to be believed, Nixon was not so wrong about the precedents he was following. See, e.g., Victor Lasky, *It Didn't Start with Watergate* (New York: Dial Press, 1977), and Seymour M. Hersh, *The Dark Side of Camelot* (Boston: Little, Brown, 1997).
7. March 14, 1972

| | |
|---|---|
| MEMORANDUM FOR: | DR. KISSINGER |
| FROM: | H. R. HALDEMAN |

I thought it might be helpful to try to summarize some of the points that we've been discussing over the last weeks that still need emphasis regarding the China trip, because as yet, they have not come through in any clear way to the general public.

The television coverage of the trip itself certainly established a basis of the dignity of the President and the manner in which he conducted the public part of the activities, and this will be very valuable in the long term.

On the other hand, there is still a great deal of mystery about how the President, Chou En-lai, and Mao Tse-tung, conducted themselves in their private meetings, and particularly, how the President handled the approach to and conduct of, these meetings.

The communique itself has been now discussed at such great length that the average person is undoubtedly tired of hearing about it. In the backgrounders and certainly on the television broadcast that you do, the background-type of information will be of much more interest to the viewer than will the substantive details of the content.

It would seem to me that some of the points we've talked about that would be well to emphasize are the following:

1. RN goes into meetings of this kind better prepared than anyone who has ever held the Presidential office. He does this by taking the voluminous briefing materials that are prepared by the NSC staff, and by the State Department, reading them all, plus reading a lot of other materials, and then he talks to a great number of people about the various aspects of the briefings in which he is particularly interested.

2. He then sits down and in painstaking detail, makes up his own mind as to what his approach should be. He does not memorize his speeches, etc. He does not follow a predictable pattern and as a result he is able to handle any of the questions that come up on the spot without being frozen into an untenable position. This, of course, is a tremendous advantage to him in all meetings, but particularly in summit meetings with skillful leaders like Chou En-lai.

3. RN has the tremendous advantage of an exceptional knowledge of world problems which he gained in his eight years in the Vice Presidency, plus eight years of travel while he was out of office, plus the three years that he has been in office as President. In other words, he has been up against big league pitching in the foreign policy field for a longer period of time than any other world leader. He has had extended conversations with the great leaders of our time—DeGaulle, DeGasperi, Adenauer, Khrushchev, Nehru, Yoshida, Sukarno, Churchill—not to mention the current batch of leaders from both the large and small countries, whom he has met as President.

4. An interesting mark of his style is that he treats all leaders whether from large or small countries, with equal dignity and respect.

5. As far as tactics are concerned, he never gives an inch on principle. As a matter of fact, he is probably more rigid on principle than many of his advisors would want him to be.

6. He never quibbles over debating points. Instead, he always keeps his eye on the main goal and constantly finds ways to bring the subject back to that goal rather than being diverted into argumentative discussions that would have no effect as far as achieving our main purpose.

7. He has great qualities of subtlety and humor—he is never belligerent—but is very tough. He has developed the quality of speaking most quietly when he is making his strongest points—a quality also observed in Chou En-lai.

8. He has the quality of knowing the other man and all of his positions as well as he knows his own. This, incidentally, also characterized Chou En-lai and was a factor which made the meeting between the two of them such a fascinating discussion.

He has a quality of absolute discipline which goes clear back to the time when he had the seven hour luncheon with Khrushchev, and has carried through all the many summits he's held as President, including the meetings with the Chinese.

He never takes a drink during the course of the meetings or prior to any important conversation, and he even carries this to the extent of resisting the temptation which was so obviously presented to him, particularly with the Chinese, of eating nuts and candies, etc., that were put before him during the course of the discussion. His personal theory is that either drinking or eating tends to dull the reaction time as far as he's concerned. Although, of course, he would not apply this same test to others for whom either eating or drinking may help their reactions, as was presumably the case with Churchill and some others.

9. He has a remarkable quality of candor, used not for the purpose of embarrassing his opposite number, but for the purpose of establishing a degree of mutual trust and confidence which is so essential for any meaningful discussion.

10. The quality of stamina. He has an ability to perform at his peak level regardless of the length of the session. This is a very important quality, of course, in dealing with the Chinese, and will be with the Soviets.

All of these above points are things that you and the President have often raised in the conversations about the summit meetings, and it would be extremely valuable if some of this kind of information would get into the public domain.

If you can, you should review your notes to see how many personal tidbits you could use to bear out these points without revealing the substance of the conversations.

I don't think you should limit this to the discussions with Chou En-lai. You could go back to specifics on the meetings with DeGaulle, Wilson, Pompidou, Ceauşescu, Tito, etc. to make some of these points.

Also, you are uniquely able to make the point that RN has acquired a great deal of respect from world leaders because of his conduct of these sessions without resorting to staff or notes.

I'm sure it's presumptuous of me to raise these points, but I thought they might be helpful. I have the very strong feeling that the most good you can do in talking with private groups and certainly in your appearance on television, will be in the area of establishing public confidence in the President as a man, and as President, rather than in the area of explaining further, the ramifications of the content of the communique, or the substance of the talks leading to it.

8. See Jonathan Aitken, *Nixon: A Life* (London: Weidenfeld & Nicolson, 1993), pp. 453, 463; William Safire, *Before the Fall* (New York: Doubleday, 1975), p. 438.

9. See Kissinger, *White House Years,* pp. 1185–86.

10. William Bundy, *A Tangled Web: The Making of Foreign Policy in the Nixon Presidency* (New York: Hill and Wang, 1998).

11. Kissinger, *White House Years,* pp. 41–44.

12. Seymour M. Hersh, *The Price of Power: Kissinger in the Nixon White House* (New York: Summit Books, 1983), p. 381, as quoted in William Bundy, *A Tangled Web: The Making of Foreign Policy in the Nixon Presidency* (New York: Hill and Wang, 1998), p. 143.

13. See Kissinger, *White House Years,* pp. 187–91.

14. See ibid., Chapter 20.

15. Ibid., p. 1154ff.

16. The following conversation from April 11, 1975, after Ford's speech urging aid for Vietnam, can serve as an example:

KISSINGER: Mr. President.

NIXON: How are you? You survived the speech last night.

KISSINGER: Yes, but it is not as bad as I thought it would be.

NIXON: Give me your quick reaction if you have the time.

KISSINGER: The *Washington Post* showed a fairly good editorial, and the others are mumbling around, but we are doing what you suggested. We are sort of blitzing around on the Hill.

NIXON: Not only blitzing around on the Hill but following up on public statements and speeches. Glad you are going to make one, and I would strongly urge that Rockefeller make one.

KISSINGER: Right. I have talked to him about it already.

NIXON: Do it publicly and strongly; having in mind that it is far better to fight and lose in the right cause than not to fight and lose in the wrong cause.

KISSINGER: Exactly. In the next year, these things will look quite different.

NIXON: Yes. I hope. You may look different from the standpoint of what we did and did not do.

KISSINGER: Exactly.

NIXON: My only purpose in calling is about the speech last night.

KISSINGER: It means so much to me.

NIXON: And to be sure that you know that the standing just has to be done and the idea that many well-intentioned advisers say—don't do anything that Congress will not give you—don't take a stand that will be unpopular. This they have to recognize —that there has to be confrontation. Accept it and enjoy it and fight like hell.

KISSINGER: I am not so sure that enjoying confrontation is the specialty of my outfit here.

NIXON: I am speaking of you and the man in the Oval Office. That is what really matters here now. No backing down simply because the Congress and Senators mumble this and this and other things. The ball is on their side of the net now. Keep hitting it. I would say a little more with regard to what is going to happen in terms of a bloodbath and who will be responsible could also be helpful.

KISSINGER: We will definitely stay on the offensive now.

NIXON: That is good, and I wish you well, and I hope—don't talk so gloomily that they are out to get you. Of course they are. That is because you are somebody. They are not going to get you. Stick in there.

17. Richard M. Nixon and Henry A. Kissinger, "An Arms Agreement—On Two Conditions," *Washington Post*, April 26, 1987.

18. "Paying the Price," Interview with President Nixon by John Stacks and Strobe Talbott, *Time*, April 2, 1990, pp. 46–49. Nixon and his friends supplied a similar version to a British biographer. See Aitken, *Nixon*, p. 463.

19. April 2, 1990

PERSONAL

Dear Mr. President:

I read your interview in *Time* with a mixture of melancholy and amazement.

Melancholy because I shall always be grateful to you for giving me the opportunity to serve my adopted country and repay it for the safe haven from persecution for my family and me. And I shall forever consider it a privilege to have worked for a President whose role in foreign policy was seminal in charting the main directions of everything that followed since. It is a pity that you permitted yourself to be drawn by *Time* into a typical journalistic trap designed to make an extraordinary record controversial by tempting its implementors to debate their respective contributions. Provocative questions of journalists should not be confused with reality. Though you seemed to go along with your interrogators' implication, the fact is that I have never—either in my memoirs or elsewhere—questioned who was in charge nor implied that I substituted my political or strategic judgement for yours.

Amazement because a host of factual inaccuracies escalated previous incorrect innuendos. If you wish, I would be happy to make available to John Taylor the various memoranda, telephone conversations and other documentation that leave no doubt of the inaccuracy of these assertions. Let me point out some flagrant examples:

*The "Peace is at Hand" press conference:* You state that you did not want to "breathe a word about negotiations" but I went public to help you politically in the "peace is at hand" press conference. But the record does not sustain this: I was as eager as you to keep the negotiations secret. However, on the morning of October 26 Hanoi broadcast the fact of the negotiations as well as the text of the agreement as it then stood. It invited you to send a representative to Paris to sign the text. Saigon soon weighed in with its own version of events. In these circumstances, it was impossible to be silent. You therefore—quite correctly—instructed me in the Oval Office to brief the media about the Administration position. Unbeknownst to me—I learned of it only after the press conference was completed—you instructed Ziegler to turn on the sound for television. Until that moment TV had not been permitted to use my voice because of the fear—to paraphrase your own remark—that my accent might jar Midwestern constituents. We can only speculate whether I would have chosen different words had I known I was on "live."

*The notion that I wanted a settlement before the election for domestic political reasons:* A review of the documents—which, again, I will happily share with John Taylor—leaves no doubt that I *never* urged *any* action for domestic political reasons. The pace of negotiations was determined largely by Hanoi. After stonewalling for three and a half years, they switched tactics in September and began to move toward our position. On October 8 they accepted the secret proposals of May 1971, which you had approved, as well as your public peace offers of January 25 and May 8. Prior to the October 8 negotiation—on September 28, to be exact—you accepted Hanoi's proposal that the October 8 talks last three days, with a view to settling by the end of October. It was the right decision. Had we refused to negotiate on that basis, Hanoi would have published its proposals immediately and our position would have become untenable. How could we refuse Hanoi's acceptance of your proposals as a basis for negotiations? How could we have broken off talks in which we had obtained greater concessions than you had publically asked for? You had approved every negotiating proposal, *all* of which were submitted to you before *every* negotiating session. You will not find in any of them or anywhere else references to their impact on the forthcoming election. Nor do they show *any* disagreement by you with the various negotiating positions.

*The implication that I was more trusting of North Vietnam than the President:* This, too, repeats previous innuendos; it is no more supported by the record than the other charges. There was indeed a difference between us concerning not Hanoi's motives but its intentions. In late August you sent me a note via Haig pointing out that you thought the deadlock could not be broken and that a continued deadlock would give ammunition to your opponent in the election. I was of the view that Hanoi would make concessions not because I trusted our adversaries but because I thought they were realists. Once Hanoi had accepted your proposals, the debate between us became moot. You knew that the negotiations with Le Duc Tho starting October 8 would be decisive. You had approved Hanoi's request for a three-day meeting. On October 2 you told Gromyko that this meeting of October 8 would represent our final effort to conclude the agreement by the end of October. In fact, in the three days starting October 8 Hanoi made concessions going beyond your public demands. In these circumstances, it was no longer possible to argue that our bargaining position would improve after the election, and you *never* did so. We were running out of money, having spent so much of the year's budget to repel Hanoi's spring offensive. Laird had already proposed a 40% reduction in aircraft sorties and a withdrawal of all forces (mostly B-52's) sent to Asia to deal with the spring offensive. Harlow had stressed that a continuing resolution to replenish funds would result in a bitter fight with uncertain outcome and would probably end with a Congressionally imposed terminal date, that is to say, our defeat. It was not clear what we would be fighting for after Hanoi had accepted and gone beyond your own proposals.

A public debate between us would be a disaster. I can think of nothing that our long-time critics would greet more joyfully than an opportunity to pit our recollections against each other. It would be all the sadder in the light of my admiration for your leadership during a tragic period. None of these tactical issues will affect what I believe must be the verdict of history: that in a desperate hour you vindicated America's honor with a foreign policy which, under your leadership, set the basic directions culminating in the revolutionary changes of last year.

> Respectfully,
> Henry

## 3: CONTROVERSY OVER DÉTENTE

1. Walter A. McDougall, "Vietnam—Legacy and Lessons," remarks presented at a panel discussion at a conference on "The Paris Agreement on Vietnam: 25 Years Later," The Nixon Center, Washington, D.C., April 24, 1998.
2. Kissinger, *White House Years*, pp. 254–56.
3. Ibid., p. 1486, n. 4.
4. First Annual Report to the Congress on United States Foreign Policy for the 1970s, February 18, 1970, in *Public Papers of the Presidents of the United States, Richard Nixon, 1970* (Washington, D.C.: U.S. Government Printing Office, 1971), p. 119.
5. See, e.g., Henry A. Kissinger, "Central Issues of American Foreign Policy," in Kermit Gordon, ed., *Agenda for the Nation* (Washington, D.C.: The Brookings Institution, 1968), pp. 607–10; Richard Nixon, *Nixon on the Issues* (New York: Nixon-Agnew Campaign Committee, 1968), pp. 28–32.
6. Kissinger, *Years of Upheaval*, pp. 242–43.
7. See Andrei Amalrik, "Will the USSR Survive Until 1984?," *Survey*, No. 73 (Autumn 1969).
8. Address, "The Western Alliance: Peace and Moral Purpose," London, June 25, 1976, inaugurating the Alastair Buchen memorial lecture series, *Department of State Bulletin*, Vol. 71, No. 1935, July 26, 1976, pp. 105–15.
9. Nixon, *Public Papers, 1970*, pp. 178–80.
10. Kissinger, *White House Years*, p. 136.
11. Nixon, *Public Papers, 1970*, p. 178.
12. Kissinger, *White House Years*, pp. 127–38.
13. "Trade with the East," *New York Times*, September 13, 1972.
14. "Trade with Moscow," *New York Times*, November 25, 1972. See also "Alliance Against Dissent," *New York Times*, September 3, 1973.
15. See Coral Bell, *Negotiation from Strength: A Study in the Politics of Power* (New York: Alfred A. Knopf, 1963).
16. See, e.g., Maurice J. Goldbloom, "Nixon So Far," *Commentary* (March 1970), pp. 30–31; Norman Podhoretz, "A Note on Vietnamization," *Commentary* (May 1971), p. 9.
17. See Kissinger, *Diplomacy*, pp. 764–85.
18. Dobrynin, *In Confidence*, p. 195.
19. See ibid., pp. 337–38.
20. Press conference, Moscow, July 3, 1974, in *Department of State Bulletin*, Vol. 71, No. 1831, July 29, 1974, p. 215. See also the discussion of this episode in *Years of Upheaval*, pp. 1174–77, and in my July 31, 1979, testimony on the SALT II treaty before the Senate Foreign Relations Committee.
21. Coral Bell, *The Diplomacy of Détente: The Kissinger Era* (London: Martin Robertson, 1977), p. 222.


## 4: JACKSON, ARMS CONTROL, AND JEWISH EMIGRATION

1. See Kissinger, *White House Years*, pp. 265–69.
2. Nineteen ninety-one figures from International Institute for Strategic Studies, *The Military Balance, 1991–1992* (London: IISS, 1991), pp. 219–20.
3. See Phyllis Schlafly and Chester Ward, *Ambush at Vladivostok* (Alton, Illinois: Père Marquette Press, 1976).
4. William G. Hyland, *Mortal Rivals: Superpower Relations from Nixon to Reagan* (New York: Random House, 1987), p. 200.
5. See Kissinger, *Years of Upheaval*, p. 991.

## 5: CHINA AND ITS LEADERS

1. See, for example, our discussions in July 1971 on the communiqué of my visit in Kissinger, *White House Years,* pp. 752–53; in October 1971 on the Shanghai Communiqué draft, pp. 781–83; and during Nixon's February 1972 visit, pp. 1071–87.
2. Ibid., p. 1060, where a slightly different translation conveying the same sense of Mao's thought was used.
3. On the "Year of Europe," see Kissinger, *Years of Upheaval,* Chapter 5.

## 6: THE NEW PRESIDENCY

1. John Osborne, *White House Watch: The Ford Years* (Washington, D.C.: New Republic Books, 1977), pp. xxiv–xxv.
2. See Kissinger, *Years of Upheaval,* p. 1155.
3. Ford, *A Time to Heal,* pp. 319–24.
4. Haig's account of his complex relationship with Nixon and me can be found in Alexander M. Haig, Jr., with Charles McCarry, *Inner Circles: How America Changed the World* (New York: Warner Books, 1992).
5. Osborne, *White House Watch,* p. xxix.
6. Ibid., p. xxviii.

## 7: CYPRUS, A CASE STUDY IN ETHNIC CONFLICT

1. Letter from President Lyndon B. Johnson, June 5, 1964, to Prime Minister Ismet Inonu of Turkey (as released by the White House on January 15, 1966), reprinted in *The Middle East Journal* (Washington, D.C.: The Middle East Institute), Summer 1966, pp. 386–93.
2. See Kissinger, *Years of Upheaval,* Chapter 24.
3. Roy Jenkins, *A Life at the Centre* (London: Macmillan, 1991), p. 441.
4. Much of the following analysis is adapted from this briefing.
5. Background briefing to reporters in San Clemente, July 20, 1974 (White House press release).
6. An excellent summary of our various telephone calls can be found in James Callahan, *Time and Chance* (London: Collins, 1987), pp. 342, 344–46.
7. Text of a statement by the Department of State issued at the noon briefing August 13, 1974, concerning Cyprus:

   The United States has been playing an active role in the negotiations. The President and the Secretary have been in daily touch about them. The Secretary has been in frequent contact with Prime Minister Ecevit, including four times by telephone during the past twenty-four hours, and with Foreign Secretary Callaghan by telephone and Prime Minister Karamanlis by letter and with Cypriot leaders.

   The United States position is as follows:
   (A) We recognize the position of the Turkish community on Cyprus requires considerable improvement and protection.
   (B) We have supported a greater degree of autonomy for them.
   (C) The parties are negotiating on one or more Turkish autonomous areas.
   The avenues of diplomacy have not been exhausted and therefore *the U.S. would consider a resort to military action unjustified. We have made this clear to all parties.*

## 8: FORD INHERITS THE DEBATE OVER DÉTENTE

1. Remarks of former Secretary of State George P. Shultz before the House-Senate committee investigating Iran-contra, July 23, 1987, in George P. Shultz, *Turmoil and Triumph: My Years as Secretary of State* (New York: Charles Scribner's Sons, 1993), p. 915.

2. "Détente: An Evaluation," reprinted for the use of the Subcommittee on Arms Control of the Committee on Armed Services, U.S. Senate, 93rd Congress, 2d Session (Washington, D.C.: U.S. Government Printing Office, 1974).

3. George F. Will, "Détente Looks a Lot Like the Cold War," *Washington Post,* October 30, 1973.

4. Hans J. Morgenthau, "Missing a Moral Consensus, The Danger of Détente," *The New Leader,* Vol. 56, No. 19 (October 1, 1973), pp. 5–7.

5. Statement before the Senate Committee on Foreign Relations, Hearings on Détente, 93rd Congress, 2d Session, September 19, 1974; reprinted "Détente with the Soviet Union: The Reality of Competition and the Imperative of Cooperation," *Department of State Bulletin,* October 14, 1974 (Washington, D.C.: U.S. Government Printing Office, 1974), p. 506.

6. Ibid.

7. Ibid.

8. "Détente," Hearings before the Senate Foreign Relations Committee, 93rd Congress, 2d Session, "On United States Relations with Communist Countries," August 15, 20, 21; September 10, 12, 18, 19, 24, 25; October 1, 8, 1974 (Washington, D.C.: U.S. Government Printing Office, 1975), p. 260.

9. Ibid., p. 269.

10. Ibid., p. 275.

11. Statement of Senator Henry M. Jackson at a press conference in the White House Briefing Room on October 18, 1974 (White House press release).

12. Following is the exchange of letters between me and Senator Henry Jackson of October 18, 1974.

October 18, 1974

Dear Senator Jackson:

I am writing to you, as the sponsor of the Jackson Amendment, in regard to the Trade Bill (H.R. 10710) which is currently before the Senate and in whose early passage the Administration is deeply interested. As you know, Title IV of that Bill, as it emerged from the House, is not acceptable to the Administration. At the same time, the Administration respects the objectives with regard to emigration from the USSR that are sought by means of the stipulations in Title IV, even if it cannot accept the means employed. It respects in particular your own leadership in this field.

To advance the purposes we share both with regard to passage of the Trade Bill and to emigration from the USSR, and on the basis of discussions that have been conducted with Soviet representatives, I should like on behalf of the Administration to inform you that we have been assured that the following criteria and practices will henceforth govern emigration from the USSR.

First, punitive actions against individuals seeking to emigrate from the USSR would be violations of Soviet laws and regulations and will therefore not be permitted by the Government of the USSR. In particular, this applies to various kinds of intimidation or reprisal, such as, for example, the firing of a person from his job, his demotion to tasks beneath his professional qualifications, and his subjection to public or other kinds of recrimination.

Second, no unreasonable or unlawful impediments will be placed in the way of persons desiring to make application for emigration, such as interference with travel or communications necessary to complete an application, the withholding of necessary documentation and other obstacles including kinds frequently employed in the past.

Third, applications for emigration will be processed in order of receipt, including those previously filed, and on a non-discriminatory basis as regards the place of residence, race, religion, national origin and professional status of the applicant. Concerning professional status, we are informed that there are limitations on emigration under Soviet law in the case of individuals holding certain security clearances, but that such individuals who desire to emigrate will be informed of the date on which they may expect to become eligible for emigration.

Fourth, hardship cases will be processed sympathetically and expeditiously; persons imprisoned who, prior to imprisonment, expressed an interest in emigrating, will be given prompt consideration for emigration upon their release; and sympathetic consideration may be given to the early release of such persons.

Fifth, the collection of the so-called emigration tax on emigrants which was suspended last year will remain suspended.

Sixth, with respect to all the foregoing points, we will be in a position to bring to the attention of the Soviet leadership indications that we may have that these criteria and practices are not being applied. Our representations, which would include but not necessarily be limited to the precise matters enumerated in the foregoing points, will receive sympathetic consideration and response.

Finally, it will be our assumption that with the application of the criteria practices and procedures set forth in this letter, the rate of emigration from the USSR would begin to rise promptly from the 1973 level and would continue to rise to correspond to the number of applicants.

I understand that you and your associates have, in addition, certain understandings incorporated in a letter dated today respecting the foregoing criteria and practices which will henceforth govern emigration from the USSR which you wish the President to accept as appropriate guidelines to determine whether the purposes sought through Title IV of the Trade Bill and further specified in our exchange of correspondence in regard to the emigration practices of non-market economy countries are being fulfilled. You have submitted this letter to me and I wish to advise you on behalf of the President that the understandings in your letter will be among the considerations to be applied by the President in exercising the authority provided for in Sec. ____* of Title IV of the Trade Bill.

I believe that the contents of this letter represent a good basis, consistent with our shared purposes, for proceeding with an acceptable formulation of Title IV of the Trade Bill, including procedures for periodic review, so that normal trading relations may go forward for the mutual benefit of the US and the USSR.

Best regards,
Henry A. Kissinger

* Statutory language authorizing the President to waive the restrictions in Title IV of the Trade Bill under certain conditions will be added as a new (and as yet undesignated) subsection.

October 18, 1974
Dear Mr. Secretary:

Thank you for your letter of October 18 which I have now had an opportunity to review. Subject to the further understandings and interpretations outlined in this letter, I agree that we have achieved a suitable basis upon which to modify Title IV by incorporating within it a provision that would enable the President to waive subsections designated (a) and (b) in Sec. 402 of Title IV as passed by the House in circumstances that would substantially promote the objectives of Title IV.

It is our understanding that the punitive actions, intimidation or reprisals that will not be permitted by the Government of the USSR include the use of punitive conscription against persons seeking to emigrate, or members of their families; and the bringing of criminal actions against persons in circumstances that suggest a relationship between their desire to emigrate and the criminal prosecution against them.

Second, we understand that among the unreasonable impediments that will no longer be placed in the way of persons seeking to emigrate is the requirement that adult applicants receive the permission of their parents or other relatives.

Third, we understand that the special regulations to be applied to persons who have had access to genuinely sensitive classified information will not constitute an unreasonable impediment to emigration. In this connection we would expect such persons to become eligible for emigration within three years of the date on which they last were exposed to sensitive and classified information.

Fourth, we understand that the actual number of emigrants would rise promptly from the 1973 level and would continue to rise to correspond to the number of applicants, and may therefore exceed 60,000 per annum. We would consider a benchmark—a minimum standard of initial compliance—to be the issuance of visas at the rate of 60,000 per annum; and we understand that the President proposes to use the same benchmark as the minimum standard of initial compliance. Until such time as the actual number of emigrants corresponds to the number of applicants the benchmark figure will not include categories of persons whose emigration has been the subject of discussion between Soviet officials and other European governments.

In agreeing to provide discretionary authority to waive the provisions of subsections designated (a) and (b) in Sec. 402 of Title IV as passed by the House, we share your anticipation of good faith in the implementation of the assurances contained in your letter of October 18 and the understandings conveyed by this letter. In particular, with respect to paragraphs three and four of your letter we wish it to be understood that the enumeration of types of punitive action and unreasonable impediments is not and cannot be considered comprehensive or complete, and that nothing in this exchange of correspondence shall be construed as permitting types of punitive action or unreasonable impediments not enumerated therein.

Finally, in order adequately to verify compliance with the standard set forth in these letters, we understand that communication by telephone, telegraph and post will be permitted.

Sincerely yours,<br>Henry M. Jackson, U.S.S.

Following is the White House clarification of October 21, 1974, issued by the White House Press Office:

The President would like to clarify one point regarding assurances on immigration as related in the exchange of letters published by Senator Jackson on October 18, a point which appears to have been widely misunderstood.

All the assurances we have received from the Soviet Union are contained in the letter from the Secretary of State to Senator Jackson. This letter, as I am sure you have already noted, does not contain specific numbers. Rather, it sets forth the principles to be applied in handling applications and visas of those wishing to immigrate.

The Senator, in his reply to the letter of the Secretary of State, set forth certain guidelines or understandings which he proposes to apply in the renewal when the President's waiver authority is considered by the Congress. With respect to these guidelines or understandings in the Senator's letter, the Administration has agreed only that, as stated in the Secretary's letter, they "will be among considerations to be applied by the President" in exercising authority provided for in the Trade Bill.

## 9: A VISIT WITH BREZHNEV

1. Dobrynin, *In Confidence*, pp. 362, 441.
2. The figure comes from an authoritative work by General Dmitri A. Volkogonov, *Stalin: Triumph and Tragedy* (London: Weidenfeld & Nicolson, 1991), p. 505.
3. See Kissinger, *White House Years*, Chapter 28.
4. Dobrynin, *In Confidence*, p. 330.
5. Eduard Shevardnadze, "The 19th All-Union CPSU Conference: Foreign Policy and Diplomacy," July 25, 1988, in *International Affairs* (Moscow), No. 10 (October 1988), pp. 8–12, 19–21. See also other examples in Peter W. Rodman, *More Precious Than Peace: The Cold War and the Struggle for the Third World* (New York: Charles Scribner's, 1994), pp. 309–11.
6. See Kissinger, *Years of Upheaval*, pp. 465–67.
7. Ibid., pp. 1173–74.
8. Text of Soviet Foreign Minister Andrei Gromyko's letter of October 26, 1974, later released

by Moscow to the media on December 18, 1974—carried by Moscow TASS in English and Moscow Domestic Service in Russian, with some variations in translation. FBIS, USSR International Affairs—United States, December 19, 1974:

Esteemed Mr State Secretary, I consider it necessary to draw your attention to the question pertaining to the publication in the United States of material known to you which touches upon the departure from the Soviet Union of a certain category of Soviet citizens.

I have to state frankly that the mentioned material, including the correspondence between you and Senator Jackson create a distorted impression regarding our position and the statement made by us to the American side on this question.

Explaining, in response to your wishes, the true state of affairs, we stress that this question in itself is entirely a matter of the internal competence of our state. We have warned that in this matter we acted and shall continue to act solely in accordance with the legislation we have in this connection.

Nothing is being said, at the present time, about this matter. At the same time attempts are being made to make the explanations we made regarding the procedure of the departure of Soviet citizens from the Soviet Union appear as some kind of assurance and almost pledge, and even some sort of figures are being mentioned regarding the supposed number of such citizens. There is talk about the expected increase in the numbers compared with past years.

We resolutely reject such an interpretation. What we said, and you Mr State Secretary know this well, concerned only the real situation on the given question.

Even when there was discussion in the way of informing you on the true state of affairs, regarding figures, the opposite was pointed out, that is the trend toward the decrease in the number of persons wishing to leave the USSR to reside permanently in other countries.

We consider it important that in view of the fundamental significance of this matter there should be no vagueness at all in relation to the Soviet Union's position.

[Signed] [Andrei] Gromyko, USSR Foreign Minister.

## 10: VLADIVOSTOK AND THE CRISIS IN AMERICAN-SOVIET RELATIONS

1. Hyland, *Mortal Rivals,* p. 76.
2. Dobrynin, *In Confidence,* p. 329.
3. Ibid., p. 330.
4. See Joint United States–Soviet Statement on the Limitation of Strategic Offensive Arms, November 24, 1974, and Joint Communiqué Following Discussions with General Secretary Brezhnev of the Soviet Union, November 24, 1974, in *Public Papers of the Presidents of the United States, Gerald R. Ford, 1974* (Washington, D.C.: U.S. Government Printing Office, 1975), pp. 657–62.
5. Public statement released by the Arms Control Association on December 11, 1974, Washington, D.C.
6. Hyland, *Mortal Rivals,* p. 100.
7. "Vladivostok Arms Pact," *New York Times,* November 29, 1974.
8. James Reston, "Ceiling but No Floor," *New York Times,* December 6, 1974.
9. "The Vladivostok Accord," *Washington Post,* December 6, 1974.
10. Press conference, December 3, 1974, *Department of State Bulletin* (Washington, D.C.: U.S. Government Printing Office), Vol. 71, No. 1853, December 30, 1974, p. 913.
11. Statement before the Senate Committee on Finance, December 3, 1974, ibid., p. 937.
12. Press conference, January 14, 1975, in *Department of State Bulletin* (Washington, D.C.: U.S. Government Printing Office), Vol. 72, No. 1858, February 3, 1975, p. 140.
13. Ibid.
14. Dobrynin, *In Confidence,* p. 338.
15. Ibid., pp. 338–39.

## 11: THE INTELLIGENCE INVESTIGATIONS

1. Comments of CIA Director Colby on December 23, 1974: "What we are talking about is the program that began many years ago of finding out if there are many connections with American businessmen. We did it a number of years ago. Not just a Nixon problem. Began in '67 or '68, something like that. You know, when the antiwar effort and the Black Panthers and stuff like that. You remember a report—you probably don't. We have written up various reports, mainly for the FBI. Then the Huston Plan was set up—remember that? That did not happen, but an interevaluation committee was set up. I think [former Justice Department official Robert] Mardian was one of the major features of that. That continued the work of that, but CIA was only involved in the foreign aspect of it. If you develop some coverage of an American abroad, you obviously have a piece of paper here with his name on it, and it would be passed to the FBI in this connection. That is what we told him. There were undoubtedly some individual misdeeds in this process. You don't run a big operation without stepping over the edge once in a while. There were undoubtedly a few. That is one track. But the second track is that, for many, many years and in great part under the rubric of the security of our operation, there were certain steps taken like—you will remember, there was a case in Georgetown where some people found some classified information; our security officers went in and entered the house and stole the classified information back. That was about '66. I have forgotten who it was. There were a series of things. About a year or so ago here in the Agency, we went out and told all our people if you know of anything questionable that CIA has ever done, you report it now, and we collected up a collection of this kind of thing. Some things that we really should not do. I bundled them together and briefed my two chairmen on it, and I let the skeletons sit quietly in the closet, hoping they would stay there. Obviously someone has gotten a smell of a certain number of those. I think a certain number of ex-employees. Hersh put those two tracks into one track."
2. Kissinger, *White House Years*, p. 653.
3. Nixon became involved because he was outraged by the refusal of the State Department and CIA to put our covert funds behind a single candidate. Because the most likely victor was considered too conservative, the money was split between two democratic parties, one of which had no chance; the split helped Allende to his narrow victory.
4. For details, see Kissinger, *White House Years*, Chapter 17, and Kissinger, *Years of Upheaval*, Chapter 9.
5. Seymour M. Hersh, "CIA Chief Tells House of $8 Million Campaign Against Allende in '70–'73," *New York Times*, September 8, 1974.
6. Seymour M. Hersh, "Senate Staff Report on Chile Accuses Helms and 3 of Contempt," *New York Times*, September 17, 1974.
7. President Ford's press conference, September 16, 1974, in Ford, *Public Papers, 1974*, p. 151.
8. Ibid., pp. 150–51.
9. Seymour M. Hersh, "CIA Is Linked to Strikes in Chile That Beset Allende," *New York Times*, September 20, 1974.
10. The members of the commission were John T. Connor, Secretary of Commerce under President Johnson; C. Douglas Dillon, Secretary of the Treasury under Presidents Kennedy and Johnson and under secretary of state under President Eisenhower; Erwin N. Griswold, former Harvard Law School dean and Solicitor General under Presidents Johnson and Nixon; Lane Kirkland, secretary-treasurer of the AFL-CIO; Lyman L. Lemnitzer, former Chairman of the Joint Chiefs of Staff; Ronald Reagan, recently retired governor of California; and Dr. Edgar F. Shannon, Jr., former president of the University of Virginia. As the executive director of the commission, the President named David W. Belin, who, in 1964, had served as assistant counsel on the President's Commission on the Assassination of President Kennedy (the Warren Commission).
11. William Colby and Peter Forbath, *Honorable Men: My Life in the CIA* (New York: Simon & Schuster, 1978), p. 402.

12. H. Res. 138, 94th Congress, 1st Session, February 19, 1975.
13. Letter from DCI W. E. Colby to Chairman Frank Church of Select Committee, dated March 11, 1975, attached to CIA Employee Bulletin No. 442, March 12, 1975.
14. Colby and Forbath, *Honorable Men*, p. 407.
15. Ibid., pp. 14–15.
16. Ibid., pp. 436–37.
17. *Report to the President by the Commission on CIA Activities Within the United States* (Washington, D.C.: U.S. Government Printing Office, 1975), p. 10 (the Rockefeller Report).
18. Ibid., pp. 161–68.
19. Ibid., pp. 81–82.
20. Comments on the "CIA and FBI Revelations" by Senator Walter Mondale, interview with *Time* editors and staff members, *Time* magazine, July 26, 1976, p. 22.
21. U.S. Senate, *Hearings Before the Select Committee to Study Governmental Operations with Respect to Intelligence Activities* (the Church Committee Report), Volume 1, 94th Congress, 1st Session (Washington, D.C.: U.S. Government Printing Office, 1975), p. 17.
22. Ibid., pp. 161–62, pp. 166–68 passim.
23. Senator Church's position as reported in Spencer Rich, "Goldwater Urges an End to Intelligence Probes," *Washington Post*, November 5, 1975.
24. U.S. Senate, *Alleged Assassination Plots Involving Foreign Leaders: An Interim Report of the Select Committee to Study Governmental Operations with Respect to Intelligence Activities*, 94th Congress, 1st Session, Report No. 94-465 (Washington, D.C.: U.S. Government Printing Office, 1975), pp. 4–5.
25. See Kissinger, *White House Years*, p. 674.
26. U.S. Senate, *Final Report of the Select Committee to Study Governmental Operations with Respect to Intelligence Activities*, 94th Congress, 2d Session, Report No. 94-755 (Washington, D.C.: U.S. Government Printing Office, 1976), p. 427.
27. Colby and Forbath, *Honorable Men*, pp. 431–32.
28. U.S. House of Representatives, Committee on Standards of Official Conduct, *Report on Investigation Pursuant to H. Res. 1042, Concerning Unauthorized Publication of the Report of the Select Committee on Intelligence*, 94th Congress, 2d Session, Report No. 94-1754 (Washington, D.C.: U.S. Government Printing Office, October 1, 1976), p. 31.
29. U.S. House of Representatives, *Hearings Before the Select Committee on Intelligence, US Intelligence Agencies and Activities: The Performance of the Intelligence Community*, 94th Congress, 1st Session, Part 2 (Washington, D.C.: U.S. Government Printing Office, 1975), p. 673.
30. "Pike Unit Shuns CIA Data Given with Restriction," including reports by Lawrence L. Knutson and George Lardner, Jr., *Washington Post*, September 18, 1975, and John M. Crewdson, "Ford Is Rebuffed by a House Panel on Offer of Data," *New York Times*, September 18, 1975.
31. House Hearings, Select Committee, *The Performance of the Intelligence Community*, Part 2, p. 683ff.
32. Ibid., pp. 913–19.
33. "Pike Urged to Drop Bid for Reports," *Washington Post*, October 18, 1975.
34. "Neo-McCarthyism?," *New York Times*, October 19, 1975.
35. Letter to the Editor from George Kennan, published in the *Washington Post*, October 14, 1975.
36. Pike Committee requests included:
    (1) All 40 Committee decisions since January 20, 1965, approving covert action projects;
    (2) Minutes of all National Security Council (NSC) Intelligence Committee, Working Group, and Economic Intelligence Subcommittee meetings held since the inception of these groups;
    (3) All Washington Special Actions Group meeting minutes relating to the October 1973 Middle East War, the 1974 Cyprus crisis, and the Portugal coup of April 24, 1974;
    (4) All intelligence reports furnished to the NSC by the CIA, the Defense Intelligence

Agency (DIA), and the National Security Agency (NSA) between October 15 and October 28, 1973, relating to the 1973 Middle East War and the military activities of the Soviet Union;

(5) All documents furnished by the Arms Control and Disarmament Agency's Standing Consultative Commission, CIA, DIA, and NSA to the NSC since May 1972 relating to adherence to the SALT agreement of 1972.

37. John M. Crewdson, "House Committee Report Finds CIA Understated Prices of Angolan Arms," *New York Times,* January 20, 1976. See also Norman Kempster, "U.S. Sent Arms to Kurds Despite CIA Opposition, House Panel Claims," *Washington Star,* January 20, 1976.

38. George Lardner, Jr., "Pike Draft Critical of Kissinger," *Washington Post,* January 21, 1976.

39. U.S. House of Representatives, *Proceedings of the Select Committee on Intelligence, US Intelligence Agencies and Activities: Committee Proceedings-II,* 94th Congress, 2d Session, Part 6 (Washington, D.C.: U.S. Government Printing Office, 1976), p. 2041.

40. Ibid., p. 2042.

41. "The Basis of CIA Oversight," *Washington Post,* January 30, 1976.

42. Schorr was suspended by CBS as a result of a controversy growing out of his reporting on this issue. For a full account, see Lesley Stahl's book *Reporting Live* (New York: Simon & Schuster, 1999), pp. 52–54.

43. Press conference of February 12, 1976, in *Department of State Bulletin,* Vol. 74, No. 1915, March 8, 1976, p. 291.

44. U.S. Senate, *Oversight of US Government Intelligence Functions, Hearings Before the Committee on Government Operations on S. 317, S. 189, S. Con. Res. 4, S. 2893, S. 2865,* 94th Congress, 2d Session, testimony on February 5, 1976 (Washington, D.C.: U.S. Government Printing Office, 1976), p. 439.

45. Stan Crock, "Schlesinger Says Leaks Curb CIA," *Washington Post,* August 3, 1975.

46. Daniel Southerland, "What's Left in CIA Bag of Tricks," *The Christian Science Monitor,* March 23, 1979.

47. Leonard Downie, Jr., "4 British Leaders Knew of Spy Deal," *Washington Post,* November 22, 1979.

48. Interview with James Schlesinger, "America Must Show 'Steadfastness and Strength,'" *Washington Post,* February 3, 1980.

49. United States Intelligence Activities, Executive Order 11905, February 18, 1976, in *Federal Register,* Vol. 41, No. 34, February 19, 1976, Part 3, pp. 7703–38. The executive order was announced and discussed by President Ford at a news conference on February 17, 1976, and cited in the President's Special Message to the Congress Proposing Legislation to Reform the United States Intelligence Community, of February 18, 1976. See Ford, *Public Papers, 1976,* pp. 348–68.

50. U.S. Senate, Government Operations Committee, *Oversight of U.S. Government Intelligence Functions,* p. 421.

51. Robert M. Gates, "CIA and the Making of American Foreign Policy," address at the Woodrow Wilson School of Public and International Affairs, Princeton University, September 29, 1987. When Gates published this speech as an article, he inserted the adverb "involuntarily" in reference to the equidistance. Robert M. Gates, "The CIA and American Foreign Policy," *Foreign Affairs,* Vol. 66, No. 2 (Winter 1987/88), p. 225.

## 12: FORD AND MIDDLE EAST DIPLOMACY

1. On the PLO charter, see Y. Harkabi, *The Palestinian Covenant and Its Meaning* (London: Vallentine, Mitchell, 1979). Harkabi, former chief of Israeli intelligence, later changed his mind and became a strong advocate of the Oslo accords.

2. See Kissinger, *Years of Upheaval,* Chapter 17.

3. Dobrynin, *In Confidence,* pp. 222, 306, 325.

4. See Kissinger, *White House Years,* especially Chapter 10, and *Years of Upheaval,* pp. 199–204.
5. See Kissinger, *White House Years,* pp. 579–80.
6. Ibid., Chapter 30, and Kissinger, *Years of Upheaval,* Chapter 6.
7. A detailed account of these negotiations can be found in Kissinger, *Years of Upheaval,* Chapters 13, 17, 18, 21, and 23.
8. See, e.g., the report of a Brookings Institution Middle East Study Group, "Toward Peace in the Middle East" (Washington, D.C.: The Brookings Institution, 1975); Zbigniew Brzezinski, François Duchene, and Kiichi Saeki, "Beyond Step by Step—Peace in an International Framework," *Foreign Policy,* No. 19 (Summer 1975); Stanley Hoffmann, "A New Policy for Israel," *Foreign Affairs,* Vol. 53, No. 3 (April 1975).
9. Yitzhak Rabin, *The Rabin Memoirs* (Berkeley: University of California Press, 1979), pp. 421–22.

## 13: ONE SHUTTLE TOO MANY

1. Harold H. Saunders and Cecilia Albin, *Sinai II: The Politics of International Mediation, 1974–1975,* FPI Case Studies No. 17 (Washington, D.C.: Foreign Policy Institute, Paul H. Nitze School of Advanced International Studies, Johns Hopkins University, 1993), pp. 60–61.
2. See, e.g., Shimon Peres and Robert Littell, *For the Future of Israel* (Baltimore: Johns Hopkins University Press, 1998).
3. See also Leah Rabin, *Rabin: Our Life, His Legacy* (New York: G. P. Putnam's Sons, 1997), pp. 157–58.

## 14: SINAI II AND THE ROAD TO PEACE

1. Ford, *Public Papers, 1975,* pp. 396–97.
2. Ford, *A Time to Heal,* p. 247.
3. Interview with Walter Cronkite, Eric Sevareid, and Bob Schieffer of CBS News, April 21, 1975, in Ford, *Public Papers, 1975,* p. 552.
4. Remarks by Prime Minister Yitzhak Rabin to President Ford, June 11, 1975, the White House: "Mr. President, I prefer to go to the problems as I see them. I want to start with this basis: If there is any country eager for peace in the area, it is Israel. Israel has fought many wars and lost many people. We know we cannot achieve peace by military means; conditions do not allow this. It happened in 1949, in 1956, in 1967, in 1973. We know that force will not bring a political settlement. Clausewitz said that war is the extension of diplomacy by other means, but the objective in war is to destroy the opposing force, to impose one's will. We cannot impose our will. Military means will not solve the problem. We have no interest in war but we have an interest in defending ourselves. Without being able to defend ourselves we will not survive. When we talk of peace, I mean by this our existence as a Jewish state with boundaries we can defend with defenses—not to depend on others to send their own troops. That would be the end of us.

"International guarantees have no meaning whatsoever with us. We have experienced them over many years. We have tried mixed armistice commissions, UNTSO, UNEF. We don't believe in putting our defense in the hands [of others]. To drag a major power into a conflict which is local would be a serious mistake. We have never asked for one American soldier to aid in our defense.

"We have tried for peace from 1949 to 1967, without results. There is an accumulation of suspicion, which must be cleared on the way to peace.

"We have two specific ways. One is the one you mentioned: we would like to solve all the problems with all of the countries at the same time and bring about a final peace. And even if such a peace could take place it would be first a peace by diplomats and governments and not by people. In order to change the attitudes in the area it would take a very long time. Even Sadat does not expect true peace; he distinguishes between the end of belligerency and normalization of relations.

"Israel has its position about peace. There are three key issues on which I fear the gap is wide open with respect to an overall settlement and has never been bridged in the past by diplomacy: First, the nature of peace. The Arabs talk about the end of the war, the end of belligerency; for us it is much more. We mean normalization of relations.

"Second, the boundaries of peace. The Arabs stress total Israeli withdrawal to the pre-June 1967 lines, which we consider practically indefensible. In the past when they moved their troops, we either had to wait for the attack or preempt. Take Egypt. Their forces have a one-and-a-quarter million, without mobilization. This would require total mobilization on our part. A half a million is the most we can mobilize. It is the highest ratio in the world. We mobilized about 40,000 in the 1973 war. We have revised our system to get the utmost. So the problem for Israel as far as an overall settlement is concerned is not to be in a position in a few years, whenever they move, we have to go to a preemptive war. The real fact that they can move near to our borders means that we have to mobilize and they can destroy our economy by requiring total mobilization.

"The third issue is the Palestinian issue.

"We cannot withdraw to the 1967 borders in the Sinai. We cannot go down from the Golan Heights even in the context of peace. There can be a stationing of forces in Sharm el-Shaykh for example, and there must be a land linkage to it. And on the Golan for example, for a period of say 10 to 20 years, until there is a change of attitudes that occurs with the Arabs. The concept of stationing forces and changing of attitudes, it is applicable to Egypt as well.

"As to the West Bank, it is more complicated. Here there is an issue both of defense as well as the Palestinian issue. What the Arabs say is not new and hasn't changed since Nasser. They say the solution is creation of what is now an Arafat state. When Arafat is asked what he has in mind, he says he has a dream of a secular state, which would eliminate the Jewish state of Israel. It would require the elimination of all Jews who have arrived since 1923 or even 1948. A Palestinian state would mean that with Strela missiles they could shoot down planes at Tel Aviv airport. Therefore, as we see it, a return to the 1967 borders and the establishment of a Palestinian state means that Israel cannot survive.

"I had five meetings with Hussein last year. I said to him, 'You have proposed a federation as a solution. If we can reach an agreement on a confederation in which Israel would be involved for about 30 years with open borders, with minimum changes—though there is a complicated problem of Jerusalem—we could also include the bulk of the Gaza Strip.' We would be prepared to make an agreement with Hussein on this basis. It was refused by Hussein. We also put to him the Allon plan as a basis for negotiation and this was refused.

"Therefore, in terms of the readiness of Israel for a final peace and the needs for Israel's security, the 1967 lines with respect to Egypt and Syria [do] not allow for security arrangements which are required for a small country of three million people against a composition of states who total 60-to-65 million. We are ready to try to achieve peace, but the gap on these three issues is wide. We have not sensed an Arab readiness to come close to the essentials of peace as we see them from our point of view.

"I recall that in 1973 Dr. Kissinger was willing to explore the concept of security and sovereignty. But Sadat had probably decided on a war. I wish that we could have reached an overall peace. That is a real peace. I don't want the Israelis to be like the Christians in Lebanon. The fate of minorities in Arab lands—Christians, Kurds, Jews—is bad. The reason why the French set up the State of Lebanon is that they wanted to save the Christian minority in Syria. Ben-Gurion said Israel can win 20 wars and it will not solve the problem; but the Arabs need to win only once and it would mean the end of Israel.

"What I have said is not popular in Israel. There are people who fought three times in the Sinai. Eisenhower, under the threat of the Soviet Union, brought about a withdrawal from the Sinai. And he said he hoped it would bring conditions of peace.

"We can consider an overall peace, but we cannot budge from the positions which I have described. If there is a Geneva Conference, we will bring our positions there and we will struggle there, because we believe in our positions.

## 15: INDOCHINA TRAGEDY—THE BEGINNING OF THE END

1. See Kissinger, *White House Years,* Chapters 8, 12, 23, 25, 27, 31, 32, 33, and 34. Also, Kissinger, *Years of Upheaval,* Chapters 2 and 8.
2. See, e.g., the illuminating memoir by David Horowitz, *Radical Son: A Generational Odyssey* (New York: Free Press, 1997), Parts 3 and 4, and James Webb, "Peace? Or Defeat? What Did the Vietnam War Protesters Want?," *The American Enterprise,* Vol. 8, No. 3 (May/June 1997), pp. 46–49.
3. My early exposure to Vietnam is described in Kissinger, *White House Years,* pp. 230–35.
4. Henry A. Kissinger, "The Viet Nam Negotiations," *Foreign Affairs,* Vol. 47, No. 2 (January 1969), pp. 211–34.
5. Kissinger, *White House Years,* p. 1432.
6. E.g., Horowitz, *Radical Son,* p. 202.
7. See, e.g., President John F. Kennedy's contribution to the genre in Kissinger, *White House Years,* p. 895 and Note 7 on p. 1488, and in Kissinger, *Years of Upheaval,* Note 5 on p. 1236.
8. Statements on United States enforcement of the Paris Agreement included the following:

*President Nixon's Address to the Nation, January 23, 1973:*
[T]he terms of the agreement must be scrupulously adhered to. We shall do everything the agreement requires of us, and we shall expect the other parties to do everything it requires of them. We shall also expect other interested nations to help insure that the agreement is carried out and peace is maintained.

*Kissinger, Press Conference. January 24, 1973:*
QUESTION: If a peace treaty is violated and if the ICC proves ineffective, will the United States ever again send troops into Vietnam?
KISSINGER: I don't want to speculate on hypothetical situations that we don't expect to arise.

*Deputy Assistant Secretary William Sullivan on NBC-TV's* Meet the Press, *January 28, 1973:*
QUESTION: There's also reports from Saigon today, Mr. Ambassador, that the United States has given official but private assurances to Saigon that we would intervene militarily again if Hanoi commits serious violations. Just what is our commitment? What would we do if a cease-fire breaks down?
SULLIVAN: I am not going to speculate on that, Mr. Rosenfeld. I think you have seen Dr. Kissinger's statement concerning the method in which the agreement has stipulated the requirements for carrying out this accord. There are no inhibitions upon us, but we are not going to discuss any hypothetical questions at this time about what the future prospects may bring.

*Kissinger, Interview on CBS News with Marvin Kalb, February 1, 1973:*
KALB: Dr. Kissinger, I think what I was trying to get at is what happens—and I suppose this question must be asked. In the best of all possible worlds the cease-fire is going to hold. In the world that we live in it may not. President Thieu said in an interview tonight on CBS that he would never call upon American airpower to go back. And Ambassador Sullivan said only last Sunday that there are no inhibitions—I believe were his words—on the use of this airpower. Is that correct?
KISSINGER: That is legally correct.
KALB: Politically and diplomatically?

KISSINGER: We have the right to do this. The question is very difficult to answer in the abstract. It depends on the extent of the challenge, on the nature of the threat, on the circumstances in which it arises; and it would be extremely unwise for a responsible American official at this stage, when the peace is in the process of being established, to give a checklist about what the United States will or will not do in every circumstance that is likely to arise.

For the future that we can foresee, the North Vietnamese are not in a position to launch an overwhelming attack on the South, even if they violate the agreement. What happens after a year or two has to be seen in the circumstances which then exist.

Most of the violations that one can now foresee should be handled by the South Vietnamese.

KALB: So that for the next year or two, if I understand you right, there would be no need for a reinvolvement of American military power?

KISSINGER: Marvin, we did not end this war in order to look for an excuse to reenter it, but it would be irresponsible for us at this moment to give a precise checklist to potential aggressors as to what they can or cannot safely do.

*President Nixon's News Conference, March 15, 1973:*

I will only suggest this: that we have informed the North Vietnamese of our concern about this infiltration and of what we believe it to be, a violation of the cease-fire, the cease-fire and the peace agreement. Our concern has also been expressed to other interested parties. And I would only suggest that based on my actions over the past four years, that the North Vietnamese should not lightly disregard such expressions of concern when they are made with regard to a violation. That is all I will say about it.

*Under Secretary for Political Affairs William Porter, speech in Grand Rapids, March 21, 1973:*

President Nixon has made clear our concern at North Vietnamese infiltration of large amounts of equipment into South Vietnam. If it continued, this infiltration could lead to serious consequences. The North Vietnamese should not lightly disregard our expressions of concern.

*President Nixon's Address to the Nation, March 29, 1973:*

There are still some problem areas. The provisions of the agreement requiring an accounting for all missing in action in Indochina, the provisions with regard to Laos and Cambodia, the provisions prohibiting infiltration from North Vietnam into South Vietnam have not been complied with. We have and will continue to comply with the agreement. We shall insist that North Vietnam comply with the agreement. And the leaders of North Vietnam should have no doubt as to the consequences if they fail to comply with the agreement.

*Defense Secretary Elliot Richardson on NBC-TV's Meet the Press, April 1, 1973:*

RON NESSEN: Mr. Secretary, can you say that the United States will never under any circumstances send military forces back to Indochina?

RICHARDSON: No. I cannot give any categorical assurance, Mr. Nessen. Obviously the future holds possible developments that are unforeseeable now. But certainly we very much hope that this will not be necessary.

NESSEN: And if I ask you the same question about, can you say whether the United States will never bomb again in North or South Vietnam, your answer would be the same?

RICHARDSON: Yes, but of course our hope and expectation is that the cease-fire agreements will be observed.

NESSEN: President Nixon has warned several times North Vietnam that it should have no doubt about the consequences if it violates the cease-fire. What does he mean, what are the consequences?

RICHARDSON: This is obviously something that cannot be spelled out in advance, Mr. Nessen. . . .

They have, I think, had some reason, looking back over the past, to know that the President has been willing to do what has been necessary in order to bring about a negotiated solution and to bring an end to the war.

*Defense Secretary Elliot Richardson to the Senate Armed Services Committee, April 2, 1973:*

QUESTION: There are reports out of South Vietnam today that President Thieu of South Vietnam says that the United States and the South Vietnamese government have an agreement that if there is an offensive, that if the North Vietnamese do come in, that the United States will come back with its airplanes and with its air support? Do we have such a commitment?

RICHARDSON: This is a question simply of very possible contingencies. I wouldn't want to try to amplify on anything he said or to subtract from it. . . .

We, of course, continue to adhere to the proposition that the cease-fire agreements not only have been signed but are in the interest of all the parties and our objective is to assure so far as is possible that they are carried out. . . .

Our job is to reinforce the considerations that will, we trust, lead them to carry out the agreement. . . .

If he [the President] had the constitutional power to carry on the war while winding it down, we think it's a natural extension of this to say that he has the constitutional power to take whatever incidental steps that are now required in order to assure that the cease-fire agreements are carried out.

*US–GVN Communiqué (San Clemente), April 3, 1973:*

Both Presidents, while acknowledging that progress was being made toward military and political settlements in South Vietnam, nevertheless viewed with great concern infiltrations of men and weapons in sizeable numbers from North Vietnam into South Vietnam in violation of the Agreement on Ending the War, and considered that actions which would threaten the basis of the agreement would call for appropriately vigorous reactions. They expressed their conviction that all the provisions of the Agreement, including in particular those concerning military forces and military supplies, must be faithfully implemented if the cease-fire is to be preserved and the prospects for a peaceful settlement are to be assured. President Nixon stated in this connection that the United States views violations of any provision of the Agreement with great and continuing concern.

*Defense Secretary Elliot Richardson, interviewed by newsmen prior to his appearance before the House Appropriations Subcommittee on Defense, April 3, 1973:*

QUESTION: Mr. Secretary, under what conditions might we have to begin bombing in support of the South Vietnamese?

RICHARDSON: It would be one of those questions that it's impossible to answer in general terms. We can only see what develops, and hopefully, what will develop is the full and complete implementation of the cease-fire agreements.

QUESTION: But is it possible that we will have to bomb either North Vietnam or in support of the South Vietnamese army again?

RICHARDSON: It's certainly something we cannot rule out at this time.

*Kissinger, Press Conference, May 2, 1973:*

QUESTION: You say if North Vietnam does not obey the call for an honorable cease-fire, it would risk revived confrontation with us. Could you spell out a little bit more clearly what you mean there [in the Foreign Policy Report]?

KISSINGER: . . . Now, on the confrontation, we have made clear that we mean to have the agreement observed. We are now engaged in an effort to discuss with the North Vietnamese what is required to bring about the strict implementation of the agreement. We have every intention and every incentive to make certain that our side of the agreement is maintained, and to use our influence wherever we can to bring about the strict implementation of the agreement.

But the United States cannot sign a solemn agreement and within weeks have major provisions violated without our making an attempt to indicate it. Now, the particular measures: some of them are, of course, obvious and we would prefer, as we state in the report and as we have stated publicly many times, to move our relationship with the North Vietnamese toward normalization, and to start a process which would accelerate, such as other processes normally have.

So the general thrust of this paragraph is that the tension existing between us certainly cannot ease as rapidly as we want if the agreement is not observed.

*President Nixon's Foreign Policy Report, May 3, 1973:*

We hope that the contending factions will now prefer to pursue their objectives through peaceful means and political competition rather than through the brutal and costly methods of the past. This choice is up to them. We shall be vigilant concerning violations of the Agreement. . . .

Hanoi has two basic choices. The first is to exploit the Vietnam Agreement and press its objectives in Indochina. In this case it would continue to infiltrate men and materiel into South Vietnam, keep its forces in Laos and Cambodia, and through pressures or outright attack renew its aggression against our friends. Such a course would endanger the hard won gains for peace in Indochina. It would risk revived confrontation with us. . . . The second course is for North Vietnam to pursue its objectives peacefully, allowing the historical trends of the region to assert themselves. . . .

The Republic of Vietnam will find us a steady friend. We will continue to deal with its government as the legitimate representative of the South Vietnamese people, while supporting efforts by the South Vietnamese parties to achieve reconciliation and shape their political future. We will provide replacement military assistance within the terms of the Agreement. We expect our friends to observe the Agreement just as we will not tolerate violations by the North Vietnamese or its allies. . . .

We have told Hanoi, privately and publicly, that we will not tolerate violations of the Agreement.

*Kissinger, Press Conference, June 13, 1973:*

QUESTION: Do you feel now that with the signing of the document you have more or less ended your work in the Indochina area or that you will still have a lot of difficulties, especially concerning Cambodia?

KISSINGER: The remaining issues in Indochina will still require significant diplomatic efforts, and we expect to continue them. Of course, we remain committed to the strict implementation of the agreement, and we will maintain our interest in it.

*President Nixon's Message to the House of Representatives, June 27, 1973, opposing the Indochina bombing halt:*

A total halt would virtually remove Communist incentive to negotiate and would thus seriously undercut ongoing diplomatic efforts to achieve a cease-fire in Cambodia. It would effectively reverse the momentum toward lasting peace in Indochina set in motion last January and renewed in the four-party communiqué signed in Paris on June 13. . . .

A Community victory in Cambodia, in turn, would threaten the fragile balance of negotiated agreements, political alignments and military capabilities upon which the overall peace in Southeast Asia depends and on which my assessment of the acceptability of the Vietnam agreements was based.

Finally, and with even more serious global implications, the legislatively imposed acceptance of the United States to Communist violations of the Paris agreements and the conquest of Cambodia by Communist forces would call into question our national commitment not only to the Vietnam settlement but to many other settlements or agreements we have reached or seek to reach with other nations. A serious blow to America's international credibility would have been struck—a blow that would be felt far beyond Indochina.

*Kissinger, Letter to Senator Edward Kennedy, March 25, 1974:*
As a signator of the Paris Agreement, the United States committed itself to strengthening the conditions which made the cease-fire possible and to the goal of the South Vietnamese people's right to self-determination. With these commitments in mind, we continue to provide to the Republic of Vietnam the means necessary for its self-defense and for its economic viability. . . .
We have . . . committed ourselves very substantially, both politically and morally.

*Interview with Tran Van Lam, former South Vietnamese Foreign Minister, April 14, 1975, Saigon (Press Report):*
Foreign Minister Lam stated that President Nixon promised to "react immediately and vigorously" to any large-scale North Vietnamese offensive. But, he added, "no secret agreement was signed."

9. Remarks by Senator Allen to a State Department official, June 25, 1974.
10. As quoted in Allan E. Goodman, *The Lost Peace, America's Search for a Negotiated Settlement of the Vietnam War* (Stanford: Hoover Institution Press, 1978), p. 177.
11. Speech by Senator Jacob Javits on the Senate floor, June 15, 1971, *Congressional Record,* p. 19, 905.
12. Courtney R. Sheldon, "Beneath Viet-blockade Cloud," *Christian Science Monitor,* May 11, 1972.
13. Senator Clifford Case *Briefing on Major Foreign Policy Questions,* Hearing before the Committee on Foreign Relations, U.S. Senate, 93rd Cong., 1st Sess., with Secretary of State William P. Rogers, February 21, 1973 (Washington, D.C.: U.S. Government Printing Office, 1973), p. 19.
14. Following are additional examples of expressions of congressional support for aid to South Vietnam after an American troop withdrawal:
Senator Hubert Humphrey had declared in favor of continued aid on February 10, 1972. The *New York Times* of February 12, 1972 (Robert B. Semple, Jr., "Democrats to Get Briefings on War"), described his position as follows:

Mr. Humphrey . . . said he would provide American military and economic aid—in the form of equipment but not men—after the United States withdraws, but only if South Vietnam comes under renewed attacks and such aid is judged to be in the United States interests.

Senator Mike Mansfield, in early 1973, had supported "backup help of an economic nature" and also "logistical support" for our allies, in accordance with the Nixon Doctrine. He viewed the Paris Agreement as achieving what he wanted—U.S. withdrawal—and acknowledged explicitly that a price had to be paid for it in terms of other commitments:

"And may I say that I would anticipate that the Nixon Doctrine, which was promulgated almost three years ago . . . would now go into effect. That means, as I interpret it, that we would gradually withdraw militarily from various countries throughout Asia and the world, that those countries would henceforth have to depend upon themselves primarily. As far as our allies are concerned, we would be willing to extend backup help of an economic nature, but would not intervene or interfere in any way in the affairs of any nation." (*Congressional Record,* January 26, 1973, p. 2202)

"The Nixon Doctrine as I understand it calls for the gradual withdrawal of our forces all over the world and a greater dependence on the nations with whom we have ties, with the United States furnishing in specific instances only logistical support. . . .

"So as I look at this picture, the things I have been arguing for have, in effect, been achieved. I realize that there is a price attached to such an agreement and after I see the details, after proposals are made to the Congress, it is my intention, insofar as I possibly can, to support proposals of that nature because I wanted the war to end. I wanted our men withdrawn. I wanted our POWs and recoverable MIAs returned home. Those are the factors in which I was most interested. Therefore, I will be most interested and, insofar as I am able, most supportive in any negotiations which led to commitments of various kinds which have not yet been finally consummated, because I think you have to balance that one against the other." ("Briefing," SFRC Hearing, February 21, 1973, pp. 16–17)

Other congressional leaders, not all of them liberals, had spoken in the same vein. Senator Robert Byrd, Democrat of West Virginia, said on the Senate floor on January 26, 1973:

"It is to America's credit . . . that, even in the face of criticism at home and abroad, she did not abandon an ally. . . . We got into this war little-by-little, unable to see where day-to-day and week-to-week events would ultimately lead us. But we became involved in behalf of an ally, and our country kept the promise of its leaders—Presidents Eisenhower, Kennedy, Johnson and Nixon—that we would not desert South Vietnam. I hope I do not live to see the day when this nation, forged in the crucible of courage, will ever forsake the pursuit of national honor. For the honor of a nation is the sum of the honor of its sons and daughters. If honor ever ceases to be a part of the American character there can be no future for our country." (*Congressional Record*, January 26, 1973, p. 2309)

Chairman George Mahon of the House Appropriations Committee was quoted as follows in the *Washington Post* on January 28, 1973:

Following the President's briefing on the Paris Agreement, Chairman Mahon . . . said "it is inherent in the cease-fire that we will continue to provide assistance to South Vietnam and rehabilitation assistance to North Vietnam." He said this must be accepted as a fact of life, and "is a better alternative than continuation of the war."

In Senate hearings in February 1973, Senator Hugh Scott, at testimony by Secretary of State William Rogers, said:

"On the question of aid to Vietnam, I agree with you [Rogers] it would be better not to be frozen into any position because we have no way of knowing what suggestion will come up in regard to possible bilateral aid or U.S. aid." ("Briefing," SFRC Hearing, February 21, 1973, p. 27)

Representative Samuel Stratton of New York made the point in general terms:

"We cannot simply abandon Asia just because we got a cease-fire. Stability in Asia will depend on our continuing participation in that area to maintain that new triangle of Russia, China, and America. If we go isolationist, then Asia polarizes again and peace goes out the window." (*Congressional Record*, January 29, 1973, p. 2519)

Senator Jesse Helms of North Carolina declared:

"We must do what we can to make the truce work. We must share our material strength with the South Vietnamese, our allies, so they can defend themselves if the truce does not work." (*Congressional Record*, January 31, 1973, p. 2732)

15. General Van Tien Dung, *Our Great Spring Victory: An Account of the Liberation of South Vietnam,* translated by John Spragens, Jr. (New York: Monthly Review Press, 1977), pp. 10–12. See also Col.-Gen. Tran Van Tra, *Vietnam: History of the Bulwark B2 Theatre, Vol. 5: Concluding the 30-Years War* (Ho Chi Minh City: Van Nghe Publishing House, 1982), translated in FBIS/JPRS 82783, Southeast Asia Report No. 1247, February 1983, pp. 45, 103.

16. Dung, *Our Great Spring Victory,* p. 15.

17. Michael Barone, Grant Ujifusa, and Douglas Matthews, *The Almanac of American Politics, 1978* (New York: E. P. Dutton, 1978), p. viii.

18. Dung, *Our Great Spring Victory,* pp. 19–20; Tra, *Vietnam: History,* p. 125.

19. Dung, *Our Great Spring Victory,* pp. 22–23. See also "How North Vietnam Won the War," interview with North Vietnamese Col. Bui Tin by Stephen Young, *Wall Street Journal,* August 3, 1995, and Bui Tin, *Following Ho Chi Minh: Memoirs of a North Vietnamese Colonel* (Honolulu: University of Hawaii Press, 1995), pp. 81–82.

20. Ron Nessen, *It Sure Looks Different from the Inside* (Chicago: Playboy Press, 1978), p. 92.

21. Murrey Marder, "U.S. Says It Plans No Reinvolvement in Indochina War," *Washington Post,* January 8, 1975.

22. Bui Tin, *Following Ho Chi Minh,* p. 79; Tra, *Vietnam: History,* p. 125.

23. Dung, *Our Great Spring Victory,* pp. 24–25.

24. Kenneth Reich, "Jackson Opposes Increase in Aid to South Vietnam," *Los Angeles Times,* January 27, 1975.

25. Dung, *Our Great Spring Victory,* p. 24.

26. "The Appalling Options," *Los Angeles Times* editorial, March 6, 1975.

## 16: THE COLLAPSE OF CAMBODIA

1. Vo Nguyen Giap, *Immediate Military Tasks for Switching Over to the General Counter-Offensive* (Ha Dong: Resistance and Administrative Committee of Ha Dong Province, 1950), p. 14, quoted in Gareth Porter, "Vietnamese Policy and the Indochina Crisis," in David W. P. Elliott, ed., *The Third Indochina Conflict* (Boulder, Colorado: Westview Press, 1981), p. 88.

2. For a fuller discussion of our policy in Cambodia, see *White House Years,* pp. 239–54, and Chapter 10.

3. Bundy, *A Tangled Web,* p. 74.

4. See also Kissinger, *Years of Upheaval,* pp. 9–18, 34–37, 335–69; Kissinger, *Diplomacy,* pp. 692–97, and Peter W. Rodman's exchange with William Shawcross in *The American Spectator,* March and July 1981.

5. President Ford's letter to Speaker of the House of Representatives Carl Albert, February 25, 1975, in Ford, *Public Papers, 1975,* pp. 279–80.

6. E.g., Sydney H. Schanberg, "Aid Request for Cambodia Said to Exceed Needs Now," *New York Times,* February 7, 1975.

7. E.g., Commentary by Eric Sevareid, CBS-TV Evening News, February 26, 1975.

8. "Congress and the Mekong," *Baltimore Sun* editorial, February 13, 1975.

9. E.g., Jim Adams, "House Leaders See Aid Losing," *Washington Star-News,* February 26, 1975; "Cambodian Climax," *New York Times* editorial, February 28, 1975.

10. E.g., "Aid for Cambodia," *Washington Post* editorial, February 5, 1975; "U.S. 'Word' Isn't at Stake in the Cambodian Civil War," *Philadelphia Inquirer* editorial, February 27, 1975.

11. E.g., "Despair of Cambodia," *New York Times* editorial, February 26, 1975; "The Sputtering Firepower," *Los Angeles Times* editorial, February 27, 1975.

12. Sydney H. Schanberg, "The Enigmatic Cambodian Insurgents: Reds Appear to Dominate Diverse Bloc," *New York Times,* March 13, 1975.

13. Staff reporter, "Ford Bid for More Arms Aid to Cambodia Is Dealt Two Severe Setbacks in Congress," *Wall Street Journal,* March 14, 1975.

14. See Kissinger, *Years of Upheaval,* p. 59.

15. For a fuller account of the following, see ibid., pp. 341–69.

16. An unrecognizable version of some of these events may be found in William Shawcross, *Sideshow: Kissinger, Nixon and the Destruction of Cambodia* (New York: Simon & Schuster, 1979), Chapter 22.

17. Ibid., p. 341.

18. Statement by Prince Norodom Sihanouk issued in Beijing on April 2, as reported in "Compromise Is Ruled Out by Sihanouk," *Baltimore Sun*, April 3, 1975.

19. Nessen, *It Sure Looks Different from the Inside*, p. 103.

20. Sydney H. Schanberg, "Indochina Without Americans: For Most, a Better Life," *New York Times*, April 13, 1975.

## 17: THE END OF VIETNAM

1. Dung, *Our Great Spring Victory*, p. 95.

2. Ford, *Public Papers, 1975*, p. 416.

3. Ibid., p. 413.

4. "Mr. Ford's Confusion," *New York Times* editorial, April 4, 1975.

5. "Vietnam: The Shell Game Goes On, and On," *Washington Post* editorial, April 4, 1975.

6. "A New Direction in Vietnam," *Los Angeles Times* editorial, April 4, 1975.

7. Press conference, April 5, 1975, in *Department of State Bulletin*, Vol. 72, No. 1870, April 28, 1975 (Washington, D.C.: U.S. Government Printing Office), p. 551.

8. Ibid., p. 555.

9. Comments by Senator Jackson, ABC-TV Evening News, Ted Koppel reporting from the State Department, April 8, 1975; see also Murrey Marder, "Jackson Cites 'Secret' U.S., Vietnam Pact," *Washington Post*, April 9, 1975.

10. Address before a Joint Session of Congress, April 10, 1975, in Ford, *Public Papers, 1975*, pp. 459–73.

11. Ford, *A Time to Heal*, p. 255.

12. Ibid.

13. "Next Steps in Vietnam After President Thieu," *New York Times* editorial, April 22, 1975; "The Departure of Nguyen Van Thieu," *Washington Post* editorial, April 22, 1975; "Mr. Thieu Steps Down," *Baltimore Sun* editorial, April 22, 1975; "After the Fall," *New York News* editorial, April 22, 1975; "After Vietnam," *Christian Science Monitor* editorial, April 22, 1975; "Exit President Thieu," *Chicago Tribune* editorial, April 22, 1975; "It Was Thieu Who Betrayed the People of Vietnam," *Philadelphia Inquirer* editorial, April 22, 1975; "Saigon's Denouement and Washington's Role," *New York Times* editorial, April 23, 1975.

14. Ford, *Public Papers, 1975*, p. 569.

15. Exchanges with President Ford:
    10:25 P.M.—April 28, 1975
    FORD: Yes, Henry.
    KISSINGER: Mr. President, the shelling seems to have substantially stopped. But now order seems to have broken down on the field and all the runways are full of people. It's getting to be like Da Nang, which is about probably what they wanted to create.
    FORD: Right.
    KISSINGER: They are trying to restore order. We've talked to Graham Martin and we've told him that if the airfield becomes unusable, he's got to go to emergency evacuation.
    FORD: I would agree in both places.
    KISSINGER: Yeah. Well, the major problem we will have now, Mr. President, is whether we can get the American personnel, if the order really has broken down at Tan Son Nhut, out of Tan Son Nhut and back to the DAO [Defense Attaché Office] compound.
    FORD: How much of a distance is there?

KISSINGER: The distance isn't far. It's only about five minutes by car if we can get them off the— You know, we have no way of knowing how intermingled they are . . .

FORD: Right.

KISSINGER: With the Vietnamese and we will just have to sit it out now.

FORD: Are the C-130s getting in?

KISSINGER: No. Because the field seems to be flooded with civilians right now.

FORD: I see.

KISSINGER: One of them was cleared for an approach but absolute bedlam broke loose when it got close, so they waved it off again. Now that shelling just created a sense of . . .

FORD: Frustration and panic.

KISSINGER: So we may just have to go to emergency evacuation in a couple of hours. But the orders are absolutely clear. The fixed-wing can't be used; we'll have to go to helicopter.

FORD: And just take ours out. Hope for the best.

KISSINGER: That's right. I don't think they'll shoot it out. And I frankly don't believe that the Russians snookered us. I think that the North Vietnamese took another reading over the weekend and decided they were going to go for broke.

FORD: Well, let's see it's 10:30—ten o'clock there, isn't it?

KISSINGER: . . . Only about six hours left.

FORD: Apparently the ARVN are not able to do anything about it.

KISSINGER: Well, we have General Smith on the ground there. He's out at Tan Son Nhut. We have Martin in town. They are in close contact and they'll just have to use their judgment. We can't run it from here.

FORD: No, I agree.

KISSINGER: Both Jim [Schlesinger] and I sent the identical messages from you through our channels.

FORD: Right.

KISSINGER: And I've talked to Graham Martin and I know that from Defense they have talked to Smith.

FORD: Right.

KISSINGER: So everybody knows what he's got to do.

FORD: So it looks like—

KISSINGER: To me it looks like an emergency evacuation right now.

FORD: With the helicopters in the two places.

KISSINGER: That's what it looks like to me. We'll keep you posted.

FORD: All right. I guess as tragic as it is, Henry, we've got to leave those five thousand there and get our people out.

KISSINGER: Yeah. The tragedy because they are all selected for the North Vietnamese right there. They are all high-risk people but we can't do anything about it.

FORD: [Long pause] Well, keep me posted and . . .

KISSINGER: Well, we have no choice, Mr. President.

FORD: No . . . in the hands of the people out there.

KISSINGER: That's right. And you've carried it to the absolute limit it could be carried and we have now just got to see how it plays out.

FORD: As I understand it now, Smith and Martin have the authority to order the helicopter operation.

KISSINGER: Anytime they decide the field is unusable.

FORD: From what you tell me, it is, so we should anticipate that action.

KISSINGER: Yes. It would be better for us if they could reopen the field at least long enough to get the Americans off with fixed-wing aircraft from out there.

FORD: Right.

KISSINGER: Because that's where all the commotion is. But since they are on the spot they really have to judge it.

FORD: But they have full authority to do it.

KISSINGER: They have full authority to do it and they are ordered to do it if they cannot get out by the end of the day.

FORD: Right.

KISSINGER: They have no authority to stay another night.

FORD: Right.

KISSINGER: They have the authority to call for the emergency airlift anytime tonight—our night—and they must call for it before the end of the day out there.

FORD: By the end of the day out there or by tomorrow morning here?

KISSINGER: By tomorrow morning here if the C-130s haven't taken them off, then the helicopters will.

FORD: That's a real shame! Twenty-four more hours—or twelve more hours?

KISSINGER: Twelve more hours and we would have saved eight thousand lives.

FORD: Henry, we did the best we could.

KISSINGER: Mr. President, you carried it single-handedly against all the advice and we played it out as far as it would play.

FORD: Well, I just hope Smith and Martin now understand where we are and will not hesitate to act.

KISSINGER: Well, we checked with Martin. I talked with him fifteen minutes ago. I can't say that he's doing it willingly but he's going to do it. He wants to stay behind with two people to take care of Americans that might come out of the woodwork. But I just don't think we can justify it.

FORD: I don't think so either, Henry.

KISSINGER: We can't give them any hostages.

FORD: No, no, no. Well—

KISSINGER: And incidentally, Mr. President, you may be pleased to know—I've told you already, the French have gotten kicked out of Cambodia, too.

FORD: Well, isn't that some consolation. Well, Henry, we've done the best we could and you and I are taking it on the chin and just hope the Good Lord is with us.

KISSINGER: Well, we'll take it on the chin for a few more days. Just a minute, they are bringing me something. Yeah—all right. They are already working on getting the Americans back to the compound.

FORD: Right.

KISSINGER: In the next thirty minutes we'll probably go to the helicopter evacuation.

FORD: Well, I'll be here. Be sure to call me and let me know how it's going.

KISSINGER: Right, Mr. President.

10:45 P.M.—April 28, 1975

FORD: Yes Henry.

KISSINGER: Mr. President, I've just talked to Graham Martin and he agrees that we ought to issue the execute for the evacuation.

FORD: From both places?

KISSINGER: That's right.

FORD: Well, I think we should too. Shortly after you called Jim Schlesinger called and I got the impression you and he were in agreement but I told him to call you to make sure that was true.

KISSINGER: Yes.

FORD: And I . . . If Martin says so, I think we should move on it.

KISSINGER: Right. And then I think that while this thing is going on I think everything ought to go through Brent or me. We'll let you know in case anything happens but so that there aren't too many nervous Nellies running loose.

FORD: Right. Do you think I ought to come over to the Situation Room?

KISSINGER: No. I don't think it's necessary. We'll keep you informed as soon as something happens. And it really doesn't require a presidential decision after the executes.

FORD: I'll be here, and by all means call me good or bad.

KISSINGER: We'll call you if there is anything at all to report. You first have to get the Americans back to the compound. That seems to be manageable from the little I've heard. But then we have to make sure Graham can get all the Americans together at the embassy. That may take him a couple of hours. I told him he had to complete it during daylight hours.

FORD: There is six hours left.

KISSINGER: About six and a half or seven hours left. I think it can be done. I just think we have no choice.

FORD: Well, tragic as it is I think this is what has to be done and tell him to do it.

KISSINGER: Well, he's under clear instructions. I'll call General Brown and him and tell them that you've ordered the thing executed. They won't fight us hard.

FORD: That's an understatement.

KISSINGER: The only thing is they'll be so eager to get out they'll get the airlift in before the people are assembled.

FORD: You tell them to make damn sure every reasonable effort is made to get everybody out.

KISSINGER: That's right.

FORD: So there's no questions about that.

KISSINGER: Right. And under these conditions we can't take any more Vietnamese.

FORD: No. Let's make sure that's in an order so that there is . . .

KISSINGER: There is no physical capability, Mr. President, but I'll make sure that is clear too.

FORD: All right. Get the order under way and it sickens me.

KISSINGER: Mr. President, we carried it as far as it could be carried and maybe a few hours beyond it and you know we need to have no regrets. It's the best that could be done.

FORD: Well, keep me posted but tell Graham to do it as quickly as possible.

KISSINGER: Right, Mr. President.

FORD: Thank you Henry.

12:22 A.M.—April 29, 1975

KISSINGER: Mr. President, I just want you to know that Big Minh [General Duong Van Minh] has just ordered all Americans out of the country within twenty-four hours.

FORD: That's helpful, isn't it?

KISSINGER: Well, he must know we are leaving, because they are doing it on open radios to collect the civilians and I think he is trying to make some points with the Communists.

FORD: I would gather that too.

KISSINGER: But actually it may be sort of a protection for the Americans too—at least they are not bugging out under these conditions. They are being ordered out.

FORD: You ordered out . . .

KISSINGER: After all we have suffered there it is a hell of a way to leave.

FORD: Yeah, big friend of ours.

KISSINGER: I think probably on the whole it will have a tendency to save lives.

FORD: I would think so. Outside of the fact you don't like it as a comment that will go down in history, but on a practical basis tonight, it might be helpful.

KISSINGER: Okay. I won't call you again until the operation has started.

FORD: All right, thanks for calling me on this, Henry.

KISSINGER: And then I'll read you also the statement we are drafting you.

FORD: That will be fine.

KISSINGER: Right, Mr. President. Bye.

FORD: Thank you very much, Henry.

16. Dung, *Our Great Spring Victory*, pp. 201–2.

17. Ibid., p. 234.

18. Press conference, April 29, 1975, in *Department of State Bulletin,* Vol. 72, No. 1873, May 19, 1975, p. 631.
19. William Shawcross, my gadfly in many treatises, seems to have had second thoughts. He had this to say in 1994: "[T]hose of us who opposed the American war in Indochina should be extremely humble in the face of the appalling aftermath: a form of genocide in Cambodia and horrific tyranny in both Vietnam and Laos. Looking back on my own coverage for *The Sunday Times* of the South Vietnamese war effort of 1970–75, I think I concentrated too easily on the corruption and incompetence of the South Vietnamese and their American allies, was too ignorant of the inhuman Hanoi regime, and far too willing to believe that a victory by the Communists would provide a better future. But after the Communist victory came the refugees to Thailand and the floods of boat people desperately seeking to escape the Cambodian killing fields and the Vietnamese gulags. Their eloquent testimony should have put paid to all illusions." (William Shawcross, "Shrugging Off Genocide," *The Times* [London], December 16, 1994). See also Horowitz, *Radical Son,* for an even more thoroughgoing recantation.

## 18: ANATOMY OF A CRISIS: THE *MAYAGUEZ*

1. Richard G. Head, Frisco W. Short, and Robert C. McFarlane, *Crisis Resolution: Presidential Decision-Making in the* Mayaguez *and Korean Confrontations* (Boulder, Colorado: Westview Press, 1978), chapter 5. This is an authoritative and detailed account.
2. *Department of State Bulletin,* Vol. 72, No. 1875, June 2, 1975, p. 720.
3. Peter Grose, "82 in *Pueblo* Crew Freed; U.S. Gives North Koreans 'Confession,' Disavows It," *New York Times,* December 23, 1968.
4. Ford, *A Time to Heal,* p. 276.
5. White House statement, May 12, 1975, in *Department of State Bulletin,* Vol. 72, No. 1875, June 2, 1975, p. 719.
6. Nessen, *It Sure Looks Different from the Inside,* pp. 118–19.
7. "The Challenge of Peace," Address before the St. Louis World Affairs Council, May 12, 1975, *Department of State Bulletin,* Vol. 72, No. 1875, June 2, 1975, pp. 711–12.
8. Associated Press report from Paris, May 13, 1975, 15:48 EDT.
9. See, e.g., Joseph Kraft, "Lessons of the *Mayaguez,*" *Washington Post,* May 18, 1975.
10. Following is the text of the initial FBIS summary of Hu Nim's statement, received in Washington May 14, 1975, at 8:06 P.M.:

BULLETIN
CAMBODIA ANNOUNCES INTENT TO RELEASE MAYAGUEZ
BK142340 FOR YOUR INFORMATION
PHNOM PENH DOMESTIC SERVICE IN CAMBODIAN AT 2307 GMT 14 MAY CARRIES A 19-MINUTE PRESS COMMUNIQUE ON THE MAYAGUEZ INCIDENT WHICH IS READ BY HU NIM, MINISTER OF INFORMATION AND PROPAGANDA.

THE COMMUNIQUE SAYS: SINCE WE LIBERATED PHNOM PENH AND THE ENTIRE COUNTRY. U.S. IMPERIALISM HAS REPEATEDLY AND SUCCESSIVELY CARRIED OUT INTELLIGENCE AND ESPIONAGE ACTIVITIES TO CONDUCT SUBVERSIVE, PROVOCATIVE ACTS AGAINST THE NEWLY LIBERATED NEW CAMBODIA IN AN APPARENT DESIRE NOT TO ALLOW THE CAMBODIAN NATION AND PEOPLE TO LIVE.

IT EXPLAINS WHY THE RGNUC HAS DETAINED U.S. IMPERIALIST SHIPS OFF THE CAMBODIAN COAST, CHARGING THAT THESE SHIPS, INCLUDING THE MAYAGUEZ, ARE CIA SPY SHIPS. IT ALSO CHARGES THE U.S. OF USING AIRPLANES TO ATTACK CAMBODIAN NAVAL VESSELS, AND THEN SAYS: "OUR RGNUC WILL ORDER THE MAYAGUEZ TO WITHDRAW FROM CAMBODIAN TERRITORIAL WATERS AND WILL WARN IT AGAINST FURTHER ESPIONAGE OR PROVOCATIVE ACTIVITIES. THIS APPLIES TO THE MAYAGUEZ OR ANY OTHER SHIPS, LIKE THE SHIP FLYING THE PANAMA FLAG WHICH WE RELEASED ON 9 MAY 1975."

For the full text of the Cambodian statement, see *New York Times,* May 16, 1976.

11. Nessen, *It Sure Looks Different from the Inside,* p. 129.
12. Ford, *A Time to Heal,* p. 284.
13. Osborne, *White House Watch,* p. 139.
14. Ford, *Public Papers, 1975,* p. 706.

## 19: TRAGEDY OF THE KURDS

1. For background, see Edmund Ghareeb, *The Kurdish Question in Iraq* (Syracuse: Syracuse University Press, 1981), pp. 87–103.
2. "The CIA Report the President Doesn't Want You to Read" (on the Pike Committee hearings), *The Village Voice,* February 16, 1976, pp. 85–88.

## 20: THE RESTORATION OF WESTERN UNITY

1. On the "Year of Europe" initiative, see Kissinger, *Years of Upheaval,* Chapters 5, 16.
2. On the Berlin negotiations, see Kissinger, *White House Years,* pp. 405–12, 823–33.
3. Marion Gräfin Dönhoff, *Von Gestern nach Übermorgen* (Hamburg: Albrecht Knaus Verlag, 1981), p. 241.
4. See Kissinger, *Years of Upheaval,* pp. 1111–23.
5. See Hans-Dietrich Genscher, *Rebuilding a House Divided: A Memoir by the Architect of Germany's Reunification,* translated by Thomas Thornton (New York: Broadway Books, 1995), pp. 52–54.
6. For Genscher's moving account, see ibid., pp. 558–60.
7. "Address by President Charles de Gaulle Outlining the Principles of French Foreign Policy Following the Failure of the Summit Conference," May 31, 1960, in *Major Addresses, Statements and Press Conferences of General Charles de Gaulle, May 19, 1958–January 31, 1964* (New York: French Embassy, Press and Information Division, 1964), p. 75.
8. From various conversations of mine with Presidents de Gaulle and Pompidou.
9. Sir Harold Nicolson, *Diplomacy* (Washington, D.C.: Institute for the Study of Diplomacy, Georgetown University, reprint of 1988), p. 81.
10. For an elaboration of these points, see my June 9, 1977, address on the subject, "Communist Parties in Western Europe: Challenges to the West," remarks at the Conference on Italy and Eurocommunism sponsored by the Hoover Institution on War, Revolution, and Peace and the American Enterprise Institute for Public Policy Research, in Washington, D.C., reprinted in Henry Kissinger, *For the Record: Selected Statements, 1977–1980* (Boston: Little, Brown, 1981), pp. 1–22.
11. These remarks were later leaked and appeared in the *New York Times* of April 7, 1976. Also reprinted in Richard P. Stebbins and Elaine P. Adam, eds., *American Foreign Relations, 1975: A Documentary Record* (New York: New York University Press, 1977), pp. 561–65.
12. See Frank C. Carlucci, "The View from the U.S. Embassy," in Hans Binnendijk, ed., with Peggy Nalle and Diane Bendahmane, *Authoritarian Regimes in Transition* (Washington, D.C.: U.S. Department of State, Foreign Service Institute, Center for the Study of Foreign Affairs, 1987), p. 209.
13. See, e.g., Leonid Brezhnev's report to the Twenty-fifth Party Congress, in L. I. Brezhnev, "Report of the CPSU Central Committee and the Immediate Tasks of the Party in Home and Foreign Policy," February 24, 1976 (Moscow: Novosti Press Agency Publishing House, 1976).
14. Carlucci, "The View from the U.S. Embassy," pp. 210–11.
15. Ford, *Public Papers, 1975,* p. 741.
16. Stebbins and Adam, *American Foreign Relations, 1975,* p. 230.
17. Helmut Schmidt, *Men and Powers: A Political Retrospective* (New York: Random House, 1989), pp. 167–68.

## 21: THE EUROPEAN SECURITY CONFERENCE

1. "Conference on Security and Cooperation in Europe: Final Act," signed in Helsinki, Finland, August 1, 1975, Section 1(a) (I), as reprinted in *Department of State Bulletin*, Vol. 73, No. 1888, September 1, 1975, p. 324.
2. Genscher, *Rebuilding a House Divided*, pp. 96–99.
3. "European 'Security,' " *New York Times* editorial, July 21, 1975.
4. "Jerry, Don't Go," *Wall Street Journal* editorial, July 23, 1975.
5. "A 'Miserable' Treaty," Letter to the Editor from Osvalds Akmentins, *New York Times*, July 25, 1975.
6. "Final Act," p. 324.
7. James M. Naughton, "Ford Sees 35-Nation Charter as a Gauge on Rights in East Europe," *New York Times*, July 26, 1975.
8. Aleksandr Solzhenitsyn, Address to the AFL-CIO, June 30, 1975, reprinted in Aleksandr Solzhenitsyn, *Warning to the West* (New York: Farrar, Straus and Giroux, 1976), p. 48.
9. See Ford, *A Time to Heal*, pp. 297–98. See also Robert T. Hartmann, *Palace Politics: An Inside Account of the Ford Years* (New York: McGraw Hill, 1980), pp. 337–39.
10. Press conference, Milwaukee, July 16, 1975, in *Department of State Bulletin*, Vol. 73, No. 1884, August 4, 1975, p. 181.
11. "The Meaning of Solzhenitsyn," *Wall Street Journal* editorial, July 18, 1975.
12. E.g., Adam B. Ulam, Letter to the Editor, *New York Times*, July 17, 1975.
13. Solzhenitsyn, *Warning to the West*, pp. 24–30.
14. Interview appearing in *Time* magazine, October 27, 1975, in *Department of State Bulletin*, Vol. 73, No. 1899, November 17, 1975, p. 693.
15. Ford statement at a meeting at the White House with seven members of Congress and representatives of East European ethnic groups, July 25, 1975, in Ford, *Public Papers, 1975*, p. 1033.
16. Solzhenitsyn, *Warning to the West*, pp. 40–41.
17. President Ford's address in Helsinki, August 1, 1975, in Ford, *Public Papers, 1975*, p. 1079.
18. Ibid., p. 1081.
19. Ford, *A Time to Heal*, p. 305.
20. "Summit in Helsinki," *Newsweek*, August 11, 1975, p. 16.
21. "American Unity and the National Interest," address before the Southern Commodity Producers Conference in Birmingham, Alabama, August 14, 1975, in *Department of State Bulletin*, Vol. 73, No. 1890, September 15, 1975, p. 392.

## 22: THE ENERGY CRISIS

1. The background can be read in more detail in Kissinger, *Years of Upheaval*, Chapters 19 and 20.
2. Interview, "Kissinger on Oil, Food, and Trade," December 23, 1974, published in *Business Week*, January 13, 1975.
3. Ford, *Public Papers, 1974*, pp. 156–61.
4. President's remarks to the Ninth World Energy Conference, Detroit, September 23, 1974, in ibid., p. 180.
5. Address, September 23, 1974, to the 29th U.N. General Assembly session, "The Age of Interdependence: Common Disaster or Community," *Department of State Bulletin*, Vol. 71, No. 1842, October 14, 1974, pp. 502–3.
6. Ibid., p. 503.
7. Paul Hoffmann, "Algerian Assails West Oil Stand," *New York Times*, October 6, 1974.
8. "The President of Venezuela Responds to the President of the United States," advertisement, *New York Times*, September 25, 1974.
9. Address, "The Energy Crisis: Strategy for Cooperative Action," November 14, 1974, *Department of State Bulletin*, Vol. 71, No. 1849, p. 753.

10. Address, "Energy: The Necessity of Decision," February 3, 1975, in *Department of State Bulletin*, Vol. 72, No. 1861, February 24, 1975, p. 242.
11. Address to the Nation on Energy and Economic Programs, January 13, 1975, in Ford, *Public Papers, 1975*, pp. 30–35.
12. *Business Week* interview, January 13, 1975.
13. Interview with Bill Moyers on January 15, 1975, for the PBS series *Bill Moyers' Journal: International Report, Department of State Bulletin*, Vol. 72, No. 1859, February 10, 1975, p. 172.
14. George P. Shultz and Kenneth W. Dam, *Economic Policy Beyond the Headlines* (New York: W. W. Norton, 1978), pp. 11–14.
15. Address, "The Industrial Democracies and the Future," November 11, 1975, Pittsburgh, Pennsylvania, *Department of State Bulletin*, Vol. 73, No. 1901, December 1, 1975, p. 758.
16. Address, "Building an Enduring Foreign Policy," November 24, 1975, Detroit, Michigan, in *Department of State Bulletin*, Vol. 73, No. 1903, p. 843.
17. Address, "Global Consensus and Economic Development," read before the Seventh Special Session of the U.N. General Assembly on September 1, 1975, by Daniel P. Moynihan, U.S. Ambassador to the United Nations, *Department of State Bulletin*, Vol. 73, No. 1891, September 22, 1975, p. 441.
18. Address, "Energy, Raw Materials, and Development: The Search for Common Ground," Paris, December 16, 1975, in *Department of State Bulletin*, Vol. 74, No. 1907, January 12, 1976, pp. 46–47.
19. Ibid., p. 37.

## 23: PANAMA, MEXICO, AND THE "NEW DIALOGUE"

1. Nelson A. Rockefeller, "The Rockefeller Report on the Americas: The Official Report of a United States Presidential Mission for the Western Hemisphere," The *New York Times* Edition (Chicago: Quadrangle Books, 1969). See also Richard Nixon, *U.S. Foreign Policy for the 1970s: A New Strategy for Peace,* February 18, 1970, Part II, pp. 41–53, on "The Western Hemisphere."
2. President Nixon's address to the Annual Meeting of the Inter-American Press Association, Washington, D.C., Hilton Hotel, October 31, 1969, in Richard Nixon, *Public Papers, 1969,* pp. 893–901.
3. My address, "A Just Consensus: A Stable Order, A Durable Peace," made before the 28th session of the United Nations General Assembly, September 24, 1973, in *Department of State Bulletin*, Vol. 69, No. 1790, October 15, 1973, pp. 469–73.
4. My toast at a luncheon I hosted for the Center for Inter-American Relations in New York, "A Western Hemisphere Relationship of Cooperation," October 5, 1973, in honor of the Latin American delegations to the United Nations General Assembly. *Department of State Bulletin,* Vol. 69, No. 1792, October 29, 1973, p. 543.
5. Ambassador Scali's statement of March 20, 1973, in *Department of State Bulletin,* Vol. 68, No. 1765, April 23, 1973, p. 497.
6. My remarks at the initialing with Juan Antonio Tack, Minister of Foreign Affairs of Panama, of a joint statement of the Principles for a new Panama Canal treaty, February 7, 1974, "U.S. and Panama Agree on Principles for Negotiation of New Panama Canal Treaty," in *Department of State Bulletin,* Vol. 70, No. 1809, p. 183.
7. The Foreign Ministers of twenty-five Western Hemisphere countries participated in the Conference of Tlateloco, Mexico City, February 18–23, 1974. My remarks, February 21, 1974, in *Department of State Bulletin,* Vol. 70, No. 1812, March 18, 1974, p. 258.
8. From the Declaration of Tlateloco, dated February 24, 1974, in *Department of State Bulletin,* Vol. 70, No. 1812, March 18, 1974, pp. 262–63.

### 24: BRAZIL, CHILE, AND WESTERN HEMISPHERE UNITY

1. Press conference, San Jose, February 24, 1976, in *Department of State Bulletin*, Vol. 74, No. 1916, March 16, 1976, p. 351.
2. See Kissinger, *White House Years*, p. 657.
3. Régis Debray, *The Chilean Revolution: Conversations with Allende* (New York: Pantheon Books, 1971), pp. 82, 122–23.
4. Kisssinger, *White House Years*, Chapter 17.
5. C. L. Sulzberger, "The Unmaking of a President," *New York Times*, November 30, 1975.
6. Kissinger, *Years of Upheaval*, Chapter 9.
7. Interview with Madred newspaper *ABC*, October 10, 1973, as quoted in *Facts on File Yearbook 1973*, Vol. 33, p. 872.
8. *La Prensa*, Santiago, Chile, October 19, 1973.
9. My toast in Santo Domingo, June 6, 1976, in *Department of State Bulletin*, Vol. 75, No. 1932, July 5, 1976, pp. 17–18.
10. My "Statement on Human Rights," Sixth Regular General Assembly of the Organization of American States, Santiago, June 8, 1976, in ibid., pp. 1–5.
11. My address, "Statement on Cooperation for Development," Santiago, ibid., pp. 5–10.
12. "A New Panama Canal Treaty Is Now Supported by Pentagon," *New York Times*, September 5, 1975.
13. Jon Nordheimer, "Reagan Sharpens His Criticism of Ford, Citing Canal Talks and Two in Cabinet," *New York Times*, February 29, 1976.
14. President's press conference, Fairmont Hotel, Dallas, April 10, 1976, in Ford, *Public Papers, 1976*, p. 1066.
15. Presidential Campaign Debate of October 6, 1976, in ibid., pp. 2430–31.
16. "Senate Roll-Call Vote Approving Canal Pact," *New York Times*, March 17, 1978; "How Senators Voted on 2d Canal Treaty," *New York Times*, April 19, 1978.

### 25: CUBAN INTERLUDE

1. Richard M. Nixon, *RN: The Memoirs of Richard Nixon* (New York: Grosset & Dunlap, 1978), pp. 220–21.
2. Ibid., p. 244.
3. Kissinger, *White House Years*, Chapter XVI.
4. Press conference, January 10, 1974, in *Department of State Bulletin*, Vol. 70, No. 1806, February 4, 1974, p. 122.
5. Some of these exchanges may be found in Peter Kornbluh and James G. Blight, "Dialogue with Castro: A Hidden History," *New York Review of Books*, Vol. XLI, No. 16, October 6, 1994, pp. 45–49.
6. Ford, *Public Papers, 1975*, p. 294.
7. Address, "The United States and Latin America: The New Opportunity," March 1, 1975, Houston, Texas, in *Department of State Bulletin*, Vol. 72, No. 1865, March 24, 1975, p. 364.
8. "Sparkman on Foreign Policy," *Wall Street Journal*, February 13, 1975.
9. Department of State Press Briefing, July 30, 1975.
10. Address, "Building an Enduring Foreign Policy," November 24, 1975, before the Detroit Economic Club, *Department of State Bulletin*, Vol. 73, No. 1903, December 15, 1975, p. 844.
11. Press conference, November 24, 1975, Detroit, ibid., p. 854.
12. Ford, *Public Papers, 1975*, p. 1988.
13. Peter Kornbluh and James G. Blight, "Dialogue with Castro," p. 49.

## 26: CIVIL WAR IN ANGOLA

1. "Sunrise for Angola?," *New York Times,* January 17, 1975.
2. Henry Giniger, "For Independent Angola, A Great Threat of Strife," *New York Times,* January 16, 1975.
3. Odd Arne Westad, "Moscow and the Angolan Crisis, 1974–1976: A New Pattern of Intervention," *Cold War International History Project Bulletin,* Issues 8–9, Winter 1996/1997 (Washington, D.C.: Woodrow Wilson International Center for Scholars), p. 24.
4. See Kissinger, *Years of Upheaval,* Chapter 9.
5. Nathaniel Davis, "The Angola Decision of 1975: A Personal Memoir," *Foreign Affairs,* Fall 1978, p. 110.
6. John Stockwell, *In Search of Enemies: A CIA Story* (New York: W. W. Norton, 1978), p. 158.
7. Dobrynin, *In Confidence,* p. 362.
8. Georgii Arbatov, *The System: An Insider's Life in Soviet Politics* (New York: Times Books, 1992), pp. 193–95.
9. Arkady N. Shevchenko, *Breaking with Moscow* (New York: Alfred A. Knopf, 1985), pp. 271–72; Westad, "Moscow and the Angolan Crisis," p. 22.
10. Westad, "Moscow and the Angolan Crisis," p. 31.
11. Jim Hershberg, "New East Bloc Evidence on the Cold War in the Third World and the Collapse of Détente in the 1970s," *Cold War International History Project Bulletin,* Issues 8–9, Winter 1996/1997, p. 1.
12. *Department of State Bulletin,* December 15, 1975, Vol. 73, No. 1903, p. 843.
13. Remarks at White House press conference, November 26, 1975, in Ford, *Public Papers,* 1975, p. 1914.
14. Piero Gleijeses, "Havana's Policy in Africa, 1959–76: New Evidence from Cuban Archives," *Cold War International History Project Bulletin,* Issues 8–9, Winter 1996/1997, p. 9; Westad, "Moscow and the Angolan Crisis," p. 26.
15. Following is a list of congressional briefings which the executive branch conducted with committees of Congress, individual members, and other congressional staff persons between July 1975 and the end of the year:

*Senate*
　　July 25—Two members of the Foreign Relations Committee and one staff aide briefed by the CIA.
　　July 30—Three members of the Intelligence Operations Subcommittee of the Appropriations Committee and two staff aides briefed by the CIA.
　　August 4—Senator Dick Clark (African Affairs Subcommittee Chairman) briefed by the CIA.
　　September 5—Three members of the Intelligence Operations Subcommittee of the Appropriations Committee and two staff aides briefed by the CIA.
　　September 23—Four members of the CIA Subcommittee of the Armed Services Committee and two staff aides briefed by the CIA.
　　October 31—Six members of the Select Committee on Intelligence Operations and twenty staff aides briefed by the CIA.
　　November 6—Nine members of the Foreign Relations Committee and three staff aides briefed by the CIA.
　　December 1—Senator Clark briefed by Deputy Secretary of State Robert S. Ingersoll; Assistant Secretary of State for African Affairs William E. Schaufele, Jr.; and Deputy Assistant Secretary of State for African Affaris Edward W. Mulcahy.
　　December 4—Ten staff members of various committees briefed by Messrs. Haverkamp, Andrew, and Fugit of State's Bureau of African Affairs (AF).
　　December 8—Senator Clark briefed by Schaufele as a follow-up of the December 1 briefing.

December 8—Two members of the Foreign Relations Committee and one staff aide briefed by the CIA.

December 12—Four members of the CIA Subcommittee of the Armed Services Committee and two staff aides briefed by the CIA.

December 16—Two members of the Intelligence Operations Subcommittee of the Appropriations Committee and two staff aides briefed by the CIA.

December 16—Ten members of the Subcommittee on Foreign Assistance and Economic Policy of the Foreign Relations Committee and several staff aides briefed by the CIA.

December 16—Senator Strom Thurmond (member of CIA Subcommittee of the Armed Services Committee) briefed by the CIA.

*House*

July 25—Three members of the Special Subcommittee on Intelligence of the Armed Services Committee and one staff aide briefed by the CIA.

July 29—Thirteen members of the Defense Subcommittee of the Appropriations Committee and two staff aides briefed by the CIA.

July 31—Six members of the Subcommittee on Oversight of the Foreign Affairs Committee and one staff aide briefed by the CIA.

September 4—Five members of the Subcommittee on Oversight of the Foreign Affairs Committee and one staff aide briefed by the CIA.

September 8—Four members of the Special Subcommittee on Intelligence of the Armed Services Committee and two staff member briefed by the CIA.

October 6—Thirteen members of the Defense Subcommittee of the Appropriations Committee and two staff aides briefed by the CIA.

October 23—Eight members of the Select Committee on Intelligence and one staff aide briefed by the CIA.

November 5—Mulcahy testified before the International Resources, Food, and Energy Subcommittee of the Foreign Affairs Committee.

November 13—Congressman Charles Diggs and nine other congressmen plus several staff aides informally briefed by Mulcahy.

December 9—Thirteen members of the Defense Subcommittee of the Appropriations Committee and three staff aides briefed by the CIA.

December 9—Seven members of the Subcommittee on Oversight of the Foreign Affairs Committee and one staff aide briefed by the CIA.

December 11—Six members of the Subcommittee on Military Affairs ([Dante] Fascell Subcommittee) briefed by Mulcahy.

December 12—Congressman [Donald] Riegle briefed by Mulcahy.

December 12—Five members of the Special Subcommittee on Intelligence of the Armed Services Committee and two staff aides briefed by the CIA.

December 15—J. Daniel O'Flaherty, staffer for Congressman [Michael] Harrington, briefed by Fugit AF.

December 16—Representative Dale Milford (member of House Select Committee) briefed by the CIA.

December 17—[George] Mahon Subcommittee briefed by CIA Director William Colby and Under Secretary of State Joseph J. Sisco.

December 17—Congressman John Burton and others (unknown) briefed by Mulcahy.

December 17—Mulcahy appeared before an informal group of twelve representatives and thirty-five staff aides.

December 17—Congressman [Robert] Leggett briefed by Colby.

December 18—Closed session of about one hundred representatives briefed by Sisco and Mulcahy.

December 19—Members of the Black Caucus briefed by Sisco and Mulcahy; Tom Doubleday of AF briefed 8 Congressional staffers in the period December 16 to December 31. ["Angola," Hearings, before the Subcommittee on African Affairs, Committee on

Foreign Relations, United States Senate, 94th Cong., 2nd Sess., on U.S. Involvement in Civil War in Angola, January 29, February 2, 3, and 6, 1976 (Washington, D.C.: GPO), 1976].

16. See Seymour Hersh, "Angola-Aid Issue Opening Rifts in State Department," *New York Times,* December 14, 1975.

17. Hearings on Foreign Assistance Authorization before the Senate Foreign Relations Sub-committee on Foreign Assistance, December 5, 1975, p. 538.

18. Hearings on Angola before the Senate Foreign Relations Subcommittee on African Affairs, January 29, 1976, p. 24.

19. Ibid., p. 38.

20. Ibid., p. 31.

21. Hearings on Angola before the Senate Foreign Relations Subcommittee on African Affairs, February 3, 1976, p. 85.

22. Hearings on Angola before the Senate Foreign Relations Subcommittee on African Affairs, January 29, 1976, p. 13.

23. Ibid., pp. 12, 16.

24. Ibid., p. 16.

25. Ford, *Public Papers, 1975,* p. 1981.

26. On the later resuscitation of American policy, see Peter W. Rodman, *More Precious than Peace: The Cold War and the Struggle for the Third World* (New York: Charles Scribner's Sons, 1994), Chapter 14; Chester A. Crocker, *High Noon in Southern Africa: Making Peace in a Rough Neighborhood* (New York: W. W. Norton, 1992).

## 27: LAST VISIT TO MOSCOW

1. Ford, *A Time to Heal,* pp. 323–24.

2. George Lardner Jr., "Jackson Blasts Kissinger Role in the Shake-up," *Washington Post,* November 3, 1976.

3. George F. Will, "Dampening Dissent," *Washington Post,* November 5, 1976.

4. "The Shake-up," editorial, *Washington Post,* November 5, 1976.

5. "Reagan: 'I Am Not Appeased,' " interview with Robert Ajemian, *Time,* November 17, 1975, p. 22.

6. Ford, *A Time to Heal,* p. 354.

7. January 22, 1976

   To:      General Scowcroft
   From:   Sonnenfeldt and Hyland
   The Secretary is sending his reply to the account of the NSC meeting, but we wanted you to know that he is being too restrained, given the outrageous performance at the NSC. It is incredible that in the middle of these negotiations, after some progress has been made, and with Brezhnev now considering our approach, that the entire agreed framework should be collapsed by new positions or 180 degree turns that were never heard before. How can Clements say that there was never any gray area, after Rumsfeld sponsored it repeatedly, or Holloway say they only want a program of a few ships with eight launchers when we have been hearing the most glowing advocacy of it, and the most scurrilous attacks on the Secretary for allegedly giving it away. Where were they all this time? We do not see how we can proceed in these weird circumstances. It is all the more devastating when you consider that the Soviets are showing a serious interest and obviously trying to find some middle ground without capitulating. If we were in the Secretary's place we would simply abandon the effort or quit, but we will certainly advise him to persevere. We could make progress here today, but not without absolute, unqualified support from Washington. What all this is doing is to drive us to a position where even if the Soviets today show some give we will have to propose deferral of the Backfire/SLCM issues which you and we know is worse for our interest than any of the options we have been negotiating. We are not, obviously, blaming you but for the first time in our careers, are giving vent

to a real outrage at what is being perpetrated to the utmost potential damage to our country.

8. See my testimony on the SALT II treaty before the Senate Foreign Relations Committee, July 31, 1979, reprinted in Kissinger, *For the Record,* pp. 189–230.
9. "America's Permanent Interests," address before the Boston World Affairs Council, March 11, 1976, in *Department of State Bulletin,* Vol. 74, No. 1919, April 5, 1976, pp. 431–32.
10. See, e.g., Rowland Evans and Robert Novak, "A Soviet-East Europe 'Organic' Union," *Washington Post,* March 22, 1976; Rowland Evans and Robert Novak, "The Sonnenfeldt Doctrine: Deflecting the Ruckus," *Washington Post,* March 30, 1976.
11. For Sonnenfeldt's account of these events, see his interview in *The Washington Quarterly* (then called *The Washington Review of Strategic and International Studies*), Vol. 1, No. 2 (April 1978), pp. 41–51, and his congressional testimony in U.S. House of Representatives, Committee on International Relations, United States National Security Policy vis-à-vis Eastern Europe (The "Sonnenfeldt Doctrine"), Hearings before the Subcommittee on International Security and Scientific Affairs, 94th Congress, 2d session, April 12, 1976, pp. 1–28.
12. "State Dept. Summary of Remarks by Sonnenfeldt," reprint of official State Department summary, *New York Times,* April 6, 1976.
13. Quoted in Coral Bell, p. 242.
14. "The Permanent Challenge to Peace: U.S. Policy toward the Soviet Union," address to the Commonwealth Club and the World Affairs Council of Northern California, San Francisco, February 3, 1976, in *Department of State Bulletin,* Vol. 74, No. 1913, February 23, 1976, pp. 201–12.
15. C. L. Sulzberger, "Mini-Metternich in a Fog," *New York Times,* March 27, 1976.
16. Evans and Novak, "Soviet–East Europe 'Organic' Union."
17. Quoted in Walter Isaacson, *Kissinger, A Biography* (New York: Simon & Schuster, 1992), p. 664.
18. "The Western Alliance: Peace and Moral Purpose," Alastair Buchan Memorial Lecture, London, June 25, 1976, in *Department of State Bulletin,* Vol. 75, No. 1935, July 26, 1976, pp. 105–15.

## 28: PRESERVING THE SINO-AMERICAN RELATIONSHIP

1. Kissinger, *Years of Upheaval,* Chapter 8, pp. 349–55.
2. Foreign Minister Qiao's toast, October 19, 1975, in *Department of State Bulletin,* Vol. 73, No. 1899, November 17, 1975, p. 681.
3. President Ford's toast, December 1, 1975, in Ford, *Public Papers, 1975,* p. 1934.
4. See Kissinger, *White House Years,* p. 1062, and Kissinger, *Years of Upheaval,* p. 692.

## 29: AN AFRICAN STRATEGY

1. See Mohamed A. El-Khawas and Barry Cohen, editors, *The Kissinger Study of Southern Africa: National Security Study Memorandum 39 (Secret)* (Westport, Connecticut: Lawrence Hill & Co., 1976); Anthony Lake, *The "Tar Baby" Option: American Policy Toward Southern Rhodesia* (New York: Columbia University Press, 1976). NSSM 39 was the White House memorandum requesting an interagency study; NSDM38 was the Presidential memorandum announcing his decision based on the study.
2. Dinner speech before the United Nations members of the Organization of African Unity, "The United States and Africa: Strengthening the Relationship," September 23, 1975, *Department of State Bulletin,* Vol. 73, No. 1894, October 13, 1975, p. 574.
3. Address before the United Nations General Assembly, "Building International Order," September 22, 1975, ibid., pp. 545–53; and dinner speech of September 23, 1975, ibid., pp. 571–75.
4. Ford, *Public Papers, 1976,* March 12, 1976, p. 641.

5. Ford interview with *Chicago Sun-Times*, March 13, 1976, excerpts of which were reprinted in *Department of State Bulletin*, Vol. 74, No. 1920, April 12, 1976, p. 497.
6. Address, "Foreign Policy and National Security," World Affairs Council of Dallas, March 22, 1976, *Department of State Bulletin*, Vol. 74, No. 1920, April 12, 1976, pp. 463–64.
7. Murray Marder, "White House, Pentagon Weigh Military Action Against Cuba," *Washington Post*, March 26, 1976.

## 30: FIRST VISIT TO AFRICA

1. Address, "United States Policy on Southern Africa," Lusaka, Zambia, April 27, 1976, *Department of State Bulletin*, Vol. 74, No. 1927, May 31, 1976, pp. 672–79.
2. Ibid., pp. 678–79.
3. Quoted in Osborne, *White House Watch*, p. 326.
4. Remarks in Dakar, Senegal, May 2, 1976, *Department of State Bulletin*, Vol. 74, No. 1927, May 31, 1976, p. 705.
5. Osborne, *White House Watch*, p. 330.
6. Ibid., p. 326.
7. Ibid., p. 330.

## 31: TOWARD MAJORITY RULE IN SOUTHERN AFRICA

1. Address, "The United States and Africa: Strengthened Ties for an Era of Challenge," August 2, 1976, before the National Urban League, Boston, Massachusetts, in *Department of State Bulletin*, Vol. 75, No. 1939, August 23, 1976, pp. 261–62.
2. President Ford's interview with Panax United Press International Television News, aboard the Presidential Express in Michigan, May 15, 1976.
3. Ibid.
4. Statement by Ambassador Albert W. Sherer, Jr., at the U.N. Security Council, June 19, 1976, *Department of State Bulletin*, Vol. 75, No. 1933, July 12, 1976, pp. 59–60.
5. Briefing by State Department spokesman Robert Funseth on Secretary Kissinger's meeting with Prime Minister Callaghan at noon at 10 Downing Street, June 25, 1976.

## 32: BREAKTHROUGH TO MAJORITY RULE

1. Following are the pertinent exchanges. Material in brackets in the September 6, 1976, "agreed" version represents my handwritten notation of modifications.

8:00 pm     9/5/76
Given to
South Africans

### BASIS FOR A PROPOSAL

1. The Constituent Assembly will be moved from Windhoek to Geneva to conduct further talks on independence.

2. All groups will be represented at the Geneva meeting.

3. The United Nations will designate observers to participate at the Geneva meeting.

4. South Africa will designate a representative who will be available for liaison with the participants to the Geneva talks.

5. The independence of Namibia will be achieved on the basis of free elections under United Nations supervision.

6. The date for the independence of Namibia will be no later than _____.

7. The work program of the Geneva talks may include any aspect of the process of independence for Namibia which any of the participants wish to raise.

*Verbal Understanding:*

The U.S. will request a list of political prisoners for the consideration of the South

African Government. It will be up to the SAG [South African Government] to decide who should be released.

September 6, 1976
10:00 am Draft (S. Afr.)

## SOUTH AFRICA'S POSITION

1. The Constitutional Conference has announced that independence should be achieved with reasonable certainty by December 31, 1978.

The South African Government has indicated that it accepts such proposals as are approved by the Conference.

Paragraphs 2, 3 and 4 of the "Basis for a Proposal" will be taken up immediately upon the Prime Minister's return to South Africa.

5. The South African Government will designate a representative to the Geneva talks who will be available for contact with the participants.

6. Not acceptable to South Africa and no commitment on South Africa's part unless the Conference should so decide.

7. Acceptable.

9/6/76
Agreed

### Basis for a Proposal

1. The Constitutional Conference will be held in Geneva to conduct further talks on independence.

2. All groups may be represented at the Geneva [Conference].

3. The United Nations will designate an observer to the Geneva [Conference].

4. South Africa will designate a representative who will be available for contact with the participants to the Geneva [Conference].

5. The [Geneva] Conference will decide the modalities of the election and the nature of its supervision prior to final independence.

6. The work program of the Geneva [Conference] may include any aspect of the process of independence which any of the participants wish to raise.

7. The South African Government indicates that it will accept such proposals as are approved by the ~~Conference~~ [Geneva talks.]

8. The South African Government accepts the proposal of the [Constitutional] Conference for independence by December 31, 1978.

Zurich
September 6, 1976

2. President Nyerere's analysis of the Namibian problem, September 15, 1976:

Let's take Namibia. I've always said Namibia is easier. Both are difficult, but Namibia may be less difficult than Rhodesia. And I've been saying so because of the problems we're facing in Rhodesia. In Namibia we have SWAPO and no disunity. And the South Africans said they're now willing to decolonize. These two factors make me think it is easier. So the answer is to get the chief actors to sit down and settle it. I found I had misled the Secretary of State. But he wasn't the only one. I was misunderstood also by the British. Surprisingly, because they're experts at constitutional conferences.

The chief actors are the South Africans—because de facto they are the colonial power. Nujoma may reject them but de facto they are the colonial power. Then we have SWAPO. The U.N. and the OAU accept them. Then the third element must be included and that is the United Nations itself. The South Africans don't like SWAPO and don't like the U.N. We can't appear to be accepting the South African positions that SWAPO is irrelevant, that the U.N. is irrelevant.

3. News conference, Dar es Salaam, September 15, 1976, *Department of State Bulletin,* Vol. 75, No. 1948, October 25, 1976, p. 512.

4. My memorandum, handed to Ian Smith, on Sunday, September 19, 1976:

    1. Rhodesia agrees to majority rule within two years.

    2. Rhodesian representatives will meet immediately at a mutually agreed place with black leaders to organize an interim government to function until majority rule is implemented.

    3. The Interim Government should consist of a Council of State, half of whose members should be black and half white, with a white chairman without a special vote.

    The European and African sides would nominate their representatives. Its functions should include:

— legislation;

— general supervisory responsibilities; and

— supervision of the process of drafting the constitution.

    The Interim Government should also have a Council of Ministers with a majority of blacks and a black first minister, decisions of the Council of Ministers to be taken by two thirds majority. Its functions should include:

— delegated legislative authorities;

— and executive responsibility.

    4. All members of the Interim Government should take an oath to work for the rapid and orderly transition to majority rule.

    5. The United Kingdom will enact enabling legislation for this process to majority rule.

    Upon enactment of that legislation, Rhodesia will repeal its constitution and also enact such legislation as may be appropriate to the process.

5. Statement, Pretoria, South Africa, September 19, 1976, *Department of State Bulletin,* Vol. 75, No. 1948, October 25, 1976, p. 519.

6. Susan Crosland, *Tony Crosland* (London: Jonathan Cape, 1982).

## 33: CIVIL WAR IN LEBANON AND MIDDLE EAST PEACE

1. Kissinger, *Years of Upheaval,* p. 789.

2. Press conference, January 14, 1976, in *Department of State Bulletin,* Vol. 74, No. 1910, February 2, 1976, p. 132.

3. "Syria Hints It Might Act to Bar Lebanon Partition," *New York Times,* November 17, 1975.

4. "Beirut Is Warned Against Partition," *New York Times,* November 29, 1975.

5. "Israeli Reconnaissance Jets Fly over Beirut, Stir Fear of Attack," *New York Times,* November 20, 1975.

6. According to the *Jerusalem Post* reporting on developments of January 9, 1976, as noted in *The Middle East Journal,* Vol. 30, No. 2, p. 213.

7. "Egypt Warns Israel to Stay Out of Lebanon," *New York Times,* January 13, 1976.

8. "Fall of Camp Sharpens Lebanese Crisis; Arab Meeting Is Urged," *New York Times,* January 15, 1976.

9. Press conference, January 20, 1976, Copenhagen, in *Department of State Bulletin,* Vol. 74, No. 1912, February 16, 1976, p. 162.

10. See Kissinger, *White House Years,* Chapter 15.

11. James M. Markham, "Rival Lebanese Deploy for Showdown; Syrians Seek a Solution Over Franjieh," *New York Times,* March 18, 1976.

12. Ibid.

13. James M. Markham, "Beirut Leftists Seize Holiday Inn in Heavy Assault," *New York Times,* March 22, 1976.

14. Ibid.

15. James M. Markham, "Beirut Rightists in Counterattack," *New York Times,* March 23, 1976.

16. Itamar Rabinovich, *The War for Lebanon, 1970–1985* (Ithaca: Cornell University Press, 1985), p. 57.

## 34: REFLECTIONS

1. I have discussed the lessons of my own experience in Kissinger, *Years of Upheaval*, p. 432ff.
2. My analysis of the Vietnam experience may be found in Kissinger, *Diplomacy*, Chapters 25, 26, and 27.

# INDEX

ABC, 318
Abplanalp, Robert, 57
Abu Rudeis oil fields, 385, 389, 402, 443, 448, 449, 453–54
Abzug, Bella, 494
Acheson, Dean, 105, 189, 190, 1062
Adenauer, Konrad, 150, 610
Afghanistan, 264, 303; Soviet invasion of, 861
AFL-CIO, 544, 649, 653; Solzhenitsyn's speech to, 649, 651
Africa, 903–24; colonial legacy in, 793–94; Cuban-Soviet interventions in, 904, 908, 909, 911, 913, 914, 915, 917–18, 919, 920, 922; government as perceived in, 906–7; Latin American concerns in, 911–13; leadership in, 904–8; Marxist appeal in, 906–7, 932; NSDM 38 and, 903; pluralistic democracy in, 906; U.S. African-American community and, 921–22; Victoria Falls meeting and, 909
African National Council, 909, 997
Africa Tour of 1976, 925–57; British and French consultations in, 925–26, 955; Cold War aspect of, 927–28; Cuban-Soviet factor in, 932, 935, 942, 950–52, 954, 956; domestic criticism of, 940–41, 949, 955–57; Gorée Island visit in, 952–953; HAK's reports on, 936, 941, 949; Kenya segment of, 928–30; Liberia segment of, 947–49; Lusaka Declaration and, 939–40, 942, 950; media and, 943–944; 1976 election and, 940, 942, 955–56; Senegal segment of, 949–53; Soviet reaction to, 942; Tanzania segment of, 931–36; UNCTAD meeting and, 953–55; U.S. Zaire policy and, 944–46; Victoria Falls incident in, 941–42; Zaire segment

of, 942–47; Zambia segment of, 937–42; see also majority rule initiative
Afrikaners, 961
Agnew, Spiro, 17, 26, 56
AHEPA, 232–33
Akalovsky, Alex, 287
Akmentins, Osvalds, 643
Albert, Carl, 491, 502–3, 722
Alessandri, Jorge, 315
Algeria, 382, 511, 534, 673, 676, 679, 735, 795, 951, 970, 1024
Allen, James, 187, 473
Allende Gossens, Salvador, 314–16, 710, 750, 751–52, 753, 754, 758, 759, 801
Alliance for Progress, 704, 706
Allon, Yigal, 347, 359, 380, 381, 386, 387, 388, 405, 407, 413, 415, 416, 419, 425, 432, 446, 451, 452; Ford's talks with, 389–91; HAK's Camp David dialogue with, 363–64; Jordanian option plan of, 361–65; Plan of, 361–65, 370, 1031; Rabin and, 375–76
*Almanac of American Politics, The,* 479
Alvor agreement, 795
Amalrik, Andrei, 100
American Foreign Service Association, 334
Americans for Democratic Action, 494
Anderson, Robert, 713, 714
Andropov, Yuri, 817
Angola crisis, 37, 108, 109, 120, 145, 172, 192, 308, 335, 340, 341, 583, 622, 629, 651, 652, 737, 739, 742, 748, 770, 798–833, 836, 861, 878, 903, 912, 914, 935, 941, 943, 944, 945, 946, 952, 960, 967, 991, 998, 1015; African Affairs Bureau and, 798, 799–800, 802–8, 809, 810, 811, 827; Alvor agreement and, 795; Brazil and, 742; Brezhnev and, 787, 816, 817, 818, 821, 845; China and, 792, 794, 807,